DEVELOPING THERAPEUTICS FOR ALZHEIMER'S DISEASE

DEVELOPING THERAPEUTICS FOR ALZHEIMER'S DISEASE

PROGRESS AND CHALLENGES

Edited by

MICHAEL S. WOLFE

Ann Romney Center for Neurologic Diseases

Brigham and Women's Hospital and Harvard Medical School

Boston, MA, United States

ELSEVIER

AMSTERDAM • BOSTON • HEIDELBERG • LONDON
NEW YORK • OXFORD • PARIS • SAN DIEGO
SAN FRANCISCO • SINGAPORE • SYDNEY • TOKYO

Academic Press is an imprint of Elsevier

AP

Academic Press is an imprint of Elsevier
125 London Wall, London EC2Y 5AS, United Kingdom
525 B Street, Suite 1800, San Diego, CA 92101-4495, United States
50 Hampshire Street, 5th Floor, Cambridge, MA 02139, United States
The Boulevard, Langford Lane, Kidlington, Oxford OX5 1GB, UK

British Library Cataloguing-in-Publication Data
A catalogue record for this book is available from the British Library

Library of Congress Cataloging-in-Publication Data
A catalog record for this book is available from the Library of Congress

ISBN: 978-0-12-802173-6

Publisher: Mica Haley
Acquisition Editor: Kristine Jones
Editorial Project Manager: Molly McLaughlin
Production Project Manager: Karen East and Kirsty Halterman
Designer: Victoria Pearson

Typeset by Thomson Digital

Dedicated to the memory of my father,
Donald Wolfe, and to all those for whom effective
Alzheimer prevention and treatment
will have come too late.

Contents

5. Therapeutic Targeting of Aβ42

T.E. GOLDE, C.B. LESSARD, Y. RAN

6. Modulators of Amyloid β-Protein (Aβ) Self-Assembly

F. RAHIMI, H. LI, S. SINHA, G. BITAN

7. Anti-Amyloid-β Immunotherapy for Alzheimer's Disease

H. CREHAN, C.A. LEMERE

8. Targeting Aβ Receptors to Modify Alzheimer's Disease Progression

L.T. HAAS, S.M. STRITTMATTER

9. Blood–Brain Barrier Transport of Alzheimer's Amyloid β-Peptide

A.R. NELSON, A.P. SAGARE, B.V. ZLOKOVIC

10. Alzheimer's Disease Therapeutics Targeting Apolipoprotein E

F. LIAO, D.M. HOLTZMAN

11. Microtubule Stabilization

C. BALLATORE, A.B. SMITH, III, V.M.-Y. LEE, J.Q. TROJANOWSKI, K.R. BRUNDEN

12. Tau Phosphorylation as a Therapeutic Target in Alzheimer's Disease

M. MEDINA, J. AVILA

13. Stimulation of Tau Degradation

R.A. QUINTANILLA, F. CABEZAS-OPAZO, S.P. PALLO, A.S. CHESSER, G.V.W. JOHNSON

14. Passive Immunotherapy for Tau Pathology

P. DAVIES

15. Inhibition of Tau Aggregation as a Basis for Treatment and Prevention of Alzheimer's Disease

C.M. WISCHIK, J.M.D. STOREY, D.J. WISCHIK, C.R. HARRINGTON

16. Neuroprotective Strategies for Alzheimer's Disease Prevention and Therapy

D.A. SIMMONS, T. YANG, S.M. MASSA, F.M. LONGO

17. Symptomatic Cognitive Enhancing Agents

J.L. CUMMINGS, K. ZHONG

18. Tackling Alzheimer's Disease by Targeting Oxidative Stress and Mitochondria

R.J. CASTELLANI, S.C. CORREIA, P.I. MOREIRA, G. PERRY

19. Clinical Issues in Alzheimer Drug Development

L.S. SCHNEIDER

20. Molecular Imaging in Alzheimer Clinical Trials

M.E. SCHMIDT, D.C. MATTHEWS, S. STAELENS

21. Fluid Biomarkers and Diagnostics

H. ZETTERBERG, K. BLENNOW

22. Nonpharmacologic Activity Interventions to Prevent Alzheimer's Disease

M.C. CARLSON

23. Prospects and Challenges for Alzheimer Therapeutics

M.S. WOLFE

List of Contributors

J. Avila CIBERNED, Madrid, Spain

C. Ballatore Department of Chemistry, School of Arts and Sciences; Center for Neurodegenerative Disease Research, Institute on Aging, University of Pennsylvania;, Philadelphia, PA, United States

G. Bitan Neurology, UCLA, Los Angeles, CA, United States

K. Blennow Clinical Neurochemistry Lab, Neuroscience and Physiology, University of Gothenburg, Mölndal, Sweden

K.R. Brunden Center for Neurodegenerative Disease Research, University of Pennsylvania, Philadelphia, PA, United States

F. Cabezas-Opazo Laboratory of Neurodegenerative Diseases, Biomedical Research Center, University of Chile, Santiago, Chile

M.C. Carlson Mental Health; Center on Aging and Health; Center for Innovative Care in Aging, Johns Hopkins Bloomberg School of Public Health, Baltimore, MD, United States

R.J. Castellani Department of Pathology, University of Maryland, Baltimore, MD, United States

A.S. Chesser Department of Anesthesiology, University of Rochester Medical Center, NY, United States

S.C. Correia CNC—Center for Neuroscience and Cell Biology; Institute for Interdisciplinary Research, University of Coimbra, Coimbra, Portugal

H. Crehan Ann Romney Center for Neurologic Diseases, Brigham and Women's Hospital; Neurology, Harvard Medical School, Boston, MA, United States

J.L. Cummings Cleveland Clinic Lou Ruvo Center for Brain Health, Cleveland Clinic, Las Vegas, NV, United States

P. Davies Litwin-Zucker Center, Feinstein Institute for Medical Research, Manhasset, NY, United States

N. Gertsik Memorial Sloan-Kettering Cancer Center, New York, NY, United States; Weill Graduate School of Medical Sciences of Cornell University, New York, NY, United States

T.E. Golde Center for Translational Research in Neurodegenerative Disease; Department of Neuroscience, University of Florida College of Medicine, Gainesville, FL, United States

L.T. Haas Cellular Neuroscience, Neurodegeneration and Repair Program, Department of Neurology, Yale University School of Medicine, New Haven, CT, United States

C.R. Harrington School of Medicine and Dentistry, College of Life Sciences and Medicine, University of Aberdeen, Aberdeen, United Kingdom

D.M. Holtzman Neurology, Washington University, St. Louis, MO, United States

B. Hooli Neurology, Massachusetts General Hospital; Neurology, Harvard Medical School, Boston, MA, United States

J.-Y. Hur Memorial Sloan-Kettering Cancer Center; Weill Graduate School of Medical Sciences of Cornell University, New York, NY, United States

D.S. Johnson Pfizer Worldwide Research and Development, Neuroscience Medicinal Chemistry and Chemical Biology, Cambridge, MA, United States

G.V.W. Johnson Department of Anesthesiology, University of Rochester Medical Center, Rochester, NY, United States

V.M.-Y. Lee Center for Neurodegenerative Disease Research, Institute on Aging, University of Pennsylvania, PA, United States

C.A. Lemere Ann Romney Center for Neurologic Diseases, Brigham and Women's Hospital; Neurology, Harvard Medical School, Boston, MA, United States

C.B. Lessard Department of Neuroscience, Center for Translational Research in Neurodegenerative Disease, McKnight Brain Institute, University of Florida, Gainesville, FL, United States

H. Li Bio-Nano Research Facilities, West Virginia University, Morgantown, VA, United States

Y.-M. Li Chemical Biology, Memorial Sloan Kettering Cancer Center, New York, NY, United States

F. Liao Department of Neurology, Hope Center for Neurological Disorders, Knight Alzheimer's Disease Research Center, Washington University School of Medicine, St. Louis, MO, United States

F.M. Longo Neurology and Neurological Sciences, Stanford University, Stanford, CA, United States

S.M. Massa Department of Neurology and Laboratory for Computational Neurochemistry and Drug Discovery, San Francisco Veterans Affairs Medical Center, and Department of Neurology, University of California San Francisco, San Francisco, CA, United States

D.C. Matthews ADM Diagnostics, LLC, Chicago, IL, United States

M. Medina CIBERNED, Madrid, Spain

P.I. Moreira CNC—Center for Neuroscience and Cell Biology; Laboratory of Physiology, Faculty of Medicine, University of Coimbra, Coimbra, Portugal

A.R. Nelson Department of Physiology and Biophysics and the Zilkha Neurogenetic Institute, Keck School of Medicine of the University of Southern California, Los Angeles, CA, United States

S.P. Pallo Department of Anesthesiology, University of Rochester Medical Center, NY, United States

G. Perry College of Sciences, The University of Texas at San Antonio, San Antonio, TX, United States

R.A. Quintanilla Laboratory of Neurodegenerative Diseases, Biomedical Research Center, University of Chile, Santiago, Chile

F. Rahimi Research School of Biology, the Australian National University, Canberra, Australia

Y. Ran Department of Neuroscience, Center for Translational Research in Neurodegenerative Disease, McKnight Brain Institute, University of Florida, Gainesville, FL, United States

A.P. Sagare Department of Physiology and Biophysics and the Zilkha Neurogenetic Institute, Keck School of Medicine of the University of Southern California, Los Angeles, CA, United States

M.E. Schmidt Neuroscience Experimental Medicine, Janssen Research & Development, Beerse, Antwerpen, Belgium

L.S. Schneider Psychiatry, Neurology, and Gerontology, Keck School of Medicine of USC, Los Angeles, CA, United States

D.J. Selkoe Neurology, Harvard Medical School; Ann Romney Center for Neurologic Diseases, Brigham and Women's Hospital, Boston, MA, United States

D.A. Simmons Department of Neurology and Neurological Sciences, Stanford University, Palo Alto, CA, United States

S. Sinha Institute of Nano Science and Technology, Habitat Centre, Mohali, Punjab, India

A.B. Smith III Department of Chemistry, School of Arts and Sciences, University of Pennsylvania, PA, United States

S. Staelens Molecular Imaging Center Antwerp, Antwerp University, Wilrijk, Antwerp, Belgium

J.M.D. Storey TauRx Therapeutics Ltd., Singapore; Department of Chemistry, University of Aberdeen, United Kingdom

S.M. Strittmatter Neurology; Cellular Neuroscience, Neurodegeneration and Repair, Yale University, New Haven, CT, United States

R.E. Tanzi Genetics and Aging Research Unit, Department of Neurology, Massachusetts General Hospital; Department of Neurology, Harvard Medical School, Boston, MA, United States

J.Q. Trojanowski Center for Neurodegenerative Disease Research, Institute on Aging, University of Pennsylvania, PA, United States

R. Vassar Department of Cell and Molecular Biology, Northwestern University, Feinberg School of Medicine, Chicago, IL, United States

C.M. Wischik School of Medicine and Dentistry, University of Aberdeen, Aberdeen, United Kingdom; TauRx Therapeutics Ltd., Singapore

D.J. Wischik Computer Science Department, University College London, UK

M.S. Wolfe Ann Romney Center for Neurologic Diseases, Brigham and Women's Hospital and Harvard Medical School, Boston, MA, United States

T. Yang Department of Neurology and Neurological Sciences, Stanford University, Palo Alto, CA, United States

H. Zetterberg Clinical Neurochemistry Laboratory, Department of Psychiatry and Neurochemistry, Institute of Neuroscience and Physiology, Molndal, Västergötland, Sweden

K. Zhong Cleveland Clinic Lou Ruvo Center for Brain Health, Las Vegas, NV, United States

B.V. Zlokavic Department of Physiology and Biophysics and the Zilkha Neurogenetic Institute, Keck School of Medicine of the University of Southern California, Los Angeles, CA, United States

Foreword

Alzheimer's disease (AD) arguably is the most important public health issue of the 21st century. In 2015 in the United States alone, it is estimated that a new AD case was diagnosed every 67 seconds. This frequency is expected to rise to every 33 seconds by 2050. It has been more than a century since Alois Alzheimer first presented the case of Auguste Deter to the South-West German Society of Alienists in 1906. Although substantial progress has been made since then in understanding the etiology and pathogenesis of AD, achieving the goal of an FDA-approved disease-modifying therapy, let alone preventives or cures, has not been achieved. Why is this so, and how can these goals be accomplished?

Answers to these questions, and many others of importance, are provided in this volume compiled and edited by one of the world's foremost authorities on AD, Dr. Michael S. Wolfe. I have had the honor of calling Mike a friend and colleague for almost two decades, since he first joined the faculty at Harvard Medical School, at which time Mike brought a magna cum laude pedigree in medicinal chemistry and fresh, innovative ideas to an AD field in desperate need of them. Groundbreaking insights by Mike culminated in the discovery of one of the holy grails of AD research, an enzyme, γ-secretase, critical for the production of the amyloid β-protein (Aβ), the protein that forms the amyloid plaques that are characteristic for AD. Mike now has assembled what one could rightly term a "dream team" of the world's most accomplished and respected AD clinicians and basic science researchers to create what currently is the most comprehensive analysis of research into the causes and treatment of AD.

The 23 chapters in this book would be an excellent syllabus for a semester course in AD. The introductory chapters on AD molecular pathology and genetics provide an overall perspective on AD and highlight its multifactorial nature and its complex genetic underpinnings. Seven chapters follow that address what can be called the "Aβ problem," namely how can Aβ production and assembly into neurotoxic structures be prevented and how can the body rid itself of such neurotoxins once formed. In these chapters, the reader will learn about the enzymes responsible for Aβ production (β- and γ-secretase) and strategies to modulate their activities, as well as exciting new work on the development of Aβ aggregation inhibitors and immunotherapeutic approaches for Aβ elimination. Two areas of research that are gaining prominence rapidly, cellular receptors for Aβ and transport of Aβ across the blood–brain barrier, conclude the Aβ section of the book.

Five chapters address tau, a microtubule-stabilizing protein whose structural alteration (eg, hyperphosphorylation) and aggregation also are tightly linked to disease pathogenesis. Strategies to stabilize microtubules in the face of impaired tau activity or to inhibit the kinases causing this impaired activity are presented. Preventing tau aggregation or facilitating tau degradation and removal also are discussed.

The strongest risk factor for late-onset AD, besides age itself, is *APOE* genotype. This fact has been useful in establishing disease risk in epidemiological and genetic studies, but more work is needed toward directly targeting this gene and its protein product. Approaches for doing so are discussed in Chapter 10.

Aβ and tau long have been central AD therapeutic targets. However, it is clear that many other factors contribute to, or affect, disease status and should be considered in strategies to prevent AD or ameliorate its symptoms. Four chapters address such factors, which include neurotrophic and neuroprotective factors, cognitive enhancers, oxidative stress and inflammation, and nonpharmacological interventions.

How does one diagnose AD? How does one determine if a new therapy is effective? The answer in both cases is the possession of biomarkers that inform the clinician and researcher of disease state. Especially useful biomarkers have come from brain imaging and analysis of body fluids (typically blood and cerebrospinal fluid). Great strides have been made in recent years in both areas, strides that have shown that incipient AD may be discovered as much as 20–30 years prior to symptoms appearing. Two chapters bring the reader up to date in these important areas.

If one chapter stands out, it is the final chapter Mike has written himself (and not only because I edited it!). This chapter, "Prospects and Challenges for Alzheimer Therapeutics," is a superb overview of where we stand in our efforts to treat AD, of the problems we have encountered and may encounter in the future, and of the promises that new insights are likely to bring. It provides both a realistic and an optimistic perspective/interpretation of the prior 22 chapters and serves as an overview of the entire book. If one reads but a single chapter in this fine book, this should be it.

Who *should* read this book and how should it be read? Scientists and clinicians involved in the study and treatment of AD certainly will find this book of value as a means of providing a broad foundation of knowledge of the most important areas of the field. Those interested in specific areas will not be disappointed by their perusal of one or more chapters of particular interest to them. Pharmaceutical scientists will gain an intuitive sense of areas attractive for therapeutic drug development. Graduate students and postdoctoral fellows new to the area of AD research should be handed this book the first day they step into a laboratory doing AD research, and should not do an experiment unless and until they have thoroughly read and thought about its content.

In conclusion, in this age of information overload, especially in science and medicine, it is difficult to keep up with developments in your own specialty, let alone other specialties. In the AD field, *this* is the book that allows one to do so.

David B. Teplow
Professor of Neurology and Director,
Biopolymer Laboratory,
David Geffen School of Medicine at UCLA,
Los Angeles, California

Preface

The problem of Alzheimer's disease (AD) needs little introduction. With over 5 million people in the United States and some 20–30 million worldwide presently affected, it seems almost everyone knows someone who has been devastated by this progressive neurodegenerative disease that inexorably destroys memory and cognitive function. Despite the severity of the problem and intense efforts to solve it, there are still no effective Alzheimer therapeutics. Only a handful of symptomatic treatments of marginal benefit have been FDA-approved, and no new agent of any kind has been approved since 2003. The purpose of this book is to convey the substantial progress as well as the major challenges in developing Alzheimer therapeutics, topics that are especially significant given the dearth of agents that have successfully made it through the drug development pipeline.

Tremendous progress has been made toward elucidating the underlying molecular and cellular basis of the disease, revealing potential therapeutic targets in the process. Small molecules and biologicals have been developed for many targets, with substantial improvements in potency, selectivity, pharmacokinetics and other drug-like properties through iterative design and testing. Major advances have also been made toward developing useful biomarkers for diagnosis, selection of subjects for human trials, and testing target engagement by experimental therapeutics. The design of clinical trials has also dramatically improved, increasing our ability to observe disease-modifying effects—slowing or halting of disease progression. The advances in diagnostics and trial design have further made possible the testing of both pharmacological and non-pharmacological approaches to disease prevention by allowing enrollment of presymptomatic individuals likely to develop AD.

Notwithstanding these advances, major challenges remain. Substantial gaps in our knowledge of disease mechanisms add uncertainty to the already risky business of drug development. Moreover, as AD targets are all human proteins or nucleic acids, the potential for mechanism-based toxicity is ever present. The special problem of delivering therapeutics to the brain presents yet another serious obstacle to Alzheimer drug developers. Moreover, progress in the area of biomarkers and diagnostics has led to the unsettling realization that the disease process apparently can begin more than two decades before the onset of symptoms, raising the concern that intervention may need to begin much farther in advance.

Given the major importance of the problem and the tremendous need to solve it before demographic shifts toward the elderly overwhelm society with Alzheimer patients, much work has gone on for many years in laboratories all over the world to understand the causes of the disease and its progression and to develop effective therapeutics, with many different approaches being taken. This book examines these diverse approaches, with internationally recognized investigators serving as authors for each chapter.

First and foremost, I thank these leaders in the field for giving their precious time, carefully putting together their chapters, and sharing their extensive knowledge and insightful perspectives on the field and where it is heading. In working with these leaders on the development of this book, I have had the privilege of learning more about their areas of investigation and gaining both a deeper and broader understanding of the field as a whole. My hope is that the readers of this book will likewise be so edified, whether students, academic researchers, industrial scientists, clinicians, science writers, or venture capitalists.

I would also like to thank the editorial staff at Elsevier who helped considerably in this process, especially Kristine Jones and Molly McLaughlin. Finally, I thank all those working in the Alzheimer field for their dedication and perseverance toward elucidating and solving this devastating disease. Because of your efforts, each day we get closer.

Michael S. Wolfe
Boston, Massachusetts

CHAPTER

1

The Complex Pathways to Mechanism-Based Therapeutics in Alzheimer's Disease

D.J. Selkoe

OUTLINE

Developing Therapeutics for Alzheimer's Disease. http://dx.doi.org/10.1016/B978-0-12-802173-6.00001-0

INTRODUCTION

Few diagnoses in modern medicine evoke greater apprehension and sadness than Alzheimer's disease (AD). Virtually unknown to the public just a generation ago, this protean disorder is now the subject of enormous concern on a personal level and represents a looming catastrophe for society. Most people have encountered victims of the disease, not infrequently within their own families, and there is a palpable sense of urgency that something be done. Yet patients told that they have AD quickly learn that no proven disease-modifying treatment exists and that they are destined to experience the insidious loss of their most human qualities—memory, reasoning, abstraction, language, and emotional stability.

Now, based on the power of reductionist biology, this bleak situation appears poised to change. Breathtaking advances in our fundamental knowledge of molecular biology and cellular function during the past half century have provided a platform on which thousands of scientists worldwide are building an understanding of how AD works. Like other new scientific subjects, research on AD has experienced its share of controversy and confusion. But there are far more advances than setbacks, and many within the field believe that a rough consensus about how the disorder begins and evolves has emerged. This chapter attempts to provide an overview of how deepening molecular understanding has led over time to a range of novel therapeutic approaches that might ultimately be used to prevent the disorder before symptoms occur. I have chosen to provide here a chronological perspective on many of the major developments in the field of mechanistic AD research over the past five decades and how the unfolding, admittedly incomplete knowledge of molecular pathogenesis has ushered in the many distinct therapeutic concepts that are the subject matter of the other chapters in this timely volume.

THE MECHANISTIC STUDY OF ALZHEIMER'S DISEASE MELDS BASIC AND APPLIED RESEARCH

Most of us interested in science have grown up with the paradigm that there are two broad areas of scientific effort: "basic" and "applied." In biology, it is understood that many programs of experimentation seek to uncover the fundamental rules by which molecules are created, interact, and give rise to cellular and organismal function. On the other hand, there is great interest in pursuing a wide range of clues about how specific human diseases begin, progress, and may ultimately be thwarted. But in the past few decades, scientists have increasingly recognized that this paradigm constitutes an inaccurate dichotomy. Many investigators whose careers have focused on normal physiology are interested in the implications of their findings for the mechanisms of unsolved diseases. In turn, those who have studied human disorders and cellular and animal models thereof have sometimes contributed novel and powerful insights into the normal functions of molecular and cellular systems. This blurring of the classical boundaries is not surprising and, indeed, is highly salutary for both aspects of biological research. Scientists principally viewed as disease-oriented should strongly support more investment in so-called fundamental research, on which understanding of disease must be based. And traditionally "basic" scientists should be encouraged to extend their knowledge and methods directly into the mechanisms of the human disorders which implicate the systems they are studying.

Research on the origins of AD and other age-related neurodegenerative disorders exemplifies this melding process. There is now an impressive list of genes and proteins the understanding of which emerged solely from an interest in AD. The amyloid β-protein precursor (APP), its homologous family members APLP-1 and APLP-2, the presenilins, and the β-secretases were all identified within programs focused on elucidating AD. The discovery of presenilin (its very name comes from its key role in "presenile" AD) as the first known intramembrane aspartyl protease and its function as a key signaling hub that processes many diverse receptors in multicellular organisms represents a signal contribution of Alzheimer research to basic protein biology. The recognition from studies of neurodegenerative disease that certain neuronal proteins (eg, tau, α-synuclein) which are normally soluble may undergo alternative folding and oligomerize to gain new functional properties has helped illustrate the inextricable relationship between normal and abnormal protein folding. These and numerous other examples in the field of human neurodegeneration underscore the relevance of disease-oriented research to normal biology. And this recognition gives added excitement and urgency to delving ever deeper into mechanisms of disease.

ALZHEIMER'S DISEASE AS A PROTOTYPE FOR THE MOLECULAR ELUCIDATION OF A CHRONIC BRAIN DISORDER

Not long ago, disorders like Alzheimer's, Parkinson's, and Huntington's diseases were often assigned to the backs of textbooks of medicine as mechanistically obscure and therapeutically intractable syndromes. But advances in two areas, *biochemical pathology* and *human genetics*, have dramatically changed this situation over just two decades. For the first 60 years after the Bavarian psychiatrist Alois Alzheimer described his index patient in 1906, virtually no progress in our understanding of the causes and mechanisms of the disorder occurred. Then, two seminal papers on the electron microscopy of Alzheimer cytopathology by Robert Terry and by Michael Kidd in the mid-1960s identified the paired helical filaments that make up the tangles and the 8 nm amyloid fibrils making up the plaques. Their imaging of the ultrastructure of the classical brain lesions heralded an upswing in scientific interest in AD. In 1968, Gary Blessed, Bernard Tomlinson, and Martin Roth published a key clinicopathological study that confirmed what some neuropathologists had long suspected: the neuropathology of many cases of common senile dementia was indistinguishable from that of AD. The latter disorder had first been described in a woman who died at age 56, and it had been thought of as a distinct "presenile" dementia. But the 1968 Blessed et al. study supported the concept that AD occurred along an age continuum, with rare cases appearing before age 60 and the incidence rising linearly through the seventh to ninth decades and beyond.

This recognition of the shared neuropathological phenotype of cases regardless of age of onset soon triggered a widespread awareness that AD, rather than being a rare presenile dementia, was a very common disorder. In 1976, Robert Katzman wrote a brief but influential piece that called attention to this fact and warned about an impending "epidemic" of cases as longevity rose in developed countries. In 1979, Jerome Stone and other lay Americans with affected family members organized the Alzheimer's Association, headquartered in Chicago. This provided an enormous boost to public recognition of the disease and the personal and societal tragedy it represents. In the area of biochemical pathology, George Glenner first isolated and partially characterized the amyloid β-protein from the brains of patients dying with AD or Down syndrome in 1984, and within 2 years, several laboratories had identified the microtubule-associated protein, tau, as the principal constituent of the neurofibrillary tangles. The cloning of the APP in 1987 and discoveries of its disease-causing mutations in 1990 and 1991 brought the field squarely into the era of molecular genetics and protein chemistry.

In this brief and incomplete overview of the emergence of modern Alzheimer research, one can sense the crescendo of public and scientific interest in the disorder. Today, hundreds of laboratories and clinics worldwide are intensely focused on applying many different approaches and techniques to characterize the Alzheimer phenotype at all levels and to search for opportunities to intervene. The array of observations, some seemingly contradictory, is daunting; it has become an enormous challenge to synthesize available findings into an accurate schema of how the disease starts, unfolds, and gradually devastates cognition, leading to the patient's premature death. Assuming that the rate of progress continues to accelerate, AD may become a salient example of the steady move from phenomenology to detailed molecular understanding in a disorder of the most advanced biological system we know, the human brain.

THE DRIVING FORCES THAT UNDERLIE AD RESEARCH

The Quest for Scientific Clarity

As in all fields of scientific inquiry, by far the strongest force for progress on AD derives from the innate curiosity of the individuals who have chosen to study the topic. Attempting to contribute to the unraveling of this very complicated riddle provides enormous stimulation to the intellect. We often find ourselves in the laboratory or the clinic at times when our friends and families expect us to put aside our work. The complexity of the problem and the diverse ways in which one might think about approaching it make for a fascinating adventure in biomedical research. In one sense, this may be surprising to colleagues in other medical fields, as AD and other brain degenerations have long been viewed with intense therapeutic nihilism. Why would one have wished to focus one's work on this (until recently) obscure and enigmatic syndrome?

One motivation arises from the fact that AD represents at its onset a remarkably pure and insidious impairment of intellect. To those who entered neuroscience because of a fascination with the mind–brain relationship, deciphering the origins of this syndrome provides a window into the anatomic and molecular substrates of clear, well-organized thinking and the subtle events that can perturb memory and reasoning. Inspired by the towering examples of 19th-century neuroscientists like Broca, Charcot, and Sherrington who used neural deficits to elucidate normal nervous system function, investigators hope to help validate some of the emerging rules of normal memory and cognitive function by understanding which circuits and signaling pathways explain the earliest symptoms of AD. This relationship is illustrated not only by the molecular dissection of the disease in the laboratory but also by clinical approaches such as functional magnetic resonance imaging (fMRI), in which one can examine in vivo the brain networks that become activated in abnormal ways when subjects destined to develop AD years later attempt to remember specific patterns such as face–name pairs.

In the past two decades, it has become apparent that AD involves changes in many overlapping molecular, cellular, and anatomical pathways. Students of the disease may choose to focus their work on neuropathology, protein folding, substrate–protease biochemistry, synaptic structure and function, signal transduction, cytoskeletal biology, inflammation, oxidative metabolism, neurotransmitter pharmacology, metal ion homeostasis, or behavioral phenotyping in murine models. In short, Alzheimer research touches upon virtually the entire range of biological inquiry. The breadth and heterogeneity of the field are evidenced by a bewildering array of findings, many seemingly unrelated, that appear in innumerable publications each month. Investigators generally tend to focus on a topic that is familiar to them and produce data that are often heralded as a critical insight into the mechanism of the disease. This experimental ferment provides intellectual stimulation but can also lead to confusion and controversy, with seemingly important observations not easily confirmed by other laboratories. Nevertheless, there has been a steady movement over the years toward mechanistic consensus, as we will discuss later.

The Personal Tragedy of Alzheimer's Disease

For many who contribute to this field, a prime motivator for their work is a painful awareness of how AD and similar progressive dementias devastate the lives of victims and their families. Among chronic diseases, Alzheimer's is particularly poignant in that it erodes the patient's intellectual and emotional life and often destroys the rewards of retirement that individuals have longingly anticipated throughout their work lives. There are few more painful experiences than to see a beloved parent or sibling slowly but inexorably become a person one can hardly recognize. In this sense, AD compounds its suffering by exacting enormous pressure and dislocation on the family of the victim.

An advantage of studying a highly prevalent disorder is that even those scientists who otherwise would have little occasion to witness the clinical syndrome firsthand are acquainted with patients harboring the disorder. The majority of researchers focused on AD globally are not clinicians caring for patients. But the frequent linkage of these scientists to centers of clinical expertise, coupled with active dissemination through professional and lay forums of what the Alzheimer phenotype is like, enables students of the problem at all levels to have an understanding of its clinical development and consequences. Those who interact professionally with patients and their loved ones and watch the disease unfold have a strong additional motivation for working on the problem beyond its scientific fascination. But one does not need to be involved in patient care to feel the enormous desire to help these individuals. All of us engaged in this endeavor are inspired to contribute in ways large and small to the relief of suffering and, ultimately, to the prevention of this most common late-life dementia.

The Societal Crisis of Alzheimer's Disease

As if the patient's personal burden were not sufficient motivation, the enormous public health impact of the rising prevalence of AD further focuses one's attention. Projections of the combined economic burden of medical care and lost productivity vary widely, but all of the estimates are alarmingly high. Assuming no meaningful disease-modifying intervention occurs, it is believed that the number of patients diagnosed with AD worldwide may rise from the current approximation of 30–35 million to perhaps three times that number by midcentury. The scientific progress described in this book makes that outcome increasingly unlikely, but a great many more cases will accrue before even optimistic predictions of early treatment and prevention show an impact on prevalence.

In the United States, the message that AD is a public health emergency has been brought forward most effectively by two entities: the National Institute on Aging (NIA) and the Alzheimer's Association. Since its founding in 1974, the NIA has expended enormous effort to bring a message of urgency to both the scientific and lay communities. Among the several NIH institutes which help fund aspects of Alzheimer research, the NIA serves as the principal funder of laboratory and clinical research nationally, and it has sponsored countless initiatives, symposia, workshops, and calls to action that have dramatically moved the effort forward. Many investigators have been trained, nurtured, and enabled by the NIA's scientific leadership over more than four decades.

Another major breakthrough in the quest to defeat the disease came from the efforts of a few affected families around 1979–80 to organize the lay public into a focused and effective force for raising public awareness, helping suffering patients in many ways, and gathering precious funds for research. The success of the Alzheimer's Association, which now sponsors the largest and most impactful international scientific meetings on the disorder, cannot be overestimated. Indeed, the example of American families organizing in this way has spawned not only chapters in all of the states and many local communities but also sister organizations in countries throughout the world. The NIA and the Alzheimer's Association often work together to move the field forward, and the scientific community is deeply indebted to their unceasing efforts on behalf of the cause.

The Competition of Ideas and Findings: A Brief Perspective on "BAPtists Versus TAUists"

To those working within the field and perhaps also to many outside of it, Alzheimer research has sometimes been viewed as unusually contentious. However, a measured examination of the trajectory of the field over the past three decades suggests that controversy arose in large part out of the newness of the topic and the initial need to focus on poorly defined phenomena of the phenotype: the imprecision of the concept of "senile dementia" and the presence of brain lesions (senile plaques and neurofibrillary tangles) that occurred in highly variable densities and patterns within the Alzheimer brain but also in seemingly unrelated disorders. The era of rigorous biological analysis of the disease arguably began in the 1960s and 1970s. In those early days, investigators started to apply electron microscopy, biochemistry, and immunohistochemistry in attempts to uncover the nature of the classical morphological lesions and their local consequences. A growing focus on plaques and tangles as important phenomena of the disease was greeted with substantial skepticism, the argument being that the lesions Alzheimer described might well represent tombstones of a decades-long process and offer little insight to etiology.

Tissue deposits of amyloid, in particular, were well known to occur in certain systemic disorders of diverse cause, where they could arise as secondary reactions to more specific pathogenic events. The idea of "secondary amyloidosis" occurring in some hosts experiencing infectious, metabolic, or inflammatory disorders implied to some that the amyloid in AD might be an end-stage reaction with little pathogenic importance, the detritus of the process. This is a concern that is still voiced by some in the field, although the application of unbiased genetic approaches to familial AD has provided unequivocal evidence that at least some cases of the disorder are directly caused by dyshomeostasis of amyloid β-protein. Nonetheless, it remains a topic of debate as to whether these rare cases are closely related mechanistically to common "idiopathic" cases of AD. Because the two major lesions are composed of distinct proteins, tau in the case of the neurofibrillary tangles and β-amyloid protein in the case of amyloid plaques, the amusing aphorism that Alzheimer research is a kind of religious war between "BAPtists" and "TAUists" has even reached the lay public. But the past decade has witnessed a palpable decrease in this tension, as inherited mutations in the APP or tau genes, mouse modeling of these genotypes, and careful analyses of the Alzheimer phenotype of Down syndrome have combined to clarify the order in which the two lesions arise in the disease. Several lines of evidence suggest that the cerebral accumulation of amyloid β-protein precedes and helps drive the deposition of the tau protein in neuronal perikarya and their processes. This recognition does nothing to diminish the pathogenic importance of tau alteration and cytoskeletal impairment in AD. Indeed, recent studies suggest that the presence of the tau protein is necessary for expression of the downstream effects of Aβ on neurons.

Although it is interesting to attempt to assemble the myriad findings about the disease into a hypothetical sequence, one must bear in mind that dynamic information about the development of the process in Alzheimer patients themselves has been difficult to acquire until recently. Almost certainly, many molecular and cellular changes occur virtually simultaneously and involve complex feedback loops, so the evolution of the disorder is likely to be far less linear than current schemes propose. Nevertheless, the temporal ordering of events based on the latest available evidence can provide heuristic arguments for debate and pathogenic hypotheses that can be tested in animal models and later in human therapeutic trials. And the rapid growth in fluid and imaging biomarker studies is particularly relevant to underpinning—or denying—the proposed cascades of pathogenesis.

ELUCIDATING THE AD MECHANISM: BIOCHEMICAL PATHOLOGY, THEN GENETICS

In AD, in striking contrast to diseases such as Huntington's disease and amyotrophic lateral sclerosis, hypotheses of the molecular mechanism were initiated by work on the biochemical pathology, not by unbiased genetic analyses of familial forms (see Fig. 1.1 for a timeline of

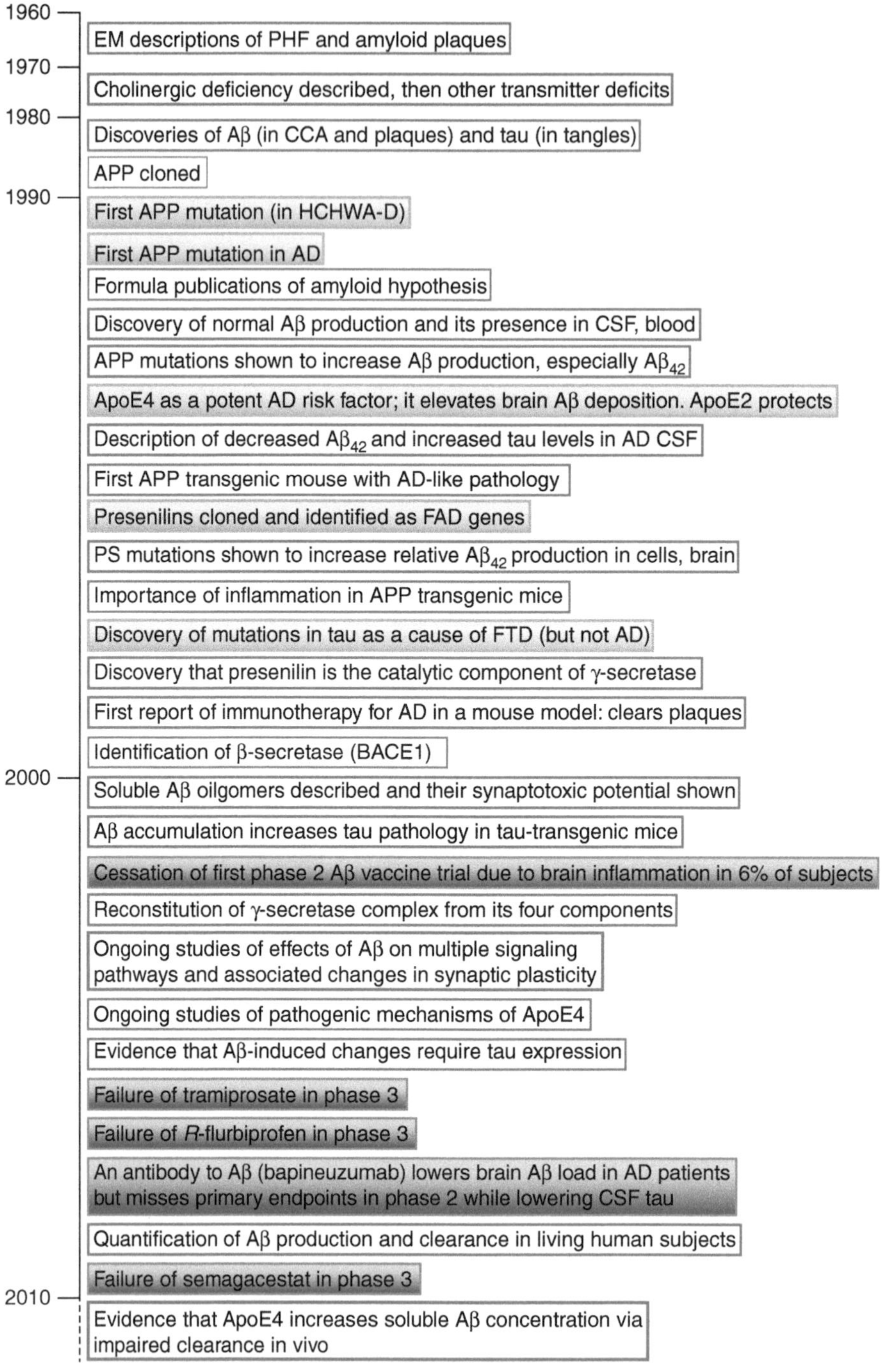

FIGURE 1.1 **Approximate timeline of some principal discoveries in AD research since 1960.** The list is by no means exhaustive and focuses on findings deemed important for the current stage of general understanding of AD pathogenesis and for the development of potentially disease-modifying agents. Abbreviations: EM, electron microscopy; HCHWA-D, hereditary cerebral hemorrhage with amyloidosis—Dutch type; CAA, Congophilic amyloid angiopathy; PS, presenilin; tg, transgenic; Ph, phase; FTD, frontotemporal dementia. Color key: light gray (pink in the web version), genetic discoveries; white (blue in the web version), discoveries about molecular pathogenesis in cells and animals; dark gray (green in the web version), clinical trials.

major developments in Alzheimer research). Subsequent genetic investigations were guided by the hypothesis arising from the biochemistry of the brain lesions, and they served to validate this hypothesis. The two canonical lesions that Alzheimer had described in 1906 became the subject of biochemical study in the early 1980s. In 1984, George Glenner isolated a protein from the meningeal vascular amyloid deposits of both AD and Down syndrome brains, provided a partial sequence (to residue 28), and dubbed the protein amyloid β-protein (Aβ), due to its presumed β-sheet content (Glenner and Wong, 1984a; Glenner and Wong, 1984b). Shortly thereafter, Colin Masters and Konrad Beyreuther isolated the subunit protein of the amyloid plaque cores, and, guided by Glenner's sequence, they showed that it had a sequence essentially indistinguishable from his β-protein (Masters et al., 1985). Work in two other labs quickly confirmed these findings (Gorevic et al., 1986; Selkoe et al., 1986), although one showed that much of the Aβ in mature plaque cores had a blocked N-terminus, exemplifying its posttranslational modification (Selkoe et al., 1986).

Based on the protein sequence through residue 28, four labs independently used pools of oligonucleotides to fish out various lengths of clones from cDNA libraries that encode the precursor protein (Goldgaber et al., 1987; Kang et al., 1987; Robakis et al., 1987; Tanzi et al., 1987). Remarkably, the cognate gene was localized to chromosome 21, fulfilling a prediction made by Glenner and providing an immediate explanation for the well-known development of typical AD neuropathology in humans with Down syndrome (trisomy 21). One lab obtained a full-length cDNA, and the structure of the predicted APP resembled a cell-surface receptor with a large ectodomain, and the Aβ region comprised 28 residues just N-terminal to the single transmembrane domain and another ~14 residues within that domain (Kang et al., 1987). This unusual locus for Aβ immediately gave rise to a conundrum: How was APP processed to release a small fragment of ~42 amino acids when the C-terminus of that fragment was in the middle of the hydrophobic transmembrane domain? This question would not be answered until more than a decade later.

Alongside this work on Aβ and its precursor, five laboratories directed their attention to the protein composition of the neurofibrillary tangles and provided evidence that the subunit of the paired helical filaments (PHF) that principally constitute the tangles was the microtubule-associated protein, tau (Brion et al., 1985; Grundke-Iqbal et al., 1986; Kosik et al., 1986; Nukina and Ihara, 1986; Wood et al., 1986). PHF had previously been discovered to be unusually insoluble and thus potentially cross-linked (Selkoe et al., 1982), so the highly soluble tau protein must have undergone substantially posttranslational modifications to become abnormally polymerized into PHF. Antibodies to certain phosphoepitopes on tau soon revealed that the tau in neurofibrillary tangles was excessively phosphorylated on a molar basis compared to normal neuronal tau. Biochemical analyses of proteolytically digested fragments obtained from insoluble PHF (Kondo et al., 1988; Wischik et al., 1988) and studies of partially soluble forms of PHF later confirmed that tau was indeed the subunit of the PHF (Lee et al., 1991).

THE FIRST GENETIC CLUES TO THE ETIOLOGY OF AD

The localization of the APP gene to the long arm of chromosome 21 and thus its implication in the early buildup of amyloid plaques in Down syndrome subjects (Lemere et al., 1996; Mann et al., 1986) made APP a leading candidate for the site of AD-causing mutations. Moreover, in 1988, two labs used anti-Aβ immunohistochemistry to recognize a multitude of apparently immature deposits of Aβ in AD brains, which they called diffuse plaques (Yamaguchi et al., 1988) or preamyloid deposits (Tagliavini et al., 1988). These apparent precursor lesions to amyloid plaques did not stain with classical amyloid dyes like Congo red and thioflavin S and were thus assumed to have little β-sheet fibrillar structure in the deposited Aβ protein. Diffuse plaques also seemed to lack surrounding activated microglial, reactive astrocytes and dystrophic neurites, thus distinguishing them from fibril-rich neuritic (senile) plaques. The latter histological evidence further suggested that Aβ deposition might be a very early feature in the development of AD neuropathology.

The first genetic mutation linked to this kind of process was discovered not in AD but in very rare families with the vascular syndrome of hereditary cerebral hemorrhage with amyloidosis—Dutch type (HCHWA-D). A missense mutation, Glu22Gln, within the Aβ region was found to segregate perfectly with affected subjects in the HCHWA-D kindreds (Fig. 1.2). Interestingly, this discovery paralleled Glenner's recovery of the Aβ peptide from the vascular deposits in AD and Down syndrome and showed that the meningovascular amyloid phenotype was strongly related to the AD parenchymal phenotype—essentially, two sides of the same coin. The finding of the "Dutch" mutation was instrumental in supporting the biochemical hypothesis that amyloid accumulation could be the principal pathogenic factor in the etiology of AD (Hardy and Allsop, 1991; Selkoe, 1991). Attention was thus focused on the APP locus in early-onset AD pedigrees, and the first mutation causing familial AD was discovered there in an English family by Goate et al. (1991). This mutation (APP Val717Ile) was not within the Aβ peptide but just beyond its C-terminus, at amino acid 46 by Aβ numbering (Fig. 1.2). The crucial discovery of an APP mutation causing AD per se solidified the amyloid cascade hypothesis (Hardy and Allsop, 1991; Hardy and Higgins, 1992; Selkoe, 1991), and its location again raised the question of what kind of proteolytic processing of the APP transmembrane domain (TMD) created the C-terminus of Aβ.

The focus on APP continued, and in 1992 two laboratories reported the surprising discovery that Aβ was a secretory product of normal APP metabolism throughout life (Haass et al., 1992; Shoji et al., 1992). Aβ was found in the conditioned medium of cultured cells both after APP transfection and at endogenous expression levels, including in normal human neurons cultured from a fetus after elective abortion (Haass et al., 1992). It was also found to be detectable in normal human cerebrospinal fluid (CSF) (Seubert et al., 1992). Prior to these papers, Aβ had been observed only by painstaking purification of the insoluble amyloid deposits from postmortem human brain tissue. The recognition that all humans normally generate Aβ throughout life had three broad implications (Selkoe, 1993). First, Aβ production and clearance could be studied dynamically in cultured cells, including fibroblasts obtained from AD and control donors, and in all mammals. Second, quantification of Aβ in the CSF suggested its potential utility as a biomarker of AD. Third and perhaps most important, APP-expressing cell lines provided the first system for performing high-throughput screening of compound libraries for Aβ-lowering agents, and these could then be tested in healthy animals. All three of these new opportunities were taken up and widely pursued in the ensuing years.

Shortly after the first two disease-causing APP mutations (ie, the "Dutch" and "London" mutations) were found, several other missense mutations were identified that all clustered in or immediately adjacent to the Aβ region of APP (Fig. 1.2). Two of these discovered in a

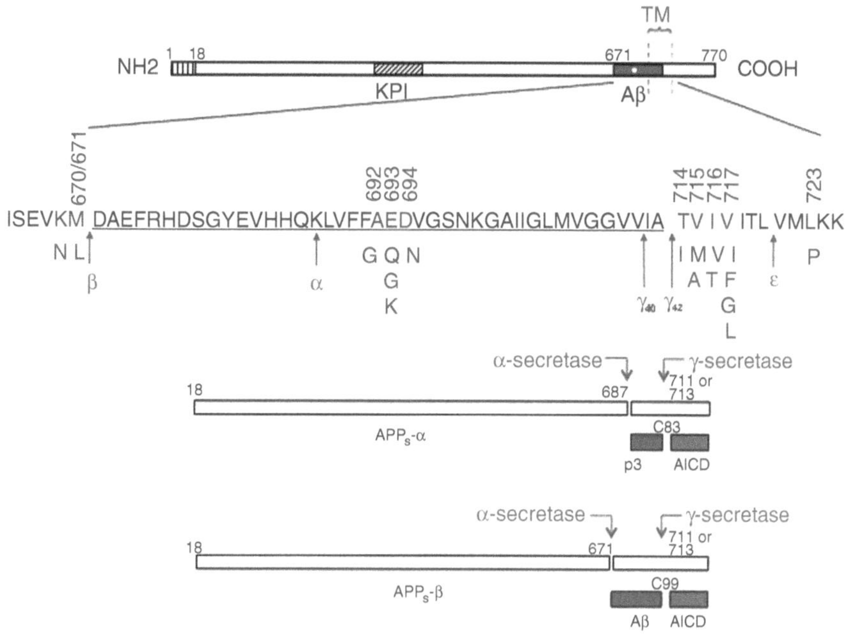

FIGURE 1.2 **Schematic diagrams of the β-amyloid precursor protein and its principal metabolic derivatives.** The first line depicts the largest of the known APP alternate splice forms, consisting of 770 amino acids. Regions of interest are indicated at their correct linear positions. A 17-residue signal peptide occurs at the N-terminus. Two alternatively spliced exons of 56 and 19 amino acids are inserted at residue 289; the first contains a serine protease inhibitor domain of the Kunitz type (KPI). A single transmembrane domain (TM) at amino acids 700–723 is indicated. The amyloid β-peptide (Aβ) includes 28 residues just outside the membrane plus the first 12–14 residues of the TM domain. In the second line, the sequence within APP that contains the Aβ and TM regions is expanded. The underlined residues represent the Aβ1-42 peptide. The large capital letters below the wild-type sequence indicate currently known missense mutations identified in certain families with AD and/or hereditary cerebral hemorrhage with amyloidosis. Three-digit numbers are codon numbers (APP770 isoform). In the third line, the first arrow indicates the site (after residue 687) of a cleavage by α-secretase that enables secretion of the large, soluble ectodomain (APP_s-α) into the medium and retention of the 83 residue C-terminal fragment (C83) in the membrane. C83 can undergo cleavage by γ-secretase principally at residue 711 or residue 713 to release the p3 peptides. The fourth line depicts the alternative proteolytic cleavage after residue 671 by β-secretase that results in the secretion of the slightly truncated APP_s-β molecule and the retention of a 99 residue C-terminal fragment in the membrane. C99 can also undergo cleavage by γ-secretase to release the Aβ peptides. Cleavage of both C83 and C99 by γ-secretase at the epsilon (**ε**) site (line 2) releases the APP intracellular domain (AICD) into the cytoplasm. The order and interdependency of the γ- and ε-cleavages are not yet established.

Swedish pedigree occurred together at the β-secretase cleavage site of APP, and modeling them in cultured cells provided the first genotype-to-phenotype relationship for AD: they markedly enhanced APP cleavage by the still-unknown β-secretase enzyme to elevate all forms of Aβ (Cai et al., 1993; Citron et al., 1992). The London mutation was shown to influence the γ-secretase cleavage of APP to enhance the relative production of the longer and more amyloidogenic Aβ42 peptides (Suzuki et al., 1994). Two other missense mutations at that same codon (APP716) did this, too. Other AD-linked and/or HCHWA-linked APP mutations occurred within the Aβ sequence itself, and these were shown in in vitro studies to enhance the aggregation propensity of the resultant Aβ peptides. Some of these mutational effects could be confirmed directly in primary cells cultured from affected carriers (Citron et al., 1994; Scheuner et al., 1996). Within 3 years of the discovery of the first APP mutation, this work supported the concept that Aβ dyshomeostasis could underlie at least rare, early-onset cases of AD.

THE DISCOVERY OF APOLIPOPROTEIN E4 AS THE MAJOR GENETIC RISK FACTOR FOR AD

A biochemical study searching for binding partners of Aβ in human CSF identified one such candidate as the circulating apolipoprotein, ApoE (Strittmatter et al., 1993). The fact that its gene was on chromosome 19 and that genetic markers on this chromosome showed linkage to AD led Strittmatter and Roses to ask whether ApoE itself was associated with AD risk. They made the striking observation that the ε4 allele of ApoE was markedly overrepresented in AD populations versus age-matched controls (Corder et al., 1993; Strittmatter et al., 1993). This major discovery was immediately replicated in populations around the world. The effect size of the ε4 allele was remarkable: humans carrying one allele had ~2- to 5-fold higher risk of developing AD than those with none, and homozygotes had as much as a ~5- to 10-fold greater risk. The allele tended to accelerate the average age of onset of late-onset AD into the mid-60s or so. Importantly, the rather infrequent ε2 allele was associated with a reduced risk of AD (Corder et al., 1993). Since the discovery of ApoE4 as the major genetic risk factor for AD, clinical trials of potentially disease-modifying therapeutics have usually been stratified according to the presence or absence of the ε4 allele.

The molecular mechanism by which the ApoE4 protein elevates the risk of AD is not fully elucidated. However, elegant studies in mice and humans by Holtzman and coworkers have shown that the clearance of Aβ from the brain is decreased by ApoE4 versus ApoE3. Mice lacking endogenous ApoE who are engineered to transgenically express human ApoE4 develop more cerebral amyloid deposits than those expressing human ApoE3 (Holtzman et al., 2000). A detailed quantitative study of Aβ homeostasis using in vivo microdialysis in hAPP × hApoE-crossed mice has shown that Aβ clearance (but not Aβ production) is decreased by ApoE4 more than E3 more than E2, closely paralleling the degree of Aβ deposition in such mice (Castellano et al., 2011). The decrease in clearance of soluble Aβ could be observed by the investigators in young mice, well before any amyloid deposition. The results strongly suggest that ApoE contributes to AD risk by differentially regulating Aβ clearance, emphasizing Aβ clearance pathways as a major therapeutic target, as discussed in detail elsewhere in this book.

PRESENILIN AS THE SITE OF MUTATIONS CAUSING AGGRESSIVE, EARLY-ONSET AD

Genetic linkage analyses in the 1980s and early 1990s indicated that familial AD was genetically heterogeneous, so that genes other than APP could cause the disease in an autosomal dominant mode of inheritance (St George-Hyslop et al., 1990). In 1995, St George-Hyslop and coworkers used linkage analysis and positional cloning to identify a gene encoding a polytopic membrane protein (originally called S182) that was the site of missense mutations in rare families with early-onset AD (Sherrington et al., 1995). This discovery led quickly to the identification of a homolog that was mutant in other FAD kindreds, including a large German-American pedigree referred to as the "Volga Germans" (Levy-Lahad et al., 1995; Rogaev et al., 1995). These genes were soon renamed the presenilins (PS1 and PS2), based on their production of an early-onset form of AD. Many missense mutations were eventually found in these genes: >200 in PS1 and >20 in PS2.

The predicted gene products are 9-TMD polytopic proteins, and how mutations in them could lead invariably to AD was obscure. But studies in *Caenorhabditis elegans* soon revealed that loss of presenilin produced a lethal phenotype closely resembling that of loss-of-function of the Notch receptor family (Levitan and Greenwald, 1995), centrally implicating presenilin in the Notch developmental pathway. In 1998, De Strooper and coworkers found that knockout of PS1 in mice markedly decreased the production of Aβ by neurons, and they postulated that it was a key cofactor for the then-unknown γ-secretase protease (De Strooper et al., 1998). But inhibitor studies by Wolfe and Selkoe suggested that γ-secretase was a type of aspartyl protease among the four classes of endopeptidases (Wolfe et al., 1999a). Close inspection of the primary sequence of presenilin revealed two and only two intramembrane aspartic acid residues predicted to be near the center of two adjacent TMDs (6 and 7) of the 9-TMD polypeptide. Mutation of either aspartate dramatically decreased Aβ production by cultured cells and also abolished the known endoproteolysis of presenilin that occurred between those two TMDs (Wolfe et al., 1999b). These data suggested that presenilin was a first-in-class intramembrane-cleaving aspartyl protease that was activated (matured) by an autoproteolytic cleavage that positioned the two aspartates correctly to perform subsequent endoproteolysis of diverse single-transmembrane proteins. In short, this work revealed that presenilin was the catalytic site of the long-sought γ-secretase. This model was highly controversial when first published, but work in many labs soon confirmed and extended it. Simultaneous overexpression of aspartate → alanine mutants in both PS1 and PS2 dropped cellular Aβ production to undetectable levels (Kimberly et al., 2000). And this mechanistic explanation was directly relevant to the requirement of presenilin for the endoproteolysis of Notch within its single TMD to support proper embryonic development of all metazoans (De Strooper et al., 1999).

THE DISCOVERY OF PRESENILIN FUNCTION SUPPORTS A MECHANISTIC HYPOTHESIS OF AD INITIATION

Taken together, the findings just reviewed indicate that all dominantly transmitted mutations causing familial AD occur in either the substrate (APP) or the protease (presenilin) of the reaction that generates Aβ. This knowledge provides a credible hypothesis for why and how AD arose in the human population. The two aspartates of presenilin are entirely conserved in metazoan evolution because they are absolutely required for the Notch signaling that mediates many cell-fate determinations during embryogenesis (and also in adulthood). This conserved proteolytic machine apparently acquired numerous other single-transmembrane substrates during evolution, one of which is APP. Normal production of its Aβ fragment throughout life allows a small fraction of the more hydrophobic Aβ42 species to aggregate over time in postreproductive life, a process that occurs in all primates and numerous lower mammals who share the specific Aβ region sequence of humans. Aβ aggregation is not energetically favored, but gradual time-dependent (age-related) accumulation of Aβ42 and related longer Aβ peptides can lead to formation of stable oligomers that have been shown to confer the key phenotypic characteristics of AD: synaptic loss, inhibition of synaptic plasticity, and interference with memory (Shankar et al., 2008). One can ask why this mechanism should lead to a chronic disease of the brain rather than other organs. The most likely answer is that β-secretase (BACE1) is principally expressed in neurons, so that lifelong neuronal Aβ production is higher in the brain than in other organs.

Of course, the mechanism of pathogenesis described here is predicated on a critical role for Aβ accumulation in the earliest stages of the disease (Fig. 1.3). In the case of APP and PS1/2 mutations, this is clear. ApoE4-related cases were once part of the large group of "sporadic" AD patients, and the credible implication of this most important risk factor in Aβ clearance (Castellano et al., 2011) further supports the previously postulated mechanism. Other risk genes for late-onset AD are being identified and their mechanisms elucidated, and each will need to be considered individually as to its relationship to the Aβ hypothesis. For example, PICALM has been linked to late-onset AD, and it appears to be involved directly in endosomal APP processing (Kanatsu et al., 2014). In addition, PICALM has recently been implicated in the transcytosis of brain Aβ across the blood–brain barrier: iPSC-derived human endothelial cells carrying an AD-protective allele exhibited higher PICALM levels and enhanced Aβ clearance (Zhao et al., 2015).

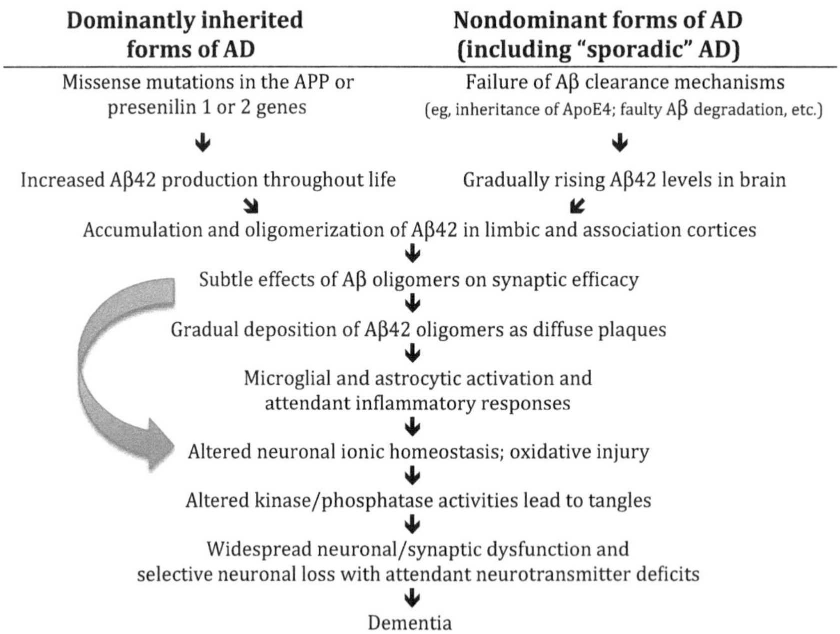

FIGURE 1.3 **The sequence of pathogenic events leading to AD proposed by the amyloid cascade hypothesis.** The curved arrow (blue in the web version) indicates that Aβ oligomers may directly injure the synapses and neurites of brain neurons, in addition to activating microglia and astrocytes.

RELATIONSHIP OF Aβ ACCUMULATION TO TAU ALTERATION AND NEUROFIBRILLARY DEGENERATION

An enduring question in AD research is the mechanistic relationship between the two canonical lesions of the disease: β-amyloid deposits and tau-positive neuronal/neuritic degeneration. A number of studies have addressed this important issue. First and foremost, human genetics has clearly indicated that mutations in APP can lead to accumulation of wild-type tau protein in neurons, whereas mutations in tau do not lead to accumulation of Aβ and the AD phenotype but rather cause a form of frontotemporal lobar degeneration (FTD), which lacks Aβ deposits (unless such patients are older than ~70 and thus have minor age-related Aβ accumulation). Thus, Aβ dyshomeostasis can occur upstream of tau-positive neurofibrillary degeneration but the converse has not been documented in humans.

As to the nature of the Aβ → tau connection, the extracellular application of Aβ oligomers isolated from AD cortex to healthy rodent neurons in culture leads to the oligomers binding to and perturbing the plasma membrane, thereby inducing AD-type hyperphosphorylation of tau and profound neuritic dystrophy (Jin et al., 2011). Preventing the neuronal binding of the oligomers by coadministering the Aβ aggregation inhibitor scyllo-inositol precludes the alteration of tau (Jin and Selkoe, 2015), and knocking down tau in such neurons largely prevents the neuritic dystrophy (Jin et al., 2011). In accord, crossing hAPP transgenic mice to mice genetically deleted of tau produces offspring that have substantially less behavioral abnormalities that the parental APP mice do (Roberson et al., 2007). Moreover, crossing hAPP mice to human mutant tau transgenic mice aggregates the tau pathology without increasing the Aβ pathology (Lewis et al., 2001), consistent with the human genetic findings.

How Aβ oligomer binding to neurons extracellularly can induce pathological signaling across the plasma membrane to alter intraneuronal tau homeostasis remains enigmatic. There have been numerous reports in the past two decades that have proposed one or another neuronal cell surface protein as a cognate receptor for Aβ oligomers, including α7-nicotinic receptors, insulin receptors, NMDA and/or AMPA receptors, the GPI-linked cellular prion protein (PrP), and several others. Whereas some experimental evidence for each of these has accrued, it often comes from just one or a few labs, and broad consensus about the identity of the cognate "Aβ oligomer receptor" is not at hand. An alternative to a protein receptor is the possibility that membrane lipids are more likely as a site of oligomer binding. Natural Aβ dimers, for example, presumably have certain exposed hydrophobic amino acids ready to accept another abnormally conformed monomer to yield a trimer, then a tetramer, and so on. The hydrophobicity of growing oligomers would make it reasonable that they bind readily to other hydrophobic surfaces, that is, the abundant local phospholipid membranes in the brain. In this regard, in vivo administration into mouse brain of soluble monomers versus dimers (through a cannula attached to a microdialysis probe) leads to much more rapid disappearance (lack of recovery in the dialysate) for the dimers than for the monomers, and the injected dimers can be recovered in membrane extracts of the brain tissue (Hong et al., 2014).

Such dynamic studies suggest that the dwell time in the interstitial fluid of dimers and oligomers that arise from dimers is very short. If this inference is correct, then there may be numerous diverse compositions of lipid membranes that could serve to bind and sequester Aβ oligomers in vivo. The concept that a discrete surface protein acts as a true, high-affinity oligomer receptor (in the way that a D2 dopamine receptor specifically binds dopamine) seems improbable, since Aβ oligomers were not present during development (they arise later in life), and a cognate receptor would not have evolved for them. It remains possible that they hijack other receptors and induce inappropriate signaling events, but this may not occur with high molecular specificity, in contrast to classical ligand–receptor interactions. In short, the mechanism by which extracellular Aβ oligomers effect neuronal alteration and microglial and astrocytic activation may be rather inelegant and lacking in specificity.

AN INCREASINGLY RECOGNIZED ROLE FOR THE INNATE IMMUNE SYSTEM IN AD

The neuropathology of AD has long suggested that the principal cellular elements of the brain's innate immune system, microglia and astrocytes, might be important determinants of the pathogenic cascade. For example, the observation by immunohistochemistry of multiple elements of the classical complement cascade, including local microglial activation, in and around neuritic plaques (Itagaki et al., 1989) and the implication of C1q as capable of binding to Aβ (Rogers et al., 1992) occurred in the early phase of modern AD research. In the past few years, genetic variability in that system has emerged as an important determinant of AD risk, implicating molecular components of innate immunity and the complement cascade as risk factors for the disease (Jones et al., 2010). Three such risk genes have been investigated in some detail: complement receptor 1 (*CR1*) (Lambert et al., 2009), *CD33* (Bertram et al., 2008), and *TREM2* (Guerreiro et al., 2013; Jonsson et al., 2013), and all three appear to be involved either directly or indirectly in the response of microglia to Aβ accumulation. Blockade of *CR1* inhibits microglial activation and potentiates microglial phagocytosis (Crehan et al., 2013). Inactivation of *CD33* in primary microglia also potentiates microglial uptake of Aβ (Griciuc et al., 2013), and *TREM2* is responsible for sustaining microglial phagocytosis of Aβ (Wang et al., 2015). In short, all three of these genetically implicated microglial proteins may be involved in helping to maintain the AD microglial phenotype of phagocytosing Aβ deposits. Accordingly, these three genes show increased expression with plaque development (Griciuc et al., 2013; Matarin et al., 2015; Wang et al., 2015). Indeed, *TREM2* expression is emerging as a central molecular determinant of the CNS response to Aβ accumulation (Forabosco et al., 2013; Matarin et al., 2015; Zhang et al., 2013). Additional genetic searches for risk alleles that predispose to the development of typical late-onset AD are under way and are likely to further implicate innate immunity. And diverse strategies are being examined in AD mouse models to modulate the microglial response in various ways that could reduce local inflammatory events in the brain.

BIOMARKERS IN LIVING HUMANS HELP ELUCIDATE THE NATURAL HISTORY OF AD

Developing a correct understanding of the sequence of events in Alzheimer pathogenesis had been hampered by the difficulty of detecting this sequence in living humans. The problem has been substantially lessened by three developments: (1) robust assays to quantify soluble Aβ monomers and tau in human CSF (Vigo-Pelfrey et al., 1995); (2) imaging fibrillar amyloid burden (but not yet soluble Aβ oligomers) by PET scanning, initially with the thioflavin T derivative Pittsburgh compound B (Klunk et al., 2004); and (3) the ability to analyze APP metabolism in humans by quantifying heavy isotope-labeled Aβ peptides in fresh CSF by mass spectrometry (Bateman et al., 2006; Mawuenyega et al., 2010).

In Vivo APP Labeling

Use of ^{13}C (heavy) leucine infusions to label all newly synthesized proteins, including APP, in presymptomatic subjects with presenilin mutations and their noncarrier sibs confirmed the extensive data in cultures and mouse models that these AD-causing mutations increase Aβ42 production (Potter et al., 2013). Further, during the period of amyloid deposition, CSF Aβ42 monomer declines in a manner suggesting it becomes bound to developing plaques (Blennow et al., 2015; Potter et al., 2013). Use of the in vivo labeling approach in ApoE3 versus E4 carriers showed that E4 subjects had lower Aβ monomer clearance (Castellano et al., 2011). Together, these data support the view that presenilin mutation carriers produce relatively more Aβ42 and that E4 carriers clear it less efficiently, each resulting in the AD phenotype.

Amyloid Imaging and CSF Biomarkers

Numerous families carrying *APP*, *PSEN1*, or *PSEN2* mutations have been studied collectively to determine the time course of fluid biomarker, neuroimaging, and clinical changes prior to the expected onset of AD symptoms, which is set as the age of symptom onset in a parent with the same mutation. Initial analyses of a familial AD cohort, the Dominantly Inherited Alzheimer Network (DIAN), suggest that Aβ42 levels in CSF may first be somewhat elevated (vs normal) and then begin to decline as early as 25 years before expected symptom onset (Bateman et al., 2012). This is followed by the appearance of fibrillar amyloid deposits in the brain (as detected by PiB-PET), increased levels of tau in CSF, and progressive brain atrophy roughly 15 years before expected symptom onset (Bateman et al., 2012). Neuronal hypometabolism (seen on FDG-PET scanning) and subtly impaired episodic verbal memory seem to begin some 10 years or so before expected symptoms (Bateman et al., 2012). If this time course is generally similar to that of "sporadic" AD, and the Australian Imaging, Biomarker & Lifestyle (AIBL) study of aging (Villemagne et al., 2013) suggests that it is, then Aβ deposition begins at least two decades before clinically noticeable cognitive decline. A key lesson which emerges from such studies of presymptomatic AD is that therapeutic interventions directed only at the mild-to-moderate clinical stage may be too late to ameliorate progression.

Overall, brain imaging and CSF biomarker studies in humans suggest that the sequence of AD pathogenic steps currently measurable in vivo broadly follows the schema proposed by Jack and coworkers (Jack and Holtzman, 2013; Jack et al., 2013). These data are consistent with early studies of AD neuropathology in Down syndrome, which documented an initial accumulation of diffuse Aβ deposits that precedes microglial and astrocytic activation, tangle formation, and neurodegeneration (eg, Lemere et al., 1996; Mann et al., 1992). The recent development of imaging agents for tangles (Chien et al., 2013; Liang et al., 2014; Maruyama et al., 2013) will help define the time course of accrual of the two major lesions, although tangles are not specific for AD in that they occur increasingly with "normal" aging and in numerous age-linked neurodegenerative diseases besides AD.

A DAUNTING ARRAY OF APPARENT DOWNSTREAM EFFECTS IN THE AMYLOID CASCADE

In recent years, an enormous number of papers have been published that describe a diverse multitude of biochemical effects of accumulating Aβ species and/or other upstream events in the complex Alzheimer pathogenic cascade (see Fig. 1.3 for a hypothetical linear scheme of the major steps in the Aβ hypothesis). These include changes in many neuronal signaling pathways, in various endocytic and autophagic trafficking pathways, in the cytoskeleton, in mitochondrial function and energy metabolism, in apoptotic cascades, in free radical formation and oxidative injury, and in numerous other molecular events. An "embarrassment of riches" with regard to possible effectors of oligomeric Aβ and/or other upstream initiating factors suggests that it will be highly challenging to devise specific compounds that effectively prevent or correct the progression of the downstream cascade. Instead, it seems more practical to attempt to neutralize or remove the offending upstream factor(s) in the first place. This is one reason why the lion's share of therapeutic approaches discussed in this book fall into the anti-Aβ realm. If oligomeric Aβ is an early bioactive agent, even if it is not *the* major cause of the disease, then attempting to remove this trigger is a rational—albeit difficult—approach to treatment and prevention.

CONCLUSION: MECHANISTIC RESEARCH OFFERS MANY AVENUES TOWARD DISEASE-MODIFYING TREATMENTS

Because laboratory and clinical research on AD over the past four decades has involved so many approaches and findings (Fig. 1.1), an attempt to incorporate these into one comprehensive model is an exercise marked by hubris. It is impossible to capture all of the complex observations and competing ideas that mark this field of inquiry.

The expansive knowledge base overviewed in this chapter and detailed in the rest of this book is likely to alter dramatically the way "Alzheimerology" is practiced within the next decade or two. We believe that the convergence of many scientific threads, particularly those from studies of fluid biomarkers and brain imaging, along with clinical genetics, should allow physicians to gauge risk with increasing accuracy and to monitor the development of the disease in its presymptomatic phase, before at least some of the irreversible neuronal injury has occurred. The paradigm we describe emphasizes screening for the disorder in midlife (perhaps earlier) and then offering a range of preventions intended to stave off—or permanently avoid—progressive cognitive decline. Such projections reveal a strong sense of optimism that emerges from extraordinary progress in deciphering the biology of AD during our lifetimes.

Acknowledgments

Portions of the beginning of this chapter were adapted from my chapter (Selkoe, DJ) in: Selkoe, Mandelkow, and Holtzman, *The Biology of Alzheimer Disease* (Cold Spring Harbor Laboratory Press, 2012). I thank my many fellows, students, and collaborators over more than three decades of research on AD for the concepts and data from our laboratory that are mentioned in this chapter. Supported by NIH grants from the National Institute on Aging.

References

Bateman RJ, Munsell LY, Morris JC, et al: Human amyloid-beta synthesis and clearance rates as measured in cerebrospinal fluid in vivo, *Nat Med* 12:856–861, 2006.

Bateman RJ, Xiong C, Benzinger TL, et al: Clinical and biomarker changes in dominantly inherited Alzheimer's disease, *N Engl J Med* 367:795–804, 2012.

Bertram L, Lange C, Mullin K, et al: Genome-wide association analysis reveals putative Alzheimer's disease susceptibility loci in addition to APOE, *Am J Hum Genet* 83:623–632, 2008.

Blennow K, Mattsson N, Scholl M, et al: Amyloid biomarkers in Alzheimer's disease, *Trends Pharmacol Sci* 36:297–309, 2015.

Brion JP, van den Bosch de Aguilar P, Flament-Durand J: *Senile dementia of the Alzheimer type: morphological and immunocytochemical studies*, Berlin, 1985, Springer-Verlag.

Cai X-D, Golde TE, Younkin GS: Release of excess amyloid β protein from a mutant amyloid β protein precursor, *Science* 259:514–516, 1993.

Castellano JM, Kim J, Stewart FR, et al: Human apoE isoforms differentially regulate brain amyloid-β peptide clearance, *Sci Transl Med* 3, 2011, 89ra57.

Chien DT, Bahri S, Szardenings AK, et al: Early clinical PET imaging results with the novel PHF-tau radioligand [F-18]-T807, *J Alzheimers Dis* 34:457–468, 2013.

Citron M, Oltersdorf T, Haass C, et al: Mutation of the β-amyloid precursor protein in familial Alzheimer's disease increases β-protein production, *Nature* 360:672–674, 1992.

Citron M, Vigo-Pelfrey C, Teplow DB, et al: Excessive production of amyloid β-protein by peripheral cells of symptomatic and presymptomatic patients carrying the Swedish familial Alzheimer's disease mutation, *Proc Natl Acad Sci USA* 91:11993–11997, 1994.

Corder EH, Saunders AM, Strittmatter WJ, et al: Gene dose of apolipoprotein E type 4 allele and the risk of Alzheimer's disease in late onset families, *Science* 261:921–923, 1993.

Crehan H, Hardy J, Pocock J: Blockage of CR1 prevents activation of rodent microglia, *Neurobiol Dis* 54:139–149, 2013.

De Strooper B, Annaert W, Cupers P, et al: A presenilin-1-dependent gamma-secretase-like protease mediates release of Notch intracellular domain, *Nature* 398:518–522, 1999.

De Strooper B, Saftig P, Craessaerts K, et al: Deficiency of presenilin-1 inhibits the normal cleavage of amyloid precursor protein, *Nature* 391:387–390, 1998.

Forabosco P, Ramasamy A, Trabzuni D, et al: Insights into TREM2 biology by network analysis of human brain gene expression data, *Neurobiol Aging* 34:2699–2714, 2013.

Glenner GG, Wong CW: Alzheimer's disease and Down's syndrome: sharing of a unique cerebrovascular amyloid fibril protein, *Biochem Biophys Res Commun* 122:1131–1135, 1984a.

Glenner GG, Wong CW: Alzheimer's disease: initial report of the purification and characterization of a novel cerebrovascular amyloid protein, *Biochem Biophys Res Commun* 120:885–890, 1984b.

Goate A, Chartier-Harlin M-C, Mullan M, et al: Segregation of a missense mutation in the amyloid precursor protein gene with familial Alzheimer's disease, *Nature* 349:704–706, 1991.

Goldgaber D, Lerman MI, McBridge OW, et al: Characterization and chromosomal localization of a cDNA encoding brain amyloid of Alzheimer's disease, *Science* 235:877–880, 1987.

Gorevic P, Goni F, Pons-Estel B, et al: Isolation and partial characterization of neurofibrillary tangles and amyloid plaque cores in Alzheimer's disease: immunohistological studies, *J Neuropathol Exp Neurol* 45:647–664, 1986.

Griciuc A, Serrano-Pozo A, Parrado AR, et al: Alzheimer's disease risk gene CD33 inhibits microglial uptake of amyloid beta, *Neuron* 78:631–643, 2013.

Grundke-Iqbal I, Iqbal K, Tung Y-C, et al: Abnormal phosphorylation of the microtubule-associated protein t (tau) in Alzheimer cytoskeletal pathology, *Proc Natl Acad Sci USA* 83:4913–4917, 1986.

Guerreiro R, Wojtas A, Bras J, et al: TREM2 variants in Alzheimer's disease, *N Engl J Med* 368:117–127, 2013.

Haass C, Schlossmacher M, Hung AY, et al: Amyloid beta-peptide is produced by cultured cells during normal metabolism, *Nature* 359:322–325, 1992.

Hardy J, Allsop D: Amyloid deposition as the central event in the aetiology of Alzheimer's disease, *Trends in Pharmacol* 12:383–388, 1991.

Hardy JA, Higgins GA: Alzheimer's disease: the amyloid cascade hypothesis, *Science* 256:184–185, 1992.

Holtzman DM, Bales KR, Tenkova T, et al: Apolipoprotein E isoform-dependent amyloid deposition and neuritic degeneration in a mouse model of Alzheimer's disease, *Proc Natl Acad Sci USA* 97:2892–2897, 2000.

Hong S, Ostaszewski BL, Yang T, et al: Soluble Abeta oligomers are rapidly sequestered from brain ISF in vivo and bind GM1 ganglioside on cellular membranes, *Neuron* 82:308–319, 2014.

Itagaki S, McGeer PL, Akiyama H, et al: Relationship of microglia and astrocytes to amyloid deposits of Alzheimer disease, *J Neuroimmunol* 24:173–182, 1989.

Jack CR Jr, Holtzman DM: Biomarker modeling of Alzheimer's disease, *Neuron* 80:1347–1358, 2013.

Jack CR Jr, Knopman DS, Jagust WJ, et al: Tracking pathophysiological processes in Alzheimer's disease: an updated hypothetical model of dynamic biomarkers, *Lancet Neurol* 12:207–216, 2013.

Jin M, Selkoe DJ: Systematic analysis of time-dependent neural effects of soluble amyloid beta oligomers in culture and in vivo: prevention by scyllo-inositol, *Neurobiol Dis* 82:152–163, 2015.

Jin M, Shepardson N, Yang T, et al: Soluble amyloid beta-protein dimers isolated from Alzheimer cortex directly induce tau hyperphosphorylation and neuritic degeneration, *Proc Natl Acad Sci USA* 108:5819–5824, 2011.

Jones L, Holmans PA, Hamshere ML, et al: Genetic evidence implicates the immune system and cholesterol metabolism in the aetiology of Alzheimer's disease, *PLoS One* 5:e13950, 2010.

Jonsson T, Stefansson H, Steinberg S, et al: Variant of TREM2 associated with the risk of Alzheimer's disease, *N Engl J Med* 368:107–116, 2013.

Kanatsu K, Morohashi Y, Suzuki M, et al: Decreased CALM expression reduces Abeta42 to total Abeta ratio through clathrin-mediated endocytosis of gamma-secretase, *Nat Commun* 5:3386, 2014.

Kang J, Lemaire H-G, Unterbeck A, et al: The precursor of Alzheimer's disease amyloid A4 protein resembles a cell-surface receptor, *Nature* 325:733–736, 1987.

Kimberly WT, Xia W, Rahmati R, et al: The transmembrane aspartates in presenilin 1 and 2 are obligatory for γ-secretase activity and amyloid β-protein generation, *J Biol Chem* 275:3173–3178, 2000.

Klunk WE, Engler H, Nordberg A, et al: Imaging brain amyloid in Alzheimer's disease with Pittsburgh compound-B, *Ann Neurol* 55:306–319, 2004.

Kondo J, Honda T, Mori H, et al: The carboxyl third of tau is tightly bound to paired helical filaments, *Neuron* 1:827–834, 1988.

Kosik KS, Joachim CL, Selkoe DJ: Microtubule-associated protein, tau, is a major antigenic component of paired helical filaments in Alzheimer's disease, *Proc Natl Acad Sci USA* 83:4044–4048, 1986.

Lambert JC, Heath S, Even G, et al: Genome-wide association study identifies variants at CLU and CR1 associated with Alzheimer's disease, *Nat Genet* 41:1094–1099, 2009.

Lee VM-Y, Balin BJ, Otvos L, et al: A68: a major subunit of paired helical filaments and derivatized forms of normal tau, *Science* 251:675–678, 1991.

Lemere CA, Blustzjan JK, Yamaguchi H, et al: Sequence of deposition of heterogeneous amyloid β-peptides and Apo E in Down syndrome: implications for initial events in amyloid plaque formation, *Neurobiol Dis* 3:16–32, 1996.

Levitan D, Greenwald I: Facilitation of *lin-12*-mediated signalling by *sel-12*, a *Caenorhabditis elegans S182* Alzheimer's disease gene, *Nature* 377:351–354, 1995.

Levy-Lahad E, Wasco W, Poorkaj P, et al: Candidate gene for the chromosome 1 familial Alzheimer's disease locus, *Science* 269:973–977, 1995.

Lewis J, Dickson DW, Lin WL, et al: Enhanced neurofibrillary degeneration in transgenic mice expressing mutant tau and APP, *Science* 293:1487–1491, 2001.

Liang SH, Yokell DL, Normandin MD, et al: First human use of a radiopharmaceutical prepared by continuous-flow microfluidic radiofluorination: proof of concept with the tau imaging agent [18F]T807, *Mol Imaging*:13, 2014.

Mann DM, Yates PO, Marcyniuk B, et al: The topography of plaques and tangles in Down's syndrome patients of different ages, *Neuropathol Appl Neurobiol* 12:447–457, 1986.

Mann DMA, Yuonis N, Jones D, et al: The time course of pathological events in Down's syndrome with particular reference to the involvement of microglial cells and deposits of β/A4, *Neurodegeneration* 1:201–215, 1992.

Maruyama M, Shimada H, Suhara T, et al: Imaging of tau pathology in a tauopathy mouse model and in Alzheimer patients compared to normal controls, *Neuron* 79:1094–1108, 2013.

Masters CL, Simms G, Weinman NA, et al: Amyloid plaque core protein in Alzheimer disease and Down syndrome, *Proc Natl Acad Sci USA* 82:4245–4249, 1985.

Matarin M, Salih DA, Yasvoina M, et al: A genome-wide gene-expression analysis and database in transgenic mice during development of amyloid or tau pathology, *Cell Rep* 10:633–644, 2015.

Mawuenyega KG, Sigurdson W, Ovod V, et al: Decreased clearance of CNS beta-amyloid in Alzheimer's disease, *Science* 330:1774, 2010.

Nukina N, Ihara Y: One of the antigenic determinants of paired helical filaments is related to tau protein, *J Biochem* 99:1541–1544, 1986.

Potter R, Patterson BW, Elbert DL, et al: Increased in vivo amyloid-beta42 production, exchange, and loss in presenilin mutation carriers, *Sci Transl Med* 5, 2013, 189ra177.

Robakis NK, Ramakrishna N, Wolfe G, et al: Molecular cloning and characterization of a cDNA encoding the cerebrovascular and the neuritic plaque amyloid peptides, *Proc Natl Acad Sci USA* 84:4190–4194, 1987.

Roberson ED, Scearce-Levie K, Palop JJ, et al: Reducing endogenous tau ameliorates amyloid beta-induced deficits in an Alzheimer's disease mouse model, *Science* 316:750–754, 2007.

Rogaev EI, Sherrington R, Rogaeva EA, et al: Familial Alzheimer's disease in kindreds with missense mutations in a gene on chromosome 1 related to the Alzheimer's disease type 3 gene, *Nature* 376:775–778, 1995.

Rogers J, Cooper NR, Webster S, et al: Complement activation by β-amyloid in Alzheimer disease, *Proc Natl Acad Sci USA* 89:10016–10020, 1992.

Scheuner D, Eckman C, Jensen M, et al: Secreted amyloid β-protein similar to that in the senile plaques of Alzheimer's disease is increased in vivo by the presenilin 1 and 2 and APP mutations linked to familial Alzheimer's disease, *Nature Med* 2:864–870, 1996.

Selkoe DJ: The molecular pathology of Alzheimer's disease, *Neuron* 6:487–498, 1991.

Selkoe DJ: Physiological production of the amyloid β-protein and the mechanism of Alzheimer's disease, *Trends in Neurosci* 16:403–409, 1993.

Selkoe DJ, Abraham CR, Podlisny MB, et al: Isolation of low-molecular-weight proteins from amyloid plaque fibers in Alzheimer's disease, *J Neurochem* 146:1820–1834, 1986.

Selkoe DJ, Ihara Y, Salazar F: Alzheimer's disease: insolubility of partially purified paired helical filaments in sodium dodecyl sulfate and urea, *Science* 215:1243–1245, 1982.

Seubert P, Vigo-Pelfrey C, Esch F, et al: Isolation and quantitation of soluble Alzheimer's β-peptide from biological fluids, *Nature* 359:325–327, 1992.

Shankar GM, Li S, Mehta TH, et al: Amyloid-beta protein dimers isolated directly from Alzheimer's brains impair synaptic plasticity and memory, *Nat Med* 14:837–842, 2008.

Sherrington R, Rogaev EI, Liang Y, et al: Cloning of a novel gene bearing missense mutations in early onset familial Alzheimer disease, *Nature* 375:754–760, 1995.

Shoji M, Golde TE, Ghiso J, et al: Production of the Alzheimer amyloid β protein by normal proteolytic processing, *Science* 258:126–129, 1992.

St George-Hyslop PH, Haines JL, Farrer LA, et al: Genetic linkage studies suggest that Alzheimer's disease is not a single homogeneous disorder, *Nature* 347:194–197, 1990.

Strittmatter WJ, Saunders AM, Schmechel D, et al: Apolipoprotein E: high-avidity binding to β-amyloid and increased frequency of type 4 allele in late-onset familial Alzheimer disease, *Proc Natl Acad Sci USA* 90: 1977–1981, 1993.

Suzuki N, Cheung TT, Cai X-D, et al: An increased percentage of long amyloid β protein secreted by familial amyloid β protein precursor (βAPP717) mutants, *Science* 264:1336–1340, 1994.

Tagliavini F, Giaccone G, Frangione B, et al: Preamyloid deposits in the cerebral cortex of patients with Alzheimer's disease and nondemented individuals, *Neurosci Lett* 93:191–196, 1988.

Tanzi RE, Gusella JF, Watkins PC, et al: Amyloid β-protein gene: cDNA, mRNA distribution, and genetic linkage near the Alzheimer locus, *Science* 235:880–884, 1987.

Vigo-Pelfrey C, Seubert P, Barbour R, et al: Elevation of microtubule-associated protein tau in the cerebrospinal fluid of patients with Alzheimer's disease, *Neurology* 45:788–793, 1995.

Villemagne VL, Burnham S, Bourgeat P, et al: Amyloid beta deposition, neurodegeneration, and cognitive decline in sporadic Alzheimer's disease: a prospective cohort study, *Lancet Neurol* 12:357–367, 2013.

Wang Y, Cella M, Mallinson K, et al: TREM2 lipid sensing sustains the microglial response in an Alzheimer's disease model, *Cell* 160:1061–1071, 2015.

Wischik CM, Novak M, Thogersen HC, et al: Isolation of a fragment of tau derived from the core of the paired helical filament of Alzheimer's disease, *Proc Natl Acad Sci USA* 85:4506–4510, 1988.

Wolfe MS, Xia W, Moore CL, et al: Peptidomimetic probes and molecular modeling suggest Alzheimer's γ-secretase is an intramembrane-cleaving aspartyl protease, *Biochemistry* 38:4720–4727, 1999a.

Wolfe MS, Xia W, Ostaszewski BL, et al: Two transmembrane aspartates in presenilin-1 required for presenilin endoproteolysis and γ-secretase activity, *Nature* 398:513–517, 1999b.

Wood JG, Mirra SS, Pollock NL, et al: Neurofibrillary tangles of Alzheimer's disease share antigenic determinants with the axonal microtubule-associated protein tau, *Proc Natl Acad Sci USA* 83:4040–4043, 1986.

Yamaguchi H, Hirai S, Morimatsu M, et al: Diffuse type of senile plaques in the brains of Alzheimer-type dementia, *Acta Neuropathol* 77:113–119, 1988.

Zhang B, Gaiteri C, Bodea LG, et al: Integrated systems approach identifies genetic nodes and networks in late-onset Alzheimer's disease, *Cell* 153:707–720, 2013.

Zhao Z, Sagare AP, Ma Q, et al: Central role for PICALM in amyloid-beta blood-brain barrier transcytosis and clearance, *Nat Neurosci* 18:978–987, 2015.

CHAPTER

2

The Genetic Basis of Alzheimer's Disease

B. Hooli, R.E. Tanzi

OUTLINE

BACKGROUND

Alzheimer's disease (AD) is the most common form of senile dementia. Broadly, the clinical symptoms of AD are characterized by progressive loss of memory and cognitive functions, dementia, and eventually death due to health complications. Postmortem neuropathological examination is the ultimate confirmation that distinguishes AD from other forms of dementia. The deposition of β-amyloid (Aβ) peptide aggregates in the form of extracellular or neuritic "plaques," crucial to initiating AD pathogenesis, and accumulation of hyperphosphorylated tau protein in the form of intracellular neurofibrillary "tangles" (NFTs) are the hallmark characteristics of postmortem AD brains. The increased synaptic load of Aβ aggregates and NFTs strongly correlates with neuronal dysfunction and disease progression (reviewed in Hooli and Tanzi, 2009). In fact, the original amyloid hypothesis proposed by George Glenner (Glenner and Wong, 1984) postulated that deposition of Aβ induces the tangles formation, eventually leading to loss of neurons, neuroinflammation, and dementia. Three decades later, Glenner's original "amyloidosis" hypothesis of AD was recently recapitulated in a 3D human

Developing Therapeutics for Alzheimer's Disease. http://dx.doi.org/10.1016/B978-0-12-802173-6.00002-2

neural culture system (Choi et al., 2014). In addition to Aβ and NFTs, there are other neuropathological signs that are reported in a subset of AD brains, including TDP-43 immunoreactivity, cerebral amyloid angiopathy (CAA), and white matter lesions (Dubois et al., 2014).

Advancing age is the biggest risk for AD, with every decade after 65 years of age doubling the risk for AD. Family history is the second strongest risk factor following age. Studies conducted over the past thirty years have illustrated that the genetic factors leading to AD are complex and heterogeneous, meaning AD risk is attributed to a complex interaction of heritable (eg, genetic) and nonheritable (eg, education, lifestyle) factors. Although environmental factors do affect AD risk, population and twin studies estimate that up to 80% of the AD cases are attributable to genetic risk factors (Gatz et al., 2006).

Traditionally, AD is classified into two dichotomous forms based on the age of onset and the associated genetic factors. The less prevalent early-onset familial form of AD (EOFAD, <5% of diagnosed AD cases, onset <60 years) is caused by the Mendelian mode of inheritance of highly penetrant, autosomal-dominant variants (n > 200 pathogenic mutations) in three genes: *APP*, *PSEN1*, and *PSEN2*. The identification and confirmation of these genes provided strong support for the "amyloid cascade hypothesis." APP is consecutively cleaved by β- and γ-secretases resulting in the Aβ peptide fragments. The majority of the known EOFAD mutations lie in the exons coding the Aβ peptide (exons 16 and 17 in *APP*) or in the presenilin genes (*PSEN1* and *PSEN2*) that are the catalytic components of the γ-secretase complex responsible for Aβ production. Functional studies on the role of pathogenic variants identified in *APP*, *PSEN1*, and *PSEN2* led to the understanding that quantitative increase in production of Aβ, and also qualitative changes to the Aβ peptides produced (Aβ42/Aβ40 ratio), cause EOFAD.

In contrast, the more predominantly diagnosed late-onset AD (LOAD, >90% of AD cases, onset age >60 years) is associated with numerous genetic risk factors that do not show obvious familial aggregation. The *APOE* gene remains the most well-established risk factor in LOAD, where the ε4 allele confers between 3.7-fold and 14-fold risk depending on the number of alleles present in the carrier (Farrer et al., 1997). The revelation of the role of APOE in AD (Corder et al., 1994; Kim et al., 2009a; Strittmatter et al., 1993) further strengthened the amyloid hypothesis by implicating the role of Aβ metabolism in AD. As a precautionary note, this broad dichotomization of early- and late-onset forms of AD is an overly simplistic perspective. Several cases of early-onset AD without Mendelian transmission of genetic risk have been reported, whereas, conversely, strong familial clustering is also observed in LOAD.

Overall, although twin and population studies estimate heritability in AD as high as 80%, the four aforementioned genes explain roughly 30–50% of heritability in AD (Bertram and Tanzi, 2012). Most important, these early genetic findings were crucial to elucidating the underlying molecular mechanism (ie, role of Aβ metabolism) in AD pathogenesis. Identification of the hitherto unknown AD genes not only will explain the missing heritability, but also will be key to revealing novel disease mechanisms, and eventually will provide new drug targets to treat this disastrous disease in the elderly.

In the past 8 years or so, about 30 additional AD genetic loci have been reported in more than a dozen GWAS carried out in multiple large study cohorts. The novel AD-GWAS genes are associated with a number of neurodegenerative pathways (Table 2.1), including Aβ production, aggregation and clearance, and tangle formation, as well as adaptive and innate immunity pathways related to neuroinflammation.

TABLE 2.1 List of Genes that are Implicated in the Pathogenesis of Early- and Late-Onset Forms of AD

Gene	Location	Marker	OR 95% CI	Possible disease pathways
EOFAD genes				
APP	21q21.3	—	—	Aβ related
PSEN1	14q24.2	—	—	Aβ related
PSEN2	1q42.13	—	—	Aβ related
AD GWAS confirmed				
APOE	19q13.32	ε4 allele	3.7–14	Aβ related
CR1	1q32.2	rs6656401	1·09–1·30	Immune response
MS4A4A and MS4A6A	11q12.2	rs983392	0.87–0.92	Immune response
PICALM	11q14.2	rs10792832	0.85–0.89	Aβ related
SORL1	11q24.1	rs11218343	0.72–0.82	Aβ related
FERMT2	14q22.1	rs17125944	1.09–1.19	Tangles related
DSG2	18q12.1	rs8093731	0.62–0.86	Aβ related; tangles related
ABCA7	19p13.3	rs4147929	1.11–1.19	Aβ related; immune response
CD33	19q13.41	rs3865444	0.91–0.96	Aβ related; immune response
BIN1	2q14.3	rs6733839	1.18–1.25	Aβ related; tangles related
INPP5D	2q37.1	rs35349669	1.05–1.11	Immune response
CASS4	20q13.31	rs7274581	0.84–0.92	Immune response
MEF2C	5q14.3	rs190982	0.90–0.95	Immune response
CD2AP	6p12.3	rs10948363	1.07–1.13	Immune response
NME8	7p14.1	rs2718058	0.90–0.95	Immune response
ZCWPW1 and NYAP1	7q22.1	rs1476679	0.89–0.94	Immune response
EPHA1	7q35	rs11771145	0.88–0.93	Immune response
CLU	8p21.1	rs9331896	0.84–0.89	Aβ related
TREM2	6p21.1	rs75932628	1.4–2.71	Immune response
AD GWAS suggestive				
DLGAP1	18p11.31	—	—	Aβ related
ECHDC3	10p14	rs7920721	1.04–1.11	Aβ related
AP2A2	11p15.5	rs10751667	0.90–0.96	Aβ related

(Continued)

TABLE 2.1 List of Genes that are Implicated in the Pathogenesis of Early- and Late-Onset Forms of AD (*cont.*)

Gene	Location	Marker	OR 95% CI	Possible disease pathways
CELF1	11p11.2	rs10838725	1.05–1.11	Aβ related; tangles related
ADAMTS20	12q12	rs7295246	1.03–1.10	Aβ related
RIN3	14q32.12	rs10498633	0.88–0.94	Aβ related
IGHV1-67	14q32.33	rs2011167	1.08–1.1	Immune response
SPPL2A	15q21.2	rs8035452	0.91–0.97	Immune response
TRIP4	15q22.31	rs74615166	1.22–1.61	Immune response
SCIMP	17p13.2	rs7225151	1.06–1.17	Immune response
ACE	17q23.3	rs1800764	0.68–0.92	Aβ related; immune response
HS3ST1	4p15.33	rs6448799	1.04–1.12	Aβ related
SQSTM1	5q35.3	rs72807343	1.15–1.58	Aβ related; immune response
ATXN1	6p22.3	rs179943	—	Aβ related
TP53INP1	8q22.1	rs1713669	1.06–1.1	Aβ related; immune response
AD functional candidate genes				
ADAM10	15q21.3	—	—	Aβ related
GGA3	17q25.1	—	—	Aβ related
TREML2	6p21.1	rs3747742	0.86–0.97	Aβ related; immune response
NRXN1	2p16.3	—	—	Aβ related; immune response
NRXN2	11q13.1	—	—	Aβ related; immune response
NRXN3	14q24.3	—	—	Aβ related; immune response

GENETICS OF EARLY-ONSET FAMILIAL AD

EOFAD is an autosomal-dominant, Mendelian form of the disease that appears in multiple first-degree relatives in the carrier families over generations. According to a recent report, up to 250,000 individuals are estimated to be currently afflicted with EOFAD in the United States (http://www.alz.org). The age of the disease onset is consistently before the age 60~65 years, and in some rare cases is also diagnosed below the age of 40 years (Acosta-Baena et al., 2011). More than 200 pathogenic variants in three genes, *APP* (Chr 21q21), *PSEN1* (14q24.2), and its homolog, *PSEN2* (1q42.13), are known to cause EOFAD (Bird, 2008; Campion et al., 1999; Cruts et al., 2012a; Rocca et al., 1991). The pathogenic mutations in these three genes cause EOFAD by altering the production or the rate of aggregation of the neurotoxic Aβ peptides. Mechanistically, full-length APP undergoes cleavage into a number of peptide fragments through a series of proteolytic cleavages by α-, β-, and γ-secretase. The majority of APP undergoes nonamyloidogenic processing via consecutive cleavage by α- and γ-secretases within the Aβ domain, resulting in nonpathogenic fragments, sAPPα, and C-terminal fragments (CTFs) (Gong et al., 2010; Vetrivel and Thinakaran, 2006). APP also undergoes sequential proteolytic cleavage by β- and γ-secretases to generate Aβ peptides as well as sAPPβ and CTF. The role of Aβ leading to AD was first proposed in 1984 (Glenner and Wong, 1984). The authors hypothesized that AD is a "cerebral amyloidosis" in which cerebral β-amyloid triggers the disease process and subsequent dementia. This cerebral amyloidosis thesis was later reinterpreted and reported as the "amyloid cascade hypothesis" of AD (Glenner and Wong, 1984; Hardy and Higgins, 1992; Tanzi and Bertram, 2005).

Following the amyloidosis theory, and taking into consideration the observation of Aβ in the AD brains as well as the trisomy of chromosome 21 (Down syndrome) patients showing AD symptoms, APP was isolated and mapped to chromosome 21 (Goldgaber et al., 1987; Kang et al., 1987; Tanzi et al., 1987a,b). The first pathogenic mutation in APP was identified in Dutch hereditary cerebral hemorrhage with amyloidosis in 1990 by analyzing exons 16 and 17 in the *APP* gene (exons coding the Aβ peptide; Levy et al., 1990). In the following year, resequencing the same exons in the AD families linked to the APP locus on chromosome 21 then led to the first EOFAD mutation (Goate et al., 1991). Numerous other studies since then have identified more than 30 pathogenic variants in *APP* to date causing 10–15% of the EOFAD cases (Hooli et al., 2012). Recently, a rare protective variant in APP, A673T, was reported in Icelandic and Finnish study subjects that confers resilience against dementia (Kero et al., 2013; Maloney et al., 2014), which is probably limited to members of the two populations from the original study (Bamne et al., 2014; Wang et al., 2015). Furthermore, apart from genomic structural variants (SVs) reported in the APP locus (APP gene duplication <1% of EOFAD cases), a comprehensive SV analysis of the genomes of AD patients is not yet available, owing mainly to technical difficulties (Hooli et al., 2014a; Tattini et al., 2015).

However, it was clear in the wake of the discovery of AD mutations in the *APP* gene that most of the EOFAD cases were not sufficiently explained, indicating the presence of other risk genes. Positional cloning of two other chromosomal loci for EOFAD, chromosome 14q24.3 (Schellenberg et al., 1992) and chromosome 1q42.13 (Levy-Lahad et al., 1995b), led to the identification of *PSEN1* and the highly homologous *PSEN2* genes with pathogenic mutations (Levy-Lahad et al., 1995a; Sherrington et al., 1995). The two presenilin genes are structurally similar integral membrane proteins that contain nine transmembrane domains with a hydrophilic intracellular loop region. The presenilins, together with nicastrin (*NCSTN*), anterior pharynx-defective-1 (*APH-1*), and presenilin enhancer 2 (*PEN2*) genes, encode the γ-secretase complex that cleaves a number of vital cell membrane proteins in addition to APP. For example, *Notch* is another γ-secretase substrate and is crucial in developmental stages (Donoviel et al., 1999; Wakabayashi and De Strooper, 2008); hence, the PSEN1 and PSEN2 double knockout is embryonically lethal in mice. Both presenilin proteins primarily localize in the endoplasmic reticulum (ER) and Golgi apparatus (De Strooper, 2003; Hansson et al., 2004; Kovacs et al., 1996), although mature, proteolytically active forms of these proteins are also found at the cell surface and in endosomes, and are key to the APP processing pathways. The *PSEN1* gene contains the most EOFAD variants (~200, 40–80% of the known EOFAD variants), while 14 pathogenic variants are reported in *PSEN2* (<5%) (Bagyinszky et al., 2014; Cruts et al., 2012a,b). Taken together, these three currently known EOFAD genes explain less than 50% of the Mendelian forms of AD, while the rest of the pathogenetic factors leading to EOFAD still remain to be determined. Interestingly, although the roles of the pathogenic variants in *APP* and the presenilin genes in EOFAD are well established, there are no confirmed reports of risk-conferring genetic variants in these three genes leading to LOAD (Hooli et al., 2012). This is remarkably different from the genes associated with other neurodegenerative disorders, such as Parkinson's disease (PD) or frontotemporal lobe dementia (FTLD), in which genes carrying rare pathogenic mutations causing Mendelian disease forms also show presence for variants that modulate susceptibility to the late-onset forms (Lill and Bertram, 2011).

GENETICS OF LATE-ONSET AD

The majority of the diagnosed AD cases (>95%) fall under the late-onset form of AD (LOAD), with the age of onset >65 years. In contrast to the genetics of EOFAD caused by autosomal-dominant pathogenic variants showing a Mendelian inheritance mode, LOAD is attributed to genetically complex and heterogeneous variants that modify disease susceptibility depending on the environmental factors and lifestyles of the individuals. The *e4* allele in the apolipoprotein E (*APOE*) (19q13.32) gene remains the most established genetic risk factor in LOAD. The risk effect of *APOE-e4* (~4- to 15-fold) has been consistently replicated in a large number of study cohorts from different ethnic groups. There are at least three major alleles in the *APOE* gene corresponding to combinations of two amino acid changes at residues 112 (rs429358) and 158 (rs7412): *e2* (Cys112/Cys158), *e3* (Cys112/Arg158), and *e4* (Arg112/Arg158). The most commonly occurring *e3* allele is present in more than half of the general population (up to 70%). Unlike the EOFAD genetic variants discussed previously, the *APOE-e4* risk allele confers risk by decreasing the age of onset in a dose-dependent manner; that is, the age of onset in the homozygous carriers is much lower than in the patients who are heterozygous for the *e4* allele. Recent studies have reported the presence of rare coding variants in *APOE* that confer risk for AD (Kamboh et al., 1999; Medway et al., 2014) but that still require confirmation from additional studies. Variants in the regulatory regions that alter APOE expression have also been found in mouse models (Bien-Ly et al., 2012; Kim et al., 2011) that lead to AD pathology by reducing plaque clearance.

Functionally, *APOE* encodes a pleiotropic glycoprotein, which is a major component of very low-density lipoproteins (VLDLs). APOE is expressed in liver, brain, and macrophages (Siest et al., 1995) and is associated with cholesterol transport pathways (Mahley and Rall, 2000). The functional consequences of APOE in AD pathogenesis are not fully obvious (Holtzman et al., 2012; Michaelson, 2014). The *APOE-e4* allele predisposes patients to vascular disease as a result of its association with increased plasma cholesterol levels (Huang, 2010) and regulates Aβ metabolism in conjunction with low-density lipoproteins (Verghese et al., 2013). In the brains of transgenic AD mice, cholesterol has also been shown to both increase Aβ production and stabilize the peptide (Kim et al., 2009b). Therefore, APOE-e4 could potentially increase AD risk via hypercholesterolemia through its influence on Aβ clearance (Castellano et al., 2011; Kanekiyo et al., 2014). APOE-e4 binds to Aβ more fervently than does APOE-e3, which leads to increased fibril formation (Hauser and Ryan, 2013; Stratman et al., 2005). Overall, the majority of data suggests that APOE contributes to LOAD risk through the Aβ metabolism pathway (Liu et al., 2013).

COMMON VARIANTS ASSOCIATED WITH LATE-ONSET AD BEYOND *APOE*

Linkage analysis in families afflicted with AD, followed by positional cloning (ie, systematic mutation screening of the genes in the linked genetic locus), led to the identification of the three EOFAD genes (*APP*, *PSEN1*, and *PSEN2*). *APOE* was identified as a LOAD susceptibility gene by using a "candidate gene" approach to analyze genes in the chromosome 19 region linked to LOAD. The candidate gene approach was used to cherry-pick or prioritize genes for investigating disease-associated variants based on the prior hypothesis on their functional role in the disease pathogenesis. Due to this early success, the search for missing heritability in LOAD beyond *APOE* using the same candidate gene approach resulted in the analyses of close to 700 different genes (resulting in ~1500 reports) over a decade. Numerous replications and refutations (http://www.alzgene.org, reviewed in Bertram and Tanzi, 2008) were published over a decade or so, but failed to reveal any novel AD genes. One of the most common obstacles in conducting AD genetic studies is having to rely on the reported "disease state" of the subjects based on psychiatric evaluation. The ultimate "definite" diagnosis of AD is possible only based on postmortem neuropathological examination, and hence a significant number of patients with other forms of dementia (eg, FTLD) also were included in the AD study cohorts. In addition, complete details of family history are almost impossible to collect since a majority of AD diagnosis takes place in older people (>65 years of age), by which time the close family members may not have survived. Therefore, it is critical to define the precise taxonomy of the disease phenotype grouped as AD using detailed information from various features, including clinical, imaging, and histological data for a more reliable association of AD subclinical phenotypes with the root genetic factors. Furthermore, accounting for the environmental and epigenetic factors that most likely contribute to disease onset is currently not possible, owing to technical difficulties in data ascertainment (Traynor and Singleton, 2010).

Nonetheless, the more recent results coming from several large GWAS and metaanalyses conducted in AD have revealed several novel genes in LOAD. While only a handful of genetic markers were utilized in the linkage and candidate gene studies, the availability of high-throughput and affordable oligonucleotide arrays made it amenable to perform a simultaneous evaluation of millions of single nucleotide polymorphisms (SNPs) routinely in thousands of samples in a typical GWAS. The SNP probes on the arrays not only are optimized to provide reliable genotypes, but also tag additional common variants in the adjacent linkage-disequilibrium (LD) region, thus making it possible to perform an unbiased genome-wide examination for association of genetic markers with the disease phenotype. In 2006 when the first wave of GWAS reports came in, GWAS was considered to hold immense potential in explaining the rest of the missing heritability of many human disorders, including AD (Thomas, 2006). The National Human Genome Research Institute (NHGRI) catalog features more than 14,000 GWAS of a variety of traits in humans to date (http://www.ebi.ac.uk).

In LOAD, more than a dozen GWAS have been reported to date implicating close to 30 different genetic loci. Some of the genes that either encompass AD GWAS markers or are in close proximity to them include (Table 2.1): triggering receptor expressed on myeloid cells 2 (*TREM2*), bridging integrator 1 (*BIN1*), clusterin (*CLU*), ATP-binding cassette transporter (*ABCA7*), complement receptor 1 (*CR1*), phosphatidylinositol binding clathrin assembly protein (*PICALM*), membrane-spanning 4A gene cluster (*MS4A4A, MS4A6A, MS4A6E*), sialic acid-binding immunoglobulin (Ig)-like lectin (*CD33*), CD2-associated protein (*CD2AP*), sortilin-related receptor (*SORL1*), fermitin family member 2 (*FERMT2*), desmoglein 2 (*DSG2*), inositol polyphosphate-5-phosphatase (*INPP5D*), Cas scaffolding protein family member 4 (*CASS4*), myocyte enhancer factor 2C (*MEF2C*), NME/NM23 family member 8 (*NME8*), CW type with PWWP domain 1 (*ZCWPW1*), ephrin receptor A1 (*EPHA1*), major histocompatibility complex, class II, DR beta (*HLA-DRB1/HLA-DRB5*), protein tyrosine kinase 2 beta (*PTK2B*), CUGBP, Elav-like family member 1 (*CELF1*), and Ras and Rab interactor 3 (*RIN3*) (Abraham et al., 2008; Beecham et al., 2009; Bertram et al., 2008; Coon et al., 2007; Grupe et al., 2007; Guerreiro et al., 2013; Harold et al., 2009; Heinzen et al., 2010; Hollingworth et al., 2011; Jonsson et al., 2013; Lambert et al., 2009, 2013; Li et al., 2008; Naj et al., 2011; Seshadri et al., 2010).

The AD GWAS era started in 2007 with publication of three GWAS using AD cases and elderly nondemented controls (Coon et al., 2007; Grupe et al., 2007; Li et al., 2008), but failed to reveal novel AD genetic loci beyond *APOE* that showed genome-wide significance. In 2008, family-based association analysis using the National Institute of Mental Health (NIMH) AD initiative study cohort (~1500 subjects from 450 families) was the first study to reveal novel AD susceptibility loci showing genome-wide significance beyond *APOE* (Bertram et al., 2008). The authors reported SNPs showing significant association in three genes that conferred risk for LOAD: ataxin 1 (*ATXN1*), *CD33*, and an uncharacterized locus on chromosome 14 (GWA_14q31.2), in addition to a highly suggestive association in the disks large-associated protein 1 (*DLGAP1*) gene. The following year, two large case–control GWAS identified three new AD genes, *CLU, CR1*, and *PICALM*, showing association with the disease (Harold et al., 2009; Lambert et al., 2009). Variants in the gene *BIN1* were reported in 2010 (Seshadri et al., 2010), which had previously failed to attain genome-wide significance in an earlier study (Lambert et al., 2009). In 2011, two large case–control studies reported variants in four additional genes that showed significant association with LOAD, including *CD2AP, MS4A6A/MS4A4E, EPHA1*, and *ABCA7* (Hollingworth et al., 2011; Naj et al., 2011). *EPHA1* gene variants reached genome-wide significance in this latter study, having failed to reach significance after corrections for multiple testing in an earlier study (Seshadri et al. 2010). Moreover, previously unreported *CD33* variants that showed protective effect in LOAD were reported in these studies—in contrast to the first report on the *CD33* variants (Bertram et al., 2008), where the associated SNP increased risk for LOAD. In 2013, a large metaanalysis of GWAS results involving 74,046 subjects from four large consortia was reported in AD (Lambert et al., 2013). In addition to demonstrating the inarguably strong association of the *APOE-ε4* allele in LOAD and confirming eight previously reported AD GWAS loci, 12 novel genetic loci showing association with LOAD were described in this study (*CASS4, CELF1, DSG2, FERMT2, HLA-DRB5-DBR1, INPP5D, MEF2C, NME8, PTK2B, SLC24H4-RIN3, SORL1*, and *ZCWPW1*) (Lambert et al., 2013).

Overall, the unbiased GWAS conducted in AD have been fruitful in identifying robust, novel risk loci in LOAD, demonstrating a much higher success rate than in the candidate gene era. However, it should be noted that the new AD loci identified in the GWAS explain a small fraction of the missing heritability in AD; the proportion of heritability including the combined effects of *APOE* and the GWAS loci most likely still explains <50% of genetic risk variants in LOAD. The rare susceptibility alleles in AD most likely still remain to be identified since the highly polymorphic markers on the GWAS array do not sufficiently tag rare SNPs. In addition, almost all the GWAS conducted in AD to date did not take into account genomic SVs, including gene deletions/duplications/inversions and large genomic rearrangements. Moreover, the effect size indicated by the odds ratios (ORs) of most of the AD GWAS-derived variants is considerably small (around 10–15%) compared to *APOE-e4* (OR between 3.7 and ~14), or the GWAS markers associated with other neurodegenerative diseases (>>2- to ~3-fold risk) (Manolio et al., 2009). Consequently, the GWAS genetic markers would not be useful in a clinical or diagnostic setting for preventive genetic testing either. Moreover, the functional variants in the GWAS genes that lead to AD are not known (Swerdlow and Corder, 2012). Therefore, most GWAS-derived AD gene candidates should be considered temporary until more in-depth genetic and functional studies provide further insight into the role of the genetic variants in AD pathogenesis.

FUNCTIONAL ROLE OF THE GWAS SUSCEPTIBILITY GENES IN AD

Although the exact functional mechanisms of the GWAS genes leading to LOAD are not known, a number of neuronal pathways are speculated to be affected that eventually lead to LOAD. Many of the pathways have been previously studied in AD, and generally the AD GWAS genes are proposed to affect at least one of the following pathways: inflammatory response (eg, *CLU, CR1, ABCA7, CD33, EPHA1, HLA*-genes, *INPP5D, TREM2*) (Griciuc et al., 2013; Tanzi, 2015), lipid metabolism pathway (*APOE, CLU,* and *ABCA7*), synaptic function (*PICALM, BIN1, CD33, MEF2C, CD2AP, PTK2B*), endocytosis (*PICALM, BIN1, CD33, CD2AP*), APP metabolism and amyloidogenesis (*CLU, PICALM, BIN1,* and *CD2AP*), and tau pathobiology (*BIN1, CELF1, NME8, CASS4, FERMT2*). Several of these GWAS susceptibility loci in LOAD are present in gene-dense regions, and consequently the genes that might be functionally involved in LOAD remain unclear. Please refer to (Hooli and Tanzi, 2016) for a detailed review of the potential functional role of the GWAS genes leading to LOAD.

RARE VARIANTS LEADING TO LATE-ONSET AD

A disintegrin and metallopeptidase domain 10 (*ADAM10*) was the first gene to be reported to carry two rare pathogenic variants in seven families showing onset of AD at an average age of 70 years (Kim et al., 2009). *ADAM10* encodes the major α-secretase in the brain (Endres and Fahrenholz, 2012), which cleaves the APP ectodomain to preclude Aβ production (Jorissen et al., 2010; Kuhn et al., 2010; Postina et al., 2004). The two ADAM10 LOAD mutations, Q170H and R181G, are located in the prodomain region and significantly impair the ability of ADAM10 to carry out α-secretase cleavage of APP, resulting in elevated

Aβ deposition (Suh et al., 2013). Variants in 5′-UTR of ADAM10 have also been implicated in posttranscriptional regulation of ADAM10 expression that consequently alter Aβ production (Lammich et al., 2010).

More recently, a rare coding SNP (rs75932628) in the *TREM2* gene, resulting in the missense coding change of arginine to histidine at position 47, has consistently shown increased LOAD risk across multiple studies (Benitez et al., 2013; Hooli et al., 2014b; Lill et al., 2015; Pottier et al., 2013). Originally found in the Icelandic population (Jonsson et al., 2013), and later in an international cohort of European population (Guerreiro et al., 2013), metaanalysis of TREM2-R47H shows the second largest effect size (2-fold increase in risk), following the *APOE-e4* allele, in LOAD (Hooli et al., 2014b). Previously, homozygous TREM2 R47H had been detected in patients afflicted with Nasu-Hakola disease, a polycystic lipomembranous osteodysplasia with sclerosing leukoencephalopathy (PLOSL) (Bianchin et al., 2004; Paloneva et al., 1993, 2003) with progressive frontal-type dementia (Bock et al., 2013; Neumann and Takahashi, 2007). Heterozygous R47H carriers have also been associated with other forms of neurodegenerative diseases, but conclusive evidence is not yet available (Lill et al., 2015).

Overall, although variants arising from GWAS have implicated several promising novel loci in LOAD, the rare functional variants identified in the AD patients have provided targets more amenable for in vitro and in vivo studies (Endres and Fahrenholz, 2012; Hickman and El Khoury, 2014; Hsieh et al., 2009; Lue et al., 2015; Suh et al., 2013), and consequently may lead to meaningful targets for development of therapeutic strategies in AD.

SUMMARY AND FUTURE

More than 200 highly penetrant pathogenic mutations in the three genes, *APP*, *PSEN1*, and *PSEN2*, cause the Mendelian form of early-onset familial AD. The genetic factors leading to late-onset AD are complex and heterogeneous. Genome-wide association studies conducted over the past 8 years have revealed several common genetic variants in more than ~30 different genomic loci showing association with AD, but with modest effects on risk. In addition, although the recent GWAS have revealed compelling new genetic loci in AD, the actual disease-causing genetic variants are yet to be determined. Genome-wide agnostic studies utilizing the next-generation sequencing technology will be the next logical step to identify and catalog the functional variants in the AD genetic loci that actually lead to the disease phenotype in affected carriers. The identification of functional variants will be key to explaining a significant proportion of the missing heritability in AD that still remains to be described.

The AD genes identified in the genetic studies to date have been fundamental to our current understanding of the molecular pathways leading to AD. The novel GWAS loci associated with LOAD in recent years are predicted to affect normal functioning of a wide range of molecular pathways, including APP metabolism and β-amyloid deposition, tangle formation, and neuroinflammation. Therefore the identification of the actual disease-causing variants will be vital to understanding the precise disease mechanism in the affected AD patient, which may ultimately lead to devising effective treatment strategies. For example, in mid- to late-stage AD patients, it may be too late to only treat β-amyloid deposition, which occurs decades prior to the clinical symptoms. Hence prescribing the right therapeutic interventions at the diagnosed stage of the disease, from prodromal asymptomatic accrual of β-amyloid to late-stage disease, in which neuroinflammation is likely to be doing most of the damage, should be a more effective treatment strategy. Identifying genetic targets such as the ones described here is the first step toward devising accurate and effective therapeutic strategies aimed at treatment and prevention of this devastating disease.

Acknowledgments

We thank all the AD patients and their families whose trust, help, and participation in the studies were crucial to making all the research summarized in this review possible. We are grateful for funding from the NIMH, NIA, Cure Alzheimer's Fund, and JPB Foundation.

References

Abraham R, Moskvina V, Sims R, Hollingworth P, Morgan A, Georgieva L, Kirov G: A genome-wide association study for late-onset Alzheimer's disease using DNA pooling, *BMC Med Genomics* 1:44, 2008.

Acosta-Baena N, Sepulveda-Falla D, Lopera-Gomez CM, Jaramillo-Elorza MC, Moreno S, Aguirre-Acevedo DC, Lopera F: Pre-dementia clinical stages in presenilin 1 E280A familial early-onset Alzheimer's disease: a retrospective cohort study, *Lancet Neurol 10*(3):213–220, 2011.

Bagyinszky E, Youn YC, An SS, Kim S: The genetics of Alzheimer's disease, *Clin Interv Aging* 9:535–551, 2014.

Bamne MN, Demirci FY, Berman S, Snitz BE, Rosenthal SL, Wang X, Kamboh MI: Investigation of an amyloid precursor protein protective mutation (A673T) in a North American case-control sample of late-onset Alzheimer's disease, *Neurobiol Aging* 35(7):1779.e15–e16, 2014.

Beecham GW, Martin ER, Li YJ, Slifer MA, Gilbert JR, Haines JL, Pericak-Vance MA: Genome-wide association study implicates a chromosome 12 risk locus for late-onset Alzheimer disease, *Am J Hum Genet* 84(1):35–43, 2009.

Benitez BA, Cooper B, Pastor P, Jin SC, Lorenzo E, Cervantes S, Cruchaga C: TREM2 is associated with the risk of Alzheimer's disease in Spanish population, *Neurobiol Aging* 34(6):1711.e15–e17, 2013.

Bertram L, Lange C, Mullin K, Parkinson M, Hsiao M, Hogan MF, Tanzi RE: Genome-wide association analysis reveals putative Alzheimer's disease susceptibility loci in addition to APOE, *Am J Hum Genet 83*(5): 623–632, 2008.

Bertram L, Tanzi RE: Thirty years of Alzheimer's disease genetics: the implications of systematic meta-analyses, *Nat Rev Neurosci* 9(10):768–778, 2008.

Bertram L, Tanzi RE: The genetics of Alzheimer's disease, *Prog Mol Biol Transl Sci* 107:79–100, 2012.

Bianchin MM, Capella HM, Chaves DL, Steindel M, Grisard EC, Ganev GG, Sakamoto AC: Nasu-Hakola disease (polycystic lipomembranous osteodysplasia with sclerosing leukoencephalopathy—PLOSL): a dementia associated with bone cystic lesions; from clinical to genetic and molecular aspects, *Cell Mol Neurobiol 24*(1):1–24, 2004.

Bien-Ly N, Gillespie AK, Walker D, Yoon SY, Huang Y: Reducing human apolipoprotein E levels attenuates age-dependent Abeta accumulation in mutant human amyloid precursor protein transgenic mice, *J Neurosci* 32(14):4803–4811, 2012.

Bird TD: Genetic aspects of Alzheimer disease, *Genet Med* 10(4):231–239, 2008.

Bock V, Botturi A, Gaviani P, Lamperti E, Maccagnano C, Piccio L, Salmaggi A: Polycystic lipomembranous osteodysplasia with sclerosing leukoencephalopathy (PLOSL): a new report of an Italian woman and review of the literature, *J Neurol Sci* 326(1–2):115–119, 2013.

Campion D, Dumanchin C, Hannequin D, Dubois B, Belliard S, Puel M, Frebourg T: Early-onset autosomal dominant Alzheimer disease: prevalence, genetic heterogeneity, and mutation spectrum, *Am J Hum Genet* 65(3): 664–670, 1999.

Castellano JM, Kim J, Stewart FR, Jiang H, DeMattos RB, Patterson BW, Holtzman DM: Human apoE isoforms differentially regulate brain amyloid-beta peptide clearance, *Sci Transl Med* 3(89): 89ra57, 2011.

Choi SH, Kim YH, Hebisch M, Sliwinski C, Lee S, D'Avanzo C, Kim DY: A three-dimensional human neural cell culture model of Alzheimer's disease, *Nature* 515(7526):274–278, 2014.

Coon KD, Myers AJ, Craig DW, Webster JA, Pearson JV, Lince DH, Stephan DA: A high-density whole-genome association study reveals that APOE is the major susceptibility gene for sporadic late-onset Alzheimer's disease, *J Clin Psychiatry* 68(4):613–618, 2007.

Corder EH, Saunders AM, Risch NJ, Strittmatter WJ, Schmechel DE, Gaskell PC, Jr, et al: Protective effect of apolipoprotein E type 2 allele for late onset Alzheimer disease, *Nat Genet* 7(2):180–184, 1994.

Cruts M, Theuns J, Broeckhoven CV: AD&FTD mutation database, 2012a. http://www.molgen.vib-ua.be/ADMutations

Cruts M, Theuns J, Van Broeckhoven C: Locus-specific mutation databases for neurodegenerative brain diseases, *Hum Mutat* 33(9):1340–1344, 2012b.

De Strooper B: Aph-1, Pen-2, and nicastrin with presenilin generate an active gamma-secretase complex, *Neuron* 38(1):9–12, 2003.

Donoviel DB, Hadjantonakis AK, Ikeda M, Zheng H, Hyslop PS, Bernstein A: Mice lacking both presenilin genes exhibit early embryonic patterning defects, *Genes Dev* 13(21):2801–2810, 1999.

Dubois B, Feldman HH, Jacova C, Hampel H, Molinuevo JL, Blennow K, Cummings JL: Advancing research diagnostic criteria for Alzheimer's disease: the IWG-2 criteria, *Lancet Neurol* 13(6):614–629, 2014.

Endres K, Fahrenholz F: Regulation of alpha-secretase ADAM10 expression and activity, *Exp Brain Res* 217(3–4): 343–352, 2012.

Farrer LA, Cupples LA, Haines JL, Hyman B, Kukull WA, Mayeux R, van Duijn CM: Effects of age, sex, and ethnicity on the association between apolipoprotein E genotype and Alzheimer disease: a meta-analysis. APOE and Alzheimer Disease Meta Analysis Consortium, *JAMA* 278(16):1349–1356, 1997.

Gatz M, Reynolds CA, Fratiglioni L, Johansson B, Mortimer JA, Berg S, Pedersen NL: Role of genes and environments for explaining Alzheimer disease, *Arch Gen Psychiatry* 63(2):168–174, 2006.

Glenner GG, Wong CW: Alzheimer's disease and Down's syndrome: sharing of a unique cerebrovascular amyloid fibril protein, *Biochem Biophys Res Commun* 122(3):1131–1135, 1984.

Goate A, Chartier-Harlin MC, Mullan M, Brown J, Crawford F, Fidani L, et al: Segregation of a missense mutation in the amyloid precursor protein gene with familial Alzheimer's disease, *Nature* 349(6311):704–706, 1991.

Goldgaber D, Lerman MI, McBride OW, Saffiotti U, Gajdusek DC: Characterization and chromosomal localization of a cDNA encoding brain amyloid of Alzheimer's disease, *Science* 235(4791):877–880, 1987.

Gong P, Vetrivel KS, Nguyen PD, Meckler X, Cheng H, Kounnas MZ, Thinakaran G: Mutation analysis of the presenilin 1 N-terminal domain reveals a broad spectrum of gamma-secretase activity toward amyloid precursor protein and other substrates, *J Biol Chem* 285(49):38042–38052, 2010.

Griciuc A, Serrano-Pozo A, Parrado AR, Lesinski AN, Asselin CN, Mullin K, Tanzi RE: Alzheimer's disease risk gene CD33 inhibits microglial uptake of amyloid beta, *Neuron* 78(4):631–643, 2013.

Grupe A, Abraham R, Li Y, Rowland C, Hollingworth P, Morgan A, Williams J: Evidence for novel susceptibility genes for late-onset Alzheimer's disease from a genome-wide association study of putative functional variants, *Hum Mol Genet* 16(8):865–873, 2007.

Guerreiro R, Wojtas A, Bras J, Carrasquillo M, Rogaeva E, Majounie E, et al: TREM2 variants in Alzheimer's disease, *N Engl J Med* 368(2):117–127, 2013.

Hansson CA, Frykman S, Farmery MR, Tjernberg LO, Nilsberth C, Pursglove SE, Ankarcrona M: Nicastrin, presenilin, APH-1, and PEN-2 form active gamma-secretase complexes in mitochondria, *J Biol Chem* 279(49): 51654–51660, 2004.

Hardy JA, Higgins GA: Alzheimer's disease: the amyloid cascade hypothesis, *Science* 256(5054):184–185, 1992.

Harold D, Abraham R, Hollingworth P, Sims R, Gerrish A, Hamshere ML, Williams J: Genome-wide association study identifies variants at CLU and PICALM associated with Alzheimer's disease, *Nat Genet* 41(10): 1088–1093, 2009.

Hauser PS, Ryan RO: Impact of apolipoprotein E on Alzheimer's disease, *Curr Alzheimer Res* 10(8):809–817, 2013.

Heinzen EL, Need AC, Hayden KM, Chiba-Falek O, Roses AD, Strittmatter WJ, Goldstein DB: Genome-wide scan of copy number variation in late-onset Alzheimer's disease, *J Alzheimers Dis* 19(1):69–77, 2010.

Hickman SE, El Khoury J: TREM2 and the neuroimmunology of Alzheimer's disease, *Biochem Pharmacol* 88(4): 495–498, 2014.

Hollingworth P, Harold D, Sims R, Gerrish A, Lambert JC, Carrasquillo MM, Williams J: Common variants at ABCA7, MS4A6A/MS4A4E, EPHA1, CD33 and CD2AP are associated with Alzheimer's disease, *Nat Genet* 43(5):429–435, 2011.

Holtzman DM, Herz J, Bu G: Apolipoprotein E and apolipoprotein E receptors: normal biology and roles in Alzheimer disease, *Cold Spring Harb Perspect Med* 2(3):a006312, 2012.

Hooli B, Tanzi RE: *The Genetic Basis of Alzheimer's Disease: findings from genome-wide studies. Genomics, circuits, and pathways in clinical neuropsychiatry*, 1st Edition, Academic Press, 2016.

Hooli BV, Kovacs-Vajna ZM, Mullin K, Blumenthal MA, Mattheisen M, Zhang C, Tanzi, RE: Rare autosomal copy number variations in early-onset familial Alzheimer's disease, *Mol Psychiatry* 19(6):676–681, 2014a.

Hooli BV, Mohapatra G, Mattheisen M, Parrado AR, Roehr JT, Shen Y, Bertram L: Role of common and rare APP DNA sequence variants in Alzheimer disease, *Neurology* 78(16):1250–1257, 2012.

Hooli BV, Parrado AR Mullin K, Yip WK, Liu T, Roehr JT, Tanzi RE: The rare TREM2 R47H variant exerts only a modest effect on Alzheimer disease risk, *Neurology* 83(15):1353–1358, 2014b.

Hooli BV, Tanzi RE: A current view of Alzheimer's disease, *F1000 Biol Rep* 1:54, 2009.

Hsieh CL, Koike M, Spusta SC, Niemi EC, Yenari M, Nakamura MC, Seaman WE: A role for TREM2 ligands in the phagocytosis of apoptotic neuronal cells by microglia, *J Neurochem* 109(4):1144–1156, 2009.

Huang Y: Mechanisms linking apolipoprotein E isoforms with cardiovascular and neurological diseases, *Curr Opin Lipidol* 21(4):337–345, 2010.

Jonsson T, Stefansson H, Steinberg S, Jonsdottir I, Jonsson PV, Snaedal J, Stefansson K: Variant of TREM2 associated with the risk of Alzheimer's disease, *N Engl J Med* 368(2):107–116, 2013.

Jorissen E, Prox J, Bernreuther C, Weber S, Schwanbeck R, Serneels L, Saftig P: The disintegrin/metalloproteinase ADAM10 is essential for the establishment of the brain cortex, *J Neurosci* 30(14):4833–4844, 2010.

Kamboh MI, Aston CE, Perez-Tur J, Kokmen E, Ferrell RE, Hardy J, DeKosky ST: A novel mutation in the apolipoprotein E gene (APOE*4 Pittsburgh) is associated with the risk of late-onset Alzheimer's disease, *Neurosci Lett* 263(2–3):129–132, 1999.

Kanekiyo T, Xu H, Bu G: ApoE and Abeta in Alzheimer's disease: accidental encounters or partners? *Neuron* 81(4):740–754, 2014.

Kang J, Lemaire HG, Unterbeck A, Salbaum JM, Masters CL, Grzeschik KH, Muller-Hill B: The precursor of Alzheimer's disease amyloid A4 protein resembles a cell-surface receptor, *Nature* 325(6106):733–736, 1987.

Kero M, Paetau A, Polvikoski T, Tanskanen M, Sulkava R, Jansson L, Tienari PJ: Amyloid precursor protein (APP) A673T mutation in the elderly Finnish population, *Neurobiol Aging* 34(5):1518 e1511–e1513, 2013.

Kim J, Basak JM, Holtzman DM: The role of apolipoprotein E in Alzheimer's disease, *Neuron* 63(3):287–303, 2009a.

Kim J, Castellano JM, Jiang H, Basak JM, Parsadanian M, Pham V, Holtzman DM: Overexpression of low-density lipoprotein receptor in the brain markedly inhibits amyloid deposition and increases extracellular A beta clearance, *Neuron* 64(5):632–644, 2009b.

Kim J, Jiang H, Park S, Eltorai AE, Stewart FR, Yoon H, Holtzman DM: Haploinsufficiency of human APOE reduces amyloid deposition in a mouse model of amyloid-beta amyloidosis, *J Neurosci* 31(49):18007–18012, 2011.

Kim M, Suh J, Romano D, Truong MH, Mullin K, Hooli B, Tanzi RE: Potential late-onset Alzheimer's disease-associated mutations in the ADAM10 gene attenuate {alpha}-secretase activity, *Hum Mol Genet* 18(20):3987–3996, 2009.

Kovacs DM, Fausett HJ, Page KJ, Kim TW, Moir RD, Merriam DE, Wasco W: Alzheimer-associated presenilins 1 and 2 neuronal expression in brain and localization to intracellular membranes in mammalian cells, *Nat Med* 2(2): 224–229, 1996.

Kuhn PH, Wang H, Dislich B, Colombo A, Zeitschel U, Ellwart JW, Lichtenthaler SF: ADAM10 is the physiologically relevant, constitutive alpha-secretase of the amyloid precursor protein in primary neurons, *EMBO J* 29(17): 3020–3032, 2010.

Lambert J, Ibrahim-Verbaas C, Harold D, Naj A, Sims R, Bellenguez C, Amouyel P: Meta-analysis of 74,046 individuals identifies 11 new susceptibility loci for Alzheimer's disease, *Nat Genet* 45(12):1452–1458, 2013.

Lambert JC, Heath S, Even G, Campion D, Sleegers K, Hiltunen M, Amouyel P: Genome-wide association study identifies variants at CLU and CR1 associated with Alzheimer's disease, *Nat Genet* 41(10):1094–1099, 2009.

Lammich S, Buell D, Zilow S, Ludwig AK, Nuscher B, Lichtenthaler SF, Haass C: Expression of the anti-amyloidogenic secretase ADAM10 is suppressed by its 5'-untranslated region, *J Biol Chem* 285(21):15753–15760, 2010.

Levy-Lahad E, Wasco W, Poorkaj P, Romano DM, Oshima J, Pettingell WH, et al: Candidate gene for the chromosome 1 familial Alzheimer's disease locus, *Science* 269(5226):973–977, 1995a.

Levy-Lahad E, Wijsman EM, Nemens E, Anderson L, Goddard KA, Weber JL, Schellenberg GD: A familial Alzheimer's disease locus on chromosome 1, *Science* 269(5226):970–973, 1995b.

Levy E, Carman MD, Fernandez-Madrid IJ, Power MD, Lieberburg I, van Duinen SG, Frangione B: Mutation of the Alzheimer's disease amyloid gene in hereditary cerebral hemorrhage, Dutch type, *Science* 248(4959): 1124–1126, 1990.

Li H, Wetten S, Li L, St Jean PL, Upmanyu R, Surh L, Roses AD: Candidate single-nucleotide polymorphisms from a genomewide association study of Alzheimer disease, *Arch Neurol* 65(1):45–53, 2008.

Lill CM, Bertram L: Towards unveiling the genetics of neurodegenerative diseases, *Semin Neurol* 31(5):531–541, 2011.

Lill CM, Rengmark A, Pihlstrom L, Fogh I, Shatunov A, Sleiman PM, Bertram L: The role of TREM2 R47H as a risk factor for Alzheimer's disease, frontotemporal lobar degeneration, amyotrophic lateral sclerosis, and Parkinson's disease, *Alzheimers Dement* 11(12):1407–1416, 2015.

Liu CC, Kanekiyo T, Xu H, Bu G: Apolipoprotein E and Alzheimer disease: risk, mechanisms and therapy, *Nat Rev Neurol* 9(2):106–118, 2013.

Lue LF, Schmitz C, Walker DG: What happens to microglial TREM2 in Alzheimer's disease: immunoregulatory turned into immunopathogenic? *Neuroscience* 302:138–150, 2015.

Mahley RW, Rall SC Jr: Apolipoprotein E: far more than a lipid transport protein, *Annu Rev Genomics Hum Genet* 1:507–537, 2000.

Maloney JA, Bainbridge T, Gustafson A, Zhang S, Kyauk R, Steiner P, Atwal JK: Molecular mechanisms of Alzheimer disease protection by the A673T allele of amyloid precursor protein, *J Biol Chem* 289(45):30990–31000, 2014.

Manolio TA, Collins FS, Cox NJ, Goldstein DB, Hindorff LA, Hunter DJ, Visscher PM: Finding the missing heritability of complex diseases, *Nature* 461(7265):747–753, 2009.

Medway CW, Abdul-Hay S, Mims T, Ma L, Bisceglio G, Zou F, Younkin SG: ApoE variant p.V236E is associated with markedly reduced risk of Alzheimer's disease, *Mol Neurodegener* 9:11, 2014.

Michaelson DM: APOE epsilon4: the most prevalent yet understudied risk factor for Alzheimer's disease, *Alzheimers Dement* 10(6):861–868, 2014.

Naj AC, Jun G, Beecham GW, Wang LS, Vardarajan BN, Buros J, Schellenberg GD: Common variants at MS4A4/MS4A6E, CD2AP, CD33 and EPHA1 are associated with late-onset Alzheimer's disease, *Nat Genet* 43(5):436–441, 2011.

Neumann H, Takahashi K: Essential role of the microglial triggering receptor expressed on myeloid cells-2 (TREM2) for central nervous tissue immune homeostasis, *J Neuroimmunol* 184(1–2):92–99, 2007.

Paloneva J, Autti T, Hakola P, Haltia MJ: In Pagon RA, Adam MP, Ardinger HH, Wallace SE, Amemiya A, Bean LJH, Bird TD, Dolan CR, Fong CT, Smith RJH, Stephens K, editors: *Polycystic lipomembranous osteodysplasia with sclerosing leukoencephalopathy (PLOSL)*, Seattle (WA), 1993, GeneReviews.

Paloneva J, Mandelin J, Kiialainen A, Bohling T, Prudlo J, Hakola P, Peltonen L: DAP12/TREM2 deficiency results in impaired osteoclast differentiation and osteoporotic features, *J Exp Med* 198(4):669–675, 2003.

Postina R, Schroeder A, Dewachter I, Bohl J, Schmitt U, Kojro E, Fahrenholz F: A disintegrin-metalloproteinase prevents amyloid plaque formation and hippocampal defects in an Alzheimer disease mouse model, *J Clin Invest* 113(10):1456–1464, 2004.

Pottier C, Wallon D, Rousseau S, Rovelet-Lecrux A, Richard AC, Rollin-Sillaire A, Hannequin D: TREM2 R47H variant as a risk factor for early-onset Alzheimer's disease, *J Alzheimers Dis* 35(1):45–49, 2013.

Rocca WA, Hofman A, Brayne C, Breteler MM, Clarke M, Copeland JR, et al: Frequency and distribution of Alzheimer's disease in Europe: a collaborative study of 1980–1990 prevalence findings. The EURODEM-Prevalence Research Group, *Ann Neurol* 30(3):381–390, 1991.

Schellenberg GD, Bird TD, Wijsman EM, Orr HT, Anderson L, Nemens E, et al: Genetic linkage evidence for a familial Alzheimer's disease locus on chromosome 14, *Science* 258(5082):668–671, 1992.

Seshadri S, Fitzpatrick AL, Ikram MA, DeStefano AL, Gudnason V, Boada M, Consortium E: Genome-wide analysis of genetic loci associated with Alzheimer disease, *JAMA* 303(18):1832–1840, 2010.

Sherrington R, Rogaev EI, Liang Y, Rogaeva EA, Levesque G, Ikeda M, St George-Hyslop PH: Cloning of a gene bearing missense mutations in early-onset familial Alzheimer's disease, *Nature* 375(6534):754–760, 1995.

Siest G, Pillot T, Regis-Bailly A, Leininger-Muller B, Steinmetz J, Galteau MM, Visvikis S: Apolipoprotein E: an important gene and protein to follow in laboratory medicine, *Clin Chem* 41(8 Pt 1):1068–1086, 1995.

Stratman NC, Castle CK, Taylor BM, Epps DE, Melchior GW, Carter DB: Isoform-specific interactions of human apolipoprotein E to an intermediate conformation of human Alzheimer amyloid-beta peptide, *Chem Phys Lipids* 137(1–2):52–61, 2005.

Strittmatter WJ, Saunders AM, Schmechel D, Pericak-Vance M, Enghild J, Salvesen GS, Roses AD: Apolipoprotein E: high-avidity binding to beta-amyloid and increased frequency of type 4 allele in late-onset familial Alzheimer disease, *Proc Natl Acad Sci USA* 90(5):1977–1981, 1993.

Suh J, Choi SH, Romano DM, Gannon MA, Lesinski AN, Kim DY, Tanzi RE: ADAM10 missense mutations potentiate beta-amyloid accumulation by impairing prodomain chaperone function, *Neuron* 80(2):385–401, 2013.

Swerdlow RH, Corder EH: For Alzheimer disease GWAS, pulling needles from the haystack is just the first step, *Neurology* 79(3):204–205, 2012.

Tanzi RE: TREM2 and risk of Alzheimer's disease—friend or foe? *N Engl J Med* 372(26):2564–2565, 2015.

Tanzi RE, Bertram L: Twenty years of the Alzheimer's disease amyloid hypothesis: a genetic perspective, *Cell* 120(4):545–555, 2005.

Tanzi RE, Gusella JF, Watkins PC, Bruns GA, St George-Hyslop P, Van Keuren ML, Neve RL: Amyloid beta protein gene: cDNA, mRNA distribution, and genetic linkage near the Alzheimer locus, *Science* 235(4791): 880–884, 1987a.

Tanzi RE, St George-Hyslop PH, Haines JL, Polinsky RJ, Nee L, Foncin JF, Gusella JF: The genetic defect in familial Alzheimer's disease is not tightly linked to the amyloid beta-protein gene, *Nature* 329(6135):156–157, 1987b.

Tattini L, D'Aurizio R, Magi A: Detection of genomic structural variants from next-generation sequencing data, *Front Bioeng Biotechnol* 3:92, 2015.

Thomas DC: Are we ready for genome-wide association studies? *Cancer Epidemiol Biomarkers Prev* 15(4):595–598, 2006.

Traynor BJ, Singleton AB: Nature versus nurture: death of a dogma, and the road ahead, *Neuron* 68(2):196–200, 2010.

Verghese PB, Castellano JM, Garai K, Wang Y, Jiang H, Shah A, Holtzman DM: ApoE influences amyloid-beta (Abeta) clearance despite minimal apoE/Abeta association in physiological conditions, *Proc Natl Acad Sci USA* 110(19): E1807–E1816, 2013.

Vetrivel KS, Thinakaran G: Amyloidogenic processing of beta-amyloid precursor protein in intracellular compartments, *Neurology* 66(2 Suppl 1):S69–S73, 2006.

Wakabayashi T, De Strooper B: Presenilins: members of the gamma-secretase quartets, but part-time soloists too, *Physiology (Bethesda)* 23:194–204, 2008.

Wang LS, Naj AC, Graham RR, Crane PK, Kunkle BW, Cruchaga C, et al: Rarity of the Alzheimer disease-protective APP A673T variant in the United States, *JAMA Neurol* 72(2):209–216, 2015.

CHAPTER

3

β-Secretase Inhibition

R. Vassar

OUTLINE

THE ROLE OF β-AMYLOID IN ALZHEIMER'S DISEASE

The extracellular accumulation of amyloid plaques composed of the β-amyloid (Aβ) peptide represents one of the two defining lesions in the Alzheimer's disease (AD) brain, the other being intracellular aggregation of hyperphosphorylated tau into neurofibrillary tangles. Recent results indicate that amyloid deposition begins ~10–20 years before the onset of dementia, suggesting that cerebral accumulation of Aβ has as a critical early role in AD pathogenesis (Hardy and Selkoe, 2002; Tanzi, 2012; Rutten and Steinbusch, 2013). If so,

Developing Therapeutics for Alzheimer's Disease. http://dx.doi.org/10.1016/B978-0-12-802173-6.00003-4

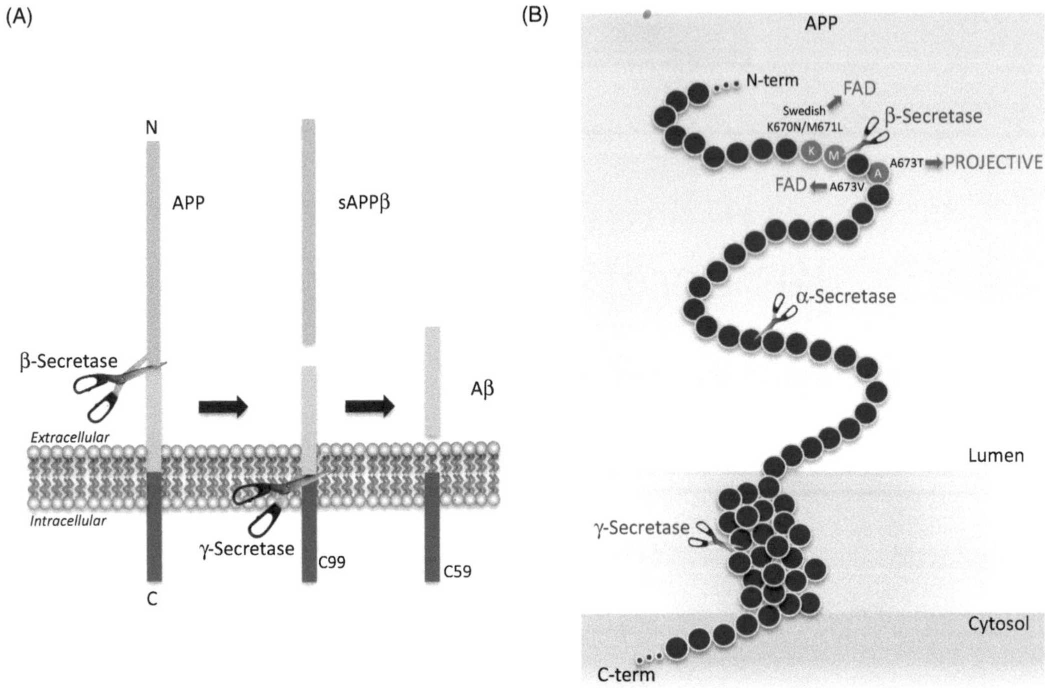

FIGURE 3.1 **APP processing and Aβ generation and mutations that affect β-secretase cleavage.** (A) APP is a type I membrane protein that is sequentially cleaved by two aspartic proteases to generate Aβ. First, the β-secretase enzyme cuts APP (1) to create the N-terminus of Aβ. Two APP fragments are produced: membrane-bound C99 and secreted sAPPβ ectodomain. Second, C99 is cleaved by the γ-secretase enzyme; and (2) to generate the C-terminus of Aβ. Aβ is then released into the lumen of the endosome and secreted into the extracellular medium. An intracellular domain, C59, is also produced. (B) The amino acids in and around the Aβ domain of APP are represented as circles. Amino acids that affect β-secretase processing of APP in humans are indicated, within circles with the wild-type residue identified by the single-letter amino acid code. The K670N/M671L (Swedish) and A673V mutations cause FAD by increasing β-secretase cleavage and Aβ production, while the A673T mutation protects against AD by doing the opposite. All three mutations occur at or within one amino acid of the β-secretase cleavage site. Scissors indicate cleavage sites of the various secretases.

then inhibition of Aβ accumulation in the brain may benefit AD, if given early enough during the course of the disease.

Neurons are the major producers of Aβ in the brain, although glia, in particular astrocytes, may also contribute to Aβ generation, particularly during physiological stress that causes glial activation as happens in AD. The formation of Aβ is a sequential proteolytic process beginning with the cleavage of amyloid precursor protein (APP) by the β-secretase enzyme, which generates the amino (N) terminus of Aβ and yields the membrane-bound C-terminal fragment C99 (Fig. 3.1A) (Vassar et al., 2009). Next, γ-secretase cuts C99 to release Aβ, which is secreted from the cell (Sisodia and St George-Hyslop, 2002; De Strooper et al., 2010; Walter and van Echten-Deckert, 2013). Interestingly, the γ-secretase cut is imprecise and creates Aβ isoforms of different lengths at the carboxy (C) terminus, of which the longer isoforms are highly associated with AD. Processing of APP by both β- and γ-secretases is necessary for the generation of Aβ, suggesting that inhibition or modulation of either or both of these proteases in the brain should decrease Aβ levels and be beneficial for AD.

Human genetics studies have greatly informed us about AD pathogenesis and strongly suggest that cerebral Aβ accumulation has an essential role in the etiology of AD (Tanzi, 2012). Thus far, over 200 autosomal dominant missense mutations have been identified in the genes for APP and presenilin (the γ-secretase catalytic subunit) that are associated with familial AD (FAD). These FAD mutations are highly penetrant and without exception increase either the generation of all Aβ isoforms (total Aβ) or the relative proportion of the 42-amino acid isoform (Aβ42) that is more neurotoxic. Notably, FAD mutations in APP are found very near to the β- and γ-secretase cleavage sites, and these mutations serve to increase APP processing and raise levels of total Aβ or Aβ42 specifically. The so-called Swedish mutation (K670N; M671L) (Mullan et al., 1992) and A673V (Di Fede et al., 2009) mutations in APP are particularly compelling because they are positioned precisely at only two amino acids C-terminal to the β-secretase cleavage site, respectively. These mutations make the cleavage of APP by the β-secretase enzyme more efficient, so greater amounts of C99 and total Aβ are generated (Fig. 3.1B). In contrast, an APP mutation, A673T, has been recently identified that confers protection against AD and cognitive decline in the elderly (Jonsson et al., 2012). This mutation, which occurs at the same position as the A673V mutation that causes FAD, is less efficiently cleaved by β-secretase so that Aβ generation is decreased by ~40% (Jonsson et al., 2012; Maloney et al., 2014; Benilova et al., 2014). Interestingly, most carriers have one copy of the A673T mutation and likely have a reduction in Aβ production of only ~20%, yet they are still protected against AD. This implies proof-of-principle of the strategy that modest reduction of brain Aβ levels may prevent AD, if started early enough. Additionally, the Swedish, A673V, and A673T mutations together strongly suggest that inhibition of β-secretase cleavage of APP should be beneficial for AD prevention.

THE IDENTIFICATION OF β-SECRETASE AS β-SITE APP CLEAVING ENZYME (BACE)

Following the discoveries of Aβ and the first APP mutations that cause FAD, it soon became clear that the β- and γ-secretase enzymes were prime therapeutic targets for the development of small molecule inhibitor drugs for the treatment of AD. Thus, their molecular identities were vigorously pursued. The properties of Aβ generation and secretase activities in cells and tissues led to the development of cell-free and cell-based assays that could be exploited for the identification of the secretases. Subsequently, five groups independently reported the molecular cloning of the β-secretase enzyme, which they variously named β-site APP cleaving enzyme (BACE), Asp2, and memapsin 2 (Vassar et al., 1999; Yan et al., 1999; Sinha et al., 1999; Hussain et al., 1999; Lin et al., 2000); "BACE" has emerged as the most common moniker in the literature. Importantly, all of the groups agreed on the same polypeptide sequence even though they used different experimental approaches to identify the β-secretase, lending strong support for the conclusion that the authentic β-secretase had been cloned.

BACE has all the molecular and cellular characteristics that had been previously predicted for the β-secretase in vitro and in vivo (Vassar et al., 2009). It is a type I transmembrane aspartic protease of 501 amino acids in length that is closely related to the pepsin family of aspartic proteases (Fig. 3.2). The catalytic domain of BACE harbors two aspartic protease signature motifs of the sequence DTGS and DSGT that come together to form the active site of the enzyme.

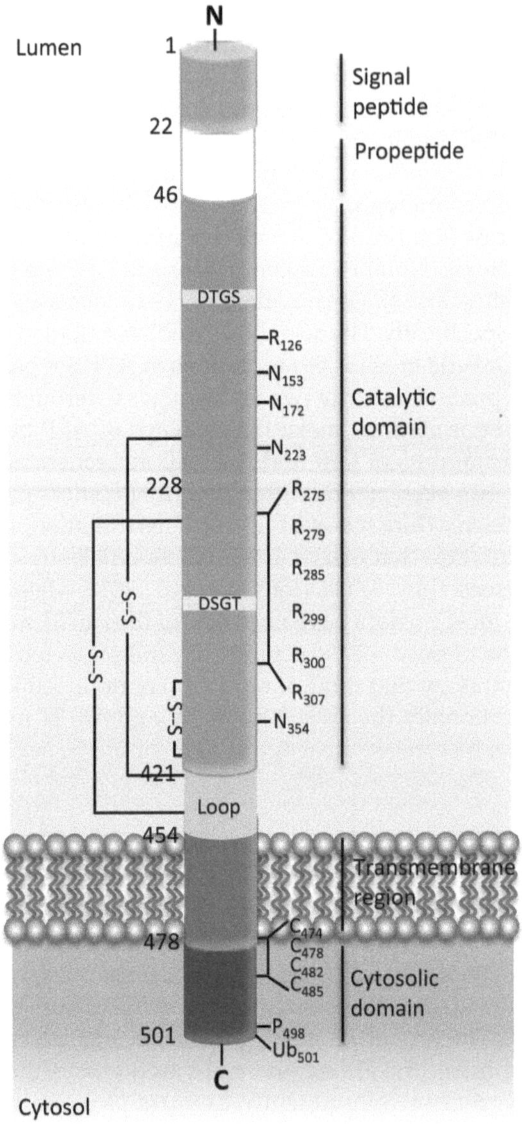

FIGURE 3.2 **Primary structure of BACE1.** BACE1 is a 501 amino acid type I transmembrane aspartic protease. The various subdomains of BACE1 are indicated by the lines to the right of the structure. Numbers refer to amino acid positions. The two signature aspartic protease active site motifs DTGS and DSGT at positions 93 and 289, respectively, are indicated. *S--S* denotes positions of disulfide bridges within the catalytic domain; *N*s represent positions of N-linked glycosylation sites; *R*s indicate positions of acetylated arginine residues; *C*s mark positions of S-palmitoylated cysteine residues; *P* indicates phosphorylation of serine 498; *Ub* denotes ubiquitination of lysine 501.

As required for β-secretase, the BACE active site is topologically oriented on the same side of the membrane as the β-secretase cleavage site in APP. Additionally, the activity of BACE has an acidic pH optimum and the catalytic domain resides within the lumen of acidic intracellular compartments, including endosomes and trans-Golgi network. Moreover, BACE levels are highest in neurons of the central nervous system (CNS), BACE has the correct sequence specificity, and BACE overexpressed in cells cleaves APP and increases Aβ production.

Soon after the discovery of BACE, a homolog, BACE2, was identified that has ~64% amino acid similarity to BACE (henceforth referred to as BACE1) (Solans et al., 2000). The extensive degree of homology between the two enzymes suggested that BACE2 might also function as a β-secretase. However, this possibility seemed unlikely because BACE2 is not expressed to a high level in neurons, in contrast to BACE1 (Bennett et al., 2000; Laird et al., 2005). Moreover, BACE2 predominantly cleaves APP within the Aβ domain, so that the generation of Aβ is precluded (Farzan et al., 2000; Yan et al., 2001; Fluhrer et al., 2002; Basi et al., 2003; Abdul-Hay et al., 2012). These data, together with the finding that BACE1 null mice are devoid of Aβ (see later discussion), suggest BACE2 is not likely to be a β-secretase in the CNS.

PHYSIOLOGICAL FUNCTIONS OF BACE1

BACE1 −/− Mice

To justify BACE1 inhibitor drug development efforts, it was necessary to provide in vivo validation that BACE1 is the primary β-secretase enzyme in the brain. To do so, gene targeting in embryonic stem cells was used to produce BACE1 knockout (−/−) mice (Luo et al., 2001; Roberds et al., 2001; Cai et al., 2001; Dominguez et al., 2005). Initial reports showed that BACE1−/− mice were viable and fertile and did not have detectable abnormalities. Their normal morphology and behavior, tissue histology, and blood cell and clinical chemistry characteristics suggested that BACE1 inhibition as a therapeutic approach for AD might lack mechanism-based toxicities. Additionally, APP overexpressing transgenic mice that also lack the BACE1 gene are devoid of cerebral Aβ, amyloid deposition, and Aβ-associated memory impairments (Ohno et al., 2004, 2007; Luo et al., 2003; Laird et al., 2005; McConlogue et al., 2007). Importantly, these data validate BACE1 as the major β-secretase in the CNS and indicate that BACE2 does not compensate for BACE1 loss of function, at least for the production of Aβ. Furthermore, they strongly suggested that BACE1 inhibition should be a safe and effective therapeutic strategy for AD.

Although initial studies of BACE1−/− mice indicated that BACE1 was not required for viability in vivo, further investigations were necessary to elucidate the physiological functions of BACE1 and fully understand the potential for mechanism-based toxicities of therapeutic BACE1 inhibition. For example, BACE1 protein is highly concentrated in presynaptic terminals of CNS neurons (Kandalepas et al., 2013; Deng et al., 2013), suggesting that BACE1 has a role in synaptic function. Moreover, in agreement with high BACE1 expression and presynaptic localization in neurons, deeper analyses of BACE1−/− mice have uncovered numerous subtle neuronal phenotypes, such as axon targeting errors (Rajapaksha et al., 2011; Cao et al., 2012; Hitt et al., 2012), reduced myelination (Willem et al., 2006; Hu et al., 2006, 2008), memory impairments (Kobayashi et al., 2008; Ohno et al., 2004, 2006, 2007; Laird et al., 2005), reduced muscle spindles (Cheret et al., 2013), neurochemical abnormalities

TABLE 3.1 Knockout Mouse Phenotypes

BACE1 knockout mouse phenotypes

Phenotype	Putative substrate	References
Astrogenesis increase; neurogenesis decrease	Jag1	Hu et al. (2013)
Axon guidance defects	CHL1	Rajapaksha et al. (2011), Cao et al. (2012), Hitt et al. (2012)
Hyperactivity	NRG1	Dominguez et al. (2005), Savonenko et al. (2008)
Hypomyelination	NRG1	Willem et al. (2006), Hu et al. (2006, 2008)
Memory deficits	Unknown	Laird et al. (2005), Ohno et al. (2004, 2006, 2007), Kobayashi et al. (2008)
Insulin sensitivity enhanced	Unknown	Dominguez et al. (2005), Meakin et al. (2012), Hoffmeister et al. (2013)
Muscle spindle reduction	NRG1	Cheret et al. (2013)
Neurochemical deficits	Unknown	Harrison et al. (2003)
Neurodegeneration with age	Unknown	Hu et al. (2010)
Postnatal lethality, growth retardation	Unknown	Dominguez et al. (2005)
Retinal abnormalities	VEGFR1	Cai et al. (2012)
Schizophrenia endophenotypes	NRG1	Savonenko et al. (2008)
Seizures	$Na_v\beta_2$	Kim et al. (2007), Kobayashi et al. (2008), Hu et al. (2010), Hitt et al. (2010)
Spine density reduction	NRG1	Savonenko et al. (2008)

BACE2 knockout mouse phenotypes

Phenotype	Putative substrate	References
Normal	—	Dominguez et al. (2005)
Pancreatic β cell increase	Tmem27	Esterhazy et al. (2011)
Pigmentation abnormalities	PMEL	Rochin et al. (2013)

BACE1/2 Double-knockout mouse phenotypes

Phenotype	Reference
Similar to BACE1 knockout, except postnatal lethality is enhanced	Dominguez et al. (2005)

(Harrison et al., 2003), alterations in neurogenesis and astrogenesis (Hu et al., 2013), increased age-related neurodegeneration (Hu et al., 2010), reduced spine density (Savonenko et al., 2008), retinal pathology (Cai et al., 2012), endophenotypes of schizophrenia (Savonenko et al., 2008), and seizures (Hitt et al., 2010; Hu et al., 2010; Kobayashi et al., 2008) (Table 3.1). Future investigations may reveal even more BACE1 null phenotypes. Any of these BACE1 null phenotypes in theory could represent mechanism-based side effects of BACE1 inhibitor drugs in humans, thus raising a note of caution that therapeutic inhibition of BACE1 might not be completely free of toxicity.

Substrates of BACE1

The varied phenotypes of the BACE1−/− mice are likely the result of abrogated β-secretase processing of different substrates of BACE1 in addition to APP. Recent proteomic analyses in cultured primary neurons have identified numerous putative BACE1 substrates that have roles in neuronal functions (Kuhn et al., 2012; Zhou et al., 2012) (Fig. 3.3). The majority of substrates of BACE1 are, like APP, type I membrane proteins, while a few, like neuregulin 1 (NRG1), have more complex membrane topologies. Cleavage of most substrates by BACE1 releases an ectodomain fragment that diffuses from the cell in the extracellular milieu. There, it may bind to another molecule on the same (autocrine) or a different (paracrine) cell to affect signal transduction or cell–cell interactions. Perhaps the best-studied example is that of BACE1 processing of type III NRG1, which releases an epidermal growth factor (EGF)-like domain that binds to the ErbB receptor on the Schwann cell for the stimulation of myelination (Fleck et al., 2013; Luo et al., 2011; Hu et al., 2006; Willem et al., 2006). Due to the lack of β-secretase processing, BACE1−/− mice have decreased shedding of the NRG1 EGF domain, which reduces instructive signals to myelinating cells and leads to hypomyelination.

Another example of β-secretase processing of a neuronal substrate involves the cleavage of the neural cell adhesion molecule close homolog of L1 (CHL1) by BACE1. Like APP, CHL1 is a type I membrane protein, and it has a well-known function in axonal outgrowth and neuronal survival (Heyden et al., 2008; Montag-Sallaz et al., 2002). Cleavage of CHL1 by BACE1 liberates a soluble ectodomain fragment that may bind to neuropilin-1 and semaphorin 3A, two molecules that are involved in axonal guidance. Thus, the lack of β-secretase processing of CHL1 might account for the presence of mistargeted axons that have been reported in the olfactory bulb and hippocampus of BACE1 null mice (Hitt et al., 2012; Kuhn et al., 2012; Zhou et al., 2012).

Although decreased β-secretase processing of many BACE1 substrates impairs their function, abrogated cleavage of other substrates may potentiate their role in a physiological process. For example, Jagged 1 (Jag1) is a type I membrane protein that is a ligand for the Notch receptor, which regulates the differentiation of many cell types in the body. Interestingly, Jag1 is also a BACE1 substrate, and reduced BACE1 cleavage of Jag1 in BACE1−/− mice increases the levels of Jag1 on the cell surface, which causes greater than normal stimulation of Notch activity in the neighboring cell. Consequently, during early development Jag1–Notch signaling is increased (Kopan and Ilagan, 2009) in radial glial neural stem cells, which promotes astrogenesis over neurogenesis (Hu et al., 2013). As additional BACE1 substrates and functions are discovered, the underlying molecular mechanisms of BACE1 null phenotypes and their implications for mechanism-based toxicities of therapeutic BACE1 inhibition will come into clearer focus.

In addition to cleavage by BACE1, a number of BACE1 substrates undergo ectodomain shedding by proteases in the A Disintegrin and Metalloproteinase Domain (ADAM) family. The extent to which a given substrate is processed by BACE1 versus an ADAM family member varies depending on the substrate (Fig. 3.3). Some substrates are almost exclusively

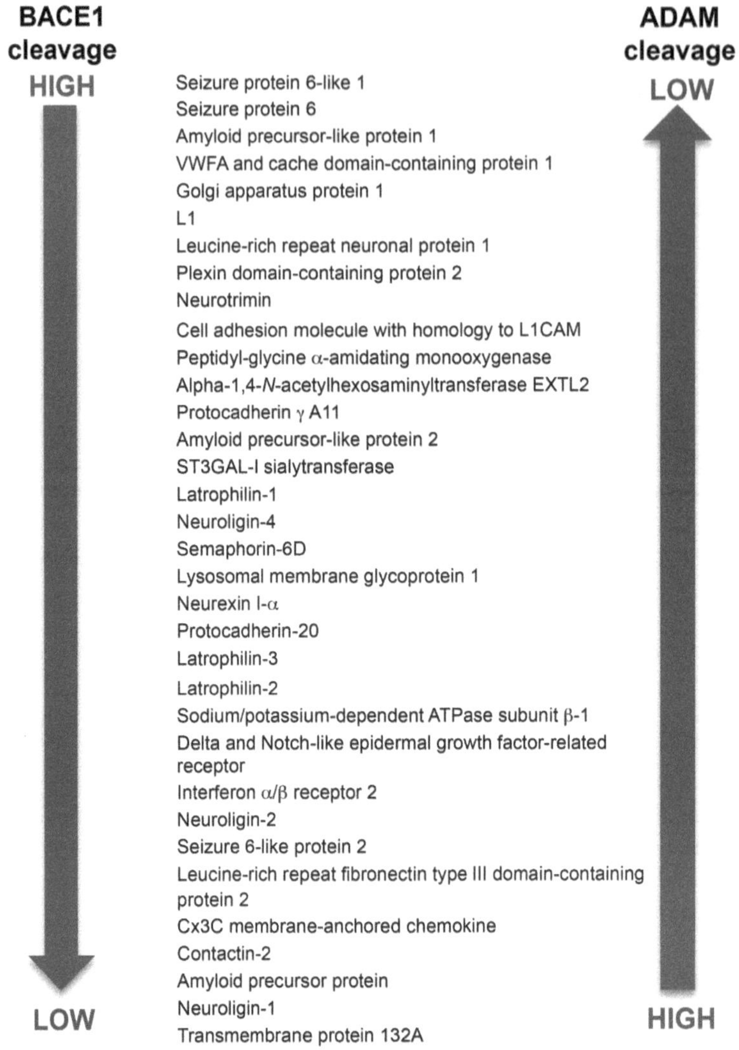

FIGURE 3.3 **Neuronal substrates of BACE1.** BACE1 substrates identified in primary cultured neurons are listed from those that are predominantly cleaved by BACE1 (BACE1 cleavage HIGH; top) to those that are processed by BACE1 at a low level (LOW; bottom). These substrates also are cleaved by other proteases in the ADAM family, but the ADAM cleavage preference is opposite to that of BACE1. *Source: Adapted from Table I, Ref. Kuhn et al. (2012).*

cut by BACE1 (eg, SEZ6, APLP1), while other substrates are primarily cleaved by the ADAMs (eg, APP, neuroligin-1) (Zhou et al., 2012; Kuhn et al., 2012). One would predict from these results that potential mechanism-based side effects that arise from therapeutic BACE1 inhibition might derive from deficient processing of substrates that predominantly undergo ectodomain shedding by BACE1 rather than the ADAMs. Conversely, potential toxicities of BACE1 inhibition may be less associated with substrates that are primarily cleaved by ADAM proteases over BACE1.

BACE2−/− Mice

The significant amino acid similarity shared by BACE1 and BACE2 suggests that it may be challenging to develop BACE1 inhibitors that do not cross-inhibit BACE2. Therefore, the possibility exists that BACE1 inhibitor drugs might also cause BACE2 mechanism-based side effects in addition to those of BACE1. To investigate this question, BACE2−/− mice were produced by gene targeting. Like BACE1 null mice, the BACE2−/− mice were initially shown to be viable and fertile with no reported phenotype (Dominguez et al., 2005). Moreover, other than enhanced early postnatal lethality, BACE1−/−, BACE2−/− double-knockout mice did not have a more severe phenotype than the BACE1−/− single knockouts (Dominguez et al., 2005). These data suggest that cross-inhibition of BACE2 with BACE1 inhibitors might not be associated with enhanced toxicity in the adult after postnatal development is completed.

Although BACE2−/− mice initially were reported to be normal, further investigations have revealed BACE2 loss-of-function phenotypes. Pancreatic β-cells express significant levels of BACE2. Interestingly, BACE2−/− mice have increased β-cell mass and insulin levels, and the mice exhibit enhanced glucose regulation (Esterhazy et al., 2011). These phenotypes appear to be the result of abrogated BACE2 cleavage of pro-proliferative type I transmembrane protein Tmem27, a protein involved in the regulation of β-cell mass. Given these results, inhibition of BACE2 may be beneficial for the treatment of type 2 diabetes, although further research into this hypothesis is necessary.

In addition to the pancreatic phenotype, BACE2−/− mice on a C57BL/6 genetic background exhibit hypopigmentation that results in a silvery coat compared to the dark coat of wild-type C57BL/6 mice. This phenotype is caused by lack of BACE2 processing of the melanocyte protein PMEL that is expressed in pigment cells of the skin and eye. BACE2 cleavage releases a fragment of PMEL into melanosomes that forms a matrix of amyloid fibrils upon which melanin is deposited (Rochin et al., 2013). Consequently, abrogated processing of PMEL in BACE2−/− mice leads to abnormal melanosome formation and hypopigmentation. These results suggest the possibility that cross-inhibition of BACE2 by BACE1 inhibitors might cause reduced pigmentation in humans.

SMALL MOLECULE BACE1 INHIBITOR DRUGS AND CLINICAL TRIALS FOR AD

The extensive validation of BACE1 as the primary β-secretase enzyme in the CNS has spurred vigorous efforts to develop small molecule inhibitors of BACE1 in both academia and industry. The first generation of BACE1 inhibitors consisted of noncleavable peptide-based transition state analogs designed after the amino-acid sequence in APP at which β-secretase cleaves (Sinha et al., 1999; Hong et al., 2002). Typically, these large peptidomimetic molecules are very potent BACE1 inhibitors in vitro, mainly because the large open active site of BACE1 has evolved to bind polypeptide substrates with high affinity. Unfortunately, the peptide-based BACE1 inhibitors did not possess favorable in vivo pharmacological properties, such as oral bioavailability, long serum half-life, or blood–brain barrier (BBB) penetration. As a consequence, investigators have turned toward designing true small molecule BACE1 inhibitor drugs. However, the development of nonpeptidic BACE1 inhibitors large enough to bind with sufficient affinity to the enzymatic active site, yet small enough to exhibit satisfactory pharmacokinetics and suitable brain penetration, has proven to be very challenging. Moreover, BACE1 inhibitors should have sufficient lipophilicity to cross both plasma and endosomal membranes for gaining access to the vesicle lumen where the BACE1 active site is located.

A crucial advance in small molecule BACE1 inhibitor development came with the first X-ray cocrystal structure of BACE1 with a peptidic BACE1 inhibitor (Hong et al., 2000). The BACE1 X-ray structure revealed important inhibitor–enzyme interactions that were exploited in rational drug design efforts. Shortly thereafter, new classes of small molecule BACE1 inhibitors were developed that exhibited improved pharmacological characteristics, including small molecular weight, plasma membrane permeability, and better pharmacokinetics (Probst and Xu, 2012; Evin et al., 2011). However, most second-generation BACE1 inhibitors were substrates of P-glycoprotein, the ATP-dependent drug efflux pump for xenobiotics in the BBB (Marques et al., 2013), and therefore could not reach high concentrations in the brain.

More recently, potent third-generation small molecule BACE1 inhibitors have been developed that achieve satisfactory brain penetration and robust cerebral Aβ reduction in preclinical animal models. Innovative diverse and complex drug development approaches have been employed to design current BACE1 inhibitors, which are described in detail in recent reviews (Evin et al., 2011; Probst and Xu, 2012). For example, in fragment-based approaches, small molecules are screened from libraries of compounds that exhibit brain penetration and other favorable druglike properties and are selected for BACE1 binding and enzyme inhibition in vitro. Hits of the screen are then cocrystalized with BACE1 and X-ray structures are determined. Small molecules exhibiting weak interactions with the BACE1 active site are bonded together to form larger molecules that strongly bind and inhibit BACE1 yet still retain favorable brain penetration and drug properties. These approaches have yielded several orally bioavailable BACE1 inhibitor drugs that have entered into human clinical trials (Table 3.2). Most are in the early clinical phases and scant information on their progress has been published, although preliminary trial results for four BACE1 inhibitor drugs have been reported at recent conferences and are summarized next.

LY2886721

The pharmaceutical company Eli Lilly was among the first to develop and test orally bioavailable nonpeptidic BACE1 inhibitors in humans. The small molecule BACE1 inhibitor LY2811376 showed satisfactory pharmacokinetic and pharmacodynamic characteristics in preclinical animal models that translated to a phase 1 clinical trial in humans (May et al., 2011). However, chronic toxicology studies in rats showing nonclinical, nontarget-associated pathology in retina and brain precluded the clinical development of this molecule. This toxicity was unlikely to result from BACE1 inhibition because similar pathologies appeared in BACE1−/− mice treated with LY2811376. Although it was discontinued, LY2811376 demonstrated the feasibility of developing a potent brain-penetrant, orally bioavailable, small molecule BACE1 inhibitor and represented the first reported translation of reduced cerebrospinal fluid (CSF) biomarkers of BACE1 cleavage from preclinical animal models to humans.

Lilly advanced a next-generation compound, LY2886721, into phase 1 and 2 clinical trials to determine its safety and tolerability, pharmacokinetics, and pharmacodynamics. Similar

TABLE 3.2 Small Molecule BACE1 Inhibitors in Clinical Trials

Company	Drug	Phase
AstraZeneca/Lilly	AZD3293	Phase 2/3
CoMentis	CTS-21166	Phase 1
Eisai/Biogen Idec	E2609	Phase 2
High Point	HPP854	Phase 1
Janssen/Shionogi	—	Phase 1
Lilly	LY2886721	Phase 2[a]
Merck	MK-8931	Phase 2/3
Novartis	—	Phase 1
Pfizer	PF-05297909	Phase 1
Roche	RG7129	Phase 1[b]
Takeda	TAK-070	Phase 1
Vitae/Boehringer Ingelheim	VTP-37948	Phase 1

[a]*Terminated due to abnormal liver biochemistry.*
[b]*Removed from pipeline.*

to LY2811376, LY2886721 was a potent, orally bioavailable, small molecule BACE1 inhibitor that robustly decreased levels of Aβ in the brains of preclinical animal models. However, unlike LY2811376, treatment with LY2886721 did not appear to be toxic to the retina or brain. Forty-seven healthy volunteers were given daily oral doses of either LY2886721 or placebo for 14 days in phase 1 (Martenyi et al., 2012). Either a multiple ascending dose (5, 15, and 35 mg) or a single dose (70 mg) followed by a multiple ascending dose was performed in two phase 1 study designs (NCT01227252, NCT01534273). Over the course of the 14-day study, LY2886721 was reported to be safe and well tolerated. Plasma half-life of LY2886721 was ~12 h, compatible with once-per-day dosing. Dose-dependent decreases of both plasma and CSF Aβ40 levels resulted from LY2886721 administration. Aβ40 levels in the CSF were decreased up to 74% with the highest dose of LY2886721. Levels of Aβ42 and sAPPβ in the CSF were both reduced to a similar extent as CSF Aβ40 by LY2886721. Interestingly, levels of sAPPα, the α-secretase cleavage product, were increased in CSF (Willis et al., 2012), an observation that is consistent with BACE1 inhibition, since β- and α-secretase compete for processing of APP. A phase 1 study of LY2886721 in patients with AD was also conducted (NCT01807026).

The positive phase 1 trials led to a 6-month phase 2 trial of 35 or 70 mg of LY2886721 dosed orally once per day in 130 patients with prodromal AD, also known as amnestic mild cognitive impairment (MCI), or mild AD (NCT01561430) (May et al., 2013). Recently, Lilly voluntarily terminated the phase 2 trial because a small number of subjects who were given LY2886721 developed abnormal liver biochemistries. The company reported that the LY2886721-related liver abnormalities did not appear to be associated with the BACE1 mechanism of action, a conclusion supported by a normal liver phenotype of BACE1−/− mice. It is not uncommon that some small molecules in clinical development are discontinued because of abnormal liver function as a nontarget-related side effect. Thus, the termination of LY2886721 does not necessarily suggest that BACE1 is not a viable drug target.

MK-8931

MK-8931, a small molecule BACE1 inhibitor developed by the pharmaceutical company Merck, was tested in 88 healthy volunteers (18–45 years old) as a two-part randomized, double-blind, placebo-controlled phase 1 clinical trial (Forman et al., 2012). Single and multiple (daily for 14 days) oral doses of MK-8931 were analyzed for safety, tolerability, pharmacokinetics, and pharmacodynamics. In healthy volunteers, MK-8931 was well tolerated and no serious adverse events were reported. Determining whether MK-8931 was able to enter the brain and engage its target, the β-secretase enzyme, was the primary goal of the study. To do so, biomarkers of BACE1 activity were measured in the CSF, including Aβ40, Aβ42, and sAPPβ, the latter being the BACE1-cleaved ectodomain of APP. MK-8931 markedly reduced levels of Aβ in the CSF in a sustained and dose-dependent manner. A single oral dose of 100 or 550 mg of MK-8931 decreased CSF Aβ40 levels by 75 or 92%, respectively, at 36 h after dosing. Levels of Aβ42 and sAPPβ in the CSF were also reduced to similar extents. Multiple oral dosing of MK-8931 lowered Aβ levels in the CSF by over 90%. MK-8931 has a plasma half-life of ~20 h, suggesting that a single daily oral dose may maintain stable drug levels in vivo.

A randomized, double-blind, placebo-controlled phase 1b trial of MK-8931 in 32 mild-to-moderate AD patients with mean age and Mini Mental State Examination (MMSE) of 73 years and 22, respectively, was also conducted for safety, tolerability, pharmacokinetics, and pharmacodynamics (NCT01496170) (Forman et al., 2013). One of the three doses (12, 40, or 60 mg) of MK-8931 or placebo was given once each day orally for 7 days, and levels of Aβ40, Aβ42, and sAPPβ in the CSF were measured. Similar to results in the healthy volunteers, MK-8931 strongly decreased levels of Aβ in the CSF in a sustained and dose-dependent fashion. Daily dosing of 12, 40, or 60 mg reduced CSF Aβ40 by 57, 79, or 84%, respectively, and resulted in similar reductions for CSF Aβ42 and sAPPβ. MK-8931 did not appear to cause serious adverse events in the AD patients during the course of the study. Importantly, the MK-8931 phase 1b results suggest that the pharmacokinetic and pharmacodynamic properties of BACE1 inhibitor drugs are not significantly altered by the presence of high amyloid loads in the brains of AD patients.

Encouraged by the positive results of the MK-8931 phase 1 and 1b studies, a phase 2/3 combined clinical trial (the EPOCH study, NCT01739348) was started in late 2012. EPOCH is a 78-week, randomized, placebo-controlled, parallel-group, double-blind clinical trial to evaluate the safety and efficacy of 12 or 40 mg/day oral dosing of MK-8931 versus placebo in mild-to-moderate AD patients. In phase 2, the trial will evaluate 200 AD patients and will enroll up to 1700 patients for phase 3. Primary efficacy outcomes are the changes from baseline in the Alzheimer's Disease Assessment Scale Cognitive Subscale (ADAS-Cog) and the Alzheimer's Disease Cooperative Study–Activities of Daily Living (ADCS-ADL) scores.

A recent interim safety analysis in 200 AD patients treated with MK-8931 for at least 3 months suggested that the drug was well tolerated and that the EPOCH study should proceed without changes to the protocol. Enrollment in the trial has continued with up to 1960 patients expected for phase 3. An additional clinical trial (the APECS study, NCT01953601) has also commenced, consisting of a 104-week randomized, placebo-controlled, parallel-group, double-blind phase 3 study to evaluate the safety and efficacy of 12 or 40 mg per day oral dosing of MK-8931 versus placebo in 1500 patients with MCI. The primary efficacy outcome in the

APECS study is the change from baseline in the Clinical Dementia Rating Scale–Sum of Boxes (CDR-SB) score. Secondary outcome substudies are included in both EPOCH and APECS to measure AD biomarkers, consisting of cortical amyloid load, CSF Aβ and tau, and hippocampal volume. The phase 3 efficacy studies for EPOCH and APECS are expected to conclude in 2017 and 2018, respectively.

AZD3293

The AstraZenica BACE1 inhibitor, AZD3293, was recently tested for safety, tolerability, pharmacokinetics, and effects on plasma and CSF Aβ levels in healthy young (18–55 years) and elderly (55–80 years) subjects (Alexander et al., 2014). Phase 1 randomized, double-blind, placebo-controlled single oral ascending dose (SAD) and multiple oral ascending dose (MAD) studies were conducted. In the SAD study (NCT01739647), 1–750 mg doses of AZD3293 were administered to seven young cohorts, while an elderly cohort received 15 mg (eight subjects/cohort). In the MAD study (NCT01795339), multiple once-daily doses of AZD3293 ranging from 15 to 70 mg were administered to five cohorts (two elderly) for 2 weeks. AZD3293 was well tolerated with no serious adverse events reported up to the highest dose given (750 mg) in the SAD study. The half-life of AZD3293 was 11–20 h and thus compatible with once-daily dosing. Pharmacokinetic parameters of AZD3293 between elderly and young subjects were indistinguishable. In the MAD study, the 15 or 50 mg doses reduced CSF Aβ40 and Aβ42 concentrations by a constant 50 or 75%, respectively. Additionally, AZD3293 administration produced dose-dependent decreases and increases of sAPPβ and sAPPα concentrations in the CSF, respectively, that had similar time lines as the reductions in CSF Aβ40 and Aβ42 (Höglund et al., 2014). The phase 1 studies of AZD3293 in healthy subjects (NCT01739647) and AD patients (NCT01795339) have been completed, and combined phase 2/3 trials in 1551 MCI and mild AD patients are planned [20 or 50 mg doses, 104-week duration, AMARANTH trial (NCT02245737)]. Recently, AstraZenica and Lilly entered into a partnership to jointly develop AZD3293 for AD.

E2609

The drug company Eisai has developed an orally bioavailable small molecule BACE1 inhibitor, E2609, that has shown robust lowering of cerebral Aβ in preclinical and clinical studies. E2609 was first clinically studied in healthy volunteers in randomized, double-blind, placebo-controlled phase 1 trials (Lai et al., 2012, 2013; Bernier et al., 2013). A SAD study (73 subjects) and a 14-day MAD study (50 subjects) tested E2609 in two separate phase 1 clinical trials (NCT01294540 and NCT01511783, respectively). The SAD study analyzed plasma Aβ levels following E2609 administration ranging from 5 to 800 mg (nine cohorts), while the MAD study measured both plasma and CSF Aβ levels in response to E2609 doses ranging from 25 to 400 mg (five cohorts). The E2609 plasma half-life of 12–16 h is compatible with once-per-day dosing. Each of the two phase 1 studies showed robust dose-dependent decreases of levels of Aβ in the CSF and/or plasma. CSF Aβ levels were reduced up to 85% at the highest dose of E2609 (400 mg) in the MAD study. Similar decreases in levels of sAPPβ in the CSF were observed, while CSF levels of sAPPα were increased. E2609 appeared to be safe and well tolerated, as no serious adverse events were reported in either phase 1 study. Eisai has recently completed a phase 1 trial of E2609 in subjects with MCI or mild AD (NCT01600859), and a phase 2 clinical trial of E2609 is planned. Recently, Eisai and Biogen Idec entered into a partnership to jointly develop E2609 for AD.

Alternative Therapeutic Approaches for BACE1 Inhibition

Although small molecules that directly inhibit BACE1 enzyme activity are leading therapeutic approaches, potential alternative strategies to reduce BACE1 processing of APP are being explored. As noted, BACE1 levels are significantly elevated in the AD brain and might accelerate the production of Aβ. Therefore, approaches to lower and normalize BACE1 levels in the brain might slow AD progression and avoid possible untoward side effects caused by direct BACE1 enzyme inhibition. Consequently, efforts are under way to elucidate the mechanisms of BACE1 elevation in AD in order to identify drug targets that could block the BACE1 increase when inhibited. BACE1 undergoes complex regulation at the transcriptional, translational, and posttranslational levels, all of which appear to have a role in elevating BACE1 levels and activity in AD (Chami and Checler, 2012; Zhao et al., 2012; Rossner et al., 2006). Much evidence suggests that BACE1 is a stress response protease that is increased by oxidative stress, inflammation, hypoxia, and trauma, among other insults that occur in AD (Chami and Checler, 2012; Sun et al., 2006; Zhang et al., 2007). Even Aβ itself increases BACE1 levels in neurons (Sadleir et al., 2014; Sadleir and Vassar, 2012), suggesting a vicious pathogenic cycle whereby Aβ could accelerate its own production through BACE1 elevation. Which, if any, of these complex multilayered regulatory mechanisms might yield therapeutic strategies for lowering BACE1 levels in AD is unclear, but continuing research in this important area may reveal promising new AD drug targets in the future.

Another class of alternative therapeutic strategy for BACE1 inhibition involves immunotherapy approaches to reduce BACE1 processing of APP. The first of these strategies employs antibodies directed against the β-secretase cleavage site of APP that sterically block access of the BACE1 active site to APP (Arbel et al., 2005; Boddapati et al., 2011). These anti-β-site APP antibodies decrease Aβ production culture cells and when injected i.v. reduce amyloid plaque pathology in the brains of APP transgenic mice (Rabinovich-Nikitin et al., 2012). Other immunotherapy approaches include anti-BACE1 antibodies that are not directed against the active site but instead target an exosite on the surface of the BACE1 catalytic domain that can allosterically regulate enzyme activity (Atwal et al., 2011; Zhou et al., 2011). This exosite is located on structurally adjacent regions of the C, D, and F loops of the enzyme (Wang et al., 2013). Exosite antibody binding to BACE1 alters structural features and dynamic characteristics near the substrate-binding cleft of the enzyme. Additionally, transport of BACE1 antibodies across the BBB has been facilitated by engineering one arm of the antibody to recognize the transferrin receptor (TfR), which shuttles transferrin across the BBB for the delivery of iron into the brain (Yu et al., 2011, 2014). These bispecific BACE1-TfR antibodies accumulate in the brain and reduce endogenous Aβ levels in mice to a much greater extent than monospecific BACE1 antibodies. Moreover, TfR bispecific antibodies could be useful for treating other neurologic diseases amenable to immunotherapy. These antibody approaches are currently in preclinical phases.

UNANSWERED QUESTIONS OF RELEVANCE TO BACE1 INHIBITOR CLINICAL TRIALS

Fifteen years after the discovery of the β-secretase enzyme, the challenges of developing brain-penetrant BACE1 inhibitors have been accomplished, and human clinical trials are under way. This promising development raises hopes that disease-modifying therapies employing BACE1 inhibition for AD are within reach. However, important questions concerning therapeutic goals and outcomes of these trials remain to be answered.

What Degree of BACE1 Inhibition Will Be Needed to Achieve Efficacy?

The level of BACE1 inhibition required for efficacy in turn should depend on how much Aβ lowering is necessary and at what stage of AD to treat (questions discussed further later). The recently discovered A673T APP mutation that protects against AD (Jonsson et al., 2012) suggests that reducing cerebral Aβ production by only a modest amount (~20%) could be preventive, if started before significant amyloid accumulation. As discussed previously, the leading BACE1 inhibitors currently in clinical trial are capable of this relatively small Aβ decrease. How BACE1 inhibition translates to Aβ reduction in the brain is difficult to estimate, although some insight into this question may be gained by considering experiments in BACE1 knockout mice. Heterozygous BACE1+/− mice that model 50% therapeutic inhibition of BACE1 exhibit ~20% lowering of cerebral Aβ levels in APP transgenic mice (McConlogue et al., 2007; Laird et al., 2005). Importantly, BACE1+/− mice appear to be normal, so 50% BACE1 inhibition may circumvent mechanism-based side effects yet provide sufficient Aβ reduction for efficacy.

As suggested by the protective A673T mutation, a therapeutic approach that reduced BACE1 activity and Aβ levels by ~50 and ~20%, respectively, would probably need to start before major amyloid deposition and be maintained for the remainder of life to prevent or delay the onset of AD. However, inhibiting BACE1 by more than 50% could be required if significant amyloid plaque load is present in the brain at the beginning of treatment. Still, the possibility exists that no level of BACE1 inhibition, no matter how strong, would be able to slow the progression of AD once a certain threshold of amyloid burden is reached. At present, these arguments are all speculative, as the levels of BACE1 inhibition and Aβ reduction necessary for efficacy in humans are as yet unknown, although insight into these parameters might be gleaned following analysis of the results from the ongoing clinical trials.

It is important to note that cerebral BACE1 levels in AD patients are increased several-fold over those in normal individuals (Li et al., 2004; Yang et al., 2003; Fukumoto et al., 2002; Holsinger et al., 2002). Both BACE1 and APP accumulate in swollen dystrophic neurites that surround amyloid plaques (Zhao et al., 2007; Kandalepas et al., 2013; Zhang et al., 2009), suggesting increased periplaque Aβ production that might accelerate amyloid deposition and induce a vicious pathogenic cycle (Torres et al., 2012). If so, normalization of BACE1 activity in periplaque dystrophic neurites may represent a modest but potentially efficacious therapeutic goal of BACE1 inhibition. However, elevated concentrations of BACE1 around plaques might necessitate the administration of very high BACE1 inhibitor doses in order to significantly reduce periplaque Aβ generation, if the amyloid burden is great.

At What Stage of AD Should We Administer BACE1 Inhibitors?

Cerebral Aβ accumulation has a crucial early role in AD pathogenesis, as suggested by more than 200 FAD mutations (Tanzi, 2012). Amyloid deposition appears to begin more than a decade before the manifestation of cognitive deficits and the clinical diagnosis of AD (Jack, 2012; Holtzman et al., 2011; Musiek and Holtzman, 2012). Aβ-lowering BACE1 inhibitors are likely to be most effective as a prevention strategy when administered early in the course of AD, before significant cerebral amyloid accumulation and neurodegeneration. Thus, BACE1 inhibitors are analogous to the cholesterol-lowering statin drugs for the prevention of heart disease: once significant amounts of cholesterol have deposited in coronary arteries and major injury to the heart has occurred, statin administration is unable to reverse the damage and provide much benefit for the patient. AD prevention trials will necessarily involve the enrollment of thousands of subjects, last for years, and incur enormous costs. As a result, AD prevention trials might be most feasible in the context of joint government–industry collaborations, such as those being conducted or planned by the Anti-Amyloid Treatment in Asymptomatic Alzheimer's Disease (A4) trial, Alzheimer's Prevention Initiative (API), and Dominantly Inherited Alzheimer Network Trials Unit (DIAN TU), all of which plan to include BACE1 inhibitor drugs. Some AD prevention trials are enrolling cognitively normal individuals that are genetically at high risk for developing AD who carry autosomal dominant FAD mutations (DIAN TU trial) or are homozygous for the apolipoprotein E ε4 allele (API trial). If BACE inhibitors are as well tolerated in chronic dosing for AD as the statins are for lowering serum cholesterol to prevent heart disease, then treating presymptomatic at-risk individuals for AD prevention is warranted.

Current BACE1 inhibitor trials have enrolled subjects with mild or moderate AD or mild cognitive impairment (MCI), the latter of which progresses to AD at a rate of ~10 to 15% per year (Tarawneh and Holtzman, 2012). A major advance has been the development of amyloid positron emission tomography (PET) imaging and CSF Aβ42 measurement as biomarkers for the diagnosis of prodromal AD (Jack and Holtzman, 2013; Rosen et al., 2013). Individuals who exhibit significant amyloid load by PET or have reduced CSF Aβ42 concentrations are likely to develop AD, even though they appear cognitively normal at the time of testing. Due to the unavailability of amyloid PET or CSF Aβ42 biomarker testing at the time, past Aβ immunotherapy trials were unable to exclude subjects who did not have cerebral amyloid accumulation, thus leading to increased variability in cognitive outcome results and ultimately contributing to the frank failure of these clinical trials (Lemere, 2013). In contrast, the BACE1 inhibitor clinical trials are enrolling only subjects who are positive by amyloid PET or have reduced CSF Aβ42, which should decrease data variability and increase the probability of observing statistically significant differences in cognition between drug and placebo groups. Periodic amyloid PET or CSF Aβ42 testing will be conducted to monitor target engagement and amyloid accumulation over the courses of the trials. Cognitive performance will also be tested, as this measure is the gold standard for efficacy in past AD clinical trials of approved palliative drugs that treat memory symptoms. However, as noted earlier, amyloid deposition appears to start years before memory deficits are detected with current tests of cognition. Thus, it might be challenging for BACE1 inhibitors to alter the trajectory of AD once a large amount of amyloid has accumulated in the brain, at least regarding the reduction of cognitive decline.

It is hoped that the levels of BACE1 inhibition and Aβ reduction necessary for disease modification could be deduced from data collected at the conclusion of the current clinical trials. Pharmacodynamic models developed from this future data might assist in the estimation of the level of BACE1 inhibition required to achieve efficacious Aβ reduction for a given cerebral amyloid load and level of cognitive impairment. These models could also be useful for the design of future primary and secondary AD prevention trials in presymptomatic individuals. At this time, the relationships between BACE1 inhibition, Aβ reduction, amyloid load, and cognitive status are not sufficiently well understood to develop accurate pharmacodynamic models for estimating the levels of BACE1 inhibition needed at a given stage of asymptomatic or symptomatic AD.

Will Treatment With BACE1 Inhibitors Cause Mechanism-Based Side Effects?

Although BACE1−/− mice were initially reported to be normal, recent studies have identified more than a dozen BACE1 null phenotypes and substantially more BACE1 substrates (Table 3.1, Fig. 3.3), suggesting that therapeutic BACE1 inhibition might cause mechanism-based toxicities. That said, it is unclear to what extent BACE1 null phenotypes in mice are able to model potential BACE1 inhibitor side effects in humans, for several reasons. First, BACE1 null phenotypes could relate to functions of BACE1 either during development or in adulthood, since BACE1−/− mice lack BACE1 from conception. For example, the major proportion of myelination occurs during development and is completed when adulthood is reached (Salzer, 2012), indicating that hypomyelination as a result of abrogated BACE1 processing of NRG1 in BACE1−/− mice is a developmental phenotype. Consequently, BACE1 inhibition in the adult might not have an impact on myelination, unless remyelination following injury becomes necessary. In contrast, neurogenesis and axon guidance are ongoing processes that occur in specific neuronal subpopulations that regenerate throughout life (Hitt et al., 2012; Hu et al., 2013), suggesting the possibility that BACE1−/− abnormalities in neurogenesis and axon targeting are adult phenotypes and that BACE1 inhibitor treatment might lead to similar defects. Additionally, it is possible that compensation from other proteases during development could mitigate the effects of BACE1 null mutation, in which case BACE1 inhibitor treatment in humans might have more severe side effects than indicated by BACE1−/− mice. Given these arguments, comprehensive analyses of BACE1−/− mice should help to parse developmental versus adult BACE1 null phenotypes for the estimation of BACE1 inhibitor side effect risk.

The risk of BACE1 mechanism-based toxicities will depend in large part on the degree of therapeutic BACE1 inhibition. At one extreme, BACE1−/− mice model 100% BACE1 inhibition, but this level of inhibition will never be achieved by BACE1 inhibitor treatment in practice, thus reducing the chances of side effects. However, AD patients are elderly and often frail, thus increasing the risk of serious adverse events caused by BACE1 inhibition. Moreover, BACE1 inhibitors must be chronically administered, necessitating a high level of safety. Ongoing and future BACE1 inhibitor clinical trials will ultimately answer these questions. It is anticipated that a therapeutic window will be discovered in which an empirically determined range of BACE1 inhibitor doses can balance tolerable mechanism-based side effects with sufficient reduction of cerebral Aβ levels for efficacy.

The statins are useful as a group for modeling the clinical development of BACE1 inhibitors, as indicated by the fact that the statin clinical trials determined a therapeutic dose window of 3-hydroxy-3-methyl-glutaryl-CoA reductase inhibitor that effectively decreased serum cholesterol levels to prevent heart disease in the presence of tolerable side effects. We are now in the early phases of this clinical development model for BACE1 inhibitors. Regardless of the final outcomes of the current BACE1 inhibitor trials, invaluable knowledge will be gained about the quantitative and temporal relationships between BACE1 inhibition, Aβ reduction, amyloid burden, and cognitive function in humans, which will be used for future clinical development of BACE1 inhibitors for AD.

CONCLUSIONS

As the β-secretase enzyme that initiates the production of Aβ, BACE1 is a key therapeutic target for AD. The protective A673T APP mutation in humans and genetic deletion of BACE1 in mice both decrease Aβ generation via reduced β-secretase processing of APP, providing strong proof of concept that BACE1 inhibition should be efficacious for AD. However, BACE1 null mice exhibit multiple complex neurological phenotypes (Table 3.1), suggesting that BACE1 inhibitor drugs might cause mechanism-based side effects involving hypomyelination, seizure, axon guidance defects, memory deficits, neurogenesis abnormalities, and neurodegeneration, and potentially others, resulting from insufficient BACE1 processing of a growing list of BACE1 substrates in neurons. Which, if any, of these BACE1 null phenotypes model BACE1 inhibitor side effects in humans remains to be determined.

Despite the challenges of BACE1 inhibitor drug development over the past 15 years since the discovery of BACE1, the recent introduction of several BACE1 inhibitors into clinical trials has refocused attention on this promising therapeutic approach for AD. To date, Merck's MK-8931 has advanced the farthest, to phase 2/3, while the other drugs, including those from AstraZeneca, Eisai, and Pfizer, among others, are in phases 1 and 2. These compounds are potent, achieving up to ~90% CSF Aβ reduction. Additionally, they are well tolerated for the most part, although two BACE1 inhibitors have recently been terminated due to toxicity that might not be related to the BACE1 mechanism of action.

The most challenging questions for BACE1 inhibitor clinical development concern the level of BACE1 inhibition and the stage of AD at which to treat for optimal efficacy. Hypothetical arguments based on the A673T APP mutation and BACE1+/− mice suggest that ~50% BACE1 inhibition might achieve ~20% Aβ reduction, which could prevent AD if begun well before significant amyloid deposition. However, it is unclear whether any level of BACE1 inhibition can be effective if major amyloid accumulation is present in the brain. Amyloid PET imaging, CSF Aβ42 measurement, and other biomarker studies suggest that amyloid deposition starts years, even decades, before the clinical diagnosis of dementia. Moreover, the relationships between amyloid burden and cognitive impairment are not sufficiently well understood to determine the stage of AD at which BACE1 inhibitor treatment would be most effective. Results from ongoing biomarker studies, future treatment and prevention trials, and pharmacodynamic modeling are expected to establish the appropriate level of BACE1 inhibition and stage of AD for optimal efficacy. Like the statins for hypercholesterolemia, the hope is that a therapeutic window of BACE1 inhibitor doses might be found that reduces cerebral Aβ levels enough for efficacy, yet maintains sufficient BACE1 activity for the avoidance of side effects. When eventually published, the results of the current BACE1 inhibitor clinical trials will prove invaluable for solving these important questions. We are at a crucial juncture in BACE1 inhibitor drug development, and the therapeutic potential of BACE1 inhibition for AD will be definitively answered in the not too distant future.

Abbreviations

AD Alzheimer's disease
Aβ β-Amyloid peptide
APP Amyloid precursor protein
BACE1 β-Site APP cleaving enzyme 1
C99 Carboxy-terminal 99 amino acid fragment of APP generated by BACE1 cleavage
sAPPβ Amino terminal ectodomain fragment of APP generated by BACE1 cleavage

Acknowledgments

I thank Dr. Patty Kandalepas for making Figs. 3.1–3.3. I would also like to acknowledge my funding sources, including the National Institutes of Health R01AG022560, R01AG030142, Cure Alzheimer's Fund, Baila Foundation, BrightFocus Foundation, and the Alzheimer's Association.

References

Abdul-Hay SO, Sahara T, McBride M, Kang D, Leissring MA: Identification of BACE2 as an avid ss-amyloid-degrading protease, *Mol Neurodegener* 7:46, 2012.

Alexander R, Budd S, Russell M, Kugler A, Cebers G, Ye N, Olsson T, Burdette D, Maltby J, Paraskos J, Elsby K, Han D, Goldwater R, Ereshefsky L: AZD3293 a novel BACE1 inhibitor: safety, tolerability, and effects on plasma and CSF Ab peptides following single- and multiple-dose administration, *Neurobiol Aging* 35:S2, 2014.

Arbel M, Yacoby I, Solomon B: Inhibition of amyloid precursor protein processing by beta-secretase through site-directed antibodies, *Proc Natl Acad Sci USA* 102:7718–7723, 2005.

Atwal JK, Chen Y, Chiu C, Mortensen DL, Meilandt WJ, Liu Y, Heise CE, Hoyte K, Luk W, Lu Y, Peng K, Wu P, Rouge L, Zhang Y, Lazarus RA, Scearce-Levie K, Wang W, Wu Y, Tessier-Lavigne M, Watts RJ: A therapeutic antibody targeting BACE1 inhibits amyloid-beta production in vivo, *Sci Transl Med* 3:84ra43, 2011.

Basi G, Frigon N, Barbour R, Doan T, Gordon G, McConlogue L, Sinha S, Zeller M: Antagonistic effects of beta-site amyloid precursor protein-cleaving enzymes 1 and 2 on beta-amyloid peptide production in cells, *J Biol Chem* 278:31512–31520, 2003.

Benilova I, Gallardo R, Ungureanu AA, Castillo Cano V, Snellinx A, Ramakers M, Bartic C, Rousseau F, Schymkowitz J, De Strooper B: The Alzheimer disease protective mutation A2T modulates kinetic and thermodynamic properties of amyloid-beta (Abeta) aggregation, *J Biol Chem* 289:30977–30989, 2014.

Bennett BD, Babu-Khan S, Loeloff R, Louis JC, Curran E, Citron M, Vassar R: Expression analysis of BACE2 in brain and peripheral tissues, *J Biol Chem* 275:20647–20651, 2000.

Bernier F, Sato Y, Matijevic M, Desmond H, McGrath S, Burns L, Kaplow JM, Albala B: Clinical study of E2609, a novel BACE1 inhibitor, demonstrates target engagement and inhibition of BACE1 activity in CSF, *Alzheimers Dement* 9(Suppl):P886, 2013.

Boddapati S, Levites Y, Sierks MR: Inhibiting beta-secretase activity in Alzheimer's disease cell models with single-chain antibodies specifically targeting APP, *J Mol Biol* 405:436–447, 2011.

Cai H, Wang Y, McCarthy D, Wen H, Borchelt DR, Price DL, Wong PC: BACE1 is the major beta-secretase for generation of Abeta peptides by neurons, *Nat Neurosci* 4:233–234, 2001.

Cai J, Qi X, Kociok N, Skosyrski S, Emilio A, Ruan Q, Han S, Liu L, Chen Z, Bowes Rickman C, Golde T, Grant MB, Saftig P, Serneels L, De Strooper B, Joussen AM, Boulton ME: Beta-secretase (BACE1) inhibition causes retinal pathology by vascular dysregulation and accumulation of age pigment, *EMBO Mol Med* 4:980–991, 2012.

Cao L, Rickenbacher GT, Rodriguez S, Moulia TW, Albers MW: The precision of axon targeting of mouse olfactory sensory neurons requires the BACE1 protease, *Sci Rep* 2:231, 2012.

Chami L, Checler F: BACE1 is at the crossroad of a toxic vicious cycle involving cellular stress and beta-amyloid production in Alzheimer's disease, *Mol Neurodegener* 7:52, 2012.

Cheret C, Willem M, Fricker FR, Wende H, Wulf-Goldenberg A, Tahirovic S, Nave KA, Saftig P, Haass C, Garratt AN, Bennett DL, Birchmeier C: BACE1 and neuregulin-1 cooperate to control formation and maintenance of muscle spindles, *EMBO J* 32:2015–2028, 2013.

De Strooper B, Vassar R, Golde T: The secretases: enzymes with therapeutic potential in Alzheimer disease, *Nat Rev Neurol* 6:99–107, 2010.

Deng M, He W, Tan Y, Han H, Hu X, Xia K, Zhang Z, Yan R: Increased expression of reticulon 3 in neurons leads to reduced axonal transport of beta site amyloid precursor protein-cleaving enzyme 1, *J Biol Chem* 288:30236–30245, 2013.

Di Fede G, Catania M, Morbin M, Rossi G, Suardi S, Mazzoleni G, Merlin M, Giovagnoli AR, Prioni S, Erbetta A, Falcone C, Gobbi M, Colombo L, Bastone A, Beeg M, Manzoni C, Francescucci B, Spagnoli A, Cantu L, Del Favero E, Levy E, Salmona M, Tagliavini F: A recessive mutation in the APP gene with dominant-negative effect on amyloidogenesis, *Science* 323:1473–1477, 2009.

Dominguez D, Tournoy J, Hartmann D, Huth T, Cryns K, Deforce S, Serneels L, Camacho IE, Marjaux E, Craessaerts K, Roebroek AJ, Schwake M, D'Hooge R, Bach P, Kalinke U, Moechars D, Alzheimer C, Reiss K, Saftig P, De Strooper B: Phenotypic and biochemical analyses of BACE1- and BACE2-deficient mice, *J Biol Chem* 280:30797–30806, 2005.

Esterhazy D, Stutzer I, Wang H, Rechsteiner MP, Beauchamp J, Dobeli H, Hilpert H, Matile H, Prummer M, Schmidt A, Lieske N, Boehm B, Marselli L, Bosco D, Kerr-Conte J, Aebersold R, Spinas GA, Moch H, Migliorini C, Stoffel M: BACE2 is a beta cell-enriched protease that regulates pancreatic beta cell function and mass, *Cell Metab* 14:365–377, 2011.

Evin G, Lessene G, Wilkins S: BACE inhibitors as potential drugs for the treatment of Alzheimer's disease: focus on bioactivity, *Recent Pat CNS Drug Discov* 6:91–106, 2011.

Farzan M, Schnitzler CE, Vasilieva N, Leung D, Choe H: BACE2, a b-secretase homolog, cleaves at the b site and within the amyloid-b region of the amyloid-b precursor protein, *Proc Natl Acad Sci USA* 97:9712–9717, 2000.

Fleck D, Van Bebber F, Colombo A, Galante C, Schwenk BM, Rabe L, Hampel H, Novak B, Kremmer E, Tahirovic S, Edbauer D, Lichtenthaler SF, Schmid B, Willem M, Haass C: Dual cleavage of neuregulin 1 type III by BACE1 and ADAM17 liberates its EGF-like domain and allows paracrine signaling, *J Neurosci* 33:7856–7869, 2013.

Fluhrer R, Capell A, Westmeyer G, Willem M, Hartung B, Condron MM, Teplow DB, Haass C, Walter J: A non-amyloidogenic function of BACE-2 in the secretory pathway, *J Neurochem* 81:1011–1020, 2002.

Forman M, Kleijn H, Dockendorf M, Palcza J, Tseng J, Canales C, Egan M, Kennedy M, Laterza O, Ma L, Scott J, Tanen M, Apter J, Backonja M, Ereshefsky L, Gevorkyan H, Jhee S, Rynders R, Zari A, Bryan E, Wagner J, Troyer M, Stone J: The novel BACE inhibitor MK-8931 dramatically lowers CSF beta-amyloid in patients with mild-to-moderate Alzheimer's disease, *Alzheimers Dement* 9(Suppl):P139, 2013.

Forman M, Palcza J, Tseng J, Leempoels J, Ramael S, Han D, Jhee S, Ereshefsky L, Tanen M, Laterza O, Dockendorf M, Krishna G, Ma L, Wagner J, Troyer M: The novel BACE inhibitor MK-8931 dramatically lowers cerebrospinal fluid Aβ peptides in health subjects following single- and multiple-dose administration, *Alzheimers Dement* 8(Suppl):P704, 2012.

Fukumoto H, Cheung BS, Hyman BT, Irizarry MC: Beta-secretase protein and activity are increased in the neocortex in Alzheimer disease, *Arch Neurol* 59:1381–1389, 2002.

Hardy J, Selkoe DJ: The amyloid hypothesis of Alzheimer's disease: progress and problems on the road to therapeutics, *Science* 297:353–356, 2002.

Harrison SM, Harper AJ, Hawkins J, Duddy G, Grau E, Pugh PL, Winter PH, Shilliam CS, Hughes ZA, Dawson LA, Gonzalez MI, Upton N, Pangalos MN, Dingwall C: BACE1 (beta-secretase) transgenic and knockout mice: identification of neurochemical deficits and behavioral changes, *Mol Cell Neurosci* 24:646–655, 2003.

Heyden A, Angenstein F, Sallaz M, Seidenbecher C, Montag D: Abnormal axonal guidance and brain anatomy in mouse mutants for the cell recognition molecules close homolog of L1 and NgCAM-related cell adhesion molecule, *Neuroscience* 155:221–233, 2008.

Hitt B, Riordan S, Kukreja L, Eimer W, Rajapaksha T, Vassar R: Beta-site amyloid precursor protein (APP) cleaving enzyme 1 (BACE1) deficient mice exhibit a close homolog of L1 (CHL1) loss-of-function phenotype involving axon guidance defects, *J Biol Chem* 287:38408–38425, 2012.

Hitt BD, Jaramillo TC, Chetkovich DM, Vassar R: BACE1−/− mice exhibit seizure activity that does not correlate with sodium channel level or axonal localization, *Mol Neurodegener* 5:31, 2010.

Hoffmeister A, Tuennemann J, Sommerer I, Mossner J, Rittger A, Schleinitz D, Kratzsch J, Rosendahl J, Kloting N, Stahl T, Rossner S, Paroni F, Maedler K, Kovacs P, Bluher M: Genetic and biochemical evidence for a functional role of BACE1 in the regulation of insulin mRNA expression, *Obesity (Silver Spring)* 21(12):E626–633, 2013.

Höglund K, Salter H, Zetterberg H, Andreason U, Olsson T, Alexander R, Kugler A, Cebers G, Ye N, Burdette D, Budd Haeberlein SL: Monitoring the soluble amyloid precursor protein alpha (sAPPa) and beta (sAPPb) fragments in plasma and CSF from healthy individuals treated with BACE inhibitor AZD3293 in a multiple ascending dose study: pharmacokinetic and pharmacodynamic correlate, *Alzheimers Dement* 10:P447, 2014.

Holsinger RM, McLean CA, Beyreuther K, Masters CL, Evin G: Increased expression of the amyloid precursor beta-secretase in Alzheimer's disease, *Ann Neurol* 51:783–786, 2002.

Holtzman DM, Morris JC, Goate AM: Alzheimer's disease: the challenge of the second century, *Sci Transl Med* 3:77sr1, 2011.

Hong L, Koelsch G, Lin X, Wu S, Terzyan S, Ghosh AK, Zhang XC, Tang J: Structure of the protease domain of memapsin 2 (beta-secretase) complexed with inhibitor, *Science* 290:150–153, 2000.

Hong L, Turner RT 3rd, Koelsch G, Shin D, Ghosh AK, Tang J: Crystal structure of memapsin 2 (beta-secretase) in complex with an inhibitor OM00-3, *Biochemistry* 41:10963–10967, 2002.

Hu X, He W, Diaconu C, Tang X, Kidd GJ, Macklin WB, Trapp BD, Yan R: Genetic deletion of BACE1 in mice affects remyelination of sciatic nerves, *FASEB J* 22:2970–2980, 2008.

Hu X, He W, Luo X, Tsubota KE, Yan R: BACE1 regulates hippocampal astrogenesis via the Jagged1-Notch pathway, *Cell Rep* 4:40–49, 2013.

Hu X, Hicks CW, He W, Wong P, Macklin WB, Trapp BD, Yan R: Bace1 modulates myelination in the central and peripheral nervous system, *Nat Neurosci* 9:1520–1525, 2006.

Hu X, Zhou X, He W, Yang J, Xiong W, Wong P, Wilson CG, Yan R: BACE1 deficiency causes altered neuronal activity and neurodegeneration, *J Neurosci* 30:8819–8829, 2010.

Hussain I, Powell D, Howlett DR, Tew DG, Meek TD, Chapman C, Gloger IS, Murphy KE, Southan CD, Ryan DM, Smith TS, Simmons DL, Walsh FS, Dingwall C, Christie G: Identification of a novel aspartic protease (Asp 2) as beta-secretase, *Mol Cell Neurosci* 14:419–427, 1999.

Jack CR Jr: Alzheimer disease: new concepts on its neurobiology and the clinical role imaging will play, *Radiology* 263:344–361, 2012.

Jack CR Jr, Holtzman DM: Biomarker modeling of Alzheimer's disease, *Neuron* 80:1347–1358, 2013.

Jonsson T, Atwal JK, Steinberg S, Snaedal J, Jonsson PV, Bjornsson S, Stefansson H, Sulem P, Gudbjartsson D, Maloney J, Hoyte K, Gustafson A, Liu Y, Lu Y, Bhangale T, Graham RR, Huttenlocher J, Bjornsdottir G, Andreassen OA, Jonsson EG, Palotie A, Behrens TW, Magnusson OT, Kong A, Thorsteinsdottir U, Watts RJ, Stefansson K: A mutation in APP protects against Alzheimer's disease and age-related cognitive decline, *Nature* 488:96–99, 2012.

Kandalepas PC, Sadleir KR, Eimer WA, Zhao J, Nicholson DA, Vassar R: The Alzheimer's beta-secretase BACE1 localizes to normal presynaptic terminals and to dystrophic presynaptic terminals surrounding amyloid plaques, *Acta Neuropathol* 126:329–352, 2013.

Kim DY, Carey BW, Wang H, Ingano LA, Binshtok AM, Wertz MH, Pettingell WH, He P, Lee VM, Woolf CJ, Kovacs DM: BACE1 regulates voltage-gated sodium channels and neuronal activity, *Nat Cell Biol* 9:755–764, 2007.

Kobayashi D, Zeller M, Cole T, Buttini M, McConlogue L, Sinha S, Freedman S, Morris RG, Chen KS: BACE1 gene deletion: impact on behavioral function in a model of Alzheimer's disease, *Neurobiol Aging* 29:861–873, 2008.

Kopan R, Ilagan MX: The canonical Notch signaling pathway: unfolding the activation mechanism, *Cell* 137:216–233, 2009.

Kuhn PH, Koroniak K, Hogl S, Colombo A, Zeitschel U, Willem M, Volbracht C, Schepers U, Imhof A, Hoffmeister A, Haass C, Rossner S, Brase S, Lichtenthaler SF: Secretome protein enrichment identifies physiological BACE1 protease substrates in neurons, *EMBO J* 31:3157–3168, 2012.

Lai R, Albala B, Kaplow JM, Aluri J, Yen M, Satlin A: First-in-human study of E2609, a novel BACE1 inhibitor, demonstrates prolonged reductions in plasma beta-amyloid levels after single dosing, *Alzheimers Dement* 8(Suppl):P96, 2012.

Lai R, Albala B, Kaplow JM, Majid O, Matijevic M, Aluri J, Satlin A: Novel BACE1 inhibitor E2609 reduces plasma and CSF amyloid in health subjects after 14 days oral administration. *The 11th International Conference on Alzheimer's & Parkinson's Diseases*, Florence, Italy.

Laird FM, Cai H, Savonenko AV, Farah MH, He K, Melnikova T, Wen H, Chiang HC, Xu G, Koliatsos VE, Borchelt DR, Price DL, Lee HK, Wong PC: BACE1, a major determinant of selective vulnerability of the brain to amyloid-beta amyloidogenesis, is essential for cognitive, emotional, and synaptic functions, *J Neurosci* 25:11693–11709, 2005.

Lemere CA: Immunotherapy for Alzheimer's disease: hoops and hurdles, *Mol Neurodegener* 8:36, 2013.

Li R, Lindholm K, Yang LB, Yue X, Citron M, Yan R, Beach T, Sue L, Sabbagh M, Cai H, Wong P, Price D, Shen Y: Amyloid beta peptide load is correlated with increased beta-secretase activity in sporadic Alzheimer's disease patients, *Proc Natl Acad Sci USA* 101:3632–3637, 2004.

Lin X, Koelsch G, Wu S, Downs D, Dashti A, Tang J: Human aspartic protease memapsin 2 cleaves the beta-secretase site of beta-amyloid precursor protein, *Proc Natl Acad Sci USA* 97:1456–1460, 2000.

Luo X, Prior M, He W, Hu X, Tang X, Shen W, Yadav S, Kiryu-Seo S, Miller R, Trapp BD, Yan R: Cleavage of neuregulin-1 by BACE1 or ADAM10 protein produces differential effects on myelination, *J Biol Chem* 286:23967–23974, 2011.

Luo Y, Bolon B, Damore MA, Fitzpatrick D, Liu H, Zhang J, Yan Q, Vassar R, Citron M: BACE1 (beta-secretase) knockout mice do not acquire compensatory gene expression changes or develop neural lesions over time, *Neurobiol Dis* 14:81–88, 2003.

Luo Y, Bolon B, Kahn S, Bennett BD, Babu-Khan S, Denis P, Fan W, Kha H, Zhang J, Gong Y, Martin L, Louis JC, Yan Q, Richards WG, Citron M, Vassar R: Mice deficient in BACE1, the Alzheimer's beta-secretase, have normal phenotype and abolished beta-amyloid generation, *Nat Neurosci* 4:231–232, 2001.

Maloney JA, Bainbridge T, Gustafson A, Zhang S, Kyauk R, Steiner P, Van der Brug M, Liu Y, Ernst JA, Watts RJ, Atwal JK: Molecular mechanisms of Alzheimer disease protection by the A673T allele of amyloid precursor protein, *J Biol Chem* 289:30990–31000, 2014.

Marques F, Sousa JC, Sousa N, Palha JA: Blood-brain-barriers in aging and in Alzheimer's disease, *Mol Neurodegener* 8:38, 2013.

Martenyi F, Dean RA, Lowe S, Nakano M, Monk S, Willis BA, Gonzales C, Mergott D, Leslie D, May P, James A, Gevorkyan H, Jhee S, Ereshefsky L, Citron M: BACE inhibitor LY2886721 safety and central and peripheral PK and PD in healthy subjects (HSs), *Alzheimers Dement* 8(Suppl):P583–P584, 2012.

May PC, Dean RA, Lowe SL, Martenyi F, Sheehan SM, Boggs LN, Monk SA, Mathes BM, Mergott DJ, Watson BM, Stout SL, Timm DE, Smith Labell E, Gonzales CR, Nakano M, Jhee SS, Yen M, Ereshefsky L, Lindstrom TD, Calligaro DO, Cocke PJ, Greg Hall D, Friedrich S, Citron M, Audia JE: Robust central reduction of amyloid-beta in humans with an orally available, non-peptidic beta-secretase inhibitor, *J Neurosci* 31:16507–16516, 2011.

May PC, Mergott DJ, Cocke PJ, Monk SA, Boggs LN, Sanchez-Felix MV, Audia JE, Calligaro DO, Citron M, Dean RA, Lowe SL, Daugherty LL, Gonzales CR, Nakano M, Willis BA, Martenyi F: Preclinical and phase I clinical characterization of LY2886721, a BACE inhibitor in phase II development Alzheimer's disease. *The 11th International Conference on Alzheimer's & Parkinson's Diseases*, Florence, Italy.

McConlogue L, Buttini M, Anderson JP, Brigham EF, Chen KS, Freedman SB, Games D, Johnson-Wood K, Lee M, Zeller M, Liu W, Motter R, Sinha S: Partial reduction of BACE1 has dramatic effects on Alzheimer plaque and synaptic pathology in APP transgenic mice, *J Biol Chem* 282:26326–26334, 2007.

Meakin PJ, Harper AJ, Hamilton DL, Gallagher J, McNeilly AD, Burgess LA, Vaanholt LM, Bannon KA, Latcham J, Hussain I, Speakman JR, Howlett DR, Ashford ML: Reduction in BACE1 decreases body weight, protects against diet-induced obesity and enhances insulin sensitivity in mice, *Biochem J* 441:285–296, 2012.

Montag-Sallaz M, Schachner M, Montag D: Misguided axonal projections, neural cell adhesion molecule 180 mRNA upregulation, and altered behavior in mice deficient for the close homolog of L1, *Mol Cell Biol* 22:7967–7981, 2002.

Mullan M, Crawford F, Houlden H, Axelman K, Lilius L, Winblad B, Lannfelt L: A pathogenic mutation for probable Alzheimer's disease in the APP gene at the N-terminus of beta-amyloid, *Nat Genet* 1:345–347, 1992.

Musiek ES, Holtzman DM: Origins of Alzheimer's disease: reconciling cerebrospinal fluid biomarker and neuropathology data regarding the temporal sequence of amyloid-beta and tau involvement, *Curr Opin Neurol* 25:715–720, 2012.

Ohno M, Chang L, Tseng W, Oakley H, Citron M, Klein WL, Vassar R, Disterhoft JF: Temporal memory deficits in Alzheimer's mouse models: rescue by genetic deletion of BACE1, *Eur J Neurosci* 23:251–260, 2006.

Ohno M, Cole SL, Yasvoina M, Zhao J, Citron M, Berry R, Disterhoft JF, Vassar R: BACE1 gene deletion prevents neuron loss and memory deficits in 5XFAD APP/PS1 transgenic mice, *Neurobiol Dis* 26:134–145, 2007.

Ohno M, Sametsky EA, Younkin LH, Oakley H, Younkin SG, Citron M, Vassar R, Disterhoft JF: BACE1 deficiency rescues memory deficits and cholinergic dysfunction in a mouse model of Alzheimer's disease, *Neuron* 41:27–33, 2004.

Probst G, Xu YZ: Small-molecule BACE1 inhibitors: a patent literature review (2006–2011), *Expert Opin Ther Pat* 22:511–540, 2012.

Rabinovich-Nikitin I, Rakover IS, Becker M, Solomon B: Beneficial effect of antibodies against beta-secretase cleavage site of APP on Alzheimer's-like pathology in triple-transgenic mice, *PLoS One* 7:e46650, 2012.

Rajapaksha TW, Eimer WA, Bozza TC, Vassar R: The Alzheimer's beta-secretase enzyme BACE1 is required for accurate axon guidance of olfactory sensory neurons and normal glomerulus formation in the olfactory bulb, *Mol Neurodegener* 6:88, 2011.

Roberds SL, Anderson J, Basi G, Bienkowski MJ, Branstetter DG, Chen KS, Freedman SB, Frigon NL, Games D, Hu K, Johnson-Wood K, Kappenman KE, Kawabe TT, Kola I, Kuehn R, Lee M, Liu W, Motter R, Nichols NF, Power M, Robertson DW, Schenk D, Schoor M, Shopp GM, Shuck ME, Sinha S, Svensson KA, Tatsuno G, Tintrup H, Wijsman J, Wright S, McConlogue L: BACE knockout mice are healthy despite lacking the primary beta-secretase activity in brain: implications for Alzheimer's disease therapeutics, *Hum Mol Genet* 10:1317–1324, 2001.

Rochin L, Hurbain I, Serneels L, Fort C, Watt B, Leblanc P, Marks MS, De Strooper B, Raposo G, Van Niel G: BACE2 processes PMEL to form the melanosome amyloid matrix in pigment cells, *Proc Natl Acad Sci USA* 110:10658–10663, 2013.

Rosen C, Hansson O, Blennow K, Zetterberg H: Fluid biomarkers in Alzheimer's disease—current concepts, *Mol Neurodegener* 8:20, 2013.

Rossner S, Sastre M, Bourne K, Lichtenthaler SF: Transcriptional and translational regulation of BACE1 expression—implications for Alzheimer's disease, *Prog Neurobiol* 79:95–111, 2006.

Rutten BP, Steinbusch HW: Current concepts in Alzheimer's disease: molecules, models and translational perspectives, *Mol Neurodegener* 8:33, 2013.

Sadleir KR, Eimer WA, Kaufman RJ, Osten P, Vassar R: Genetic inhibition of phosphorylation of the translation initiation factor eIF2α does not block Aβ-dependent elevation of BACE1 and APP levels or reduce amyloid pathology in a mouse model of Alzheimer's disease, *PLoS One* 9:e110914, 2014.

Sadleir KR, Vassar R: Cdk5 protein inhibition and Abeta42 increase BACE1 protein level in primary neurons by a post-transcriptional mechanism: implications of CDK5 as a therapeutic target for Alzheimer disease, *J Biol Chem* 287:7224–7235, 2012.

Salzer JL: Axonal regulation of Schwann cell ensheathment and myelination, *J Peripher Nerv Syst* 17(Suppl 3):14–19, 2012.

Savonenko AV, Melnikova T, Laird FM, Stewart KA, Price DL, Wong PC: Alteration of BACE1-dependent NRG1/ErbB4 signaling and schizophrenia-like phenotypes in BACE1-null mice, *Proc Natl Acad Sci USA* 105:5585–5590, 2008.

Sinha S, Anderson JP, Barbour R, Basi GS, Caccavello R, Davis D, Doan M, Dovey HF, Frigon N, Hong J, Jacobson-Croak K, Jewett N, Keim P, Knops J, Lieberburg I, Power M, Tan H, Tatsuno G, Tung J, Schenk D, Seubert P, Suomensaari SM, Wang S, Walker D, Zhao J, McConlogue L, John V: Purification and cloning of amyloid precursor protein beta-secretase from human brain, *Nature* 402:537–540, 1999.

Sisodia SS, St George-Hyslop PH: Gamma-secretase, Notch, Abeta and Alzheimer's disease: where do the presenilins fit in? *Nat Rev Neurosci* 3:281–290, 2002.

Solans A, Estivill X, De la Luna S: A new aspartyl protease on 21q22.3, BACE2, is highly similar to Alzheimer's amyloid precursor protein beta-secretase, *Cytogenet Cell Genet* 89:177–184, 2000.

Sun X, He G, Qing H, Zhou W, Dobie F, Cai F, Staufenbiel M, Huang LE, Song W: Hypoxia facilitates Alzheimer's disease pathogenesis by up-regulating BACE1 gene expression, *Proc Natl Acad Sci USA* 103:18727–18732, 2006.

Tanzi RE: The genetics of Alzheimer disease, *Cold Spring Harb Perspect Med* 2:a006296, 2012.

Tarawneh R, Holtzman DM: The clinical problem of symptomatic Alzheimer disease and mild cognitive impairment, *Cold Spring Harb Perspect Med* 2:a006148, 2012.

Torres M, Jimenez S, Sanchez-Varo R, Navarro V, Trujillo-Estrada L, Sanchez-Mejias E, Carmona I, Davila JC, Vizuete M, Gutierrez A, Vitorica J: Defective lysosomal proteolysis and axonal transport are early pathogenic events that worsen with age leading to increased APP metabolism and synaptic Abeta in transgenic APP/PS1 hippocampus, *Mol Neurodegener* 7:59, 2012.

Vassar R, Bennett BD, Babu-Khan S, Kahn S, Mendiaz EA, Denis P, Teplow DB, Ross S, Amarante P, Loeloff R, Luo Y, Fisher S, Fuller J, Edenson S, Lile J, Jarosinski MA, Biere AL, Curran E, Burgess T, Louis JC, Collins F, Treanor J, Rogers G, Citron M: Beta-secretase cleavage of Alzheimer's amyloid precursor protein by the transmembrane aspartic protease BACE, *Science* 286:735–741, 1999.

Vassar R, Kovacs DM, Yan R, Wong PC: The beta-secretase enzyme BACE in health and Alzheimer's disease: regulation, cell biology, function, and therapeutic potential, *J Neurosci* 29:12787–12794, 2009.

Walter J, van Echten-Deckert G: Cross-talk of membrane lipids and Alzheimer-related proteins, *Mol Neurodegener* 8:34, 2013.

Wang W, Liu Y, Lazarus RA: Allosteric inhibition of BACE1 by an exosite-binding antibody, *Curr Opin Struct Biol* 23:797–805, 2013.

Willem M, Garratt AN, Novak B, Citron M, Kaufmann S, Rittger A, Destrooper B, Saftig P, Birchmeier C, Haass C: Control of peripheral nerve myelination by the beta-secretase BACE1, *Science* 314:664–666, 2006.

Willis B, Martenyi F, Dean R, Lowe S, Nakano M, Monk S, Gonzales C, Mergott D, Daugherty L, Citron M, May P: Central BACE1 inhibition by LY2886721 produces opposing effects on APP processing as reflected by cerebrospinal fluid sAPPalpha and sAPPbeta, *Alzheimers Dement* 8(Suppl):P582, 2012.

Yan R, Bienkowski MJ, Shuck ME, Miao H, Tory MC, Pauley AM, Brashier JR, Stratman NC, Mathews WR, Buhl AE, Carter DB, Tomasselli AG, Parodi LA, Heinrikson RL, Gurney ME: Membrane-anchored aspartyl protease with Alzheimer's disease beta-secretase activity, *Nature* 402:533–537, 1999.

Yan R, Munzner JB, Shuck ME, Bienkowski MJ: BACE2 functions as an alternative alpha-secretase in cells, *J Biol Chem* 276:34019–34027, 2001.

Yang LB, Lindholm K, Yan R, Citron M, Xia W, Yang XL, Beach T, Sue L, Wong P, Price D, Li R, Shen Y: Elevated beta-secretase expression and enzymatic activity detected in sporadic Alzheimer disease, *Nat Med* 9:3–4, 2003.

Yu YJ, Atwal JK, Zhang Y, Tong RK, Wildsmith KR, Tan C, Bien-Ly N, Hersom M, Maloney JA, Meilandt WJ, Bumbaca D, Gadkar K, Hoyte K, Luk W, Lu Y, Ernst JA, Scearce-Levie K, Couch JA, Dennis MS, Watts RJ: Therapeutic bispecific antibodies cross the blood–brain barrier in nonhuman primates, *Sci Transl Med* 6:261ra154, 2014.

Yu YJ, Zhang Y, Kenrick M, Hoyte K, Luk W, Lu Y, Atwal J, Elliott JM, Prabhu S, Watts RJ, Dennis MS: Boosting brain uptake of a therapeutic antibody by reducing its affinity for a transcytosis target, *Sci Transl Med* 3:84ra44, 2011.

Zhang X, Zhou K, Wang R, Cui J, Lipton SA, Liao FF, Xu H, Zhang YW: Hypoxia-inducible factor 1alpha (HIF-1alpha)-mediated hypoxia increases BACE1 expression and beta-amyloid generation, *J Biol Chem* 282:10873–10880, 2007.

Zhang XM, Cai Y, Xiong K, Cai H, Luo XG, Feng JC, Clough RW, Struble RG, Patrylo PR, Yan XX: Beta-secretase-1 elevation in transgenic mouse models of Alzheimer's disease is associated with synaptic/axonal pathology and amyloidogenesis: implications for neuritic plaque development, *Eur J Neurosci* 30:2271–2283, 2009.

Zhao J, Fu Y, Yasvoina M, Shao P, Hitt B, O'Connor T, Logan S, Maus E, Citron M, Berry R, Binder L, Vassar R: Beta-site amyloid precursor protein cleaving enzyme 1 levels become elevated in neurons around amyloid plaques: implications for Alzheimer's disease pathogenesis, *J Neurosci* 27:3639–3649, 2007.

Zhao Y, Wang Y, Yang J, Wang X, Zhao Y, Zhang X, Zhang YW: Sorting nexin 12 interacts with BACE1 and regulates BACE1-mediated APP processing, *Mol Neurodegener* 7:30, 2012.

Zhou L, Barao S, Laga M, Bockstael K, Borgers M, Gijsen H, Annaert W, Moechars D, Mercken M, Gevaer K, De Strooper B: The neural cell adhesion molecules L1 and CHL1 are cleaved by BACE1 protease in vivo, *J Biol Chem* 287:25927–25940, 2012.

Zhou L, Chavez-Gutierrez L, Bockstael K, Sannerud R, Annaert W, May PC, Karran E, De Strooper B: Inhibition of beta-secretase in vivo via antibody binding to unique loops (D and F) of BACE1, *J Biol Chem* 286:8677–8687, 2011.

CHAPTER

4

γ-Secretase Inhibitors: From Chemical Probes to Drug Development

J.-Y. Hur, N. Gertsik, D.S. Johnson, Y.-M. Li

OUTLINE

THE γ-SECRETASE COMPLEX

γ-Secretase has been on the frontier of biomedical research due to its critical role in normal physiology as well as in the pathology of Alzheimer's disease (AD) (Crump et al., 2013; Esler and Wolfe, 2001; Li, 2001; Wolfe and Kopan, 2004). γ-Secretase functions as a macromolecular intramembrane protease complex containing presenilin (PS), nicastrin (Nct), anterior pharynx defective-1 (Aph1), and presenilin enhancer-2 (Pen2) (De Strooper, 2003; Gertsik et al., 2014) (Fig. 4.1). Formation of the active γ-secretase complex relies on the assembly and trafficking of these subunits, as well as on the endoproteolytic processing of PS upon assembly (Takasugi et al., 2003). Recently, the cryo-EM structures of human γ-secretase at 4.5 and 4.32 Å resolution showed the horseshoe-shaped transmembrane domain of the complex and the way in which the subunits are assembled (Lu et al., 2014; Sun et al., 2015), offering a structural basis for γ-secretase function and regulation. Of note, Pen2 appears to possess

Developing Therapeutics for Alzheimer's Disease. http://dx.doi.org/10.1016/B978-0-12-802173-6.00004-6

a unique topology (Lu et al., 2014; Sun et al., 2015). Changes in γ-secretase structure and activity can be deleterious: mutations in its subunits are associated with AD (Levy Lahad et al., 1995; Sherrington et al., 1995), acne inversa (Wang et al., 2010), and myeloid leukemia (Klinakis et al., 2011).

PS, Nct, Aph1, AND Pen2

Presenilins

Presenilin-1 (PS1) and presenilin-2 (PS2) are two genes that are associated with familial AD (FAD), a condition that often leads to early onset of disease. Autosomal-dominant inheritance of mutations in the PS1 gene is the most common cause of FAD (Sherrington et al., 1995). Mutations in PS2 can also lead to FAD (Levy Lahad et al., 1995). PS1 and PS2 are polytopic membrane proteins that are synthesized as single polypeptide chains (PS-FL) with nine transmembrane domains. Both the PS1 and PS2 polypeptides undergo autocatalytic endoproteolysis, an internal cleavage event that generates amino- and carboxy-terminal cleavage products (PS-NTF and PS-CTF), which remain associated as heterodimeric integral membrane proteins (Thinakaran et al., 1996) (Fig. 4.1).

The discovery of the PS proteins provided critical insight into γ-secretase, its function in important molecular pathways, and its role in disease. Given that γ-secretase cleaves the amyloid precursor protein (APP) to generate heterogeneous C-terminuses of Aβ peptides, the following data are proof that PS is the catalytic subunit of the γ-secretase complex. First, FAD mutations in PS1 and PS2 caused an increase in the ratio of Aβ42/Aβ40 in transfected cells and in transgenic mice (Borchelt et al., 1996; Duff et al., 1996; Scheuner et al., 1996), implying that PS plays a role in APP processing. Second, isolated cultured neurons derived from PS1-deficient mice showed significantly reduced Aβ production and accumulation of APP fragments, suggesting that PS1 participates in γ-secretase cleavage of APP (De Strooper et al., 1998; Naruse et al., 1998). Third, γ-secretase activity was abolished in cultured cells derived from mice that are deficient in both PS1 and PS2 (Herreman et al., 2000; Zhang et al., 2000), revealing that PS1 and PS2 have overlapping functions and are required for γ-secretase activity and APP processing. Fourth, mutagenesis of two conserved aspartates in the transmembrane region of PS1 significantly reduced Aβ production (Wolfe et al., 1999b),

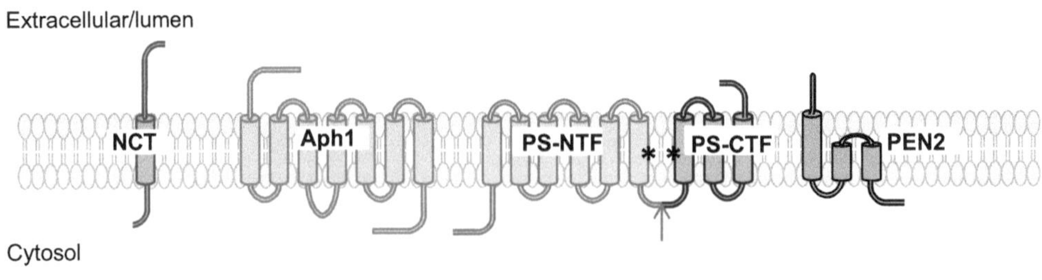

FIGURE 4.1 **Schematic representation of the γ-secretase subunits.** The two catalytic aspartyl residues (indicated by *) are located on transmembrane domains 6 and 7 of PS. Full-length PS undergoes endoproteolysis (*arrow*) to form the PS-NTF/PS-CTF heterodimer.

pointing to the requirement of the aspartyl protease activity of PS for γ-secretase activity. Fifth, γ-secretase activity is directly associated with PS1-containing macromolecular complexes (Li et al., 2000a). Sixth, active site-directed γ-secretase inhibitors directly bind to PS1 and PS2 (Esler et al., 2000; Li et al., 2000b; Xu et al., 2002). Finally, a PS1 variant alone can reconstitute γ-secretase activity, providing a final proof that PS1 is the catalytic subunit of γ-secretase (Ahn et al., 2010).

Nicastrin

Nct encodes a 78 kDa type I single pass transmembrane protein that is highly glycosylated, resulting in an apparent molecular weight of ~120 kDa. Blockage of Nct glycosylation in cells using mannosidase I inhibitors did not suppress γ-secretase activity but led to an incorporation of immature Nct into the γ-secretase complex (Herreman et al., 2003). It appears that glycosylation of Nct is required for proper trafficking of the mature complex but is not required for enzymatic activity (Herreman et al., 2003). Nct is required for stabilization and assembly of PS into the γ-secretase complex (Li et al., 2003). Nct is also postulated to act as a substrate receptor (Shah et al., 2005).

Aph1

Aph1 is a ~30 kDa integral membrane protein with seven transmembrane domains. Aph1 is implicated in γ-secretase complex stability, activity, and selectivity (Lee et al., 2002; Takasugi et al., 2003). A highly conserved GXXXG motif in transmembrane domain 4 of Aph1 mediates critical protein–protein interactions with PS and is thought to contribute to γ-secretase stability (Lee et al., 2004; Niimura et al., 2005).

Aph1 exists as two conserved homologs, Aph1a and Aph1b, which are expressed in both peripheral and neuronal tissues (Francis et al., 2002; Shirotani et al., 2004). Aph1a is the principal isoform present in γ-secretase complexes during embryonic development (Ma et al., 2005). In addition, Aph1a can undergo alternative splicing to produce Aph1a-long (Aph1aL) and Aph1a-short (Aph1aS) with Aph1aS being the more abundantly expressed isoform in most tissues. However, while Aph1aS is more abundant, Aph1aL is more commonly found associated with γ-secretase complexes (Farmery et al., 2003; Lee et al., 2002). Expression of these isoforms appears to be coordinately regulated (Gu et al., 2003). Regardless of expression, all isoforms and homologs of Aph1 can be found as functional components of mutually exclusive γ-secretase complexes. Like PS, Aph1 homologs share overlapping but also nonredundant roles in γ-secretase activity. Aph1a$^{-/-}$ mice are embryonically lethal, and Aph1a deficiency in cell models results in a total loss of γ-secretase activity. Aph1b$^{-/-}$ mice are viable but have γ-secretase substrate processing defects, and therefore it appears that Aph1b fulfills a partially redundant role (Serneels et al., 2005; Shirotani et al., 2004). However, Aph1b may contribute to γ-secretase substrate selectivity (Coolen et al., 2005a,b). Genetic knockout of Aph1b γ-secretase in a mouse AD model improved the disease-relevant phenotypic features without Notch-related side effects (Serneels et al., 2009). Therefore, it has been suggested that inhibitors that target the Aph1b-containing γ-secretase complexes could be developed for AD therapy (Serneels et al., 2009).

Pen2

Pen2 is a ~12 kDa integral membrane protein with three transmembrane domains (Sun et al., 2015). Pen2 is critical for the final maturation of γ-secretase as it promotes endoproteolysis of PS-FL into PS-NTF and PS-CTF. Biochemical reconstitution studies showed that Pen2 is necessary and sufficient to promote the endoproteolysis of PS1 to generate the active form of γ-secretase (Ahn et al., 2010). In addition, Pen2 is required for stability of the γ-secretase complex (Francis et al., 2002; Luo et al., 2003; Prokop et al., 2004; Shiraishi et al., 2004; Steiner et al., 2002; Takasugi et al., 2003).

γ-SECRETASE INHIBITORS

γ-Secretase inhibitors (GSIs) have extensively been developed as molecular probes and therapeutic agents (Golde et al., 2013; Josien, 2002; Wolfe, 2012). Distinct classes of small molecules that target γ-secretase have been reported (Crump et al., 2013; Golde et al., 2013; Josien, 2002; Wolfe, 2012). γ-Secretase cleaves more than 90 different substrates (Haapasalo and Kovacs, 2011), of which APP and Notch are the most heavily studied due to their roles in AD and cancer, respectively. Complete inhibition of γ-secretase, as achieved by nonselective GSIs, abolishes all γ-secretase activity so that there is a decrease in Aβ production and Notch signaling.

ACTIVE SITE-DIRECTED GSIs

Wolfe et al. found that a substrate-based difluoro ketone peptidomimetic compound ($IC_{50} = 13 \pm 5\ \mu M$) inhibited γ-secretase activity in APP-expressing cells (Wolfe et al., 1998). Shearman et al. reported a potent γ-secretase inhibitor, L-685,458 (L-458), which contains a hydroxyethylene dipeptide isostere directed to the active site of aspartyl proteases (Shearman et al., 2000) (Fig. 4.2). Active site-directed small molecule inhibitors have been developed as activity-based probes for identification, localization, and isolation of γ-secretase and detection of conformational changes within the active site (Beher et al., 2003; Chau et al., 2012; Chun et al., 2004; Crump et al., 2011; Esler et al., 2000, 2002, 2004; Gertsik et al., 2015; Kimberly et al., 2003; Kornilova et al., 2003, 2005; Li et al., 2000a,b; Moore et al., 2000; Placanica et al., 2009a,b, 2010; Shelton et al., 2009; Tarassishin et al., 2004; Teranishi et al., 2010; Tian et al., 2010; Vetrivel et al., 2007, 2008; Wolfe et al., 1999a; Yang et al., 2009). These probes interact with the PS-NTF/PS-CTF heterodimer, but not with PS full length (Ahn et al., 2010; Li et al., 2000b).

FIRST-GENERATION GSIs

Compound E, DAPT, and LY-411,575 are early first-generation GSIs that continue to be used for investigation of γ-secretase. Compound E ($IC_{50} = 300$ pM) was shown to inhibit Aβ production by binding to PS1 and PS2 (Seiffert et al., 2000). DAPT ($IC_{50} = 20$ nM) was one of

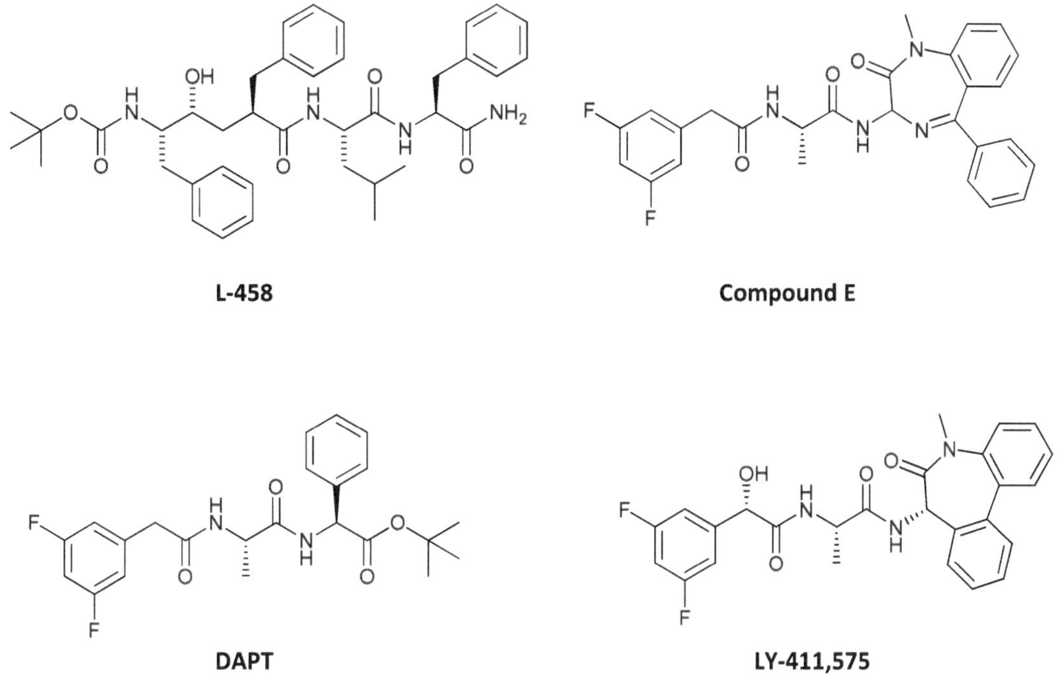

FIGURE 4.2 **Structures of L-458 and first-generation GSIs.**

the first compounds to show reduction of Aβ in vivo (Dovey et al., 2001). When DAPT was orally administered to PDAPP mice (harboring human APP with the "Indiana" mutation [V717F]), brain Aβ levels decreased in a dose-dependent manner within 3 h and APP-CTFs accumulated (Dovey et al., 2001). Similarly, DAPT decreased Aβ levels in the plasma and cerebrospinal fluid (CSF) of Tg2576 mice (harboring human APP with the "Swedish" mutation) (Lanz et al., 2003). Administration of LY-411,575 (IC_{50} = 30 pM) for 15 days in a murine model of AD also led to a reduction in Aβ levels (Wong et al., 2004). However, side effects on lymphocyte development and the intestine were observed due to the inhibition of Notch signaling by this GSI (Wong et al., 2004).

CLINICAL GSIs FOR AD

Nonselective GSIs

LY450139 (semagacestat, Eli Lilly) is a potent GSI that pan-inhibits γ-secretase cleavage of its substrates (Fig. 4.3) and was the first GSI to enter phase 3 clinical trials. The most surprising outcome of the clinical trial of semagacestat was the worsening of memory in patients (Doody et al., 2013). The other major adverse effect of the trial was the increased risk of skin cancer, which likely resulted from inhibition of Notch signaling (Nicolas et al., 2003; Xia et al., 2001). While the Notch-associated side effects are somewhat understood, the mechanism of cognitive decline is elusive.

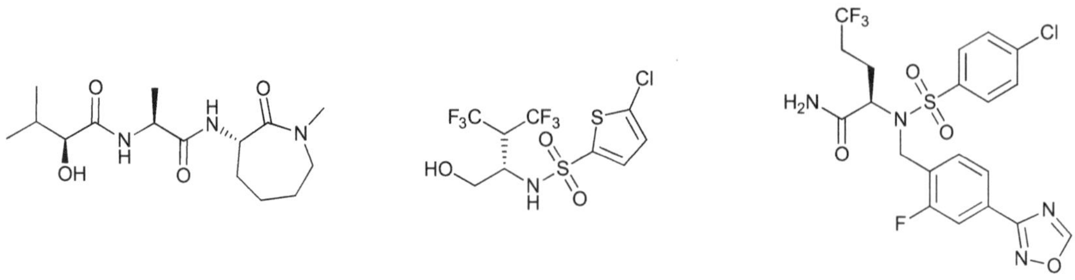

Semagacestat (LY450139) **Begacestat (GSI-953)** **Avagacestat (BMS-708163)**

FIGURE 4.3 **Structures of GSIs that have advanced into clinical studies for AD.**

"Notch-Sparing" GSIs

"Notch-sparing" GSIs, in contrast, are intended to inhibit Aβ production while leaving some Notch signaling intact (Kreft et al., 2008; Mayer et al., 2008). GSI-953 (begacestat, Wyeth [now Pfizer]) is a thiophene sulfonamide GSI (Martone et al., 2009). It is 16 times more potent for inhibition of APP cleavage versus Notch cleavage in the assays used and was optimized for improved stability in humans ($t_{1/2} > 90$ min) compared to other Wyeth compounds (Hopkins, 2012; Martone et al., 2009). Begacestat was reported to decrease plasma, brain, and CSF Aβ levels in Tg2576 mice overexpressing APP and also reduce plasma Aβ levels in a dose-dependent manner in healthy humans (Martone et al., 2009). While begacestat appeared to have a higher selectivity for APP over Notch than semagacestat, it was discontinued in the phase 1 trial in 2010 for unknown reasons.

BMS-708163 (avagacestat, Bristol-Myers Squibb) is a sulfonamide-based GSI that has a preference for inhibition of APP processing over Notch processing (Gillman et al., 2010). Initially, avagacestat was reported to have 193-fold selectivity for APP over Notch in cell culture (Gillman et al., 2010). Although the major adverse effects of the avagacestat phase 2 trial were gastrointestinal and dermatologic complications, which probably stemmed from Notch inhibition, the 100 mg and 125 mg dose arms also led to a trend for cognitive worsening (Coric et al., 2012), suggesting that avagacestat may share a common mechanism of toxicity with semagacestat. While avagacestat was initially reported as a Notch-sparing inhibitor (Gillman et al., 2010), two groups were unable to reproduce this result using different assay formats (Chavez-Gutierrez et al., 2012; Crump et al., 2012). Therefore, the toxicity can be partially attributed to the inhibition of Notch signaling (Chavez-Gutierrez et al., 2012; Crump et al., 2012; De Strooper, 2014). A recent study suggested that the worsening in cognition by treatment with semagacestat and avagacestat could be due to the accumulation of APP-CTF in the presynaptic terminals of the hippocampus (Mitani et al., 2012).

PS1 Isoform-Selective GSIs

Another approach toward developing a more selective GSI has been to screen for differences in PS1/PS2 selectivity with the intention of making GSIs specific for one or the other isoform. In fact, studies show that PS1 and PS2 do exhibit different activities (Lai et al., 2003) and these activities can be specifically targeted by small molecule inhibitors. $PS1^{-/-}$ mice have a severe phenotype, and embryos suffer from brain hemorrhage and late embryonic lethality (Shen et al., 1997; Wong et al., 1997), while $PS2^{-/-}$ mice are viable and fertile and develop only mild pulmonary fibrosis and hemorrhage with age (Donoviel et al., 1999). These studies demonstrate that PS2 is redundant for normal Notch signaling during mammalian embryological development. Furthermore, observations from PS1 and PS2 knockout mice indicate that PS1-comprised γ-secretase is responsible for ~80% of total Aβ production in brain, whereas PS2-comprised γ-secretase contributes to the formation of the remaining 20% (De Strooper et al., 1998). It has been shown using blastocyst-derived (BD) cells and membranes from $PS1^{+/-}PS2^{-/-}$ and $PS1^{-/-}PS2^{+/+}$ mice that the PS1 γ-secretase is more active than PS2 γ-secretase toward the APP C100 substrate (Lai et al., 2003). Furthermore, the PS1- and PS2-mediated activities display different sensitivities to GSIs, suggesting that PS1 and PS2 have unique active sites and may have different substrate preferences. For example, L-458 inhibited PS1-mediated γ-secretase activity 5.4-fold more than PS2-mediated γ-secretase activity (Lai et al., 2003). Using transformed fibroblasts from PS double-knockout mice transfected with APPsw/PS1 or APPsw/PS2, investigators at Elan were the first to report that certain sulfonamide GSIs, including ELN318463 and BMS299897, have selectivity for inhibition of PS1-containing γ-secretase (Zhao et al., 2008) (Fig. 4.4). These data underscore the feasibility of selectively inhibiting one or the other PS isoform in spite of their highly homologous nature.

The reconstitution of four γ-secretase complexes composed of different PS (PS1 or PS2) and Aph1 (Aph1a and Aph1b) isoforms along with Nct and Pen2 in Sf9 cells provided additional insight into their distinct behaviors (Lee et al., 2011). γ-Secretase complexes containing PS1 produced a higher proportion of the toxic species Aβ42 than γ-secretase complexes containing PS2, suggesting that a PS1 subtype-selective GSI could be attractive for AD. Using the reconstituted system and C99 as a substrate, Lee et al. screened several GSIs and identified MRK-560 and SCH 1500022 as selective inhibitors of PS1 γ-secretase activity. The fold selectivity for inhibition (PS2/PS1 IC_{50} ratio) of PS1 over PS2 complexes was 37 (MRK-560) and 250 (SCH 1500022). Despite the subtype selectivity, MRK-560 and SCH 1500022 did not show selectivity between inhibition of APP and Notch processing in vitro. However, chronic dosing with MRK-560 in wild-type mice did not cause Notch-mediated side effects at drug exposure levels and resulted in a substantial decrease in brain Aβ levels (Best et al., 2007). In contrast, MRK-560 did cause dose-dependent Notch-related side effects in PS2-deficient mice suggesting that PS2 plays an important role in mediating Notch signaling when PS1-γ-secretase activity is inhibited (Borgegard et al., 2012). This explains why a GSI with strong preference for PS1 avoids Notch-related toxicity in vivo. Nonetheless, it remains to be seen if PS1-selective GSIs can overcome the major liabilities associated with nonselective GSIs that have failed in clinical testing. One important question to consider in assessing the feasibility of this approach is whether elevated APP CTFs lead to cognitive worsening. If so, then treatment with any GSI, including a PS1-selective GSI, causes an accumulation of APP CTFs that may lead to such side effect. Moreover, a deeper understanding of the role of individual γ-secretase complexes is needed to facilitate the development of these subtype-selective GSIs.

Aβ IC_{50} (nM)

ELN318463

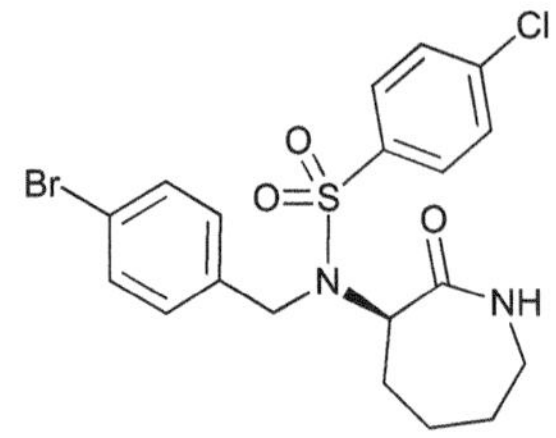

PS1: 12
PS2: 656

BMS299897

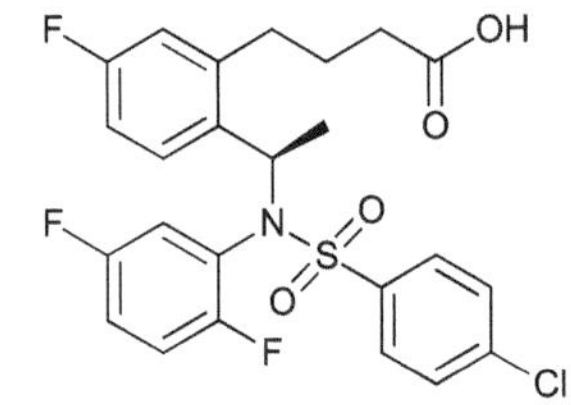

PS1: 8
PS2: 308

MRK-560

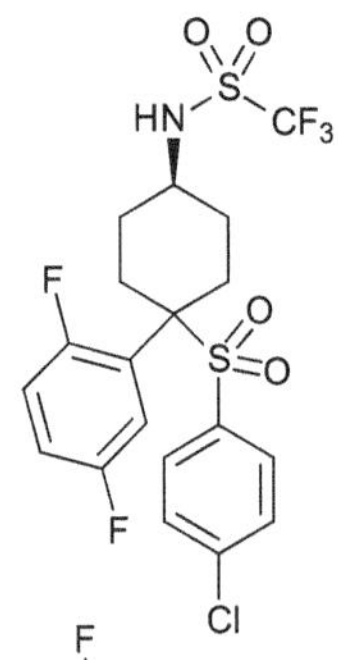

PS1: 0.14
PS2: 5

SCH 1500022

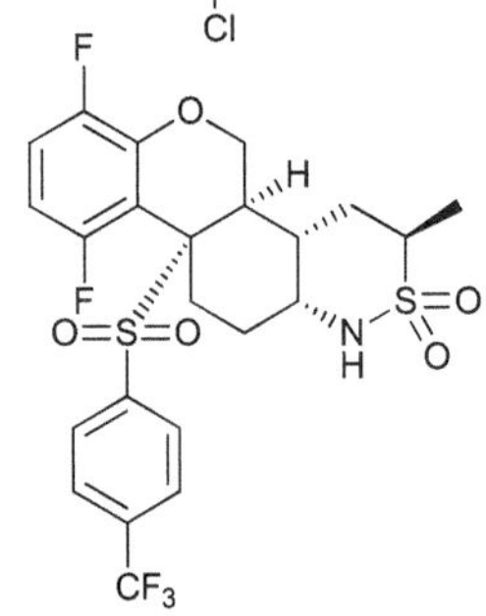

PS1: 1
PS2: 275

FIGURE 4.4 **Structures of PS1 isoform-selective GSIs and their IC_{50}s (nM).**

CONCLUDING REMARKS

While all clinical trials for treating AD with GSIs have failed to date, there is reason to believe that a successful Aβ-reducing therapy is around the corner. Recent analyses and discussion questioned whether GSIs, such as semagacestat or avagacestat, were the best candidates for clinical studies (Chavez-Gutierrez et al., 2012; Crump et al., 2012; De Strooper, 2014), and suggested that the failed clinical trials do not disqualify γ-secretase as a target for AD drug development (Alzforum, 2015; De Strooper, 2014; De Strooper and Chavez Gutierrez, 2015). Past failures with GSIs appear to have been a result of suboptimal compound selection and poorly designed trials (De Strooper, 2014). For example, the once-a-day dosing regimen of semagacestat resulted in abrupt inhibition of γ-secretase followed by a rebound in activity and Aβ production. This not only led to spikes in Aβ, but also may have interfered severely with Notch signaling. A constant, moderate dose treatment may have improved trial results. By taking into account the lessons we have learned, it may be possible to design efficacious, minimally toxic drug candidates to slow or arrest disease progression. In fact, clinical investigation of aducanumab (BIIB037) suggested that targeting Aβ is a valid strategy for AD drug development (Biogen, 2015). There is an urgent need to develop a better understanding of the structure and function of γ-secretase in order to elucidate the disease mechanism and develop effective AD therapies (Alzforum, 2015; De Strooper, 2014; De Strooper and Chavez Gutierrez, 2015). The major challenge lies in retaining the physiological activity of γ-secretase while decreasing its pathological activity, a feat that may be attained through development of selective GSIs or γ-secretase modulators, compounds that lower formation of the toxic Aβ42 without affecting formation of other γ-secretase cleavage products. We have witnessed recent success in the advancement of cancer immunotherapy after decades of disappointments (Mellman et al., 2011), and there is hope that safe and effective AD therapies will become available in the near future with the aid of a deeper understanding of targets and disease mechanisms.

Acknowledgments

This work is supported by NIH Grant R01AG026660 (Y.M.L.), R01NS076117 (Y.M.L.), Alzheimer Association IIRG-12-242137 (Y.M.L.), the MetLife Foundation (Y.M.L.), the JPB Foundation (Y.M.L.), William H. Goodwin and Alice Goodwin, the Commonwealth Foundation for Cancer Research, the Experimental Therapeutics Center of MSKCC, and the William Randolph Hearst Fund in Experimental Therapeutics.

References

Ahn K, Shelton CC, Tian Y, Zhang X, Gilchrist ML, Sisodia SS, Li Y-M: Activation and intrinsic γ-secretase activity of presenilin 1, *Proc Natl Acad Sci USA* 107:21435–21440, 2010.

Alzforum: Semagacestat failure analysis: should γ-secretase remain a target?, 2015. Available from: http://wwwalzforumorg/news/research-news/semagacestat-failure-analysis-should-g-secretase-remain-target

Beher D, Fricker M, Nadin A, Clarke EE, Wrigley JD, Li YM, Culvenor JG, Masters CL, Harrison T, Shearman MS: In vitro characterization of the presenilin-dependent gamma-secretase complex using a novel affinity ligand, *Biochemistry* 42:8133–8142, 2003.

Best JD, Smith DW, Reilly MA, O'Donnell R, Lewis HD, Ellis S, Wilkie N, Rosahl TW, Laroque PA, Boussiquet-Leroux C, Churcher I, Atack JR, Harrison T, Shearman MS: The novel gamma secretase inhibitor N-[cis-4-[(4-chlorophenyl)sulfonyl]-4-(2,5-difluorophenyl)cyclohexyl]-1,1,1-trifluoromethanesulfonamide (MRK-560) reduces amyloid plaque deposition without evidence of Notch-related pathology in the Tg2576 mouse, *J Pharmacol Exp Ther* 320:552–558, 2007.

Biogen: Biogen Idec presents positive interim results from phase 1B study of investigational Alzheimer's disease treatment aducanumab (BIIB037) at 2015 AD/PD™ Conference, 2015. Available from: http://mediabiogencom/press-release/corporate/biogen-idec-presents-positive-interim-results-phase-1b-study-investigational

Borchelt DR, Thinakaran G, Eckman CB, Lee MK, Davenport F, Ratovitsky T, Prada CM, Kim G, Seekins S, Yager D, Slunt HH, Wang R, Seeger M, Levey AI, Gandy SE, Copeland NG, Jenkins NA, Price DL, Younkin SG, Sisodia SS: Familial Alzheimer's disease-linked presenilin 1 variants elevate Abeta1-42/1-40 ratio in vitro and in vivo, *Neuron* 17:1005–1013, 1996.

Borgegard T, Gustavsson S, Nilsson C, Parpal S, Klintenberg R, Berg AL, Rosqvist S, Serneels L, Svensson S, Olsson F, Jin S, Yan H, Wanngren J, Jureus A, Ridderstad-Wollberg A, Wollberg P, Stockling K, Karlstrom H, Malmberg A, Lund J, Arvidsson PI, De Strooper B, Lendahl U, Lundkvist J: Alzheimer's disease: presenilin 2-sparing gamma-secretase inhibition is a tolerable Abeta peptide-lowering strategy, *J Neurosci* 32:17297–17305, 2012.

Chau DM, Crump CJ, Villa JC, Scheinberg DA, Li YM: Familial Alzheimer disease presenilin-1 mutations alter the active site conformation of gamma-secretase, *J Biol Chem* 287:17288–17296, 2012.

Chavez-Gutierrez L, Bammens L, Benilova I, Vandersteen A, Benurwar M, Borgers M, Lismont S, Zhou L, Van Cleynenbreugel S, Esselmann H, Wiltfang J, Serneels L, Karran E, Gijsen H, Schymkowitz J, Rousseau F, Broersen K, De Strooper B: The mechanism of gamma-secretase dysfunction in familial Alzheimer disease, *EMBO J* 31:2261–2274, 2012.

Chun J, Yin YI, Yang G, Tarassishin L, Li YM: Stereoselective synthesis of photoreactive peptidomimetic gamma-secretase inhibitors, *J Org Chem* 69:7344, 2004.

Coolen MW, van Loo KM, van Bakel NN, Ellenbroek BA, Cools AR, Martens GJ: Reduced Aph-1b expression causes tissue- and substrate-specific changes in gamma-secretase activity in rats with a complex phenotype, *FASEB J*:175–177, 2005a.

Coolen MW, Van Loo KM, Van Bakel NN, Pulford DJ, Serneels L, De Strooper B, Ellenbroek BA, Cools AR, Martens GJ: Gene dosage effect on gamma-secretase component Aph-1b in a rat model for neurodevelopmental disorders, *Neuron* 45:497–503, 2005b.

Coric V, van Dyck CH, Salloway S, Andreasen N, Brody M, Richter RW, Soininen H, Thein S, Shiovitz T, Pilcher G, Colby S, Rollin L, Dockens R, Pachai C, Portelius E, Andreasson U, Blennow K, Soares H, Albright C, Feldman HH, Berman RM: Safety and tolerability of the gamma-secretase inhibitor avagacestat in a phase 2 study of mild to moderate Alzheimer disease, *Arch Neurol* 69:1430–1440, 2012.

Crump CJ, Castro SV, Wang F, Pozdnyakov N, Ballard TE, Sisodia SS, Bales KR, Johnson DS, Li YM: BMS-708,163 targets presenilin and lacks Notch-sparing activity, *Biochemistry* 51:7209–7211, 2012.

Crump CJ, Fish BA, Castro SV, Chau DM, Gertsik N, Ahn K, Stiff C, Pozdnyakov N, Bales KR, Johnson DS, Li YM: Piperidine acetic acid based gamma-secretase modulators directly bind to presenilin-1, *ACS Chem Neurosci* 2:705–710, 2011.

Crump CJ, Johnson DS, Li Y-M: Development and mechanism of γ-secretase modulators for Alzheimer's disease, *Biochemistry* 52:3197–3216, 2013.

De Strooper B: Aph-1, Pen-2, and nicastrin with presenilin generate an active gamma-secretase complex, *Neuron* 38:9–12, 2003.

De Strooper B: Lessons from a failed gamma-secretase Alzheimer trial, *Cell* 159:721–726, 2014.

De Strooper B, Chavez Gutierrez L: Learning by failing: ideas and concepts to tackle gamma-secretases in Alzheimer's disease and beyond, *Annu Rev Pharmacol Toxicol* 55:419–437, 2015.

De Strooper B, Saftig P, Craessaerts K, Vanderstichele H, Guhde G, Annaert W, Von Figura K, Van Leuven F: Deficiency of presenilin-1 inhibits the normal cleavage of amyloid precursor protein, *Nature* 391:387–390, 1998.

Donoviel DB, Hadjantonakis AK, Ikeda M, Zheng H, Hyslop PS, Bernstein A: Mice lacking both presenilin genes exhibit early embryonic patterning defects, *Genes Dev* 13:2801–2810, 1999.

Doody RS, Raman R, Farlow M, Iwatsubo T, Vellas B, Joffe S, Kieburtz K, He F, Sun X, Thomas RG, Aisen PS, Alzheimer's Disease Cooperative Study Steering Committee, Siemers E, Sethuraman G, Mohs R: Semagacestat Study Group: A phase 3 trial of semagacestat for treatment of Alzheimer's disease, *N Engl J Med* 369:341–350, 2013.

Dovey HF, John V, Anderson JP, Chen LZ, de Saint Andrieu P, Fang LY, Freedman SB, Folmer B, Goldbach E, Holsztynska EJ, Hu KL, Johnson-Wood KL, Kennedy SL, Kholodenko D, Knops JE, Latimer LH, Lee M, Liao Z, Lieberburg IM, Motter RN, Mutter LC, Nietz J, Quinn KP, Sacchi KL, Seubert PA, Shopp GM, Thorsett ED, Tung JS, Wu J, Yang S, Yin CT, Schenk DB, May PC, Altstiel LD, Bender MH, Boggs LN, Britton TC, Clemens JC, Czilli DL, Dieckman-McGinty DK, Droste JJ, Fuson KS, Gitter BD, Hyslop PA, Johnstone EM, Li WY, Little SP, Mabry TE, Miller FD, Audia JE: Functional gamma-secretase inhibitors reduce beta-amyloid peptide levels in brain, *J Neurochem* 76:173–181, 2001.

Duff K, Eckman C, Zehr C, Yu X, Prada CM, Perez-tur J, Hutton M, Buee L, Harigaya Y, Yager D, Morgan D, Gordon MN, Holcomb L, Refolo L, Zenk B, Hardy J, Younkin S: Increased amyloid-beta42(43) in brains of mice expressing mutant presenilin 1, *Nature* 383:710–713, 1996.

Esler WP, Das C, Wolfe MS: Probing pockets S2-S4′ of the gamma-secretase active site with (hydroxyethyl)urea peptidomimetics, *Bioorg Med Chem Lett* 14:1935–1938, 2004.

Esler WP, Kimberly WT, Ostaszewski BL, Diehl TS, Moore CL, Tsai JY, Rahmati T, Xia W, Selkoe DJ, Wolfe MS: Transition-state analogue inhibitors of gamma-secretase bind directly to presenilin-1, *Nat Cell Biol* 2:428–434, 2000.

Esler WP, Kimberly WT, Ostaszewski BL, Ye W, Diehl TS, Selkoe DJ, Wolfe MS: Activity-dependent isolation of the presenilin-gamma-secretase complex reveals nicastrin and a gamma substrate, *Proc Natl Acad Sci USA* 99:2720–2725, 2002.

Esler WP, Wolfe MS: A portrait of Alzheimer secretases—new features and familiar faces, *Science* 293:1449–1454, 2001.

Farmery MR, Tjernberg LO, Pursglove SE, Bergman A, Winblad B, Naslund J: Partial purification and characterization of gamma-secretase from post mortem human brain, *J Biol Chem* 278(27):24277–24284, 2003.

Francis R, McGrath G, Zhang J, Ruddy DA, Sym M, Apfeld J, Nicoll M, Maxwell M, Hai B, Ellis MC, Parks AL, Xu W, Li J, Gurney M, Myers RL, Himes CS, Hiebsch R, Ruble C, Nye JS, Curtis D: Aph-1 and pen-2 are required for Notch pathway signaling, gamma-secretase cleavage of betaAPP, and presenilin protein accumulation, *Dev Cell* 3:85–97, 2002.

Gertsik N, Chau DM, Li YM: Gamma-secretase inhibitors and modulators induce distinct conformational changes in the active sites of gamma-secretase and signal peptide peptidase, *ACS Chem Biol* 10(8):1925–1931, 2015.

Gertsik N, Chiu D, Li YM: Complex regulation of gamma-secretase: from obligatory to modulatory subunits, *Front Aging Neurosci* 6:342, 2014.

Gillman KW, Starrett JE, Parker MF, Xie K, Bronson JJ, Marcin LR, McElhone KE, Bergstrom CP, Mate RA, Williams R, Meredith JE, Burton CR, Barten DM, Toyn JH, Roberts SB, Lentz KA, Houston JG, Zaczek R, Albright CF, Decicco CP, Macor JE, Olson RE: Discovery and evaluation of BMS-708163, a potent, selective and orally bioavailable gamma-secretase inhibitor, *ACS Med Chem Lett* 1:120–124, 2010.

Golde TE, Koo EH, Felsenstein KM, Osborne BA, Miele L: Gamma-secretase inhibitors and modulators, *Biochim Biophys Acta* 1828:2898–2907, 2013.

Gu Y, Chen F, Sanjo N, Kawarai T, Hasegawa H, Duthie M, Li W, Ruan X, Luthra A, Mount HT, Tandon A, Fraser PE, St George-Hyslop P: APH-1 interacts with mature and immature forms of presenilins and nicastrin and may play a role in maturation of presenilin.nicastrin complexes, *J Biol Chem* 278:7374–7380, 2003.

Haapasalo A, Kovacs DM: The many substrates of presenilin/gamma-secretase, *J Alzheimers Dis* 25:3–28, 2011.

Herreman A, Serneels L, Annaert W, Collen D, Schoonjans L, De Strooper B: Total inactivation of gamma-secretase activity in presenilin-deficient embryonic stem cells, *Nat Cell Biol* 2:461–462, 2000.

Herreman A, Van Gassen G, Bentahir M, Nyabi O, Craessaerts K, Mueller U, Annaert W, De Strooper B: Gamma-secretase activity requires the presenilin-dependent trafficking of nicastrin through the Golgi apparatus but not its complex glycosylation, *J Cell Sci* 116:1127–1136, 2003.

Hopkins CR: ACS chemical neuroscience molecule spotlight on Begacestat (GSI-953), *ACS Chem Neurosci* 3:3–4, 2012.

Josien H: Recent advances in the development of gamma-secretase inhibitors, *Curr Opin Drug Discov Devel* 5:513–525, 2002.

Kimberly WT, LaVoie MJ, Ostaszewski BL, Ye W, Wolfe MS, Selkoe DJ: Gamma-secretase is a membrane protein complex comprised of presenilin, nicastrin, Aph-1, and Pen-2, *Proc Natl Acad Sci USA* 100:6382–6387, 2003.

Klinakis A, Lobry C, Abdel-Wahab O, Oh P, Haeno H, Buonamici S, van De Walle I, Cathelin S, Trimarchi T, Araldi E, Liu C, Ibrahim S, Beran M, Zavadil J, Efstratiadis A, Taghon T, Michor F, Levine RL, Aifantis I: A novel tumour-suppressor function for the Notch pathway in myeloid leukaemia, *Nature* 473:230–233, 2011.

Kornilova AY, Bihel F, Das C, Wolfe MS: The initial substrate-binding site of gamma-secretase is located on presenilin near the active site, *Proc Natl Acad Sci USA* 102:3230–3235, 2005.

Kornilova AY, Das C, Wolfe MS: Differential effects of inhibitors on the gamma-secretase complex: mechanistic implications, *J Biol Chem* 278:16470–16473, 2003.

Kreft A, Harrison B, Aschmies S, Atchison K, Casebier D, Cole DC, Diamantidis G, Ellingboe J, Hauze D, Hu Y, Huryn D, Jin M, Kubrak D, Lu P, Lundquist J, Mann C, Martone R, Moore W, Oganesian A, Porte A, Riddell DR, Sonnenberg-Reines J, Stock JR, Sun SC, Wagner E, Woller K, Xu Z, Zhou H, Jacobsen JS: Discovery of a novel series of Notch-sparing gamma-secretase inhibitors, *Bioorg Med Chem Lett* 18:4232–4236, 2008.

Lai MT, Chen E, Crouthamel MC, DiMuzio-Mower J, Xu M, Huang Q, Price E, Register RB, Shi XP, Donoviel DB, Bernstein A, Hazuda D, Gardell SJ, Li YM: Presenilin-1 and presenilin-2 exhibit distinct yet overlapping γ-secretase activities, *J Biol Chem* 278:22475–22481, 2003.

Lanz TA, Himes CS, Pallante G, Adams L, Yamazaki S, Amore B, Merchant KM: The gamma-secretase inhibitor N-[N-(3,5-difluorophenacetyl)-L-alanyl]-S-phenylglycine t-butyl ester reduces A beta levels in vivo in plasma and cerebrospinal fluid in young (plaque-free) and aged (plaque-bearing) Tg2576 mice, *J Pharmacol Exp Ther* 305:864–871, 2003.

Lee J, Song L, Terracina G, Bara T, Josien H, Asberom T, Sasikumar TK, Burnett DA, Clader J, Parker EM, Zhang L: Identification of presenilin 1-selective gamma-secretase inhibitors with reconstituted gamma-secretase complexes, *Biochemistry* 50:4973–4980, 2011.

Lee SF, Shah S, Li H, Yu C, Han W, Yu G: Mammalian APH-1 interacts with presenilin and nicastrin and is required for intramembrane proteolysis of amyloid-beta precursor protein and Notch, *J Biol Chem* 277:45013–45019, 2002.

Lee SF, Shah S, Yu C, Wigley WC, Li H, Lim M, Pedersen K, Han W, Thomas P, Lundkvist J, Hao YH, Yu G: A conserved GXXXG motif in APH-1 is critical for assembly and activity of the gamma-secretase complex, *J Biol Chem* 279:4144–4152, 2004.

Levy Lahad E, Wasco W, Poorkaj P, Romano DM, Oshima J, Pettingell WH, Yu CE, Jondro PD, Schmidt SD, Wang K, et al: Candidate gene for the chromosome 1 familial Alzheimer's disease locus, *Science* 269:973–977, 1995.

Li T, Ma G, Cai H, Price DL, Wong PC: Nicastrin is required for assembly of presenilin/gamma-secretase complexes to mediate Notch signaling and for processing and trafficking of beta-amyloid precursor protein in mammals, *J Neurosci* 23:3272–3277, 2003.

Li YM: Gamma-secretase: a catalyst of Alzheimer disease and signal transduction, *Mol Interv* 1:198–207, 2001.

Li YM, Lai MT, Xu M, Huang Q, DiMuzio-Mower J, Sardana MK, Shi XP, Yin KC, Shafer JA, Gardell SJ: Presenilin 1 is linked with gamma-secretase activity in the detergent solubilized state, *Proc Natl Acad Sci USA* 97:6138–6143, 2000a.

Li YM, Xu M, Lai MT, Huang Q, Castro JL, DiMuzio-Mower J, Harrison T, Lellis C, Nadin A, Neduvelil JG, Register RB, Sardana MK, Shearman MS, Smith AL, Shi XP, Yin KC, Shafer JA, Gardell SJ: Photoactivated gamma-secretase inhibitors directed to the active site covalently label presenilin 1, *Nature* 405:689–694, 2000b.

Lu P, Bai XC, Ma D, Xie T, Yan C, Sun L, Yang G, Zhao Y, Zhou R, Scheres SH, Shi Y: Three-dimensional structure of human gamma-secretase, *Nature* 512:166–170, 2014.

Luo WJ, Wang H, Li H, Kim BS, Shah S, Lee HJ, Thinakaran G, Kim TW, Yu G, Xu H: PEN-2 and APH-1 coordinately regulate proteolytic processing of presenilin 1, *J Biol Chem* 278:7850–7854, 2003.

Ma G, Li T, Price DL, Wong PC: APH-1a is the principal mammalian APH-1 isoform present in gamma-secretase complexes during embryonic development, *J Neurosci* 25:192–198, 2005.

Martone RL, Zhou H, Atchison K, Comery T, Xu JZ, Huang X, Gong X, Jin M, Kreft A, Harrison B, Mayer SC, Aschmies S, Gonzales C, Zaleska MM, Riddell DR, Wagner E, Lu P, Sun SC, Sonnenberg-Reines J, Oganesian A, Adkins K, Leach MW, Clarke DW, Huryn D, Abou-Gharbia M, Magolda R, Bard J, Frick G, Raje S, Forlow SB, Balliet C, Burczynski ME, Reinhart PH, Wan HI, Pangalos MN, Jacobsen JS: Begacestat (GSI-953): a novel, selective thiophene sulfonamide inhibitor of amyloid precursor protein gamma-secretase for the treatment of Alzheimer's disease, *J Pharmacol Exp Ther* 331:598–608, 2009.

Mayer SC, Kreft AF, Harrison B, Abou-Gharbia M, Antane M, Aschmies S, Atchison K, Chlenov M, Cole DC, Comery T, Diamantidis G, Ellingboe J, Fan K, Galante R, Gonzales C, Ho DM, Hoke ME, Hu Y, Huryn D, Jain U, Jin M, Kremer K, Kubrak D, Lin M, Lu P, Magolda R, Martone R, Moore W, Oganesian A, Pangalos MN, Porte A, Reinhart P, Resnick L, Riddell DR, Sonnenberg-Reines J, Stock JR, Sun SC, Wagner E, Wang T, Woller K, Xu Z, Zaleska MM, Zeldis J, Zhang M, Zhou H, Jacobsen JS: Discovery of begacestat, a Notch-1-sparing gamma-secretase inhibitor for the treatment of Alzheimer's disease, *J Med Chem* 51:7348–7351, 2008.

Mellman I, Coukos G, Dranoff G: Cancer immunotherapy comes of age, *Nature* 480:480–489, 2011.

Mitani Y, Yarimizu J, Saita K, Uchino H, Akashiba H, Shitaka Y, Ni K, Matsuoka N: Differential effects between gamma-secretase inhibitors and modulators on cognitive function in amyloid precursor protein-transgenic and nontransgenic mice, *J Neurosci* 32:2037–2050, 2012.

Moore CL, Leatherwood DD, Diehl TS, Selkoe DJ, Wolfe MS: Difluoro ketone peptidomimetics suggest a large S1 pocket for Alzheimer's gamma-secretase: implications for inhibitor design, *J Med Chem* 43:3434–3442, 2000.

Naruse S, Thinakaran G, Luo JJ, Kusiak JW, Tomita T, Iwatsubo T, Qian X, Ginty DD, Price DL, Borchelt DR, Wong PC, Sisodia SS: Effects of PS1 deficiency on membrane protein trafficking in neurons, *Neuron* 21:1213–1221, 1998.

Nicolas M, Wolfer A, Raj K, Kummer JA, Mill P, Van Noort M, Hui CC, Clevers H, Dotto GP, Radtke F: Notch1 functions as a tumor suppressor in mouse skin, *Nat Genet* 33:416–421, 2003.

Niimura M, Isoo N, Takasugi N, Tsuruoka M, Ui-Tei K, Saigo K, Morohashi Y, Tomita T, Iwatsubo T: Aph-1 contributes to the stabilization and trafficking of the gamma-secretase complex through mechanisms involving intermolecular and intramolecular interactions, *J Biol Chem* 280:12967–12975, 2005.

Placanica L, Chien JW, Li YM: Characterization of an atypical gamma-secretase complex from hematopoietic origin, *Biochemistry* 49:2796–2804, 2010.

Placanica L, Tarassishin L, Yang G, Peethumnongsin E, Kim SH, Zheng H, Sisodia SS, Li YM: Pen2 and presenilin-1 modulate the dynamic equilibrium of presenilin-1 and presenilin-2 γ-secretase complexes, *J Biol Chem* 284:2967–2977, 2009a.

Placanica L, Zhu L, Li YM: Gender- and age-dependent gamma-secretase activity in mouse brain and its implication in sporadic Alzheimer disease, *PLoS One* 4:e5088, 2009b.

Prokop S, Shirotani K, Edbauer D, Haass C, Steiner H: Requirement of PEN-2 for stabilization of the presenilin N-/C-terminal fragment heterodimer within the gamma-secretase complex, *J Biol Chem* 279:23255–23261, 2004.

Scheuner D, Eckman C, Jensen M, Song X, Citron M, Suzuki N, Bird TD, Hardy J, Hutton M, Kukull W, Larson E, Levy-Lahad E, Viitanen M, Peskind E, Poorkaj P, Schellenberg G, Tanzi R, Wasco W, Lannfelt L, Selkoe D, Younkin

S: Secreted amyloid beta-protein similar to that in the senile plaques of Alzheimer's disease is increased in vivo by the presenilin 1 and 2 and APP mutations linked to familial Alzheimer's disease, *Nat Med* 2:864–870, 1996.

Seiffert D, Bradley JD, Rominger CM, Rominger DH, Yang F, Meredith JE Jr, Wang Q, Roach AH, Thompson LA, Spitz SM, Higaki JN, Prakash SR, Combs AP, Copeland RA, Arneric SP, Hartig PR, Robertson DW, Cordell B, Stern AM, Olson RE, Zaczek R: Presenilin-1 and -2 are molecular targets for gamma-secretase inhibitors, *J Biol Chem* 275:34086–34091, 2000.

Serneels L, Dejaegere T, Craessaerts K, Horre K, Jorissen E, Tousseyn T, Hebert S, Coolen M, Martens G, Zwijsen A, Annaert W, Hartmann D, De Strooper B: Differential contribution of the three Aph1 genes to gamma-secretase activity in vivo, *Proc Natl Acad Sci USA* 102:1719–1724, 2005.

Serneels L, Van Biervliet J, Craessaerts K, Dejaegere T, Horre K, Van Houtvin T, Esselmann H, Paul S, Schafer MK, Berezovska O, Hyman BT, Sprangers B, Sciot R, Moons L, Jucker M, Yang Z, May PC, Karran E, Wiltfang J, D'Hooge R, De Strooper B: Gamma-secretase heterogeneity in the Aph1 subunit: relevance for Alzheimer's disease, *Science* 324:639–642, 2009.

Shah S, Lee SF, Tabuchi K, Hao YH, Yu C, LaPlant Q, Ball H, Dann CE 3rd, Sudhof T, Yu G: Nicastrin functions as a gamma-secretase-substrate receptor, *Cell* 122:435–447, 2005.

Shearman MS, Beher D, Clarke EE, Lewis HD, Harrison T, Hunt P, Nadin A, Smith AL, Stevenson G, Castro JL: L-685,458, an aspartyl protease transition state mimic, is a potent inhibitor of amyloid beta-protein precursor gamma-secretase activity, *Biochemistry* 39:8698–8704, 2000.

Shelton CC, Zhu L, Chau D, Yang L, Wang R, Djaballah H, Zheng H, Li YM: Modulation of gamma-secretase specificity using small molecule allosteric inhibitors, *Proc Natl Acad Sci USA* 106:20228–20233, 2009.

Shen J, Bronson RT, Chen DF, Xia W, Selkoe DJ, Tonegawa S: Skeletal and CNS defects in presenilin-1-deficient mice, *Cell* 89:629–639, 1997.

Sherrington R, Rogaev EI, Liang Y, Rogaeva EA, Levesque G, Ikeda M, Chi H, Lin C, Li G, Holman K, et al: Cloning of a gene bearing missense mutations in early-onset familial Alzheimer's disease, *Nature* 375:754–760, 1995.

Shiraishi H, Sai X, Wang HQ, Maeda Y, Kurono Y, Nishimura M, Yanagisawa K, Komano H: PEN-2 enhances gamma-cleavage after presenilin heterodimer formation, *J Neurochem* 90:1402–1413, 2004.

Shirotani K, Edbauer D, Prokop S, Haass C, Steiner H: Identification of distinct γ-secretase complexes with different APH-1 variants, *J Biol Chem* 279:41340–41345, 2004.

Steiner H, Winkler E, Edbauer D, Prokop S, Basset G, Yamasaki A, Kostka M, Haass C: PEN-2 is an integral component of the gamma-secretase complex required for coordinated expression of presenilin and nicastrin, *J Biol Chem* 277:39062–39065, 2002.

Sun L, Zhao L, Yang G, Yan C, Zhou R, Zhou X, Xie T, Zhao Y, Wu S, Li X, Shi Y: Structural basis of human gamma-secretase assembly, *Proc Natl Acad Sci USA* 112:6003–6008, 2015.

Takasugi N, Tomita T, Hayashi I, Tsuruoka M, Niimura M, Takahashi Y, Thinakaran G, Iwatsubo T: The role of presenilin cofactors in the gamma-secretase complex, *Nature* 422:438–441, 2003.

Tarassishin L, Yin YI, Bassit B, Li YM: Processing of Notch and amyloid precursor protein by gamma-secretase is spatially distinct, *Proc Natl Acad Sci USA* 101:17050–17055, 2004.

Teranishi Y, Hur JY, Welander H, Franberg J, Aoki M, Winblad B, Frykman S, Tjernberg LO: Affinity pulldown of gamma-secretase and associated proteins from human and rat brain, *J Cell Mol Med* 14:2675–2686, 2010.

Thinakaran G, Borchelt DR, Lee MK, Slunt HH, Spitzer L, Kim G, Ratovitsky T, Davenport F, Nordstedt C, Seeger M, Hardy J, Levey AI, Gandy SE, Jenkins NA, Copeland NG, Price DL, Sisodia SS: Endoproteolysis of presenilin 1 and accumulation of processed derivatives in vivo, *Neuron* 17:181–190, 1996.

Tian Y, Bassit B, Chau D, Li YM: An APP inhibitory domain containing the Flemish mutation residue modulates gamma-secretase activity for Abeta production, *Nat Struct Mol Biol* 17:151–158, 2010.

Vetrivel KS, Gong P, Bowen JW, Cheng H, Chen Y, Carter M, Nguyen PD, Placanica L, Wieland FT, Li YM, Kounnas MZ, Thinakaran G: Dual roles of the transmembrane protein p23/TMP21 in the modulation of amyloid precursor protein metabolism, *Mol Neurodegener* 2:4, 2007.

Vetrivel KS, Zhang X, Meckler X, Cheng H, Lee S, Gong P, Lopes KO, Chen Y, Iwata N, Yin KJ, Lee JM, Parent AT, Saido TC, Li YM, Sisodia SS, Thinakaran G: Evidence that CD147 modulation of beta-amyloid (Abeta) levels is mediated by extracellular degradation of secreted Abeta, *J Biol Chem* 283:19489–19498, 2008.

Wang B, Yang W, Wen W, Sun J, Su B, Liu B, Ma D, Lv D, Wen Y, Qu T, Chen M, Sun M, Shen Y, Zhang X: Gamma-secretase gene mutations in familial acne inversa, *Science* 330:1065, 2010.

Wolfe MS: Gamma-secretase inhibitors and modulators for Alzheimer's disease, *J Neurochem* 120(Suppl 1):89–98, 2012.

Wolfe MS, Citron M, Diehl TS, Xia W, Donkor IO, Selkoe DJ: A substrate-based difluoro ketone selectively inhibits Alzheimer's gamma-secretase activity, *J Med Chem* 41:6–9, 1998.

Wolfe MS, Kopan R: Intramembrane proteolysis: theme and variations, *Science* 305:1119–1123, 2004.

Wolfe MS, Xia W, Moore CL, Leatherwood DD, Ostaszewski B, Rahmati T, Donkor IO, Selkoe DJ: Peptidomimetic probes and molecular modeling suggest that Alzheimer's gamma-secretase is an intramembrane-cleaving aspartyl protease, *Biochemistry* 38:4720–4727, 1999a.

Wolfe MS, Xia W, Ostaszewski BL, Diehl TS, Kimberly WT, Selkoe DJ: Two transmembrane aspartates in presenilin-1 required for presenilin endoproteolysis and gamma-secretase activity, *Nature* 398:513–517, 1999b.

Wong GT, Manfra D, Poulet FM, Zhang Q, Josien H, Bara T, Engstrom L, Pinzon-Ortiz M, Fine JS, Lee HJ, Zhang L, Higgins GA, Parker EM: Chronic treatment with the gamma-secretase inhibitor LY-411,575 inhibits beta-amyloid peptide production and alters lymphopoiesis and intestinal cell differentiation, *J Biol Chem* 279:12876–12882, 2004.

Wong PC, Zheng H, Chen H, Becher MW, Sirinathsinghji DJ, Trumbauer ME, Chen HY, Price DL, Van der Ploeg LH, Sisodia SS: Presenilin 1 is required for Notch1 and DII1 expression in the paraxial mesoderm, *Nature* 387:288–292, 1997.

Xia X, Qian S, Soriano S, Wu Y, Fletcher AM, Wang XJ, Koo EH, Wu X, Zheng H: Loss of presenilin 1 is associated with enhanced beta-catenin signaling and skin tumorigenesis, *Proc Natl Acad Sci USA* 98:10863–10868, 2001.

Xu M, Lai MT, Huang Q, DiMuzio-Mower J, Castro JL, Harrison T, Nadin A, Neduvelil JG, Shearman MS, Shafer JA, Gardell SJ, Li YM: Gamma-secretase: characterization and implication for Alzheimer disease therapy, *Neurobiol Aging* 23:1023–1030, 2002.

Yang G, Yin YI, Chun J, Shelton CC, Ouerfelli O, Li YM: Stereo-controlled synthesis of novel photoreactive gamma-secretase inhibitors, *Bioorg Med Chem Lett* 19:922–925, 2009.

Zhang Z, Nadeau P, Song W, Donoviel D, Yuan M, Bernstein A, Yankner BA: Presenilins are required for gamma-secretase cleavage of beta-APP and transmembrane cleavage of Notch-1, *Nat Cell Biol* 2:463–465, 2000.

Zhao B, Yu M, Neitzel M, Marugg J, Jagodzinski J, Lee M, Hu K, Schenk D, Yednock T, Basi G: Identification of gamma-secretase inhibitor potency determinants on presenilin, *J Biol Chem* 283:2927–2938, 2008.

CHAPTER

5

Therapeutic Targeting of Aβ42

T.E. Golde, C.B. Lessard, Y. Ran

OUTLINE

INTRODUCTION

Following the definitive identification of the ~4 kDa Aβ as the principal component of both plaque core and vascular amyloid in Alzheimer's disease (AD) (Glenner and Wong, 1984; Masters et al., 1985a, 1985b), the gene encoding Aβ was subsequently identified (Dyrks et al., 1988; Kang et al., 1987; Robakis et al., 1987; Tanzi et al., 1987). Sequencing of the cDNA encoding Aβ revealed that Aβ was an internal sequence within the much larger amyloid β precursor protein (APP) whose major alternatively spliced isoforms were 695–770 amino acids in length (Dyrks et al., 1988; Golde et al., 1990; Kang et al., 1987). Modeling of APP indicated it was likely to be a type 1 membrane protein and that the amino terminus of the Aβ peptide is part of the large ectodomain and ~28 residues from the membrane, whereas the carboxyl terminus of Aβ is well into the transmembrane domain (Kang et al., 1987). These topological models were rapidly confirmed, and following a seminal study from Beyreuther and coworkers describing the processing of APP (Weidemann et al., 1989) a number of questions about how Aβ could be generated were raised. In that study, it was shown that in cell lines, APP was processed by a protease or proteases to release a large ectodomain that contained a small portion of the amino terminus of Aβ (Weidemann et al., 1989). This finding was viewed as a potential conundrum by the field, as it appeared that the constitutive processing of APP would preclude generation of Aβ by essentially cutting it into fragments that had not been detected in human brain amyloid. Further, as the carboxyl terminus of Aβ lay within the

Developing Therapeutics for Alzheimer's Disease. http://dx.doi.org/10.1016/B978-0-12-802173-6.00005-8

transmembrane domain of APP, and there was no precedence at that time for proteases that cleaved in such an environment, it was postulated that Aβ was produced only in a disease state and that membrane damage had to occur before Aβ could be released from the APP (Weidemann et al., 1989).

Although many groups rapidly pursued the hypothesis that generation of Aβ would occur only in the AD state and required some sort of cellular stress, it soon became apparent that this was not the case (Busciglio et al., 1993; Haass et al., 1991; Seubert et al., 1992; Shoji et al., 1992). Collectively, these studies demonstrated that normal constitutive processing of APP produced Aβ peptides that were identical to the two principal forms of Aβ (Aβ1-40 and Aβ1-42) identified in the human brain. Further study of Aβ peptides in human cerebrospinal fluid (CSF) revealed that numerous ~4 kDa Aβ peptides could be detected in both normal and AD CSF (Seubert et al., 1992), a finding that has since been replicated many times and extended to include evidence that multiple species of Aβ are normally found in AD and control brains (Golde et al., 2000; Lue et al., 1999; Moore et al., 2012). Indeed, species detected from CSF and brain include: Aβ1-17, 19, 22, 26–31, 33–43; Aβ2-42, 43; Aβ3-41; Aβ pyroglutamate (pE3)-40, 42; Aβ4-40, 42; Aβ5-42; Aβ7-40; Aβ8-40; and AβpE11-40, 42 (Albertini et al., 2012; Bibl et al., 2006; Lewczuk et al., 2003; Maddalena et al., 2004; Moore et al., 2012).

APP PROCESSING PATHWAYS

Today, we typically describe the processing of APP in two general pathways, the nonamyloidogenic α-secretase pathway that precludes Aβ generation and the amyloidogenic β-secretase pathway that leads to the production of Aβ (reviewed in De Strooper et al., 2010; Hooper et al., 2000; Selkoe, 2001; Golde et al., 2000). In both cases, the membrane-bound stubs of APP referred to either as CTFα or CTFβ (or C83 and C99, respectively) were cleaved by a third secretase activity, γ-secretase, to generate a fragment called p3 from CTFα or Aβ from CTFβ (Fig. 5.1). In truth, this simple dichotomy of amyloidogenic (β-secretase) and nonamyloidogenic (α-secretase) pathways is a vast oversimplification, as APP processing is much more complex, with numerous additional cleavages of both the cytoplasmic and ectodomain of APP occurring in both the secretory and endosomal lysosomal pathways.

At the time these processing pathways were initially described, the proteases responsible for these various "secretase" activities were unknown. But over the next decade and a half the identity of the proteases responsible for these cleavages was uncovered. Multiple proteases within the ADAM family of metalloprotease disintegrins, including ADAM10 and 17 (Fahrenholz et al., 2000; Kojro and Fahrenholz, 2005), have been shown to contribute to α-secretase activity. BACE1, a transmembrane aspartyl protease, is responsible for β-secretase activity (Cai et al., 2001; Vassar et al., 1999; Yan et al., 1999), and presenilin (PSEN1 and PSEN2) has been shown to be the catalytic core of the multiprotein γ-secretase complex (Edbauer et al., 2003; Kimberly et al., 2003; Wolfe et al., 1999b). BACE1 and its homolog BACE2 can also cleave APP within the Aβ sequence, with BACE1 producing Aβ peptides beginning at position 11 and BACE2 cleaving within the Aβ sequence at positions 19 and 20 (Hong et al., 2000).

The characterization of the processing of APP into Aβ, by itself, did not inform the field with respect to any potential pathogenic role of Aβ in AD; however, roughly coincident with the elaboration of the processing pathways that produce Aβ as a normal metabolite, genetic

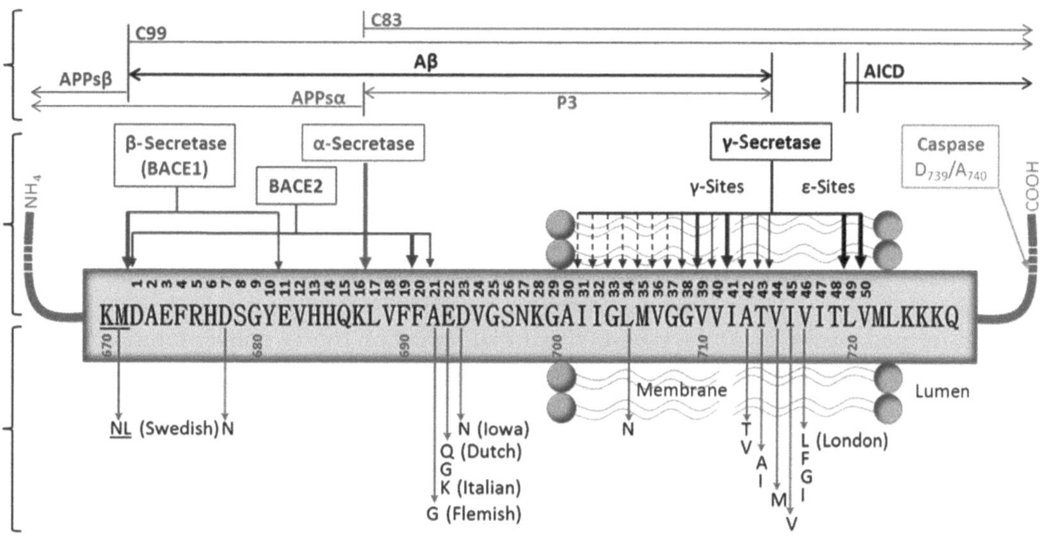

FIGURE 5.1 **Major proteolysis of amyloid precursor protein and inherited mutations in the TMD and adjacent domain.** The main proteases involved are boxed. Cleavage sites are indicated by solid arrows. Arrow weight indicates the relative yield of each fragment. The top panel lists major observed proteolysis products. Vertical short lines indicate each fragment's start or end position. The bottom panel lists a number of inherited mutations observed around the proteolysis sites.

studies identified causal mutations in *APP*, *PSEN1*, and *PSEN2* that were linked to early-onset familial Alzheimer's disease (FAD) (reviewed in Golde, 2006; Selkoe, 2001). Together with emerging modeling, pathology, and biophysical studies of Aβ, these genetic linkages firmly established a "triggering," causal role for Aβ and Aβ aggregation in AD pathogenesis (Hardy and Higgins, 1992).

In the early 1990s, biophysical studies of synthetic Aβ demonstrated that Aβ1-42 aggregated rapidly into amyloid fibrils with physical properties similar to those of the Aβ amyloid fibrils found in the human brain (Jarrett et al., 1993a, 1993b; Kirschner et al., 1987). Further, Aβ1-42 was shown to aggregate much more rapidly than Aβ1-40 (Jarrett et al., 1993a,b). Akin to other amyloids, Aβ formation into amyloid was found to occur through a nucleation-dependent conformational templating mechanism that was concentration dependent (Jarrett and Lansbury, 1993). Aβ1-42 aggregated faster because it nucleated more quickly. Once nucleated, at least in vitro, there was little difference in subsequent kinetics of aggregation between the species. Further, although in most systems Aβ1-40 was found to be the major Aβ species normally produced, in the AD brain Aβ1-42 or NH_2-terminally truncated Aβx-42 species were shown to be both the most abundant and the earliest species deposited (Gravina et al., 1995; Iwatsubo et al., 1994; Saido et al., 1995). Thus, both biophysical and pathological studies provided significant clues that the pathogenicity of the various Aβ peptides may not be equivalent.

As this pathological and biophysical framework for understanding the properties of different Aβ peptides was emerging, the field rapidly elucidated the likely mechanisms of how the FAD-linked mutations in the APP caused AD. The first mutation for which cell modeling studies provided insights into the mechanism of pathogenicity was the KM670/671NL or "Swedish" mutant (Mullan et al., 1992). Cells transfected with this mutant showed increased levels of Aβ, with increases typically ranging from two- to three-fold compared to wild-type APP (Cai et al., 1993; Citron et al., 1992). This increase in Aβ was later shown to be attributable to the fact that Swedish APP was a better substrate for BACE1-mediated β-secretase cleavage (Haass et al., 1995) (Fig. 5.1). Subsequent studies in transgenic mice, human plasma, human CSF, and cultured primary fibroblasts also confirmed that the major effect of this mutation was to increase β-secretase cleavage and total Aβ levels (reviewed in Golde et al., 2011; Price et al., 1998). Presumably because amyloid formation is concentration dependent, increasing total levels of Aβ as observed with this mutation would accelerate the rate at which amyloid formed; however, at the time of the initial report on the Swedish mutations, several other mutations had been identified, and these—rather than flanking the NH_2-terminus of Aβ—flanked the COOH-terminus of Aβ. In similar cell culture studies, these mutations [eg, V717I (London), V717G, V7171F] did not increase total Aβ levels (Cai et al., 1993); however, building off the hypothesis derived from the biophysical studies that small shifts in production toward Aβ1-42 would drive amyloid deposition, it was soon shown that these mutations at the COOH-terminus of Aβ increased the relative amount Aβ1-42 produced (Suzuki et al., 1994). This finding has since been consistently reproduced and, like the effects of the Swedish mutations on total Aβ production, many of these COOH-terminal mutations have been shown to alter Aβ42 production in humans, transgenic mice, cultured primary human fibroblasts, and even neurons derived from human pluripotent stem cells (Liu et al., 2014; Israel, 2012; Younkin, 1998).

Although the studies of these rare FAD-linked APP mutants was incredibly informative, collectively they accounted for a very small percentage of all the familial early-onset cases of AD and an even smaller percentage of all AD (Hardy, 1996). Thus, there remained some skepticism in the field as to the generalization of these findings. However, following the identification of mutations in the PSEN1 and PSEN2 genes as much more common causes of early-onset FAD (Rogaev et al., 1995; Campion et al., 1995; Levy-Lahad et al., 1995; Wasco et al., 1995), and biological studies into how these mutations altered Aβ (Duff et al., 1996; Holcomb et al., 1998; Scheuner et al., 1996), this skepticism was largely abated. Indeed, biological studies showed that, like the COOH-terminal APP mutations, these FAD-linked PSEN mutations had a common effect on APP processing that resulted in an increased ratio of Aβ42:Aβ40 (reviewed in Younkin, 1998). Of note, there have now been more than 250 mutations in PSEN1 and PSEN2 that have been linked to FAD. Though a very limited number of mutations have been shown to alter other cellular functions (Kelleher and Shen, 2010), for mutations that are truly causal the consistent biological finding has been that *PSEN* mutations increase the relative production of Aβ42 (De Strooper et al., 2012). Because measuring and comparing absolute levels of Aβ can be challenging, especially if comparing across multiple experiments and multiple laboratories, the most reliable finding is that *APP* and *PSEN* mutants shift APP processing to favor relative production of Aβ1-42 (Golde et al., 2000). Such a shift in ratio could occur either by increasing Aβ42 production, decreasing Aβ40, or some combination of the two. In well-controlled model systems, it appears that different PSEN mutations do in fact function differently in this regard (Chavez-Gutierrez et al., 2012; De Strooper et al., 2012; Fernandez et al., 2014; Quintero-Monzon et al., 2011; Wolfe, 2012). Some simply increase the relative production of Aβ1-42, others can decrease Aβ1-40 selectively, and still others produce more complex effects that still result in an altered Aβ42:Aβ40 ratio. Because some in the field still find it conceptually difficult to accept that more than a hundred different mutations alter function in a common way, these findings on the effects of PSEN mutations on Aβ40 and Aβ42 production are important. PSEN mutations do have subtly different effects on APP processing, but the net biological effect is similar.

In addition to the Swedish APP mutation, there are additional exceptions to the generalization that FAD-linked mutations cause AD by increasing the relative Aβ42 levels. Mutations within *APP* that directly alter the sequence of Aβ are linked to AD or hereditary cerebral hemorrhage with amyloidosis or result in pathology and clinical phenotype that is a mix of these two diseases (Levy et al., 1990; Selkoe, 2001; Van Broeckhoven et al., 1990). These internal Aβ mutations appear to increase the rate of Aβ assembly into aggregates, alter processing to favor relative production of Aβ1-42, or do some combination of the two. Thus, although the vast majority of *APP* and *PSEN1* mutations increase the relative levels Aβ42, other mutations have other effects on Aβ; however, all of these mutations result in an increased likelihood that Aβ will aggregate—a finding that has served as pivotal support for the amyloid hypothesis of AD.

Following these seminal findings that emerged largely during the 1990s, additional evidence has accrued that Aβ42 and the biophysically similar Aβ43 are the key pathogenic species of Aβ. In multiple in vivo model systems, Aβ42 can be shown to have pathologic effects, whereas Aβ40 is either much less toxic or not toxic at all. For example, when expressed in the eye of *Drosophila*, Aβ42 results in a dramatic phenotype whereas Aβ40 is largely benign (Finelli et al., 2004; Iijima et al., 2004; Tan et al., 2008; Treusch et al., 2011). Similar findings are noted in other model organism such as *Caenorhabditis elegans* and *Saccharomyces cerevisiae* in which Aβ42 expression is highly toxic (Link, 2005). Further, in transgenic mice engineered to express either Aβ40 or Aβ42 in the secretory pathway, expression of Aβ42 results in parenchymal and cerebrovascular amyloid deposition, but expression of Aβ40—even at levels ~10-fold higher than the level of Aβ42—does not (Kim et al., 2007; McGowan et al., 2005). Moreover, in mice Aβ40 can be shown to attenuate amyloid deposition (Kim et al., 2007). Thus, not only may Aβ42 be highly pathogenic, but under some circumstances Aβ40 may be protective.

Given the importance of the heterogeneity in the COOH-terminus of Aβ in determining its pathogenicity, one of the key questions for the field was the biological basis for that heterogeneity. This was especially perplexing following two observations that were difficult to reconcile. Knockout studies demonstrated that both PSEN1 and PSEN2 played a role in generation of Aβ and were key regulators of γ-secretase activity (De Strooper et al., 1999; Herreman, 2000; Herreman, 1999); however, pharmacological studies suggested that the γ-secretase activities that generated Aβ40 and Aβ42 were distinct (Citron et al., 1996; Murphy et al., 1999, 2000). As knockout of *PSEN1* or *PSEN2* equivalently reduced Aβ40 and Aβ42 production and PSENs did not resemble any known protease, some in the field, including Dr. Golde, postulated that PSENs must be upstream regulators of multiple distinct γ-secretase activities; however, seminal studies from Wolfe and coworkers and other groups provided evidence that PSENs were the target of various γ-secretase inhibitors (GSIs) and indeed intramembrane-cleaving proteases with two aspartates in opposing transmembrane domains; that is, PSENs are aspartyl-type proteases capable of cleaving proteins within their transmembrane domains (Li et al., 2000; Seiffert et al., 2000; Wolfe et al., 1999a, 1999b). Though some in the field were reluctant to accept these data, over the next few years a number of additional observations established that PSENs, acting in concert with three additional proteins (APH1, PEN2, and NCT), were bona fide proteases. Indeed, (1) γ-secretase could be purified to homogeneity and shown to consist of these four proteins (Fraering et al., 2004; Kimberly et al., 2003), and (2) γ-secretase activity could be reconstituted in heterologous expression systems by expressing these four proteins together (Edbauer et al., 2003; Takasugi et al., 2003; Zhang et al., 2005). Further, the identification of the signal peptide peptidase family of multipass membrane proteins as intramembrane-cleaving proteases with homology to PSENs also served to convince the vast majority in the field that PSENs were indeed the catalytic subunits of the γ-secretase complex (Ponting et al., 2002; Weihofen et al., 2002).

After the molecular composition of γ-secretase was elucidated, several perplexing questions remained, including: How did a single protease generate a spectrum of Aβ peptides with differing carboxyl termini? How did AD-associated mutations either in APP or PSEN alter the spectrum of those peptides? What was the specificity of γ-secretase? Where does it cleave in the cell? Does the composition of the membrane alter activity? From a therapeutic perspective, a major concern that had already been recognized was that γ-secretase cleaved a number of other type 1 transmembrane proteins and that cleavage by γ-secretase regulated intramembrane signaling pathways (a process often referred to by the acronym RIP) (De Strooper et al., 1999; Haapasalo and Kovacs, 2011; Huppert and Kopan, 2001). Indeed, of major concern therapeutically was the effect of γ-secretase on Notch1 signaling (De Strooper et al., 1999; Hadland et al., 2001; Schroeter et al., 1998). The transmembrane receptor Notch1 is essential for many cell fate determinations. Upon ligand binding to Notch1, the ectodomain is shed, followed by cleavage of the membrane-bound CTF by γ-secretase. This cleavage then releases the intracellular domain of Notch1 from the membrane, enabling it to translocate to the nucleus, where, in combination with other proteins, it can regulate expression of numerous genes. Blocking Notch signaling by inhibition of γ-secretase or knockout of PSEN1 or other components of the γ-secretase complex produced a severe, lethal phenotype during development that was very similar to the phenotype of a Notch1 knockout (Curry et al., 2005; De Strooper et al., 1999; Kopan and Goate, 2002; Searfoss et al., 2003; Selkoe and Kopan, 2003; Shen et al., 1997; Wong et al., 1997). Further, in adult mice γ-secretase inhibition or PSEN conditional knockout also results in severe phenotypes, including gastrointestinal, immune, skin, and cognitive abnormalities, many of which can be linked at least in part to blockade of Notch1 signaling (Curry et al., 2005; Saura et al., 2004; Searfoss et al., 2003); however, it is now recognized that there are well over 100 γ-secretase substrates and the list of actual substrates is likely longer as γ-secretase cleaves virtually any type 1 membrane protein that is undergoing ectodomain shedding (Haapasalo and Kovacs, 2011). Thus, it is likely that phenotypic alterations observed by inhibition or knockout of PSEN/γ-secretase are the net result of complex signaling alterations resulting from changes in PSEN-mediated RIP.

TARGETING Aβ42

As we have gained insight into the natural history of AD, it has become increasingly clear that therapeutic strategies targeting Aβ are likely to have the most efficacy when employed either in a primary prevention setting or in the very earliest phases of amyloid deposition (Golde et al., 2011). Such prophylactic therapy would thus need to be initiated 10, 15, or even

20+ years before an individual would be predicted to develop AD. This means that the therapy must be very safe, as it will be given to cognitively normal individuals, and probably will need to be taken for long periods of time. Indeed, given the current regulatory environment, one could posit that such a therapy would need to be at least as safe as approved statins. Additional issues besides a "safe enough" therapy remain for any prophylactic approach to AD. These issues largely relate to trial design and end points for these early intervention trials. The hope is that new clinical trial paradigms that address these issues will emerge from the recently initiated early-intervention studies that are testing therapies in both genetically at-risk individuals and other individuals who are asymptomatic, but have a positive amyloid scan (Carrillo et al., 2013; Khachaturian et al., 2010; Moulder et al., 2013; Reiman et al., 2011, 2014; Sperling et al., 2014).

Given the pathological importance of Aβ42 in AD, there has been extensive work devoted to developing methods to selectively target this species. Indeed, though γ-secretase is easily targeted by small molecules, pan-inhibition of γ-secretase cleavage is not well tolerated (Curry et al., 2005; Doody et al., 2013; Searfoss et al., 2003). Thus, conceptually, the notion of selectively altering γ-secretase cleavages that produce Aβ42 is very attractive. As with generally targeting Aβ, therapies targeting Aβ42 are almost certainly going to be most efficacious when administered prophylactically (Golde et al., 2011). The hope is that as optimized therapies targeting Aβ42 emerge, these will be tested as prophylactics using novel clinical paradigms that have emerged from the ongoing prevention studies mentioned earlier.

γ-SECRETASE MODULATORS

As noted previously, following the development of assays that enabled the specific detection of Aβ40 and Aβ42, several groups identified small molecules that could selectively lower Aβ40 production, but increased Aβ42 as well as other longer Aβ peptides (Citron et al., 1996; Murphy et al., 1999, 2000). These studies raised the possibility that small molecules could be identified that would selectively lower Aβ42, but not inhibit the initial cleavage of APP by γ-secretase that is referred to as ε-cleavage (Fig. 5.1), inhibit release of intracellular domains from other substrates, or alter the total level of Aβ generated. Indeed, such compounds were identified and over time were referred to as γ-secretase modulators (GSMs). The initial report showing that select nonsteroidal antiinflammatory drugs (NSAIDs) such as ibuprofen, sulindac sulfide, and indomethacin were GSMs and lowered Aβ42 selectively was published in 2001 (Eriksen et al., 2003; Weggen et al., 2001, 2003a). These first-generation GSMs did not alter total Aβ production or increase APP CTFs, but instead decreased Aβ1-42 levels and increased Aβ1-38 (Weggen et al., 2001). Further, these compounds had no effect on intracellular domain release from Notch1. These data were viewed with excitement by the field, as many hypothesized that GSMs could be therapeutic agents for AD, as they would selectively target the longer, more pathogenic forms of Aβ. In addition to GSMs, compounds referred to as inverse GSMs (iGSMs) were also identified (Gasparini et al., 2004; Kukar et al., 2005). These compounds were often structurally related to the first-generation GSMs, but typically lacked an acidic group, and increased, rather than lowered, Aβ1-42. These compounds also variably decreased levels of the short Aβ peptides including Aβ1-37, 38, and 39. iGSMs might be predicted to accelerate Aβ deposition and thus increase risk for AD;

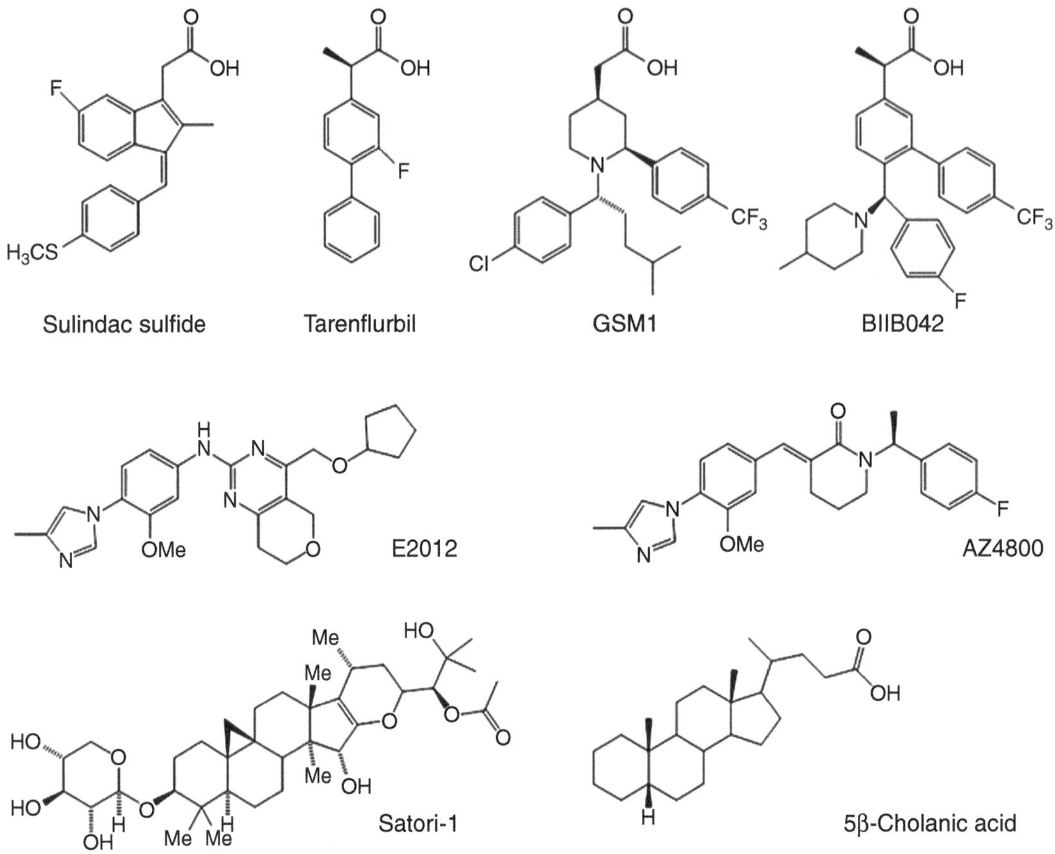

FIGURE 5.2 **Structure of selected GSMs.** The top row shows the structures of NSAID (sulindac sulfide and tarenflurbil) and NSAID-derived GSMs with the acetic acid functional group. The middle row depicts a popular scaffold for second-generation GSMs with arylimidazole substructure, found in E2012 and AZ4800. The bottom row shows the structure of two natural GSMs with distinct structural scaffolds.

however, this potential untoward effect of iGSMs has never been formally tested, in part because a potent (<1 μM EC50 for raising Aβ42) brain-penetrant iGSM has not been identified.

Following the identification of NSAID-based, "first-generation" GSMs, numerous academic, biotech, and pharmaceutical groups made major efforts to improve their potency and pharmacokinetic properties as well as attempt to find new classes of GSMs. Acidic GSMs with dramatic increases in potency and brain penetrance have now been identified, as well as highly potent brain-penetrant nonacidic GSMs (Bischoff et al., 2012; Gijsen and Mercken, 2012; Hall et al., 2010; Imbimbo et al., 2007b; Imbimbo and Giardina, 2011; Kounnas et al., 2010; Li et al., 2013; Lubbers et al., 2011; Narlawar et al., 2007; Portelius et al., 2010; Qin et al., 2011; Rivkin et al., 2010a, b; Rogers et al., 2012; Stanton et al., 2010; Sun et al., 2012; Van Broeck et al., 2011; Xin et al., 2011) (Fig. 5.2). More recently, both steroid-based and triterpenoid natural-product-derived GSMs have been identified (Hubbs et al., 2012; Jung et al., 2013, 2015; Loureiro et al., 2013). Notably, two of the more potent steroid-based GSMs,

TABLE 5.1 Proposed Targets of GSMs and iGSMs

GSM	Target	References
Fenofibrate	APP	Kukar et al. (2008)
	PS1–APP complex	Uemura et al. (2010)
Tarenflurbil	APP	Kukar et al. (2008)
	γ-Secretase	Beher et al. (2004)
	PS1–APP complex	Lleo et al. (2004)
Ibuprofen	PS1–APP complex	Lleo et al. (2004)
Indomethacin	PS1–APP complex	Lleo et al. (2004)
Sulindac sulfide	CTF100	Botev et al. (2011), Richter et al. (2010)
	Aβ	Yesuvadian et al. (2014)
	Membrane architecture	Gamerdinger et al. (2008)
	γ-Secretase	Beher et al. (2004), Takahashi et al. (2003)
Sulindac sulfone	γ-Secretase	Beher et al. (2004)
GSM1	PS1	Ohki et al. (2011), Crump et al. (2011)
Diarylaminothiazoles	Pen2 and lesser PS1	Kounnas et al. (2010)
BB25 (AR243)	PS1–NTF	Jumpertz et al. (2012)
AstraZeneca GSMs	γ-Secretase	Borgegard et al. (2012)
RO-57	PS1, PS2–NTF	Ebke et al. (2011)
E2012	PS1–NTF	Pozdnyakov et al. (2013)
	Aβ	Yesuvadian et al. (2014)
ST1120	PS1–NTF	Takeo et al. (2014)

lithocholic and cholestenoic acid, are endogenous cholesterol metabolites (Jung et al., 2013, 2015), raising the intriguing possibility that endogenous metabolites may modulate Aβ42 levels. In addition to potential pharmacokinetic differences, these GSMs have pharmacological differences that may have therapeutic relevance. All acidic GSMs—including steroid-based GSMs—show the classic GSM signature of lowering Aβ1-42 and increasing Aβ1-38 (Page et al., 2008), while nonacidic GSMs increase Aβ1-37 and 1-38 and lower both Aβ1-40 and 1-42 (Kounnas et al., 2010). In contrast, the triterpenoid GSM appears to be even more distinct, lowering both Aβ1-38 and 1-42 (Hubbs et al., 2012; Loureiro et al., 2013).

As opposed to reasonably well understood active site or allosteric mechanisms of inhibition that have been proposed and experimentally supported for various GSIs, it has been more challenging to identify the mechanism of action for GSMs. Binding studies have shown that GSMs can interact with various components of the γ-secretase complex (Table 5.1). First-generation acidic GSMs were shown to bind substrate (Kounnas et al., 2010; Kukar et al., 2008; Richter et al., 2010), whereas more potent acidic GSMs and nonacidic GSMs have been shown to bind PSEN1 or PEN-2 (Crump et al., 2011; Kounnas et al., 2010; Ohki et al., 2011; Pozdnyakov et al., 2013). The target of the triterpenoid natural product has not been established. Notably, the identification of various steroids as GSMs together with data showing that cholesterol—albeit at low affinity—interacts with APP CTFβ at a site similar to the NSAID-based GSM binding site on APP is intriguing, as it again supports the concept that GSMs may interact with substrate (Barrett et al., 2012; Beel et al., 2010). Extending this concept, we have proposed that GSMs likely alter γ-secretase cleavage through a complex interaction involving both substrate and γ-secretase and possibly even other lipid membrane components (Jung et al., 2013, 2014; Kukar and Golde, 2008; Kukar et al., 2005). This tripartite interaction model is consistent with data showing that GSM effects are very sensitive to substrate mutations and could explain the differential binding of GSM affinity probes (Jung et al., 2014). Of note, binding with such probes to a particular γ-secretase component does not rule out interaction with the other components. Inferences from such studies are not definitive because of restrictions on where the reactive cross-linking groups can be placed on the GSM affinity probes and still allow the compound to maintain its GSM activity. Indeed, as the photoaffinity label must be in very close proximity to the target protein to bind, showing binding to one protein in γ-secretase simply means that the GSM interacts with that component, but does not exclude interaction with other components of the γ-secretase complex or substrate.

Regardless of where the GSM may bind, significant progress has been made with respect to understanding how GSMs and iGSMs shift as opposed to inhibit γ-secretase cleavage. This understanding leverages insights provided by the sequential cleavage model initially proposed and experimentally supported by Ihara and coworkers (Takami et al., 2009) (Fig. 5.3). In this model, γ-secretase first cleaves APP at one of the three ε-sites within the APP transmembrane domain, but very close to the cytoplasmic face of the membrane. Subsequently, there is successive stepwise cleavage of the substrate that is referred to as processive cleavage. Typically, three to five processive cleavages occur, producing multiple different Aβ peptides. Notably, for APP the initial γ-cleavage at the ε-sites results in preferential—but not absolute—processing along specific product lines (Takami et al., 2009). Cleavage generating Aβ48 or Aβ50 preferentially leads to Aβ42 production and cleavage generating Aβ49 preferentially leads to Aβ40 production. Neither acidic/nonacidic GSMs nor iGSMS significantly alter the initial γ-secretase cleavage at the ε-site in APP (Czirr et al., 2008; Dimitrov et al., 2013; Jung et al., 2014; Ran et al., 2014; Sagi et al., 2011; Weggen et al., 2001, 2003a,b), but alter the subsequent number of processivity cleavage events. Thus, there is evidence that GSMs act as processivity enhancers and iGSMs as inhibitors of processivity (Chavez-Gutierrez et al., 2012; De Strooper et al., 2012; Fernandez et al., 2014; Quintero-Monzon et al., 2011; Wolfe, 2012).

For the more well-studied GSMs, there is ample evidence that these compounds do not alter Notch1 processing to any great extent (Eriksen et al., 2003; Sagi et al., 2011; Weggen et al., 2001, 2003b). They preserve Notch1 signaling and thus are thought to be inherently safe, which as noted earlier is essential given that they likely need to be clinically used as prophylactic therapies. Such substrate selectivity and lack of effect on the initial γ-secretase substrate cleavage is further reinforced by studies showing that point mutations in APP can significantly alter sensitivity to GSM action. Although some GSMs may modulate cleavage of some other γ-secretase substrates, there is no evidence that such modulation will have significant biological impact. One area of continued debate is whether APP and PS1 mutations influence the potency of GSMs. Potency of GSMs has been variably reported to be altered by AD-linked PS1 and APP mutations (Czirr et al., 2007; Mertens et al., 2013; Page

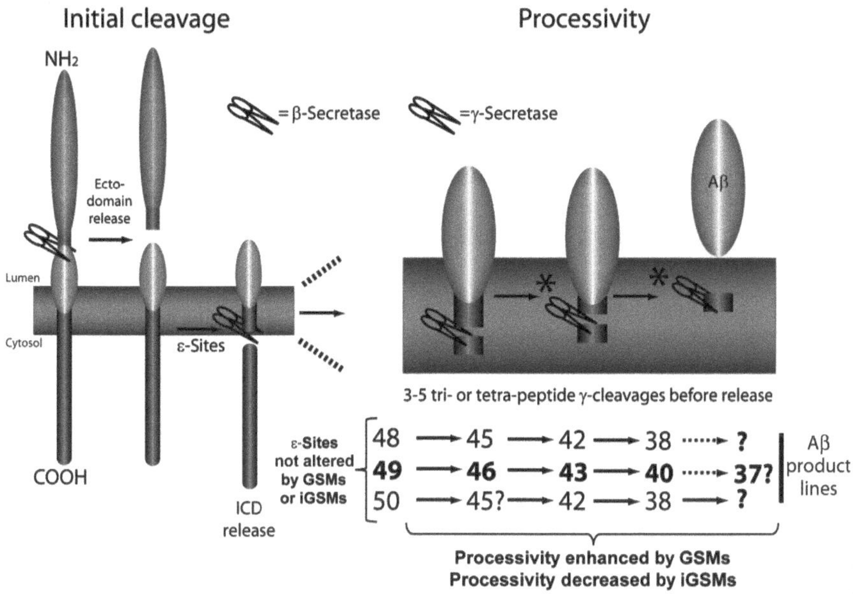

FIGURE 5.3 **Schematic model of APP stepwise cleavage by the γ-secretase.** Left: APP cleavages by β-secretase in the lumen and by the γ-secretase complex at the transmembrane ε-site will result in release of multiple potentially bioactive protein fragments. Right: The γ-secretase activity generates potentially bioactive fragments by processive stepwise cleavages every 3–5 amino acids. GSIs inhibit the initial cleavage, and GSMs alter processivity.

et al., 2008). If GSMs are ever tested in patients with PSEN or APP mutations, it will be important to empirically test for alterations in potency of the GSM with that particular PSEN or APP mutation. More recent studies have also suggested that human iPSC-derived neurons may be less sensitive to some GSMs; however, no mechanistic insight to this effect has been provided (Liu et al., 2014). Again prior to advancing a given GSM candidate to the clinic, it will be important to evaluate its action in such model systems. There are few published long-term studies of GSMs in APP transgenic mice (Kounnas et al., 2010; Rogers et al., 2012), though there are numerous studies showing acute lowering of Aβ42 following dosing of various GSMs. As expected when potent brain-penetrant GSMs are chronically dosed in these APP models, a reduction in amyloid loads and other AD-relevant phenotypes is observed.

CLINICAL DEVELOPMENT OF GSMs

No benefit on cognitive or functional outcomes was observed in a phase 3 study of the NSAID-based GSM tarenflurbil (R-flurbiprofen) in patients with mild AD (Green et al., 2009); however, tarenflurbil is a weak GSM with low CNS penetrance. Thus, results from this trial should not be generalized in any way to predict potential clinical efficacy of more potent, CNS-penetrant GSMs (De Strooper et al., 2010; Eriksen et al., 2003; Gijsen and Mercken, 2012; Kukar et al., 2007). There are a small number of ongoing GSM development programs and more potent GSMs continue to be tested in early-phase clinical trials. One GSM, CHF5074, developed by Chiesi Pharmaceuticals, has completed phase 2 testing in humans (Imbimbo et al., 2007a). Though this compound may possess GSM activity, it appears to have a rich pharmacology; these other activities have been postulated to contribute to its potential efficacy (Poli et al., 2012; Sivilia et al., 2013). A clear challenge in the development of optimized GSMs is the balance between potency and lipophilicity (Gijsen and Mercken, 2012). Though both potency and pharmacokinetic properties with respect to CNS exposure have been dramatically improved in second- and third-generation GSMs, this optimization has been associated with increases in lipophilicity of the compounds. Lipophilicity as well as glucuronidation of acidic GSMs are thought to contribute to off-target, toxic effects; therefore, additional optimization of GSMs will be necessary to develop the "safe enough" GSMs needed for prophylactic therapy (Gijsen and Mercken, 2012).

Although Aβ1-42 or other longer Aβ peptides are critical for initiating Aβ deposition, shorter Aβ species can accumulate in the AD brain as well (Moore et al., 2012). Thus, shifting Aβ cleavage after nucleation events have occurred is not likely to dramatically alter Aβ deposition kinetics, again indicating that GSMs are best considered as a prophylactic therapy. Another clinically relevant issue relates to the biology of the shorter Aβ peptides. There has been little systematic investigation of these peptides to determine their potential pathogenicity. One report suggested that Aβ1-38 may behave in vitro like Aβ1-42, but this important finding has not been reproduced (Kuperstein et al., 2010). Additional study of these short Aβ peptides may reveal select properties that might help to guide development of GSMs. Indeed, Aβ1-40 appears to act as an inhibitor of Aβ42 nucleation and aggregation in vivo (Kim et al., 2007; Wang et al., 2006), but whether Aβ36, 37, 38, or 39 inhibit aggregation in vivo is unknown. As nonacidic GSMs decrease Aβ40 whereas acidic GSMs do not, the distinct action of these two classes of GSMs could have a major impact on efficacy.

BIOLOGICAL APPROACHES TO TARGET Aβ42

An alternative to GSMs and small molecules is to use antibodies to directly and selectively target Aβ42. There are several proof-of-concept studies showing that (1) peripheral administration of anti-Aβ42 selective monoclonal antibodies (Asami-Odaka et al., 2005; Levites et al., 2006) or (2) intracerebral expression of recombinant anti-Aβ42 selective single-chain variable-fragment antibodies to APP transgenic mice can attenuate Aβ deposition; however, in one of these studies it was found that the anti-Aβ42 monoclonal antibody was effective only if used as preventive therapy and had no efficacy when delivered to mice with preexisting amyloid deposits. Given that the COOH-terminus of Aβ42 is thought to be buried when it assembles into oligomers or amyloid, it may be hard to target this epitope once aggregate formation has begun (Tycko, 2015; Walsh and Selkoe, 2004). A very recent study also shows that anti-Aβ42 selective single-chain variable-fragment antibodies expressed in a *Drosophila* model of Aβ42 toxicity could suppress the toxic effects of Aβ. Further, when expressed together with a pan-Aβ single-chain variable fragment, a synergistic neuroprotective effect was observed (Fernandez-Funez et al., 2015). There has been no report of active vaccination to selectively target Aβ42. Although selective antibodies to Aβ42 can be generated following immunization with Aβ35-42 or Aβ32-42 peptides conjugated to various carriers, these immunizations typically result in a polyclonal anti-Aβ response and only a small subset of the antibodies generated following immunization are Aβ42 specific. These are isolated by extensive screening of hybridomas for secretion of antibodies which bind Aβ42 but not other secreted Aβs. Given that only two hydrophobic amino acids distinguish Aβ42 from 40, there seem to be significant challenges to developing an active vaccination strategy that would generate only Aβ42 selective antibodies. In any case, given the encouraging preclinical data and the huge amount of interest in pan-Aβ immunotherapies (see Chapter 7), it is somewhat surprising that there has been such limited focus on further development of anti-Aβ42 selective immunotherapies (Golde et al., 2010).

SUMMARY AND FUTURE DIRECTIONS

Critical clinical tests of the amyloid hypothesis in preclinical AD are currently under way. Given the previous failures of anti-Aβ therapies in clinical trials, these ongoing prevention trials are pivotal studies that will have long-lasting influence on the field. If even minimally successful, then they will pave the way for renewed efforts to develop optimal anti-Aβ treatments. If unsuccessful, then it may be very challenging to move any new anti-Aβ therapy forward without clear demonstration that the new therapy is far superior to previous therapies. Despite the theoretical attractiveness of selective targeting of Aβ42 because of (1) uncertainties regarding efficacy and toxicity of the current clinical GSMs and (2) the current focus on β-secretase inhibitors, future investments in developing novel GSMs may be attentuated, at least for the immediate future. Given the large number of compounds developed around existing scaffolds, it will be difficult to develop optimal clinical GSM candidates through additional chemistry efforts. Thus, our own efforts in this area are focused on identifying new lead GSMs that are novel and not structurally similar to the current classes of GSMs described previously.

Although the initial GSMs identified were a subset of clinically used NSAIDs, there is little evidence that in humans these NSAID-based GSMs would reach sufficient levels to alter brain Aβ42 (Galasko et al., 2007). Indeed, recent rigorous studies in nonhuman primates indicate that ibuprofen even when dosed at 100 mg/kg intravenously could not acutely lower Aβ42 in vivo. In contrast, the more potent compound GSM-1 could lower both plasma and CSF Aβ42 (Ling et al., 2015). These data are important as they suggest that the proposed protective effects of NSAIDs that have been deduced from multiple epidemiologic studies are likely not attributable to the GSM activity of certain NSAIDs (Anthony et al., 2000; Breitner et al., 1994, 1995; in 't Veld et al., 1998, 2001; McGeer et al., 1996; Stewart et al., 1997; Zandi and Breitner, 2001). Thus, the field should explore other mechanisms by which long-term NSAID use might confer protection from developing AD.

We personally remain optimistic that selective targeting of Aβ42 as a prophylactic therapy for AD is a realistic approach. Like any prophylactic approach, such therapy will require a high degree of safety. It will also be challenging to prove efficacy. Unlike other approaches to the targeting of Aβ, GSMs appear to be inherently safe from a mechanistic point of view. We believe that additional work in this area, although challenging, will overcome the limitations of current GSMs and could also identify new approaches to selectively targeting Aβ42. For example, to our knowledge no one has ever systematically used genetic or chemical screens to identify other factors that could alter Aβ42 production. As there is a great deal of individual variability in Aβ42 levels, which appears to be genetically regulated in part (Ertekin-Taner et al., 2000), one might predict that other unknown factors can selectively regulate Aβ42 levels. Identification of such factors could provide new avenues for selective Aβ42 targeting that could overcome limitations of current approaches.

References

Albertini V, Benussi L, Paterlini A, et al: Distinct cerebrospinal fluid amyloid-beta peptide signatures in cognitive decline associated with Alzheimer's disease and schizophrenia, *Electrophoresis* 33:3738–3744, 2012.

Anthony JC, Breitner JC, Zandi PP, et al: Reduced prevalence of AD in users of NSAIDs and H2 receptor antagonists: the Cache County study, *Neurology* 54:2066–2071, 2000.

Asami-Odaka A, Obayashi-Adachi Y, Matsumoto Y, et al: Passive immunization of the Abeta42(43) C-terminal-specific antibody BC05 in a mouse model of Alzheimer's disease, *Neurodegener Dis* 2:36–43, 2005.

Barrett PJ, Song Y, Van Horn WD, et al: The amyloid precursor protein has a flexible transmembrane domain and binds cholesterol, *Science* 336:1168–1171, 2012.

Beel AJ, Sakakura M, Barrett PJ, et al: Direct binding of cholesterol to the amyloid precursor protein: an important interaction in lipid-Alzheimer's disease relationships? *Biochim Biophys Acta* 1801:975–982, 2010.

Beher D, Clarke EE, Wrigley JD, et al: Selected non-steroidal anti-inflammatory drugs and their derivatives target gamma-secretase at a novel site—evidence for an allosteric mechanism, *J Biol Chem* 279(42):43419–43426, 2004.

Bibl M, Mollenhauer B, Esselmann H, et al: CSF amyloid-beta-peptides in Alzheimer's disease, dementia with Lewy bodies and Parkinson's disease dementia, *Brain* 129:1177–1187, 2006.

Bischoff F, Berthelot D, De Cleyn M, et al: Design and synthesis of a novel series of bicyclic heterocycles as potent gamma-secretase modulators, *J Med Chem* 55:9089–9106, 2012.

Borgegard T, Gustavsson S, Nilsson C, et al: Alzheimer's disease: presenilin 2-sparing gamma-secretase inhibition is a tolerable Abeta peptide-lowering strategy, *J Neurosci* 32:17297–17305, 2012.

Botev A, Munter LM, Wenzel R, et al: The amyloid precursor protein C-terminal fragment C100 occurs in monomeric and dimeric stable conformations and binds gamma-secretase modulators, *Biochemistry* 50:828–835, 2011.

Breitner JC, Gau BA, Welsh KA, et al: Inverse association of anti-inflammatory treatments and Alzheimer's disease: initial results of a co-twin control study, *Neurology* 44:227–232, 1994.

Breitner JC, Welsh KA, Helms MJ, et al: Delayed onset of Alzheimer's disease with nonsteroidal anti-inflammatory and histamine H2 blocking drugs, *Neurobiol Aging* 16:523–530, 1995.

Busciglio J, Gabuzda DH, Matsudaira P, et al: Generation of beta-amyloid in the secretory pathway in neuronal and nonneuronal cells, *Proc Natl Acad Sci USA* 90:2092–2096, 1993.

Cai H, Wang Y, McCarthy D, et al: BACE1 is the major beta-secretase for generation of Abeta peptides by neurons, *Nat Neurosci* 4:233–234, 2001.

Cai XD, Golde TE, Younkin SG: Release of excess amyloid beta protein from a mutant amyloid beta protein precursor, *Science* 259:514–516, 1993.

Campion D, Flaman JM, Brice A, et al: Mutations of the presenilin I gene in families with early-onset Alzheimer's disease, *Hum Mol Genet* 4:2373–2377, 1995.

Carrillo MC, Brashear HR, Logovinsky V, et al: Can we prevent Alzheimer's disease? Secondary "prevention" trials in Alzheimer's disease, *Alzheimers Dement* 9:123–131.e1, 2013.

Chavez-Gutierrez L, Bammens L, Benilova I, et al: The mechanism of gamma-secretase dysfunction in familial Alzheimer disease, *EMBO J* 31:2261–2274, 2012.

Citron M, Diehl TS, Gordon G, et al: Evidence that the 42- and 40-amino acid forms of amyloid beta protein are generated from the beta-amyloid precursor protein by different protease activities, *Proc Natl Acad Sci USA* 93:13170–13175, 1996.

Citron M, Oltersdorf T, Haass C, et al: Mutation of the beta-amyloid precursor protein in familial Alzheimer's disease increases beta-protein production, *Nature* 360:672–674, 1992.

Crump CJ, Fish BA, Castro SV, et al: Piperidine acetic acid based gamma-secretase modulators directly bind to presenilin-1, *ACS Chem Neurosci* 2:705–710, 2011.

Curry CL, Reed LL, Golde TE, et al: Gamma secretase inhibitor blocks Notch activation and induces apoptosis in Kaposi's sarcoma tumor cells, *Oncogene* 24(42):6333–6344, 2005.

Czirr E, Cottrell BA, Leuchtenberger S, et al: Independent generation of Abeta 42 and Abeta 38 peptide species by gamma-secretase, *J Biol Chem* 283(25):17049–17054, 2008.

Czirr E, Leuchtenberger S, Dorner-Ciossek C, et al: Insensitivity to Abeta42-lowering nonsteroidal anti-inflammatory drugs and gamma-secretase inhibitors is common among aggressive presenilin-1 mutations, *J Biol Chem* 282:24504–24513, 2007.

De Strooper B, Annaert W, Cupers P, et al: A presenilin-1-dependent gamma-secretase-like protease mediates release of Notch intracellular domain, *Nature* 398:518–522, 1999.

De Strooper B, Iwatsubo T, Wolfe MS: Presenilins and gamma-secretase: structure, function, and role in Alzheimer disease, *Cold Spring Harb Perspect Med* 2:a006304, 2012.

De Strooper B, Vassar R, Golde T: The secretases: enzymes with therapeutic potential in Alzheimer disease, *Nat Rev Neurol* 6:99–107, 2010.

Dimitrov M, Alattia JR, Lemmin T, et al: Alzheimer's disease mutations in APP but not gamma-secretase modulators affect epsilon-cleavage-dependent AICD production, *Nat Commun* 4:2246, 2013.

Doody RS, Raman R, Farlow M, et al: A phase 3 trial of semagacestat for treatment of Alzheimer's disease, *N Engl J Med* 369:341–350, 2013.

Duff K, Eckman C, Zehr C, et al: Increased amyloid-beta42(43) in brains of mice expressing mutant presenilin 1, *Nature* 383:710–713, 1996.

Dyrks T, Weidemann A, Multhaup G, et al: Identification, transmembrane orientation and biogenesis of the amyloid A4 precursor of Alzheimer's disease, *EMBO J* 7:949–957, 1988.

Ebke A, Luebbers T, Fukumori A, et al: Novel gamma-secretase enzyme modulators directly target presenilin protein, *J Biol Chem* 286:37181–37186, 2011.

Edbauer D, Winkler E, Regula JT, et al: Reconstitution of gamma-secretase activity, *Nat Cell Biol* 5:486–488, 2003.

Eriksen JL, Sagi SA, Smith TE, et al: NSAIDs and enantiomers of flurbiprofen target gamma-secretase and lower Abeta 42 in vivo, *J Clin Invest* 112:440–449, 2003.

Ertekin-Taner N, Graff-Radford N, Younkin LH, et al: Linkage of plasma Abeta42 to a quantitative locus on chromosome 10 in late-onset Alzheimer's disease pedigrees, *Science* 290:2303–2304, 2000.

Fahrenholz F, Gilbert S, Kojro E, et al: Alpha-secretase activity of the disintegrin metalloprotease ADAM 10: influences of domain structure, *Ann NY Acad Sci* 920:215–222, 2000.

Fernandez MA, Klutkowski JA, Freret T, et al: Alzheimer presenilin-1 mutations dramatically reduce trimming of long amyloid beta-peptides (Abeta) by gamma-secretase to increase 42-to-40-residue Abeta, *J Biol Chem* 289:31043–31052, 2014.

Fernandez-Funez P, Zhang Y, Sanchez-Garcia J, et al: Anti-Abeta single chain variable fragment antibodies exert synergistic neuroprotective activities in Drosophila models of Alzheimer's disease, *Hum Mol Genet* 24(21):6093–6105, 2015.

Finelli A, Kelkar A, Song HJ, et al: A model for studying Alzheimer's Abeta42-induced toxicity in Drosophila melanogaster, *Mol Cell Neurosci* 26:365–375, 2004.

Fraering PC, Ye W, Strub JM, et al: Purification and characterization of the human gamma-secretase complex, *Biochemistry* 43:9774–9789, 2004.

Galasko DR, Graff-Radford N, May S, et al: Safety, tolerability, pharmacokinetics, and Abeta levels after short-term administration of R-flurbiprofen in healthy elderly individuals, *Alzheimer Dis Assoc Disord* 21:292–299, 2007.

Gamerdinger M, Clement AB, Behl C: Effects of sulindac sulfide on the membrane architecture and the activity of gamma-secretase, *Neuropharmacology* 54:998–1005, 2008.

Gasparini L, Rusconi L, Xu H, et al: Modulation of beta-amyloid metabolism by non-steroidal anti-inflammatory drugs in neuronal cell cultures, *J Neurochem* 88:337–348, 2004.

Gijsen HJ, Mercken M: Gamma-secretase modulators: can we combine potency with safety? *Int J Alzheimers Dis* 2012:295207, 2012.

Glenner GG, Wong CW: Alzheimer's disease and Down's syndrome: sharing of a unique cerebrovascular amyloid fibril protein, *Biochem Biophys Res Commun* 122:1131–1135, 1984.

Golde TE: Disease modifying therapy for AD? *J Neurochem* 99:689–707, 2006.

Golde TE, Eckman CB, Younkin SG: Biochemical detection of Abeta isoforms: implications for pathogenesis, diagnosis, and treatment of Alzheimer's disease, *Biochim Biophys Acta* 1502:172–187, 2000.

Golde TE, Estus SG, Usiak M, et al: Expression of β amyloid protein precursor mRNAs: recognition of a novel alternatively spliced form and quantitation in Alzheimer's disease using PCR, *Neuron* 4:253–267, 1990.

Golde TE, Petrucelli L, Lewis J: Targeting Abeta and tau in Alzheimer's disease, an early interim report, *Exp Neurol* 223:252–266, 2010.

Golde TE, Schneider LS, Koo EH: Anti-abeta therapeutics in Alzheimer's disease: the need for a paradigm shift, *Neuron* 69:203–213, 2011.

Gravina SA, Ho L, Eckman CB, et al: Amyloid beta protein (A beta) in Alzheimer's disease brain: biochemical and immunocytochemical analysis with antibodies specific for forms ending at A beta 40 or A beta 42(43), *J Biol Chem* 270:7013–7016, 1995.

Green RC, Schneider LS, Amato DA, et al: Effect of tarenflurbil on cognitive decline and activities of daily living in patients with mild Alzheimer disease: a randomized controlled trial, *J Amer Med Assoc* 302:2557–2564, 2009.

Haapasalo A, Kovacs DM: The many substrates of presenilin/gamma-secretase, *J Alzheimers Dis* 25(1):3–28, 2011.

Haass C, Hung AY, Selkoe DJ: Processing of β-amyloid precursor protein in microglia and astrocytes favors an internal localization over constitutive secretion, *J Neurosci* 11:3783–3793, 1991.

Haass C, Lemere CA, Capell A, et al: The Swedish mutation causes early-onset Alzheimer's disease by beta-secretase cleavage within the secretory pathway, *Nat Med* 1:1291–1296, 1995.

Hadland BK, Manley NR, Su D, et al: Gamma-secretase inhibitors repress thymocyte development, *Proc Natl Acad Sci USA* 98:7487–7491, 2001.

Hall A, Elliott RL, Giblin GM, et al: Piperidine-derived gamma-secretase modulators, *Bioorg Med Chem Lett* 20:1306–1311, 2010.

Hardy J: New insights into the genetics of Alzheimer's disease, *Ann Med* 28:255–258, 1996.

Hardy JA, Higgins GA: Alzheimer's disease: the amyloid cascade hypothesis, *Science* 256:184–185, 1992.

Herreman A, Hartmann D, Annaert W, et al: Presenilin 2 deficiency causes a mild pulmonary phenotype and no changes in amyloid precursor protein processing but enhances the embryonic lethal phenotype of presenilin 1 deficiency, *Proc Natl Acad Sci USA* 96:11872–11877, 1999.

Herreman A, Serneels L, Annaert W, et al: Total inactivation of gamma-secretase activity in presenilin-deficient embryonic stem cells, *Nat Cell Biol* 2:461–462, 2000.

Holcomb L, Gordon MN, McGowan E, et al: Accelerated Alzheimer-type phenotype in transgenic mice carrying both mutant amyloid precursor protein and presenilin 1 transgenes, *Nat Med* 4:97–100, 1998.

Hong L, Koelsch G, Lin X, et al: Structure of the protease domain of memapsin 2 (beta-secretase) complexed with inhibitor [in process citation], *Science* 290:150–153, 2000.

Hooper NM, Trew AJ, Parkin ET, et al: The role of proteolysis in Alzheimer's disease [in process citation], *Adv Exp Med Biol* 477:379–390, 2000.

Hubbs JL, Fuller NO, Austin WF, et al: Optimization of a natural product-based class of gamma-secretase modulators, *J Med Chem* 55:9270–9282, 2012.

Huppert S, Kopan R: Regulated intramembrane proteolysis takes another twist, *Dev Cell* 1:590–592, 2001.

Iijima K, Liu HP, Chiang AS, et al: Dissecting the pathological effects of human Abeta40 and Abeta42 in Drosophila: a potential model for Alzheimer's disease, *Proc Natl Acad Sci USA* 101:6623–6628, 2004.

Imbimbo BP, Del Giudice E, Cenacchi V, et al: In vitro and in vivo profiling of CHF5022 and CHF5074: two beta-amyloid1-42 lowering agents, *Pharmacol Res* 55:318–328, 2007a.

Imbimbo BP, Del Giudice E, Colavito D, et al: 1-(3′,4′-Dichloro-2-fluoro[1,1′-biphenyl]-4-yl)-cyclopropanecarboxylic acid (CHF5074), a novel gamma-secretase modulator, reduces brain beta-amyloid pathology in a transgenic mouse model of Alzheimer's disease without causing peripheral toxicity, *J Pharmacol Exp Ther* 323:822–830, 2007b.

Imbimbo BP, Giardina GA: Gamma-secretase inhibitors and modulators for the treatment of Alzheimer's disease: disappointments and hopes, *Curr Top Med Chem* 11:1555–1570, 2011.

in 't Veld BA, Launer LJ, Hoes AW, et al: NSAIDs and incident Alzheimer's disease: the Rotterdam Study [see comments], *Neurobiol Aging* 19:607–611, 1998.

in 't Veld BA, Ruitenberg A, Hofman A, et al: Nonsteroidal antiinflammatory drugs and the risk of Alzheimer's disease, *N Engl J Med* 345:1515–1521, 2001.

Israel MA, Yuan SH, Bardy C, et al: Probing sporadic and familial Alzheimer's disease using induced pluripotent stem cells, *Nature* 482:216–220, 2012.

Iwatsubo T, Odaka A, Suzuki N, et al: Visualization of A beta 42(43) and A beta 40 in senile plaques with end-specific A beta monoclonals: evidence that an initially deposited species is A beta 42(43), *Neuron* 13:45–53, 1994.

Jarrett JT, Berger EP, Lansbury PT Jr: The carboxy terminus of β amyloid protein is critical for the seeding of amyloid formation: implications for pathogenesis of Alzheimer's disease, *Biochem* 32:4693–4697, 1993a.

Jarrett JT, Berger EP, Lansbury PT Jr: The C-terminus of the beta protein is critical in amyloidogenesis. [Review], *Ann NY Acad Sci* 695:144–148, 1993b.

Jarrett JT, Lansbury PT Jr: Seeding "one dimensional crystallization" of amyloid: a pathogenic mechanism in Alzheimer's disease and scrapie? *Cell* 73:1055–1058, 1993.

Jumpertz T, Rennhack A, Ness J, et al: Presenilin is the molecular target of acidic gamma-secretase modulators in living cells, *PLoS One* 7:e30484, 2012.

Jung JI, Ladd TB, Kukar T, et al: Steroids as gamma-secretase modulators, *FASEB J* 27:3775–3785, 2013.

Jung JI, Price AR, Ladd TB, et al: Cholestenoic acid, an endogenous cholesterol metabolite, is a potent gamma-secretase modulator, *Mol Neurodegener* 10:29, 2015.

Jung JI, Ran Y, Cruz PE, et al: Complex relationships between substrate sequence and sensitivity to alterations in gamma-secretase processivity induced by gamma-secretase modulators, *Biochemistry* 53:1947–1957, 2014.

Kang J, Lemaire H-G, Unterbeck A, et al: The precursor of Alzheimer's disease amyloid A4 protein resembles a cell-surface receptor, *Nature* 325:733–736, 1987.

Kelleher RJ 3rd, Shen J: Genetics. Gamma-secretase and human disease, *Science* 330:1055–1056, 2010.

Khachaturian ZS, Barnes D, Einstein R, et al: Developing a national strategy to prevent dementia: Leon Thal Symposium 2009, *Alzheimers Dement* 6:89–97, 2010.

Kim J, Onstead L, Randle S, et al: Abeta40 inhibits amyloid deposition in vivo, *J Neurosci* 27:627–633, 2007.

Kimberly WT, LaVoie MJ, Ostaszewski BL, et al: Gamma-secretase is a membrane protein complex comprised of presenilin, nicastrin, Aph-1, and Pen-2, *Proc Natl Acad Sci USA* 100:6382–6387, 2003.

Kirschner DA, Inouye H, Duffy LK, et al: Synthetic peptide homologous to β protein from Alzheimer disease forms amyloid-like fibrils in vitro, *Proc Natl Acad Sci USA* 84:6953–6957, 1987.

Kojro E, Fahrenholz F: The non-amyloidogenic pathway: structure and function of alpha-secretases, *Subcell Biochem* 38:105–127, 2005.

Kopan R, Goate A: Aph-2/nicastrin: an essential component of gamma-secretase and regulator of Notch signaling and presenilin localization, *Neuron* 33:321–324, 2002.

Kounnas MZ, Danks AM, Cheng S, et al: Modulation of gamma-secretase reduces beta-amyloid deposition in a transgenic mouse model of Alzheimer's disease, *Neuron* 67:769–780, 2010.

Kukar T, Golde TE: Possible mechanisms of action of NSAIDs and related compounds that modulate gamma-secretase cleavage, *Curr Top Med Chem* 8:47–53, 2008.

Kukar T, Murphy MP, Eriksen JL, et al: Diverse compounds mimic Alzheimer disease-causing mutations by augmenting Abeta42 production, *Nat Med* 11:545–550, 2005.

Kukar T, Prescott S, Eriksen JL, et al: Chronic administration of R-flurbiprofen attenuates learning impairments in transgenic amyloid precursor protein mice, *BMC Neurosci* 8:54, 2007.

Kukar TL, Ladd TB, Bann MA, et al: Substrate-targeting gamma-secretase modulators, *Nature* 453:925–929, 2008.

Kuperstein I, Broersen K, Benilova I, et al: Neurotoxicity of Alzheimer's disease Abeta peptides is induced by small changes in the Abeta42 to Abeta40 ratio, *EMBO J* 29:3408–3420, 2010.

Levites Y, Das P, Price RW, et al: Anti-Abeta42- and anti-Abeta40-specific mAbs attenuate amyloid deposition in an Alzheimer disease mouse model, *J Clin Invest* 116:193–201, 2006.

Levy E, Carman MD, Fernandez-Madrid IJ, et al: Mutation of the Alzheimer's disease amyloid gene in hereditary cerebral hemorrhage, Dutch type, *Science* 248:1124–1126, 1990.

Levy-Lahad E, Wijsman EM, Nemens E, et al: A familial Alzheimer's disease locus on chromosome 1, *Science* 269:970–973, 1995.

Lewczuk P, Esselmann H, Meyer M, et al: The amyloid-beta (Abeta) peptide pattern in cerebrospinal fluid in Alzheimer's disease: evidence of a novel carboxyterminally elongated Abeta peptide, *Rapid Commun Mass Spectrom* 17:1291–1296, 2003.

Li H, Qin J, Dhondi P, et al: The discovery of fused oxadiazepines as gamma secretase modulators for treatment of Alzheimer's disease, *Bioorg Med Chem Lett* 23:466–471, 2013.

Li YM, Xu M, Lai MT, et al: Photoactivated gamma-secretase inhibitors directed to the active site covalently label presenilin 1, *Nature* 405:689–694, 2000.

Ling IF, Golde TE, Galasko DR, et al: Modulation of Abeta42 in vivo by gamma-secretase modulator in primates and humans, *Alzheimers Res Ther* 7:55, 2015.

Link CD: Invertebrate models of Alzheimer's disease, *Genes Brain Behav* 4:147–156, 2005.

Liu Q, Waltz S, Woodruff G, et al: Effect of potent gamma-secretase modulator in human neurons derived from multiple presenilin 1-induced pluripotent stem cell mutant carriers, *JAMA Neurol* 71:1481–1489, 2014.

Lleo A, Berezovska O, Herl L, et al: Nonsteroidal anti-inflammatory drugs lower Abeta42 and change presenilin 1 conformation, *Nat Med* 10:1065–1066, 2004.

Loureiro RM, Dumin JA, McKee TD, et al: Efficacy of SPI-1865, a novel gamma-secretase modulator, in multiple rodent models, *Alzheimers Res Ther* 5:19, 2013.

Lubbers T, Flohr A, Jolidon S, et al: Aminothiazoles as gamma-secretase modulators, *Bioorg Med Chem Lett* 21:6554–6558, 2011.

Lue LF, Kuo YM, Roher AE, et al: Soluble amyloid beta peptide concentration as a predictor of synaptic change in Alzheimer's disease, *Am J Pathol* 155:853–862, 1999.

Maddalena AS, Papassotiropoulos A, Gonzalez-Agosti C, et al: Cerebrospinal fluid profile of amyloid beta peptides in patients with Alzheimer's disease determined by protein biochip technology, *Neurodegener Dis* 1:231–235, 2004.

Masters CL, Multhaup G, Simms G, et al: Neuronal origin of a cerebral amyloid: neurofibrillary tangles of Alzheimer's disease contain the same protein as the amyloid of plaque cores and blood vessels, *EMBO J* 4:2757–2763, 1985a.

Masters CL, Simms G, Weinman NA, et al: Amyloid plaque core protein in Alzheimer disease and Down syndrome, *Proc Natl Acad Sci USA* 82:4245–4249, 1985b.

McGeer PL, Schulzer M, McGeer EG: Arthritis and anti-inflammatory agents as possible protective factors for Alzheimer's disease: a review of 17 epidemiologic studies [see comments], *Neurology* 47:425–432, 1996.

McGowan E, Pickford F, Kim J, et al: Abeta42 is essential for parenchymal and vascular amyloid deposition in mice, *Neuron* 47:191–199, 2005.

Mertens J, Stuber K, Wunderlich P, et al: APP processing in human pluripotent stem cell-derived neurons is resistant to NSAID-based gamma-secretase modulation, *Stem Cell Reports* 1:491–498, 2013.

Moore BD, Chakrabarty P, Levites Y, et al: Overlapping profiles of Abeta peptides in the Alzheimer's disease and pathological aging brains, *Alzheimers Res Ther* 4:18, 2012.

Moulder KL, Snider BJ, Mills SL, et al: Dominantly inherited Alzheimer network: facilitating research and clinical trials, *Alzheimers Res Ther* 5:48, 2013.

Mullan M, Crawford F, Axelman K, et al: A pathogenic mutation for probable Alzheimer's disease in the APP gene at the N-terminus of β-amyloid, *Nat Genet* 1:345–347, 1992.

Murphy MP, Hickman LJ, Eckman CB, et al: Gamma-secretase, evidence for multiple proteolytic activities and influence of membrane positioning of substrate on generation of amyloid beta peptides of varying length, *J Biol Chem* 274:11914–11923, 1999.

Murphy MP, Uljon SN, Fraser PE, et al: Presenilin 1 regulates pharmacologically distinct gamma-secretase activities: implications for the role of presenilin in gamma-secretase cleavage, *J Biol Chem* 275:26277–26284, 2000.

Narlawar R, Perez Revuelta BI, Baumann K, et al: N-substituted carbazolyloxyacetic acids modulate Alzheimer associated gamma-secretase, *Bioorg Med Chem Lett* 17:176–182, 2007.

Ohki Y, Higo T, Uemura K, et al: Phenylpiperidine-type gamma-secretase modulators target the transmembrane domain 1 of presenilin 1, *EMBO J* 30:4815–4824, 2011.

Page RM, Baumann K, Tomioka M, et al: Generation of A 38 and A 42 is independently and differentially affected by familial Alzheimer disease-associated presenilin mutations and γ-secretase modulation, *J Biol Chem* 283:677–683, 2008.

Poli G, Corda E, Lucchini B, et al: Therapeutic effect of CHF5074, a new gamma-secretase modulator, in a mouse model of scrapie, *Prion* 6:62–72, 2012.

Ponting CP, Hutton M, Nyborg A, et al: Identification of a novel family of presenilin homologues, *Hum Mol Genet* 11:1037–1044, 2002.

Portelius E, Van Broeck B, Andreasson U, et al: Acute effect on the Abeta isoform pattern in CSF in response to gamma-secretase modulator and inhibitor treatment in dogs, *J Alzheimers Dis* 21:1005–1012, 2010.

Pozdnyakov N, Murrey HE, Crump CJ, et al: Gamma-secretase modulator (GSM) photoaffinity probes reveal distinct allosteric binding sites on presenilin, *J Biol Chem* 288:9710–9720, 2013.

Price DL, Tanzi RE, Borchelt DR, et al: Alzheimer's disease: genetic studies and transgenic models, *Annu Rev Genet* 32:461–493, 1998.

Qin J, Zhou W, Huang X, et al: Discovery of a potent pyrazolopyridine series of gamma-secretase modulators, *ACS Med Chem-Lett* 2:471–476, 2011.

Quintero-Monzon O, Martin MM, Fernandez MA, et al: Dissociation between the processivity and total activity of gamma-secretase: implications for the mechanism of Alzheimer's disease-causing presenilin mutations, *Biochemistry* 50:9023–9035, 2011.

Ran Y, Cruz PE, Ladd TB, et al: Gamma-secretase processing and effects of gamma-secretase inhibitors and modulators on long Abeta peptides in cells, *J Biol Chem* 289:3276–3287, 2014.

Reiman EM, Langbaum JB, Fleisher AS, et al: Alzheimer's Prevention Initiative: a plan to accelerate the evaluation of presymptomatic treatments, *J Alzheimers Dis* 26(Suppl 3):321–329, 2011.

Reiman EM, Langbaum JB, Tariot PN: Endpoints in preclinical Alzheimer's disease trials, *J Clin Psychiat* 75:661–662, 2014.

Richter L, Munter LM, Ness J, et al: Amyloid beta 42 peptide (Abeta42)-lowering compounds directly bind to Abeta and interfere with amyloid precursor protein (APP) transmembrane dimerization, *Proc Natl Acad Sci USA* 107:14597–14602, 2010.

Rivkin A, Ahearn SP, Chichetti SM, et al: Purine derivatives as potent gamma-secretase modulators, *Bioorg Med Chem Lett* 20:2279–2282, 2010a.

Rivkin A, Ahearn SP, Chichetti SM, et al: Piperazinyl pyrimidine derivatives as potent gamma-secretase modulators, *Bioorg Med Chem Lett* 20:1269–1271, 2010b.

Robakis NK, Ramakrishna N, Wolfe G, et al: Molecular cloning and characterization of a cDNA encoding the cerebrovascular and the neuritic plaque amyloid peptides, *Proc Natl Acad Sci USA* 84:4190–4194, 1987.

Rogaev EI, Sherrington R, Levesque G, et al: Familial Alzheimer's disease in kindreds with missense mutations in a gene on chromosome 1 related to the Alzheimer's disease type 3 gene, *Nature* 376:775–778, 1995.

Rogers K, Felsenstein KM, Hrdlicka L, et al: Modulation of gamma-secretase by EVP-0015962 reduces amyloid deposition and behavioral deficits in Tg2576 mice, *Mol Neurodegener* 7:61, 2012.

Sagi SA, Lessard CB, Winden KD, et al: Substrate sequence influences gamma-secretase modulator activity, role of the transmembrane domain of the amyloid precursor protein, *J Biol Chem* 286:39794–39803, 2011.

Saido TC, Iwatsubo T, Mann DM, et al: Dominant and differential deposition of distinct beta-amyloid peptide species, A beta N3(pE), in senile plaques, *Neuron* 14:457–466, 1995.

Saura CA, Choi SY, Beglopoulos V, et al: Loss of presenilin function causes impairments of memory and synaptic plasticity followed by age-dependent neurodegeneration, *Neuron* 42:23–36, 2004.

Scheuner D, Eckman C, Jensen M, et al: Secreted amyloid beta-protein similar to that in the senile plaques of Alzheimer's disease is increased in vivo by the presenilin 1 and 2 and APP mutations linked to familial Alzheimer's disease, *Nat Med* 2:864–870, 1996.

Schroeter EH, Kisslinger JA, Kopan R: Notch-1 signalling requires ligand-induced proteolytic release of intracellular domain [see comments], *Nature* 393:382–386, 1998.

Searfoss GH, Jordan WH, Calligaro DO, et al: Adipsin, a biomarker of gastrointestinal toxicity mediated by a functional gamma-secretase inhibitor, *J Biol Chem* 278:46107–46116, 2003.

Seiffert D, Bradley JD, Rominger CM, et al: Presenilin-1 and -2 are molecular targets for gamma-secretase inhibitors [in process citation], *J Biol Chem* 275:34086–34091, 2000.

Selkoe D, Kopan R: Notch and presenilin: regulated intramembrane proteolysis links development and degeneration, *Annu Rev Neurosci* 26:565–597, 2003.

Selkoe DJ: Alzheimer's disease: genes, proteins, and therapy, *Physiol Rev* 81:741–766, 2001.

Seubert P, Vigo-Pelfrey C, Esch F, et al: Isolation and quantitation of soluble Alzheimer's β-peptide from biological fluids, *Nature* 359:325–327, 1992.

Shen J, Bronson RT, Chen DF, et al: Skeletal and CNS defects in presenilin-1-deficient mice, *Cell* 89:629–639, 1997.

Shoji M, Golde TE, Ghiso J, et al: Production of the Alzheimer amyloid beta protein by normal proteolytic processing, *Science* 258:126–129, 1992.

Sivilia S, Lorenzini L, Giuliani A, et al: Multi-target action of the novel anti-Alzheimer compound CHF5074: in vivo study of long term treatment in Tg2576 mice, *BMC Neurosci* 14:44, 2013.

Sperling RA, Rentz DM, Johnson KA, et al: The A4 study: stopping AD before symptoms begin? *Sci Transl Med* 6:228fs13, 2014.

Stanton MG, Hubbs J, Sloman D, et al: Fluorinated piperidine acetic acids as gamma-secretase modulators, *Bioorg Med Chem Lett* 20:755–758, 2010.

Stewart WF, Kawas C, Corrada M, et al: Risk of Alzheimer's disease and duration of NSAID use [see comments], *Neurology* 48:626–632, 1997.

Sun ZY, Asberom T, Bara T, et al: Cyclic hydroxyamidines as amide isosteres: discovery of oxadiazolines and oxadiazines as potent and highly efficacious gamma-secretase modulators in vivo, *J Med Chem* 55:489–502, 2012.

Suzuki N, Cheung TT, Cai X-D, et al: An increased percentage of long amyloid β protein is secreted by familial amyloid β protein precursor (βAPP_{717}) mutants, *Science* 264:1336–1340, 1994.

Takahashi Y, Hayashi I, Tominari Y, et al: Sulindac sulfide is a noncompetitive gamma-secretase inhibitor that preferentially reduces Abeta 42 generation, *J Biol Chem* 278:18664–18670, 2003.

Takami M, Nagashima Y, Sano Y, et al: Gamma-secretase: successive tripeptide and tetrapeptide release from the transmembrane domain of beta-carboxyl terminal fragment, *J Neurosci* 29:13042–13052, 2009.

Takasugi N, Tomita T, Hayashi I, et al: The role of presenilin cofactors in the gamma-secretase complex, *Nature* 422:438–441, 2003.

Takeo K, Tanimura S, Shinoda T, et al: Allosteric regulation of gamma-secretase activity by a phenylimidazole-type gamma-secretase modulator, *Proc Natl Acad Sci USA* 111:10544–10549, 2014.

Tan L, Schedl P, Song HJ, et al: The Toll→NFkappaB signaling pathway mediates the neuropathological effects of the human Alzheimer's Abeta42 polypeptide in Drosophila, *PLoS One* 3:e3966, 2008.

Tanzi RE, Gusella JF, Watkins PC, et al: Amyloid β protein gene: cDNA, mRNA distribution and genetic linkage near the Alzheimer locus, *Science* 235:880–884, 1987.

Treusch S, Hamamichi S, Goodman JL, et al: Functional links between Abeta toxicity, endocytic trafficking, and Alzheimer's disease risk factors in yeast, *Science* 334:1241–1245, 2011.

Tycko R: Amyloid polymorphism: structural basis and neurobiological relevance, *Neuron* 86:632–645, 2015.

Uemura K, Farner KC, Hashimoto T, et al: Substrate docking to gamma-secretase allows access of gamma-secretase modulators to an allosteric site, *Nat Commun* 1:130, 2010.

Van Broeck B, Chen JM, Treton G, et al: Chronic treatment with a novel gamma-secretase modulator, JNJ-40418677, inhibits amyloid plaque formation in a mouse model of Alzheimer's disease, *Br J Pharmacol* 163:375–389, 2011.

Van Broeckhoven C, Haan J, Bakker E, et al: Amyloid beta protein precursor gene and hereditary cerebral hemorrhage with amyloidosis (Dutch), *Science* 248:1120–1122, 1990.

Vassar R, Bennett B, Babu-Khan S, et al: Beta-secretase cleavage of Alzheimer's amyloid precursor protein by the transmembrane aspartic protease BACE, *Science* 286:735–740, 1999.

Walsh DM, Selkoe DJ: Oligomers on the brain: the emerging role of soluble protein aggregates in neurodegeneration, *Protein Pept Lett* 11:213–228, 2004.

Wang R, Wang B, He W, et al: Wild-type presenilin 1 protects against Alzheimer disease mutation-induced amyloid pathology, *J Biol Chem* 281:15330–15336, 2006.

Wasco W, Pettingell WP, Jondro PD, et al: Familial Alzheimer chromosome-14 mutations, *Nat Med* 1:848, 1995.

Weggen S, Eriksen JL, Das P, et al: A subset of NSAIDs lower amyloidogenic Abeta42 independently of cyclooxygenase activity, *Nature* 414:212–216, 2001.

Weggen S, Eriksen JL, Sagi SA, et al: Abeta42-lowering nonsteroidal anti-inflammatory drugs preserve intramembrane cleavage of the amyloid precursor protein (APP) and ErbB-4 receptor and signaling through the APP intracellular domain, *J Biol Chem* 278:30748–30754, 2003a.

Weggen S, Eriksen JL, Sagi SA, et al: Evidence that nonsteroidal anti-inflammatory drugs decrease amyloid beta 42 production by direct modulation of gamma-secretase activity, *J Biol Chem* 278:31831–31837, 2003b.

Weidemann A, Konig G, Bunke D, et al: Identification, biogenesis, and localization of precursors of Alzheimer's disease A4 amyloid protein, *Cell* 57:115–126, 1989.

Weihofen A, Binns K, Lemberg MK, et al: Identification of signal peptide peptidase, a presenilin-type aspartic protease, *Science* 296:2215–2218, 2002.

Wolfe MS: Processive proteolysis by gamma-secretase and the mechanism of Alzheimer's disease, *Biol Chem* 393:899–905, 2012.

Wolfe MS, Xia WM, Moore CL, et al: Peptidomimetic probes and molecular modeling suggest that Alzheimer's gamma-secretase is an intramembrane-cleaving aspartyl protease, *Biochemistry* 38:4720–4727, 1999a.

Wolfe MS, Xia WM, Ostaszewski BL, et al: Two transmembrane aspartates in presenilin-1 required for presenilin endoproteolysis and gamma-secretase activity, *Nature* 398:513–517, 1999b.

Wong PC, Zheng H, Chen H, et al: Presenilin 1 is required for Notch1 and DII1 expression in the paraxial mesoderm, *Nature* 387:288–292, 1997.

Xin Z, Peng H, Zhang A, et al: Discovery of 4-aminomethylphenylacetic acids as gamma-secretase modulators via a scaffold design approach, *Bioorg Med Chem Lett* 21:7277–7280, 2011.

Yan R, Bienkowski MJ, Shuck ME, et al: Membrane-anchored aspartyl protease with Alzheimer's disease beta-secretase activity, *Nature* 402:533–537, 1999.

Yesuvadian R, Krishnamoorthy J, Ramamoorthy A, et al: Potent gamma-secretase inhibitors/modulators interact with amyloid-beta fibrils but do not inhibit fibrillation: a high-resolution NMR study, *Biochem Biophys Res Commun* 447:590–595, 2014.

Younkin SG: The role of A beta 42 in Alzheimer's disease, *J Physiology-Paris* 92:289–292, 1998.

Zandi PP, Breitner JC: Do NSAIDs prevent Alzheimer's disease? And, if so, why? The epidemiological evidence, *Neurobiol Aging* 22:811–817, 2001.

Zhang L, Lee J, Song L, et al: Characterization of the reconstituted gamma-secretase complex from Sf9 cells co-expressing presenilin 1, nicastrin, aph-1a, and pen-2, *Biochemistry* 44:4450–4457, 2005.

CHAPTER

6

Modulators of Amyloid β-Protein (Aβ) Self-Assembly

F. Rahimi, H. Li, S. Sinha, G. Bitan

OUTLINE

INTRODUCTION

Amyloid β-protein (Aβ) is produced mainly as 40- or 42-amino acid polypeptides from the amyloid β-protein precursor (APP) through sequential cleavage by enzymatic activities called β- and γ-secretases (Esler and Wolfe, 2001; Martins et al., 1991). It is produced in a monomeric form as part of normal physiology by different cells in the body throughout life (Haass et al., 1993); yet, although the peptide was discovered in the 1980s (Glenner and Wong, 1984; Masters et al., 1985), more than 30 years later its physiological role is poorly understood. Most studies of Aβ have focused on its pathogenic role in disease. The original discovery of Aβ was in brain extracts from patients with Alzheimer's disease (AD). Today, AD still is the main

Developing Therapeutics for Alzheimer's Disease. http://dx.doi.org/10.1016/B978-0-12-802173-6.00006-X

disease associated with Aβ, though deleterious effects of Aβ aggregates also have been found in other diseases, including Down syndrome (Wilcock and Griffin, 2013), inclusion-body myositis (Askanas et al., 2012), and age-related macular degeneration (Ratnayaka et al., 2015).

Following the discovery that Aβ was the main proteinaceous component of amyloid plaques, the amyloid cascade hypothesis posited that formation of Aβ fibrils along with their deposition in amyloid plaques was the key event initiating the disease process, and that all the other pathologic processes, including abnormal tau hyperphosphorylation and aggregation, oxidative stress, and inflammation, were consequences of Aβ fibrillation (Hardy and Higgins, 1992). Later, this original hypothesis was revised when it became clear that elusive, metastable oligomers were substantially more neurotoxic than amyloid fibrils (Dahlgren et al., 2002; Lambert et al., 1998), and oligomer concentration showed high correlation with the progression of AD, whereas fibril abundance and location did not (Hardy, 2002; Selkoe, 2004).

Over the past three decades, major progress has been made in elucidating the central role of Aβ in AD and uncovering the contribution of specific forms of Aβ. In addition to the increasing understanding that oligomers are the proximal neurotoxins acting in AD, research has shown that the 42-amino-acid-long form of Aβ, Aβ42, is substantially more toxic than the shorter form, Aβ40. Aβ40 is ~10 times more abundant than Aβ42, yet because of its lower toxicity, it is believed to be a lesser contributor to AD pathology (Rahimi and Bitan, 2012). Alongside these shifts in conception and understanding of the rank order of importance of different Aβ species, the search for therapeutic intervention has been shifting slowly from fibrils to oligomers and from Aβ in general to Aβ42.

Therapeutic approaches targeting Aβ generally have focused on three main strategies—inhibition of Aβ production, enhancement of Aβ clearance, and inhibition/modulation of Aβ assembly. Theoretically, inhibition of Aβ formation would be the most straightforward approach. A major strength of the pharmaceutical industry has been discovering and optimizing enzyme inhibitors. Thus, searching for inhibitors of β- and γ-secretases appeared to be a promising strategy after the major enzymes responsible for these enzymatic activities were identified as presenilin 1 (Wolfe et al., 1999) and β-site APP-cleaving enzyme 1 (BACE1) (Vassar et al., 1999). However, in both cases, efforts of more than a decade have not led to effective drugs, primarily due to the fact that each enzyme is responsible for processing multiple substrates. Thus, discovering inhibitors with sufficient specificity and safety has been challenging (Pollack and Lewis, 2005; Wolfe, 2012; Yan and Vassar, 2014). γ-Secretase therapy suffered a major recent setback with the failure of semagacestat, which not only did not improve symptoms in patients with AD, but actually worsened symptoms (Doody et al., 2013). β-Secretase inhibitors are currently being tested in several clinical trials (Vassar, 2014), yet recent research showing that these inhibitors may lead to accumulation of N-terminally extended APP fragments with substantial neurotoxicity are worrisome (Kaneko et al., 2014; Willem et al., 2015).

Clearance of Aβ from the brain has been the most advanced therapeutic strategy explored to date following initial discoveries showing that antibodies targeting Aβ could reduce Aβ burden dramatically in animal models (Frenkel et al., 2000; Schenk, 2002). Early attempts to immunize patients with AD with fibrillar Aβ were halted abruptly after some patients developed subacute meningoencephalitis (Orgogozo et al., 2003). Subsequently, several clinical trials used passive immunization with antibodies targeting different Aβ epitopes. Unfortunately, these trials have not been successful due to lack of efficacy and/or because of safety issues, decreasing hope for a breakthrough therapy (Cummings et al., 2014; Doody et al., 2014; Salloway et al., 2014). Very recently, results reported in the 2015 Alzheimer's Association International Conference provided cautious hope with news of possible delayed cognitive decline in patients with mild AD treated by Eli Lilly's monoclonal antibody, solanezumab, and positive target engagement by Roche's gantenerumab. These reports followed positive data from a small phase 1 trial showing efficacy of Biogen's aducanumab earlier in the year, yet safety issues with this antibody are a concern (https://www.alz.org/aaic/releases_2015/wed-7amET.asp). Current trepidation exists regarding the general approach using antibody clearance of Aβ due to fear that finding the right balance between efficacy and safety may be more difficult than previously perceived. Another general worry is that virtually all the major trials conducted to date were done too late in the disease process to have an effect. New clinical trials in asymptomatic patients (A4 NCT02008357) or patients with familial AD (DIAN-TU NCT01760005, PSEN1 E280A NCT01998841) are expected to address this concern and potentially provide hope for effective disease-modifying therapy in the next few years. Other strategies for enhancement of Aβ clearance, such as increased autophagy (Maiese, 2014) or induction of efflux from the brain (Paganetti et al., 2014; Roberts et al., 2014) have been explored but are not as advanced as immunological approaches.

A general strategic caveat in inhibition of Aβ production and enhancement of Aβ clearance is that they affect normal physiological processes. The limited understanding of the physiological role of Aβ itself increases this concern even further (Rajasekhar et al., 2015). In contrast, because Aβ self-assembly is a purely pathologic process, targeting this process, at least conceptually, is a highly attractive strategy. The problem here is that the therapeutic target—the metastable toxic oligomers—is an unusual and highly challenging one. The oligomers exist in mixtures of constantly changing structures, and the conformational stability of each monomer in these oligomers is low, making targeting the oligomers using typical strategies, for example, screening of small molecules, a frustrating endeavor.

Monomeric Aβ is nontoxic. Upon Aβ self-assembly, the toxicity increases substantially as oligomers form and then decreases with formation of fibrils. Because assembly state has such a strong impact on toxicity, researchers have asked whether particular oligomers are the most toxic or most important pathologic determinants in AD (Reed et al., 2011). However, despite intense research, no consensus has emerged, and it appears that most oligomers ranging from dimers to protofibrils are indeed toxic, increasing the complexity of the problem and the difficulty of developing effective inhibitors of Aβ oligomer toxicity. An even more confusing aspect of the problem is that because the oligomers are metastable structures, even molecules that interact with them with moderate affinity can affect their structure and assembly state. Many examples of such molecules are discussed in this chapter. However, to date, there are no clear criteria allowing the prediction of whether modulation in a particular direction would be therapeutically viable.

Despite these difficulties, but also perhaps because obtaining an initial effect is relatively easy and low-potency hits are easy to find, multiple groups have examined natural products, peptides, peptidomimetics, and various synthetic compounds as potential modulators of Aβ assembly and inhibitors of its toxicity (Liu and Bitan, 2012). In this chapter we review prominent examples of each category, emphasizing molecules that have "made it" to clinical trials or to advanced preclinical studies, yet also highlighting other compounds and interesting strategies that are still in their early stages.

PEPTIDIC OR PEPTIDOMIMETIC MODULATORS OF Aβ ASSEMBLY

Several strategies have been used to design and discover peptides and peptidomimetics that modulate Aβ assembly and inhibit its toxicity (summarized in Table 6.1). These strategies include using fragments of Aβ itself based on the principle of self-recognition, generation of sequences mimicking the binding domains of Aβ-binding proteins/peptides, de novo peptide design, peptide–small-molecule conjugates, and screening of random peptide libraries. Many comprehensive reviews have discussed peptide inhibitors previously, and readers are encouraged to refer to these reviews (Doig and Derreumaux, 2015; Kumar and Sim, 2014; Luo and Abrahams, 2014; Sciarretta et al., 2006; Soto and Estrada, 2005; Takahashi and Mihara, 2008) in addition to this chapter.

Aβ Fragments or Aβ Derivatives

Self-aggregation is a predominant characteristic of amyloid proteins. An attractive strategy for developing amyloid aggregation inhibitors is to use fragments of the wild-type peptide, particularly those derived from sequences known to mediate aggregation because of their known tendency to self-assemble. Thus, the Aβ fragments 17–21 (central hydrophobic cluster, CHC) and 29–42 (C-terminus) have been used frequently as starting points for developing inhibitors.

CHC-Derived Sequences

Tjernberg et al. (1996) were the first to show that Aβ(16–21), KLVFFA, bound full-length Aβ, thereby preventing its fibrillization. Subsequently, the β-sheet breaker LPFFD (termed iAβ5), an analog of Aβ(17–21), was designed with Val17→Pro and Ala21→Asp substitutions to reduce the aggregation propensity of the peptide (Soto et al., 1998). This peptide inhibited Aβ fibrillization and prevented the neurotoxic effect of Aβ fibrils in cultured cells (Poduslo et al., 1999; Soto et al., 1998). The C- and N-terminal-protected version of iAβ5 (Ac–LPFFD–NH_2), referred to as iAβ5p, and one of its *N*-methylated derivatives, iAβ5p-A1 (Ac–LP–(NMe) F–FD–NH_2), also inhibited Aβ fibrillization and Aβ-induced neuron death. These peptides also significantly reduced Aβ deposition in a transgenic mouse model. In addition, most of the *N*-methylated derivatives were highly stable against enzymatic degradation in human plasma and in 10% rat brain homogenates (Adessi et al., 2003; Permanne et al., 2002).

Building on the pioneering studies of Tjernberg and Soto, various peptides and peptide derivatives subsequently were synthetized based on the CHC sequence. For example, three trehalose-conjugated peptide derivatives of iAβ5p were prepared, in which the disaccharide was covalently attached to different sites of the LPFFD peptide chain, including the N-terminus (Th-NT), C-terminus (Th-CT), or the Asp side chain (Th-SC) (De Bona et al., 2009). All the sugar–peptide conjugates were more stable in 10% rat brain homogenates than iAβ5p. Th-NT or Th-CT at 500 μM effectively inhibited β-sheet formation of 100 μM Aβ42 in *N*-ethylmaleimide buffer, but not in phosphate-buffered saline, in thioflavin T (ThT) fluorescence experiments (De Bona et al., 2009). The reason for the difference in activity between the two buffer systems was not discussed. About 50% of Aβ42 formed fibrils longer than 100 nm, whereas in the presence of fivefold excess Th-NT or Th-CT, only 27 and 30% of Aβ42, respectively, formed fibrils as seen by scanning-force microscopy. All three peptides protected ~80–95% of primary cortical

TABLE 6.1 Peptidic or Peptidomimetic Modulators of Aβ Assembly

		In vitro studies		Animal studies		
Compound	Type	Inhibition of Aβ-induced cytotoxicity	Modulation of Aβ assembly	Decrease of pathological Aβ	Effect on behavioral deficits	Human studies/ clinical trials
LPFFD (iAβ5) and derivatives	CHC-derived sequence, β-sheet breaker	Yes	Inhibit Aβ fibrillization	Reduce Aβ deposition in a transgenic mouse model	Unknown	Unknown
Th-NT, Th-CT, and Th-SC	CHC-derived sequence, β-sheet breaker	Yes	Th-NT and Th-CT inhibit β-sheet formation and fibril formation	Unknown	Unknown	Unknown
iAβ5–PEG5000	CHC-derived sequence, β-sheet breaker	Unknown	Inhibits Aβ42 fibrillization more strongly than iAβ5–PEG3200 and similarly to iAβ5	Unknown	Unknown	Unknown
OR1 and OR2	CHC-derived sequence, β-sheet breaker	Yes (OR2)	Both inhibit fibrillization; OR2 inhibits oligomerization	Unknown	Unknown	Unknown
RI-OR2	CHC-derived sequence	Yes	Prevents formation of Aβ fibrils and oligomers	Unknown	Unknown	Unknown
RI-OR2–TAT	CHC-derived sequence conjugated to TAT	Yes	Inhibits Aβ42 oligomer and fibril formation	Reduces cortical Aβ oligomer levels, amyloid plaque count, activated microglia, and oxidative damage	Unknown	Unknown
Fc-KLVFF	CHC-derived sequence, β-sheet breaker	Unknown	Inhibits Aβ aggregation similar to KLVFF	Unknown	Unknown	Unknown
Ac-L-D(OBzl)-F-F-D-NH_2	CHC-derived sequence, β-sheet breaker	Unknown	Inhibits Aβ40 fibrillization	Unknown	Unknown	Unknown
H102	CHC-derived sequence, β-sheet breaker	Yes	Inhibits Aβ42 fibrillization	Unknown	Improves memory in transgenic mice	Unknown

(*Continued*)

TABLE 6.1 Peptidic or Peptidomimetic Modulators of Aβ Assembly (*cont.*)

		In vitro studies		Animal studies		
Compound	**Type**	**Inhibition of Aβ-induced cytotoxicity**	**Modulation of Aβ assembly**	**Decrease of pathological Aβ**	**Effect on behavioral deficits**	**Human studies/ clinical trials**
Ac-L-Ant-FFD-NH_2	CHC-derived sequence	Unknown	Inhibits Aβ40 fibrillization	Unknown	Unknown	Unknown
Aβ(16–22)m and Aβ(16–22)mR	CHC-derived sequence	Unknown	Inhibit Aβ40 fibril formation and disassemble preformed Aβ40 fibrils	Unknown	Unknown	Unknown
SEN304	CHC-derived sequence	Yes, and protects LTP in rat hippocampal slices	Delays β-sheet formation, and remodels toxic oligomers into nontoxic aggregates	Unknown	Unknown	Unknown
inD and inrD	CHC-derived sequence	Yes	Inhibit Aβ fibrillization	Unknown	Unknown	Unknown
ABSM-1a and ABSM-1b	CHC-derived sequence	Yes	Inhibit Aβ40 fibrillization	Unknown	Unknown	Unknown
Compound 17	Small molecule based on CHC-derived cyclic peptide	Unknown	Inhibits Aβ42 oligomerization and fibrillization	Unknown	Unknown	Unknown
Aβ(31–42) and Aβ(39–42)	C-terminal fragments	Yes, and prevent disruptions of synaptic activity	Inhibits Aβ42 oligomerization	Unknown	Unknown	Unknown
N-methylated Aβ(32–37)	C-terminal fragment	Yes	Penta-*N*-methylated peptide inhibits Aβ aggregation	Unknown	Penta-*N*-methylated peptide increases *Drosophila* longevity and improves locomotion	Unknown

RIIGLa	C-terminal fragment	Yes and prevents disruptions of synaptic activity	Inhibits Aβ fibril formation	Unknown	Unknown	Unknown
G16	Mimicking the binding domain of Aβ-binding proteins	Yes	Moderately inhibits Aβ40 fibrillization; promotes formation of large, nonfibrillar aggregates	Unknown	Unknown	Unknown
PP-Leu	Shares common structural features with Aβ fragments	Yes	Inhibits Aβ42 oligomerization and fibrillization	Unknown	Unknown	Unknown
D-Trp-Aib	Rationally designed small peptides	Yes	Inhibits Aβ oligomerization	Reduces cerebral amyloid deposits in transgenic mice	Improves cognitive performance of transgenic mice	Unknown
RR (RYYAAFFARR)	Rationally designed peptide	Yes	Inhibits Aβ40 fibrillization	Unknown	Unknown	Unknown
CILFWG, CTLWWG, CTIYWG	De novo design	Yes	Inhibit Aβ42 fibrillization	Unknown	Unknown	Unknown

"Yes" means protection to a statistically significant extent from Aβ-induced reduction of cell viability.

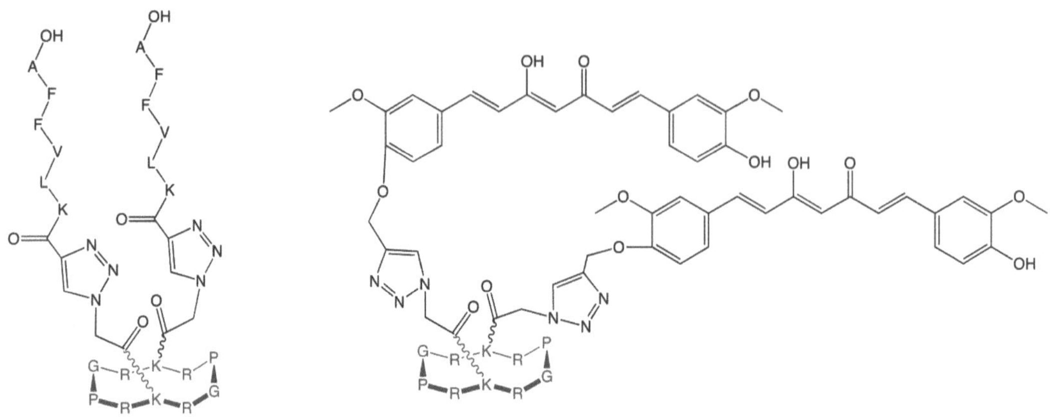

FIGURE 6.1 **Structures of KLVFFA or curcumin with cyclopeptide scaffold conjugates.** *Source: Modified from Ouberai et al. (2009).*

neurons against Aβ42 toxicity in the 3-(4,5-dimethylthiazol-2-yl)-2,5-diphenyltetrazolium bromide (MTT) assay, but only when added at fivefold molar excess to 25 μM Aβ42, first upon Aβ42 addition to cultured cells and then again 48 h later (De Bona et al., 2009).

In another study, two copies of an Aβ-binding motifs [either curcumin (see section: Curcumin and Curcumin Derivatives) or KLVFFA] were conjugated to a constrained cyclopeptide scaffold designed to interfere with Aβ aggregation (Fig. 6.1) (Ouberai et al., 2009). The conjugates strongly inhibited Aβ40 fibrillization at low molar ratios relative to Aβ (eg, 1:50 in the case of the KLVFFA conjugate), whereas the nonconjugated compounds, curcumin or KLVFFA, were inactive in ThT and atomic-force microscopy (AFM) experiments under the same conditions.

iAβ5 also was linked to polyethylene glycol (PEG) with the goal to reduce its immunogenicity and increase its molecular weight, and, as a result, to prolong its half-life in vivo (Rocha et al., 2009). In a binding competition assay, the pegylated iAβ5 had similar affinity to iAβ5 for Aβ42. Using transmission electron microscopy (TEM), iAβ5–PEG5000 inhibited Aβ42 fibrillization more strongly than iAβ5–PEG3200 and similarly to iAβ5. Caspase-3 activation by Aβ42 in SH-SY5Y neuroblastoma cells was inhibited by treatment with both pegylated iAβ5 derivatives. This work showed that pegylation of the β-sheet-breaker peptides effectively maintained antiamyloidogenic properties of iAβ5 (Rocha et al., 2009). However, the half-lives of the pegylated compounds were not determined.

Other potential peptide-based aggregation inhibitors were designed to contain the KLVFF sequence with Arg–Gly and Gly–Arg residues added at N- and C-terminal ends, respectively, to aid solubility (Austen et al., 2008). Two peptides, RGKLVFFGR, named OR1, and RGKLVFFGR–NH_2, named OR2, inhibited Aβ40 fibrillization effectively in ThT and TEM assays, but only OR2 inhibited Aβ oligomer formation in an enzyme-linked immunosorbent assay (ELISA) using monoclonal antibody 6E10 for capture and a biotinylated form of the same antibody for detection. This antibody was produced against a peptide comprising the first 16 amino acid residues of Aβ (Kim et al., 1988, 1990). OR2 also inhibited Aβ40 toxicity in human SH-SY5Y cells using the MTT assay.

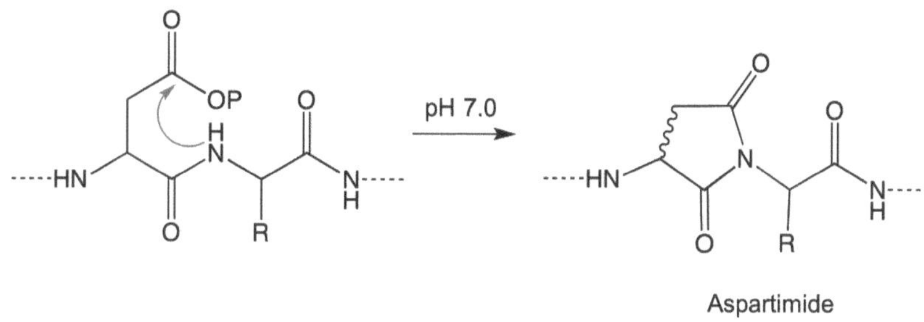

FIGURE 6.2 Chemical transformation of Asp(OP)–Axx to aspartimide-containing peptide. *Source: Adapted from Nadimpally et al. (2014).*

A ferrocenoyl (Fc) group was conjugated to the N-terminus of KLVFF (Fc-KLVFF) (Wei et al., 2011) to increase the hydrophobicity and stability toward proteolysis of the conjugated compound. Ferrocene was chosen because of its high prevalence in different types of drugs, including antimalarial, antitumor, and antibacterial drugs. Using the ThT assay, Fc-KLVFF inhibited Aβ42 aggregation with a similar potency to KLVFF. AFM and TEM confirmed the inhibitory effect on Aβ42 fibrillization. Even after 5 months of incubation at room temperature, there was no sign of fibril formation. As expected, Fc-KLVFF showed improved lipophilicity and significant resistance toward proteolytic degradation compared to its parent peptide.

A series of β-sheet-breaker dipeptides (BBDPs) was designed with the general formula Asp(OP)–Axx as the β-sheet-breaker unit, where P designates a suitable side-chain-protecting group of the Asp residue, and Axx can be any amino acid (Nadimpally et al., 2014). Conceptually, Asp could be replaced by Glu or artificial amino acids bearing a carboxyl group at a suitable position of their side chains. The BBDPs incorporated into β-sheet-breaker sequences, for example, Aβ(17–21), and then chemically transformed into aspartimide-containing peptides at physiological pH (Fig. 6.2), generating a kink in the peptide backbone in situ and thereby breaking the aggregation pattern. One designed model peptide, Ac–L–D(OBzl)–F–F–D–NH_2, was found to increase fibril formation at the initial reaction stages (until ~24 h). As the reaction progressed, a gradual decrease in ThT fluorescence was observed, and TEM showed amorphous aggregates after 4 days of incubation, suggesting that the peptide might have incorporated into the fibrils, but then gradually disrupted them as the aspartimide moiety formed.

A 10-residue β-sheet-breaker called H102, HKQLPFFED, was reported to inhibit Aβ42 aggregation in the ThT fluorescence assay and Aβ42-induced toxicity effectively in SH-SY5Y cells (Lin et al., 2014; Xu et al., 2008). In the Morris water-maze test, 3 μL of 80 mM of H102 in a saline solution injected into the lateral ventricle of APP695 mice daily improved memory performance compared to vehicle-treated mice. This transgenic model expresses human APP695 containing the Swedish (KM670/671/NL) and Indiana (V717F) mutations under the control of the hamster prion gene promoter (Chishti et al., 2001). No significant difference was found between wild-type animals and H102-treated mice, indicating that H102 improved learning and memory in the transgenic mice to the level of wild-type mice (Lin et al., 2014). Expression of inflammatory factors, including inducible nitric oxide synthase, interleukin-1β, and tumor necrosis factor-α in the CA1 hippocampal region, was lower, and apoptosis was reduced in the H102-treated APP transgenic mice as assessed by immunohistochemistry for BCL2-associated X protein, a regulator of apoptosis (Lin et al., 2014).

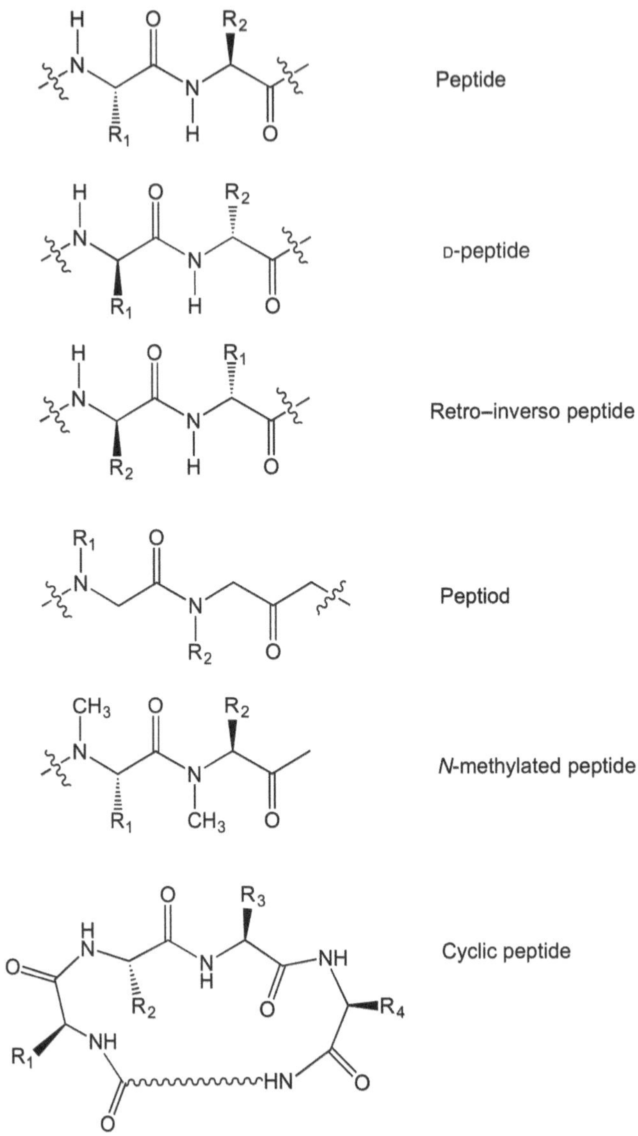

FIGURE 6.3 **Examples of structure-restricting strategies as tools for peptide-based drug design.**

CONFORMATIONALLY RESTRICTED PEPTIDES

Conformationally restricted peptides have emerged as an important peptide-based drug-design strategy by stabilizing peptides of interest in an active conformation, which simultaneously protects them against proteases. Most reported conformation-restricting strategies include modified α-amino acids or β-amino acids, *N*-methylation, and/or cyclization by linking together two compatible groups in the peptide, such as two cysteines in a disulfide bond, or a carboxyl and an amine in a lactam ring (Luo and Abrahams, 2014). See Fig. 6.3 for general

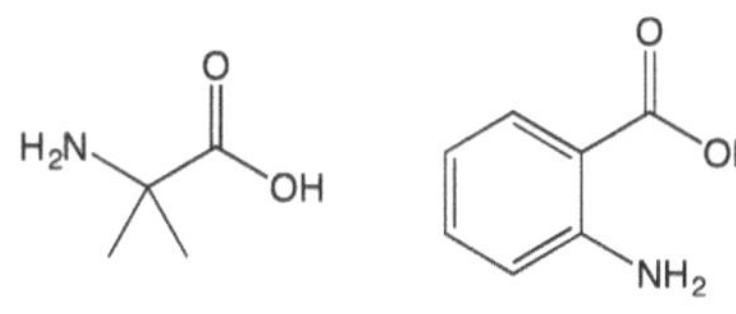

FIGURE 6.4 **Structures of α-aminoisobutyric acid (Aib) and *o*-aminobenzoic acid (Ant).**

examples of chemical modifications that confer conformational stability on peptides or otherwise change their backbones to increase metabolic stability.

MODIFIED AMINO ACIDS Substituted α-amino acids or β-amino acids may limit a peptide's conformational space, for example, favoring an α-helical conformation to a β-strand. These structures can be effective β-sheet-breaker elements. For example, α-aminoisobutyric acid (Aib) (Gilead and Gazit, 2004) and anthranilic acid (Ant, Fig. 6.4) (Paul et al., 2015) have been introduced into short peptides for this purpose. The known propensity of Ant to induce either a helix or a turn conformation and its stability toward proteolytic degradation prompted Paul et al. to use it as a novel β-breaker element in peptides. Ac–L-Ant-FFD–NH_2 was found to resist aggregation itself and at 10-fold excess reduced Aβ40 fibril formation by ~72% at physiological pH and temperature using the ThT assay. This inhibitory effect was higher than that of iAβ5p, which was used as a positive control and inhibited Aβ40 fibril formation by 48% under the same conditions. In a disaggregation assay, Ac–L-Ant-FFD–NH_2 also performed substantially better than iAβ5p (Paul et al., 2015).

N-*METHYLATED PEPTIDES* *N*-methylated peptides are a common class of aggregation inhibitors. Because the *N*-methyl group replaces a backbone N—H group, the hydrogen bonds that stabilize the cross-β structure of amyloid fibrils cannot form at the *N*-methylated site. Thus, the *N*-methylated peptide can join a growing fibril and cap it, preventing further growth.

Gordon et al. (2001) described an *N*-methylated derivative of Aβ(16–22), termed Aβ(16–22)m, which incorporated *N*-methyl residues in alternating positions: K–(NMe)L–V–(NMe)F–F–(NMe)A–E–NH_2, and its reverse sequence, Aβ(16–22)mR, E–(NMe)L–V–(NMe)F–F–(NMe)A–K–NH_2, both of which inhibited Aβ40 fibril formation and disassembled preformed Aβ40 fibrils as observed by ThT fluorescence assay and TEM. In contrast, nonmethylated Aβ(16–22) and an analog methylated in consecutive positions (ie, K–L–(NMe)V–(NMe)F–(NMe)F–(NMe)A–E–NH_2), showed weak or no inhibition of Aβ fibrillization. Aβ(16–22)m and Aβ(16–22)mR were highly soluble in aqueous media and resistant to chymotrypsin digestion (Gordon et al., 2001), and Aβ(16–20)m passed spontaneously through natural and artificial phospholipid bilayers, suggesting good potential for drug development (Gordon et al., 2002).

Aβ(16–20) was used in later studies as a template for five libraries with variations in peptide length, *N*-methylation sites, N-terminal acetylation and/or C-terminal amidation, side-chain identity, and chirality (Kokkoni et al., 2006). Multiple assays, including ThT fluorescence, Aβ-affinity chromatography, TEM, and MTT, were used to test the inhibitory activity. Favorable structures for inhibiting Aβ aggregation included all-D chirality, a free N-terminus, an

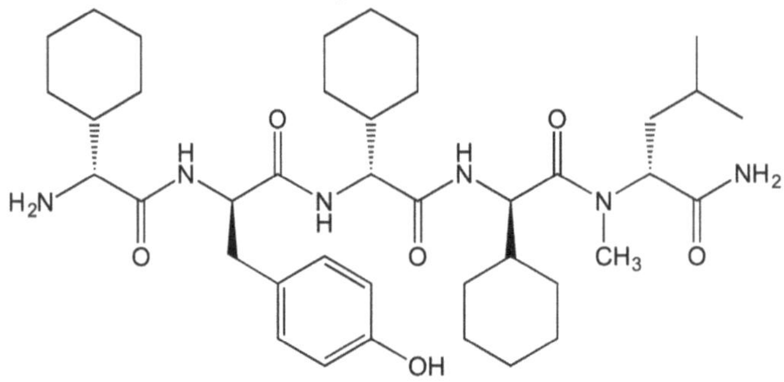

FIGURE 6.5 **Structure of SEN 304.**

amidated C-terminus, large branched hydrophobic side chains at positions 1–4, and a single *N*-methyl group. An analog termed SEN304, D-[chG–Y–chG–chG–(NMe)L]–NH_2 (chG stands for cyclohexylglycine) (Fig. 6.5) was the most active inhibitor of Aβ40 and Aβ42 aggregation by the ThT assay and an effective inhibitor of Aβ42-induced toxicity by the MTT assay in rat pheochromocytoma (PC-12) cells (Kokkoni et al., 2006). Circular dichroism (CD) spectroscopy measurements suggested that SEN304 caused only a subtle change in β structure, yet size-exclusion chromatography (SEC) experiments using equimolar concentrations (10 μM) of Aβ42 and SEN304 showed that SEN304 slowed Aβ42 aggregation and prevented formation of Aβ42 oligomers. Using surface-plasmon resonance (SPR), SEN304 was found to bind directly to monomeric Aβ40 and Aβ42 and to oligomeric Aβ42, with $K_d = 14$, 2.5, and 11 μM, respectively. TEM data showed that SEN304 did not stop fibril formation, but changed the morphology of the resulting fibrils, which were noticeably wider than those formed by Aβ42 alone. In addition, SEN304 was found to inhibit Aβ42-induced cytotoxicity in human SH-SHY5Y cells, Aβ42-induced decrease of synaptophysin in cortical neurons, and both Aβ40-induced and Aβ42-induced inhibition of long-term potentiation (LTP) in rat hippocampal slices (Amijee et al., 2012).

Giralt and coworkers applied the retro–inverso (RI) concept (Goodman and Chorev, 1979) to design an *N*-methylated peptide inhibitor of Aβ42 aggregation (Grillo-Bosch et al., 2009). The RI strategy flips both the chirality of the residue from L to D and the direction of the peptide bond, thus maintaining the overall topology of the native peptides. Previously, this group identified a peptide they termed inL (KKLVF–(NMe)F–A–NH_2), which decreased Aβ42-induced cytotoxicity in PC-12 cells in the MTT assay (Cruz et al., 2004). Considering developing a proteolysis-resistant, active version of the peptide, they designed and synthesized two analogs of inL composed of all-D amino acids, inD (kklvf–(NMe)f–a–NH_2) (lowercase letters represent D-amino acids) and an RI analog, inrD (a–(NMe)f–fvlkk–NH_2) (Grillo-Bosch et al., 2009). ThT and TEM experiments showed that inD and inrD inhibited Aβ42 fibrillization more efficiently than inL. InD and inrD strongly lowered the ThT plateau value of Aβ42 aggregation, whereas inL did not lower the plateau. Using photo-induced cross-linking of unmodified proteins (PICUP) experiments (Bitan, 2006; Fancy and Kodadek, 1999), monomers, dimers, and pentamers were found to be more abundant in Aβ42 solutions incubated with inD or inrD than in Aβ42 solution treated with inL. Both inD and inrD reduced Aβ42 toxicity in SH-SY5Y cells using the [3-(4,5-dimethylthiazol-2-yl)-5-(3

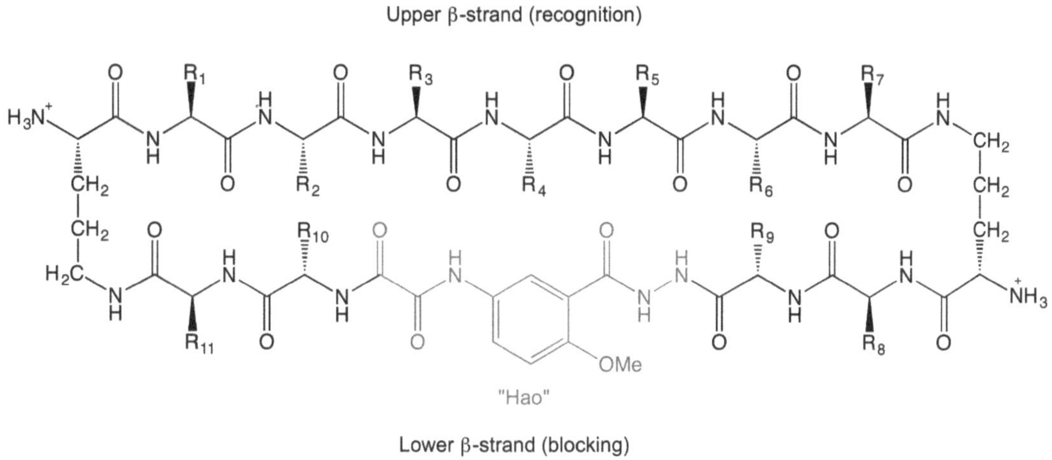

FIGURE 6.6 General structure of an amyloid β-sheet mimic (ABSM) peptide. *Source: Reproduced from Cheng et al. (2012).*

carboxymethoxyphenyl)-2(4-sulfophenyl)-2H-tetrazolium salt] (MTS) assay. Both inD and inrD also were found to be stable in cerebrospinal fluid (CSF), indicating their therapeutic potential in the central nervous system (CNS) (Grillo-Bosch et al., 2009).

CYCLIC PEPTIDES Another way to achieve conformational restriction is by cyclization. Cyclization may stabilize peptide structures into bioactive conformations, and cyclic peptides often are more biostable than their noncyclic analogs because of their resistance to enzymatic proteolysis. Therefore, cyclization is an attractive method for developing peptides into drugs.

Cheng and coworkers investigated an "amyloid β-sheet mimic" (ABSM), which was composed of a heptapeptide β-strand (the upper strand) and one "Hao" unit [an unnatural amino acid containing hydrazine, 5-amino-2-methoxybenzoic acid, and oxalic acid groups, designated as Hao (Nowick et al., 2000), a tripeptide β-strand mimic] flanked by dipeptides (the lower strand) and two δ-linked ornithine turns (Fig. 6.6) (Cheng et al., 2012). The upper β-strand of ABSM-1 incorporated different heptapeptide fragments from Aβ or other amyloid proteins. For Aβ, fragments derived from the CHC and C-terminal regions were selected. The lower strand was expected to serve as a template for intramolecular hydrogen bonding, assuming the designed cyclic peptide would fold well. The structural design of "Hao" helped prevent the cyclic peptides from aggregating in solution (Nowick et al., 2000). Fulfilling the expectation, ABSM-1a, incorporating Aβ(16–22), and ABSM-1b, incorporating Aβ(17–23), inhibited Aβ40 aggregation in the ThT assay. In contrast, ABSMs incorporating C-terminal fragments (CTFs) showed little or no inhibition. ABSM-1a reduced Aβ40- and Aβ42-induced toxicity in PC-12 cells using the MTT assay.

Starting from cyclic Aβ(16–20), Arai et al. synthesized cyclo-D-peptides, RI peptides, Ala-substituted peptides, and single D-amino-acid-substituted peptides, and evaluated their inhibitory effects on Aβ fibrillization using the ThT assay. Based on their structure–activity relationship studies, they then simplified the structure into a small molecule, designated compound 17, containing isopentyl carboxamide (Leu side-chain mimic), benzyl (Phe side-chain

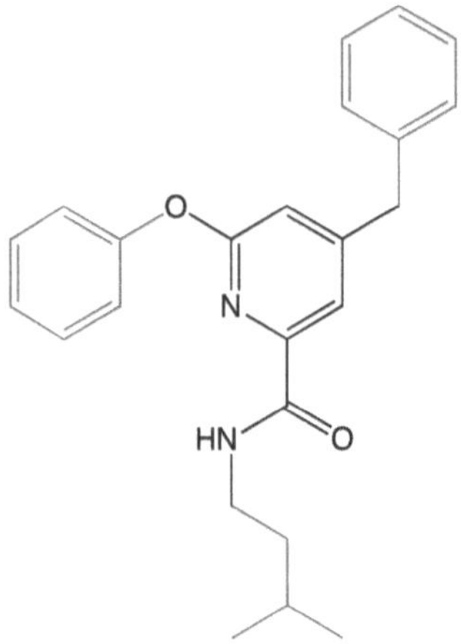

Compound 17

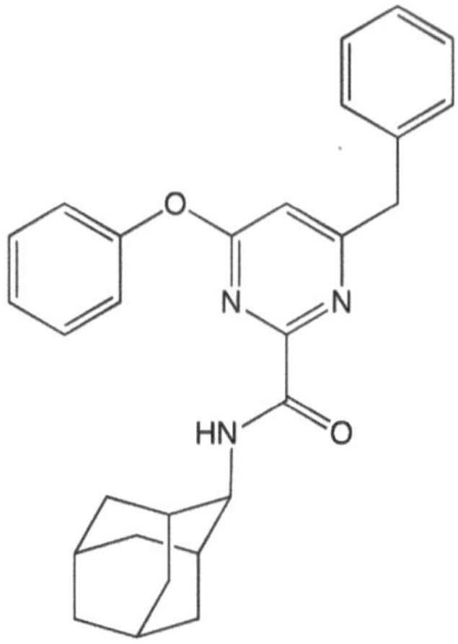

Compound 18

FIGURE 6.7 **Structures of compounds 17 and 18.** *Source: Reproduced from Arai et al. (2014).*

mimic), and phenoxy (Phe side-chain mimic) groups arranged at positions 2, 4, and 6 of a pyridine ring core, respectively (Fig. 6.7) (Arai et al., 2014). Using ThT and AFM experiments, the compound was found to inhibit Aβ42 aggregation. In ThT experiments, fivefold excess of compound 17 coincubated with Aβ42 at 10 μM decreased the fluorescence intensity to ~71% relative to Aβ42 alone. A follow-up analog, termed compound 18 (Fig. 6.7), decreased the fluorescence to ~47%. In comparison, the parent peptide cyclo-[klvff] and its analog cyclo-[klaff] reduced ThT fluorescence to 39 and 58%, respectively.

D-PEPTIDES

D-Peptides are less susceptible to enzymatic degradation than native L-peptides, making them attractive candidates for drug discovery; for a recent review in the context of AD, see Kumar and Sim (2014). In that review, the authors categorized the D-peptides into two types (Kumar and Sim, 2014): (1) those preventing fibril formation, such as an 11-residue peptide called D-iAβ1 (rdlpffpvpid) prepared by Soto et al. (1998), D versions of Aβ(16–20) or Aβ(16–22), and derivatives thereof, and (2) those promoting the formation of stable, nontoxic, off-pathway assemblies, including 12-residue D-peptides, qshyrhispaqv and rprtrlhthrnr, discovered through screening of a mirror-image phage display (see section: Peptide Library Screening), and the short pentapeptide, SEN304, discussed in section: *N*-Methylated Peptides. However, this division likely is misleading and simply based on incomplete information with regard to the first class. Inhibition of fibril formation typically yields nonfibrillogenic assemblies, such as those defined in the second class, but this may have not been characterized in early studies that simply reported inhibition of fibril formation without asking what the resulting structures were.

Austen et al. designed an RI peptide (RI-OR2, Ac–[rGffvlkGr]–NH_2) (Taylor et al., 2010) based on a previously described inhibitor of Aβ oligomer formation (OR2, RGKLVFFGR–NH_2) (Austen et al., 2008). RI-OR2 was highly stable to proteolysis and completely resisted degradation in human plasma and brain extracts, in contrast to the parent peptide, OR2, which was almost completely degraded under the same conditions. RI-OR2 blocked the formation of oligomers and fibrils of Aβ40 or Aβ42, as assessed by ThT fluorescence, an immunoassay for Aβ oligomers, sodium dodecyl sulfate–polyacrylamide gel electrophoresis (SDS–PAGE) fractionation of "stable oligomers," and AFM, and was more effective against Aβ42 than against Aβ40. In SPR experiments, RI-OR2 bound to immobilized Aβ42 monomers and fibrils, with K_d = 9–12 μM, and also inhibited Aβ42 fibril extension. In two different cytotoxicity assays, lactate dehydrogenase (LDH) release and MTS, RI-OR2 reduced Aβ42 toxicity significantly in SH-SY5Y cells.

In subsequent experiments, an RI version of the HIV protein transduction domain TAT was attached to RI-OR2, with the goal to target this new inhibitor, RI-OR2–TAT (Ac–[rGffvlkGrrrrqrrkkrGy]–NH_2), into the brain (Parthsarathy et al., 2013). The fluorescein-tagged peptide crossed the blood–brain barrier, and bound to amyloid plaques and to activated microglial cells present in the cerebral cortex of 17-month-old APP_{SWE}/PS1ΔE9 transgenic mice—PSAPP mice bearing exon-9-deleted presenilin 1 and the Swedish $APP_{K595N/M596L}$ mutations (Jankowsky et al., 2001, 2004). Daily intraperitoneal injection of 266 mg/kg RI-OR2–TAT for 21 days into 10-month-old APP_{SWE}/PS1ΔE9 mice resulted in a 25% reduction ($p < 0.01$) of Aβ oligomer levels in the cerebral cortex detected by a sandwich ELISA after ultracentrifugation at 100,000*g* at 4°C for 1 h to remove fibrils. The treatment also led to significant 32% reduction in amyloid plaque count detected by Aβ immunostaining, 44% reduction in the number of activated microglial cells shown by Iba-1 immunostaining, and 25% reduction in oxidative damage shown in 8-oxoguanine immunostaining, whereas the number of young neurons in the dentate gyrus was significantly increased by 210%.

Jagota and Rajadas (2013) examined the effects of D-peptides, pgklvya, kklvffarrrra, and kklvffa, derived from the Aβ CHC, on Aβ aggregation in vitro and on toxicity in a transgenic *Caenorhabditis elegans* model expressing human Aβ42. ThT, CD, and 4,4′-*bis*(1-anilinonaphthalene 8-sulfonate) (*bis*-ANS) binding assays suggested that kklvffarrrra and kklvffa effectively inhibited Aβ fibrillization. Of the three peptides, pgklvya and kklvffa, but not kklvffarrrra, prolonged survival of the transgenic *C. elegans* by ~20%.

C-Terminal Fragments

The C-terminus of Aβ42 is a key region controlling oligomerization (Bitan et al., 2003). Aβ42 differs from Aβ40 by having two extra C-terminal amino acids, Ile41 and Ala42. Aβ42 is more toxic (Dahlgren et al., 2002) and its C-terminus more rigid than that of Aβ40 (Yan and Wang, 2006). Discrete molecular dynamics studies suggested that oligomerization of Aβ42, but not Aβ40, was driven primarily by intermolecular interactions involving the C-terminal region (Ile31–Ala42) (Urbanc et al., 2004, 2010). Based on these data, our group hypothesized that peptides derived from the C-terminus of Aβ42 may coassemble with the full-length peptide and thereby disrupt oligomer formation and inhibit Aβ42-induced neurotoxicity. We prepared a series of CTFs with the general formula Aβ($x - 42$), $x = 28-39$ (Condron et al., 2008), and evaluated their capability to disrupt Aβ42 assembly and neurotoxicity (Fradinger et al., 2008). A cell-viability screen identified Aβ(31–42) (IIGLMVGGVVIA) as the most potent inhibitor. In addition, the shortest peptide, Aβ(39–42) (VVIA), also had surprisingly high activity. Both Aβ(31–42) and Aβ(39–42), at micromolar concentrations, inhibited Aβ-induced cell death by the MTT and LDH assays in differentiated PC-12 cells and prevented disruption of synaptic activity by Aβ42 oligomers in experiments measuring miniature excitatory postsynaptic currents in primary hippocampal mouse neurons.

Investigation of the biophysical properties of this peptide series revealed that CTFs up to eight residues long were soluble at concentrations >100 μM and had a low propensity to aggregate (Li et al., 2010a). Longer CTFs were soluble at ~1–80 μM, and most but not all readily formed β-sheet-rich fibrils. Dynamic light scattering (DLS) experiments showed that inhibition of Aβ42-induced toxicity correlated with stabilization of small oligomers with hydrodynamic radius (R_H) ≈ 8–12 nm and attenuation of formation of larger oligomers with R_H ≈ 20–60 nm (Li et al., 2010b). In contrast, inhibition of Aβ42 hexamer formation, analyzed by PICUP, correlated with CTF solubility and the degree to which CTFs formed amyloid fibrils themselves, but not with inhibition of Aβ42-induced toxicity (Li et al., 2010b).

The amphipathic nature and small size of Aβ(39–42) suggested that it could be used as a drug lead. Therefore, we explored the effects of structural modifications on inhibitory activity to determine the key structural features, including D-configuration, Ala-substitution, N-terminal acetylation, and C-terminal amidation (Li et al., 2011). We found that an L-configuration, bulky side chains, and a free N-terminus were important for inhibition of neurotoxicity. Thus, despite the small size of Aβ(39–42) and the hydrophobic, aliphatic nature of all four side chains, the interaction of Aβ(39–42) with Aβ42 was controlled by specific intermolecular contacts requiring a combination of hydrophobic and electrostatic interactions and a particular stereochemistry.

To elucidate the binding site(s) of Aβ(39–42) on Aβ42, intrinsic Tyr fluorescence of Aβ42 was measured in analogs containing Tyr at positions 1, 10, 20, 30, or 40, in the presence or absence of Aβ(39–42). In addition, solution-state nuclear magnetic resonance (NMR), as well as $^{15}N–^{1}H$ and $^{13}C–^{1}H$ heteronuclear single-quantum coherence (HSQC), were used to study the interaction between Aβ(39–42) and Aβ42. Both Tyr fluorescence and NMR data suggested that Aβ(39–42) bound at several sites, of which the predominant one was located at the Aβ42 N-terminus. These data agreed with modeling studies (Urbanc et al., 2011) predicting that Aβ(39–42) bound to several regions of Aβ42, including the Ala2–Phe4 region. The findings of predominant binding sites at the Aβ42 N-terminus were surprising and did not agree with our original rationale for preparing CTFs, which postulated that they would interrupt the intermolecular association of Aβ C-termini into a hydrophobic oligomer core.

Interestingly, ion-mobility spectroscopy–mass-spectrometry (IM–MS), ThT fluorescence, and TEM experiments indicated that Aβ(39–42) disrupted the early assembly of full-length Aβ42, but did not prevent fibril formation (Gessel et al., 2012). Specifically, the IM–MS results showed that Aβ(39–42) prevented the formation of large decamer/dodecamer Aβ42 species. At the same time, ThT fluorescence and TEM results showed that the CTF did not inhibit fibril formation, lending strong support to the hypothesis that oligomers and not amyloid fibrils are responsible for toxicity.

These data recently were corroborated by a study of Aβ(39–42) analogs in which either the N-terminus was acetylated or the C-terminus was amidated (Zheng et al., 2015b). Previously, acetylation of the N-terminus was found to abrogate the inhibitory activity of the peptide against Aβ42-induced toxicity, whereas amidation of the C-terminus yielded an active analog (Li et al., 2011). The new study used IM–MS and TEM, and showed that the difference between these two analogs was subtle. Both disrupted formation of Aβ42 dodecamers, but they bound to different regions and different assembly sizes of Aβ42. Similarly to the parent peptide, neither analog affected fibril formation (Zheng et al., 2015b).

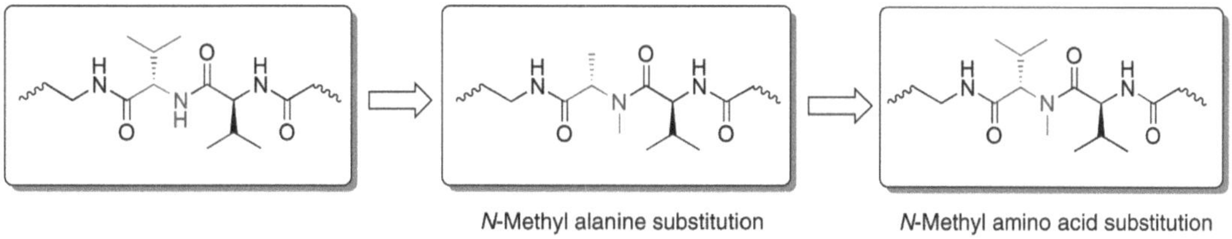

FIGURE 6.8 **A two-step strategy for identifying positions sensitive to *N*-methylation.** In the first step, each residue is replaced by *N*-Me-Ala. In the second step, in positions found sensitive to the substitutions, the original side chain is restored, leaving the *N*-Me group intact.

As mentioned earlier, *N*-methylation helps inhibit aggregation of peptides and often yields highly soluble analogs due to disruption of hydrogen bonding and β-sheet formation. We used this approach to increase the solubility of Aβ(31−42), which was the strongest inhibitor of Aβ42-induced toxicity in our original study (Fradinger et al., 2008), using a two-step substitution strategy (Li et al., 2012). In the first step, to achieve a systematic structural study and to improve aqueous solubility, each residue was replaced by NMe-Ala. In the second step, to distinguish between the effects of side-chain minimization and *N*-methylation, side chains with substantial effects on activity were reintroduced, while keeping the *N*-Me moiety in that position (Fig. 6.8). We found that introduction of *N*-Me amino acid substitution at position 9 or 11 improved the aqueous solubility and increased the inhibitory activity relative to the parent peptide. The data suggested that inhibition of Aβ42 toxicity by short peptides was highly structure specific, providing a basis for the design of new peptidomimetic inhibitors with improved activity, physicochemical properties, and metabolic stability.

The effect of peptides derived from Aβ(32–37), with none, two, three, or five *N*-methylated amino acids (Fig. 6.9) on Aβ40 and Aβ42 aggregation was assessed using CD (Pratim Bose et al., 2009). Deconvoluted Aβ42 CD spectra in the absence or presence of inhibitors showed that peptide 4 (containing five *N*-methylated amino acids) increased unordered structures significantly. Peptide 4 also reduced the formation of Congo red (CR)-positive assemblies of Aβ40 or Aβ42 in agreement with the CD results. Peptides 1–3 (Fig. 6.9) were less effective than peptide 4 in this assay. The authors also found that increasing the extent of *N*-methylation improved the efficiency of the peptides in inhibiting Aβ-mediated toxicity in PC-12 cells in the MTT assay (Pratim Bose et al., 2009). The tri-*N*-methylated and penta-*N*-methylated peptides were the strongest inhibitors, and the latter protected the cells to the same level as the untreated cells (Pratim Bose et al., 2009). In a *Drosophila melanogaster* model expressing Aβ42 in the CNS, 300 μM peptide 4 increased the longevity by 13% relative to untreated flies ($n \approx 100$, $p = 0.004$) and improved locomotion. This effect was specific to the action of the peptide on Aβ42 because no effect on life span was observed in peptide-treated wild-type *Drosophila* (Pratim Bose et al., 2009).

Peptides derived from the region Aβ(31–34), including Pr-IIGLa (propionyl–IIGL–NH_2) and RIIGLa (RIIGL–NH_2), were studied by Penke and coworkers (Fülöp et al., 2004; Harkany et al., 1999; Laskay et al., 1997; Szegedi et al., 2005). The two peptides were tested in CR-binding assay to study whether they could influence the process of Aβ42 aggregation. RIIGLa strongly inhibited CR binding to Aβ42 fibrils, and was more effective than Pr-IIGLa. Fivefold

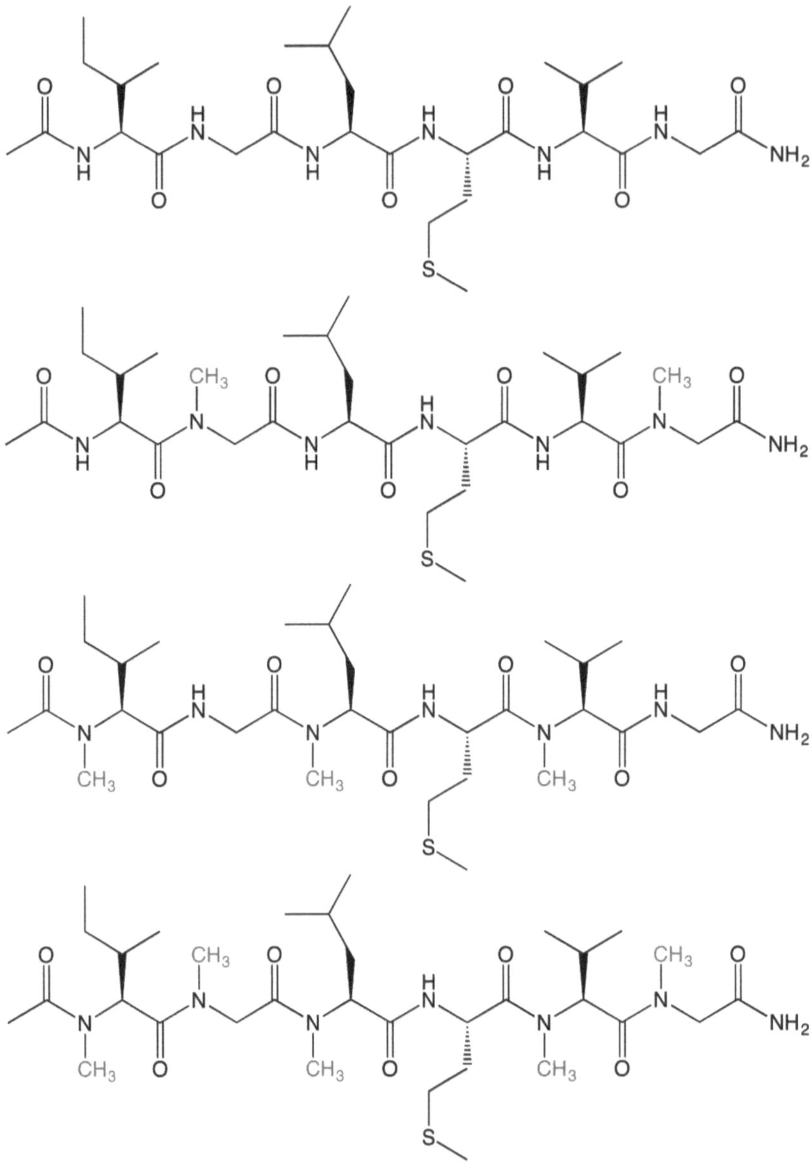

(A) 1

(B) 2

(C) 3

(D) 4

FIGURE 6.9 **Structure of *N*-methylated Aβ(32–37) peptides.** *Source: Reproduced from Pratim Bose et al. (2009).*

molar excess RIIGLa completely inhibited Aβ42 fibril formation over a 6-day coincubation with Aβ42 as observed by TEM (Fülöp et al., 2004). RIIGLa inhibited Aβ42-induced cytotoxicity significantly using the MTT assay in SH-SY5Y cells. In contrast, Pr–IIGLa itself was found to be toxic and thus did not show any protective effect (Fülöp et al., 2004). Electrophysiological experiments in rat brain slices demonstrated that RIIGLa prevented the attenuation of field excitatory postsynaptic potential by Aβ42 (Szegedi et al., 2005).

Peptides and Peptidomimetics From Other Sources

Mimicking the Binding Domain of Aβ-Binding Proteins

Due to Aβ's propensity to self-assemble, Aβ-derived peptides are highly likely to interact with Aβ and interrupt its aggregation, as discussed in the preceding section. By the same token, peptides mimicking, or derived from, the Aβ-binding regions of Aβ ligands would be expected to have a high potential to interact with Aβ and inhibit its aggregation and toxicity.

Transthyretin, a stably folded homotetrameric protein abundant in the plasma and CSF, has been shown to inhibit Aβ aggregation and reduce its toxicity (Buxbaum et al., 2008). Strand G of the inner β-sheet of transthyretin was identified and characterized as a specific Aβ-binding domain (Cho et al., 2014). A 12-mer peptide, TIAALLSPYSYS, corresponding to transthyretin residues 106–117, was identified as the strongest Aβ binder of all the contiguous sequences tested (Cho et al., 2014). The authors further studied the minimal sequence length required for Aβ40 binding and single-amino-acid substitution using this peptide as a starting point to identify individual amino acids required for binding. These experiments eventually led to a modified and somewhat longer peptide, G16 (PRRYTLAALLSPYSWS), and control peptides, which were synthesized and studied in Aβ40-binding and cytotoxicity assays. G16 was found to interact with Aβ40 in PICUP experiments, in which a smear of oligomers (~30 to ~100 kDa) was observed in G16–Aβ40 mixtures but not in Aβ alone, indicating that G16 bound Aβ40 and promoted its self-assembly. These observations were corroborated by DLS data showing that G16 dramatically increased the average size and growth rate of Aβ40 aggregates. At the same time, G16 moderately inhibited Aβ40 fibrillization observed by TEM and reduced cross-β-sheet formation in ThT experiments, suggesting that it promoted formation of large nonfibrillar aggregates. G16 inhibited Aβ40 toxicity dose dependently in primary cortical neurons examined by the MTS assay. Inhibition of cytotoxicity by G16 was less potent than by the recombinant human transthyretin mutant F87M/L110M, which inhibited Aβ40 oligomerization, rather than enhancing Aβ40 aggregation. The study introduced a general strategy for designing inhibitors of Aβ toxicity. Other proteins, such as cystatin C or clusterin, also are present in the CSF and bind Aβ oligomers. Thus, peptides derived from these proteins may also protect against Aβ-induced cytotoxicity.

Peptides Sharing Common Structural Features With Aβ Fragments

A peptide or a protein that shares with Aβ fragments such characteristics as hydrophobicity and propensity to incorporate into β-sheet structures may interact with, and inhibit, Aβ42 aggregation. Based on this rationale, Teplow and coworkers described a *θ*-defensin analog, a 13-residue peptide hairpin, called PP-Leu, as a potential inhibitor of Aβ42 oligomerization and fibrillization. The PP-Leu structure was stabilized by a C_2—C_{13} disulfide bond and a type II β-turn formed by a D-P_7–L-P_8 moiety (Fig. 6.10) (Yamin et al., 2009). PP-Leu lowered the rate of Aβ42 assembly in a concentration-dependent manner in ThT experiments. In a

FIGURE 6.10 **Structure of PP-Leu.** *Source: Reproduced from Yamin et al. (2009).*

mixture containing respective 5:1 or 10:1 molar ratios of PP-Leu and Aβ42 ThT, fluorescence did not increase significantly up to 300 h, whereas under the same conditions, Aβ42 alone displayed a rapid increase in ThT florescence which plateaued after ~24 h. Addition of fivefold PP-Leu excess to preformed Aβ42 fibrils resulted in an immediate and significant drop in ThT fluorescence. In this case, a mesh-like assembly instead of fibrils was observed by TEM. PICUP experiments showed that fivefold molar excess PP-Leu blocked Aβ42 paranucleus formation completely and produced an oligomer size distribution similar to that of noncrosslinked Aβ42.

Rationally Designed Small Peptides

Gazit and coworkers demonstrated that a hybrid molecule composed of an aromatic moiety and α-amino-isobutyric acid (Aib) inhibited Aβ fibrillization (Frydman-Marom et al., 2009). The dipeptide D-Trp-Aib interacted with early and intermediate Aβ assemblies and inhibited their further growth into toxic oligomers. Intraperitoneally administered D-Trp-Aib reduced the extent of cerebral amyloid deposits and improved cognitive performance in the Morris water maze in male APP_{SweLon} mice. These mice overexpress human APP containing the Swedish double mutation (K670M/N671L) and the London mutation (V717I) (Lamb et al., 1997). D-Trp-Aib was completely stable in both mouse and human sera for 24 h as determined by LC–MS/MS, and showed excellent bioavailability upon oral (39%) and intranasal (55%) administration to mice (Frydman-Marom et al., 2009).

Liu et al. (2014) identified a decapeptide inhibitor of Aβ40 aggregation, nicknamed RR (RYYAAFFARR). They reasoned that the relatively weak inhibitory activity of some CHC β-sheet breakers, which merely prolong the lag time of Aβ aggregation but do not completely inhibit the aggregation, may be due to low affinity of these agents for Aβ. RR was designed by using molecular simulations targeting the Aβ(11−23) sequence, which was expected to bind Aβ40 by hydrophobic and electrostatic interactions and hydrogen bonding. RR had substantially stronger affinity for Aβ40 (K_d = 1.1 μM) than iAβ5 (K_d = 156 μM) by SPR. TEM showed that RR inhibited Aβ40 fibrillization completely at fourfold molar excess, and by ~75% at equimolar concentration. In the MTT assay, when used at fourfold molar excess to Aβ40, RR reduced Aβ40-induced cytotoxicity and rescued the viability of differentiated PC-12 cells to ~95% of untreated cells.

De Novo Design

Computer-aided modeling and characterization of the binding sites of a target protein could be used to construct an "ideal drug" by docking experiments using the target binding sites and evaluating their interactions, provided that a stable structure exists and is known. The de novo design method using this strategy has been applied broadly in peptide-based drug discovery campaigns of anticancer, antiangiogenic, and antiinflammatory agents (Kliger, 2010). In the case of Aβ, applying this strategy is challenging because the most toxic species, Aβ oligomers, do not have a stable structure. Nonetheless, the popularity of the approach has motivated some researchers to explore ways of modeling the interaction between potential inhibitors and Aβ, mostly based on the common structural motifs of Aβ fibrils.

Wang et al. (2014a) developed a hybrid, high-throughput computational method to screen and design hexapeptides against Aβ aggregation and toxicity. Considering that all amyloid peptides have a strong self-aggregating propensity and share common β-sheet structural characteristics, they proposed a "like-interacts-like" hypothesis to design peptide-based amyloid inhibitors. They combined bioinformatics, molecular dynamics simulations, and in vitro experiments to test the principles they used for selecting new peptide-based aggregation inhibitors from a large pool of sequences, unrelated to the Aβ sequence. Of the 8000 sequences with self-assembling propensity predicted by quantitative structure–activity relationship, they randomly selected 35 hexapeptides with predicted high, moderate, or low self-assembly propensity determined by molecular dynamics simulations. The simulations showed that 11 out of 35 peptide dimers had relatively high structural stability. Of the 11 selected hexapeptides, three different effects (inhibition, promotion, or no effect) were observed on Aβ42 fibrillization using the ThT fluorescence assay and AFM, but their effects on Aβ42 fibrillization did not correlate with their binding affinity for Aβ42 measured by SPR. In cell-culture experiments, three moderate-to-high-affinity peptides (CILFWG, CTLWWG, CTIYWG) strongly suppressed Aβ-induced cytotoxicity in SH-SY5Y cells in the MTT assay.

Peptide Library Screening

Using phage display, combinatorial chemistry, or existing/virtual libraries, a large number of peptides could be produced for drug screening. If an efficient high-throughput screening method were established, the library screening method would be a powerful tool for finding potential drug candidates with structural variation (Bratkovic, 2010; Lazo and Wipf, 2000; Smith, 1985). With that in mind, a variation of a novel protein-fragment-complementation assay was used to generate and screen peptide libraries in bacterial cells (Acerra et al., 2013). Aβ(25–35) was used in the design scaffold as the target, and the selection peptide library was based on Aβ(29–35), a peptide known to self-associate into toxic fibrils (Hughes et al., 2000; Hung et al., 2008; Pike et al., 1995). The Aβ(25–35) sequence was fused to one half of an essential murine enzyme, dihydrofolate reductase, and the peptide library fused to the other half of the same enzyme. Following expression in *Escherichia coli*, binding of a library component to Aβ(25–35) could reconstitute murine dihydrofolate reductase, which was used as an indicator of expression, and result in bacterial growth and colony formation under the selection conditions. Using this protein-fragment-complementation assay and a library containing 8000 peptides led to selection of an initial pool of sequences interacting with Aβ(25–35). A second library of 160,000 peptides based on the first hit (GA<u>KAT</u>LM) as a design scaffold yielded two additional novel interacting sequences (L2P1, FS<u>KAT</u>SN, and L2P2, PV<u>KAT</u>TA). These peptides shared no homology with the starting Aβ(29–35) design template. All selected peptides bound Aβ42, inhibited its fibril formation, and disaggregated preformed fibrils. In follow-up work, Acerra et al. (2014) generated RI analogs of these peptides to increase their metabolic stability. The RI peptides KAR-R1 (mltakag–NH_2), L2P1a-RI (nstaksf–NH_2), L2P1b-RI (pagnstaksfsa–NH_2), L2P2a-RI (attakvp–NH_2), and L2P2b-RI (ragattakvpsa–NH_2) blocked fibrillization and disaggregated Aβ fibrils efficiently, similarly to the parent peptides, as shown by ThT fluorescence, CD spectroscopy, and oblique angle fluorescence microscopy. They also modestly reduced Aβ42-induced cytotoxicity in PC-12 cells in the MTT assay and restored locomotion in a *Drosophila* model of Aβ toxicity (Acerra et al., 2014).

Biyani et al. (2014) applied a progressive library method to obtain Aβ42-binding peptide aptamers. In the primary and secondary library selections, peptides with a moderate binding affinity to Aβ42 (K_d in the micromolar range) were found (Tsuji-Ueno et al., 2011). Then, the peptides were further evolved by the paired-peptide method (Ghimire Gautam et al., 2014), in which the library was constructed by random shuffling of peptide blocks selected from the primary and secondary libraries. The evolved peptide aptamers contained two peptide moieties, which were combined arbitrarily through a linker sequence. The selected two peptides (P84, CGILDPIPWGGSGGSCGILDPIPW, and P131, GCPCIGIIGGSGGSDCSSDLTPS, where GGSGGS is a linker) had higher binding affinity for Aβ42 (K_d = 20 nM and 12 nM, respectively), as determined by SPR experiments, than the primary and secondary Aβ42-binding peptides. Both peptides at 10 μM inhibited Aβ42 (100 μM) fibrillization as shown by ThT fluorescence and AFM experiments. P84 inhibited Aβ42 oligomerization evidenced by AFM experiments. Both P84 and P131 inhibited the toxic effects of Aβ42 fibrils and Aβ42 oligomers, yet P84 was significantly more effective than P131, in PC-12 cells using the cell-counting kit-8, CCK-8, and water-soluble tetrazolium salt-8 assays.

Kawasaki et al. (2010) constructed a random heptapeptide library (XX–P–XXXX) using phage display to search inhibitors specific against formation of globulomers, which are 37–48 kDa oligomers of Aβ42 formed in the presence of SDS. Pro was introduced into the sequences as a β-sheet-breaker element. An antibody raised against globulomers showed increased reactivity in the brains of patients with AD versus healthy individuals, suggesting that globulomers or similar structures exist in the AD brain (Barghorn et al., 2005). Eight peptides selected after the fifth round of panning revealed that a common feature was the presence of Arg residues. The strongest binder (RGPRGRV) was used in an inhibition test against formation of globulomers. Using SDS–PAGE and SEC, the peptide strongly inhibited formation of globulomers, but did not affect formation of low-molecular-weight oligomers. To reduce the peptide length, 3-residue and 4-residue random libraries prepared by phage display were tested. The 3-residue peptides did not significantly inhibit globulomer formation, likely because they were too small. In contrast, the tetrapeptide RFRK inhibited globulomer formation similarly to the best heptapeptide. Interestingly, RFRK had little effect on Aβ fibrillization (Kawasaki et al., 2011), similarly to the activity of SEN304 (Kokkoni et al., 2006) or Aβ(39–42) and its analogs (Li et al., 2011; Zheng et al., 2015b). To discover a small molecule that might inhibit formation of both Aβ42-derived globulomers and fibrils, Kawasaki et al. then searched for Arg-containing small molecules and tested their inhibitory activity against Aβ42 aggregation by SDS–PAGE and ThT fluorescence assay. The search yielded Arg-Arg-7-amino-4-trifluoromethylcoumarin (RR-AFC) (Fig. 6.11), which was found to inhibit Aβ42-derived globulomer formation (37- and 48-kDa bands on SDS–PAGE) at fivefold excess and was a weak inhibitor of Aβ42 aggregation at the same concentrations in the ThT fluorescence assay (Kawasaki and Kamijo, 2012).

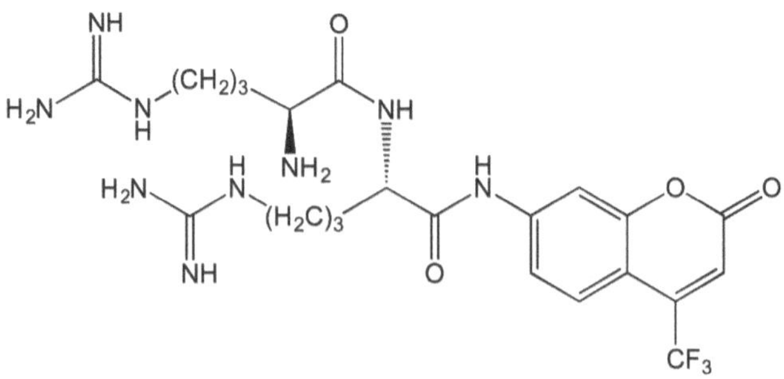

FIGURE 6.11 **Structure of Arg-Arg-7-amino-4-trifluoromethylcoumarin (RR-AFC).**

Luo et al. (2013) synthesized an on-bead library consisting of 38,416 unique peptoids, which are *N*-substituted glycine oligomers (Fig. 6.3), to develop selective and high-affinity Aβ42 ligands. The generated peptoid library was screened and arrays of Aβ42-selective peptoid ligands were identified. One of those ligands, IAM1, was evaluated further by different biochemical assays. ELISA experiments determined that IAM1 was approximately 10-fold more selective for Aβ42 than for Aβ40. IAM1 inhibited Aβ42 aggregation in a concentration-dependent manner in the ThT assay. To increase the binding affinity, the authors prepared a dimeric form of IAM1, designated $(IAM1)_2$. Using the same ELISA, a K_d value = 0.06 ± 0.04 μM for Aβ42 was determined, indicating a 7.4-fold increase in affinity relative to the monomeric IAM1. However, affinity for Aβ40 was also increased, resulting in some loss of specificity. $(IAM1)_2$, but not IAM1, protected primary hippocampal neurons against Aβ42-induced toxicity. In this experiment, mouse hippocampal neurons were incubated for 3 days with Aβ-containing conditioned media (Luo et al., 2013) and then fixed, permeabilized, and stained for the neuronal marker MAP2. A 73% decrease in neuronal viability was found in neurons incubated with Aβ compared to control cells incubated with media alone.

Rahimipour and coworkers hypothesized that due to the strong similarities between self-assembled cyclic D,L-α-peptides and amyloids, such peptides likely would bind to, and stabilize, nontoxic forms of Aβ (Richman et al., 2013). By screening a focused library of 6-residue head-to-tail cyclic D,L-α-peptides containing Lys, Glu, Ser, Leu, Trp, and His, and by optimizing the activity of the lead peptide, the authors discovered the peptide CP-2, cyclo-[l–J–w–H–s–K] (J denotes L-norleucine), which interacted strongly with Aβ40 or Aβ42 and inhibited their aggregation. By TEM, ThT fluorescence, and cytotoxicity assays, CP-2 inhibited both Aβ40 and Aβ42 assembly, entirely disassembled preformed fibrillar Aβ40, and protected PC-12 cells from Aβ40-induced or Aβ42-induced toxicity, without showing toxicity itself. NMR spectroscopy indicated that CP-2, likely in a self-assembled form, interacted with monomeric and low-oligomeric Aβ40 and induced weak secondary structures (α-helix) in Aβ40 during the initial stage of aggregation, followed by a shift to a parallel β-sheet structure. The NMR data suggested that CP-2 might promote the conformational transition of Aβ from a more toxic antiparallel β-sheet to the less toxic parallel β-sheet.

Conclusions

During the past 20 years, peptide-based Aβ protein aggregation inhibitors were discovered using many sources and strategies, including Aβ fragments, sequences sharing common structural features with Aβ, sequences mimicking the binding domain of Aβ-binding proteins, de novo designed peptides, and library screening. Sequences based on Aβ itself have been the most popular method, especially those derived from the central hydrophobic region. Regardless of the chosen strategy, peptides made of natural amino acids serve as leads but require subsequent optimization due to poor bioavailability and metabolic stability. Introduction of unnatural amino acid, backbone modification, cyclization, and unnatural secondary structural mimics are popular directions to pursue. Currently, there are no guidelines or algorithms that can predict what modification is likely to succeed. Rather, modifications typically are screened and sometimes combined with other strategies. Structural modification directions are all geared to fulfill biological and biophysical criteria. Therefore, correct evaluation of the structure–activity relationship is important for optimization of the compounds so they can best fulfill these criteria. Reviewing the methods used by different labs reveals large variations in sample preparation and testing methods, which often makes comparison of results difficult. We therefore would like to emphasize the need for standardized protocols for Aβ preparation for biophysical and biological tests, and for standard positive controls, which may allow comparing the activities of inhibitors from different laboratories.

Aβ ASSEMBLY MODULATORS DERIVED FROM NATURAL SOURCES

Molecules derived from natural foods likely are the largest group of nonpeptidic compounds explored as modulators of Aβ assembly. These "nutraceutical" compounds are appealing because they have been consumed for thousands of years and therefore are expected to be safe and bioavailable. Compounds from sources including tea, coffee, wine, or spices such as turmeric or cinnamon are attractive due to their abundance and the perception that consuming them may begin immediately, without the need for approval by regulatory agencies, and be beneficial and protective in one's lifetime. It is important to note, however, that the safety and bioavailability of *purified* compounds likely differ from their safety and bioavailability in the context of a consumed beverage or spice. Not only can the dose of a pure compound taken, for example, as a dietary supplement be substantially different from the dose consumed through food intake, but also the combination or interaction of the compound with other alimentary ingredients, which is what we have become accustomed to through thousands or millions of years of evolution, may be required to elicit a desirable outcome.

In this chapter, we have classified the nutraceutical compounds into five groups: polyphenols, inositol derivatives, vitamins, natural proteins or peptides (as opposed to the synthetic peptides discussed in section: Peptidic or Peptidomimetic Modulators of Aβ Assembly), and other compounds. The examples we discuss are summarized in Table 6.2.

Polyphenols

Polyphenols are organic compounds with multiple phenol groups in their structure. They are a major component of the naturally occurring, plant-derived phytochemicals. Polyphenols have received much attention in health research because they are free-radical scavengers and antioxidants. More than 8000 naturally occurring polyphenols have been categorized as flavonoids, phenolic acids, lignans, and stilbenes. Some polyphenols that inhibit Aβ assembly and/or toxicity are discussed next.

Curcumin and Curcumin Derivatives

Curcumin (diferuloylmethane, Fig. 6.12A) is a natural compound that has been studied extensively among potential therapeutics for AD. It is the principal antioxidant component of the spice turmeric (*Curcuma longa*) and is also responsible for its yellow color. It was first demonstrated by Lim et al. (2001) that curcumin substantially reduced Aβ plaque burden in the transgenic Tg2576 mouse model of AD (Hsiao et al., 1996). This mouse model bears the isoform 695 of the human APP gene containing the double mutation K670N/M671L (Swedish mutation) under the control of the hamster prion protein (Hsiao et al., 1996). Lim et al. (2001) used 24 mg or 744 mg of curcumin per kilogram of body weight and monitored inflammation,

TABLE 6.2 Modulatory Effects of Naturally Sourced Compounds on Aβ Assembly and Toxicity

		In vitro, cell culture, and ex vivo studies		Animal studies		
Compound	**Type**	**Inhibition of Aβ-induced cytotoxicity**	**Modulation of Aβ assembly**	**Decrease of pathological Aβ**	**Effect on behavioral deficits**	**Human studies/ clinical trials**
Curcumin and derivatives	Polyphenol	Yes	Prevent oligomerization	Reduce plaques in model mice; stain plaques; FMeC1 binds plaques in model mice	Improve life span and locomotion in flies; improve spatial memory and learning in mice; nanoparticle-conjugated preparations reverse learning and memory deficits in a rat model of AD	Curumin C3 Complex® used in trials with minimal effect due to poor bioavailability
Inositol derivatives	Sugars	Yes and rescue LTP in mouse hippocampal slices	Some isoforms cause micelle formation whereas others cause β-sheet formation	Reduce plaque burden in mice	Improve learning in rats; improve cognitive deficits in mice; fluorinated derivatives improve spatial memory in mice	Clinical trials inconclusive because of toxicity at high doses and lack of effectiveness at low doses
EGCG	Polyphenol	Yes	Causes formation of nontoxic assemblies; reduces Aβ levels in cultured cells	Reduces Aβ oligomerization and aggregation in a *C. elegans* model; reduces Aβ42 levels in the hippocampus of a mouse model measured by ELISA	Rescues cognitive deficits in senescence-accelerated mice by intragastric administration (5 and 15 mg/kg) for 60 days; improves learning and memory in APP/PS1 mice	A phase 2/phase 3 trial is ongoing with EGCG formulation Sunphenon; results expected in 2015
Brazilin	Polyphenol	Yes	Inhibits fibrillization by redirecting the misfolding pathway toward nontoxic assemblies	Unknown	Unknown	Unknown

(Continued)

TABLE 6.2 Modulatory Effects of Naturally Sourced Compounds on Aβ Assembly and Toxicity (*cont.*)

		In vitro, cell culture, and ex vivo studies		Animal studies		
Compound	**Type**	**Inhibition of Aβ-induced cytotoxicity**	**Modulation of Aβ assembly**	**Decrease of pathological Aβ**	**Effect on behavioral deficits**	**Human studies/ clinical trials**
Myricetin	Flavonoid	Yes and inhibits synaptotoxicity in hippocampal slices	Interferes with oligomerization	No effect on plaque burden but reduces levels of soluble Aβ and A11-positive oligomers	Unknown	Unknown
Quercetin and derivatives	Flavonoid	Inhibit cytotoxicity and synaptotoxicity	Inhibit aggregation	Reverse AD pathology	Restore spatial memory in an AD model	Unknown
Taxifolin	Flavonoid	Yes	Inhibits aggregation	Unknown	Unknown	Unknown
Rosmarinic acid	Similar to polyphenols	Yes	Inhibits Aβ fibrillization and oligomerization; disintegrates preformed fibrils	Decreases Aβ deposition in brain of a mouse model	Unknown	Unknown
Tannic acid	Similar to polyphenols	Yes	Inhibits Aβ fibrillization; disintegrates preformed fibrils	Reduces brain parenchymal and cerebral vascular Aβ deposits; reduces Aβ oligomers in a mouse model	Prevents behavioral impairment, including hyperactivity, decreased object recognition, and defective spatial reference memory in a mouse model of AD	Unknown
Theaflavins	Polyphenol	Yes	Remodel preformed toxic Aβ fibrils into nontoxic spherical assemblies	Unknown	Unknown	Unknown

Ginkgo biloba	Mixture of flavonoids and terpenoids	Inhibits Aβ-induced cytotoxicity in cultured cells, primary hippocampal neurons, and in *C. elegans*	Inhibits formation of Aβ-derived diffusible ligands	Did not affect plaque burden	Recovers spatial memory deficits in mice	Rates of decline of memory, attention, visuospatial abilities, language, and executive functions did not differ between treated and placebo groups
Vitamin A	Vitamins	Yes	Inhibits oligomerization, fibrillization, and fibril extension; disintegrates preformed fibrils	Reduces Aβ deposition	Rescues memory deficits in two mouse models of AD	Dietary supplementation has shown improvement of clinical symptoms of AD
Vitamin C	Vitamins	Yes	Suppresses A11-positive Aβ oligomers in cultured cells	Supplementation reduces Aβ plaque deposition in a rodent model deficient of vitamin C	Improves spatial memory in a mouse model of AD	Inconclusive
Vitamin E	Vitamins	Yes	α-Tocopherolquinone, a derivative of vitamin E, inhibits Aβ42 fibrillization, disaggregates preformed fibrils, and interferes with intracellular Aβ oligomerization	Vitamin E administered at a younger age caused a significant reduction in Aβ levels and amyloid deposition in mouse model of AD, but mice supplemented with vitamin E at a later age did not show any significant difference from placebo	Combination with vitamin C supplementation rescued behavioral deficits in a mouse model of AD	Inconclusive

(Continued)

TABLE 6.2 Modulatory Effects of Naturally Sourced Compounds on Aβ Assembly and Toxicity (*cont.*)

		In vitro, cell culture, and ex vivo studies		Animal studies		
Compound	**Type**	**Inhibition of Aβ-induced cytotoxicity**	**Modulation of Aβ assembly**	**Decrease of pathological Aβ**	**Effect on behavioral deficits**	**Human studies/ clinical trials**
Colostrinin	Polypeptide	Yes	Changes fibril morphology	Unknown	Improves life span and motor and sensory parameters in a mouse model	Improves outcomes in patients with mild or moderate dementia
Laminin	Polypeptide	Yes	Inhibits aggregation; disaggregates preformed fibrils	Unknown	Unknown	Unknown
Docosahexaenoic acid (DHA)	Miscellaneous	No. Forms toxic oligomers. Some studies suggest DHA inhibits and reverses formation of toxic Aβ oligomers	Prevents fibrillization by stabilizing Aβ protofibrils	Reduces Aβ plaque density	Improves cognitive function in a mouse model	Unknown
Melatonin	Miscellaneous	Yes	Inhibits Aβ aggregation	Decreases Aβ in organotypic cultures; improves neuroplasticity in a rat model of sporadic AD; attenuates Aβ pathology	Improves memory in mouse models of AD	A prolonged-release formulation was shown to improve cognitive function and sleep maintenance in AD patients compared with placebo

(A)

(B)

(C)

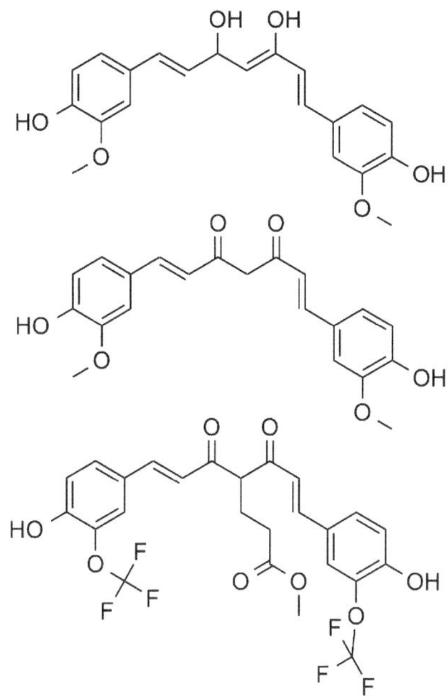

FIGURE 6.12 Chemical structures of the enol (A) and keto (B) forms of curcumin, and of the curcumin derivative FMeC1 (C).

oxidative damage, and plaque pathology in the treated model mice. Curcumin reduced insoluble Aβ by 43–50% without affecting APP levels. In the same year, curcumin derivatives (curcumin, demethoxycurcumin, and bisdemethoxycurcumin) also were reported to prevent Aβ-induced toxicity in cultured cells (Kim et al., 2001).

These initial results inspired many follow-up studies, which investigated the effects and mechanisms of action of curcumin in relation to AD (Balasubramanian, 2006; Banerjee, 2014; Garcia-Alloza et al., 2007; Kumaraswamy et al., 2013; Masuda et al., 2011; Mithu et al., 2014; Ngo and Li, 2012; Thapa et al., 2013; Yang et al., 2005a; Zhao et al., 2012). Curcumin was found to have antioxidant, antiinflammatory, neurogenic, neuroprotective, and immunomodulatory effects along with modulatory effects on Aβ oligomerization and aggregation. During in vitro aggregation, curcumin inhibited Aβ40 aggregation (IC_{50} = 0.8 μM) and disaggregated fibrillar Aβ40 (IC_{50} = 1 μM). It also prevented Aβ42 oligomerization and cytotoxicity between 0.1 and 1 μM (Yang et al., 2005a; Ye and Zhang, 2012).

Curcumin crossed the blood–brain barrier and stained Aβ plaques, further demonstrating direct binding to Aβ (Yang et al., 2005a). Ab initio density functional theory studies showed that penetration of curcumin through the blood–brain barrier and curcumin binding to Aβ plaques were facilitated by critical hydrophobic–hydrophilic balance involving the polar enolic and two phenolic moieties separated by an aliphatic bridge (Balasubramanian, 2006). The polar enol form of curcumin is favored structurally over the keto form (Fig. 6.12A) when crossing the blood–brain barrier and when binding to Aβ.

In a transgenic *Drosophila* model of Aβ, toxicity, life span, and locomotion were improved by 75% in flies treated with curcumin compared to control flies. Interestingly, this effect did not correlate with a significant decrease in Aβ deposition. In fact, flies treated with curcumin had accelerated Aβ42 deposition, suggesting that faster kinetics of fibrillization and lower steady-state concentrations of toxic low-molecular-weight assemblies were responsible for the improved life span and phenotype (Caesar et al., 2012).

An accelerating effect on Aβ aggregation has been observed in many additional studies. However, the therapeutic potential of this effect in AD is questionable because, unlike the human disease, most animal models do not develop cerebral amyloid angiopathy (CAA), which would be exacerbated by accelerated Aβ aggregation, potentially leading to microhemorrhage, increasing the risk of vascular dementia (Thal et al., 2008).

Curcumin interacts with Aβ at several sites. In monomeric Aβ40, two-dimensional, ^{1}H–^{15}N HSQC NMR spectroscopy showed that curcumin interacts with Arg5, Ser8, Gly9, His13, Lys16, Leu17, Asp23, and Ile31 (Ono et al., 2012). Solid-state NMR studies of curcumin-induced Aβ42 aggregates indicated major structural changes in the Asp23–Lys28 salt bridge and near the C-terminus, similar to structural changes in the presence of Zn^{2+} (Mithu et al., 2014). Solid-state NMR using dipolar-assisted rotational resonance of curcumin-complexed Aβ42 fibrils showed that curcumin interacted with Val12 and the CHC region of Aβ, which makes up part of the β-sheet structure in the Aβ42 fibrils (Masuda et al., 2011). The methoxy and hydroxyl groups attached to the aromatic rings of curcumin were found to be important for the binding to Aβ42 fibrils (Masuda et al., 2011).

Although curcumin is a potent inhibitor of Aβ cytotoxicity in vivo, its poor bioavailability and low solubility in water have restricted its use as a drug for AD. In a short pilot study of AD patients, curcumin did not significantly improve the Mini Mental State Examination (MMSE) score (Baum et al., 2008). MMSE is a test used extensively in clinical or research settings to measure cognitive impairment. In a different 24-week phase 2 trial, no significant score improvement ensued in the MMSE, Alzheimer's Disease Assessment Scale Cognitive portion (ADAS-Cog), neuropsychiatric inventory, and Alzheimer's Disease Cooperative Study–Activities of Daily Living (ADCS-ADL). No appreciable differences in plasma or CSF biomarkers of Aβ40, Aβ42, total tau, or hyperphosphorylated tau were observed in this trial (Ringman et al., 2008). In another 24-month-long clinical study of 30 patients with AD, curcumin was well tolerated except in three patients who suffered gastrointestinal symptoms. Unfortunately, in this trial, again the efficacy of the curcumin formulation (curcumin C3 Complex®) was minimal (Ringman et al., 2012), possibly due to its poor bioavailability. These findings inspired attempts to improve the water solubility of curcumin derivatives (Endo et al., 2014). To improve the bioavailability and efficacy of curcumin, use was made of formulations containing carriers, such as liposomes, poly(lactic-*co*-glycolic acid), or gold nanoparticles (AuNPs) (Hoppe et al., 2013; Lazar et al., 2013; Palmal et al., 2014; Tsai et al., 2011); curcumin nanoparticles (80 nm, prepared by flash precipitation of curcumin, polyethylene glycol-polylactic acid coblock polymer, and polyvinylpyrrolidone, followed by freeze-drying with β-cyclodextrin) (Cheng et al., 2013); chemically modified curcumin derivatives (eg, FMeC1; Fig. 6.12B) (Yanagisawa et al., 2015); or curcumin conjugates with other compounds, such as melatonin, cyclodextrin, sugars, or metals (Al(III), Cu(II), or Zn(II)) (Banerjee, 2014; Chojnacki et al., 2014; Dolai et al., 2011; Gautam et al., 2014; Picciano and Vaden, 2013). An inhalable aerosolized formulation of FMeC1 led to binding of the compound to hippocampal and cortical plaques in 5 × FAD mice (McClure et al., 2015). The 5 × FAD mice bear two transgenes: (1) mutant human APP with the Swedish (K670N/M671L), Florida (I716V), and London (V717I) mutations, and (2) mutant human *PSEN1* including M146L and L286V mutations. Both transgenes are driven by the mouse Thy1 promoter (Oakley et al., 2006).

In APP_{SWE}/PS1ΔE9 transgenic mice (Jankowsky et al., 2001, 2004) treated with 200 mg/kg or 400 mg/kg body weight per day of a curcumin preparation, spatial learning and memory were improved compared with untreated mice tested by the Morris water maze (Wang et al., 2014d). In the same study, SDS–PAGE and Western blotting of hippocampal tissue extracts and immunohistochemistry of hippocampal tissue sections of mice treated with curcumin showed lower Aβ40 or Aβ42 levels, and lower A11-reactive species than those measured in samples of vehicle-treated control mice (Wang et al., 2014d). A11 recognizes a common secondary structure shared by toxic assemblies of a number of amyloid proteins (Kayed et al., 2003). Besides changes in Aβ levels, Western blotting and immunohistochemistry showed that treated transgenic mice expressed low levels of the γ-secretase component, presenilin 2, and higher levels of Aβ-degrading enzymes—insulin-degrading enzyme and neprilysin (Wang et al., 2014d). Overall, Wang et al. (2014d) described curcumin's action mechanisms that are distinct from its potential modulatory effects on Aβ self-assembly, but are likely clearing Aβ through presenilin 2 inhibition and expression of Aβ-degrading enzymes.

In rats treated intraperitoneally with curcumin-encapsulated poly(lactic-*co*-glycolic acid) nanoparticles (Cur-PLGA-NPs) at 5, 10, or 20 mg/kg body weight, nanoparticles could cross the blood–brain barrier, act as prolonged-release curcumin carriers, and induce hippocampal stem cell proliferation and neurogenesis (Tiwari et al., 2014). Mechanistically, the Wnt/β-catenin pathway was activated while the glycogen kinase-3β pathway was inhibited in the treated rats. The Wnt/β-catenin pathway is involved in survival, proliferation, and differentiation of neural stem cells during embryonic and adult neurogenesis (Machon et al., 2003; Zhang et al., 2011). To assess whether curcumin nanoparticles could reverse Aβ effects in the brain, anesthetized rats were injected stereotactically with 2 μL of 0.2 μg/μL Aβ42 in bilateral hippocampi and then treated with 20 mg/kg body weight curcumin nanoparticles. As a result of this treatment, Aβ-induced inhibition of neurogenesis and the ensuing learning and memory deficits were prevented by Cur-PLGA-NP treatment (Tiwari et al., 2014). This study did not investigate the modulation of Aβ self-assembly but described other mechanisms of curcumin action.

In addition to using curcumin as a drug, owing to its affinity for Aβ, curcumin derivatives have been used for diagnostic applications in AD (Asti et al., 2014; Lee et al., 2011; Liu et al., 2012; Zhang et al., 2014). For example, radiolabeled fluorinated and pegylated curcumin derivatives could cross the blood–brain barrier better than the fluorinated derivatives (Lee et al., 2011; Rokka et al., 2014). In addition, intravenously administered curcumin was shown to detect retinal Aβ plaques by noninvasive optical imaging applied in live, anesthetized, APP_{SWE}/PS1ΔE9 transgenic mice (Koronyo-Hamaoui et al., 2011).

Several factors may limit the use of curcumin as an AD therapeutic. Curcumin interferes with certain physiological functions, including actin and tubulin polymerization, and corneal neovascularization and angiogenesis (Bhandarkar and Arbiser, 2007; Dhar et al., 2015). Curcumin interaction with actin causes loosening of the actin structure, leading to destabilization of filaments and reduced cell proliferation and angiogenesis (Arbiser et al., 1998). Hence, testing curcumin as an anti-AD drug must be explored with caution.

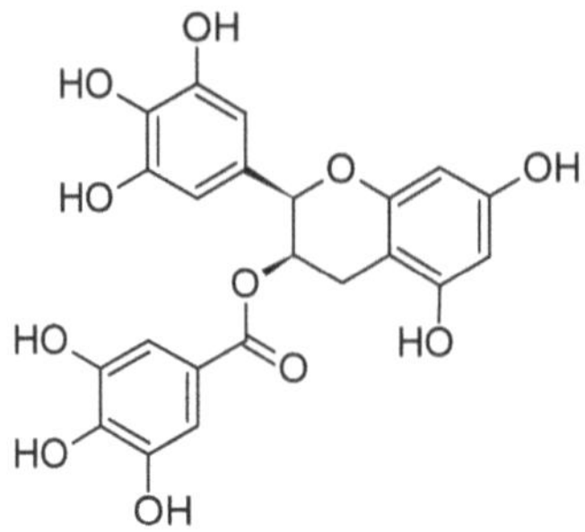

FIGURE 6.13 **Structure of (−)-epigallocatechin-3-gallate.**

(−)-Epigallocatechin-3-Gallate

(−)-Epigallocatechin-3-gallate (EGCG; Fig. 6.13) is a natural polyphenol and a key bioactive ingredient of green tea (*Camellia sinensis*). EGCG was found to inhibit Aβ assembly and toxicity by directing its aggregation pathway toward formation of nontoxic assemblies (Ehrnhoefer et al., 2008). Electron micrographs of Aβ aged in the presence of EGCG showed amorphous aggregates in contrast to long fibrils that formed in the absence of the polyphenol. The amorphous Aβ aggregates formed in the presence of EGCG did not react with the oligomer-specific antibody A11 (Sinha et al., 2012a), which recognizes a common secondary structure shared by toxic assemblies of various amyloid proteins (Kayed et al., 2003). In cytotoxicity experiments using PC-12 cells, fivefold excess EGCG to Aβ completely inhibited Aβ oligomer toxicity (Bieschke et al., 2010; Ehrnhoefer et al., 2008). Similar results were observed in primary rat hippocampal neurons and mixed glial and neuronal cultures (Sinha et al., 2012a).

Several experimental and theoretical studies have attempted to clarify the mechanisms underlying Aβ–EGCG interaction. Isothermal calorimetry and molecular dynamics simulations showed that Aβ42–EGCG interactions depend on their concentration ratio (m = [EGCG]/[Aβ42]) (Wang et al., 2010). The binding stoichiometry N is linearly related to m. At $m < 16$, the process is always enthalpy driven, suggesting that it is driven predominantly by hydrogen bonding. At $m > 46$, binding is entropy driven, suggesting increased hydrophobic interactions. At m values between 16 and 46, both hydrogen bonding and hydrophobic interactions are involved. The study also showed that at pH values close to the isoelectric point of Aβ42 (pI = 5.5), Aβ42 self-association became dominant due to low repulsive electrostatic forces, and the aforementioned trend for Aβ42–EGCG interaction did not hold (Wang et al., 2010).

Solution-state two-dimensional NMR showed that EGCG interacted with the entire peptide backbone (Sinha et al., 2012a), in agreement with previous studies (Ehrnhoefer et al., 2008). Magic angle spinning solid-state NMR showed that EGCG interacted with the aromatic hydrophobic core of Aβ. In the EGCG-induced oligomeric Aβ structure, the C-terminal residues (22–39) assumed a β-sheet conformation, the N-terminal Aβ residues 1–20 were unstructured, and the salt bridge between Asp23 and Lys28 was retained (Lopez del Amo et al., 2012).

Another report showed that EGCG autooxidation was critical for remodeling Aβ40 fibril structures (Palhano et al., 2013). Here, a centrifugation–wash protocol was used, whereby the soluble unbound EGCG was removed from fibrillar Aβ by centrifugation before taking measurements. Using this protocol, when ThT was added to Aβ fibrils incubated with EGCG, no change in ThT fluorescence was observed immediately after ThT addition, yet the ThT fluorecence signal decreased substantially after 24 h. In the unwashed samples, there was an initial rapid decrease in ThT fluorescence followed by a gradual decrease. This suggested that EGCG interfered with ThT fluorescence either by competitively binding to ThT binding sites on the fibrils or by quenching the ThT fluorescence. The color of the mixture of Aβ aggregates with EGCG became brown, and Aβ aggregates inspected by AFM were amorphous. The authors hypothesized that upon oxidation, EGCG-derived quinones covalently interacted with free amines and formed Schiff bases. Presumably, such covalent binding prevents formation of small toxic oligomeric species and drives the equilibrium toward nontoxic assemblies (Palhano et al., 2013).

EGCG also reduced Aβ aggregation, oligomerization, and toxicity in a transgenic *C. elegans* model of AD (Abbas and Wink, 2010), and significantly reduced cell-secreted Aβ levels detected by immunoprecipitation and Western blotting using the 6E10 antibody in Chinese hamster ovarian (CHO) cells (Reznichenko et al., 2006). EGCG treatment in N2a cells overexpressing the Swedish mutant of human APP, or in primary neurons from transgenic mice bearing the Swedish APP mutation, demonstrated reduction in Aβ levels assessed by immunohistochemistry using monoclonal antibody 4G8 (Rezai-Zadeh et al., 2005), which recognizes residues 18–22 of Aβ (Kim et al., 1988).

In a different report, 16 or 32 μM EGCG treatment caused proliferation of an Aβ42-overproducing cell model (M146L) which was established by overexpressing APP and mutant PS1 genes into CHO cells; EGCG did not affect proliferation of the CHO cells themselves, and untreated M146L cells normally undergo slow growth rates compared to CHO cells (Chang et al., 2015). In the same report, EGCG significantly prevented Aβ42 accumulation in the hippocampi of SAM-P/8 mice (Yagi et al., 1988) and in M146L model cells measured by Western blotting and ELISA (Chang et al., 2015). It was also found that EGCG treatment upregulated neprilysin expression in M146L cells and in the hippocampi of SAM-P/8 mice, suggesting that EGCG-induced neprilysin could potentially prevent Aβ accumulation in this cell and animal model. SAM-P/8 is a senescence-accelerated mouse line that occurs naturally (Yagi et al., 1988). SAM-P/8 mice suffer from marked spatial learning and memory deficits in the Morris water maze test. EGCG treatment improved spatial learning and memory in these mice (Chang et al., 2015).

When APP/PS1 mice (Borchelt et al., 1996, 1997) were treated with EGCG at 6 mg/kg body weight per day by gavage, and spatial memory was assessed by the Morris water maze, treated mice recovered their spatial learning and memory (Jia et al., 2013). When levels of soluble and insoluble Aβ42 were measured by ELISA in the hippocampal extracts of the same mice, EGCG at 2 mg/kg per day or at 6 mg/kg per day reduced soluble Aβ42 levels in the hippocampi of transgenic mice by 25 or 38% in comparison with vehicle-treated transgenic mice, respectively (Jia et al., 2013). Insoluble Aβ42 levels were reduced by 18 or 31%, respectively (Jia et al., 2013). Mechanistically, these observations were ascribed to inactivation of hippocampal TNFα/JNK signaling (antiinflammatory), restoration of dysregulated Akt/GSK3β signaling (gluconeogenic), improved insulin signaling, and reduction of hippocampal Aβ42 levels in this AD mouse model (Jia et al., 2013). GSK3β, has been associated with tau phosphorylation, APP–Aβ cascades, and neurodegeneration in AD (Kaytor and Orr, 2002; Phiel et al., 2003; Planel et al., 2002).

A phase 2/3 clinical trial (NCT00951834) with an EGCG formulation called Sunphenon in early-stage AD cases was completed in Aug. 2015, but the results have not yet reported at the completion of writing this chapter.

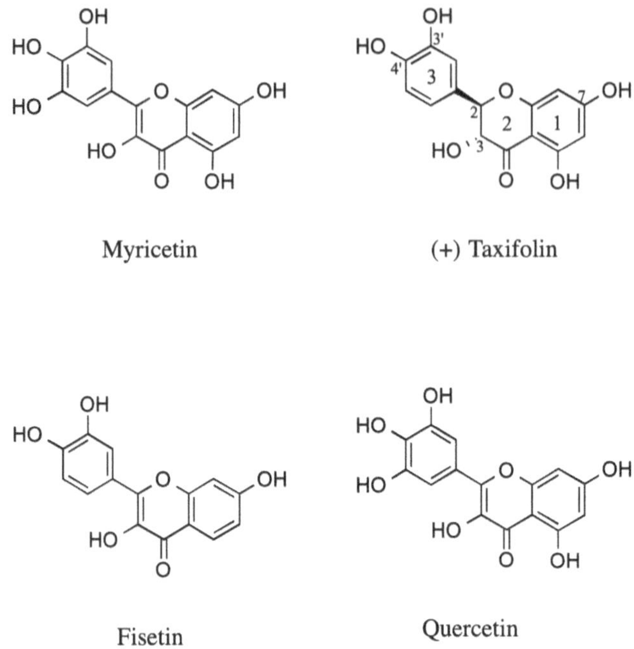

FIGURE 6.14 **Structures of common flavonoids.**

Flavonoids—Myricetin, Quercetin, Taxifolin, and Fisetin

Flavonoids are described as secondary metabolites in plants. They perform important functions, including antioxidation, chelation of redox-active metals, regulation of cell growth and differentiation, and imparting colors to plant petals or other components. Several flavonoids have been tested for their efficacy against AD symptoms based on their ability to interfere with Aβ assembly.

Myricetin (Fig. 6.14), which is derived from vegetables, fruits, nuts, berries, and tea (Ross and Kasum, 2002) and is also present in red wine (Basli et al., 2012), was shown to alter Aβ assembly and interfere with its oligomerization patterns as examined by CD spectroscopy, ThT fluorescence, PICUP, SEC, and AFM experiments (Ono et al., 2012). At a peptide–myricetin concentration ratio of 5:2, myricetin completely inhibited the self-assembly of Aβ40 and moderately that of Aβ42. At a 1:4 ratio, respectively, Aβ42 oligomerization, examined by PICUP and AFM, also was completely inhibited (Ono et al., 2012). At the same concentration ratio, curcumin (section: Curcumin and Curcumin Derivatives) and rosmarinic acid (section: Rosmarinic Acid and Tannic Acid) failed to inhibit Aβ oligomerization. Solution-state NMR studies showed that myricetin stabilized the statistical-coil structures in Aβ42 by binding to the monomeric peptide. The chemical shifts of monomeric ^{15}N-labeled Aβ42 peptide in the presence of myricetin (1:10, Aβ42–myricetin concentration ratio) showed preferential binding to Aβ(16–24) and Aβ(31–33) (Ono et al., 2012). Myricetin prevented the toxicity of crosslinked or noncrosslinked Aβ40 and Aβ42 oligomers in HEK293 cells in the MTT assay. In electrophysiological experiments, myricetin reversed Aβ42-induced inhibition of LTP (97.5 ± 7.6%) to baseline values (157 ± 5.1%) in mouse CA1 hippocampal slices (Ono et al., 2012). Myricetin was found to be more potent against Cu^{2+}-associated or Zn^{2}-associated Aβ40 than metal-free Aβ40 species. The compound inhibited metal-induced Aβ40 assembly in vitro ([Aβ40] = 25 μM, [$CuCl_2$] or [$ZnCl_2$] = 25 μM, [myricetin] = 50 μM) and neurotoxicity in human neuroblastoma SK-N-BE(2)-M17 cells at twofold excess to Aβ40 ([Aβ40] = 10 μM, [$CuCl_2$ or $ZnCl_2$] = 10 μM, [myricetin] = 20 μM) (DeToma et al., 2011). These observations suggest that myricetin may inhibit Aβ40 assembly by metal chelation similar to clioquinol or PBT2 (Crouch et al., 2011); however, there is no experimental evidence to support this hypothesis.

Tg2576 mice fed a diet containing 0.5% myricetin showed high levels of soluble Aβ (detected by antibodies against human Aβ40, Aβ42, or aggregated Aβ) and low levels of A11-reactive oligomers (using immunohistochemistry), with no substantial reduction in Aβ plaque deposition (Hamaguchi et al., 2009). These results suggest that myricetin can induce formation of nontoxic Aβ structures and supports its future therapeutic development for AD.

Another flavonoid, (+)-taxifolin (Fig. 6.14), also was reported to inhibit Aβ assembly and toxicity (Sato et al., 2013a,b). ThT experiments showed that taxifolin (50 μM) oxidized with sodium periodate (100 μM) inhibited Aβ42 (25 μM) aggregation more effectively than unoxidized taxifolin (Sato et al., 2013b). The combination of taxifolin and periodate did not suppress Aβ40 fibrillization under anaerobic or reducing conditions (Sato et al., 2013b). The exact mechanism of (+)-taxifolin action on Aβ is unclear; however, it was suggested that oxidation of the catechol moiety of taxifolin to an *o*-quinone may be responsible. This change subsequently causes formation of covalent conjugates with susceptible side chains in Aβ and leads to inhibition of Aβ assembly (Sato et al., 2013b). This inhibition mechanism is similar to the data reported for EGCG (section: (−)-Epigallocatechin-3-Gallate) and is likely to be the same for all the catechol-containing categories of flavonoids.

The 3′- and 4′-hydroxyl groups of taxifolin (Fig. 6.14) are critical for inhibition of Aβ aggregation, whereas the 7-hydroxyl group and the stereochemistry at positions 2 and 3 are not, as was shown by methylation of these hydroxyl groups. (+)-Taxifolin–Aβ adducts were analyzed by an ion-trap-type LC–MS equipped with a time-of-flight mass analyzer. These experiments showed oxidized Aβ42–taxifolin adducts that resulted from the Michael addition of the *o*-quinone groups to Lys or Arg residues (Sato et al., 2013b).

To identify residues involved in adduct formation, Aβ42 isoforms with Arg5, Lys16, or Lys28 mutated to norleucine (Nle) were examined. Five different Aβ42 mutants, Arg5Nle–Aβ42, Lys16Nle–Aβ42, Lys28Nle–Aβ42, Lys16Nle/K28Nle–Aβ42, and Arg5Nle/Lys16Nle/Lys28Nle–Aβ42, were generated. The intensity of ThT-positive aggregates of the singly mutated Lys16Nle–Aβ42 was similar in the presence or absence of (+)-taxifolin, whereas that of the singly mutated Lys28Nle–Aβ42 in the presence of (+)-taxifolin was slightly lower than that in its absence. (+)-Taxifolin did not alter the aggregation pattern of the doubly mutated Lys16Nle/Lys28Nle–Aβ42 and the triply mutated Arg5Nle/Lys16Nle/Lys28Nle–Aβ42. However, (+)-taxifolin predominantly blocked the aggregation of the singly mutated Arg5Nle–Aβ42. Taken together, these results showed that Lys residues at positions 16 and 28 likely are the targets of oxidized taxifolin. Lys16, which is believed to be exposed to the solvent (Zhang et al., 1998, 2000), appears to be the primary target, as (+)-taxifolin could not alter the aggregation profiles of Lys16Nle–Aβ42 or Lys16Nle/Lys28Nle–Aβ42. Moreover, ThT assays done in the presence of catechol-type flavonoids (dihydromyricetin, (+)-taxifolin, myricetin, or quercetin) or noncatechol-type flavonols (morin, kaempferol, or datiscetin) using Lys16Nle–Aβ42, Lys16Nle/Lys28Nle–Aβ42, and Aβ42 showed that catechol-type flavonoids suppressed

Aβ42 aggregation by forming covalent adducts on Lys residues. The study suggested that Lys residues are important determinants of Aβ42 assembly and toxicity, and may be targets for therapeutic approaches developed against abnormal self-assembly of amyloidogenic proteins in AD and other amyloidoses (Sato et al., 2013b). These findings dovetail with studies in our group showing that substitution of the Lys residues by Ala dramatically decreased the neurotoxicity of both Aβ40 and Aβ42 (Sinha et al., 2012b), and that labile complexation of Lys residues in multiple amyloidogenic proteins by molecular tweezers (section: Molecular Tweezers) inhibited the aggregation and cytotoxicity of these proteins (Sinha et al., 2011).

Fisetin (Fig. 6.14) has been found to be neurotrophic (Maher, 2006), induce neuron differentiation (Sagara et al., 2004), enhance memory (Maher et al., 2006), and inhibit Aβ aggregation (Kim et al., 2005). Fisetin also inhibited Aβ42 aggregation and toxicity in cultured hippocampal neurons (Akaishi et al., 2008). Similarly to the findings with taxifolin, a comparative study of several related flavonoids suggested that the 3′,4′-dihydroxyl group, and not the 3-hydroxyl or 7-hydroxyl group, were essential for fisetin's inhibitory activity (Akaishi et al., 2008). Although no direct studies of the mechanism of interaction between fisetin and Aβ have been published to our knowledge, the compound likely targets Lys residues on Aβ covalently as in the case of most catechol-type flavonoids.

Quercetin and its derivatives reportedly have many beneficial biochemical and pharmacological properties, including free-radical scavenging (Fiorani et al., 2010) and effects on immune and inflammatory functions (Garcia-Mediavilla et al., 2007). They could also have beneficial effects in AD by reducing age-associated cellular damage that causes metabolic by-production of reactive oxygen species (Weinreb et al., 2004). Quercetin and its derivatives were tested as modifiers of Aβ assembly to find out whether they could reverse the primary pathological hallmarks of AD as an additive outcome to their other beneficial properties (Sabogal-Guaqueta et al., 2015). Quercetin (Fig. 6.14) and its derivatives, such as quercetin-3′-*O*-glucoside and quercetin-3-*O*-rutinoside, were found to inhibit Aβ42 aggregation as seen in ThT and TEM assays, and attenuated Aβ42-induced cytotoxicity in SH-SY5Y neuroblastoma cells (Jimenez-Aliaga et al., 2011; Wang et al., 2012). In a triple-transgenic (3 × Tg) AD mouse model, which expresses human APP (KM670/671NL), PSEN1 (M146V), and tau (P301L) (Oddo et al., 2003), quercetin reversed AD pathology and restored spatial memory tested by the elevated plus maze (Sabogal-Guaqueta et al., 2015). In this study, quercetin administered via intraperitoneal injection every 48 h at 25 mg/kg for 3 months decreased significantly hippocampal and amygdala Aβ40 and Aβ42 deposition in 3 × Tg AD mice.

Quercetin-3-*O*-glucuronide significantly decreased Aβ in primary corticohippocampal neurons derived from the Tg2576 AD mouse model (Ho et al., 2013). PICUP experiments showed that quercetin-3-*O*-glucuronide interacted with Aβ monomers and inhibited Aβ self-assembly and oligomer formation. In electrophysiologic assays, quercetin-3-*O*-glucuronide significantly rescued deficits in basal neuronal transmission in the CA1 region of hippocampal slices compared to vehicle-treated hippocampal slices from Tg2576 mice (Ho et al., 2013).

Rosmarinic Acid and Tannic Acid

Several natural antioxidants such as rosmarinic acid and tannic acid have neuroprotective properties. These compounds structurally resemble the polyphenols and flavonoids discussed earlier, suggesting that they may have similar activity, modifying Aβ assembly and reducing its toxicity.

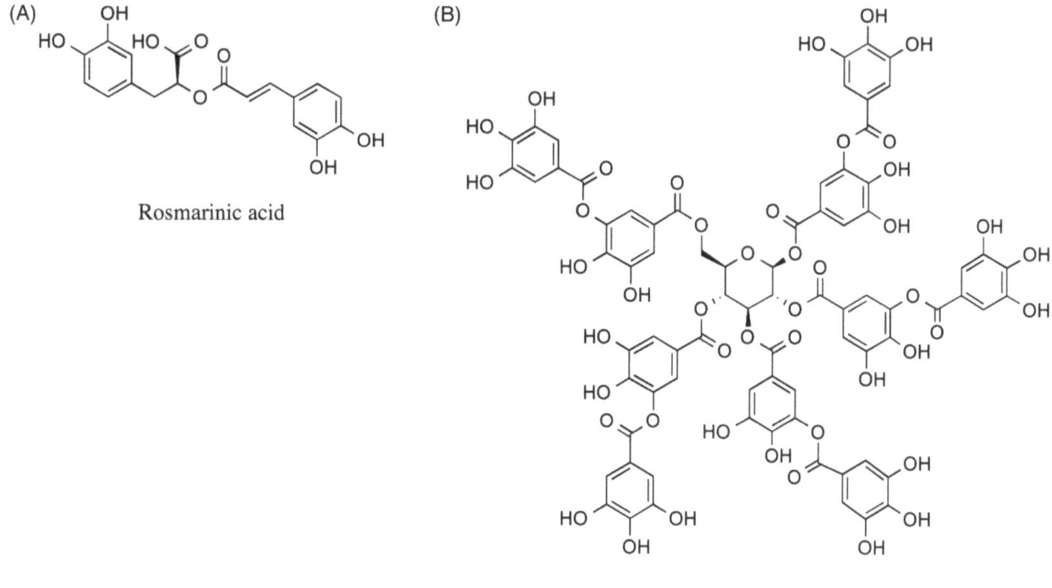

Tannic acid

FIGURE 6.15 Structures of (A) rosmarinic acid and (B) tannic acid.

Rosmarinic acid (Fig. 6.15A) inhibited the formation of β-sheet-rich fibrils of Aβ40 and Aβ42 in ThT fluorescence and TEM experiments. The compound also disintegrated preformed Aβ fibrils with $EC_{50} = 0.1–1\ \mu M$ (Ishigaki et al., 2013; Ono et al., 2004b), prevented the formation of A11-positive oligomers, and inhibited Aβ-induced neurotoxicity in PC-12 cells with significant inhibition at 0.1 μM (Camilleri et al., 2013; Hamaguchi et al., 2009; Iuvone et al., 2006). Rosmarinic acid included at 0.5% in the diet of a Tg2576 mouse model of AD (Hsiao et al., 1996) significantly reduced the total Aβ plaque burden in the brain as assessed by immunohistochemistry using the antibody 4G8 (Hamaguchi et al., 2009). This monoclonal antibody recognizes residues 18–22 of Aβ (Kim et al., 1988). Solution state 2D HSQC-NMR studies with monomeric ^{15}N-labeled Aβ42 in the presence of 20-fold excess rosmarinic acid showed no substantial movement of crosspeaks compared to the Aβ42 peptide alone, suggesting that rosmarinic acid does not bind to specific regions in monomeric Aβ42 (Ono et al., 2012), similarly to EGCG (section: (−)-Epigallocatechin-3-Gallate). In contrast, there was substantial binding of myricetin to Aβ42 under similar conditions (see section: Flavonoids—Myricetin, Quercetin, Taxifolin, and Fisetin).

Tannic acid (Fig. 6.15B) dose dependently inhibited Aβ40 and Aβ42 fibrillization and disintegrated preformed fibrils (Ono et al., 2004a). Tannic acid did not extend the length of the lag phase, but decreased the rate of aggregation in Aβ40 and Aβ42. In samples seeded with sonicated Aβ42 fibrils, tannic acid completely inhibited ThT-fluorescence increase, suggesting that it bound to fibril ends. Electron micrographs of tannic acid-treated Aβ40 or Aβ42 fibrils showed smaller disintegrated fibrils compared to the untreated preparations (Ono et al., 2004a). When administered by gavage at 30 mg/kg body weight for 6 months (Mori et al., 2012), tannic acid reduced brain parenchymal and cerebral vascular

Aβ deposits (visualized by immunohistochemistry) and reduced Aβ oligomers (measured by ELISA in SDS-containing extracts) in the PSAPP mouse model of cerebral amyloidosis [bearing exon-9-deleted presenilin 1 and the Swedish $APP_{K595N/M596L}$ mutations (Jankowsky et al., 2001, 2004)]. Behaviorally, hyperactivity, perturbed object recognition, and defective spatial reference memory were also prevented by tannic acid treatment in the mice. Mechanistically, these findings were ascribed to inhibition of β-secretase activity and dampening of neuroinflammation resulting in reduced Aβ burden (Mori et al., 2012).

Theaflavins

Theaflavins, the major polyphenolic components of fermented black tea, include theaflavin 1, theaflavin 2a, theaflavin 2b, and theaflavin 3 (Fig. 6.16). These compounds were reported to remodel preformed toxic Aβ fibrils into nontoxic, ThT-negative assemblies. Aβ toxicity was measured in PC-12 cells (Grelle et al., 2011). AFM experiments showed formation of spherical Aβ aggregates in the presence of theaflavins, as opposed to fibrils forming by Aβ alone. Theaflavins, especially theaflavin 3, were found to be less susceptible to oxidation than EGCG and flavonoids (sections: (−)-Epigallocatechin-3-Gallate; Flavonoids—Myricetin, Quercetin, Taxifolin, and Fisetin) (Grelle et al., 2011). To determine the potential theaflavin-binding sites of Aβ, an array of 33 Aβ-derived overlapping peptides covering the sequence of Aβ42 was used, and binding was determined using dot blots followed by densitometric analysis. Theaflavin 3 preferentially was found to interact with the regions Aβ(12–23) and Aβ(24–36) with different affinities, yet the binding mainly was based on nonspecific hydrophobic interactions rather than sequence specificity (Grelle et al., 2011).

Ginkgo Biloba Extract

Ginkgo biloba extract from the medicinal maidenhair tree is a mixture of flavonoids and terpenoids (isoprenoids). EGb 761® is a standard, proprietary extract of *G. biloba* (DeFeudis, 2003; Adis R&D Profile, 2003). The extract was tested in a number of small-to-medium clinical trials for dementia or specifically for AD, and has shown mild positive effects (Itil and Martorano, 1995; Kanowski et al., 1996; Le Bars et al., 1997; Maurer et al., 1997). Based on these results, several mechanistic studies tested the direct effect of EGb 761 on Aβ assembly and toxicity. The extract was shown to prevent Aβ-mediated toxicity in PC-12 cells, human neuroblastoma cells, rat hippocampal cell lines, primary hippocampal neurons, and in *C. elegans* (Bastianetto et al., 2000; Smith and Luo, 2003; Wu et al., 2006; Yao et al., 2001). Interestingly, in the study by Smith and Luo (2003), pretreatment with EGb 761 did not prevent Aβ-induced toxicity but prevented generation of Aβ-induced reactive oxygen species. However, in a different study using PC-12 cells, EGb 761 was reported to interact directly with Aβ and inhibit formation of Aβ-derived diffusible ligands (ADDLs) dose dependently (Yao et al., 2001). ADDLs are particular Aβ42 oligomers originally reported by Klein and coworkers (Lambert et al., 1998; Oda et al., 1995). They are highly toxic in cell culture and in vivo (Gong et al., 2003; Wang et al., 2002). EGb 761 (10–100 μg/mL) also protected hippocampal neurons against toxicity induced by Aβ40 or Aβ42 dose dependently with complete protection achieved at 100 μg/mL.

Treatment of Tg2576 mice with *G. biloba* extract in water led to spatial memory recovery to comparable levels measured in wild-type mice, without affecting soluble Aβ levels or plaque burden (Stackman et al., 2003). The reported dose was 70 mg/kg per day, yet this is an

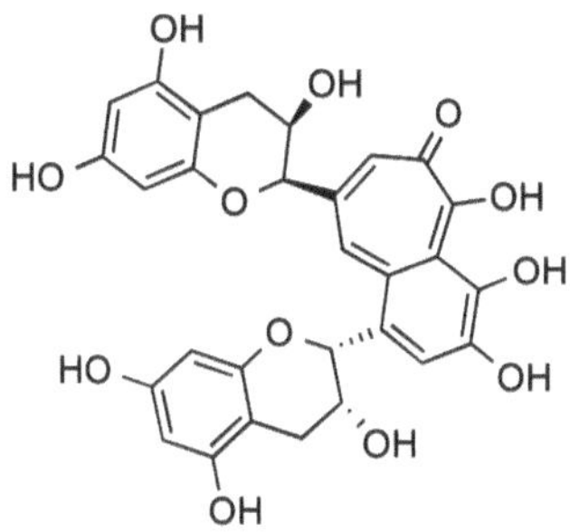

Theaflavin (TF1)

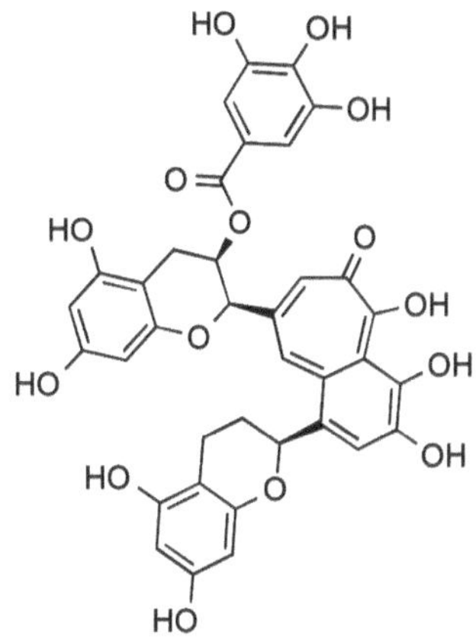

Theaflavin-3-gallate (TF2a)

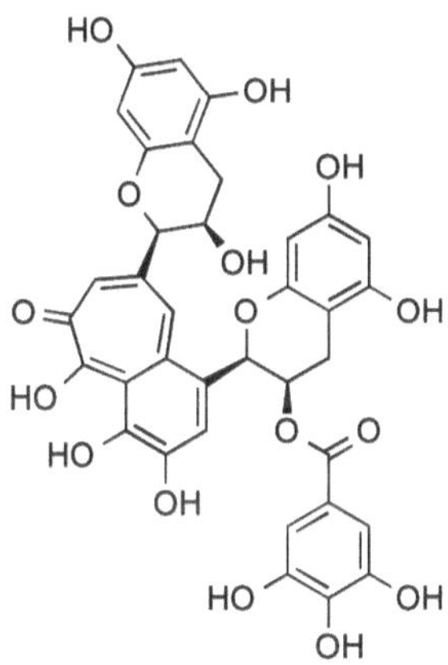

Theaflavin-3'-gallate (TF2b)

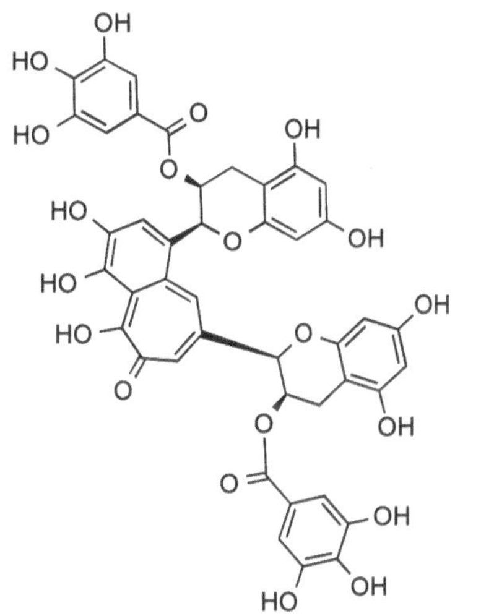

Theaflavin-3,3'-gallate (TF3)

FIGURE 6.16 **Structures of different theaflavins, major polyphenols derived from fermented black tea.**

estimate because the *G. biloba* extract in the water was administered ad libitum. Surprisingly, the brain levels of protein carbonyls were elevated in the treated mice (Stackman et al., 2003). If certain compounds in the extract undergo self-oxidation, similar to the process described earlier for EGCG (section: (−)-Epigallocatechin-3-Gallate) and certain flavonoids (section: Flavonoids—Myricetin, Quercetin, Taxifolin, and Fisetin) and form Schiff-base adducts with lysine residues, they may contribute to oxidative stress and explain the observation of increased carbonyls in the mice.

A 2009 clinical trial showed that compared with placebo (n = 1524), the use of *G. biloba* at 120 mg twice daily (n = 1545), did not change the rate of cognitive decline in older adults

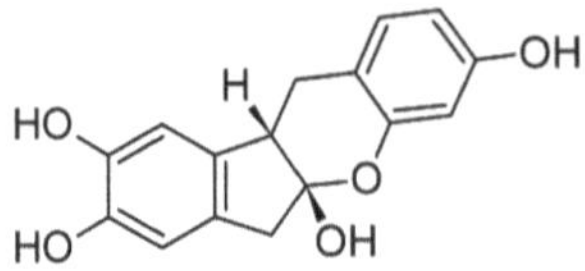

FIGURE 6.17 **Structure of brazilin.**

(72–96 years of age) with normal cognition or with mild cognitive impairment (Snitz et al., 2009). The annual rates of decline did not differ between the *G. biloba* and placebo groups in all the measured parameters, including memory, attention, visuospatial abilities, language, and executive functions (Snitz et al., 2009). Thus, overall, in multiple trials the effect of *G. biloba* on patients with AD has been underwhelming. The extract is available as an over-the-counter supplement but is not expected to have a significant therapeutic effect on patients with AD.

Brazilin

Brazilin (Fig. 6.17) is a red pigment obtained from the wood of *Caesalpinia spinosa*. It was part of a >600 compound library screened virtually by Du et al. (2015) for docking onto a fibrillar Aβ(17–42) pentamer. Out of the hits discovered, bicuculline and brazilin were chosen for further characterization based on their hydropathy characteristics. ThT fluorescence experiments suggested that brazilin was a stronger inhibitor than bicuculline, and therefore subsequent exepriments focused on brazilin only.

ThT, TEM, and CD suggested that, similarly to EGCG, brazilin inhibited Aβ42 fibrillization by redirecting the misfolding pathway toward nontoxic assemblies. Brazilin reduced Aβ42-induced toxicity in the LDH release assay. Molecular dynamics simulations suggested that brazilin inhibited Aβ42 fibrillization by directly binding to Aβ42 species using hydrophobic interactions and hydrogen bonding, and altered the structure of mature Aβ42 fibrils by disrupting the Asp23–Lys28 salt bridge (Du et al., 2015).

Inositol Derivatives

Inositol exists as nine potential stereoisomers, which are involved in diverse physiological functions, including gene expression, fat metabolism, maintenance of membrane potential, regulation of intracellular calcium levels, cytoskeletal assembly, control of telomere length, and insulin secretion (Michell, 2008). They are synthesized physiologically by the enzymatic conversion of glucose-6-phosphate—a glycolysis metabolite (Parthasarathy et al., 2006).

Four physiologically active stereoisomers of inositol (cyclohexane-1,2,3,4,5,6-hexol) (*epi-*, *scyllo-*, *myo-*, and *chiro*-inositol, Fig. 6.18) had been tested for their ability to modulate Aβ assembly and toxicity (McLaurin et al., 2000). *Myo*-inositol bound to Aβ42 in vitro forming small, stable micelles, whereas *epi-* and *scyllo*-inositol induced β-sheet formation in Aβ42. *Chiro*-inositol did not induce structural changes in Aβ42 (Fenili et al., 2007). *Myo-*, *epi-*, *chiro-*, and *scyllo*-inositol reduced Aβ42 oligomers' toxicity to different degrees when tested in differentiated PC-12 cells (McLaurin et al., 2000). *Scyllo*-inositol was the most potent inhibitor, and therefore subsequent studies focused mainly on this stereoisomer.

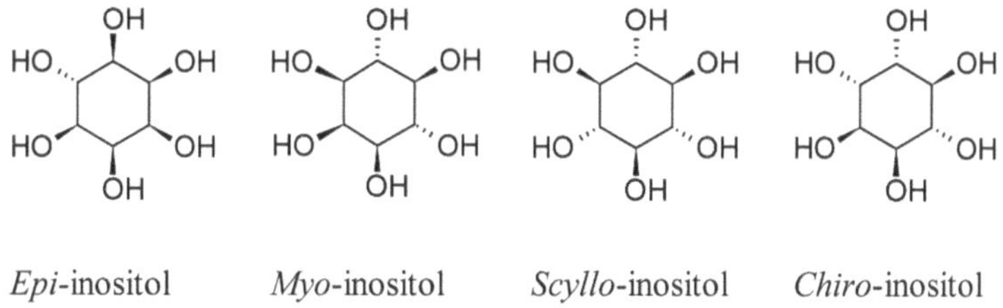

FIGURE 6.18 **Structures of four physiologically active isoforms of inositol.**

Scyllo-inositol dose dependently rescued LTP in mouse hippocampal slices treated with soluble assemblies of cell-derived human Aβ (Townsend et al., 2006). In vivo, *scyllo*-inositol given in drinking water completely rescued the learning deficits caused by Aβ oligomers injected intracerebroventricularly in rats (Townsend et al., 2006). Orally administered *scyllo*- or *myo*-inositol reversed the cognitive deficits and substantially reduced Aβ plaque burden in the TgCRND8 mouse model of AD (Fenili et al., 2007). This transgenic model expresses human APP695 containing the Swedish (KM670/671/NL) and Indiana (V717F) mutations under the control of the hamster prion gene promoter (Chishti et al., 2001). Administration of *scyllo*-inositol at 10-fold excess over endogenous concentration levels (1 mM) did not interfere with general physiological functions, such as phospholipid synthesis, suggesting that *scyllo*-inositol could be used therapeutically at higher concentrations than the endogenous levels (Fenili et al., 2007; Townsend et al., 2006). However, administration of high doses of *scyllo*-inositol was found to be lethal in a clinical trial (see following discussion).

To understand the nature of interactions between *scyllo*-inositol and Aβ, a series of deoxy-inositol derivatives was used (Sun et al., 2008). Aβ42 aggregated in the presence of 1-deoxy-*scyllo*-inositol or 1,4-dideoxy-*scyllo*-inositol, suggesting that both the equatorial and axial hydroxyl groups were important for inhibiting aggregation. Incubation of Aβ42 with 1-deoxy-1-fluoro-*scyllo*-inositol resulted in ThT-positive, amorphous aggregates, similar to those in the presence of *scyllo*-inositol, whereas Aβ42 incubation with 1,4-dideoxy-1,4-difluoro-*scyllo*-inositol showed both amorphous aggregates and fibrils. Later in vivo studies showed that 1-deoxy-1-fluoro-*scyllo*-inositol dose-dependently improved spatial memory in TgCRND8 mice (Hawkes et al., 2012). The compound did not change the overall cerebral Aβ40 or Aβ42 concentration, but decreased Aβ plaque burden (Hawkes et al., 2012).

The derivative 1,4-di-*O*-methyl-*scyllo*-inositol inhibited Aβ42 fibrillization in vitro by stabilizing Aβ42 protofibril-like structures (Hawkes et al., 2010; Shaw et al., 2012). However, unlike protofibrils of Aβ itself, which are highly neurotoxic (Nilsberth et al., 1999; O'Nuallain et al., 2010; Walsh et al., 1999), the structures formed in the presence of 1,4-di-*O*-methyl-*scyllo*-inositol apparently were nontoxic. Thus, in the TgCRND8 AD mouse model, 1,4-di-*O*-methyl-*scyllo*-inositol improved spatial memory measured by the Morris water-maze test and significantly decreased cerebral amyloid pathology (Hawkes et al., 2010). In agreement with the in vitro data, the total Aβ plaque burden decreased by 30%, whereas soluble Aβ levels increased (Hawkes et al., 2010; Shaw et al., 2012). As oligomeric Aβ forms are more toxic than the mature fibrils, and those found in the mice were not well characterized, the data suggested caution in testing 1,4-di-*O*-methyl-*scyllo*-inositol in humans.

A randomized, 78-week, phase 2 trial using *scyllo*-inositol was conducted in 353 patients with mild or moderate AD who received 250, 1000, or 2000 mg/day. Clinical scores of the "neuropsychological test battery" and ADCS-ADL tests were used as primary outcome measures. The high doses of 1000 and 2000 mg/day, however, were discontinued due to significant incidence of adverse reactions in patients. These included nine deaths, in addition to less severe side effects, such as falls, depression, and confusion. The trial continued with only the low dose, 250 mg/day, which did not lead to significant cognitive or functional improvement (Salloway et al., 2011). In this trial, *scyllo*-inositol concentrations increased in the CSF, and cerebral and CSF Aβ concentrations decreased significantly compared to the placebo group ($p = 0.009$), suggesting that these parameters may not serve as meaningful pharmacodynamics biomarkers for the treatment's efficacy since the clinical outcome measures were insignificant. Alternatively, the reason for the lack of efficacy might be that the trial was conducted too late in the disease.

The insignificant effect of *scyllo*-inositol in the clinical trial correlated with an in vitro/cell-culture study by our group, in which the effects of *scyllo*-inositol on Aβ42 oligomerization, aggregation, and toxicity were substantially weaker than those of EGCG (section: (−)-Epigallocatechin-3-Gallate) or CLR01 (section: Molecular Tweezers) (Sinha et al., 2012a).

Vitamins

Vitamins are essential nutrients our body cannot synthesize in sufficient quantities and thus are acquired through food. Vitamins play diverse functions in growth, development, immune regulation (vitamin A), metabolism (vitamin B), mineral absorption (vitamin D), and antioxidant defense (vitamins C and E). In AD patients, levels of several vitamins are lower than normal. These include particularly vitamins A, C, and E. Supplementation of some vitamins in AD patients could improve AD symptoms clinically and therefore has been researched as a potential treatment for AD. Perhaps as a fashionable addition, in some cases the effect of certain vitamins on Aβ assembly also has been explored.

Vitamin A

Vitamin A is a mixture of retinol, retinal, retinoic acid, and β-carotene (Fig. 6.19). It is important for human growth, development, and visual sensation. In AD patients, plasma and CSF levels of vitamin A reportedly are lower than those in age-matched normal individuals

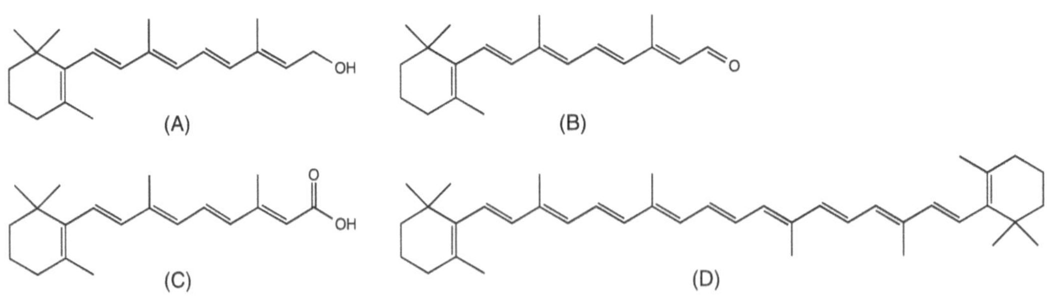

FIGURE 6.19 Components of vitamin A, which is a mixture of retinol (A), retinal (B), retinoic acid (C), and β-carotene (D).

(Lopes da Silva et al., 2014; Ono and Yamada, 2012). Dietary supplementation of vitamin A has been shown to improve clinical AD symptoms (Obulesu et al., 2011). To test if there is a correlation between decrease in levels of vitamin A and Aβ aggregation, inhibition of Aβ assembly by vitamin A was examined. Vitamin A inhibited oligomerization, fibrillization, and fibril extension of Aβ40 or Aβ42 dose dependently in ThT fluorescence and TEM experiments. Vitamin A also disintegrated fibrillar Aβ dose dependently (Ono et al., 2004c; Takasaki et al., 2011). All-*trans* retinoic acid, an active metabolite of vitamin A, was found to decrease cerebral Aβ deposition and rescue memory deficits in APP/PS1 transgenic mice (Ding et al., 2008) and in a streptozotocin-induced model of dementia of Alzheimer type in Swiss albino mice (Sodhi and Singh, 2013). Immunodetection using 6E10 and CR staining were used to assess amyloid plaque burden in APP/PS1 and in albino mice, respectively (Sodhi and Singh, 2013).

Vitamin C

Vitamin C (L-ascorbic acid, Fig. 6.20A), is an important cofactor in several different physiological processes, including collagen synthesis, wound healing, and scavenging of reactive oxygen species. It is a powerful antioxidant and plays an important role in prevention of cancer and cardiovascular diseases, which involve oxidative damage. In AD, plasma vitamin C levels are significantly reduced (0.56 mg/dL vs 0.8 mg/dL in control individuals) (Charlton et al., 2004). However, it is unclear whether vitamin C deficiency is a cause or an effect of AD pathogenesis. In several in vivo and cell-culture assays, vitamin C acted as a potent inhibitor of Aβ-induced insults. Vitamin C completely prevented Aβ-induced increase of cellular calcium levels, suppressed A11-positive Aβ oligomers in Tg2576 fibroblasts, and prevented Aβ-induced death of PC-12 cells (Cheng et al., 2011; Yallampalli et al., 1998). Studying vitamin C deficiency in rodents has been difficult because, unlike humans, rodents produce sufficient endogenous amounts of vitamin C. To overcome this practical challenge, 5 × FAD mice (Oakley et al., 2006) were cross-bred with mice lacking the enzyme L-gulono-γ-lactone oxidase (EC 1.1.3.8), which produces vitamin C in rodents, but is nonfunctional in haplorrhines,

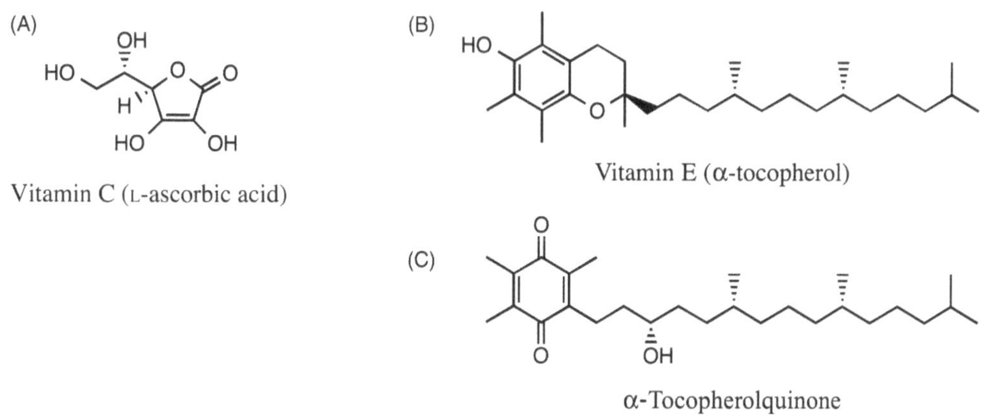

FIGURE 6.20 **Structures of vitamins C and E.** (A) L-ascorbic acid, (B) α-tocopherol, (C) α-tocopherolquinone.

including humans (Nishikimi et al., 1988). This animal model was tested for the effect of vitamin C in AD. The crossbred mice, which could not synthesize vitamin C, showed heavy amyloid plaque deposition in the brain (Kook et al., 2014). The mice were supplemented with low (0.66 g/L) or high (3.3 g/L) doses of vitamin C. The higher dose reduced the amyloid plaque burden in the cortical and hippocampal regions of these mice, suggesting a prospective potential for using vitamin C for AD prevention (Kook et al., 2014). Vitamin C treatment was shown to improve memory performance in the middle-aged APP/PS1 mouse model of AD and in wild-type mice (Kennard and Harrison, 2014). Human data, however, calls for caution regarding vitamin C treatment (Arlt et al., 2012) (and see section: Vitamin E).

Vitamin E

Vitamin E (α-tocopherol, Fig. 6.20B) is an antioxidant, which scavenges reactive oxygen species upon oxidation of lipids. It plays other important physiological roles in gene expression, cell signaling, and inhibition of platelet aggregation (Azzi, 2007; Bell, 1987; Zingg and Azzi, 2004). Although endogenous vitamin E levels are not altered in patients with AD, exogenous vitamin E reportedly reversed Aβ-induced damage in several experimental paradigms. α-Tocopherolquinone (Fig. 6.20C), an important derivative of α-tocopherol, inhibited Aβ42 fibrillization and Aβ42-induced neurotoxicity in SH-SY5Y neuroblastoma cells, disaggregated preformed fibrils, and interfered with intracellular Aβ oligomerization (Yang et al., 2010). In the Tg2576 transgenic mouse model of AD, vitamin E treatment as 2 IU/g diet, which was started at 5 months of age and continued until 13 months, significantly reduced lipid peroxidation, Aβ levels, and Aβ deposition (Sung et al., 2004). By contrast, mice taking diet-supplemented vitamin E at 14 months of age until month 20 did not show any significant difference when compared with placebo (Sung et al., 2004). In a different study, combined vitamin E (400 IU/kg diet) and vitamin C (1 g/kg diet) treatment prevented spatial memory deficits in APP/PS1 mice tested in the water maze. However, Aβ deposition was not reduced by this treatment (Harrison et al., 2009). A clinical trial of vitamin E for AD was carried out in 341 patients with moderate or severe AD (Sano et al., 1997). Patients received 2000 IU of vitamin E a day for 2 years. However, no effect was observed in the MMSE test. In another study, 769 patients with mild cognitive impairment received the same dose of vitamin E. Unfortunately, there were no significant differences in the rate of AD progression between vitamin E and placebo groups (Petersen et al., 2005). Negative results were reported in AD patients taking a cholinesterase inhibitor supplemented with 1000 mg/day vitamin C and 400 IU/day vitamin E (Arlt et al., 2012).

In a clinical trial that included 78 patients with mild-to-moderate AD, the patients were given a combination of antioxidants, including vitamin E, vitamin C, α-lipoic acid, and coenzyme Q3. The treatment was well tolerated by the subjects but showed no effect on the CSF biomarkers related to amyloid or tau pathology. Moreover, in certain groups, there was accelerated decline in MMSE scores, suggesting against this strategy for AD treatment (Galasko et al., 2012).

Proteins or Peptides

Though we dedicated section: Peptidic or Peptidomimetic Modulators of Aβ Assembly to peptides and peptidomimetics, those are *synthetic* compounds synthesized and tested based on specific rationales. Here, we discuss two examples of *natural* peptides and proteins tested as inhibitors of Aβ assembly and toxicity, and therefore we include them in the section dealing with molecules of natural sources.

Colostrinin

Colostrinin is a proline-rich polypeptide mixture derived from mammalian colostrum. Reportedly, colostrinin is made up of 32 polypeptides (molecular weight 500–3000 Da) resulting from the proteolytic cleavage of colostrum proteins, for example, β-casein. These peptides contain 25% proline and 40% hydrophobic residues (Janusz and Zablocka, 2013). In primary rat hippocampal cells, colostrinin alleviated Aβ42-induced toxicity (Froud et al., 2010). Upon treatment with 0.25 μM colostrinin, 25 μM preparations of Aβ40 formed shorter and less dense fibrils than untreated Aβ40 as documented by TEM experiments (Schuster et al., 2005). When given orally to mice, colostrinin increased the life span and improved various motor and sensory activities (Boldogh and Kruzel, 2008). However, the exact mechanism of colostrinin action is still unclear (Boldogh and Kruzel, 2008; Rocha et al., 2010). In a double-blind, placebo-controlled study to test the effect of colostrinin on daily activities of AD patients, orally administered colostrinin improved cognitive AD outcomes in patients with mild or moderate dementia. This trial consisted of 105 patients and comprised a 15-week double-blind phase comparing colostrinin with placebo, followed by a second 15-week period in which all patients received colostrinin. The patients received 100 μg drug on alternate days for 3 weeks followed by no drug for 2 weeks. At week 15 and week 30, parameters were evaluated for ADAS-Cog, Clinical Global Impression of Change (CGIC), instrumental activities of daily living (IADL), MMSE, ADAS Noncognitive test (ADAS-Noncog), and overall patient response. Colostrinin showed an alleviating effect on cognitive function in ADAS-Cog and on daily function in IADL. The overall patient response was also in favor of the drug (Bilikiewicz and Gaus, 2004). Colostrinin is used as a nutraceutical for treating the early stages of cognitive decline in North America, Australia, and Europe (Stewart, 2008).

Laminin

Extracellular matrix (ECM) proteins can serve as important traps for extracellular Aβ. Laminin, which is a major component of the basement membrane, is a high-molecular-weight extracellular membrane protein, which was found to bind Aβ40 with nanomolar affinity (Castillo et al., 2000) and colocalize with Aβ in senile plaques. Among several other ECM components, laminin inhibited Aβ40 aggregation significantly better than perlecan, type IV collagen, or fibronectin (Castillo et al., 2000). Inhibition of Aβ40 aggregation by other ECM proteins was not statistically significant. Laminin caused a ninefold inhibition by day 3, and a 21-fold inhibition 1 week after initiation of Aβ40 assembly, measured by ThT fluorescence. Incubation of Aβ40 with laminin resulted in formation of amorphous aggregates and preformed Aβ40 fibrils were disassembled upon incubation with laminin as detected by TEM.

The potential Aβ-interacting domains of laminin were investigated using proteolysis with a combination of V8 protease and elastase, which identified 55-kDa globular repeats in laminin that bound Aβ40 (Castillo et al., 2000). Interestingly, laminin receptor precursors/laminin receptors (LPR/LR) were shown to bind and internalize Aβ42. The LPR–/LR–Aβ complexes facilitated endocytosis of the peptide, thus enhancing neurotoxicity and accumulation. In view of a recent report suggesting that cellular internalization and accumulation of Aβ are

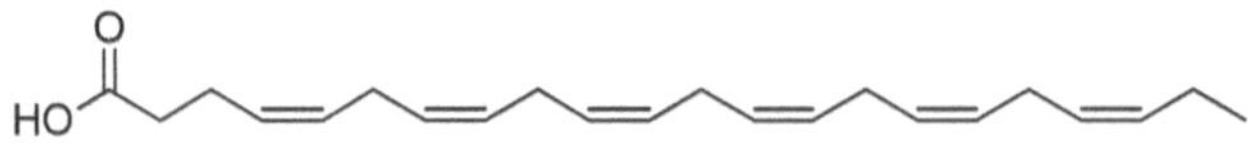

FIGURE 6.21 **Structure of docosahexaenoic acid (DHA).**

critical for induction of synaptotoxicity (Ripoli et al., 2014), anti-LPR/LR antibodies and LPR/LR-based gene therapy could serve as potential strategies for treating AD (Da Costa Dias et al., 2014).

Other Compounds

Docosahexaenoic Acid

Docosahexaenoic acid (DHA, Fig. 6.21) is a polyunsaturated ω-3 fatty acid present in high amounts in fish oil and breast milk. DHA is a major component of the human eye, brain, skin, and sperm. Elevated levels of DHA have been linked with decreased risk of dementia (Cole and Frautschy, 2010; Laurin et al., 2003). This instigated further investigations on the use of DHA as a therapeutic agent for AD. ThT fluorescence and TEM showed that DHA inhibited Aβ42 fibril formation (Hossain et al., 2009). In viability assays using SH-S5Y5 cells or brain endothelial cells, DHA reduced Aβ42-induced toxicity (Hossain et al., 2009; Veszelka et al., 2013). In Tg2576 mice, DHA supplementation noticeably reduced Aβ42 accumulation and oxidative damage, corrected synaptic deficits, and improved cognitive function (Cole and Frautschy, 2006). In the APP/PS1 rat model of AD, rats fed a DHA-supplemented diet showed lower hippocampal Aβ plaque density and modest behavioral improvements relative to those animals fed a DHA-lacking diet. But DHA supplementation also increased overall fibrillar Aβ in the hippocampus (Teng et al., 2015). On the other hand, previous in vitro assays had shown that DHA micelles stabilized protofibrillar Aβ42, preventing further fibrillization (Johansson et al., 2007). Unfortunately, these protofibrils induced toxicity in PC-12 cells, suggesting that DHA may act as a double-edged sword and, depending on the context, may actually exacerbate AD pathology (Cole and Frautschy, 2006; Hashimoto et al., 2008; Johansson et al., 2007).

Melatonin

Melatonin (Fig. 6.22) is a hormone produced by the pineal gland. It is involved in many physiological processes, including circadian rhythm, blood pressure regulation, oncogenesis, retinal physiology, reproduction, ovarian physiology, immune regulation, and osteoblast differentiation (Altun and Ugur-Altun, 2007). Melatonin also acts as a potent free-radical scavenger and an antioxidant by direct and indirect mechanisms (Hardeland, 2005). Melatonin

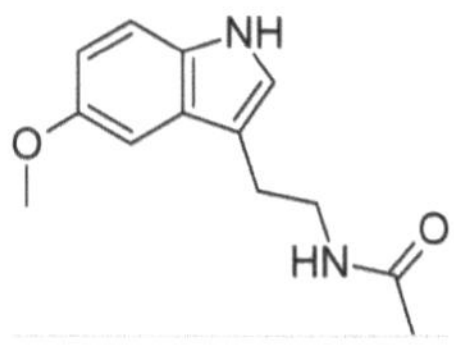

FIGURE 6.22 **Structure of melatonin.**

levels tend to decline with aging. Although no direct correlation between melatonin levels and AD pathogenesis has been established, the antioxidant activity of the hormone and its declining concentration levels with aging prompted its investigation in the context of AD.

Melatonin inhibited Aβ aggregation in CD, TEM, and NMR experiments. Electrospray ionization–mass spectrometry and proteolysis experiments showed that melatonin bound to the 29–40 region of Aβ40, mainly by hydrophobic interactions (Pappolla et al., 1998; Skribanek et al., 2001). Pretreatment of PC-12 cells with melatonin rescued them from Aβ42-induced apoptotic insults as evident from MTT cell viability assay, Hoechst 33342 nuclear staining, DNA fragmentation analysis, and flow cytometry (Feng and Zhang, 2004). However, the neuroprotective effect observed for melatonin was reduced considerably when picrotoxin, an antagonist of the γ-amino butyric acid (GABA) receptor, was added to the system. Therefore, the neuroprotective effect of melatonin actually might be mediated by its action on the GABA receptor rather than directly on Aβ (Paula-Lima et al., 2003). Melatonin was reportedly neuroprotective in organotypic hippocampal cultures maximally at 1 μM in combination with 1 μM galantamine, an acetylcholinesterase inhibitor. Mechanistically, this treatment caused antiapoptotic effects and reduced oxidative stress, neuroinflammation, tau phosphorylation, and aggregates positively stained with thioflavin S (Buendia et al., 2015). In a recent study, melatonin rescued Aβ-induced memory deficits in mice. Wild-type male C57BL/6N mice (25–30 g, 8 weeks old) were stereotactically administered human Aβ42 (aggregated for 4 days at 37°C at a concentration of 1 mg/mL) intracerebroventricularly (Ali and Kim, 2015). Using Y-maze, Morris water maze, and immunohistochemistry, the authors showed that melatonin had protective effects against Aβ42-induced neurotoxicity by decreasing memory impairment, synaptic disorder, and tau hyperphosphorylation. In another study using Tg2576 mice, melatonin treatment improved pathology and memory performance in 4- to 12-month-old mice by targeting activated GSK3β (Peng et al., 2013). Melatonin supplementation decreased Aβ42 and Aβ40 levels in the hippocampus and Aβ42 levels in the frontal cortex of OXYS rats, and improved treated rats' reference memory function (Rudnitskaya et al., 2015). OXYS rat is a model of senescence-accelerated sporadic AD that suffers from deficient melatonin secretion (Kolosova et al., 2014; Stefanova et al., 2014a,b).

Excess melatonin is associated with several physiological disorders, including seasonal affective disorder, mood changes, abnormalities in thyroid and adrenal function, cancer, cardiovascular diseases, and hypertension. Thus because melatonin affects multiple physiological systems, its therapeutic use probably will be difficult and is not likely to be a viable option for AD. However, a prolonged-release formulation containing 2 mg melatonin was recently tested in 80 patients who suffered from mild-to-moderate AD, with or without insomnia comorbidity, but receiving standard therapy (acetylcholinesterase inhibitors with or without memantine) (Wade et al., 2014). In this randomized, double-blind, parallel-group study, patients were treated for 2 weeks with placebo and subsequently received 2 mg of prolonged-release melatonin or placebo nightly for 24 weeks, followed by 2 weeks placebo treatment. In the comorbid AD–insomnia subgroup, prolonged-release melatonin resulted in significant and better effects than the placebo when patients' performances were scored by IADL, MMSE, ADAS-Cog, and sleep efficiency. Prolonged-release melatonin was well tolerated by the patients. The authors concluded that melatonin positively affected cognitive functioning and sleep regulation in AD patients, particularly in those suffering insomnia (Wade et al., 2014).

Aβ ASSEMBLY MODULATORS FROM NONNATURAL SOURCES

In this section, we discuss typical and atypical small molecules, as well as large molecules or molecular complexes used to modulate Aβ assembly and toxicity (summarized in Table 6.3). Although most typical small molecules are ≤500 Da according to Lipinski's guidelines (Lipinski et al., 2001) because Aβ self-assembly is an atypical target, we define small molecules as those ranging from ~300 to 1000 Da in molecular mass, and large molecules as those whose molecular mass is ≥1000 Da.

Small-Molecule Modulators of Aβ Assembly and Toxicity

Methylene Blue

Methylene blue or methylthioninium chloride (3,7-*bis*(dimethylamino)-phenothiazin-5-ium chloride, trade name: Rember™, Fig. 6.23A) belongs to the tricyclic phenothiazine family (reviewed by Guerrero-Muñoz et al., 2014; Schirmer et al., 2011). It is used in a wide range of clinical indications, including methemoglobinemia, ifosfamide-induced neurotoxicity in cancer patients, urinary tract infections in the elderly, vasoplegic adrenalin-resistant shock, and pediatric malaria (Guerrero-Muñoz et al., 2014; Schirmer et al., 2011). It is also used for intraoperative visualization of nerves, nerve tissues, endocrine glands, parathyroid glands, or pathologic fistulae (Guerrero-Muñoz et al., 2014; Schirmer et al., 2011).

Methylene blue or its derivatives currently are in phase 2 clinical trials for AD (Wischik et al., 2015), and patient recruitment is under way for phase 3 trials. These clinical trials are based on the evidence that methylene blue functions as a tau aggregation modulator/inhibitor (Taniguchi et al., 2005; Wischik et al., 1996, 2008, 2015). Because our chapter does not focus on modulators of tau aggregation (see Chapter 15), here we summarize studies related to the effects of methylene blue on Aβ aggregation and discuss experimental animal studies that showed reduction in Aβ levels following methylene blue treatment.

In 2007, azure C (3-amino-7-methylaminophenothiazin-5-ium chloride, Fig. 6.23B), an oxidation product of methylene blue (Marshall, 1976), was shown to modulate Aβ42 oligomerization and promote fibrillization in vitro when tested by dot-blotting using the oligomer-targeting antibody, A11 (Necula et al., 2007b). Rather than completely inhibiting oligomerization, azure C modulated oligomerization such that A11 reactivity was lost but fibrillization still continued; Aβ formed 6E10-positive, high-molecular-weight species which could not enter the SDS–PAGE gels (Necula et al., 2007b). These findings were further confirmed by TEM experiments (Necula et al., 2007a).

A different study showed modulation of Aβ42 oligomerization, enhanced disappearance of nonaggregated Aβ42, and formation of larger, potentially fibrillar aggregates using capillary electrophoresis (Brinet et al., 2014). However, this study did not specify the exact chemical name or source of methylene blue, or whether its derivatives or oxidation products were used.

In 2014, effects of methylene blue on AD-like pathology and behavioral deficits were tested (Mori et al., 2014) in PSAPP mice bearing exon-9-deleted presenilin 1 and Swedish $APP_{K595N/M596L}$ (APP_{SWE}) (Jankowsky et al., 2001, 2004), modeling cerebral amyloidosis. The authors administered methylene blue at 3 mg/kg once daily for 3 months to 15-month-old transgenic mice by gavage and examined the effect of the treatment on cognitive function, behavior,

TABLE 6.3 Aβ Assembly and Toxicity Modulators from Nonnatural Sources

		In vitro studies		Animal studies		
Compound	**Type**	**Inhibition of Aβ-induced cytotoxicity**	**Modulation of Aβ assembly**	**Decrease of pathological Aβ**	**Effect on behavioral deficits**	**Human studies/ clinical trials**
Methylene blue	Small molecule	Yes, and also reduces APP processing in cultured cells	Promotes fibrillization (azure C)	Reduces brain parenchymal and vascular Aβ deposits; reduces levels of extracted Aβ in treated mice compared to vehicle-treated mice	Prevents behavioral deficits in mouse models of AD	Currently in clinical trials based on its inhibition of tau aggregation, not its effects on Aβ
Mitoxantrone, bithionol, and hexachlorophene	Small molecule	Bithionol alone is nontoxic; mitoxantrone and hexachlorophene reduce cell viability, mitoxantrone or bithionol reduce cytotoxicity significantly	Inhibit seeded Aβ fibrillization and fibrillization of nonaggregated Aβ preparations	Transgenic mice treated with bithionol or mitoxantrone showed diffuse Aβ plaques and significantly lower Aβ42 in the frontal cortex and in the hippocampus (only biothionol) than untreated APPtg mice. Both compounds protected neurons and synapses; hexachlorophene was ineffective	Unknown	Unknown
D737	Small molecule	Inhibits cytotoxicity of high-molecular-weight Aβ42 oligomers but not that caused by low-molecular-weight oligomers	Inhibits fibril formation	Unknown	Improves life span and locomotion in a fly model of AD	Unknown
D737 analogs D744 and D830	Small molecule	Expected similar to parent compound	Expected similar to parent compound	Unknown	More effective than D737	Unknown
Cromolyn sodium	Small molecule	Increases Aβ clearance by microglial activation	Inhibits Aβ fibrillization and oligomerization but does not dissociate preexisting assemblies	Lowers soluble Aβ levels but not insoluble Aβ burden in a mouse model; enhances microglial activation and microglia-mediated Aβ clearance in vivo	Unknown	Unknown

(Continued)

TABLE 6.3 Aβ Assembly and Toxicity Modulators From Nonnatural Sources (*cont.*)

		In vitro studies		Animal studies		
Compound	**Type**	**Inhibition of Aβ-induced cytotoxicity**	**Modulation of Aβ assembly**	**Decrease of pathological Aβ**	**Effect on behavioral deficits**	**Human studies/ clinical trials**
Aminopyrazole derivatives	Small molecule	Yes	Some derivatives suppress fibril formation more efficiently than others	Unknown	Unknown	Unknown
Ruthenium complexes, for example, PRMU20	Small molecule	Yes	Inhibits Aβ fibrillization	Unknown	Unknown	Unknown
Molecular tweezers	Small molecule	Inhibit Aβ-induced cell death, retraction of dendritic spines, impairment of basal synaptic activity, and suppression of LTP	Inhibit Aβ fibril formation and oligomerization; dissociate preformed fibrils	Reduce Aβ plaques in transgenic AD mice and rats	Unknown in AD models Rescue disease phenotype and improve behavioral deficits in models of Parkinson's disease	Unknown
Cucurbit[7]uril	Large molecule	Yes	Inhibits fibrillization	Unknown	Unknown	Unknown
Metallohelical complexes	Large molecule	Yes	Inhibit fibrillization	Unknown	Unknown	Unknown
Polyoxometalates (POMs)	Large molecule	Yes but after a long, 7-day incubation with Aβ; some derivatives dissociate preformed fibrils	Wells–Dawson POMs were more effective than other POMs	Unknown	Unknown	Unknown
Artificial molecular chaperones	Large molecule	Yes	Attenuates nucleation and elongation of Aβ fibrillization; does not affect preformed aggregates/fibrils	Unknown	Unknown	Unknown

(A)

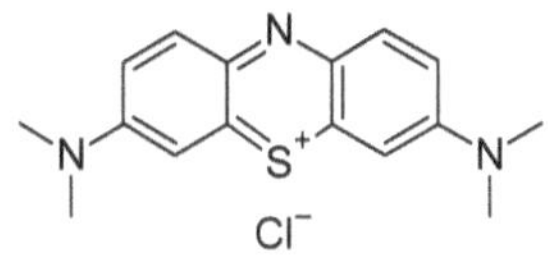

Methylene blue

(B)

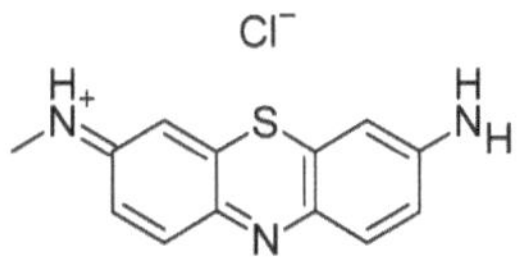

Azure C

FIGURE 6.23 Structures of (A) methylene blue and (B) azure C, a methylene blue derivative.

CAA, and APP processing. Transgene-associated behavioral deficits, including hyperactivity and impaired spatial, working, and reference memory, were prevented upon treatment (Mori et al., 2014). Moreover, brain parenchymal and vascular Aβ deposits and levels of extracted Aβ were reduced in methylene blue-treated mice compared to vehicle-treated mice (Mori et al., 2014). Mechanistically, the reported beneficial effects in this animal model were attributed to inhibition of amyloidogenic APP proteolysis, whereby protein expression of β-carboxyl-terminal APP fragment and expression and activity of BACE1 were found to be reduced (Mori et al., 2014). Although these mechanisms are not directly relevant to our chapter, which deals with inhibition and/or modulation of Aβ self-assembly rather than Aβ production, we mention them here briefly for completeness of the discussion. Methylene blue treatment of CHO cells overexpressing wild-type human APP also significantly decreased Aβ production and proteolytic APP processing (Mori et al., 2014).

The therapeutic or preventive uses of oral or intraperitoneal methylene blue treatment against Aβ pathology also was tested (Paban et al., 2014) in the transgenic mouse model APP/PS1, bearing the chimeric human–mouse APP gene with the Swedish mutation (K549N/M595L) and the human presenilin 1 A246E variant, APP_{SWE}/PS1 (A246E) (Borchelt et al., 1996, 1997). Cognitive impairment assessed by social, learning, or exploratory tasks was prevented in treated transgenic mice in this study (Paban et al., 2014). Correlating with the behavioral findings, immunoreactive hippocampal and cortical Aβ deposition was significantly reduced in treated mice, again likely reflecting effects on Aβ production rather than assembly.

Besides methylene blue's effects on Aβ and tau aggregation, it partially improves mitochondrial function (Paban et al., 2014) and cellular metabolism, and influences cholinergic, serotonergic, and glutamatergic neurotransmitters, all of which are involved in AD pathogenesis (Oz et al., 2009). Collective evidence suggests that the combination of methylene blue's diverse roles likely mediates its potentially beneficial effects in animal models and disease settings.

The aforementioned studies used a multifaceted rationale for employing methylene blue as a modulator of Aβ and/or tau aggregation:

- Methylene blue is a small molecule with many properties suitable for a drug that can enter and act in the brain.
- It has high aqueous solubility.

- It has low toxicity in rats and humans (Kupfer et al., 1994; Riha et al., 2005).
- It can cross the blood–brain barrier in rats, and it yields high cerebral levels irrespective of its administration route (O'Leary et al., 1968; Peter et al., 2000; Walter-Sack et al., 2009).
- It has been approved for use in humans (DiSanto and Wagner, 1972; Guerrero-Muñoz et al., 2014; Kupfer et al., 1994; Schirmer et al., 2011). However, it should never be given intrathecally in humans (Schirmer et al., 2011); when administered through this route, it can reportedly cause reversible paraplegia with residual perineal anesthesia and bladder dysfunction (Evans, 1959; Sivak, 1959).

The major caveat in using methylene blue for treating AD is that the compound accelerates Aβ fibrillization. This may provide initial relief due to reduction in the steady-state concentration of oligomers, which are the most toxic Aβ species and are more toxic than fibrils. However, fibrils form amyloid plaques and accumulate therein; plaques impinge on functional neurites, take up parenchymal space, and resist proteolysis and clearance as AD progresses. In addition, fibrillar Aβ deposits in the brain vasculature lead to CAA (Ellis et al., 1996), a major comorbidity in AD that may lead to microhemorrhage and stroke, and complicates use of Aβ-targeting strategies (Sperling et al., 2011). Also, Aβ normally regulates brain function and memory at picomolar physiological levels (Morley and Farr, 2014), and lowering free Aβ by hastening fibrillization may compromise Aβ's potential physiological role. Thus, a therapeutic strategy based on increasing fibril load is questionable.

Mitoxantrone, Bithionol, and Hexachlorophene

Addition of preformed Aβ fibril "seeds" to a fibrillization reaction shortens the nucleation-dependent lag phase of Aβ self-assembly, and accelerates fibrillization in vitro and in vivo (Harper and Lansbury, 1997; Stöhr et al., 2012, 2014). Seeded Aβ fibrillization in vivo likely is crucial for Aβ plaque formation (Walker et al., 2013) and Aβ dissemination by a potential prion-like mechanism of propagation (Frost and Diamond, 2010).

Seeded fibrillization of Aβ42 was targeted to identify molecules that could disrupt this process, prevent Aβ42 toxicity, and potentially prevent the prion-like spread of Aβ plaques (Eleuteri et al., 2015). A library of 1040 compounds (80% of which were approved by the US Food and Drug Administration) was screened in a high-throughput seeded fibrillization assay in vitro. Fibril fragments of 100–300 nm length were added to monomeric Aβ42 solutions at molar ratio 4:10, respectively, in 384-well plates. The test compounds were added to the reaction mixture at 10 μM final concentration per well and incubated at 37°C for 3 h under agitation. Fibrillization kinetics was assayed by ThT fluorescence. Three compounds were found to inhibit seeded Aβ fibrillization at low micromolar concentrations: mitoxantrone (IC_{50} = 1.7 μM, Fig. 6.24A), bithionol (IC_{50} = 5.33 μM, Fig. 6.24B), and hexachlorophene (IC_{50} = 5.9 μM, Fig. 6.24C). They also strongly inhibited fibrillization of freshly prepared monomeric Aβ42 by SEC (Di Giovanni et al., 2010) with similar IC_{50} values.

The potential protective effect of the three compounds against Aβ42-induced toxicity was tested in primary murine cortical neurons. Although bithionol alone was nontoxic, mitoxantrone and hexachlorophene reduced cell viability at 20 and 50 μM, respectively. Primary neurons were ~50–60% less viable when treated for 24 h with crude Aβ42 preparations (40 μM), which contained predominantly monomeric and protofibrillar species. In the presence of 5 or 10 μM mitoxantrone or bithionol, Aβ42 cytotoxicity was significantly reduced. According to the authors, this was consistent with the proposed inhibitory action of the compounds

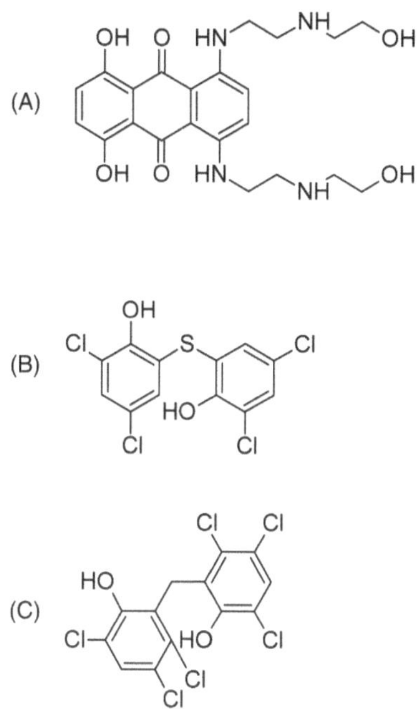

FIGURE 6.24 Structures of mitoxantrone (A), bithionol (B), and hexachlorophene (C).

that target fibril growth rather than stabilizing monomeric Aβ42. However, stabilization of Aβ42 monomers also would be consistent with inhibition of toxicity when oligomerization is prevented. Hexachlorophene only modestly protected against Aβ42-induced cytotoxicity despite inhibiting conversion of protofibrils to fibrils and inhibiting seeded fibrillization.

In view of the strong antiamyloidogenic and neuroprotective properties of bithionol and mitoxantrone and the modest effects of hexachlorophene observed in vitro and in tissue culture, the authors examined the compounds next in an APP transgenic mouse model of AD (mThy1–APPtg; Rockenstein et al., 2001, 2002). Each compound was administered intravenously at 10 mg/kg to 8-month-old mice, and their pharmacokinetic properties were studied in plasma and brain extracts by liquid chromatography–mass spectrometry (LC–MS/MS). Bithionol showed 20% brain penetration with plasma and brain half-lives of 7.62 and 1.77 h, respectively. Mitoxantrone surprisingly showed 100% brain penetration. Hexachlorophene showed 50% brain permeability with plasma and brain half-lives of 4.4 and 5.64 h, respectively (Eleuteri et al., 2015; DiMeco et al., 2002; Green et al., 1988).

The authors then examined the effects of the three compounds on Aβ42 deposition, Aβ42 oligomer levels, synaptic loss, neuronal damage, and astrogliosis, as representative neuropathological hallmarks of AD, and compared the corresponding data among the treated animals, vehicle-treated APP transgenic mice, and the nontransgenic vehicle-treated control mice. Because bithionol and mitoxantrone cross the blood–brain barrier, they were administered daily by intraperitoneal injection for 1 month at 10 and 1 mg/kg, respectively. A confusing point in the report is that despite finding 50% brain permeability for hexachlorophene, it was treated as if it could not cross the blood–brain barrier and thus was administered intracerebroventricularly (Eleuteri et al., 2015).

Aβ42 immunohistochemistry using antibody 6E10 and thioflavin S staining in vehicle-treated tissue sections from the APPtg mice showed dense amyloid plaques in the frontal cortex and the hippocampus. Treated mice showed diffuse Aβ plaques in the frontal and hippocampal regions and significantly lower Aβ42 immunoreactivity in the frontal cortex when treated with bithionol or mitoxantrone and in the hippocampus when treated with bithionol, relative to untreated APPtg mice. In contrast, hexachlorophene-treated APPtg mice showed dense plaques and high Aβ42 immunoreactivity.

Bithionol- or mitoxantrone-treated APPtg mouse brains also showed significantly reduced Aβ monomers and intermediate species. Total Aβ levels in membrane fractions and in guanidine–HCl-extracted samples were dramatically reduced following administration of bithionol or mitoxantrone compared with that in vehicle-treated APPtg mice as measured by ELISA. Hexachlorophene did not significantly reduce Aβ42 levels. Together, immunoblotting and ELISA confirmed that bithionol and mitoxantrone strongly reduced Aβ42 levels in brain tissue extracts from treated mice. In addition, these compounds protected neuronal and synaptic integrity in the APPtg mice, as shown by immunohistochemistry and/or Western blotting of several markers, including synaptophysin, a major membrane constituent of the presynaptic vesicles; postsynaptic density-95 protein; the neuronal marker microtubule-associated protein 2; and NeuN, a vertebrate neuron-specific nuclear protein.

D737

The discovery of D737 ensued from screening of 65,000 small molecules in a high-throughput fluorescence assay to isolate those that modulate Aβ42 assembly; the fluorescence assay used a recombinant fusion system of Aβ and green fluorescent protein (GFP) (McKoy et al., 2012). In this system, aggregation and/or insolubility of the upstream Aβ42 in the fusion sequence prevents correct folding of the downstream GFP, whereby Aβ42–GFP fusion expressed in *E. coli* does not fold properly or fluoresce. Thus, compounds that inhibit Aβ42 assembly and allow proper GFP folding can be found by fluorescence screening (Kim et al., 2006; Waldo et al., 1999). Of all the screened compounds, 269 constituted positive hits. From these, eight commercially available compounds were chosen for further testing, and D737 (Fig. 6.25A) was identified by ThT fluorescence to interfere with Aβ fibrillization more significantly than the others. This effect depended on D737 concentration; 10 μM D737 inhibited ThT fluorescence of 20 μM Aβ42 by 50%. In cytotoxicity assays using the MTT reduction assay, D737 inhibited cytotoxicity of high-molecular-weight Aβ42 oligomers but did not affect that caused by low-molecular-weight oligomers formed after 1 h of incubation. D737 also inhibited the cytotoxicity of insoluble high-molecular-weight oligomers formed after 2–24 h of incubation and of fibrils formed after 8 h of incubation.

D737 significantly improved both the life span and locomotive ability of transgenic *Drosophila* expressing either wild-type Aβ42 or Aβ42(E22G) in their CNS, thus confirming D737's effect in vivo. D737 at 20 μM increased the median life span of Aβ42-expressing transgenic flies to 43 days, compared with control flies with a median life span of 37 days. The median life span for untreated transgenic flies expressing Aβ42(E22G) was 30 days whereas treatment with 20 μM D737 extended the median life span to 34 days. The flies' locomotive activity was assessed using a climbing assay (Crowther et al., 2006). Transgenic flies treated with 20 μM D737 showed dramatically improved climbing ability relative to untreated flies (McKoy et al., 2012).

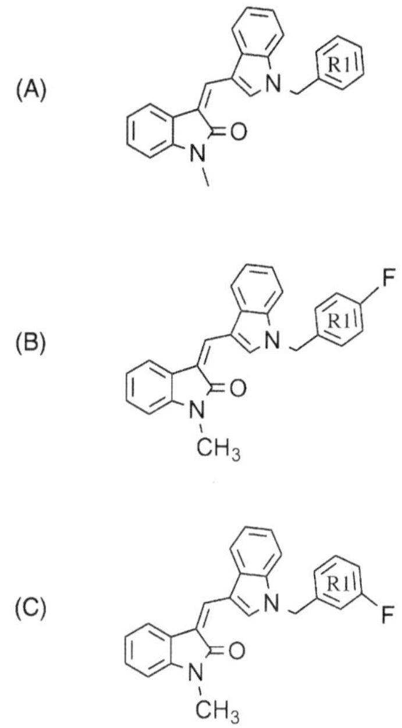

FIGURE 6.25 Structures of D737 (A), D744 (B), and D830 (C), with fluorine substitutions at the *para-* and *meta-*positions in the R1 phenyl group of D737, respectively. A methyl group in the R2 position was essential for the function of all three compounds.

In a follow-up study, structure–activity relationships of 11 commercially available D737 analogs were reported (McKoy et al., 2014). D744 (Fig. 6.25B) and D830 (Fig. 6.25C), containing fluorine substitutions at the *para-* and *meta-*positions, respectively, in the R1 phenyl group of D737, were found to be more effective than the parent compound in extending the life span and in improving the locomotive ability of Aβ42-expressing flies (McKoy et al., 2014).

Cromolyn Sodium (Disodium Cromoglycate)

Cromolyn sodium (Fig. 6.26) was tested for modulation of Aβ self-assembly based on the rationale that its structure is similar to that of fisetin (Fig. 6.14) (Hori et al., 2015). Furthermore, pharmacological use of cromolyn sodium in asthma and other diseases (Ammit et al., 2009; Castells et al., 2011; Daniels et al., 2013; Ng and Ohlsson, 2012) and its ability to cross the blood–brain barrier after injection in rodent addiction models (Leza et al., 1995; San-Martin-Clark et al., 1993, 1995) provided additional incentives to study the compound in relation to AD.

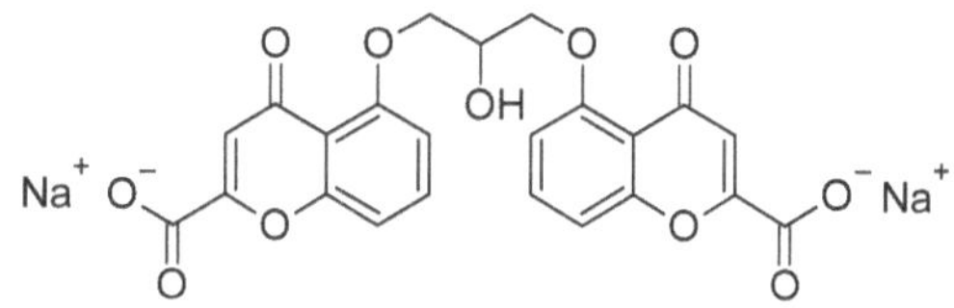

FIGURE 6.26 **Structure of cromolyn sodium.**

ThT assays were used first to assess the role of cromolyn sodium in modulating Aβ40 and Aβ42 self-assembly. Increasing concentrations of cromolyn sodium (5, 50, 500 nM) inhibited ThT fluorescence over 1 h, and TEM confirmed that fibrillization of Aβ42 at 0.2 mg/mL (~44 μM) was inhibited by 500 nM of the compound (Hori et al., 2015). Next, a split luciferase complementation assay (Hashimoto et al., 2011) was used for indirectly monitoring Aβ oligomer formation. HEK293 cells overexpressing both N-terminally or C-terminally luciferase-conjugated Aβ42 showed a significantly lower, dose-dependent luminescence signal when treated with cromolyn sodium compared to untreated cells (Hori et al., 2015). However, cromolyn sodium inhibited intracellular Aβ oligomerization only at concentrations >10 μM in cells expressing the split luciferase system. Addition of cromolyn sodium to preformed luciferase-conjugated Aβ oligomers did not abrogate the luminescence signal. Altogether, the authors concluded that cromolyn sodium prevented Aβ self-assembly into high-order oligomers or fibrils, but could not dissociate preexisting assemblies (Hori et al., 2015).

To extend these findings in vivo, APP/PS1 mice were treated with increasing doses of cromolyn sodium (1.05, 2.1, 3.15 mg/kg), injected daily intraperitoneally (Hori et al., 2015). A 7-day treatment of mice with 2.1 or 3.15 mg/kg cromolyn sodium significantly reduced buffer-soluble Aβx–40 and Aβx–42 species by >50%. Treating mice with the highest dose of cromolyn sodium, 3.15 mg/kg, also led to significantly lower concentrations of "detergent-resistant" Aβ (Aβx–40 and Aβx–42) species, extracted sequentially in buffers containing 2% Triton or 2% SDS, than in control animals treated with phosphate-buffered saline. In contrast, in mice treated with cromolyn sodium, levels of insoluble Aβ species extracted in formic acid, and the overall Aβ plaque burden assessed by immunohistochemistry, were unaffected by the treatment. Because cromolyn sodium treatment only lowered soluble Aβ levels and did not affect insoluble Aβ burden in APP/PS1 mouse brain treated for 1 week, the authors concluded that cromolyn sodium predominantly modulated Aβ aggregation rather than dissociating preformed Aβ assemblies, similar to their in vitro findings (Hori et al., 2015). Reduction of the concentration of soluble Aβ would be expected to induce disaggregation of plaques, but such disaggregation was not observed, leaving the in vivo mechanism of action of cromolyn sodium unclear.

Because treatment with cromolyn sodium decreased the amount of soluble Aβ rather than aggregated species in mice, the authors measured soluble Aβ species in the hippocampal interstitial fluid (ISF) using an in vivo microdialysis system (Hori et al., 2015). Treating the APP/PS1 mice with cromolyn sodium at 3.15 mg/kg daily for 1 week decreased ISF Aβx–40 by 30% (control, 387 pM; cromolyn-treated mice, 283 pM). ISF Aβx–42 and Aβ oligomers followed a similar trend, but the changes were not statistically significant.

Besides modulating Aβ assembly, cromolyn sodium reportedly enhanced microglial activation and microglia-mediated Aβ clearance in vivo. These postulates were based on a 50% reduction in Aβ half-life in ISF of mice treated with cromolyn sodium compared with that in control mice, and a higher percentage of overlapping immunoreactivity of microglia and Aβ in brain sections of mice treated with 3.15 mg/kg cromolyn sodium compared with untreated animals. These findings were supported by tissue-culture experiments in which cromolyn-sodium-treated microglia cleared Aβ40 or Aβ42 levels dose dependently after 16 h. Microglia treated with 1 mM cromolyn sodium decreased Aβ40 or Aβ42 levels 1.5-fold or 2-fold, respectively, more efficiently than untreated cells. Thus, the combination of in vivo and in vitro results suggests that cromolyn sodium may modulate Aβ self-assembly and promote microglial activation and resultant Aβ clearance (Hori et al., 2015).

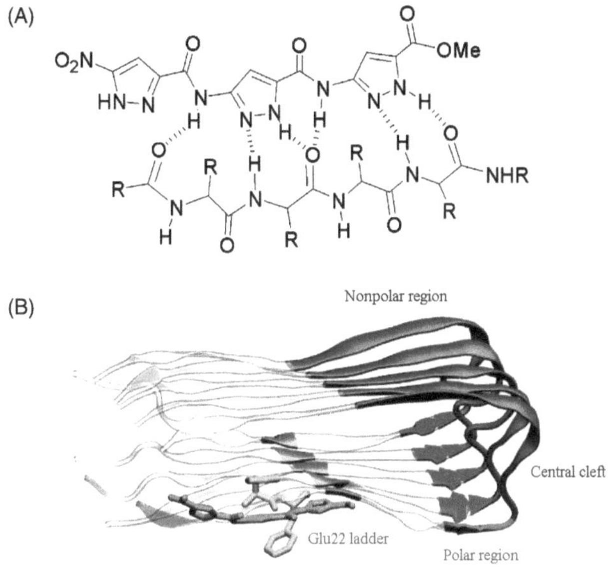

FIGURE 6.27 **Interaction of aminopyrazole trimers with an extended β-strand.** (A) Hydrogen-bonding interactions of an aminopyrazole trimer with Aβ(17–21). (B) Aβ42 fibrils stacked as a pentameric unit. Aβ42 fibril structure was determined by NMR (Lührs et al., 2005). Four regions likely to interact with C-terminally extended aminopyrazole trimers are indicated in *dark gray*. The aminopyrazole moiety and the interacting phenylalanine residues are shown in *light gray stick models*, respectively. *Adapted with permission from Hochdörffer K, März-Berberich J, Nagel-Steger L, Epple M, Meyer-Zaika W, Horn AH, Sticht H, Sinha S, Bitan G, Schrader T: Rational design of β-sheet ligands against Aβ42-induced toxicity,* J Am Chem Soc *133:4348–4358, 2011; Copyright 2011 American Chemical Society.*

Aminopyrazole Derivatives

Aminopyrazole derivatives are a class of rationally designed, β-sheet-binding, small molecules with specific hydrogen bonding donor–acceptor–donor configurations that interact complementarily with hydrogen bonding groups of a peptide in a β-sheet configuration (Kirsten and Schrader, 1997; Schrader and Kirsten, 1996). As such, aminopyrazole derivatives were shown initially to stabilize β-sheet structures by forming cooperative hydrogen bonds (Schrader and Kirsten, 1996). An example of such interactions is presented in Fig. 6.27A. Since then, several different aminopyrazole-containing derivatives have been generated and tested with the aim of increasing their length for providing more hydrogen bonding or π-stacking groups for interactions with β-sheet peptide (Hellmert et al., 2015; Hochdörffer et al., 2011; Kroth et al., 2012; Rzepecki et al., 2003, 2004; Rzepecki and Schrader, 2005). For example, with consideration of complementary binding sites on the Aβ42 protofilament structure determined previously by NMR (Lührs et al., 2005), also shown in Fig. 6.27B, "trimeric" aminopyrazoles were designed to feature various C-terminal extensions (Hochdörffer et al., 2011). These extended "trimers" (Fig. 6.28) were designed to bestow additional favorable interacting groups besides hydrogen bonding and π-stacking by targeting specific Aβ regions (Fig. 6.27B):

- For binding to the polar Aβ42 region spanning residues Glu22–Lys28 (Fig. 6.27B), carboxylate and ammonium groups were placed close to the aminopyrazoles, for example, trimer-diamine, trimer-GABA-OH, and trimer TEG-OH (Fig. 6.28).

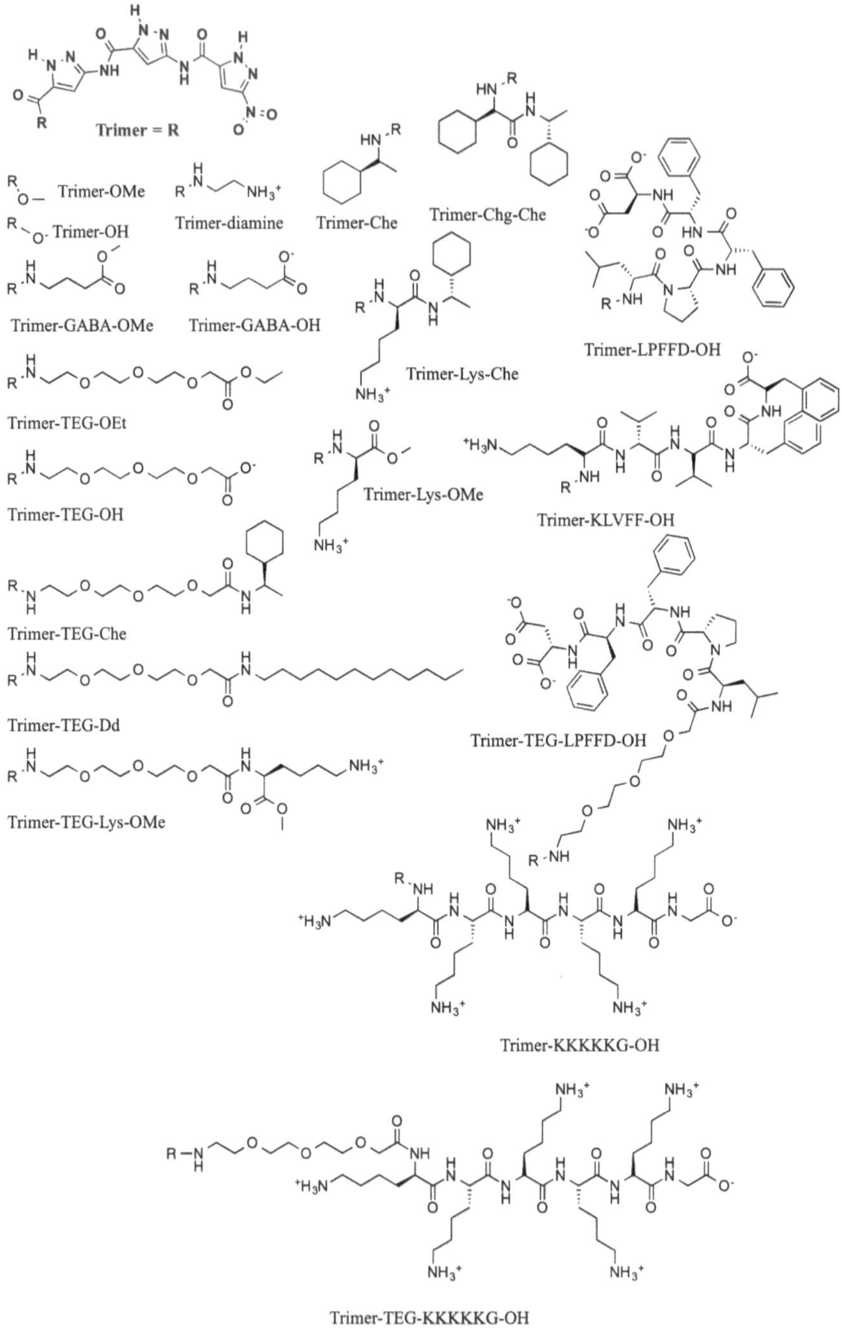

FIGURE 6.28 **Structures of unprotected aminopyrazole trimer derivatives.** Small neutral, anionic, and cationic moieties, and nonpolar and TEG-spacer groups are shown on the left. Peptidic attachments are shown on the right. R = aminopyrazole trimer moiety.

- For binding to the Glu22 ladder (Fig. 6.27B) formed by the Glu22 side chains on adjacent cross-β-sheet layers, pentacationic groups (eg, five Lys residues) were added, for example, trimer-KKKKKG-OH and trimer-TEG-KKKKKG-OH (Fig. 6.28).
- For potential binding to the central U-shaped turn of Aβ joining its polar and nonpolar regions (Fig. 6.27B), a triethyleneglycol unit was added for extended van der Waals interactions, for example, trimer-TEG-OEt, trimer-TEG-OH, trimer-TEG-Che, trimer-TEG-Dd, and trimer-TEG-Lys-OMe (Fig. 6.28).
- For binding to the nonpolar residues Ile31–Val36 (Fig. 6.27B), flexible, branched hydrocarbons such as cyclohexylglycine were included (for hydrophobic and dispersive interactions), for example, trimer-Che, trimer-Lys-Che, trimer-TEG-Che, and trimer-Chg-Che (Fig. 6.28).
- Small peptides from the CHC also were attached to aminopyrazole trimers for promoting self-recognition, for example, trimer-LPFFD-OH, trimer-KLVFF-OH, and trimer-TEG-LPFFD-OH (Fig. 6.28).

Overall, the derivatives were divided into type A (polar), type B (very polar), and type C (nonpolar). Molecular dynamics simulations suggested that extended aminopyrazole trimers interacted with the Aβ42 fibril structure as expected (Hochdörffer et al., 2011). To confirm the simulations experimentally, some of the designed aminopyrazole derivatives were synthesized and tested in ThT, CD, TEM, and cytotoxicity assays. Of all the tested aminopyrazole trimers, the trimer TEG-K-OMe (Fig. 6.28) suppressed Aβ fibril formation most efficiently. However, of all tested trimer aminopyrazoles, this ligand was found to form colloidal aggregates. Colloidal aggregates have been reported to inhibit amyloid formation in a nonspecific manner (Feng et al., 2008) and therefore are not considered viable therapeutics candidates.

In ThT assays assessing disaggregation, the percentage of remaining ThT fluorescence for most trimer derivatives was identical to the final ThT fluorescence in aggregation assays (Table 6.4). This observation led the authors to conclude that aminopyrazoles functioned in a reversible fashion, ultimately reaching an open equilibrium where the most thermodynamically stable complexes with Aβ were favored (Hochdörffer et al., 2011).

Generally, the various trimer aminopyrazoles did not prevent fibrillization but caused formation of compact and thin fibrils of 5–10 nm diameter and 800 nm length, in some cases with

TABLE 6.4 Reported Experimental Results of Aminopyrazole Derivatives

	Glu22 ladder (polylysines)	Polar region (single charged groups)	Nonpolar region (extended alkyl residues)	Central pore (TEG derivatives)
ThT (inhibition)[a]	24%	25%	27–50%	48–54%
ThT (disaggregation)[a]	28%	21%	35–62%	42–68%
TEM	Amorphous material	Unstructured material and thin bent fibrils	Thick twisted fibrils (70 × 600 nm)	Thin, delicate structures
MTT[b]	$IC_{50} > 80\ \mu M$	$IC_{50} \geq 22\ \mu M$	$IC_{50} \geq 3\ \mu M$	$IC_{50} \geq 35\ \mu M$

[a]*Percent ThT fluorescence of a mixture containing 10 μM Aβ42 and 60 μM of an aminopyrazole derivative.*
[b]*PC-12 cells treated with 10 μM Aβ42 and aminopyrazoles at 0.3–100 μM.*
From Hochdörffer K, März-Berberich J, Nagel-Steger L, Epple M, Meyer-Zaika W, Horn AH, Sticht H, Sinha S, Bitan G, Schrader T: Rational design of β-Sheet ligands against $A\beta_{42}$-induced toxicity, J Am Chem Soc *133:4348–4358, 2011.*

no typical helical twist (Hochdörffer et al., 2011). For example, presence of trimer-TEG-OH or trimer-OMe caused formation of delicate thin fibrillar structures with no helical twist (Table 6.4). The authors postulated that the compact nature of these structures prevented ThT binding.

In cytotoxicity assays, all compounds were screened at 100 μM using the MTT assay in differentiated PC-12 cells. The compounds by themselves did not reduce cell viability at this concentration. When treated for 24 h with 10 μM Aβ42 in the presence of 100 μM of each compound, the cells were completely protected against Aβ42-induced toxicity by most of the derivatives except for trimer-OMe and trimer-OH, which only increased viability by <10% (Hochdörffer et al., 2011).

Two important binding motifs greatly enhanced the β-sheet-breaker ability of the aminopyrazoles. Lipophilic moieties interacted with nonpolar amino acid clusters between Ile31 and Val36, and the oligo-Lys residues interacted with the Glu22 ladder.

Ruthenium Complexes

Messori et al. (2013) used the rationale that metal-containing complexes, such as platinum–phenanthrolines, bind Aβ42, interfere with its self-assembly, and protect against Aβ42-induced cytotoxicity (Barnham et al., 2008; Kenche and Barnham, 2011; Valensin et al., 2011). However, they decided to test various ruthenium complexes because they posited that ruthenium-containing compounds are less cytotoxic than platinum complexes (Messori et al., 2013). Ruthenium compounds have affinity toward His residues and may modulate Aβ42 assembly by interacting with His6, His13, and His14 residues (Messori et al., 2013). Three representative ruthenium compounds were tested, namely NAMI-A (Alessio et al., 2004), KP1019 (Hartinger et al., 2008), and PMRU20 (Mura et al., 2005). NAMI-A ([ImH][*trans*-$RuCl_4$(DMSO-S)(Im)], where DMSO is dimethyl sulfoxide and Im is imidazole; Fig. 6.29A) and KP1019 (indazolium *trans*-[tetrachlorobis(^{1}H-indazole)ruthenate(III)]; Fig. 6.29B) are two experimental anticancer compounds. PMRU20 (2-aminothiazolium [*trans*-tetrachlorobis(2-aminothiazole) ruthenate(III)]; Fig. 6.29C), which is a relatively new compound, was prepared and characterized by the same group (Mura et al., 2005).

The activity of the three compounds was tested against Aβ42-induced cytotoxicity using the MTT assay in rat primary cortical neurons. PMRU20 was active whereas NAMI-A was poorly active and KP1019 was nearly inactive in the MTT assay (Messori et al., 2013). To

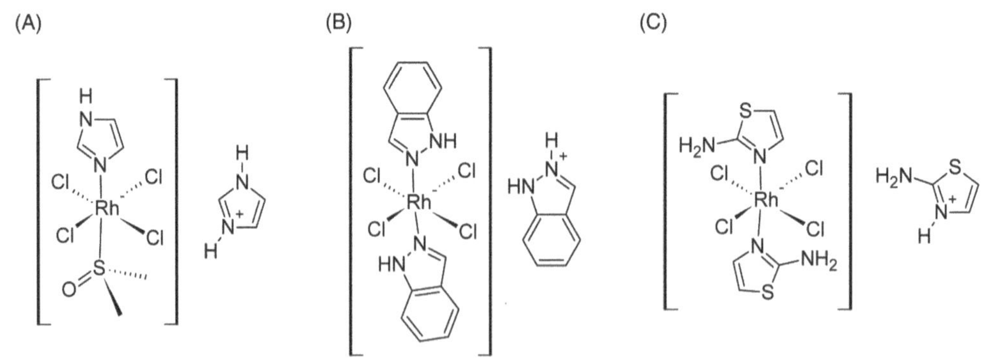

FIGURE 6.29 Structures of ruthenium complexes, including NAMI-A (A), KP1019 (B), and PMRU20 (C).

test whether the protective effect of PMRU20 was due to the metal-containing center of the compound and not due to the antioxidant properties that were shown for aminothiazole derivatives (Uchikawa et al., 1996), its counter-ion, 2-aminothiazole, was tested in the presence of Aβ42. Because 2-aminothiazole alone was ineffective, the authors concluded that the protective effects of the compound were primarily due to the metal-containing center. However, using only the aminothiazole counter-ion in these experiments does not necessarily demonstrate that the protective activity is specific to the metal-containing center of the molecule.

The authors used the ThT assays to compare the effects of the ruthenium compounds on Aβ42 aggregation. PMRU20 addition at twofold molar excess to Aβ42 caused a large decrease in ThT fluorescence after 10 h of incubation, whereas NAMI-A was less effective and KP1019 reacted with ThT and precipitated. In contrast to the aforementioned report, a different study found that KP1019 at ≥0.5 equivalents to Aβ42 (5 μM in the assay) limited ThT fluorescence and caused formation of amorphous Aβ42 assemblies observed by TEM (Jones et al., 2015).

To explore the binding site of KP1019, reactivity of antibodies 6E10 and 4G8 with Aβ42 in the presence of KP1019 was assessed (Jones et al., 2015). At a 1:1 KP1019-to-Aβ42 ratio over 24, 48, or 72 h incubation, 6E10 still bound Aβ42. However, at 2:1, 4:1, or 10:1 ratios, 6E10 reactivity was reduced, possibly due to saturated binding of KP1019 at the Aβ42 N-terminus. In contrast, 4G8 reactivity to the peptide was unaffected on dot blots over time, suggesting that the binding site of KP1019 was not near the CHC of Aβ42. Native PAGE and Western blotting showed that increasing concentrations of KP1019 (0.25–2 molar equivalents to Aβ) caused disappearance of monomeric Aβ and small oligomeric Aβ42 bands but increased the intensity of high-molecular-weight species between 37 and 250 kDa, and higher aggregates that did not enter the gel. These results combined with TEM experiments showed that KP1019 drove formation of large Aβ aggregates but prevented formation of small oligomeric Aβ42 assemblies. Induction of formation of high-molecular-weight assemblies might have been responsible for the change in 6E10 reactivity. When preincubated with Aβ42 from 5 min to 24 h, KP1019 rescued SH-SY5Y cells from Aβ42 toxicity when used at ≥0.1 molar equivalents to Aβ42 (Jones et al., 2015).

Molecular Tweezers

Molecular tweezers are supramolecular compounds prepared originally by Klärner et al. (1996). They have a rigid hydrocarbon skeleton comprising alternating aromatic and aliphatic rings. The aliphatic rings are constrained in norbornene-like structures forcing the molecules into a horseshoe-shape structure (Fig. 6.30A). This structure creates a high electron density in the cavity of the tweezers (Fig. 6.30B), making them welcoming "hosts" for electron-deficient "guests" (Klärner et al., 1996, 2000). Attachment of negatively charged groups, for example, phosphonates and phosphates by Schrader and coworkers to the central aromatic ring of the tweezers has rendered them water soluble, allowing examination of potential biological applications and leading to the discovery that these compounds bound with low micromolar affinity and high selectivity to Lys residues (Fokkens et al., 2005; Talbiersky et al., 2008). The molecular tweezers also bound Arg, yet with 5–10 times lower affinity, and did not bind to other amino acid residues or small, positively charged biological cofactors (Fokkens et al., 2005).

The selectivity of the molecular tweezers for Lys (and Arg) is due to inclusion of the alkyl chain of these residues inside the cavity of the tweezer, facilitating hydrophobic interaction

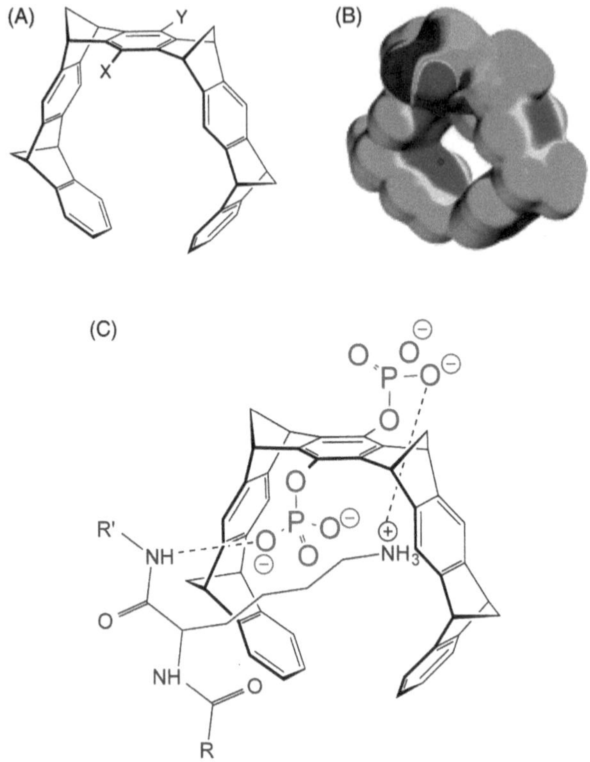

FIGURE 6.30 **Molecular tweezers.** (A) A schematic structure of water-soluble molecular tweezers. At least one of the X and Y groups must be negatively charged. (B) Electrostatic potential surface showing the high electron density inside the tweezer cavity. Color code: −25 kcal/mol: *dark gray*; +25 kcal/mol: *black*. (C) Schematic structure of the complex between CLR01 and Lys. *Source: Part B, adapted from Fokkens et al. (2005).*

between the tweezer's side arms and the butylene chain of Lys, and simultaneous strong electrostatic attraction between the ε-NH_3^+ group of Lys and the negatively charged groups of the molecular tweezer (Fig. 6.30C).

Importantly, binding of the molecular tweezers to their target amino acids is labile and has a high on–off rate (Bier et al., 2013). Our group discovered that these characteristics allow the molecular tweezers to disrupt selectively the abnormal self-assembly process of amyloid-forming proteins without affecting normal proteins, even though their binding is not selective to a particular protein (Attar and Bitan, 2014). This somewhat counterintuitive selectivity profile is due to the difference between normal protein and abnormal proteins assemblies. Stable proteins, whose structure was optimized by millions of years of evolution, are unaffected by the gentle binding of the molecular tweezers, whereas the weak forces mediating formation of metastable oligomers and nuclei, which (mis)fold considerably more slowly and through a rougher energy landscape (Yu et al., 2015), are disrupted by the molecular tweezers' binding. Moreover, there is a profound difference between freely accessible Lys on unstructured proteins, which can all be complexed by CLR01—the derivative in which both polar groups are phosphates (depicted in Fig. 6.30C), and folded proteins whose surface often does not allow the sterically demanding tweezer to approach a Lys residue close enough for binding. This was evidenced by X-ray crystallography, isothermal titration calorimetry, and molecular dynamics simulations of the complex between the molecular tweezer CLR01, which has two phosphate groups attached to the central aromatic ring (Fig. 6.30C), and the small adapter protein, 14-3-3, in which only 5 of 17 surface Lys residues were complexed by CLR01 (Bier et al., 2013). In contrast, in unfolded proteins, virtually all lysine residues are expected to be accessible to the molecular tweezers.

ThT fluorescence and TEM showed that CLR01 prevented fibril formation by Aβ40 or Aβ42, tau, and six other disease-associated proteins (Sinha et al., 2011). Additional experiments showed that CLR01 inhibited formation of Aβ42 oligomers in dot blots using the oligomer-specific antibody, A11 (Kayed et al., 2003), attenuated the transition from an unstructured conformation to β-sheet measured (using CD spectroscopy), and prevented formation of large aggregates observed by DLS. ThT and TEM studies also showed that CLR01 dissociated preformed fibrils of Aβ40 or Aβ42 (Sinha et al., 2011). Recently, using IM–MS, CLR01 was shown to directly decrease the formation of Aβ42 hexamers and dodecamers (Zheng et al., 2015a). Previously, these oligomers have been shown to form selectively by Aβ42 (Bernstein et al., 2009; Bitan et al., 2003), and dodecamers were found to correlate with AD pathology in human brain and transgenic mouse brain (Gong et al., 2003; Lesné et al., 2006).

The predicted binding sites for CLR01 in Aβ are Lys16 and Lys28, and to a lower extent Arg5. Binding to these three sites was confirmed by two independent methods—2D heteronuclear solution-state NMR, and top-down, electron-capture dissociation–mass spectrometry (Sinha et al., 2011). Lys16 and Lys28 were found to be the primary and secondary binding sites, respectively, because the former is exposed to the solvent, whereas the latter is involved in a salt bridge with Glu22 and/or Asp23 (Lazo et al., 2005).

Experiments using the MTT-reduction assay in differentiated PC-12 cells showed that CLR01 prevented the toxicity induced by 20 μM Aβ40 or 10 μM Aβ42 oligomers with $IC_{50} = 14 \pm 11$ and 52 ± 18 μM, respectively (Sinha et al., 2011). In the same cells, inhibition of 5 μM Aβ42 toxicity was achieved with $IC_{50} = 9 \pm 4$ μM in the LDH assay (unpublished data), likely reflecting the fact that decreasing the protein's concentration reduced the concentration of toxic oligomers nonlinearly.

Subsequent experiments in rat or mouse primary neurons showed that CLR01 inhibited synaptotoxic effects of Aβ42 (Attar et al., 2012), including hippocampal dendritic-spine retraction, reduction in frequency and amplitude of basal synaptic activity, and suppression of LTP, a cellular correlate of learning and memory.

To test the hypothesis that CLR01 would disrupt aberrant protein self-assembly but not normal assembly, we compared the protein–CLR01 concentration ratio needed for inhibiting aggregation of amyloid proteins to that required for interfering with a normal assembly process—tubulin polymerization. In experiments examining what ratio would be necessary for inhibition of amyloidogenic proteins, the protein–CLR01 concentration ratios needed for complete inhibition of different amyloid proteins were mostly in the range 1:0.1 to 1:3 (Lopes et al., 2015; Prabhudesai et al., 2012; Sinha et al., 2011). These concentration ratios had no effect on tubulin polymerization. Only at a tubulin:CLR01 concentration ratio of 1:55 was some disruption observed, but not complete inhibition of the process (Attar et al., 2014). Schrader and coworkers also have tested CLR01 as an inhibitor of enzymes containing key Lys residues at or near the active site. The enzyme:CLR01 ratios needed for inhibiting the activity of alcohol dehydrogenase and PARP-1 were 1:865 (Talbiersky et al., 2008) and 1:1435 (T. Schrader, personal communication), respectively.

The selectivity of CLR01 also was demonstrated in cultured cells, in which CLR01 itself reduced cell viability only at concentrations 1–3 orders of magnitude higher than those needed for inhibition of toxicity by Aβ or other amyloidogenic proteins. CLR01 toxicity depended on the cell type tested. For example, in differentiated PC-12 cells, no toxicity was observed at ≤200 μM CLR01, and ~15% viability reduction (MTT assay) occurred at 400 μM (Sinha et al., 2011). In recent experiments, no reduction in viability (XTT assay) was found at ≤500 μM in the HIV reporter cell line TZM-bl (a HeLa cell line that enables quantitative analysis of HIV using β-gal or luciferase as reporter genes) (Lump et al., 2015).

CLR01 was evaluated in the 3 × Tg mouse model of AD (Oddo et al., 2003). Mixed-gender, 15-month-old mice were treated for 28 days with 0.04 mg/kg per day CLR01 in saline (vehicle), or with vehicle alone, applied subcutaneously, continuously using osmotic minipumps (Attar et al., 2012). Immunohistochemistry of brain sections of vehicle-treated mice using antibody 6E10 showed extracellular amyloid plaques deposited predominantly in the subiculum and CA1 regions of the hippocampus, as reported previously (Oddo et al., 2003). In addition, the mice showed neurofibrillary tangles detected by the anti-p-tau mAb AT8, predominantly in the CA1 and CA3 regions.

Mice treated with CLR01 showed a significant decrease in Aβ in multiple brain regions. Similarly, reduction in AT8-positive p-tau was observed in the CA1 (33%) and CA3 (46%) regions (Attar et al., 2012). Therapeutic effects of CLR01 were also observed in animal models of other diseases (Ferreira et al., 2014; Prabhudesai et al., 2012), and CLR01 was shown to have a high safety margin in mice (Attar et al., 2014). In the context of AD, the ability of the compound to affect both Aβ and tau is particularly attractive.

Large Molecules That Modulate Aβ Assembly and Toxicity

In this section, cyclic molecules such as cucurbit[7]uril, metal-containing complexes such as POMs and helical metallocomplexes, and artificial molecular chaperones are discussed. These compounds are mainly experimental, with most data available only in vitro and in cell culture.

Three important potential concerns must be considered, especially in relation to the compounds described later:

1. Are their molecular weights prohibitive of blood–brain barrier penetration?
2. Do these compounds form colloids?
3. If they form colloids, does the colloidal mechanism of inhibition apply?

As discussed previously in section: Aminopyrazole Derivatives, the colloidal mechanism of inhibition (Feng et al., 2008) is relevant when assessing whether certain modulators or inhibitors of Aβ assembly have the potential to become drug candidates. This is important because excess of other proteins, such as albumin, can prevent the colloidal inhibition of amyloid assembly by sequestering the colloid aggregates (Feng et al., 2008). This mechanism can be tested by addition of a nonionic detergent, such as Triton X-100, in the system. Detergents disrupt the colloidal aggregates and thus prevent their nonspecific, promiscuous inhibitory activity toward an enzyme, for example, β-lactamase. Assaying for the detergent-sensitive inhibition of β-lactamase activity thus can be used to determine which molecules likely act through a colloidal mechanism of inhibition (Coan and Shoichet, 2007; Feng et al., 2005, 2008; McGovern et al., 2003). Recently, electrospray ionization–ion-mobility spectrometry–mass spectrometry (ESI–IMS–MS) was used successfully to identify the colloidal mechanism of inhibition in the context of Aβ and amylin (Young et al., 2014, 2015a,b).

Cucurbit[7]uril

Cucurbituril designates a family of macrocyclic supramolecular compounds that derives its name from its physical resemblance to a gourd or pumpkin (botanical family Cucurbitaceae) and to a cucurbit, a vessel connected to a distillation alembic used by Persian alchemists (Mandadapu et al., 2014). The rigid and symmetrical cucurbituril structure is made of two identical hydrophilic portals surrounded by partially negative carbonyl groups, and a hydrophobic cavity (Fig. 6.31) (Gürbüz et al., 2015; Mandadapu et al., 2014). Nanomaterials, including nanoparticles, nanocomposites, vesicles, and rods, can be prepared by altering the cavity size of cucurbituril homologs (Gürbüz et al., 2015). Cucurbituril homologs take the cucurbit[*n*]uril ($n = 5$–8, 10, 14) composition (Mandadapu et al., 2014). Of the different homologs, cucurbit[7]uril binds specifically and avidly ($K_a = 10^4$–$10^7\ M^{-1}$) to phenylalanine residues in peptides and proteins (Chinai et al., 2011; Mandadapu et al., 2014). It was hypothesized that capturing the phenylalanine residues by cucurbit[7]uril would block phenylalanine-mediated hydrophobic interactions in amyloid proteins (Lee et al., 2014). Effectively, this interaction could prevent amyloid fibrillization because phenylalanine residues may initiate and enhance hydrophobic clustering in amyloid proteins (Vivekanandan et al., 2011).

Based on the aforementioned rationale, cucurbit[7]uril (1163 Da) was used to target Aβ40 or Aβ42 self-assembly (Lee et al., 2014). Cucurbit[7]uril was found to inhibit Aβ self-assembly effectively by increasing the kinetic energy barrier to fibrillization. The authors tested

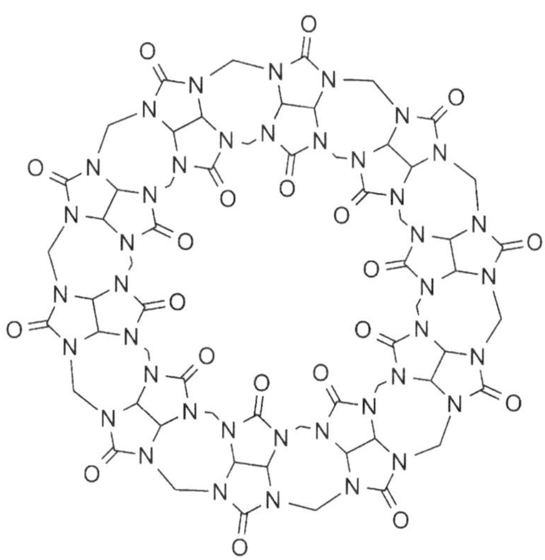

FIGURE 6.31 Cucurbit[n]uril has a rigid and symmetrical structure which is made of two identical hydrophilic portals surrounded by partially negative carbonyl groups and a hydrophobic cavity.

cucurbit[7]uril in a ThT fluorescence assay first. Without cucurbit[7]uril, Aβ40 aggregation led to an increase in the ThT fluorescence signal to a plateau in 4 h. When 50-fold or 100-fold excess cucurbit[7]uril was added to Aβ40, Aβ40 fibrils were not observed (ThT and TEM). In experiments with Aβ42, the time-dependent ThT fluorescence intensity decreased with increasing concentration ratios of added cucurbit[7]uril, thus showing slowing down of Aβ42 fibrillization. In accordance with the ThT experiments, the morphology of Aβ40 and Aβ42, assessed by TEM, changed from fibrillar to amorphous aggregates with increasing concentrations of cucurbit[7]uril. However, cucurbit[7]uril was effective only when added before initiation of fibrillization.

Using fluorescence titration, the K_a of interactions between cucurbit[7]uril and Aβ40 was calculated to be $7.1 \times 10^4\ M^{-1}$ (Lee et al., 2014). Structure–activity relationship analysis using Aβ40 analogs, in which the Phe, Tyr, or His residues were substituted by Ala, showed that the three Phe residues (at positions 4, 19, and 20) contributed equally to the interaction with cucurbit[7]uril. Next, cucurbit[7]uril was examined for its ability to protect SH-SY5Y cells from Aβ-mediated cytotoxicity using the MTT reduction assay. Aβ40 or Aβ42 fibrils reduced SH-SY5Y cell viability to ~75% of control. Applying cucurbit[7]uril at 50-fold or 100-fold molar excess to Aβ40 and at 500-fold molar excess to Aβ42 restored the viability of treated SH-SY5Y cells to values comparable to untreated cells, 90 and 100%, respectively.

Helical Metallocomplexes

Stereochemistry and enantioselectivity importantly determine the therapeutic efficacy of a drug. Generally, one of any two hypothetical enantiomers of a compound is therapeutically active whereas the other is inactive or likely bears unwanted side effects (Nakanishi et al., 2004; Schapira et al., 2009). Considering stereochemistry and enantioselectivity, two triple helical, dinuclear, chiral metallosupramolecular complexes were designed and synthesized (Li et al., 2014). The aim was to modulate Aβ aggregation (Li et al., 2014). The study rationale was that these metallohelicates could bind to α-helical Aβ regions and prevent or modulate Aβ oligomerization and self-assembly. The authors postulated that the α-helical structure of these complexes could target early stages of aggregation at α/β discordant Aβ stretches—segments predicted to form a β-strand but preferentially form an α-helix (Kallberg et al., 2001). An α/β discordant segment in Aβ spans amino acids 13–23 (Kallberg et al., 2001).

The designed helicate complexes were thermodynamically stable and composed of single enantiomers of monometallic units connected by organic linkers: Λ1, Δ1 and Λ2, Δ2 (Fig. 6.32). Fluorescence screening and other biophysical and biochemical techniques were used to test these compounds. In the fluorescence assay, Aβ42 fused to enhanced cyan fluorescent protein (ECFP) through a short linker sequence (Aβ–ECFP) was used to measure fluorescence, which depends on the fused Aβ42's folding and solubility. Similar to the Aβ–GFP system (see section: D737), ECFP fluoresces when it folds normally but fails to fluoresce if the fused Aβ42 aggregates or precipitates. Thus, blocking or preventing Aβ42 aggregation would allow normal ECFP folding and resultant ECFP fluorescence. The design of this probe system follows the original work of Hecht and coworkers, who used Aβ fused to GFP for the same purpose (Kim et al., 2006; Wurth et al., 2002).

When testing the compounds, complex 1 ($[Fe_2L^1_3]Cl_4$) was more potent than complex 2 ($[Fe_2L^2_3]Cl_4$) and enantiomers Λ1 ($\Lambda Fe,S_C$-$[Fe_2L^1_3]Cl_4$) and Λ2 ($\Lambda Fe,R_C$-$[Fe_2L^2_3]Cl_4$) were more effective than their corresponding mirror images, Δ1 ($\Delta Fe,R_C$-$[Fe_2L^1_3]Cl_4$) and Δ2

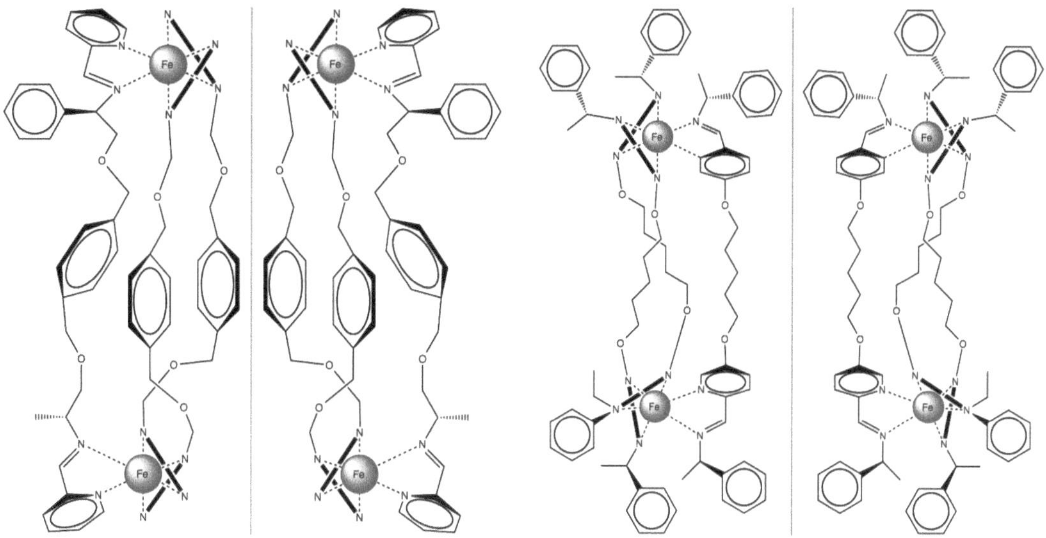

Λ1 Δ1 Λ2 Δ2

FIGURE 6.32 Structures of helical metallocomplexes, Λ1 (ΛFe,SC-[Fe2L13]Cl4), Δ1 (ΔFe,RC-[Fe2L13]Cl4), Λ2 (ΛFe,RC-[Fe2L23]Cl4), and Δ2 (ΔFe,SC-[Fe2L23]Cl4).

(ΔFe,S_C-[$Fe_2L_3^2$]Cl_4). Thus, less polar complexes (complex 1) were more effective than polar complexes, ΛFe enantiomers were more effective than the ΔFe enantiomers, and ThT fluorescence plunged to the lowest values with equimolar concentration of metal complexes. The latter finding was consistent with the postulate that Aβ40 and metal complexes interacted at an equimolar ratio. Thus, the authors speculated that the metal complexes could interact with monomeric Aβ before early oligomers formed. They used ESI–MS experiments to show masses corresponding to Aβ–metal complexes of a 1:1 ratio. AFM and CD data also showed that Λ1 and Λ2 prevented Aβ40 fibrillization more effectively than the corresponding mirror images, Δ1 and Δ2. These findings were supported by dialysis experiments, which showed enrichment of Λ1 and Λ2 in dialysis tubes containing Aβ40, suggesting preferential binding of the Λ compounds to Aβ40. NMR experiments showed that complex Λ2 interacted with Phe19 and Phe20. Similarly, less polar complexes (complex 1) were more effective than polar complexes in destabilizing preformed Aβ40 fibrils. The most effective complex, Λ1, dissociated Aβ40 fibrils with IC_{50} = 1.97 μM. Again in these experiments, ΛFe enantiomers were more effective than ΔFe enantiomers (Li et al., 2014).

Because the complexes modulated Aβ assembly, the authors postulated that they could also inhibit Aβ-induced cytotoxicity, and measured their effect using the MTT assay. Complex 1 or 2 (1–5 μM) inhibited Aβ40-induced cytotoxicity dose dependently and did not affect cell viability on their own; aged Aβ40 was used at 5 μM in these experiments. ΛFe enantiomers were more effective than the ΔFe enantiomers, in agreement with their stronger ability to modulate Aβ40 aggregation. In addition, ΛFe enantiomers inhibited Aβ40-mediated intracellular calcium changes more effectively than ΔFe enantiomers.

To test whether the complexes could cross the blood–brain barrier, mice were injected with the compounds and levels of CSF iron were measured, as an indirect indicator for complexes, using inductively coupled plasma–mass spectrometry (ICP–MS) analysis. Iron accumulation was more than that in control mice by 1.5 and 0.7% for complexes 1 and 2, respectively. To draw solid conclusions, however, experiments should measure the complexes directly in the CSF.

In contrast to the aforementioned study, stereospecific interactions cannot be generalized to other enantiomeric molecules potentially interacting with Aβ. As an example, a previous study (Sood et al., 2009), which assessed the effects of enantiomeric trifluoromethyl-indolyl-acetic acid ethyl esters on Aβ self-assembly, found that both enantiomers inhibited Aβ self-assembly with apparently similar potencies, suggesting lack of stereospecific interactions between these small molecules and Aβ (Sood et al., 2009).

Polyoxometalates

POMs are synthetic, nonbiological clusters of oxygen anions and certain transition metals (especially Mo, W, and V). POMs can be used to construct versatile nanoscale molecular structures with important catalytic, electronic, magnetic, interactive, or structural properties (Hasenknopf, 2005; Miras et al., 2012). POMs are effective antiviral, antibiotic, and anticancer agents (Leon et al., 2014; Wang et al., 2014b,c). Most of the transition metals within the composition of POMs are generally toxic and tolerated only at low concentrations (Barceloux, 1999; Imtiaz et al., 2015; Okamoto et al., 2015; Vyskocil and Viau, 1999; Witten et al., 2012). Despite the toxicity of transition metals within POMs, Qu and coworkers recently assessed POMs for modulating Aβ aggregation and fibrillization in a number of articles (Gao et al., 2014, 2015; Geng et al., 2011; Li et al., 2013a,b). Their rationale for testing POMs for this purpose included POMs' catalytic, electronic, and structural versatility and researchers' knowledge of how to control POMs' physicochemical properties (Rhule et al., 1998); previous work showing their interaction with proteins (Judd et al., 2001; Sarafianos et al., 1996; Seko et al., 2009) and their structural similarity to fullerene derivatives that have antiamyloid activity (Geng et al., 2011; Kim and Lee, 2003).

Initially, a screening method based on bacterial expression of Aβ fused to ECFP (Kim et al., 2006) was used to test different POMs with Wells–Dawson ($K_8[P_2CoW_{17}O_{61}]$), Keggin ($\alpha Na_9H[SiW_9O_{34}]$), or Anderson ($Na_5[IMo_6O_{24}]$) structures (Geng et al., 2011). The Wells–Dawson phosphotungstate ($K_8[P_2CoW_{17}O_{61}]$; POMD–Co) inhibited Aβ aggregation more effectively than the others in the Aβ–ECFP system; POMs with Keggin structure caused moderate to high inhibition of Aβ aggregation; POMs with Anderson structure, for example, $Na_5[IMo_6O_{24}]$, were inactive. The inhibitory effect related to the size and surface charge of the POMs. Thus, POMs with the largest structure and strongest binding affinity to Aβ, commensurate with their electrostatic interactions, were the most active (Geng et al., 2011). Complementary methods such as ThT fluorescence assay, native gel electrophoresis, and TEM also confirmed the initial findings by the Aβ–ECFP aggregation screening (Geng et al., 2011).

The authors next used trypsin digestion, competition experiments using *bis*-ANS, and a shorter Aβ fragment, Aβ12–28 (VHHQKLVFFAEDVGSNK), to investigate how POMs interacted with Aβ (Geng et al., 2011). POMD–Co prevented trypsin digestion of Aβ dose dependently and completely inhibited trypsin digestion at twofold molar excess to Aβ. The authors tested whether POMD–Co could inhibit trypsin digestion of lysozyme under similar conditions. They showed that lysozyme could be digested by trypsin in the presence of

POMD–Co. They concluded that the positively charged Lys or Arg residues of Aβ likely were important in POMD–Co–Aβ interactions (Geng et al., 2011). Further, POMD–Co competed off *bis*-ANS binding to Aβ concentration dose dependently. Thus, the study suggested that POMD–Co could bind close to the *bis*-ANS binding site on Aβ. Reportedly, *bis*-ANS binds to the Aβ CHC near the HHQK segment (Ferrão-Gonzales et al., 2005; LeVine, 2002); thus, the authors postulated the same region as the POMD–Co binding site. POMD–Co also rescued Aβ12–28 from trypsin digestion and competed off *bis*-ANS binding, suggesting that POMD–Co likely binds to His13–Lys16 of Aβ. However, the authors did not test whether POMD–Co could form colloidal aggregates and cause colloidal sequestration (Feng et al., 2008) of Aβ rather than specifically interacting with it, as was discussed also in section: Aminopyrazole Derivatives.

The authors suggested two possible mechanisms whereby POMDs could inhibit Aβ fibrillization. First, POMDs likely bind Aβ monomers, shifting the equilibrium away from oligomerization and fibrillization. Second, POMDs likely block the self-contact points among monomers or among other prefibrillar Aβ assemblies, rendering nucleation and fibrillization less favorable (Geng et al., 2011). The authors postulated that this could be because of the large size and electrostatic interactions of POMD–Co (Geng et al., 2011). Such interactions likely also could sequester Aβ molecules by the colloidal mechanism of inhibition, as described previously (Feng et al., 2008).

After determining the effect of POMs on Aβ self-assembly, the authors tested whether POMs could block Aβ-mediated cytotoxicity in PC-12 cells by the MTT reduction assay. POMs by themselves were nontoxic, and they rescued viability of PC-12 cells to 90%, the level of untreated cells after a 7-day preincubation with Aβ (Geng et al., 2011). This requirement for long preincubation suggests that POMs are not strong inhibitors of Aβ-mediated toxicity.

Because POM–Aβ interactions depended mainly on POM size and nonspecific electrostatic properties, Qu and coworkers aimed to improve POM specificity for Aβ in their following studies (Gao et al., 2015; Li et al., 2013b). One of their approaches was to modify POMs by introducing specific Aβ self-recognition motifs. Thus, the peptide Ac–QKLVFF–NH_2 of Aβ was conjugated to POMD–Co, and the conjugate used to target Aβ40 self-assembly (Li et al., 2013b). This POMD–Co–Aβ(15–20) complex was compared with POMD–Co or the peptide alone using the ThT fluorescence assay. The conjugate, which self-assembles when aqueous solutions of Aβ(15–20) and POMD–Co are mixed and matured at room temperature for 6 h, was approximately twice as effective as either component alone in inhibiting β-sheet formation by Aβ40 (Li et al., 2013b).

In cytotoxicity assays, the POMD–Co–peptide conjugate was nontoxic. Aβ fibrils (10 μM) reduced cell viability to 46%. Addition of POMD–Co–Aβ(15–20) (6 μM), POMD–Co (10 μM), or Aβ15–20 (6 μM) increased the cell viability to 82, 72, or 69%, respectively. Next, the authors conjugated the CR dye to the POMD–Co–Aβ(15–20) complex, and tested the ability of POMD–Co–Aβ(15–20)–CR to affect Aβ fibrillization in murine CSF. Aβ40 incubated with CR in the CSF for 7 days showed birefringent particles by polarized microscopy. Aβ40 samples incubated with POMD–Co–Aβ(15–20)–CR in the CSF under the same conditions showed less CR-positive deposits (Li et al., 2013b). However, the CR component of POMD–Co–Aβ(15–20)–CR could compete with CR binding at the same sites, thus reducing CR fluorescence without affecting fibrils. Moreover, CR was one of the first molecules to show colloidal inhibition (McGovern et al., 2002).

Because POMDs presumably engage the cationic HHQK cluster of Aβ (Geng et al., 2011), it was proposed that the two neighboring His residues of this cluster likely act as specific chelators of POMDs' transition metal ions (such as Ni(II) or Co(II)) to achieve specific Aβ recognition (Gao et al., 2014). They hypothesized that POMDs with a defined His-binding site would greatly inhibit Aβ fibrillization and toxicity (Gao et al., 2014). Thus the authors used a semirational approach to test a series of POMDs, functionalized with different known His-chelating metals (Cu, Fe, Ni, Co, or Mn), by using the same high-throughput Aβ–ECFP screening method (Geng et al., 2011). The aim was to verify binding affinity of the tested POMDs to Aβ.

Among the tested derivatives of POMDs (POMD–Mn, POMD–Cu, and POMD–Fe) and unmodified Wells–Dawson POM, only those with Ni or Co inhibited Aβ42 aggregation; thus, only $K_8P_2NiW_{17}O_{61}$ (POMD–Ni) and $K_8P_2CoW_{17}O_{61}$ (POMD–Co) were used in the following tests. The compounds suppressed ThT fluorescence with the following potencies: POMD–Ni > POMD–Co > POMD derivatives. Native-gel electrophoresis of Aβ40, AFM experiments, and IC_{50} calculations confirmed these findings; IC_{50} values of POMD–Ni and POMD–Co were approximately 4.5-fold and 1.8-fold lower than that of POMD, respectively. The authors also tested whether POMDs could inhibit Aβ oligomerization following a 24 h Cu^{2+} treatment at 37°C. Native PAGE showed that in Aβ treated with Cu^{2+} the monomer band was absent, whereas when POMD–Co or POMD–Ni were incubated with Aβ samples, a strong monomer band and weaker oligomers appeared (Gao et al., 2014).

The enhanced binding affinity of POMDs to Aβ was attributed to two features: First, there were high electrostatic interactions between POMDs and Aβ because POMs have six negative charges and POMDs have eight; the two additional negative charges would increase electrostatic interactions with the cationic HHQK cluster. Second, His binding was improved by the metal-chelated POMDs to recognize the HHQK cluster. This postulate was confirmed by the higher apparent K_a value of POMD–Ni than that of POMD–Co. The authors suggested two possible mechanisms whereby POMDs could interfere with Aβ aggregation and fibrillization: binding between POMDs and Aβ assemblies could substantially lower the concentration of the monomeric Aβ in solution, thus tilting the equilibrium away from aggregation. In addition, interactions between POMDs and oligomeric Aβ species could block the contact points between various Aβ species, effecting unfavorable conditions for further nucleation or fibril growth.

In cytotoxicity assays using the MTT assay in PC-12 cells, Aβ was incubated in the presence or absence of POMD, POMD–Ni, or POMD–Co again for 7 days, and subsequently the cells were exposed to different Aβ–POMD mixtures. POMD–Ni was more efficacious than POMD or POMD–Co, while they were all nontoxic by themselves (Gao et al., 2014). The long, 7-day duration of preincubation with Aβ was used by the authors presumably because ThT experiments and Aβ fibril formation were monitored that long. However, this long incubation suggests an unfavorable therapeutic potential for these compounds, which would likely require continual administration or a durable pharmacokinetic availability. This therapeutic postulate is notwithstanding their potential systemic toxicity (yet to be determined), which would more likely emerge with prolonged pharmacokinetic availability.

Because the blood–brain barrier is a major impediment for experimental compounds for AD treatment (100% of large-molecule drugs and 98% of small-molecule drugs fail to cross the blood–brain barrier; see Pardridge, 2009), POMDs were tested to determine whether they cross the blood–brain barrier, by treating wild-type mice with POMD–Ni, which was the most effective in vitro. In the test, 25 mg/kg of POMD–Ni was administered to mice intravenously (Gao et al., 2014). Plasma and brain tissue were collected 5, 10, 30, and 60 min after POMD–Ni treatment. Tungsten levels were then measured as an indirect indicator of POMD–Ni in brain homogenates and in plasma by ICP–MS. Tungsten levels in the plasma rapidly increased and plateaued in POMD–Ni-treated animals after 5 min (~8.9 mg/kg). However, peak tungsten levels in the brain did not coincide at the same time as in the plasma but rather 10 min after POMD–Ni administration; the brain tungsten level (~0.0231 mg/kg) was extremely low, 0.26% of that in the blood at 5 min. Thereafter, brain and plasma tungsten concentrations markedly decreased and returned to initial levels after 48 h.

In similar experiments, wild-type Wistar rats were treated with POMD–Ni intravenously at 25 mg/kg of body weight. Rats' CSF was collected 60 min after dosing and analyzed by high-performance liquid chromatography. The samples contained POMD–Ni at the same retention time as the pure POMD–Ni. Thus the authors concluded that POMD–Ni entered the brain, distributed extracellularly in the brain, and appeared in the CSF where Aβ could exist in different aggregation states.

In a recent study, the Wells–Dawson POMs (POMDs) were conjugated to AuNPs (Gao et al., 2015). The AuNPs already were conjugated using sulfur–gold chemistry to a β-sheet-breaker peptide derived from the Aβ sequence, LPFFD, and containing a Cys residue at its N-terminus (*N*-acetyl–Cys–LPFFD) for Au–S conjugation to AuNPs. The authors postulated that the POMD–AuNP–peptide conjugate could inhibit Aβ fibrillization, dissociate preformed fibrils, and easily cross the blood–brain barrier because the AuNPs could efficiently deliver the drug through the blood–brain barrier (Yang et al., 2005b). After confirming the POMD–AuNP–peptide synthesis success, the substances were tested by ThT fluorescence assays. The 40 nM POMD–AuNP–peptide with 40 μM Aβ40 reduced ThT fluorescence by ~47%, and POMD–AuNP–peptide dissociated preformed Aβ fibrils; these results were confirmed using TEM experiments, DLS, and native PAGE. Trypsin digestion experiments using Aβ12–28 showed that the POMD–AuNP–peptide bound this Aβ fragment and inhibited its degradation by trypsin.

Similar to studies conducted by Qu and coworkers, three different multimolybdenum POM anionic nanoclusters were used against Aβ40 assembly (Chen et al., 2014). By using ThT fluorescence, native PAGE, turbidity, CD, and TEM, it was shown that the three tested POM complexes significantly inhibited Aβ40 self-assembly and metal-induced Aβ40 assembly (Chen et al., 2014). They also reported that PC-12 cell viability, which was reduced by 20 μM Aβ40 in the absence or presence of 40 μM Cu^{2+} or 40 μM Zn^{2+}, was rescued by 10 μg/mL POM complexes to up to 80% of control levels (Chen et al., 2014). Morphological studies assessing cell shape and dendritic processes also confirmed that POM complexes protected cells from the toxic effects of Zn^{2+}–Aβ40 or Cu^{2+}–Aβ40 complexes. Flow cytometry and annexin V staining confirmed that POM complexes protected cells against metal-induced apoptosis, and fluorescence staining indicated that cells were protected against insults by reactive oxygen species induced by Aβ40 assemblies or metal–Aβ40 complexes (Chen et al., 2014).

Artificial Molecular Chaperones

Molecular chaperones control protein misfolding and maintain protein homeostasis in vivo (Kim et al., 2013; Smith et al., 2015). Chaperones, including heat-shock proteins, chaperonins,

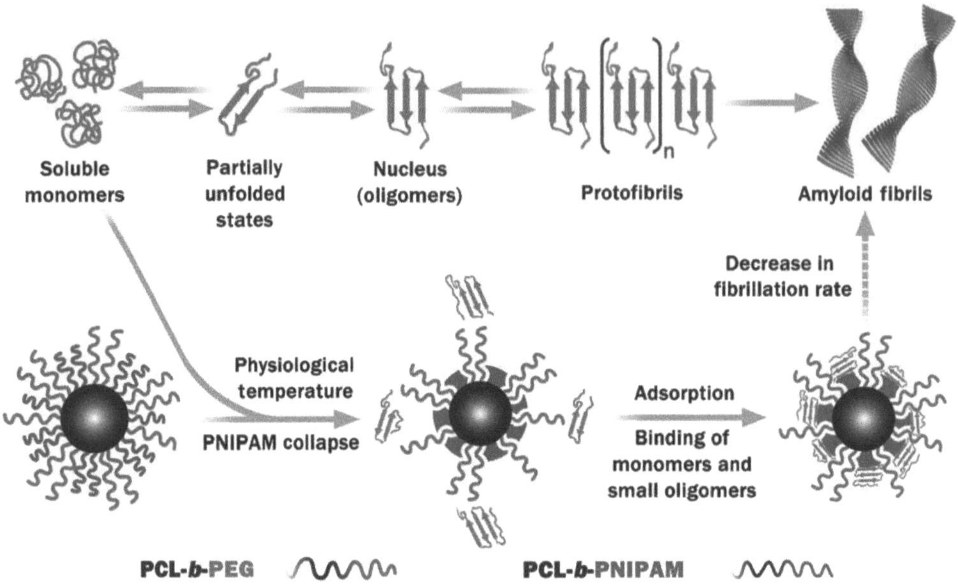

FIGURE 6.33 **Depiction of a possible mechanism underlying interactions between mixed-shell polymeric micelles and Aβ peptide.**

apolipoproteins, DNAJB6, heparan sulfate proteoglycans, and αB crystalin, to name a few, can modulate pathological neurodegenerative processes by targeting misfolded proteins for refolding or degradation (Holtzman, 2004; Kim et al., 2013; Mansson et al., 2014; Niforou et al., 2014; Shammas et al., 2011; Smith et al., 2015; Wilhelmus et al., 2007).

In an attempt to mimic endogenous chaperones, artificial molecular chaperones were developed to modulate Aβ self-assembly (Huang et al., 2014). These chaperones were synthesized by self-assembly of two amphiphilic di-block copolymers, poly(ε-caprolactone)–*block*–poly(ethylene oxide) (PCL–*b*–PEG) and poly(ε-caprolactone)–*block*–poly(*N*-isopropylacrylamide) (PCL–*b*–PNIPAM) in aqueous solution. The self-assembly process resulted in complex micelles composing a PCL core and a mixed shell comprising PEG and PNIPAM (Fig. 6.33) (Huang et al., 2014). At 37°C, the PNIPAM chains, which form the micellar shell, transition from hydrophilic to hydrophobic character spontaneously and fold to form hydrophobic domains on the PCL core. These hydrophobic domains were thought to bind to Aβ monomers or oligomers through hydrophobic interactions, whereas the extended hydrophilic PEG chains likely repel excessive Aβ to prevent aggregation of the micelles themselves. Importantly, the PNIPAM surfaces could be altered by changing the proportion of the two hydrophilic–hydrophobic copolymers on the surface of the mixed-shell polymeric micelles (MSPM) to enhance their antiaggregative effects. Adjusting this ratio modulated MSPMs' surface properties and controlled their effect on Aβ fibrillization. Moreover, MSPMs with an optimal surface hydrophilicity–hydrophobicity balance had advantageous circulatory pharmacokinetics (Gao et al., 2013), a critical characteristic for potential in vivo applications as amyloid modulators. The same authors had shown previously that such MSPMs did not interact or affect functions of other proteins (Gao et al., 2013; Liu et al., 2013).

When MSPMs were added to Aβ, the lag phase of ThT fluorescence was prolonged and the final intensity at plateau was reduced, suggesting that the artificial chaperones attenuated both the nucleation and the elongation of Aβ fibrillization (Huang et al., 2014). Among the different MSPMs with varying PEG–PNIPAM ratios, MSPM–50PNIPAM was the best inhibitor of Aβ fibrillization, suggesting that controlling the balance between PEG chains and PNIPAM domains was essential for preventing Aβ self-assembly. MSPMs abrogated Aβ aggregation in a concentration-dependent manner. For example, MSPM–70PNIPAM was most effective at 0.4 mg/mL and least effective at 0.05 mg/mL. In the presence of MSPMs, Aβ showed an α-helical structure for 48 h by CD, and eventually converted to the spectral characteristic of the Aβ transition state from α-helical to β-sheet structure (decreased intensity at 222 nm and disappearance of the dip at 208 nm), suggesting that MSPMs fixed Aβ structures in the conformational transition state, and typical β-sheet spectra were not observed for the duration of the experiment (144 h) (Huang et al., 2014).

Using DLS, the authors showed that immediately after dissolution, Aβ particles of ~10 nm R_H predominated, consistent with Aβ oligomers, which changed over time to larger aggregates as Aβ fibrillized. When MSPMs were mixed with Aβ, the hydrodynamic radius, R_H, was similar to that of MSPMs initially, but over time increased from ~65 to ~98 nm, indicating formation of MSPM–Aβ complexes. These complexes, examined by TEM, showed dark spherical structures, whereas MSPMs alone formed distinctly white structures (Huang et al., 2014). Furthermore, the authors used a quartz crystal microbalance with dissipation monitoring (QCM-D) as a mass sensor to determine the adsorption/desorption and binding kinetics of MSPMs for Aβ. A QCM comprises a thin quartz disk sandwiched between two electrodes. When an alternative electrical current is applied across the electrodes, the disk oscillates at its acoustic resonance frequency. When the voltage is cut off, the disk oscillation decays exponentially. This decay is recorded, and the resonance frequency (f) and the energy dissipation factor (D) are calculated.

When surface-adsorbed MSPMs at different hydrophilic–hydrophobic ratios were exposed to Aβ preparations at 37°C, resonance frequency rapidly decreased. The largest decrease of frequency was for MSPM–50PNIPAM, entailing that MSPM–50PNIPAM interacted with Aβ most avidly, in agreement with ThT results. All types of MSPMs bound unaggregated Aβ preparations more preferably than Aβ oligomers and showed negligible binding to fibrils. It was thus hypothesized that the PEG chains triggered adsorption of Aβ by MSPMs and the PNIPAM domains then strongly captured the peptides, signifying the synergistic roles of hydrophilic PEG chains and hydrophobic PNIPAM domains in modulating Aβ assembly (Huang et al., 2014).

MSPMs at concentrations ranging from 6.25 to 400 μg/mL were negligibly toxic to PC-12 or SH-SY5Y cells (~90% cell viability) and rescued cell survival to ~80% of control when used at fourfold excess to Aβ (40 μM) in the MTT assay. Although MSPMs modulated Aβ fibrillization, they could not decrease Aβ-induced cytotoxicity completely. This effect can be attributed to the inherent cytotoxic effect of the MSPMs, averaging 10% cell death at almost all the different concentrations used.

The authors also performed proteinase-K proteolysis experiments to compare the stability of Aβ fibrils and MSPM–Aβ complexes. ThT fluorescence intensity of MSPM–Aβ complexes treated with proteinase K decreased with time, whereas mature amyloid fibrils showed a slight reduction in the first 16 h and then the relative fluorescence intensity climbed again. Thus, MSPM–Aβ complexes were more susceptible to proteinase K than amyloid fibrils in vitro. Moreover, the authors demonstrated that MSPMs did not have any effect on 7-day-matured amyloid fibrils in a disaggregation ThT assay (Huang et al., 2014). Thus, the two aforementioned observations suggest that MSPMs would not affect preexisting amyloid plaque if they were to successfully pass through the blood–brain barrier. This makes their potential as an AD therapeutic unlikely.

CONCLUSIONS

In this chapter, we surveyed more than 50 peptides and peptidomimetics, about 30 natural compounds (of which two-thirds were polyphenols), and approximately the same number of nonnatural molecules tested for their ability to modulate Aβ assembly and inhibit Aβ toxicity. Yet we are far from covering this vast field. A PubMed search for the terms "amyloid*" and "inhibit*" in the Title field yielded 1718 hits in Sep. 2015. Even if we assume arbitrarily that 50% of these hits do not discuss unique inhibitors of Aβ assembly or toxicity, the number of remaining articles is much larger than could be covered in a typical review.

Despite the major effort dedicated to discovery, design, optimization, and characterization of "Aβ inhibitors" (a term we use hereafter to convey modulators and/or inhibitors of Aβ assembly and inhibitors of Aβ-induced toxicity), none of the compounds studied thus far has yielded a drug for AD. So are we, as a field, barking up the wrong tree as some have questioned in recent years? In agreement with others in the field (Karran and Hardy, 2014; Lo et al., 2014), we believe that Aβ self-assembly and toxicity play a central role in AD and most likely are the causative pathologic event, yet the efforts targeting the self-assembly process have not been effective to date.

Reading through this chapter, several trends can be pointed out. First, although peptides and peptidomimetics are the largest group of molecules explored as Aβ inhibitors, none of them has progressed to clinical trials, and the frequency of publication of peptide-based Aβ inhibitors studies seems to have declined in recent years compared to the previous decade. This trend may reflect the boundaries posed by the known limitations of peptides as drug leads—low bioavailability and metabolic stability compared to nonpeptidic small molecules. Have we exhausted the attempts to turn peptides into effective Aβ inhibitors? Some of the peptidomimetics reviewed in this chapter actually did show relatively high metabolic stability and bioavailability (eg, sections: D-Peptides; Rationally Designed Small Peptides), yet to the best of our knowledge, they have not been pursued further, possibly due to lack of continued research funding and/or lack of interest by the pharmaceutical industry.

We suggest that there are important lessons to be learned here. The pharmaceutical industry may be too conservative and miss important opportunities offered by peptidomimetics that fulfill druggability criteria. On the other side of the equation, academic scientists considering using peptide-based strategies for development of Aβ inhibitors should consider pharmacokinetic and toxicity factors early, rather than the traditional approach of focusing on efficacy with the assumption that pharmacokinetic and safety characteristics can be improved later. The same considerations should be taken into account when designing nonpeptidic compounds, such as those discussed in section: Aβ Assembly Modulators From Nonnatural Sources. The common side to most of the compounds discussed in sections: Peptidic or Peptidomimetic Modulators of Aβ Assembly; Aβ Assembly Modulators From Nonnatural Sources is the existence of a scientific rationale for making and testing them. At the same time, similarly to peptides, some of the nonnatural, nonpeptidic compounds explored, especially the ones discussed toward the end of section: Aβ Assembly Modulators From Nonnatural Sources, have obvious liabilities, such as large size and incorporation of metal ions, which would be expected to limit their translation potential into drugs.

In section: Aβ Assembly Modulators Derived From Natural Sources, the broad use of polyphenolic compounds is an obvious trend. Of the different compounds we reviewed, compounds in this group most often have reached clinical trials. Yet the reason for this higher rate of success likely is simply the relative ease of reaching the point of human studies due to low toxicity, rather than compelling rationales or preclinical data. As the public health need is increasingly overwhelming, testing compounds with a potential to provide even moderate improvement is understood, though we must remember that the resources are limited, and dedicating much effort and funding to compounds expected to have only a moderate effect may come at the expense of developing a disease-modifying therapy for AD. Funding agencies must keep the need for balance between these approaches in mind.

As section: Polyphenols illustrates, the popularity of polyphenols may be related to the ease of obtaining them and the hope that due to their abundance in natural sources they would be easy to develop into drugs. However, to date, these premises have not proven successful (we note that this statement will change dramatically if the anticipated Sunphenon results show significant disease-modifying effects). The realization that flavonoids tend to form covalent adducts with susceptible amino groups in Aβ (and likely those in off-targets) is a concern that should be taken into account in every study considering these compounds.

Despite many doubts in the validity of Aβ assembly and toxicity as a therapeutic target for AD in recent years, the genetic evidence for the causative role of Aβ in AD, including both familial-AD-causing mutations (Attar et al., 2013) and the recently discovered rare, protective mutation in an Icelandic kindred (Jonsson et al., 2012), is very strong. We maintain that targeting Aβ assembly as a purely pathogenic process is an attractive therapeutic approach. That said, we emphasize two important considerations: (1) Because the most relevant species, the highly toxic yet structurally elusive oligomers, are held together by weak forces, many compounds will interact with them nonspecifically and will affect their structure and aggregation kinetics. But this does not mean that the compounds can become useful drugs for AD. In particular, as discussed in the Introduction, compounds that accelerate aggregation are poor candidates for drug development. (2) AD is a complex disease involving multiple pathologic mechanisms. Therefore, a single therapeutic approach focused only on Aβ is unlikely to be successful in isolation. Developing effective therapy for AD, and ultimately a prevention strategy or a cure, most likely will require a multipronged approach targeting Aβ, tau, inflammation, and possibly other mechanisms.

Abbreviations

ABSM Amyloid β-sheet mimic
Aβ Amyloid β-protein
AD Alzheimer's disease
ADAS-Cog Alzheimer's Disease Assessment Scale–Cognitive portion
ADCS-ADL Alzheimer's Disease Cooperative Study–Activities of Daily Living
AFM Atomic-force microscopy
ANS 1-Anilinonaphthalene 8-sulfonate
APP Amyloid β-protein precursor

AuNPs Gold nanoparticles
BBDPs β-Sheet-breaker dipeptides
CAA Cerebral amyloid angiopathy
CD Circular dichroism
CHC Central hydrophobic cluster
CHO Chinese hamster ovarian cells
CR Congo red
CSF Cerebrospinal fluid
CTFs C-terminal fragments
Cur-PLGA-NPs Curcumin-encapsulated poly(lactic-*co*-glycolic acid) nanoparticles
DHA Docosahexaenoic acid
DLS Dynamic light scattering
ECFP Enhanced cyan fluorescent protein
ECM Extracellular matrix
EGCG (−)-Epigallocatechin-3-gallate
ELISA Enzyme-linked immunosorbent assay
ESI Electrospray ionization
GABA γ-Amino butyric acid
GFP Green fluorescent protein
HSQC Heteronuclear single-quantum coherence
IADLs Instrumental activities of daily living
ICP–MS Inductively coupled plasma–mass spectrometry
IM–MS Ion-mobility–mass spectrometry
ISF Interstitial fluid
LDH Lactate dehydrogenase
LPR/LR Laminin receptor precursors/laminin receptors
LTP Long-term potentiation
MMSE Mini Mental State Examination
MSPM Mixed-shell polymeric micelles
MTS [3-(4,5-Dimethylthiazol-2-yl)-5-(3 carboxymethoxyphenyl)-2(4-sulfophenyl)-2H-tetrazolium salt]
MTT 3-(4,5-Dimethylthiazol-2-yl)-2,5-diphenyltetrazolium bromide
NMR Nuclear magnetic resonance
PAGE Polyacrylamide gel electrophoresis
PCL Poly(ε-caprolactone)
PEG Polyethylene glycol
PICUP Photo-induced crosslinking of unmodified proteins
PNIPAM Poly(*N*-isopropylacrylamide)
POM Polyoxometalate
POMD The Wells–Dawson polyoxometalate
QCM-D Quartz crystal microbalance with dissipation monitoring
R_H Hydrodynamic radius
RI Retro–inverso
SDS Sodium dodecyl sulfate
SEC Size-exclusion chromatography
SPR Surface-plasmon resonance
TEM Transmission electron microscopy
ThT Thioflavin T

References

Abbas S, Wink M: Epigallocatechin gallate inhibits β amyloid oligomerization in *Caenorhabditis elegans* and affects the daf-2/insulin-like signaling pathway, *Phytomedicine* 17:902–909, 2010.

Acerra N, Kad NM, Mason JM: Combining intracellular selection with protein-fragment complementation to derive Aβ interacting peptides, *Protein Eng Des Sel* 26:463–470, 2013.

Acerra N, Kad NM, Griffith DA, Ott S, Crowther DC, Mason JM: Retro-inversal of intracellular selected β-amyloid-interacting peptides: implications for a novel Alzheimer's disease treatment, *Biochemistry* 53:2101–2111, 2014.

Adessi C, Frossard MJ, Boissard C, Fraga S, Bieler S, Ruckle T, Vilbois F, Robinson SM, Mutter M, Banks WA, Soto C: Pharmacological profiles of peptide drug candidates for the treatment of Alzheimer's disease, *J Biol Chem* 278:13905–13911, 2003.

Adis R&D Profile: EGb 761 *Ginkgo biloba* extract, Ginkor, *Drugs R&D* 4:188–193, 2003.

Akaishi T, Morimoto T, Shibao M, Watanabe S, Sakai-Kato K, Utsunomiya-Tate N, Abe K: Structural requirements for the flavonoid fisetin in inhibiting fibril formation of amyloid β protein, *Neurosci Lett* 444:280–285, 2008.

Alessio E, Mestroni G, Bergamo A, Sava G: Ruthenium antimetastatic agents, *Curr Top Med Chem* 4:1525–1535, 2004.

Ali T, Kim MO: Melatonin ameliorates amyloid β-induced memory deficits, tau hyperphosphorylation and neurodegeneration via PI3/Akt/GSk3β pathway in the mouse hippocampus, *J Pineal Res* 59:47–59, 2015.

Altun A, Ugur-Altun B: Melatonin: therapeutic and clinical utilization, *Int J Clin Pract* 61:835–845, 2007.

Amijee H, Bate C, Williams A, Virdee J, Jeggo R, Spanswick D, Scopes DI, Treherne JM, Mazzitelli S, Chawner R, Eyers CE, Doig AJ: The *N*-methylated peptide SEN304 powerfully inhibits Aβ(1–42) toxicity by perturbing oligomer formation, *Biochemistry* 51:8338–8352, 2012.

Ammit AJ, Burgess JK, Hirst SJ, Hughes JM, Kaur M, Lau JY, Zuyderduyn S: The effect of asthma therapeutics on signalling and transcriptional regulation of airway smooth muscle function, *Pulm Pharmacol Ther* 22:446–454, 2009.

Arai T, Araya T, Sasaki D, Taniguchi A, Sato T, Sohma Y, Kanai M: Rational design and identification of a non-peptidic aggregation inhibitor of amyloid-β based on a pharmacophore motif obtained from cyclo[-Lys-Leu-Val-Phe-Phe-], *Angew Chem Int Ed Engl* 53:8236–8239, 2014.

Arbiser JL, Klauber N, Rohan R, van Leeuwen R, Huang MT, Fisher C, Flynn E, Byers HR: Curcumin is an in vivo inhibitor of angiogenesis, *Mol Med* 4:376–383, 1998.

Arlt S, Muller-Thomsen T, Beisiegel U, Kontush A: Effect of one-year vitamin C- and E-supplementation on cerebrospinal fluid oxidation parameters and clinical course in Alzheimer's disease, *Neurochem Res* 37:2706–2714, 2012.

Askanas V, Engel WK, Nogalska A: Pathogenic considerations in sporadic inclusion-body myositis, a degenerative muscle disease associated with aging and abnormalities of myoproteostasis, *J Neuropathol Exp Neurol* 71:680–693, 2012.

Asti M, Ferrari E, Croci S, Atti G, Rubagotti S, Iori M, Capponi PC, Zerbini A, Saladini M, Versari A: Synthesis and characterization of ^{68}Ga-labeled curcumin and curcuminoid complexes as potential radiotracers for imaging of cancer and Alzheimer's disease, *Inorg Chem* 53:4922–4933, 2014.

Attar A, Bitan G: Disrupting self-assembly and toxicity of amyloidogenic protein oligomers by "molecular tweezers"—from the test tube to animal models, *Curr Pharm Des* 20:2469–2483, 2014.

Attar A, Ripoli C, Riccardi E, Maiti P, Li Puma DD, Liu T, Hayes J, Jones MR, Lichti-Kaiser K, Yang F, Gale GD, Tseng CH, Tan M, Xie CW, Straudinger JL, Klärner FG, Schrader T, Frautschy SA, Grassi C, Bitan G: Protection of primary neurons and mouse brain from Alzheimer's pathology by molecular tweezers, *Brain* 135:3735–3748, 2012.

Attar A, Meral D, Urbanc B, Bitan G: Assembly of amyloid β-protein variants containing familial Alzheimer's disease-linked amino acid substitutions. In Uversky VN, Lyubchenko V, editors: *Bionanoimaging: protein misfolding & aggregation*, USA, 2013, Elsevier, pp 429–442.

Attar A, Chan WT, Klärner FG, Schrader T, Bitan G: Safety and pharmacological characterization of the molecular tweezer CLR01—a broad-spectrum inhibitor of amyloid proteins' toxicity, *BMC Pharmacol Toxicol* 15:23, 2014.

Austen BM, Paleologou KE, Ali SA, Qureshi MM, Allsop D, El-Agnaf OM: Designing peptide inhibitors for oligomerization and toxicity of Alzheimer's β-amyloid peptide, *Biochemistry* 47:1984–1992, 2008.

Azzi A: Molecular mechanism of α-tocopherol action, *Free Radic Biol Med* 43:16–21, 2007.

Balasubramanian K: Molecular orbital basis for yellow curry spice curcumin's prevention of Alzheimer's disease, *J Agric Food Chem* 54:3512–3520, 2006.

Banerjee R: Effect of curcumin on the metal ion induced fibrillization of amyloid-β peptide, *Spectrochim Acta A* 117:798–800, 2014.

Barceloux DG: Molybdenum, *J Toxicol Clin Toxicol* 37:231–237, 1999.

Barghorn S, Nimmrich V, Striebinger A, Krantz C, Keller P, Janson B, Bahr M, Schmidt M, Bitner RS, Harlan J, Barlow E, Ebert U, Hillen H: Globular amyloid β-peptide oligomer—a homogenous and stable neuropathological protein in Alzheimer's disease, *J Neurochem* 95:834–847, 2005.

Barnham KJ, Kenche VB, Ciccotosto GD, Smith DP, Tew DJ, Liu X, Perez K, Cranston GA, Johanssen TJ, Volitakis I, Bush AI, Masters CL, White AR, Smith JP, Cherny RA, Cappai R: Platinum-based inhibitors of amyloid-β as therapeutic agents for Alzheimer's disease, *Proc Natl Acad Sci USA* 105:6813–6818, 2008.

Basli A, Soulet S, Chaher N, Merillon JM, Chibane M, Monti JP, Richard T: Wine polyphenols: potential agents in neuroprotection, *Oxid Med Cell Longev* 2012:805762, 2012.

Bastianetto S, Ramassamy C, Dore S, Christen Y, Poirier J, Quirion R: The Ginkgo biloba extract (EGb 761) protects hippocampal neurons against cell death induced by β-amyloid, *Eur J Neurosci* 12:1882–1890, 2000.

Baum L, Lam CW, Cheung SK, Kwok T, Lui V, Tsoh J, Lam L, Leung V, Hui E, Ng C, Woo J, Chiu HF, Goggins WB, Zee BC, Cheng KF, Fong CY, Wong A, Mok H, Chow MS, Ho PC, Ip SP, Ho CS, Yu XW, Lai CY, Chan MH, Szeto S, Chan IH, Mok V: Six-month randomized, placebo-controlled, double-blind, pilot clinical trial of curcumin in patients with Alzheimer disease, *J Clin Psychopharmacol* 28:110–113, 2008.

Bell EF: History of vitamin E in infant nutrition, *Am J Clin Nutr* 46:183–186, 1987.

Bernstein SL, Dupuis NF, Lazo ND, Wyttenbach T, Condron MM, Bitan G, Teplow DB, Shea JE, Ruotolo BT, Robinson CV, Bowers MT: Amyloid-β protein oligomerization and the importance of tetramers and dodecamers in the aetiology of Alzheimer's disease, *Nat Chem* 1:326–331, 2009.

Bhandarkar SS, Arbiser JL: Curcumin as an inhibitor of angiogenesis, *Adv Exp Med Biol* 595:185–195, 2007.

Bier D, Rose R, Bravo-Rodriguez K, Bartel M, Ramirez-Anguita JM, Dutt S, Wilch C, Klärner FG, Sanchez-Garcia E, Schrader T, Ottmann C: Molecular tweezers modulate 14-3-3 protein–protein interactions, *Nat Chem* 5:234–239, 2013.

Bieschke J, Russ J, Friedrich RP, Ehrnhoefer DE, Wobst H, Neugebauer K, Wanker EE: EGCG remodels mature α-synuclein and amyloid-β fibrils and reduces cellular toxicity, *Proc Natl Acad Sci USA* 107:7710–7715, 2010.

Bilikiewicz A, Gaus W: Colostrinin (a naturally occurring, proline-rich, polypeptide mixture) in the treatment of Alzheimer's disease, *J Alzheimers Dis* 6:17–26, 2004.

Bitan G: Structural study of metastable amyloidogenic protein oligomers by photo-induced cross-linking of unmodified proteins, *Methods Enzymol* 413:217–236, 2006.

Bitan G, Kirkitadze MD, Lomakin A, Vollers SS, Benedek GB, Teplow DB: Amyloid β-protein (Aβ) assembly: Aβ40 and Aβ42 oligomerize through distinct pathways, *Proc Natl Acad Sci USA* 100:330–335, 2003.

Biyani M, Nishigaki K, Biyani M: Biomolecular display technology: a new tool for drug discovery. In Verma AS, Singh A, editors: *Aminal biotechnology models in discovery and translation*, Oxford, UK, 2014, Academic Press, pp 369–384.

Boldogh I, Kruzel ML: Colostrinin: an oxidative stress modulator for prevention and treatment of age-related disorders, *J Alzheimers Dis* 13:303–321, 2008.

Borchelt DR, Thinakaran G, Eckman CB, Lee MK, Davenport F, Ratovitsky T, Prada CM, Kim G, Seekins S, Yager D, Slunt HH, Wang R, Seeger M, Levey AI, Gandy SE, Copeland NG, Jenkins NA, Price DL, Younkin SG, Sisodia SS: Familial Alzheimer's disease-linked presenilin 1 variants elevate Aβ1–42/1–40 ratio in vitro and in vivo, *Neuron* 17:1005–1013, 1996.

Borchelt DR, Ratovitski T, Vanlare J, Lee MK, Gonzales V, Jenkins NA, Copeland NG, Price DL, Sisodia SS: Accelerated amyloid deposition in the brains of transgenic mice coexpressing mutant presenilin 1 and amyloid precursor proteins, *Neuron* 19:939–945, 1997.

Bratkovic T: Progress in phage display: evolution of the technique and its application, *Cell Mol Life Sci* 67:749–767, 2010.

Brinet D, Kaffy J, Oukacine F, Glumm S, Ongeri S, Taverna M: An improved capillary electrophoresis method for in vitro monitoring of the challenging early steps of Aβ1–42 peptide oligomerization: application to anti-Alzheimer's drug discovery, *Electrophoresis* 35:3302–3309, 2014.

Buendia I, Parada E, Navarro E, Leon R, Negredo P, Egea J, Lopez MG: Subthreshold concentrations of melatonin and galantamine improves pathological AD-hallmarks in hippocampal organotypic cultures, *Mol Neurobiol* June, 2015, pp 1–11.

Buxbaum JN, Ye Z, Reixach N, Friske L, Levy C, Das P, Golde T, Masliah E, Roberts AR, Bartfai T: Transthyretin protects Alzheimer's mice from the behavioral and biochemical effects of Aβ toxicity, *Proc Natl Acad Sci USA* 105:2681–2686, 2008.

Caesar I, Jonson M, Nilsson KP, Thor S, Hammarstrom P: Curcumin promotes A-beta fibrillation and reduces neurotoxicity in transgenic *Drosophila*, *PLoS One* 7:e31424, 2012.

Camilleri A, Zarb C, Caruana M, Ostermeier U, Ghio S, Hogen T, Schmidt F, Giese A, Vassallo N: Mitochondrial membrane permeabilisation by amyloid aggregates and protection by polyphenols, *Biochim Biophys Acta* 1828:2532–2543, 2013.

Castells M, Metcalfe DD, Escribano L: Diagnosis and treatment of cutaneous mastocytosis in children: practical recommendations, *Am J Clin Dermatol* 12:259–270, 2011.

Castillo GM, Lukito W, Peskind E, Raskind M, Kirschner DA, Yee AG, Snow AD: Laminin inhibition of β-amyloid protein (Aβ) fibrillogenesis and identification of an Aβ binding site localized to the globular domain repeats on the laminin A chain, *J Neurosci Res* 62:451–462, 2000.

Chang X, Rong C, Chen Y, Yang C, Hu Q, Mo Y, Zhang C, Gu X, Zhang L, He W, Cheng S, Hou X, Su R, Liu S, Dun W, Wang Q, Fang S: (−)-Epigallocatechin-3-gallate attenuates cognitive deterioration in Alzheimer's disease model mice by upregulating neprilysin expression, *Exp Cell Res* 334:136–145, 2015.

Charlton KE, Rabinowitz TL, Geffen LN, Dhansay MA: Lowered plasma vitamin C, but not vitamin E, concentrations in dementia patients, *J Nutr Health Aging* 8:99–107, 2004.

Chen Q, Yang L, Zheng C, Zheng W, Zhang J, Zhou Y, Liu J: Mo polyoxometalate nanoclusters capable of inhibiting the aggregation of Aβ-peptide associated with Alzheimer's disease, *Nanoscale* 6:6886–6897, 2014.

Cheng F, Cappai R, Ciccotosto GD, Svensson G, Multhaup G, Fransson LA, Mani K: Suppression of amyloid β A11 antibody immunoreactivity by vitamin C: possible role of heparan sulfate oligosaccharides derived from glypican-1 by ascorbate-induced, nitric oxide (NO)-catalyzed degradation, *J Biol Chem* 286:27559–27572, 2011.

Cheng PN, Liu C, Zhao M, Eisenberg D, Nowick JS: Amyloid β-sheet mimics that antagonize protein aggregation and reduce amyloid toxicity, *Nat Chem* 4:927–933, 2012.

Cheng KK, Yeung CF, Ho SW, Chow SF, Chow AH, Baum L: Highly stabilized curcumin nanoparticles tested in an in vitro blood–brain barrier model and in Alzheimer's disease Tg2576 mice, *AAPS J* 15:324–336, 2013.

Chinai JM, Taylor AB, Ryno LM, Hargreaves ND, Morris CA, Hart PJ, Urbach AR: Molecular recognition of insulin by a synthetic receptor, *J Am Chem Soc* 133:8810–8813, 2011.

Chishti MA, Yang DS, Janus C, Phinney AL, Horne P, Pearson J, Strome R, Zuker N, Loukides J, French J, Turner S, Lozza G, Grilli M, Kunicki S, Morissette C, Paquette J, Gervais F, Bergeron C, Fraser PE, Carlson GA, George-Hyslop PS, Westaway D: Early-onset amyloid deposition and cognitive deficits in transgenic mice expressing a double mutant form of amyloid precursor protein 695, *J Biol Chem* 276:21562–21570, 2001.

Cho PY, Joshi G, Johnson JA, Murphy RM: Transthyretin-derived peptides as β-amyloid inhibitors, *ACS Chem Neurosci* 5:542–551, 2014.

Chojnacki JE, Liu K, Yan X, Toldo S, Selden T, Estrada M, Rodriguez-Franco MI, Halquist MS, Ye D, Zhang S: Discovery of 5-(4-hydroxyphenyl)-3-oxo-pentanoic acid [2-(5-methoxy-1H-indol-3-yl)-ethyl]-amide as a neuroprotectant for Alzheimer's disease by hybridization of curcumin and melatonin, *ACS Chem Neurosci* 5:690–699, 2014.

Coan KE, Shoichet BK: Stability and equilibria of promiscuous aggregates in high protein milieus, *Mol Biosyst* 3:208–213, 2007.

Cole GM, Frautschy SA: Docosahexaenoic acid protects from amyloid and dendritic pathology in an Alzheimer's disease mouse model, *Nutr Health* 18:249–259, 2006.

Cole GM, Frautschy SA: DHA may prevent age-related dementia, *J Nutr* 140:869–874, 2010.

Condron MM, Monien BH, Bitan G: Synthesis and purification of highly hydrophobic peptides derived from the C-terminus of amyloid β-protein, *Open Biotechnol J* 2:87–93, 2008.

Crouch PJ, Savva MS, Hung LW, Donnelly PS, Mot AI, Parker SJ, Greenough MA, Volitakis I, Adlard PA, Cherny RA, Masters CL, Bush AI, Barnham KJ, White AR: The Alzheimer's therapeutic PBT2 promotes amyloid-β degradation and GSK3 phosphorylation via a metal chaperone activity, *J Neurochem* 119:220–230, 2011.

Crowther DC, Page R, Chandraratna D, Lomas DA: A *Drosophila* model of Alzheimer's disease, *Methods Enzymol* 412:234–255, 2006.

Cruz M, Tusell JM, Grillo-Bosch D, Albericio F, Serratosa J, Rabanal F, Giralt E: Inhibition of β-amyloid toxicity by short peptides containing *N*-methyl amino acids, *J Pept Res* 63:324–328, 2004.

Cummings JL, Morstorf T, Zhong K: Alzheimer's disease drug-development pipeline: few candidates, frequent failures, *Alzheimers Res Ther* 6:37, 2014.

Da Costa Dias B, Jovanovic K, Gonsalves D, Moodley K, Reusch U, Knackmuss S, Weinberg MS, Little M, Weiss SF: The 37kDa/67kDa laminin receptor acts as a receptor for $A\beta_{42}$ internalization, *Sci Rep* 4:5556, 2014.

Dahlgren KN, Manelli AM, Stine WB Jr, Baker LK, Krafft GA, LaDu MJ: Oligomeric and fibrillar species of amyloid-β peptides differentially affect neuronal viability, *J Biol Chem* 277:32046–32053, 2002.

Daniels T, Mills N, Whitaker P: Nebuliser systems for drug delivery in cystic fibrosis, *Cochrane Database Syst Rev* 4:Cd007639, 2013.

De Bona P, Giuffrida ML, Caraci F, Copani A, Pignataro B, Attanasio F, Cataldo S, Pappalardo G, Rizzarelli E: Design and synthesis of new trehalose-conjugated pentapeptides as inhibitors of Aβ(1–42) fibrillogenesis and toxicity, *J Pept Sci* 15:220–228, 2009.

DeFeudis FV: A brief history of EGb 761® and its therapeutic uses, *Pharmacopsychiatry* 36(Suppl 1):S2–S7, 2003.

DeToma AS, Choi JS, Braymer JJ, Lim MH: Myricetin: a naturally occurring regulator of metal-induced amyloid-β aggregation and neurotoxicity, *ChemBioChem* 12:1198–1201, 2011.

Dhar G, Chakravarty D, Hazra J, Dhar J, Poddar A, Pal M, Chakrabarti P, Surolia A, Bhattacharyya B: Actin–curcumin interaction: insights into the mechanism of actin polymerization inhibition, *Biochemistry* 54:1132–1143, 2015.

Di Giovanni S, Eleuteri S, Paleologou KE, Yin G, Zweckstetter M, Carrupt PA, Lashuel HA: Entacapone and tolcapone, two catechol *O*-methyltransferase inhibitors, block fibril formation of α-synuclein and β-amyloid and protect against amyloid-induced toxicity, *J Biol Chem* 285:14941–14954, 2010.

DiMeco F, Li KW, Tyler BM, Wolf AS, Brem H, Olivi A: Local delivery of mitoxantrone for the treatment of malignant brain tumors in rats, *J Neurosurg* 97:1173–1178, 2002.

Ding Y, Qiao A, Wang Z, Goodwin JS, Lee ES, Block ML, Allsbrook M, McDonald MP, Fan GH: Retinoic acid attenuates β-amyloid deposition and rescues memory deficits in an Alzheimer's disease transgenic mouse model, *J Neurosci* 28:11622–11634, 2008.

DiSanto AR, Wagner JG: Pharmacokinetics of highly ionized drugs. II. Methylene blue—absorption, metabolism, and excretion in man and dog after oral administration, *J Pharm Sci* 61:1086–1090, 1972.

Doig AJ, Derreumaux P: Inhibition of protein aggregation and amyloid formation by small molecules, *Curr Opin Struct Biol* 30:50–56, 2015.

Dolai S, Shi W, Corbo C, Sun C, Averick S, Obeysekera D, Farid M, Alonso A, Banerjee P, Raja K: "Clicked" sugar–curcumin conjugate: modulator of amyloid-β and tau peptide aggregation at ultralow concentrations, *ACS Chem Neurosci* 2:694–699, 2011.

Doody RS, Raman R, Farlow M, Iwatsubo T, Vellas B, Joffe S, Kieburtz K, He F, Sun X, Thomas RG, Aisen PS, Alzheimer's Disease Cooperative Study Steering Committee, Siemers E, Sethuraman G, Mohs R: Semagacestat Study Group: A phase 3 trial of semagacestat for treatment of Alzheimer's disease, *N Engl J Med* 369:341–350, 2013.

Doody RS, Thomas RG, Farlow M, Iwatsubo T, Vellas B, Joffe S, Kieburtz K, Raman R, Sun X, Aisen PS, Siemers E, Liu-Seifert H, Mohs R, Alzheimer's Disease Cooperative Study Steering Committee, Solanezumab Study Group: Phase 3 trials of solanezumab for mild-to-moderate Alzheimer's disease, *N Engl J Med* 370:311–321, 2014.

Du WJ, Guo JJ, Gao MT, Hu SQ, Dong XY, Han YF, Liu FF, Jiang S, Sun Y: Brazilin inhibits amyloid β-protein fibrillogenesis, remodels amyloid fibrils and reduces amyloid cytotoxicity, *Sci Rep* 5:7992, 2015.

Ehrnhoefer DE, Bieschke J, Boeddrich A, Herbst M, Masino L, Lurz R, Engemann S, Pastore A, Wanker EE: EGCG redirects amyloidogenic polypeptides into unstructured, off-pathway oligomers, *Nat Struct Mol Biol* 15:558–566, 2008.

Eleuteri S, Di Giovanni S, Rockenstein E, Mante M, Adame A, Trejo M, Wrasidlo W, Wu F, Fraering PC, Masliah E, Lashuel HA: Novel therapeutic strategy for neurodegeneration by blocking Aβ seeding mediated aggregation in models of Alzheimer's disease, *Neurobiol Dis* 74:144–157, 2015.

Ellis RJ, Olichney JM, Thal LJ, Mirra SS, Morris JC, Beekly D, Heyman A: Cerebral amyloid angiopathy in the brains of patients with Alzheimer's disease: the CERAD experience, Part XV, *Neurology* 46:1592–1596, 1996.

Endo H, Nikaido Y, Nakadate M, Ise S, Konno H: Structure activity relationship study of curcumin analogues toward the amyloid-β aggregation inhibitor, *Bioorg Med Chem Lett* 24:5621–5626, 2014.

Esler WP, Wolfe MS: A portrait of Alzheimer secretases—new features and familiar faces, *Science* 293:1449–1454, 2001.

Evans JP: Warning against intrathecal use of methylene blue, *J Amer Med Assoc* 169:526, 1959.

Fancy DA, Kodadek T: Chemistry for the analysis of protein–protein interactions: rapid and efficient cross-linking triggered by long wavelength light, *Proc Natl Acad Sci USA* 96:6020–6024, 1999.

Feng Z, Zhang JT: Melatonin reduces amyloid β-induced apoptosis in pheochromocytoma (PC12) cells, *J Pineal Res* 37:257–266, 2004.

Feng BY, Shelat A, Doman TN, Guy RK, Shoichet BK: High-throughput assays for promiscuous inhibitors, *Nat Chem Biol* 1:146–148, 2005.

Feng BY, Toyama BH, Wille H, Colby DW, Collins SR, May BC, Prusiner SB, Weissman J, Shoichet BK: Small-molecule aggregates inhibit amyloid polymerization, *Nat Chem Biol* 4:197–199, 2008.

Fenili D, Brown M, Rappaport R, McLaurin J: Properties of *scyllo*-inositol as a therapeutic treatment of AD-like pathology, *J Mol Med* 85:603–611, 2007.

Ferrão-Gonzales AD, Robbs BK, Moreau VH, Ferreira A, Juliano L, Valente AP, Almeida FC, Silva JL, Foguel D: Controlling β-amyloid oligomerization by the use of naphthalene sulfonates: trapping low molecular weight oligomeric species, *J Biol Chem* 280:34747–34754, 2005.

Ferreira N, Pereira-Henriques A, Attar A, Klärner FG, Schrader T, Bitan G, Gales L, Saraiva MJ, Almeida MR: Molecular tweezers targeting transthyretin amyloidosis, *Neurotherapeutics* 11:450–461, 2014.

Fiorani M, Guidarelli A, Blasa M, Azzolini C, Candiracci M, Piatti E, Cantoni O: Mitochondria accumulate large amounts of quercetin: prevention of mitochondrial damage and release upon oxidation of the extramitochondrial fraction of the flavonoid, *J Nutr Biochem* 21:397–404, 2010.

Fokkens M, Schrader T, Klärner FG: A molecular tweezer for lysine and arginine, *J Am Chem Soc* 127:14415–14421, 2005.

Fradinger EA, Monien BH, Urbanc B, Lomakin A, Tan M, Li H, Spring SM, Condron MM, Cruz L, Xie CW, Benedek GB, Bitan G: C-terminal peptides coassemble into Aβ42 oligomers and protect neurons against Aβ42-induced neurotoxicity, *Proc Natl Acad Sci USA* 105:14175–14180, 2008.

Frenkel D, Solomon B, Benhar I: Modulation of Alzheimer's β-amyloid neurotoxicity by site-directed single-chain antibody, *J Neuroimmunol* 106:23–31, 2000.

Frost B, Diamond MI: Prion-like mechanisms in neurodegenerative diseases, *Nat Rev Neurosci* 11:155–159, 2010.

Froud KE, Wardhaugh T, Banks D, Saffrey MJ, Stewart MG: Colostrinin alleviates amyloid-β induced toxicity in rat primary hippocampal cultures, *J Alzheimers Dis* 20:423–426, 2010.

Frydman-Marom A, Rechter M, Shefler I, Bram Y, Shalev DE, Gazit E: Cognitive-performance recovery of Alzheimer's disease model mice by modulation of early soluble amyloidal assemblies, *Angew Chem Int Ed Engl* 48:1981–1986, 2009.

Fülöp L, Zarandi M, Datki Z, Soos K, Penke B: β-Amyloid-derived pentapeptide RIIGLa inhibits Aβ(1–42) aggregation and toxicity, *Biochem Biophys Res Commun* 324:64–69, 2004.

Galasko DR, Peskind E, Clark CM, Quinn JF, Ringman JM, Jicha GA, Cotman C, Cottrell B, Montine TJ, Thomas RG, Aisen P, Alzheimer's Disease Cooperative Study: Antioxidants for Alzheimer disease: a randomized clinical trial with cerebrospinal fluid biomarker measures, *Arch Neurol* 69:836–841, 2012.

Gao H, Xiong J, Cheng T, Liu J, Chu L, Liu J, Ma R, Shi L: In vivo biodistribution of mixed shell micelles with tunable hydrophilic/hydrophobic surface, *Biomacromolecules* 14:460–467, 2013.

Gao N, Sun H, Dong K, Ren J, Duan T, Xu C, Qu X: Transition-metal-substituted polyoxometalate derivatives as functional anti-amyloid agents for Alzheimer's disease, *Nat Commun* 5:3422, 2014.

Gao N, Sun H, Dong K, Ren J, Qu X: Gold-nanoparticle-based multifunctional amyloid-β inhibitor against Alzheimer's disease, *Chemistry* 21:829–835, 2015.

Garcia-Alloza M, Borrelli LA, Rozkalne A, Hyman BT, Bacskai BJ: Curcumin labels amyloid pathology in vivo, disrupts existing plaques, and partially restores distorted neurites in an Alzheimer mouse model, *J Neurochem* 102:1095–1104, 2007.

Garcia-Mediavilla V, Crespo I, Collado PS, Esteller A, Sanchez-Campos S, Tunon MJ, Gonzalez-Gallego J: The anti-inflammatory flavones quercetin and kaempferol cause inhibition of inducible nitric oxide synthase, cyclooxygenase-2 and reactive C-protein, and down-regulation of the nuclear factor kappaB pathway in Chang liver cells, *Eur J Pharmacol* 557:221–229, 2007.

Gautam S, Karmakar S, Bose A, Chowdhury PK: β-Cyclodextrin and curcumin, a potent cocktail for disaggregating and/or inhibiting amyloids: a case study with α-synuclein, *Biochemistry* 53:4081–4083, 2014.

Geng J, Li M, Ren J, Wang E, Qu X: Polyoxometalates as inhibitors of the aggregation of amyloid β peptides associated with Alzheimer's disease, *Angew Chem Int Ed Engl* 50:4184–4188, 2011.

Gessel MM, Wu C, Li H, Bitan G, Shea JE, Bowers MT: Aβ(39–42) modulates Aβ oligomerization but not fibril formation, *Biochemistry* 51:108–117, 2012.

Ghimire Gautam S, Komatsu M, Nishigaki K: Strong inhibition of β-amyloid peptide aggregation realized by two-steps evolved peptides, *Chem Biol Drug Des* 85:356–368, 2014.

Gilead S, Gazit E: Inhibition of amyloid fibril formation by peptide analogues modified with α-aminoisobutyric acid, *Angew Chem Int Ed Engl* 43:4041–4044, 2004.

Glenner GG, Wong CW: Alzheimer's disease: initial report of the purification and characterization of a novel cerebrovascular amyloid protein, *Biochem Biophys Res Commun* 120:885–890, 1984.

Gong Y, Chang L, Viola KL, Lacor PN, Lambert MP, Finch CE, Krafft GA, Klein WL: Alzheimer's disease-affected brain: presence of oligomeric Aβ ligands (ADDLs) suggests a molecular basis for reversible memory loss, *Proc Natl Acad Sci USA* 100:10417–10422, 2003.

Goodman M, Chorev M: On the concept of linear modified retro-peptide structures, *Acc Chem Res* 12:1–7, 1979.

Gordon DJ, Sciarretta KL, Meredith SC: Inhibition of β-amyloid(40) fibrillogenesis and disassembly of β-amyloid(40) fibrils by short β-amyloid congeners containing *N*-methyl amino acids at alternate residues, *Biochemistry* 40:8237–8245, 2001.

Gordon DJ, Tappe R, Meredith SC: Design and characterization of a membrane permeable *N*-methyl amino acid-containing peptide that inhibits Aβ(1–40) fibrillogenesis, *J Pept Res* 60:37–55, 2002.

Green RM, Stewart DJ, Hugenholtz H, Richard MT, Thibault M, Montpetit V: Human central nervous system and plasma pharmacology of mitoxantrone, *J Neurooncol* 6:75–83, 1988.

Grelle G, Otto A, Lorenz M, Frank RF, Wanker EE, Bieschke J: Black tea theaflavins inhibit formation of toxic amyloid-β and α-synuclein fibrils, *Biochemistry* 50:10624–10636, 2011.

Grillo-Bosch D, Carulla N, Cruz M, Sanchez L, Pujol-Pina R, Madurga S, Rabanal F, Giralt E: Retro-enantio *N*-methylated peptides as β-amyloid aggregation inhibitors, *ChemMedChem* 4:1488–1494, 2009.

Guerrero-Muñoz MJ, Castillo-Carranza DL, Kayed R: Therapeutic approaches against common structural features of toxic oligomers shared by multiple amyloidogenic proteins, *Biochem Pharmacol* 88:468–478, 2014.

Gürbüz S, Idris M, Tuncel D: Cucurbituril-based supramolecular engineered nanostructured materials, *Org Biomol Chem* 13:330–347, 2015.

Haass C, Hung AY, Schlossmacher MG, Oltersdorf T, Teplow DB, Selkoe DJ: Normal cellular processing of the β-amyloid precursor protein results in the secretion of the amyloid β peptide and related molecules, *Ann NY Acad Sci* 695:109–116, 1993.

Hamaguchi T, Ono K, Murase A, Yamada M: Phenolic compounds prevent Alzheimer's pathology through different effects on the amyloid-β aggregation pathway, *Am J Pathol* 175:2557–2565, 2009.

Hardeland R: Antioxidative protection by melatonin: multiplicity of mechanisms from radical detoxification to radical avoidance, *Endocrine* 27:119–130, 2005.

Hardy J: Testing times for the "amyloid cascade hypothesis", *Neurobiol Aging* 23:1073–1074, 2002.

Hardy JA, Higgins GA: Alzheimer's disease: the amyloid cascade hypothesis, *Science* 256:184–185, 1992.

Harkany T, Abraham I, Laskay G, Timmerman W, Jost K, Zarandi M, Penke B, Nyakas C, Luiten PG: Propionyl-IIGL tetrapeptide antagonizes β-amyloid excitotoxicity in rat nucleus basalis, *Neuroreport* 10:1693–1698, 1999.

Harper JD, Lansbury PT Jr: Models of amyloid seeding in Alzheimer's disease and scrapie: mechanistic truths and physiological consequences of the time-dependent solubility of amyloid proteins, *Annu Rev Biochem* 66:385–407, 1997.

Harrison FE, Allard J, Bixler R, Usoh C, Li L, May JM, McDonald MP: Antioxidants and cognitive training interact to affect oxidative stress and memory in APP/PSEN1 mice, *Nutr Neurosci* 12:203–218, 2009.

Hartinger CG, Jakupec MA, Zorbas-Seifried S, Groessl M, Egger A, Berger W, Zorbas H, Dyson PJ, Keppler BK: KP1019, a new redox-active anticancer agent—preclinical development and results of a clinical phase I study in tumor patients, *Chem Biodivers* 5:2140–2155, 2008.

Hasenknopf B: Polyoxometalates: introduction to a class of inorganic compounds and their biomedical applications, *Front Biosci* 10:275–287, 2005.

Hashimoto M, Shahdat HM, Yamashita S, Katakura M, Tanabe Y, Fujiwara H, Gamoh S, Miyazawa T, Arai H, Shimada T, Shido O: Docosahexaenoic acid disrupts in vitro amyloid $\beta_{1\text{-}40}$ fibrillation and concomitantly inhibits amyloid levels in cerebral cortex of Alzheimer's disease model rats, *J Neurochem* 107:1634–1646, 2008.

Hashimoto T, Adams KW, Fan Z, McLean PJ, Hyman BT: Characterization of oligomer formation of amyloid-β peptide using a split-luciferase complementation assay, *J Biol Chem* 286:27081–27091, 2011.

Hawkes CA, Deng LH, Shaw JE, Nitz M, McLaurin J: Small molecule β-amyloid inhibitors that stabilize protofibrillar structures in vitro improve cognition and pathology in a mouse model of Alzheimer's disease, *Eur J Neurosci* 31:203–213, 2010.

Hawkes CA, Deng L, Fenili D, Nitz M, McLaurin J: In vivo uptake of β-amyloid by non-plaque associated microglia, *Curr Alzheimer Res* 9:890–901, 2012.

Hellmert M, Muller-Schiffmann A, Peters MS, Korth C, Schrader T: Hybridization of an Aβ-specific antibody fragment with aminopyrazole-based β-sheet ligands displays striking enhancement of target affinity, *Org Biomol Chem* 13:2974–2979, 2015.

Ho L, Ferruzzi MG, Janle EM, Wang J, Gong B, Chen TY, Lobo J, Cooper B, Wu QL, Talcott ST, Percival SS, Simon JE, Pasinetti GM: Identification of brain-targeted bioactive dietary quercetin-3-O-glucuronide as a novel intervention for Alzheimer's disease, *FASEB J* 27:769–781, 2013.

Hochdörffer K, März-Berberich J, Nagel-Steger L, Epple M, Meyer-Zaika W, Horn AH, Sticht H, Sinha S, Bitan G, Schrader T: Rational design of β-sheet ligands against $A\beta_{42}$-induced toxicity, *J Am Chem Soc* 133:4348–4358, 2011.

Holtzman DM: In vivo effects of ApoE and clusterin on amyloid-β metabolism and neuropathology, *J Mol Neurosci* 23:247–254, 2004.

Hoppe JB, Coradini K, Frozza RL, Oliveira CM, Meneghetti AB, Bernardi A, Pires ES, Beck RC, Salbego CG: Free and nanoencapsulated curcumin suppress β-amyloid-induced cognitive impairments in rats: involvement of BDNF and Akt/GSK-3β signaling pathway, *Neurobiol Learn Mem* 106:134–144, 2013.

Hori Y, Takeda S, Cho H, Wegmann S, Shoup TM, Takahashi K, Irimia D, Elmaleh DR, Hyman BT, Hudry E: A Food and Drug Administration–approved asthma therapeutic agent impacts amyloid β in the brain in a transgenic model of Alzheimer disease, *J Biol Chem* 290:1966–1978, 2015.

Hossain S, Hashimoto M, Katakura M, Miwa K, Shimada T, Shido O: Mechanism of docosahexaenoic acid-induced inhibition of in vitro Aβ1–42 fibrillation and Aβ1–42-induced toxicity in SH-S5Y5 cells, *J Neurochem* 111:568–579, 2009.

Hsiao K, Chapman P, Nilsen S, Eckman C, Harigaya Y, Younkin S, Yang F, Cole G: Correlative memory deficits, Aβ elevation, and amyloid plaques in transgenic mice, *Science* 274:99–102, 1996.

Huang F, Wang J, Qu A, Shen L, Liu J, Liu J, Zhang Z, An Y, Shi L: Maintenance of amyloid β peptide homeostasis by artificial chaperones based on mixed-shell polymeric micelles, *Angew Chem Int Ed Engl* 53:8985–8990, 2014.

Hughes E, Burke RM, Doig AJ: Inhibition of toxicity in the β-amyloid peptide fragment β-(25–35) using *N*-methylated derivatives: a general strategy to prevent amyloid formation, *J Biol Chem* 275:25109–25115, 2000.

Hung LW, Ciccotosto GD, Giannakis E, Tew DJ, Perez K, Masters CL, Cappai R, Wade JD, Barnham KJ: Amyloid-β peptide (Aβ) neurotoxicity is modulated by the rate of peptide aggregation: Aβ dimers and trimers correlate with neurotoxicity, *J Neurosci* 28:11950–11958, 2008.

Imtiaz M, Rizwan MS, Xiong S, Li H, Ashraf M, Shahzad SM, Shahzad M, Rizwan M, Tu S: Vanadium, recent advancements and research prospects: a review, *Environ Int* 80:79–88, 2015.

Ishigaki Y, Tanaka H, Akama H, Ogara T, Uwai K, Tokuraku K: A microliter-scale high-throughput screening system with quantum-dot nanoprobes for amyloid-β aggregation inhibitors, *PLoS One* 8:e72992, 2013.

Itil T, Martorano D: Natural substances in psychiatry (*Ginkgo biloba* in dementia), *Psychopharmacol Bull* 31:147–158, 1995.

Iuvone T, De Filippis D, Esposito G, D'Amico A, Izzo AA: The spice sage and its active ingredient rosmarinic acid protect PC12 cells from amyloid-β peptide-induced neurotoxicity, *J Pharmacol Exp Ther* 317:1143–1149, 2006.

Jagota S, Rajadas J: Synthesis of D-amino acid peptides and their effect on β-amyloid aggregation and toxicity in transgenic *Caenorhabditis elegans*, *Med Chem Res* 22:3991–4000, 2013.

Jankowsky JL, Slunt HH, Ratovitski T, Jenkins NA, Copeland NG, Borchelt DR: Co-expression of multiple transgenes in mouse CNS: a comparison of strategies, *Biomol Eng* 17:157–165, 2001.

Jankowsky JL, Fadale DJ, Anderson J, Xu GM, Gonzales V, Jenkins NA, Copeland NG, Lee MK, Younkin LH, Wagner SL, Younkin SG, Borchelt DR: Mutant presenilins specifically elevate the levels of the 42 residue β-amyloid peptide in vivo: evidence for augmentation of a 42-specific γ secretase, *Hum Mol Genet* 13:159–170, 2004.

Janusz M, Zablocka A: Colostrinin: a proline-rich polypeptide complex of potential therapeutic interest, *Cell Mol Biol* 59:4–11, 2013.

Jia N, Han K, Kong JJ, Zhang XM, Sha S, Ren GR, Cao YP: (−)-Epigallocatechin-3-gallate alleviates spatial memory impairment in APP/PS1 mice by restoring IRS-1 signaling defects in the hippocampus, *Mol Cell Biochem* 380:211–218, 2013.

Jimenez-Aliaga K, Bermejo-Bescos P, Benedi J, Martin-Aragon S: Quercetin and rutin exhibit antiamyloidogenic and fibril-disaggregating effects in vitro and potent antioxidant activity in APPswe cells, *Life Sci* 89:939–945, 2011.

Johansson AS, Garlind A, Berglind-Dehlin F, Karlsson G, Edwards K, Gellerfors P, Ekholm-Pettersson F, Palmblad J, Lannfelt L: Docosahexaenoic acid stabilizes soluble amyloid-β protofibrils and sustains amyloid-β-induced neurotoxicity in vitro, *FEBS J* 274:990–1000, 2007.

Jones MR, Mu C, Wang MC, Webb MI, Walsby CJ, Storr T: Modulation of the Aβ peptide aggregation pathway by KP1019 limits Aβ-associated neurotoxicity, *Metallomics* 7:129–135, 2015.

Jonsson T, Atwal JK, Steinberg S, Snaedal J, Jonsson PV, Bjornsson S, Stefansson H, Sulem P, Gudbjartsson D, Maloney J, Hoyte K, Gustafson A, Liu Y, Lu Y, Bhangale T, Graham RR, Huttenlocher J, Bjornsdottir G, Andreassen OA, Jonsson EG, Palotie A, Behrens TW, Magnusson OT, Kong A, Thorsteinsdottir U, Watts RJ, Stefansson K: A mutation in APP protects against Alzheimer's disease and age-related cognitive decline, *Nature* 488:96–99, 2012.

Judd DA, Nettles JH, Nevins N, Snyder JP, Liotta DC, Tang J, Ermolieff J, Schinazi RF, Hill CL: Polyoxometalate HIV-1 protease inhibitors. A new mode of protease inhibition, *J Am Chem Soc* 123:886–897, 2001.

Kallberg Y, Gustafsson M, Persson B, Thyberg J, Johansson J: Prediction of amyloid fibril-forming proteins, *J Biol Chem* 276:12945–12950, 2001.

Kaneko N, Nakamura A, Washimi Y, Kato T, Sakurai T, Arahata Y, Bundo M, Takeda A, Niida S, Ito K, Toba K, Tanaka K, Yanagisawa K: Novel plasma biomarker surrogating cerebral amyloid deposition, *Proc Jpn Acad Ser B* 90:353–364, 2014.

Kanowski S, Herrmann WM, Stephan K, Wierich W, Horr R: Proof of efficacy of the *Ginkgo biloba* special extract EGb 761 in outpatients suffering from mild to moderate primary degenerative dementia of the Alzheimer type or multi-infarct dementia, *Pharmacopsychiatry* 29:47–56, 1996.

Karran E, Hardy J: A critique of the drug discovery and phase 3 clinical programs targeting the amyloid hypothesis for Alzheimer disease, *Ann Neurol* 76:185–205, 2014.

Kawasaki T, Kamijo S: Inhibition of aggregation of amyloid β42 by arginine-containing small compounds, *Biosci Biotechnol Biochem* 76:762–766, 2012.

Kawasaki T, Onodera K, Kamijo S: Selection of peptide inhibitors of soluble $A\beta_{1-42}$ oligomer formation by phage display, *Biosci Biotechnol Biochem* 74:2214–2219, 2010.

Kawasaki T, Onodera K, Kamijo S: Identification of novel short peptide inhibitors of soluble 37/48 kDa oligomers of amyloid β42, *Biosci Biotechnol Biochem* 75:1496–1501, 2011.

Kayed R, Head E, Thompson JL, McIntire TM, Milton SC, Cotman CW, Glabe CG: Common structure of soluble amyloid oligomers implies common mechanism of pathogenesis, *Science* 300:486–489, 2003.

Kaytor MD, Orr HT: The GSK3 β signaling cascade and neurodegenerative disease, *Curr Opin Neurobiol* 12:275–278, 2002.

Kenche VB, Barnham KJ: Alzheimer's disease & metals: therapeutic opportunities, *Br J Pharmacol* 163:211–219, 2011.

Kennard JA, Harrison FE: Intravenous ascorbate improves spatial memory in middle-aged APP/PSEN1 and wild type mice, *Behav Brain Res* 264:34–42, 2014.

Kim JE, Lee M: Fullerene inhibits β-amyloid peptide aggregation, *Biochem Biophys Res Commun* 303:576–579, 2003.

Kim KS, Miller DL, Sapienza VJ, Chen CMJ, Bai C, Grundke-Iqbal I, Currie JR, Wisniewski HM: Production and characterization of monoclonal antibodies reactive to synthetic cerebrovascular amyloid peptide, *Neurosci Res Commun* 2:121–130, 1988.

Kim KS, Wen GY, Bancher C, Chen CMJ, Sapienza VJ, Hong H, Wisniewski HM: Detection and quantitation of amyloid β-peptide with two monoclonal antibodies, *Neurosci Res Commun* 7:113–122, 1990.

Kim DS, Park SY, Kim JK: Curcuminoids from *Curcuma longa* L. (Zingiberaceae) that protect PC12 rat pheochromocytoma and normal human umbilical vein endothelial cells from βA(1–42) insult, *Neurosci Lett* 303:57–61, 2001.

Kim H, Park BS, Lee KG, Choi CY, Jang SS, Kim YH, Lee SE: Effects of naturally occurring compounds on fibril formation and oxidative stress of β-amyloid, *J Agric Food Chem* 53:8537–8541, 2005.

Kim W, Kim Y, Min J, Kim DJ, Chang YT, Hecht MH: A high-throughput screen for compounds that inhibit aggregation of the Alzheimer's peptide, *ACS Chem Biol* 1:461–469, 2006.

Kim YE, Hipp MS, Bracher A, Hayer-Hartl M, Hartl FU: Molecular chaperone functions in protein folding and proteostasis, *Annu Rev Biochem* 82:323–355, 2013.

Kirsten CN, Schrader TH: Intermolecular β-sheet stabilization with aminopyrazoles, *J Am Chem Soc* 119:12061–12068, 1997.

Klärner FG, Benkhoff J, Boese R, Burkert U, Kamieth M, Naatz U: Molecular tweezers as synthetic receptors in host–guest chemistry: inclusion of cyclohexane and self-assembly of aliphatic side chains, *Angew Chem Int Ed Engl* 35:1130–1133, 1996.

Klärner FG, Burkert U, Kamieth M, Boese R: Molecular tweezers as synthetic receptors: molecular recognition of neutral and cationic aromatic substrates; a comparison between the supramolecular structures in crystal and in solution, *J Phys Org Chem* 13:604–611, 2000.

Kliger Y: Computational approaches to therapeutic peptide discovery, *Biopolymers* 94:701–710, 2010.

Kokkoni N, Stott K, Amijee H, Mason JM, Doig AJ: *N*-methylated peptide inhibitors of β-amyloid aggregation and toxicity: optimization of the inhibitor structure, *Biochemistry* 45:9906–9918, 2006.

Kolosova NG, Stefanova NA, Korbolina EE, Fursova A, Kozhevnikova OS: The senescence-accelerated oxys rats—a genetic model of premature aging and age-dependent degenerative diseases, *Adv Gerontol* 27:336–340, 2014.

Kook SY, Lee KM, Kim Y, Cha MY, Kang S, Baik SH, Lee H, Park R, Mook-Jung I: High-dose of vitamin C supplementation reduces amyloid plaque burden and ameliorates pathological changes in the brain of 5XFAD mice, *Cell Death Dis* 5:e1083, 2014.

Koronyo-Hamaoui M, Koronyo Y, Ljubimov AV, Miller CA, Ko MK, Black KL, Schwartz M, Farkas DL: Identification of amyloid plaques in retinas from Alzheimer's patients and noninvasive in vivo optical imaging of retinal plaques in a mouse model, *NeuroImage* 54(Suppl 1):S204–S217, 2011.

Kroth H, Ansaloni A, Varisco Y, Jan A, Sreenivasachary N, Rezaei-Ghaleh N, Giriens V, Lohmann S, Lopez-Deber MP, Adolfsson O, Pihlgren M, Paganetti P, Froestl W, Nagel-Steger L, Willbold D, Schrader T, Zweckstetter M, Pfeifer A, Lashuel HA, Muhs A: Discovery and structure activity relationship of small molecule inhibitors of toxic β-amyloid-42 fibril formation, *J Biol Chem* 287:34786–34800, 2012.

Kumar J, Sim V: D-Amino acid-based peptide inhibitors as early or preventative therapy in Alzheimer disease, *Prion* 8:119–124, 2014.

Kumaraswamy P, Sethuraman S, Krishnan UM: Mechanistic insights of curcumin interactions with the core-recognition motif of β-amyloid peptide, *J Agric Food Chem* 61:3278–3285, 2013.

Kupfer A, Aeschlimann C, Wermuth B, Cerny T: Prophylaxis and reversal of ifosfamide encephalopathy with methylene-blue, *Lancet* 343:763–764, 1994.

Lamb BT, Call LM, Slunt HH, Bardel KA, Lawler AM, Eckman CB, Younkin SG, Holtz G, Wagner SL, Price DL, Sisodia SS, Gearhart JD: Altered metabolism of familial Alzheimers-disease-linked amyloid precursor protein variants in yeast artificial chromosome transgenic mice, *Hum Mol Genet* 6:1535–1541, 1997.

Lambert MP, Barlow AK, Chromy BA, Edwards C, Freed R, Liosatos M, Morgan TE, Rozovsky I, Trommer B, Viola KL, Wals P, Zhang C, Finch CE, Krafft GA, Klein WL: Diffusible, nonfibrillar ligands derived from Aβ_{1-42} are potent central nervous system neurotoxins, *Proc Natl Acad Sci USA* 95:6448–6453, 1998.

Laskay G, Zarandi M, Varga J, Jost K, Fonagy A, Torday C, Latzkovits L, Penke B: A putative tetrapeptide antagonist prevents β-amyloid-induced long-term elevation of $[Ca^{2+}]_i$ in rat astrocytes, *Biochem Biophys Res Commun* 235:479–481, 1997.

Laurin D, Verreault R, Lindsay J, Dewailly E, Holub BJ: Omega-3 fatty acids and risk of cognitive impairment and dementia, *J Alzheimers Dis* 5:315–322, 2003.

Lazar AN, Mourtas S, Youssef I, Parizot C, Dauphin A, Delatour B, Antimisiaris SG, Duyckaerts C: Curcumin-conjugated nanoliposomes with high affinity for Aβ deposits: possible applications to Alzheimer disease, *Nanomedicine* 9:712–721, 2013.

Lazo JS, Wipf P: Combinatorial chemistry and contemporary pharmacology, *J Pharmacol Exp Ther* 293:705–709, 2000.

Lazo ND, Grant MA, Condron MC, Rigby AC, Teplow DB: On the nucleation of amyloid β-protein monomer folding, *Protein Sci* 14:1581–1596, 2005.

Le Bars PL, Katz MM, Berman N, Itil TM, Freedman AM, Schatzberg AF: A placebo-controlled, double-blind, randomized trial of an extract of *Ginkgo biloba* for dementia. North American EGb Study Group, *J Amer Med Assoc* 278:1327–1332, 1997.

Lee I, Yang J, Lee JH, Choe YS: Synthesis and evaluation of 1-(4-[^{18}F]fluoroethyl)-7-(4′-methyl)curcumin with improved brain permeability for β-amyloid plaque imaging, *Bioorg Med Chem Lett* 21:5765–5769, 2011.

Lee HH, Choi TS, Lee SJ, Lee JW, Park J, Ko YH, Kim WJ, Kim K, Kim HI: Supramolecular inhibition of amyloid fibrillation by cucurbit[7]uril, *Angew Chem Int Ed Engl* 53:7461–7465, 2014.

Leon IE, Porro V, Astrada S, Egusquiza MG, Cabello CI, Bollati-Fogolin M, Etcheverry SB: Polyoxometalates as antitumor agents: bioactivity of a new polyoxometalate with copper on a human osteosarcoma model, *Chem Biol Interact* 222C:87–96, 2014.

Lesné S, Koh MT, Kotilinek L, Kayed R, Glabe CG, Yang A, Gallagher M, Ashe KH: A specific amyloid-β protein assembly in the brain impairs memory, *Nature* 440:352–357, 2006.

LeVine H: 4,4′-Dianilino-1,1′-binaphthyl-5,5′-disulfonite: report on non-β-sheet conformers of Alzheimer's peptide β(1–40), *Arch Biochem Biophys* 404:106–115, 2002.

Leza JC, Lizasoain I, San-Martin-Clark O, Lorenzo P: Morphine-induced changes in cerebral and cerebellar nitric oxide synthase activity, *Eur J Pharmacol* 285:95–98, 1995.

Li H, Monien BH, Fradinger EA, Urbanc B, Bitan G: Biophysical characterization of Aβ42 C-terminal fragments: inhibitors of Aβ42 neurotoxicity, *Biochemistry* 49:1259–1267, 2010a.

Li H, Monien BH, Lomakin A, Zemel R, Fradinger EA, Tan M, Spring SM, Urbanc B, Xie CW, Benedek GB, Bitan G: Mechanistic investigation of the inhibition of Aβ42 assembly and neurotoxicity by Aβ42 C-terminal fragments, *Biochemistry* 49:6358–6364, 2010b.

Li H, Du Z, Lopes DH, Fradinger EA, Wang C, Bitan G: C-terminal tetrapeptides inhibit Aβ42-induced neurotoxicity primarily through specific interaction at the N-terminus of Aβ42, *J Med Chem* 54:8451–8460, 2011.

Li H, Zemel R, Lopes DH, Monien BH, Bitan G: A two-step strategy for structure-activity relationship studies of *N*-methylated Aβ42 C-terminal fragments as Aβ42 toxicity inhibitors, *ChemMedChem* 7:515–522, 2012.

Li M, Xu C, Ren J, Wang E, Qu X: Photodegradation of β-sheet amyloid fibrils associated with Alzheimer's disease by using polyoxometalates as photocatalysts, *Chem Commun* 49:11394–11396, 2013a.

Li M, Xu C, Wu L, Ren J, Wang E, Qu X: Self-assembled peptide–polyoxometalate hybrid nanospheres: two in one enhances targeted inhibition of amyloid β-peptide aggregation associated with Alzheimer's disease, *Small* 9:3455–3461, 2013b.

Li M, Howson SE, Dong K, Gao N, Ren J, Scott P, Qu X: Chiral metallohelical complexes enantioselectively target amyloid β for treating Alzheimer's disease, *J Am Chem Soc* 136:11655–11663, 2014.

Lim GP, Chu T, Yang FS, Beech W, Frautschy SA, Cole GM: The curry spice curcumin reduces oxidative damage and amyloid pathology in an Alzheimer transgenic mouse, *J Neurosci* 21:8370–8377, 2001.

Lin LX, Bo XY, Tan YZ, Sun FX, Song M, Zhao J, Ma ZH, Li M, Zheng KJ, Xu SM: Feasibility of β-sheet breaker peptide-H102 treatment for Alzheimer's disease based on β-amyloid hypothesis, *PLoS One* 9:e112052, 2014.

Lipinski CA, Lombardo F, Dominy BW, Feeney PJ: Experimental and computational approaches to estimate solubility and permeability in drug discovery and development settings, *Adv Drug Del Rev* 46:3–26, 2001.

Liu T, Bitan G: Modulating self-assembly of amyloidogenic proteins as a therapeutic approach for neurodegenerative diseases: strategies and mechanisms, *ChemMedChem* 7:359–374, 2012.

Liu K, Guo TL, Chojnacki J, Lee HG, Wang X, Siedlak SL, Rao W, Zhu X, Zhang S: Bivalent ligand containing curcumin and cholesterol as fluorescence probe for Aβ plaques in Alzheimer's disease, *ACS Chem Neurosci* 3:141–146, 2012.

Liu X, Liu Y, Zhang Z, Huang F, Tao Q, Ma R, An Y, Shi L: Temperature-responsive mixed-shell polymeric micelles for the refolding of thermally denatured proteins, *Chemistry* 19:7437–7442, 2013.

Liu J, Wang W, Zhang Q, Zhang S, Yuan Z: Study on the efficiency and interaction mechanism of a decapeptide inhibitor of β-amyloid aggregation, *Biomacromolecules* 15:931–939, 2014.

Lo AW, Ho C, Cummings J, Kosik KS: Parallel discovery of Alzheimer's therapeutics, *Sci Transl Med* 6:241–245, 2014.

Lopes da Silva S, Vellas B, Elemans S, Luchsinger J, Kamphuis P, Yaffe K, Sijben J, Groenendijk M, Stijnen T: Plasma nutrient status of patients with Alzheimer's disease: systematic review and meta-analysis, *Alzheimers Dement* 10:485–502, 2014.

Lopes DH, Attar A, Nair G, Hayden EY, Du Z, McDaniel K, Dutt S, Bravo-Rodriguez K, Mittal S, Klärner FG, Wang C, Sanchez-Garcia E, Schrader T, Bitan G: Molecular tweezers inhibit islet amyloid polypeptide assembly and toxicity by a new mechanism, *ACS Chem Biol* 10:1555–1569, 2015.

Lopez del Amo JM, Fink U, Dasari M, Grelle G, Wanker EE, Bieschke J, Reif B: Structural properties of EGCG-induced, nontoxic Alzheimer's disease Aβ oligomers, *J Mol Biol* 421:517–524, 2012.

Lührs T, Ritter C, Adrian M, Riek-Loher D, Bohrmann B, Döbeli H, Schubert D, Riek R: 3D structure of Alzheimer's amyloid-β(1–42) fibrils, *Proc Natl Acad Sci USA* 102:17342–17347, 2005.

Lump E, Castellano LM, Meier C, Seeliger J, Erwin N, Sperlich B, Stürzel CM, Usmani S, Hammond RM, von Einem J, Gerold G, Kreppel F, Bravo-Rodriguez K, Pietschmann T, Holmes VM, Palesch D, Zirafi O, Weissman D, Sowislok A, Wettig B, Heid C, Kirchhoff F, Weil T, Klarner FG, Schrader T, Bitan G, Sanchez-Garcia E, Winter R, Shorter J, Münch J: A molecular tweezer antagonizes seminal amyloids and HIV infection, *Elife* August:4, 2015.

Luo J, Abrahams JP: Cyclic peptides as inhibitors of amyloid fibrillation, *Chemistry* 20:2410–2419, 2014.

Luo Y, Vali S, Sun S, Chen X, Liang X, Drozhzhina T, Popugaeva E, Bezprozvanny I: Aβ42-binding peptoids as amyloid aggregation inhibitors and detection ligands, *ACS Chem Neurosci* 4:952–962, 2013.

Machon O, van den Bout CJ, Backman M, Kemler R, Krauss S: Role of β-catenin in the developing cortical and hippocampal neuroepithelium, *Neuroscience* 122:129–143, 2003.

Maher P: A comparison of the neurotrophic activities of the flavonoid fisetin and some of its derivatives, *Free Radic Res* 40:1105–1111, 2006.

Maher P, Akaishi T, Abe K: Flavonoid fisetin promotes ERK-dependent long-term potentiation and enhances memory, *Proc Natl Acad Sci USA* 103:16568–16573, 2006.

Maiese K: Taking aim at Alzheimer's disease through the mammalian target of rapamycin, *Ann Med* 46:587–596, 2014.

Mandadapu V, Day AI, Ghanem A: Cucurbituril: chiral applications, *Chirality* 26:712–723, 2014.

Mansson C, Arosio P, Hussein R, Kampinga HH, Hashem RM, Boelens WC, Dobson CM, Knowles TP, Linse S, Emanuelsson C: Interaction of the molecular chaperone DNAJB6 with growing amyloid-β 42 (Aβ42) aggregates leads to sub-stoichiometric inhibition of amyloid formation, *J Biol Chem* 289:31066–31076, 2014.

Marshall PN: The composition of stains produced by the oxidation of methylene blue, *Histochem J* 8:431–442, 1976.

Martins RN, Robinson PJ, Chleboun JO, Beyreuther K, Masters CL: The molecular pathology of amyloid deposition in Alzheimer's disease, *Mol Neurobiol* 5:389–398, 1991.

Masters CL, Simms G, Weinman NA, Multhaup G, McDonald BL, Beyreuther K: Amyloid plaque core protein in Alzheimer disease and Down syndrome, *Proc Natl Acad Sci USA* 82:4245–4249, 1985.

Masuda Y, Fukuchi M, Yatagawa T, Tada M, Takeda K, Irie K, Akagi K, Monobe Y, Imazawa T, Takegoshi K: Solid-state NMR analysis of interaction sites of curcumin and 42-residue amyloid β-protein fibrils, *Bioorg Med Chem* 19:5967–5974, 2011.

Maurer K, Ihl R, Dierks T, Frolich L: Clinical efficacy of Ginkgo biloba special extract EGb 761 in dementia of the Alzheimer type, *J Psychiatr Res* 31:645–655, 1997.

McClure R, Yanagisawa D, Stec D, Abdollahian D, Koktysh D, Xhillari D, Jaeger R, Stanwood G, Chekmenev E, Tooyama I, Gore JC, Pham W: Inhalable curcumin: offering the potential for translation to imaging and treatment of Alzheimer's disease, *J Alzheimers Dis* 44:283–295, 2015.

McGovern SL, Caselli E, Grigorieff N, Shoichet BK: A common mechanism underlying promiscuous inhibitors from virtual and high-throughput screening, *J Med Chem* 45:1712–1722, 2002.

McGovern SL, Helfand BT, Feng B, Shoichet BK: A specific mechanism of nonspecific inhibition, *J Med Chem* 46:4265–4272, 2003.

McKoy AF, Chen J, Schupbach T, Hecht MH: A novel inhibitor of amyloid β (Aβ) peptide aggregation: from high throughput screening to efficacy in an animal model of Alzheimer disease, *J Biol Chem* 287:38992–39000, 2012.

McKoy AF, Chen J, Schupbach T, Hecht MH: Structure–activity relationships for a series of compounds that inhibit aggregation of the Alzheimer's peptide Aβ42, *Chem Biol Drug Des* 84:505–512, 2014.

McLaurin J, Golomb R, Jurewicz A, Antel JP, Fraser PE: Inositol stereoisomers stabilize an oligomeric aggregate of Alzheimer amyloid β peptide and inhibit Aβ-induced toxicity, *J Biol Chem* 275:18495–18502, 2000.

Messori L, Camarri M, Ferraro T, Gabbiani C, Franceschini D: Promising in vitro anti-Alzheimer properties for a ruthenium(III) complex, *ACS Med Chem Lett* 4:329–332, 2013.

Michell RH: Inositol derivatives: evolution and functions, *Nat Rev Mol Cell Biol* 9:151–161, 2008.

Miras HN, Yan J, Long DL, Cronin L: Engineering polyoxometalates with emergent properties, *Chem Soc Rev* 41:7403–7430, 2012.

Mithu VS, Sarkar B, Bhowmik D, Das AK, Chandrakesan M, Maiti S, Madhu PK: Curcumin alters the salt bridge-containing turn region in amyloid β(1–42) aggregates, *J Biol Chem* 289:11122–11131, 2014.

Mori T, Rezai-Zadeh K, Koyama N, Arendash GW, Yamaguchi H, Kakuda N, Horikoshi-Sakuraba Y, Tan J, Town T: Tannic acid is a natural β-secretase inhibitor that prevents cognitive impairment and mitigates Alzheimer-like pathology in transgenic mice, *J Biol Chem* 287:6912–6927, 2012.

Mori T, Koyama N, Segawa T, Maeda M, Maruyama N, Kinoshita N, Hou H, Tan J, Town T: Methylene blue modulates β-secretase, reverses cerebral amyloidosis, and improves cognition in transgenic mice, *J Biol Chem* 289:30303–30317, 2014.

Morley JE, Farr SA: The role of amyloid-β in the regulation of memory, *Biochem Pharmacol* 88:479–485, 2014.

Mura P, Piccioli F, Gabbiani C, Camalli M, Messori L: Structure–function relationships within Keppler-type antitumor ruthenium(III) complexes: the case of 2-aminothiazolium[*trans*-tetrachlorobis(2-aminothiazole)ruthenate(III)], *Inorg Chem* 44:4897–4899, 2005.

Nadimpally KC, Paul A, Mandal B: Reversal of aggregation using β-breaker dipeptide containing peptides: application to Aβ(1–40) self-assembly and its inhibition, *ACS Chem Neurosci* 5:400–408, 2014.

Nakanishi T, Yamakawa N, Asahi T, Shibata N, Ohtani B, Osaka T: Chiral discrimination between thalidomide enantiomers using a solid surface with two-dimensional chirality, *Chirality* 16(Suppl):S36–S39, 2004.

Necula M, Breydo L, Milton S, Kayed R, van der Veer WE, Tone P, Glabe CG: Methylene blue inhibits amyloid Aβ oligomerization by promoting fibrillization, *Biochemistry* 46:8850–8860, 2007a.

Necula M, Kayed R, Milton S, Glabe CG: Small molecule inhibitors of aggregation indicate that amyloid β oligomerization and fibrillization pathways are independent and distinct, *J Biol Chem* 282:10311–10324, 2007b.

Ng G, Ohlsson A: Cromolyn sodium for the prevention of chronic lung disease in preterm infants, *Cochrane Database Syst Rev* 6:Cd003059, 2012.

Ngo ST, Li MS: Curcumin binds to Aβ1–40 peptides and fibrils stronger than ibuprofen and naproxen, *J Phys Chem B* 116:10165–10175, 2012.

Niforou K, Cheimonidou C, Trougakos IP: Molecular chaperones and proteostasis regulation during redox imbalance, *Redox Biol* 2:323–332, 2014.

Nilsberth C, Forsell C, Axelman K, Gustafsson C, Luthman J, Näslund J, Lannfelt L: A novel APP mutation (E693G)—the Arctic mutation, causing Alzheimer's disease with vascular symptoms, *Soc Neurosci Abstr* 25:297, 1999.

Nishikimi M, Koshizaka T, Ozawa T, Yagi K: Occurrence in humans and guinea pigs of the gene related to their missing enzyme L-gulono-γ-lactone oxidase, *Arch Biochem Biophys* 267:842–846, 1988.

Nowick JS, Chung DM, Maitra K, Maitra S, Stigers KD, Sun Y: An unnatural amino acid that mimics a tripeptide β-strand and forms β-sheetlike hydrogen-bonded dimers, *J Am Chem Soc* 122:7654–7661, 2000.

O'Leary JL, Petty J, Harris AB, Inukai J: Supravital staining of mammalian brain with intra-arterial methylene blue followed by pressurized oxygen, *Stain Technol* 43:197–201, 1968.

O'Nuallain B, Freir DB, Nicoll AJ, Risse E, Ferguson N, Herron CE, Collinge J, Walsh DM: Amyloid β-protein dimers rapidly form stable synaptotoxic protofibrils, *J Neurosci* 30:14411–14419, 2010.

Oakley H, Cole SL, Logan S, Maus E, Shao P, Craft J, Guillozet-Bongaarts A, Ohno M, Disterhoft J, Van Eldik L, Berry R, Vassar R: Intraneuronal β-amyloid aggregates, neurodegeneration, and neuron loss in transgenic mice with five familial Alzheimer's disease mutations: potential factors in amyloid plaque formation, *J Neurosci* 26:10129–10140, 2006.

Obulesu M, Dowlathabad MR, Bramhachari PV: Carotenoids and Alzheimer's disease: an insight into therapeutic role of retinoids in animal models, *Neurochem Int* 59:535–541, 2011.

Oda T, Wals P, Osterburg HH, Johnson SA, Pasinetti GM, Morgan TE, Rozovsky I, Stine WB, Snyder SW, Holzman TF, et al: Clusterin (apoJ) alters the aggregation of amyloid β-peptide ($A\beta_{1-42}$) and forms slowly sedimenting Aβ complexes that cause oxidative stress, *Exp Neurol* 136:22–31, 1995.

Oddo S, Caccamo A, Shepherd JD, Murphy MP, Golde TE, Kayed R, Metherate R, Mattson MP, Akbari Y, LaFerla FM: Triple-transgenic model of Alzheimer's disease with plaques and tangles: intracellular Aβ and synaptic dysfunction, *Neuron* 39:409–421, 2003.

Okamoto A, Yamamuro M, Tatarazako N: Acute toxicity of 50 metals to *Daphnia magna*, *J Appl Toxicol* 35:824–830, 2015.

Ono K, Yamada M: Vitamin A and Alzheimer's disease, *Geriatr Gerontol Int* 12:180–188, 2012.

Ono K, Hasegawa K, Naiki H, Yamada M: Anti-amyloidogenic activity of tannic acid and its activity to destabilize Alzheimer's β-amyloid fibrils in vitro, *Biochim Biophys Acta* 1690:193–202, 2004a.

Ono K, Hasegawa K, Naiki H, Yamada M: Curcumin has potent anti-amyloidogenic effects for Alzheimer's β-amyloid fibrils in vitro, *J Neurosci Res* 75:742–750, 2004b.

Ono K, Yoshiike Y, Takashima A, Hasegawa K, Naiki H, Yamada M: Vitamin A exhibits potent antiamyloidogenic and fibril-destabilizing effects in vitro, *Exp Neurol* 189:380–392, 2004c.

Ono K, Li L, Takamura Y, Yoshiike Y, Zhu L, Han F, Mao X, Ikeda T, Takasaki J, Nishijo H, Takashima A, Teplow DB, Zagorski MG, Yamada M: Phenolic compounds prevent amyloid β-protein oligomerization and synaptic dysfunction by site-specific binding, *J Biol Chem* 287:14631–14643, 2012.

Orgogozo JM, Gilman S, Dartigues JF, Laurent B, Puel M, Kirby LC, Jouanny P, Dubois B, Eisner L, Flitman S, Michel BF, Boada M, Frank A, Hock C: Subacute meningoencephalitis in a subset of patients with AD after Aβ42 immunization, *Neurology* 61:46–54, 2003.

Ouberai M, Dumy P, Chierici S, Garcia J: Synthesis and biological evaluation of clicked curcumin and clicked KLVFFA conjugates as inhibitors of β-amyloid fibril formation, *Bioconjug Chem* 20:2123–2132, 2009.

Oz M, Lorke DE, Petroianu GA: Methylene blue and Alzheimer's disease, *Biochem Pharmacol* 78:927–932, 2009.

Paban V, Manrique C, Filali M, Maunoir-Regimbal S, Fauvelle F, Alescio-Lautier B: Therapeutic and preventive effects of methylene blue on Alzheimer's disease pathology in a transgenic mouse model, *Neuropharmacology* 76(Pt A):68–79, 2014.

Paganetti P, Antoniello K, Devraj K, Toni N, Kieran D, Madani R, Pihlgren M, Adolfsson O, Froestl W, Schrattenholz A, Liebner S, Havas D, Windisch M, Cirrito JR, Pfeifer A, Muhs A: Increased efflux of amyloid-β peptides through the blood–brain barrier by muscarinic acetylcholine receptor inhibition reduces pathological phenotypes in mouse models of brain amyloidosis, *J Alzheimers Dis* 38:767–786, 2014.

Palhano FL, Lee J, Grimster NP, Kelly JW: Toward the molecular mechanism(s) by which EGCG treatment remodels mature amyloid fibrils, *J Am Chem Soc* 135:7503–7510, 2013.

Palmal S, Maity AR, Singh BK, Basu S, Jana NR, Jana NR: Inhibition of amyloid fibril growth and dissolution of amyloid fibrils by curcumin-gold nanoparticles, *Chemistry* 20:6184–6191, 2014.

Pappolla M, Bozner P, Soto C, Shao HY, Robakis NK, Zagorski M, Frangione B, Ghiso J: Inhibition of Alzheimer β-fibrillogenesis by melatonin, *J Biol Chem* 273:7185–7188, 1998.

Pardridge WM: Alzheimer's disease drug development and the problem of the blood–brain barrier, *Alzheimers Dement* 5:427–432, 2009.

Parthasarathy LK, Seelan RS, Tobias C, Casanova MF, Parthasarathy RN: Mammalian inositol 3-phosphate synthase: its role in the biosynthesis of brain inositol and its clinical use as a psychoactive agent, *Subcell Biochem* 39:293–314, 2006.

Parthsarathy V, McClean PL, Holscher C, Taylor M, Tinker C, Jones G, Kolosov O, Salvati E, Gregori M, Masserini M, Allsop D: A novel retro-inverso peptide inhibitor reduces amyloid deposition, oxidation and inflammation and stimulates neurogenesis in the APPswe/PS1ΔE9 mouse model of Alzheimer's disease, *PLoS One* 8:e54769, 2013.

Paul A, Nadimpally KC, Mondal T, Thalluri K, Mandal B: Inhibition of Alzheimer's amyloid-β peptide aggregation and its disruption by a conformationally restricted α/β hybrid peptide, *Chem Commun* 51:2245–2248, 2015.

Paula-Lima AC, Louzada PR, De Mello FG, Ferreira ST: Neuroprotection against Aβ and glutamate toxicity by melatonin: are GABA receptors involved? *Neurotox Res* 5:323–327, 2003.

Peng CX, Hu J, Liu D, Hong XP, Wu YY, Zhu LQ, Wang JZ: Disease-modified glycogen synthase kinase-3β intervention by melatonin arrests the pathology and memory deficits in an Alzheimer's animal model, *Neurobiol Aging* 34:1555–1563, 2013.

Permanne B, Adessi C, Saborio GP, Fraga S, Frossard MJ, Van Dorpe J, Dewachter I, Banks WA, Van Leuven F, Soto C: Reduction of amyloid load and cerebral damage in a transgenic mouse model of Alzheimer's disease by treatment with Aβ-sheet breaker peptide, *FASEB J* 16:860–862, 2002.

Peter C, Hongwan D, Kupfer A, Lauterburg BH: Pharmacokinetics and organ distribution of intravenous and oral methylene blue, *Eur J Clin Pharmacol* 56:247–250, 2000.

Petersen RC, Thomas RG, Grundman M, Bennett D, Doody R, Ferris S, Galasko D, Jin S, Kaye J, Levey A, Pfeiffer E, Sano M, van Dyck CH, Thal LJ: Vitamin E and donepezil for the treatment of mild cognitive impairment, *N Engl J Med* 352:2379–2388, 2005.

Phiel CJ, Wilson CA, Lee VMY, Klein PS: GSK-3 α regulates production of Alzheimer's disease amyloid-β peptides, *Nature* 423:435–439, 2003.

Picciano AL, Vaden TD: Complexation between Cu(II) and curcumin in the presence of two different segments of amyloid β, *Biophys Chem* 184:62–67, 2013.

Pike CJ, Walencewicz-Wasserman AJ, Kosmoski J, Cribbs DH, Glabe CG, Cotman CW: Structure-activity analyses of β-amyloid peptides: contributions of the β25–35 region to aggregation and neurotoxicity, *J Neurochem* 64:253–265, 1995.

Planel E, Sun XY, Takashima A: Role of GSK-3 β in Alzheimer's disease pathology, *Drug Dev Res* 56:491–510, 2002.

Poduslo JF, Curran GL, Kumar A, Frangione B, Soto C: β-sheet breaker peptide inhibitor of Alzheimer's amyloidogenesis with increased blood–brain barrier permeability and resistance to proteolytic degradation in plasma, *J Neurobiol* 39:371–382, 1999.

Pollack SJ, Lewis H: Secretase inhibitors for Alzheimer's disease: challenges of a promiscuous protease, *Curr Opin Investig Drugs* 6:35–47, 2005.

Prabhudesai S, Sinha S, Attar A, Kotagiri A, Fitzmaurice AG, Lakshmanan R, Ivanova MI, Loo JA, Klärner FG, Schrader T, Stahl M, Bitan G, Bronstein JM: A novel "molecular tweezer" inhibitor of α-synuclein neurotoxicity in vitro and in vivo, *Neurotherapeutics* 9:464–476, 2012.

Pratim Bose P, Chatterjee U, Nerelius C, Govender T, Norstrom T, Gogoll A, Sandegren A, Gothelid E, Johansson J, Arvidsson PI: Poly-*N*-methylated amyloid β-peptide (Aβ) C-terminal fragments reduce Aβ toxicity in vitro and in *Drosophila melanogaster*, *J Med Chem* 52:8002–8009, 2009.

Rahimi F, Bitan G: The structure and function of fibrillar and oligomeric assemblies of amyloidogenic proteins. In Rahimi F, Bitan G, editors: *Non-fibrillar amyloidogenic protein assemblies—common cytotoxins underlying degenerative diseases*, Dordrecht, 2012, Springer Science+Business Media B.V., pp 1–36.

Rajasekhar K, Chakrabarti M, Govindaraju T: Function and toxicity of amyloid β and recent therapeutic interventions targeting amyloid β in Alzheimer's disease, *Chem Commun* 51:13434–13450, 2015.

Ratnayaka JA, Serpell LC, Lotery AJ: Dementia of the eye: the role of amyloid β in retinal degeneration, *Eye* 29:1013–1026, 2015.

Reed MN, Hofmeister JJ, Jungbauer L, Welzel AT, Yu C, Sherman MA, Lesne S, LaDu MJ, Walsh DM, Ashe KH, Cleary JP: Cognitive effects of cell-derived and synthetically derived Aβ oligomers, *Neurobiol Aging* 32:1784–1794, 2011.

Rezai-Zadeh K, Shytle D, Sun N, Mori T, Hou H, Jeanniton D, Ehrhart J, Townsend K, Zeng J, Morgan D, Hardy J, Town T, Tan J: Green tea epigallocatechin-3-gallate (EGCG) modulates amyloid precursor protein cleavage and reduces cerebral amyloidosis in Alzheimer transgenic mice, *J Neurosci* 25:8807–8814, 2005.

Reznichenko L, Amit T, Zheng H, Avramovich-Tirosh Y, Youdim MB, Weinreb O, Mandel S: Reduction of iron-regulated amyloid precursor protein and β-amyloid peptide by (−)-epigallocatechin-3-gallate in cell cultures: implications for iron chelation in Alzheimer's disease, *J Neurochem* 97:527–536, 2006.

Rhule JT, Hill CL, Judd DA, Schinazi RF: Polyoxometalates in medicine, *Chem Rev* 98:327–358, 1998.

Richman M, Wilk S, Chemerovski M, Warmlander SK, Wahlstrom A, Graslund A, Rahimipour S: In vitro and mechanistic studies of an antiamyloidogenic self-assembled cyclic D,L-α-peptide architecture, *J Am Chem Soc* 135:3474–3484, 2013.

Riha PD, Bruchey AK, Echevarria DJ, Gonzalez-Lima F: Memory facilitation by methylene blue: dose-dependent effect on behavior and brain oxygen consumption, *Eur J Pharmacol* 511:151–158, 2005.

Ringman JM, Cole G, Teng E, Badmaev V, Bardens J, Frautschy S, Rosario E, Fein J, Porter V, Vanek Z, Sugar C, Yau A, Cummings JL: P4-344: oral curcumin for the treatment of mild-to-moderate Alzheimer's disease: tolerability and clinical and biomarker efficacy results of a placebo-controlled 24-week study, *Alzheimers Dement* 4:T774, 2008.

Ringman JM, Frautschy SA, Teng E, Begum AN, Bardens J, Beigi M, Gylys KH, Badmaev V, Heath DD, Apostolova LG, Porter V, Vanek Z, Marshall GA, Hellemann G, Sugar C, Masterman DL, Montine TJ, Cummings JL, Cole GM: Oral curcumin for Alzheimer's disease: tolerability and efficacy in a 24-week randomized, double blind, placebo-controlled study, *Alzheimers Res Ther* 4:43, 2012.

Ripoli C, Cocco S, Li Puma DD, Piacentini R, Mastrodonato A, Scala F, Puzzo D, D'Ascenzo M, Grassi C: Intracellular accumulation of amyloid-β (Aβ) protein plays a major role in Aβ-induced alterations of glutamatergic synaptic transmission and plasticity, *J Neurosci* 34:12893–12903, 2014.

Roberts KF, Elbert DL, Kasten TP, Patterson BW, Sigurdson WC, Connors RE, Ovod V, Munsell LY, Mawuenyega KG, Miller-Thomas MM, Moran CJ, Cross DT III, Derdeyn CP, Bateman RJ: Amyloid-β efflux from the central nervous system into the plasma, *Ann Neurol* 76:837–844, 2014.

Rocha S, Cardoso I, Borner H, Pereira MC, Saraiva MJ, Coelho M: Design and biological activity of β-sheet breaker peptide conjugates, *Biochem Biophys Res Commun* 380:397–401, 2009.

Rocha M, Hernandez-Mijares A, Garcia-Malpartida K, Banuls C, Bellod L, Victor VM: Mitochondria-targeted antioxidant peptides, *Curr Pharm Des* 16:3124–3131, 2010.

Rockenstein E, Mallory M, Mante M, Sisk A, Masliaha E: Early formation of mature amyloid-β protein deposits in a mutant APP transgenic model depends on levels of Aβ(1–42), *J Neurosci Res* 66:573–582, 2001.

Rockenstein E, Mallory M, Mante M, Alford M, Windisch M, Moessler H, Masliah E: Effects of Cerebrolysin™ on amyloid-β deposition in a transgenic model of Alzheimer's disease, *J Neural Transm Suppl* 62:327–336, 2002.

Rokka J, Snellman A, Zona C, La Ferla B, Nicotra F, Salmona M, Forloni G, Haaparanta-Solin M, Rinne JO, Solin O: Synthesis and evaluation of a ^{18}F-curcumin derivate for β-amyloid plaque imaging, *Bioorg Med Chem* 22:2753–2762, 2014.

Ross JA, Kasum CM: Dietary flavonoids: bioavailability, metabolic effects, and safety, *Annu Rev Nutr* 22:19–34, 2002.

Rudnitskaya EA, Muraleva NA, Maksimova KY, Kiseleva E, Kolosova NG, Stefanova NA: Melatonin attenuates memory impairment, amyloid-β accumulation, and neurodegeneration in a rat model of sporadic Alzheimer's disease, *J Alzheimers Dis* 47:103–116, 2015.

Rzepecki P, Schrader T: β-Sheet ligands in action: KLVFF recognition by aminopyrazole hybrid receptors in water, *J Am Chem Soc* 127:3016–3025, 2005.

Rzepecki P, Wehner M, Molt O, Zadmard R, Harms K, Schrader T: Aminopyrazole oligomers for β-sheet stabilization of peptides, *Synthesis-Stuttgart* (12):1815–1826, 2003.

Rzepecki P, Nagel-Steger L, Feuerstein S, Linne U, Molt O, Zadmard R, Aschermann K, Wehner M, Schrader T, Riesner D: Prevention of Alzheimer's disease-associated Aβ aggregation by rationally designed nonpeptidic β-sheet ligands, *J Biol Chem* 279:47497–47505, 2004.

Sabogal-Guaqueta AM, Munoz-Manco JI, Ramirez-Pineda JR, Lamprea-Rodriguez M, Osorio E, Cardona-Gomez GP: The flavonoid quercetin ameliorates Alzheimer's disease pathology and protects cognitive and emotional function in aged triple transgenic Alzheimer's disease model mice, *Neuropharmacology* 93C:134–145, 2015.

Sagara Y, Vanhnasy J, Maher P: Induction of PC12 cell differentiation by flavonoids is dependent upon extracellular signal-regulated kinase activation, *J Neurochem* 90:1144–1155, 2004.

Salloway S, Sperling R, Keren R, Porsteinsson AP, van Dyck CH, Tariot PN, Gilman S, Arnold D, Abushakra S, Hernandez C, Crans G, Liang E, Quinn G, Bairu M, Pastrak A, Cedarbaum JM, ELND005-AD201 Investigators: A phase 2 randomized trial of ELND005, *scyllo*-inositol, in mild to moderate Alzheimer disease, *Neurology* 77:1253–1262, 2011.

Salloway S, Sperling R, Fox NC, Blennow K, Klunk W, Raskind M, Sabbagh M, Honig LS, Porsteinsson AP, Ferris S, Reichert M, Ketter N, Nejadnik B, Guenzler V, Miloslavsky M, Wang D, Lu Y, Lull J, Tudor IC, Liu E, Grundman M, Yuen E, Black R, Brashear HR: Bapineuzumab Clinical Trial Investigators: Two phase 3 trials of bapineuzumab in mild-to-moderate Alzheimer's disease, *N Engl J Med* 370:322–333, 2014.

San-Martin-Clark O, Leza JC, Lizasoain I, Lorenzo P: Changes induced by sodium cromoglycate on brain serotonin turnover in morphine dependent and abstinent mice, *Psychopharmacology* 111:233–238, 1993.

San-Martin-Clark O, Cuellar B, De Alba J, Leza JC, Lorenzo P: Changes induced by sodium cromoglycate in brain catecholamine turnover in morphine dependent and abstinent mice, *Psychopharmacology* 118:347–353, 1995.

Sano M, Ernesto C, Thomas RG, Klauber MR, Schafer K, Grundman M, Woodbury P, Growdon J, Cotman CW, Pfeiffer E, Schneider LS, Thal LJ: A controlled trial of selegiline, α-tocopherol, or both as treatment for Alzheimer's disease: the Alzheimer's Disease Cooperative Study [see comments], *N Engl J Med* 336:1216–1222, 1997.

Sarafianos SG, Kortz U, Pope MT, Modak MJ: Mechanism of polyoxometalate-mediated inactivation of DNA polymerases: an analysis with HIV-1 reverse transcriptase indicates specificity for the DNA-binding cleft, *Biochem J* 319(Pt 2):619–626, 1996.

Sato M, Murakami K, Uno M, Ikubo H, Nakagawa Y, Katayama S, Akagi K, Irie K: Structure–activity relationship for (+)-taxifolin isolated from silymarin as an inhibitor of amyloid β aggregation, *Biosci Biotechnol Biochem* 77:1100–1103, 2013a.

Sato M, Murakami K, Uno M, Nakagawa Y, Katayama S, Akagi K, Masuda Y, Takegoshi K, Irie K: Site-specific inhibitory mechanism for amyloid β42 aggregation by catechol-type flavonoids targeting the Lys residues, *J Biol Chem* 288:23212–23224, 2013b.

Schapira AH, Emre M, Jenner P, Poewe W: Levodopa in the treatment of Parkinson's disease, *Eur J Neurol* 16:982–989, 2009.

Schenk D: Amyloid-β immunotherapy for Alzheimer's disease: the end of the beginning, *Nat Rev Neurosci* 3:824–828, 2002.

Schirmer RH, Adler H, Pickhardt M, Mandelkow E: Lest we forget you—methylene blue, *Neurobiol Aging* 32, 2011, 2325 e2327-2316.

Schrader T, Kirsten C: Intermolecular stabilisation of the β-sheet conformation in dipeptides, *Chem Commun*: 2089–2090, 1996.

Schuster D, Rajendran A, Hui SW, Nicotera T, Srikrishnan T, Kruzel ML: Protective effect of colostrinin on neuroblastoma cell survival is due to reduced aggregation of β-amyloid, *Neuropeptides* 39:419–426, 2005.

Sciarretta KL, Gordon DJ, Meredith SC: Peptide-based inhibitors of amyloid assembly, *Methods Enzymol* 413:273–312, 2006.

Seko A, Yamase T, Yamashita K: Polyoxometalates as effective inhibitors for sialyl- and sulfotransferases, *J Inorg Biochem* 103:1061–1066, 2009.

Selkoe DJ: Alzheimer disease: mechanistic understanding predicts novel therapies, *Ann Intern Med* 140:627–638, 2004.

Shammas SL, Waudby CA, Wang S, Buell AK, Knowles TP, Ecroyd H, Welland ME, Carver JA, Dobson CM, Meehan S: Binding of the molecular chaperone αB-crystallin to Aβ amyloid fibrils inhibits fibril elongation, *Biophys J* 101:1681–1689, 2011.

Shaw JE, Chio J, Dasgupta S, Lai AY, Mo GC, Pang F, Thomason LA, Yang AJ, Yip CM, Nitz M, McLaurin J: Aβ(1–42) assembly in the presence of *scyllo*-inositol derivatives: identification of an oxime linkage as important for the development of assembly inhibitors, *ACS Chem Neurosci* 3:167–177, 2012.

Sinha S, Lopes DH, Du Z, Pang ES, Shanmugam A, Lomakin A, Talbiersky P, Tennstaedt A, McDaniel K, Bakshi R, Kuo PY, Ehrmann M, Benedek GB, Loo JA, Klärner FG, Schrader T, Wang C, Bitan G: Lysine-specific molecular tweezers are broad-spectrum inhibitors of assembly and toxicity of amyloid proteins, *J Am Chem Soc* 133:16958–16969, 2011.

Sinha S, Du Z, Maiti P, Klärner FG, Schrader T, Wang C, Bitan G: Comparison of three amyloid assembly inhibitors: the sugar *scyllo*-inositol, the polyphenol epigallocatechin gallate, and the molecular tweezer CLR01, *ACS Chem Neurosci* 3:451–458, 2012a.

Sinha S, Lopes DH, Bitan G: A key role for lysine residues in amyloid β-protein folding, assembly, and toxicity, *ACS Chem Neurosci* 3:473–481, 2012b.

Sivak BJ: Intrathecal use of methylene blue, *J Amer Med Assoc* 170:2232, 1959.

Skribanek Z, Balaspiri L, Mak M: Interaction between synthetic amyloid-β-peptide (1–40) and its aggregation inhibitors studied by electrospray ionization mass spectrometry, *J Mass Spectrom* 36:1226–1229, 2001.

Smith GP: Filamentous fusion phage: novel expression vectors that display cloned antigens on the virion surface, *Science* 228:1315–1317, 1985.

Smith JV, Luo Y: Elevation of oxidative free radicals in Alzheimer's disease models can be attenuated by *Ginkgo biloba* extract EGb 761, *J Alzheimers Dis* 5:287–300, 2003.

Smith HL, Li W, Cheetham ME: Molecular chaperones and neuronal proteostasis, *Semin Cell Dev Biol* 40:142–152, 2015.

Snitz BE, O'Meara ES, Carlson MC, Arnold AM, Ives DG, Rapp SR, Saxton J, Lopez OL, Dunn LO, Sink KM, DeKosky ST: Ginkgo biloba for preventing cognitive decline in older adults: a randomized trial, *J Amer Med Assoc* 302:2663–2670, 2009.

Sodhi RK, Singh N: All-*trans* retinoic acid rescues memory deficits and neuropathological changes in mouse model of streptozotocin-induced dementia of Alzheimer's type, *Prog Neuropsychopharmacol Biol Psychiatr* 40:38–46, 2013.

Sood A, Abid M, Hailemichael S, Foster M, Torok B, Torok M: Effect of chirality of small molecule organofluorine inhibitors of amyloid self-assembly on inhibitor potency, *Bioorg Med Chem Lett* 19:6931–6934, 2009.

Soto C, Estrada L: Amyloid inhibitors and β-sheet breakers, *Subcell Biochem* 38:351–364, 2005.

Soto C, Sigurdsson EM, Morelli L, Kumar RA, Castano EM, Frangione B: β-sheet breaker peptides inhibit fibrillogenesis in a rat brain model of amyloidosis: implications for Alzheimer's therapy, *Nat Med* 4:822–826, 1998.

Sperling RA, Jack CR Jr, Black SE, Frosch MP, Greenberg SM, Hyman BT, Scheltens P, Carrillo MC, Thies W, Bednar MM, Black RS, Brashear HR, Grundman M, Siemers ER, Feldman HH, Schindler RJ: Amyloid-related imaging abnormalities in amyloid-modifying therapeutic trials: recommendations from the Alzheimer's Association Research Roundtable Workgroup, *Alzheimers Dement* 7:367–385, 2011.

Stackman RW, Eckenstein F, Frei B, Kulhanek D, Nowlin J, Quinn JF: Prevention of age-related spatial memory deficits in a transgenic mouse model of Alzheimer's disease by chronic *Ginkgo biloba* treatment, *Exp Neurol* 184:510–520, 2003.

Stefanova NA, Kozhevnikova OS, Vitovtov AO, Maksimova KY, Logvinov SV, Rudnitskaya EA, Korbolina EE, Muraleva NA, Kolosova NG: Senescence-accelerated OXYS rats: a model of age-related cognitive decline with relevance to abnormalities in Alzheimer disease, *Cell Cycle* 13:898–909, 2014a.

Stefanova NA, Muraleva NA, Skulachev VP, Kolosova NG: Alzheimer's disease-like pathology in senescence-accelerated OXYS rats can be partially retarded with mitochondria-targeted antioxidant SkQ1, *J Alzheimers Dis* 38:681–694, 2014b.

Stewart MG: Colostrinin: a naturally occurring compound derived from mammalian colostrum with efficacy in treatment of neurodegenerative diseases, including Alzheimer's, *Expert Opin Pharmacother* 9:2553–2559, 2008.

Stöhr J, Watts JC, Mensinger ZL, Oehler A, Grillo SK, DeArmond SJ, Prusiner SB, Giles K: Purified and synthetic Alzheimer's amyloid β (Aβ) prions, *Proc Natl Acad Sci USA* 109:11025–11030, 2012.

Stöhr J, Condello C, Watts JC, Bloch L, Oehler A, Nick M, DeArmond SJ, Giles K, DeGrado WF, Prusiner SB: Distinct synthetic Aβ prion strains producing different amyloid deposits in bigenic mice, *Proc Natl Acad Sci USA* 111:10329–10334, 2014.

Sun Y, Zhang G, Hawkes CA, Shaw JE, McLaurin J, Nitz M: Synthesis of *scyllo*-inositol derivatives and their effects on amyloid β peptide aggregation, *Bioorg Med Chem* 16:7177–7184, 2008.

Sung S, Yao Y, Uryu K, Yang H, Lee VM, Trojanowski JQ, Pratico D: Early vitamin E supplementation in young but not aged mice reduces Abeta levels and amyloid deposition in a transgenic model of Alzheimer's disease, *FASEB J* 18:323–325, 2004.

Szegedi V, Fülöp L, Farkas T, Rozsa E, Robotka H, Kis Z, Penke Z, Horvath S, Molnar Z, Datki Z, Soos K, Toldi J, Budai D, Zarandi M, Penke B: Pentapeptides derived from Aβ1–42 protect neurons from the modulatory effect of Aβ fibrils—an in vitro and in vivo electrophysiological study, *Neurobiol Dis* 18:499–508, 2005.

Takahashi T, Mihara H: Peptide and protein mimetics inhibiting amyloid β-peptide aggregation, *Acc Chem Res* 41:1309–1318, 2008.

Takasaki J, Ono K, Yoshiike Y, Hirohata M, Ikeda T, Morinaga A, Takashima A, Yamada M: Vitamin A has anti-oligomerization effects on amyloid-β in vitro, *J Alzheimers Dis* 27:271–280, 2011.

Talbiersky P, Bastkowski F, Klärner FG, Schrader T: Molecular clip and tweezer introduce new mechanisms of enzyme inhibition, *J Am Chem Soc* 130:9824–9828, 2008.

Taniguchi S, Suzuki N, Masuda M, Hisanaga S, Iwatsubo T, Goedert M, Hasegawa M: Inhibition of heparin-induced tau filament formation by phenothiazines, polyphenols, and porphyrins, *J Biol Chem* 280:7614–7623, 2005.

Taylor M, Moore S, Mayes J, Parkin E, Beeg M, Canovi M, Gobbi M, Mann DM, Allsop D: Development of a proteolytically stable retro-inverso peptide inhibitor of β-amyloid oligomerization as a potential novel treatment for Alzheimer's disease, *Biochemistry* 49:3261–3272, 2010.

Teng E, Taylor K, Bilousova T, Weiland D, Pham T, Zuo X, Yang F, Chen PP, Glabe CG, Takacs A, Hoffman DR, Frautschy SA, Cole GM: Dietary DHA supplementation in an APP/PS1 transgenic rat model of AD reduces behavioral and Aβ pathology and modulates Aβ oligomerization, *Neurobiol Dis* 82:552–560, 2015.

Thal DR, Griffin WS, de Vos RA, Ghebremedhin E: Cerebral amyloid angiopathy and its relationship to Alzheimer's disease, *Acta Neuropathol* 115:599–609, 2008.

Thapa A, Vernon BC, De la Pena K, Soliz G, Moreno HA, Lopez GP, Chi EY: Membrane-mediated neuroprotection by curcumin from amyloid-β-peptide-induced toxicity, *Langmuir* 29:11713–11723, 2013.

Tiwari SK, Agarwal S, Seth B, Yadav A, Nair S, Bhatnagar P, Karmakar M, Kumari M, Chauhan LK, Patel DK, Srivastava V, Singh D, Gupta SK, Tripathi A, Chaturvedi RK, Gupta KC: Curcumin-loaded nanoparticles potently induce adult neurogenesis and reverse cognitive deficits in Alzheimer's disease model via canonical Wnt/β-catenin pathway, *ACS Nano* 8:76–103, 2014.

Tjernberg LO, Näslund J, Lindqvist F, Johansson J, Karlstrom AR, Thyberg J, Terenius L, Nordstedt C: Arrest of β-amyloid fibril formation by a pentapeptide ligand, *J Biol Chem* 271:8545–8548, 1996.

Townsend M, Cleary JP, Mehta T, Hofmeister J, Lesne S, O'Hare E, Walsh DM, Selkoe DJ: Orally available compound prevents deficits in memory caused by the Alzheimer amyloid-β oligomers, *Ann Neurol* 60:668–676, 2006.

Tsai YM, Chien CF, Lin LC, Tsai TH: Curcumin and its nano-formulation: the kinetics of tissue distribution and blood–brain barrier penetration, *Int J Pharm* 416:331–338, 2011.

Tsuji-Ueno S, Komatsu M, Iguchi K, Takahashi M, Yoshino S, Suzuki M, Nemoto N, Nishigaki K: Novel high-affinity Aβ-binding peptides identified by an advanced in vitro evolution, progressive library method, *Protein Pept Lett* 18:642–650, 2011.

Uchikawa O, Fukatsu K, Suno M, Aono T, Doi T: In vivo biological activity of antioxidative aminothiazole derivatives, *Chem Pharm Bull* 44:2070–2077, 1996.

Urbanc B, Cruz L, Yun S, Buldyrev SV, Bitan G, Teplow DB, Stanley HE: In silico study of amyloid β-protein folding and oligomerization, *Proc Natl Acad Sci USA* 101:17345–17350, 2004.

Urbanc B, Betnel M, Cruz L, Bitan G, Teplow DB: Elucidation of amyloid β-protein oligomerization mechanisms: discrete molecular dynamics study, *J Am Chem Soc* 132:4266–4280, 2010.

Urbanc B, Betnel M, Cruz L, Li H, Fradinger EA, Monien BH, Bitan G: Structural basis for Aβ(1–42) toxicity inhibition by Aβ C-terminal fragments: discrete molecular dynamics study, *J Mol Biol* 410:316–328, 2011.

Valensin D, Migliorini C, Valensin G, Gaggelli E, La Penna G, Kozlowski H, Gabbiani C, Messori L: Exploring the reactions of β-amyloid (Aβ) peptide 1–28 with Al(III) and Fe(III) ions, *Inorg Chem* 50:6865–6867, 2011.

Vassar R: BACE1 inhibitor drugs in clinical trials for Alzheimer's disease, *Alzheimers Res Ther* 6:89, 2014.

Vassar R, Bennett BD, Babu-Khan S, Kahn S, Mendiaz EA, Denis P, Teplow DB, Ross S, Amarante P, Loeloff R, Luo Y, Fisher S, Fuller L, Edenson S, Lile J, Jarosinski MA, Biere AL, Curran E, Burgess T, Louis JC, Collins F, Treanor J, Rogers G, Citron M: β-secretase cleavage of Alzheimer's amyloid precursor protein by the transmembrane aspartic protease BACE, *Science* 286:735–741, 1999.

Veszelka S, Toth AE, Walter FR, Datki Z, Mozes E, Fulop L, Bozso Z, Hellinger E, Vastag M, Orsolits B, Kornyei Z, Penke B, Deli MA: Docosahexaenoic acid reduces amyloid-β induced toxicity in cells of the neurovascular unit, *J Alzheimers Dis* 36:487–501, 2013.

Vivekanandan S, Brender JR, Lee SY, Ramamoorthy A: A partially folded structure of amyloid-β(1–40) in an aqueous environment, *Biochem Biophys Res Commun* 411:312–316, 2011.

Vyskocil A, Viau C: Assessment of molybdenum toxicity in humans, *J Appl Toxicol* 19:185–192, 1999.

Wade AG, Farmer M, Harari G, Fund N, Laudon M, Nir T, Frydman-Marom A, Zisapel N: Add-on prolonged-release melatonin for cognitive function and sleep in mild to moderate Alzheimer's disease: a 6-month, randomized, placebo-controlled, multicenter trial, *Clin Interv Aging* 9:947–961, 2014.

Waldo GS, Standish BM, Berendzen J, Terwilliger TC: Rapid protein-folding assay using green fluorescent protein, *Nat Biotechnol* 17:691–695, 1999.

Walker LC, Diamond MI, Duff KE, Hyman BT: Mechanisms of protein seeding in neurodegenerative diseases, *JAMA Neurol* 70:304–310, 2013.

Walsh DM, Hartley DM, Kusumoto Y, Fezoui Y, Condron MM, Lomakin A, Benedek GB, Selkoe DJ, Teplow DB: Amyloid β-protein fibrillogenesis: structure and biological activity of protofibrillar intermediates, *J Biol Chem* 274:25945–25952, 1999.

Walter-Sack I, Rengelshausen J, Oberwittler H, Burhenne J, Mueller O, Meissner P, Mikus G: High absolute bioavailability of methylene blue given as an aqueous oral formulation, *Eur J Clin Pharmacol* 65:179–189, 2009.

Wang HW, Pasternak JF, Kuo H, Ristic H, Lambert MP, Chromy B, Viola KL, Klein WL, Stine WB, Krafft GA, Trommer BL: Soluble oligomers of β amyloid (1–42) inhibit long-term potentiation but not long-term depression in rat dentate gyrus, *Brain Res* 924:133–140, 2002.

Wang SH, Liu FF, Dong XY, Sun Y: Thermodynamic analysis of the molecular interactions between amyloid β-peptide 42 and (−)-epigallocatechin-3-gallate, *J Phys Chem B* 114:11576–11583, 2010.

Wang SW, Wang YJ, Su YJ, Zhou WW, Yang SG, Zhang R, Zhao M, Li YN, Zhang ZP, Zhan DW, Liu RT: Rutin inhibits β-amyloid aggregation and cytotoxicity, attenuates oxidative stress, and decreases the production of nitric oxide and proinflammatory cytokines, *Neurotoxicology* 33:482–490, 2012.

Wang Q, Liang G, Zhang M, Zhao J, Patel K, Yu X, Zhao C, Ding B, Zhang G, Zhou F, Zheng J: De novo design of self-assembled hexapeptides as β-amyloid (Aβ) peptide inhibitors, *ACS Chem Neurosci* 5:972–981, 2014a.

Wang J, Liu Y, Xu K, Qi Y, Zhong J, Zhang K, Li J, Wang E, Wu Z, Kang Z: Broad-spectrum antiviral property of polyoxometalate localized on a cell surface, *ACS Appl Mater Interf* 6:9785–9789, 2014b.

Wang J, Qu X, Qi Y, Li J, Song X, Li L, Yin D, Xu K, Li J: Pharmacokinetics of anti-HBV polyoxometalate in rats, *PLoS One* 9:e98292, 2014c.

Wang P, Su C, Li R, Wang H, Ren Y, Sun H, Yang J, Sun J, Shi J, Tian J, Jiang S: Mechanisms and effects of curcumin on spatial learning and memory improvement in APPswe/PS1dE9 mice, *J Neurosci Res* 92:218–231, 2014d.

Wei CW, Peng Y, Zhang L, Huang Q, Cheng M, Liu YN, Li J: Synthesis and evaluation of ferrocenoyl pentapeptide (Fc-KLVFF) as an inhibitor of Alzheimer's Aβ(1–42) fibril formation in vitro, *Bioorg Med Chem Lett* 21:5818–5821, 2011.

Weinreb O, Mandel S, Amit T, Youdim MB: Neurological mechanisms of green tea polyphenols in Alzheimer's and Parkinson's diseases, *J Nutr Biochem* 15:506–516, 2004.

Wilcock DM, Griffin WS: Down's syndrome, neuroinflammation, and Alzheimer neuropathogenesis, *J Neuroinflamm* 10:84, 2013.

Wilhelmus MM, de Waal RM, Verbeek MM: Heat shock proteins and amateur chaperones in amyloid-β accumulation and clearance in Alzheimer's disease, *Mol Neurobiol* 35:203–216, 2007.

Willem M, Tahirovic S, Busche MA, Ovsepian SV, Chafai M, Kootar S, Hornburg D, Evans LD, Moore S, Daria A, Hampel H, Muller V, Giudici C, Nuscher B, Wenninger-Weinzierl A, Kremmer E, Heneka MT, Thal DR, Giedraitis V, Lannfelt L, Muller U, Livesey FJ, Meissner F, Herms J, Konnerth A, Marie H, Haass C: η-Secretase processing of APP inhibits neuronal activity in the hippocampus, *Nature* 526:443–447, 2015.

Wischik CM, Edwards PC, Lai RY, Roth M, Harrington CR: Selective inhibition of Alzheimer disease-like tau aggregation by phenothiazines, *Proc Natl Acad Sci USA* 93:11213–11218, 1996.

Wischik CM, Bentham P, Wischik DJ, Seng KM: O3-04-07: Tau aggregation inhibitor (TAI) therapy with Rember™ arrests disease progression in mild and moderate Alzheimer's disease over 50 weeks, *Alzheimers Dement* 4:T167, 2008.

Wischik CM, Staff RT, Wischik DJ, Bentham P, Murray AD, Storey JM, Kook KA, Harrington CR: Tau aggregation inhibitor therapy: an exploratory phase 2 study in mild or moderate Alzheimer's disease, *J Alzheimers Dis* 44:705–720, 2015.

Witten ML, Sheppard PR, Witten BL: Tungsten toxicity, *Chem Biol Interact* 196:87–88, 2012.

Wolfe MS: γ-Secretase inhibitors and modulators for Alzheimer's disease, *J Neurochem* 120(Suppl 1):89–98, 2012.

Wolfe MS, Xia WM, Ostaszewski BL, Diehl TS, Kimberly WT, Selkoe DJ: Two transmembrane aspartates in presenilin-1 required for presenilin endoproteolysis and γ-secretase activity, *Nature* 398:513–517, 1999.

Wu Y, Wu Z, Butko P, Christen Y, Lambert MP, Klein WL, Link CD, Luo Y: Amyloid-β-induced pathological behaviors are suppressed by *Ginkgo biloba* extract EGb 761 and ginkgolides in transgenic *Caenorhabditis elegans*, *J Neurosci* 26:13102–13113, 2006.

Wurth C, Guimard NK, Hecht MH: Mutations that reduce aggregation of the Alzheimer's Aβ 42 peptide: an unbiased search for the sequence determinants of Aβ amyloidogenesis, *J Mol Biol* 319:1279–1290, 2002.

Xu S, Zhou G, Wang W, Tianjin Medical University: β-sheet inhibiting peptides for preventing and/or treating Alzheimer's disease. CN2008. US 8,361,967 B2.

Yagi H, Katoh S, Akiguchi I, Takeda T: Age-related deterioration of ability of acquisition in memory and learning in senescence accelerated mouse: SAM-P/8 as an animal model of disturbances in recent memory, *Brain Res* 474:86–93, 1988.

Yallampalli S, Micci MA, Taglialatela G: Ascorbic acid prevents β-amyloid-induced intracellular calcium increase and cell death in PC12 cells, *Neurosci Lett* 251:105–108, 1998.

Yamin G, Ruchala P, Teplow DB: A peptide hairpin inhibitor of amyloid β-protein oligomerization and fibrillogenesis, *Biochemistry* 48:11329–11331, 2009.

Yan R, Vassar R: Targeting the β secretase BACE1 for Alzheimer's disease therapy, *Lancet Neurol* 13:319–329, 2014.

Yan Y, Wang C: Aβ42 is more rigid than Aβ40 at the C terminus: implications for Aβ aggregation and toxicity, *J Mol Biol* 364:853–862, 2006.

Yanagisawa D, Ibrahim NF, Taguchi H, Morikawa S, Hirao K, Shirai N, Sogabe T, Tooyama I: Curcumin derivative with the substitution at C-4 position, but not curcumin, is effective against amyloid pathology in APP/PS1 mice, *Neurobiol Aging* 36:201–210, 2015.

Yang F, Lim GP, Begum AN, Ubeda OJ, Simmons MR, Ambegaokar SS, Chen PP, Kayed R, Glabe CG, Frautschy SA, Cole GM: Curcumin inhibits formation of amyloid β oligomers and fibrils, binds plaques, and reduces amyloid in vivo, *J Biol Chem* 280:5892–5901, 2005a.

Yang PH, Sun X, Chiu JF, Sun H, He QY: Transferrin-mediated gold nanoparticle cellular uptake, *Bioconjug Chem* 16:494–496, 2005b.

Yang SG, Wang WY, Ling TJ, Feng Y, Du XT, Zhang X, Sun XX, Zhao M, Xue D, Yang Y, Liu RT: α-Tocopherol quinone inhibits β-amyloid aggregation and cytotoxicity, disaggregates preformed fibrils and decreases the production of reactive oxygen species NO and inflammatory cytokines, *Neurochem Int* 57:914–922, 2010.

Yao ZX, Drieu K, Papadopoulos V: The *Ginkgo biloba* extract EGb 761 rescues the PC12 neuronal cells from β-amyloid-induced cell death by inhibiting the formation of β-amyloid-derived diffusible neurotoxic ligands, *Brain Res* 889:181–190, 2001.

Ye J, Zhang Y: Curcumin protects against intracellular amyloid toxicity in rat primary neurons, *Int J Clin Exp Med* 5:44–49, 2012.

Young LM, Cao P, Raleigh DP, Ashcroft AE, Radford SE: Ion mobility spectrometry–mass spectrometry defines the oligomeric intermediates in amylin amyloid formation and the mode of action of inhibitors, *J Am Chem Soc* 136:660–670, 2014.

Young LM, Saunders JC, Mahood RA, Revill CH, Foster RJ, Ashcroft AE, Radford SE: ESI-IMS-MS: a method for rapid analysis of protein aggregation and its inhibition by small molecules, *Methods* 95:62–69, 2015a.

Young LM, Saunders JC, Mahood RA, Revill CH, Foster RJ, Tu LH, Raleigh DP, Radford SE, Ashcroft AE: Screening and classifying small-molecule inhibitors of amyloid formation using ion mobility spectrometry–mass spectrometry, *Nat Chem* 7:73–81, 2015b.

Yu H, Dee DR, Liu X, Brigley AM, Sosova I, Woodside MT: Protein misfolding occurs by slow diffusion across multiple barriers in a rough energy landscape, *Proc Natl Acad Sci USA* 112:8308–8313, 2015.

Zhang S, Casey N, Lee JP: Residual structure in the Alzheimer's disease peptide: probing the origin of a central hydrophobic cluster, *Fold Des* 3:413–422, 1998.

Zhang S, Iwata K, Lachenmann MJ, Peng JW, Li S, Stimson ER, Lu Y, Felix AM, Maggio JE, Lee JP: The Alzheimer's peptide Aβ adopts a collapsed coil structure in water, *J Struct Biol* 130:130–141, 2000.

Zhang L, Yang X, Yang S, Zhang J: The Wnt/β-catenin signaling pathway in the adult neurogenesis, *Eur J Neurosci* 33:1–8, 2011.

Zhang X, Tian Y, Yuan P, Li Y, Yaseen MA, Grutzendler J, Moore A, Ran C: A bifunctional curcumin analogue for two-photon imaging and inhibiting crosslinking of amyloid β in Alzheimer's disease, *Chem Commun* 50:11550–11553, 2014.

Zhao LN, Chiu SW, Benoit J, Chew LY, Mu Y: The effect of curcumin on the stability of Aβ dimers, *J Phys Chem B* 116:7428–7435, 2012.

Zheng X, Liu D, Klärner FG, Schrader T, Bitan G, Bowers MT: Amyloid β-protein assembly: the effect of molecular tweezers CLR01 and CLR03, *J Phys Chem B* 119:4831–4841, 2015a.

Zheng X, Wu C, Liu D, Li H, Bitan G, Shea JE, Bowers MT: Mechanism of C-terminal fragments of amyloid β-protein as Aβ inhibitors: do C-terminal interactions play a key role in their inhibitory activity?, *J Phys Chem B* 120:1615–1623, 2016.

Zingg JM, Azzi A: Non-antioxidant activities of vitamin E, *Curr Med Chem* 11:1113–1133, 2004.

CHAPTER

7

Anti-Amyloid-β Immunotherapy for Alzheimer's Disease

H. Crehan, C.A. Lemere

OUTLINE

INTRODUCTION TO ALZHEIMER'S DISEASE

Alzheimer's disease (AD), the leading form of dementia, currently affects 44 million people worldwide and is rapidly increasing (http://www.brightfocus.org). The United States alone accounts for 5.3 million of these people, that is, 1 in 9 elderly individuals over the age of 65 years. These staggering numbers lead to substantial costs in health care, long-term care,

Developing Therapeutics for Alzheimer's Disease. http://dx.doi.org/10.1016/B978-0-12-802173-6.00007-1

and hospice requirements, of which the total expense in 2015 was reported at $226 billion (US dollars) (Alzheimer's Association, 2015). AD is characterized by progressive memory impairment accompanied by language dysfunction, impairment of visiospatial skills, and changes in personality leading to intensive caregiving requirements (Marczinski and Kertesz, 2006; Hamilton et al., 2009; Peters et al., 2009; Savva et al., 2009; Wagner et al., 2012).

AD Genetics

There are both genetic and nongenetic risk factors for the development of AD. Familial early-onset AD (EOAD) is typically inherited in an autosomal-dominant fashion, and three genes have been found to harbor AD causative mutations: the amyloid precursor protein (*APP*), presenilin 1 (*PS1*), and presenilin 2 (*PS2*) genes (Chartier-Harlin et al., 1991; Goate et al., 1991; Levy-Lahad et al., 1995; Sherrington et al., 1995; Walker et al., 2005). Until recently, the genetics of late-onset AD (LOAD) were not well understood, and the ε4 allele of the apolipoprotein E gene (*ApoE*) was the only confirmed risk factor (Chartier-Harlin et al., 1994). However, genome-wide association studies (GWAS) have revealed common genetic variations in *CLU, CR1, TREM2, PICALM, ABCA7, BIN1, EPHA1, CD33, CD2AP, PTK2B, SORL1, MEF2C, ZCWPN1, CASS4*, and the *MS4A* gene cluster as additional risk factors contributing to the development of LOAD (Harold et al., 2009; Lambert et al., 2009; Hollingworth et al., 2011; Naj et al., 2011; Guerreiro et al., 2013; Beecham et al., 2014). In addition, people with Down syndrome have an increased risk of AD owing to the trisomy of chromosome 21, which encompasses hundreds of genes, including the gene for APP, as reviewed by Hartley et al. (2015). Age is the greatest risk factor for developing AD, with the prevalence of AD increasing exponentially with age after roughly 65 years (Prince et al., 2013). Cerebrovascular disease and type II diabetes mellitus have also been reported as nongenetic risk factors for the disease (Luchsinger et al., 2001; Lindsay et al., 2002; Reitz and Mayeux, 2014).

AD Pathogenesis

There are a number of changes that occur in the AD brain such as synaptic pathology, neuron loss, neuroinflammation, and brain atrophy (Scheff and Price, 2003; Donev et al., 2009; Leung et al., 2013; Heneka et al., 2015); however, the commonly known neuropathological hallmarks of AD are amyloid-β (Aβ) plaques and neurofibrillary tangles (NFTs) (Wisniewski et al., 1973; Mirra, 1997; Hardy and Selkoe, 2002). The amino-terminus of Aβ is generated by proteolytic cleavage of β-amyloid precursor protein (βAPP) by β-secretase, and its C-terminus is generated by γ-secretase. In AD, Aβ aggregates into oligomers and fibrils, the initial step of the amyloid cascade hypothesis (Hardy and Selkoe, 2002). Ensuing events include tau hyperphosphorylation and aggregation, gliosis, oxidative stress, synaptic dysfunction, NFT formation, neuron loss, and eventually cognitive decline. Senile plaques are primarily composed of Aβ in its fibrillar form, which can lead to a number of pathologies resulting in dysfunctional neuronal activity and neurodegeneration (Deshpande et al., 2006). Aβ undergoes a number of conformational changes prior to fibrillization which can also be toxic at lower nanomolar concentrations (Sakono and Zako, 2010). These soluble Aβ species, which have been found in the cerebrospinal fluid (CSF) of AD patients, consist of forms such as monomers, oligomers, and protofibrils (Georganopoulou et al., 2005). It is important to note that different conformations of Aβ can contribute to the pathogenesis of AD through distinct mechanisms (Walsh et al., 2002; Hartley et al., 2015). The formation of Aβ through endopeptidase cleavage of APP can result in a number of Aβ species being formed. The Aβ species ending at position 40 (Aβ40) is the most abundant, but the slightly longer Aβ species ending at position 42 (Aβ42) is the main species deposited in the AD brain (Selkoe, 2001; Murphy and LeVine, 2010). In addition to differences in the C-terminus, the N-terminus can be truncated and modified, forming less abundant but highly toxic variants such as pyroGlu-3 Aβ and pyroGlu-11 Aβ (Saido et al., 1995; Schilling et al., 2006), which have been found in the brains of humans with AD and animal models (Frost et al., 2013).

Another relatively common feature of AD is cerebral amyloid angiopathy (CAA) in which amyloid forms in the walls of blood vessels of the central nervous system (CNS). Carriers of the ApoE ε4 allele show a tighter correlation with high CAA burden than with parenchymal Aβ plaque burden (Premkumar et al., 1996; Chalmers et al., 2003).

Aβ plaques mainly accumulate in the isocortex, and although the progression of plaque deposition is poorly predicted, there are two main staging systems commonly used: the three Braak and Braak stages and the five Thal stages (Braak and Braak, 1991; Thal et al., 2002). Although the total amyloid burden does not correlate with the severity of dementia (Arriagada et al., 1992; Giannakopoulos et al., 2003; Ingelsson et al., 2004), sequential accumulation of Aβ deposits in the cerebral cortex has been observed. In a study investigating the relationship between Braak and Braak stages with topographical distribution of Aβ deposits and neuritic plaques (deteriorating neuronal fragments surrounding Aβ deposits) in the entorhinal and perirhinal cortices and the hippocampus, it was found that the number of subregions within these areas that displayed such pathologies increased in correlation with Braak and Braak stage (Yilmazer-Hanke and Hanke, 1999).

Glial cells are commonly found surrounding Aβ plaques, suggesting that Aβ is a trigger for neuroinflammation (Itagaki et al., 1989; Vehmas et al., 2003). Although microglial activity may be beneficial under certain circumstances, chronic activation and a progressive microglial response may result in accelerated neurodegeneration. Deregulation of the complement system has also been attributed to the progression of neurodegeneration observed in AD (Stoltzner et al., 2000; Crehan et al., 2012). Loss of synaptic function in the AD brain is a key characteristic of AD that was first described from postmortem studies of AD brains (Masliah et al., 1989; Scheff and Price, 1993). The exact process by which synapses degenerate remains to be fully understood; however, oligomeric Aβ appears to accumulate around neurons early in the disease and cause synaptic dysfunction (Selkoe, 2008; Pozueta et al., 2013).

AD Biomarkers

Tracking pathological changes early in the disease can be difficult, which can in turn make diagnosis and subsequent treatment of AD more problematic. There are three established and validated biomarkers that have been measured in CSF to help diagnose AD: Aβ1–42, total tau, and phospho-tau-181 (Blennow, 2004; Marksteiner et al., 2007). However, a correct early clinical diagnosis is difficult to decipher between AD and mild cognitive impairment (MCI) and other dementias; therefore, imaging markers have been developed and used in parallel with methods such as magnetic resonance imaging (MRI), which can calculate brain atrophy, and positron emission tomography (PET) scans, which can measure neuritic plaque load and amyloid plaque surface area (Galton et al., 2005; Burton et al., 2009; Vandenberghe et al., 2013). Other radiolabeled PET tracers, such as those targeting the translocator protein (TSPO), have been developed and are currently undergoing validation for the monitoring of neuroinflammatory changes in AD (Wadsworth et al., 2012; Liu et al., 2014); these tools may prove useful during treatment as well as in diagnosis.

Current Approved Therapeutics

With the exceedingly growing number of people being diagnosed with AD, it is clear that there is a great need for effective therapeutics. Currently, the therapies offered to AD patients include symptomatic treatments such as acetylcholinesterase inhibitors (eg, donepezil, rivastigmine, and metrifonate) and an NMDA receptor blocker (eg, memantine) (Cummings et al., 1998; Rogers et al., 1998; Rosler et al., 1999; Reisberg et al., 2003). There is a considerable need for therapeutics that alter disease progression. Development of these therapies has largely focused on targeting Aβ peptide or aggregates in AD, as the amyloid cascade hypothesis is strongly supported by pathology, genetics, and biochemistry (Hardy and Higgins, 1992; Hardy and Selkoe, 2002). Here, we describe the evolution of immunotherapies targeting the Aβ protein. We will provide an overview of the preclinical trials in animals and clinical trials, past and present, including what has been learned and where these therapies may be most beneficial.

Aβ IMMUNOTHERAPY—AN INTRODUCTION

Aβ immunotherapy uses anti-Aβ antibodies (or fragments thereof) in an attempt to reduce Aβ aggregates and deposits in the AD brain. A number of mechanisms have been postulated that may vary depending on the specific Aβ vaccine and stage of disease when administered. These mechanisms may work individually or in combination and include: (1) decreasing or modulating Aβ production, (2) degrading Aβ aggregates or enhancing their clearance, (3) blocking Aβ aggregation, and (4) neutralizing toxic Aβ aggregates (Fig. 7.1).

The two approaches used in immunotherapy are active and passive immunization, each of which has its own pros and cons (Fig. 7.2). Active immunization, which involves the administration of an antigen, and often an adjuvant, to induce a host immune response to produce antibodies, is advantageous in that it provides a long-term response, therefore requiring fewer treatments. This method has some disadvantages, however, such as a polyclonal response that might result in antibodies that lower many forms of Aβ and/or crossreact with other proteins, including APP, a widely abundant protein in the body. Moreover, the different Ig isotypes produced have different immune effector functions. Also, the long-term response could potentially be a disadvantage if there are adverse reactions to the treatment, as it may be difficult to "shut off" the humoral immune response. Passive immunization involves the direct administration of externally generated antibodies or antibody fragments as a treatment. Although this method results in more precise targeting of the epitope, it requires frequent administration, which would be disadvantageous for a long-term condition such as AD (Lemere, 2013).

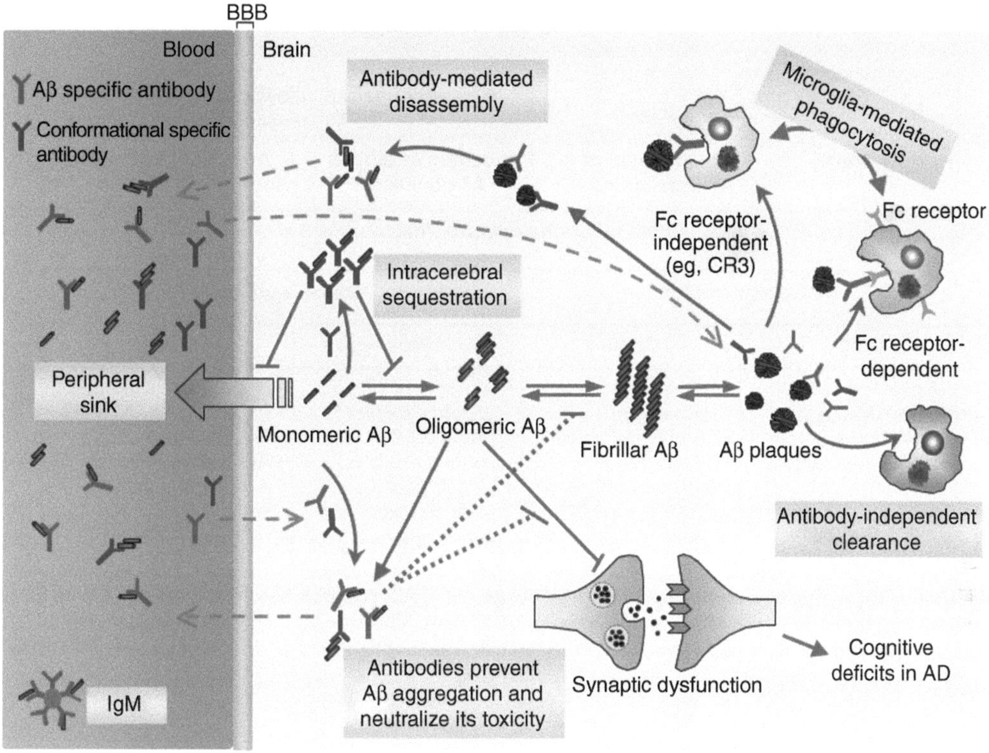

FIGURE 7.1 **Schematic of possible mechanism(s) of action of anti-Aβ immunotherapy treatments in AD models.** Mechanisms that may clear Aβ plaques either independently or in combination include: antibody-mediated microglial phagocytosis; antibody-independent microglial phagocytosis; sequestration of Aβ in a monomeric state; disassembly of Aβ to prevent plaque aggregation; peripheral sink; IgM-mediated hydrolysis of Aβ, neutralization of Aβ toxicity, and prevention of aggregation. *Source: Courtesy of Fu HJ, Liu B, Frost JL, Lemere CA: Amyloid-beta immunotherapy for Alzheimer's disease,* CNS Neurol Disord Drug Targets *9(2):197–206, 2010.*

PRECLINICAL STUDIES

AD-Like Transgenic Mouse Models

There are many genetic mouse models from which to choose when studying AD mechanisms and treatments, and no model is considered the best, as none of the models demonstrate every clinical and pathological feature of AD. The mouse models primarily used when studying amyloidosis in AD are concentrated around familial mutations in *APP*, *PS1*, and *PS2* genes. There are a number of transgenic (Tg) mouse lines overexpressing the human *APP* gene incorporating familial mutations which develop age- and region-specific Aβ plaque and vascular deposits, gliosis, synaptic damage, and neuritic dystrophy.

Commonly used mouse models used include the PDAPP mouse model, which expresses the V717F Indiana mutation under the PDGF promoter. The PDAPP model was the first Tg mouse developed and exhibits both Aβ plaques similar to those observed in AD as well as cognitive deficits from 6 months of age (Games et al., 1995; Dodart et al., 1999). The next AD

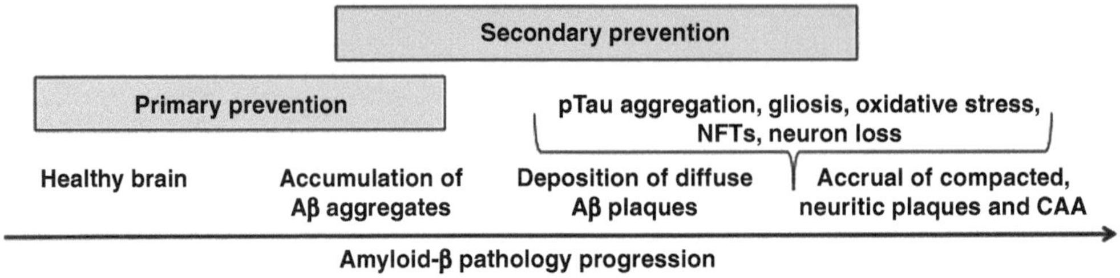

Active vaccination		Passive vaccination	
Pros	**Cons**	**Pros**	**Cons**
• Long-lasting • Multiple epitopes • Cost-effective • Feasible for a large population • Fewer physician's visits	• Immune risks due to self-antigen • Need for adjuvant • Difficult to terminate • Too many epitopes?	• No humoral immune response required • Treatment can be stopped easily • Targets specific epitopes and/or conformations	• Repeated injections • Expensive • Frequent physician's visits • ARIA (mAb specific) • Antidrug neutralizing antibodies

FIGURE 7.2 **Timeline schematic depicting possible points of intervention before and during AD for primary and secondary prevention by anti-Aβ immunotherapy.** Both anti-Aβ treatments, active and passive immunization, have advantages and disadvantages associated with them and should be carefully considered together with disease stage when choosing treatment.

mouse model developed, Tg2576, overexpresses human APP containing the Swedish mutation, APP695swe, under the hamster prion promoter (Hsiao et al., 1996; Sturchler-Pierrat et al., 1997). This mouse model demonstrates AD plaque pathology from about 11–13 months of age throughout the cortex and hippocampus, and exhibits progressive cognitive deficits from 6 months of age (Westerman et al., 2002). APP23 is a widely used model that has an overexpression of human APP carrying the Swedish mutation, APP751swe, under the murine Thy1 promoter (Sturchler-Pierrat et al., 1997). These mice show extensive amyloid pathology that first presents at 6 months of age followed by glial activation surrounding the plaques, dystrophic neurites containing hyperphosphorylated tau, and CAA. Like other APP and APP/PS1 Tg mouse models, APP23 mice do not develop neurofibrillary tangles and have only mild neuron loss; however, cognitive deficits are seen in older animals (Sturchler-Pierrat et al., 1997; Kelly et al., 2003). Another popular AD transgenic animal model includes the J20 mouse model, which overexpresses human APP with the Swedish mutation, KM670/671NL, and the Indiana mutation, V717F, under the PDGF promoter (Mucke et al., 2000). These mice start to develop Aβ plaques at about 5 months of age, which become widespread by 8–9 months of age, and show significant cognitive deficits by 6 months of age (Mucke et al., 2000; Palop et al., 2003). The discovery of a number of mutations in the *PS1* gene which cause an aggressive form of early-onset AD have led to the development of mice overexpressing mutant human PS1 (Sherrington et al., 1995; Borchelt et al., 1996; Duff et al., 1996). In general, these mouse models exhibit elevated levels of Aβ42 in the brain; however, when crossed with APP transgenic mouse lines, they display extensive plaque deposition and behavioral deficits (eg, Borchelt et al., 1996; Dewachter et al., 2000; Jankowsky et al., 2001; Casas et al., 2004; Savonenko et al., 2005; Oakley et al., 2006; Radde et al., 2006; Saito et al., 2011). One of the most commonly used APP/PS1 mouse lines is APPswe/PS1ΔE9, generated by coinjecting two vectors, one encoding human mutant APP with the Swedish mutation and the other mutant PS1 containing the ΔE9 mutation, so that they breed as a single transgene (Jankowsky et al., 2004). These mice have plaque deposition and gliosis starting at 5–6 months of age (Kamphuis et al., 2012), impaired spatial learning at 12 months of age (Lalonde et al., 2005), and synaptic plasticity and neuronal activity deficits from 3 months of age (Meyer-Luehmann et al., 2009; Volianskis et al., 2010).

Active Aβ Immunotherapy in Mice

The first beneficial study using Aβ immunotherapy in mice was reported by Schenk et al. in 1999 using the PDAPP mouse model. Active immunization—using full-length human Aβ peptide and adjuvant—generated Aβ antibodies that prevented Aβ plaque formation, neuritic dystrophy, and astrogliosis in young PDAPP mice and reduced the extent of these pathologies in older PDAPP mice (Schenk et al., 1999). A similar reduction in cerebral Aβ was observed in PDAPP mice following 7 months of intranasal Aβ1–40 treatment (Lemere et al., 2000; Weiner et al., 2000). Morgan et al. (2000) reported that active immunization with subcutaneous injections of Aβ1–42 peptide with Freund's complete adjuvant in Tg2576 and PDAPP mice for 8 months, starting at 7.5 months, resulted in improvements in behavior to wild-type mouse levels and prevented plaque deposition.

The AN1792 phase 2 active immunization clinical trial was halted in 2002 as a result of meningoencephalitis in ≈6% of the AD patients (see later discussion). Subsequently, a number of studies have sought to design second- and third-generation active vaccines to avoid such adverse events. In particular, short Aβ peptides containing B-cell epitopes in the N-terminus but avoiding Aβ-specific T-cell epitopes in the midregion and C-terminus have been developed. For example, we demonstrated that multiple copies of Aβ1–15 peptide reduced plaque burden and spared cognition without eliciting an Aβ-specific T-cell response in J20 hAPP Tg mice (Maier et al., 2006). In addition, alternative adjuvants have been tested to bias the immune response. In one such study, we immunized APPswe/PS1ΔE9 mice with an Aβ B-cell epitope vaccine, MER5101, composed of multiple copies of Aβ1–15 conjugated to an immunogenic carrier protein, diphtheria toxoid, and formulated in a nanoparticular emulsion-based adjuvant, MAS-1, which primarily provokes a Th2 response. We found a reduction in Aβ plaque burden, attenuation of microglial activation, and sparing of both synapse loss and cognitive decline (Liu et al., 2013). Carrera et al. (2012) demonstrated that another vaccine targeting Aβ1–42, EB101, using a novel immunogenic adjuvant, liposomes, resulted in a reduction in plaque burden, as well as a reduction of T-cell-mediated immune system activation and amyloid-induced inflammation in APPswe/PS1ΔE9. Other second- and third-generation active anti-Aβ vaccines have been tested preclinically (reviewed in Lemere, 2013; Wisniewski and Goni, 2015).

DNA-Based Aβ Vaccines

DNA-based vaccination is a technique that employs the method of directly injecting a plasmid DNA that is encoded with the genes for protein or peptide antigens (Donnelly et al., 2005). The advantages of this method of vaccination are that there is an increased ability for prolonged and endogenous antigen synthesis within the host. There are, however, drawbacks to this method such as insertion of foreign DNA (which can result in the cell becoming cancerous), induction of antibodies against DNA, and poor immunogenicity (Khan, 2013). Combining the DNA-based method with a short Aβ peptide as a vaccine or administering a vaccine against multiple Aβ epitopes are other alternatives that may result in less adverse effects and increased humoral and cellular response against the antigens. Early preclinical studies testing immunization with a DNA epitope vaccine involved the development of a plasmid encoding three copies of the self-B cell epitope of $A\beta_{42}$, a foreign nonself T helper cell epitope, and a macrophage-derived cytokine as a molecular adjuvant (Movsesyan et al., 2008). Reports have shown a reduction in Aβ pathology and glial activation as well as prevention of behavioral deficits in the 3xTg-AD transgenic mouse model using this DNA epitope vaccine (Movsesyan et al., 2008). A recent report showed that treatment every 4 weeks with a DNA vaccine composed of a construct containing 10 random repeats of Aβ3–10 fused with IL-4 as a molecular adjuvant in 8-month-old APP/PS1 mice for a total of nine injections demonstrated a decrease in Aβ deposition with no evidence of microhemorrhage (Xing et al., 2015). To our knowledge, this promising method has not yet been used in human clinical trials.

Passive Aβ Immunotherapy in Mice

Bard et al. (2000) were the first to demonstrate that weekly intraperitoneal injections of an N-terminal-specific monoclonal antibody (mAb) against Aβ, 3D6, for 6 months in PDAPP mice resulted in a reduction in Aβ and an increase in Fc receptor-mediated phagocytosis. Passive immunization with an anti-Aβ mAb directed against the central domain of Aβ, m266, administered to PDAPP mice, demonstrated a significant reduction in Aβ deposition without binding to Aβ deposits in the brain (DeMattos et al., 2001) and rapid cognitive improvement in aged mice (Dodart et al., 2002). This antibody was shown to preferentially bind to soluble Aβ to reduce Aβ burden by altering the equilibrium between CNS and plasma Aβ, a process commonly referred to as clearance by peripheral sink. However, another preclinical study investigating treatment of J20 mice with m266 reported no change in cognition and no change in Aβ oligomer levels in the brain (Mably et al., 2015). Studies comparing Aβ antibodies targeting different epitopes (N-terminal vs midregion) by passive immunization in PDAPP mice have demonstrated that targeting Aβ1–5 (3D6) at a high dose (7.5 mg/kg) prevented or cleared vascular Aβ. However, these mice also had an increased incidence of microhemorrhage (Schroeter et al., 2008), which was observed by others in this mouse model as a transient event that was reduced over the treatment period (Zago et al., 2013). Other immunization studies using these mice have also demonstrated that microglia may mediate the clearance observed by certain Aβ immunotherapies (Koenigsknecht-Talboo et al., 2008). Similarly, plaque lowering was observed following 5 months of passive immunization treatment with an anti-Aβ mAb that recognizes Aβ3–6 in aged APP23 mice; however, Aβ clearance was accompanied by cerebral microhemorrhages (Pfeifer et al., 2002). Increased microhemorrhage following treatment with this antibody was also observed in other preclinical studies (Wilcock et al., 2004; Racke et al., 2005).

Passive vaccination with monoclonal antibodies specifically targeting the highly toxic N-terminally truncated pyroglutamate-3 Aβ have demonstrated plaque clearance in the absence of microhemorrhages in APPswe/PS1ΔE9 mice and PDAPP mice (Bayer and Wirths, 2011; Frost et al., 2012, 2015; Demattos et al., 2012). Although it is a minor species in the brain, pyroglutamate-3 Aβ, once formed, is highly resistant to degradation and may act as a seed for aggregation for other Aβ species (Nussbaum et al., 2012). In addition, unlike full-length Aβ, pyroglutamate-3 Aβ is not detected in plasma. Thus, antipyroglutamate-3 antibodies are unlikely to be saturated in the periphery and therefore may have a better chance of reaching the brain.

Catalytic antibodies occur naturally in the innate immune system and can specifically target and digest Aβ without disrupting APP and without involvement of inflammatory proteins (Paul et al., 2010). The innate immune system is composed of much catalytic activity in the immunoglobulin variable (IgV) domain, and constructs from the IgV domain can be used to induce degradation and clearance of Aβ (Planque et al., 2015). Isolation of human catalytic autoantibodies to Aβ can provide a useful therapeutic tool in AD treatment. Catalytic IgMs purified from pooled human serum have been found to hydrolyze Aβ, and, when these IgM were administered intravenously to 8-month-old APPswe/PS1ΔE9 mice with one additional repeated injection 7 days later, Aβ was elevated in peripheral blood collected days following the last IgM injection compared to before treatment, suggesting an Aβ efflux from the brain (Taguchi et al., 2008).

Immunotherapy studies to test prevention continue to be pursued in the various mouse models, as genetic evidence points to Aβ playing an initiating role in the disease. Although these mouse models are unable to completely recapitulate AD pathology, they provide useful tools to gain insight into the neurobiology of AD and provide proof of concept for a number of different anti-Aβ immunotherapy treatments, especially in terms of Aβ lowering as an indication of target engagement.

HUMAN CLINICAL TRIALS: ACTIVE Aβ VACCINES

AN1792

Based on initial Aβ vaccine results in AD-like transgenic mice, which showed a reduction in amyloid deposition following active immunization against Aβ (Schenk et al., 1999), an Aβ1–42 peptide vaccine, AN1792, was brought to clinical trials in moderate to severe AD patients. AN1792, consisting of synthetic full-length Aβ peptide with the helper T-cell Th1-activating QS-21 adjuvant, was expected to generate anti-Aβ antibodies that would bind Aβ and enhance its clearance. However, a multinational phase 2a trial was suspended after approximately 6% (18/300) of the patients developed subacute meningoencephalitis (Orgogozo et al., 2003), a side effect that was never seen in the preclinical mouse studies. Interestingly, a small group of patients (~19%) generated a significant antibody titer, primarily directed against the N-terminus of Aβ, following one to three doses of vaccine (Lee et al., 2005). Later postmortem pathological analysis of a small number of individuals in the AN1792 trial who generated antibody titers revealed focal areas of the brain almost completely devoid of plaques. Fewer than expected tau-positive dystrophic neurites associated with plaques were also observed; however, NFTs remained abundant (Holmes et al., 2008; Boche et al., 2010). Despite the apparent clearance of plaques, these individuals were severely demented at death.

A subset of the remaining patients was followed after the trial ended, and those who had generated anti-Aβ titers were found to have slower cognitive decline compared to patients receiving placebo (Hock et al., 2003). Another long-term follow-up study revealed that most of the antibody responders in the phase 2a trial had detectable antibody titers 4.6 years after immunization with AN1792, and these responders showed significantly reduced cognitive decline compared to placebo-treated controls (Vellas et al., 2009).

Despite these somewhat beneficial outcomes from the treatment (excluding the subacute meningoencephalitis), there appeared to be a surprisingly paradoxical outcome in terms of brain volume. Using volumetric MRI, Fox et al. (2005) determined that the antibody responders had a greater reduction in brain volume compared to the placebo-control patients in the AN1792 trial. This dissociation between antibody generation in responders and brain shrinkage is still not fully understood, although several possible explanations were suggested by the authors. One is that the change in brain volume may be due to the removal of plaque from the brain, although this may not fully account for the extent of brain volume shrinkage exhibited. Another is that a dispersal of glial cells or proteins may have led to shifts in fluid from the brain parenchyma to the CSF. Ultimately, these are still untested hypotheses, and the underlying cause remains unknown.

It is important to note that the patients in the AN1792 trial had moderate to severe AD dementia, suggesting that the clearance of Aβ may have been too late in the disease (ie, after significant neuron loss). Although the trial was terminated, data from the trial were useful for the development of future, safer immunotherapy studies and suggested that this form of treatment may have merit for AD. In the wake of the AN1792 trial, there has been a shift toward targeting smaller epitopes in the N-terminus of Aβ to avoid activating an Aβ-specific, self-antigen T-cell response, considered a possible cause of the meningoencephalitis observed in this study.

Shortly after the halting of the AN1792 trial, a number of companies began developing active vaccines that avoided the Aβ T-cell epitopes within Aβ16–42 (Table 7.1).

Vanutide Cridificar

Janssen, in collaboration with Pfizer, brought forward an alternative active Aβ vaccine called vanutide cridificar, otherwise known as ACC-001 or PF-05236806, into clinical trials 5 years following the halting of AN1792. This vaccine, a conjugate of multiple short Aβ1–7 fragments linked to a nontoxic, inactivated diphtheria toxin with the adjuvant QS-21, is designed to avoid the safety issues previously seen with AN1792. Preclinical data reported that ACC-001 generated antibodies directed to the Aβ N-terminus in the absence of an Aβ T-cell response in nonhuman primates (Hagen et al., 2011). There have been a number of phase 2 clinical trials with this vaccine testing repeated injections of multiple doses with and without adjuvant. A study based on Japanese patients with mild-to-moderate AD demonstrated high anti-Aβ antibody titer responses following intramuscular injections every 3 months for 12 months of three doses of ACC-001, 3, 10, and 30 μg with and without adjuvant. These phase 2 trials found ACC-001 to be safe and well tolerated but required adjuvant to induce high antibody titers (Arai et al., 2013). Recently, this treatment was discontinued from clinical development for reasons that are not disclosed (http://www.pfizer.com).

TABLE 7.1 Active Immunization Trials for Anti-Aβ Treatment of Alzheimer's Disease

Sponsor	Vaccine	Target	Stage	Enrollment	Country	Duration (months)	Completion date	Outcomes
Élan/Wyeth	AN1792	Full-length Aβ	Phase 2	375 (mild–moderate AD)	USA	4	02/2002	Phase 2: Six patients developed meningoencephalitis; plaque clearance; T-cell infiltration.
Janssen/Pfizer	ACC-001	Aβ1–6	Phase 2	40 (mild–moderate AD)	Japan	24	07/2012	Phase 2: Safe and well tolerated; small number of patients developed meningoencephalitis.
Janssen/Pfizer	ACC-001	Aβ1–6	Phase 2	86 (mild–moderate AD)	France, Germany, Spain	24	01/2013	
Janssen/Pfizer	ACC-001	Aβ1–6	Phase 2	245 (mild–moderate AD)	USA	24	02/2013	
Janssen/Pfizer	ACC-001	Aβ1–6	Phase 2	50 (mild–moderate AD)	France, Germany, Spain	24	12/2013	Development discontinued.
Janssen/Pfizer	ACC-001	Aβ1–6	Phase 2	111 (mild–moderate AD)	USA	24	12/2013	
Janssen/Pfizer	ACC-001	Aβ1–6	Phase 2	67 (mild–moderate AD)	France, Germany, Spain	24	09/2014	
Janssen/Pfizer	ACC-001	Aβ1–6	Phase 2	63 (early AD)	USA	24	02/2014	
Janssen/Pfizer	ACC-001	Aβ1–6	Phase 2	108 (mild–moderate AD)	USA	24	02/2014	
Novartis	CAD106	Aβ1–6	Phase 2	27 (mild AD)	France, Sweden, Switzerland, UK	12	02/2010	Phase 1: Safe and well tolerated.
Novartis	CAD106	Aβ1–6	Phase 2	31 (mild AD)	USA	12	11/2010	Phase 2: Incidences of amyloid-related imaging abnormalities (ARIA); biomarker study saw reduction in amyloid load and phosphorylated tau in the SSRs compared to controls.
Novartis	CAD106	Aβ1–6	Phase 2	21 (AD)	France, Sweden, Switzerland, UK	12	06/2011	
Novartis	CAD106	Aβ1–6	Phase 2	24 (AD)	USA	16	02/2012	
Novartis	CAD106	Aβ1–6	Phase 2	177 (mild AD)	USA, Belgium, Canada, Germany, Italy, Netherlands, Norway, Spain, Sweden, Switzerland	22	12/2012	
Novartis	*CAD106*	*Aβ1–6*	*Phase 2/3*	*1340 (prodromal AD)*	*Australia, Belgium, Canada, Finland, France, Germany, Italy, Netherlands, Spain, Switzerland, UK, USA*	*85*	*08/2023*	

(Continued)

TABLE 7.1 Active Immunization Trials for Anti-Aβ Treatment of Alzheimer's Disease (*cont.*)

Sponsor	Vaccine	Target	Stage	Enrollment	Country	Duration (months)	Completion date	Outcomes
Affiris	AD02	Asp-1 Aβ	Phase 1	24 (AD)	Austria	24	09/2009	Phase 1: Safe and well tolerated.
Affiris	AD02	Asp-1 Aβ	Phase 2	335 (early AD)	Austria, Croatia, Czech Republic, France, Germany, Slovakia	12	12/2013	Phase 2: No cognitive improvements compared to placebo.
Affiris	AD03	Aβ N-terminus	Phase 1	28 (mild–moderate AD)	Austria	12	09/2011	Phase 1: Safe and well tolerated.
AC Immune	ACI-24	Aβ1–15	Phase 1/2a	198 (mild–moderate AD)	N/A	12	12/2010	Phase 1/2a: Trial ongoing.
AC Immune	*ACI-24*	*Aβ1–15*	*Phase 1/2a*	*N/A*	*N/A*	*N/A*	*N/A*	

Italics represent ongoing trials.
Available from: http://www.clinicaltrials.gov

CAD106

Following a reduction in amyloid accumulation in the brains of APP transgenic mice (Wiessner et al., 2011), Novartis/BioArctic assessed CAD106 in a 52-week randomized, double-blind, placebo-controlled study in patients (Winblad et al., 2009, 2012). CAD106 is comprised of Aβ1–6 peptide coupled to a Qβ virus-like particle and may be advantageous as it is able to induce antibody titers without activating Aβ-specific T-cells. When testing two doses (50 and 150 μg) of CAD106 for 52 weeks, no meningoencephalitis was observed. A study investigating CNS biomarkers following immunotherapy with CAD106 comparing strong serological responders (SSR; ie, generated high anti-Aβ titers) versus nonresponders and placebo controls revealed a reduction in amyloid load and phosphorylated tau in the SSRs compared to controls, coupled with no safety issues (Riviere et al., 2014). CAD106 is currently in phase 2 trials. Evaluation of the safety and tolerability of repeated injections of CAD106 in 47 patients (and in 11 patients who received placebo), from two 52-week phase 2a studies and two 66-week open-label extension studies, showed that CAD106 was safe and tolerable (Farlow et al., 2015). In addition, Novartis and the Banner Health Institute plan to test CAD106 and a BACE inhibitor, an inhibitor of an enzyme important for Aβ production, in the Alzheimer's Prevention Initiative APOE4 trial (http://www.alzforum.org). Presymptomatic, cognitively healthy adults between 60 and 75 years old who possess two copies of the ApoE4 gene—and therefore are at much higher risk of developing AD—will be treated.

Affitope AD02

AffiRiS AG developed an active vaccine comprised of a synthetic hexapeptide that mimics the N-terminus of Aβ, called Affitope AD02 (Schneeberger et al., 2009), without sharing sequence identity with other human proteins. This active vaccine is unique in that synthetic hexapeptides, considered "foreign," can easily elicit an immune response, allowing the use of aluminum hydroxide as an adjuvant, which has been shown to have a very good safety profile. The specificity of using Affitope technology is also advantageous as it targets a precise part of the Aβ N-terminus neoepitope that is not present in APP or other human proteins. Clinical studies with Affitope AD02 began in 2008. Because the safety and toxicity profile was favorable, a phase 2 trial was initiated in Sep. 2010 in patients with early AD. At the Alzheimer's Association International Conference (AAIC) in 2015, AffiRiS AG reported that Affitope AD02 did not provide any improvement in the AD patients. A scheduled follow-up study has since been terminated (http://www.clinicaltrials.gov). Surprisingly, the placebo group, injected with only the immunomodulator portion (2 mg alum) of the Affitope AD02, showed slowed cognitive decline in patients with a Mini Mental State Examination (MMSE) score of 23 or higher (mildly impaired), an effect that correlated with reduced hippocampal shrinkage. While this result is interesting, follow-up studies are needed to confirm and determine the mechanism by which alum alone might mediate improvements in AD patients.

ACI-24

AC Immune developed a vaccine, ACI-24, likewise in an attempt to avoid the T-cell mediated response that had previously led to the adverse events in the AN1792 trial. ACI-24 is a liposome-based vaccine that contains the Aβ1–15 sequence to exclude the T-cell epitopes (Muhs et al., 2007). The Aβ peptide is anchored on the liposome by palmitoylated lysines to form a conformational epitope which induces β-sheet conformation-specific antibodies. Following successful reduction of soluble and insoluble Aβ and improvements in cognition in preclinical studies with transgenic mice (Muhs et al., 2007; Hickman et al., 2011), ACI-24 is currently being tested in a phase 1/2 double-blind, randomized, placebo-controlled study investigating the safety, tolerability, immunogenicity, and efficacy in patients with mild-to-moderate AD (http://www.clinicaltrialsregister.eu). AC Immune is also planning to investigate ACI-24 as a treatment for AD in Down syndrome patients (http://www.acimmune.com).

HUMAN CLINICAL TRIALS: PASSIVE Aβ IMMUNIZATIONS

Passive immunization, or direct injection of anti-Aβ antibodies, although more costly in the long run, may be an easier and safer method to treat AD, as it avoids the complications involved with eliciting a Th-1-mediated response. There are several therapies that have advanced to anti-Aβ passive immunization trials (Table 7.2).

Bapineuzumab

Bapineuzumab is a humanized form of the murine mAb 3D6, targeting the N-terminus of Aβ, which, as previously mentioned, was shown in Tg mice to bind to plaques and induce Fc-receptor-mediated microglial phagocytosis (Bard et al., 2000). This treatment, first developed by Élan and Wyeth and then Janssen and Pfizer, advanced into phase 1, 2, and 3 trials. After overall safety and tolerance were established in phase 1, a phase 2 trial tested four doses of the antibody or placebo in patients with mild-to-moderate AD who were either carriers or noncarriers for the AD risk-factor allele, ApoE4. Post hoc analyses showed some cognitive benefits in the ApoE4 noncarriers, prompting advancement of bapineuzumab into phase 3 trials. A phase 2 study, including 28 patients assigned to bapineuzumab treatment and 8 patients assigned to placebo treatment, demonstrated that Aβ plaque burden was lowered when measured by ^{11}C-PiB PET imaging, which identifies cortical fibrillar Aβ load (Rinne et al., 2010). A number of phase 3 trials were initiated between 2007 and 2009. However, four of these were terminated following failure in the first two completed trials due to no significant treatment effect on cognitive outcomes among either ApoE4 carriers or noncarriers. Amyloid-related imaging abnormalities (ARIA) were observed in a subset of AD patients receiving bapineuzumab, which worsened with increasing dose and ApoE4 carrier status (Salloway et al., 2014). Although biomarker results demonstrated that the antibody modified Aβ accumulation in patients carrying the ApoE4 risk allele, this did not lead to improved clinical function. Amyloid ^{11}C-PiB-PET imaging substudies were carried out on 115 ApoE4 carriers and 39 noncarriers and showed a reduction of fibrillar Aβ accumulation in patients who received bapineuzumab treatment (Liu et al., 2015). Evidence suggests that the pathological process of AD begins long before clinical symptoms manifest. Therefore, treatment may need to start much earlier to be efficacious (Lemere and Masliah, 2010; Sperling et al., 2011b). The presence of full-blown (mild-to-moderate) AD and the inclusion of some

TABLE 7.2 Passive Immunization Trials for Anti-Aβ Treatment of Alzheimer's Disease

Sponsor	Antibody	Target	Stage	Enrollment	Country	Duration	Completion date	Outcomes
Pfizer	Bapineuzumab	Aβ N-terminus	Phase 1	80 (mild–moderate AD)	Japan	12 months	02/2010	Phase 1: Safe and well tolerated.
Pfizer	Bapineuzumab	Aβ N-terminus	Phase 2	79 (mild–moderate AD)	USA	6 months	10/2010	Phase 2: No significant differences in primary cognitive outcome measures; Aβ plaque burden lowered.
Janssen	Bapineuzumab	Aβ N-terminus	Phase 2	146 (mild–moderate AD)	USA	24 months	01/2013	
Janssen/Pfizer	Bapineuzumab	Aβ N-terminus	Phase 3	1121 (mild–moderate AD & ApoE4 carrier)	USA	18 months	04/2012	Phase 3: No significant differences in primary cognitive measures; Aβ accumulation reduced in ApoE4 carriers; incidences of ARIA.
Janssen/Pfizer	Bapineuzumab	Aβ N-terminus	Phase 3	1331 (mild–moderate AD & non-ApoE4 carrier)	USA, Austria, Canada, Germany	18 months	06/2012	
Janssen/Pfizer	Bapineuzumab	Aβ N-terminus	Phase 3	234 (mild–moderate AD)	USA	18 months	11/2008	Development discontinued.
Eli Lilly	Solanezumab	Middomain soluble Aβ	Phase 2	25 (mild–moderate AD & healthy individuals)	USA	12 months	05/2008	Phase 1: Safe and well tolerated.
Eli Lilly	Solanezumab	Middomain soluble Aβ	Phase 2	33 (mild–moderate AD)	Japan	6 months	07/2009	Phase 2: Dose-dependent increases of Aβ in plasma and CSF; no effect on cognition.
Eli Lilly	Solanezumab	Middomain soluble Aβ	Phase 2	55 (mild AD & healthy individuals)	USA	4 months	08/2012	Phase 3: Improved cognition in mild AD.
Eli Lilly	Solanezumab	Middomain soluble Aβ	Phase 3	1000 (mild–moderate AD)	USA, Argentina, Brazil, Canada, Japan	19 months	04/2012	Further trials ongoing.
Eli Lilly	Solanezumab	Middomain soluble Aβ	Phase 3	1040 (mild–moderate AD)	USA, Australia, France, Germany, Italy, Japan, Rep. of Korea, Poland, Russian Federation, Spain, Sweden, Taiwan, UK	19 months	06/2012	

(*Continued*)

TABLE 7.2 Passive Immunization Trials for Anti-Aβ Treatment of Alzheimer's Disease (*cont.*)

Sponsor	Antibody	Target	Stage	Enrollment	Country	Duration	Completion date	Outcomes
Eli Lilly	*Solanezumab*	*Middomain soluble Aβ*	*Phase 3*	*1275 (probable AD)*	*USA, Argentina, Brazil, Canada, France, Germany, Italy, Japan, Rep. of Korea, Poland, Russian Federation, Spain, Sweden, Taiwan, UK*	*24 months*	*06/2016*	
Washington University School of Medicine (DIAN Network)	*Solanezumab*	*Middomain soluble Aβ*	*Phase 3*	*210 (individuals with genetic predisposition for AD)*	*USA, Australia, Canada, France, Italy, Puerto Rico, Spain, UK*	*52 months*	*09/2019*	
Eli Lilly	*Solanezumab*	*Middomain soluble Aβ*	*Phase 3*	*2100 (mild AD)*	*USA, Australia, Canada, France, Germany, Italy, Japan, Poland, Spain, Sweden, UK*	*20 months*	*10/2016*	
Eli Lilly/Alzheimer's Disease Cooperative Study (A4)	*Solanezumab*	*Middomain soluble Aβ*	*Phase 3*	*1150 [older individulas at risk of AD (A4)]*	*USA, Australia, Canada*	*42 months*	*04/2020*	
Chugai Pharmaceutical	Gantenerumab	N-terminal and middomain fibrillar Aβ	Phase 1	28 (prodromal AD)	Japan	21 months	03/2014	Phase 1: Generally safe and well tolerated; incidences of ARIA.
Hoffmann-La Roche	Gantenerumab	N-terminal and midterminal fibrillar Aβ	Phase 1	60 (mild–moderate AD)	Denmark, Israel, Netherlands, Sweden, UK	3 months	09/2010	Phase 2/3: DIAN network trial is ongoing. Phase 3: Trial in mild AD is ongoing.
Washington University School of Medicine (DIAN Network)	*Gantenerumab*	*N-terminal and middomain fibrillar Aβ*	*Phase 2/3*	*210 (individuals with genetic predisposition for AD)*	*USA, Australia, Canada, France, Italy, Puerto Rico, Spain, UK*	*24 months*	*12/2016*	

Hoffmann-La Roche	*Gantenerumab*	*N-terminal and middomain fibrillar Aβ*	*Phase 3*	*1000 (mild AD)*	*USA, Argentina, Australia, Belgium, Brazil, Bulgaria, Canada, Denmark, Finland, France, Germany, Guatemala, Hungary, Italy, Japan, Rep. of Korea, Netherlands, Poland, Portugal, Russian Federation, Spain, Sweden, Switzerland, Turkey, UK*	*26 months*	*03/2019*	
Hoffmann-La Roche	Gantenerumab	N-terminal and midterminal fibrillar Aβ	Phase 3	799 (prodromal AD)	USA, Argentina, Australia, Belgium, Brazil, Canada, Chile, Czech Republic, Denmark, Finland, France, Germany, Israel, Italy, Rep. of Korea, Mexico, Netherlands, Poland, Portugal, Russian Federation, Spain, Sweden, Switzerland, Turkey, UK	24 months	12/2015 Discontinued (12/2014)	
Hoffmann-La Roche	*Gantenerumab*	*N-terminal and midterminal fibrillar Aβ*	*Phase 2*	*210 (individuals with genetic predisposition for AD)*	*USA, Australia, Canada, France, Italy, Puerto Rico, Spain, UK*	*52 months*	*09/2019*	
Genentech	Crenezumab (MABT5102A)	Soluble Aβ Oligomeric Aβ Fibrillar Aβ	Phase 2	72 (mild–moderate AD)	USA, France, Spain	16 months	02/2014	Phase 1: Safe and well tolerated. Phase 2: No significant differences in coprimary cognitive and functional measures; trend for cognitive benefit in mild patients in prespecified subanalyses. Further trials ongoing.
Genentech	Crenezumab (MABT5102A)	Soluble Aβ Oligomeric Aβ Fibrillar Aβ	Phase 2	372 (mild–moderate AD)	USA, Canada, France, Germany, Spain, UK	17 months	06/2014	
Genentech	*Crenezumab (MABT5102A)*	*Soluble Aβ Oligomeric Aβ Fibrillar Aβ*	*Phase 2*	*360 (mild–moderate AD)*	*USA, Canada, France, Germany, Spain, UK*	*24 months*	*02/2017*	
Genentech/Banner/NIH	*Crenezumab (MABT5102A)*	*Soluble Aβ Oligomeric Aβ Fibrillar Aβ*	*Phase 2*	*300 (presymptomatic PS1 E280A FAD carrier)*	*Colombia*	*60 months*	*09/2020*	

(*Continued*)

TABLE 7.2 Passive Immunization Trials for Anti-Aβ Treatment of Alzheimer's Disease (*cont.*)

Sponsor	Antibody	Target	Stage	Enrollment	Country	Duration	Completion date	Outcomes
Biogen Idec	Aducanumab (BIIB037)	Aβ aggregates	Phase 1	53 (mild–moderate AD)	USA	6 months	09/2013	Phase 1: Safe and well tolerated; no new incidences of ARIA beyond baseline.
Biogen Idec	*Aducanumab (BIIB037)*	*Aβ aggregates*	*Phase 1*	*197 (prodromal–mild AD)*	*USA, Australia, Belgium*	*29 months*	*04/2016*	
Biogen Idec	*Aducanumab (BIIB037)*	*Aβ aggregates*	*Phase 1*	*25 (mild–moderate AD)*	*Japan*	*10 months*	*07/2017*	Phase 3: Interim report of reduced cognitive decline and reduced amyloid plaque burden with high dose (10 mg/kg).
Biogen Idec	*Aducanumab (BIIB037)*	*Aβ aggregates*	*Phase 3*	*1350 (early AD)*	*USA, Australia, Austria, Canada, Denmark, France, Germany, Hungary, Italy, Rep. of Korea, Portugal, Spain, Taiwan, UK*	*19 months*	*02/2022*	Further trials ongoing.
Biogen Idec	*Aducanumab (BIIB037)*	*Aβ aggregates*	*Phase 3*	*1350 (early AD)*	*USA, Belgium, Canada, France, Germany, Italy, Netherlands, Poland, Spain, Sweden, Switzerland, UK*	*19 months*	*02/2022*	
GlaxoSmithKline (GSK)	GSK933776	Aβ N-terminus	Phase 1	19 (mild AD–MCI)	Germany, Sweden	22 h	12/2011	Phase 1: Initial increase in plasma Aβ and tau; however, no significant differences following all doses.
GlaxoSmithKline (GSK)	GSK933776	Aβ N-terminus	Phase 1	50 (mild AD)	Australia, Norway, Sweden	12 months	05/2011	
Pfizer	Ponezumab (PF-04360365)	Aβ40	Phase 1	15 (mild–moderate AD)	USA	6 months	07/2009	Phase 1: Safe and well tolerated; no incidences of ARIA.
Pfizer	Ponezumab (PF-04360365)	Aβ40	Phase 1	8 (mild–moderate AD)	Japan	6 months	08/2009	Phase 2: No effect on primary end points of brain and CSF Aβ burden.
Pfizer	Ponezumab (PF-04360365)	Aβ40	Phase 1	20 (mild–moderate AD)	Japan	12 months	08/2010	Development discontinued for AD.
Pfizer	Ponezumab (PF-04360365)	Aβ40	Phase 1	17 (mild–moderate AD)	USA, Sweden	36 h	09/2012	Under investigation for CAA.

Pfizer	Ponezumab (PF-04360365)	Aβ40	Phase 2	37 (mild–moderate AD)	Australia, Canada, Sweden, UK	90 months	09/2009	
Pfizer	Ponezumab (PF-04360365)	Aβ40	Phase 2	36 (mild–moderate AD)	Sweden	18 months	06/2011	
Pfizer	Ponezumab (PF-04360365)	Aβ40	Phase 2	198 (mild–moderate AD)	USA, Australia, Belgium, Canada, Rep. of Korea, UK	24 months	09/2011	
Pfizer	Ponezumab (PF-04360365)	Aβ40	Phase 2	36 (probable CAA)	USA, Canada, France, Netherlands, UK	8 months	09/2015	
Eisai/BioArctic	BAN2401	Aβ protofibrils	Phase 1	26 (mild AD)	Japan	3.5 months	05/2015	Phase 1: Safe and well tolerated; no incidences of ARIA.
Eisai/BioArctic	BAN2401	Aβ protofibrils	Phase 1	80 (mild–moderate AD)	USA	9 months	02/2013	Phase 2: Ongoing.
Eisai/BioArctic	*BAN2401*	*Aβ protofibrils*	*Phase 2*	*800 (MCI & mild AD)*	*USA*	*18 months*	*07/2018*	
Cornell University/Baxter	Gammagard IVIG	Not determined	Phase 2	24 (mild–moderate AD)	USA	6 months	01/2009	Phase 2: Safe and well tolerated; slow cognitive decline; reduced brain shrinkage.
Baxter	Gammagard IVIG	Not determined	Phase 3	390 (mild–moderate AD)	USA, Canada	18 months	12/2012	Phase 3: No effect on primary end point of slowing cognitive decline. Development discontinued.
Grifols Biologicals	*Albumin and Ig (IVIG)*	*Not determined*	*Phase 2/3*	*350 (mild–moderate AD)*	*USA, Spain*	*14 months*	*12/2016*	Phase 2/3: Ongoing.
Sutter Health	*NewGam 10% IVIG*	*Not determined*	*Phase 2*	*50 (MCI)*	*USA*	*24 months*	*11/2017*	Phase 2: Ongoing.

Italics represent ongoing trials.
Available from: http://www.clinicaltrials.gov

ApoE4 noncarriers who were amyloid-negative (and therefore perhaps not AD patients) may have contributed to the failure of the clinical trials with bapineuzumab. In addition, reduced dosing due to ARIA may have limited the amount of antibody penetrating the CNS, thereby lowering efficacy.

Solanezumab

Another anti-Aβ immunotherapy treatment currently being tested in clinical trials is solanezumab. This antibody, developed by Eli Lilly, is an mAb that recognizes a linear epitope in the middomain of the Aβ peptide and recognizes only soluble Aβ. As mentioned, preclinical investigations with the murine version of the antibody, m266, observed a rapid normalization of the cognitive deficits in 24-month-old PDAPP transgenic mice (Dodart et al., 2002). The hypothesis behind this treatment is that removal of small, toxic soluble Aβ may reduce or inhibit synaptic toxicity or promote efflux of Aβ from the brain to plasma, a process otherwise referred to as the peripheral sink. Phase 1 and 2 studies demonstrated that solanezumab was well tolerated in both healthy controls and mild-to-moderate AD patients, with no microhemorrhages or severe adverse events (Siemers et al., 2010; Farlow et al., 2012). These studies also revealed dose-related increases in plasma Aβ, suggesting target engagement and increased efflux of Aβ from brain to blood, consistent with "peripheral sink" effects. Eli Lilly conducted two phase 3 double-blind clinical trials on solanezumab, which, overall, did not show significant beneficial effects. Similar to bapineuzumab, the late intervention with anti-Aβ immunotherapy may have contributed to the failure of this therapy in clinical trials. Prespecified analysis of a subgroup of patients with mild cognitive impairment within phase 3 trials showed significant stabilization of cognition, which prompted Eli Lilly to conduct a third phase 3 trial that started in 2013 to further confirm whether solanezumab is able to slow cognitive and functional decline in patients with mild AD. This trial is expected to reach completion by the end of 2016. In addition, solanezumab has been selected as a therapeutic agent in a phase 2/3 trial conducted by the Dominantly Inherited Alzheimer's Network (DIAN) in patients with mild symptoms who are carriers of autosomal-dominant *APP*, *PS1*, and *PS2* mutations. This trial is also scheduled to end at the end of 2016 (http://www.clinicaltrials.gov).

Ponezumab

Ponezumab is a humanized mAb that binds to amino acids 33–40—the C-terminus of Aβ1–40—that was developed by Rinat Neuroscience and acquired by Pfizer in 2006. Preclinical studies with 2H6, a murine mAb that similarly binds to the C-terminus of Aβ1–40, demonstrated reduced amyloid deposition in the Tg2576 AD transgenic mouse model (Karlnoski et al., 2009). Ponezumab is an IgG2 antibody with two mutations in the Fc portion rendering the antibody void of an effector function, thus eliminating possible antibody-dependent cell-mediated toxicity or complement-dependent cytotoxicity (La Porte et al., 2012). This antibody is thought to work by a peripheral sink mechanism to remove Aβ from the brain. Phase 1 trials of ponezumab showed that it was safe and well tolerated with no incidences of microhemorrhages or ARIA. Ponezumab was brought to phase 2 clinical trials in 198 mild-to-moderate AD patients, where a peripheral sink effect was suggested by an increase in plasma Aβ1–40 levels. However, a second phase 2 clinical trial in a similar cohort of patients did not show any change in brain or CSF Aβ levels. The development of this antibody for AD therapy has since been discontinued. However, a phase 2 clinical trial is under way for the treatment of CAA (http://www.clinicaltrials.gov).

GSK933776

GlaxoSmithKline developed an AD therapeutic candidate for passive immunotherapy, GSK933776, which is a humanized mouse anti-Aβ IgG1 antibody that binds the N-terminus of Aβ with an altered Fc region to reduce Fc receptor binding and complement activation and consequently reduce complement-dependent cytotoxicity (Leyhe et al., 2014). Analysis of a phase 1 trial with GSK933776 reported an immediate slight increase in plasma Aβ concentrations; however, no overall significant change was observed. The same was also reported for tau levels in the CSF. The development of GSK933776 for AD treatment has since been discontinued. However, clinical trials are under way for geographic atrophy (advanced dry), a type of late-stage age-related macular degeneration (http://www.clinicaltrials.gov).

BAN2401

An AD-causing pathogenic mutation found to be located within the Aβ sequence at codon 693 (E693G) and that forms Aβ protofibrils has led to an immunotherapy approach that targets this type of Aβ assembly (Nilsberth et al., 2001). BAN2401 is a humanized IgG1 mAb developed by BioArctic, now licensed to Eisai, that selectively targets large, soluble Aβ protofibrils. This antibody was found to be safe and well tolerated, with no reports of ARIA, in a multicenter phase 1 trial in 80 people with mild-to-moderate AD. BAN2401 is currently in a phase 2 trial in patients with MCI due to AD or mild AD, testing three doses (2.5 mg/kg, 5 mg/kg, or 10 mg/kg). This trial is currently ongoing and is expected to reach completion by 2018.

Gantenerumab

Gantenerumab, developed by Hoffmann-La Roche, is a conformation-specific human anti-Aβ mAb that binds with subnanomolar affinity to both an N-terminal and a midregion epitope on Aβ folded into a fibrillar conformation. This antibody is thought to reduce plaque burden in the brain by glial recruitment and phagocytosis. Preclinical studies investigating the effect of this antibody in an APP transgenic mouse model showed binding to cerebral Aβ and a reduction in small plaques following chronic treatment (Bohrmann et al., 2012). In addition, Aβ was internalized into lysosomal vesicles indicating microglial phagocytosis as a mechanism of Aβ removal. Phase 1 trials deemed this antibody safe and well tolerated, aside from some transient incidences of ARIA. A multicenter, randomized, double-blind, placebo-controlled PET study in AD patients with mild-to-moderate AD was carried out using varying doses of gantenerumab. A dose-dependent reduction of amyloid in the brain was observed (Ostrowitzki et al., 2012). This study also reported that two ApoE4 carriers who received the high dose of gantenerumab (200 mg) developed microhemorrhages and inflammation or vasogenic edema, which quickly dissipated following termination of treatment. These patients had the highest amyloid reduction in the areas of the brain that had increased inflammation.

Further studies with gantenerumab have been closely monitored with additional MRI scanning. Phase 2/3 trials were initiated, and new selection criteria helped to provide a homogeneous population of early-stage, symptomatic people who had evidence of amyloid and were given subcutaneous injections of gantenerumab at one of two doses. However, surprisingly, the trial was discontinued based on an interim futility analysis. Since then, Roche has initiated another phase 3 trial in patients with a mild clinical AD diagnosis. This study is currently ongoing and is scheduled to finish in early 2019.

Crenezumab

Crenezumab is a fully humanized anti-Aβ mAb that binds multiple forms of Aβ—soluble, oligomeric, and fibrillar—but, unlike other anti-Aβ mAbs tested for Aβ immunotherapy, this mAb is in the IgG4 class. The antibody was designed with this IgG isotype to limit inflammatory cytokine release from microglia while conserving phagocytic functions. This was to avoid the ARIA previously observed in other mAb passive immunotherapy clinical trials (Adolfsson et al., 2012) and to avoid effector functions such as complement-dependent cytotoxicity (van der Zee et al., 1986). Genentech, which licensed crenezumab from AC Immune, demonstrated that this antibody has a good safety profile with no vasogenic edema or cerebral microhemorrhage in two phase 1 safety trials. This led to a phase 2 trial that tested a higher concentration (15 mg/kg) of the antibody intravenously administered every 4 weeks in patients with mild-to-moderate AD for 73 weeks. Unfortunately, this proof-of-concept study did not meet its coprimary end points of significantly reduced cognitive decline or stabilization of global function. Subanalyses of patients with mild-to-moderate AD who were intravenously administered a 15 mg/kg dose of crenezumab demonstrated a 16.8% reduction in cognitive decline ($p = 0.19$), while those with mild AD had a 23.8% reduction ($p = 0.13$) and those with even milder AD symptoms demonstrated a 35.4% reduction ($p = 0.036$); patients who received 300 mg by subcutaneous injection every other week showed no differences in cognition (Roche, 2014). This would suggest that timing and route of treatment plays an important role in AD therapy. As such, crenezumab has been included in the Alzheimer Prevention Initiative (API), sponsored by Genentech and the Banner Institute in a PS1 E280A early-onset AD family in Colombia and was the first immunotherapy treatment to be investigated for its ability to prevent or delay cognitive decline in presymptomatic carriers of autosomal-dominant presenilin mutations. This trial is currently ongoing and is scheduled to reach completion in 2020 (http://www.clinicaltrials.gov).

BIIB037 (Aducanumab)

Biogen's aducanumab or BIIB037, originally developed by Neurimmune, is a high-affinity, fully human mAb that binds aggregated forms of Aβ and also preferentially binds parenchymal amyloid over vascular amyloid (http://www.neurimmune.com). It was generated by a reverse translational medical approach whereby the antibody was derived from older individuals who have not developed AD, with the idea that they may have an unusual resistance to developing the disease. In Tg2576 mice, intraperitoneal injection of aducanumab was found to bind and aid in clearance of parenchymal plaques without causing microhemorrhages (Dunstan et al., 2011). The researchers also observed an accumulation of brain macrophages around the remaining plaques, suggesting phagocytosis as a possible mechanism of removal. Biogen brought aducanumab to a phase 1 trial in 2011 whereby giving a single ascending dose by intravenous infusion to participants with mild-to-moderate AD demonstrated a good safety profile when compared to those receiving the placebo dose. Biogen next conducted a phase 1b randomized, double-blind, placebo-controlled, multiple-dose trial evaluating aducanumab at 1, 3, 6, and 10 mg/kg in participants with prodromal (amyloid-positive by PET but asymptomatic) and mild AD. The promising results from this trial were presented at two conferences in 2015 (Alzheimer's & Parkinson's Diseases Congress [AD/PD] and AAIC) and demonstrated dramatic dose- and time-dependent reduction of amyloid plaque burden over 54 weeks of treatment, as measured by amyloid PET. Incidences of ARIA were observed with increasing dose and ApoE4 genotype. A prespecified analysis of placebo and all doses revealed a statistically significant overall dose-dependent slowing of clinical decline in the Clinical Dementia Rating sum of boxes (CDR-SB) and the MMSE. Based on these relatively positive results, Biogen recently began two phase 3 multicenter trials (ENGAGE and EMERGE) in 20 countries in North America, Europe, and Asia for the evaluation of aducanumab at two undisclosed doses (high and low) in 2700 people with early AD (http://www.clinicaltrials.gov).

Intravenous Immunoglobulins

There are also a number of AD clinical trials that use intravenous immunoglobulins (IVIGs) prepared from purified plasma immunoglobulins from healthy donors. The hypothesized mechanism by which this treatment works is through targeted clearance of Aβ by polyclonal anti-Aβ antibodies from the healthy non-AD donors, with possible reduced Aβ-induced synaptic toxicity (Szabo et al., 2010). Dr. Norman Relkin of Weill Medical College, Cornell University, New York, suggested at the International Conference for Alzheimer's Disease in 2008 that IVIG treatment may also have immunomodulatory effects on patients' phagocytic microglial phenotype, which may in turn increase Aβ clearance. Baxter Healthcare's Gammagard is one such treatment whereby an 18-month dose-finding study with eight patients with mild AD demonstrated decreased CSF Aβ and stabilization of MMSE scores (Relkin et al., 2009). MRI data from a phase 2 clinical trial demonstrated that Gammagard protected against brain atrophy and positively altered plasma cytokine levels. However, no treatment effect on primary end points, including cognitive decline, was observed in phase 3 clinical trials, leading to discontinuation of the development of Gammagard. Griffols Biologicals and Sutter Health both currently have an IVIG treatment in phase 2/3 clinical trials, which are expected to reach completion in 2016 and 2017, respectively. Griffols Biologicals' Flebogamma IVIG is being evaluated in combination with albumin in a phase 2/3 trial. Sutter Health's NewGam IVIG is currently in phase 2 trial in patients with MCI to determine if it reduces their risk of developing AD.

SUMMARY AND CONCLUSIONS

Despite the initial setback following the AN1972 trial, immunotherapy still remains a promising therapeutic approach for AD. The field has expanded over the past 15 years, and although there have been some promising results, a number of hurdles remain. Target engagement has been demonstrated in many of the clinical trials, although intervention may have come too late to save neurons lost long ago to the disease. ARIA has occurred with several passive anti-Aβ vaccines as a transient adverse effect that is dose- and ApoE4-dependent. Thus far, there has been a lack of robust cognitive or functional efficacy in moderate or severe AD patients. However, evidence for cognitive efficacy has been observed in prodromal and mild AD patients as demonstrated in the recent trials with solanuzumab and aducanumab.

Penetration of the antibodies into the brain prevails as a major challenge with this type of treatment, as only a small percentage (0.1%) of antibodies have the ability to cross the blood–brain barrier (BBB) (Banks et al., 2002). Approaches to address this transport issue are being investigated, including different methods of delivery such as mAb-containing liposomes, which are coated with an antitransferrin receptor antibody, aiding in the passage across the BBB (Salvati et al., 2013). The transferrin receptor is normally present on endothelial cells and mediates the transfer of iron from the blood into the brain by endocytosis (Fishman et al., 1987). Interaction with this receptor may be leveraged to develop anti-Aβ drugs that have better access to the brain. The development of bispecific antibodies, otherwise known as brain shuttle constructs, whereby one Fab region targets Aβ and the other Fab region targets the transferrin receptor, has been investigated in a PS2-APP double transgenic mouse model of amyloidosis. In this model, the bispecific mAb demonstrated a greater penetration into the brain paranchyma and reduction in Aβ compared to monospecific anti-Aβ antibody (Niewoehner et al., 2014).

It is now widely known that the pathophysiological process of AD starts years before clinical diagnosis of AD (Sperling et al., 2011a), which poses a huge obstacle to successful treatment. A number of anti-Aβ immunotherapy clinical trials have tested these agents in cohorts consisting of mild-to-moderate AD patients. The failure of these agents to provide fully efficacious results is most likely due to the late stage of administration and/or the ability of sufficient antibodies to enter the brain. The Anti-Amyloid Treatment in Asymptomatic Alzheimer's (A4) study is novel in that the overall goal is to test antiamyloid treatments in the "correct" population. This study, headed by Dr. Reisa Sperling (Brigham and Women's Hospital) and sponsored by the National Institutes of Health (NIH), Eli Lilly, the Alzheimer's Association, and others, will test Aβ immunotherapy using solanezumab in older people without dementia but with amyloid-positive PET scans, a cohort at high risk for AD (http://www.a4study.org). Other trials are following suit and seeking to recruit prodromal AD study cohorts. The high costs involved with continuous passive immunotherapy with externally generated antibodies make this therapy more applicable to secondary prevention in AD following the deposition of Aβ plaques rather than long-term primary prevention in people without plaques, unless they are at high genetic risk for AD. The ability to quickly cease treatment makes this an alluring method, especially with the documented ARIA and microhemorrhage cases reported during treatment in trials.

Active vaccination may be a suitable early treatment method for preventing the downstream neurotoxicity and neuronal death observed in AD and subsequent cognitive deficits by clearance of Aβ prior to its aggregation and deposition. This long-lasting treatment would be similar to preventive vaccinations currently available for other conditions such as hepatitis B. Moreover, vaccination against Aβ would require fewer injections due to the activated immune response elicited, making it an attractive, cost-effective therapy. Active immunotherapy as a preventive AD therapy would need to be used with caution, as it may be difficult to terminate the immune response to the vaccine. However, the safety issues may be less of a concern in preplaque and pre-CAA individuals, and it is likely that younger people may generate more robust titers than their elder counterparts. In general, active Aβ immunotherapy may represent an effective and efficient way to prevent AD if given prior to or in the very early stages of the onset of Aβ pathogenesis.

The need for an effective treatment is obvious, considering the increasingly growing medical and economic burden of AD. Investigating anti-Aβ immunotherapy in a prodromal AD population together with improving the vaccines' targets may lead to more successful outcomes in the clinic. We remain optimistic that earlier treatment with anti-Aβ vaccines may protect against AD.

References

Adolfsson O, Pihlgren M, Toni N, Varisco Y, Buccarello AL, Antoniello K, Lohmann S, Piorkowska K, Gafner V, Atwal JK, Maloney J, Chen M, Gogineni A, Weimer RM, Mortensen DL, Friesenhahn M, Ho C, Paul R, Pfeifer A, Muhs A, Watts RJ: An effector-reduced anti-beta-amyloid (Abeta) antibody with unique Abeta binding properties promotes neuroprotection and glial engulfment of Abeta, *J Neurosci* 32:9677–9689, 2012.

Alzheimer's Association: Alzheimer's disease facts and figures, *Alzheimers Dement* 11(3):332–384, 2015.

Arai H, Hideo S, Tamotsu Y, Lobello K, Yahong P, Enchi L, Nzeera K, Margolin R, Jackson N, Fujimoto Y: Safety, tolerability, and immunogenicity of an immunotherapeutic vaccine (vanutide cridificar [ACC-001]) and the QS-21 adjuvant in Japanese subjects with mild to moderate Alzheimer's disease: a phase 2a, multicenter, randomized, adjuvant- and placebo-controlled, multiple-ascending-dose study, *Presented at the International Conference on Alzheimer's Disease (ICAD)*, Boston, MA, 2013.

Arriagada PV, Growdon JH, Hedley-Whyte ET, Hyman BT: Neurofibrillary tangles but not senile plaques parallel duration and severity of Alzheimer's disease, *Neurology* 42:631–639, 1992.

Banks WA, Terrell B, Farr SA, Robinson SM, Nonaka N, Morley JE: Passage of amyloid beta protein antibody across the blood–brain barrier in a mouse model of Alzheimer's disease, *Peptides* 23:2223–2226, 2002.

Bard F, Cannon C, Barbour R, Burke RL, Games D, Grajeda H, Guido T, Hu K, Huang J, Johnson-Wood K, Khan K, Kholodenko D, Lee M, Lieberburg I, Motter R, Nguyen M, Soriano F, Vasquez N, Weiss K, Welch B, Seubert P, Schenk D, Yednock T: Peripherally administered antibodies against amyloid beta-peptide enter the central nervous system and reduce pathology in a mouse model of Alzheimer disease, *Nat Med* 6:916–919, 2000.

Bayer TA, Wirths O: Intraneuronal Abeta as a trigger for neuron loss: can this be translated into human pathology? *Biochem Soc Trans* 39:857–861, 2011.

Beecham GW, Hamilton K, Naj AC, Martin ER, Huentelman M, Myers AJ, Corneveaux JJ, Hardy J, Vonsattel JP, Younkin SG, Bennett DA, De Jager PL, Larson EB, Crane PK, Kamboh MI, Kofler JK, Mash DC, Duque L, Gilbert JR, Gwirtsman H, Buxbaum JD, Kramer P, Dickson DW, Farrer LA, Frosch MP, Ghetti B, Haines JL, Hyman BT, Kukull WA, Mayeux RP, Pericak-Vance MA, Schneider JA, Trojanowski JQ, Reiman EM, Schellenberg GD, Montine TJ: Genome-wide association meta-analysis of neuropathologic features of Alzheimer's disease and related dementias, *PLoS Genet* 10:e1004606, 2014.

Blennow K: CSF biomarkers for mild cognitive impairment, *J Intern Med* 256:224–234, 2004.

Boche D, Donald J, Love S, Harris S, Neal JW, Holmes C, Nicoll JA: Reduction of aggregated tau in neuronal processes but not in the cell bodies after Abeta42 immunisation in Alzheimer's disease, *Acta Neuropathol* 120:13–20, 2010.

Bohrmann B, Baumann K, Benz J, Gerber F, Huber W, Knoflach F, Messer J, Oroszlan K, Rauchenberger R, Richter WF, Rothe C, Urban M, Bardroff M, Winter M, Nordstedt C, Loetscher H: Gantenerumab: a novel human anti-Abeta antibody demonstrates sustained cerebral amyloid-beta binding and elicits cell-mediated removal of human amyloid-beta, *J Alzheimers Dis* 28:49–69, 2012.

Borchelt DR, Thinakaran G, Eckman CB, Lee MK, Davenport F, Ratovitsky T, Prada CM, Kim G, Seekins S, Yager D, Slunt HH, Wang R, Seeger M, Levey AI, Gandy SE, Copeland NG, Jenkins NA, Price DL, Younkin SG, Sisodia SS: Familial Alzheimer's disease-linked presenilin 1 variants elevate Abeta1–42/1–40 ratio in vitro and in vivo, *Neuron* 15:1005–1013, 1996.

Braak H, Braak E: Neuropathological stageing of Alzheimer-related changes, *Acta Neuropathol* 82:239–259, 1991.

Burton EJ, Barber R, Mukaetova-Ladinska EB, Robson J, Perry RH, Jaros E, Kalaria RN, O'Brien JT: Medial temporal lobe atrophy on MRI differentiates Alzheimer's disease from dementia with Lewy bodies and vascular cognitive impairment: a prospective study with pathological verification of diagnosis, *Brain* 132:195–203, 2009.
Carrera I, Etcheverria I, Fernandez-Novoa L, Lombardi V, Cacabelos R, Vigo C: Vaccine development to treat Alzheimer's disease neuropathology in APP/PS1 transgenic mice, *Int J Alzheimers Dis* 2012:376138, 2012.
Casas C, Sergeant N, Itier JM, Blanchard V, Wirths O, van der Kolk N, Vingtdeux V, van de Steeg E, Ret G, Canton T, Drobecq H, Clark A, Bonici B, Delacourte A, Benavides J, Schmitz C, Tremp G, Bayer TA, Benoit P, Pradier L: Massive CA1/2 neuronal loss with intraneuronal and N-terminal truncated Abeta42 accumulation in a novel Alzheimer transgenic model, *Am J Pathol* 165:1289–1300, 2004.
Chalmers K, Wilcock GK, Love S: APOE epsilon 4 influences the pathological phenotype of Alzheimer's disease by favouring cerebrovascular over parenchymal accumulation of A beta protein, *Neuropathol Appl Neurobiol* 29:231–238, 2003.
Chartier-Harlin MC, Crawford F, Houlden H, Warren A, Hughes D, Fidani L, Goate A, Rossor M, Roques P, Hardy J, et al: Early-onset Alzheimer's disease caused by mutations at codon 717 of the beta-amyloid precursor protein gene, *Nature* 353:844–846, 1991.
Chartier-Harlin MC, Parfitt M, Legrain S, Perez-Tur J, Brousseau T, Evans A, Berr C, Vidal O, Roques P, Gourlet V, et al: Apolipoprotein E, epsilon 4 allele as a major risk factor for sporadic early and late-onset forms of Alzheimer's disease: analysis of the 19q13 2 chromosomal region, *Hum Mol Genet* 3:569–574, 1994.
Crehan H, Hardy J, Pocock J: Microglia, Alzheimer's disease, and complement, *Int J Alzheimers Dis* 2012:983640, 2012.
Cummings JL, Cyrus PA, Bieber F, Mas J, Orazem J, Gulanski B: Metrifonate treatment of the cognitive deficits of Alzheimer's disease. Metrifonate Study Group, *Neurology* 50:1214–1221, 1998.
DeMattos RB, Bales KR, Cummins DJ, Dodart JC, Paul SM, Holtzman DM: Peripheral anti-A beta antibody alters CNS and plasma A beta clearance and decreases brain A beta burden in a mouse model of Alzheimer's disease, *Proc Natl Acad Sci USA* 98:8850–8855, 2001.
DeMattos RB, Lu J, Tang Y, Racke MM, Delong CA, Tzaferis JA, Hole JT, Forster BM, McDonnell PC, Liu F, Kinley RD, Jordan WH, Hutton ML: A plaque-specific antibody clears existing beta-amyloid plaques in Alzheimer's disease mice, *Neuron* 76:908–920, 2012.
Deshpande A, Mina E, Glabe C, Busciglio J: Different conformations of amyloid beta induce neurotoxicity by distinct mechanisms in human cortical neurons, *J Neurosci* 26:6011–6018, 2006.
Dewachter I, Van Dorpe J, Smeijers L, Gilis M, Kuiperi C, Laenen I, Caluwaerts N, Moechars D, Checler F, Vanderstichele H, Van Leuven F: Aging increased amyloid peptide and caused amyloid plaques in brain of old APP/V717I transgenic mice by a different mechanism than mutant presenilin 1, *J Neurosci* 20:6452–6458, 2000.
Dodart JC, Meziane H, Mathis C, Bales KR, Paul SM, Ungerer A: Behavioral disturbances in transgenic mice overexpressing the V717F beta-amyloid precursor protein, *Behav Neurosci* 113:982–990, 1999.
Dodart JC, Bales KR, Gannon KS, Greene SJ, DeMattos RB, Mathis C, DeLong CA, Wu S, Wu X, Holtzman DM, Paul SM: Immunization reverses memory deficits without reducing brain Abeta burden in Alzheimer's disease model, *Nat Neurosci* 5:452–457, 2002.
Donev R, Kolev M, Millet B, Thome J: Neuronal death in Alzheimer's disease and therapeutic opportunities, *J Cell Mol Med* 13:4329–4348, 2009.
Donnelly JJ, Wahren B, Liu MA: DNA vaccines: progress and challenges, *J Immunol* 175:633–639, 2005.
Duff K, Eckman C, Zehr C, Yu X, Prada CM, Perez-tur J, Hutton M, Buee L, Harigaya Y, Yager D, Morgan D, Gordon MN, Holcomb L, Refolo L, Zenk B, Hardy J, Younkin S: Increased amyloid-beta42(43) in brains of mice expressing mutant presenilin 1, *Nature* 383:710–713, 1996.
Dunstan R, Bussiere T, Engber T, Weinreb P, Maier M, Grimm J, Rhodes K, Arastu M, Li M, Zhang X: The role of brain macrophages on the clearance of amyloid plaques following the treatment of Tg2576 with BIIB037, *Alzheimers Dement* l 7(4):S700, 2011.
Farlow M, Arnold SE, van Dyck CH, Aisen PS, Snider BJ, Porsteinsson AP, Friedrich S, Dean RA, Gonzales C, Sethuraman G, DeMattos RB, Mohs R, Paul SM, Siemers ER: Safety and biomarker effects of solanezumab in patients with Alzheimer's disease, *Alzheimers Dement* 8:261–271, 2012.
Farlow MR, Andreasen N, Riviere ME, Vostiar I, Vitaliti A, Sovago J, Caputo A, Winblad B, Graf A: Long-term treatment with active Abeta immunotherapy with CAD106 in mild Alzheimer's disease, *Alzheimers Res Ther* 7:23, 2015.
Fishman JB, Rubin JB, Handrahan JV, Connor JR, Fine RE: Receptor-mediated transcytosis of transferrin across the blood–brain barrier, *J Neurosci Res* 18:299–304, 1987.
Fox NC, Black RS, Gilman S, Rossor MN, Griffith SG, Jenkins L, Koller M: Effects of Abeta immunization (AN1792) on MRI measures of cerebral volume in Alzheimer disease, *Neurology* 64:1563–1572, 2005.

Frost JL, Liu B, Kleinschmidt M, Schilling S, Demuth HU, Lemere CA: Passive immunization against pyroglutamate-3 amyloid-beta reduces plaque burden in Alzheimer-like transgenic mice: a pilot study, *Neurodegener Dis* 10:265–270, 2012.

Frost JL, Le KX, Cynis H, Ekpo E, Kleinschmidt M, Palmour RM, Ervin FR, Snigdha S, Cotman CW, Saido TC, Vassar RJ, St George-Hyslop P, Ikezu T, Schilling S, Demuth HU, Lemere CA: Pyroglutamate-3 amyloid-beta deposition in the brains of humans, non-human primates, canines, and Alzheimer disease-like transgenic mouse models, *Am J Pathol* 183:369–381, 2013.

Frost JL, Liu B, Rahfeld JU, Kleinschmidt M, O'Nuallain B, Le KX, Lues I, Caldarone BJ, Schilling S, Demuth HU, Lemere CA: An anti-pyroglutamate-3 Aβ vaccine reduces plaques and improves cognition in APP_{SWE}/PS1dE9 mice, *Neurobiol Aging* 36(12):3187–3199, 2015.

Galton CJ, Erzinclioglu S, Sahakian BJ, Antoun N, Hodges JR: A comparison of the Addenbrooke's Cognitive Examination (ACE), conventional neuropsychological assessment, and simple MRI-based medial temporal lobe evaluation in the early diagnosis of Alzheimer's disease, *Cogn Behav Neurol* 18:144–150, 2005.

Games D, Adams D, Alessandrini R, Barbour R, Berthelette P, Blackwell C, Carr T, Clemens J, Donaldson T, Gillespie F, et al: Alzheimer-type neuropathology in transgenic mice overexpressing V717F beta-amyloid precursor protein, *Nature* 373:523–527, 1995.

Georganopoulou DG, Chang L, Nam JM, Thaxton CS, Mufson EJ, Klein WL, Mirkin CA: Nanoparticle-based detection in cerebral spinal fluid of a soluble pathogenic biomarker for Alzheimer's disease, *Proc Natl Acad Sci USA* 102:2273–2276, 2005.

Giannakopoulos P, Herrmann FR, Bussiere T, Bouras C, Kovari E, Perl DP, Morrison JH, Gold G, Hof PR: Tangle and neuron numbers, but not amyloid load, predict cognitive status in Alzheimer's disease, *Neurology* 60:1495–1500, 2003.

Goate A, Chartier-Harlin MC, Mullan M, Brown J, Crawford F, Fidani L, Giuffra L, Haynes A, Irving N, James L, et al: Segregation of a missense mutation in the amyloid precursor protein gene with familial Alzheimer's disease, *Nature* 349:704–706, 1991.

Guerreiro R, Wojtas A, Bras J, Carrasquillo M, Rogaeva E, Majounie E, Cruchaga C, Sassi C, Kauwe JS, Younkin S, Hazrati L, Collinge J, Pocock J, Lashley T, Williams J, Lambert JC, Amouyel P, Goate A, Rademakers R, Morgan K, Powell J, St George-Hyslop P, Singleton A, Hardy J: TREM2 variants in Alzheimer's disease, *N Engl J Med* 368:117–127, 2013.

Hagen M, Seubert P, Jacobsen S, Schenk D, Pride M, Arumugham R, Warner G, Kinney G: The Aβ peptide conjugate vaccine, ACC-001, generates N-terminal anti-Aβ antibodies in the absence of Aβ directed T-cell responses, *Alzheimers Dement* 7:S460-S461, 2011.

Hamilton L, Fay S, Rockwood K: Misplacing objects in mild to moderate Alzheimer's disease: a descriptive analysis from the VISTA clinical trial, *J Neurol Neurosurg Psychiatr* 80:960–965, 2009.

Hardy JA, Higgins GA: Alzheimer's disease: the amyloid cascade hypothesis, *Science* 256:184–185, 1992.

Hardy J, Selkoe DJ: The amyloid hypothesis of Alzheimer's disease: progress and problems on the road to therapeutics, *Science* 297:353–356, 2002.

Harold D, Abraham R, Hollingworth P, Sims R, Gerrish A, Hamshere ML, Pahwa JS, Moskvina V, Dowzell K, Williams A, Jones N, Thomas C, Stretton A, Morgan AR, Lovestone S, Powell J, Proitsi P, Lupton MK, Brayne C, Rubinsztein DC, Gill M, Lawlor B, Lynch A, Morgan K, Brown KS, Passmore PA, Craig D, McGuinness B, Todd S, Holmes C, Mann D, Smith AD, Love S, Kehoe PG, Hardy J, Mead S, Fox N, Rossor M, Collinge J, Maier W, Jessen F, Schurmann B, Heun R, van den Bussche H, Heuser I, Kornhuber J, Wiltfang J, Dichgans M, Frolich L, Hampel H, Hull M, Rujescu D, Goate AM, Kauwe JS, Cruchaga C, Nowotny P, Morris JC, Mayo K, Sleegers K, Bettens K, Engelborghs S, De Deyn PP, Van Broeckhoven C, Livingston G, Bass NJ, Gurling H, McQuillin A, Gwilliam R, Deloukas P, Al-Chalabi A, Shaw CE, Tsolaki M, Singleton AB, Guerreiro R, Muhleisen TW, Nothen MM, Moebus S, Jockel KH, Klopp N, Wichmann HE, Carrasquillo MM, Pankratz VS, Younkin SG, Holmans PA, O'Donovan M, Owen MJ, Williams J: Genome-wide association study identifies variants at CLU and PICALM associated with Alzheimer's disease, *Nat Genet* 41:1088–1093, 2009.

Hartley D, Blumenthal T, Carrillo M, DiPaolo G, Esralew L, Gardiner K, Granholm AC, Iqbal K, Krams M, Lemere C, Lott I, Mobley W, Ness S, Nixon R, Potter H, Reeves R, Sabbagh M, Silverman W, Tycko B, Whitten M, Wisniewski T: Down syndrome and Alzheimer's disease: common pathways, common goals, *Alzheimers Dement* 11:700–709, 2015.

Heneka MT, Carson MJ, El Khoury J, Landreth GE, Brosseron F, Feinstein DL, Jacobs AH, Wyss-Coray T, Vitorica J, Ransohoff RM, Herrup K, Frautschy SA, Finsen B, Brown GC, Verkhratsky A, Yamanaka K, Koistinaho J, Latz E, Halle A, Petzold GC, Town T, Morgan D, Shinohara ML, Perry VH, Holmes C, Bazan NG, Brooks DJ, Hunot S,

Joseph B, Deigendesch N, Garaschuk O, Boddeke E, Dinarello CA, Breitner JC, Cole GM, Golenbock DT, Kummer MP: Neuroinflammation in Alzheimer's disease, *Lancet Neurol* 14:388–405, 2015.

Hickman DT, Lopez-Deber MP, Ndao DM, Silva AB, Nand D, Pihlgren M, Giriens V, Madani R, St-Pierre A, Karastaneva H, Nagel-Steger L, Willbold D, Riesner D, Nicolau C, Baldus M, Pfeifer A, Muhs A: Sequence-independent control of peptide conformation in liposomal vaccines for targeting protein misfolding diseases, *J Biol Chem* 286:13966–13976, 2011.

Hock C, Konietzko U, Streffer JR, Tracy J, Signorell A, Muller-Tillmanns B, Lemke U, Henke K, Moritz E, Garcia E, Wollmer MA, Umbricht D, de Quervain DJ, Hofmann M, Maddalena A, Papassotiropoulos A, Nitsch RM: Antibodies against beta-amyloid slow cognitive decline in Alzheimer's disease, *Neuron* 38:547–554, 2003.

Hollingworth P, Harold D, Sims R, Gerrish A, Lambert JC, Carrasquillo MM, Abraham R, Hamshere ML, Pahwa JS, Moskvina V, Dowzell K, Jones N, Stretton A, Thomas C, Richards A, Ivanov D, Widdowson C, Chapman J, Lovestone S, Powell J, Proitsi P, Lupton MK, Brayne C, Rubinsztein DC, Gill M, Lawlor B, Lynch A, Brown KS, Passmore PA, Craig D, McGuinness B, Todd S, Holmes C, Mann D, Smith AD, Beaumont H, Warden D, Wilcock G, Love S, Kehoe PG, Hooper NM, Vardy ER, Hardy J, Mead S, Fox NC, Rossor M, Collinge J, Maier W, Jessen F, Ruther E, Schurmann B, Heun R, Kolsch H, van den Bussche H, Heuser I, Kornhuber J, Wiltfang J, Dichgans M, Frolich L, Hampel H, Gallacher J, Hull M, Rujescu D, Giegling I, Goate AM, Kauwe JS, Cruchaga C, Nowotny P, Morris JC, Mayo K, Sleegers K, Bettens K, Engelborghs S, De Deyn PP, Van Broeckhoven C, Livingston G, Bass NJ, Gurling H, McQuillin A, Gwilliam R, Deloukas P, Al-Chalabi A, Shaw CE, Tsolaki M, Singleton AB, Guerreiro R, Muhleisen TW, Nothen MM, Moebus S, Jockel KH, Klopp N, Wichmann HE, Pankratz VS, Sando SB, Aasly JO, Barcikowska M, Wszolek ZK, Dickson DW, Graff-Radford NR, Petersen RC, van Duijn CM, Breteler MM, Ikram MA, DeStefano AL, Fitzpatrick AL, Lopez O, Launer LJ, Seshadri S, Berr C, Campion D, Epelbaum J, Dartigues JF, Tzourio C, Alperovitch A, Lathrop M, Feulner TM, Friedrich P, Riehle C, Krawczak M, Schreiber S, Mayhaus M, Nicolhaus S, Wagenpfeil S, Steinberg S, Stefansson H, Stefansson K, Snaedal J, Bjornsson S, Jonsson PV, Chouraki V, Genier-Boley B, Hiltunen M, Soininen H, Combarros O, Zelenika D, Delepine M, Bullido MJ, Pasquier F, Mateo I, Frank-Garcia A, Porcellini E, Hanon O, Coto E, Alvarez V, Bosco P, Siciliano G, Mancuso M, Panza F, Solfrizzi V, Nacmias B, Sorbi S, Bossu P, Piccardi P, Arosio B, Annoni G, Seripa D, Pilotto A, Scarpini E, Galimberti D, Brice A, Hannequin D, Licastro F, Jones L, Holmans PA, Jonsson T, Riemenschneider M, Morgan K, Younkin SG, Owen MJ, O'Donovan M, Amouyel P, Williams J: Common variants at ABCA7, MS4A6A/MS4A4E, EPHA1, CD33 and CD2AP are associated with Alzheimer's disease, *Nat Genet* 43:429–435, 2011.

Holmes C, Boche D, Wilkinson D, Yadegarfar G, Hopkins V, Bayer A, Jones RW, Bullock R, Love S, Neal JW, Zotova E, Nicoll JA: Long-term effects of Abeta42 immunisation in Alzheimer's disease: follow-up of a randomised, placebo-controlled phase I trial, *Lancet* 372:216–223, 2008.

Hsiao K, Chapman P, Nilsen S, Eckman C, Harigaya Y, Younkin S, Yang F, Cole G: Correlative memory deficits, Abeta elevation, and amyloid plaques in transgenic mice, *Science* 274:99–102, 1996.

Ingelsson M, Fukumoto H, Newell KL, Growdon JH, Hedley-Whyte ET, Frosch MP, Albert MS, Hyman BT, Irizarry MC: Early Abeta accumulation and progressive synaptic loss, gliosis, and tangle formation in AD brain, *Neurology* 62:925–931, 2004.

Itagaki S, McGeer PL, Akiyama H, Zhu S, Selkoe D: Relationship of microglia and astrocytes to amyloid deposits of Alzheimer disease, *J Neuroimmunol* 24:173–182, 1989.

Jankowsky JL, Slunt HH, Ratovitski T, Jenkins NA, Copeland NG, Borchelt DR: Co-expression of multiple transgenes in mouse CNS: a comparison of strategies, *Biomol Eng* 17:157–165, 2001.

Jankowsky JL, Fadale DJ, Anderson J, Xu GM, Gonzales V, Jenkins NA, Copeland NG, Lee MK, Younkin LH, Wagner SL, Younkin SG, Borchelt DR: Mutant presenilins specifically elevate the levels of the 42 residue beta-amyloid peptide in vivo: evidence for augmentation of a 42-specific gamma secretase, *Hum Mol Genet* 13:159–170, 2004.

Kamphuis W, Mamber C, Moeton M, Kooijman L, Sluijs JA, Jansen AH, Verveer M, de Groot LR, Smith VD, Rangarajan S, Rodriguez JJ, Orre M, Hol EM: GFAP isoforms in adult mouse brain with a focus on neurogenic astrocytes and reactive astrogliosis in mouse models of Alzheimer disease, *PLoS One* 7:e42823, 2012.

Karlnoski RA, Rosenthal A, Kobayashi D, Pons J, Alamed J, Mercer M, Li Q, Gordon MN, Gottschall PE, Morgan D: Suppression of amyloid deposition leads to long-term reductions in Alzheimer's pathologies in Tg2576 mice, *J Neurosci* 29:4964–4971, 2009.

Kelly PH, Bondolfi L, Hunziker D, Schlecht HP, Carver K, Maguire E, Abramowski D, Wiederhold KH, Sturchler-Pierrat C, Jucker M, Bergmann R, Staufenbiel M, Sommer B: Progressive age-related impairment of cognitive behavior in APP23 transgenic mice, *Neurobiol Aging* 24:365–378, 2003.

Khan KH: DNA vaccines: roles against diseases, *Germs* 3:26–35, 2013.

Koenigsknecht-Talboo J, Meyer-Luehmann M, Parsadanian M, Garcia-Alloza M, Finn MB, Hyman BT, Bacskai BJ, Holtzman DM: Rapid microglial response around amyloid pathology after systemic anti-Abeta antibody administration in PDAPP mice, *J Neurosci* 28:14156–14164, 2008.

La Porte SL, Bollini SS, Lanz TA, Abdiche YN, Rusnak AS, Ho WH, Kobayashi D, Harrabi O, Pappas D, Mina EW, Milici AJ, Kawabe TT, Bales K, Lin JC, Pons J: Structural basis of C-terminal beta-amyloid peptide binding by the antibody ponezumab for the treatment of Alzheimer's disease, *J Mol Biol* 421:525–536, 2012.

Lalonde R, Kim HD, Maxwell JA, Fukuchi K: Exploratory activity and spatial learning in 12-month-old APP(695) SWE/co+PS1/DeltaE9 mice with amyloid plaques, *Neurosci Lett* 390:87–92, 2005.

Lambert JC, Heath S, Even G, Campion D, Sleegers K, Hiltunen M, Combarros O, Zelenika D, Bullido MJ, Tavernier B, Letenneur L, Bettens K, Berr C, Pasquier F, Fievet N, Barberger-Gateau P, Engelborghs S, De Deyn P, Mateo I, Franck A, Helisalmi S, Porcellini E, Hanon O, de Pancorbo MM, Lendon C, Dufouil C, Jaillard C, Leveillard T, Alvarez V, Bosco P, Mancuso M, Panza F, Nacmias B, Bossu P, Piccardi P, Annoni G, Seripa D, Galimberti D, Hannequin D, Licastro F, Soininen H, Ritchie K, Blanche H, Dartigues JF, Tzourio C, Gut I, Van Broeckhoven C, Alperovitch A, Lathrop M, Amouyel P: Genome-wide association study identifies variants at CLU and CR1 associated with Alzheimer's disease, *Nat Genet* 41:1094–1099, 2009.

Lee M, Bard F, Johnson-Wood K, Lee C, Hu K, Griffith SG, Black RS, Schenk D, Seubert P: Abeta42 immunization in Alzheimer's disease generates Abeta N-terminal antibodies, *Ann Neurol* 58:430–435, 2005.

Lemere CA: Immunotherapy for Alzheimer's disease: hoops and hurdles, *Mol Neurodegener* 8:36, 2013.

Lemere CA, Masliah E: Can Alzheimer disease be prevented by amyloid-beta immunotherapy? *Nat Rev Neurol* 6:108–119, 2010.

Lemere CA, Maron R, Spooner ET, Grenfell TJ, Mori C, Desai R, Hancock WW, Weiner HL, Selkoe DJ, Nasal A: Beta treatment induces anti-A beta antibody production and decreases cerebral amyloid burden in PD-APP mice, *Ann NY Acad Sci* 920:328–331, 2000.

Leung KK, Bartlett JW, Barnes J, Manning EN, Ourselin S, Fox NC: Cerebral atrophy in mild cognitive impairment and Alzheimer disease: rates and acceleration, *Neurology* 80:648–654, 2013.

Levy-Lahad E, Wasco W, Poorkaj P, Romano DM, Oshima J, Pettingell WH, Yu CE, Jondro PD, Schmidt SD, Wang K, et al: Candidate gene for the chromosome 1 familial Alzheimer's disease locus, *Science* 269:973–977, 1995.

Leyhe T, Andreasen N, Simeoni M, Reich A, von Arnim CA, Tong X, Yeo A, Khan S, Loercher A, Chalker M, Hottenstein C, Zetterberg H, Hilpert J, Mistry P: Modulation of beta-amyloid by a single dose of GSK933776 in patients with mild Alzheimer's disease: a phase I study, *Alzheimers Res Ther* 6:19, 2014.

Lindsay J, Laurin D, Verreault R, Hebert R, Helliwell B, Hill GB, McDowell I: Risk factors for Alzheimer's disease: a prospective analysis from the Canadian Study of Health and Aging, *Am J Epidemiol* 156:445–453, 2002.

Liu B, Frost JL, Sun J, Fu H, Grimes S, Blackburn P, Lemere CA: MER5101, a novel Abeta 1-15:DT conjugate vaccine, generates a robust anti-Abeta antibody response and attenuates Abeta pathology and cognitive deficits in APPswe/PS1DeltaE9 transgenic mice, *J Neurosci* 33:7027–7037, 2013.

Liu GJ, Middleton RJ, Hatty CR, Kam WW, Chan R, Pham T, Harrison-Brown M, Dodson E, Veale K, Banati RB: The 18 kDa translocator protein, microglia and neuroinflammation, *Brain Pathol* 24:631–653, 2014.

Liu E, Schmidt ME, Margolin R, Sperling R, Koeppe R, Mason NS, Klunk WE, Mathis CA, Salloway S, Fox NC, Hill DL, Les AS, Collins P, Gregg KM, Di J, Lu Y, Tudor IC, Wyman BT, Booth K, Broome S, Yuen E, Grundman M, Brashear HR: Amyloid-beta 11C-PiB-PET imaging results from 2 randomized bapineuzumab phase 3 AD trials, *Neurology* 85:692–700, 2015.

Luchsinger JA, Tang MX, Stern Y, Shea S, Mayeux R: Diabetes mellitus and risk of Alzheimer's disease and dementia with stroke in a multiethnic cohort, *Am J Epidemiol* 154:635–641, 2001.

Mably AJ, Liu W, Mc Donald JM, Dodart JC, Bard F, Lemere CA, O'Nuallain B, Walsh DM: Anti-Abeta antibodies incapable of reducing cerebral Abeta oligomers fail to attenuate spatial reference memory deficits in J20 mice, *Neurobiol Dis* 82:372–384, 2015.

Maier M, Seabrook TJ, Lazo ND, Jiang L, Das P, Janus C, Lemere CA: Short amyloid-beta (Abeta) immunogens reduce cerebral Abeta load and learning deficits in an Alzheimer's disease mouse model in the absence of an Abeta-specific cellular immune response, *J Neurosci* 26:4717–4728, 2006.

Marczinski CA, Kertesz A: Category and letter fluency in semantic dementia, primary progressive aphasia, and Alzheimer's disease, *Brain Lang* 93:258–265, 2006.

Marksteiner J, Hinterhuber H, Humpel C: Cerebrospinal fluid biomarkers for diagnosis of Alzheimer's disease: beta-amyloid 1-42 tau, phospho-tau-181 and total protein, *Drugs Today* 43:423–431, 2007.

Masliah E, Terry RD, DeTeresa RM, Hansen LA: Immunohistochemical quantification of the synapse-related protein synaptophysin in Alzheimer disease, *Neurosci Lett* 103:234–239, 1989.

Meyer-Luehmann M, Mielke M, Spires-Jones TL, Stoothoff W, Jones P, Bacskai BJ, Hyman BT: A reporter of local dendritic translocation shows plaque-related loss of neural system function in APP-transgenic mice, *J Neurosci* 29:12636–12640, 2009.

Mirra SS: The CERAD neuropathology protocol and consensus recommendations for the postmortem diagnosis of Alzheimer's disease: a commentary, *Neurobiol Aging* 18:S91–S94, 1997.

Morgan D, Diamond DM, Gottschall PE, Ugen KE, Dickey C, Hardy J, Duff K, Jantzen P, DiCarlo G, Wilcock D, Connor K, Hatcher J, Hope C, Gordon M, Arendash GW: A beta peptide vaccination prevents memory loss in an animal model of Alzheimer's disease, *Nature* 408:982–985, 2000.

Movsesyan N, Ghochikyan A, Mkrtichyan M, Petrushina I, Davtyan H, Olkhanud PB, Head E, Biragyn A, Cribbs DH, Agadjanyan MG: Reducing AD-like pathology in 3xTg-AD mouse model by DNA epitope vaccine—a novel immunotherapeutic strategy, *PLoS One* 3:e2124, 2008.

Mucke L, Masliah E, Yu GQ, Mallory M, Rockenstein EM, Tatsuno G, Hu K, Kholodenko D, Johnson-Wood K, McConlogue L: High-level neuronal expression of abeta 1-42 in wild-type human amyloid protein precursor transgenic mice: synaptotoxicity without plaque formation, *J Neurosci* 20:4050–4058, 2000.

Muhs A, Hickman DT, Pihlgren M, Chuard N, Giriens V, Meerschman C, van der Auwera I, van Leuven F, Sugawara M, Weingertner MC, Bechinger B, Greferath R, Kolonko N, Nagel-Steger L, Riesner D, Brady RO, Pfeifer A, Nicolau C: Liposomal vaccines with conformation-specific amyloid peptide antigens define immune response and efficacy in APP transgenic mice, *Proc Natl Acad Sci USA* 104:9810–9815, 2007.

Murphy MP, LeVine H III: Alzheimer's disease and the amyloid-beta peptide, *J Alzheimers Dis* 19:311–323, 2010.

Naj AC, Jun G, Beecham GW, Wang LS, Vardarajan BN, Buros J, Gallins PJ, Buxbaum JD, Jarvik GP, Crane PK, Larson EB, Bird TD, Boeve BF, Graff-Radford NR, De Jager PL, Evans D, Schneider JA, Carrasquillo MM, Ertekin-Taner N, Younkin SG, Cruchaga C, Kauwe JS, Nowotny P, Kramer P, Hardy J, Huentelman MJ, Myers AJ, Barmada MM, Demirci FY, Baldwin CT, Green RC, Rogaeva E, St George-Hyslop P, Arnold SE, Barber R, Beach T, Bigio EH, Bowen JD, Boxer A, Burke JR, Cairns NJ, Carlson CS, Carney RM, Carroll SL, Chui HC, Clark DG, Corneveaux J, Cotman CW, Cummings JL, DeCarli C, DeKosky ST, Diaz-Arrastia R, Dick M, Dickson DW, Ellis WG, Faber KM, Fallon KB, Farlow MR, Ferris S, Frosch MP, Galasko DR, Ganguli M, Gearing M, Geschwind DH, Ghetti B, Gilbert JR, Gilman S, Giordani B, Glass JD, Growdon JH, Hamilton RL, Harrell LE, Head E, Honig LS, Hulette CM, Hyman BT, Jicha GA, Jin LW, Johnson N, Karlawish J, Karydas A, Kaye JA, Kim R, Koo EH, Kowall NW, Lah JJ, Levey AI, Lieberman AP, Lopez OL, Mack WJ, Marson DC, Martiniuk F, Mash DC, Masliah E, McCormick WC, McCurry SM, McDavid AN, McKee AC, Mesulam M, Miller BL, Miller CA, Miller JW, Parisi JE, Perl DP, Peskind E, Petersen RC, Poon WW, Quinn JF, Rajbhandary RA, Raskind M, Reisberg B, Ringman JM, Roberson ED, Rosenberg RN, Sano M, Schneider LS, Seeley W, Shelanski ML, Slifer MA, Smith CD, Sonnen JA, Spina S, Stern RA, Tanzi RE, Trojanowski JQ, Troncoso JC, Van Deerlin VM, Vinters HV, Vonsattel JP, Weintraub S, Welsh-Bohmer KA, Williamson J, Woltjer RL, Cantwell LB, Dombroski BA, Beekly D, Lunetta KL, Martin ER, Kamboh MI, Saykin AJ, Reiman EM, Bennett DA, Morris JC, Montine TJ, Goate AM, Blacker D, Tsuang DW, Hakonarson H, Kukull WA, Foroud TM, Haines JL, Mayeux R, Pericak-Vance MA, Farrer LA, Schellenberg GD: Common variants at MS4A4/MS4A6E, CD2AP, CD33 and EPHA1 are associated with late-onset Alzheimer's disease, *Nat Genet* 43:436–441, 2011.

Niewoehner J, Bohrmann B, Collin L, Urich E, Sade H, Maier P, Rueger P, Stracke JO, Lau W, Tissot AC, Loetscher H, Ghosh A, Freskgard PO: Increased brain penetration and potency of a therapeutic antibody using a monovalent molecular shuttle, *Neuron* 81:49–60, 2014.

Nilsberth C, Westlind-Danielsson A, Eckman CB, Condron MM, Axelman K, Forsell C, Stenh C, Luthman J, Teplow DB, Younkin SG, Naslund J, Lannfelt L: The "Arctic" APP mutation (E693G) causes Alzheimer's disease by enhanced Abeta protofibril formation, *Nat Neurosci* 4:887–893, 2001.

Nussbaum JM, Schilling S, Cynis H, Silva A, Swanson E, Wangsanut T, Tayler K, Wiltgen B, Hatami A, Ronicke R, Reymann K, Hutter-Paier B, Alexandru A, Jagla W, Graubner S, Glabe CG, Demuth HU, Bloom GS: Prion-like behaviour and tau-dependent cytotoxicity of pyroglutamylated amyloid-beta, *Nature* 485:651–655, 2012.

Oakley H, Cole SL, Logan S, Maus E, Shao P, Craft J, Guillozet-Bongaarts A, Ohno M, Disterhoft J, Van Eldik L, Berry R, Vassar R: Intraneuronal beta-amyloid aggregates, neurodegeneration, and neuron loss in transgenic mice with five familial Alzheimer's disease mutations: potential factors in amyloid plaque formation, *J Neurosci* 26:10129–10140, 2006.

Orgogozo JM, Gilman S, Dartigues JF, Laurent B, Puel M, Kirby LC, Jouanny P, Dubois B, Eisner L, Flitman S, Michel BF, Boada M, Frank A, Hock C: Subacute meningoencephalitis in a subset of patients with AD after Abeta42 immunization, *Neurology* 61:46–54, 2003.

Ostrowitzki S, Deptula D, Thurfjell L, Barkhof F, Bohrmann B, Brooks DJ, Klunk WE, Ashford E, Yoo K, Xu ZX, Loetscher H, Santarelli L: Mechanism of amyloid removal in patients with Alzheimer disease treated with gantenerumab, *Arch Neurol* 69:198–207, 2012.

Palop JJ, Jones B, Kekonius L, Chin J, Yu GQ, Raber J, Masliah E, Mucke L: Neuronal depletion of calcium-dependent proteins in the dentate gyrus is tightly linked to Alzheimer's disease-related cognitive deficits, *Proc Natl Acad Sci USA* 100:9572–9577, 2003.

Paul S, Planque S, Nishiyama Y: Beneficial catalytic immunity to Abeta peptide, *Rejuvenation Res* 13:179–187, 2010.

Peters F, Collette F, Degueldre C, Sterpenich V, Majerus S, Salmon E: The neural correlates of verbal short-term memory in Alzheimer's disease: an fMRI study, *Brain* 132:1833–1846, 2009.

Pfeifer M, Boncristiano S, Bondolfi L, Stalder A, Deller T, Staufenbiel M, Mathews PM, Jucker M: Cerebral hemorrhage after passive anti-Abeta immunotherapy, *Science* 298:1379, 2002.

Planque SA, Nishiyama Y, Sonoda S, Lin Y, Taguchi H, Hara M, Kolodziej S, Mitsuda Y, Gonzalez V, Sait HB, Fukuchi K, Massey RJ, Friedland RP, O'Nuallain B, Sigurdsson EM, Paul S: Specific amyloid beta clearance by a catalytic antibody construct, *J Biol Chem* 290:10229–10241, 2015.

Pozueta J, Lefort R, Shelanski ML: Synaptic changes in Alzheimer's disease and its models, *Neuroscience* 251:51–65, 2013.

Premkumar DR, Cohen DL, Hedera P, Friedland RP, Kalaria RN: Apolipoprotein E-epsilon4 alleles in cerebral amyloid angiopathy and cerebrovascular pathology associated with Alzheimer's disease, *Am J Pathol* 148:2083–2095, 1996.

Prince M, Bryce R, Albanese E, Wimo A, Ribeiro W, Ferri CP: The global prevalence of dementia: a systematic review and metaanalysis, *Alzheimers Dement* 9:63–75, 2013, e2.

Racke MM, Boone LI, Hepburn DL, Parsadainian M, Bryan MT, Ness DK, Piroozi KS, Jordan WH, Brown DD, Hoffman WP, Holtzman DM, Bales KR, Gitter BD, May PC, Paul SM, DeMattos RB: Exacerbation of cerebral amyloid angiopathy-associated microhemorrhage in amyloid precursor protein transgenic mice by immunotherapy is dependent on antibody recognition of deposited forms of amyloid beta, *J Neurosci* 25:629–636, 2005.

Radde R, Bolmont T, Kaeser SA, Coomaraswamy J, Lindau D, Stoltze L, Calhoun ME, Jaggi F, Wolburg H, Gengler S, Haass C, Ghetti B, Czech C, Holscher C, Mathews PM, Jucker M: Abeta42-driven cerebral amyloidosis in transgenic mice reveals early and robust pathology, *EMBO Rep* 7:940–946, 2006.

Reisberg B, Doody R, Stoffler A, Schmitt F, Ferris S, Mobius HJ: Memantine in moderate-to-severe Alzheimer's disease, *N Engl J Med* 348:1333–1341, 2003.

Reitz C, Mayeux R: Alzheimer disease: epidemiology, diagnostic criteria, risk factors and biomarkers, *Biochem Pharmacol* 88:640–651, 2014.

Relkin NR, Szabo P, Adamiak B, Burgut T, Monthe C, Lent RW, Younkin S, Younkin L, Schiff R, Weksler ME: 18-Month study of intravenous immunoglobulin for treatment of mild Alzheimer disease, *Neurobiol Aging* 30:1728–1736, 2009.

Rinne JO, Brooks DJ, Rossor MN, Fox NC, Bullock R, Klunk WE, Mathis CA, Blennow K, Barakos J, Okello AA, Rodriguez Martinez de Liano S, Liu E, Koller M, Gregg KM, Schenk D, Black R, Grundman M: 11C-PiB PET assessment of change in fibrillar amyloid-beta load in patients with Alzheimer's disease treated with bapineuzumab: a phase 2, double-blind, placebo-controlled, ascending-dose study, *Lancet Neurol* 9:363–372, 2010.

Riviere M-E, Caputo A, Laurent N, Vostiar I, Andreasen N, Cohen S, Kressig RW, Ryan JM, Graf A: Active AB immunotherapy CAD106 phase II dose-adjuvant finding study: immune response, *Alzheimers Dement*: 447–448, 2014.

Roche: Roche announces phase II clinical results of crenezumab in Alzheimer's disease, 2014. Available from: http://www.roche.com/investors/updates/inv-update-2014-07-16.htm

Rogers SL, Farlow MR, Doody RS, Mohs R, Friedhoff LT: A 24-week, double-blind, placebo-controlled trial of donepezil in patients with Alzheimer's disease. Donepezil Study Group, *Neurology* 50:136–145, 1998.

Rosler M, Anand R, Cicin-Sain A, Gauthier S, Agid Y, Dal-Bianco P, Stahelin HB, Hartman R, Gharabawi M: Efficacy and safety of rivastigmine in patients with Alzheimer's disease: international randomised controlled trial, *Br Med J* 318:633–638, 1999.

Saido TC, Iwatsubo T, Mann DM, Shimada H, Ihara Y, Kawashima S: Dominant and differential deposition of distinct beta-amyloid peptide species, A beta N3(pE), in senile plaques, *Neuron* 14:457–466, 1995.

Saito T, Suemoto T, Brouwers N, Sleegers K, Funamoto S, Mihira N, Matsuba Y, Yamada K, Nilsson P, Takano J, Nishimura M, Iwata N, Van Broeckhoven C, Ihara Y, Saido TC: Potent amyloidogenicity and pathogenicity of Abeta43, *Nat Neurosci* 14:1023–1032, 2011.

Sakono M, Zako T: Amyloid oligomers: formation and toxicity of Abeta oligomers, *FEBS J* 277:1348–1358, 2010.

Salloway S, Sperling R, Fox NC, Blennow K, Klunk W, Raskind M, Sabbagh M, Honig LS, Porsteinsson AP, Ferris S, Reichert M, Ketter N, Nejadnik B, Guenzler V, Miloslavsky M, Wang D, Lu Y, Lull J, Tudor IC, Liu E, Grundman

M, Yuen E, Black R, Brashear HR: Two phase 3 trials of bapineuzumab in mild-to-moderate Alzheimer's disease, *N Engl J Med* 370:322–333, 2014.

Salvati E, Re F, Sesana S, Cambianica I, Sancini G, Masserini M, Gregori M: Liposomes functionalized to overcome the blood–brain barrier and to target amyloid-beta peptide: the chemical design affects the permeability across an in vitro model, *Int J Nanomed* 8:1749–1758, 2013.

Savonenko A, Xu GM, Melnikova T, Morton JL, Gonzales V, Wong MP, Price DL, Tang F, Markowska AL, Borchelt DR: Episodic-like memory deficits in the APPswe/PS1dE9 mouse model of Alzheimer's disease: relationships to beta-amyloid deposition and neurotransmitter abnormalities, *Neurobiol Dis* 18:602–617, 2005.

Savva GM, Zaccai J, Matthews FE, Davidson JE, McKeith I, Brayne C: Prevalence, correlates and course of behavioural and psychological symptoms of dementia in the population, *Br J Psychiatry* 194:212–219, 2009.

Scheff SW, Price DA: Synapse loss in the temporal lobe in Alzheimer's disease, *Ann Neurol* 33:190–199, 1993.

Scheff SW, Price DA: Synaptic pathology in Alzheimer's disease: a review of ultrastructural studies, *Neurobiol Aging* 24:1029–1046, 2003.

Schenk D, Barbour R, Dunn W, Gordon G, Grajeda H, Guido T, Hu K, Huang J, Johnson-Wood K, Khan K, Kholodenko D, Lee M, Liao Z, Lieberburg I, Motter R, Mutter L, Soriano F, Shopp G, Vasquez N, Vandevert C, Walker S, Wogulis M, Yednock T, Games D, Seubert P: Immunization with amyloid-beta attenuates Alzheimer-disease-like pathology in the PDAPP mouse, *Nature* 400:173–177, 1999.

Schilling S, Lauber T, Schaupp M, Manhart S, Scheel E, Bohm G, Demuth HU: On the seeding and oligomerization of pGlu-amyloid peptides (in vitro), *Biochemistry* 45:12393–12399, 2006.

Schneeberger A, Mandler M, Otawa O, Zauner W, Mattner F, Schmidt W: Development of AFFITOPE vaccines for Alzheimer's disease (AD)—from concept to clinical testing, *J Nutr Health Aging* 13:264–267, 2009.

Schroeter S, Khan K, Barbour R, Doan M, Chen M, Guido T, Gill D, Basi G, Schenk D, Seubert P, Games D: Immunotherapy reduces vascular amyloid-beta in PDAPP mice, *J Neurosci* 28:6787–6793, 2008.

Selkoe DJ: Alzheimer's disease results from the cerebral accumulation and cytotoxicity of amyloid beta-protein, *J Alzheimers Dis* 3:75–80, 2001.

Selkoe DJ: Soluble oligomers of the amyloid beta-protein impair synaptic plasticity and behavior, *Behav Brain Res* 192:106–113, 2008.

Sherrington R, Rogaev EI, Liang Y, Rogaeva EA, Levesque G, Ikeda M, Chi H, Lin C, Li G, Holman K, Tsuda T, Mar L, Foncin JF, Bruni AC, Montesi MP, Sorbi S, Rainero I, Pinessi L, Nee L, Chumakov I, Pollen D, Brookes A, Sanseau P, Polinsky RJ, Wasco W, Da Silva HA, Haines JL, Perkicak-Vance MA, Tanzi RE, Roses AD, Fraser PE, Rommens JM, St George-Hyslop PH: Cloning of a gene bearing missense mutations in early-onset familial Alzheimer's disease, *Nature* 375:754–760, 1995.

Siemers ER, Friedrich S, Dean RA, Gonzales CR, Farlow MR, Paul SM, Demattos RB: Safety and changes in plasma and cerebrospinal fluid amyloid beta after a single administration of an amyloid beta monoclonal antibody in subjects with Alzheimer disease, *Clin Neuropharmacol* 33:67–73, 2010.

Sperling RA, Aisen PS, Beckett LA, Bennett DA, Craft S, Fagan AM, Iwatsubo T, Jack CR Jr, Kaye J, Montine TJ, Park DC, Reiman EM, Rowe CC, Siemers E, Stern Y, Yaffe K, Carrillo MC, Thies B, Morrison-Bogorad M, Wagster MV, Phelps CH: Toward defining the preclinical stages of Alzheimer's disease: recommendations from the National Institute on Aging–Alzheimer's Association workgroups on diagnostic guidelines for Alzheimer's disease, *Alzheimers Dement* 7:280–292, 2011a.

Sperling RA, Jack CR Jr, Aisen PS: Testing the right target and right drug at the right stage, *Sci Transl Med* 3:111–133, 2011b.

Stoltzner SE, Grenfell TJ, Mori C, Wisniewski KE, Wisniewski TM, Selkoe DJ, Lemere CA: Temporal accrual of complement proteins in amyloid plaques in Down's syndrome with Alzheimer's disease, *Am J Pathol* 156:489–499, 2000.

Sturchler-Pierrat C, Abramowski D, Duke M, Wiederhold KH, Mistl C, Rothacher S, Ledermann B, Burki K, Frey P, Paganetti PA, Waridel C, Calhoun ME, Jucker M, Probst A, Staufenbiel M, Sommer B: Two amyloid precursor protein transgenic mouse models with Alzheimer disease-like pathology, *Proc Natl Acad Sci USA* 94:13287–13292, 1997.

Szabo P, Mujalli DM, Rotondi ML, Sharma R, Weber A, Schwarz HP, Weksler ME, Relkin N: Measurement of anti-beta amyloid antibodies in human blood, *J Neuroimmunol* 227:167–174, 2010.

Taguchi H, Planque S, Nishiyama Y, Szabo P, Weksler ME, Friedland RP, Paul S: Catalytic antibodies to amyloid beta peptide in defense against Alzheimer disease, *Autoimmun Rev* 7:391–397, 2008.

Thal DR, Rub U, Orantes M, Braak H: Phases of A beta-deposition in the human brain and its relevance for the development of AD, *Neurology* 58:1791–1800, 2002.

van der Zee JS, van Swieten P, Aalberse RC: Inhibition of complement activation by IgG4 antibodies, *Clin Exp Immunol* 64:415–422, 1986.

Vandenberghe R, Adamczuk K, Van Laere K: The interest of amyloid PET imaging in the diagnosis of Alzheimer's disease, *Curr Opin Neurol* 26:646–655, 2013.

Vehmas AK, Kawas CH, Stewart WF, Troncoso JC: Immune reactive cells in senile plaques and cognitive decline in Alzheimer's disease, *Neurobiol Aging* 24:321–331, 2003.

Vellas B, Black R, Thal LJ, Fox NC, Daniels M, McLennan G, Tompkins C, Leibman C, Pomfret M, Grundman M: Long-term follow-up of patients immunized with AN1792: reduced functional decline in antibody responders, *Curr Alzheimer Res* 6:144–151, 2009.

Volianskis A, Kostner R, Molgaard M, Hass S, Jensen MS: Episodic memory deficits are not related to altered glutamatergic synaptic transmission and plasticity in the CA1 hippocampus of the APPswe/PS1deltaE9-deleted transgenic mice model of ss-amyloidosis, *Neurobiol Aging*: 1173–1187, 2010.

Wadsworth H, Jones PA, Chau WF, Durrant C, Fouladi N, Passmore J, O'Shea D, Wynn D, Morisson-Iveson V, Ewan A, Thaning M, Mantzilas D, Gausemel I, Khan I, Black A, Avory M, Trigg W: [(1)(8)F]GE-180: a novel fluorine-18 labelled PET tracer for imaging translocator protein 18 kDa (TSPO), *Bioorg Med Chem Lett* 22:1308–1313, 2012.

Wagner M, Wolf S, Reischies FM, Daerr M, Wolfsgruber S, Jessen F, Popp J, Maier W, Hull M, Frolich L, Hampel H, Perneczky R, Peters O, Jahn H, Luckhaus C, Gertz HJ, Schroder J, Pantel J, Lewczuk P, Kornhuber J, Wiltfang J: Biomarker validation of a cued recall memory deficit in prodromal Alzheimer disease, *Neurology* 78:379–386, 2012.

Walker ES, Martinez M, Brunkan AL, Goate A: Presenilin 2 familial Alzheimer's disease mutations result in partial loss of function and dramatic changes in Abeta 42/40 ratios, *J Neurochem*:294–301, 2005.

Walsh DM, Klyubin I, Fadeeva JV, Cullen WK, Anwyl R, Wolfe MS, Rowan MJ, Selkoe DJ: Naturally secreted oligomers of amyloid beta protein potently inhibit hippocampal long-term potentiation in vivo, *Nature* 416:535–539, 2002.

Weiner HL, Lemere CA, Maron R, Spooner ET, Grenfell TJ, Mori C, Issazadeh S, Hancock WW, Selkoe DJ: Nasal administration of amyloid-beta peptide decreases cerebral amyloid burden in a mouse model of Alzheimer's disease, *Ann Neurol* 48:567–579, 2000.

Westerman MA, Cooper-Blacketer D, Mariash A, Kotilinek L, Kawarabayashi T, Younkin LH, Carlson GA, Younkin SG, Ashe KH: The relationship between Abeta and memory in the Tg2576 mouse model of Alzheimer's disease, *J Neurosci* 22:1858–1867, 2002.

Wiessner C, Wiederhold KH, Tissot AC, Frey P, Danner S, Jacobson LH, Jennings GT, Luond R, Ortmann R, Reichwald J, Zurini M, Mir A, Bachmann MF, Staufenbiel M: The second-generation active Abeta immunotherapy CAD106 reduces amyloid accumulation in APP transgenic mice while minimizing potential side effects, *J Neurosci* 31:9323–9331, 2011.

Wilcock DM, Rojiani A, Rosenthal A, Subbarao S, Freeman MJ, Gordon MN, Morgan D: Passive immunotherapy against Abeta in aged APP-transgenic mice reverses cognitive deficits and depletes parenchymal amyloid deposits in spite of increased vascular amyloid and microhemorrhage, *J Neuroinflammation* 1:24, 2004.

Winblad B, Minthon L, Floesser A, Imbert G, Dumortier T, He Y, Maguire P, Karlsson M, Östlund H, Lundmark J, Orgogozo JM, Andreasen AGN: Results of the first-in-man study with the active Aβ immunotherapy CAD106 in Alzheimer patients, *Alzheimers Dement* 11:113–114, 2009.

Winblad B, Andreasen N, Minthon L, Floesser A, Imbert G, Dumortier T, Maguire RP, Blennow K, Lundmark J, Staufenbiel M, Orgogozo JM, Graf A: Safety, tolerability, and antibody response of active Abeta immunotherapy with CAD106 in patients with Alzheimer's disease: randomised, double-blind, placebo-controlled, first-in-human study, *Lancet Neurol* 11:597–604, 2012.

Wisniewski T, Goni F: Immunotherapeutic approaches for Alzheimer's disease, *Neuron* 85:1162–1176, 2015.

Wisniewski HM, Ghetti B, Terry RD: Neuritic (senile) plaques and filamentous changes in aged rhesus monkeys, *J Neuropathol Exp Neurol* 32:566–584, 1973.

Xing XN, Sha S, Chen XH, Guo WS, Guo R, Jiang TZ, Cao YP: Active immunization with DNA vaccine reduced cerebral inflammation and improved cognitive ability in APP/PS1 transgenic mice by in vivo electroporation, *Neurochem Res* 40:1032–1041, 2015.

Yilmazer-Hanke DM, Hanke J: Progression of Alzheimer-related neuritic plaque pathology in the entorhinal region, perirhinal cortex and hippocampal formation, *Dement Geriatr Cogn Disord* 10:70–76, 1999.

Zago W, Schroeter S, Guido T, Khan K, Seubert P, Yednock T, Schenk D, Gregg KM, Games D, Bard F, Kinney GG: Vascular alterations in PDAPP mice after anti-Abeta immunotherapy: implications for amyloid-related imaging abnormalities, *Alzheimers Dement* 9:S105–S115, 2013.

Internet Resources

http://www.a4study.org
http://www.acimmune.com
http://www.alzforum.org
http://www.brightfocus.org
http://www.clinicaltrials.gov
http://www.clinicaltrialsregister.eu
http://www.neurimmune.com
http://www.pfizer.com

CHAPTER

8

Targeting Aβ Receptors to Modify Alzheimer's Disease Progression

L.T. Haas, S.M. Strittmatter

OUTLINE

Developing Therapeutics for Alzheimer's Disease. http://dx.doi.org/10.1016/B978-0-12-802173-6.00008-3

INTRODUCTION

Alzheimer's disease (AD) is a progressive dementing neurodegenerative disease and a major public health problem due to the advancing average age of the human population. An urgent need for novel therapeutic strategies for AD exists. Genetic analysis of dominantly inherited AD cases as well as biomarker studies of patients support the amyloid hypothesis of AD, which states that amyloid-β (Aβ) peptide triggers the disease. Aβ-induced synaptotoxicity and neuronal dysfunction are well established (Lambert et al., 1998; Shankar et al., 2008). However, it is still a matter of active investigation as to how extracellular Aβ peptides induce intracellular changes that lead to synaptic alterations and neurotoxicity. It has been demonstrated that Aβ can trigger synaptotoxicity rapidly, specifically, and reversibly. Thus, Aβ must interact with synapses, and the existence of a receptor for Aβ has long been proposed to link extracellular Aβ to intracellular signaling. The aim of this chapter is to provide an overview of different cell-surface receptors for Aβ as well as their therapeutic tractability for pharmaceutical disease intervention. Binding of Aβ to a receptor is thought to be a crucial step in triggering intracellular signaling cascades that lead to synaptotoxicity and neuronal dysfunction. Further, binding of Aβ to receptors might induce toxicity by altering the endogenous function of receptor signaling itself. Multiple proteins have reached our attention as potential receptors for Aβ, and several receptors might act synergistically in causing Aβ-induced deficits.

GENERAL ASPECTS OF Aβ RECEPTORS

Which Isoforms of Aβ Should a Functional Receptor Bind Selectively?

One of the key pathological features of AD is the accumulation of insoluble fibrillar amyloid-β (Aβ) in the form of extracellular plaques. However, the poor correlation between levels of either monomeric Aβ or insoluble amyloid plaques with the severity of dementia suggests that alternative forms of Aβ are most disease-relevant (Dickson et al., 1995; Josephs et al., 2008; Katzman et al., 1988; Lue et al., 1999; McLean et al., 1999; Terry et al., 1991). Hydrophobic Aβ peptides associate to form soluble, prefibrillar amyloid-β oligomers (Aβo). Aβo correlate well with disease severity and have been proposed to be key mediators of AD pathophysiology (Lue et al., 1999; McLean et al., 1999; Wang et al., 1999). Aβo can be derived from human AD patients or produced synthetically. Both forms of Aβo have been shown to cause synaptic dysfunction, bring about dendritic spine loss, and impair learning and memory in behavioral tasks in mice (Berman et al., 2008; Cleary et al., 2005; Lacor et al., 2007; Lambert et al., 1998; Lesne et al., 2006; Li et al., 2009; Palop and Mucke, 2010; Shankar et al., 2008; Walsh et al., 2002). Notably, AD brain-derived Aβo are more potent than synthetic Aβo to inhibit synaptic plasticity, trigger hyperphosphorylation of tau, initiate neuritic degeneration, and impair behavior in rats (Jin et al., 2011; Reed et al., 2011; Townsend et al., 2006). The exact mechanism(s) underlying Aβo-induced neurotoxicity remain(s) incompletely understood. Some studies demonstrated direct interaction of Aβo with lipids and gangliosides (Hong et al., 2014; Small et al., 2007; Williams and Serpell, 2011). Additional work suggests Aβo insertion into the lipid bilayer and uptake by neurons as primary trigger of synaptotoxicity (Ashley et al., 2006; Lai and McLaurin, 2010; Valincius et al., 2008). Alternatively, a cell-surface proteinaceous receptor for Aβo could mediate Aβo-dependent neurotoxicity and has the potential for even greater specificity of action. The latter will be discussed in more detail later.

How can we Define a Protein as Receptor for Aβo?

In order to propose a protein as a receptor for a certain ligand, this protein must bind the ligand selectively and with high affinity. The first potential receptors identified to bind Aβ peptides were so-called Aβ scavenger receptors located on microglia and macrophages (El Khoury et al., 1996; Paresce et al., 1996). These receptors might be involved in some aspects of Aβ toxicity by generating free radicals (Munch et al., 1998). Chronically, nonneuronal cells are likely contributing to neuronal dysfunction. However, the rapid induction of Aβo-induced synaptotoxicity in vitro cannot fully be explained by nonneuronal receptors for Aβo. Multiple neuronal receptors for Aβ have been reported to directly bind certain isoforms of Aβ. These include cellular prion protein (PrP^C), neuronal acetylcholinergic receptor subunit alpha 7 (nAchRα7), ephrin type-B receptor 2 (EphB2), ephrin type-A receptor 4 (EphA4), Nogo-66 receptor 1 (NgR1), receptor for advanced glycation end products (RAGE), leukocyte immunoglobulin-like receptor B2 (LilrB2), Fcγ receptor IIb (FcγRIIb), epidermal growth factor receptor (EGFR), sigma-2 receptor/progesterone receptor membrane component 1 (σ_2R/PGRMC1), sortilin, low-affinity nerve growth factor receptor ($p75^{NTR}$), and insulin receptor (IR) (Carlo et al., 2013; Cissé et al., 2011a; Du Yan et al., 1996; Fu et al., 2014; Izzo et al., 2014a,b; Kam et al., 2013; Kim et al., 2013; Kuner et al., 1998; Lambert et al., 2013; Lauren et al., 2009; Park et al., 2006a; Wang et al., 2000b, 2012; Xie et al., 2002; Zhao et al., 2008). Some of these potential receptors will be discussed in more detail later. Notably, knockout or knockdown of the specific receptor should prevent Aβ binding to neurons. Unfortunately, this has been demonstrated for only two of the listed receptors, PrP^C and σ_2R/PGRMC1. Genetic deletion of *prnp*, the gene encoding PrP^C, reduces Aβo binding to neurons to 50% (Lauren et al., 2009). Other studies showed that knockdown of σ_2R/PGRMC1 resulted in almost complete reduction of Aβo binding to neurons.

How can we Define a Candidate Disease-Relevant Receptor?

Once a receptor for Aβo has been identified, it is necessary to characterize its functional role in disease pathogenesis. If the receptor plays a role in Aβo-induced neurotoxicity, genetic removal or pharmacological blockade of the receptor should prevent Aβo phenotypes. One of the key features of Aβo toxicity is inhibition of synaptic plasticity. Data support a role for multiple proposed receptors to be involved in mediating Aβo-induced inhibition of long-term potentiation (LTP). Aβo-triggered synaptic impairment may be mediated at least in part by PrP^C, EphB2, EphA4, FcγRIIb, and LilrB2 (Cissé et al., 2011a; Fu et al., 2006; Gimbel et al., 2010; Kam et al., 2013; Kim et al., 2013). Model mice expressing human AD transgenes show enhanced Aβ1–42 production, which leads to increased Aβo levels and amyloid plaque load. AD transgenic mice have substantial synapse loss compared to wild-type littermates. This phenotype can be rescued by blocking the binding of Aβo to PrP^C, EphA4, and FcγRIIb (Fu et al., 2014; Gimbel et al., 2010; Kam et al., 2013). Another characteristic symptom of AD transgenic model mice is memory deficits compared to wild-type littermates. This can be tested in behavioral assessments like the radial arm maze or Morris water maze. Here, mice whose spatial memory is impaired take a longer time to orient themselves within spatial cues

TABLE 8.1 Characterization of Aβ-Binding Receptors

Receptor (alphabetical order)	Estimated affinity for Aβ oligomers (monomer equivalents)	Absence/ blockade of receptor restores synaptic plasticity?	Absence/ blockade of receptor rescues synapse loss?	Absence/ blockade of receptor rescues memory deficits?	In vivo effectiveness of pharmacological approaches
EGFR	Not quantified	N/A	N/A	+	Inhibition: +
EphA4	Not quantified	+	+	N/A	N/A
EphB2	Not quantified	Rescue by increasing EphB2 expression	N/A	Rescue by increasing EphB2 expression	N/A
FcγRIIb	57 nM (~0.5 nM oligomer)	+	+	+	N/A
LilrB2/PirB	250 nM (~2.5 nM oligomer)	+	N/A	+	N/A
mGluR5	Coreceptor for PrP^C	+	+	+	Inhibition: +
nAchRα7	N/A (Aβ monomers studied)	+	+	Variable results	Activation: +
NgR1	N/A (Aβ monomers studied)	N/A	N/A	N/A	Nogo receptor decoy protein: +
PrP^C	50–100 nM (~0.5 nM oligomer)	+	+	+	Immunotherapy: +
RAGE	N/A (Aβ monomers studied)	N/A	N/A	–	Inhibition of Aβ-RAGE interaction: – (clinical)
σ_2R/ PGRMC1	Not quantified	N/A	N/A	+	Inhibition: +

The different receptors discussed in this chapter are characterized by their affinity for Aβo as well as their functional role in AD symptoms. The effectiveness of pharmacologically targeting the respective receptor in AD is listed. Symbols: +, specifies a positive outcome of experimental studies; −, a negative outcome. N/A indicates that the study has not yet been performed or reported.

to find the target of behavioral tasks. If a receptor for Aβ mediates signaling involved in memory impairment, genetic removal of the Aβ receptor should be beneficial for mouse memory. This has been demonstrated in at least one mouse transgenic model for PrP^C, EphB2, FcγRIIb, and LilrB2 (Cissé et al., 2011a; Gimbel et al., 2010; Kam et al., 2013; Kim et al., 2013). Table 8.1 summarizes main characteristics of the Aβ-binding receptors discussed later.

POTENTIAL ADVANTAGES OF TARGETING AN Aβo RECEPTOR

AD pharmaceutical approaches aim at targeting different aspects of the disease at diverse intervention points. Yet, so far only four approved AD therapeutics exist. Three of these are cholinesterase inhibitors (donepezil, rivastigmine, and galantamine), which were approved by the US Food and Drug Administration from 1993 to 2001. In 2003, an *N*-methyl-D-aspartate receptor (NMDAR) antagonist (memantine) was approved as a symptomatic cognitive enhancer (Lipton, 2006). No further drugs have been approved for the treatment of AD. When studying all AD trials performed from 2002 to 2012 (413 trials in total), the high failure rate of 99.6% is striking (Cummings et al., 2014). Many of these failed trials aim at reducing Aβ or tau levels. Aβ is generated by sequential proteolytical cleavage of the amyloid precursor protein (APP) by two secretases, β- and γ-secretase. Multiple specific β- and γ-secretase inhibitors potently inhibit Aβ generation. However, both secretases involved in Aβ generation have many substrates. Thus, targeting secretases can alter many physiological pathways, which explains the toxicity of most secretase inhibitors. Another approach for intervention in AD is the removal of Aβ from the brain. This can be achieved immunotherapeutically by targeting Aβ with therapeutic antibodies. Unfortunately, Aβ peptides are highly prevalent in the brain, which requires massive intervention with molecules aiming at their clearance. Consequently, alternative approaches are needed to interfere with the disease. One promising approach includes targeting receptors, which have a high affinity and are selective for Aβ. Targeting receptors that have a high preference for Aβo over Aβ can specifically prevent neurotoxic signals from propagating from extracellular Aβo to intracellular targets. Since the concentration of receptors is limited, receptors can be targeted with lower concentration of drugs compared to their ligand, Aβ. Using lower drug doses reduces the risk for potential side effects. Nonetheless, it is important to target Aβo receptors without altering the physiological function of the receptor. Ideally, the interaction between Aβo and the receptor should be targeted specifically without altering the interaction of physiological ligands with the same receptor. Thus, after many attempts to alter Aβ or tau levels, targeting Aβo receptors remains untested clinically but holds great promise as an alternative. Eventually, these approaches may provide synergistic efficacy.

CELLULAR PRION PROTEIN (PrP^C) AS NEURONAL CELL-SURFACE RECEPTOR FOR Aβo

Evidence for PrP^C as a Functional Receptor for Aβo

PrP^C was identified in an unbiased genome-wide screen as a high-affinity cell-surface receptor for extracellular Aβo (Lauren et al., 2009). In this screen, biotin-conjugated synthetic Aβo were exposed to COS-7 cells that expressed a genome-wide adult mouse brain library. The 225,000 cDNA clones that were screened revealed only two positive clones. Both clones encoded full-length PrP^C. While Aβo do not bind to untransfected COS-7 cells, overexpression of PrP^C generates high-affinity binding to COS-7 cells, indistinguishable from that of hippocampal neurons. PrP^C also demonstrated a pronounced selectivity for Aβo over monomeric Aβ. However, genetic deletion of PrP^C removes only 50% of Aβo binding to neurons. Thus, both PrP^C and other receptors for Aβo must exist in neurons.

The structure of PrP^C has been studied extensively (Antonyuk et al., 2009). PrP^C is attached to the membrane of lipid rafts by a glycosylphosphatidylinositol (GPI) anchor (Agostini et al., 2013; Yusa et al., 2012). The protein consists of an intrinsically unstructured part (region 23–111), which is subdivided into the so-called octarepeat region (residues 60–91), a charged cluster (residues 91–111), and a hydrophobic region (residues 112–134). The C-terminal domain of PrP^C contains three individual α-helices (Antonyuk et al., 2009). Using a series of PrP^C deletion mutants, the binding site of Aβo in PrP^C was mapped to residues 95–110, which lie

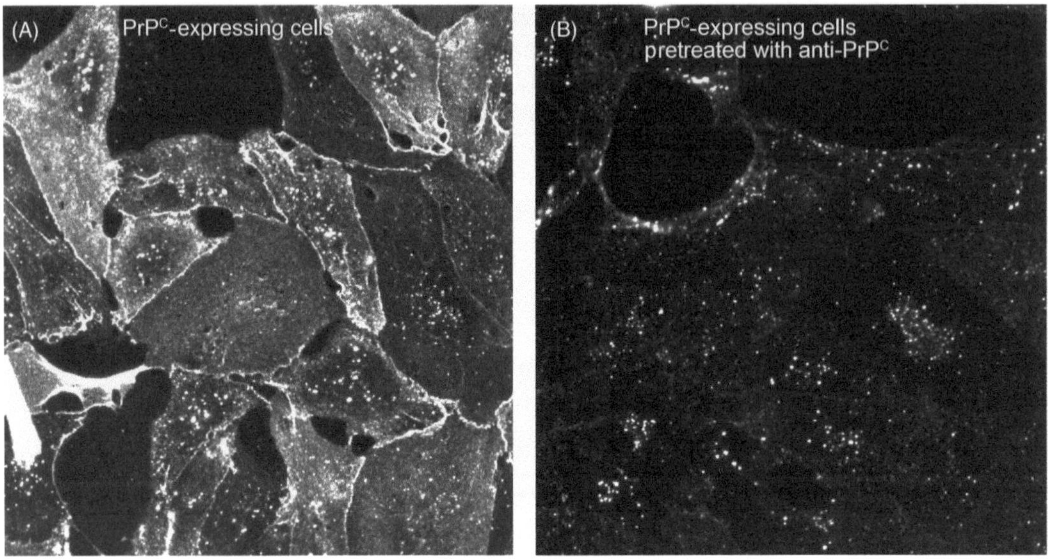

FIGURE 8.1 **Aβo binding to cell surface PrP^C.** The binding of 200 nM biotin-Aβ-oligomer to PrP^C-expressing CV-1 (*Cercopithecus aethiops* kidney) cells is detected by fluorescent avidin (A) and is blocked by pretreatment with 1 μg/mL of 6D11 anti-PrP^C antibody (B).

within the intrinsically unstructured region of PrP^C. Further studies used surface plasmon resonance to confirm region 95–110 and identify a second binding site at the amino terminus (residues 23–27) (Chen et al., 2010). Aβo binding to PrP^C with nanomolar affinity was confirmed both in vivo and in vitro using coimmunoprecipitation, surface plasmon resonance (SPR), and immunocytochemistry (Balducci et al., 2010; Chen et al., 2010; Lauren et al., 2009; Zou et al., 2011).

Fig. 8.1 shows biotin-Aβo binding to PrP^C-overexpressing CV-1 (*C. aethiops* kidney) cells. Binding of biotin-Aβo is blocked by preincubation of cells with antibody 6D11, which targets one of the two Aβo-binding sites on PrP^C (region 95–110).

Multiple studies confirmed PrP^C to be essentially involved in mediating AD-related deficits in vitro and in vivo. Genetic deletion of *prnp*, the gene encoding PrP^C, prevents Aβo-induced inhibition of synaptic plasticity, Aβo-triggered cell death in vitro and in vivo, dendritic spine and synapse loss, serotonin axon degeneration, epileptiform discharges, early death events, and learning and memory deficits in at least some AD transgenic mouse models (Barry et al., 2011; Bate and Williams, 2011; Chung et al., 2010; Fluharty et al., 2013; Freir et al., 2011; Gimbel et al., 2010; Hu et al., 2014; Klyubin et al., 2014; Kudo et al., 2012; Lauren et al., 2009; Ostapchenko et al., 2013; Resenberger et al., 2011; Rushworth et al., 2013; Um et al., 2012; Zou et al., 2011).

However, some studies revealed AD-related phenotypes independent of the presence of PrP^C. As such, one study described behavioral deficits in hAPPJ20 AD transgenic mice that were independent of PrP^C (Cissé et al., 2011b). Notably, hAPPJ20 exhibits early onset of behavioral deficits, and these might be independent of PrP^C (Cissé et al., 2011b). The role of PrP^C in mediating AD was also called into question in studies that found Aβo-induced impairment of hippocampal LTP independent of PrP^C (Calella et al., 2010; Kessels et al., 2010). However, the study by Kessels et al. (2010) utilized incompletely characterized Aβo and detected Aβo-induced inhibition of baseline synaptic function. This baseline inhibition raises the possibility of a more generalized cytotoxic response triggered by alternate Aβ forms. Subsequent studies with a well-characterized preparation of Aβo verified that Aβo-triggered inhibition was dependent on *prnp* (Freir et al., 2011; Nicoll et al., 2013). The study by Calella et al. (2010) used *prnp* null mice crossed to APP/PS1$^+$ mice. These transgenic mice demonstrated impairment of LTP at 4 months of age, independent of the genetic presence of *prnp*. One explanation for this might be the very high degree of Aβ production at an early age in this particular mouse line with effects separate from mature age-dependent neurodegeneration. Once PrP^C is saturated with Aβo, Aβo might bind to other receptors and induce neurotoxicity independent of PrP^C. Notably, the same group also examined APP/PS1$^+$ mice overexpressing a secreted version of PrP^C that was lacking its GPI anchor. Transgenic mice expressing truncated PrP^C were protected from Aβo-dependent impairment of LTP. Thus, excess secreted PrP^C ectodomain has a dominant negative action, sequestering Aβo to rescue synaptic impairment (Calella et al., 2010).

One study suggested that acute focal brain injections of Aβo impaired object recognition memory independently of PrP^C (Balducci et al., 2010). However, other acute Aβo injection paradigms have shown that PrP^C mediates Aβo action in the brain (Barry et al., 2011; Fluharty et al., 2013; Klyubin et al., 2014). These differences may relate to the fact that a large number of different isoforms of Aβo exist and the composition of Aβo preparations varies greatly between studies (Freir et al., 2011). Recent work has shown that nearly all soluble Aβo species from human AD brain or from transgenic mouse brain are high molecular weight assemblies, and that approximately 50% have strong affinity for PrP^C (Kostylev et al., 2015). Moreover, the level of PrP^C-interacting Aβo is closely correlated with progression of memory deficits in AD transgenic mice (Kostylev et al., 2015).

In conclusion, some isoforms of Aβo seem to trigger specific AD-related toxic effects that are independent of PrP^C (Cheng et al., 2007; Gandy et al., 2010; Lesne et al., 2006; Reed et al., 2011). In contrast, a number of well-characterized species of Aβo consistently show an involvement of PrP^C in mediating neurotoxicity (Barry et al., 2011; Bate and Williams, 2011; Chung et al., 2010; Fluharty et al., 2013; Freir et al., 2011; Gimbel et al., 2010; Hu et al., 2014; Klyubin et al., 2014; Kudo et al., 2012; Lauren et al., 2009; Ostapchenko et al., 2013; Resenberger et al., 2011; Rushworth et al., 2013; Shankar et al., 2008; Um et al., 2012; Um and Strittmatter, 2013; Zou et al., 2011). Most critically, the deleterious actions triggered by Aβo isolated from human AD brain require PrP^C (Barry et al., 2011; Klyubin et al., 2014).

Targeting PrP^C as Therapeutic Strategy

Therapeutic intervention studies in preclinical models further support the hypothesis that binding of Aβo to PrP^C is essential for AD-related synaptotoxicity. Barry et al. (2011) injected mice with AD brain extracts containing Aβo in combination with antibodies targeting different epitopes on PrP^C (Barry et al., 2011). AD brain extracts cause synaptotoxicity in mice, which is prevented by immunodepletion of Aβ. Critically, antibody blockade of one of the Aβo-binding sites on PrP^C (residues 95–110) abrogates Aβo-dependent synaptic impairment. In contrast, immunotargeting the C-terminal region of PrP^C did not affect Aβo-triggered deficits in LTP

(Barry et al., 2011). In another study, rats were treated systemically with humanized antibodies targeting the binding site between Aβo and PrP^C. These rats exhibited a complete rescue of AD brain extract-induced synaptic impairment (Klyubin et al., 2014). Moreover, treatment of AD transgenic mice with antibodies targeting the binding of Aβo to PrP^C reversed their preexisting memory deficit (Chung et al., 2010). In addition, soluble "decoy" PrP^C fragments prevent APP/Aβ-induced deficits (Calella et al., 2010; Fluharty et al., 2013). While the anti-PrP^C antibody studies are quite encouraging, translation of these approaches to the AD clinic will require adequate penetration of antibody across the human blood–brain barrier. Small molecules that competitively block Aβo binding to PrP^C are a promising secondary alternative to anti-PrP^C antibodies, and are actively under development.

Separate from strategies that aim to prevent Aβo binding to PrP^C, treatments may be developed to reduce the cell-surface expression of PrP^C. For example, pentosan polysulfate (PPS) is known to induce internalization and redistribution of PrP^C from the plasma membrane toward late endosomes (Shyng et al., 1995). Other studies reported a decrease in total PrP^C levels at higher concentrations of PPS (eg, 100 μg/mL) (Yamaguchi et al., 2006). Similarly, chlorpromazine (CPZ) has been described to redistribute PrP^C from the plasma membrane and to reduce PrP^C levels (Yamasaki et al., 2014). Both PPS and CPZ are under investigation as therapeutic agents for prion disease. Further preclinical studies are needed to analyze whether drugs like PPS or CPZ are beneficial for AD disease pathogenesis.

METABOTROPIC GLUTAMATE RECEPTOR 5 AS CORECEPTOR FOR Aβo BOUND TO PrP^C

Evidence for Metabotropic Glutamate Receptor 5 as Coreceptor for Aβo

Located on the extracellular site of the postsynaptic density (PSD), PrP^C requires a coreceptor to affect intracellular signaling. To identify the coreceptor involved in the transmission of Aβo onto intracellular targets, 61 transmembrane PSD proteins were screened to trigger Aβo-dependent activation of intracellular proteins. This event is naturally occurring in cortical neurons but not in HEK-293T cells. Overexpression of both PrP^C and metabotropic glutamate receptor 5 (mGluR5) renders HEK-293T cells responsive to Aβo to induce enhanced calcium response, dendritic spine loss, and lactate dehydrogenase (LDH) release (Um et al., 2013).

Fig. 8.2 illustrates the topography of membrane-inserted PrP^C and the seven transmembrane-spanning receptor mGluR5. The binding site of mGluR5 on PrP^C is mapped to region 91–153, which is partly overlapping with one of the Aβo-binding sites (region 95–110).

The receptor mGluR5 belongs in the class of G-protein coupled receptors, which are well known for transduction of extracellular signals onto intracellular protein mediators. The finding of mGluR5 as mediator of Aβo-induced signaling is consistent with several studies that demonstrated the recovery of Aβo-induced inhibition of LTP by mGluR5-directed antagonists (Bruno et al., 2000; Rammes et al., 2011; Shankar et al., 2008; Wang et al., 2004). Further support for the role of mGluR5 in Aβo-induced signaling comes from a comparison of glutamate-induced mGluR5- and Aβo-triggered intracellular signaling. Both mGluR1 and mGluR5 belong in group I mGluRs, which are coupled to $G_{q/11}$ proteins. Activation of

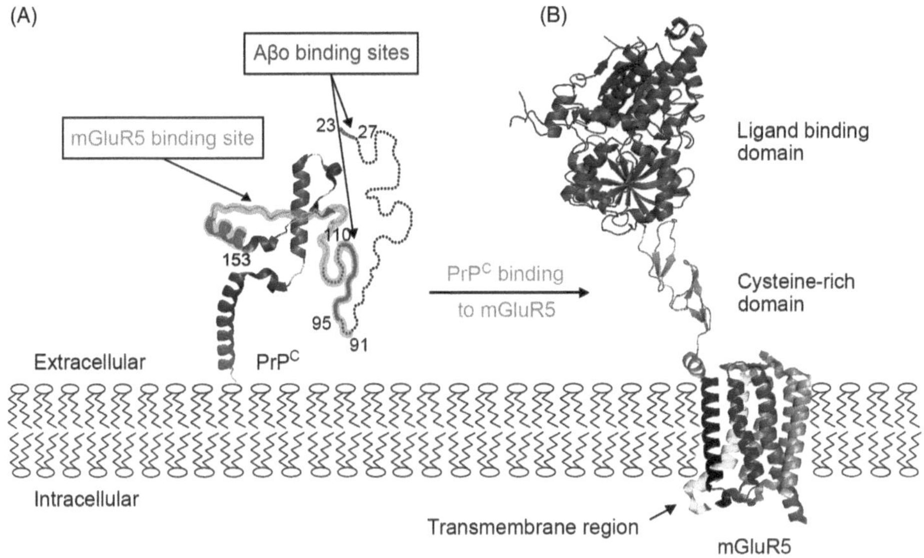

FIGURE 8.2 Three-dimensional model of membrane-anchored PrP^C and membrane-inserted mGluR5. (A) PrP^C is composed of an intrinsically unstructured region composed of residues 23–118, followed by a mainly α-helical folded structure. The Aβo binding sites in PrP^C have been mapped to residues 23–27 and 95–110. The metabotropic glutamate receptor 5 (mGluR5) binds to region 91–153 of PrP^C. (B) The extracellular N-terminal region of mGluR5 is divided into ligand-binding domain (residues 25–508) and cysteine-rich domain (residues 509–575). Note, the ligand-binding domain in this model is shown in its closed conformation. The transmembrane spanning domain of mGluR5 is composed of seven individual transmembrane domains. The structure of the intracellular C-terminal domain of mGluR5 is not shown in this model, since it has not been characterized yet. This model was generated using the pdb codes 1I4M, 2E4U, and 4OO9.

this class of receptors mediates a signal transduction with activation of phospholipase Cβ1 (PLCβ1) and inositol-1,4,5-trisphosphate (IP_3)/Ca^{2+} signaling (Ribeiro et al., 2010). These events activate protein kinase C (PKC), which phosphorylates downstream target proteins (Luscher and Huber, 2010; Pin and Duvoisin, 1995). Interestingly, incubation of mature neurons with Aβo mimics signaling induced by glutamate stimulation of mGlu class I receptors (Berman et al., 2008; Um et al., 2012, 2013).

Fig. 8.3 summarizes main aspects of the Aβo-PrP^C-mGluR5 pathway. Binding of Aβo-PrP^C to mGluR5 activates intracellular mediators like Fyn kinase and the $G_{q/11}$ protein. This results in a net rise of intracellular Ca^{2+}, initiated by both the IP_3/Ca^{2+} pathway and Ca^{2+} influx through NMDA receptors. Subsequently, the microtubule-associated protein tau is phosphorylated by different kinases, including Fyn kinase. Hyperphosphorylated tau is cytotoxic for reducing microtubule stability and triggering loss of axonal transport. Different aspects of the pathway finally manifest in forms of synaptic toxicity, synapse loss, and neuronal death.

PrP^C and mGluR5 receptors are localized to lipid raft-like domains, where Aβo-triggered induction of synaptotoxicity occurs (Agostini et al., 2013; Francesconi et al., 2009; Zampagni et al., 2010). Single-particle tracking of labeled Aβo confirmed the PrP^C- and mGluR5-dependence

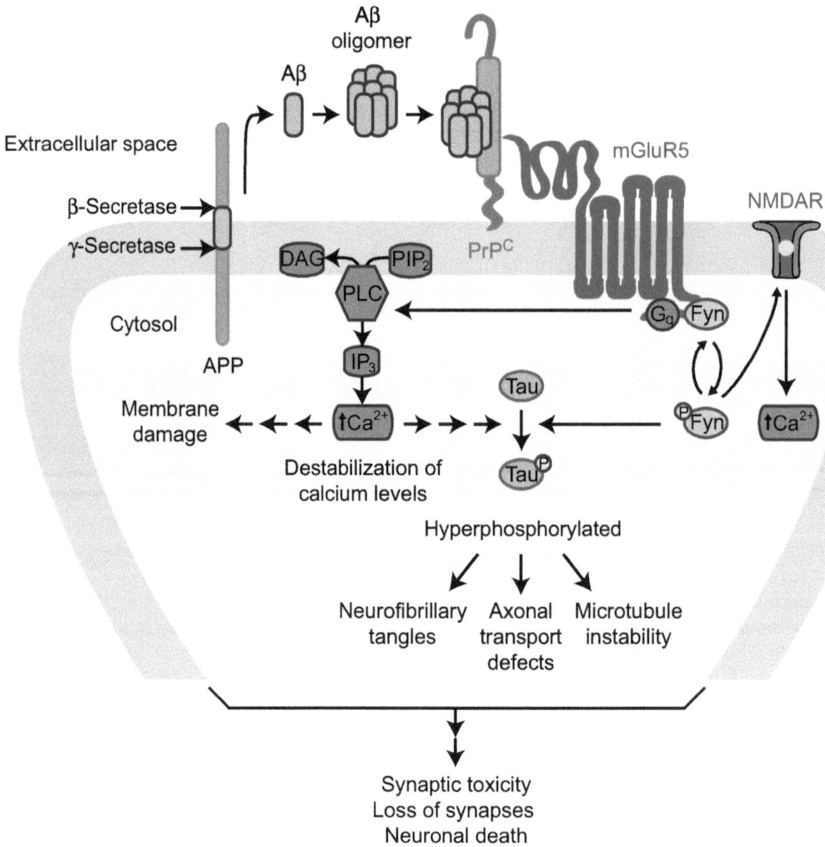

FIGURE 8.3 **The Aβo-PrP^C-mGluR5 signaling cascade.** Processing of the membrane-embedded amyloid precursor protein (APP) generates amyloid-β peptides (Aβ), which associate to form amyloid-β oligomers (Aβo). Aβo bind to cellular prion protein (PrP^C), which associates with metabotropic glutamate receptor 5 (mGluR5). This triggers activation of intracellular protein mediators like Fyn kinase and the $G_{q/11}$ protein. A rise of intracellular Ca^{2+} and activated Fyn kinase contribute to hyperphosphorylation of tau. Tau is a microtubule-associated protein that loses its function when hyperphosphorylated. Different aspects of the signaling cascade contribute to synaptotoxicity, synapse loss, and neurodegeneration. *NMDAR*, *N*-methyl-D-aspartate receptor; *PLC*, phospholipase C; *DAG*, diacylglycerol; *PIP$_2$*, phosphatidylinositol 4,5-bisphosphate; *IP$_3$*, inositol 1,4,5-trisphosphate.

of Aβo binding to synapses (Renner et al., 2010). The authors propose that Aβo impair synaptic function by inducing clustering and overstabilization of mGluR5 receptors within the membrane. The mGluR1/5-mediated transmission of signals from PrP^C to cytosolic partners has been demonstrated in a similar way for laminin binding to PrP^C (Beraldo et al., 2011).

Multiple Aβo-induced AD-related deficits are dependent on the presence of both PrP^C and mGluR5. Some examples include Aβo-triggered deficits of synaptic plasticity, activation of intracellular protein mediators, dendritic spine loss, and learning and memory impairments of AD transgenic model mice (Hu et al., 2014; Larson et al., 2012; Um et al., 2012, 2013).

Targeting mGluR5 as Therapeutic Strategy

The tractability of mGluR5 as a pharmacological target has been studied extensively, since mGluR5 is implicated to be involved in multiple neurodegenerative and psychiatric CNS disorders. These include fragile X syndrome, Parkinson's disease, amyotrophic lateral sclerosis, multiple sclerosis, Huntington's disease, epilepsy, schizophrenia, AD, and drug addiction (Bruno et al., 2001; Gasparini and Spooren, 2007; Gregory et al., 2011, 2012; Molck et al., 2014; Ribeiro et al., 2010; Sheffler et al., 2011). The mGluRs belong in the class of seven transmembrane-spanning receptors, which harbor an extracellular region, a transmembrane region, and an intracellular C-terminal loop (Muto et al., 2007; Pin et al., 2003; Wu et al., 2014). Recently, different domains of the structure of mGluRs were characterized by X-ray crystallography (Muto et al., 2007; Wu et al., 2014).

Different classes of mGluR therapeutics exist and will be described in more detail later. The mGluR agonists and antagonists target the receptor in its orthosteric binding pocket and alter glutamate signaling. Progress in the field led to the development of a second class of pharmaceutical molecules that target mGluRs, so-called allosteric modulators (Conn et al., 2009). Rapid characterization and optimization of these allosteric modulators has generated promising new approaches for CNS therapeutics. These modulators offer the advantage of greater selectivity for specific receptors as well as better control over off-target effects (Conn et al., 2014). Allosteric modulators bind to transmembrane allosteric binding pockets that are topographically distinct from endogenous ligands, rendering them noncompetitive over physiological signaling (Conn et al., 2009; Melancon et al., 2012). They function by stabilizing the structure of the receptor in specific conformations, which changes the response of the receptor to endogenous ligands or other allosteric modulators (Nickols and Conn, 2014). Allosteric modulators can differentially affect intracellular Ca^{2+} mobilization and other signaling pathways. As an example, mGluR5 activation triggers an increase in both net Ca^{2+} and extracellular signal-regulated kinase 1/2 (ERK1/2) signaling. Certain allosteric modulators show functional selectivity by altering Ca^{2+} mobilization and ERK1/2 signaling differentially (Zhang et al., 2005). Other mGluR5 agents differentiate G-protein-mediated signaling from NMDAR regulation (Isherwood et al., 2015).

The class of allosteric modulators can be further divided into positive allosteric modulators (PAMs), negative allosteric modulators (NAMs), and silent allosteric modulators (SAMs). While PAMs and NAMs affect glutamate-induced Ca^{2+} mobilization similarly to agonists and antagonists, SAMs do not alter endogenous glutamate signaling. Since physiological mGluR5 signaling is essential for normal brain function, the optimal AD drug candidate for this target should not alter endogenous signaling (Luscher and Huber, 2010; Xu et al., 2009). SAMs neither potentiate nor inhibit endogenous glutamate signaling, suggesting a greater potential therapeutic window for AD. Yet SAMs alter the conformation of mGlu receptors, which can be demonstrated by using multiple allosteric modulators simultaneously, whose action is blocked in the presence of SAMs (O'Brien et al., 2003).

One class of allosteric mGluR5 modulators is related to picolinamide-methoxy-PEPy (so-called MPEP class of allosteric mGluR5 modulators). Notably, minor chemical changes of allosteric modulators exert major alterations in functionality. As such, differences in functionality between, for example, the NAM MPEP and the SAM 5-MPEP are achieved by translocating a methyl group from position 6 to position 5 of the pyridine ring of MPEP (Gregory et al., 2010).

This translocation prevents the compound 5-MPEP from altering glutamate-induced Ca^{2+} mobilization. Further, 5-MPEP blocks negative and positive allosteric modulation of mGluR5 by other allosteric modulators targeting the same binding pocket (Gregory et al., 2010). Therapeutic molecules like SAMs of mGluR5 have previously been shown to inhibit Aβo-triggered enhanced binding of PrP^C to mGluR5 (Haas et al., 2014). Future research is necessary to investigate the efficacy of SAMs to prevent Aβo/PrP^C binding to mGluR5 and prohibit neurotoxic Aβo signaling in AD.

Alternative Coreceptors for Aβo/PrP^C Complexes

The endocytic receptor low-density lipoprotein receptor-related protein 1 (LRP-1) is recognized to be involved in PrP^C cellular trafficking. Recent data suggest it also has the potential to function as a signaling coreceptor for Aβo/PrP^C complexes (Rushworth et al., 2013). While mGluR5 may have a more central role at synapses described previously, a coreceptor role for LRP-1 has the potential to link Aβo signaling to apolipoprotein E and genetic risk for AD. This possible link has not yet been examined experimentally.

nAchRα7 AS RECEPTOR FOR Aβ

Evidence for nAchRα7 as Receptor for Aβ

A characteristic feature of AD is the loss of cholinergic neurons (Davies and Maloney, 1976). This led Wang et al. (2000b) to investigate the relationship between cholinergic signaling and Aβ. They proposed the ionotropic acetylcholine receptor nAchRα7 as receptor for the most aggregation-prone species of Aβ, $A\beta_{1-42}$. The receptor nAchRα7 belongs in the receptor family of pentameric ligand-gated ion channels (Gotti et al., 2006). Competition binding assays with radiolabeled $A\beta_{1-42}$ revealed that nAchRα7 binds $A\beta_{1-42}$ monomers at two different binding sites with high affinity (Wang et al., 2000b). Anti-Aβ immunoblots of Aβ-treated, nAchRα-overexpressing neuroblastoma cells suggested SDS-resistant binding of a single $A\beta_{1-42}$ monomer per nAchRα7 polypeptide (Wang et al., 2000b). Interestingly, nAchRα7-overexpressing neuroblastoma cells show enhanced cell death in vitro when treated with $A\beta_{1-42}$, which was blocked with nicotine. Further, $A\beta_{1-42}$ treatment reduces Ca^{2+} mobilization and acetylcholine release. The authors proposed this to be the underlying mechanism of cognitive dysfunction in AD (Wang et al., 2000a). Notably, the binding site of nAchRα7 on $A\beta_{1-42}$ was mapped to residues 12–28 inside the Aβ sequence (Wang et al., 2000a). Further studies showed that $A\beta_{1-42}$ induces tau phosphorylation in vitro at Ser-202, Thr-181, and Thr-231 via the extracellular signal-regulated kinase (ERK) and JNK-1 pathways in an nAchRα7-dependent manner (Wang et al., 2003). Preincubation of cells with antisense-nAchRα7 oligonucleotides or of hippocampal synaptosome preparations with nAchRα7 antagonists prevented $A\beta_{1-42}$-induced tau phosphorylation. The authors further revealed that nAchRα7 agonists trigger a similar pattern of tau phosphorylation compared to $A\beta_{1-42}$ (Wang et al., 2003). Thus, they proposed that Aβ induces enhanced tau phosphorylation via nAchRα7.

Dineley et al. (2001) further analyzed the role of nAchRα7 in $A\beta_{1-42}$ signaling. Incubation of rat brain slices with $A\beta_{1-42}$ induces ERK2 signaling in a Ca^{2+}-dependent manner, as does incubation of slices with nicotine (Dineley et al., 2001). Further, blocking nAchRα7 with the selective antagonist MLA prevents $A\beta_{1-42}$-induced ERK2 activation, and $A\beta_{1-42}$ can desensitize nAchRα7. As such, preincubation of slices with $A\beta_{1-42}$ does not elicit enhanced Erk2 activation by subsequent nicotine treatment (Dineley et al., 2001). The authors further found an age-dependent increase of nAchRα7 in CA1 and dentate gyrus of Tg2576 transgenic AD-model mice (Dineley et al., 2001). Additionally, a negative correlation between performance in the Morris water maze spatial memory task and the amount of brain nAchRα7 was described (Dineley et al., 2001). They concluded that monomeric $A\beta_{1-42}$ associates with nAchRα7 and induces ERK pathway signaling.

Another study showed that $A\beta_{1-42}$ binding to nAchRα7 induces neurotoxicity. In contrast, binding of nicotinic ligands to nAchRα7 promotes neuroprotection (Buckingham et al., 2009). Thus, the effects of $A\beta_{1-42}$ binding to nAchRα7 seem to be independent of nAchRα7 activation by endogenous ligands. Both $A\beta_{1-42}$ and nicotine signal through the same intracellular pathways. These include the ERK/mitogen-activated protein kinase (MAPK), the Janus kinase 2 (JAK-2)/signal transducer and activator of transcription 3 (STAT-3), and the phosphatidylinositol 3-kinase (P13K)/v-akt murine thymoma viral oncogene homolog (AKT) pathways. Differential activation of those pathways might explain why nicotine as ligand offers neuroprotection, whereas $A\beta_{1-42}$ induces neurotoxicity (Buckingham et al., 2009).

The differential activation of nAchRα7 by $A\beta_{1-42}$ and nicotine has been studied (Khan et al., 2010). Here, the authors found that disruption of lipid-raft-like domains prevented $A\beta_{1-42}$-induced nAchRα7 signaling. In contrast, this did not affect nicotine-dependent signaling. The nAchRα7 may also function as a carrier of Aβ across the plasma membrane, causing internalization of Aβ (Nagele et al., 2002). Thus, Khan et al. (2010) speculate that neurotoxic $A\beta_{1-42}$-dependent effects occur after $A\beta_{1-42}$ internalization, whereas nicotine-signaling occurs only by activation of nAchRα7 at the plasma membrane (Khan et al., 2010).

Contradictory results were found in AD transgenic model mice deficient in nAchRα7. When Hernandez et al. crossed APP transgenic mice to nAchRα7 null mice, they observed elevated Aβ levels and more severe learning and memory deficits. Strikingly, the level of Aβo was highly enhanced in APP transgenic nAchRα7 null mice compared to pure APP transgenic mice at 5 months of age. These results further support the role of Aβo underlying learning and memory impairments in APP transgenic mice (Hernandez et al., 2010). In distinction to these findings, when Dziewczapolski et al. crossed APP transgenic mice to nAchRα7 null mice, they found similar levels of Aβ in $nAchR\alpha7^{-/-}$ and $nAchR\alpha7^{+/+}$ transgenic mice. Additionally, they observed a rescue of synapse loss, dendrite loss, enhanced gliosis and synaptic deficits in 19- to 22-month-old APPα7KO mice (Dziewczapolski et al., 2009). Moreover, they found a recovery of behavioral deficits in 13- to 16-month-old APPα7KO mice. Interestingly, amyloid plaque load and soluble Aβ levels were unchanged. Thus, the authors concluded that amelioration is fully dependent on targeting signaling pathways of Aβ (Dziewczapolski et al., 2009).

Targeting nAchRα7 as Therapeutic Strategy

At this point, direct binding of $A\beta_{1-42}$ to nAchRα7 has not been reverified or further investigated by follow-up studies from other groups after the original report (Wang et al., 2000b). It remains unclear whether nAchRα7 binds only monomeric or also other forms of Aβ.

The nAchRα7 is a well-characterized pharmacological target, but preliminary findings of targeting nAchRα7 for AD therapeutics have not been extended. Potent, tolerable, and specific nAchRα7 orthosteric ligands exist and could be tested in the context of AD pathophysiology. As such, the partial agonist 2-[2-(4-bromophenyl)-2-oxoethyl]-1-methyl pyridinium (S 24795) has been shown to release $A\beta_{1-42}$ from nAchRα7 after $A\beta_{1-42}$-nAchRα7 complexes had formed (Wang et al., 2009). Unfortunately, these findings have not yet been followed by studies where S 24795 was used to treat AD transgenic mice in order to rescue AD phenotypes. Similarly, the original study demonstrated that nAchRα7 ligands such as nicotine and epibatidine successfully prevented $A\beta_{1-42}$ binding to nAchRα7 and neurotoxicity (Wang et al., 2000b). Yet no data show that these compounds can protect AD transgenic model mice from AD symptoms. To conclude, evidence for nAchRα7 as a receptor for $A\beta_{1-42}$ remains partial, and no preclinical study has demonstrated that blocking the $A\beta_{1-42}$ binding to nAchRα7 can ameliorate AD phenotypes. Nonetheless, the use of the selective nAchRα7 partial agonist encenicline (EVP-6124) as cognitive enhancer in AD is currently under clinical investigation. Encenicline is brain-penetrant and well tolerated. Orally administered encenicline has shown significant cognitive improvement in mild to cognitive AD in a phase 2b trial (Barbier et al., 2015). Thus, the outcome of the phase 3 clinical trial is greatly anticipated.

THE INTERACTION BETWEEN Eph RECEPTORS AND Aβ

Evidence for Eph Proteins as Receptors for Aβ

Multiple genome-wide association studies (GWAS) identified EphA1 as a risk factor for AD. While no studies demonstrate direct binding of Aβ to EphA1, this protein is closely related to the receptor tyrosine kinases EphB2 and EphA4, both of which have been shown to bind Aβo.

EphB2 attracted attention for activating Src family kinases and thereby regulating the surface levels of NMDAR (Dalva et al., 2000; Henderson et al., 2001; Takasu et al., 2002). EphB2 is reduced specifically in the hippocampus of AD patients compared to age-matched healthy controls as well as in AD model mice compared to wild-type mice (Simon et al., 2009). Aβo bind to the fibronectin repeats of EphB2, which causes internalization and proteasomal degradation of EphB2 (Cissé et al., 2011a). The authors propose that this event is responsible for Aβo-dependent synaptic impairment. Notably, Lenti-sh-EphB2-GFP knockdown of EphB2 in the mouse hippocampus induces synaptic deficits comparable to those triggered acutely by Aβo. Interestingly, when the authors increased neuronal EphB2 levels in hAPP mouse granule cells, Aβo-dependent inhibition of LTP in the dentate gyrus was rescued. Enhanced EphB2 expression in granule cells also recovered behavioral deficits in Morris water maze, novel object/place recognition, and passive avoidance test in hAPP transgenic mice compared to wild-type mice (Cissé et al., 2011a).

Separate studies demonstrated Aβo binding to EphA4 in a cell-free pull-down assay. Activation of EphA4 by ephrin A4 triggers cyclin-dependent kinase 5 (CDK5)-induced RhoA activation (Bourgin et al., 2007; Fu et al., 2006; Richter et al., 2007). CDK5 is also known to be deregulated in AD and to phosphorylate tau (Hernandez et al., 2009; Noble et al., 2003). Thus, Aβo binding to EphA4 could potentially link Aβo to hyperphosphorylation of tau.

Interestingly, EphA4 is altered in human AD patients compared to age-matched controls and in AD model mice compared to wild-type mice (Fu et al., 2014; Simon et al., 2009).

Targeting Eph Receptors as a Therapeutic Strategy

EphB2 might be considered a pharmacological target for AD. Targeting EphB2 would require methods to increase EphB2 expression or EphB2 activity in human AD patients. As such, the proteasomal degradation of EphB2 induced by Aβo might be targeted. Alternatively, beneficial intervention might be achieved with small molecules that block Aβo binding to the fibronectin repeats of EphB2. Interestingly, phosphorylation of the NMDAR subunit NR1 by EphB2 regulates the surface expression of NR1. Aβo binding to EphB2 triggers a cascade that reduces surface levels of EphB2, which subsequently also decreases surface levels of the NMDAR subunit NR1. Thus, another approach could aim at increasing the interaction between EphB2 and NMDARs to boost surface expression of NR1 subunits and prevent synaptic impairment (Cissé et al., 2011a).

EphA4 is also a potential target for disease-intervening therapy of AD. Aβo-dependent inhibition of hippocampal LTP can be rescued by an inhibitor of the EphA4 ligand binding domain (Fu et al., 2014). The same inhibitor was effective to prevent synaptic deficits in APP/PS1$^+$ transgenic model mice compared to wild-type mice. Thus, potent inhibitors of EphA4 exist and should be tested in the context of learning and memory in AD model mice.

In summary, certain Eph receptors bind Aβo and seem to be involved in synaptic dysfunction induced by Aβo. Further work is necessary to address targeting Eph receptors as a potential intervention strategy for AD.

BINDING OF APP AND Aβ TO NOGO-RECEPTOR 1 (NgR1)

APP was shown to colocalize with cell-surface NgR1 in Cos-7 cells and in primary cultures of dorsal root ganglia (Park et al., 2006a). NgR1 is a receptor for Nogo, MAG, and OMgp (Fournier et al., 2001; Liu et al., 2002; Wang et al., 2002), and is known to gate synaptic plasticity in the adult brain (Akbik et al., 2012, 2013; McGee et al., 2005; Schwab and Strittmatter, 2014). A physical interaction between APP and NgR1 was demonstrated by coimmunoprecipitation in transfected cell lines and rat brains. Interestingly, Aβ plaques in human AD patient postmortem brains colocalize with NgR1. Further studies revealed binding of Aβ to NgR1 with a binding affinity of 62 ± 10 nM (Park et al., 2006a). When APP/PS1$^+$ mice were treated peripherally or intracerebroventricular with the soluble ectodomain of NgR1 (NgR(310)ecto-Fc), both Aβ plaque burden and Aβ40 and Aβ42 were reduced (Park et al., 2006b). Notably, behavioral deficits in APP/PS1$^+$ mice were rescued by treatment with NgR(310)ecto-Fc. To further underline the role of NgR1 in AD pathogenesis, the authors studied APP/PS1$^+$ NgR1 null mice. Genetic deletion of NgR1 caused a more severe pathology with increased Aβ levels, increased amyloid plaque burden, and enhanced dystrophic neurites. Thus, NgR1 is a regulator of APP metabolism as well as Aβ binding (Park et al., 2006b). More research is necessary to better characterize NgR1 as a potential pharmaceutical target for AD.

EVIDENCE FOR OTHER Aβ RECEPTORS

One of the first proteins proposed to act as a receptor for Aβ was RAGE, a member of the immunoglobulin superfamily (Du Yan et al., 1996). Overexpression of RAGE induces enhanced AD pathology, which might be due to internalization of Aβ and thus intracellular accumulation (Du Yan et al., 1996; Takuma et al., 2009). A clinical trial for a small molecule inhibitor of the RAGE-Aβ interaction was performed. This trial did not meet the primary end points, even though a low-dose therapeutic approach indicated some beneficial results (Galasko et al., 2014).

Another potential receptor for Aβo is LilrB2, the human homolog of murine-paired immunoglobulin-like receptor B (PirB) (Kim et al., 2013). LilrB2/PirB is known to localize to growth cones in neurons and is associated with synapses. It interacts physically with Nogo-66 and regulates plasticity (Atwal et al., 2008). Deletion of PirB prevents Aβo-induced synaptic impairment of CA1 hippocampal LTP (Kim et al., 2013). Further, APP/PS1^{+} AD transgenic model mice are characterized by impaired behavioral memory tasks and reduced ocular dominance plasticity during postnatal day 22 (P22) to P32 in the visual cortex (William et al., 2012). Both phenotypes are rescued by genetic deletion of PirB. Signaling through Aβo-LilR2B/PirB might occur via the actin-severing protein cofilin and protein phosphatases PP2A and PP2B/calcineurin pathways, which are known to contribute to dendritic spine loss and synaptic defects (Kim et al., 2013).

Aβo has also been shown to interact with FcγRIIb in cell lysates and in human AD brain extracts (Kam et al., 2013). Genetic deletion of FcγRIIb prevents neuronal death, synapse loss, and decreased dendritic spine density when primary hippocampal neurons are exposed to Aβo. Similar findings were made by incubation of neurons with both Aβo and the soluble FcγRIIb ectodomain, or by overexpression of the FcγRIIb I232T loss-of-function mutant protein (Kam et al., 2013). Interestingly, absence of FcγRIIb in transgenic AD model mice prevents Aβo-dependent inhibition of LTP and learning and memory deficits (Kam et al., 2013).

The epidermal growth factor receptor (EGFR) has been studied extensively as a cancer therapy target. An interaction of EGFR with Aβo was shown by immunoprecipitation (Wang et al., 2012). Interestingly, treating AD transgenic model mice with EGFR inhibitors rescues behavioral deficits (Wang et al., 2012).

In a more recent drug screening for prevention of Aβo-induced neuronal exocytosis phenotypes, multiple compounds with high affinity for the σ_2R/PGRMC1 receptor were identified (Izzo et al., 2014a,b). In these studies, a 30% knockdown of σ_2R/PGRMC1 resulted in a 90% decrease in Aβo binding to neurons (Izzo et al., 2014b). Moreover, treatment of AD transgenic model mice with σ_2R/PGRMC1 antagonists prevented memory and learning deficits in behavioral assessments (Izzo et al., 2014a). Understanding the mechanisms that underlie σ_2R/PGRMC1-dependent Aβo-induced toxicity remains a priority, and targeting the σ_2R/PGRMC1 receptor is a strategy that is under active investigation.

MECHANISMS INDEPENDENT OF Aβ BINDING TO SPECIFIC PROTEIN RECEPTORS

A collection of studies show that Aβ assemblies can interact with lipids and glycolipids, irrespective of protein-binding sites in the plasma membrane. Surface plasmon resonance studies demonstrate direct Aβ interaction with lipids (Small et al., 2007; Williams and

Serpell, 2011). Interaction of Aβo with gangliosides of the plasma membrane can rapidly trap diffusible Aβo (Hong et al., 2014). Further studies demonstrated Aβo insertion into the lipid bilayer (Ashley et al., 2006; Lai and McLaurin, 2010; Valincius et al., 2008). We hypothesize that Aβo interaction with lipids and glycolipids plays a key role in concentrating Aβ assemblies at the neuronal cell surface to facilitate signaling via protein partners.

CONCLUDING REMARKS

Identifying receptors that bind Aβo and trigger the signaling cascades underlying neurotoxicity has the potential to enable novel approaches to slow or halt the progression of AD when excess Aβo has already been formed. So far, the most extensively validated downstream signaling cascade of Aβo is mediated by the PrP^C/mGluR5 pathway. This pathway has been shown to induce Aβo-dependent aberrant intracellular signaling, dendritic spine loss, synapse loss, synaptic plasticity, and learning and memory deficits. However, more work is necessary to better understand the role of additional receptors for Aβo as well as to fully characterize and develop interventions to modify the course of AD by targeting Aβo receptors.

Acknowledgments

This work was supported by grants from NIH, BrightFocus Foundation, Alzheimer's Association, and Falk Medical Research Trust to S.M.S.

Disclosure

S.M.S. is a cofounder of Axerion Therapeutics seeking to develop PrP-based therapeutics for Alzheimer's disease.

References

Agostini F, Dotti CG, Perez-Canamas A, Ledesma MD, Benetti F, Legname G: Prion protein accumulation in lipid rafts of mouse aging brain, *PLoS One* 8:e74244, 2013.

Akbik F, Cafferty WB, Strittmatter SM: Myelin associated inhibitors: a link between injury-induced and experience-dependent plasticity, *Exp Neurol* 235:43–52, 2012.

Akbik FV, Bhagat SM, Patel PR, Cafferty WB, Strittmatter SM: Anatomical plasticity of adult brain is titrated by Nogo receptor 1, *Neuron* 77:859–866, 2013.

Antonyuk SV, Trevitt CR, Strange RW, Jackson GS, Sangar D, Batchelor M, Cooper S, Fraser C, Jones S, Georgiou T, Khalili-Shirazi A, Clarke AR, Hasnain SS, Collinge J: Crystal structure of human prion protein bound to a therapeutic antibody, *Proc Natl Acad Sci USA* 106:2554–2558, 2009.

Ashley RH, Harroun TA, Hauss T, Breen KC, Bradshaw JP: Autoinsertion of soluble oligomers of Alzheimer's Abeta(1–42) peptide into cholesterol-containing membranes is accompanied by relocation of the sterol towards the bilayer surface, *BMC Struct Biol* 6:21, 2006.

Atwal JK, Pinkston-Gosse J, Syken J, Stawicki S, Wu Y, Shatz C, Tessier-Lavigne M: PirB is a functional receptor for myelin inhibitors of axonal regeneration, *Science* 322:967–970, 2008.

Balducci C, Beeg M, Stravalaci M, Bastone A, Sclip A, Biasini E, Tapella L, Colombo L, Manzoni C, Borsello T, Chiesa R, Gobbi M, Salmona M, Forloni G: Synthetic amyloid-beta oligomers impair long-term memory independently of cellular prion protein, *Proc Natl Acad Sci USA* 107:2295–2300, 2010.

Barbier AJ, Hilhorst M, Van Vliet A, Snyder P, Palfreyman MG, Gawryl M, Dgetluck N, Massaro M, Tiessen R, Timmerman W, Hilt DC: Pharmacodynamics, pharmacokinetics, safety, and tolerability of encenicline, a selective alpha7 nicotinic receptor partial agonist, in single ascending-dose and bioavailability studies, *Clin Ther* 37:311–324, 2015.

Barry AE, Klyubin I, Mc Donald JM, Mably AJ, Farrell MA, Scott M, Walsh DM, Rowan MJ: Alzheimer's disease brain-derived amyloid-beta-mediated inhibition of LTP in vivo is prevented by immunotargeting cellular prion protein, *J Neurosci* 31:7259–7263, 2011.

Bate C, Williams A: Amyloid-beta-induced synapse damage is mediated via cross-linkage of cellular prion proteins, *J Biol Chem* 286:37955–37963, 2011.

Beraldo FH, Arantes CP, Santos TG, Machado CF, Roffe M, Hajj GN, Lee KS, Magalhaes AC, Caetano FA, Mancini GL, Lopes MH, Americo TA, Magdesian MH, Ferguson SS, Linden R, Prado MA, Martins VR: Metabotropic glutamate receptors transduce signals for neurite outgrowth after binding of the prion protein to laminin gamma1 chain, *FASEB J* 25:265–279, 2011.

Berman DE, Dall'Armi C, Voronov SV, McIntire LB, Zhang H, Moore AZ, Staniszewski A, Arancio O, Kim TW, Di Paolo G: Oligomeric amyloid-beta peptide disrupts phosphatidylinositol-4,5-bisphosphate metabolism, *Nat Neurosci* 11:547–554, 2008.

Bourgin C, Murai KK, Richter M, Pasquale EB: The EphA4 receptor regulates dendritic spine remodeling by affecting beta1-integrin signaling pathways, *J Cell Biol* 178:1295–1307, 2007.

Bruno V, Battaglia G, Copani A, D'Onofrio M, Di Iorio P, De Blasi A, Melchiorri D, Flor PJ, Nicoletti F: Metabotropic glutamate receptor subtypes as targets for neuroprotective drugs, *J Cerebr Blood Flow Metabol* 21: 1013–1033, 2001.

Bruno V, Ksiazek I, Battaglia G, Lukic S, Leonhardt T, Sauer D, Gasparini F, Kuhn R, Nicoletti F, Flor PJ: Selective blockade of metabotropic glutamate receptor subtype 5 is neuroprotective, *Neuropharmacology* 39:2223–2230, 2000.

Buckingham SD, Jones AK, Brown LA, Sattelle DB: Nicotinic acetylcholine receptor signalling: roles in Alzheimer's disease and amyloid neuroprotection, *Pharmacol Rev* 61:39–61, 2009.

Calella AM, Farinelli M, Nuvolone M, Mirante O, Moos R, Falsig J, Mansuy IM, Aguzzi A: Prion protein and Abeta-related synaptic toxicity impairment, *EMBO Molecular Med* 2:306–314, 2010.

Carlo A-S, Gustafsen C, Mastrobuoni G, Nielsen MS, Burgert T, Hartl D, Rohe M, Nykjaer A, Herz J, Heeren J: The pro-neurotrophin receptor sortilin is a major neuronal apolipoprotein E receptor for catabolism of amyloid-β peptide in the brain, *J Neurosci* 33:358–370, 2013.

Chen S, Yadav SP, Surewicz WK: Interaction between human prion protein and amyloid-beta (Abeta) oligomers: role of N-terminal residues, *J Biol Chem* 285:26377–26383, 2010.

Cheng IH, Scearce-Levie K, Legleiter J, Palop JJ, Gerstein H, Bien-Ly N, Puolivali J, Lesne S, Ashe KH, Muchowski PJ, Mucke L: Accelerating amyloid-beta fibrillization reduces oligomer levels and functional deficits in Alzheimer disease mouse models, *J Biol Chem* 282:23818–23828, 2007.

Chung E, Ji Y, Sun Y, Kascsak RJ, Kascsak RB, Mehta PD, Strittmatter SM, Wisniewski T: Anti-PrP^C monoclonal antibody infusion as a novel treatment for cognitive deficits in an Alzheimer's disease model mouse, *BMC Neurosci* 11:130, 2010.

Cissé M, Halabisky B, Harris J, Devidze N, Dubal DB, Sun B, Orr A, Lotz G, Kim DH, Hamto P, Ho K, Yu GQ, Mucke L: Reversing EphB2 depletion rescues cognitive functions in Alzheimer model, *Nature* 469:47–52, 2011a.

Cissé M, Sanchez PE, Kim DH, Ho K, Yu G-Q, Mucke L: Ablation of cellular prion protein does not ameliorate abnormal neural network activity or cognitive dysfunction in the J20 line of human amyloid precursor protein transgenic mice, *J Neurosci* 31:10427–10431, 2011b.

Cleary JP, Walsh DM, Hofmeister JJ, Shankar GM, Kuskowski MA, Selkoe DJ, Ashe KH: Natural oligomers of the amyloid-beta protein specifically disrupt cognitive function, *Nat Neurosci* 8:79–84, 2005.

Conn PJ, Christopoulos A, Lindsley CW: Allosteric modulators of GPCRs: a novel approach for the treatment of CNS disorders, *Nat Rev Drug Discov* 8:41–54, 2009.

Conn PJ, Lindsley CW, Meiler J, Niswender CM: Opportunities and challenges in the discovery of allosteric modulators of GPCRs for treating CNS disorders, *Nat Rev Drug Discov* 13:692–708, 2014.

Cummings JL, Morstorf T, Zhong K: Alzheimer's disease drug-development pipeline: few candidates, frequent failures, *Alzheimers Res Therapy* 6:37, 2014.

Dalva MB, Takasu MA, Lin MZ, Shamah SM, Hu L, Gale NW, Greenberg ME: EphB receptors interact with NMDA receptors and regulate excitatory synapse formation, *Cell* 103:945–956, 2000.

Davies P, Maloney AJ: Selective loss of central cholinergic neurons in Alzheimer's disease, *Lancet* 2:1403, 1976.

Dickson DW, Crystal HA, Bevona C, Honer W, Vincent I, Davies P: Correlations of synaptic and pathological markers with cognition of the elderly, *Neurobiol Aging* 16:285–298, 1995, discussion 298–304.

Dineley KT, Westerman M, Bui D, Bell K, Ashe KH, Sweatt JD: Beta-amyloid activates the mitogen-activated protein kinase cascade via hippocampal alpha7 nicotinic acetylcholine receptors: in vitro and in vivo mechanisms related to Alzheimer's disease, *J Neurosci* 21:4125–4133, 2001.

Du Yan S, Chen X, Fu J, Chen M, Zhu H, Roher A, Slattery T, Zhao L, Nagashima M, Morser J: RAGE and amyloid-β peptide neurotoxicity in Alzheimer's disease, *Nature* 382:685–691, 1996.

Dziewczapolski G, Glogowski CM, Masliah E, Heinemann SF: Deletion of the alpha 7 nicotinic acetylcholine receptor gene improves cognitive deficits and synaptic pathology in a mouse model of Alzheimer's disease, *J Neurosci* 29:8805–8815, 2009.

El Khoury J, Hickman SE, Thomas CA, Cao L, Silverstein SC, Loike JD: Scavenger receptor-mediated adhesion of microglia to beta-amyloid fibrils, *Nature* 382:716–719, 1996.

Fluharty BR, Biasini E, Stravalaci M, Sclip A, Diomede L, Balducci C, La Vitola P, Messa M, Colombo L, Forloni G, Borsello T, Gobbi M, Harris DA: An N-terminal fragment of the prion protein binds to amyloid-beta oligomers and inhibits their neurotoxicity in vivo, *J Biol Chem* 288:7857–7866, 2013.

Fournier AE, GrandPre T, Strittmatter SM: Identification of a receptor mediating Nogo-66 inhibition of axonal regeneration, *Nature* 409:341–346, 2001.

Francesconi A, Kumari R, Zukin RS: Regulation of group I metabotropic glutamate receptor trafficking and signaling by the caveolar/lipid raft pathway, *J Neurosci* 29:3590–3602, 2009.

Freir DB, Nicoll AJ, Klyubin I, Panico S, Mc Donald JM, Risse E, Asante EA, Farrow MA, Sessions RB, Saibil HR, Clarke AR, Rowan MJ, Walsh DM, Collinge J: Interaction between prion protein and toxic amyloid beta assemblies can be therapeutically targeted at multiple sites, *Nat Commun* 2:336, 2011.

Fu AK, Hung KW, Huang H, Gu S, Shen Y, Cheng EY, Ip FC, Huang X, Fu WY, Ip NY: Blockade of EphA4 signaling ameliorates hippocampal synaptic dysfunctions in mouse models of Alzheimer's disease, *Proc Natl Acad Sci USA* 111:9959–9964, 2014.

Fu W-Y, Chen Y, Sahin M, Zhao X-S, Shi L, Bikoff JB, Lai K-O, Yung W-H, Fu AK, Greenberg ME: Cdk5 regulates EphA4-mediated dendritic spine retraction through an ephexin1-dependent mechanism, *Nat Neurosci* 10:67–76, 2006.

Galasko D, Bell J, Mancuso JY, Kupiec JW, Sabbagh MN, van Dyck C, Thomas RG, Aisen PSS: Clinical trial of an inhibitor of RAGE–Abeta interactions in Alzheimer disease: Alzheimer's disease cooperative study, *Neurology* 82:1536–1542, 2014.

Gandy S, Simon AJ, Steele JW, Lublin AL, Lah JJ, Walker LC, Levey AI, Krafft GA, Levy E, Checler F, Glabe C, Bilker WB, Abel T, Schmeidler J, Ehrlich ME: Days to criterion as an indicator of toxicity associated with human Alzheimer amyloid-beta oligomers, *Ann Neurol* 68:220–230, 2010.

Gasparini F, Spooren W: Allosteric modulators for mGlu receptors, *Curr Neuropharmacol* 5:187–194, 2007.

Gimbel DA, Nygaard HB, Coffey EE, Gunther EC, Lauren J, Gimbel ZA, Strittmatter SM: Memory impairment in transgenic Alzheimer mice requires cellular prion protein, *J Neurosci* 30:6367–6374, 2010.

Gotti C, Riganti L, Vailati S, Clementi F: Brain neuronal nicotinic receptors as new targets for drug discovery, *Curr Pharm Des* 12:407–428, 2006.

Gregory KJ, Dong EN, Meiler J, Conn PJ: Allosteric modulation of metabotropic glutamate receptors: structural insights and therapeutic potential, *Neuropharmacology* 60:66–81, 2011.

Gregory KJ, Malosh C, Turlington M, Morrison R, Vinson P, Daniels JS, Jones C, Niswender CM, Conn PJ, Lindsley CW, Stauffer SR: Identification of a high affinity MPEP-site silent allosteric modulator (SAM) for the metabotropic glutamate subtype 5 receptor (mGlu5). *In* Probe Reports from the NIH Molecular Libraries Program, Bethesda, 2010, MD.

Gregory KJ, Noetzel MJ, Rook JM, Vinson PN, Stauffer SR, Rodriguez AL, Emmitte KA, Zhou Y, Chun AC, Felts AS, Chauder BA, Lindsley CW, Niswender CM, Conn PJ: Investigating metabotropic glutamate receptor 5 allosteric modulator cooperativity, affinity, and agonism: enriching structure-function studies and structure-activity relationships, *Mol Pharmacol* 82:860–875, 2012.

Haas LT, Kostylev MA, Strittmatter SM: Therapeutic molecules and endogenous ligands regulate the interaction between brain cellular prion protein (PrP^C) and metabotropic glutamate receptor 5 (mGluR5), *J Biol Chem* 289:28460–28477, 2014.

Henderson JT, Georgiou J, Jia Z, Robertson J, Elowe S, Roder JC, Pawson T: The receptor tyrosine kinase EphB2 regulates NMDA-dependent synaptic function, *Neuron* 32:1041–1056, 2001.

Hernandez CM, Kayed R, Zheng H, Sweatt JD, Dineley KT: Loss of alpha7 nicotinic receptors enhances beta-amyloid oligomer accumulation, exacerbating early-stage cognitive decline and septohippocampal pathology in a mouse model of Alzheimer's disease, *J Neurosci* 30:2442–2453, 2010.

Hernandez P, Lee G, Sjoberg M, Maccioni RB: Tau phosphorylation by cdk5 and Fyn in response to amyloid peptide Abeta (25–35): involvement of lipid rafts, *J Alzheimers Dis* 16:149–156, 2009.

Hong S, Ostaszewski BL, Yang T, O'Malley TT, Jin M, Yanagisawa K, Li S, Bartels T, Selkoe DJ: Soluble Abeta oligomers are rapidly sequestered from brain ISF in vivo and bind GM1 ganglioside on cellular membranes, *Neuron* 82:308–319, 2014.

Hu NW, Nicoll AJ, Zhang D, Mably AJ, O'Malley T, Purro SA, Terry C, Collinge J, Walsh DM, Rowan MJ: mGlu5 receptors and cellular prion protein mediate amyloid-beta-facilitated synaptic long-term depression in vivo, *Nat Commun* 5:3374, 2014.

Isherwood SN, Pekcec A, Nicholson JR, Robbins TW, Dalley JW: Dissociable effects of mGluR5 allosteric modulation on distinct forms of impulsivity in rats: interaction with NMDA receptor antagonism, *Psychopharmacology (Berl)*, 232:3327–3344, 2015.

Izzo NJ, Staniszewski A, To L, Fa M, Teich AF, Saeed F, Wostein H, Walko T, Vaswani A, Wardius M, Syed Z, Ravenscroft J, Mozzoni K, Silky C, Rehak C, Yurko R, Finn P, Look G, Rishton G, Safferstein H, Miller M, Johanson C, Stopa E, Windisch M, Hutter-Paier B, Shamloo M, Arancio O, LeVine H, Catalano SM: Alzheimer's therapeutics targeting amyloid beta 1-42 oligomers I: abeta 42 oligomer binding to specific neuronal receptors is displaced by drug candidates that improve cognitive deficits, *PLoS One* 9:e111898, 2014a.

Izzo NJ, Xu J, Zeng C, Kirk MJ, Mozzoni K, Silky C, Rehak C, Yurko R, Look G, Rishton G, Safferstein H, Cruchaga C, Goate A, Cahill MA, Arancio O, Mach RH, Craven R, Head E, LeVine H 3rd, Spires-Jones TL, Catalano SM: Alzheimer's therapeutics targeting amyloid beta 1-42 oligomers II: sigma-2/PGRMC1 receptors mediate Abeta 42 oligomer binding and synaptotoxicity, *PLoS One* 9:e111899, 2014b.

Jin M, Shepardson N, Yang T, Chen G, Walsh D, Selkoe DJ: Soluble amyloid beta-protein dimers isolated from Alzheimer cortex directly induce tau hyperphosphorylation and neuritic degeneration, *Proc Natl Acad Sci USA* 108:5819–5824, 2011.

Josephs KA, Whitwell JL, Ahmed Z, Shiung MM, Weigand SD, Knopman DS, Boeve BF, Parisi JE, Petersen RC, Dickson DW, Jack CR Jr: Beta-amyloid burden is not associated with rates of brain atrophy, *Ann Neurol* 63:204–212, 2008.

Kam TI, Song S, Gwon Y, Park H, Yan JJ, Im I, Choi JW, Choi TY, Kim J, Song DK, Takai T, Kim YC, Kim KS, Choi SY, Choi S, Klein WL, Yuan J, Jung YK: FcgammaRIIb mediates amyloid-beta neurotoxicity and memory impairment in Alzheimer's disease, *J Clin Invest* 123:2791–2802, 2013.

Katzman R, Terry R, DeTeresa R, Brown T, Davies P, Fuld P, Renbing X, Peck A: Clinical, pathological, and neurochemical changes in dementia: a subgroup with preserved mental status and numerous neocortical plaques, *Ann Neurol* 23:138–144, 1988.

Kessels HW, Nguyen LN, Nabavi S, Malinow R: The prion protein as a receptor for amyloid-beta, *Nature* 466:E4–5, 2010, E3–4; discussion.

Khan GM, Tong M, Jhun M, Arora K, Nichols RA: Beta-amyloid activates presynaptic alpha7 nicotinic acetylcholine receptors reconstituted into a model nerve cell system: involvement of lipid rafts, *Eur J Neurosci* 31:788–796, 2010.

Kim T, Vidal GS, Djurisic M, William CM, Birnbaum ME, Garcia KC, Hyman BT, Shatz CJ: Human LilrB2 is a β-amyloid receptor and its murine homolog PirB regulates synaptic plasticity in an Alzheimer's model, *Science* 341:1399–1404, 2013.

Klyubin I, Nicoll AJ, Khalili-Shirazi A, Farmer M, Canning S, Mably A, Linehan J, Brown A, Wakeling M, Brandner S, Walsh DM, Rowan MJ, Collinge J: Peripheral administration of a humanized anti-PrP antibody blocks Alzheimer's disease Abeta synaptotoxicity, *J Neurosci* 34:6140–6145, 2014.

Kostylev MA, Kaufman AC, Nygaard HB, Patel P, Haas LT, Gunther EC, Vortmeyer A, Strittmatter SM: Prion-protein-interacting amyloid-beta oligomers of high molecular weight are tightly correlated with memory impairment in multiple Alzheimer mouse models, *J Biol Chem* 290:17415–17438, 2015.

Kudo W, Lee HP, Zou WQ, Wang X, Perry G, Zhu X, Smith MA, Petersen RB, Lee HG: Cellular prion protein is essential for oligomeric amyloid-beta-induced neuronal cell death, *Hum Mol Genet* 21:1138–1144, 2012.

Kuner P, Schubenel R, Hertel C: β-amyloid binds to p75NTR and activates NFκB in human neuroblastoma cells, *J Neurosci Res* 54:798–804, 1998.

Lacor PN, Buniel MC, Furlow PW, Clemente AS, Velasco PT, Wood M, Viola KL, Klein WL: Abeta oligomer-induced aberrations in synapse composition, shape, and density provide a molecular basis for loss of connectivity in Alzheimer's disease, *J Neurosci* 27:796–807, 2007.

Lai AY, McLaurin J: Mechanisms of amyloid-beta peptide uptake by neurons: the role of lipid rafts and lipid raft-associated proteins, *Int J Alzheimers Dis* 2011:548380, 2010.

Lambert JC, Ibrahim-Verbaas CA, Harold D, Naj AC, Sims R, Bellenguez C, DeStafano AL, Bis JC, Beecham GW, Grenier-Boley B, Russo G, Thorton-Wells TA, Jones N, Smith AV, Chouraki V, Thomas C, Ikram MA, Zelenika D, Vardarajan BN, Kamatani Y, Lin CF, Gerrish A, Schmidt H, Kunkle B, Dunstan ML, Ruiz A, Bihoreau MT, Choi SH, Reitz C, Pasquier F, Cruchaga C, Craig D, Amin N, Berr C, Lopez OL, De Jager PL, Deramecourt V, Johnston JA, Evans D, Lovestone S, Letenneur L, Moron FJ, Rubinsztein DC, Eiriksdottir G, Sleegers K, Goate AM, Fievet N, Huentelman MW, Gill M, Brown K, Kamboh MI, Keller L, Barberger-Gateau P, McGuiness B, Larson EB, Green R, Myers AJ, Dufouil C, Todd S, Wallon D, Love S, Rogaeva E, Gallacher J, St George-Hyslop P, Clarimon J, Lleo A, Bayer A, Tsuang DW, Yu L, Tsolaki M, Bossu P, Spalletta G, Proitsi P, Collinge J, Sorbi S, Sanchez-Garcia F, Fox NC, Hardy J, Deniz Naranjo MC, Bosco P, Clarke R, Brayne C, Galimberti D, Mancuso M, Matthews F, European Alzheimer's Disease Initiative (EADI); Genetic and Environmental Risk in Alzheimer's Disease; Alzheimer's Disease Genetic Consortium; Cohorts for Heart and Aging Research in Genomic Epidemiology, Moebus S, Mecocci P, Del Zompo M, Maier W, Hampel H, Pilotto A, Bullido M, Panza F, Caffarra P, et al: 2013. Meta-analysis of 74,046 individuals identifies 11 new susceptibility loci for Alzheimer's disease. *Nat Genet*. 45:1452–1458.

Lambert MP, Barlow AK, Chromy BA, Edwards C, Freed R, Liosatos M, Morgan TE, Rozovsky I, Trommer B, Viola KL, Wals P, Zhang C, Finch CE, Krafft GA, Klein WL: Diffusible, nonfibrillar ligands derived from Abeta1-42 are potent central nervous system neurotoxins, *Proc Natl Acad Sci USA* 95:6448–6453, 1998.

Larson M, Sherman MA, Amar F, Nuvolone M, Schneider JA, Bennett DA, Aguzzi A, Lesne SE: The complex PrP(c)-Fyn couples human oligomeric Abeta with pathological tau changes in Alzheimer's disease, *J Neurosci* 32:16857–16871a, 2012.

Lauren J, Gimbel DA, Nygaard HB, Gilbert JW, Strittmatter SM: Cellular prion protein mediates impairment of synaptic plasticity by amyloid-beta oligomers, *Nature* 457:1128–1132, 2009.

Lesne S, Koh MT, Kotilinek L, Kayed R, Glabe CG, Yang A, Gallagher M, Ashe KH: A specific amyloid-beta protein assembly in the brain impairs memory, *Nature* 440:352–357, 2006.

Li S, Hong S, Shepardson NE, Walsh DM, Shankar GM, Selkoe D: Soluble oligomers of amyloid beta protein facilitate hippocampal long-term depression by disrupting neuronal glutamate uptake, *Neuron* 62:788–801, 2009.

Lipton SA: Paradigm shift in neuroprotection by NMDA receptor blockade: memantine and beyond, *Nat Rev Drug Discov* 5:160–170, 2006.

Liu BP, Fournier A, GrandPre T, Strittmatter SM: Myelin-associated glycoprotein as a functional ligand for the Nogo-66 receptor, *Science* 297:1190–1193, 2002.

Lue LF, Kuo YM, Roher AE, Brachova L, Shen Y, Sue L, Beach T, Kurth JH, Rydel RE, Rogers J: Soluble amyloid beta peptide concentration as a predictor of synaptic change in Alzheimer's disease, *Am J Pathol* 155:853–862, 1999.

Luscher C, Huber KM: Group 1 mGluR-dependent synaptic long-term depression: mechanisms and implications for circuitry and disease, *Neuron* 65:445–459, 2010.

McGee AW, Yang Y, Fischer QS, Daw NW, Strittmatter SM: Experience-driven plasticity of visual cortex limited by myelin and Nogo receptor, *Science* 309:2222–2226, 2005.

McLean CA, Cherny RA, Fraser FW, Fuller SJ, Smith MJ, Beyreuther K, Bush AI, Masters CL: Soluble pool of Abeta amyloid as a determinant of severity of neurodegeneration in Alzheimer's disease, *Ann Neurol* 46:860–866, 1999.

Melancon BJ, Hopkins CR, Wood MR, Emmitte KA, Niswender CM, Christopoulos A, Conn PJ, Lindsley CW: Allosteric modulation of seven transmembrane spanning receptors: theory, practice, and opportunities for central nervous system drug discovery, *J Med Chem* 55:1445–1464, 2012.

Molck C, Harpsoe K, Gloriam DE, Mathiesen JM, Nielsen SM, Brauner-Osborne H: mGluR5: exploration of orthosteric and allosteric ligand binding pockets and their applications to drug discovery, *Neurochem Res* 39:1862–1875, 2014.

Munch G, Schinzel R, Loske C, Wong A, Durany N, Li JJ, Vlassara H, Smith MA, Perry G, Riederer P: Alzheimer's disease—synergistic effects of glucose deficit, oxidative stress and advanced glycation endproducts, *J Neural Transm* 105:439–461, 1998.

Muto T, Tsuchiya D, Morikawa K, Jingami H: Structures of the extracellular regions of the group II/III metabotropic glutamate receptors, *Proc Natl Acad Sci USA* 104:3759–3764, 2007.

Nagele RG, D'Andrea MR, Anderson WJ, Wang HY: Intracellular accumulation of beta-amyloid(1-42) in neurons is facilitated by the alpha 7 nicotinic acetylcholine receptor in Alzheimer's disease, *Neuroscience* 110:199–211, 2002.

Nickols HH, Conn PJ: Development of allosteric modulators of GPCRs for treatment of CNS disorders, *Neurobiol Dis* 61:55–71, 2014.

Nicoll AJ, Panico S, Freir DB, Wright D, Terry C, Risse E, Herron CE, O'Malley T, Wadsworth JD, Farrow MA, Walsh DM, Saibil HR, Collinge J: Amyloid-beta nanotubes are associated with prion protein-dependent synaptotoxicity, *Nat Commun* 4:2416, 2013.

Noble W, Olm V, Takata K, Casey E, Mary O, Meyerson J, Gaynor K, LaFrancois J, Wang L, Kondo T, Davies P, Burns M, Veeranna, Nixon R, Dickson D, Matsuoka Y, Ahlijanian M, Lau LF, Duff K: Cdk5 is a key factor in tau aggregation and tangle formation in vivo, *Neuron* 38:555–565, 2003.

O'Brien JA, Lemaire W, Chen TB, Chang RS, Jacobson MA, Ha SN, Lindsley CW, Schaffhauser HJ, Sur C, Pettibone DJ, Conn PJ, Williams DL Jr: A family of highly selective allosteric modulators of the metabotropic glutamate receptor subtype 5, *Mol Pharmacol* 64:731–740, 2003.

Ostapchenko VG, Beraldo FH, Mohammad AH, Xie YF, Hirata PH, Magalhaes AC, Lamour G, Li H, Maciejewski A, Belrose JC, Teixeira BL, Fahnestock M, Ferreira ST, Cashman NR, Hajj GN, Jackson MF, Choy WY, MacDonald JF, Martins VR, Prado VF, Prado MA: The prion protein ligand, stress-inducible phosphoprotein 1, regulates amyloid-beta oligomer toxicity, *J Neurosci* 33:16552–16564, 2013.

Palop JJ, Mucke L: Amyloid-beta-induced neuronal dysfunction in Alzheimer's disease: from synapses toward neural networks, *Nat Neurosci* 13:812–818, 2010.

Paresce DM, Ghosh RN, Maxfield FR: Microglial cells internalize aggregates of the Alzheimer's disease amyloid beta-protein via a scavenger receptor, *Neuron* 17:553–565, 1996.

Park JH, Gimbel DA, GrandPre T, Lee JK, Kim JE, Li W, Lee DH, Strittmatter SM: Alzheimer precursor protein interaction with the Nogo-66 receptor reduces amyloid-beta plaque deposition, *J Neurosci* 26:1386–1395, 2006a.

Park JH, Widi GA, Gimbel DA, Harel NY, Lee DH, Strittmatter SM: Subcutaneous Nogo receptor removes brain amyloid-beta and improves spatial memory in Alzheimer's transgenic mice, *J Neurosci* 26:13279–13286, 2006b.

Pin JP, Duvoisin R: The metabotropic glutamate receptors: structure and functions, *Neuropharmacology* 34:1–26, 1995.

Pin JP, Galvez T, Prezeau L: Evolution, structure, and activation mechanism of family 3/C G-protein-coupled receptors, *Pharmacol Therapeut* 98:325–354, 2003.

Rammes G, Hasenjager A, Sroka-Saidi K, Deussing JM, Parsons CG: Therapeutic significance of NR2B-containing NMDA receptors and mGluR5 metabotropic glutamate receptors in mediating the synaptotoxic effects of beta-amyloid oligomers on long-term potentiation (LTP) in murine hippocampal slices, *Neuropharmacology* 60:982–990, 2011.

Reed MN, Hofmeister JJ, Jungbauer L, Welzel AT, Yu C, Sherman MA, Lesne S, LaDu MJ, Walsh DM, Ashe KH, Cleary JP: Cognitive effects of cell-derived and synthetically derived Abeta oligomers, *Neurobiol Aging* 32:1784–1794, 2011.

Renner M, Lacor PN, Velasco PT, Xu J, Contractor A, Klein WL, Triller A: Deleterious effects of amyloid beta oligomers acting as an extracellular scaffold for mGluR5, *Neuron* 66:739–754, 2010.

Resenberger UK, Harmeier A, Woerner AC, Goodman JL, Muller V, Krishnan R, Vabulas RM, Kretzschmar HA, Lindquist S, Hartl FU, Multhaup G, Winklhofer KF, Tatzelt J: The cellular prion protein mediates neurotoxic signalling of beta-sheet-rich conformers independent of prion replication, *EMBO J* 30:2057–2070, 2011.

Ribeiro FM, Paquet M, Cregan SP, Ferguson SS: Group I metabotropic glutamate receptor signalling and its implication in neurological disease, *CNS Neurol Disord-Dr* 9:574–595, 2010.

Richter M, Murai KK, Bourgin C, Pak DT, Pasquale EB: The EphA4 receptor regulates neuronal morphology through SPAR-mediated inactivation of Rap GTPases, *J Neurosci* 27:14205–14215, 2007.

Rushworth JV, Griffiths HH, Watt NT, Hooper NM: Prion protein-mediated toxicity of amyloid-beta oligomers requires lipid rafts and the transmembrane LRP1, *J Biol Chem* 288:8935–8951, 2013.

Schwab ME, Strittmatter SM: Nogo limits neural plasticity and recovery from injury, *Curr Opin Neurobiol* 27:53–60, 2014.

Shankar GM, Li S, Mehta TH, Garcia-Munoz A, Shepardson NE, Smith I, Brett FM, Farrell MA, Rowan MJ, Lemere CA, Regan CM, Walsh DM, Sabatini BL, Selkoe DJ: Amyloid-beta protein dimers isolated directly from Alzheimer's brains impair synaptic plasticity and memory, *Nat Medicine* 14:837–842, 2008.

Sheffler DJ, Gregory KJ, Rook JM, Conn PJ: Allosteric modulation of metabotropic glutamate receptors, *Adv Pharmacol* 62:37–77, 2011.

Shyng SL, Lehmann S, Moulder KL, Harris DA: Sulfated glycans stimulate endocytosis of the cellular isoform of the prion protein, PrP^C, in cultured cells, *J Biol Chem* 270:30221–30229, 1995.

Simon AM, de Maturana RL, Ricobaraza A, Escribano L, Schiapparelli L, Cuadrado-Tejedor M, Perez-Mediavilla A, Avila J, Del Rio J, Frechilla D: Early changes in hippocampal Eph receptors precede the onset of memory decline in mouse models of Alzheimer's disease, *J Alzheimers Dis* 17:773–786, 2009.

Small DH, Maksel D, Kerr ML, Ng J, Hou X, Chu C, Mehrani H, Unabia S, Azari MF, Loiacono R, Aguilar MI, Chebib M: The beta-amyloid protein of Alzheimer's disease binds to membrane lipids but does not bind to the alpha7 nicotinic acetylcholine receptor, *J Neurochem* 101:1527–1538, 2007.

Takasu MA, Dalva MB, Zigmond RE, Greenberg ME: Modulation of NMDA receptor-dependent calcium influx and gene expression through EphB receptors, *Science* 295:491–495, 2002.

Takuma K, Fang F, Zhang W, Yan S, Fukuzaki E, Du H, Sosunov A, McKhann G, Funatsu Y, Nakamichi N, Nagai T, Mizoguchi H, Ibi D, Hori O, Ogawa S, Stern DM, Yamada K, Yan SS: RAGE-mediated signaling contributes to intraneuronal transport of amyloid-beta and neuronal dysfunction, *Proc Natl Acad Sci USA* 106:20021–20026, 2009.

Terry RD, Masliah E, Salmon DP, Butters N, DeTeresa R, Hill R, Hansen LA, Katzman R: Physical basis of cognitive alterations in Alzheimer's disease: synapse loss is the major correlate of cognitive impairment, *Ann Neurol* 30:572–580, 1991.

Townsend M, Shankar GM, Mehta T, Walsh DM, Selkoe DJ: Effects of secreted oligomers of amyloid beta-protein on hippocampal synaptic plasticity: a potent role for trimers, *J Physiol* 572:477–492, 2006.

Um JW, Kaufman AC, Kostylev M, Heiss JK, Stagi M, Takahashi H, Kerrisk ME, Vortmeyer A, Wisniewski T, Koleske AJ, Gunther EC, Nygaard HB, Strittmatter SM: Metabotropic glutamate receptor 5 is a coreceptor for Alzheimer abeta oligomer bound to cellular prion protein, *Neuron* 79:887–902, 2013.

Um JW, Nygaard HB, Heiss JK, Kostylev MA, Stagi M, Vortmeyer A, Wisniewski T, Gunther EC, Strittmatter SM: Alzheimer amyloid-beta oligomer bound to postsynaptic prion protein activates Fyn to impair neurons, *Nat Neurosci* 15:1227–1235, 2012.

Um JW, Strittmatter SM: Amyloid-beta induced signaling by cellular prion protein and Fyn kinase in Alzheimer disease, *Prion* 7:37–41, 2013.

Valincius G, Heinrich F, Budvytyte R, Vanderah DJ, McGillivray DJ, Sokolov Y, Hall JE, Losche M: Soluble amyloid beta-oligomers affect dielectric membrane properties by bilayer insertion and domain formation: implications for cell toxicity, *Biophys J* 95:4845–4861, 2008.

Walsh DM, Klyubin I, Fadeeva JV, Cullen WK, Anwyl R, Wolfe MS, Rowan MJ, Selkoe DJ: Naturally secreted oligomers of amyloid beta protein potently inhibit hippocampal long-term potentiation in vivo, *Nature* 416:535–539, 2002.

Wang HY, Lee DH, D'Andrea MR, Peterson PA, Shank RP, Reitz AB: Beta-amyloid(1–42) binds to alpha7 nicotinic acetylcholine receptor with high affinity: implications for Alzheimer's disease pathology, *J Biol Chem* 275:5626–5632, 2000a.

Wang HY, Lee DH, Davis CB, Shank RP: Amyloid peptide Aβ1–42 binds selectively and with picomolar affinity to α7 nicotinic acetylcholine receptors, *J Neurochem* 75:1155–1161, 2000b.

Wang HY, Li W, Benedetti NJ, Lee DH: Alpha 7 nicotinic acetylcholine receptors mediate beta-amyloid peptide-induced tau protein phosphorylation, *J Biol Chem* 278:31547–31553, 2003.

Wang HY, Stucky A, Liu J, Shen C, Trocme-Thibierge C, Morain P: Dissociating beta-amyloid from alpha 7 nicotinic acetylcholine receptor by a novel therapeutic agent, S 24795 normalizes alpha 7 nicotinic acetylcholine and NMDA receptor function in Alzheimer's disease brain, *J Neurosci* 29:10961–10973, 2009.

Wang J, Dickson DW, Trojanowski JQ, Lee VM: The levels of soluble versus insoluble brain Abeta distinguish Alzheimer's disease from normal and pathologic aging, *Exp Neurol* 158:328–337, 1999.

Wang KC, Koprivica V, Kim JA, Sivasankaran R, Guo Y, Neve RL, He Z: Oligodendrocyte-myelin glycoprotein is a Nogo receptor ligand that inhibits neurite outgrowth, *Nature* 417:941–944, 2002.

Wang L, Chiang H-C, Wu W, Liang B, Xie Z, Yao X, Ma W, Du S, Zhong Y: Epidermal growth factor receptor is a preferred target for treating amyloid-β-induced memory loss, *Proc Natl Acad Sci USA* 109:16743–16748, 2012.

Wang Q, Walsh DM, Rowan MJ, Selkoe DJ, Anwyl R: Block of long-term potentiation by naturally secreted and synthetic amyloid beta-peptide in hippocampal slices is mediated via activation of the kinases c-Jun N-terminal kinase, cyclin-dependent kinase 5, and p38 mitogen-activated protein kinase as well as metabotropic glutamate receptor type 5, *J Neurosci* 24:3370–3378, 2004.

William CM, Andermann ML, Goldey GJ, Roumis DK, Reid RC, Shatz CJ, Albers MW, Frosch MP, Hyman BT: Synaptic plasticity defect following visual deprivation in Alzheimer's disease model transgenic mice, *J Neurosci* 32:8004–8011, 2012.

Williams TL, Serpell LC: Membrane and surface interactions of Alzheimer's Abeta peptide—insights into the mechanism of cytotoxicity, *FEBS J* 278:3905–3917, 2011.

Wu H, Wang C, Gregory KJ, Han GW, Cho HP, Xia Y, Niswender CM, Katritch V, Meiler J, Cherezov V, Conn PJ, Stevens RC: Structure of a class C GPCR metabotropic glutamate receptor 1 bound to an allosteric modulator, *Science* 344:58–64, 2014.

Xie L, Helmerhorst E, Taddei K, Plewright B, Van Bronswijk W, Martins R: Alzheimer's beta-amyloid peptides compete for insulin binding to the insulin receptor, *J Neurosci* 22:RC221, 2002.

Xu J, Zhu Y, Contractor A, Heinemann SF: mGluR5 has a critical role in inhibitory learning, *J Neurosci* 29:3676–3684, 2009.

Yamaguchi S, Nishida Y, Sasaki K, Kambara M, Kim CL, Ishiguro N, Nagatsuka T, Uzawa H, Horiuchi M: Inhibition of PrPSc formation by synthetic O-sulfated glycopyranosides and their polymers, *Biochem Biophys Res Commun* 349:485–491, 2006.

Yamasaki T, Suzuki A, Hasebe R, Horiuchi M: Comparison of the anti-prion mechanism of four different anti-prion compounds, anti-PrP monoclonal antibody 44B1, pentosan polysulfate, chlorpromazine, and U18666A, in prion-infected mouse neuroblastoma cells, *PLoS One* 9:e106516, 2014.

Yusa S, Oliveira-Martins JB, Sugita-Konishi Y, Kikuchi Y: Cellular prion protein: from physiology to pathology, *Viruses* 4:3109–3131, 2012.

Zampagni M, Evangelisti E, Cascella R, Liguri G, Becatti M, Pensalfini A, Uberti D, Cenini G, Memo M, Bagnoli S, Nacmias B, Sorbi S, Cecchi C: Lipid rafts are primary mediators of amyloid oxidative attack on plasma membrane, *J Mol Med* 88:597–608, 2010.

Zhang Y, Rodriguez AL, Conn PJ: Allosteric potentiators of metabotropic glutamate receptor subtype 5 have differential effects on different signaling pathways in cortical astrocytes, *J Pharmacol Exp Ther* 315:1212–1219, 2005.

Zhao WQ, De Felice FG, Fernandez S, Chen H, Lambert MP, Quon MJ, Krafft GA, Klein WL: Amyloid beta oligomers induce impairment of neuronal insulin receptors, *FASEB J* 22:246–260, 2008.

Zou WQ, Xiao X, Yuan J, Puoti G, Fujioka H, Wang X, Richardson S, Zhou X, Zou R, Li S, Zhu X, McGeer PL, McGeehan J, Kneale G, Rincon-Limas DE, Fernandez-Funez P, Lee HG, Smith MA, Petersen RB, Guo JP: Amyloid-beta42 interacts mainly with insoluble prion protein in the Alzheimer brain, *J Biol Chem* 286:15095–15105, 2011.

CHAPTER

9

Blood–Brain Barrier Transport of Alzheimer's Amyloid β-Peptide

A.R. Nelson, A.P. Sagare, B.V. Zlokovic

OUTLINE

INTRODUCTION

Alzheimer's disease (AD) is associated with elevated levels of amyloid β-peptide (Aβ) in the brain. Brain Aβ is normally regulated by its production (Haass et al., 2012; Wolfe, 2008) and clearance from the brain (Zlokovic, 2011). The majority of AD cases are sporadic late-onset AD, and <5% of cases are early-onset autosomal-dominant AD (ADAD) (Tanzi, 2012). In sporadic AD, Aβ accumulates in the brain mainly because of its faulty clearance from the brain (Mawuenyega et al., 2010; Zlokovic, 2011). In ADAD, however, there is increased production of Aβ caused by mutations in Aβ precursor protein (*APP*) and presenilin (*PSEN*) genes (Bateman et al., 2011).

Developing Therapeutics for Alzheimer's Disease. http://dx.doi.org/10.1016/B978-0-12-802173-6.00009-5

The blood–brain barrier (BBB) prevents uncontrolled entry of blood-derived neurotoxic molecules, cells, and pathogens into the brain, and regulates the concentrations of ions, nutrients, and energy metabolites in the brain interstitial fluid (ISF) via highly specialized substrate-specific transporters at the luminal and abluminal membranes of the brain endothelium (Daneman and Prat, 2015; Ramanathan et al., 2015; Zlokovic, 1995; Zlokovic et al., 1985; Zloković et al., 1987). Receptor-mediated transcytosis across the BBB is crucial for efficient removal of potentially toxic proteinaceous molecules from the brain such as Aβ. Using mathematical models, it has been calculated that under physiological conditions it will take approximately 13 min for all Aβ40 to be removed from the brain via transport across the BBB into the bloodstream by the low-density lipoprotein receptor-related protein 1 (LRP1)-dependent transcytosis, in the case when Aβ production from APP and influx of circulating Aβ into the brain are inhibited (Deane and Zlokovic, 2007). In contrast, the microtubule-stabilizing protein tau, currently without a known transporter at the BBB, is eliminated from the brain ISF via ISF-cerebrospinal fluid (CSF) bulk flow at a much slower rate, with a half-life of approximately 11 days (Yamada et al., 2014). This example illustrates the importance of rapid transvascular clearance of proteinaceous, potentially toxic molecules across the BBB, which is critical for preventing their accumulation in the brain and is required for proper neuronal functioning.

Previous studies in mice have shown that normally ~85% of Aβ is cleared by transvascular transport across the BBB, and a smaller amount by the ISF bulk flow (Bading et al., 2002; Bell et al., 2007; Deane et al., 2004, 2008; Shibata et al., 2000). These findings have been confirmed by other studies, as recently reviewed (Sagare et al., 2012). Brain-derived Aβ is cleared across the BBB principally via LRP1-mediated transcytosis (Deane et al., 2004; Shibata et al., 2000; Zlokovic et al., 2010) and is taken up into the brain across the BBB by the receptor for advanced glycation end products (RAGE), particularly under pathophysiological conditions when RAGE expression is increased in brain endothelium (Deane et al., 2003, 2012). Here, we examine Aβ transcytosis across the BBB via LRP1 and Aβ uptake across the BBB by RAGE, and discuss how alterations within these pathways can contribute to Aβ accumulation in the brain in AD. We also review potential therapeutic opportunities based on restoring the function of Aβ BBB transporters in dementia and AD.

Aβ CLEARANCE FROM BRAIN

LRP1

LRP1 is localized mainly to the abluminal side of the BBB and is the key receptor mediating Aβ transcytosis across the BBB into the circulation (Bell et al., 2007; Deane et al., 2004; Shibata et al., 2000; Zhao et al., 2015). LRP1 is also expressed in other cell types of the neurovascular unit, including pericytes (Sagare et al., 2013b), astrocytes (Koistinaho et al., 2004), vascular smooth muscle cells (VSMCs) (Bell et al., 2009), and neurons (Kanekiyo and Bu, 2014). In addition to Aβ, the extracellular binding domains of LRP1 also bind >40 different ligands, including some proteins implicated in AD pathogenesis, such as, to name a few, APP, apolipoprotein E (ApoE), and α2-macroglobulin (Lillis et al., 2008; Ramanathan et al., 2015; Zlokovic, 2008, 2010). The species of Aβ determines the rate of their transport by LRP1-mediated clearance; for example, Aβ40 is cleared at the fastest rate, and Aβ42 is cleared at a faster rate than the vasculotropic

Dutch Aβ mutants (Bell et al., 2007; Deane et al., 2004). Besides its cargo transport function, LRP1 has different signal transduction functions (van der Geer, 2002).

LRP1 is present in cells as a cell-surface membrane receptor and circulates in blood as a truncated shed form or soluble LRP1 (sLRP1) (Zlokovic et al., 2010). LRP1 is composed of two subunits, including an extracellular α-chain (515 kDa) and a β-chain (85 kDa). The β-chain consists of a short extracellular extension, a single transmembrane domain, and a 100-amino-acid intracellular domain (Emonard et al., 2014). The cytoplasmic C-terminal tail of LRP1 has two NPXY motifs, one YXXL motif, and two dileucine motifs that bind endocytic and scaffold adaptors, whereas the extracellular N-terminal domain has four ligand-binding domains that bind ligands like Aβ (Deane et al., 2004, 2008; Li et al., 2001).

The molecular steps mediating clearance of LRP1-Aβ complexes across the BBB have been recently elucidated (Zhao et al., 2015). Briefly, brain-derived Aβ binds to LRP1 at the abluminal side of the BBB, and is rapidly internalized into endothelial cells and cleared into the bloodstream (Fig. 9.1). This process involves endothelial cell-dependent clathrin/phosphatidylinositol-binding clathrin assembly protein (PICALM)-mediated internalization of LRP1-Aβ complexes (Zhao et al., 2015). After rapid dissociation of clathrin from the internalized vesicles, PICALM continues to guide intracellular trafficking of Aβ-containing endocytic vesicles across the endothelium for fusion with Rab5-positive early endosomes, and then Rab11-positive sorting endosomes mediating Aβ exocytosis at the luminal side of the BBB (Zhao et al., 2015). PICALM directs Aβ endocytic vesicles away from Rab7-positive late endosomes that normally guide endocytic vesicles to lysosomes, which results in minimal degradation of Aβ during its transcytosis across the BBB (Zhao et al., 2015).

Factors Influencing LRP1-Mediated Aβ Clearance

In the following we describe AD genetic risk factors and brain endothelial genes that can influence LRP1-mediated Aβ clearance.

ApoE: ApoE, produced in the brain mainly by astrocytes, plays an important role in regulating lipid metabolism (Huang and Mahley, 2014; Mahley, 1988). Human *APOE* exists in three isoforms, *APOE2*, *APOE3*, and *APOE4*, which differ from each other by either one or two amino acids at positions 112 and 158 (Huang and Mahley, 2014). *APOE4* has been repeatedly identified as a major genetic risk factor for AD (Corder et al., 1993; Saunders et al., 1993; Tanzi, 2012). APOE4 contributes to vascular and neuronal dysfunction by Aβ-dependent and Aβ-independent pathways (Bell et al., 2012; Casey et al., 2015; Deane et al., 2008; Halliday et al., 2016; Huang and Mahley, 2014; Hudry et al., 2013). APOE isoforms interact with Aβ and differentially regulate its metabolism and transport at the BBB (Bell et al., 2007; Castellano et al., 2011; Deane et al., 2008; DeMattos et al., 2004; Holtzman et al., 2000; Jiang et al., 2008; Tai et al., 2014; Wisniewski and Frangione, 1992; Zlokovic, 2013) (Fig. 9.1). The lipidation of ApoE also affects binding and clearance of Aβ across the BBB (Bell et al., 2007; Deane et al., 2008; Martel et al., 1997). Rapid BBB clearance of Aβ complexes with ApoE2 and ApoE3 is mediated by LRP1, whereas ApoE4-Aβ complexes do not interact with LRP1 and are removed by the much slower, very low-density lipoprotein receptor (VLDLR)-mediated internalization and transcytosis (Fig. 9.1) (Bell et al., 2007; Deane et al., 2008). This slow removal may in turn contribute to Aβ accumulation in the brain.

PICALM: *PICALM* is crucial for endocytotic internalization of cell-surface receptors (Sorkin and von Zastrow, 2009; Treusch et al., 2011) including LRP1 after binding of Aβ to LRP1

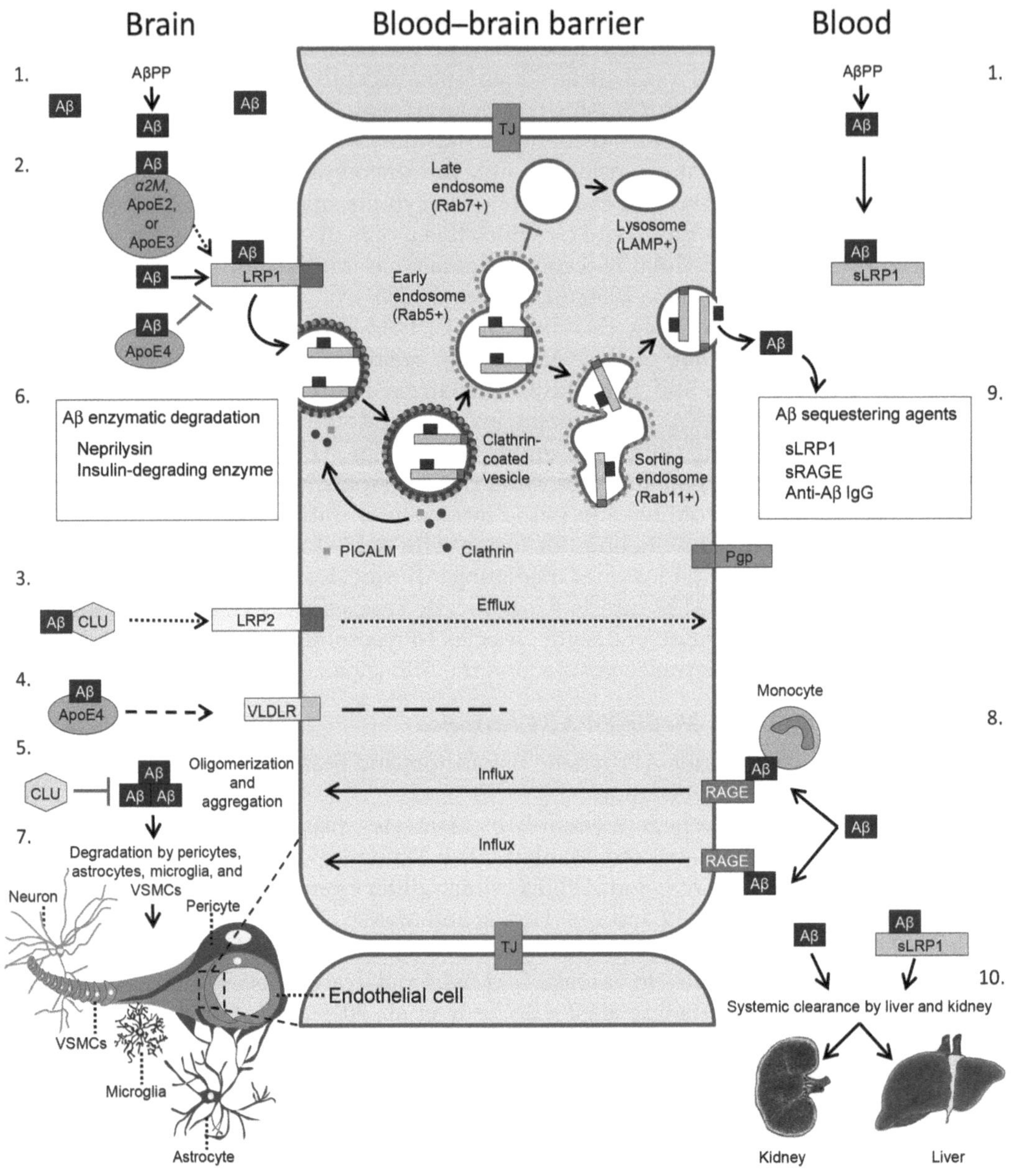

FIGURE 9.1 Aβ transport at the blood–brain barrier (BBB). (1) Aβ is produced from amyloid-β precursor protein (AβPP) in the brain and in the periphery. (2) Brain-derived Aβ is cleared across the BBB primarily by the low-density lipoprotein receptor-related protein 1 (LRP1)-mediated transcytosis. LRP1 binds free Aβ, as well as Aβ bound to apolipoprotein E2 (ApoE2), ApoE3, or α2-macroglobulin but not ApoE4. Aβ binding to LRP1 at the abluminal side of the BBB leads to a rapid PICALM/clathrin-dependent endocytosis of Aβ-LRP1 complexes. In contrast to clathrin that rapidly dissociates from the internalized vesicles, PICALM continues to guide transport of Aβ-LRP1-containing endocytic vesicles for fusion with Rab5-positive early endosomes, and then Rab11-positive sorting endosomes leading to Aβ exocytosis. PICALM directs Aβ away from Rab7 late endosomes and lysosomes. (3) Clusterin (CLU) aids in ▶

(Fig. 9.1). Several genome-wide association studies (GWAS) have suggested that PICALM is a highly validated risk factor for AD (Carrasquillo et al., 2010, 2015; Chen et al., 2012; Harold et al., 2009; Lambert et al., 2009; Liu et al., 2013; Morgen et al., 2014; Tanzi, 2012). All single-nucleotide polymorphisms (SNPs) of *PICALM* identified by GWAS are localized upstream of the coding region of the gene (Carrasquillo et al., 2010, 2015; Chen et al., 2012; Harold et al., 2009; Lambert et al., 2009; Liu et al., 2013; Morgen et al., 2014; Tanzi, 2012).

Recent studies have shown that PICALM levels are reduced in AD brain endothelium, which can potentially lead to Aβ accumulation in the brain by hindering LRP1-mediated Aβ transport (Zlokovic et al., 2010). It has been reported that some AD-associated SNPs influence *PICALM* expression (Raj et al., 2012). Additionally, it has been shown that the *rs3851179 PICALM* variants in which the $rs3851179^{A}$ allele lowers the risk of AD compared to the $rs3851179^{G}$ allele (Lambert et al., 2013) leads to increased expression of PICALM (Zhao et al., 2015). Using inducible pluripotent stem cell (iPSC)-derived endothelial cells, it has been shown that the protective $rs3851179^{A}$ allele increases *PICALM* expression and Aβ clearance across an in vitro model of the human BBB compared to the nonprotective allele, suggesting the vascular link between *PICALM*, Aβ clearance, and AD pathogenesis (Zhao et al., 2015).

MEOX2: Whole genome transcriptional profiling of AD-derived human brain endothelial cells has shown substantial reduction in the expression of mesenchyme homeobox gene 2 (*MEOX2*), a regulator of vascular differentiation and remodeling (Wu et al., 2005). The down-regulation of *MEOX2* is associated with altered angiogenesis, cerebral hypoperfusion, and accumulation of Aβ in the brain (Wu et al., 2005). *MEOX2* expression affects Aβ homeostasis by regulating LRP1 expression. Low levels of *MEOX2*, as studied in in vivo and in vitro BBB models, have been shown to lead to diminished LRP1 levels at the BBB by promoting its proteasomal degradation (Fig. 9.2) (Wu et al., 2005).

GLUT1: The brain receives its supply of glucose across the BBB through the glucose transporter, GLUT1 (encoded by *SLC2A1*). In AD, there is a reduction in GLUT1 levels in cerebral microvessels, particularly in brain endothelium (Mooradian et al., 1997). Also in AD patients, there is a decreased glucose uptake by the brain as measured by positron emission tomography (PET) using 18F-2-fluoro-2-deoxy-D-glucose (FDG) that is associated with brain atrophy (Hunt et al., 2007). Decreased glucose uptake has been observed in individuals with a genetic risk for AD, in those with a positive familial AD history, and in those with mild cognitive deficits who later in life develop AD (Herholz, 2010; Hunt et al., 2007).

Recently it was demonstrated that brain endothelial GLUT1 deficiency accelerates amyloid load and aggravates Aβ accumulation in transgenic AD mice overexpressing human

◀ FIGURE 9.1 the efflux of Aβ42 across the BBB via LRP2. (4) Aβ bound to ApoE4 cannot use rapid LRP1-dependent transcytosis, and is cleared by the very low-density lipoprotein receptor (VLDLR) at a substantially slower rate than free Aβ or Aβ bound to ApoE2 or ApoE3. (5) Clusterin prevents the oligomerization and aggregation of Aβ. (6) Several enzymes, including neprilysin and insulin-degrading enzyme (IDE), contribute to Aβ enzymatic degradation. (7) In addition to Aβ clearance across the BBB, different cell types of the neurovascular unit, for example, pericytes, astrocytes, microglia, and vascular smooth muscle cells [VSMCs]) and neurons contribute to Aβ clearance. (8) The receptor for advanced glycation end products (RAGE) mediates influx of circulating Aβ or Aβ bound to monocytes into the brain across the BBB. (9) Sequestering Aβ in plasma with agents like soluble LRP1 (sLRP1), soluble RAGE (sRAGE), and/or some antibodies against Aβ (anti-Aβ) contribute to Aβ clearance from the brain by creating a concentration gradient favoring Aβ efflux from the brain known as a "peripheral sink" for Aβ. (10) Elimination of circulating Aβ by excretory organs such as liver and kidney leads to its systemic clearance from the body.

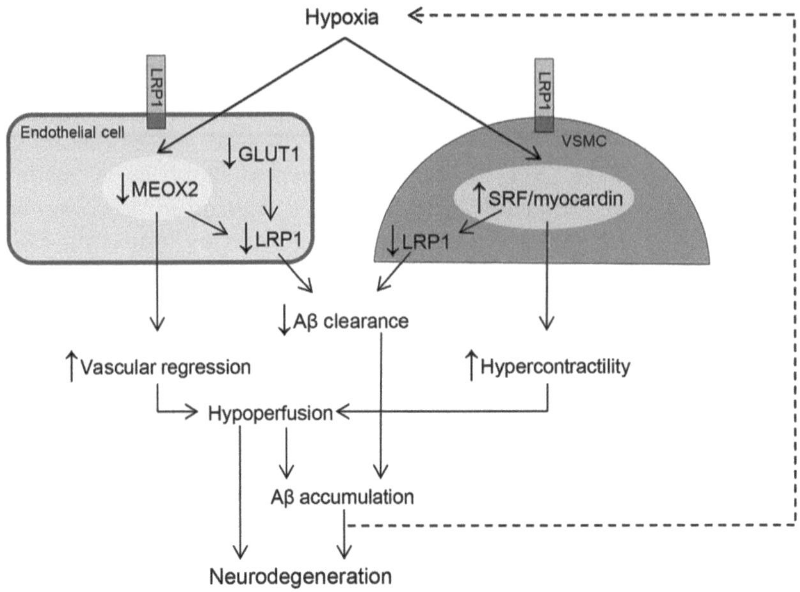

FIGURE 9.2 **Molecular pathways in endothelial cells and vascular smooth muscle cells linking hypoxia to brain hypoperfusion and diminished Aβ clearance and Aβ accumulation in the brain.** *Endothelial cell.* Hypoxia downregulates mesenchyme homeobox gene-2 (MEOX2) expression in brain endothelial cells. Reduced MEOX2 levels in brain endothelium lead to aberrant angiogenesis, vascular regression, and endothelial hypoplasia on the one hand, and accelerated proteasomal degradation of LRP1 on the other, contributing to brain hypoperfusion and decreased LRP1-mediated Aβ clearance from the brain, respectively. Reductions in endothelial glucose transporter GLUT1 expression lead to sterol binding protein-2 (SREBP2)-dependent transcriptional downregulation of LRP1, contributing to decreased LRP1-mediated Aβ clearance. *Vascular smooth muscle cell (VSMC).* Hypoxia increases expression of serum response factor (SRF) and myocardin (MYOCD) in VSMCs, resulting in increased expression of several VSMC contractile proteins and Ca^{2+} homeostasis genes and leading to arteriolar hypercontractility on the one hand, and expression of SREBP2, a major transcriptional suppressor of LRP1, on the other, contributing to brain hypoperfusion and diminished Aβ clearance by VSMCs and leading to deposition of Aβ along the arteriole wall, known as cerebral amyloid angiopathy, respectively. Reduced brain perfusion with blood (hypoperfusion) and diminished Aβ clearance causing Aβ accumulation in the brain can independently and/or synergistically initiate and/or contribute to development of neurodegenerative changes.

APP Swedish mutant, $APP^{sw/0}$ (Winkler et al., 2015). Surprisingly, GLUT1 heterozygous mice ($Slc2a1^{+/-}$) express lower levels of LRP1 at the BBB than control mice ($Slc2a1^{+/+}$), and $Slc2a1^{+/-}APP^{Sw/0}$ mice develop even further reductions in LRP1 BBB levels (Fig. 9.2) (Winkler et al., 2015). The link between GLUT1 and LRP1 was supported by the findings showing that reexpression of *Slc2a1* increases LRP1 levels in brain endothelium, whereas silencing *Slc2a1* decreases LRP1 levels (Winkler et al., 2015). Mechanistically, these studies found that *Slc2a1* deficiency upregulates sterol regulatory element binding protein 2 (*SREBP2*), which is a well-known transcriptional suppressor of LRP1 expression (Llorente-Cortés et al., 2006, 2007). Whether the observed reductions in GLUT1 levels at the BBB as seen in AD cases (Horwood and Davies, 1994; Kalaria and Harik, 1989; Mooradian et al., 1997; Simpson et al., 1994) can also diminish Aβ clearance by downregulating LRP1 in humans in vivo, as they do in an animal model of AD and a human model of the BBB (Winkler et al., 2015), remains to be seen.

SRF/Myocardin: Serum response factor (SRF) and myocardin (MYOCD), a tandem of transcription factors that regulate differentiation of vascular smooth muscle cells (VSMC), are upregulated in VSMCs derived from AD patients (Bell et al., 2009; Chow et al., 2007). Overexpression of SRF/MYOCD initiates a hypercontractile phenotype in cerebral arteries by increasing the expression of SRF/MYOCD-regulated contractile proteins and Ca^{2+} homeostasis genes, leading to cerebral hypoperfusion, diminished neurovascular coupling, and eventually cerebral amyloid angiopathy (CAA) (Fig. 9.2) (Bell et al., 2009; Chow et al., 2007). SRF/MYOCD overexpression in VSMCs downregulates LRP1 levels by transactivation of *SREBP2*, a transcriptional suppressor of LRP1, thus reducing LRP1 expression and diminishing Aβ clearance by VSMCs in small penetrating cerebral arteries (Fig. 9.2) (Bell et al., 2009).

Clusterin

The clusterin gene (*CLU*; also known as *APOJ*) on chromosome 8p21.1 encodes the 75 kDa heterodimeric secreted chaperone glycoprotein, which is the most abundantly expressed apolipoprotein in the brain (Calero et al., 2000). It is a multifunctional protein, involved in clearance of extracellular misfolded proteins (Wyatt et al., 2011), regulation of apoptosis, inflammation, and cancer (Lord and Morgan, 2013; McLaughlin et al., 2000). Clusterin binds different proteinaceous molecules in biological fluids, including Aβ (Calero et al., 2005; Ghiso et al., 1993; Matsubara et al., 1995; Wilson and Easterbrook-Smith, 2000), and prevents their aggregation (Hammad et al., 1997; Magalhães and Saraiva, 2011; Matsubara et al., 1996; Narayan et al., 2012a,b, 2014). Clusterin-Aβ complexes are transported across the BBB and blood–CSF barrier via LRP2 (also known as megalin) (Fig. 9.1) (Bell et al., 2007; Chun et al., 1999; Zlokovic, 2011; Zlokovic et al., 1994, 1996). Aβ42 binding to clusterin significantly accelerates its LRP2-mediated clearance across the BBB (Bell et al., 2007). Prior studies have found that lack of clusterin in transgenic AD mice increases the levels of soluble Aβ in the brain (DeMattos et al., 2004).

The *rs11136000* SNP located in the intron region of the *CLU* gene was identified as one of the risk factors for late-onset AD (Harold et al., 2009; Lambert et al., 2009). The minor protective *rs11136000*^{T} allele reduces the risk of AD compared to the nonprotective allele (Harold et al., 2009; Lambert et al., 2009; Roussotte et al., 2014). Several recent studies confirmed association of *CLU* variants with AD (Bettens et al., 2012, 2015; Carrasquillo et al., 2010; Corneveaux et al., 2010; Jun et al., 2010; Kamboh et al., 2012; Lambert et al., 2013; Liu et al., 2013; Seshadri et al., 2010). The minor AD protective *rs11136000*^{T} allele is associated with increased clusterin expression (Ling et al., 2012), and missense mutations in the β-chain coding region of *CLU* have been demonstrated to reduce clusterin secretion (Bettens et al., 2012, 2015). However, the mechanism and functional impact of *CLU* polymorphisms on Aβ clearance remain elusive (Karch and Goate, 2015; Tanzi, 2012).

VLDLR

Very low-density lipoprotein receptor (VLDLR) has a substantially slower endocytotic rate compared to LRP1 (Li et al., 2001) (Fig. 9.1). Importantly, Aβ clearance at the BBB is influenced in an ApoE isoform-specific manner where ApoE4-Aβ complexes are redirected from LRP1 to the slower VLDLR-mediated transport, thereby reducing the Aβ clearance rate (Deane et al., 2008).

Aβ UPTAKE BY RAGE

RAGE is a cell-surface receptor of the immunoglobulin (IgG) superfamily (Neeper et al., 1992; Schmidt, 2015). It transports Aβ into the brain and accelerates Aβ pathology in an AD mouse model (Deane et al., 2003, 2012) (Fig. 9.1). In the brain, RAGE is expressed normally at relatively low levels in endothelial cells, VSMCs, pericytes, glial cells, and neurons (Sturchler et al., 2008; Yan et al., 1996, 2010). RAGE contains one V-type IgG domain and two constant (C)-type ligand-binding domains, and a short, highly charged 43-amino-acid cytoplasmic tail that is essential for RAGE-mediated signaling (Yan et al., 2010). RAGE binds multiple and structurally diverse ligands, including Aβ, advanced glycation end products (AGEs), the products of nonenzymatically glycated proteins or lipids, amphoterin, S100B/calgranulins, advanced oxidation protein products, and high-mobility group box 1 (Goldin et al., 2006; Neeper et al., 1992; Schmidt, 2015; Yan et al., 2010). The X-ray crystallographic, biochemical, and NMR data suggest that RAGE–ligand binding is driven largely by electrostatic interaction between the positively charged surface of the ectodomain and negatively charged ligands (Fritz, 2011; Koch et al., 2010; Park et al., 2010). RAGE binds monomeric and oligomeric Aβ via its V domain and aggregated Aβ via its C1 domain (Deane et al., 2012; Sturchler et al., 2008; Yan et al., 1996, 2010) and mediates Aβ-induced neurotoxicity directly by causing oxidant stress and indirectly by activating microglia (Yan et al., 1996). Intraneuronal Aβ transport via RAGE leads to mitochondrial dysfunction (Takuma et al., 2009). Targeted expression of RAGE in neurons in *APP* transgenic mice accelerates cognitive decline and Aβ-induced neuronal perturbation (Arancio et al., 2004).

RAGE mediates transport of circulating Aβ from the luminal side of endothelial cells across the BBB into the brain (Deane et al., 2003, 2012; Mackic et al., 1998) and also contributes to monocyte trafficking across the BBB (Giri et al., 2000) (Fig. 9.1). Additionally, RAGE-Aβ interaction at the BBB initiates NF-κB-dependent endothelial cell activation resulting in neuroinflammatory response and generation of endothelin-1, which causes suppression of cerebral blood flow (CBF) (Deane et al., 2003). RAGE expression is increased in endothelium and neurons in an Aβ-rich and/or AGE-rich environment (Yan et al., 1995), which exacerbates RAGE-mediated pathological responses. Therefore, blocking RAGE or reducing its endothelial expression may potentially control Aβ-mediated toxicity in AD.

Factors Promoting RAGE

RAGE expression is increased in brain microvascular endothelial cells in AD animal models and AD postmortem brain tissue (Bierhaus et al., 2005; Bucciarelli et al., 2002; Deane et al., 2003; Donahue et al., 2006; Schmidt et al., 2009; Yan et al., 1995, 1996). Experimental studies in rats showed that microvessel RAGE expression gradually increases with normal aging from 9 to 36 months of age (Silverberg et al., 2010). RAGE–ligand interaction in chronic diseases such as diabetes, peripheral inflammation, and AD leads to increased cellular stress and vascular dysfunction (Deane et al., 2003, 2012; Stern et al., 2002; Yan et al., 2010; Zlokovic, 2011).

sRAGE

The soluble extracellular domain of RAGE (sRAGE) circulates in plasma and may act as a decoy receptor sequestering circulating RAGE ligands, including Aβ, and thereby preventing their interaction with cell-surface RAGE (Srikanth et al., 2011) (Fig. 9.1). Levels of plasma sRAGE are significantly reduced in AD patients compared to cognitively normal controls (Emanuele et al., 2005). Experimental studies found that treating young AD mice with sRAGE inhibited RAGE-dependent BBB influx of Aβ and its accumulation in brain parenchyma (Deane et al., 2003). Therefore, sRAGE has been considered as a potential therapeutic target for AD (Geroldi et al., 2006).

PERIPHERAL SINK AND SYSTEMIC CLEARANCE OF Aβ

Soluble LRP1 (sLRP1) released into the extracellular fluid after cleavage of the LRP1 β-chain has been found to be a major peripheral Aβ binding protein (Sagare et al., 2007) (Fig. 9.1). Several proteases are involved in the shedding of LRP1, including β-secretase 1 (BACE-1), ADAM (a disintegrin and metalloprotease) 10, ADAM12, ADAM17, membrane type-1 matrix metalloprotease, and tissue plasminogen activator (An et al., 2008; Liu et al., 2009b; Polavarapu et al., 2007; Rozanov et al., 2004; Selvais et al., 2011; von Arnim et al., 2005). The sLRP1 circulates freely in plasma (Quinn et al., 1997) and sequesters unbound Aβ in the bloodstream (Sagare et al., 2007, 2011).

In human plasma, sLRP1 normally sequesters >70% of circulating Aβ (Sagare et al., 2007, 2011). In AD patients, the levels of plasma sLRP1 are reduced (Liang et al., 2013; Sagare et al., 2007) and sLRP1-Aβ binding is diminished due to sLRP1 oxidation (Sagare et al., 2007, 2011). One cross-sectional study found that increased levels of oxidized sLRP1 in patients with mild cognitive impairment who progressed to AD were associated with a significant increase in free Aβ40 and Aβ42 levels in plasma (Sagare et al., 2011). The free Aβ in plasma can reenter the brain via brain endothelial RAGE, which is upregulated in AD (Deane et al., 2003; Donahue et al., 2006; Mackic et al., 2002; Miller et al., 2008; Ujiie et al., 2003). These studies suggest that sLRP1 in plasma might likely provide an endogenous "peripheral sink" for plasma Aβ in healthy individuals to drive Aβ removal from the brain similarly to what has been shown in animal models (Sagare et al., 2007).

LRP1 is highly expressed in the liver and mediates a rapid clearance of Aβ from the systemic circulation (Fig. 9.1) (Tamaki et al., 2006, 2007). Moreover, reduced expression of LRP1 in the liver in aged rats results in decreased peripheral clearance of Aβ (Tamaki et al., 2006, 2007). Others studies also suggested that the liver can regulate brain Aβ levels (Sagare et al., 2011; Sutcliffe et al., 2011). In addition to the liver, Aβ has been detected in human urine, suggesting clearance by the kidney (Ghiso et al., 1997). Interestingly, patients with a chronic kidney disease have increased serum Aβ levels (Liu et al., 2015). Recent clinical studies have shown that dialysis effectively removes Aβ from the circulation (Kitaguchi et al., 2011, 2015) and found that patients on hemodialysis have reduced plasma Aβ42 levels that positively correlate with cognitive improvement (Kato et al., 2012). Altogether, these studies support that the "peripheral sink" can potentially lower brain Aβ levels and possibly improve cognition.

Aβ DEGRADATION

Aβ can be degraded by neprilysin and neprilysin-like peptidases (Farris et al., 2007; Guan et al., 2009; Liu et al., 2009a) and insulin-degrading enzyme (Fig. 9.1) (Morelli et al., 2005; Qiu and Folstein, 2006). Other Aβ-degrading enzymes include endothelin converting enzyme-1 and -2 (Pacheco-Quinto and Eckman, 2013; Palmer et al., 2009), angiotensin converting enzyme (Hemming and Selkoe, 2005), acylpeptide hydrolase (Yamin et al., 2009), presequence peptidase (Malito et al., 2008), cathepsin (Cat) B (Mueller-Steiner et al., 2006), CatD (Tian et al., 2014), plasmin 3 (Jacobsen et al., 2008), matrix metalloproteinases (Hernandez-Guillamon et al., 2015), and tissue plasminogen activator (Oh et al., 2014).

Many of the cellular components of the neurovascular unit participate in Aβ clearance, including astrocytes, microglia, pericytes, and neurons (Fig. 9.1). For example, extracellular Aβ aggregates can be phagocytozed and/or taken up by microglia (Wyss-Coray et al., 2001), astrocytes (Koistinaho et al., 2004), pericytes (Sagare et al., 2013b), and VSMCs (Kanekiyo et al., 2012). Intracellular Aβ can be degraded by the ubiquitin-proteosome pathway, the autophagy-lysosome pathway, and the endosome-lysosome pathway (Tarasoff-Conway et al., 2015). Furthermore, Aβ is degraded in neurons via the ubiquitin-proteosome pathway (Tarasoff-Conway et al., 2015).

REGULATION AND RESTORATION OF BBB CLEARANCE

Upregulation of LRP1

Increasing LRP1 levels in endothelial cells, pericytes, and VSMCs may increase Aβ clearance and slow down development of Aβ-dependent pathologies. Interestingly, diet and exercise have been demonstrated to increase LRP1 levels in the brain microvessels. For example, oleocanthal, a component of extra-virgin olive oil, was found to increase LRP1 levels at the BBB in AD transgenic mice and decrease Aβ load in hippocampal parenchyma and microvessels (Qosa et al., 2015). Additionally, physical activity increases BBB LRP1 levels in brain microvessels and promotes Aβ clearance (Herring et al., 2008; Prince et al., 2014). Also, treatment with *Withania somnifera* root extract increased LRP1 expression in brain microvessels and liver, as well as circulating sLRP1 levels in plasma, resulting in reduced brain Aβ pathology in AD transgenic mice (Sehgal et al., 2012). Future studies should examine novel therapeutic drugs and/or gene therapy vectors to reestablish LRP1 levels in endothelial cells and pericytes at the BBB. In addition to recovering LRP1 in cerebral microvessels, restoration or selective enhancement of LRP1 by gene therapy in the liver may function to increase "peripheral sink" and the concentration gradient driving Aβ out of the brain (Zlokovic et al., 2010).

Upregulation of PICALM

PICALM controls several transcytosis steps mediating Aβ clearance across the BBB, and PICALM levels are reduced in AD-derived endothelial cells (Zhao et al., 2015). To date, there are no known drugs or gene therapy vectors that increase PICALM expression levels. Future studies are needed to determine the benefit of increasing PICALM levels in AD.

sLRP1 Therapy

The receptor sLRP1 and its wild-type recombinant ligand-binding domain cluster IV (WT-LRPIV) have been reported to effectively bind free Aβ in plasma of AD patients in vitro and AD mice in vivo, resulting in reduced Aβ brain pathology in mice (Fig. 9.1) (Sagare et al., 2007). A new recombinant mutant LRPIV-D3674G cluster was recently generated with improved affinity for Aβ compared with WT-LRPIV (Sagare et al., 2013a). These data show that LRPIV-D3674G binds other known ligands of LRP1 with less affinity and clears Aβ from the brain in AD mice (Sagare et al., 2013a).

Inhibition of RAGE

Two low-molecular-weight, high-affinity RAGE inhibitors, FPS2 and FPS-ZM1, were recently developed (Deane et al., 2012). FPS-ZM1, a novel multimodal RAGE blocker which crosses the BBB, reduced influx of Aβ into the brain, improved blood-flow responses, downregulated β-secretase activity, decreased amyloid load, suppressed neuroinflammatory responses, and reduced behavioral deficits in a mouse model of AD (Deane et al., 2012). In a rodent model of hypertension, RAGE inhibition by FPS-ZM1 significantly reduced hypertension-induced AD pathology as shown by improved cognitive performance and reduced parenchymal Aβ deposition (Carnevale et al., 2012). RAGE inhibitors are currently being examined in a phase 3 clinical trial in mild-to-moderate AD (NCT02080364) (Burstein et al., 2014; Galasko et al., 2014).

Downregulation of RAGE

RAGE expression could be controlled by diet and exercise. For example, resveratrol has been shown to reduce RAGE expression in vascular cells (Jing et al., 2010). Glucagon-like peptide 1 (GLP-1) is an incretin and gut hormone secreted by L cells in the intestine in response to food intake (Holst, 2007). GLP-1 and GLP-1 analogs inhibit RAGE expression and exhibit antiinflammatory properties in cultured endothelial cells (Shiraki et al., 2012). Additionally, physical activity was found to downregulate RAGE expression at the BBB (Herring et al., 2008).

Gammagard

Intravenous immunoglobulins (IVIG, gammagard) are prepared using pooled plasma from a large number of healthy donors (Kazatchkine and Kaveri, 2001; Loeffler, 2014). Although recent clinical trials have shown beneficial effects of IVIG treatment in patients with mild AD (Relkin et al., 2009; Shayan et al., 2012), the mechanisms through which IVIG produces its therapeutic benefits are not completely understood. A recent study demonstrated the presence of natural human anti-Aβ IgG in Baxter's IVIG preparation which binds with high affinity specifically to synthetic Aβ dimers and protofibrils but not to synthetic Aβ monomers or fragments (Welzel et al., 2012). Passive immunization has been proposed to sequester Aβ and markedly reduce brain Aβ levels (Wolfe, 2002) (see Chapter 7). Given the limited success with anti-Aβ monoclonal antibodies solanezumab and bapineuzumab in recent AD clinical trials in delaying the progression of the disease (Doody et al., 2014; Salloway et al., 2014), it is probably essential to develop antibodies which target diverse Aβ conformers to treat AD (Welzel et al., 2012). Earlier studies demonstrated the presence of neuroprotective natural antibodies, not only to toxic Aβ species but also to other non-Aβ amyloidogenic peptides in plasma of AD patients and healthy age-matched controls (Britschgi et al., 2009; Szabo et al., 2010). Apart from Aβ conformer-specific IgG autoantibodies, Baxter's IVIG preparation has also been shown to contain sLRP1 and antibodies against RAGE (anti-RAGE IgG) which can block Aβ uptake into the brain (Weber et al., 2009). In addition, presence of an anti-RAGE antibody may also explain the antiinflammatory activity of IVIG (Nimmerjahn and Ravetch, 2008). The presence of anti-RAGE and sLRP1 in gammagard could also contribute in lowering brain Aβ levels and inflammation in AD (Deane et al., 2003, 2012; Sagare et al., 2007).

Young Plasma

Recent studies found that plasma from young mice may be beneficial to cognition, whereas plasma from aged mice may be detrimental (Villeda et al., 2014). These intriguing findings have prompted discussion about the possible components in young plasma that provide this beneficial effect (Jawaid et al., 2015). One beneficial component proposed to be in young plasma is that it could replenish sLRP1 levels and restore the "peripheral sink" for Aβ in old mice (Jawaid et al., 2015).

CONCLUSIONS

There is growing appreciation that AD is a multifactorial disease that has vascular contributions. This has led to the neurovascular hypothesis of AD, which states that damage to the neurovasculature can contribute to the onset and progression of cognitive decline and the pathogenic events leading to dementia. Here, we reviewed vascular disruption to BBB transporters in AD, including LRP1, involved in Aβ transvascular clearance out of the brain, and RAGE, involved in Aβ influx into the brain. These receptors are converging points between vascular damage and Aβ pathology and thus represent potentially important therapeutic targets to control β-amyloidosis in AD. To date, no drugs are available to halt or reverse the progression of AD. Therefore, research must move forward at a rapid pace to develop therapies to restore and/or maintain healthy brain vasculature.

Some important scientific directions to be pursued by future studies will be to find out (1) methodologies and/or drugs to safely upregulate LRP1 and PICALM in the brain, (2) the benefit of recombinant LRPIV-D3674 therapy in AD patients, (3) the benefit of RAGE inhibitors in AD patients, (4) IVIG preparations with concentrated individual components (eg, sLRP1 and sRAGE) to restore the Aβ transport at the BBB, and (5) the identity of the beneficial factors in young plasma. Potential methodologies to increase LRP1 and PICALM levels in brain endothelial cells include small molecules and gene therapy. Furthermore, lifestyles, including diet and exercise, have been implicated in regulation of LRP1 and RAGE expression and should be further explored. When considering LRP1 and RAGE as therapeutic targets, it is important to also consider an individualized, multifaceted approach tailored to the patient. The development of biomarkers that clearly indicate the disease pathogenesis and progression is crucial for designing patient-specific AD treatments (Sweeney et al., 2015).

Acknowledgments

The work of B.V.Z. is supported by the National Institutes of Health grants R01AG023084, R01NS090904, R01NS034467, R01AG039452 and the Cure for Alzheimer's Fund.

References

An J, Zhang C, Polavarapu R, Zhang X, Zhang X, Yepes M: Tissue-type plasminogen activator and the low-density lipoprotein receptor-related protein induce Akt phosphorylation in the ischemic brain, *Blood* 112:2787–2794, 2008.

Arancio O, Zhang HP, Chen X, Lin C, Trinchese F, Puzzo D, et al: RAGE potentiates Abeta-induced perturbation of neuronal function in transgenic mice, *EMBO J* 23:4096–4105, 2004.

Bading JR, Yamada S, Mackic JB, Kirkman L, Miller C, Calero M, et al: Brain clearance of Alzheimer's amyloid-beta40 in the squirrel monkey: a SPECT study in a primate model of cerebral amyloid angiopathy, *J Drug Target* 10:359–368, 2002.

Bateman RJ, Aisen PS, De Strooper B, Fox NC, Lemere CA, Ringman JM, et al: Autosomal-dominant Alzheimer's disease: a review and proposal for the prevention of Alzheimer's disease, *Alzheimers Res Ther* 3:1, 2011.

Bell RD, Sagare AP, Friedman AE, Bedi GS, Holtzman DM, Deane R, et al: Transport pathways for clearance of human Alzheimer's amyloid beta-peptide and apolipoproteins E and J in the mouse central nervous system, *J Cereb Blood Flow Metab* 27:909–918, 2007.

Bell RD, Deane R, Chow N, Long X, Sagare A, Singh I, et al: SRF and myocardin regulate LRP-mediated amyloid-beta clearance in brain vascular cells, *Nat Cell Biol* 11:143–153, 2009.

Bell RD, Winkler EA, Singh I, Sagare AP, Deane R, Wu Z, et al: Apolipoprotein E controls cerebrovascular integrity via cyclophilin A, *Nature* 485:512–516, 2012.

Bettens K, Brouwers N, Engelborghs S, Lambert J-C, Rogaeva E, Vandenberghe R, et al: Both common variations and rare non-synonymous substitutions and small insertion/deletions in CLU are associated with increased Alzheimer risk, *Mol Neurodegener* 7:3, 2012.

Bettens K, Vermeulen S, Van Cauwenberghe C, Heeman B, Asselbergh B, Robberecht C, et al: Reduced secreted clusterin as a mechanism for Alzheimer-associated CLU mutations, *Mol Neurodegener* 10:30, 2015.

Bierhaus A, Humpert PM, Stern DM, Arnold B, Nawroth PP: Advanced glycation end product receptor-mediated cellular dysfunction, *Ann NY Acad Sci* 1043:676–680, 2005.

Britschgi M, Olin CE, Johns HT, Takeda-Uchimura Y, LeMieux MC, Rufibach K, et al: Neuroprotective natural antibodies to assemblies of amyloidogenic peptides decrease with normal aging and advancing Alzheimer's disease, *Proc Natl Acad Sci USA* 106:12145–12150, 2009.

Bucciarelli LG, Wendt T, Rong L, Lalla E, Hofmann MA, Goova MT, et al: RAGE is a multiligand receptor of the immunoglobulin superfamily: implications for homeostasis and chronic disease, *Cell Mol Life Sci* 59:1117–1128, 2002.

Burstein AH, Grimes I, Galasko DR, Aisen PS, Sabbagh M, Mjalli AM: Effect of TTP488 in patients with mild to moderate Alzheimer's disease, *BMC Neurol* 14:12, 2014.

Calero M, Rostagno A, Matsubara E, Zlokovic B, Frangione B, Ghiso J: Apolipoprotein J (clusterin) and Alzheimer's disease, *Microsc Res Tech* 50:305–315, 2000.

Calero M, Rostagno A, Frangione B, Ghiso J: Clusterin and Alzheimer's disease, *Subcell Biochem* 38:273–298, 2005.

Carnevale D, Mascio G, D'Andrea I, Fardella V, Bell RD, Branchi I, et al: Hypertension induces brain β-amyloid accumulation, cognitive impairment, and memory deterioration through activation of receptor for advanced glycation end products in brain vasculature, *Hypertension* 60:188–197, 2012.

Carrasquillo MM, Belbin O, Hunter TA, Ma L, Bisceglio GD, Zou F, et al: Replication of CLU, CR1, and PICALM associations with Alzheimer disease, *Arch Neurol* 67:961–964, 2010.

Carrasquillo MM, Crook JE, Pedraza O, Thomas CS, Pankratz VS, Allen M, et al: Late-onset Alzheimer's risk variants in memory decline, incident mild cognitive impairment, and Alzheimer's disease, *Neurobiol Aging* 36:60–67, 2015.

Casey CS, Atagi Y, Yamazaki Y, Shinohara M, Tachibana M, Fu Y, et al: Apolipoprotein E inhibits cerebrovascular pericyte mobility through a RhoA-mediated pathway, *J Biol Chem* 290:14208–14217, 2015.

Castellano JM, Kim J, Stewart FR, Jiang H, DeMattos RB, Patterson BW, et al: Human apoE isoforms differentially regulate brain amyloid-β peptide clearance, *Sci Transl Med* 3:89ra57, 2011.

Chen LH, Kao PYP, Fan YH, Ho DTY, Chan CSY, Yik PY, et al: Polymorphisms of CR1 CLU and PICALM confer susceptibility of Alzheimer's disease in a southern Chinese population, *Neurobiol Aging* 33:210, 2012, e1–e7.

Chow N, Bell RD, Deane R, Streb JW, Chen J, Brooks A, et al: Serum response factor and myocardin mediate arterial hypercontractility and cerebral blood flow dysregulation in Alzheimer's phenotype, *Proc Natl Acad Sci USA* 104:823–828, 2007.

Chun JT, Wang L, Pasinetti GM, Finch CE, Zlokovic BV: Glycoprotein 330/megalin (LRP-2) has low prevalence as mRNA and protein in brain microvessels and choroid plexus, *Exp Neurol* 157:194–201, 1999.

Corder EH, Saunders AM, Strittmatter WJ, Schmechel DE, Gaskell PC, Small GW, et al: Gene dose of apolipoprotein E type 4 allele and the risk of Alzheimer's disease in late onset families, *Science* 261:921–923, 1993.

Corneveaux JJ, Myers AJ, Allen AN, Pruzin JJ, Ramirez M, Engel A, et al: Association of CR1 CLU and PICALM with Alzheimer's disease in a cohort of clinically characterized and neuropathologically verified individuals, *Hum Mol Genet* 19:3295–3301, 2010.

Daneman R, Prat A: The blood–brain barrier, *Cold Spring Harb Perspect Biol* 7:a020412, 2015.

Deane R, Zlokovic BV: Role of the blood–brain barrier in the pathogenesis of Alzheimer's disease, *Curr Alzheimer Res* 4:191–197, 2007.

Deane R, Du Yan S, Submamaryan RK, LaRue B, Jovanovic S, Hogg E, et al: RAGE mediates amyloid-beta peptide transport across the blood–brain barrier and accumulation in brain, *Nat Med* 9:907–913, 2003.

Deane R, Wu Z, Sagare A, Davis J, Du Yan S, Hamm K, et al: LRP/amyloid beta-peptide interaction mediates differential brain efflux of Abeta isoforms, *Neuron* 43:333–344, 2004.

Deane R, Sagare A, Hamm K, Parisi M, Lane S, Finn MB, et al: ApoE isoform-specific disruption of amyloid beta peptide clearance from mouse brain, *J Clin Invest* 118:4002–4013, 2008.

Deane R, Singh I, Sagare AP, Bell RD, Ross NT, LaRue B, et al: A multimodal RAGE-specific inhibitor reduces amyloid β-mediated brain disorder in a mouse model of Alzheimer disease, *J Clin Invest* 122:1377–1392, 2012.

DeMattos RB, Cirrito JR, Parsadanian M, May PC, O'Dell MA, Taylor JW, et al: ApoE and clusterin cooperatively suppress Abeta levels and deposition: evidence that ApoE regulates extracellular Abeta metabolism in vivo, *Neuron* 41:193–202, 2004.

Donahue JE, Flaherty SL, Johanson CE, Duncan JA, Silverberg GD, Miller MC, et al: RAGE, LRP-1, and amyloid-beta protein in Alzheimer's disease, *Acta Neuropathol* 112:405–415, 2006.

Doody RS, Thomas RG, Farlow M, Iwatsubo T, Vellas B, Joffe S, et al: Phase 3 trials of solanezumab for mild-to-moderate Alzheimer's disease, *N Engl J Med* 370:311–321, 2014.

Emanuele E, D'Angelo A, Tomaino C, Binetti G, Ghidoni R, Politi P, et al: Circulating levels of soluble receptor for advanced glycation end products in Alzheimer disease and vascular dementia, *Arch Neurol* 62:1734–1736, 2005.

Emonard H, Théret L, Bennasroune AH, Dedieu S: Regulation of LRP-1 expression: make the point, *Pathol Biol* 62:84–90, 2014.

Farris W, Schütz SG, Cirrito JR, Shankar GM, Sun X, George A, et al: Loss of neprilysin function promotes amyloid plaque formation and causes cerebral amyloid angiopathy, *Am J Pathol* 171:241–251, 2007.

Fritz G: RAGE: a single receptor fits multiple ligands, *Trends Biochem Sci* 36:625–632, 2011.

Galasko D, Bell J, Mancuso JY, Kupiec JW, Sabbagh MN, van Dyck C, et al: Clinical trial of an inhibitor of RAGE-Aβ interactions in Alzheimer disease, *Neurology* 82:1536–1542, 2014.

Geroldi D, Falcone C, Emanuele E: Soluble receptor for advanced glycation end products: from disease marker to potential therapeutic target, *Curr Med Chem* 13:1971–1978, 2006.

Ghiso J, Matsubara E, Koudinov A, Choi-Miura NH, Tomita M, Wisniewski T, et al: The cerebrospinal-fluid soluble form of Alzheimer's amyloid beta is complexed to SP-40,40 (apolipoprotein J), an inhibitor of the complement membrane-attack complex, *Biochem J* 293(Pt 1):27–30, 1993.

Ghiso J, Calero M, Matsubara E, Governale S, Chuba J, Beavis R, et al: Alzheimer's soluble amyloid beta is a normal component of human urine, *FEBS Lett* 408:105–108, 1997.

Giri R, Shen Y, Stins M, Du Yan S, Schmidt AM, Stern D, et al: Beta-amyloid-induced migration of monocytes across human brain endothelial cells involves RAGE and PECAM-1, *Am J Physiol Cell Physiol* 279:C1772–C1781, 2000.

Goldin A, Beckman JA, Schmidt AM, Creager MA: Advanced glycation end products: sparking the development of diabetic vascular injury, *Circulation* 114:597–605, 2006.

Guan H, Liu Y, Daily A, Police S, Kim M-H, Oddo S, et al: Peripherally expressed neprilysin reduces brain amyloid burden: a novel approach for treating Alzheimer's disease, *J Neurosci Res* 87:1462–1473, 2009.

Haass C, Kaether C, Thinakaran G, Sisodia S: Trafficking and proteolytic processing of APP, *Cold Spring Harb Perspect Med* 2:205–229, 2012.

Halliday MR, Rege SV, Ma Q, Zhao Z, Miller CA, Winkler EA, et al: Accelerated pericyte degeneration and blood–brain barrier breakdown in apolipoprotein E4 carriers with Alzheimer's disease, *J Cereb Blood Flow Metab* 36:216–227, 2016.

Hammad SM, Ranganathan S, Loukinova E, Twal WO, Argraves WS: Interaction of apolipoprotein J-amyloid beta-peptide complex with low density lipoprotein receptor-related protein-2/megalin A mechanism to prevent pathological accumulation of amyloid beta-peptide, *J Biol Chem* 272:18644–18649, 1997.

Harold D, Abraham R, Hollingworth P, Sims R, Gerrish A, Hamshere ML, et al: Genome-wide association study identifies variants at CLU and PICALM associated with Alzheimer's disease, *Nat Genet* 41:1088–1093, 2009.

Hemming ML, Selkoe DJ: Amyloid beta-protein is degraded by cellular angiotensin-converting enzyme (ACE) and elevated by an ACE inhibitor, *J Biol Chem* 280:37644–37650, 2005.

Herholz K: Cerebral glucose metabolism in preclinical and prodromal Alzheimer's disease, *Expert Rev Neurother* 10:1667–1673, 2010.

Hernandez-Guillamon M, Mawhirt S, Blais S, Montaner J, Neubert TA, Rostagno A, et al: Sequential amyloid-β degradation by the matrix metalloproteases MMP-2 and MMP-9, *J Biol Chem* 290:15078–15091, 2015.

Herring A, Yasin H, Ambrée O, Sachser N, Paulus W, Keyvani K: Environmental enrichment counteracts Alzheimer's neurovascular dysfunction in TgCRND8 mice, *Brain Pathol* 18:32–39, 2008.

Holst JJ: The physiology of glucagon-like peptide 1, *Physiol Rev* 87:1409–1439, 2007.

Holtzman DM, Bales KR, Tenkova T, Fagan AM, Parsadanian M, Sartorius LJ, et al: Apolipoprotein E isoform-dependent amyloid deposition and neuritic degeneration in a mouse model of Alzheimer's disease, *Proc Natl Acad Sci USA* 97:2892–2897, 2000.

Horwood N, Davies DC: Immunolabelling of hippocampal microvessel glucose transporter protein is reduced in Alzheimer's disease, *Virchows Arch Int J Pathol* 425:69–72, 1994.

Huang Y, Mahley RW: Apolipoprotein E: structure and function in lipid metabolism, neurobiology, and Alzheimer's diseases, *Neurobiol Dis* 72(Pt A):3–12, 2014.

Hudry E, Dashkoff J, Roe AD, Takeda S, Koffie RM, Hashimoto T, et al: Gene transfer of human ApoE isoforms results in differential modulation of amyloid deposition and neurotoxicity in mouse brain, *Sci Transl Med* 5:212ra161, 2013.

Hunt A, Schönknecht P, Henze M, Seidl U, Haberkorn U, Schröder J: Reduced cerebral glucose metabolism in patients at risk for Alzheimer's disease, *Psychiatr Res* 155:147–154, 2007.

Jacobsen JS, Comery TA, Martone RL, Elokdah H, Crandall DL, Oganesian A, et al: Enhanced clearance of Abeta in brain by sustaining the plasmin proteolysis cascade, *Proc Natl Acad Sci USA* 105:8754–8759, 2008.

Jawaid A, Kremer EA, Piatek A, Schulz PE: Improvement of age-related memory impairment with infusion of young plasma: a role for the peripheral amyloid sink? *J Am Geriatr Soc* 63:419–420, 2015.

Jiang Q, Lee CYD, Mandrekar S, Wilkinson B, Cramer P, Zelcer N, et al: ApoE promotes the proteolytic degradation of Abeta, *Neuron* 58:681–693, 2008.

Jing Y-H, Chen K-H, Yang S-H, Kuo P-C, Chen J-K: Resveratrol ameliorates vasculopathy in STZ-induced diabetic rats: role of AGE-RAGE signalling, *Diabetes Metab Res Rev* 26:212–222, 2010.

Jun G, Naj AC, Beecham GW, Wang L-S, Buros J, Gallins PJ, et al: Meta-analysis confirms CR1, CLU, and PICALM as Alzheimer disease risk loci and reveals interactions with APOE genotypes, *Arch Neurol* 67:1473–1484, 2010.

Kalaria RN, Harik SI: Reduced glucose transporter at the blood–brain barrier and in cerebral cortex in Alzheimer disease, *J Neurochem* 53:1083–1088, 1989.

Kamboh MI, Minster RL, Demirci FY, Ganguli M, Dekosky ST, Lopez OL, et al: Association of CLU and PICALM variants with Alzheimer's disease, *Neurobiol Aging* 33:518–521, 2012.

Kanekiyo T, Bu G: The low-density lipoprotein receptor-related protein 1 and amyloid-β clearance in Alzheimer's disease, *Front Aging Neurosci* 6:93, 2014.

Kanekiyo T, Liu C-C, Shinohara M, Li J, Bu G: LRP1 in brain vascular smooth muscle cells mediates local clearance of Alzheimer's amyloid-β, *J Neurosci* 32:16458–16465, 2012.

Karch CM, Goate AM: Alzheimer's disease risk genes and mechanisms of disease pathogenesis, *Biol Psychiatr* 77:43–51, 2015.

Kato M, Kawaguchi K, Nakai S, Murakami K, Hori H, Ohashi A, et al: Potential therapeutic system for Alzheimer's disease: removal of blood Aβs by hemodialyzers and its effect on the cognitive functions of renal-failure patients, *J Neural Transm* 1996(119):1533–1544, 2012.

Kazatchkine MD, Kaveri SV: Immunomodulation of autoimmune and inflammatory diseases with intravenous immune globulin, *N Engl J Med* 345:747–755, 2001.

Kitaguchi N, Kawaguchi K, Nakai S, Murakami K, Ito S, Hoshino H, et al: Reduction of Alzheimer's disease amyloid-β in plasma by hemodialysis and its relation to cognitive functions, *Blood Purif* 32:57–62, 2011.

Kitaguchi N, Hasegawa M, Ito S, Kawaguchi K, Hiki Y, Nakai S, et al: A prospective study on blood Aβ levels and the cognitive function of patients with hemodialysis: a potential therapeutic strategy for Alzheimer's disease, *J Neural Transm* 122:1593–1607, 2015.

Koch M, Chitayat S, Dattilo BM, Schiefner A, Diez J, Chazin WJ, et al: Structural basis for ligand recognition and activation of RAGE, *Structure* 18:1342–1352, 2010, 1993.

Koistinaho M, Lin S, Wu X, Esterman M, Koger D, Hanson J, et al: Apolipoprotein E promotes astrocyte colocalization and degradation of deposited amyloid-beta peptides, *Nat Med* 10:719–726, 2004.

Lambert J-C, Heath S, Even G, Campion D, Sleegers K, Hiltunen M, et al: Genome-wide association study identifies variants at CLU and CR1 associated with Alzheimer's disease, *Nat Genet* 41:1094–1099, 2009.

Lambert JC, Ibrahim-Verbaas CA, Harold D, Naj AC, Sims R, Bellenguez C, et al: Meta-analysis of 74,046 individuals identifies 11 new susceptibility loci for Alzheimer's disease, *Nat Genet* 45:1452–1458, 2013.

Li Y, Lu W, Marzolo MP, Bu G: Differential functions of members of the low density lipoprotein receptor family suggested by their distinct endocytosis rates, *J Biol Chem* 276:18000–18006, 2001.

Liang F, Jia J, Wang S, Qin W, Liu G: Decreased plasma levels of soluble low density lipoprotein receptor-related protein-1 (sLRP) and the soluble form of the receptor for advanced glycation end products (sRAGE) in the clinical diagnosis of Alzheimer's disease, *J Clin Neurosci* 20:357–361, 2013.

Lillis AP, Van Duyn LB, Murphy-Ullrich JE, Strickland DK: LDL receptor-related protein 1 unique tissue-specific functions revealed by selective gene knockout studies, *Physiol Rev* 88:887–918, 2008.

Ling I-F, Bhongsatiern J, Simpson JF, Fardo DW, Estus S: Genetics of clusterin isoform expression and Alzheimer's disease risk, *PLoS One* 7:e33923, 2012.

Liu Y, Studzinski C, Beckett T, Guan H, Hersh MA, Murphy MP, et al: Expression of neprilysin in skeletal muscle reduces amyloid burden in a transgenic mouse model of Alzheimer disease, *Mol Ther J Am Soc Gene Ther* 17:1381–1386, 2009a.

Liu Q, Zhang J, Tran H, Verbeek MM, Reiss K, Estus S, et al: LRP1 shedding in human brain: roles of ADAM10 and ADAM17, *Mol Neurodegener* 4:17, 2009b.

Liu G, Zhang S, Cai Z, Ma G, Zhang L, Jiang Y, et al: PICALM gene rs3851179 polymorphism contributes to Alzheimer's disease in an Asian population, *Neuromolecular Med* 15:384–388, 2013.

Liu Y-H, Xiang Y, Wang Y-R, Jiao S-S, Wang Q-H, Bu X-L, et al: Association between serum amyloid-beta and renal functions: implications for roles of kidney in amyloid-beta clearance, *Mol Neurobiol* 52:115–119, 2015.

Llorente-Cortés V, Costales P, Bernués J, Camino-Lopez S, Badimon L: Sterol regulatory element-binding protein-2 negatively regulates low density lipoprotein receptor-related protein transcription, *J Mol Biol* 359:950–960, 2006.

Llorente-Cortés V, Royo T, Otero-Viñas M, Berrozpe M, Badimon L: Sterol regulatory element binding proteins downregulate LDL receptor-related protein (LRP1) expression and LRP1-mediated aggregated LDL uptake by human macrophages, *Cardiovasc Res* 74:526–536, 2007.

Loeffler DA: Should development of Alzheimer's disease-specific intravenous immunoglobulin be considered? *J Neuroinflammation* 11:198, 2014.

Lord J, Morgan K: Clusterin [Internet]. In Morgan K, Carrasquillo MM, editors: *Genetic variants in Alzheimer's disease*, New York, NY, 2013, Springer, pp 25–51.

Mackic JB, Stins M, McComb JG, Calero M, Ghiso J, Kim KS, et al: Human blood–brain barrier receptors for Alzheimer's amyloid-beta 1-40: asymmetrical binding, endocytosis, and transcytosis at the apical side of brain microvascular endothelial cell monolayer, *J Clin Invest* 102:734–743, 1998.

Mackic JB, Bading J, Ghiso J, Walker L, Wisniewski T, Frangione B, et al: Circulating amyloid-beta peptide crosses the blood–brain barrier in aged monkeys and contributes to Alzheimer's disease lesions, *Vascul Pharmacol* 38:303–313, 2002.

Magalhães J, Saraiva MJ: Clusterin overexpression and its possible protective role in transthyretin deposition in familial amyloidotic polyneuropathy, *J Neuropathol Exp Neurol* 70:1097–1106, 2011.

Mahley RW: Apolipoprotein E: cholesterol transport protein with expanding role in cell biology, *Science* 240:622–630, 1988.

Malito E, Hulse RE, Tang W-J: Amyloid beta-degrading cryptidases: insulin degrading enzyme, presequence peptidase, and neprilysin, *Cell Mol Life Sci* 65:2574–2585, 2008.

Martel CL, Mackic JB, Matsubara E, Governale S, Miguel C, Miao W, et al: Isoform-specific effects of apolipoproteins E2, E3, and E4 on cerebral capillary sequestration and blood–brain barrier transport of circulating Alzheimer's amyloid beta, *J Neurochem* 69:1995–2004, 1997.

Matsubara E, Frangione B, Ghiso J: Characterization of apolipoprotein J–Alzheimer's A beta interaction, *J Biol Chem* 270:7563–7567, 1995.

Matsubara E, Soto C, Governale S, Frangione B, Ghiso J: Apolipoprotein J and Alzheimer's amyloid beta solubility, *Biochem J* 316 (Pt 2):671–679, 1996.

Mawuenyega KG, Sigurdson W, Ovod V, Munsell L, Kasten T, Morris JC, et al: Decreased clearance of CNS beta-amyloid in Alzheimer's disease, *Science* 330:1774, 2010.

McLaughlin L, Zhu G, Mistry M, Ley-Ebert C, Stuart WD, Florio CJ, et al: Apolipoprotein J/clusterin limits the severity of murine autoimmune myocarditis, *J Clin Invest* 106:1105–1113, 2000.

Miller MC, Tavares R, Johanson CE, Hovanesian V, Donahue JE, Gonzalez L, et al: Hippocampal RAGE immunoreactivity in early and advanced Alzheimer's disease, *Brain Res* 1230:273–280, 2008.

Mooradian AD, Chung HC, Shah GN: GLUT-1 expression in the cerebra of patients with Alzheimer's disease, *Neurobiol Aging* 18:469–474, 1997.

Morelli L, Llovera RE, Alonso LG, Frangione B, de Prat-Gay G, Ghiso J, et al: Insulin-degrading enzyme degrades amyloid peptides associated with British and Danish familial dementia, *Biochem Biophys Res Commun* 332:808–816, 2005.

Morgen K, Ramirez A, Frölich L, Tost H, Plichta MM, Kölsch H, et al: Genetic interaction of PICALM and APOE is associated with brain atrophy and cognitive impairment in Alzheimer's disease, *Alzheimers Dement* 10:S269–S276, 2014.

Mueller-Steiner S, Zhou Y, Arai H, Roberson ED, Sun B, Chen J, et al: Antiamyloidogenic and neuroprotective functions of cathepsin B: implications for Alzheimer's disease, *Neuron* 51:703–714, 2006.

Narayan P, Meehan S, Carver JA, Wilson MR, Dobson CM, Klenerman D: Amyloid-β oligomers are sequestered by both intracellular and extracellular chaperones, *Biochemistry* 51:9270–9276, 2012a.

Narayan P, Orte A, Clarke RW, Bolognesi B, Hook S, Ganzinger KA, et al: The extracellular chaperone clusterin sequesters oligomeric forms of the amyloid-β(1–40) peptide, *Nat Struct Mol Biol* 19:79–83, 2012b.

Narayan P, Holmström KM, Kim D-H, Whitcomb DJ, Wilson MR, St George-Hyslop P, et al: Rare individual amyloid-β oligomers act on astrocytes to initiate neuronal damage, *Biochemistry* 53:2442–2453, 2014.

Neeper M, Schmidt AM, Brett J, Yan SD, Wang F, Pan YC, et al: Cloning and expression of a cell surface receptor for advanced glycosylation end products of proteins, *J Biol Chem* 267:14998–15004, 1992.

Nimmerjahn F, Ravetch JV: Anti-inflammatory actions of intravenous immunoglobulin, *Ann Rev Immunol* 26:513–533, 2008.

Oh SB, Byun CJ, Yun J-H, Jo D-G, Carmeliet P, Koh J-Y, et al: Tissue plasminogen activator arrests Alzheimer's disease pathogenesis, *Neurobiol Aging* 35:511–519, 2014.

Pacheco-Quinto J, Eckman EA: Endothelin-converting enzymes degrade intracellular β-amyloid produced within the endosomal/lysosomal pathway and autophagosomes, *J Biol Chem* 288:5606–5615, 2013.

Palmer JC, Baig S, Kehoe PG, Love S: Endothelin-converting enzyme-2 is increased in Alzheimer's disease and up-regulated by Abeta, *Am J Pathol* 175:262–270, 2009.

Park H, Adsit FG, Boyington JC: The 1.5 Å crystal structure of human receptor for advanced glycation endproducts (RAGE) ectodomains reveals unique features determining ligand binding, *J Biol Chem* 285:40762–40770, 2010.

Polavarapu R, Gongora MC, Yi H, Ranganthan S, Lawrence DA, Strickland D, et al: Tissue-type plasminogen activator-mediated shedding of astrocytic low-density lipoprotein receptor-related protein increases the permeability of the neurovascular unit, *Blood* 109:3270–3278, 2007.

Prince M, Albanese E, Guerchet M, Prina M: World Alzheimer Report 2014: dementia and risk reduction: an analysis of protective and modifiable factors. Alzheimer's Disease International, 2014, pp 1–99.

Qiu WQ, Folstein MF: Insulin, insulin-degrading enzyme and amyloid-beta peptide in Alzheimer's disease: review and hypothesis, *Neurobiol Aging* 27:190–198, 2006.

Qosa H, Batarseh YS, Mohyeldin MM, El Sayed KA, Keller JN, Kaddoumi A: Oleocanthal enhances amyloid-β clearance from the brains of TgSwDI mice and in vitro across a human blood–brain barrier model, *ACS Chem Neurosci* 6:1849–1859, 2015.

Quinn KA, Grimsley PG, Dai YP, Tapner M, Chesterman CN, Owensby DA: Soluble low density lipoprotein receptor-related protein (LRP) circulates in human plasma, *J Biol Chem* 272:23946–23951, 1997.

Raj T, Shulman JM, Keenan BT, Chibnik LB, Evans DA, Bennett DA, et al: Alzheimer disease susceptibility loci: evidence for a protein network under natural selection, *Am J Hum Genet* 90:720–726, 2012.

Ramanathan A, Nelson AR, Sagare AP, Zlokovic BV: Impaired vascular-mediated clearance of brain amyloid beta in Alzheimer's disease: the role, regulation and restoration of LRP1, *Front Aging Neurosci* 7:136, 2015.

Relkin NR, Szabo P, Adamiak B, Burgut T, Monthe C, Lent RW, et al: 18-Month study of intravenous immunoglobulin for treatment of mild Alzheimer disease, *Neurobiol Aging* 30:1728–1736, 2009.

Roussotte FF, Gutman BA, Madsen SK, Colby JB, Thompson PM: Alzheimer's Disease Neuroimaging Initiative: combined effects of Alzheimer risk variants in the CLU and ApoE genes on ventricular expansion patterns in the elderly, *J Neurosci* 34:6537–6545, 2014.

Rozanov DV, Hahn-Dantona E, Strickland DK, Strongin AY: The low density lipoprotein receptor-related protein LRP is regulated by membrane type-1 matrix metalloproteinase (MT1-MMP) proteolysis in malignant cells, *J Biol Chem* 279:4260–4268, 2004.

Sagare A, Deane R, Bell RD, Johnson B, Hamm K, Pendu R, et al: Clearance of amyloid-beta by circulating lipoprotein receptors, *Nat Med* 13:1029–1031, 2007.

Sagare AP, Deane R, Zetterberg H, Wallin A, Blennow K, Zlokovic BV: Impaired lipoprotein receptor-mediated peripheral binding of plasma amyloid-β is an early biomarker for mild cognitive impairment preceding Alzheimer's disease, *J Alzheimers Dis* 24:25–34, 2011.

Sagare AP, Deane R, Zlokovic BV: Low-density lipoprotein receptor-related protein a physiological Aβ homeostatic mechanism with multiple therapeutic opportunities, *Pharmacol Ther* 136:94–105, 2012.

Sagare AP, Bell RD, Srivastava A, Sengillo JD, Singh I, Nishida Y, et al: A lipoprotein receptor cluster IV mutant preferentially binds amyloid-β and regulates its clearance from the mouse brain, *J Biol Chem* 288:15154–15166, 2013a.

Sagare AP, Bell RD, Zhao Z, Ma Q, Winkler EA, Ramanathan A, et al: Pericyte loss influences Alzheimer-like neurodegeneration in mice, *Nat Commun* 4:2932, 2013b.

Salloway S, Sperling R, Fox NC, Blennow K, Klunk W, Raskind M, et al: Two phase 3 trials of bapineuzumab in mild-to-moderate Alzheimer's disease, *N Engl J Med* 370:322–333, 2014.

Saunders AM, Strittmatter WJ, Schmechel D, George-Hyslop PH, Pericak-Vance MA, Joo SH, et al: Association of apolipoprotein E allele epsilon 4 with late-onset familial and sporadic Alzheimer's disease, *Neurology* 43:1467–1472, 1993.

Schmidt AM: Soluble RAGEs—prospects for treating & tracking metabolic and inflammatory disease, *Vascul Pharmacol* 72:1–8, 2015.

Schmidt AM, Sahagan B, Nelson RB, Selmer J, Rothlein R, Bell JM: The role of RAGE in amyloid-beta peptide-mediated pathology in Alzheimer's disease, *Curr Opin Investig Drugs* 10:672–680, 2009.

Sehgal N, Gupta A, Valli RK, Joshi SD, Mills JT, Hamel E, et al: Withania somnifera reverses Alzheimer's disease pathology by enhancing low-density lipoprotein receptor-related protein in liver, *Proc Natl Acad Sci USA* 109:3510–3515, 2012.

Selvais C, D'Auria L, Tyteca D, Perrot G, Lemoine P, Troeberg L, et al: Cell cholesterol modulates metalloproteinase-dependent shedding of low-density lipoprotein receptor-related protein-1 (LRP-1) and clearance function, *FASEB J* 25:2770–2781, 2011.

Seshadri S, Fitzpatrick AL, Ikram MA, DeStefano AL, Gudnason V, Boada M, et al: Genome-wide analysis of genetic loci associated with Alzheimer disease, *J Am Med Assoc* 303:1832–1840, 2010.

Shayan G, Adamiak B, Relkin NR, Lee KH: Longitudinal analysis of novel Alzheimer's disease proteomic cerebrospinal fluid biomarkers during intravenous immunoglobulin therapy, *Electrophoresis* 33:1975–1979, 2012.

Shibata M, Yamada S, Kumar SR, Calero M, Bading J, Frangione B, et al: Clearance of Alzheimer's amyloid-ss(1-40) peptide from brain by LDL receptor-related protein-1 at the blood–brain barrier, *J Clin Invest* 106:1489–1499, 2000.

Shiraki A, Oyama J, Komoda H, Asaka M, Komatsu A, Sakuma M, et al: The glucagon-like peptide 1 analog liraglutide reduces TNF-α-induced oxidative stress and inflammation in endothelial cells, *Atherosclerosis* 221:375–382, 2012.

Silverberg GD, Miller MC, Messier AA, Majmudar S, Machan JT, Donahue JE, et al: Amyloid deposition and influx transporter expression at the blood–brain barrier increase in normal aging, *J Neuropathol Exp Neurol* 69:98–108, 2010.

Simpson IA, Chundu KR, Davies-Hill T, Honer WG, Davies P: Decreased concentrations of GLUT1 and GLUT3 glucose transporters in the brains of patients with Alzheimer's disease, *Ann Neurol* 35:546–551, 1994.

Sorkin A, von Zastrow M: Endocytosis and signalling: intertwining molecular networks, *Nat Rev Mol Cell Biol* 10:609–622, 2009.

Srikanth V, Maczurek A, Phan T, Steele M, Westcott B, Juskiw D, et al: Advanced glycation endproducts and their receptor RAGE in Alzheimer's disease, *Neurobiol Aging* 32:763–777, 2011.

Stern DM, Yan SD, Yan SF, Schmidt AM: Receptor for advanced glycation endproducts (RAGE) and the complications of diabetes, *Ageing Res Rev* 1:1–15, 2002.

Sturchler E, Galichet A, Weibel M, Leclerc E, Heizmann CW: Site-specific blockade of RAGE-Vd prevents amyloid-beta oligomer neurotoxicity, *J Neurosci* 28:5149–5158, 2008.

Sutcliffe JG, Hedlund PB, Thomas EA, Bloom FE, Hilbush BS: Peripheral reduction of β-amyloid is sufficient to reduce brain β-amyloid: implications for Alzheimer's disease, *J Neurosci Res* 89:808–814, 2011.

Sweeney MD, Sagare AP, Zlokovic BV: Cerebrospinal fluid biomarkers of neurovascular dysfunction in mild dementia and Alzheimer's disease, *J Cereb Blood Flow Metab* 35:1055–1068, 2015.

Szabo P, Mujalli DM, Rotondi ML, Sharma R, Weber A, Schwarz H-P, et al: Measurement of anti-beta amyloid antibodies in human blood, *J Neuroimmunol* 227:167–174, 2010.

Tai LM, Mehra S, Shete V, Estus S, Rebeck GW, Bu G, et al: Soluble apoE/Aβ complex: mechanism and therapeutic target for APOE4-induced AD risk, *Mol Neurodegener* 9:2, 2014.

Takuma K, Fang F, Zhang W, Yan S, Fukuzaki E, Du H, et al: RAGE-mediated signaling contributes to intraneuronal transport of amyloid-beta and neuronal dysfunction, *Proc Natl Acad Sci USA* 106:20021–20026, 2009.

Tamaki C, Ohtsuki S, Iwatsubo T, Hashimoto T, Yamada K, Yabuki C, et al: Major involvement of low-density lipoprotein receptor-related protein 1 in the clearance of plasma free amyloid beta-peptide by the liver, *Pharm Res* 23:1407–1416, 2006.

Tamaki C, Ohtsuki S, Terasaki T: Insulin facilitates the hepatic clearance of plasma amyloid beta-peptide (1 40) by intracellular translocation of low-density lipoprotein receptor-related protein 1 (LRP-1) to the plasma membrane in hepatocytes, *Mol Pharmacol* 72:850–855, 2007.

Tanzi RE: The genetics of Alzheimer disease, *Cold Spring Harb Perspect Med* 2:a006296, 2012.

Tarasoff-Conway JM, Carare RO, Osorio RS, Glodzik L, Butler T, Fieremans E, et al: Clearance systems in the brain—implications for Alzheimer disease, *Nat Rev Neurol* 11:457–470, 2015.

Tian L, Zhang K, Tian Z-Y, Wang T, Shang D-S, Li B, et al: Decreased expression of cathepsin D in monocytes is related to the defective degradation of amyloid-β in Alzheimer's disease, *J Alzheimers Dis* 42:511–520, 2014.

Treusch S, Hamamichi S, Goodman JL, Matlack KES, Chung CY, Baru V, et al: Functional links between Aβ toxicity, endocytic trafficking, and Alzheimer's disease risk factors in yeast, *Science* 334:1241–1245, 2011.

Ujiie M, Dickstein DL, Carlow DA, Jefferies WA: Blood–brain barrier permeability precedes senile plaque formation in an Alzheimer disease model, *Microcirculation* 10:463–470, 2003.

van der Geer P: Phosphorylation of LRP1: regulation of transport and signal transduction, *Trends Cardiovasc Med* 12:160–165, 2002.

Villeda SA, Plambeck KE, Middeldorp J, Castellano JM, Mosher KI, Luo J, et al: Young blood reverses age-related impairments in cognitive function and synaptic plasticity in mice, *Nat Med* 20:659–663, 2014.

von Arnim CAF, Kinoshita A, Peltan ID, Tangredi MM, Herl L, Lee BM, et al: The low density lipoprotein receptor-related protein (LRP) is a novel beta-secretase (BACE1) substrate, *J Biol Chem* 280:17777–17785, 2005.

Weber A, Engelmaier A, Teschner W, Ehrlich HJ, Schwarz HP: Intravenous immunoglobulin (IVIg) gammagard liquid contains anti-RAGE IgG and sLRP, *Alzheimers Dement* 5:P416, 2009.

Welzel AT, Williams AD, McWilliams-Koeppen HP, Acero L, Weber A, Blinder V, et al: Human anti-Aβ IgGs target conformational epitopes on synthetic dimer assemblies and the AD brain-derived peptide, *PLoS One* 7:e50317, 2012.

Wilson MR, Easterbrook-Smith SB: Clusterin is a secreted mammalian chaperone, *Trends Biochem Sci* 25:95–98, 2000.

Winkler EA, Nishida Y, Sagare AP, Rege SV, Bell RD, Perlmutter D, et al: GLUT1 reductions exacerbate Alzheimer's disease vasculo-neuronal dysfunction and degeneration, *Nat Neurosci* 18:521–530, 2015.

Wisniewski T, Frangione B: Apolipoprotein E: a pathological chaperone protein in patients with cerebral and systemic amyloid, *Neurosci Lett* 135:235–238, 1992.

Wolfe MS: Therapeutic strategies for Alzheimer's disease, *Nat Rev Drug Discov* 1:859–866, 2002.

Wolfe MS: Inhibition and modulation of gamma-secretase for Alzheimer's disease, *Neurotherapeutics* 5:391–398, 2008.

Wu Z, Guo H, Chow N, Sallstrom J, Bell RD, Deane R, et al: Role of the MEOX2 homeobox gene in neurovascular dysfunction in Alzheimer disease, *Nat Med* 11:959–965, 2005.

Wyatt AR, Yerbury JJ, Berghofer P, Greguric I, Katsifis A, Dobson CM, et al: Clusterin facilitates in vivo clearance of extracellular misfolded proteins, *Cell Mol Life Sci* 68:3919–3931, 2011.

Wyss-Coray T, Lin C, Yan F, Yu GQ, Rohde M, McConlogue L, et al: TGF-beta1 promotes microglial amyloid-beta clearance and reduces plaque burden in transgenic mice, *Nat Med* 7:612–618, 2001.

Yamada K, Holth JK, Liao F, Stewart FR, Mahan TE, Jiang H, et al: Neuronal activity regulates extracellular tau in vivo, *J Exp Med* 211:387–393, 2014.

Yamin R, Zhao C, O'Connor PB, McKee AC, Abraham CR: Acyl peptide hydrolase degrades monomeric and oligomeric amyloid-beta peptide, *Mol Neurodegener* 4:33, 2009.

Yan SD, Yan SF, Chen X, Fu J, Chen M, Kuppusamy P, et al: Non-enzymatically glycated tau in Alzheimer's disease induces neuronal oxidant stress resulting in cytokine gene expression and release of amyloid beta-peptide, *Nat Med* 1:693–699, 1995.

Yan SD, Chen X, Fu J, Chen M, Zhu H, Roher A, et al: RAGE and amyloid-beta peptide neurotoxicity in Alzheimer's disease, *Nature* 382:685–691, 1996.

Yan SF, Ramasamy R, Schmidt AM: Soluble RAGE: therapy and biomarker in unraveling the RAGE axis in chronic disease and aging, *Biochem Pharmacol* 79:1379–1386, 2010.

Zhao Z, Sagare AP, Ma Q, Halliday MR, Kong P, Kisler K, et al: Central role for PICALM in amyloid-β blood–brain barrier transcytosis and clearance, *Nat Neurosci* 18:978–987, 2015.

Zlokovic BV: Cerebrovascular permeability to peptides: manipulations of transport systems at the blood–brain barrier, *Pharm Res* 12:1395–1406, 1995.

Zlokovic BV: New therapeutic targets in the neurovascular pathway in Alzheimer's disease, *Neurotherapeutics* 5:409–414, 2008.

Zlokovic BV: Neurodegeneration and the neurovascular unit, *Nat Med* 16:1370–1371, 2010.

Zlokovic BV: Neurovascular pathways to neurodegeneration in Alzheimer's disease and other disorders, *Nat Rev Neurosci* 12:723–738, 2011.
Zlokovic BV: Cerebrovascular effects of apolipoprotein E: implications for Alzheimer disease, *JAMA Neurol* 70:440–444, 2013.
Zlokovic BV, Begley DJ, Chain-Eliash DG: Blood–brain barrier permeability to leucine-enkephalin, D-alanine2-D-leucine5-enkephalin and their N-terminal amino acid (tyrosine), *Brain Res* 336:125–132, 1985.
Zlokovic BV, Martel CL, Mackic JB, Matsubara E, Wisniewski T, McComb JG, et al: Brain uptake of circulating apolipoproteins J and E complexed to Alzheimer's amyloid beta, *Biochem Biophys Res Commun* 205:1431–1437, 1994.
Zlokovic BV, Martel CL, Matsubara E, McComb JG, Zheng G, McCluskey RT, et al: Glycoprotein 330/megalin: probable role in receptor-mediated transport of apolipoprotein J alone and in a complex with Alzheimer disease amyloid beta at the blood–brain and blood–cerebrospinal fluid barriers, *Proc Natl Acad Sci USA* 93:4229–4234, 1996.
Zlokovic BV, Deane R, Sagare AP, Bell RD, Winkler EA: Low-density lipoprotein receptor-related protein-1: a serial clearance homeostatic mechanism controlling Alzheimer's amyloid β-peptide elimination from the brain, *J Neurochem* 115:1077–1089, 2010.
Zloković BV, Lipovac MN, Begley DJ, Davson H, Rakić L: Transport of leucine-enkephalin across the blood–brain barrier in the perfused guinea pig brain, *J Neurochem* 49:310–315, 1987.

CHAPTER

10

Alzheimer's Disease Therapeutics Targeting Apolipoprotein E

F. Liao, D.M. Holtzman

OUTLINE

INTRODUCTION

Alzheimer's disease (AD) is the most common cause of dementia, affecting more than 5 million people in the United States alone. AD is characterized by the progressive impairment of memory and thinking, the presence of extracellular amyloid plaques, intracellular neurofibrillary tangles, and selective neuronal and synaptic loss. Currently, there is no effective therapeutic that delays the onset or slows progression of AD. Amyloid β (Aβ), a 38- to 43-amino-acid peptide, is the primary component of amyloid plaques and cerebral amyloid angiopathy (CAA). There is substantial evidence that Aβ plays a key role in the initiation

Developing Therapeutics for Alzheimer's Disease. http://dx.doi.org/10.1016/B978-0-12-802173-6.00010-1

and development of AD (Hardy and Selkoe, 2002). Aβ is generated by sequential cleavage of amyloid precursor protein (APP) by β- and γ-secretases. Most autosomal-dominant inherited missense mutations, in APP or components of the γ-secretase complex presenilin 1 (PS1) or presenilin 2 (PS2) that cause rare autosomal-dominant forms of AD, result in an increase in production of total Aβ species or a shift to a greater relative production of an aggregation-prone form of Aβ ($A\beta_{42}$) (Hardy and Selkoe, 2002). Some mutations in APP that cause autosomal-dominant AD or CAA are in the Aβ sequence itself and do not affect Aβ production but alter the aggregation propensity and clearance of Aβ (Tsubuki et al., 2003). Also, a recently discovered mutation in APP just N-terminal to the β-secretase site results in decreased Aβ production and protects against AD (Jonsson et al., 2012). Thus, substantial genetic and biochemical evidence implicates Aβ in instigating autosomal-dominant AD as well as CAA.

However, less than 1% of AD cases are caused by autosomal-dominant mutations (Bateman et al., 2011). The majority of cases of AD clinically begin after the age of 60. This form of AD is known as late-onset AD (LOAD). In contrast to the dysregulation in Aβ production which characterizes most cases of autosomal-dominant AD, deficits in Aβ clearance or increased aggregation appear to be a major cause of LOAD (Selkoe, 2001; Mawuenyega et al., 2010). Most genetic risk factors for LOAD identified during the past 20 years have a very small relative impact on AD. However, beginning in 1993 and in numerous subsequent studies the apolipoprotein E gene (*APOE*) has been shown to have a very large impact on risk for LOAD (http://www.alzgene.org; Corder et al., 1993, 1994; Strittmatter et al., 1993a). The *APOE* gene, located on chromosome 19, encodes the apoE protein, which is 299 amino acids in length and glycosylated (Olaisen et al., 1982). In humans, there are three common isoforms of apoE: ε2, ε3, and ε4. In a healthy population, the most common apoE allele is ε3 with a 77% allele frequency, while the frequencies of ε2 and ε4 are 8 and 15%, respectively (Farrer et al., 1997). Although apoE2 (Cys112, Cys158), apoE3 (Cys112, Arg158), and apoE4 (Arg112, Arg158) differ by only one or two amino acids at residue 112 or 158, their impact on AD is very different. The presence of apoE4 is associated with an increased risk and earlier age of onset for LOAD, whereas apoE2 is protective relative to apoE3. More than 50% of LOAD patients carry at least one copy of the ε4 allele. *APOE* ε4/ε4 homozygous individuals occupy about 15% of the LOAD population, although only 2% of the healthy population are ε4/ε4 (Farrer et al., 1997). Individuals carrying one copy or two copies of ε4 allele have an ~4 or 12 times higher risk to develop AD, respectively, relative to the presence of two copies of the ε3 allele (http://www.alzgene.org; Farrer et al., 1997). The age of highest probability of AD for apoE4 carriers is 5–10 years earlier than for apoE3 carriers (Raber et al., 2004) (Fig. 10.1).

PHYSIOLOGICAL FUNCTION OF apoE

The primary physiological functions of apoE are the maintenance of the structure of specific lipoprotein particles and the transport of lipids among different organs or different cell types. In the periphery, apoE is one of the apolipoproteins associated with lipoproteins of different size classes, including very low-density lipoproteins, chylomicron remnants, intermediate density lipoproteins, and a subclass of high-density lipoproteins (HDLs) (Mahley, 1988). The liver is the major source of peripheral apoE. Since apoE produced in the periphery cannot cross the blood–brain barrier (BBB) and enter the central nervous system (CNS) to any significant

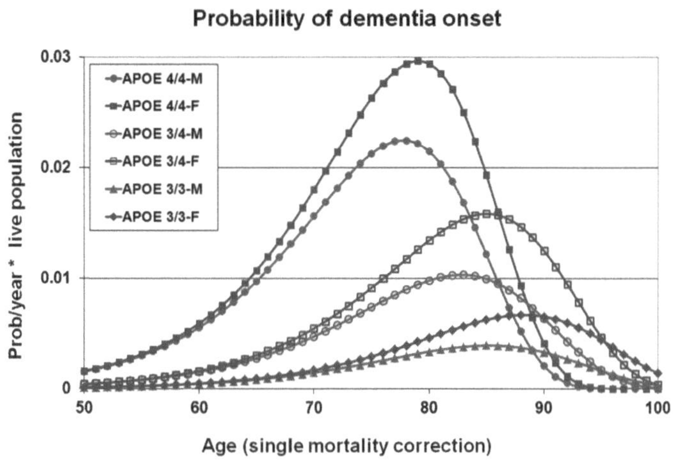

FIGURE 10.1 **The influence of apoE genotypes on probability of AD onset.** The effect of apoE genotype on the US population of the 2000 Census for probability of AD onset in a year is shown as age-specific risk × proportion of original population at 50 years of age living at the age. Abbreviations: *AD*, Alzheimer's disease; *apoE*, apolipoprotein E; *M*, male; *F*, female. *Adapted from Raber et al. (2004).*

degree (Linton et al., 1991; Zlokovic et al., 1994; Liu et al., 2012), the apoE in the CNS is synthesized locally within the CNS. Brain apoE is expressed primarily by astrocytes (Pitas et al., 1987; Grehan et al., 2001) and to some extent by microglia. Neurons do not express apoE under normal conditions but they appear to be able to express apoE in response to excitotoxic injury (Xu et al., 2006). Unlike in the periphery, the only lipoproteins in the CNS are HDL-like in size and apoE is present only in a class of HDL-like lipoproteins in both the cerebrospinal fluid (CSF) and interstitial fluid (ISF) of the brain (LaDu et al., 1998; Ulrich et al., 2013).

The mechanisms of how apoE functions in the periphery and in the brain are quite different. Plasma cholesterol levels in mice that express different human apoE isoforms follow the trend of apoE2 > apoE3 > apoE4, while brain cholesterol levels are not affected by apoE genotype (Mann et al., 2004). Mice (Zhang et al., 1992) and humans (Mak et al., 2014) lacking apoE have marked peripheral hypercholesterolemia. However, brain function in the absence of apoE appears normal for the most part in the absence of injury (Anderson et al., 1998; Fagan et al., 1998; Mak et al., 2014), suggesting that either apoE is not important for normal brain function or the function of brain apoE can be fulfilled by other surrogate proteins/apoproteins. Although apoE is the most abundant apolipoprotein in the CNS (Neely and Montine, 2002), apoA-I, apoA-II, apoA-IV, apoD, apoH, and apoJ are also found in the brain (Kim et al., 2009a). Among them, the most abundant are apoA-I and apoJ (clusterin). Clusterin in the CNS is expressed locally by glia (Charnay et al., 2008), but apoA-I is derived from the periphery (Sorci-Thomas et al., 1988).

ApoE AND apoE RECEPTORS

ApoE fulfills its function of transporting lipids by functioning as a ligand in receptor-mediated endocytosis of lipoprotein particles in the periphery and CNS. Several apoE receptors are members of the low-density lipoprotein receptor (LDLR) family, including LDLR, lipoprotein receptor-related protein 1 (LRP1), very low-density lipoprotein receptor (VLDLR), and ApoER2. The LDLR family is a highly conserved receptor family that performs diverse biological functions in cellular physiology (Lane-Donovan et al., 2014). ApoE receptors are expressed in neurons, astrocytes, oligodendrocytes, smooth muscle cells, pericytes, cerebral endothelial cells, and microglia. When apoE lipoprotein particles bind to the receptors, the lipoprotein particles, including the lipids in the particles, are taken up into the cells, where they are utilized in cell metabolism and biomembrane synthesis (Mahley, 1988). In addition, upon binding with the ligands, some of the apoE receptors can elicit intracellular signal transduction and cause a series of downstream events. The effects of apoE/receptor binding depend on the cell types and receptor types. LDLR and LRP1, the main apoE-lipoprotein metabolic receptors in the brain, regulate apoE levels (Fryer et al., 2005b; Liu et al., 2007). ApoER2 and VLDLR initiate signal transduction upon binding with apoE or other ligands such as reelin (Holtzman et al., 2012). Reelin signaling is important for neural development, synaptic function, and tau phosphorylation (Hiesberger et al., 1999; Trommsdorff et al., 1999; Niu et al., 2008). In addition to the LDLR family, cell-surface heparan sulfate proteoglycans also bind apoE, either directly (Saito et al., 2003; Futamura et al., 2005) or cooperatively with LRP1 (Ji et al., 1993) to regulate Aβ cellular uptake (Kanekiyo et al., 2011).

ApoE LEVELS IN PERIPHERY AND CNS

Since *APOE* is the strongest genetic risk factor for LOAD, apoE level has been investigated extensively to see whether it is correlated with AD status. In humans, plasma apoE ranges from 10 to 80 μg/mL (Wildsmith et al., 2012). CSF apoE ranges from 5 to 9 μg/mL (Cruchaga et al., 2012). In most studies, there is no correlation between plasma and CSF apoE levels (Fagan et al., 2000; Cruchaga et al., 2012; Wildsmith et al., 2012; Martinez-Morillo et al., 2014), supporting the observations that apoE does not cross the BBB (Linton et al., 1991; Zlokovic et al., 1994; Liu et al., 2012). Here we summarize the previous studies on the plasma, CSF, and brain tissue apoE levels regarding isoform effect and AD association. Since there has been a long debate regarding whether an increase or decrease in apoE should be employed as a therapeutic strategy, more effort needs to be made to understand the relationship between apoE levels (especially before disease onset) and development of AD pathology and brain function. The utilization of human apoE knockin mice that express different human apoE isoforms under control of the mouse apoE regulatory elements has helped to address this question.

ApoE Levels in Plasma

The apoE levels in plasma are isoform dependent with the pattern of ε2/ε2 > ε3/ε3 > ε4/ε4 (Mooijaart et al., 2006; Martinez-Morillo et al., 2014) due to the faster turnover rate of plasma apoE4 (Wildsmith et al., 2012) and lower binding affinity between apoE2 and lipoprotein receptors. Some studies show that lower plasma apoE is associated with AD, but this association might be largely driven by apoE genotype since apoE4 individuals have lower plasma apoE. When the genotype was included as a covariate, there was no significant difference in plasma apoE levels between control and AD patients (Cruchaga et al., 2012; Simon et al., 2012).

However, in a recent study, lower plasma apoE is found to be associated with AD even after adjusting for apoE genotype (Rasmussen et al., 2014). To date, there is no solid relationship established between plasma apoE and AD status.

ApoE Levels in CSF

CSF apoE might be more closely related to brain pathology. In CSF, there is no significant difference in total apoE levels across all apoE genotypes reported in many but not all studies (Landen et al., 1996; Wahrle et al., 2007; Cruchaga et al., 2012; Martinez-Morillo et al., 2014). ApoE ε3/ε4 heterozygotes have a higher proportion of apoE4 as compared to apoE3, whereas in plasma the relationship is reversed (Fukumoto et al., 2003; Simon et al., 2012; Martinez-Morillo et al., 2014). These observations suggested differential metabolism of the apoE isoforms in CSF versus plasma. CSF apoE levels have generally not been found to be different in controls and clinically defined AD cases (Wahrle et al., 2007; Cruchaga et al., 2012; Simon et al., 2012; Martinez-Morillo et al., 2014). However, a recent study found that CSF apoE level is positively correlated with the AD biomarker, CSF $A\beta_{42}$, independent of *APOE* genotype (Cruchaga et al., 2012). Another study showed that higher CSF apoE levels were associated with higher total and phosphorylated CSF tau levels as well as longitudinal cognitive decline (Toledo et al., 2014). In the future, more studies with larger sample size and quantitative assays are needed to confirm the relationship between CSF apoE and AD status.

ApoE Levels in Brain Parenchyma

Previous studies of brain parenchymal apoE levels in humans have not reached consensus on whether apoE levels are affected by AD status or apoE genotype. Some earlier studies observed reductions in the level of apoE protein levels in the AD hippocampus (Bertrand et al., 1995; Beffert et al., 1999b), whereas another study showed the same apoE levels (Harr et al., 1996) or even elevated apoE levels in AD brain depending on the brain region and what pool of apoE is measured (Arold et al., 2012). The effects of genotype on apoE levels are also conflicting in different studies. ApoE4 levels have been reported to be lower (Beffert et al., 1999b), similar (Harr et al., 1996), or even slightly higher when compared with apoE3 (Bray et al., 2004). These studies could be affected by several factors, including small sample sizes, postmortem delay, and, most importantly, changes related to different disease stages. Recently, the apoE levels in different regions of postmortem brain from nondemented humans were assessed. ApoE levels were highly correlated with an astrocyte marker GFAP, agreeing with the fact that astrocytes are the major cells generating apoE in the brain (Shinohara et al., 2013). In addition, regional brain apoE levels are negatively correlated with $A\beta_{40}$ (Shinohara et al., 2013). Since $A\beta_{40}$ is produced predominantly by neurons and is positively correlated with the synaptic marker PSD95 (Shinohara et al., 2013), the negative correlation between apoE and $A\beta_{40}$ in different brain regions could reflect the ratio of neurons versus astrocytes within brain regions. In the future, additional longitudinal studies starting prior to the onset of AD pathology are needed to answer the question of whether apoE levels are correlated in any way with the development of AD pathology and how this role is affected by apoE genotype.

Studies on apoE Metabolism in Mouse Models

Mouse models provide a good opportunity to study the level of apoE under a variety of physiological conditions. Genetically modified mice that express different human apoE isoforms in different CNS cells have been generated in the past 15 years (Sullivan et al., 1997; Raber et al., 1998; Cambon et al., 2000; Hartman et al., 2001; White et al., 2001; Lanz et al., 2003). Among these, apoE knockin mice expressing human apoE under the control of the endogenous murine apoE regulatory sequences have been heavily utilized (Sullivan et al., 1997; Hamanaka et al., 2000; Bien-Ly et al., 2012). These mice have allowed scientists to study apoE metabolism in ways that are likely physiologically and pathologically relevant.

In apoE knockin mice, plasma apoE levels follow the pattern $\varepsilon2/\varepsilon2 \geq \varepsilon3/\varepsilon3 > \varepsilon4/\varepsilon4$, a pattern also seen in humans (Sullivan et al., 2004; Riddell et al., 2008). In CSF, apoE protein levels are significantly higher in apoE2 mice than in apoE3 and apoE4 mice (Fryer et al., 2005b), while the apoE3 and apoE4 protein levels are very similar, with apoE4 found to be lower in some studies (Fryer et al., 2005a, b; Riddell et al., 2008). Recently, a more sensitive assay shows that CSF apoE3 is higher than apoE4 (Sullivan et al., 2011).

In mouse brain parenchyma, the genotype effects on apoE levels are less consistent across different studies depending on the sensitivity of the assays used (Mann et al., 2004; Sullivan et al., 2004, 2011; Ramaswamy et al., 2005; Riddell et al., 2008; Bales et al., 2009). In most studies, including a recent study using a novel mass-spectrometry method (Sullivan et al., 2011), apoE2 levels tend to be the highest among the three isoforms, with apoE3 being intermediate and apoE4 being lowest (Bales et al., 2009).

Since Aβ deposition occurs in the extracellular space in the brain parenchyma, the pool of apoE that directly interacts with extracellular Aβ is likely to be apoE that is present in the ISF as well as what is bound to the extracellular matrix and cell surfaces. Our laboratory utilized an in vivo microdialysis technique to characterize ISF apoE in the mouse brain (Takeda et al., 2013; Ulrich et al., 2013). Native gel electrophoresis analysis showed that ISF apoE was present in HDL-like lipoprotein particles that are 8–12 nm in size (Ulrich et al., 2013). The ISF apoE levels in the apoE-targeted replacement mice follow the trend of $\varepsilon2/\varepsilon2 > \varepsilon3/\varepsilon3 > \varepsilon4/\varepsilon4$, a pattern very similar to that seen in CSF apoE (Ulrich et al., 2013).

ApoE levels are the result of production and clearance (Fig. 10.2). ApoE gene transcription is regulated in part by transcription factor peroxisome proliferator-activated receptors (PPARs), liver X receptors (LXRs), and retinoid X receptors (RXRs). The expression of apoE in brain parenchyma is similar across all the apoE isoforms in apoE-targeted replacement mice as measured by mRNA (Riddell et al., 2008; Sullivan et al., 2011), suggesting a different turnover rate of different apoE protein isoforms in the brain.

ApoE clearance in the brain is 3–6 times slower than that in the periphery (Wildsmith et al., 2012). ApoE is cleared from the brain through several pathways, including receptor-mediated cellular uptake, proteolysis (Harris et al., 2003; Brecht et al., 2004), ISF to CSF and lymphatic clearance, and transport across the BBB (Fig. 10.2). LDLR and LRP1 play primary roles in regulating brain apoE levels. Endogenous murine apoE half-life in mouse brain parenchyma is ~7 h as measured using bolus stable isotope labeling (Basak et al., 2012a). LDLR hastens the apoE clearance rate by almost 3 times in an APP transgenic mouse model (Basak et al., 2012b). Deletion of the LDLR gene in the mouse brain results in higher apoE levels in the brain and CSF (Fryer et al., 2005b), whereas overexpression of LDLR in the brain decreases

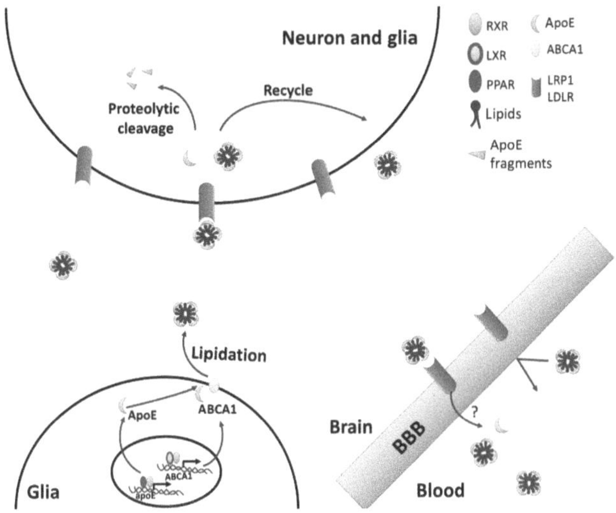

FIGURE 10.2 **ApoE metabolism in the brain.** ApoE levels in the CNS are the net balance of apoE synthesis and clearance. Brain apoE is locally expressed within the brain (Linton et al., 1991; Liu et al., 2012). Under normal conditions, astrocytes play a dominant role in the synthesis and secretion of apoE although apoE is also synthesized in microglia (Pitas et al., 1987; Grehan et al., 2001). Neurons appear to express apoE only in response to stress (Xu et al., 2006). The transcription of the *APOE* gene is regulated by the heterodimers formed by ligand-activated nuclear receptors RXR with PPAR or LXR. PPAR:RXR and LXR:RXR also regulate the expression of ABCA1, a transmembrane protein that transports cellular cholesterol and phospholipids from cells to apoE. Upon lipidation, apoE is secreted into the extracellular space and carries lipids to other cells. ApoE lipoprotein particles are readily taken by cells via apoE receptors. LDLR and LRP1 are the major metabolic receptors for apoE (Holtzman et al., 2012). After being taken up into cells, apoE can be degraded through proteolysis or recycled back to the cell surface. The clearance of apoE is affected by apoE isoform and lipidation status (Huang and Mahley, 2014). Whether an increase or a decrease of apoE will be beneficial remains a controversial topic; both increases and decreases of apoE were explored as potential strategies for AD. An increase in apoE levels can be achieved by using LXR and RXR agonists (Cramer et al., 2012). Decrease of apoE can be mediated by overexpression of apoE metabolic receptors (Kim et al., 2009b) as well as producing mice with 0, 1, or 2 copies of each apoE isoform of interest. Abbreviations: *apoE*, apolipoprotein E; *ABCA1*, ATP-binding cassette transporter A1; *AD*, Alzheimer's disease; *RXR*, retinoid X receptor; *LXR*, liver X receptor; *PPAR*, peroxisome proliferator-activated receptor; *LRP1*, low-density lipoprotein receptor-related protein 1; *LDLR*, low-density lipoprotein receptor.

brain apoE (Kim et al., 2009b). Similarly, deletion (Liu et al., 2007) or overexpression (Zerbinatti et al., 2006) of LRP1 causes increases or decreases, respectively, of brain apoE levels. The lipidation status of apoE also modifies apoE proteolysis, receptor-binding properties, and BBB transport (Bell et al., 2007; Deane et al., 2008; Huang and Mahley, 2014). Theoretically, apoE isoform could also affect apoE clearance due to having a different susceptibility to proteolysis (Harris et al., 2003; Brecht et al., 2004) and different binding affinity to lipoprotein receptors (Hatters et al., 2006). However, a recent study shows that the turnover rates of human CSF apoE (1.5~2.5%/h) are similar between apoE genotypes in cognitively normal adults as measured by an in vivo stable isotope labeling technique (Wildsmith et al., 2012). In future studies, it may be worth determining whether apoE metabolism differs between control and AD cases to better understand the role that apoE level plays in AD pathogenesis.

ApoE AND Aβ

There is evidence supporting the possibility that apoE may also contribute to the AD process via Aβ-independent mechanisms that include, among others, influencing neuronal plasticity, neurotoxicity caused by neuronal apoE fragments, tau hyperphosphorylation, mitochondrial dysfunction, neuroinflammation, and impairment of brain vascular integrity (Kim et al., 2009a; Huang, 2010; Bell et al., 2012) (Fig. 10.3). However, many of the previous apoE-based AD therapeutic strategies focus on the effects of apoE on Aβ pathology because of the compelling evidence showing that apoE greatly influences the amount, onset, location, and aggregation state of Aβ deposition both in parenchymal Aβ deposits and in the form of CAA. ApoE appears to affect AD pathogenesis by affecting both Aβ aggregation as well as soluble Aβ clearance. The apoE4 allele is associated with greater Aβ plaque load in AD patients. Importantly, it leads to earlier and greater plaque onset in cognitively normal middle-aged and older adults (Drzezga et al., 2009; Reiman et al., 2009; Morris et al., 2010; Kantarci et al., 2012). Consistent with its role in being a protective factor, apoE2 leads to a strong delay in Aβ deposition (Morris et al., 2010). In addition, apoE4 is also a risk factor for CAA in which

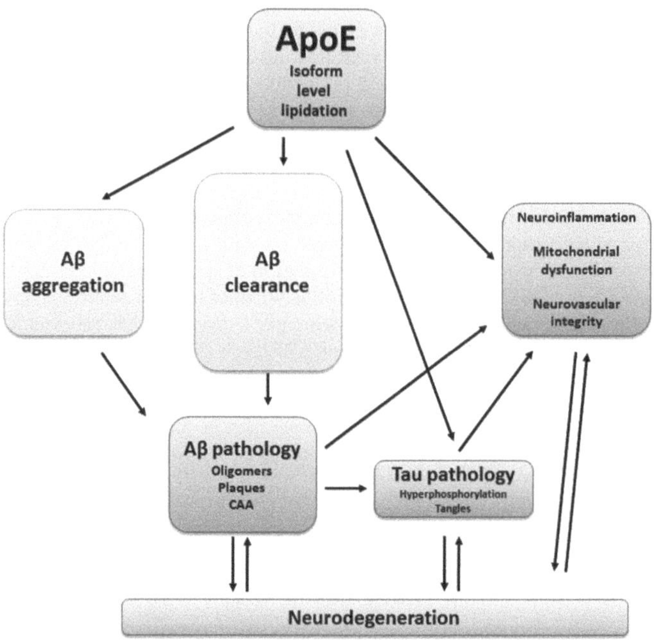

FIGURE 10.3 **The effects of apoE on AD pathogenesis.** Currently, compelling evidence suggests that apoE influences AD pathogenesis in large part via affecting Aβ aggregation and clearance. The accumulation of Aβ in soluble oligomeric forms, in amyloid plaques, and in CAA initiates local toxicity and inflammation. Other evidence also indicates that apoE may affect tau pathology, neuroinflammation, mitochondrial dysfunction, and neurovascular integrity. Differences in apoE isoform, level, and lipidation status can affect these processes. Abbreviations: *Aβ*, amyloid-β; *AD*, Alzheimer's disease; *apoE*, apolipoprotein E.

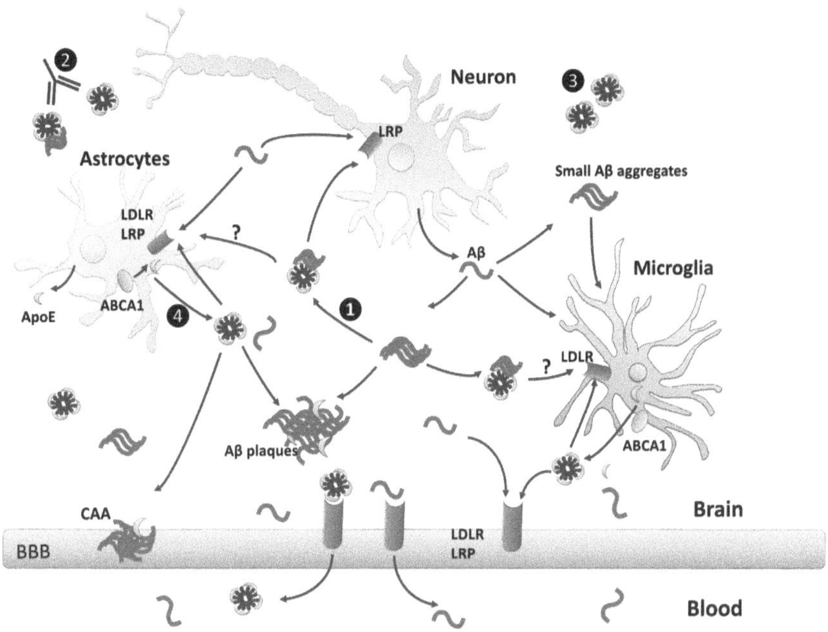

FIGURE 10.4 **The effects of apoE on Aβ metabolism.** ApoE affects Aβ pathology primarily by affecting its aggregation and clearance. ApoE is expressed in astrocytes and microglia in the brain. After being lipidated by ABCA1, it is secreted into the interstitial space as HDL-like lipoprotein particles. ApoE coaggregates with Aβ in amyloid plaques and CAA (Namba et al., 1991). The binding affinity of lipidated apoE to soluble Aβ follows the pattern of apoE2 > apoE3 > apoE4 (Tokuda et al., 2000). The interaction between apoE and Aβ may affect Aβ fibrillization, although it is still not clear whether apoE inhibits or promotes Aβ fibrillization (Ma et al., 1994; Sanan et al., 1994; Evans et al., 1995; Garai and Frieden, 2010). ApoE influences Aβ clearance through several possible pathways. ApoE was shown to affect enzymatic degradation of Aβ (Jiang et al., 2008). Aβ is transported across the BBB via LDLR- and LRP1-mediated mechanisms (Deane et al., 2008; Castellano et al., 2012). ApoE can also influence endocytosis of Aβ by astrocytes and microglia via modifying the activation state of the glial cells (Baitsch et al., 2011; Yang et al., 2013). The cellular uptake of Aβ is also affected by apoE-receptor-mediated endocytosis (Koistinaho et al., 2004; Basak et al., 2012b). It was proposed that apoE and Aβ are internalized as a complex into the astrocytes through LDLR. However, recent evidence suggests that Aβ can bind to LDLR directly and be internalized. ApoE may affect this process by competing LDLR with Aβ (Basak et al., 2012b). The effects of apoE on Aβ clearance are influenced by apoE isoform, apoE level, and lipidation status. Current strategies that modify the Aβ metabolism through apoE include ❶ Aβ peptides that block the interaction between apoE and Aβ (Sadowski et al., 2006; Yang et al., 2011), ❷ apoE antibodies that suppress Aβ plaque growth (Liao et al., 2014), ❸ manipulation of apoE levels (Kim et al., 2009b; Cramer et al., 2012), and ❹ modification of apoE lipidation status via ABCA1 (Koldamova et al., 2005a; Riddell et al., 2007; Wahrle et al., 2008; Boehm-Cagan and Michaelson, 2014). Abbreviations: *Aβ*, amyloid-β; *ABCA1*, ATP-binding cassette transporter A1; *apoE*, apolipoprotein E; *LDLR*, low-density lipoprotein receptor; *LRP1*, low-density lipoprotein receptor-related protein 1.

amyloid deposits form in brain arterioles (Greenberg et al., 1995). In many in vitro and in vivo experiments, apoE has been demonstrated to influence aggregation and clearance of Aβ (Kim et al., 2009a). Herein, we will mainly focus on discussing how the interactions between apoE and Aβ affect AD pathology and the potential strategies to interfere with these processes (Fig. 10.4).

ApoE and Aβ Aggregation

In Vivo Aggregation Studies in Human Brains and Mouse Models

ApoE is a component of amyloid plaques in the human brain (Namba et al., 1991; Wisniewski and Frangione, 1992). The colocalization of apoE within newly formed amyloid plaques is isoform dependent, being seen more frequently in ε4/ε4 than in non-apoE ε4/ε4 individuals (Thal et al., 2005). In APP transgenic mice, deletion of endogenous murine apoE leads to significantly less Aβ deposition and almost no fibrillar Aβ deposits in brain parenchyma, and no CAA, suggesting that apoE is essential for Aβ to aggregate into a fibrillar form (Bales et al., 1997, 1999; Holtzman et al., 2000b). Interestingly, introduction of human apoE into APP mice lacking endogenous mouse apoE leads to a delayed Aβ deposition in comparison to when murine apoE is present (Holtzman et al., 1999; Fagan et al., 2002). Importantly, as in humans, Aβ deposition, including in fibrillar plaques, eventually does occur in the presence of human apoE, and it is in the order apoE4 > apoE3 > apoE2 in PDAPP transgenic mice crossed to human apoE knockin mice (Bales et al., 2009; Castellano et al., 2011). The reasons that human apoE results in delayed but eventually fibrillar Aβ deposition relative to murine apoE may be that human apoE both affects monomeric Aβ clearance as well as influencing the process of Aβ aggregation. In several other APP transgenic mouse models, it was also observed that apoE4 is associated with higher Aβ plaque deposition as compared to apoE3 (Holtzman et al., 2000a; Dolev and Michaelson, 2004; Fryer et al., 2005a; Kim et al., 2011; Bien-Ly et al., 2012; Youmans et al., 2012). The CAA load in APP transgenic mice carrying different human apoE isoforms also follows the pattern of apoE4 > apoE3 (Fryer et al., 2005a). However, the distribution of amyloid deposition to plaques or CAA is different in APP mice expressing murine apoE versus those expressing human apoE4. Murine apoE is more amyloidogenic, with Aβ depositing earlier and to a greater extent in brain parenchyma. In contrast, human apoE4 leads to later Aβ aggregation but to a much greater percentage of CAA versus parenchymal plaques in mice (Fryer et al., 2005a; Oddo et al., 2009), suggesting that apoE may influence plaque and CAA formation via different mechanisms. In addition to isoform effects on amyloid deposition, the dose of apoE also modifies Aβ pathology. There is significantly less Aβ plaque deposition in mice expressing one copy of apoE as compared to mice that express two copies of the same apoE isoform (Kim et al., 2011; Bien-Ly et al., 2012). This information may be very important since there has been a long debate about whether increasing or decreasing apoE will be beneficial for AD pathology. These data would suggest that lowering apoE3 or apoE4 would be beneficial in regard to lowering Aβ-related pathology. Whether the same findings would be seen if apoE3 or apoE4 is lowered in an adult brain is not yet clear. Interestingly, there are data that, unlike apoE3 and apoE4, indicate that overexpression of apoE2 leads to less Aβ deposition (Dodart et al., 2005; Hudry et al., 2013). However, the mechanism by which different apoE isoforms affect Aβ aggregation is not yet completely clear.

In the past 20 years, efforts have been made to identify an apoE/Aβ complex in human biological samples. ApoE/Aβ complexes have been seen in the biochemically soluble fraction of human tissue homogenates (Naslund et al., 1995; Russo et al., 1998; Hashimoto et al., 2012; Tai et al., 2013). In CSF of healthy subjects, an apoE/Aβ complex has been detected but the abundance is inconsistent between studies. One study found that most CSF Aβ cofractionates with CSF lipoprotein particles (LaDu et al., 2012), whereas a study from our group shows that there is minimal association of Aβ with lipoprotein particles or apoE in either CSF or cell culture under physiological conditions (Verghese et al., 2013). The difference between these two studies is likely due to the fact that in one study CSF was concentrated prior to fractionation (LaDu et al., 2012) whereas in the other it was not (Verghese et al., 2013). While apoE present in physiological fluids such as CSF may not be in complex with Aβ, there is no question that once Aβ aggregates in the brain parenchyma or in CAA in the form of fibrils, apoE is then found in complex with amyloid fibrils. When different apoE isoforms have been compared in their binding to Aβ, some studies have found that apoE3 binds to Aβ to a greater extent than apoE4 does (Russo et al., 1998; Yamauchi et al., 1999; Tai et al., 2013), whereas others found no difference in their binding (Naslund et al., 1995; Verghese et al., 2013). The binding between Aβ and apoE appears to require amino acids 12–28 of Aβ and amino acids 244–272 of apoE (Strittmatter et al., 1993a).

In Vitro Studies on apoE/Aβ Binding

The binding between apoE and Aβ under in vitro conditions has been extensively studied to understand how apoE isoforms could affect Aβ aggregation differentially. An initial study shows that CSF apoE bound to immobilized Aβ peptides (Strittmatter et al., 1993a). Binding between nonlipidated apoE4 and Aβ occurred faster than binding with apoE3 (Strittmatter et al., 1993b). However, the formation of a complex between astrocyte-derived apoE with Aβ follows the pattern apoE3 > apoE4 in another study (LaDu et al., 1994). In fact, most studies demonstrate that the efficiency of complex formation between lipidated apoE and Aβ follows the order of apoE2 > apoE3 ≫ apoE4 (Zhou et al., 1996; Yang et al., 1997; Tokuda et al., 2000; Kim et al., 2009a; Petrlova et al., 2011).

Effects of apoE on In Vitro Aβ Fibrillization

ApoE also influences the kinetics of Aβ fibrillization in vitro. As with binding, the observations are not consistent across different studies. Despite this, most reports in which apoE is shown to promote Aβ aggregation have found that apoE4 causes greater Aβ fibril formation than other apoE isoforms. Some studies show that all three apoE isoforms promoted $A\beta_{42}$ aggregation (Ma et al., 1994). The profibrillization effects of apoE isoforms follow the order apoE4 > apoE3 > apoE2 (Ma et al., 1994; Sanan et al., 1994; Wisniewski et al., 1994). However, other studies suggest that apoE isoforms inhibit Aβ aggregation, with apoE4 being least effective (Evans et al., 1995; Wood et al., 1996; Beffert and Poirier, 1998; Garai et al., 2014). The inconsistency of the effects of apoE isoform on Aβ binding fibrillization observed in different studies may be caused by the experimental conditions, including the species of Aβ used ($A\beta_{40}$ or $A\beta_{42}$), preparation of Aβ and apoE (lipidated vs nonlipidated), and incubation conditions (Kim et al., 2009a). In the future, more effort needs to be made to clarify the impact of apoE on Aβ aggregation since this is an essential point to address in determining part of the mechanism as to how apoE influences Aβ deposition, as well as in developing ways to target this interaction.

ApoE and Aβ Clearance

Aβ deposition depends on not only the propensity for Aβ to aggregate, but also the concentration of monomeric Aβ. Aβ monomer concentration is a net balance of Aβ production and Aβ clearance. In cell culture, several studies suggest that apoE affects APP processing through ApoER2 (He et al., 2007) or LRP1-regulated endocytic trafficking (Ulery et al., 2000;

Cam et al., 2005). When different apoE isoforms were compared in cell culture, some studies suggested that apoE4 enhances Aβ production (Ye et al., 2005), whereas other studies showed that there is no apoE-isoform-specific effect on APP processing (Biere et al., 1995; Cedazo-Minguez et al., 2001; Irizarry et al., 2004). In APP transgenic mice expressing human apoE isoforms, neither amyloidogenic processing of APP nor Aβ synthesis rates vary according to human apoE isoforms (Castellano et al., 2011). Despite the lack of evidence that apoE isoforms influence Aβ production differently, substantial evidence suggests that apoE isoforms affect monomeric Aβ clearance. Aβ is cleared from the brain by several mechanisms, including enzymatic degradation, transport across the blood–brain barrier, ISF–CSF bulk flow, and cellular uptake. ApoE seems to influence multiple pathways to change Aβ clearance.

ApoE and Enzymatic Degradation of Aβ

There are several proteases that contribute to Aβ degradation in the brain. Among them, neprilysin (NEP) and insulin-degrading enzyme have received the most attention. NEP degrades Aβ that associates with the cell membrane, whereas insulin-degrading enzyme acts both intracellularly or extracellularly since it can be secreted into the extracellular fluid (Nalivaeva et al., 2012). In cell culture, extracellular degradation of soluble Aβ by insulin-degrading enzyme is enhanced when apoE is present. In addition, lipidated apoE has greater effects than nonlipidated apoE (Jiang et al., 2008).

ApoE and BBB Transport of Aβ

The BBB is a highly selective permeability barrier that separates the blood from brain ISF. It is formed by continuous capillary endothelial cells connected by tight junctions. The endothelial cells are surrounded by basal lamina, astrocytic perivascular end feet, and pericytes. Aβ is actively transported from brain ISF to the blood across the BBB through transporters, including P-glycoprotein (Cirrito et al., 2005), LRP1 (Shibata et al., 2000), and LDLR (Castellano et al., 2012). LRP1 appears to be a major Aβ efflux transporter at the BBB. In an in vitro model of BBB cells, LRP1 is found to mediate the uptake of Aβ (Yamada et al., 2008). Blocking LRP1 function with antibodies leads to reduction of Aβ clearance from the brain to the blood (Shibata et al., 2000). When Aβ aggregates alone or in the presence of other molecules such as apoE, Aβ clearance across the BBB is impaired (Ito et al., 2007; Deane et al., 2008). Importantly, apoE has been found to disrupt monomeric Aβ clearance across the BBB in an isoform-specific manner such that apoE4 had a greater disruptive effect than either apoE3 or apoE2 (Deane et al., 2008). Consistent with the effect of apoE inhibiting monomeric Aβ clearance across the BBB are data showing that in PDAPP mice expressing apoE2, E3, or E4, clearance of Aβ from the brain is in the order of fastest to slowest E2 > E3 > E4 (Castellano et al., 2011). Lipidation status of apoE also affects Aβ transport across the BBB (Bachmeier et al., 2013). In the future, more studies are needed to understand the mechanism by which apoE affects Aβ cross-BBB clearance and whether there is an isoform-dependent effect. A recent study from our group suggests that apoE inhibits Aβ clearance by competing for apoE receptors such as LDLR and LRP1 (Verghese et al., 2013). In addition to affecting the BBB clearance of Aβ via receptor-mediated mechanisms, apoE4 may also disrupt normal BBB function by impairing BBB integrity. Studies indicate that apoE4 impairs the function of tight junctions between endothelial cells (Nishitsuji et al., 2011) or activates a destructive inflammatory response in pericytes (Bell et al., 2012).

ApoE and Cellular Metabolism of Aβ

A variety of cells, including neurons (Paresce et al., 1996, 1997), astrocytes (Koistinaho et al., 2004), microglia (Mandrekar et al., 2009), endothelial cells, and smooth muscle cells (Kanekiyo et al., 2012), along the brain vasculature have been shown to internalize Aβ. The ability to internalize Aβ is not equal for these cell types. In addition, whether internalization of Aβ is beneficial or detrimental largely depends on the efficiency of intracellular Aβ degradation mechanisms in different cell types. Neurons are able to take up Aβ in the absence (Saavedra et al., 2007) or presence (Beffert et al., 1999a) of ApoE. In hippocampal neuronal culture, apoE3 was able to clear Aβ from the extracellular space better than apoE4. However, neurons have more intracellular Aβ in the presence of apoE4, suggesting impaired intracellular Aβ degradation (Beffert et al., 1999a). Several studies have shown that Aβ is concentrated upon internalization into neurons (Zerbinatti et al., 2006; Hu et al., 2009), suggesting that neurons are not able to degrade Aβ efficiently. Instead, microglia and astrocytes appear to degrade Aβ more efficiently and are likely the major brain cells that clear Aβ from the interstitial space.

The role of microglia, the resident macrophages in the brain, in AD pathogenesis is still under intense study. Microglia can promote proinflammatory pathways that enhance Aβ accumulation and neurotoxicity (Hickman et al., 2008). On the other hand, microglia can internalize Aβ and reduce the Aβ level in the ISF. Microglia are able to engulf Aβ fibrils through phagocytosis, although the ability to digest fibrillar Aβ appears limited under most conditions (Paresce et al., 1996, 1997). Soluble Aβ has been shown to be internalized by microglia through fluid phase micropinocytosis, and the internalized Aβ is rapidly degraded though the late endocytic pathway (Mandrekar et al., 2009). Although LRP1 is expressed in microglia, the LRP1-mediated endocytosis does not appear to be the major pathway for soluble Aβ uptake by microglia (Mandrekar et al., 2009). ApoE is more likely to influence the intracellular degradation of Aβ by neprilysin and related enzymes in microglia (Jiang et al., 2008). In addition, apoE may influence the microglial Aβ clearance pathway through converting microglia from a more proinflammatory M1-like state to the antiinflammatory M2-like state (Baitsch et al., 2011) or affect the migration speed of activated microglia. ApoE4 is associated with a lower efficiency of antiinflammatory function (Baitsch et al., 2011; Yang et al., 2013) and a slower microglial migration rate (Cudaback et al., 2011).

Immunostaining for Aβ suggests that astrocytes are able to internalize Aβ in the brain (Funato et al., 1998; Thal et al., 2000). Cultured astrocytes are able to internalize and degrade Aβ in both soluble (Shaffer et al., 1995; Nielsen et al., 2009) and fibrillar forms (Wyss-Coray et al., 2003; Koistinaho et al., 2004). ApoE can contribute to this process by stimulating activity of astrocytes. A previous study showed that the absence of apoE leads to impairment of endocytosis and degradation of aggregated Aβ by astrocytes (Koistinaho et al., 2004). The effects of apoE-mediated uptake of Aβ seem to be receptor mediated. An antagonist against the LDLR family blocked Aβ degradation by astrocytes (Koistinaho et al., 2004). However, a recent study shows that LDLR can bind directly to soluble Aβ and facilitates the uptake, endocytosis, and transport of Aβ to lysosomes in astrocytes (Basak et al., 2012b). This effect is intact in the absence of apoE, suggesting an apoE-independent phenomenon (Basak et al., 2012b). ApoE can compete for this Aβ binding and uptake (Verghese et al., 2013). In the future, more studies are needed to clarify the roles that apoE plays in the uptake and degradation of different forms of Aβ by different cell types.

AD THERAPEUTIC OPPORTUNITIES TARGETING apoE

Based on the potential roles that apoE plays in AD pathogenesis as discussed previously in this chapter, different therapeutic modalities targeting apoE have been proposed. Some of these concepts have been tested in cell culture and animal models. These strategies include Aβ fragments that block the interaction between apoE and Aβ, different ways to manipulate apoE levels, monoclonal antibodies against apoE, small molecules that modify apoE structure, compounds that change apoE lipidation status, and apoE mimetic peptides (Table 10.1).

TABLE 10.1 Summary of apoE-Targeted Therapeutic Strategies for Alzheimer Disease

Strategy	Method and rationale	Example	References
Disrupt ApoE/Aβ interaction	Aβ peptide or apoE fragment that blocks binding sites to reduce Aβ aggregation	Aβ12-28P, Aβ17-21, ApoE249-256	Sadowski et al. (2006), Liu et al. (2011), Yang et al. (2011), Kuszczyk et al. (2013)
Increase apoE levels	Stimulate expression of endogenous apoE or increase apoE2 specifically to enhance protective effects of apoE	Bexarotene	Cramer et al. (2012), Fitz et al. (2013), Price et al. (2013), Tesseur et al. (2013), Veeraraghavalu et al. (2013)
		Gene delivery	Dodart et al. (2005), Hudry et al. (2013)
Decrease apoE levels	Clearance of apoE out of the brain by overexpression of apoE receptors, monoclonal antibodies to apoE, or gene inhibition to decrease detrimental effects of apoE	ApoE receptor overexpression	Kim et al. (2009b)
ApoE immunotherapy	Passive immunization of monoclonal apoE antibody to slow growth of plaques and activate antiinflammatory response of microglia	Anti-ApoE antibody	Kim et al. (2012), Liao et al. (2014)
ApoE structure corrector	Conversion of apoE4 to an apoE3-like structure to increase apoE3-related function and decrease apoE4-related function	GIND25, PH002, CB9032258	Brodbeck et al. (2011), Chen et al. (2012)
ApoE lipidation modification	Increase ABCA1 expression to modify apoE/Aβ binding and enhance apoE clearance	PPAR, LXR, RXR agonists	Koldamova et al. (2005a), Riddell et al. (2007), Donkin et al. (2010), Fitz et al. (2010)
Block apoE fragmentation	Inhibit protease involved in apoE fragmentation or antibody target to C-terminal apoE fragments to decrease tau hyperphosphorylation and mitochondrial toxicity		
ApoE mimetic peptide	ApoE mimetic peptides to compete with full-length protein for receptor binding to suppress microglial activation and maintain neuroprotective properties of full-length apoE	apoE133-149 analogs	Laskowitz et al. (2007), Wang et al. (2007), Vitek et al. (2012)

Aβ, amyloid-β; *ABCA1*, ATP-binding cassette transporter A1; *AD*, Alzheimer's disease; *apoE*, apolipoprotein E; *LDLR*, low-density lipoprotein receptor; *LRP1*, low-density lipoprotein receptor-related protein 1; *LXR*, liver X receptor; *PPAR*, peroxisome proliferator-activated receptors; *RNAi*, RNA interference; *RXR*, retinoid X receptor.

Aβ Peptides or apoE Fragments That Block Interaction Between apoE and Aβ

Since amino acids 12–28 of Aβ are suggested to be the region that binds apoE (Strittmatter et al., 1993b), Aβ-mimicking peptides that block the Aβ/apoE interaction have been assessed as potential AD therapeutics. Aβ12-28P, a BBB-permeable nontoxic and nonfibrillogenic synthetic peptide homologous to the apoE binding site on full-length Aβ, binds to lipidated human apoE and abolishes its effect on Aβ aggregation and toxicity in cell culture (Ma et al., 1996; Sadowski et al., 2006). When given systemically to APP transgenic mice, it was shown to reduce amyloid deposition in plaques and CAA, reduce microhemorrhages, inhibit synaptic degeneration, and prevent memory decline (Sadowski et al., 2006; Yang et al., 2011; Kuszczyk et al., 2013). Recently, more effort has been made to identify smaller amino acid regions that are essential for the apoE/Aβ interaction, and Aβ17–21 has been found to inhibit the apoE/Aβ interaction efficiently (Liu et al., 2011). ApoE249–256 segment was also a potent inhibitor of apoE/Aβ interaction in vitro (Liu et al., 2011). However, the in vivo effects of apoE249–256 on Aβ deposition have not yet been reported.

Manipulation of apoE Levels

There has been a long debate regarding whether apoE4 is a risk for AD because of a gain of detrimental effects or a loss of protective effects. There is no general agreement regarding the level of apoE in humans of different apoE genotype. The measurement of apoE levels in mice suggested that the level of the most pathogenic isoform, apoE4, is somewhat lower than apoE3 or apoE2 in the brain of apoE knockin mice (Riddell et al., 2008; Sullivan et al., 2011). However, the key issue from a therapeutic standpoint is whether increasing or decreasing the level of apoE would be beneficial or detrimental with regard to key aspects of AD pathogenesis. In animal studies, when the same isoform of apoE is compared, APP transgenic mice that express one copy of human apoE have much lower amyloid plaque deposition than mice that express two copies of apoE (Kim et al., 2011; Bien-Ly et al., 2012). The latter findings strongly argue that reducing apoE will be beneficial to reducing Aβ deposition. It will be important in proof of concept experiments to reduce apoE3 and apoE4 in adult mice to see if the same effect is observed.

A possible side effect of reducing apoE is abnormal lipid metabolism. However, studies have shown that less than 10% of normal serum apoE is sufficient to maintain normal serum cholesterol level in the mouse (Hasty et al., 1999). This implies that reducing apoE level within a reasonable range, even peripherally, is not likely to cause abnormal peripheral lipid metabolism. In addition, there are no clear brain abnormalities either in human apoE knockin mice or in humans with one copy of functional apoE. As mentioned earlier, while lowering apoE3 or apoE4 has been reported to be beneficial in lowering Aβ deposition, increasing expression of apoE2 in the brain has also been reported to decrease Aβ deposition (Dodart et al., 2005; Hudry et al., 2013). Why these opposite effects of apoE4 and apoE4 versus apoE2 in this regard are found is not yet clear. We will next discuss the potential approaches, including both increasing and decreasing apoE levels.

Strategies That Increase apoE Levels

When considering strategies to increase apoE levels, stimulating the expression of endogenous apoE is a straightforward idea. However, there are no compounds known to selectively increase apoE but not have effects on other molecules. Bexarotene is a drug which is an RXR agonist which increases apoE mRNA and protein levels, and was recently reported to rapidly decrease monomeric Aβ, remove amyloid plaques, and improve behavioral performance (Cramer et al., 2012). However, there is some inconsistency in that different groups of scientists have not been able to replicate the rapid plaque-removing effect (Fitz et al., 2013; Price et al., 2013; Tesseur et al., 2013; Veeraraghavalu et al., 2013). The effect of bexarotene on lowering ISF Aβ has been seen by other groups (Fitz et al., 2013; Ulrich et al., 2013). It is not clear whether the potential beneficial effects of bexarotene are mediated by improvement of apoE lipidation status versus elevation of apoE levels since RXR also controls the expression of ATP-binding cassette A1 (ABCA1), a protein that is responsible for apoE lipidation. More details about bexarotene, ABCA1, and apoE lipidation will be discussed later in the section: ApoE Lipidation Modification.

Gene delivery approaches were used to virally express human apoE in APP transgenic mice in the presence of endogenous murine apoE (Dodart et al., 2005; Hudry et al., 2013). The expression of apoE2 significantly reduced amyloid plaque load while apoE4 increased plaque load. Plaque growth was suppressed by apoE2 whereas it tended to be accelerated by apoE4 as monitored by in vivo multiphoton imaging technique (Hudry et al., 2013). These studies suggest that generally stimulating the expression of endogenous apoE may not be a good strategy because over 50% of the LOAD patients are apoE4 carriers. If an increase of apoE level will be used as a therapeutic strategy, the protective isoform of apoE2 will likely need to be specifically increased. If a strategy is designed to target the endogenous apoE of the apoE4 carriers, reducing the apoE level clearly appears to be a better choice, at least in regard to influencing Aβ-related pathology.

Strategies That Decrease apoE Levels

Since the clearance of apoE both within the brain as well as out of the brain is in large part dependent on apoE receptors (Fig. 10.2), apoE-receptor-based strategies were used to lower apoE levels. LDLR is a major receptor that regulates apoE metabolism. LDLR is more highly expressed on glial cells as compared to neurons in vivo. Overexpression of LDLR in astrocytes significantly reduces extracellular apoE concentration and increases Aβ uptake (Basak et al., 2012b). Overexpression of LDLR in an APP transgenic mouse brain significantly reduces brain apoE levels and amyloid deposition (Kim et al., 2009b). LRP1 is another lipoprotein receptor that is important for apoE metabolism. Overexpression of a functional LRP1 minireceptor in APP transgenic mice increases Aβ cellular uptake (Zerbinatti et al., 2006). However, since LRP1 is highly expressed on neurons and to a lesser extent in glia (Rapp et al., 2006), the functional outcome of increasing LRP1 needs to be carefully evaluated due to the poor ability of neurons to degrade the accumulating Aβ (Zerbinatti et al., 2006). In the future, if the manipulation of LRP1 in the CNS is employed as an AD therapeutic approach, the overexpression of LRP1 needs to be directed into cells that have a good capacity to clear Aβ—for example, vascular smooth muscle cells (Kanekiyo et al., 2012) or endothelial cells (Yamada et al., 2008).

Monoclonal antibodies against apoE can also reduce apoE levels as measured by immunostaining (Liao et al., 2014). Decrease of apoE levels could be one of the mechanisms by which apoE antibodies reduce Aβ pathology (Kim et al., 2012; Liao et al., 2014). In the future, antibodies specific to the detrimental apoE4 isoform could be generated and tested in APP transgenic mice. In addition, gene knockdown techniques such as RNA interference and antisense oligonucleotides could be utilized to decrease apoE levels in the CNS.

ApoE Passive Immunotherapy

Since the first report that Aβ immunization attenuates AD-like pathology in APP transgenic mice (Schenk et al., 1999), active and passive immunization approaches against Aβ have been explored to design treatments appropriate for human use. This approach has been successful in animal models and is being tested and remains promising in humans. However, certain types of active and passive immunization have resulted in significant side effects such as brain edema and hemorrhages. Given that Aβ metabolism is regulated by other proteins, immunization against proteins which regulate Aβ metabolism or are complexed with Aβ aggregates could also provide another treatment avenue, perhaps with less significant side effects. Since apoE colocalizes with Aβ in amyloid plaques, apoE antibodies have been tested to see whether they can reduce Aβ pathology (Kim et al., 2012; Liao et al., 2014). A monoclonal antibody against murine apoE (HJ6.3) was shown to reduce amyloid plaque load by more than 50% when given to an APP transgenic mouse model by weekly intraperitoneal injection starting before the onset of plaque deposition (Kim et al., 2012). When given to mice after plaque deposition, apoE antibodies also suppressed amyloid deposition and improved brain functional connectivity and cognition, yet did not alter plasma total cholesterol (Liao et al., 2014). The effects of apoE monoclonal antibodies are likely to be mediated through multiple mechanisms. ApoE antibodies were able to activate an antiinflammatory response of microglia in an acute treatment paradigm (Kim et al., 2012). The growth of individual plaques on the brain surface was monitored over a 14-day period of time using in vivo imaging. The plaques that were bound by apoE antibodies grew significantly more slowly than those not bound by antibodies, likely because either apoE antibodies interfere with the apoE and Aβ interaction or they increased microglial apoE/Aβ uptake (Liao et al., 2014).

One potential side effect of apoE antibody therapy is that targeting apoE might change systemic lipid metabolism. However, no significant changes in total cholesterol were observed in both published studies to date (Kim et al., 2012; Liao et al., 2014). In addition, the mice treated with apoE antibody did not have an alteration in CAA load, which often occurs with Aβ passive immunotherapy. In the future, studies with antibodies that are specific for human apoE, especially apoE4, would be very useful to determine the effect of passive immunotherapy targeting human apoE. The efficacy and side effects would then need to be evaluated in the mice expressing both human apoE and human Aβ.

ApoE Structure Correctors

Although the three major apoE isoforms differ by only one or two amino acids in composition, the intrinsic biophysical and structural features appear to be different between apoE isoforms and to account for the dramatic differences in disease risk for AD. Due to the high self-aggregation propensity occurring through the C-terminal domain, including its lipid binding and highly hydrophobic nature, the structure of full-length wild-type apoE protein is difficult to determine. Lipid-free apoE contains two independent structural domains (Wetterau et al., 1988). Initial efforts to understand apoE structure used the strategy of determining the N-terminal (residues 1–191) and C-terminal (residues 216–299) structural domains separately. The N-terminal domain is an elongated four-helix bundle, as determined by X-ray crystallography (Wilson et al., 1991). The regions between helices are flexible loops

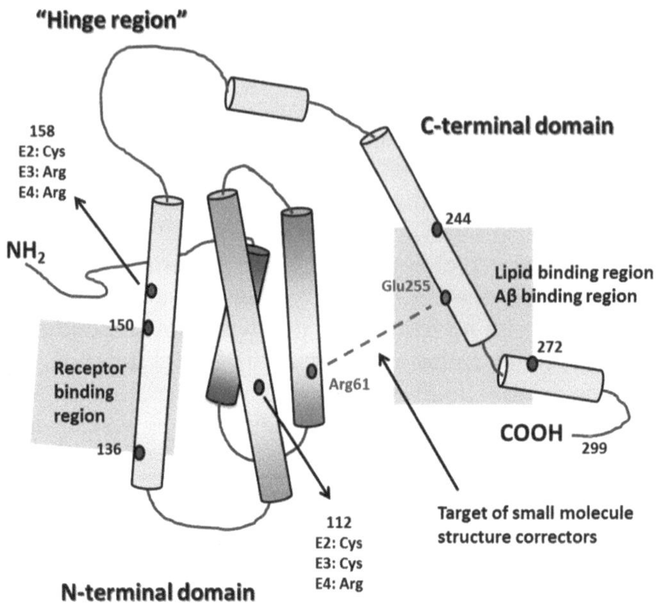

FIGURE 10.5 **Domain structure of human apoE3.** The lipid-free apoE3 protein contains two independent domains which are connected by a "hinge region." The N-terminal domain structure is a four-helix bundle as determined by X-ray crystallography (Wilson et al., 1991). The C-terminal domain contains three helices as predicted by computer modeling (Hatters et al., 2006) or determined on a C-terminal-mutated apoE3 using NMR (Chen et al., 2011). The LDLR binding region (136–150) is located on the fourth helix in the N-terminal domain. The difference in residue 158 influences the nearby LDLR binding region in apoE2, leading to a low binding affinity between apoE2 with receptors. The lipid binding region is located on residues 244–272 in the C-terminal domain (Strittmatter et al., 1993b). The same region also interacts with residues 12–28 on Aβ peptide (Strittmatter et al., 1993b). It is proposed that Arg112 in apoE4 exposes nearby Arg61 which forms a salt bridge with Glu255 in the C-terminal domain and leads to closer contact between the N- and C-terminal domains. This unique "domain interaction" in apoE4 may result in different folding status, lipidation, resistance to proteolysis, and apoE/Aβ interaction (Mahley and Huang, 2012). Based on this hypothesis, small-molecule structure correctors have been designed (Brodbeck et al., 2011; Chen et al., 2012). Abbreviations: *Aβ*, amyloid-β; *apoE*, apolipoprotein E; *LDLR*, low-density lipoprotein receptor. *Modified from Hatters et al. (2006).*

rather than tight turns. The C-terminal domain is predicted to be highly α-helical using a structural prediction program (Aggerbeck et al., 1988). The N- and C-terminal domains have been proposed to be linked by a flexible hinge region (Hatters et al., 2006) (Fig. 10.5). Later, the full-length apoE structure was determined by NMR based on a biologically functional form of apoE which contains five mutations in the C-terminal domain to prevent self-aggregation (Chen et al., 2011). The overall structures determined by the two different approaches are similar in that both structural models propose that apoE contains a four-helix-bundle N-terminal domain connected with a helical C-terminal domain. However, the interactions between N-terminal and C-terminal domains are different in these two models. For example, in the model proposed by Hatters et al. (2006) there is no interaction between N- and C-terminal domains in apoE3, whereas in apoE4, Arg112 orients the side chain of Arg61 to form a salt bridge with the Glu255 of the C-terminal region, resulting in an interaction between the

N- and C-terminal domains. In the structure of full-length apoE3 determined by Chen et al., apoE3 displays extensive domain interaction mediated by multiple H-bonds and salt bridges between N- and C-terminal domains. In addition, Glu255 forms a salt bridge with Lys95 instead of Arg61 within the N-terminal domain (Chen et al., 2011). It is not yet clear whether the five C-terminal mutations in the full-length apoE in the latter model affect the interactions between N- and C-terminal domains or the effect of Arg61 in the previous model is indirect (Frieden and Garai, 2013). This will be very important to sort out.

In vivo, the majority of apoE protein is lipidated. ApoE binds to lipids through the lipid binding region located within the C-terminal domain (residues 244–272). It can then act as a ligand to bind with apoE receptors through the receptor binding region (residues 136–150) at the fourth helix within the N-terminal domain and mediate lipid transport (Hatters et al., 2006). This receptor binding region is also the predominant binding region with heparin, although the C-terminal domain also contains a heparin binding region (Saito et al., 2003). ApoE also binds with Aβ at residues 244–272 of apoE, part of the same C-terminal region important for lipid binding (Strittmatter et al., 1993b).

ApoE polymorphisms may affect apoE structure and function in several ways. The difference between apoE2 and apoE3 at residue 158 appears to be involved in regulating the conformation of the receptor binding region since apoE2 (Cys158) has much lower binding affinity with LDLR than apoE3 (Arg158) and apoE4 (Arg158) have. According to the model proposed by Hatters et al., apoE polymorphism at residue 112 might play a role in modifying the N- and C-domain interaction since it is spatially located very close to Arg61, a residue within the second helix of the N-terminal domain which forms a salt bridge with Glu255 within the C-terminal domain and stabilizes closer contact between the N- and C-terminal domains in apoE4 (Raffai et al., 2001; Hatters et al., 2006). The different folding status of apoE3 (Cys112) and apoE4 (Arg112) as supported by data from Weisgraber and coworkers results in different lipoprotein-binding preference, protein stability, and interaction with Aβ (Morrow et al., 2000; Raffai et al., 2001; Acharya et al., 2002; Bentley et al., 2002; Hatters et al., 2006). Although the exact mechanism of how apoE polymorphism affects AD pathogenesis is not completely clear, small-molecule apoE4 structure correctors (apoE4SCs) targeting domain interaction were identified and tested in cell cultures. GIND25 and PH002, two apoE4SCs converting a more closed apoE4 structure to a more open apoE3-like structure, were shown to rescue the impaired intracellular trafficking of apoE4 (Brodbeck et al., 2011). Another apoE4SC called CB9032258 rescued apoE4-mediated impairments of mitochondrial motility and neurite outgrowth in a neuronal cell line (Chen et al., 2012). In the future, additional studies are needed to test the effects of these apoE4SCs in vivo on different phenotypes associated with apoE pathophysiology related to AD.

ApoE Lipidation Modification

The function of apoE is greatly dependent on its lipidation status. To date, the most studied molecule that lipidates apoE is ABCA1. ABCA1 is a transmembrane protein that utilizes ATP hydrolysis to transport cellular cholesterol and phospholipids from cells to lipid-poor apolipoproteins, including apoE. Loss of ABCA1 function is the cause of Tangier disease, which is characterized by significantly reduced levels of normal apoA-I containing HDL in the blood (Lawn et al., 1999). In the brain, astrocytes secrete the majority of apoE in

HDL-like lipoprotein particles. Astrocytes that lack ABCA1 secrete very poorly lipidated apoE, resulting in an intracellular lipid accumulation and a decrease of apoE levels in the brain and CSF (Hirsch-Reinshagen et al., 2004; Wahrle et al., 2004). Surprisingly, decreased apoE levels in the ABCA1 knockout mice were not associated with decreased Aβ plaque load in APP mouse models as expected. Instead, studies from three independent groups demonstrated that deletion of ABCA1 leads to an increase of amyloid plaque burden (Hirsch-Reinshagen et al., 2005; Koldamova et al., 2005b; Wahrle et al., 2005). In agreement with the ABCA1 deletion study, ABCA1 overexpression in APP mouse models results in a significantly decreased Aβ plaque burden (Wahrle et al., 2008). These studies suggested that ABCA1 may affect Aβ pathology through apoE lipidation; poorly lipidated apoE is more amyloidogenic, whereas highly lipidated apoE is less amyloidogenic. Interestingly, losing one copy of ABCA1 resulted in increased amyloid plaque burden and exacerbated memory deficits in APP/E4 but not in APP/E3 mice (Fitz et al., 2012), suggesting that lipidation deficiency has different effects depending on apoE isoform.

Since Aβ production is not altered in APP transgenic mice lacking ABCA1 (Koldamova et al., 2005b; Morikawa et al., 2005), the effect of ABCA1 on amyloid deposition is probably mediated through Aβ clearance or aggregation. When looking into the details about how ABCA1 affects Aβ pathology, conflicting data on the effect of ABCA1 on Aβ clearance were observed using different methods. It was shown that ABCA1 deficiency leads to a slower ISF Aβ clearance in APP/E4 mice using an in vivo Aβ microdialysis approach (Fitz et al., 2012). In contrast, a study using a bolus stable isotope labeling kinetics technique shows that ABCA1 affects apoE clearance but does not affect Aβ clearance directly (Basak et al., 2012a). Interestingly, both over-expressing and deletion of ABCA1 lead to a faster clearance rate of apoE (Basak et al., 2012a). It is known that poorly lipidated lipoprotein particles have lower stability, probably accounting for faster apoE clearance in the poorly lipidated state (Schaefer et al., 1981, 2001). On the other hand, the lipidation of apoE also significantly enhances its propensity to bind to LDLR (Innerarity and Mahley, 1978), which would likely result in a faster clearance rate. Therefore, deletion or overexpression of ABCA1 both result in a faster apoE clearance rate, depending on which mechanism is dominant. ABCA1 can also modify the binding between apoE and Aβ through apoE lipidation. Previous studies show conflicting results regarding whether apoE lipidation promotes or inhibits apoE/Aβ binding. Nonlipidated apoE was found to interact with immobilized Aβ with a higher affinity than lipidated apoE particles (Verghese et al., 2013). However, in another study, nonlipidated apoE had lower affinity as compared to lipidated apoE (Tokuda et al., 2000). While the details still need to be worked out, it does seem clear that upregulation of ABCA1 expression or function is a potentially attractive target for increasing apoE lipidation and decreasing Aβ pathology if it can be done selectively.

The expression of ABCA1 and apoE are both under the control of transcription factors PPAR, LXR, and RXR (Perez et al., 2012). Chronic treatment of different LXR and PPAR agonists reduces Aβ pathology and improves cognitive function in APP mouse models (Koldamova et al., 2005a; Riddell et al., 2007; Donkin et al., 2010; Fitz et al., 2010; Terwel et al., 2011; Cramer et al., 2012; Yamanaka et al., 2012; Boehm-Cagan and Michaelson, 2014; Tai et al., 2014). Among them, the RXR agonist bexarotene received the most attention because it is highly selective, BBB permeable, and approved by the US Food and Drug Administration. An initial report demonstrated that bexarotene can rapidly remove amyloid deposition and improve brain function (Cramer et al., 2012). Later, replications of this study were carried out by different groups of scientists using different AD mouse models. There is some discrepancy among the replications and the initial report, which may be due to the different mouse models, ages, and formulation and treatment schedule of the drug (Fitz et al., 2013; Price et al., 2013; Tesseur et al., 2013; Veeraraghavalu et al., 2013). In addition to the inconsistency of the data regarding bexarotene's efficacy, dyslipidemia caused by bexarotene could be a considerable side effect (de Vries-van der Weij et al., 2009). Therefore, more studies are needed to validate the efficiency and side effects before bexarotene can be used to treat AD patients.

Recently, another member of ATP-binding cassette subfamily A, ABCA7, was associated with late-onset AD in genome-wide association studies (Hollingworth et al., 2011; Naj et al., 2011; Reitz et al., 2013). The risk for AD is conferred by loss-of-function variants in ABCA7 (Steinberg et al., 2015). In humans, the ABCA7 AD susceptibility loci rs3764650 is associated with increased neuritic plaque pathology (Shulman et al., 2013). How ABCA7 impacts AD pathology is not yet understood. In fetal human brain, ABCA7 is expressed at highest levels by microglia followed by oligodendrocytes, although it is also detected in neurons (Kim et al., 2006). ABCA7 mediates the efflux of lipids from cells to lipid receptors such as apoA-I or apoE (Abe-Dohmae et al., 2004; Chan et al., 2008). It also plays a key role in phagocytosis (Kim et al., 2008). In APP transgenic mice, deletion of ABCA7 leads to increased amyloid plaque load (Kim et al., 2013). However, no difference in APP processing, brain apoE level, and brain microglia/macrophage markers was detected in these APP/ABCA7 knockout mice as compared to control APP mice (Kim et al., 2013). In the future, more work is needed to explore how ABCA7 confers AD risk and whether the mechanisms are related to apoE lipidation.

Block apoE Fragmentation

Although the majority of the apoE in the CNS is synthesized in glia, neurons appear to be able to generate apoE under stressful conditions. Neuronal apoE can be cleaved by proteolysis to generate C-terminal-truncated fragments which have been shown to mediate tau hyperphosphorylation and mitochondrial toxicity (Huang and Mucke, 2012). Due to its domain interaction, apoE4 is more susceptible to proteolysis than is apoE3 (Harris et al., 2003; Brecht et al., 2004). C-terminal-truncated fragments generated by proteolysis have been shown to accumulate in neurons (Brecht et al., 2004), cause mitochondrial dysfunction (Chang et al., 2005), promote tau hyperphosphorylation (Huang et al., 2001), form NFT-like tangles (Harris et al., 2003), cause dendritic spine loss (Brodbeck et al., 2008), and impair learning and memory in mice (Harris et al., 2003). In the future, the protease that cleaves apoE4 and generates neurotoxic apoE fragments needs to be identified. If so, specific protease inhibitors could potentially be developed to reduce the formation of neurotoxic apoE fragments (Huang and Mucke, 2012). In addition, specific antibodies targeting the fragments of apoE could be developed to block detrimental effects.

ApoE Mimetic Peptides

BBB-permeable apoE mimetic peptides composed of the receptor binding region apoE133–149 are proposed to compete with the full-length protein for receptor binding, suppress microglial activation, and maintain the neuroprotective properties of full-length apoE. The results show that the apoE mimetic peptides were able to reduce microglial activation and brain inflammation, decrease endogenous murine $A\beta_{42}$, and improve functional outcome in brain-injury mouse models (Laskowitz et al., 2007; Wang et al., 2007). Later, studies were extended to an APP transgenic mouse model, and apoE mimetic peptides were shown to attenuate plaque deposition and reduce behavioral deficits (Vitek et al., 2012). The mechanism by which the apoE mimetic peptides conduct neuroprotective effects is not fully understood, but it seems to be apoE isoform dependent even though the peptide does not contain the isoform-specific apoE158 residue. The effects are likely mediated by the ability of the apoE peptides to activate a neuroprotective cellular signaling pathway. ApoE mimetic peptides containing the receptor binding sequence have very little effects in apoE4 mice while the effects are much more significant in apoE2 mice even though apoE2 has a very low affinity to lipoprotein receptors to begin with (Wang et al., 2007). Furthermore, upon binding to lipoprotein receptors, these peptides may block the uptake of lipoproteins containing lipidated full-length apoE. Therefore, the lipid profile in the brain and blood of the treated animals will need to be characterized to see whether the treatment is associated with a disturbance of lipid metabolism.

CONCLUSIONS

As *APOE* is the strongest genetic regulator of AD risk, the role of *APOE* gene polymorphism in AD pathogenesis has been extensively explored over the past 20 years. Compelling evidence has demonstrated that apoE influences AD pathogenesis in large part by affecting Aβ pathology. There is also evidence suggesting that apoE may contribute to AD pathogenesis via Aβ-independent mechanisms as well, though there is less unanimity about which of the Aβ-independent mechanisms are most relevant. ApoE appears to influence Aβ deposition by affecting both the aggregation and the clearance of Aβ. It is known that apoE can interact with certain forms of Aβ (likely oligomeric and fibrillar) and change Aβ aggregation kinetics. ApoE appears to affect Aβ clearance by influencing monomeric Aβ enzymatic degradation, Aβ transport across the BBB, Aβ transport and flow in the ISF and CSF, and Aβ cellular uptake by local cells in the CNS such as astrocytes and microglia. The effects of apoE on Aβ largely depend on apoE isoform, concentration, and lipidation status. Due to the lack of understanding of the exact role that apoE plays in AD pathogenesis, current strategies targeting apoE are still at an early preclinical stage. However, given the strong association between apoE4 and AD risk, apoE genotype status is already being used for subgroup analyses in clinical trials and could certainly be used to target specific apoE-directed therapies designed to work more effectively in the presence of specific apoE genotypes. In the future, understanding the mechanism by which apoE modifies AD pathogenesis will guide scientists to design new and—it is hoped—effective therapeutic strategies that target apoE.

References

Abe-Dohmae S, Ikeda Y, Matsuo M, Hayashi M, Okuhira K, Ueda K, Yokoyama S: Human ABCA7 supports apolipoprotein-mediated release of cellular cholesterol and phospholipid to generate high density lipoprotein, *J Biol Chem* 279:604–611, 2004.

Acharya P, Segall ML, Zaiou M, Morrow J, Weisgraber KH, Phillips MC, Lund-Katz S, Snow J: Comparison of the stabilities and unfolding pathways of human apolipoprotein E isoforms by differential scanning calorimetry and circular dichroism, *Biochim Biophys Acta* 1584:9–19, 2002.

Aggerbeck LP, Wetterau JR, Weisgraber KH, Wu CS, Lindgren FT: Human apolipoprotein E3 in aqueous solution: II. Properties of the amino- and carboxyl-terminal domains, *J Biol Chem* 263:6249–6258, 1988.

Anderson R, Barnes JC, Bliss TV, Cain DP, Cambon K, Davies HA, Errington ML, Fellows LA, Gray RA, Hoh T, Stewart M, Large CH, Higgins GA: Behavioural, physiological and morphological analysis of a line of apolipoprotein E knockout mouse, *Neuroscience* 85:93–110, 1998.

Arold S, Sullivan P, Bilousova T, Teng E, Miller CA, Poon WW, Vinters HV, Cornwell LB, Saing T, Cole GM, Gylys KH: Apolipoprotein E level and cholesterol are associated with reduced synaptic amyloid beta in Alzheimer's disease and apoE TR mouse cortex, *Acta Neuropathol* 123:39–52, 2012.

Bachmeier C, Beaulieu-Abdelahad D, Crawford F, Mullan M, Paris D: Stimulation of the retinoid X receptor facilitates beta-amyloid clearance across the blood–brain barrier, *J Mol Neurosci* 49:270–276, 2013.

Baitsch D, Bock HH, Engel T, Telgmann R, Muller-Tidow C, Varga G, Bot M, Herz J, Robenek H, von Eckardstein A, Nofer JR: Apolipoprotein E induces antiinflammatory phenotype in macrophages, *Arterioscler Thromb Vasc Biol* 31:1160–1168, 2011.

Bales KR, Verina T, Dodel RC, Du Y, Altstiel L, Bender M, Hyslop P, Johnstone EM, Little SP, Cummins DJ, Piccardo P, Ghetti B, Paul SM: Lack of apolipoprotein E dramatically reduces amyloid beta-peptide deposition, *Nat Genet* 17:263–264, 1997.

Bales KR, Verina T, Cummins DJ, Du Y, Dodel RC, Saura J, Fishman CE, DeLong CA, Piccardo P, Petegnief V, Ghetti B, Paul SM: Apolipoprotein E is essential for amyloid deposition in the APP(V717F) transgenic mouse model of Alzheimer's disease, *Proc Natl Acad Sci USA* 96:15233–15238, 1999.

Bales KR, Liu F, Wu S, Lin S, Koger D, DeLong C, Hansen JC, Sullivan PM, Paul SM: Human APOE isoform-dependent effects on brain beta-amyloid levels in PDAPP transgenic mice, *J Neurosci* 29:6771–6779, 2009.

Basak JM, Kim J, Pyatkivskyy Y, Wildsmith KR, Jiang H, Parsadanian M, Patterson BW, Bateman RJ, Holtzman DM: Measurement of apolipoprotein E and amyloid beta clearance rates in the mouse brain using bolus stable isotope labeling, *Mol Neurodegener* 7:14, 2012a.

Basak JM, Verghese PB, Yoon H, Kim J, Holtzman DM: Low-density lipoprotein receptor represents an apolipoprotein E-independent pathway of Abeta uptake and degradation by astrocytes, *J Biol Chem* 287:13959–13971, 2012b.

Bateman RJ, Aisen PS, De Strooper B, Fox NC, Lemere CA, Ringman JM, Salloway S, Sperling RA, Windisch M, Xiong C: Autosomal-dominant Alzheimer's disease: a review and proposal for the prevention of Alzheimer's disease, *Alzheimers Res Ther* 3:1, 2011.

Beffert U, Poirier J: ApoE associated with lipid has a reduced capacity to inhibit beta-amyloid fibril formation, *Neuroreport* 9:3321–3323, 1998.

Beffert U, Aumont N, Dea D, Lussier-Cacan S, Davignon J, Poirier J: Apolipoprotein E isoform-specific reduction of extracellular amyloid in neuronal cultures, *Brain Res Mol Brain Res* 68:181–185, 1999a.

Beffert U, Cohn JS, Petit-Turcotte C, Tremblay M, Aumont N, Ramassamy C, Davignon J, Poirier J: Apolipoprotein E and beta-amyloid levels in the hippocampus and frontal cortex of Alzheimer's disease subjects are disease-related and apolipoprotein E genotype dependent, *Brain Res* 843:87–94, 1999b.

Bell RD, Sagare AP, Friedman AE, Bedi GS, Holtzman DM, Deane R, Zlokovic BV: Transport pathways for clearance of human Alzheimer's amyloid beta-peptide and apolipoproteins E and J in the mouse central nervous system, *J Cereb Blood Flow Metab* 27:909–918, 2007.

Bell RD, Winkler EA, Singh I, Sagare AP, Deane R, Wu Z, Holtzman DM, Betsholtz C, Armulik A, Sallstrom J, Berk BC, Zlokovic BV: Apolipoprotein E controls cerebrovascular integrity via cyclophilin A, *Nature* 485:512–516, 2012.

Bentley NM, Ladu MJ, Rajan C, Getz GS, Reardon CA: Apolipoprotein E structural requirements for the formation of SDS-stable complexes with beta-amyloid-(1–40): the role of salt bridges, *Biochem J* 366:273–279, 2002.

Bertrand P, Poirier J, Oda T, Finch CE, Pasinetti GM: Association of apolipoprotein E genotype with brain levels of apolipoprotein E and apolipoprotein J (clusterin) in Alzheimer disease, *Brain Res Mol Brain Res* 33:174–178, 1995.

Bien-Ly N, Gillespie AK, Walker D, Yoon SY, Huang Y: Reducing human apolipoprotein E levels attenuates age-dependent Abeta accumulation in mutant human amyloid precursor protein transgenic mice, *J Neurosci* 32:4803–4811, 2012.

Biere AL, Ostaszewski B, Zhao H, Gillespie S, Younkin SG, Selkoe DJ: Co-expression of beta-amyloid precursor protein (betaAPP) and apolipoprotein E in cell culture: analysis of betaAPP processing, *Neurobiol Dis* 2:177–187, 1995.

Boehm-Cagan A, Michaelson DM: Reversal of apoE4-driven brain pathology and behavioral deficits by bexarotene, *J Neurosci* 34:7293–7301, 2014.

Bray NJ, Jehu L, Moskvina V, Buxbaum JD, Dracheva S, Haroutunian V, Williams J, Buckland PR, Owen MJ, O'Donovan MC: Allelic expression of APOE in human brain: effects of epsilon status and promoter haplotypes, *Hum Mol Genet* 13:2885–2892, 2004.

Brecht WJ, Harris FM, Chang S, Tesseur I, Yu GQ, Xu Q, Dee Fish J, Wyss-Coray T, Buttini M, Mucke L, Mahley RW, Huang Y: Neuron-specific apolipoprotein e4 proteolysis is associated with increased tau phosphorylation in brains of transgenic mice, *J Neurosci* 24:2527–2534, 2004.

Brodbeck J, Balestra ME, Saunders AM, Roses AD, Mahley RW, Huang Y: Rosiglitazone increases dendritic spine density and rescues spine loss caused by apolipoprotein E4 in primary cortical neurons, *Proc Natl Acad Sci USA* 105:1343–1346, 2008.

Brodbeck J, McGuire J, Liu Z, Meyer-Franke A, Balestra ME, Jeong DE, Pleiss M, McComas C, Hess F, Witter D, Peterson S, Childers M, Goulet M, Liverton N, Hargreaves R, Freedman S, Weisgraber KH, Mahley RW, Huang Y: Structure-dependent impairment of intracellular apolipoprotein E4 trafficking and its detrimental effects are rescued by small-molecule structure correctors, *J Biol Chem* 286:17217–17226, 2011.

Cam JA, Zerbinatti CV, Li Y, Bu G: Rapid endocytosis of the low density lipoprotein receptor-related protein modulates cell surface distribution and processing of the beta-amyloid precursor protein, *J Biol Chem* 280:15464–15470, 2005.

Cambon K, Davies HA, Stewart MG: Synaptic loss is accompanied by an increase in synaptic area in the dentate gyrus of aged human apolipoprotein E4 transgenic mice, *Neuroscience* 97:685–692, 2000.

Castellano JM, Kim J, Stewart FR, Jiang H, DeMattos RB, Patterson BW, Fagan AM, Morris JC, Mawuenyega KG, Cruchaga C, Goate AM, Bales KR, Paul SM, Bateman RJ, Holtzman DM: Human apoE isoforms differentially regulate brain amyloid-beta peptide clearance, *Sci Transl Med* 3:89ra57, 2011.

Castellano JM, Deane R, Gottesdiener AJ, Verghese PB, Stewart FR, West T, Paoletti AC, Kasper TR, DeMattos RB, Zlokovic BV, Holtzman DM: Low-density lipoprotein receptor overexpression enhances the rate of brain-to-blood Abeta clearance in a mouse model of beta-amyloidosis, *Proc Natl Acad Sci USA* 109:15502–15507, 2012.

Cedazo-Minguez A, Wiehager B, Winblad B, Huttinger M, Cowburn RF: Effects of apolipoprotein E (apoE) isoforms, beta-amyloid (Abeta) and apoE/Abeta complexes on protein kinase C-alpha (PKC-alpha) translocation and amyloid precursor protein (APP) processing in human SH-SY5Y neuroblastoma cells and fibroblasts, *Neurochem Int* 38:615–625, 2001.

Chan SL, Kim WS, Kwok JB, Hill AF, Cappai R, Rye KA, Garner B: ATP-binding cassette transporter A7 regulates processing of amyloid precursor protein in vitro, *J Neurochem* 106:793–804, 2008.

Chang S, ran Ma T, Miranda RD, Balestra ME, Mahley RW, Huang Y: Lipid- and receptor-binding regions of apolipoprotein E4 fragments act in concert to cause mitochondrial dysfunction and neurotoxicity, *Proc Natl Acad Sci USA* 102:18694–18699, 2005.

Charnay Y, Imhof A, Vallet PG, Hakkoum D, Lathuiliere A, Poku N, Aronow B, Kovari E, Bouras C, Giannakopoulos P: Clusterin expression during fetal and postnatal CNS development in mouse, *Neuroscience* 155:714–724, 2008.

Chen J, Li Q, Wang J: Topology of human apolipoprotein E3 uniquely regulates its diverse biological functions, *Proc Natl Acad Sci USA* 108:14813–14818, 2011.

Chen HK, Liu Z, Meyer-Franke A, Brodbeck J, Miranda RD, McGuire JG, Pleiss MA, Ji ZS, Balestra ME, Walker DW, Xu Q, Jeong DE, Budamagunta MS, Voss JC, Freedman SB, Weisgraber KH, Huang Y, Mahley RW: Small molecule structure correctors abolish detrimental effects of apolipoprotein E4 in cultured neurons, *J Biol Chem* 287:5253–5266, 2012.

Cirrito JR, Deane R, Fagan AM, Spinner ML, Parsadanian M, Finn MB, Jiang H, Prior JL, Sagare A, Bales KR, Paul SM, Zlokovic BV, Piwnica-Worms D, Holtzman DM: P-glycoprotein deficiency at the blood–brain barrier increases amyloid-beta deposition in an Alzheimer disease mouse model, *J Clin Invest* 115:3285–3290, 2005.

Corder EH, Saunders AM, Strittmatter WJ, Schmechel DE, Gaskell PC, Small GW, Roses AD, Haines JL, Pericak-Vance MA: Gene dose of apolipoprotein E type 4 allele and the risk of Alzheimer's disease in late onset families, *Science* 261:921–923, 1993.

Corder EH, Saunders AM, Risch NJ, Strittmatter WJ, Schmechel DE, Gaskell PC Jr, Rimmler JB, Locke PA, Conneally PM, Schmader KE, et al: Protective effect of apolipoprotein E type 2 allele for late onset Alzheimer disease, *Nat Genet* 7:180–184, 1994.

Cramer PE, Cirrito JR, Wesson DW, Lee CY, Karlo JC, Zinn AE, Casali BT, Restivo JL, Goebel WD, James MJ, Brunden KR, Wilson DA, Landreth GE: ApoE-directed therapeutics rapidly clear beta-amyloid and reverse deficits in AD mouse models, *Science* 335:1503–1506, 2012.

Cruchaga C, Kauwe JS, Nowotny P, Bales K, Pickering EH, Mayo K, Bertelsen S, Hinrichs A, Fagan AM, Holtzman DM, Morris JC, Goate AM: Alzheimer's Disease Neuroimaging Initiative: Cerebrospinal fluid APOE levels: an endophenotype for genetic studies for Alzheimer's disease, *Hum Mol Genet* 21:4558–4571, 2012.

Cudaback E, Li X, Montine KS, Montine TJ, Keene CD: Apolipoprotein E isoform-dependent microglia migration, *FASEB J* 25:2082–2091, 2011.

de Vries-van der Weij J, de Haan W, Hu L, Kuif M, Oei HL, van der Hoorn JW, Havekes LM, Princen HM, Romijn JA, Smit JW, Rensen PC: Bexarotene induces dyslipidemia by increased very low-density lipoprotein production and cholesteryl ester transfer protein-mediated reduction of high-density lipoprotein, *Endocrinology* 150:2368–2375, 2009.

Deane R, Sagare A, Hamm K, Parisi M, Lane S, Finn MB, Holtzman DM, Zlokovic BV: apoE isoform-specific disruption of amyloid beta peptide clearance from mouse brain, *J Clin Invest* 118:4002–4013, 2008.

Dodart JC, Marr RA, Koistinaho M, Gregersen BM, Malkani S, Verma IM, Paul SM: Gene delivery of human apolipoprotein E alters brain Abeta burden in a mouse model of Alzheimer's disease, *Proc Natl Acad Sci USA* 102:1211–1216, 2005.

Dolev I, Michaelson DM: A nontransgenic mouse model shows inducible amyloid-beta (Abeta) peptide deposition and elucidates the role of apolipoprotein E in the amyloid cascade, *Proc Natl Acad Sci USA* 101:13909–13914, 2004.

Donkin JJ, Stukas S, Hirsch-Reinshagen V, Namjoshi D, Wilkinson A, May S, Chan J, Fan J, Collins J, Wellington CL: ATP-binding cassette transporter A1 mediates the beneficial effects of the liver X receptor agonist GW3965 on object recognition memory and amyloid burden in amyloid precursor protein/presenilin 1 mice, *J Biol Chem* 285:34144–34154, 2010.

Drzezga A, Grimmer T, Henriksen G, Muhlau M, Perneczky R, Miederer I, Praus C, Sorg C, Wohlschlager A, Riemenschneider M, Wester HJ, Foerstl H, Schwaiger M, Kurz A: Effect of APOE genotype on amyloid plaque load and gray matter volume in Alzheimer disease, *Neurology* 72:1487–1494, 2009.

Evans KC, Berger EP, Cho CG, Weisgraber KH, Lansbury PT Jr: Apolipoprotein E is a kinetic but not a thermodynamic inhibitor of amyloid formation: implications for the pathogenesis and treatment of Alzheimer disease, *Proc Natl Acad Sci USA* 92:763–767, 1995.

Fagan AM, Murphy BA, Patel SN, Kilbridge JF, Mobley WC, Bu G, Holtzman DM: Evidence for normal aging of the septo-hippocampal cholinergic system in apoE (−/−) mice but impaired clearance of axonal degeneration products following injury, *Exp Neurol* 151:314–325, 1998.

Fagan AM, Younkin LH, Morris JC, Fryer JD, Cole TG, Younkin SG, Holtzman DM: Differences in the Abeta40/Abeta42 ratio associated with cerebrospinal fluid lipoproteins as a function of apolipoprotein E genotype, *Ann Neurol* 48:201–210, 2000.

Fagan AM, Watson M, Parsadanian M, Bales KR, Paul SM, Holtzman DM: Human and murine ApoE markedly alters A beta metabolism before and after plaque formation in a mouse model of Alzheimer's disease, *Neurobiol Dis* 9:305–318, 2002.

Farrer LA, Cupples LA, Haines JL, Hyman B, Kukull WA, Mayeux R, Myers RH, Pericak-Vance MA, Risch N, van Duijn CM: Effects of age, sex, and ethnicity on the association between apolipoprotein E genotype and Alzheimer disease: a meta-analysis. APOE and Alzheimer Disease Meta Analysis Consortium, *JAMA* 278:1349–1356, 1997.

Fitz NF, Cronican A, Pham T, Fogg A, Fauq AH, Chapman R, Lefterov I, Koldamova R: Liver X receptor agonist treatment ameliorates amyloid pathology and memory deficits caused by high-fat diet in APP23 mice, *J Neurosci* 30:6862–6872, 2010.

Fitz NF, Cronican AA, Saleem M, Fauq AH, Chapman R, Lefterov I, Koldamova R: Abca1 deficiency affects Alzheimer's disease-like phenotype in human ApoE4 but not in ApoE3-targeted replacement mice, *J Neurosci* 32:13125–13136, 2012.

Fitz NF, Cronican AA, Lefterov I, Koldamova R: Comment on "ApoE-directed therapeutics rapidly clear beta-amyloid and reverse deficits in AD mouse models", *Science* 340:924-c, 2013.

Frieden C, Garai K: Concerning the structure of apoE, *Protein Sci* 22:1820–1825, 2013.

Fryer JD, Simmons K, Parsadanian M, Bales KR, Paul SM, Sullivan PM, Holtzman DM: Human apolipoprotein E4 alters the amyloid-beta 40:42 ratio and promotes the formation of cerebral amyloid angiopathy in an amyloid precursor protein transgenic model, *J Neurosci* 25:2803–2810, 2005a.

Fryer JD, Demattos RB, McCormick LM, O'Dell MA, Spinner ML, Bales KR, Paul SM, Sullivan PM, Parsadanian M, Bu G, Holtzman DM: The low density lipoprotein receptor regulates the level of central nervous system human and murine apolipoprotein E but does not modify amyloid plaque pathology in PDAPP mice, *J Biol Chem* 280:25754–25759, 2005b.

Fukumoto H, Ingelsson M, Garevik N, Wahlund LO, Nukina N, Yaguchi Y, Shibata M, Hyman BT, Rebeck GW, Irizarry MC: APOE epsilon 3/epsilon 4 heterozygotes have an elevated proportion of apolipoprotein E4 in cerebrospinal fluid relative to plasma, independent of Alzheimer's disease diagnosis, *Exp Neurol* 183:249–253, 2003.

Funato H, Yoshimura M, Yamazaki T, Saido TC, Ito Y, Yokofujita J, Okeda R, Ihara Y: Astrocytes containing amyloid beta-protein (Abeta)-positive granules are associated with Abeta40-positive diffuse plaques in the aged human brain, *Am J Pathol* 152:983–992, 1998.

Futamura M, Dhanasekaran P, Handa T, Phillips MC, Lund-Katz S, Saito H: Two-step mechanism of binding of apolipoprotein E to heparin: implications for the kinetics of apolipoprotein E-heparan sulfate proteoglycan complex formation on cell surfaces, *J Biol Chem* 280:5414–5422, 2005.

Garai K, Frieden C: The association–dissociation behavior of the ApoE proteins: kinetic and equilibrium studies, *Biochemistry* 49:9533–9541, 2010.

Garai K, Verghese PB, Baban B, Holtzman DM, Frieden C: The binding of apoE to oligomers and fibrils of amyloid-beta alters the kinetics of amyloid aggregation, *Biochemistry* 53, 2014, 6323-6231.

Greenberg SM, Rebeck GW, Vonsattel JP, Gomez-Isla T, Hyman BT: Apolipoprotein E epsilon 4 and cerebral hemorrhage associated with amyloid angiopathy, *Ann Neurol* 38:254–259, 1995.

Grehan S, Tse E, Taylor JM: Two distal downstream enhancers direct expression of the human apolipoprotein E gene to astrocytes in the brain, *J Neurosci* 21:812–822, 2001.

Hamanaka H, Katoh-Fukui Y, Suzuki K, Kobayashi M, Suzuki R, Motegi Y, Nakahara Y, Takeshita A, Kawai M, Ishiguro K, Yokoyama M, Fujita SC: Altered cholesterol metabolism in human apolipoprotein E4 knock-in mice, *Hum Mol Genet* 9:353–361, 2000.

Hardy J, Selkoe DJ: The amyloid hypothesis of Alzheimer's disease: progress and problems on the road to therapeutics, *Science* 297:353–356, 2002.

Harr SD, Uint L, Hollister R, Hyman BT, Mendez AJ: Brain expression of apolipoproteins E, J, and A-I in Alzheimer's disease, *J Neurochem* 66:2429–2435, 1996.

Harris FM, Brecht WJ, Xu Q, Tesseur I, Kekonius L, Wyss-Coray T, Fish JD, Masliah E, Hopkins PC, Scearce-Levie K, Weisgraber KH, Mucke L, Mahley RW, Huang Y: Carboxyl-terminal-truncated apolipoprotein E4 causes Alzheimer's disease-like neurodegeneration and behavioral deficits in transgenic mice, *Proc Natl Acad Sci USA* 100:10966–10971, 2003.

Hartman RE, Wozniak DF, Nardi A, Olney JW, Sartorius L, Holtzman DM: Behavioral phenotyping of GFAP-apoE3 and -apoE4 transgenic mice: apoE4 mice show profound working memory impairments in the absence of Alzheimer's-like neuropathology, *Exp Neurol* 170:326–344, 2001.

Hashimoto T, Serrano-Pozo A, Hori Y, Adams KW, Takeda S, Banerji AO, Mitani A, Joyner D, Thyssen DH, Bacskai BJ, Frosch MP, Spires-Jones TL, Finn MB, Holtzman DM, Hyman BT: Apolipoprotein E, especially apolipoprotein E4, increases the oligomerization of amyloid beta peptide, *J Neurosci* 32:15181–15192, 2012.

Hasty AH, Linton MF, Swift LL, Fazio S: Determination of the lower threshold of apolipoprotein E resulting in remnant lipoprotein clearance, *J Lipid Res* 40:1529–1538, 1999.

Hatters DM, Peters-Libeu CA, Weisgraber KH: Apolipoprotein E structure: insights into function, *Trends Biochem Sci* 31:445–454, 2006.

He X, Cooley K, Chung CH, Dashti N, Tang J: Apolipoprotein receptor 2 and X11 alpha/beta mediate apolipoprotein E-induced endocytosis of amyloid-beta precursor protein and beta-secretase, leading to amyloid-beta production, *J Neurosci* 27:4052–4060, 2007.

Hickman SE, Allison EK, El Khoury J: Microglial dysfunction and defective beta-amyloid clearance pathways in aging Alzheimer's disease mice, *J Neurosci* 28:8354–8360, 2008.

Hiesberger T, Trommsdorff M, Howell BW, Goffinet A, Mumby MC, Cooper JA, Herz J: Direct binding of reelin to VLDL receptor and ApoE receptor 2 induces tyrosine phosphorylation of disabled-1 and modulates tau phosphorylation, *Neuron* 24:481–489, 1999.

Hirsch-Reinshagen V, Zhou S, Burgess BL, Bernier L, McIsaac SA, Chan JY, Tansley GH, Cohn JS, Hayden MR, Wellington CL: Deficiency of ABCA1 impairs apolipoprotein E metabolism in brain, *J Biol Chem* 279:41197–41207, 2004.

Hirsch-Reinshagen V, Maia LF, Burgess BL, Blain JF, Naus KE, McIsaac SA, Parkinson PF, Chan JY, Tansley GH, Hayden MR, Poirier J, Van Nostrand W, Wellington CL: The absence of ABCA1 decreases soluble ApoE levels but does not diminish amyloid deposition in two murine models of Alzheimer disease, *J Biol Chem* 280:43243–43256, 2005.

Hollingworth P, et al: Common variants at ABCA7, MS4A6A/MS4A4E, EPHA1 CD33 and CD2AP are associated with Alzheimer's disease, *Nat Genet* 43:429–435, 2011.

Holtzman DM, Bales KR, Wu S, Bhat P, Parsadanian M, Fagan AM, Chang LK, Sun Y, Paul SM: Expression of human apolipoprotein E reduces amyloid-beta deposition in a mouse model of Alzheimer's disease, *J Clin Invest* 103:R15–R21, 1999.

Holtzman DM, Bales KR, Tenkova T, Fagan AM, Parsadanian M, Sartorius LJ, Mackey B, Olney J, McKeel D, Wozniak D, Paul SM: Apolipoprotein E isoform-dependent amyloid deposition and neuritic degeneration in a mouse model of Alzheimer's disease, *Proc Natl Acad Sci USA* 97:2892–2897, 2000a.

Holtzman DM, Fagan AM, Mackey B, Tenkova T, Sartorius L, Paul SM, Bales K, Ashe KH, Irizarry MC, Hyman BT: Apolipoprotein E facilitates neuritic and cerebrovascular plaque formation in an Alzheimer's disease model, *Ann Neurol* 47:739–747, 2000b.

Holtzman DM, Herz J, Bu G: Apolipoprotein E and apolipoprotein E receptors: normal biology and roles in Alzheimer disease, *Cold Spring Harb Perspect Med* 2:a006312, 2012.

Hu X, Crick SL, Bu G, Frieden C, Pappu RV, Lee JM: Amyloid seeds formed by cellular uptake, concentration, and aggregation of the amyloid-beta peptide, *Proc Natl Acad Sci USA* 106:20324–20329, 2009.

Huang Y: Abeta-independent roles of apolipoprotein E4 in the pathogenesis of Alzheimer's disease, *Trends Mol Med* 16:287–294, 2010.

Huang Y, Mahley RW: Apolipoprotein E: structure and function in lipid metabolism, neurobiology, and Alzheimer's diseases, *Neurobiol Dis* 72(Pt A):3–12, 2014.

Huang Y, Mucke L: Alzheimer mechanisms and therapeutic strategies, *Cell* 148:1204–1222, 2012.

Huang Y, Liu XQ, Wyss-Coray T, Brecht WJ, Sanan DA, Mahley RW: Apolipoprotein E fragments present in Alzheimer's disease brains induce neurofibrillary tangle-like intracellular inclusions in neurons, *Proc Natl Acad Sci USA* 98:8838–8843, 2001.

Hudry E, Dashkoff J, Roe AD, Takeda S, Koffie RM, Hashimoto T, Scheel M, Spires-Jones T, Arbel-Ornath M, Betensky R, Davidson BL, Hyman BT: Gene transfer of human Apoe isoforms results in differential modulation of amyloid deposition and neurotoxicity in mouse brain, *Sci Transl Med* 5:212ra161, 2013.

Innerarity TL, Mahley RW: Enhanced binding by cultured human fibroblasts of apo-E-containing lipoproteins as compared with low density lipoproteins, *Biochemistry* 17:1440–1447, 1978.

Irizarry MC, Deng A, Lleo A, Berezovska O, Von Arnim CA, Martin-Rehrmann M, Manelli A, LaDu MJ, Hyman BT, Rebeck GW: Apolipoprotein E modulates gamma-secretase cleavage of the amyloid precursor protein, *J Neurochem* 90:1132–1143, 2004.

Ito S, Ohtsuki S, Kamiie J, Nezu Y, Terasaki T: Cerebral clearance of human amyloid-beta peptide (1–40) across the blood–brain barrier is reduced by self-aggregation and formation of low-density lipoprotein receptor-related protein-1 ligand complexes, *J Neurochem* 103:2482–2490, 2007.

Ji ZS, Brecht WJ, Miranda RD, Hussain MM, Innerarity TL, Mahley RW: Role of heparan sulfate proteoglycans in the binding and uptake of apolipoprotein E-enriched remnant lipoproteins by cultured cells, *J Biol Chem* 268:10160–10167, 1993.

Jiang Q, Lee CY, Mandrekar S, Wilkinson B, Cramer P, Zelcer N, Mann K, Lamb B, Willson TM, Collins JL, Richardson JC, Smith JD, Comery TA, Riddell D, Holtzman DM, Tontonoz P, Landreth GE: ApoE promotes the proteolytic degradation of Abeta, *Neuron* 58:681–693, 2008.

Jonsson T, et al: A mutation in APP protects against Alzheimer's disease and age-related cognitive decline, *Nature* 488:96–99, 2012.

Kanekiyo T, Zhang J, Liu Q, Liu CC, Zhang L, Bu G: Heparan sulphate proteoglycan and the low-density lipoprotein receptor-related protein 1 constitute major pathways for neuronal amyloid-beta uptake, *J Neurosci* 31:1644–1651, 2011.

Kanekiyo T, Liu CC, Shinohara M, Li J, Bu G: LRP1 in brain vascular smooth muscle cells mediates local clearance of Alzheimer's amyloid-beta, *J Neurosci* 32:16458–16465, 2012.

Kantarci K, Lowe V, Przybelski SA, Weigand SD, Senjem ML, Ivnik RJ, Preboske GM, Roberts R, Geda YE, Boeve BF, Knopman DS, Petersen RC, Jack CR Jr: APOE modifies the association between Abeta load and cognition in cognitively normal older adults, *Neurology* 78:232–240, 2012.

Kim WS, Guillemin GJ, Glaros EN, Lim CK, Garner B: Quantitation of ATP-binding cassette subfamily-A transporter gene expression in primary human brain cells, *Neuroreport* 17:891–896, 2006.

Kim WS, Weickert CS, Garner B: Role of ATP-binding cassette transporters in brain lipid transport and neurological disease, *J Neurochem* 104:1145–1166, 2008.

Kim J, Basak JM, Holtzman DM: The role of apolipoprotein E in Alzheimer's disease, *Neuron* 63:287–303, 2009a.

Kim J, Castellano JM, Jiang H, Basak JM, Parsadanian M, Pham V, Mason SM, Paul SM, Holtzman DM: Overexpression of low-density lipoprotein receptor in the brain markedly inhibits amyloid deposition and increases extracellular A beta clearance, *Neuron* 64:632–644, 2009b.

Kim J, Jiang H, Park S, Eltorai AE, Stewart FR, Yoon H, Basak JM, Finn MB, Holtzman DM: Haploinsufficiency of human APOE reduces amyloid deposition in a mouse model of amyloid-beta amyloidosis, *J Neurosci* 31:18007–18012, 2011.

Kim J, Eltorai AE, Jiang H, Liao F, Verghese PB, Stewart FR, Basak JM, Holtzman DM: Anti-apoE immunotherapy inhibits amyloid accumulation in a transgenic mouse model of Abeta amyloidosis, *J Exp Med* 209:2149–2156, 2012.

Kim WS, Li H, Ruberu K, Chan S, Elliott DA, Low JK, Cheng D, Karl T, Garner B: Deletion of Abca7 increases cerebral amyloid-beta accumulation in the J20 mouse model of Alzheimer's disease, *J Neurosci* 33:4387–4394, 2013.

Koistinaho M, Lin S, Wu X, Esterman M, Koger D, Hanson J, Higgs R, Liu F, Malkani S, Bales KR, Paul SM: Apolipoprotein E promotes astrocyte colocalization and degradation of deposited amyloid-beta peptides, *Nat Med* 10:719–726, 2004.

Koldamova RP, Lefterov IM, Staufenbiel M, Wolfe D, Huang S, Glorioso JC, Walter M, Roth MG, Lazo JS: The liver X receptor ligand T0901317 decreases amyloid beta production in vitro and in a mouse model of Alzheimer's disease, *J Biol Chem* 280:4079–4088, 2005a.

Koldamova R, Staufenbiel M, Lefterov I: Lack of ABCA1 considerably decreases brain ApoE level and increases amyloid deposition in APP23 mice, *J Biol Chem* 280:43224–43235, 2005b.

Kuszczyk MA, Sanchez S, Pankiewicz J, Kim J, Duszczyk M, Guridi M, Asuni AA, Sullivan PM, Holtzman DM, Sadowski MJ: Blocking the interaction between apolipoprotein E and Abeta reduces intraneuronal accumulation of Abeta and inhibits synaptic degeneration, *Am J Pathol* 182:1750–1768, 2013.

LaDu MJ, Falduto MT, Manelli AM, Reardon CA, Getz GS, Frail DE: Isoform-specific binding of apolipoprotein E to beta-amyloid, *J Biol Chem* 269:23403–23406, 1994.

LaDu MJ, Gilligan SM, Lukens JR, Cabana VG, Reardon CA, Van Eldik LJ, Holtzman DM: Nascent astrocyte particles differ from lipoproteins in CSF, *J Neurochem* 70:2070–2081, 1998.

LaDu MJ, Munson GW, Jungbauer L, Getz GS, Reardon CA, Tai LM, Yu C: Preferential interactions between ApoE-containing lipoproteins and Abeta revealed by a detection method that combines size exclusion chromatography with non-reducing gel-shift, *Biochim Biophys Acta* 1821:295–302, 2012.

Landen M, Hesse C, Fredman P, Regland B, Wallin A, Blennow K: Apolipoprotein E in cerebrospinal fluid from patients with Alzheimer's disease and other forms of dementia is reduced but without any correlation to the apoE4 isoform, *Dementia* 7:273–278, 1996.

Lane-Donovan C, Philips GT, Herz J: More than cholesterol transporters: lipoprotein receptors in CNS function and neurodegeneration, *Neuron* 83:771–787, 2014.

Lanz TA, Carter DB, Merchant KM: Dendritic spine loss in the hippocampus of young PDAPP and Tg2576 mice and its prevention by the ApoE2 genotype, *Neurobiol Dis* 13:246–253, 2003.

Laskowitz DT, McKenna SE, Song P, Wang H, Durham L, Yeung N, Christensen D, Vitek MP: COG1410, a novel apolipoprotein E-based peptide, improves functional recovery in a murine model of traumatic brain injury, *J Neurotrauma* 24:1093–1107, 2007.

Lawn RM, Wade DP, Garvin MR, Wang X, Schwartz K, Porter JG, Seilhamer JJ, Vaughan AM, Oram JF: The Tangier disease gene product ABC1 controls the cellular apolipoprotein-mediated lipid removal pathway, *J Clin Invest* 104:R25–R31, 1999.

Liao F, Hori Y, Hudry E, Bauer AQ, Jiang H, Mahan TE, Lefton KB, Zhang TJ, Dearborn JT, Kim J, Culver JP, Betensky R, Wozniak DF, Hyman BT, Holtzman DM: Anti-ApoE antibody given after plaque onset decreases Abeta accumulation and improves brain function in a mouse model of Abeta amyloidosis, *J Neurosci* 34:7281–7292, 2014.

Linton MF, Gish R, Hubl ST, Butler E, Esquivel C, Bry WI, Boyles JK, Wardell MR, Young SG: Phenotypes of apolipoprotein B and apolipoprotein E after liver transplantation, *J Clin Invest* 88:270–281, 1991.

Liu Q, Zerbinatti CV, Zhang J, Hoe HS, Wang B, Cole SL, Herz J, Muglia L, Bu G: Amyloid precursor protein regulates brain apolipoprotein E and cholesterol metabolism through lipoprotein receptor LRP1, *Neuron* 56:66–78, 2007.

Liu Q, Wu WH, Fang CL, Li RW, Liu P, Lei P, Hu J, Sun X, Zheng YZ, Zhao YF, Li YM: Mapping ApoE/Abeta binding regions to guide inhibitor discovery, *Mol Biosyst* 7:1693–1700, 2011.

Liu M, Kuhel DG, Shen L, Hui DY, Woods SC: Apolipoprotein E does not cross the blood–cerebrospinal fluid barrier, as revealed by an improved technique for sampling CSF from mice, *Am J Physiol Regul Integr Comp Physiol* 303:R903–R908, 2012.

Ma J, Yee A, Brewer HB Jr, Das S, Potter H: Amyloid-associated proteins alpha 1-antichymotrypsin and apolipoprotein E promote assembly of Alzheimer beta-protein into filaments, *Nature* 372:92–94, 1994.

Ma J, Brewer HB Jr, Potter H: Alzheimer A beta neurotoxicity: promotion by antichymotrypsin ApoE4; inhibition by A beta-related peptides, *Neurobiol Aging* 17:773–780, 1996.

Mahley RW: Apolipoprotein E: cholesterol transport protein with expanding role in cell biology, *Science* 240:622–630, 1988.

Mahley RW, Huang Y: Small-molecule structure correctors target abnormal protein structure and function: structure corrector rescue of apolipoprotein E4-associated neuropathology, *J Med Chem* 55:8997–9008, 2012.

Mak AC, et al: Effects of the absence of apolipoprotein E on lipoproteins, neurocognitive function, and retinal function, *JAMA Neurol* 71:1228–1236, 2014.

Mandrekar S, Jiang Q, Lee CY, Koenigsknecht-Talboo J, Holtzman DM, Landreth GE: Microglia mediate the clearance of soluble Abeta through fluid phase macropinocytosis, *J Neurosci* 29:4252–4262, 2009.

Mann KM, Thorngate FE, Katoh-Fukui Y, Hamanaka H, Williams DL, Fujita S, Lamb BT: Independent effects of APOE on cholesterol metabolism and brain Abeta levels in an Alzheimer disease mouse model, *Hum Mol Genet* 13:1959–1968, 2004.

Martinez-Morillo E, Hansson O, Atagi Y, Bu G, Minthon L, Diamandis EP, Nielsen HM: Total apolipoprotein E levels and specific isoform composition in cerebrospinal fluid and plasma from Alzheimer's disease patients and controls, *Acta Neuropathol* 127:633–643, 2014.

Mawuenyega KG, Sigurdson W, Ovod V, Munsell L, Kasten T, Morris JC, Yarasheski KE, Bateman RJ: Decreased clearance of CNS beta-amyloid in Alzheimer's disease, *Science* 330:1774, 2010.

Mooijaart SP, Berbee JF, van Heemst D, Havekes LM, de Craen AJ, Slagboom PE, Rensen PC, Westendorp RG: ApoE plasma levels and risk of cardiovascular mortality in old age, *PLoS Med* 3:e176, 2006.

Morikawa M, Fryer JD, Sullivan PM, Christopher EA, Wahrle SE, DeMattos RB, O'Dell MA, Fagan AM, Lashuel HA, Walz T, Asai K, Holtzman DM: Production and characterization of astrocyte-derived human apolipoprotein E isoforms from immortalized astrocytes and their interactions with amyloid-beta, *Neurobiol Dis* 19:66–76, 2005.

Morris JC, Roe CM, Xiong C, Fagan AM, Goate AM, Holtzman DM, Mintun MA: APOE predicts amyloid-beta but not tau Alzheimer pathology in cognitively normal aging, *Ann Neurol* 67:122–131, 2010.

Morrow JA, Segall ML, Lund-Katz S, Phillips MC, Knapp M, Rupp B, Weisgraber KH: Differences in stability among the human apolipoprotein E isoforms determined by the amino-terminal domain, *Biochemistry* 39:11657–11666, 2000.

Naj AC, et al: Common variants at MS4A4/MS4A6E, CD2AP CD33 and EPHA1 are associated with late-onset Alzheimer's disease, *Nat Genet* 43:436–441, 2011.

Nalivaeva NN, Beckett C, Belyaev ND, Turner AJ: Are amyloid-degrading enzymes viable therapeutic targets in Alzheimer's disease? *J Neurochem* 120(Suppl 1):167–185, 2012.

Namba Y, Tomonaga M, Kawasaki H, Otomo E, Ikeda K: Apolipoprotein E immunoreactivity in cerebral amyloid deposits and neurofibrillary tangles in Alzheimer's disease and kuru plaque amyloid in Creutzfeldt-Jakob disease, *Brain Res* 541:163–166, 1991.

Naslund J, Thyberg J, Tjernberg LO, Wernstedt C, Karlstrom AR, Bogdanovic N, Gandy SE, Lannfelt L, Terenius L, Nordstedt C: Characterization of stable complexes involving apolipoprotein E and the amyloid beta peptide in Alzheimer's disease brain, *Neuron* 15:219–228, 1995.

Neely MD, Montine TJ: CSF lipoproteins and Alzheimer's disease, *J Nutr Health Aging* 6:383–391, 2002.

Nielsen HM, Veerhuis R, Holmqvist B, Janciauskiene S: Binding and uptake of A beta1-42 by primary human astrocytes in vitro, *Glia* 57:978–988, 2009.

Nishitsuji K, Hosono T, Nakamura T, Bu G, Michikawa M: Apolipoprotein E regulates the integrity of tight junctions in an isoform-dependent manner in an in vitro blood–brain barrier model, *J Biol Chem* 286:17536–17542, 2011.

Niu S, Yabut O, D'Arcangelo G: The reelin signaling pathway promotes dendritic spine development in hippocampal neurons, *J Neurosci* 28:10339–10348, 2008.

Oddo S, Caccamo A, Cheng D, LaFerla FM: Genetically altering Abeta distribution from the brain to the vasculature ameliorates tau pathology, *Brain Pathol* 19:421–430, 2009.

Olaisen B, Teisberg P, Gedde-Dahl T Jr: The locus for apolipoprotein E (apoE) is linked to the complement component C3 (C3) locus on chromosome 19 in man, *Hum Genet* 62:233–236, 1982.

Paresce DM, Ghosh RN, Maxfield FR: Microglial cells internalize aggregates of the Alzheimer's disease amyloid beta-protein via a scavenger receptor, *Neuron* 17:553–565, 1996.

Paresce DM, Chung H, Maxfield FR: Slow degradation of aggregates of the Alzheimer's disease amyloid beta-protein by microglial cells, *J Biol Chem* 272:29390–29397, 1997.

Perez E, Bourguet W, Gronemeyer H, de Lera AR: Modulation of RXR function through ligand design, *Biochim Biophys Acta* 1821:57–69, 2012.

Petrlova J, Hong HS, Bricarello DA, Harishchandra G, Lorigan GA, Jin LW, Voss JC: A differential association of apolipoprotein E isoforms with the amyloid-beta oligomer in solution, *Proteins* 79:402–416, 2011.

Pitas RE, Boyles JK, Lee SH, Foss D, Mahley RW: Astrocytes synthesize apolipoprotein E and metabolize apolipoprotein E-containing lipoproteins, *Biochim Biophys Acta* 917:148–161, 1987.

Price AR, Xu G, Siemienski ZB, Smithson LA, Borchelt DR, Golde TE, Felsenstein KM: Comment on "ApoE-directed therapeutics rapidly clear beta-amyloid and reverse deficits in AD mouse models", *Science* 340:24-d, 2013.

Raber J, Wong D, Buttini M, Orth M, Bellosta S, Pitas RE, Mahley RW, Mucke L: Isoform-specific effects of human apolipoprotein E on brain function revealed in ApoE knockout mice: increased susceptibility of females, *Proc Natl Acad Sci USA* 95:10914–10919, 1998.

Raber J, Huang Y, Ashford JW: ApoE genotype accounts for the vast majority of AD risk and AD pathology, *Neurobiol Aging* 25:641–650, 2004.

Raffai RL, Dong LM, Farese RV Jr, Weisgraber KH: Introduction of human apolipoprotein E4 "domain interaction" into mouse apolipoprotein E, *Proc Natl Acad Sci USA* 98:11587–11591, 2001.

Ramaswamy G, Xu Q, Huang Y, Weisgraber KH: Effect of domain interaction on apolipoprotein E levels in mouse brain, *J Neurosci* 25:10658–10663, 2005.

Rapp A, Gmeiner B, Huttinger M: Implication of apoE isoforms in cholesterol metabolism by primary rat hippocampal neurons and astrocytes, *Biochimie* 88:473–483, 2006.

Rasmussen KL, Tybjaerg-Hansen A, Nordestgaard BG, Frikke-Schmidt R: Plasma levels of apolipoprotein E and risk of dementia in the general population, *Ann Neurol* 77:301–311, 2014.

Reiman EM, Chen K, Liu X, Bandy D, Yu M, Lee W, Ayutyanont N, Keppler J, Reeder SA, Langbaum JB, Alexander GE, Klunk WE, Mathis CA, Price JC, Aizenstein HJ, DeKosky ST, Caselli RJ: Fibrillar amyloid-beta burden in cognitively normal people at 3 levels of genetic risk for Alzheimer's disease, *Proc Natl Acad Sci USA* 106:6820–6825, 2009.

Reitz C, et al: Variants in the ATP-binding cassette transporter (ABCA7) apolipoprotein E 4 and the risk of late-onset Alzheimer disease in African Americans, *JAMA* 309:1483–1492, 2013.

Riddell DR, et al: The LXR agonist TO901317 selectively lowers hippocampal Abeta42 and improves memory in the Tg2576 mouse model of Alzheimer's disease, *Mol Cell Neurosci* 34:621–628, 2007.

Riddell DR, Zhou H, Atchison K, Warwick HK, Atkinson PJ, Jefferson J, Xu L, Aschmies S, Kirksey Y, Hu Y, Wagner E, Parratt A, Xu J, Li Z, Zaleska MM, Jacobsen JS, Pangalos MN, Reinhart PH: Impact of apolipoprotein E (ApoE) polymorphism on brain ApoE levels, *J Neurosci* 28:11445–11453, 2008.

Russo C, Angelini G, Dapino D, Piccini A, Piombo G, Schettini G, Chen S, Teller JK, Zaccheo D, Gambetti P, Tabaton M: Opposite roles of apolipoprotein E in normal brains and in Alzheimer's disease, *Proc Natl Acad Sci USA* 95:15598–15602, 1998.

Saavedra L, Mohamed A, Ma V, Kar S, de Chaves EP: Internalization of beta-amyloid peptide by primary neurons in the absence of apolipoprotein E, *J Biol Chem* 282:35722–35732, 2007.

Sadowski MJ, Pankiewicz J, Scholtzova H, Mehta PD, Prelli F, Quartermain D, Wisniewski T: Blocking the apolipoprotein E/amyloid-beta interaction as a potential therapeutic approach for Alzheimer's disease, *Proc Natl Acad Sci USA* 103:18787–18792, 2006.

Saito H, Dhanasekaran P, Nguyen D, Baldwin F, Weisgraber KH, Wehrli S, Phillips MC, Lund-Katz S: Characterization of the heparin binding sites in human apolipoprotein E, *J Biol Chem* 278:14782–14787, 2003.

Sanan DA, Weisgraber KH, Russell SJ, Mahley RW, Huang D, Saunders A, Schmechel D, Wisniewski T, Frangione B, Roses AD, et al: Apolipoprotein E associates with beta amyloid peptide of Alzheimer's disease to form novel monofibrils: isoform apoE4 associates more efficiently than apoE3, *J Clin Invest* 94:860–869, 1994.

Schaefer EJ, Anderson DW, Zech LA, Lindgren FT, Bronzert TB, Rubalcaba EA, Brewer HB Jr: Metabolism of high density lipoprotein subfractions and constituents in Tangier disease following the infusion of high density lipoproteins, *J Lipid Res* 22:217–228, 1981.

Schaefer EJ, Brousseau ME, Diffenderfer MR, Cohn JS, Welty FK, O'Connor J Jr, Dolnikowski GG, Wang J, Hegele RA, Jones PJ: Cholesterol and apolipoprotein B metabolism in Tangier disease, *Atherosclerosis* 159:231–236, 2001.

Schenk D, et al: Immunization with amyloid-beta attenuates Alzheimer-disease-like pathology in the PDAPP mouse, *Nature* 400:173–177, 1999.

Selkoe DJ: Clearing the brain's amyloid cobwebs, *Neuron* 32:177–180, 2001.

Shaffer LM, Dority MD, Gupta-Bansal R, Frederickson RC, Younkin SG, Brunden KR: Amyloid beta protein (A beta) removal by neuroglial cells in culture, *Neurobiol Aging* 16:737–745, 1995.

Shibata M, Yamada S, Kumar SR, Calero M, Bading J, Frangione B, Holtzman DM, Miller CA, Strickland DK, Ghiso J, Zlokovic BV: Clearance of Alzheimer's amyloid-β(1–40) peptide from brain by LDL receptor-related protein-1 at the blood–brain barrier, *J Clin Invest* 106:1489–1499, 2000.

Shinohara M, Petersen RC, Dickson DW, Bu G: Brain regional correlation of amyloid-beta with synapses and apolipoprotein E in non-demented individuals: potential mechanisms underlying regional vulnerability to amyloid-beta accumulation, *Acta Neuropathol* 125:535–547, 2013.

Shulman JM, Chen K, Keenan BT, Chibnik LB, Fleisher A, Thiyyagura P, Roontiva A, McCabe C, Patsopoulos NA, Corneveaux JJ, Yu L, Huentelman MJ, Evans DA, Schneider JA, Reiman EM, De Jager PL, Bennett DA: Genetic susceptibility for Alzheimer disease neuritic plaque pathology, *JAMA Neurol* 70:1150–1157, 2013.

Simon R, Girod M, Fonbonne C, Salvador A, Clement Y, Lanteri P, Amouyel P, Lambert JC, Lemoine J: Total ApoE and ApoE4 isoform assays in an Alzheimer's disease case-control study by targeted mass spectrometry (n = 669): a pilot assay for methionine-containing proteotypic peptides, *Mol Cell Proteomics* 11:1389–1403, 2012.

Sorci-Thomas M, Prack MM, Dashti N, Johnson F, Rudel LL, Williams DL: Apolipoprotein (apo) A-I production and mRNA abundance explain plasma apoA-I and high density lipoprotein differences between two nonhuman primate species with high and low susceptibilities to diet-induced hypercholesterolemia, *J Biol Chem* 263:5183–5189, 1988.

Steinberg S, et al: Loss-of-function variants in ABCA7 confer risk of Alzheimer's disease, *Nat Genet* 47:445–447, 2015.

Strittmatter WJ, Saunders AM, Schmechel D, Pericak-Vance M, Enghild J, Salvesen GS, Roses AD: Apolipoprotein E: high-avidity binding to beta-amyloid and increased frequency of type 4 allele in late-onset familial Alzheimer disease, *Proc Natl Acad Sci USA* 90:1977–1981, 1993a.

Strittmatter WJ, Weisgraber KH, Huang DY, Dong LM, Salvesen GS, Pericak-Vance M, Schmechel D, Saunders AM, Goldgaber D, Roses AD: Binding of human apolipoprotein E to synthetic amyloid beta peptide: isoform-specific effects and implications for late-onset Alzheimer disease, *Proc Natl Acad Sci USA* 90:8098–8102, 1993b.

Sullivan PM, Mezdour H, Aratani Y, Knouff C, Najib J, Reddick RL, Quarfordt SH, Maeda N: Targeted replacement of the mouse apolipoprotein E gene with the common human APOE3 allele enhances diet-induced hypercholesterolemia and atherosclerosis, *J Biol Chem* 272:17972–17980, 1997.

Sullivan PM, Mace BE, Maeda N, Schmechel DE: Marked regional differences of brain human apolipoprotein E expression in targeted replacement mice, *Neuroscience* 124:725–733, 2004.

Sullivan PM, Han B, Liu F, Mace BE, Ervin JF, Wu S, Koger D, Paul S, Bales KR: Reduced levels of human apoE4 protein in an animal model of cognitive impairment, *Neurobiol Aging* 32:791–801, 2011.

Tai LM, Bilousova T, Jungbauer L, Roeske SK, Youmans KL, Yu C, Poon WW, Cornwell LB, Miller CA, Vinters HV, Van Eldik LJ, Fardo DW, Estus S, Bu G, Gylys KH, Ladu MJ: Levels of soluble apolipoprotein E/amyloid-beta (Abeta) complex are reduced and oligomeric Abeta increased with APOE4 and Alzheimer disease in a transgenic mouse model and human samples, *J Biol Chem* 288:5914–5926, 2013.

Tai LM, Koster KP, Luo J, Lee SH, Wang YT, Collins NC, Ben Aissa M, Thatcher GR, LaDu MJ: Amyloid-beta pathology and APOE genotype modulate retinoid X receptor agonist activity in vivo, *J Biol Chem* 289:30538–30555, 2014.

Takeda S, Hashimoto T, Roe AD, Hori Y, Spires-Jones TL, Hyman BT: Brain interstitial oligomeric amyloid beta increases with age and is resistant to clearance from brain in a mouse model of Alzheimer's disease, *FASEB J* 27:3239–3248, 2013.

Terwel D, Steffensen KR, Verghese PB, Kummer MP, Gustafsson JA, Holtzman DM, Heneka MT: Critical role of astroglial apolipoprotein E and liver X receptor-alpha expression for microglial Abeta phagocytosis, *J Neurosci* 31:7049–7059, 2011.

Tesseur I, Lo AC, Roberfroid A, Dietvorst S, Van Broeck B, Borgers M, Gijsen H, Moechars D, Mercken M, Kemp J, D'Hooge R, De Strooper B: Comment on "ApoE-directed therapeutics rapidly clear beta-amyloid and reverse deficits in AD mouse models", *Science* 340:924-e, 2013.

Thal DR, Schultz C, Dehghani F, Yamaguchi H, Braak H, Braak E: Amyloid beta-protein (Abeta)-containing astrocytes are located preferentially near N-terminal-truncated Abeta deposits in the human entorhinal cortex, *Acta Neuropathol* 100:608–617, 2000.

Thal DR, Capetillo-Zarate E, Schultz C, Rub U, Saido TC, Yamaguchi H, Haass C, Griffin WS, Del Tredici K, Braak H, Ghebremedhin E: Apolipoprotein E co-localizes with newly formed amyloid beta-protein (Abeta) deposits lacking immunoreactivity against N-terminal epitopes of Abeta in a genotype-dependent manner, *Acta Neuropathol* 110:459–471, 2005.

Tokuda T, Calero M, Matsubara E, Vidal R, Kumar A, Permanne B, Zlokovic B, Smith JD, Ladu MJ, Rostagno A, Frangione B, Ghiso J: Lipidation of apolipoprotein E influences its isoform-specific interaction with Alzheimer's amyloid beta peptides, *Biochem J* 348(Pt 2):359–365, 2000.

Toledo JB, Da X, Weiner MW, Wolk DA, Xie SX, Arnold SE, Davatzikos C, Shaw LM, Trojanowski JQ: Alzheimer's Disease Neuroimaging Initiative: CSF Apo-E levels associate with cognitive decline and MRI changes, *Acta Neuropathol* 127:621–632, 2014.

Trommsdorff M, Gotthardt M, Hiesberger T, Shelton J, Stockinger W, Nimpf J, Hammer RE, Richardson JA, Herz J: Reeler/disabled-like disruption of neuronal migration in knockout mice lacking the VLDL receptor and ApoE receptor 2, *Cell* 97:689–701, 1999.

Tsubuki S, Takaki Y, Saido TC: Dutch, Flemish, Italian, and Arctic mutations of APP and resistance of Abeta to physiologically relevant proteolytic degradation, *Lancet* 361:1957–1958, 2003.

Ulery PG, Beers J, Mikhailenko I, Tanzi RE, Rebeck GW, Hyman BT, Strickland DK: Modulation of beta-amyloid precursor protein processing by the low density lipoprotein receptor-related protein (LRP): evidence that LRP contributes to the pathogenesis of Alzheimer's disease, *J Biol Chem* 275:7410–7415, 2000.

Ulrich JD, Burchett JM, Restivo JL, Schuler DR, Verghese PB, Mahan TE, Landreth GE, Castellano JM, Jiang H, Cirrito JR, Holtzman DM: In vivo measurement of apolipoprotein E from the brain interstitial fluid using microdialysis, *Mol Neurodegener* 8:13, 2013.

Veeraraghavalu K, Zhang C, Miller S, Hefendehl JK, Rajapaksha TW, Ulrich J, Jucker M, Holtzman DM, Tanzi RE, Vassar R, Sisodia SS: Comment on "ApoE-directed therapeutics rapidly clear beta-amyloid and reverse deficits in AD mouse models", *Science* 340:924-f, 2013.

Verghese PB, Castellano JM, Garai K, Wang Y, Jiang H, Shah A, Bu G, Frieden C, Holtzman DM: ApoE influences amyloid-beta (Abeta) clearance despite minimal apoE/Abeta association in physiological conditions, *Proc Natl Acad Sci USA* 110:E1807–E1816, 2013.

Vitek MP, Christensen DJ, Wilcock D, Davis J, Van Nostrand WE, Li FQ, Colton CA: APOE-mimetic peptides reduce behavioral deficits, plaques and tangles in Alzheimer's disease transgenics, *Neurodegener Dis* 10:122–126, 2012.

Wahrle SE, Jiang H, Parsadanian M, Legleiter J, Han X, Fryer JD, Kowalewski T, Holtzman DM: ABCA1 is required for normal central nervous system ApoE levels and for lipidation of astrocyte-secreted apoE, *J Biol Chem* 279:40987–40993, 2004.

Wahrle SE, Jiang H, Parsadanian M, Hartman RE, Bales KR, Paul SM, Holtzman DM: Deletion of Abca1 increases Abeta deposition in the PDAPP transgenic mouse model of Alzheimer disease, *J Biol Chem* 280:43236–43242, 2005.

Wahrle SE, Shah AR, Fagan AM, Smemo S, Kauwe JS, Grupe A, Hinrichs A, Mayo K, Jiang H, Thal LJ, Goate AM, Holtzman DM: Apolipoprotein E levels in cerebrospinal fluid and the effects of ABCA1 polymorphisms, *Mol Neurodegener* 2:7, 2007.

Wahrle SE, Jiang H, Parsadanian M, Kim J, Li A, Knoten A, Jain S, Hirsch-Reinshagen V, Wellington CL, Bales KR, Paul SM, Holtzman DM: Overexpression of ABCA1 reduces amyloid deposition in the PDAPP mouse model of Alzheimer disease, *J Clin Invest* 118:671–682, 2008.

Wang H, Durham L, Dawson H, Song P, Warner DS, Sullivan PM, Vitek MP, Laskowitz DT: An apolipoprotein E-based therapeutic improves outcome and reduces Alzheimer's disease pathology following closed head injury: evidence of pharmacogenomic interaction, *Neuroscience* 144:1324–1333, 2007.

Wetterau JR, Aggerbeck LP, Rall SC Jr, Weisgraber KH: Human apolipoprotein E3 in aqueous solution. I. Evidence for two structural domains, *J Biol Chem* 263:6240–6248, 1988.

White F, Nicoll JA, Roses AD, Horsburgh K: Impaired neuronal plasticity in transgenic mice expressing human apolipoprotein E4 compared to E3 in a model of entorhinal cortex lesion, *Neurobiol Dis* 8:611–625, 2001.

Wildsmith KR, Basak JM, Patterson BW, Pyatkivskyy Y, Kim J, Yarasheski KE, Wang JX, Mawuenyega KG, Jiang H, Parsadanian M, Yoon H, Kasten T, Sigurdson WC, Xiong C, Goate A, Holtzman DM, Bateman RJ: In vivo human apolipoprotein E isoform fractional turnover rates in the CNS, *PLoS One* 7:e38013, 2012.

Wilson C, Wardell MR, Weisgraber KH, Mahley RW, Agard DA: Three-dimensional structure of the LDL receptor-binding domain of human apolipoprotein E, *Science* 252:1817–1822, 1991.

Wisniewski T, Frangione B: Apolipoprotein E: a pathological chaperone protein in patients with cerebral and systemic amyloid, *Neurosci Lett* 135:235–238, 1992.

Wisniewski T, Castano EM, Golabek A, Vogel T, Frangione B: Acceleration of Alzheimer's fibril formation by apolipoprotein E in vitro, *Am J Pathol* 145:1030–1035, 1994.

Wood SJ, Chan W, Wetzel R: Seeding of A beta fibril formation is inhibited by all three isotypes of apolipoprotein E, *Biochemistry* 35:12623–12628, 1996.

Wyss-Coray T, Loike JD, Brionne TC, Lu E, Anankov R, Yan F, Silverstein SC, Husemann J: Adult mouse astrocytes degrade amyloid-beta in vitro and in situ, *Nat Med* 9:453–457, 2003.

Xu Q, Bernardo A, Walker D, Kanegawa T, Mahley RW, Huang Y: Profile and regulation of apolipoprotein E (ApoE) expression in the CNS in mice with targeting of green fluorescent protein gene to the ApoE locus, *J Neurosci* 26:4985–4994, 2006.

Yamada K, Hashimoto T, Yabuki C, Nagae Y, Tachikawa M, Strickland DK, Liu Q, Bu G, Basak JM, Holtzman DM, Ohtsuki S, Terasaki T, Iwatsubo T: The low density lipoprotein receptor-related protein 1 mediates uptake of amyloid beta peptides in an in vitro model of the blood–brain barrier cells, *J Biol Chem* 283:34554–34562, 2008.

Yamanaka M, Ishikawa T, Griep A, Axt D, Kummer MP, Heneka MT: PPARgamma/RXRalpha-induced and CD36-mediated microglial amyloid-beta phagocytosis results in cognitive improvement in amyloid precursor protein/presenilin 1 mice, *J Neurosci* 32:17321–17331, 2012.

Yamauchi K, Tozuka M, Nakabayashi T, Sugano M, Hidaka H, Kondo Y, Katsuyama T: Higher avidity binding of apolipoprotein (E-AII) complex than of apolipoprotein E monomer to beta-amyloid, *J Neurosci Res* 58:301–307, 1999.

Yang DS, Smith JD, Zhou Z, Gandy SE, Martins RN: Characterization of the binding of amyloid-beta peptide to cell culture-derived native apolipoprotein E2, E3, and E4 isoforms and to isoforms from human plasma, *J Neurochem* 68:721–725, 1997.

Yang J, Ji Y, Mehta P, Bates KA, Sun Y, Wisniewski T: Blocking the apolipoprotein E/amyloid-beta interaction reduces fibrillar vascular amyloid deposition and cerebral microhemorrhages in TgSwDI mice, *J Alzheimers Dis* 24:269–285, 2011.

Yang Y, Cudaback E, Jorstad NL, Hemingway JF, Hagan CE, Melief EJ, Li X, Yoo T, Khademi SB, Montine KS, Montine TJ, Keene CD: APOE3, but not APOE4, bone marrow transplantation mitigates behavioral and pathological changes in a mouse model of Alzheimer disease, *Am J Pathol* 183:905–917, 2013.

Ye S, Huang Y, Mullendorff K, Dong L, Giedt G, Meng EC, Cohen FE, Kuntz ID, Weisgraber KH, Mahley RW: Apolipoprotein (apo) E4 enhances amyloid beta peptide production in cultured neuronal cells: apoE structure as a potential therapeutic target, *Proc Natl Acad Sci USA* 102:18700–18705, 2005.

Youmans KL, Tai LM, Nwabuisi-Heath E, Jungbauer L, Kanekiyo T, Gan M, Kim J, Eimer WA, Estus S, Rebeck GW, Weeber EJ, Bu G, Yu C, Ladu MJ: APOE4-specific changes in Abeta accumulation in a new transgenic mouse model of Alzheimer disease, *J Biol Chem* 287:41774–41786, 2012.

Zerbinatti CV, Wahrle SE, Kim H, Cam JA, Bales K, Paul SM, Holtzman DM, Bu G: Apolipoprotein E and low density lipoprotein receptor-related protein facilitate intraneuronal Abeta42 accumulation in amyloid model mice, *J Biol Chem* 281:36180–36186, 2006.

Zhang SH, Reddick RL, Piedrahita JA, Maeda N: Spontaneous hypercholesterolemia and arterial lesions in mice lacking apolipoprotein E, *Science* 258:468–471, 1992.

Zhou Z, Smith JD, Greengard P, Gandy S: Alzheimer amyloid-beta peptide forms denaturant-resistant complex with type epsilon 3 but not type epsilon 4 isoform of native apolipoprotein E, *Mol Med* 2:175–180, 1996.

Zlokovic BV, Martel CL, Mackic JB, Matsubara E, Wisniewski T, McComb JG, Frangione B, Ghiso J: Brain uptake of circulating apolipoproteins J and E complexed to Alzheimer's amyloid beta, *Biochem Biophys Res Commun* 205:1431–1437, 1994.

Internet Resource

http://www.alzgene.org

CHAPTER

11

Microtubule Stabilization

C. Ballatore, A.B. Smith, III, V.M.-Y. Lee, J.Q. Trojanowski, K.R. Brunden

OUTLINE

INTRODUCTION

Alzheimer's disease (AD) is characterized by the progressive accumulation of characteristic protein aggregates in the brains of affected individuals. These aggregate structures are known as senile plaques (SPs), which are made of Aβ peptides and are found within the extracellular interstitial space, and neurofibrillary tangles (NFTs) and dystrophic neurites, composed of hyperphosphorylated tau proteins that appear inside neurons. Although the precise mechanism(s) linking these lesions remain the focus of ongoing studies, the preponderance of available data clearly indicates that tau and Aβ aggregates participate directly or indirectly in the onset and progression of AD. This chapter summarizes literature reports that underpin a promising AD therapeutic strategy based on the use of brain-penetrant microtubule (MT)-stabilizing molecules to treat the neuropathological consequences of the sequestration of tau proteins into aggregate structures. If successful, such a strategy may provide a viable approach to treat AD and possibly other related tau-mediated neurodegenerative diseases.

Developing Therapeutics for Alzheimer's Disease. http://dx.doi.org/10.1016/B978-0-12-802173-6.00011-3

MICROTUBULES AND TAU PROTEIN

MTs, hollow structures that result from the polymerization of α- and β-tubulin heterodimers, are ubiquitous in all eukaryotic cells and are known to play a number of structural and regulatory functions in different cell types. One of the characteristic properties of MTs is their dynamic instability, which derives in part from the fact that MTs spontaneously alternate between growing and shrinking phases (Fig. 11.1) (Desai and Mitchison, 1997).

Posttranslational modifications of tubulin, as well as interactions with MT-associated proteins, can affect both the dynamics and overall organization of the MT structure. This enables the MT lattice to carry out a variety of functions in different cell types, or even within different cellular compartments. In the axons of neurons, for example, the particular organization of MTs provides both structural support and directionality to the motor proteins (ie, kinesins and dyneins) that transport various cellular cargoes along the axon to and from the cell body (*see later*).

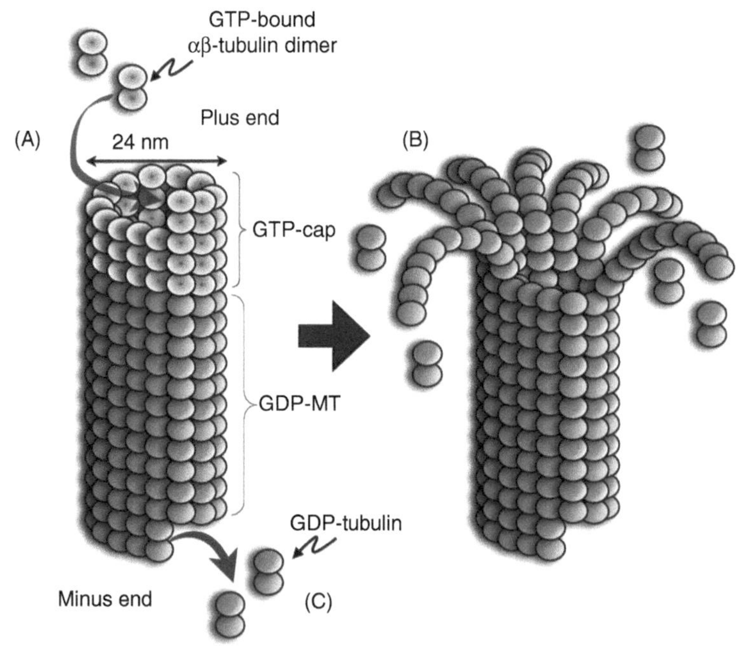

FIGURE 11.1 **Dynamic instability of MTs.** (A) Guanosine 5′-triphosphate (GTP)-bound α,β-tubulin heterodimers are added at the polymerizing end of the MT (plus end). After incorporation into the MT, GTP bound to β-tubulin is hydrolyzed to the corresponding diphosphate (GDP-MT). The GTP to GDP hydrolysis is not required for MT polymerization; however, as GTP-tubulin forms comparatively more stable interactions than GDP-tubulin, this conversion is believed to be an important factor that determines the dynamic instability of the MT. The presence of a GTP-bound tubulin at the growing end of the MT, commonly known as the GTP cap, protects the MT from depolymerization. Removal of the GTP cap can result in a rapid depolymerization event (B). Tubulin heterodimers released during depolymerization can reenter the polymerization cycle after exchange of GDP with GTP (C).

Among the different MT-associated proteins, tau, which is particularly abundant in the axons of neurons, promotes MT assembly and stabilization (Drechsel et al., 1992; Buee et al., 2000). This protein exhibits little or no secondary structure when not bound to MTs (Schweers et al., 1994), and thus is considered natively unfolded (Tompa, 2002). Six human tau isoforms have been identified that result from alternative splicing of a single gene product (Goedert et al., 1989; Himmler et al., 1989; Lee et al., 1991). From a structural standpoint, tau isoforms contain either three or four MT-binding domains composed of highly conserved but nonidentical amino acid repeats, a basic proline-rich region, and an acidic N-terminal sequence known as the projection domain (Figs. 11.2 and 11.3). As shown in Fig. 11.2, tau isoforms differ not only in the number of MT-binding repeats (ie, 3R for three-repeat and 4R for four-repeat tau isoforms), but also in the presence or absence of either one or two 29-amino-acid inserts in the N-terminal region (0N, 1N, 2N). In the adult brain, there is an approximately 1:1 ratio of 3R and 4R isoforms, and certain mutations that cause autosomal-dominant inherited forms of frontotemporal lobar degeneration (FTLD) lead to an imbalance in this ratio.

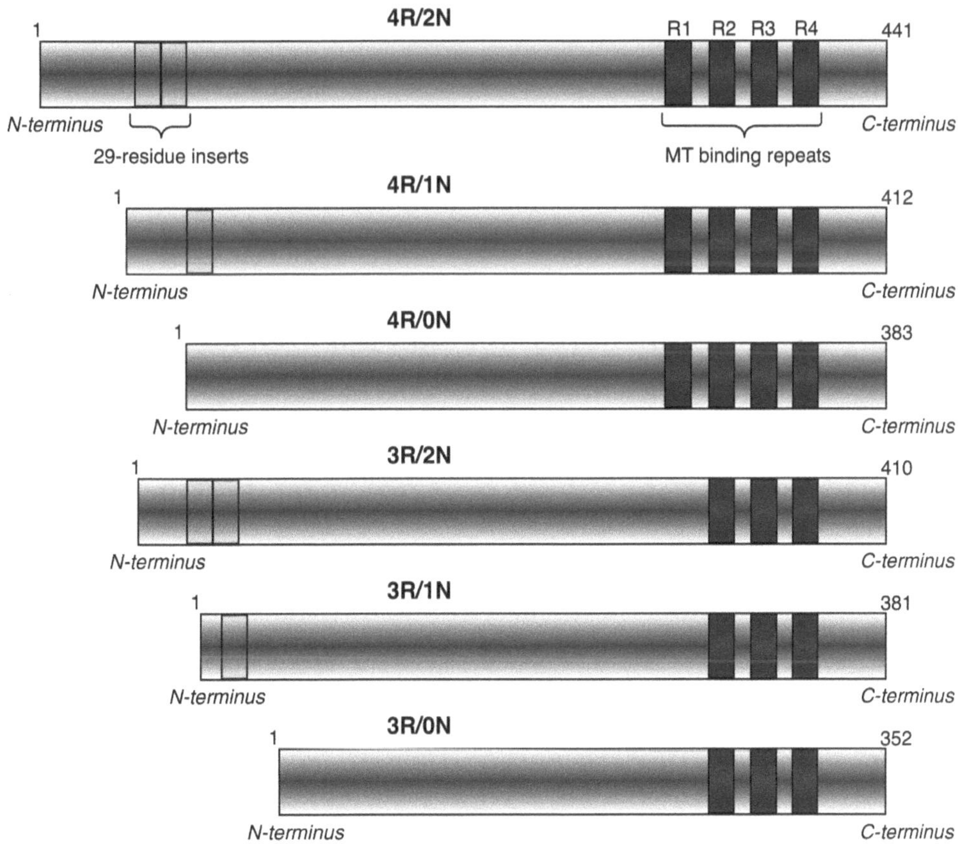

FIGURE 11.2 **The six isoforms of tau.**

The MT-stabilizing ability of tau is primarily mediated by the MT-binding domains, with each of the amino acid repeats bound to β-tubulin subunits of adjacent protofilaments at a binding site that is believed to overlap with the binding region of paclitaxel and other related MT-stabilizing natural products (Kar et al., 2003). In addition to the MT-binding domains, other sections of the protein, such as the proline-rich region, are likely to participate in the stabilization of the MT structure via electrostatic interactions with the negatively charged surface of the MTs (Amos, 2004). Different studies suggest that the binding mode of tau with MTs may be substantially different depending on whether tau coassembles with tubulin heterodimers or binds to preformed MTs (Makrides et al., 2004). In the former case, coassembly of tau with tubulin results in an irreversible interaction, as tau becomes intercalated in the MT structure (Fig. 11.3A). Conversely, interaction of tau with preformed MTs leads to a readily reversible mode of binding in which tau interacts with the surface of MTs (Fig. 11.3B). Importantly, the affinity of tau for MTs is known to be affected by the phosphorylation state of the

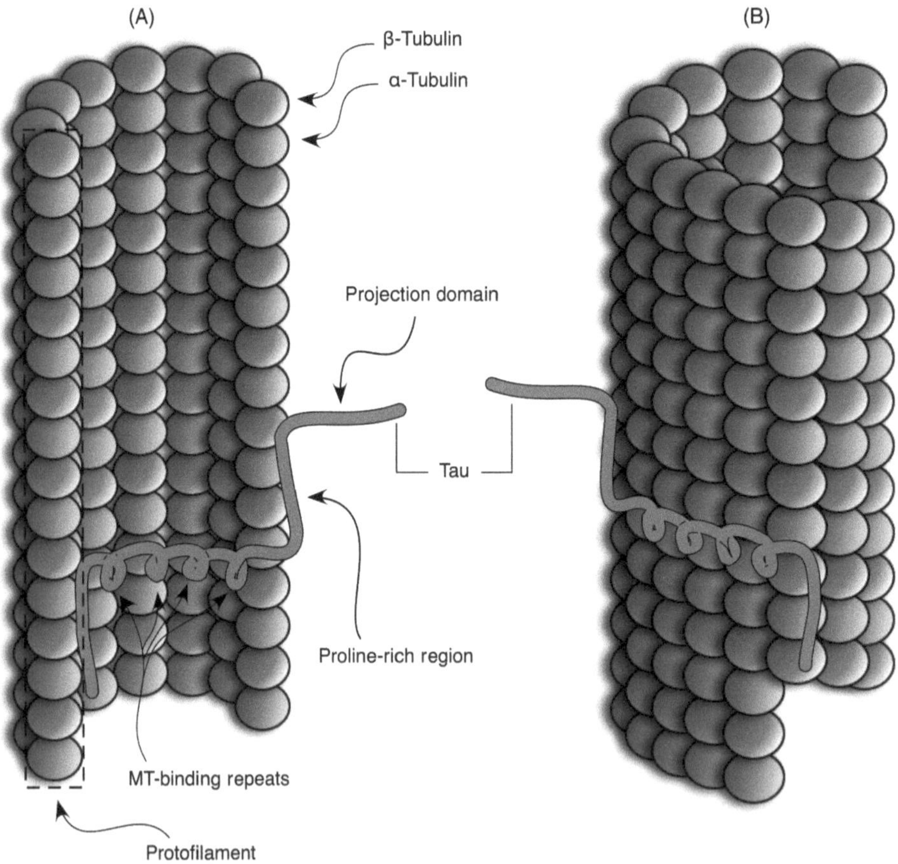

FIGURE 11.3 The interaction of tau with MTs may be irreversible if tau coassembles with tubulin (A), or reversible if tau associates with preassembled MTs (B).

protein, and the hyperphosphorylation of tau that is observed in AD and related tauopathies significantly reduces MT-binding affinity (Drechsel et al., 1992).

In addition to the MT-stabilizing function, tau may play additional roles that affect axonal transport, including modulating MT binding of molecular motors required for the movement of organelles and vesicles along MTs. For example, there is evidence in cultured cells over-expressing tau that the protein can regulate kinesin binding to the MTs (Stamer et al., 2002; Doshi et al., 2009). Similarly, it has been suggested that tau may bind to dynactin, and as a result may affect dynein-mediated axonal transport (Magnani et al., 2007). Thus, the disengagement of hyperphosphorylated tau from the MTs in the diseased brain could alter axonal transport by multiple mechanisms.

RATIONALE FOR THERAPEUTIC INTERVENTION

Tau is particularly abundant in the axons of neurons, and the MT-stabilizing function of this protein is believed to play an important role in the axonal transport of proteins, organelles, and other cellular constituents. As summarized in Fig. 11.4, the axonal transport machinery is composed of three essential constituents: (1) the MTs, which provide structural support and directionality; (2) the motor proteins, dyneins and kinesins, which move cellular cargo toward the cell body (retrograde movement) and the synapses (anterograde movement), respectively; and (3) the cargo vesicles. In this context, tau-mediated MT stabilization is likely to be essential in that it ensures an appropriate organization of axonal MTs. However, as the presence of tau along the MT tracks may also alter the movement of motor proteins and cargoes, the interaction of tau with MTs is likely to be in an equilibrium in which the concerted action of tau kinases and phosphatases modulate the binding affinity of the protein for MTs. Under normal conditions, the equilibrium of tau on and off MTs is believed to be shifted toward MT-bound tau (Congdon et al., 2008). However, under pathological conditions typical of tauopathies, hyperphosphorylation of tau, caused presumably by an imbalance between tau kinase and phosphatase activities (Mazanetz and Fischer, 2007), leads to an excessive detachment of tau from MTs. This deviation from the physiological equilibrium between the MT-bound and -unbound tau fractions affects both the normal structure and dynamics of axonal MTs as well as the normal interaction of MT motors with axons, which in turn causes a disruption of axonal transport (Fig. 11.4). In this regard, studies with purified MTs reveal that tau binding can affect dynein- and kinesin-mediated axonal transport, and it has been suggested that the redistribution of tau to somatodendritic compartments in tauopathies alters normal kinesin-mediated axonal transport (Dixit et al., 2008).

Evidence in support of this model of tau-mediated neurodegeneration is the relative reduction in MT density that has been observed both in the AD brain (Cash et al., 2003) as well as in tau transgenic (Tg) mice (Ishihara et al., 2001; Brunden et al., 2010). In addition, an inverse correlation between the number of NFTs and markers of stable MTs has been observed in brain tissue samples collected postmortem from AD patients (Hempen and Brion, 1996). Moreover, studies from Barten et al. (2012) revealed that MTs isolated from the rTg4510 and 3xTg mouse models of tauopathy exchange more soluble tubulin dimers than MTs from control mice, suggesting that tau pathology is associated with hyperdynamic MTs.

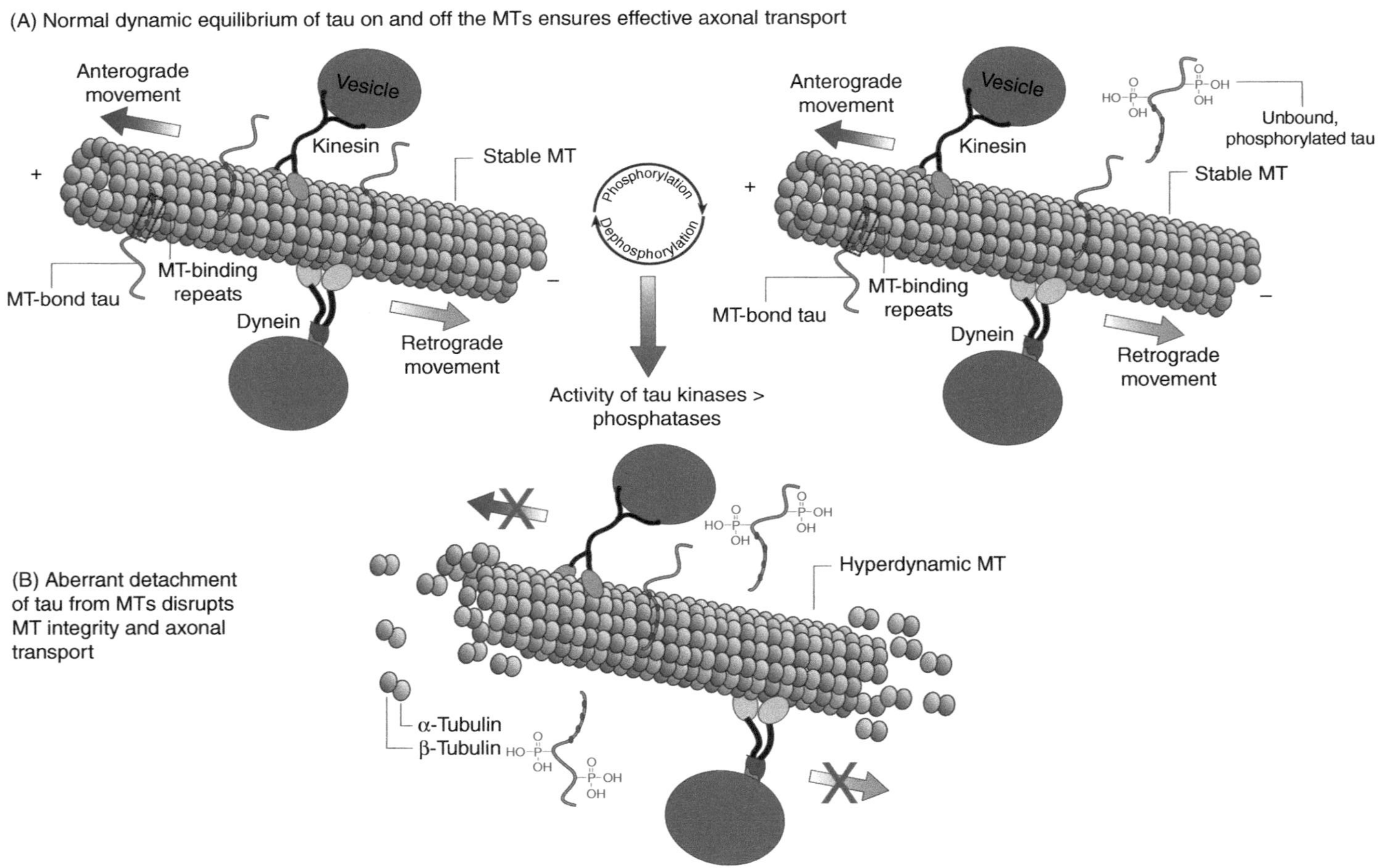

FIGURE 11.4 Schematic representation of normal (A) and disrupted (B) axonal transport. Under normal conditions, tau is mostly bound to MTs, and the MT-stabilizing function of tau ensures that axonal MTs are appropriately organized for effective axonal transport. The normal equilibrium of tau on and off MTs is regulated by the phosphorylation state of the protein. Imbalances between the activity of tau kinases and phosphatases can cause hyperphosphorylation of tau, leading to an excessive disengagement of tau from MTs and consequent disruption in MT dynamics and axonal transport.

Based on the likely relationship in tauopathies between increased disengagement of tau from MTs and altered axonal MT dynamics, with consequent axonal transport deficits leading to axonal degeneration, a potential therapeutic strategy was hypothesized more than 20 years ago (Lee et al., 1994). It was proposed that exogenous MT-stabilizing molecules might be employed to compensate for the loss of MT-stabilizing function of tau and thus restore or maintain effective axonal transport. Despite the logical rationale for this strategy, such a therapeutic approach faced significant challenges. MT-stabilizing agents have been employed extensively in cancer chemotherapy due to the ability of these compounds to trigger apoptosis in rapidly dividing cancer cells (Jordan and Wilson, 2004). Although highly effective in the treatment of a number of tumors, this class of therapeutics is known to have a relatively narrow safety margin, in large part due to on-target toxicities related to the inhibition of normal cell division. As a result, long-term or chronic treatment of elderly patients with doses of MT-stabilizing compounds that are near the chemotherapeutic dose would likely cause significant morbidities, including neutropenia and immunosuppression (Bedard et al., 2010). Furthermore, another common dose-limiting side effect encountered in cancer chemotherapy regimens employing MT-targeting agents is peripheral neuropathy (Lee and Swain, 2006), a form of neurotoxicity that has been linked to a disruption of the axonal transport machinery of peripheral nerves caused by MT-stabilizing and -destabilizing drugs (LaPointe et al., 2013). Thus, the therapeutic potential of molecules of this type for neurodegenerative tauopathies is likely to depend, at least in part, on whether the doses required to normalize MTs and restore axonal transport in the brain are significantly lower than those typically used in cancer chemotherapy. In this regard, MT-stabilizing agents are known to influence MT dynamics at low molar ratios (ie, as low as 1:1000) with tubulin (Derry et al., 1995), indicating that a therapeutic suppression of MT dynamics in the treatment of neurodegenerative tauopathies may be achievable at doses that are considerably lower than that required for inhibition of mitosis. Evidence in support of this possibility came first from a key study (Zhang et al., 2005) in which the MT-stabilizing drug paclitaxel (Taxol, **1**, Table 11.1), at doses below those commonly used for cancer chemotherapy, was found to improve the neurodegenerative phenotype of tau Tg mice that exhibit tau pathology and axonal transport deficits primarily in the brain stem and in motor neurons. Of note, the improvements of axonal function observed in this first proof-of-concept study resulted from drug absorption at the neuromuscular junctions of motor neurons harboring tau pathology. As a result, paclitaxel, which is not a brain-penetrant compound, was not required to cross the blood–brain barrier (BBB) in order to be effective. Thus, the further advancement of this therapeutic strategy required testing and validation of brain-penetrant candidate compounds.

THE IDENTIFICATION OF EPOTHILONE D AS A POTENTIAL CLINICAL CANDIDATE

As noted, paclitaxel is not a brain-penetrant compound, and different reports have indicated that the limited uptake of this compound into the CNS might be directly linked to the action of the P-glycoprotein (Pgp) (Fellner et al., 2002; Gallo et al., 2003; Kemper et al., 2003), an active transporter that is highly expressed in the endothelial cells of the BBB. In the BBB, the combined action of the tight junctions, which prevent the diffusion of molecules through the

TABLE 11.1 The Different Classes of MT-Stabilizing Natural Products

Class Name	Typifying structure	Key references: Isolation	Key references: Synthesis	Key references: Mode of action
Taxane	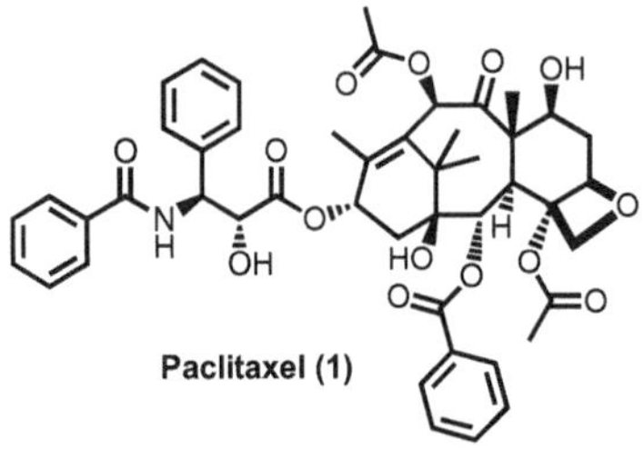 Paclitaxel (1)	Wani et al. (1971)	Semisynthesis (Holton, 1992; Ojima et al., 1992; Ojima, 1995); for a review, see also Kingston et al. (2002)	Schiff et al. (1979), Nogales et al. (1995)
Epothilones	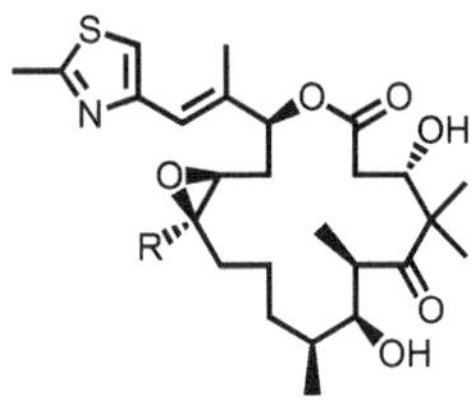 R = H : Epothilone A R = Me : Epothilone B (9)	Hofle and Reichenbach (2005)	Balog et al. (1996), Schinzer et al. (1997), Yang et al. (1997); for a review, see also Altmann et al. (2009)	Bollag et al. (1995), Prota et al. (2013)
Discodermolide	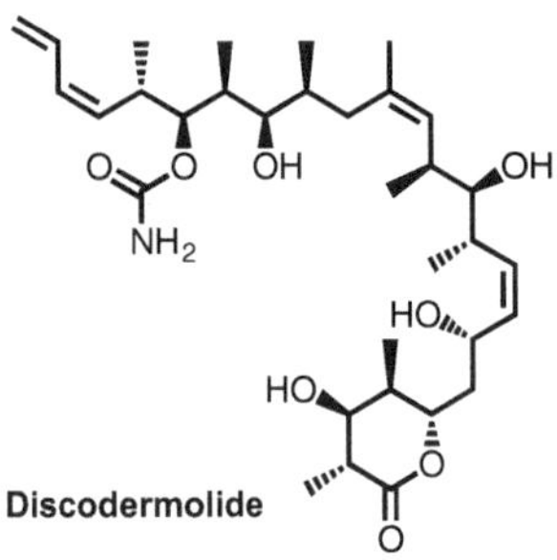 Discodermolide	Gunasekera et al. (1990)	Hung et al. (1996b), Paterson et al. (2000), Smith et al. (2000); for a review, see also Smith and Freeze (2008)	Hung et al. (1996a), ter Haar et al. (1996), Kowalski et al. (1997), Xia et al. (2006)
Dictyostatin	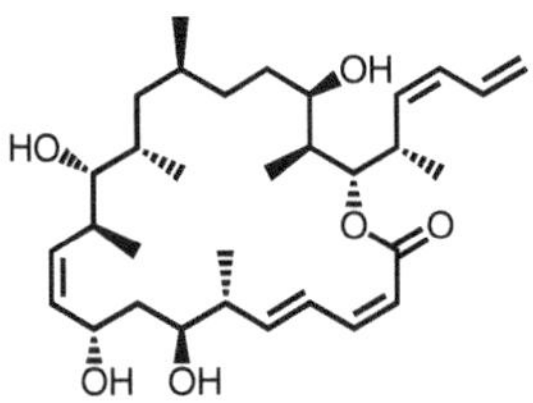 Dictyostatin (10)	Pettit et al. (1994)	Paterson et al. (2004, 2010), Shin et al. (2004), O'Nei and Phillips (2006), Ramachandran et al. (2006), Ho et al. (2013)	Isbrucker et al. (2003), Madiraju et al. (2005)

TABLE 11.1 The Different Classes of MT-Stabilizing Natural Products (*cont.*)

		Key references		
Class Name	**Typifying structure**	**Isolation**	**Synthesis**	**Mode of action**
Eleuthesides	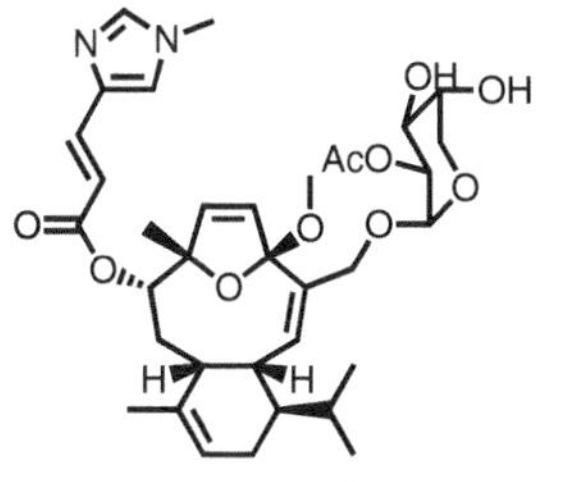 **Eleutherobin**	Lindel et al. (1997)	Nicolaou et al. (1997a, 1998a Chen et al. (1998a,b), Chen et al. (1999)	Lindel et al. (1997), Long et al. (1998), Hamel et al. (1999)
Sarcodyctins	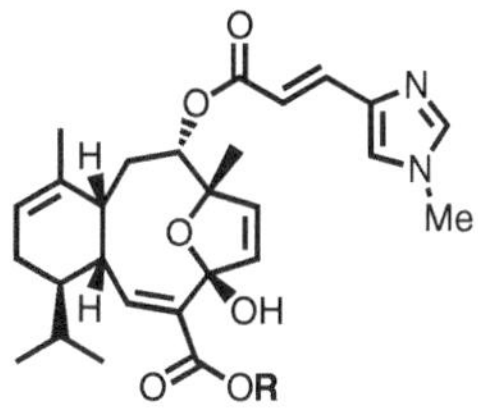 **R** = CH_3, **Sarcodyctin A** **R** = CH_2CH_3, **Sarcodyctin B**	D'Ambrosio et al. (1987, 1988), Ciomei et al. (1997)	Nicolaou et al. (1997b, 1998b)	Ciomei et al. (1997), Hamel et al. (1999)
Laulimalide	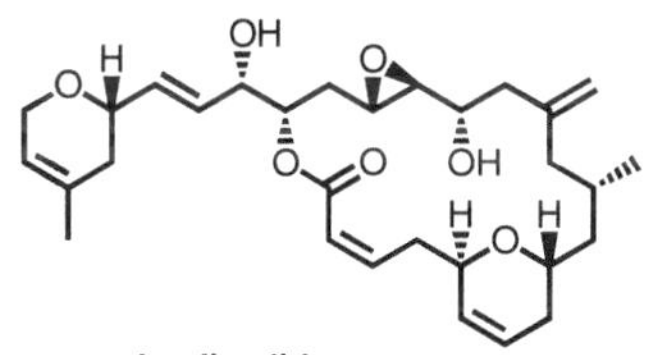 **Laulimalide**	Corley et al. (1988), Quinoa et al. (1988), Jefford et al. (1996)	For a review of other approaches, see Mulzer and Ohler (2003)	Mooberry et al. (1999), Pryor et al. (2002), Hamel et al. (2006), Bennett et al. (2010)
Peloruside	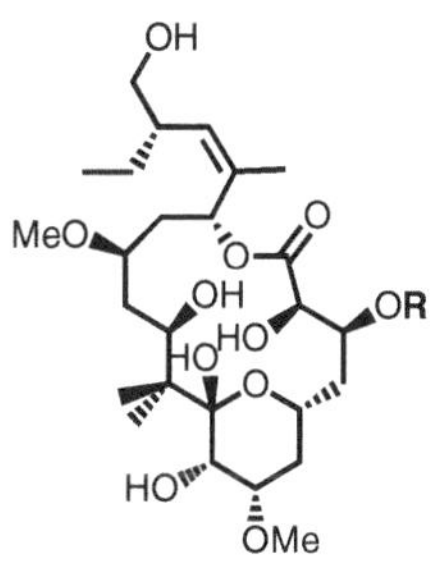 **R** = CH_3, **Peloruside A** **R** = H, **Peloruside B**	West et al. (2000), Hood et al. (2001)	Liao et al. (2003), Jin and Taylor (2005), Ghosh et al. (2008), Smith et al. (2008), Evans et al. (2009), Dalby and Paterson (2010), Hoye et al. (2010), McGowan et al. (2010)	Gaitanos et al. (2004), Hamel et al. (2006), Huzil et al. (2008)

(Continued)

TABLE 11.1 The Different Classes of MT-Stabilizing Natural Products (*cont.*)

		Key references		
Class Name	**Typifying structure**	**Isolation**	**Synthesis**	**Mode of action**
Cyclostreptin	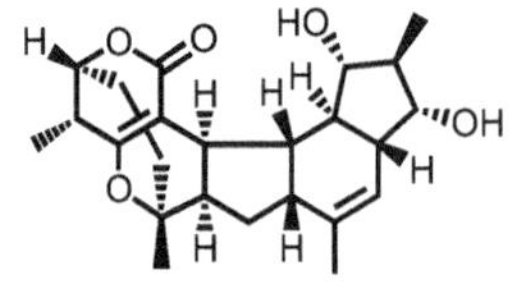 **Cyclostreptin**	Sato et al. (2000a)	Evans and Starr (2002), Vosburg et al. (2002), Vanderwal et al. (2003)	Sato et al. (2000b), Edler et al. (2005), Buey et al. (2007), Bai et al. (2008)
Taccalonolides	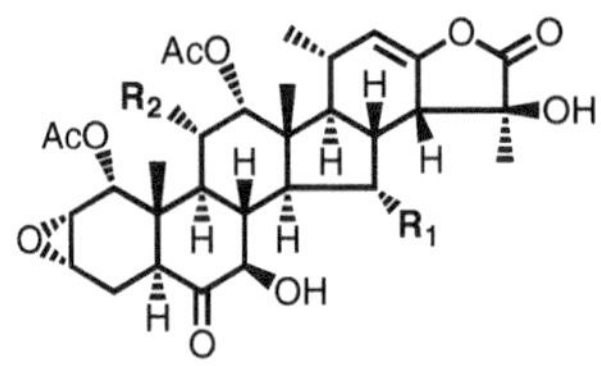 R	Scheuer et al. (1963), Chen et al. (1987)	None	Tinley et al. (2003), Risinger and Mooberry (2010, 2011), Risinger et al. (2013)
Zampanolide	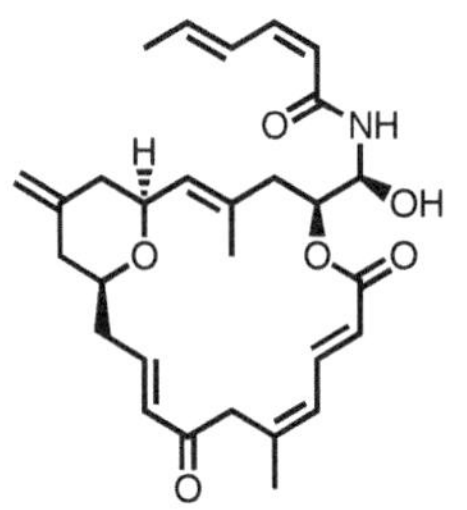 **Zampanolide**	Tanaka and Higa (1996)	Smith et al. (2001, 2002), Uenishi et al. (2009), Ghosh et al. (2012)	Field et al. (2012), Prota et al. (2013)
Dactylolide	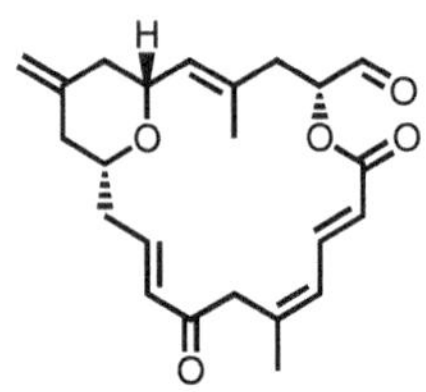 **Dactylolide**	Cutignano et al. (2001)	Smith and Safonov (2002), Smith et al. (2002), Hoye and Hu (2003), Aubele et al. (2005)	Zurwerra et al. (2010)
Ceratamines	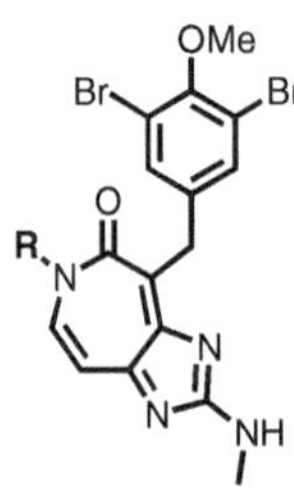 R = CH_3, **Ceratamine A** R = H, **Ceratamine B**	Manzo et al. (2003)	Coleman et al. (2009), Nodwell et al. (2009)	Karjala et al. (2005)

intercellular space, and the active efflux mechanism provided by transporters such as Pgp, ensure that the CNS is protected from most endogenous and exogenous substances, including the vast majority of drugs and drug candidates (Pardridge, 2005). Given that Pgp-mediated efflux is also a well-understood mechanism of multidrug resistance (MDR) in cancer chemotherapy (Gottesman and Pastan, 1993), considerable effort by the biomedical research community had already identified MT-stabilizing natural products, or derivatives thereof, that could effectively overcome the MDR phenotype associated with the overexpression of Pgp; for a series of examples, see Ballatore et al. (2012). Although the ability of these compounds to overcome Pgp-mediated efflux in cancer cell lines cannot be used as an entirely reliable predictor of BBB permeability, this subset of compounds was initially prioritized, as these molecules were thought to be less likely to be actively effluxed from the CNS by Pgp (Ballatore et al., 2007, 2008). However, subsequent investigations revealed that taxanes lacking Pgp interaction were still generally incapable of crossing the BBB (Brunden et al., 2011).

The first important break in the search for brain-penetrant MT-stabilizing agents came from the evaluation of selected members of the epothilone class of MT-stabilizing compounds (ie, **2–8**, Fig. 11.5). Among the different members of the epothilones that, based on cytotoxicity studies, were likely to exhibit limited Pgp-substrate potential, the 12,13-desoxy congeners were prioritized as structure–activity relationship (SAR) studies had established that the epoxide moiety was not essential for MT-stabilizing activity (Altmann et al., 2007), and we considered that the presence of this functional group may be a potential safety liability. Thus, with the exception of ixabepilone (**2**), which was selected because this was the only member of the epothilone class to have reached regulatory approval for cancer treatment (Conlin et al., 2007), we restricted our studies to the 12,13-desoxy series, such as epothilone D (**3**), **4**, and **5**, as well as the corresponding 9,10-dehydro congeners (**6–8**). Of note, while the resynthesis of these selected epothilones was ongoing in our laboratories, conducted following the synthesis developed by Danishefsky and coworkers (Rivkin et al., 2003, 2004), a report appeared which suggested that epothilone D could cross the BBB, as this compound was found to have activity in an animal model of schizophrenia (Andrieux et al., 2006). Later, the brain penetration of epothilone B (**9**, Fig. 11.5) was also determined (O'Reilly et al., 2008).

Interestingly, bidirectional permeability studies with epothilones **3–8** indicated that compounds **3**, **4**, and **5** were poor substrates for the Pgp, as demonstrated by efflux ratio values near unity (Brunden et al., 2011). However, further investigation demonstrated that these congeners inhibit Pgp function, as revealed by the fact that these compounds interfered with the Pgp-mediated transport of digoxin. Evaluation of brain-to-plasma concentration ratios (B/P) 2 h after intraperitoneal (i.p.) administration of compounds **2–8** revealed that, with the exception of **2**, all tested epothilones exhibited B/P values >1 (Brunden et al., 2011). Furthermore, evaluation of brain and plasma PK revealed that these selected epothilones exhibit brain half-lives that are longer than the plasma half-lives, indicating the existence of brain-tissue-specific interactions that sequester these compounds within the CNS. Similarly, prolonged brain retention was also described for **9** (O'Reilly et al., 2008).

To determine whether these brain-penetrant epothilones could interact with MTs and promote MT stabilization in CNS neurons, a series of pharmacodynamic (PD) studies was conducted to monitor for compound-induced increase of acetylated α-tubulin (AcTub), a marker of stable MTs (Baas and Black, 1990), in CNS tissue (ie, optic nerve or whole brain homogenates) (Brunden et al., 2011). Interestingly, among the congeners evaluated, **3** was

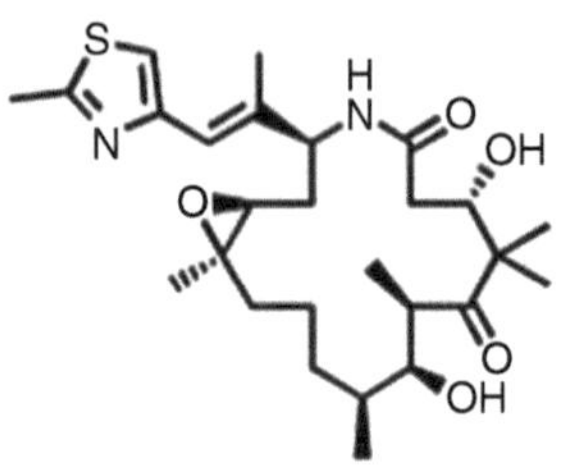

Ixabepilone (**2**)

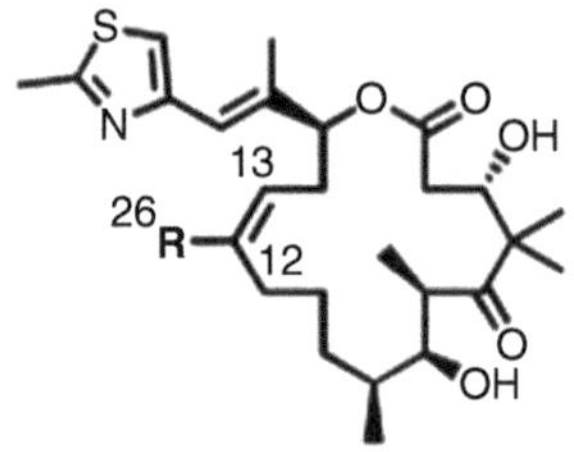

R = CH_3, Epothilone D (**3**)
R = CF_3, 26-F_3-12,13-desoxy-EpoB (**4**)

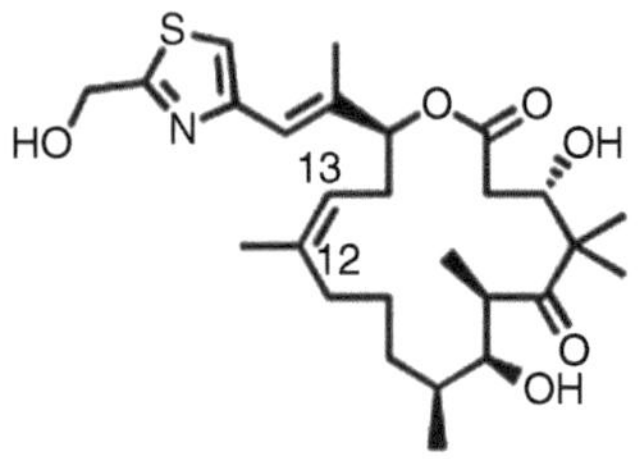

12, 13-desoxy-EpoF (**5**)

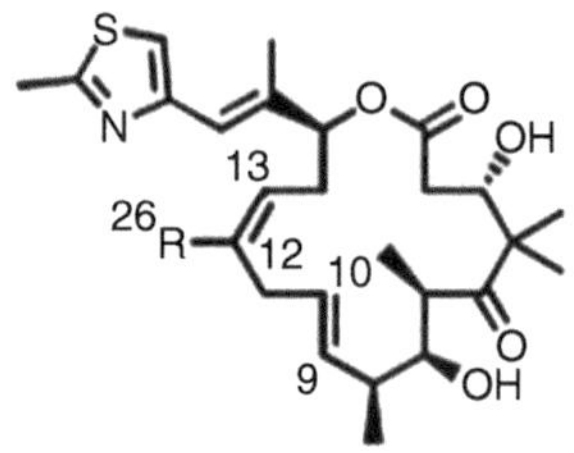

R = CH_3, (E)-9 10-dehydro-12,13-desoxy-EpoB (**6**)
R = CF_3, Fludelone (**7**)

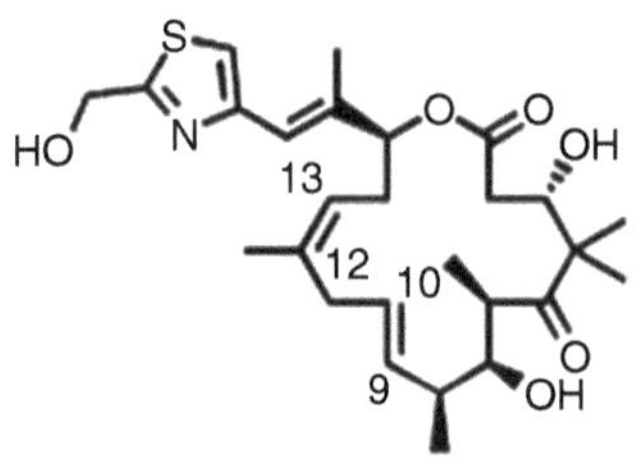

(E)-9,10-dehydro-12,13-desoxy-EpoF (**8**)

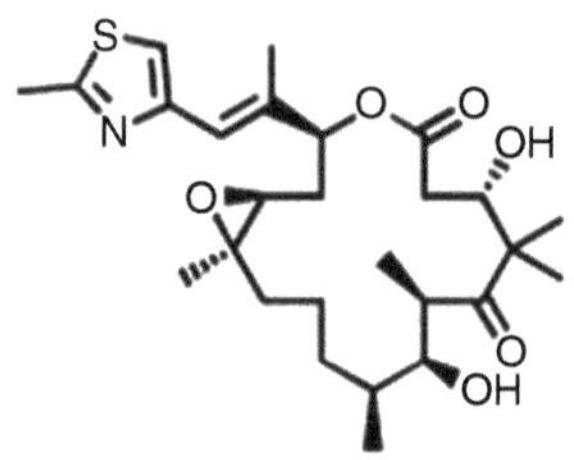

Epothilone B (**9**)

FIGURE 11.5 **The structures of epothilone B, ixabepilone, and epothilone D, as well as other selected congeners.**

found to be the most promising compound as significant increases in the AcTub marker of stable MTs in CNS samples could be observed after a single administration of 1 mg/kg of the test compound (Brunden et al., 2011). As 1 mg/kg is equivalent to 1/30th of the recommended chemotherapeutic dose of **3**, these results were particularly encouraging as they demonstrated that MT stabilization within the CNS could be obtained at relatively low and thus potentially more tolerable doses. In addition, the prolonged retention of epothilone D in the brain implied that relatively infrequent dosing schedules, such as once weekly, could be sufficient to obtain a sustained PD effect while minimizing peripheral exposure. Thus, based on the favorable PK/PD profiles, **3** was selected to evaluate whether a brain-penetrant MT-stabilizing agent could be therapeutically beneficial in a Tg mouse model of tauopathy.

The PS19 tau Tg mouse model was selected for these studies, as these mice overexpress the human 4R-tau isoform bearing the P301S mutation found in familial tauopathies

(Hutton et al., 1998; Hong et al., 1998) and begin to develop tau inclusions in the CNS between 3 and 6 months of age, with more extensive NFT-like lesions and cognitive impairments observed at >9 months of age (Yoshiyama et al., 2007). The therapeutic potential of epothilone D was thus investigated in the PS19 mice in both preventive (Brunden et al., 2010) and interventional (Zhang et al., 2012) study designs. For the former, **3** was administered to 3-month-old mice at 1 or 3 mg/kg once weekly via i.p. injections for a total of 3 months. These studies revealed that epothilone D-treated mice exhibited improved MT density and axonal integrity in CNS neurons, with a consequent reduction of the mild cognitive impairment that develops by 6 months of age in these mice (Brunden et al., 2010). Furthermore, in line with the fact that the doses used in this study were a fraction of the previously utilized chemotherapeutic doses, no notable side effects were elicited, such as the hallmark neutropenia and peripheral neuropathy that are typically observed when MT-stabilizing agents are used in oncology (Brunden et al., 2010). Interestingly, the lower dose of 1 mg/kg was found to be more effective than the 3 mg/kg dose. Thus, the doses of epothilone D were lowered to 0.1 and 1 mg/kg for an interventional study in which epothilone D was administered to 9-month-old PS19 mice for 3 months. The results of this investigation confirmed that 1 mg/kg of epothilone D was the optimal dose to restore axonal transport and reduce axonal dystrophy in PS19 mice with preexisting tau pathology (Zhang et al., 2012). Furthermore, particularly promising was the observation that the tau Tg mice that received epothilone D exhibited a significant decrease in both tau neuropathology and hippocampal neuron loss (Zhang et al., 2012). These compound-mediated effects ultimately led to a significant improvement of cognitive performance by the epothilone D-treated tau Tg mice compared to those receiving vehicle only. Again, no overt signs of toxicities, including peripheral neuropathy or neutropenia, were observed in these studies. Collectively, these preventive and interventional studies provide compelling evidence that compensation for the loss of an MT-stabilizing function of tau may be a viable therapeutic strategy for the treatment of AD and related tauopathies. Following these promising results and those from a set of related studies in which epothilone D was evaluated in different Tg mouse models of human tauopathies (Barten et al., 2012), Bristol-Myers Squibb (BMS) launched a phase 1b clinical trial with epothilone D in AD patients.

Other Brain-Penetrant MT-Stabilizing Agents

Although epothilone D proved to be instrumental to validate the therapeutic potential of MT-stabilizing agents for the treatment of tauopathies, this compound is only the first brain-penetrant example that has undergone in vivo efficacy studies in tau Tg animal models. Furthermore, this compound exhibits potential limitations as an AD drug candidate, including an intravenous (i.v.) route of administration, as well as the inhibition of Pgp, which upon prolonged dosing could result in CNS toxicities and/or drug–drug interactions (Fromm, 2000). As a result, the evaluation of additional CNS-active MT-stabilizing agents is clearly desirable to identify the most promising subset of candidates for future clinical development. MT-stabilizing compounds make up a large and growing group of molecules that, although functionally related, exhibit a rather remarkable degree of structural diversity and complexity (Table 11.1). Among the different classes of MT-stabilizing natural products and derivatives thereof, selected brain-penetrant examples have been identified.

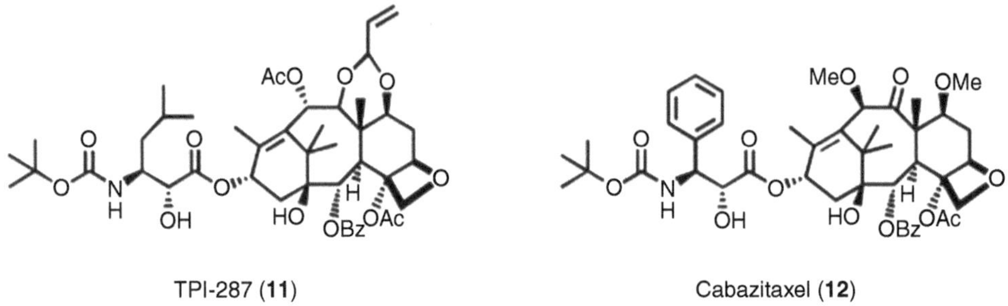

FIGURE 11.6 **The structures of TPI-287 and cabazitaxel.**

These include the highly potent marine natural product dictyostatin (**10**, Table 11.1) (Brunden et al., 2013), as well as selected nonnaturally occurring taxanes, such as TPI-287 (**11**, Fig. 11.6) (Fitzgerald et al., 2012) and cabazitaxel (**12**, Fig. 11.6) (Bouchet and Galmarini, 2010; Galsky et al., 2010). Of note, **11** is undergoing safety and tolerability studies at present in patients with mild to moderate AD (see ClinicalTrials.gov identifier NCT01966666) and in patients affected by other tauopathies, such as primary four-repeat tauopathies, corticobasal degeneration, or progressive supranuclear palsy (see ClinicalTrials.gov identifier NCT02133846).

Nonnaturally Occurring MT-Stabilizing Agents

While the vast majority of MT-stabilizing molecules are either natural products or derivatives thereof, in recent years progress has been made in the development of structurally simpler synthetic small molecules that exhibit relatively potent MT-stabilizing activity and at the same time are endowed with a potentially favorable set of druglike properties that may ultimately facilitate drug development efforts (Ballatore et al., 2012). Among nonnaturally occurring small molecules with reported MT-stabilizing activity, particularly promising are a series of triazolopyrimidines (eg, **14**, Fig. 11.7) and phenylpyrimidines (eg, **15**, Fig. 11.7) that had been originally identified as antifungal agents and then developed as potential

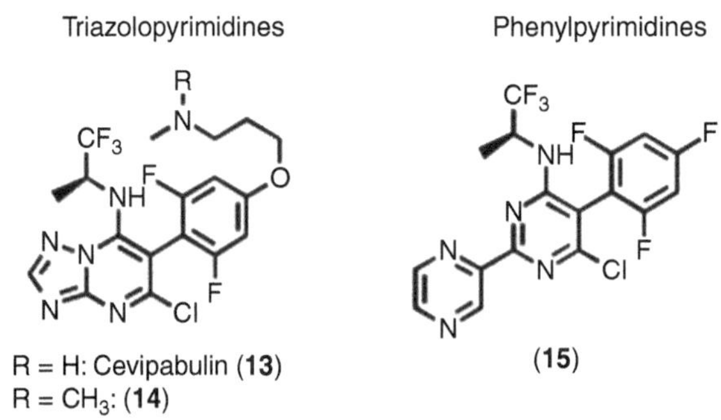

FIGURE 11.7 **The structures of representative brain-penetrant and orally bioavailable MT-stabilizing triazolopyrimidines and phenylpyrimidines.**

anticancer drugs (Zhang et al., 2007, 2009). Interestingly, although the mode of action of these classes of small molecule MT-stabilizing agents has not been fully elucidated, an evaluation of MT-stabilizing activity of representative compounds in a cell-based AcTub assay revealed that several of these small molecules exhibit activity that is comparable to that of epothilone D (**3**, Fig. 11.5) (Lou et al., 2014). Furthermore, selected examples of these heterocyclic compounds (eg, **14** and **15**) have been identified that are both brain-penetrant and orally bioavailable, while PD studies confirmed that these representative compounds can enhance MT stabilization in the CNS (Lou et al., 2014). As a result, given the generally favorable drug-like properties and the synthetic accessibility, these nonnaturally occurring heterocyclic compounds may have potential advantages over MT-stabilizing natural products. However, as noted earlier, the mode of action of these compounds has not been fully elucidated, although published reports highlighted a series of important differences in the mechanism of action of triazolopyrimidines when compared to those of other classes of MT-binding natural products (Beyer et al., 2008, 2009). For example, MT binding experiments with cevipabulin (**13**, Fig. 11.7), the most potent compound within the triazolopyrimidine series, revealed that this molecule does not compete with [^{3}H]paclitaxel, but rather it appears to interfere with the binding of the MT-depolymerizing agent [^{3}H]vincristine (Beyer et al., 2008). Although the results from these competition binding experiments could not determine whether cevipabulin competes with [^{3}H]vincristine by binding orthosterically within the vinca site or possibly allosterically at a distinct binding region, it was noted that, similar to vincristine and other vinca-domain ligands, **13** reduces the exchange rate of GTP at the exchangeable nucleotide site of the tubulin heterodimer (Beyer et al., 2009). This observation appears to be consistent with an orthosteric interaction of **13** within the vinca binding site (Beyer et al., 2009). If confirmed, these results would indicate that cevipabulin, and thus possibly other related congeners, can stabilize MTs via a rather unique mode of action. As a result, further studies, ongoing in our laboratories at present, are exploring whether this class of MT-targeting compounds could be employed to normalize hyperdynamic MTs and ultimately improve axonal transport in tauopathy neurons.

CONCLUDING REMARKS

Although tau-mediated neurodegeneration is likely to involve multiple mechanisms, there is compelling evidence to suggest that the disengagement of hyperphosphorylated tau from MTs and the subsequent sequestration of tau into insoluble aggregates can disrupt MT dynamics and thereby trigger or exacerbate axonal transport deficits. Thus, the development of CNS-directed, MT-stabilizing therapies holds considerable promise as potential treatments for AD and related neurodegenerative tauopathies. Epothilone D has been the first example of a brain-penetrant MT-stabilizing compound to undergo efficacy and safety studies in animal models of human tauopathies. The promising results obtained with this natural product led to epothilone D being evaluated as a clinical candidate. Other MT-stabilizing molecules, including the natural product dictyostatin, the paclitaxel analogs TPI-287, as well as the different nonnaturally occurring triazolopyrimidines and phenylpyrimidines that are currently under evaluation, may provide alternative drug candidates for the treatment of tau-mediated neurodegeneration.

Acknowledgments

These studies were supported by NIH grants AG17586, AG029213, and AG044332, as well as the Karen Cohen Segal and Christopher S. Segal Alzheimer Drug Discovery Initiative Fund, the Paula C. Schmerler Fund for Alzheimer's Research, the Barrist Neurodegenerative Disease Research Fund, the Eleanor Margaret Kurtz Endowed Fund, the Mary Rasmus Endowed Fund for Alzheimer's Research, Mrs Gloria J. Miller, and Arthur Peck, MD.

References

Altmann KH, Hofle G, Muller R, Mulzer J, Prantz K: *Epothilones: an outstanding family of anti-tumor agents: from soil to the clinic*, New York, 2009, Springer.

Altmann KH, Pfeiffer B, Arseniyadis S, Pratt BA, Nicolaou KC: The chemistry and biology of epothilones—the wheel keeps turning, *Chem Med Chem* 2(4):396–424, 2007.

Amos LA: Microtubule structure and its stabilisation, *Org Biomol Chem* 2(15):2153–2160, 2004.

Andrieux A, Salin P, Schweitzer A, Begou M, Pachoud B, Brun P, Gory-Faure S, Kujala P, Suaud-Chagny MF, Hofle G, Job D: Microtubule stabilizer ameliorates synaptic function and behavior in a mouse model for schizophrenia, *Biol Psychiat* 60(11):1224–1230, 2006.

Aubele DL, Wan S, Floreancig PE: Total synthesis of (+)-dactylolide through an efficient sequential Peterson olefination and Prins cyclization reaction, *Angew Chem Int Ed* 44(22):3485–3488, 2005.

Baas PW, Black MM: Individual microtubules in the axon consist of domains that differ in both composition and stability, *J Cell Biol* 111(2):495–509, 1990.

Bai R, Vanderwal CD, Diaz JF, Hamel E: Interaction of a cyclostreptin analogue with the microtubule taxoid site: the covalent reaction rapidly follows binding, *J Nat Prod* 71(3):370–374, 2008.

Ballatore C, Brunden KR, Huryn DM, Trojanowski JQ, Lee VMY, Smith AB: Microtubule stabilizing agents as potential treatment for Alzheimer's disease and related neurodegenerative tauopathies, *J Med Chem* 55(21):8979–8996, 2012.

Ballatore C, Hyde E, Deiches RF, Lee VMY, Trojanowski JQ, Huryn D, Smith AB III: Paclitaxel C-10 carbamates: potential candidates for the treatment of neurodegenerative tauopathies, *Bioorg Med Chem Lett* 17(13):3642–3646, 2007.

Ballatore C, Zhang B, Trojanowski JQ, Lee VM, Smith AB 3rd: In situ blood–brain barrier permeability of a C-10 paclitaxel carbamate, *Bioorg Med Chem Lett* 18(23):6119–6121, 2008.

Balog A, Meng D, Kamenecka T, Bertinato P, Su D-S, Sorensen EJ, Danishefsky SJ: Total synthesis of (−)-epothilone A, *Angew Chem Int Ed Engl* 35(23–24):2801–2803, 1996.

Barten DM, Fanara P, Andorfer C, Hoque N, Wong PYA, Husted KH, Cadelina GW, DeCarr LB, Yang L, Liu L, Fessler C, Protassio J, Riff T, Turner H, Janus CG, Sankaranarayanan S, Polson C, Meredith JE, Gray G, Hanna A, Olson RE, Kim SH, Vite GD, Lee FY, Albright CF: Hyperdynamic microtubules, cognitive deficits, and pathology are improved in tau transgenic mice with low doses of the microtubule-stabilizing agent BMS-241027, *J Neurosci* 32(21):7137–7145, 2012.

Bedard PL, Di Leo A, Piccart-Gebhart MJ: Taxanes: optimizing adjuvant chemotherapy for early-stage breast cancer, *Nat Rev Clin Oncol* 7(1):22–36, 2010.

Bennett MJ, Barakat K, Huzil JT, Tuszynski J, Schriemer DC: Discovery and characterization of the laulimalide-microtubule binding mode by mass shift perturbation mapping, *Chem Biol* 17(7):725–734, 2010.

Beyer CF, Zhang N, Hernandez R, Vitale D, Lucas J, Nguyen T, Discafani C, Ayral-Kaloustian S, Gibbons JJ: TTI-237: a novel microtubule-active compound with in vivo antitumor activity, *Cancer Res* 68(7):2292–2300, 2008.

Beyer CF, Zhang N, Hernandez R, Vitale D, Nguyen T, Ayral-Kaloustian S, Gibbons JJ: The microtubule-active antitumor compound TTI-237 has both paclitaxel-like and vincristine-like properties, *Cancer Chemother Pharmacol* 64(4):681–689, 2009.

Bollag DM, McQueney PA, Zhu J, Hensens O, Koupal L, Liesch J, Goetz M, Lazarides E, Woods CM: Epothilones, a new class of microtubule-stabilizing agents with a Taxol-like mechanism of action, *Cancer Res* 55(11):2325–2333, 1995.

Bouchet BP, Galmarini CM: Cabazitaxel, a new taxane with favorable properties, *Drugs Today (Barc)* 46(10):735–742, 2010.

Brunden KR, Gardner NM, James MJ, Yao Y, Trojanowski JQ, Lee VMY, Paterson I, Ballatore C, Smith AB: MT-stabilizer, dictyostatin, exhibits prolonged brain retention and activity: potential therapeutic implications, *ACS Med Chem Lett* 4(9):886–889, 2013.

Brunden KR, Yao Y, Potuzak JS, Ferrer NI, Ballatore C, James MJ, Hogan AM, Trojanowski JQ, Smith AB, Lee VM: The characterization of microtubule-stabilizing drugs as possible therapeutic agents for Alzheimer's disease and related tauopathies, *Pharmacol Res* 63(4):341–351, 2011.

Brunden KR, Zhang B, Carroll J, Yao Y, Potuzak JS, Hogan AM, Iba M, James MJ, Xie SX, Ballatore C, Smith AB, Lee VM, Trojanowski JQ: Epothilone D improves microtubule density, axonal integrity, and cognition in a transgenic mouse model of tauopathy, *J Neurosci* 30(41):13861–13866, 2010.

Buee L, Bussiere T, Buee-Scherrer V, Delacourte A, Hof PR: Tau protein isoforms, phosphorylation and role in neurodegenerative disorders, *Brain Res Rev* 33(1):95–130, 2000.

Buey RM, Calvo E, Barasoain I, Pineda O, Edler MC, Matesanz R, Cerezo G, Vanderwal CD, Day BW, Sorensen EJ, Lopez JA, Andreu JM, Hamel E, Diaz JF: Cyclostreptin binds covalently to microtubule pores and lumenal taxoid binding sites, *Nat Chem Biol* 3(2):117–125, 2007.

Cash AD, Aliev G, Siedlak SL, Nunomura A, Fujioka H, Zhu X, Raina AK, Vinters HV, Tabaton M, Johnson AB, Paula-Barbosa M, Avíla J, Jones PK, Castellani RJ, Smith MA, Perry G: Microtubule reduction in Alzheimer's disease and aging is independent of tau filament formation, *Am J Pathol* 162(5):1623–1627, 2003.

Chen X-T, Bhattacharya SK, Zhou B, Gutteridge CE, Pettus TRR, Danishefsky SJ: The total synthesis of eleutherobin, *J Am Chem Soc* 121(28):6563–6579, 1999.

Chen X-T, Gutteridge CE, Bhattacharya SK, Zhou B, Pettus TRR, Hascall T, Danishefsky SJ: A convergent route for the total synthesis of the eleuthesides, *Angew Chem Int Ed* 37(1–2):185–186, 1998a.

Chen X-T, Zhou B, Bhattacharya SK, Gutteridge CE, Pettus TRR, Danishefsky SJ: The total synthesis of eleutherobin: a surprise ending, *Angew Chem Int Ed* 37(6):789–792, 1998b.

Chen Z, Wang B, Chen M: Steroidal bitter principles from Tacca plantaginea structures of taccalonolide A and B, *Tetrahedron Lett* 28(15):1673–1675, 1987.

Ciomei M, Albanese C, Pastori W, Grandi M, Pietra F, D'Ambrosio M, Guerriero A, Battistini C: Sarcodictyins: a new class of marine derivatives with mode of action similar to Taxol; abstract 30, *Proc Am Ass Canc Res* 38:5, 1997.

Coleman RS, Campbell EL, Carper DJ: A direct and efficient total synthesis of the tubulin-binding agents ceratamine A and B: use of IBX for a remarkable heterocycle dehydrogenation, *Org Lett* 11(10):2133–2136, 2009.

Congdon EE, Kim S, Bonchak J, Songrug T, Matzavinos A, Kuret J: Nucleation-dependent tau filament formation: the importance of dimerization and an estimation of elementary rate constants, *J Biol Chem* 283(20):13806–13816, 2008.

Conlin A, Fornier M, Hudis C, Kar S, Kirkpatrick P: Ixabepilone, *Nat Rev Drug Discov* 6(12):953–954, 2007.

Corley DG, Herb R, Moore RE, Scheuer PJ, Paul VJ: Laulimalide: new potent cytotoxic macrolides from a marine sponge and a nudibranch predator, *J Org Chem* 53:3644–3646, 1988.

Cutignano A, Bruno I, Bifulco G, Casapullo A, Debitus C, Gomez-Paloma L, Riccio R: Dactylolide, a new cytotoxic macrolide from the Vanuatu sponge Dactylospongia sp, *Eur J Org Chem* 2001(4):775–778, 2001.

Dalby SM, Paterson I: Synthesis of polyketide natural products and analogs as promising anticancer agents, *Curr Opin Drug Discov Devel* 13(6):777–794, 2010.

D'Ambrosio M, Guerriero A, Pietra F: Sarcodictyin A and sarcodictyin B, novel diterpenoidic alcohols esterified by (E)-N(1)-methylurocanic acid: isolation from the Mediterranean stolonifer *Sarcodictyon roseum*, *Helv Chim Acta* 70(8):2019–2027, 1987.

D'Ambrosio M, Guerriero A, Pietra F: Isolation from the Mediterranean stolonifern coral *Sarcodictyon roseum* of sarcodictyin C, D, E, and F, novel diterpenodic alcohols esterified by (E)- or (Z)-N(1)-methylurocanic acid: failure of the carbon-skeleton type as a classification criterion, *Helv Chim Acta* 71(5):964–976, 1988.

Derry WB, Wilson L, Jordan MA: Substoichiometric binding of Taxol suppresses microtubule dynamics, *Biochemistry* 34(7):2203–2211, 1995.

Desai A, Mitchison TJ: Microtubule polymerization dynamics, *Annu Rev Cell Dev Biol* 13:83–117, 1997.

Dixit R, Ross JL, Goldman YE, Holzbaur EL: Differential regulation of dynein and kinesin motor proteins by tau, *Science* 319(5866):1086–1089, 2008.

Doshi LS, Brahma MK, Sayyed SG, Dixit AV, Chandak PG, Pamidiboina V, Motiwala HF, Sharma SD, Nemmani KV: Acute administration of GPR40 receptor agonist potentiates glucose-stimulated insulin secretion in vivo in the rat, *Metabolism* 58(3):333–343, 2009.

Drechsel DN, Hyman AA, Cobb MH, Kirschner MW: Modulation of the dynamic instability of tubulin assembly by the microtubule-associated protein tau, *Mol Biol Cell* 3(10):1141–1154, 1992.

Edler MC, Buey RM, Gussio R, Marcus AI, Vanderwal CD, Sorensen EJ, Diaz JF, Giannakakou P, Hamel E: Cyclostreptin (FR182877), an antitumor tubulin-polymerizing agent deficient in enhancing tubulin assembly despite its high affinity for the taxoid site, *Biochemistry* 44(34):11525–11538, 2005.

Evans DA, Starr JT: A cascade cycloaddition strategy leading to the total synthesis of (−)-FR182877, *Angew Chem Int Ed* 41(10):1787–1790, 2002.

Evans DA, Welch DS, Speed AW, Moniz GA, Reichelt A, Ho S: An aldol-based synthesis of (+)-peloruside a, a potent microtubule stabilizing agent, *J Am Chem Soc* 131(11):3840–3841, 2009.

Fellner S, Bauer B, Miller DS, Schaffrik M, Fankhanel M, Spruss T, Bernhardt G, Graeff C, Farber L, Gschaidmeier H, Buschauer A, Fricker G: Transport of paclitaxel (Taxol) across the blood–brain barrier in vitro and in vivo, *J Clin Invest* 110(9):1309–1318, 2002.

Field JJ, Pera B, Calvo E, Canales A, Zurwerra D, Trigili C, Rodríguez-Salarichs J, Matesanz R, Kanakkanthara A, Wakefield SJ, Singh AJ, Jiménez-Barbero J, Northcote P, Miller JH, López JA, Hamel E, Barasoain I, Altmann K-H, Díaz JF: Zampanolide, a potent new microtubule-stabilizing agent, covalently reacts with the taxane luminal site in tubulin α,β-heterodimers and microtubules, *Chem Biol* 19(6):686–698, 2012.

Fitzgerald DP, Emerson DL, Qian YZ, Anwar T, Liewehr DJ, Steinberg SM, Silberman S, Palmieri D, Steeg PS: TPI-287, a new taxane family member, reduces the brain metastatic colonization of breast cancer cells, *Mol Cancer Ther* 11(9):1959–1967, 2012.

Fromm MF: P-glycoprotein: a defense mechanism limiting oral bioavailability and CNS accumulation of drugs, *Int J Clin Pharmacol Ther* 38(2):69–74, 2000.

Gaitanos TN, Buey RM, Diaz JF, Northcote PT, Teesdale-Spittle P, Andreu JM, Miller JH: Peloruside A does not bind to the taxoid site on beta-tubulin and retains its activity in multidrug-resistant cell lines, *Cancer Res* 64(15):5063–5067, 2004.

Gallo JM, Li S, Guo P, Reed K, Ma J: The effect of P-glycoprotein on paclitaxel brain and brain tumor distribution in mice, *Cancer Res* 63(16):5114–5117, 2003.

Galsky MD, Dritselis A, Kirkpatrick P, Oh WK: Cabazitaxel, *Nat Rev Drug Discov* 9(9):677–678, 2010.

Ghosh AK, Cheng X, Bai R, Hamel E: Total synthesis of potent antitumor macrolide (−)-zampanolide: an oxidative intramolecular cyclization-based strategy, *Eur J Org Chem*:4130–4139, 2012.

Ghosh AK, Xu X, Kim J-H, Xu C-X: Enantioselective total synthesis of peloruside A: a potent microtubule stabilizer, *Org Lett* 10(5):1001–1004, 2008.

Goedert M, Spillantini MG, Jakes R, Rutherford D, Crowther RA: Multiple isoforms of human microtubule-associated protein tau: sequences and localization in neurofibrillary tangles of Alzheimer's disease, *Neuron* 3(4):519–526, 1989.

Gottesman MM, Pastan I: Biochemistry of multidrug-resistance mediated by the multidrug transporter, *Ann Rev Biochem* 62:385–427, 1993.

Gunasekera SP, Gunasekera M, Longley RE, Schulte GK: Discodermolide: a new bioactive polyhydroxylated lactone from the marine sponge Discodermia dissoluta, *J Org Chem* 55(16):4912–4915, 1990.

Hamel E, Day BW, Miller JH, Jung MK, Northcote PT, Ghosh AK, Curran DP, Cushman M, Nicolaou KC, Paterson I: Synergistic effects of peloruside A and laulimalide with taxoid site drugs, but not with each other, on tubulin assembly, *Mol Pharmacol* 70(5):1555, 2006.

Hamel E, Sackett DL, Vourloumis D, Nicolaou KC: The coral-derived natural products eleutherobin and sarcodictyins A and B: effects on the assembly of purified tubulin with and without microtubule-associated proteins and binding at the polymer taxoid site, *Biochemistry* 38(17):5490–5498, 1999.

Hempen B, Brion JP: Reduction of acetylated alpha-tubulin immunoreactivity in neurofibrillary tangle-bearing neurons in Alzheimer's disease, *J Neuropathol Exp Neurol* 55(9):964–972, 1996.

Himmler A, Drechsel D, Kirschner MW, Martin DW Jr: Tau consists of a set of proteins with repeated C-terminal microtubule-binding domains and variable N-terminal domains, *Mol Cell Biol* 9(4):1381–1388, 1989.

Ho S, Bucher C, Leighton JL: A highly step-economical synthesis of dictyostatin, *Angew Chem Int Ed* 52:6757–6761, 2013.

Hofle G, Reichenbach H: *Anticancer agents from natural products*, Boca Raton, FL, 2005, CRC Press, 413–450.

Holton RA. Method for preparation of Taxol using beta lactam. US005175315A, 1992.

Hong M, Zhukareva V, Vogelsberg-Ragaglia V, Wszolek Z, Reed L, Miller BI, Geschwind DH, Bird TD, McKeel D, Goate A, Morris JC, Wilhelmsen KC, Schellenberg GD, Trojanowski JQ, Lee VM: Mutation-specific functional impairments in distinct tau isoforms of hereditary FTDP-17, *Science* 282(5395):1914–1917, 1998.

Hood KA, Bäckström BT, West LM, Northcote PT, Berridge MV, Miller JH: The novel cytotoxic sponge metabolite peloruside A, structurally similar to bryostatin-1, has unique bioactivity independent of protein kinase C, *Anticancer Drug Des* 16(2–3):155–166, 2001.

Hoye TR, Hu M: Macrolactonization via Ti(IV)-mediated epoxy-acid coupling: a total synthesis of (–)-dactylolide [and zampanolide], *J Am Chem Soc* 125(32):9576–9577, 2003.

Hoye TR, Jeon J, Kopel LC, Ryba TD, Tennakoon MA, Wang Y: Total synthesis of peloruside A through kinetic lactonization and relay ring-closing metathesis cyclization reactions, *Angew Chem Int Ed* 49(35):6151–6155, 2010.

Hung DT, Chen J, Schreiber SL: (+)-Discodermolide binds to microtubules in stoichiometric ratio to tubulin dimers, blocks Taxol binding and results in mitotic arrest, *Chem Biol* 3(4):287–293, 1996a.

Hung DT, Nerenberg JB, Schreiber SL: Syntheses of discodermolides useful for investigating microtubule binding and stabilization, *J Am Chem Soc* 118(45):11054–11080, 1996b.

Hutton M, Lendon CL, Rizzu P, Baker M, Froelich S, Houlden H, Pickering-Brown S, Chakraverty S, Isaacs A, Grover A, Hackett J, Adamson J, Lincoln S, Dickson D, Davies P, Petersen RC, Stevens M, de Graaff E, Wauters E, van Baren J, Hillebrand M, Joosse M, Kwon JM, Nowotny P, Che LK, Norton J, Morris JC, Reed LA, Trojanowski J, Basun H, Lannfelt L, Neystat M, Fahn S, Dark F, Tannenberg T, Dodd PR, Hayward N, Kwok JB, Schofield PR, Andreadis A, Snowden J, Craufurd D, Neary D, Owen F, Oostra BA, Hardy J, Goate A, van Swieten J, Mann D, Lynch T, Heutink P: Association of missense and 5′-splice-site mutations in tau with the inherited dementia FTDP-17, *Nature* 393(6686):702–705, 1998.

Huzil JT, Chik JK, Slysz GW, Freedman H, Tuszynski J, Taylor RE, Sackett DL, Schriemer DC: A unique mode of microtubule stabilization induced by peloruside A, *J Mol Biol* 378(5):1016–1030, 2008.

Isbrucker RA, Cummins J, Pomponi SA, Longley RE, Wright AE: Tubulin polymerizing activity of dictyostatin-1, a polyketide of marine sponge origin, *Biochem Pharmacol* 66(1):75–82, 2003.

Ishihara T, Zhang B, Higuchi M, Yoshiyama Y, Trojanowski JQ, Lee VMY: Age-dependent induction of congophilic neurofibrillary tau inclusions in tau transgenic mice, *Am J Pathol* 158(2):555–562, 2001.

Jefford CW, Bernardinelli G, Tanaka J-I, Higa T: Structures and absolute configurations of the marine toxins, latrunculin A and laulimalide, *Tetrahedron Lett* 37:159–162, 1996.

Jin M, Taylor RE: Total synthesis of (+)-peloruside A, *Org Lett* 7(7):1303–1305, 2005.

Jordan MA, Wilson L: Microtubules as a target for anticancer drugs, *Nat Rev Cancer* 4(4):253–265, 2004.

Kar S, Florence GJ, Paterson I, Amos LA: Discodermolide interferes with the binding of tau protein to microtubules, *FEBS Lett* 539(1–3):34–36, 2003.

Karjala G, Chan Q, Manzo E, Andersen RJ, Roberge M: Ceratamines, structurally simple microtubule-stabilizing antimitotic agents with unusual cellular effects, *Cancer Res* 65(8):3040–3043, 2005.

Kemper EM, van Zandbergen AE, Cleypool C, Mos HA, Boogerd W, Beijnen JH, van Tellingen O: Increased penetration of paclitaxel into the brain by inhibition of P-glycoprotein, *Clin Cancer Res* 9(7):2849–2855, 2003.

Kingston DG, Jagtap PG, Yuan H, Samala L: The chemistry of Taxol and related taxoids, *Fortschr Chem Org Naturst* 84:53–225, 2002.

Kowalski RJ, Giannakakou P, Gunasekera SP, Longley RE, Day BW, Hamel E: The microtubule-stabilizing agent discodermolide competitively inhibits the binding of paclitaxel (Taxol) to tubulin polymers, enhances tubulin nucleation reactions more potently than paclitaxel, and inhibits the growth of paclitaxel-resistant cells, *Mol Pharmacol* 52(4):613–622, 1997.

LaPointe NE, Morfini G, Brady ST, Feinstein SC, Wilson L, Jordan MA: Effects of eribulin, vincristine, paclitaxel and ixabepilone on fast axonal transport and kinesin-1 driven microtubule gliding: implications for chemotherapy-induced peripheral neuropathy, *Neurotoxicology* 37:231–239, 2013.

Lee JJ, Swain SM: Peripheral neuropathy induced by microtubule-stabilizing agents, *J Clin Oncol* 24(10):1633–1642, 2006.

Lee VM, Balin BJ, Otvos L Jr, Trojanowski JQ: A68: a major subunit of paired helical filaments and derivatized forms of normal tau, *Science* 251(4994):675–678, 1991.

Lee VMY, Daughenbaugh R, Trojanowski JQ: Microtubule stabilizing drugs for the treatment of Alzheimer's disease, *Neurobiol Aging* 15(Suppl 2):S87–S89, 1994.

Liao X, Wu Y, De Brabander JK: Total synthesis and absolute configuration of the novel microtubule-stabilizing agent peloruside A, *Angew Chem Int Ed Engl* 42(14):1648–1652, 2003.

Lindel T, Jensen PR, Fenical W, Long BH, Casazza AM, Carboni J, Fairchild CR: Eleutherobin, a new cytotoxin that mimics paclitaxel (Taxol) by stabilizing microtubules, *J Am Chem Soc* 119(37):8744–8745, 1997.

Long BH, Carboni JM, Wasserman AJ, Cornell LA, Casazza AM, Jensen PR, Lindel T, Fenical W, Fairchild CR: Eleutherobin, a novel cytotoxic agent that induces tubulin polymerization, is similar to paclitaxel (Taxol®), *Cancer Res* 58(6):1111, 1998.

Lou K, Yao Y, Hoye AT, James MJ, Cornec AS, Hyde E, Gay B, Lee VM, Trojanowski JQ, Smith AB 3rd, Brunden KR, Ballatore C: Brain-penetrant, orally bioavailable microtubule-stabilizing small molecules are potential candidate therapeutics for Alzheimer's disease and related tauopathies, *J Med Chem* 57(14):6116–6127, 2014.

Madiraju C, Edler MC, Hamel E, Raccor BS, Balachandran R, Zhu G, Giuliano KA, Vogt A, Shin Y, Fournier JH, Fukui Y, Bruckner AM, Curran DP, Day BW: Tubulin assembly, taxoid site binding, and cellular effects of the microtubule-stabilizing agent dictyostatin, *Biochemistry* 44(45):15053–15063, 2005.

Magnani E, Fan J, Gasparini L, Golding M, Williams M, Schiavo G, Goedert M, Amos LA, Spillantini MG: Interaction of tau protein with the dynactin complex, *EMBO J* 26(21):4546–4554, 2007.

Makrides V, Massie MR, Feinstein SC, Lew J: Evidence for two distinct binding sites for tau on microtubules, *Proc Natl Acad Sci USA* 101(17):6746–6751, 2004.

Manzo E, van Soest R, Matainaho L, Roberge M, Andersen RJ: Ceratamines A and B, antimitotic heterocyclic alkaloids isolated from the marine sponge Pseudoceratina sp. collected in Papua New Guinea, *Org Lett* 5(24):4591–4594, 2003.

Mazanetz MP, Fischer PM: Untangling tau hyperphosphorylation in drug design for neurodegenerative diseases, *Nat Rev Drug Discov* 6(6):464–479, 2007.

McGowan MA, Stevenson CP, Schiffler MA, Jacobsen EN: An enantioselective total synthesis of (+)-peloruside A, *Angew Chem* 122(35):6283–6286, 2010.

Mooberry SL, Tien G, Hernandez AH, Plubrukarn A, Davidson BS: Laulimalide and isolaulimalide, new paclitaxel-like microtubule-stabilizing agents, *Cancer Res* 59(3):653, 1999.

Mulzer J, Ohler E: Microtubule-stabilizing marine metabolite laulimalide and its derivatives: synthetic approaches and antitumor activity, *Chem Rev* 103(9):3753–3786, 2003.

Nicolaou KC, Ohshima T, Hosokawa S, van Delft FL, Vourloumis D, Xu JY, Pfefferkorn J, Kim S: Total synthesis of eleutherobin and eleuthosides A and B, *J Am Chem Soc* 120(34):8674–8680, 1998a.

Nicolaou KC, van Delft F, Ohshima T, Vourloumis D, Xu J, Hosokawa S, Pfefferkorn J, Kim S, Li T: Total synthesis of eleutherobin, *Angew Chem Int Ed Engl* 36(22):2520–2524, 1997a.

Nicolaou KC, Xu JY, Kim S, Ohshima T, Hosokawa S, Pfefferkorn J: Synthesis of the tricyclic core of eleutherobin and sarcodictyins and total synthesis of sarcodictyin A, *J Am Chem Soc* 119(46):11353–11354, 1997b.

Nicolaou KC, Xu JY, Kim S, Pfefferkorn J, Ohshima T, Vourloumis D, Hosokawa S: Total synthesis of sarcodictyins A and B, *J Am Chem Soc* 120(34):8661–8673, 1998b.

Nodwell M, Pereira A, Riffell JL, Zimmerman C, Patrick BO, Roberge M, Andersen RJ: Synthetic approaches to the microtubule-stabilizing sponge alkaloid ceratamine A and desbromo analogues, *J Org Chem* 74(3):995–1006, 2009.

Nogales E, Wolf SG, Khan IA, Luduena RF, Downing KH: Structure of tubulin at 6.5 A and location of the Taxol-binding site, *Nature* 375(6530):424–427, 1995.

Ojima I: Recent advances in the beta-lactam synthon method, *Acc Chem Res* 28(9):383–389, 1995.

Ojima I, Habus I, Zhao M, Zucco M, Park YH, Sun CM, Brigaud T: New and efficient approaches to the semisynthesis of Taxol and its C-13 side chain analogs by means of β-lactam synthon method, *Tetrahedron* 48(34):6985–7012, 1992.

O'Nei GW, Phillips AJ: Total synthesis of (−)-dictyostatin, *J Am Chem Soc* 128(16):5340–5341, 2006.

O'Reilly T, Wartmann M, Brueggen J, Allegrini PR, Floersheimer A, Maira M, McSheehy PM: Pharmacokinetic profile of the microtubule stabilizer patupilone in tumor-bearing rodents and comparison of anti-cancer activity with other MTS in vitro and in vivo, *Cancer Chemother Pharmacol* 62(6):1045–1054, 2008.

Pardridge WM: The blood–brain barrier: bottleneck in brain drug development, *NeuroRx* 2(1):3–14, 2005.

Paterson I, Britton R, Delgado O, Gardner NM, Meyer A, Naylor GJ, Poullennec KG: Total synthesis of (−)-dictyostatin, a microtubule-stabilising anticancer macrolide of marine sponge origin, *Tetrahedron* 66(33):6534–6545, 2010.

Paterson I, Britton R, Delgado O, Meyer A, Poullennec KG: Total synthesis and configurational assignment of (−)-dictyostatin, a microtubule-stabilizing macrolide of marine sponge origin, *Angew Chem Int Ed* 43(35):4629–4633, 2004.

Paterson I, Florence GJ, Gerlach K, Scott JP: Total synthesis of the antimicrotubule agent (+)-discodermolide using boron-mediated aldol reactions of chiral ketones, *Angew Chem Int Ed Engl* 39(2):377–380, 2000.

Pettit GR, Cichacz ZA, Gao F, Boyd MR, Schmidt JM: Isolation and structure of the cancer cell growth inhibitor dictyostatin 1, *J Chem Soc Chem Commun*:1111–1112, 1994.

Prota AE, Bargsten K, Zurwerra D, Field JJ, Díaz JF, Altmann KH, Steinmetz MO: Molecular mechanism of action of microtubule-stabilizing anticancer agents, *Science* 339(6119):587–590, 2013.

Pryor DE, O'Brate A, Bilcer G, Diaz JF, Wang Y, Kabaki M, Jung MK, Andreu JM, Ghosh AK: The microtubule stabilizing agent laulimalide does not bind in the taxoid site, kills cells resistant to paclitaxel and epothilones, and may not require its epoxide moiety for activity, *Biochemistry* 41(29):9109–9115, 2002.

Quinoa E, Kakou Y, Crews P: Fijianolides, polyketide heterocyclics from a marine sponge, *J Org Chem* 53:3642–3644, 1988.

Ramachandran PV, Srivastava A, Hazra D: Total synthesis of potential antitumor agent, (−)-dictyostatin, *Org Lett* 9(1):157–160, 2006.

Risinger AL, Li J, Bennett MJ, Rohena CC, Peng J, Schriemer DC, Mooberry SL: Taccalonolide binding to tubulin imparts microtubule stability and potent in vivo activity, *Cancer Res* 73(22):6780–6792, 2013.

Risinger AL, Mooberry SL: Taccalonolides: novel microtubule stabilizers with clinical potential, *Cancer Lett* 291(1):14–19, 2010.

Risinger AL, Mooberry SL: Cellular studies reveal mechanistic differences between taccalonolide A and paclitaxel, *Cell Cycle* 10(13):2162–2171, 2011.

Rivkin A, Yoshimura F, Gabarda AE, Cho YS, Chou TC, Dong H, Danishefsky SJ: Discovery of (E)-9,10-dehydroepothilones through chemical synthesis: on the emergence of 26-trifluoro-(E)-9,10-dehydro-12,13-desoxyepothilone B as a promising anticancer drug candidate, *J Am Chem Soc* 126(35):10913–10922, 2004.

Rivkin A, Yoshimura F, Gabarda AE, Chou TC, Dong H, Tong WP, Danishefsky SJ: Complex target-oriented total synthesis in the drug discovery process: the discovery of a highly promising family of second generation epothilones, *J Am Chem Soc* 125(10):2899–2901, 2003.

Sato B, Muramatsu H, Miyauchi M, Hori Y, Takase S, Hino M, Hashimoto S, Terano H: A new antimitotic substance, FR182877. I. Taxonomy, fermentation, isolation, physico-chemical properties and biological activities, *J Antibiot (Tokyo)* 53(2):123–130, 2000a.

Sato B, Nakajima H, Hori Y, Hino M, Hashimoto S, Terano H: A new antimitotic substance, FR182877. II. The mechanism of action, *J Antibiot (Tokyo)* 53(2):204–206, 2000b.

Scheuer PJ, Swanholm CE, Madamba LA, Hudgins WR: The constituents of tacca leontopetaloides, *Lloydia* 26:133–140, 1963.

Schiff PB, Fant J, Horwitz SB: Promotion of microtubule assembly in vitro by Taxol, *Nature* 277(5698):665–667, 1979.

Schinzer D, Limberg A, Bauer A, Böhm OM, Cordes M: Total synthesis of (−)-epothilone A, *Angew Chem Int Ed Engl* 36(5):523–524, 1997.

Schweers O, Schönbrunn-Hanebeck E, Marx A, Mandelkow E: Structural studies of tau protein and Alzheimer paired helical filaments show no evidence for beta-structure, *J Biol Chem* 269(39):24290–24297, 1994.

Shin Y, Fournier JH, Fukui Y, Bruckner AM, Curran DP: Total synthesis of (–)-dictyostatin: confirmation of relative and absolute configurations, *Angew Chem Int Ed* 43(35):4634–4637, 2004.

Smith AB III, Freeze BS: (+)-Discodermolide: total synthesis, construction of novel analogues, and biological evaluation, *Tetrahedron* 64(2):261–298, 2008.

Smith AB, Safonov IG: Total synthesis of (+)-dactylolide, *Org Lett* 4(4):635–637, 2002.

Smith AB 3rd, Beauchamp TJ, LaMarche MJ, Kaufman MD, Qiu Y, Arimoto H, Jones DR, Kobayashi K: Evolution of a gram-scale synthesis of (+)-discodermolide, *J Am Chem Soc* 122(36):8654–8664, 2000.

Smith AB, Cox JM, Furuichi N, Kenesky CS, Zheng J, Atasoylu O, Wuest WM: Total synthesis of (−)-2-epi-peloruside A, *Org Lett* 10(24):5501–5504, 2008.

Smith AB, Safonov IG, Corbett RM: Total synthesis of (+)-zampanolide, *J Am Chem Soc* 123(49):12426–12427, 2001.

Smith AB 3rd, Safonov IG, Corbett RM: Total syntheses of (+)-zampanolide and (+)-dactylolide exploiting a unified strategy, *J Am Chem Soc* 124(37):11102–11113, 2002.

Stamer K, Vogel R, Thies E, Mandelkow E, Mandelkow EM: Tau blocks traffic of organelles, neurofilaments, and APP vesicles in neurons and enhances oxidative stress, *J Cell Biol* 156(6):1051–1063, 2002.

Tanaka J-I, Higa T: Zampanolide, a new cytotoxic marcrolide from a marine sponge, *Tetrahedron Lett* 37(31):5535–5538, 1996.

ter Haar E, Kowalski RJ, Hamel E, Lin CM, Longley RE, Gunasekera SP, Rosenkranz HS, Day BW: Discodermolide, a cytotoxic marine agent that stabilizes microtubules more potently than Taxol, *Biochemistry* 35(1):243–250, 1996.

Tinley TL, Randall-Hlubek DA, Leal RM, Jackson EM, Cessac JW, Quada JC Jr, Hemscheidt TK, Mooberry SL: Taccalonolides E and A: plant-derived steroids with microtubule-stabilizing activity, *Cancer Res* 63(12):3211–3220, 2003.

Tompa P: Intrinsically unstructured proteins, *Trends Biochem Sci* 27(10):527–533, 2002.

Uenishi J, Iwamoto T, Tanaka J: Total synthesis of (–)-zampanolide and questionable existence of (–)-dactylolide as the elusive biosynthetic precursor of (–)-zampanolide in an Okinawan sponge, *Org Lett* 11(15):3262–3265, 2009.

Vanderwal CD, Vosburg DA, Weiler S, Sorensen EJ: An enantioselective synthesis of FR182877 provides a chemical rationalization of its structure and affords multigram quantities of its direct precursor, *J Am Chem Soc* 125(18):5393–5407, 2003.

Vosburg DA, Vanderwal CD, Sorensen EJ: A synthesis of (+)-FR182877, featuring tandem transannular Diels–Alder reactions inspired by a postulated biogenesis, *J Am Chem Soc* 124(17):4552–4553, 2002.

Wani MC, Taylor HL, Wall ME, Coggon P, McPhail AT: Plant antitumor agents. VI. The isolation and structure of Taxol, a novel antileukemic and antitumor agent from Taxus brevifolia, *J Am Chem Soc* 93(9):2325–2327, 1971.

West LM, Northcote PT, Battershill CN: Peloruside A: a potent cytotoxic macrolide isolated from the New Zealand marine sponge Mycale sp, *J Org Chem* 65(2):445–449, 2000.

Xia S, Kenesky CS, Rucker PV, Smith AB, Orr GA, Horwitz SB: A photoaffinity analogue of discodermolide specifically labels a peptide in beta-tubulin, *Biochemistry* 45(39):11762–11775, 2006.

Yang Z, He Y, Vourloumis D, Vallberg H, Nicolaou KC: Total synthesis of epothilone A: the olefin metathesis approach, *Angew Chem Int Ed Engl* 36(1/2):166–168, 1997.

Yoshiyama Y, Higuchi M, Zhang B, Huang S, Iwata N, Saido T, Maeda J, Suhara T, Trojanowski J, Lee V: Synapse loss and microglial activation precede tangles in a P301S tauopathy mouse model, *Neuron* 53:337–351, 2007.

Zhang B, Carroll J, Trojanowski JQ, Yao Y, Iba M, Potuzak JS, Hogan AM, Xie SX, Ballatore C, Smith AB 3rd, Lee VM, Brunden KR: The microtubule-stabilizing agent, epothilone D, reduces axonal dysfunction, neurotoxicity, cognitive deficits, and Alzheimer-like pathology in an interventional study with aged tau transgenic mice, *J Neurosci* 32(11):3601–3611, 2012.

Zhang B, Maiti A, Shively S, Lakhani F, McDonald-Jones G, Bruce J, Lee EB, Xie SX, Joyce S, Li C, Toleikis PM, Lee VMY, Trojanowski JQ: Microtubule-binding drugs offset tau sequestration by stabilizing microtubules and reversing fast axonal transport deficits in a tauopathy model, *Proc Natl Acad Sci USA* 102(1):227–231, 2005.

Zhang N, Ayral-Kaloustian S, Nguyen T, Afragola J, Hernandez R, Lucas J, Gibbons J, Beyer C: Synthesis and SAR of [1,2,4]triazolo[1,5-a]pyrimidines, a class of anticancer agents with a unique mechanism of tubulin inhibition, *J Med Chem* 50(2):319–327, 2007.

Zhang N, Ayral-Kaloustian S, Nguyen T, Hernandez R, Lucas J, Discafani C, Beyer C: Synthesis and SAR of 6-chloro-4-fluoroalkylamino-2-heteroaryl-5-(substituted)phenylpyrimidines as anti-cancer agents, *Bioorg Med Chem* 17(1):111–118, 2009.

Zurwerra D, Gertsch J, Altmann K-H: Synthesis of (−)-dactylolide and 13-desmethylene-(−)-dactylolide and their effects on tubulin, *Org Lett* 12(10):2302–2305, 2010.

CHAPTER

12

Tau Phosphorylation as a Therapeutic Target in Alzheimer's Disease

M. Medina, J. Avila

OUTLINE

INTRODUCTION

The two classical hallmark pathological lesions present in Alzheimer's disease (AD) brains are extracellular "senile plaques" (SPs) consisting of β-amyloid (Aβ) peptide, and intracellular neurofibrillary "tangles" (NFTs) made up of hyperphosphorylated tau protein. These hallmarks are inseparable and remain diagnostic as described by Dr. Alzheimer more than a century ago. Both SPs and NFTs accumulate in a consistent pattern reflecting a hierarchic vulnerability of individual cells or brain regions, although with a different regional distribution within the diseased brain (Braak and Braak, 1991). Tau pathology in AD seems to correlate with the neurodegeneration observed during the disease progression, which also correlates with the appearance of phosphorylated tau (Delacourte et al., 1999). Furthermore, the severity of dementia seems to be positively correlated with NFT rather than with SP (Arriagada et al., 1992; Gomez-Isla et al., 1997; Terry, 2004). Despite the fact that the presence of extensive tau pathology is central to the disease, little attention has been placed on tau-based therapeutic approaches until recently.

Furthermore, the occurrence of filamentous structures of aggregated, hyperphosphorylated tau is a constant, common feature in various neurodegenerative disorders, generally

Developing Therapeutics for Alzheimer's Disease. http://dx.doi.org/10.1016/B978-0-12-802173-6.00012-5

associated with synaptic loss and neuronal death but also within glial cells (Medina and Avila, 2015). Because of this shared histopathological feature, they are referred to collectively as tauopathies, although they constitute a group of etiologically heterogeneous, clinically and neuropathologically overlapping entities (Spillantini and Goedert, 2013).

Our current understanding of tau cellular functions goes beyond its classical role in the stabilization of microtubules to unveil novel physiological tau functions that may also play a role in pathogenesis. Moreover, a significant effort is being made at the preclinical level to validate a number of tau-related targets and to develop novel ways for the treatment of these conditions, and thus a number of different strategies targeting several aspects of the tau pathogenesis are being actively pursued, broadening our range of potentially useful therapeutic tools to treat AD and other tauopathies. Among them, the strong correlation that exists between phosphorylation and tau pathology has laid the foundation to look for inhibitors of the protein kinases responsible for tau phosphorylation as potential therapeutics, which will be the focus of this chapter.

TAU PROTEIN STRUCTURE

Tau protein was first isolated from porcine brain as a heat-stable protein essential for microtubule assembly (Weingarten et al., 1975). The protein is expressed in humans from a single *MAPT* gene located at chromosome 17q21 (Neve et al., 1986), which comprises 16 exons. In the human brain, transcription of the tau gene results in a nuclear RNA that generates different mRNAs by alternative splicing of exons 2, 3, and 10 and are then translated into up to six different tau protein isoforms (Goedert et al., 1989a; Himmler, 1989) (Fig. 12.1). Thus, regulated inclusion of exons 2 and 3 gives rise to tau isoforms with 0, 1, or 2 N-terminal

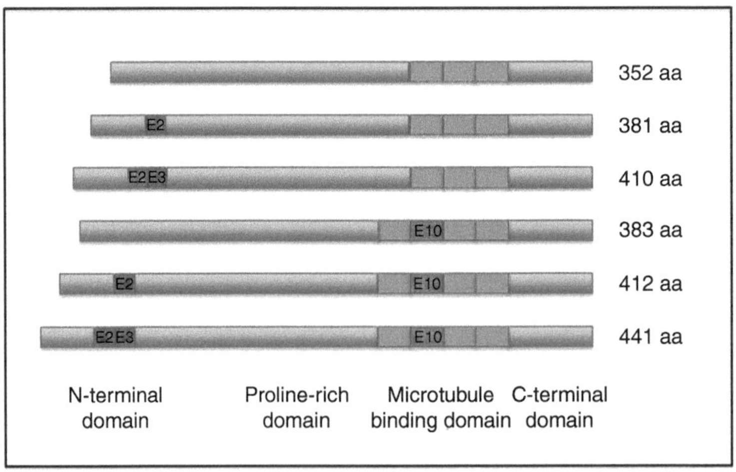

FIGURE 12.1 **The six tau isoforms expressed in the adult human brain.** They are all produced from a single gene by alternative splicing of exons 2, 3, and 10 (E2, E3, E10). Exons 2 and 3 code for N-terminal inserts whereas exon 10 codes for the second repeat within the microtubule binding domain. The longest isoform (441 aa) is also known as 2N4R (two N-terminal inserts plus four repeats).

inserts, whereas alternative splicing of exon 10 leads to tau molecules containing three (3R) or four (4R) microtubule-binding repeats (Lee et al., 1988). These tubulin binding domains consist of similar but not identical 31- or 32-residue repeats involved in the direct binding to tubulin. In the adult human brain, the 3R/4R ratio is approximately 1:1, whereas in many tauopathies other than AD this ratio is altered. Moreover, an additional tau isoform containing an extra exon (exon 4a) resulting in a much larger isoform known as "big tau" is expressed in the peripheral nervous system (PNS) (Goedert et al., 1992).

The largest CNS tau protein contains 441 residues (Goedert et al., 1989b) encompassing four main domains: (1) the N-terminal domain, enriched in acidic residues; (2) the proline-rich domain; (3) the microtubule binding domain, which contains a relatively high proportion of basic residues; and (4) the C-terminal domain, where acidic residues are mainly present (Fig. 12.1). A main characteristic of the tau molecule is the high proportion (around 20% of the total) of serine and threonine residues. If the molecule is split into two halves and the human tau molecule is compared to that from other organisms, a higher variability can be found in the N-terminal half than in the C-terminal one (Nelson et al., 1996). The most conserved region in the tau molecule is that containing the tubulin-binding repeats located close to the C-terminal region. That low variability might reflect a selective pressure to preserve the binding of this microtubule-associated protein to the conserved structure of tubulin.

The Thr/Ser ratio is much higher in the N-terminal half than in the rest of the molecule, and some of the threonine residues (17, 30, 39, 50, 52, and 95) (Fig. 12.2) are not always conserved in other species, but whether any of those residues play a role in a human-specific

1 MAEPRQEFEV MEDHAGTYGL GDRKDQGGYT MHQDQEGDTD AGLKESPLQT PTEDGSEEPG

61 SETSDAKSTP TAEDVTAPLV DEGAPGKQAA AQPHTEIPEG TTAEEAGIGD TPSLEDEAAG

121 HVTQARMVSK SKDGTGSDDK KAKGADGKTK IATPRGAAPP GQKGQANATR IPAKTPPAPK

181 TPPSSGEPPK SGDRSGYSSP GSPGTPGSRS RTPSLPTPPT REPKKVAVVR TPPKSPSSAK

241 SRLQTAPVPM PDLKNVKSKI GSTENLKHQP GGGKVQIINK KLDLSNVQSK CGSKDNIKHV

301 PGGGSVQIVY KPVDLSKVTS KCGSLGNIHH KPGGGQVEVK SEKLDFKDRV QSKIGSLDNI

361 THVPGGGNKK IETHKLTFRE NAKAKTDHGA EIVYKSPVVS GDTSPRHLSN VSSTGSIDMV

421 DSPQLATLAD EVSASLAKQG L

FIGURE 12.2 **Primary peptide sequence from the largest CNS human tau isoform (441 residues).** All potential phosphorylation sites are indicated: five tyrosines, 35 threonines (*bold*), and 45 serines. Residues encompassing the two N-terminal inserts and the four microtubule binding domains are underlined. NCBI reference sequence: NP_005901.2.

TABLE 12.1 Protein Kinase Consensus Phosphorylation Motifs Present in the Human Tau Molecule

Consensus phosphorylation motifs	
Protein kinase A (cAMP-dependent kinase)	RXS RRXS RXXS
Casein kinase II (CK2)	S/T XX E/D
Calmodulin-dependent protein kinase E (CaMKII)	XRXX S/T
Glycogen synthase kinase (GSK-3)	S/T XXX S(P)/T(P)
Cyclin-dependent kinase 5 (cdk5)	X S/T PX
Mitogen-activated protein kinase (MAPK)	X S/T PX
Protein kinase C (PKC)	S/T X K/R K/R XX S/T K/R X S/T

Two main groups of kinases are indicated: proline-directed protein kinases (PDPKs) such as GSK-3, cdk5, or MAPK, and nonproline-directed protein kinases such as PKA A, PKC, CK2, or CaMKII.

tau protein function is unknown. Threonine, serine, and tyrosine residues can be modified by phosphorylation, and the presence of specific phosphorylatable residues in the human tau molecule could suggest a possible human-specific function. Also, depending on the area where the phosphorylatable residues are present, close to acidic, basic, or proline residues, its modification by phosphorylation will be performed by different protein kinases having different recognition motifs enriched in acidic, basic, or proline residues (Pearson and Kemp, 1991) (Table 12.1). In addition, the localization of those phosphorylatable residues will affect the regulation of specific functions. Thus, the modification of those residues located at the microtubule binding domain may affect the interaction of tau protein with tubulin; for a review, see Avila et al. (2004).

Regarding the secondary structure of the protein, it is known that tau behaves in solution like an unfolded protein (Cleveland et al., 1977), able to interact with other molecules, including itself, practically through any residue(s) along the whole length of the molecule. However, when the protein is posttranslationally modified or when it interacts with other proteins, a partial folding of the protein might take place. On the other hand, it has been suggested that tau could fold in a "paper-clip" manner, in which the N-terminal and C-terminal ends are able to interact with the tubulin repeats (Schwalbe et al., 2013).

TAU PHOSPHORYLATION

Regulation of tau behavior and function under physiological and pathological conditions is mainly achieved through posttranslational modifications such as phosphorylation, acetylation, O-GlcNAcylation, glycation, glycosylation, ubiquitination, sumoylation, nitrosylation, or truncation (Avila et al., 2004), which has significant implications for the development of novel therapeutic approaches in a number of neurodegenerative disorders.

Some residues can be modified in different ways. For example, lysine can be acetylated, ubiquitinated, or subjected to sumoylation. Moreover, there could be competition between different types of modifications (glycosylation or phosphorylation) for the same residue, for instance in serine or threonine residues. On the other hand, some modifications may facilitate others, as is the case for tau sumoylation at lysine 340, which appears to inhibit its ubiquitination while stimulating its phosphorylation (Luo et al., 2014).

Without a doubt, the most studied posttranslational modification of tau protein is phosphorylation. There are up to 85 putative phosphorylation sites in the longest human tau isoform: 45 serines, 35 threonines, and 5 tyrosines (Hanger et al., 2009) (Fig. 12.2). The phosphorylation state of a protein is a consequence of a dynamic equilibrium between the protein kinases that incorporate phosphate in one or several residues and the protein phosphatases that remove them. In view of the central role that phosphorylation plays in tau physiological and pathological functions, considerable effort has been made for many years in identifying the protein kinases and phosphatases involved in tau phosphorylation, laying the ground for searching for tau kinase inhibitors as potential therapeutic agents (Medina and Avila, 2015).

Notwithstanding, there is not a single but rather multiple kinases involved in phosphorylating tau in vitro (Moreno et al., 1995; Medina et al., 1996; Medina and Avila, 2014) or in vivo (Hanger et al., 2009; Wang et al., 2013), raising the issue of whether reducing tau hyperphosphorylation will be more effective by targeting specific kinases or distinct groups of kinases (Zhang et al., 2013). Several tau kinases, including glycogen synthase kinase-3 (GSK-3, also known as tau kinase 1), cyclin-dependent kinase 5 (cdk5, also known as tau kinase 2), casein kinase (CK) I/II, extracellular regulated kinase/mitogen-activated protein kinase (ERK/MAPK), cyclic AMP-dependent kinase (PKA), protein kinase C (PKC), c-jun N-terminal kinase (JNK), dual-specificity tyrosine phosphorylated-regulated kinase 1A (DYRK1A), and microtubule affinity regulating kinase (MARK), among others, have all been implicated as potential kinase targets for tau therapeutics (Schneider and Mandelkow, 2008). While a number of efforts are under way at the preclinical level to develop tau kinase inhibitors, so far the most advanced strategy in the clinic has mostly focused on GSK-3 inhibition (Hooper et al., 2008; Medina and Castro, 2008), as discussed later in the chapter.

TAU LOCALIZATION AND TAU FUNCTIONS

It has become increasingly clear in recent years that, apart from the well-established classical functions of tau in regulating microtubule dynamics and stabilization, as well as in axonal transport (Dawson et al., 2001; Li et al., 2011; Tortosa et al., 2013), tau also displays other cellular functions (Medina and Avila, 2015). Thus, tau has been reported to interact with a number of other proteins and to be present in various subcellular localizations (Morris et al., 2011). For instance, tau can associate with the plasma membrane through its amino-terminal domain (Brandt et al., 1995; Arrasate et al., 2000), an interaction that can be modulated by phosphorylation. It has also been reported in the nucleus, where it could play a role in DNA protection (Sultan et al., 2011). Furthermore, tau phosphorylation regulates axonal transport and modulates interaction with other proteins such as 14.3.3, Pin-1, Fyn, and many others (Hanger et al., 2009). Inside a neuron, tau is mainly present in the axon, but it can also be found at the somato-dendritic compartment in neurodegenerative disorders like AD (Gotz et al., 1995). In addition, tau can be found in dendritic spines, where it may play an important role interacting with glutamate/NMDA receptors through PSD95 protein

(Ittner et al., 2010), or even interacting extracellularly with muscarinic receptors M1/M3 (Gomez-Ramos et al., 2008).

It has been suggested that increased tau phosphorylation could facilitate tau acetylation within the MT repeat domain to further impair tau binding to MTs, suggesting complex regulation of tau–MT dynamics (Cohen et al., 2011). Interestingly, tau has been most recently reported to display an intrinsic acetyltransferase activity capable of catalyzing self-acetylation by using catalytic cysteine residues in the microtubule binding domain to facilitate tau lysine acetylation (Cohen et al., 2013).

As already mentioned, tau is a phosphoprotein that could be modified at different sites of its molecule with different consequences. During development, tau is phosphorylated during the embryogenesis, decreases its level of phosphorylation during maturation of the organism, and, in aging, it can increase again its level of phosphorylation in some specific regions of the human brain (Avila et al., 2004). Moreover, the level of tau phosphorylation in aging further increases in some diseases.

The presence of tau in the brain parenchyma or in the cerebrospinal fluid (CSF) has traditionally been considered as a consequence of tau protein being released upon cell death. However, this has recently been challenged by a number of studies showing extracellular tau being released from cell lines and neurons via multiple pathways, strongly supporting the notion that secretion of tau protein may be an important part of its biological function, especially in disease (Medina and Avila, 2014). Thus, mounting evidence suggests that extracellular tau might be the result of a physiological process independent of cell death. The precise relationship between tau release and pathology spreading during AD and other tauopathies remains to be sorted out.

Some tau posttranslational modifications have been related to cell toxicity and neurodegeneration: tau aggregation, phosphorylation, and truncation. The toxicity of tau aggregates remains under discussion, in particular regarding which tau aggregates (oligomers, fibers, etc.) are actually responsible for toxicity. Interestingly, some reports suggest that higher-order tau polymers such as paired helical filaments or NFTs could indeed have a protective role (Avila, 2010). Actually, tau hyperphosphorylation also occurs in specific physiological processes such as hibernation in rodents like Syrian hamsters or ground squirrels (Arendt et al., 2003; Leon-Espinosa et al., 2013) in which a protective role has also been proposed (Su et al., 2008), or during anesthesia as well (Planel et al., 2007). Toxicity of phosphotau will be further discussed later in the chapter. More recently, it has also been described that tau truncated by asparagine endopeptidase cleavage promotes neurodegeneration (Zhang et al., 2014).

MODULATION OF TAU FUNCTION BY PHOSPHORYLATION

Almost all tau biological functions mentioned so far in the chapter are modulated by phosphorylation of the protein at different sites. Thus, tau phosphorylation might result in its detachment from microtubules, impairment of axonal transport, or lack of interaction with several proteins. Furthermore, tau phosphorylation could regulate its self-aggregation (Avila et al., 2004). Neurofibrillary degeneration correlates with abnormal hyperphosphorylation of all isoforms of tau protein (Grundke-Iqbal et al., 1986) so that tau phosphorylation is a pivotal event in AD (and other tauopathies) pathogenesis. The adult brain from a nondemented person contains around three phosphate groups per molecule, whereas that amount increases three times in the brain of an AD patient (Ksiezak-Reding et al., 1992; Kopke et al., 1993). In AD, around 40% of the abnormally phosphorylated tau is in an oligomeric form, not incorporated into NFTs.

Mounting evidence strongly suggests that tau phosphorylation during neurodegeneration results from a combination of loss of function as well as gain of (toxic) function. On the one hand, tau detachment from microtubules after hyperphosphorylation causes impaired microtubule function, axonal transport, and subsequently synaptic dysfunction and neuronal loss (Takashima et al., 1993). On the other hand, hyperphosphorylated tau molecules tend to self-assemble into filaments, can no longer interact with tubulin, and are able to sequester normal tau molecules into oligomeric filaments, a process which can be reversed by phosphatase treatment (Iqbal et al., 2014). Other posttranslational modifications such as truncation, glycosylation, O-GlcNAcylation, and ubiquitination might occur at some point after detaching from microtubules and during the aggregation process, which could also contribute to the pathology.

The increased levels of tau observed in interstitial fluid and CSF in AD may not be due solely to tau release from dying neurons (Yamada et al., 2011; Nedergaard, 2013), but rather to a normal physiological process of secretion (Simon et al., 2013). Released tau seems to exist in a relatively dephosphorylated state, compared to that of intracellular tau (Pooler et al., 2013). Interestingly, tau released from cortical neurons under physiological conditions is regulated by neuronal activity, as release is enhanced by glutamate receptor stimulation induced by the agonist S-AMPA, a process also modulated by phosphorylation (Pooler et al., 2013). Furthermore, tau subcellular localization and secretion have recently been reported to be mediated by mTor signaling and phosphorylation in a human neuronal cell line (Tang et al., 2015).

Moreover, tau can be toxic when applied extracellularly to cultured cells (Gomez-Ramos et al., 2006; Kopeikina et al., 2012), and extracellular tau might provoke a receptor-activated increase in intracellular calcium through the stimulation of M1/M3 muscarinic receptors (Gomez-Ramos et al., 2008; Diaz-Hernandez et al., 2010), leading to endocytosis of extracellular tau. Remarkably, tau phosphorylation could inhibit its interaction with M1/M3 receptors, and it has been proposed that such alterations might be involved in the transmission of tau pathology (Simon et al., 2013).

Finally, it must be stressed that although tau hyperphosphorylation takes place in various human neurodegenerative disorders, phosphorylation signatures for different diseases might share similar features but not necessarily be identical (Lee et al., 2001; Steinhilb et al., 2007; Rabano et al., 2014). It is also worth mentioning that tau phosphorylation at threonine 181 and total tau levels in CSF are considered useful biomarkers of neuronal degeneration or injury in the recent National Institute on Aging-Alzheimer's Association revised criteria for the diagnosis of AD (Jack et al., 2012).

PHOSPHOTAU TOXICITY AND DISEASE

A critical issue is whether tau hyperphosphorylation is correlative but not causative in the neurodegenerative process and also whether phosphorylation precedes aggregation. The mechanisms responsible for tau aggregation are still largely unknown. Therefore, understanding how tau is regulated may be essential to identify the origin of tau aggregate formation and to sort out the role of phosphotau in toxicity. A number of studies have suggested that phosphorylation at some specific sites on the tau molecule might facilitate aggregation (Perez et al., 2003; Noble et al., 2005), whereas phosphorylation at the microtubule binding region of tau molecule prevents its self-assembly (Liu et al., 2007). In this regard, evidence suggests that the microtubule binding domain of the tau molecule is the region mainly involved in the self-assembly of tau protein and that modification of that region prevents protein aggregation (Perez et al., 1996).

AD is the most prevalent tauopathy and, as previously indicated, in the brains of AD patients tau can be found abnormally hyperphosphorylated at some specific residues. Some of these phosphosites, but not all of them, are present in the different tauopathies, and the possibility has been suggested of different specific phosphosites signatures for different tauopathies (Lee et al., 2001). A similar picture has been indicated for tau aggregates in various tauopathies. Indeed, the formation of different aggregates in diseases like AD, Pick's disease, or argylophilic grain disease (AGD) is well known. In Pick's disease, for instance, tau is not phosphorylated at serine 262 (Probst et al., 1996), whereas that residue is modified in AD. In AGD, apart from some differences in phosphorylation with regard to AD, there are other AD tau modifications such as acetylation that do not occur (Grinberg et al., 2013).

Regarding the toxicity of phosphotau and its role in pathology, a number of reports provide substantial support for the toxicity of phosphotau, mainly at specific residues (Alonso et al., 1997; Avila et al., 2004; Gotz et al., 2013), whereas the toxicity of insoluble tau aggregates remains under discussion (de Calignon et al., 2010; Cowan and Mudher, 2013). Thus, for instance, it has been shown in a fly model that phosphotau by itself may cause neurodegeneration (Steinhilb et al., 2007). As already mentioned, tau phosphorylation could result in changes in microtubule dynamics, axonal transport, impairment of synaptic activity (due to its presence in dendritic spines), and neuronal death by apoptosis, and the presence of phosphotau unbound to microtubules could sequester normal tau and other MAPs to produce toxic effects (Alonso et al., 1996, 1997; Alonso Adel et al., 2006). Like tau purified from AD brains, in vitro hyperphosphorylated recombinant tau is capable of sequestering normal tau and inhibiting microtubule assembly (Alonso et al., 2001). Furthermore, treatment of hyperphosphorylated tau with phosphatase inhibits its polymerization in filaments and restores its binding to tubulin and microtubule assembly, whereas in vitro phosphorylation promotes its self-assembly into filaments (Wang et al., 2007). On the other hand, since extracellular tau and cell-to-cell transferred tau appear to be largely dephosphorylated, it has been recently proposed that hyperphosphorylated tau aggregates may differ from those tau forms that propagate (reviewed in Holmes and Diamond, 2014).

Hence, it is important to correlate toxicity with the phosphorylation at specific sites of tau protein that may take place in vivo at different times. In the case of some mouse models, tau phosphorylation in the proline-rich region and recognized by an antibody known as AT8 (Hernandez et al., 2003) occurs earlier than that occurring at the C-terminal region and recognized by the antibody PHF-1 (Otvos et al., 1994). Phosphorylation at the PHF-1 epitope has been recently correlated with loss of dendritic spines by looking at human postmortem brain tissue (Merino-Serrais et al., 2013), although the molecular mechanism linking both processes remains to be elucidated.

Considering our current understanding of the tau pathological pathway, it is clear that not only does tau phosphorylation play a critical role in regulating tau function at different subcellular locations, but a growing body of evidence suggests that tau phosphorylation is critical for its toxicity (Gotz et al., 2013). Thus, inhibition of tau phosphorylation is indeed a point of therapeutic intervention with disease-modifying potential on AD and tauopathies.

TAU KINASE INHIBITORS

As mentioned earlier, there is not a single but multiple kinases involved in generating hyperphosphorylated tau in vivo (Grundke-Iqbal et al., 1986), raising the issue of whether targeting specific kinases or distinct groups of kinases will be more effective in reducing tau hyperphosphorylation (Zhang et al., 2013). Several tau kinases, including GSK-3β, CDK5, and MARK, among others, have all been implicated as potential kinase targets for tau therapeutics (reviewed by Schneider and Mandelkow, 2008). Despite the challenges faced by this approach with respect to toxicity and specificity, numerous kinase inhibitors have been developed, some of which have even made it to the clinic (Medina and Castro, 2008).

AD was one of the earliest disorders linked to GSK-3 dysfunction, so the discovery of small molecule GSK-3 inhibitors has attracted significant attention as a therapeutic approach in AD and related disorders (Medina and Avila, 2010). GSK-3 (also known as tau kinase I) (Ishiguro et al., 1993) is a serine-threonine protein kinase that is encoded in mammals by two different genes (GSK3α and GSK3β), giving rise to two similar but not identical proteins, with the sequence differences located mainly at their N-terminal regions (Woodgett, 1991). GSK-3β is the isoform more abundant in the brain, where its function and activity can be regulated through its phosphorylation by other kinases or its interaction with other proteins. GSK-3β appears to act as a cellular nexus, integrating several signaling systems, including several second messengers and a wide selection of cellular stimulants, playing a role in processes such as morphogenesis, axonal polarity, synaptogenesis, and cell survival (Medina and Wandosell, 2011).

A few observational pilot studies have addressed the potential clinical effect of the mood-stabilizing drug lithium, a reference GSK-3 inhibitor, in patients with AD, so far with mixed results due in part to the low number of subjects and low compliance (reviewed by Medina et al., 2011). Interestingly, a couple of recent studies have suggested that lithium (most likely through GSK-3 inhibition) might have disease-modifying properties in AD and perhaps other tauopathies. Forlenza et al. (2011) reported a significant decrease in CSF concentrations of pTau and with a better performance in cognitive tasks in 45 people with amnestic mild cognitive impairment after lithium treatment for 12 months. More recently, Nunes et al. (2013) have also reported a stabilization of clinical cognitive outcomes after a microdose lithium treatment, reinforcing its therapeutic potential to treat AD using very low doses.

The small molecule tideglusib (Dominguez et al., 2012) is one of the few kinase inhibitors that has advanced to clinical trials for treating AD. This GSK-3 inhibitor was tested in a double-blind, placebo-controlled, randomized, escalating dose phase 2 clinical trial on 30 mild-to-moderate AD patients treated for up to 20 weeks. Although the primary objective was to evaluate the safety and tolerability, some efficacy measures were assessed as secondary objectives. Tideglusib oral administration was well tolerated and showed encouraging positive effects in the Mini Mental State Examination (MMSE), Alzheimer's Disease Assessment

Scale–Cognitive subscale (ADAS-Cog+), word fluency, Geriatric Depression Scale (GDS), and a final Global Clinical Assessment (GCA) without statistical significance in this small sample (del Ser et al., 2013). However, in a subsequent 26-week phase 2b trial to evaluate the efficacy of tideglusib versus placebo plus standard of care for the treatment of more than 300 mild-to-moderate AD patients, tideglusib failed to meet the primary cognitive end point and two of the secondary end points (Lovestone et al., 2015). Unfortunately, no data on target engagement or brain/CSF drug levels have been reported.

The same compound received the orphan drug status from the US Food and Drug Administration and European Medicines Agency and was assessed in a placebo-controlled, yearlong phase 2 efficacy trial on progressive supranuclear palsy (PSP), a pure tauopathy. The trial tested oral treatment with tideglusib versus placebo in 146 patients with possible or probable mild-to-moderate PSP for 52 weeks at 24 sites in Europe and the United States. Although the drug failed to meet the prespecified clinical end points (Tolosa et al., 2014), an MRI substudy showed a significant slowdown of the brain atrophy rate in tideglusib-treated patients (Hoglinger et al., 2014).

Cdk5 (also known as tau kinase II) (Ishiguro et al., 1994; Morfini et al., 2004) is a neuronal kinase that is involved in neuronal maturation and that phosphorylates tau in various sites. This protein is activated by another protein known as p35 or its fragment p25. Like GSK-3, cdk5 has many other substrates in the neuron, in addition to tau. Interestingly, there is a link between these two kinases, since a novel cdk5-dependent pathway for regulating GSK-3 has been proposed (Morfini et al., 2004). Many inhibitors from various chemical families targeting cdk5 and a number of other kinases involved in tau phosphorylation have been tested in preclinical models of AD and tauopathies (Puzzo et al., 2015), but none of them has reached a clinical trial so far (Tell and Hilgeroth, 2013).

Although not the main focus of this chapter, it is worth mentioning that as an alternative to kinase inhibition, activation of phosphatases has also been proposed as a strategy for reducing tau phosphorylation, especially in the case of protein phosphatase 2A (PP2A), which seems to be the main brain phosphatase involved in tau phosphorylation (Liu et al., 2005; Gong and Iqbal, 2008). It has a quaternary structure composed of three subunits (Lambrecht et al., 2013), a structural A subunit, a regulatory B subunit, and the catalytic C subunit. The A and C subunits show a well-conserved structure, whereas the B subunit is more heterogeneous. In the case of tau dephosphorylation by PP2A, B subunits known as PPP2R2A and PPP2R5D may play a role (Xu et al., 2008; Yu et al., 2014).

Activating PP2A has its own challenges, though, as it has broad substrate specificity and a number of regulatory subunits, which make it difficult to target the right pool of PP2A to the right extent. The activity of PP2A is regulated by several posttranslational modifications, including phosphorylation and methylation, but also by two noncompetitive inhibitor proteins known as I1PP2A and I2PP2A (Tanimukai et al., 2009) that can bind directly to the catalytic subunit of PP2A (Arif et al., 2014). Inhibition of these inhibitors results in the activation of the phosphatase activity. Recently, a novel etiopathogenic mechanism of AD mediated by the cleavage of I2PP2A has been suggested (Wang et al., 2010), opening the possibility of new therapeutic approaches for AD (Iqbal et al., 2014).

Despite the fact that other tau protein kinases are considered targets for reducing tau phosphorylation, no tau kinase inhibitors other than GSK-3 inhibitors have entered clinical trials to date. Besides the general challenges faced by drug discovery and development programs in diseases of this type (crossing the blood–brain barrier, target engagement, pharmacokinetics, chronic administration, etc.), developing kinase inhibitors also has its own challenges regarding kinase specificity (single kinase vs multitarget approaches), occurrence of multiple substrates (hence, potential side effects), or extent of inhibition (most tau kinases have many other key cellular functions), to name a few.

In summary, although there is a large body of evidence supporting the notion that inhibiting tau phosphorylation might have widespread disease-modifying effects on AD and other tauopathies, development of rational tau-based drug therapies calls for a deep understanding of the role of phosphorylation in regulating tau functions, including kinases/phosphatases as well as specific phosphorylation sites involved in each process leading to neurodegeneration.

References

Alonso Adel C, Li B, Grundke-Iqbal I, Iqbal K: Polymerization of hyperphosphorylated tau into filaments eliminates its inhibitory activity, *Proc Natl Acad Sci USA* 103:8864–8869, 2006.

Alonso AC, Grundke-Iqbal I, Iqbal K: Alzheimer's disease hyperphosphorylated tau sequesters normal tau into tangles of filaments and disassembles microtubules, *Nat Med* 2:783–787, 1996.

Alonso AD, Grundke-Iqbal I, Barra HS, Iqbal K: Abnormal phosphorylation of tau and the mechanism of Alzheimer neurofibrillary degeneration: sequestration of microtubule-associated proteins 1 and 2 and the disassembly of microtubules by the abnormal tau, *Proc Natl Acad Sci USA* 94:298–303, 1997.

Alonso AD, Zaidi T, Novak M, Barra HS, Grundke-Iqbal I, Iqbal K: Interaction of tau isoforms with Alzheimer's disease abnormally hyperphosphorylated tau and in vitro phosphorylation into the disease-like protein, *J Biol Chem* 276:37967–37973, 2001.

Arendt T, Stieler J, Strijkstra AM, Hut RA, Rudiger J, Van der Zee EA, Harkany T, Holzer M, Hartig W: Reversible paired helical filament-like phosphorylation of tau is an adaptive process associated with neuronal plasticity in hibernating animals, *J Neurosci* 23:6972–6981, 2003.

Arif M, Wei J, Zhang Q, Liu F, Basurto-Islas G, Grundke-Iqbal I, Iqbal K: Cytoplasmic retention of protein phosphatase 2A inhibitor 2 (I2PP2A) induces Alzheimer-like abnormal hyperphosphorylation of tau, *J Biol Chem* 289:27677–27691, 2014.

Arrasate M, Perez M, Avila J: Tau dephosphorylation at tau-1 site correlates with its association to cell membrane, *Neurochem Res* 25:43–50, 2000.

Arriagada PV, Growdon JH, Hedley-Whyte ET, Hyman BT: Neurofibrillary tangles but not senile plaques parallel duration and severity of Alzheimer's disease, *Neurology* 42:631–639, 1992.

Avila J: Alzheimer disease: caspases first, *Nat Rev Neurol* 6:587–588, 2010.

Avila J, Lucas JJ, Perez M, Hernandez F: Role of tau protein in both physiological and pathological conditions, *Physiol Rev* 84:361–384, 2004.

Braak H, Braak E: Neuropathological staging of Alzheimer-related changes, *Acta Neuropathol* 82:239–259, 1991.

Brandt R, Leger J, Lee G: Interaction of tau with the neural plasma membrane mediated by tau's amino-terminal projection domain, *J Cell Biol* 131:1327–1340, 1995.

Cleveland DW, Hwo SY, Kirschner MW: Purification of tau, a microtubule-associated protein that induces assembly of microtubules from purified tubulin, *J Mol Biol* 116:207–225, 1977.

Cohen TJ, Guo JL, Hurtado DE, Kwong LK, Mills IP, Trojanowski JQ, Lee VM: The acetylation of tau inhibits its function and promotes pathological tau aggregation, *Nat Commun* 2:252, 2011.

Cohen TJ, Friedmann D, Hwang AW, Marmorstein R, Lee VM: The microtubule-associated tau protein has intrinsic acetyltransferase activity, *Nat Struct Mol Biol* 20:756–762, 2013.

Cowan CM, Mudher A: Are tau aggregates toxic or protective in tauopathies? *Front Neurol* 4:114, 2013.

Dawson HN, Ferreira A, Eyster MV, Ghoshal N, Binder LI, Vitek MP: Inhibition of neuronal maturation in primary hippocampal neurons from tau deficient mice, *J Cell Sci* 114:1179–1187, 2001.

de Calignon A, Fox LM, Pitstick R, Carlson GA, Bacskai BJ, Spires-Jones TL, Hyman BT: Caspase activation precedes and leads to tangles, *Nature* 464:1201–1204, 2010.

del Ser T, Steinwachs KC, Gertz HJ, Andres MV, Gomez-Carrillo B, Medina M, Vericat JA, Redondo P, Fleet D, Leon T: Treatment of Alzheimer's disease with the GSK-3 inhibitor tideglusib: a pilot study, *J Alzheimers Dis* 33:205–215, 2013.

Delacourte A, David JP, Sergeant N, Buee L, Wattez A, Vermersch P, Ghozali F, Fallet-Bianco C, Pasquier F, Lebert F, Petit H, Di Menza C: The biochemical pathway of neurofibrillary degeneration in aging and Alzheimer's disease, *Neurology* 52:1158–1165, 1999.

Diaz-Hernandez M, Gomez-Ramos A, Rubio A, Gomez-Villafuertes R, Naranjo JR, Miras-Portugal MT, Avila J: Tissue-nonspecific alkaline phosphatase promotes the neurotoxicity effect of extracellular tau, *J Biol Chem* 285:32539–32548, 2010.

Dominguez JM, Fuertes A, Orozco L, del Monte-Millan M, Delgado E, Medina M: Evidence for irreversible inhibition of glycogen synthase kinase-3beta by tideglusib, *J Biol Chem* 287:893–904, 2012.

Forlenza OV, Diniz BS, Radanovic M, Santos FS, Talib LL, Gattaz WF: Disease-modifying properties of long-term lithium treatment for amnestic mild cognitive impairment: randomised controlled trial, *Br J Psychiatr* 198:351–356, 2011.

Goedert M, Spillantini MG, Jakes R, Rutherford D, Crowther RA: Multiple isoforms of human microtubule-associated protein tau: sequences and localization in neurofibrillary tangles of Alzheimer's disease, *Neuron* 3:519–526, 1989a.

Goedert M, Spillantini MG, Potier MC, Ulrich J, Crowther RA: Cloning and sequencing of the cDNA encoding an isoform of microtubule-associated protein tau containing four tandem repeats: differential expression of tau protein mRNAs in human brain, *EMBO J* 8:393–399, 1989b.

Goedert M, Spillantini MG, Crowther RA: Cloning of a big tau microtubule-associated protein characteristic of the peripheral nervous system, *Proc Natl Acad Sci USA* 89:1983–1987, 1992.

Gomez-Isla T, Hollister R, West H, Mui S, Growdon JH, Petersen RC, Parisi JE, Hyman BT: Neuronal loss correlates with but exceeds neurofibrillary tangles in Alzheimer's disease, *Ann Neurol* 41:17–24, 1997.

Gomez-Ramos A, Diaz-Hernandez M, Cuadros R, Hernandez F, Avila J: Extracellular tau is toxic to neuronal cells, *FEBS Lett* 580:4842–4850, 2006.

Gomez-Ramos A, Diaz-Hernandez M, Rubio A, Miras-Portugal MT, Avila J: Extracellular tau promotes intracellular calcium increase through M1 and M3 muscarinic receptors in neuronal cells, *Mol Cell Neurosci* 37:673–681, 2008.

Gong CX, Iqbal K: Hyperphosphorylation of microtubule-associated protein tau: a promising therapeutic target for Alzheimer disease, *Curr Med Chem* 15:2321–2328, 2008.

Gotz J, Probst A, Spillantini MG, Schafer T, Jakes R, Burki K, Goedert M: Somatodendritic localization and hyperphosphorylation of tau protein in transgenic mice expressing the longest human brain tau isoform, *EMBO J* 14:1304–1313, 1995.

Gotz J, Xia D, Leinenga G, Chew YL, Nicholas H: What renders tau toxic, *Front Neurol* 4:72, 2013.

Grinberg LT, Wang X, Wang C, Sohn PD, Theofilas P, Sidhu M, Arevalo JB, Heinsen H, Huang EJ, Rosen H, Miller BL, Gan L, Seeley WW: Argyrophilic grain disease differs from other tauopathies by lacking tau acetylation, *Acta Neuropathol* 125:581–593, 2013.

Grundke-Iqbal I, Iqbal K, Tung YC, Quinlan M, Wisniewski HM, Binder LI: Abnormal phosphorylation of the microtubule-associated protein tau (tau) in Alzheimer cytoskeletal pathology, *Proc Natl Acad Sci USA* 83:4913–4917, 1986.

Hanger DP, Anderton BH, Noble W: Tau phosphorylation: the therapeutic challenge for neurodegenerative disease, *Trends Mol Med* 15:112–119, 2009.

Hernandez F, Lucas JJ, Cuadros R, Avila J: GSK-3 dependent phosphoepitopes recognized by PHF-1 and AT-8 antibodies are present in different tau isoforms, *Neurobiol Aging* 24:1087–1094, 2003.

Himmler A: Structure of the bovine tau gene: alternatively spliced transcripts generate a protein family, *Mol Cell Biol* 9:1389–1396, 1989.

Hoglinger GU, Huppertz HJ, Wagenpfeil S, Andres MV, Belloch V, Leon T, Del Ser T: TAUROS MRI Investigators: tideglusib reduces progression of brain atrophy in progressive supranuclear palsy in a randomized trial, *Mov Disord* 29:479–487, 2014.

Holmes BB, Diamond MI: Prion-like properties of tau protein: the importance of extracellular tau as a therapeutic target, *J Biol Chem* 289:19855–19861, 2014.

Hooper C, Killick R, Lovestone S: The GSK3 hypothesis of Alzheimer's disease, *J Neurochem* 104:1433–1439, 2008.

Iqbal K, Gong CX, Liu F: Microtubule-associated protein tau as a therapeutic target in Alzheimer's disease, *Expert Opin Ther Targets* 18:307–318, 2014.

Ishiguro K, Shiratsuchi A, Sato S, Omori A, Arioka M, Kobayashi S, Uchida T, Imahori K: Glycogen synthase kinase 3 beta is identical to tau protein kinase I generating several epitopes of paired helical filaments, *FEBS Lett* 325:167–172, 1993.

Ishiguro K, Kobayashi S, Omori A, Takamatsu M, Yonekura S, Anzai K, Imahori K, Uchida T: Identification of the 23 kDa subunit of tau protein kinase II as a putative activator of cdk5 in bovine brain, *FEBS Lett* 342:203–208, 1994.

Ittner LM, Ke YD, Delerue F, Bi M, Gladbach A, van Eersel J, Wölfing H, Chieng BC, Christie MJ, Napier IA, Eckert A, Staufenbiel M, Hardeman E, Götz J: Dendritic function of tau mediates amyloid-beta toxicity in Alzheimer's disease mouse models, *Cell* 142:387–397, 2010.

Jack CR Jr, Knopman DS, Weigand SD, Wiste HJ, Vemuri P, Lowe V, Kantarci K, Gunter JL, Senjem ML, Ivnik RJ, Roberts RO, Rocca WA, Boeve BF, Petersen RC: An operational approach to National Institute on Aging–Alzheimer's Association criteria for preclinical Alzheimer disease, *Ann Neurol* 71:765–775, 2012.

Kopeikina KJ, Hyman BT, Spires-Jones TL: Soluble forms of tau are toxic in Alzheimer's disease, *Transl Neurosci* 3:223–233, 2012.

Kopke E, Tung YC, Shaikh S, Alonso AC, Iqbal K, Grundke-Iqbal I: Microtubule-associated protein tau: abnormal phosphorylation of a non-paired helical filament pool in Alzheimer disease, *J Biol Chem* 268:24374–24384, 1993.

Ksiezak-Reding H, Liu WK, Yen SH: Phosphate analysis and dephosphorylation of modified tau associated with paired helical filaments, *Brain Res* 597:209–219, 1992.

Lambrecht C, Haesen D, Sents W, Ivanova E, Janssens V: Structure, regulation, and pharmacological modulation of PP2A phosphatases, *Methods Mol Biol* 1053:283–305, 2013.

Lee G, Cowan N, Kirschner M: The primary structure and heterogeneity of tau protein from mouse brain, *Science* 239:285–288, 1988.

Lee VM, Goedert M, Trojanowski JQ: Neurodegenerative tauopathies, *Ann Rev Neurosci* 24:1121–1159, 2001.

Leon-Espinosa G, Garcia E, Garcia-Escudero V, Hernandez F, Defelipe J, Avila J: Changes in tau phosphorylation in hibernating rodents, *J Neurosci Res* 91:954–962, 2013.

Li X, Kumar Y, Zempel H, Mandelkow EM, Biernat J, Mandelkow E: Novel diffusion barrier for axonal retention of tau in neurons and its failure in neurodegeneration, *EMBO J* 30:4825–4837, 2011.

Liu F, Grundke-Iqbal I, Iqbal K, Gong CX: Contributions of protein phosphatases PP1, PP2A, PP2B and PP5 to the regulation of tau phosphorylation, *Eur J Neurosci* 22:1942–1950, 2005.

Liu F, Li B, Tung EJ, Grundke-Iqbal I, Iqbal K, Gong CX: Site-specific effects of tau phosphorylation on its microtubule assembly activity and self-aggregation, *Eur J Neurosci* 26:3429–3436, 2007.

Lovestone S, Boada M, Dubois B, Hull M, Rinne JO, Huppertz HJ, Calero M, Andres MV, Gomez-Carrillo B, Leon T, del Ser T: ARGO Investigators: a phase II trial of tideglusib in Alzheimer's disease, *J Alzheimers Dis* 45:75–88, 2015.

Luo HB, Xia YY, Shu XJ, Liu ZC, Feng Y, Liu XH, Yu G, Yin G, Xiong YS, Zeng K, Jiang J, Ye K, Wang XC, Wang JZ: SUMOylation at K340 inhibits tau degradation through deregulating its phosphorylation and ubiquitination, *Proc Natl Acad Sci USA* 111:16586–16591, 2014.

Medina M, Avila J: Glycogen synthase kinase-3 (GSK-3) inhibitors for the treatment of Alzheimer's disease, *Curr Pharm Des* 16:2790–2798, 2010.

Medina M, Avila J: New perspectives on the role of tau in Alzheimer's disease: implications for therapy, *Biochem Pharmacol* 88:540–547, 2014.

Medina M, Avila J: Further understanding of tau phosphorylation: implications for therapy, *Expert Rev Neurother* 15:115–122, 2015.

Medina M, Castro A: Glycogen synthase kinase-3 (GSK-3) inhibitors reach the clinic, *Curr Opin Drug Discov Devel* 11:533–543, 2008.

Medina M, Wandosell F: Deconstructing GSK-3: the fine regulation of its activity, *Int J Alzheimers Dis* 2011:479249, 2011.

Medina M, Garcia-Rocha M, Padilla R, Perez M, Montejo de Garcini E, Avila J: Protein kinases involved in the phosphorylation of human tau protein in transfected COS-1 cells, *Biochim Biophys Acta* 1316:43–50, 1996.

Medina M, Garrido JJ, Wandosell FG: Modulation of GSK-3 as a therapeutic strategy on tau pathologies, *Front Mol Neurosci* 4:24, 2011.

Merino-Serrais P, Benavides-Piccione R, Blazquez-Llorca L, Kastanauskaite A, Rabano A, Avila J, DeFelipe J: The influence of phospho-tau on dendritic spines of cortical pyramidal neurons in patients with Alzheimer's disease, *Brain* 136:1913–1928, 2013.

Moreno FJ, Medina M, Perez M, Montejo de Garcini E, Avila J: Glycogen synthase kinase 3 phosphorylates recombinant human tau protein at serine-262 in the presence of heparin (or tubulin), *FEBS Lett* 372:65–68, 1995.

Morfini G, Szebenyi G, Brown H, Pant HC, Pigino G, DeBoer S, Beffert U, Brady ST: A novel CDK5-dependent pathway for regulating GSK3 activity and kinesin-driven motility in neurons, *EMBO J* 23:2235–2245, 2004.

Morris M, Maeda S, Vossel K, Mucke L: The many faces of tau, *Neuron* 70:410–426, 2011.

Nedergaard M: Neuroscience: garbage truck of the brain, *Science* 340:1529–1530, 2013.

Nelson PT, Stefansson K, Gulcher J, Saper CB: Molecular evolution of tau protein: implications for Alzheimer's disease, *J Neurochem* 67:1622–1632, 1996.

Neve RL, Harris P, Kosik KS, Kurnit DM, Donlon TA: Identification of cDNA clones for the human microtubule-associated protein tau and chromosomal localization of the genes for tau and microtubule-associated protein 2, *Brain Res* 387:271–280, 1986.

Noble W, Planel E, Zehr C, Olm V, Meyerson J, Suleman F, Gaynor K, Wang L, LaFrancois J, Feinstein B, Burns M, Krishnamurthy P, Wen Y, Bhat R, Lewis J, Dickson D, Duff K: Inhibition of glycogen synthase kinase-3 by lithium correlates with reduced tauopathy and degeneration in vivo, *Proc Natl Acad Sci USA* 102:6990–6995, 2005.

Nunes MA, Viel TA, Buck HS: Microdose lithium treatment stabilized cognitive impairment in patients with Alzheimer's disease, *Curr Alzheimer Res* 10:104–107, 2013.

Otvos L Jr, Feiner L, Lang E, Szendrei GI, Goedert M, Lee VM: Monoclonal antibody PHF-1 recognizes tau protein phosphorylated at serine residues 396 and 404, *J Neurosci Res* 39:669–673, 1994.

Pearson RB, Kemp BE: Protein kinase phosphorylation site sequences and consensus specificity motifs: tabulations, *Methods Enzymol* 200:62–81, 1991.

Perez M, Valpuesta JM, Medina M, Montejo de Garcini E, Avila J: Polymerization of tau into filaments in the presence of heparin: the minimal sequence required for tau–tau interaction, *J Neurochem* 67:1183–1190, 1996.

Perez M, Hernandez F, Lim F, Diaz-Nido J, Avila J: Chronic lithium treatment decreases mutant tau protein aggregation in a transgenic mouse model, *J Alzheimers Dis* 5:301–308, 2003.

Planel E, Richter KE, Nolan CE, Finley JE, Liu L, Wen Y, Krishnamurthy P, Herman M, Wang L, Schachter JB, Nelson RB, Lau LF, Duff KE: Anesthesia leads to tau hyperphosphorylation through inhibition of phosphatase activity by hypothermia, *J Neurosci* 27:3090–3097, 2007.

Pooler AM, Phillips EC, Lau DH, Noble W, Hanger DP: Physiological release of endogenous tau is stimulated by neuronal activity, *EMBO Rep* 14:389–394, 2013.

Probst A, Tolnay M, Langui D, Goedert M, Spillantini MG: Pick's disease: hyperphosphorylated tau protein segregates to the somatoaxonal compartment, *Acta Neuropathol* 92:588–596, 1996.

Puzzo D, Gulisano W, Palmeri A, Arancio O: Rodent models for Alzheimer's disease drug discovery, *Expert Opin Drug Discov* 10:703–711, 2015.

Rabano A, Rodal I, Cuadros R, Calero M, Hernandez F, Avila J: Argyrophilic grain pathology as a natural model of tau propagation, *J Alzheimers Dis* 40(Suppl 1):S123–S133, 2014.

Schneider A, Mandelkow E: Tau-based treatment strategies in neurodegenerative diseases, *Neurotherapeutics* 5:443–457, 2008.

Schwalbe M, Biernat J, Bibow S, Ozenne V, Jensen MR, Kadavath H, Blackledge M, Mandelkow E, Zweckstetter M: Phosphorylation of human tau protein by microtubule affinity-regulating kinase 2, *Biochemistry* 52:9068–9079, 2013.

Simon D, Hernandez F, Avila J: The involvement of cholinergic neurons in the spreading of tau pathology, *Front Neurol* 4:74, 2013.

Spillantini MG, Goedert M: Tau pathology and neurodegeneration, *Lancet Neurol* 12:609–622, 2013.

Steinhilb ML, Dias-Santagata D, Fulga TA, Felch DL, Feany MB: Tau phosphorylation sites work in concert to promote neurotoxicity in vivo, *Mol Biol Cell* 18:5060–5068, 2007.

Su B, Wang X, Drew KL, Perry G, Smith MA, Zhu X: Physiological regulation of tau phosphorylation during hibernation, *J Neurochem* 105:2098–2108, 2008.

Sultan A, Nesslany F, Violet M, Begard S, Loyens A, Talahari S, Mansuroglu Z, Marzin D, Sergeant N, Humez S, Colin M, Bonnefoy E, Buee L, Galas MC: Nuclear tau, a key player in neuronal DNA protection, *J Biol Chem* 286:4566–4575, 2011.

Takashima A, Noguchi K, Sato K, Hoshino T, Imahori K: Tau protein kinase I is essential for amyloid beta-protein-induced neurotoxicity, *Proc Natl Acad Sci USA* 90:7789–7793, 1993.

Tang Z, Ioja E, Bereczki E, Hultenby K, Li C, Guan Z, Winblad B, Pei JJ: mTor mediates tau localization and secretion: implication for Alzheimer's disease, *Biochim Biophys Acta* 1853:1646–1657, 2015.

Tanimukai H, Kudo T, Tanaka T, Grundke-Iqbal I, Iqbal K, Takeda M: Novel therapeutic strategies for neurodegenerative disease, *Psychogeriatrics* 9:103–109, 2009.

Tell V, Hilgeroth A: Recent developments of protein kinase inhibitors as potential AD therapeutics, *Front Cell Neurosci* 7:189, 2013.

Terry RD: Tangles precede plaques but don't cause them, *Neurobiol Aging* 25:741–742, 2004 (discussion 743–746).

Tolosa E, Litvan I, Hoglinger GU, Burn D, Lees A, Andres MV, Gomez-Carrillo B, Leon T, Del Ser T, TAUROS Investigators: A phase 2 trial of the GSK-3 inhibitor tideglusib in progressive supranuclear palsy, *Mov Disord* 29:470–478, 2014.

Tortosa E, Galjart N, Avila J, Sayas CL: MAP1B regulates microtubule dynamics by sequestering EB1/3 in the cytosol of developing neuronal cells, *EMBO J* 32:1293–1306, 2013.

Wang JZ, Grundke-Iqbal I, Iqbal K: Kinases and phosphatases and tau sites involved in Alzheimer neurofibrillary degeneration, *Eur J Neurosci* 25:59–68, 2007.

Wang X, Blanchard J, Kohlbrenner E, Clement N, Linden RM, Radu A, Grundke-Iqbal I, Iqbal K: The carboxy-terminal fragment of inhibitor-2 of protein phosphatase-2A induces Alzheimer disease pathology and cognitive impairment, *FASEB J* 24:4420–4432, 2010.

Wang JZ, Xia YY, Grundke-Iqbal I, Iqbal K: Abnormal hyperphosphorylation of tau: sites, regulation, and molecular mechanism of neurofibrillary degeneration, *J Alzheimers Dis* 33(Suppl 1):S123–S139, 2013.

Weingarten MD, Lockwood AH, Hwo SY, Kirschner MW: A protein factor essential for microtubule assembly, *Proc Natl Acad Sci USA* 72:1858–1862, 1975.

Woodgett JR: cDNA cloning and properties of glycogen synthase kinase-3, *Methods Enzymol* 200:564–577, 1991.

Xu Y, Chen Y, Zhang P, Jeffrey PD, Shi Y: Structure of a protein phosphatase 2A holoenzyme: insights into B55-mediated tau dephosphorylation, *Mol Cell* 31:873–885, 2008.

Yamada K, Cirrito JR, Stewart FR, Jiang H, Finn MB, Holmes BB, Binder LI, Mandelkow EM, Diamond MI, Lee VM, Holtzman DM: In vivo microdialysis reveals age-dependent decrease of brain interstitial fluid tau levels in P301S human tau transgenic mice, *J Neurosci* 31:13110–13117, 2011.

Yu UY, Yoo BC, Ahn JH: Regulatory B subunits of protein phosphatase 2A are involved in site-specific regulation of tau protein phosphorylation, *Kor J Physiol Pharmacol* 18:155–161, 2014.

Zhang X, Hernandez I, Rei D, Mair W, Laha JK, Cornwell ME, Cuny GD, Tsai LH, Steen JA, Kosik KS: Diaminothiazoles modify tau phosphorylation and improve the tauopathy in mouse models, *J Biol Chem* 288:22042–22056, 2013.

Zhang Z, Song M, Liu X, Kang SS, Kwon IS, Duong DM, Seyfried NT, Hu WT, Liu Z, Wang JZ, Cheng L, Sun YE, Yu SP, Levey AI, Ye K: Cleavage of tau by asparagine endopeptidase mediates the neurofibrillary pathology in Alzheimer's disease, *Nat Med* 20:1254–1262, 2014.

CHAPTER

13

Stimulation of Tau Degradation

R.A. Quintanilla, F. Cabezas-Opazo, S.P. Pallo, A.S. Chesser, G.V.W. Johnson

OUTLINE

INTRODUCTION

The accumulation of pathological tau species as insoluble, fibrillar, intraneuronal aggregates called neurofibrillary tangles (NFTs) is a defining hallmark of the AD brain (Braak and Braak, 1991). In addition, it is evident that NFT pathology is predictive of the cognitive state of an AD patient (Duyckaerts et al., 1997; Murray et al., 2015). NFTs are composed of tau molecules with posttranslational modifications. The predominant modification of tau found in NFTs is phosphorylation; however, numerous other modifications have been noted, including truncation, acetylation, and nitration (Gamblin et al., 2003; Min et al., 2010; Cohen et al., 2011; Reynolds et al., 2007; Arnold et al., 1996). Historically, NFTs, as opposed to soluble tau species, were considered to be the primary damage-causing agent in AD, but a seminal study in 2005 started a paradigm shift. In this study a mouse model was made to express a frontotemporal dementia with parkinsonism linked to chromosome 17 (FTDP17) mutant

Developing Therapeutics for Alzheimer's Disease. http://dx.doi.org/10.1016/B978-0-12-802173-6.00013-7

form of human tau (P301L tau) in a doxycycline-regulatable manner. In these transgenic mice (denoted as the tg4510 mouse line), tau levels were more than 13-fold higher than endogenous levels in the absence of doxycycline, and the mice developed significant numbers of NFTs, had neuronal loss, and exhibited behavioral deficits. Turning expression "off" via doxycycline administration reduced P301L tau levels to only ~three-fold higher than endogenous levels and resulted in the prevention of further neuronal loss and in improved behavior. However, NFT numbers were unchanged or even increased (Santacruz et al., 2005). These findings strongly indicated that NFTs are not the primary toxic entity, and subsequent studies have provided evidence that pathologically modified monomeric and/or soluble oligomeric forms of tau are likely to be the harmful species (Kopeikina et al., 2012; Ward et al., 2012; Lasagna-Reeves et al., 2012). Given significant evidence that tau is an important effector of pathology in AD, clearing pathological tau species is generally expected to have beneficial effects in AD. In this context, there is a growing interest in defining the degradative pathways that remove tau from the cell. Indeed, compelling evidence suggests that reduction of overall tau levels early in the disease process would be sufficient to reduce tau toxicity and slow progression of AD, and thus would be of therapeutic value as part of the treatment regimen (Gotz et al., 2013).

The two primary protein clearance pathways in neurons are the ubiquitin proteasome system (UPS) and the autophagy and lysosome pathway (ALP). In this chapter we will review what is known about the functioning of these pathways in neurons and their contribution to tau clearance. Evidence for defects in these pathways in AD will also be presented, along with a discussion of different therapeutic strategies to enhance tau degradation through each pathway.

THE UBIQUITIN PROTEASOME SYSTEM

Overview of the UPS Pathway

The UPS is one of the primary degradative pathways, and as such plays a crucial role in the maintenance of a functional neuronal proteome. In general, the UPS is involved in the clearance of short-lived proteins as well as certain soluble proteins that have been damaged (Schmidt and Finley, 2014). The targeting of proteins to the proteasome for degradation usually involves the covalent addition of the 76 amino acid polypeptide, ubiquitin, to the substrate. This is a multistep process that is governed by a ubiquitin-activating enzyme (E1), a ubiquitin-conjugating enzyme (E2), and a ubiquitin ligase (E3). The initial step involves activation of ubiquitin by the E1 enzyme in an ATP-dependent reaction, followed by transfer of the E1-bound ubiquitin to E2. The E2–ubiquitin complex subsequently interacts with the E3 ubiquitin ligase. The E3 ligase, which binds the substrate directly or indirectly, catalyzes the ligation of ubiquitin to the substrate protein. The isopeptide bond formed involves the C-terminal glycine (Gly76) of ubiquitin and a lysine residue in the target protein (Amm et al., 2014). This basic reaction is repeated to add additional ubiquitin molecules to the primary ubiquitin at internal lysine residues. A minimum of four ubiquitin molecules is normally required for targeting of a substrate to the proteasome. The interubiquitin isopeptide bonds usually occur at Lys48, which is considered the classical motif for recognition by the proteasome. However, it is now evident that ubiquitin chains containing linkages through other lysine residues (eg, Lys63 or Lys29) can also target substrates to the proteasome (Kravtsova-Ivantsiv and Ciechanover, 2012). Once the substrate has been appropriately targeted, deubiquitylating enzymes (DUBs) remove the chain from the substrate (Reyes-Turcu et al., 2009); hence, the polyubiquitin chains are not themselves degraded by the proteasome, but can be recycled for further use.

The target organelle for polyubiquitylated proteins is the 26S proteasome, which is composed of a central barrel-shaped catalytic 20S core that contains the proteolytic enzymes, and regulatory particles that cap the ends of the 20S core. Although the 19S regulatory particle is the most studied, the 20S proteasome core can also be capped with two other activator complexes, either the 11S regulatory particle (REG/PA28) or PA200/Blm10. Unlike the 19S particle, neither of these regulatory peptides contains ATPases (Layfield et al., 2003; Savulescu and Glickman, 2011; Schmidt and Finley, 2014). The regulatory caps are primarily responsible for recognizing the polyubiquitylated substrate and facilitating the unfolding of the attached protein for entry into the 20S proteolytic core for degradation into small peptides (Liu et al., 2006). The eukaryotic 20S proteasome has three proteases; one exhibits a chymotrypsin-like activity with preference for Tyr or Phe in the P1 position, another has trypsin-like activity with preference for Arg or Lys at the P1 position, and a third is caspase-like with a preference for Glu or other acidic residues at the P1 position (Schmidt and Finley, 2014). These proteolytic activities of the proteasome result in cleavage of the substrates to short peptides in a highly defined manner, with mean lengths between 6 and 10 amino acids, which can then be further processed to free amino acids by other cytosolic proteases (Hegde and Upadhya, 2011).

Evidence indicates that the polyubiquitin chain alone may not always be sufficient to efficiently target substrates to the 26S proteasome, as chaperones and proteins containing ubiquitin-like (UBL) and ubiquitin-associated (UBA) domains have been implicated in the recognition and delivery of substrates to the 26S proteasome for degradation (Su and Lau, 2009). For example, the adaptor protein p62, which has a UBA domain, has been reported to bind polyubiquitylated substrates and facilitate targeting to the proteasome. This is likely accomplished through the binding of p62 to regulatory protein triphosphatase 1 (Rpt1), a subunit of the 19S particle, through its PB1 domain (Babu et al., 2005; Geetha et al., 2008).

It should be noted that the 20S proteasome can also degrade substrates which lack a ubiquitin tag. Substrates that are directly degraded by the 20S (or 26S) proteasome without being ubiquitylated have regions that are unstructured either due to intrinsic structural properties or from unfolding in response to stressors. Numerous proteins have intrinsically disordered regions, including tau, making them potential substrates of the 20S proteasome (Ben-Nissan and Sharon, 2014), and a significant proportion of cellular proteins have been shown to be degraded by the proteasome in a ubiquitin-independent manner (Baugh et al., 2009). Therefore, although studies have largely focused on ubiquitin-mediated degradation of substrates by the proteasome, the fact that ubiquitin-independent proteasome degradation of proteins contributes to the clearance mechanisms of the cell needs to be kept in mind.

Evidence of Defects in UPS in AD

There is evidence that the UPS is impaired in AD. For example, an early study reported that proteasome activity was significantly decreased in lysates prepared from regions of AD brain that are involved in the disease process (including the hippocampus and superior and middle temporal gyri), while no decreases were observed in the cerebellum or occipital lobe—areas which do not show significant pathology in AD (Keller et al., 2000). In contrast, a later study reported that the activity of isolated 20S proteasomes was not decreased in AD brains compared to controls. It was suggested that the observed decreases in the earlier study may be due to the presence of inhibitory molecules in crude brain homogenates (Gillardon et al., 2007), including paired helical filament (PHF)-tau (Keck et al., 2003), as will be discussed later. Further, it has been hypothesized that the increased oxidative stress present in AD brain could result in selective protein oxidation that may indirectly (or possibly directly) impair proteasome function (Riederer et al., 2011). Extensively oxidized proteins cannot be properly degraded by the proteasome and thus decrease proteolytic efficiency (Dunlop et al., 2009). Further, 19S and 20S subunits are susceptible to oxidative modifications which can impair activity (Aiken et al., 2011). Overall, it is unclear whether the proteasomes themselves are less efficient in AD; nevertheless, there is evidence that the cellular milieu in AD is not conducive to proteasomal degradation, leading to an overall inhibition of proteasome function.

Ubiquitin itself may be defective in AD, which would interfere with proteasomal degradation. In AD brain the NFTs and amyloid plaques contain a mutant form of ubiquitin, UBB+1, which is generated by a molecular misread and a dinucleotide deletion resulting in a 19-amino acid C-terminal extension (van Leeuwen et al., 1998; Oddo, 2008). The presence of UBB+1 is not unique to AD as it has been found in other neurodegenerative conditions such as Huntington's disease and argyrophilic grain disease (Dennissen et al., 2010; Ferrer et al., 2008). This mutant form of ubiquitin can be ubiquitylated itself and form polyubiquitin chains, but cannot be processed by DUBs. This prevents protein degradation, as evidenced by a study showing that expression of UBB+1 in neuroblastoma cells inhibits ubiquitin-dependent proteolysis (Lindsten et al., 2002). Proteomic analysis of transgenic mice that express UBB+1 in neurons revealed UPS impairment and changes in proteins involved in energy metabolism and cytoskeleton organization. This was reported to be similar to the proteomic profiles of both human AD brain and several AD mouse models. However, these UBB+1 mice do not have an overt neurological phenotype, although some cognitive deficits were noted (Fischer et al., 2009). Furthermore, the underlying mechanisms that result in production of UBB+1, and the disease stage at which this process first appears, are not known. Therefore, it remains to be determined whether this is a contributory event or collateral process in AD.

Finally, the processing of ubiquitin may be impaired in AD. The protein ubiquitin carboxyl-terminal hydrolase L 1 (UCH-L1) was originally identified as a DUB but also has ubiquitin ligase activity. It has been shown to be downregulated in the AD brain and the remaining protein is oxidatively modified, which impairs its function (Choi et al., 2004; Kabuta et al., 2008). Reduced or inhibited function of UCH-L1 would prevent efficient untagging of ubiquitylated proteins, both preventing their degradation and reducing the pool of free ubiquitin that could be used to tag additional proteins for UPS processing.

Tau Processing by the UPS and Pathological Alterations in AD

As discussed previously, tau fits many of the criteria for a proteasomal substrate, including its size and the presence of intrinsically unorganized regions. Indeed, there is evidence that tau can be degraded by the proteasome through both ubiquitin-independent and ubiquitin-dependent processes. In an early study using SH-SY5Y human neuroblastoma cells that either were untransfected or were stably transfected with a human tau construct, it was shown that inhibition of the proteasome using lactacystin (a specific inhibitor of the 20S core) blocked the degradation of tau (David et al., 2002). Moreover, in the same study a cell-free in vitro system was used to show that tau could be directly degraded by the 20S proteasome without ubiquitylation, indicating the existence of ubiquitin-independent pathways for the proteasomal degradation of unfolded proteins (David et al., 2002). In support of these early findings, ubiquitin-independent tau degradation by the proteasome has been reported in neurons (Carrettiero et al., 2009). A subsequent study provided further evidence for ubiquitin-independent proteasomal degradation of tau in HT22 cells (an immortalized mouse hippocampal cell line), and in E36 cells (which are derived from hamster lung) transfected with tau (Grune et al., 2010). However, a role for ubiquitylation also has been reported in proteasome-mediated tau clearance using tau-transfected human embryonic kidney (HEK) cells. In this study, when tau and the E3 ligase carboxy-terminus of Hsp70 interaction protein (CHIP) were transiently cotransfected into HEK cells and subsequently treated with proteasome inhibitors, the amount of multimeric ubiquitylated tau increased, suggesting that tau is being ubiquitylated and degraded by the proteasome (Petrucelli et al., 2004). However, it is interesting to note that when primary neurons are treated with proteasome inhibitors the level of tau actually decreases. Data indicate that this is likely due to an upregulation of autophagy and tau being degraded through this pathway (see later discussion) (Kruger et al., 2012; Lei et al., 2014).

The aforementioned studies utilized cells with intact protein control mechanisms. However, as described previously, protein clearance mechanisms may be impaired in AD. This may alter the normal route of clearance, or may change the reliance on tagging signals such as ubiquitin. Indeed, in the context of AD specifically, it appears that ubiquitylation plays a role in tau pathology. Early evidence showed that ubiquitin was present in the PHFs, NFTs, and amyloid plaques in the AD brain (Mori et al., 1987; Perry et al., 1987). A subsequent study confirmed that tau in PHFs was ubiquitylated but showed it was primarily monoubiquitylation that occurred, with only a small portion of the associated ubiquitin being in a polyubiquitin chain (Morishima-Kawashima et al., 1993). Mass-spectrometry analysis confirmed that PHF-tau isolated from AD brain is ubiquitylated in its microtubule-binding region at Lys254, Lys311, and Lys353. This occurs as a combination of mono- and polyubiquitylation modifications, with polyubiquitylation occurring mostly via Lys48 linkages, but also through Lys11 and Lys6 intraubiquitin bonds (Cripps et al., 2006). Interestingly, it has been suggested that Lys6 linkages inhibit ubiquitin-dependent protein degradation, and it was postulated that this might play a role in initiating the formation of degradation-resistant PHFs (Cripps et al., 2006).

Although in the AD brain tau appears to be targeted for clearance by the proteasome, it seems clear that efficient degradation does not occur, as ubiquitylated tau is deposited in the AD brain. This may in part be due to a direct inhibitory effect on proteasomal function by pathologic tau (Keck et al., 2003). This in vitro study showed that PHF-tau isolated from AD brain inhibited the activity of purified proteasomes. Furthermore, the reported decrease of proteasome activity in homogenates from AD brains was not associated with changes in the proteasomal proteins but rather an association of PHF-tau with proteasomes (Keck et al., 2003). In support of this hypothesis, misfolded, pathological tau species were deposited at synapses in the AD brain along with a concomitant buildup of ubiquitylated proteins and protein components of the UPS. This further suggests that pathological tau may inhibit the UPS, which in turn may inhibit the normal turnover of tau, to enhance the formation of additional misfolded species (Tai et al., 2012).

Heat-Shock Proteins and Their Roles in the UPS

Heat-shock proteins (Hsps) are an ancient and evolutionarily conserved family of proteins that function as molecular chaperones. These proteins play an essential role in determining the fate of client proteins by either facilitating their folding/refolding or by targeting them for degradation (Abisambra et al., 2011). Thus, their involvement in the processing of tau has been of interest. Two important Hsps are hsp70 and hsc70, which are very similar isoforms but may play different roles in determining the fate of client proteins (refolding or targeting for degradation). Hsc70 (HSPA8/Hsp73) is constitutively expressed and found at high levels in cells, while hsp70 (HSPA1A/Hsp72) is induced by different stressors (Brocchieri et al., 2008; Kampinga and Craig, 2010; Kim et al., 2013). Hsps, particularly hsp90, hsp70, and hsc70, often work cooperatively in protein triage decisions, in part utilizing a balance of the chaperone proteins themselves to determine client protein fate. For example, inhibition of hsp90 with geldanamycin or its derivatives (which block the refolding/release of client proteins by hsp90) results in upregulation of hsp70 in mouse cortical neurons, and of hsp70, hsp40, and hsp27 in CHO cells (Dickey et al., 2006a). The upregulation of these Hsps in response to hsp90 inhibition is because hsp90 represses the activity of heat-shock transcription factor 1 (Hsf1), and inhibition of hsp90 relieves this repression (Zou et al., 1998). These changes in Hsps can then promote the clearance of client proteins, including tau. For example, when hsp90 in inhibited, the shift in the balance of the Hsps results in decreases in particular forms of tau in CHO cells transfected with mutant P301L tau. Hsp90 inhibition specifically caused a decrease in tau phosphorylated at Ser/Thr-Pro sites, but not at Ser262/356 within the microtubule binding region, which are non-Ser/Thr-Pro sites (KXGS motifs) (Dickey et al., 2006a). Further studies indicated that this degradation of phospho-tau species involved the recruitment of the hsp70–CHIP complex, leading to the ubiquitylation of tau and its subsequent targeting to the proteasome. These latter studies were carried out in tau-transfected HeLa and HEK cells (Dickey et al., 2007). Similar studies using both in vitro assays and cell models showed that when CHIP forms a complex with hsc70 (HSPA8), this also facilitated the ubiquitylation of phosphorylated tau species (Shimura et al., 2004). However, another study found that only expression of inducible hsp70 (HSPA1A) resulted in a decrease in tau, while the highly and constitutively expressed hsc70 (HSPA8) either had no effect or increased tau levels. It was indicated that this was because hsp70 in the presence of tau was able to recruit in CHIP, which presumably would result in the ubiquitylation of tau and targeting to the proteasome for degradation, whereas hsc70 was unable to recruit CHIP into a complex with tau (Jinwal et al., 2013). The reason for the differences in the two studies is not known, and further studies are warranted.

In vivo studies also provide evidence that hsp90 and hsp70 play a role in mediating tau clearance. Administration of an hsp90 inhibitor in an hTau mouse model—which was generated by crossing mice that express a tau transgene derived from a human P1-derived artificial chromosome (PAC), H1 haplotype (8c mice), with mice in which GFP was knocked into the tau locus, resulting in expression of a GFP fusion protein containing the first 31 amino acids of tau (Andorfer et al., 2003)—reduced phosphorylated tau levels (Dickey et al., 2007). Interestingly, in this model the hsp90 inhibitor did not affect the clearance of tau phosphorylated at Ser262/356 (KXGS motif), which is similar to what had been seen in a cell line. In this same study, HEK cells transiently transfected with different tau constructs were used to show that CHIP was unable to bind or ubiquitylate tau that was phosphorylated at the KXGS motif or contained alanine phospho-null mutations at KXGS motifs. Thus, both phosphorylation and alanine substitutions that block phosphorylation at Ser262/356 blocked CHIP binding to tau and subsequent ubiquitylation. The reason why both phosphorylation and alanine mutations blocked CHIP binding is unknown, but it was speculated that it could be that KXGS may be a recognition consensus for both MARK2/PAR-1 (which phosphorylates the Ser in this motif) and CHIP (Dickey et al., 2007). In CHIP$^{-/-}$ mice the levels of soluble, ubiquitin-negative, phosphorylated tau species were increased (Dickey et al., 2006b). In contrast, 30-month-old mice that overexpress hsp70 exhibit decreased levels of total soluble and insoluble tau relative to age-matched controls (Petrucelli et al., 2004). Overall, these results suggest that CHIP is likely a mediator of tau ubiquitylation and that Hsps play an important role in facilitating this process and targeting the protein for degradation (Dickey et al., 2006b, 2007).

Treatment Strategies to Increase UPS-Dependent Tau Clearance

The development of therapeutic approaches that target components of the UPS pathway to increase tau clearance is an emerging area of research. Inhibition of the DUB, Usp14, using the small molecule, IU1, in cell models was reported to result in increased proteasome activity and the clearance of ubiquitylated substrates, including tau (Lee et al., 2010a). However, acute administration of IU1 in wild-type mice reduced neuromuscular junction synaptic transmission, indicating that Usp14 plays a fundamentally important role in modulating synaptic activity (Vaden et al., 2015). Furthermore, a Usp14-deficient mouse model (ax(J)) exhibited no decreases in total tau levels; rather, the levels of phospho-tau species were increased (Jin et al., 2012). These studies indicate that Usp14 may be a necessary protein for maintaining the general health of the nervous system, and thus inhibitory strategies may not be ideal. Clearly, further studies are necessary before Usp14 inhibitors can be tested as a treatment strategy in AD.

Another area of investigation is the use of hsp90 and hsp70 inhibitors to facilitate clearance of tau by the proteasome as a therapeutic strategy for AD. As described earlier, treatment of hTau mice with an hsp90 inhibitor reduced the levels of tau phosphorylated at Ser396/404 and Ser202/Thr205. The drug used was EC102, which inhibits the ATPase activity of hsp90 and is able to cross the blood–brain barrier (BBB). Interestingly, EC102 appears to have higher affinity for hsp90 in a disease state as hsp90 expressed in the cortex of human AD cases bound EC102 more strongly than that found in the cortex of control cases or the cerebellum which is not significantly affected in the disease (Dickey et al., 2007). In contrast, another hsp90 inhibitor, 17-AAG, had no significant effect on tau pathology in mice expressing P301L mutant tau (JNPL3 mice) (Lewis et al., 2000) after 3 months of intraperitoneal administration three times per week (Ho et al., 2013). The differences between these studies could be due to differences in the mouse models used (hTau vs JNPL3), the bioavailability of the inhibitors, or differences in efficacy. Thus additional studies would be beneficial.

Alternate treatment strategies are also being developed that do not involve inhibiting hsp90 directly, but rather are aimed at promoting hsp90-mediated degradation indirectly. One such strategy is targeting cochaperones of hsp90 such as CHIP that are involved in promoting degradation of client proteins (Blair et al., 2014). Another is to target modifications to hsp90 that control its activity. Histone deacetylase 6 (HDAC6) deacetylates hsp90, which then favors refolding of client proteins rather than targeting for degradation. Treatment of mice that inducibly overexpress P301L tau (tg4510 mice) with the HDAC6 inhibitor tubastatin resulted in a decrease in total P301L tau levels (Selenica et al., 2014). Further, knocking down HDAC6 enhances the efficacy of hsp90 inhibitors to increase tau clearance. Thus inhibiting both HDAC6 and hsp90 may be a more efficacious approach that needs to be explored more thoroughly (Cook et al., 2012). These preliminary studies suggest that hsp90-directed therapies may hold promise for the treatment of AD. It should be noted that numerous hsp90 inhibitors are currently in different phases of clinical trials; however, none of the trials are for AD or other neurodegenerative diseases, but rather the majority are cancer therapy trials (see clinicaltrials.gov).

Hsp70-targeted therapies are also being pursued. Similar to what is being studied for hsp90, inhibition of the ATPase activity of hsp70 is now being considered as a therapeutic strategy for AD, as hsp70 inhibition has been shown to decrease tau levels in several models, presumably by facilitating the targeting of tau to the proteasome (Jinwal et al., 2010). In an initial study it was found that methylene blue, azure C, and myricetin all inhibited the ATPase activity of hsp70, and reduced tau levels in clonal cells expressing transfected tau. This was suggested to be primarily due to increased clearance through the UPS (Jinwal et al., 2009). In contrast, activators of hsp70 ATPase activity preserved tau levels in the same systems, providing further evidence that the activity of hsp70 is critical in determining tau proteostasis (Jinwal et al., 2009). In a subsequent study, the allosteric inhibitor MKT-077 was found to bind to ADP-bound hsp70 and lock it in this inactive state, which resulted in increased tau clearance in transfected Hela cells. MKT-077 (as well as derivatives) phenocopies the effects of Hsp70 interacting protein (Hip), which stabilizes hsp70 in its ADP-bound state and thus increases binding to clients and targets them for degradation rather than refolding (Wang et al., 2013). MKT-077 is a potent antitumor agent, and it entered a phase 1 clinical trial but was found to have renal toxicity, and thus the trial was discontinued (Rousaki et al., 2011). In addition to the renal toxicity, MKT-077 is not BBB permeable, making it a poor candidate for an AD trial. Therefore, a modified derivative of MKT-077 was synthesized and tested in a mouse model. This compound, YM-08, was found to cross the BBB with a brain/plasma ratio of approximately 0.25, as well as to be quickly cleared from the kidney (reducing the opportunity for renal damage). Further, in tau-transfected Hela cells, as well as in brain slices from tg4510 mice, YM-08 was able to reduce tau levels and is thus considered a promising lead compound (Miyata et al., 2013). YM-01 is another allosteric hsp70 inhibitor that has been evaluated. YM-01 significantly reduces tau levels in a number of clonal cell models, as well as in primary neurons from tg5410 mice. In this study, the implicated mechanism was direct binding of YM-01 to hsc70 to direct tau to the proteasome for degradation. In brain slices from wild-type mice, YM-01 did not cause a decrease in endogenous tau levels unless the slices were first treated with nocodazole to depolymerize the microtubules, suggesting that hsc70 with YM-01 preferentially interacts with free tau (Abisambra et al., 2013). Overall, these studies indicate that further development

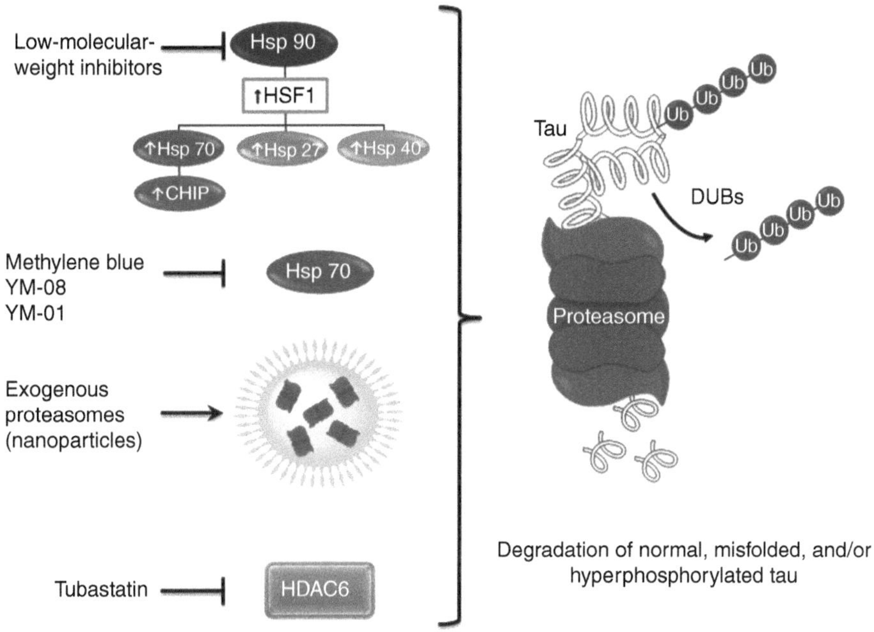

FIGURE 13.1 **Potential therapeutic strategies to increase tau clearance by the proteasome.** A promising approach to reduce the accumulation of pathological forms of tau is the inhibition of Hsps. For example, the inhibition of hsp90 activity by low-molecular-weight molecules (eg, EC102) that cross the BBB results in the selective degradation of aberrant forms of tau in AD mouse models (Dickey et al., 2007). This is likely due in part to activation of Hsf1 and increased expression of other Hsps. In addition, an increase in Hsp70/CHIP complexes may facilitate tau ubiquitylation and degradation by the proteasome (Jinwal et al., 2013). Also, the inhibition of the ATPase activity of hsp70 by methylene blue, YM-01, or YM-08 reduces tau levels and increases their clearance through the UPS (Abisambra et al., 2013; Jinwal et al., 2009, Miyata et al., 2013). Moreover, increasing proteasome activity may also be a valid therapeutic target, since current studies showed that exogenous delivery of proteasomes in the form of nanoparticles increased the clearance of tau (Han et al., 2014). Inhibition of HDAC6 activity can also be a relevant target. HDAC6 can bind polyubiquitin chains and decrease proteasomal degradation of substrates (Sadoul et al., 2008). Promising studies showed that tubastatin (an HDAC6 inhibitor) decreased total levels of tau in an AD mouse model (Selenica et al., 2014).

of hsp70 inhibitors as an AD therapeutic strategy to reduce tau levels through the UPS may be warranted.

Given that enhancing proteasome activity is likely to be beneficial in AD, direct delivery of human 26S proteasomes into cells has been explored. To do so, purified proteasomes were loaded onto nanoparticles through noncovalent interactions. The proteasome–nanoparticle complexes were transported into cells by endocytosis, and the exogenous proteasomes enhanced the degradation of transfected tau in various cell models. Since the silica-based nanoparticles are nonantigenic and can be modified to cross the BBB, this approach may represent a new therapeutic strategy for increasing the clearance of tau in AD (Han et al., 2014). The effects of these different proteasome-directed treatment strategies to increase tau clearance are summarized in Fig. 13.1.

THE AUTOPHAGY AND LYSOSOME PATHWAY

Overview of the ALP

Autophagy, which literally means "self-eating," is a basic catabolic system that involves targeting damaged cellular components to the lysosome for degradation. Three general forms have been described: microautophagy, which involves direct lysosomal engulfment of substrates (Sahu et al., 2011); chaperone-mediated autophagy (CMA), where substrates containing an exposed KFERQ motif are recognized by chaperone complexes and directly targeted to lysosomes through a lamp2a-mediated process (Kaushik and Cuervo, 2012); and macroautophagy, which involves the formation of a double-membrane phagophore containing substrates to be degraded and subsequent fusion of the fully formed vesicular autophagosome with a lysosome. Substrates can become entrapped within the autophagosome via two methods—either nonspecific engulfment by the developing phagophore of a region of cytoplasm containing the substrate(s) to be degraded or selective targeting of clients via autophagy adaptors and chaperones (Nixon, 2013). In the context of AD, the majority of studies have focused on macroautophagy, and the same is true of studies examining the role of autophagy in the clearance of tau. One study has shown that CMA may be able to clear tau fragments in vitro (Wang et al., 2009b); however, at this point no studies have examined a possible role for microautophagy in AD or in vivo tau clearance. Therefore, in this section we will focus on macroautophagy (and hereafter refer to it as "autophagy" for simplicity).

Autophagy induction can be by a mammalian target of rapamycin (mTOR)-dependent or independent pathway. The mTOR-dependent pathway has been extensively studied and involves inhibition of mTOR followed by phosphorylation and activation of ULK1 and phosphorylation of other members of the Ulk1-Atg13-FIP200 complex, which regulates autophagosome biosynthesis. The regulators of autophagosome formation in mTOR-independent pathways are less clear, although a number of different players have been implicated. Here we will describe the dynamic process of autophagy, but will not detail all the different proteins involved. For a more complete discussion of the mTOR-dependent and mTOR-independent regulatory machinery, see a more comprehensive review (Sarkar, 2013).

Autophagy starts with a preautophagosomal structure which transitions into the isolation membrane or phagophore that engulfs the substrates and then becomes a double membrane vacuole called an autophagosome. The autophagosome either fuses next with a late endosome/multivesicular body (MVB) to form an amphisome, which then fuses with a lysosome, or autophagosomes can fuse directly with lysosomes. The contents of the resulting autolysosomes are degraded by lysosomal hydrolases in the acidic lumen of the organelle. The products of the digestive processes are then released for reutilization by the cell (Nixon, 2013; Stolz et al., 2014).

Autophagy was initially described as a nonselective process in response to cellular stressors such as starvation that resulted in bulk degradation of proteins and organelles in order to maintain the nutrient status of the cell (Klionsky, 2007). However, it is now apparent that autophagy has a significant selective component, in that specific proteins or organelles are targeted to the autophagic machinery for degradation during normal cell homeostasis (Stolz et al., 2014). Autophagy adaptor proteins play a pivotal role in selective autophagy as they recognize and interact with damaged proteins or organelles and tether them to the core autophagic machinery by binding to the autophagosome surface protein, LC3-II (Nixon, 2013). These autophagy adaptors include p62, NBR1, Traf 6 binding protein, optineurin, and NDP52 (Johansen and Lamark, 2011; Stolz et al., 2014; Tumbarello et al., 2013; Boyle and Randow, 2013). Although cargos that are targeted to the autophagy pathway by the adaptor proteins are often ubiquitylated, ubiquitylation does not appear to be a prerequisite for clearance by the ALP (Gal et al., 2009; Gibbings et al., 2012; Korac et al., 2013; Watanabe and Tanaka, 2011). Autophagy adaptors also can work in concert with chaperones and cochaperones to facilitate recognition of damaged or defective substrates and efficient targeting to the autophagy machinery. For example, the cochaperone Bcl-2 associated athanogene 3 (BAG3) in concert with hsp70, as well as the small Hsp, hspB8, and the autophagy adaptor, p62, can target specific clients for autophagic degradation (Carra et al., 2008; Crippa et al., 2010; Ulbricht et al., 2013).

Autophagy occurs in all cell types to varying degrees. Initially, it was postulated that baseline autophagy in neurons was low because it was difficult to detect autophagosomes and other vacuolar structures of the autophagy pathway in healthy neurons. However, it was found that the efficient formation and clearance of autophagosomes, which is referred to as autophagic flux, occurs constitutively and to a high degree in healthy neurons (Boland et al., 2008). In neurons, it is now clear that autophagy is a critical pathway for normal cellular maintenance, and neurons are very efficient at clearing defective proteins and organelles. Because neurons are highly dependent on autophagy to maintain a healthy proteome, dysfunctional clearance mechanisms and impaired induction of autophagy are likely to be contributors to the pathogenic processes in AD and other neurodegenerative diseases (Nixon, 2013).

Evidence of Defects in ALP in AD

There is significant evidence of defective autophagy in AD. A seminal electron microscopic study revealed accumulation of autophagosomes, MVBs, autophagolysosomes, and other autophagy-related vacuoles in the AD brain, occurring most predominantly in dystrophic neurites (Nixon et al., 2005). Treatment of ex vivo hippocampal slice cultures with lysosomal disruptors results in the formation of enlarged, dystrophic neurites filled with autophagic vacuoles and lysosomes (Bi et al., 1999, 2000), similar to what is seen in mouse AD models and human AD tissue (Nixon et al., 2005; Yang et al., 2011b; Sanchez-Varo et al., 2012). In mouse models of AD, autophagic defects are also evident (Nixon, 2013; Tan et al., 2014). For example, in 4- to 6-month-old transgenic mice expressing AD-related mutations in amyloid precursor protein (APP) and presenilin 1 (PS1), indications of increased autophagy were evident, including elevated levels of LC3 in dystrophic neurites and numerous autophagic vacuoles present at presynaptic terminals (Sanchez-Varo et al., 2012).

Further evidence for a link between PS1 and autophagic dysfunction exists. It has been demonstrated that PS1 plays a crucial role in targeting the v-ATPase V0a1 subunit to lysosomes, which is essential for appropriate acidification and efficient hydrolase activity. PS1 mutations that cause familial AD produce a lysosomal/autophagy phenotype that is similar to what is observed in fibroblasts from AD patients. Overall, the data indicate that PS1 plays an important role in v-ATPase targeting to lysosomes, lysosome acidification, and proteolysis during autophagy. PS1 mutations lead to familial AD, and hence these findings suggest that defective acidification of lysosomes and thus decreased proteolysis of cargos engulfed during autophagosome formation could be a contributing factor in nonfamilial AD pathogenesis as well (Lee et al., 2010b; Nixon and Yang, 2011; Nixon, 2013). Interestingly, in the TgCRND8 mice, which expresses mutant APP only, increased staining for LC3-II, as well as an increase in cathepsin D-positive lysosomes, were detected along with defective proteolytic clearance of neuronal autophagic substrates. These data suggest that in the absence of mutant PS1, AD-associated impairment in autophagy occurs and thus is due to other factors (Yang et al., 2011a).

As described before, mTOR is a critical regulator of autophagy. Its kinase activity suppresses autophagy, and thus inhibition results in an upregulation of autophagy. Inhibition of mTOR can result in an increase in Beclin 1. Beclin 1 is involved in the initiation of autophagophore formation, and thus increased levels often result in increased autophagy (Wang et al., 2009a). In mild cognitive impairment (MCI) cases, as well as in AD, quantitative immunoblotting for phosphorylated substrates of mTOR revealed that the activity of the kinase was likely increased and this occurred concurrently with decreases in autophagy-related proteins including Beclin 1 (Tramutola et al., 2015).

Although it is well documented that Beclin 1 is involved in the initiation of autophagy, there is also evidence indicating that it could play a role in later maturation steps as well, thus making it a critical autophagy protein (Peric and Annaert, 2015; Jaeger and Wyss-Coray, 2010). Beclin 1 levels are decreased in the AD brain, and genetic reduction of Beclin 1 in mice that express human APP results in an exacerbation of Aβ-related pathology. Conversely, lentiviral expression of Beclin 1 in APP mice ameliorated Aβ pathology (Pickford et al., 2008). In cell models, reduction of Beclin 1 has resulted in increased APP levels as well as the C-terminal fragment of APP and Aβ (Jaeger et al., 2010). It was noted that in both mice and cell models, APP overexpression did not alter Beclin 1 levels, and therefore it was suggested that defects in autophagy can lead to disruptions in APP processing, but not the converse (Jaeger and Wyss-Coray, 2010).

Overall, the studies described here, as well as others, strongly indicate that deficiencies in the ALP are involved in AD pathogenesis. In addition, data suggest that deficits in the ALP occur early in the development of AD and thus are likely contributory factors in the progression of the disease. For this reason, the initiation and progression of autophagy and lysosomal function are all potential therapeutic targets.

Tau Processing by the ALP and Dysfunction in AD

There is a great deal of evidence that tau is degraded through the ALP. An initial study examined tau proteolysis directly in a cell-free system using the lysosomal protease cathepsin D. Cathepsin D is an acidic protease, and incubation with tau at pH 4.0 resulted in a decrease in full-length tau and a concomitant increase in cleaved fragments (Bednarski and Lynch, 1996). Several subsequent studies demonstrated that inhibiting lysosomal function with the compound chloroquine (which raises the pH of lysosomes and impairs the function of the acid hydrolases) led to increased levels of tau in multiple models, including hippocampal slices and human neuroblastoma cells engineered to express tau (Bednarski and Lynch, 1996; Bendiske and Bahr, 2003). In human neuroblastoma BE(2)-M17D cells that inducibly express human tau (M1C cells), inhibition of cathepsins using a selective inhibitor also resulted in increases in tau levels (Hamano et al., 2008). Further, in the same cell model, inhibiting autophagy upstream using 3-methyladenine (3-MA), a PI3 kinase inhibitor which blocks autophagosome formation, also resulted in tau accumulation (Hamano et al., 2008). Conversely, stimulating autophagy in SH-SY5Y cells overexpressing aggregation-prone P301L tau led to a substantial reduction in aggregates, an effect that was prevented by 3-MA (Wong et al., 2008). 3-MA treatment of mouse neuroblastoma N2a cells overexpressing only the microtubule binding repeat region of tau containing an FTDP17 mutation ($Tau_{RD}\Delta K280$) (which is prone to aggregation) led to an increase in both soluble and insoluble tau (Wang et al., 2009b).

Animal studies have also provided evidence for tau clearance by autophagy. In a *Drosophila* tauopathy model, cathepsin D is upregulated with age. Genetic ablation of cathepsin D causes enhanced neurotoxicity and a shorter life span in these flies (Khurana et al., 2010). In a functional genomic screen using a fly model where wild-type tau was expressed in the eye, a loss of function of Beclin 1 (Atg6) significantly increased tau toxicity (Ambegaokar and Jackson, 2011). Age-dependent neurodegeneration occurs in mice in which the essential autophagy gene Atg7 has been knocked out in forebrain neurons concurrent with an accumulation of phosphorylated tau within intracellular inclusions (Inoue et al., 2012). Finally, additional supporting evidence for the role of autophagy in clearing tau was surprisingly generated during an attempt to elucidate the role of the proteasome in tau degradation in neurons. Treatment of rat primary neurons with a proteasome inhibitor resulted in a significant reduction in total tau. This decrease in tau levels was likely due to a compensatory upregulation of autophagy, as evidenced by increased LC3-II levels and an increased number of autophagosomes in treated cells (Kruger et al., 2012). This finding was confirmed in a subsequent study (Lei et al., 2014).

Human genetic studies have provided evidence that autophagy and tau clearance are impaired in AD. Genome-wide association studies (GWAS) have identified PICALM/CALM (phosphatidylinositol binding clathrin assembly protein) as a risk locus for AD (Harold et al., 2009; Jun et al., 2010). Adaptor protein 2 together with PICALM bind to LC3-II and facilitate the clearance of the C-terminal fragment of APP by autophagy (Tian et al., 2013). However, another study indicated that PICALM likely plays a more complex role in regulating autophagy and tau clearance, as both reduced and elevated levels result in impaired tau clearance. In flies, expression of low levels of wild-type human tau results in no discernible phenotype; however, if the *Drosophila* homolog of PICALM is reduced, the levels of tau apparently increase. Conversely, if PICALM is overexpressed in a zebra fish model where tau is expressed in the eye, degeneration increases concurrently with increases in phosphorylated tau and thioflavin-S-positive tau inclusions (Moreau et al., 2014). Further implicating this protein in AD pathogenesis, PICALM is abnormally cleaved in the AD brain and is found to colocalize with NFTs (Ando et al., 2013). This may suggest that defects in PICALM and subsequent autophagy/tau clearance deficiencies are a feature of AD. However, given the differences in these studies, further studies are need to clarify the mechanisms whereby PICALM affects autophagy.

Transcription factor EB (TFEB) has been shown to regulate the expression of genes involved in lysosome biogenesis (Settembre et al., 2011, 2012). In addition, TFEB translocates from the cytoplasm to the nucleus in response to starvation, and increases the expression of genes involved in autophagy (eg, p62SQSTM1, MAP1LC3, and UVRAG)—thus facilitating autophagosome formation and autophagic flux (Settembre and Ballabio, 2011). Furthermore, intracerebroventricular administration of AAV-TFEB in tg4510 mice that inducibly express P301L tau resulted in decreases in the level of phosphorylated P301L tau, but did not alter the levels of total tau. TFEB administration had no effect on endogenous tau in wild-type mice. In HEK cells transfected with P301L tau and TFEB-FLAG, an inverse correlation between the levels of TFEB-FLAG and tau phosphorylated at Ser396/404 (as detected by PHF1 immunoreactivity) was observed. In addition, TFEB expression promoted increased autophagosome formation in this cell model. The results of these studies suggest that upregulation of TFEB results in the selective clearance of phosphorylated P301L tau, while not affecting the degradation of wild-type tau (Polito et al., 2014).

The expression of specific autophagy adaptor proteins is essential to appropriately target substrates for degradation by selective autophagy (Johansen and Lamark, 2011). In neurons, the autophagy adaptor protein, NDP52, facilitates the clearance of tau. Further, the expression of NDP52 is strongly regulated by the stress-activated transcription factor Nrf2. In $Nrf2^{-/-}$ mice, levels of tau and phospho-tau are significantly increased, and activation of Nrf2 results in decreases in phospho-tau levels in primary neurons, an effect that is blocked when NDP52 is knocked down. Increasing expression of NDP52 in neurons also facilitates trehalose-induced autophagy-dependent clearance of tau (Jo et al., 2014a).

Overall, given the strong evidence that basal autophagy is normally high in neurons (Boland et al., 2008) and contributes to tau turnover, the defects in the ALP that occur in AD are likely to contribute to tau accumulation and toxicity. Therefore, strategies that upregulate autophagy are likely to be beneficial in the context of AD.

Treatment Strategies That Increase ALP-Dependent Tau Clearance

A number of in vitro and in vivo studies have provided evidence that activating autophagy increases tau clearance. In brain slices from JNPL3 mice (which express P301L tau), treatment with methylene blue resulted in decreases in phospho-tau levels, as well as increases in cathepsin D, Beclin 1, and LC3-II, indicating an increase in autophagy. In the same study, treatment of primary neurons with methylene blue resulted in an increase in the number of autophagic vacuoles, and tau was found to colocalize with the vacuoles (Congdon et al., 2012). Treatment of primary neurons with the disaccharide trehalose, which increases autophagy through an mTOR-independent pathway (Sarkar et al., 2007), results in a significant decrease in tau levels concurrent with a robust increase in LC3-II (Kruger et al., 2012; Lei et al., 2014).

Trehalose has also shown promise in animal models. Initiating trehalose treatment at weaning in a mouse model expressing the FTDP17 tau mutant P301S resulted in a significant reduction in insoluble tau, as well as soluble tau phosphorylated at Thr212/Ser214 (AT100) at 20 weeks of age (Schaeffer et al., 2012). Trehalose treatment also improved neuronal survival in cortical layers I–III (Schaeffer et al., 2012). In a mouse model with parkin deleted that also expresses mutant tau with three FTDP17 mutations (G272V, P301L, R406W) ($PK^{-/-}/tau^{VLW}$), chronic administration of trehalose in the drinking water decreased phospho-tau levels and tau pathology (Rodriguez-Navarro et al., 2010).

In the same P301S transgenic mice used for the trehalose study described earlier (Schaeffer et al., 2012), long-term treatment with the autophagy activator rapamycin (which is an mTOR inhibitor) resulted in decreased phospho-tau levels as well as a significant decrease in the amount of sarkosyl insoluble tau (Caccamo et al., 2013; Ozcelik et al., 2013). Rapamycin also decreased the levels of tau phosphorylated at Thr181 in 3xTg-AD mice (Caccamo et al., 2010) expressing mutant APP, PS1, and tau (P301L) that develop both amyloid plaque and tau pathology (Oddo et al., 2003). Treatment of FTDP17 tau mutant P301S mice with temsirolimus, a rapamycin analog approved by the US Food and Drug Administration for treating renal cell carcinoma, increased autophagy and clearance of phospho-tau, and attenuated learning and memory deficits (Jiang et al., 2014). Similarly, temsirolimus treatment of Tg30 mice, which overexpress tau with a double FTDP17 mutation (P301S/G272V), resulted in increased indicators of autophagy, including LC3-II and Rab7. Further, the density of NFTs was decreased when treatments were started prior to the onset of motor deficits (Frederick et al., 2015).

Increasing the expression of autophagy adaptors is another strategy that could be used to facilitate tau clearance. Since Nrf2 increases the expression of NDP52, which targets tau for degradation by autophagy (Jo et al., 2014a), it would be expected that treatment with Nrf2 agonists may facilitate tau clearance and thus these could have potential as AD therapeutic agents (Tarozzi et al., 2013). The isothiocyanate, sulforaphane, comes from plants of the *Brassica* genus (eg, brussels sprouts, broccoli, kohlrabi, etc.) and is a well-documented Nrf2 activator (Tarozzi et al., 2013). Treatment of neurons with sulforaphane results in decreased tau levels, an effect that is dependent on NDP52 expression (Jo et al., 2014a). Sulforaphane also increases autophagy (Jo et al., 2014b). Therefore the combined effect of increases in bulk autophagy as well as increased targeting of tau for clearance makes sulforaphane a phytochemical that could be considered for further development as a prophylactic AD treatment.

Another strategy for increasing tau clearance by autophagy has involved increasing energy bioavailability. In one study, 3xTgAD mice were used to determine if improving neuronal bioenergetics by providing nicotinamide would ameliorate autophagy deficits. Nicotinamide crosses the BBB and is converted to NAD^+. Treatment of these mice with nicotinamide (provided in the drinking water at 40 μg/g body weight per day) for 8 months resulted in improved autophagic flux by enhancing lysosome/autolysosome acidification, reduced the levels of tau phosphorylated at Thr231 (AT180 epitope), and attenuated the cognitive decline (Liu et al., 2013). Given that defects in lysosome acidification have been implicated in AD pathology, improving autophagy at this step in the ALP has the potential for being a treatment strategy.

Immunotherapy to increase tau clearance is an emerging area of investigation. Passive immunization of JNPL3 mice with an antibody to the PHF1 (phosphorylated Ser396/404) epitope resulted in decreases in the levels of insoluble tau species (Boutajangout et al., 2011). In another study, two different monoclonal antibodies to the PHF1 epitope were developed. In JNPL3 brain slice cultures, it was found that neurons were the primary cell type that internalized the monoclonal antibodies. Within the neurons, the antibodies colocalized with pathological tau species and with endosomal/lysosomal/autophagy markers, indicating that the ALP is likely to be involved in facilitating the clearance of antibody-bound tau (Gu et al., 2013). These studies suggest that immunotherapy approaches to decrease tau levels are likely to depend on a functional ALP. Therefore, immunotherapy may be useful when combined with strategies that enhance autophagic processes.

Lithium has been used to treat bipolar disorder for decades and has been shown to have neuroprotective effects in various models (Jope and Nemeroff, 2013). Lithium inhibits GSK-3 and inositol monophosphatase, as well as other targets (Jope and Nemeroff, 2013; Klein and Melton, 1996; Malhi et al., 2013). In 2005, Sarkar and coworkers showed that lithium-induced autophagy, and this involved inhibition of inositol monophosphatase. In cell-based models, lithium enhanced the clearance of mutant huntingtin and α-synuclein (Sarkar et al., 2005). When lithium was administered over a 4-month period to JNPL3 mice, indicators of increased autophagy were observed. Furthermore, the levels of both total and phosphorylated forms of the exogenously expressed P301L tau were significantly decreased (Shimada et al., 2012). Given that lithium can decrease tau phosphorylation and the levels of insoluble tau in different AD mouse models (Caccamo et al., 2007; Leroy et al., 2010) and can increase autophagy and tau clearance (Motoi et al., 2014), these data indicate that it could be a useful therapeutic for treating AD. However, a 10-week study with 71 AD patients found that lithium treatment did not alter phospho-tau levels in the CSF, nor did it have an effect on cognitive performance (Hampel et al., 2009). But in a 12-month randomized controlled trial with 45 amnestic MCI patients, lithium treatment did significantly decrease CSF phospho-tau levels, and improvements in certain cognitive measures were also noted (Forlenza et al., 2011). This later clinical trial would suggest that lithium may be useful to increase autophagy and tau clearance, though perhaps only at earlier stages of disease.

It has also been shown that GSK-3 inhibitors are able to attenuate mTOR activity depending on the TSC1/TSC2 complex, which is a negative regulator of mTOR activity (Tomasoni and Mondino, 2011). GSK-3 inhibitors also enhance lysosomal acidification and thus increase autophagy in nonneuronal cells (Azoulay-Alfaguter et al., 2014). Chronic nasal treatment of 5xFAD mice, which cooverexpress five familial AD mutations (Oakley et al., 2006), with a GSK-3 inhibitor resulted in decreases in lysosomal pH (Avrahami et al., 2013). Since low lysosomal pH is necessary for efficient hydrolase activity, these data suggest that inhibiting GSK-3 activity may improve autophagic flux, which would likely enhance tau clearance, as we have previously discussed. However, at this time no studies have directly examined the effect of GSK-3 inhibitors on tau clearance specifically.

There is evidence that inhibiting the deacetylase, HDAC6, could facilitate tau clearance. HDAC6 deacetylates a number of substrates, including tubulin, hsp90, and tau. Knockdown of HDAC6 in HeLa cells expressing P301L-tau resulted in decreases in tau phosphorylated at Ser396/404 (PHF1 epitope); however, changes in total tau levels were not shown. In addition, HDAC6 inhibition in neurons from wild-type mice also resulted in decreases in PHF1 immunoreactivity (Cook et al., 2012). In this initial study, it was suggested that inhibition of HDAC6 resulted in increased hsp90 acetylation, which favored the formation of a "degradation complex" followed by clearance of tau (Cook et al., 2012). However, a subsequent study by the same group using a selective HDAC6 inhibitor in wild-type mice showed increases in acetylation of tau at the KXGS motif in the microtubule binding region, along with decreases in tau phosphorylated at Ser262 (12E8 epitope) and Ser396/404 (PHF1 epitope), but without changes in total tau levels. It was therefore suggested that the increase in tau acetylation was responsible for decreases in phospho-tau species in response to HDAC6 inhibition (Cook et al., 2014). In another study, administration of HDAC6 inhibitors to a mouse model of AD resulted in increased clearance of phosphorylated tau by autophagy (Zhang et al., 2014). Additionally, HDAC6 has been reported to increase autophagy by facilitating autophagosome–lysosome fusion, although these mechanistic studies were carried out in mouse embryonic fibroblasts (Lee et al., 2010c). Overall, further studies are needed to determine if HDAC6 inhibitors can increase autophagy and promote tau clearance, or simply alter the phosphorylation state of the protein. Also, the role of tau acetylation in promoting or decreasing tau clearance is not that straightforward. For example, in another study it was reported that

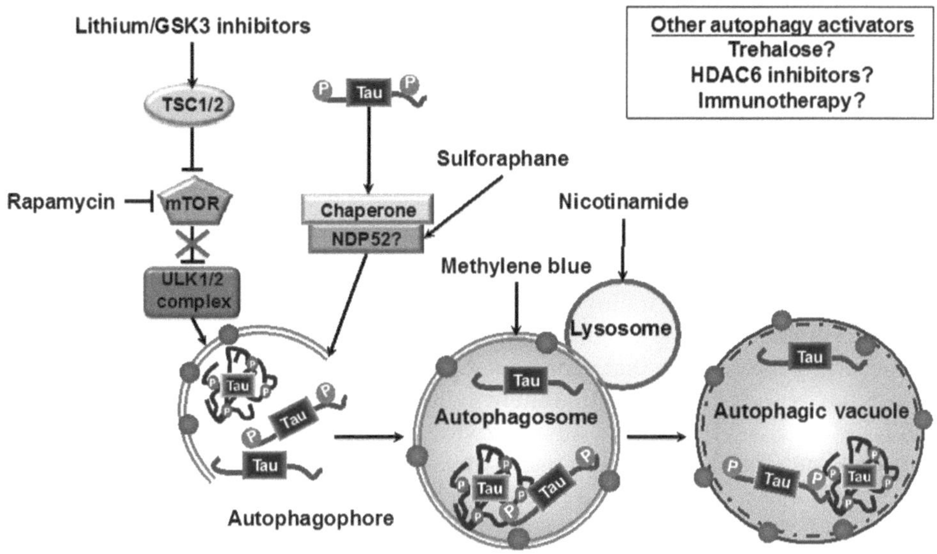

FIGURE 13.2 **Potential therapeutic strategies to increase tau clearance by autophagy.** TSC1/2 is a negative regulator of mTOR, and GSK-3 inhibitors result in decreases in mTOR activity in a TSC1/2-dependent manner and also can enhance lysosomal acidification and thus increase autophagy in nonneuronal cells (Azoulay-Alfaguter et al., 2014). Lithium may also increase autophagy by inhibiting inositol monophosphatase (Sarkar et al., 2005). Rapamycin, and analogs such as temsirolimus, inhibit mTOR and thus increase autophagy and phosphorylated tau clearance in tauopathy mouse models (Frederick et al., 2015; Jiang et al., 2014). The isothiocyanate sulforaphane increases the expression of the autophagy adaptor NDP52 in an Nrf2-dependent manner, as well as increasing autophagy, which results in increased tau clearance (Jo et al., 2014a,b). Methylene blue treatment increases the number of autophagic vacuoles concurrent with increases in cathepsin D, Beclin 1, and LC3II, indicating an increase in autophagy (Congdon et al., 2012). Treatment of a mouse AD model with nicotinamide for 8 months resulted in improved autophagic flux by enhancing lysosome/autolysosome acidification. A reduction in tau phosphorylated at Thr231 was also observed (Liu et al., 2013). Trehalose increases autophagy through an mTOR-independent pathway and reduces phosphorylated tau in tauopathy mouse models (Rodriguez-Navarro et al., 2010; Schaeffer and Goedert, 2012). Studies suggest that HDAC6 inhibitors may increase autophagy and clearance of phosphorylated tau, but the mechanisms are unclear (Zhang et al., 2014). Finally, immunotherapy using antibodies to specific tau phosphoepitopes may involve autophagic clearance of the immune complexes (Gu et al., 2013).

tau can be acetylated at sites outside of the microtubule binding region, and that increased acetylation of these sites, which are deacetylated by SIRT1 instead of HDAC6, results in increased levels of phospho-tau species, possibly by blocking proteasome degradation (Min et al., 2010). These data indicate that site-specific acetylation of tau differentially affects its ability to be targeted for degradation. The effects of these different autophagy-directed treatment strategies to increase tau clearance are summarized in Fig. 13.2.

COOPERATION BETWEEN UPS AND ALP IN CLEARING TAU

There is significant evidence that the UPS and ALP cooperate to facilitate the clearance of substrates, including tau. Furthermore, it is likely that the relative contribution of each pathway is determined by a number of factors, including age, and may change over time. Indeed, it has been speculated that during aging the cell switches from being primarily dependent on the proteasome for maintaining protein homeostasis to a reliance on autophagy (Behl, 2011; Morawe et al., 2012). However, the exact timing of this switch and the factors that govern it have not been fully elucidated. Given this situation, using cell-based model systems may not give an accurate view of the contribution of each pathway to the clearance of tau in vivo, and may not account for changes seen as the organism ages.

It is clear that inhibition of the UPS results in a compensatory upregulation of autophagy (Kruger et al., 2012; Pandey et al., 2007), but autophagy inhibition actually results in an impairment of the UPS (Korolchuk et al., 2009, 2010), indicating that although there is cooperation between the two catabolic pathways, the interactions are not straightforward. Therefore, it needs to be emphasized that a lack of involvement of the proteasome in tau clearance cannot be inferred by the finding that proteasome inhibition results in increased tau clearance, similar to what is seen following treatment with agents that increase autophagy (Kruger et al., 2012; Lei et al., 2014). These findings provide evidence that normal tau can be degraded by autophagy, and that if proteasome activity is impaired, autophagy is upregulated in a compensatory manner. However, it is still highly likely that the proteasome contributes to the clearance of tau under normal conditions, and this could occur independent of ubiquitylation (Lee et al., 2013). However, if tau is oligomerized or aggregated, it is likely that it is mostly cleared through autophagy (Wong et al., 2008) as the process of proteasome-mediated degradation is not optimal for multimeric protein complexes, and protein aggregates have been reported to inhibit proteasome function (Bence et al., 2001).

Of interest is the fact that ubiquitylation of substrates can result in targeting to both pathways. As discussed earlier, Lys48 linkages are the most common linkages in a polyubiquitin chain that results in targeting of a client protein to the proteasome (Nathan et al., 2013). Interestingly, although purified 26S proteasomes can degrade ubiquitylated substrates with Lys63 linkages, within the living cell substrates with Lys63 polyubiquitin chains are invariably targeted to the ALP. This was due in part to ESCRT0 (endosomal sorting complex required for transport) associating with Lys63-ubiquitylated proteins and preventing their association with the proteasome (Nathan et al., 2013). Transfection of HEK cells with tau and ubiquitin Lys48 or Lys63 mutants demonstrated that in the presence of the E3 ligase CHIP, tau could be ubiquitylated through both Lys48 and Lys63 linkages (Petrucelli et al., 2004). Thus if ubiquitin is the signal for targeting to degradation, tau would have the potential to be cleared either through the proteasome or by autophagy, although the physical structure of the ubiquitin chain is unlikely to be a sufficient signal for the selective targeting of tau to either degradative pathway. Indeed, the involvement of chaperones, cochaperones, and adaptor proteins probably contribute significantly to the targeting of tau to the different pathways. As discussed previously, these auxiliary proteins can direct tau to either the proteasome or autophagy, depending on the context. For instance, p62 binds ubiquitylated substrates, and data suggest that it can facilitate targeting of tau to the proteasome (Babu et al., 2005), as well as to autophagy (Ozcelik et al., 2013; Schaeffer et al., 2012). In the case of autophagy, p62 has been shown to bind both ubiquitylated substrates and LC3-II, resulting in targeting of the client to the ALP for degradation (Pankiv et al., 2007). Whether p62 facilitates the targeting of tau to degradation by the proteasome or autophagy is likely to depend on the presence of other proteins such as Hsps and cochaperones such as BAG3 (Dickey et al., 2006a; Lei et al., 2014; Ulbricht et al., 2013), as well as the state of tau (phosphorylated, acetylated, oligomeric, etc.).

For example, the preferential degradation of specific phospho-forms of tau by a particular pathway has been reported. In CHO cells transfected with P301L mutant tau, treatment with the Hsp90 inhibitor geldanamycin resulted in a proteasome-dependent reduction in tau phosphorylated at Ser/Thr-Pro sites. However, the levels of tau phosphorylated at KXGS sites within the repeat domain were not altered by geldanamycin (Dickey et al., 2006a). In contrast, inhibiting autophagy in primary rat cortical neurons with 3-MA resulted in the selective accumulation of tau phosphorylated at the KXGS motif Ser262 (12E8 epitope) (Dolan et al., 2011; Wang et al., 2009b). These findings suggest that both pathways cooperate to clear different tau species.

Since the evidence strongly suggests that tau is cleared by both the proteasome and autophagy, strategies that upregulate the functioning of either or both systems would likely have favorable effects in AD. The development of agents that increase the targeting of tau to degradation by either pathway, or facilitate the functioning of the different proteolytic systems, is ongoing. Currently, numerous different approaches are either in the early stages of development or in preclinical phases. Given the contribution of the UPS and ALP to tau clearance, combination treatment strategies that enhance the functioning of both pathways are likely to be more efficacious in ameliorating the progression of AD than just targeting one or the other system.

Acknowledgments

The work from the authors' laboratory was supported by NIH grants (GVWJ) and FONDECYT Grant #1140968 (RAQ). Acknowledgment is also made to the donors of the ADR, a program of BrightFocus Foundation for support of the research in the lab of GVW Johnson.

References

Abisambra J, Jinwal UK, Miyata Y, Rogers J, Blair L, Li X, Seguin SP, Wang L, Jin Y, Bacon J, Brady S, Cockman M, Guidi C, Zhang J, Koren J, Young ZT, Atkins CA, Zhang B, Lawson LY, Weeber EJ, Brodsky JL, Gestwicki JE, Dickey CA: Allosteric heat shock protein 70 inhibitors rapidly rescue synaptic plasticity deficits by reducing aberrant tau, *Biol Psychiatry* 74:367–374, 2013.

Abisambra JF, Jinwal UK, Jones JR, Blair LJ, Koren J 3rd, Dickey CA: Exploiting the diversity of the heat-shock protein family for primary and secondary tauopathy therapeutics, *Curr Neuropharmacol* 9:623–631, 2011.

Aiken CT, Kaake RM, Wang X, Huang L: Oxidative stress-mediated regulation of proteasome complexes, *Mol Cell Proteomics* 10, 2011, R110 006924.

Ambegaokar SS, Jackson GR: Functional genomic screen and network analysis reveal novel modifiers of tauopathy dissociated from tau phosphorylation, *Hum Mol Genet* 20:4947–4977, 2011.

Amm I, Sommer T, Wolf DH: Protein quality control and elimination of protein waste: the role of the ubiquitin-proteasome system, *Biochim Biophys Acta* 1843:182–196, 2014.

Ando K, Brion JP, Stygelbout V, Suain V, Authelet M, Dedecker R, Chanut A, Lacor P, Lavaur J, Sazdovitch V, Rogaeva E, Potier MC, Duyckaerts C: Clathrin adaptor CALM/PICALM is associated with neurofibrillary tangles and is cleaved in Alzheimer's brains, *Acta Neuropathol* 125:861–878, 2013.

Andorfer C, Kress Y, Espinoza M, De Silva R, Tucker KL, Barde YA, Duff K, Davies P: Hyperphosphorylation and aggregation of tau in mice expressing normal human tau isoforms, *J Neurochem* 86:582–590, 2003.

Arnold CS, Johnson GV, Cole RN, Dong DL, Lee M, Hart GW: The microtubule-associated protein tau is extensively modified with O-linked N-acetylglucosamine, *J Biol Chem* 271:28741–28744, 1996.

Avrahami L, Farfara D, Shaham-Kol M, Vassar R, Frenkel D, Eldar-Finkelman H: Inhibition of glycogen synthase kinase-3 ameliorates beta-amyloid pathology and restores lysosomal acidification and mammalian target of rapamycin activity in the Alzheimer disease mouse model: in vivo and in vitro studies, *J Biol Chem* 288:1295–1306, 2013.

Azoulay-Alfaguter I, Elya R, Avrahami L, Katz A, Eldar-Finkelman H: Combined regulation of mTORC1 and lysosomal acidification by GSK-3 suppresses autophagy and contributes to cancer cell growth, *Oncogene* 34:4613–4623, 2014.

Babu JR, Geetha T, Wooten MW: Sequestosome 1/p62 shuttles polyubiquitinated tau for proteasomal degradation, *J Neurochem* 94:192–203, 2005.

Baugh JM, Viktorova EG, Pilipenko EV: Proteasomes can degrade a significant proportion of cellular proteins independent of ubiquitination, *J Mol Biol* 386:814–827, 2009.

Bednarski E, Lynch G: Cytosolic proteolysis of tau by cathepsin D in hippocampus following suppression of cathepsins B and L, *J Neurochem* 67:1846–1855, 1996.

Behl C: BAG3 and friends: co-chaperones in selective autophagy during aging and disease, *Autophagy* 7:795–798, 2011.

Bence NF, Sampat RM, Kopito RR: Impairment of the ubiquitin-proteasome system by protein aggregation, *Science* 292:1552–1555, 2001.

Bendiske J, Bahr BA: Lysosomal activation is a compensatory response against protein accumulation and associated synaptopathogenesis—an approach for slowing Alzheimer disease? *J Neuropathol Exp Neurol* 62:451–463, 2003.

Ben-Nissan G, Sharon M: Regulating the 20S proteasome ubiquitin-independent degradation pathway, *Biomolecules* 4:862–884, 2014.

Bi X, Haque TS, Zhou J, Skillman AG, Lin B, Lee CE, Kuntz ID, Ellman JA, Lynch G: Novel cathepsin D inhibitors block the formation of hyperphosphorylated tau fragments in hippocampus, *J Neurochem* 74:1469–1477, 2000.

Bi X, Zhou J, Lynch G: Lysosomal protease inhibitors induce meganeurites and tangle-like structures in entorhino-hippocampal regions vulnerable to Alzheimer's disease, *Exp Neurol* 158:312–327, 1999.

Blair LJ, Sabbagh JJ, Dickey CA: Targeting Hsp90 and its co-chaperones to treat Alzheimer's disease, *Expert Opin Ther Targets* 18:1219–1232, 2014.

Boland B, Kumar A, Lee S, Platt FM, Wegiel J, Yu WH, Nixon RA: Autophagy induction and autophagosome clearance in neurons: relationship to autophagic pathology in Alzheimer's disease, *J Neurosci* 28:6926–6937, 2008.

Boutajangout A, Ingadottir J, Davies P, Sigurdsson EM: Passive immunization targeting pathological phospho-tau protein in a mouse model reduces functional decline and clears tau aggregates from the brain, *J Neurochem* 118:658–667, 2011.

Boyle KB, Randow F: The role of "eat-me" signals and autophagy cargo receptors in innate immunity, *Curr Opin Microbiol* 16:339–348, 2013.

Braak H, Braak E: Neuropathological stageing of Alzheimer-related changes, *Acta Neuropathol* 82:239–259, 1991.

Brocchieri L, Conway de Macario E, Macario AJ: hsp70 genes in the human genome: conservation and differentiation patterns predict a wide array of overlapping and specialized functions, *BMC Evol Biol* 8:19, 2008.

Caccamo A, Magri A, Medina DX, Wisely EV, Lopez-Aranda MF, Silva AJ, Oddo S: mTOR regulates tau phosphorylation and degradation: implications for Alzheimer's disease and other tauopathies, *Aging Cell* 12:370–380, 2013.

Caccamo A, Majumder S, Richardson A, Strong R, Oddo S: Molecular interplay between mammalian target of rapamycin (mTOR), amyloid-beta, and tau: effects on cognitive impairments, *J Biol Chem* 285:13107–13120, 2010.

Caccamo A, Oddo S, Tran LX, Laferla FM: Lithium reduces tau phosphorylation but not A beta or working memory deficits in a transgenic model with both plaques and tangles, *Am J Pathol* 170:1669–1675, 2007.

Carra S, Seguin SJ, Landry J: HspB8 and Bag3: a new chaperone complex targeting misfolded proteins to macroautophagy, *Autophagy* 4:237–239, 2008.

Carrettiero DC, Hernandez I, Neveu P, Papagiannakopoulos T, Kosik KS: The cochaperone BAG2 sweeps paired helical filament-insoluble tau from the microtubule, *J Neurosci* 29:2151–2161, 2009.

Choi J, Levey AI, Weintraub ST, Rees HD, Gearing M, Chin LS, Li L: Oxidative modifications and down-regulation of ubiquitin carboxyl-terminal hydrolase L1 associated with idiopathic Parkinson's and Alzheimer's diseases, *J Biol Chem* 279:13256–13264, 2004.

Cohen TJ, Guo JL, Hurtado DE, Kwong LK, Mills IP, Trojanowski JQ, Lee VM: The acetylation of tau inhibits its function and promotes pathological tau aggregation, *Nat Commun* 2:252, 2011.

Congdon EE, Wu JW, Myeku N, Figueroa YH, Herman M, Marinec PS, Gestwicki JE, Dickey CA, Yu WH, Duff KE: Methylthioninium chloride (methylene blue) induces autophagy and attenuates tauopathy in vitro and in vivo, *Autophagy* 8:609–622, 2012.

Cook C, Carlomagno Y, Gendron TF, Dunmore J, Scheffel K, Stetler C, Davis M, Dickson D, Jarpe M, Deture M, Petrucelli L: Acetylation of the KXGS motifs in tau is a critical determinant in modulation of tau aggregation and clearance, *Hum Mol Genet* 23:104–116, 2014.

Cook C, Gendron TF, Scheffel K, Carlomagno Y, Dunmore J, Deture M, Petrucelli L: Loss of HDAC6, a novel CHIP substrate, alleviates abnormal tau accumulation, *Hum Mol Genet* 21:2936–2945, 2012.

Crippa V, Carra S, Rusmini P, Sau D, Bolzoni E, Bendotti C, De Biasi S, Poletti A: A role of small heat shock protein B8 (HspB8) in the autophagic removal of misfolded proteins responsible for neurodegenerative diseases, *Autophagy* 6:958–960, 2010.

Cripps D, Thomas SN, Jeng Y, Yang F, Davies P, Yang AJ: Alzheimer disease-specific conformation of hyperphosphorylated paired helical filament-tau is polyubiquitinated through Lys-48, Lys-11, and Lys-6 ubiquitin conjugation, *J Biol Chem* 281:10825–10838, 2006.

David DC, Layfield R, Serpell L, Narain Y, Goedert M, Spillantini MG: Proteasomal degradation of tau protein, *J Neurochem* 83:176–185, 2002.

Dennissen FJ, Kholod N, Steinbusch HW, Van Leeuwen FW: Misframed proteins and neurodegeneration: a novel view on Alzheimer's and Parkinson's diseases, *Neurodegener Dis* 7:76–79, 2010.

Dickey CA, Dunmore J, Lu B, Wang JW, Lee WC, Kamal A, Burrows F, Eckman C, Hutton M, Petrucelli L: HSP induction mediates selective clearance of tau phosphorylated at proline-directed Ser/Thr sites but not KXGS (MARK) sites, *FASEB J* 20:753–755, 2006a.

Dickey CA, Kamal A, Lundgren K, Klosak N, Bailey RM, Dunmore J, Ash P, Shoraka S, Zlatkovic J, Eckman CB, Patterson C, Dickson DW, Nahman NS Jr, Hutton M, Burrows F, Petrucelli L: The high-affinity HSP90-CHIP complex recognizes and selectively degrades phosphorylated tau client proteins, *J Clin Invest* 117:648–658, 2007.

Dickey CA, Yue M, Lin WL, Dickson DW, Dunmore JH, Lee WC, Zehr C, West G, Cao S, Clark AM, Caldwell GA, Caldwell KA, Eckman C, Patterson C, Hutton M, Petrucelli L: Deletion of the ubiquitin ligase CHIP leads to the accumulation, but not the aggregation, of both endogenous phospho- and caspase-3-cleaved tau species, *J Neurosci* 26:6985–6996, 2006b.

Dolan PJ, Jin YN, Hwang W, Johnson GV: Decreases in valosin-containing protein result in increased levels of tau phosphorylated at Ser262/356, *FEBS Lett* 585:3424–3429, 2011.

Dunlop RA, Brunk UT, Rodgers KJ: Oxidized proteins: mechanisms of removal and consequences of accumulation, *IUBMB Life* 61:522–527, 2009.

Duyckaerts C, Bennecib M, Grignon Y, Uchihara T, He Y, Piette F, Hauw JJ: Modeling the relation between neurofibrillary tangles and intellectual status, *Neurobiol Aging* 18:267–273, 1997.

Ferrer I, Santpere G, Van Leeuwen FW: Argyrophilic grain disease, *Brain* 131:1416–1432, 2008.

Fischer DF, Van Dijk R, Van Tijn P, Hobo B, Verhage MC, Van Der Schors RC, Li KW, Van Minnen J, Hol EM, Van Leeuwen FW: Long-term proteasome dysfunction in the mouse brain by expression of aberrant ubiquitin, *Neurobiol Aging* 30:847–863, 2009.

Forlenza OV, Diniz BS, Radanovic M, Santos FS, Talib LL, Gattaz WF: Disease-modifying properties of long-term lithium treatment for amnestic mild cognitive impairment: randomised controlled trial, *Br J Psychiatry* 198:351–356, 2011.

Frederick C, Ando K, Leroy K, Heraud C, Suain V, Buee L, Brion JP: Rapamycin ester analog CCI-779/temsirolimus alleviates tau pathology and improves motor deficit in mutant tau transgenic mice, *J Alzheimers Dis* 44:1145–1156, 2015.

Gal J, Strom AL, Kwinter DM, Kilty R, Zhang J, Shi P, Fu W, Wooten MW, Zhu H: Sequestosome 1/p62 links familial ALS mutant SOD1 to LC3 via an ubiquitin-independent mechanism, *J Neurochem* 111:1062–1073, 2009.

Gamblin TC, Chen F, Zambrano A, Abraha A, Lagalwar S, Guillozet AL, Lu M, Fu Y, Garcia-Sierra F, Lapointe N, Miller R, Berry RW, Binder LI, Cryns VL: Caspase cleavage of tau: linking amyloid and neurofibrillary tangles in Alzheimer's disease, *Proc Natl Acad Sci USA* 100:10032–10037, 2003.

Geetha T, Seibenhener ML, Chen L, Madura K, Wooten MW: p62 serves as a shuttling factor for TrkA interaction with the proteasome, *Biochem Biophys Res Commun* 374:33–37, 2008.

Gibbings D, Mostowy S, Jay F, Schwab Y, Cossart P, Voinnet O: Selective autophagy degrades DICER and AGO2 and regulates miRNA activity, *Nat Cell Biol* 14:1314–1321, 2012.

Gillardon F, Kloss A, Berg M, Neumann M, Mechtler K, Hengerer B, Dahlmann B: The 20S proteasome isolated from Alzheimer's disease brain shows post-translational modifications but unchanged proteolytic activity, *J Neurochem* 101:1483–1490, 2007.

Gotz J, Xia D, Leinenga G, Chew YL, Nicholas H: What renders tau toxic, *Front Neurol* 4:72, 2013.

Grune T, Botzen D, Engels M, Voss P, Kaiser B, Jung T, Grimm S, Ermak G, Davies KJ: Tau protein degradation is catalyzed by the ATP/ubiquitin-independent 20S proteasome under normal cell conditions, *Arch Biochem Biophys* 500:181–188, 2010.

Gu J, Congdon EE, Sigurdsson EM: Two novel tau antibodies targeting the 396/404 region are primarily taken up by neurons and reduce tau protein pathology, *J Biol Chem* 288:33081–33095, 2013.

Hamano T, Gendron TF, Causevic E, Yen SH, Lin WL, Isidoro C, Deture M, Ko LW: Autophagic-lysosomal perturbation enhances tau aggregation in transfectants with induced wild-type tau expression, *Eur J Neurosci* 27:1119–1130, 2008.

Hampel H, Ewers M, Burger K, Annas P, Mortberg A, Bogstedt A, Frolich L, Schroder J, Schonknecht P, Riepe MW, Kraft I, Gasser T, Leyhe T, Moller HJ, Kurz A, Basun H: Lithium trial in Alzheimer's disease: a randomized, single-blind, placebo-controlled, multicenter 10-week study, *J Clin Psychiatry* 70:922–931, 2009.

Han DH, Na HK, Choi WH, Lee JH, Kim YK, Won C, Lee SH, Kim KP, Kuret J, Min DH, Lee MJ: Direct cellular delivery of human proteasomes to delay tau aggregation, *Nat Commun* 5:5633, 2014.

Harold D, Abraham R, Hollingworth P, Sims R, Gerrish A, Hamshere ML, Pahwa JS, Moskvina V, Dowzell K, Williams A, Jones N, Thomas C, Stretton A, Morgan AR, Lovestone S, Powell J, Proitsi P, Lupton MK, Brayne C, Rubinsztein DC, Gill M, Lawlor B, Lynch A, Morgan K, Brown KS, Passmore PA, Craig D, McGuinness B, Todd S, Holmes C, Mann D, Smith AD, Love S, Kehoe PG, Hardy J, Mead S, Fox N, Rossor M, Collinge J, Maier W, Jessen F, Schurmann B, Heun R, Van Den Bussche H, Heuser I, Kornhuber J, Wiltfang J, Dichgans M, Frolich L, Hampel H, Hull M, Rujescu D, Goate AM, Kauwe JS, Cruchaga C, Nowotny P, Morris JC, Mayo K, Sleegers K, Bettens K, Engelborghs S, De Deyn PP, Van Broeckhoven C, Livingston G, Bass NJ, Gurling H, McQuillin A, Gwilliam R, Deloukas P, Al-Chalabi A, Shaw CE, Tsolaki M, Singleton AB, Guerreiro R, Muhleisen TW, Nothen MM, Moebus S, Jockel KH, Klopp N, Wichmann HE, Carrasquillo MM, Pankratz VS, Younkin SG, Holmans PA, O'Donovan M, Owen MJ, Williams J: Genome-wide association study identifies variants at CLU and PICALM associated with Alzheimer's disease, *Nat Genet* 41:1088–1093, 2009.

Hegde AN, Upadhya SC: Role of ubiquitin-proteasome-mediated proteolysis in nervous system disease, *Biochim Biophys Acta* 1809:128–140, 2011.

Ho SW, Tsui YT, Wong TT, Cheung SK, Goggins WB, Yi LM, Cheng KK, Baum L: Effects of 17-allylamino-17-demethoxygeldanamycin (17-AAG) in transgenic mouse models of frontotemporal lobar degeneration and Alzheimer's disease, *Transl Neurodegener* 2:24, 2013.

Inoue K, Rispoli J, Kaphzan H, Klann E, Chen EI, Kim J, Komatsu M, Abeliovich A: Macroautophagy deficiency mediates age-dependent neurodegeneration through a phospho-tau pathway, *Mol Neurodegener* 7:48, 2012.

Jaeger PA, Pickford F, Sun CH, Lucin KM, Masliah E, Wyss-Coray T: Regulation of amyloid precursor protein processing by the Beclin 1 complex, *PLoS One* 5:e11102, 2010.

Jaeger PA, Wyss-Coray T: Beclin 1 complex in autophagy and Alzheimer disease, *Arch Neurol* 67:1181–1184, 2010.

Jiang T, Yu JT, Zhu XC, Zhang QQ, Cao L, Wang HF, Tan MS, Gao Q, Qin H, Zhang YD, Tan L: Temsirolimus attenuates tauopathy in vitro and in vivo by targeting tau hyperphosphorylation and autophagic clearance, *Neuropharmacology* 85:121–130, 2014.

Jin YN, Chen PC, Watson JA, Walters BJ, Phillips SE, Green K, Schmidt R, Wilson JA, Johnson GV, Roberson ED, Dobrunz LE, Wilson SM: Usp14 deficiency increases tau phosphorylation without altering tau degradation or causing tau-dependent deficits, *PLoS One* 7:e47884, 2012.

Jinwal UK, Akoury E, Abisambra JF, O'Leary JC 3rd, Thompson AD, Blair LJ, Jin Y, Bacon J, Nordhues BA, Cockman M, Zhang J, Li P, Zhang B, Borysov S, Uversky VN, Biernat J, Mandelkow E, Gestwicki JE, Zweckstetter M, Dickey CA: Imbalance of Hsp70 family variants fosters tau accumulation, *FASEB J* 27:1450–1459, 2013.

Jinwal UK, Koren J, O'Leary JC, Jones JR, Abisambra JF, Dickey CA: Hsp70 ATPase modulators as therapeutics for Alzheimer's and other neurodegenerative diseases, *Mol Cell Pharmacol* 2:43–46, 2010.

Jinwal UK, Miyata Y, Koren J 3rd, Jones JR, Trotter JH, Chang L, O'Leary J, Morgan D, Lee DC, Shults CL, Rousaki A, Weeber EJ, Zuiderweg ER, Gestwicki JE, Dickey CA: Chemical manipulation of hsp70 ATPase activity regulates tau stability, *J Neurosci* 29:12079–12088, 2009.

Jo C, Gundemir S, Pritchard S, Jin YN, Rahman I, Johnson GV: Nrf2 reduces levels of phosphorylated tau protein by inducing autophagy adaptor protein NDP52, *Nat Commun* 5:3496, 2014a.

Jo C, Kim S, Cho SJ, Choi KJ, Yun SM, Koh YH, Johnson GV, Park SI: Sulforaphane induces autophagy through ERK activation in neuronal cells, *FEBS Lett* 588:3081–3088, 2014b.

Johansen T, Lamark T: Selective autophagy mediated by autophagic adapter proteins, *Autophagy* 7:279–296, 2011.

Jope RS, Nemeroff CB: The ups and downs of bipolar disorder research, *Biol Psychiatry* 73:597–599, 2013.

Jun G, Naj AC, Beecham GW, Wang LS, Buros J, Gallins PJ, Buxbaum JD, Ertekin-Taner N, Fallin MD, Friedland R, Inzelberg R, Kramer P, Rogaeva E, St George-Hyslop P, Alzheimer's Disease Genetics Consortium, Cantwell LB, Dombroski BA, Saykin AJ, Reiman EM, Bennett DA, Morris JC, Lunetta KL, Martin ER, Montine TJ, Goate AM,

Blacker D, Tsuang DW, Beekly D, Cupples LA, Hakonarson H, Kukull W, Foroud TM, Haines J, Mayeux R, Farrer LA, Pericak-Vance MA, Schellenberg GD: Meta-analysis confirms CR1, CLU, and PICALM as Alzheimer disease risk loci and reveals interactions with APOE genotypes, *Arch Neurol* 67:1473–1484, 2010.

Kabuta T, Setsuie R, Mitsui T, Kinugawa A, Sakurai M, Aoki S, Uchida K, Wada K: Aberrant molecular properties shared by familial Parkinson's disease-associated mutant UCH-L1 and carbonyl-modified UCH-L1, *Hum Mol Genet* 17:1482–1496, 2008.

Kampinga HH, Craig EA: The HSP70 chaperone machinery: J proteins as drivers of functional specificity, *Nat Rev Mol Cell Biol* 11:579–592, 2010.

Kaushik S, Cuervo AM: Chaperone-mediated autophagy: a unique way to enter the lysosome world, *Trends Cell Biol* 22:407–417, 2012.

Keck S, Nitsch R, Grune T, Ullrich O: Proteasome inhibition by paired helical filament-tau in brains of patients with Alzheimer's disease, *J Neurochem* 85:115–122, 2003.

Keller JN, Hanni KB, Markesbery WR: Impaired proteasome function in Alzheimer's disease, *J Neurochem* 75:436–439, 2000.

Khurana V, Elson-Schwab I, Fulga TA, Sharp KA, Loewen CA, Mulkearns E, Tyynela J, Scherzer CR, Feany MB: Lysosomal dysfunction promotes cleavage and neurotoxicity of tau in vivo, *PLoS Genet* 6:e1001026, 2010.

Kim YE, Hipp MS, Bracher A, Hayer-Hartl M, Hartl FU: Molecular chaperone functions in protein folding and proteostasis, *Annu Rev Biochem* 82:323–355, 2013.

Klein PS, Melton DA: A molecular mechanism for the effect of lithium on development, *Proc Natl Acad Sci USA* 93:8455–8459, 1996.

Klionsky DJ: Autophagy: from phenomenology to molecular understanding in less than a decade, *Nat Rev Mol Cell Biol* 8:931–937, 2007.

Kopeikina KJ, Hyman BT, Spires-Jones TL: Soluble forms of tau are toxic in Alzheimer's disease, *Transl Neurosci* 3:223–233, 2012.

Korac J, Schaeffer V, Kovacevic I, Clement AM, Jungblut B, Behl C, Terzic J, Dikic I: Ubiquitin-independent function of optineurin in autophagic clearance of protein aggregates, *J Cell Sci* 126:580–592, 2013.

Korolchuk VI, Mansilla A, Menzies FM, Rubinsztein DC: Autophagy inhibition compromises degradation of ubiquitin-proteasome pathway substrates, *Mol Cell* 33:517–527, 2009.

Korolchuk VI, Menzies FM, Rubinsztein DC: Mechanisms of cross-talk between the ubiquitin–proteasome and autophagy–lysosome systems, *FEBS Lett* 584:1393–1398, 2010.

Kravtsova-Ivantsiv Y, Ciechanover A: Non-canonical ubiquitin-based signals for proteasomal degradation, *J Cell Sci* 125:539–548, 2012.

Kruger U, Wang Y, Kumar S, Mandelkow EM: Autophagic degradation of tau in primary neurons and its enhancement by trehalose, *Neurobiol Aging* 33:2291–2305, 2012.

Lasagna-Reeves CA, Castillo-Carranza DL, Sengupta U, Sarmiento J, Troncoso J, Jackson GR, Kayed R: Identification of oligomers at early stages of tau aggregation in Alzheimer's disease, *FASEB J* 26:1946–1959, 2012.

Layfield R, Cavey JR, Lowe J: Role of ubiquitin-mediated proteolysis in the pathogenesis of neurodegenerative disorders, *Ageing Res Rev* 2:343–356, 2003.

Lee BH, Lee MJ, Park S, Oh DC, Elsasser S, Chen PC, Gartner C, Dimova N, Hanna J, Gygi SP, Wilson SM, King RW, Finley D: Enhancement of proteasome activity by a small-molecule inhibitor of USP14, *Nature* 467:179–184, 2010a.

Lee JH, Yu WH, Kumar A, Lee S, Mohan PS, Peterhoff CM, Wolfe DM, Martinez-Vicente M, Massey AC, Sovak G, Uchiyama Y, Westaway D, Cuervo AM, Nixon RA: Lysosomal proteolysis and autophagy require presenilin 1 and are disrupted by Alzheimer-related PS1 mutations, *Cell* 141:1146–1158, 2010b.

Lee JY, Koga H, Kawaguchi Y, Tang W, Wong E, Gao YS, Pandey UB, Kaushik S, Tresse E, Lu J, Taylor JP, Cuervo AM, Yao TP: HDAC6 controls autophagosome maturation essential for ubiquitin-selective quality-control autophagy, *EMBO J* 29:969–980, 2010c.

Lee MJ, Lee JH, Rubinsztein DC: Tau degradation: the ubiquitin–proteasome system versus the autophagy–lysosome system, *Prog Neurobiol* 105:49–59, 2013.

Lei Z, Brizzee C, Johnson GV: BAG3 facilitates the clearance of endogenous tau in primary neurons, *Neurobiol Aging* 36:241–248, 2014.

Leroy K, Ando K, Heraud C, Yilmaz Z, Authelet M, Boeynaems JM, Buee L, De Decker R, Brion JP: Lithium treatment arrests the development of neurofibrillary tangles in mutant tau transgenic mice with advanced neurofibrillary pathology, *J Alzheimers Dis* 19:705–719, 2010.

Lewis J, McGowan E, Rockwood J, Melrose H, Nacharaju P, Van Slegtenhorst M, Gwinn-Hardy K, Paul Murphy M, Baker M, Yu X, Duff K, Hardy J, Corral A, Lin WL, Yen SH, Dickson DW, Davies P, Hutton M: Neurofibrillary tangles, amyotrophy and progressive motor disturbance in mice expressing mutant (P301L) tau protein, *Nat Genet* 25:402–405, 2000.

Lindsten K, De Vrij FM, Verhoef LG, Fischer DF, Van Leeuwen FW, Hol EM, Masucci MG, Dantuma NP: Mutant ubiquitin found in neurodegenerative disorders is a ubiquitin fusion degradation substrate that blocks proteasomal degradation, *J Cell Biol* 157:417–427, 2002.

Liu CW, Li X, Thompson D, Wooding K, Chang TL, Tang Z, Yu H, Thomas PJ, Demartino GN: ATP binding and ATP hydrolysis play distinct roles in the function of 26S proteasome, *Mol Cell* 24:39–50, 2006.

Liu D, Pitta M, Jiang H, Lee JH, Zhang G, Chen X, Kawamoto EM, Mattson MP: Nicotinamide forestalls pathology and cognitive decline in Alzheimer mice: evidence for improved neuronal bioenergetics and autophagy procession, *Neurobiol Aging* 34:1564–1580, 2013.

Malhi GS, Tanious M, Das P, Coulston CM, Berk M: Potential mechanisms of action of lithium in bipolar disorder: current understanding, *CNS Drugs* 27:135–153, 2013.

Min SW, Cho SH, Zhou Y, Schroeder S, Haroutunian V, Seeley WW, Huang EJ, Shen Y, Masliah E, Mukherjee C, Meyers D, Cole PA, Ott M, Gan L: Acetylation of tau inhibits its degradation and contributes to tauopathy, *Neuron* 67:953–966, 2010.

Miyata Y, Li X, Lee HF, Jinwal UK, Srinivasan SR, Seguin SP, Young ZT, Brodsky JL, Dickey CA, Sun D, Gestwicki JE: Synthesis and initial evaluation of YM-08, a blood–brain barrier permeable derivative of the heat shock protein 70 (Hsp70) inhibitor MKT-077, which reduces tau levels, *ACS Chem Neurosci* 4:930–939, 2013.

Morawe T, Hiebel C, Kern A, Behl C: Protein homeostasis, aging and Alzheimer's disease, *Mol Neurobiol* 46:41–54, 2012.

Moreau K, Fleming A, Imarisio S, Lopez Ramirez A, Mercer JL, Jimenez-Sanchez M, Bento CF, Puri C, Zavodszky E, Siddiqi F, Lavau CP, Betton M, O'Kane CJ, Wechsler DS, Rubinsztein DC: PICALM modulates autophagy activity and tau accumulation, *Nat Commun* 5:4998, 2014.

Mori H, Kondo J, Ihara Y: Ubiquitin is a component of paired helical filaments in Alzheimer's disease, *Science* 235:1641–1644, 1987.

Morishima-Kawashima M, Hasegawa M, Takio K, Suzuki M, Titani K, Ihara Y: Ubiquitin is conjugated with amino-terminally processed tau in paired helical filaments, *Neuron* 10:1151–1160, 1993.

Motoi Y, Shimada K, Ishiguro K, Hattori N: Lithium and autophagy, *ACS Chem Neurosci* 5:434–442, 2014.

Murray ME, Lowe VJ, Graff-Radford NR, Liesinger AM, Cannon A, Przybelski SA, Rawal B, Parisi JE, Petersen RC, Kantarci K, Ross OA, Duara R, Knopman DS, Jack CR Jr, Dickson DW: Clinicopathologic and 11C-Pittsburgh compound B implications of Thal amyloid phase across the Alzheimer's disease spectrum, *Brain* 138:1370–1381, 2015.

Nathan JA, Kim HT, Ting L, Gygi SP, Goldberg AL: Why do cellular proteins linked to K63-polyubiquitin chains not associate with proteasomes? *EMBO J* 32:552–565, 2013.

Nixon RA: The role of autophagy in neurodegenerative disease, *Nat Med* 19:983–997, 2013.

Nixon RA, Wegiel J, Kumar A, Yu WH, Peterhoff C, Cataldo A, Cuervo AM: Extensive involvement of autophagy in Alzheimer disease: an immuno-electron microscopy study, *J Neuropathol Exp Neurol* 64:113–122, 2005.

Nixon RA, Yang DS: Autophagy failure in Alzheimer's disease—locating the primary defect, *Neurobiol Dis* 43:38–45, 2011.

Oakley H, Cole SL, Logan S, Maus E, Shao P, Craft J, Guillozet-Bongaarts A, Ohno M, Disterhoft J, Van Eldik L, Berry R, Vassar R: Intraneuronal beta-amyloid aggregates, neurodegeneration, and neuron loss in transgenic mice with five familial Alzheimer's disease mutations: potential factors in amyloid plaque formation, *J Neurosci* 26:10129–10140, 2006.

Oddo S: The ubiquitin-proteasome system in Alzheimer's disease, *J Cell Mol Med* 12:363–373, 2008.

Oddo S, Caccamo A, Shepherd JD, Murphy MP, Golde TE, Kayed R, Metherate R, Mattson MP, Akbari Y, Laferla FM: Triple-transgenic model of Alzheimer's disease with plaques and tangles: intracellular Abeta and synaptic dysfunction, *Neuron* 39:409–421, 2003.

Ozcelik S, Fraser G, Castets P, Schaeffer V, Skachokova Z, Breu K, Clavaguera F, Sinnreich M, Kappos L, Goedert M, Tolnay M, Winkler DT: Rapamycin attenuates the progression of tau pathology in P301S tau transgenic mice, *PLoS One* 8:e62459, 2013.

Pandey UB, Nie Z, Batlevi Y, McCray BA, Ritson GP, Nedelsky NB, Schwartz SL, Diprospero NA, Knight MA, Schuldiner O, Padmanabhan R, Hild M, Berry DL, Garza D, Hubbert CC, Yao TP, Baehrecke EH, Taylor JP: HDAC6 rescues neurodegeneration and provides an essential link between autophagy and the UPS, *Nature* 447:859–863, 2007.

Pankiv S, Clausen TH, Lamark T, Brech A, Bruun JA, Outzen H, Overvatn A, Bjorkoy G, Johansen T: p62/SQSTM1 binds directly to Atg8/LC3 to facilitate degradation of ubiquitinated protein aggregates by autophagy, *J Biol Chem* 282:24131–24145, 2007.

Peric A, Annaert W: Early etiology of Alzheimer's disease: tipping the balance toward autophagy or endosomal dysfunction? *Acta Neuropathol* 129:363–381, 2015.

Perry G, Friedman R, Shaw G, Chau V: Ubiquitin is detected in neurofibrillary tangles and senile plaque neurites of Alzheimer disease brains, *Proc Natl Acad Sci USA* 84:3033–3036, 1987.

Petrucelli L, Dickson D, Kehoe K, Taylor J, Snyder H, Grover A, De Lucia M, McGowan E, Lewis J, Prihar G, Kim J, Dillmann WH, Browne SE, Hall A, Voellmy R, Tsuboi Y, Dawson TM, Wolozin B, Hardy J, Hutton M: CHIP and Hsp70 regulate tau ubiquitination, degradation and aggregation, *Hum Mol Genet* 13:703–714, 2004.

Pickford F, Masliah E, Britschgi M, Lucin K, Narasimhan R, Jaeger PA, Small S, Spencer B, Rockenstein E, Levine B, Wyss-Coray T: The autophagy-related protein Beclin 1 shows reduced expression in early Alzheimer disease and regulates amyloid beta accumulation in mice, *J Clin Invest* 118:2190–2199, 2008.

Polito VA, Li H, Martini-Stoica H, Wang B, Yang L, Xu Y, Swartzlander DB, Palmieri M, Di Ronza A, Lee VM, Sardiello M, Ballabio A, Zheng H: Selective clearance of aberrant tau proteins and rescue of neurotoxicity by transcription factor EB, *EMBO Mol Med* 6:1142–1160, 2014.

Reyes-Turcu FE, Ventii KH, Wilkinson KD: Regulation and cellular roles of ubiquitin-specific deubiquitinating enzymes, *Annu Rev Biochem* 78:363–397, 2009.

Reynolds MR, Berry RW, Binder LI: Nitration in neurodegeneration: deciphering the "Hows" "nYs", *Biochemistry* 46:7325–7336, 2007.

Riederer BM, Leuba G, Vernay A, Riederer IM: The role of the ubiquitin proteasome system in Alzheimer's disease, *Exp Biol Med* 236:268–276, 2011.

Rodriguez-Navarro JA, Rodriguez L, Casarejos MJ, Solano RM, Gomez A, Perucho J, Cuervo AM, Garcia De Yebenes J, Mena MA: Trehalose ameliorates dopaminergic and tau pathology in parkin deleted/tau overexpressing mice through autophagy activation, *Neurobiol Dis* 39:423–438, 2010.

Rousaki A, Miyata Y, Jinwal UK, Dickey CA, Gestwicki JE, Zuiderweg ER: Allosteric drugs: the interaction of antitumor compound MKT-077 with human Hsp70 chaperones, *J Mol Biol* 411:614–632, 2011.

Sadoul K, Boyault C, Pabion M, Khochbin S: Regulation of protein turnover by acetyltransferases and deacetylases, *Biochimie* 90:306–312, 2008.

Sahu R, Kaushik S, Clement CC, Cannizzo ES, Scharf B, Follenzi A, Potolicchio I, Nieves E, Cuervo AM, Santambrogio L: Microautophagy of cytosolic proteins by late endosomes, *Dev Cell* 20:131–139, 2011.

Sanchez-Varo R, Trujillo-Estrada L, Sanchez-Mejias E, Torres M, Baglietto-Vargas D, Moreno-Gonzalez I, De Castro V, Jimenez S, Ruano D, Vizuete M, Davila JC, Garcia-Verdugo JM, Jimenez AJ, Vitorica J, Gutierrez A: Abnormal accumulation of autophagic vesicles correlates with axonal and synaptic pathology in young Alzheimer's mice hippocampus, *Acta Neuropathol* 123:53–70, 2012.

Santacruz K, Lewis J, Spires T, Paulson J, Kotilinek L, Ingelsson M, Guimaraes A, Deture M, Ramsden M, Mcgowan E, Forster C, Yue M, Orne J, Janus C, Mariash A, Kuskowski M, Hyman B, Hutton M, Ashe KH: Tau suppression in a neurodegenerative mouse model improves memory function, *Science* 309:476–481, 2005.

Sarkar S: Regulation of autophagy by mTOR-dependent and mTOR-independent pathways: autophagy dysfunction in neurodegenerative diseases and therapeutic application of autophagy enhancers, *Biochem Soc Trans* 41:1103–1130, 2013.

Sarkar S, Davies JE, Huang Z, Tunnacliffe A, Rubinsztein DC: Trehalose, a novel mTOR-independent autophagy enhancer, accelerates the clearance of mutant huntingtin and alpha-synuclein, *J Biol Chem* 282:5641–5652, 2007.

Sarkar S, Floto RA, Berger Z, Imarisio S, Cordenier A, Pasco M, Cook LJ, Rubinsztein DC: Lithium induces autophagy by inhibiting inositol monophosphatase, *J Cell Biol* 170:1101–1111, 2005.

Savulescu AF, Glickman MH: Proteasome activator 200: the heat is on, *Mol Cell Proteomics* 10, 2011, R110 006890.

Schaeffer V, Goedert M: Stimulation of autophagy is neuroprotective in a mouse model of human tauopathy, *Autophagy* 8:1686–1687, 2012.

Schaeffer V, Lavenir I, Ozcelik S, Tolnay M, Winkler DT, Goedert M: Stimulation of autophagy reduces neurodegeneration in a mouse model of human tauopathy, *Brain* 135:2169–2177, 2012.

Schmidt M, Finley D: Regulation of proteasome activity in health and disease, *Biochim Biophys Acta* 1843:13–25, 2014.

Selenica ML, Benner L, Housley SB, Manchec B, Lee DC, Nash KR, Kalin J, Bergman JA, Kozikowski A, Gordon MN, Morgan D: Histone deacetylase 6 inhibition improves memory and reduces total tau levels in a mouse model of tau deposition, *Alzheimers Res Ther* 6:12, 2014.

Settembre C, Ballabio A: TFEB regulates autophagy: an integrated coordination of cellular degradation and recycling processes, *Autophagy* 7:1379–1381, 2011.

Settembre C, Di Malta C, Polito VA, Garcia Arencibia M, Vetrini F, Erdin S, Erdin SU, Huynh T, Medina D, Colella P, Sardiello M, Rubinsztein DC, Ballabio A: TFEB links autophagy to lysosomal biogenesis, *Science* 332:1429–1433, 2011.

Settembre C, Zoncu R, Medina DL, Vetrini F, Erdin S, Erdin S, Huynh T, Ferron M, Karsenty G, Vellard MC, Facchinetti V, Sabatini DM, Ballabio A: A lysosome-to-nucleus signalling mechanism senses and regulates the lysosome via mTOR and TFEB, *EMBO J* 31:1095–1108, 2012.

Shimada K, Motoi Y, Ishiguro K, Kambe T, Matsumoto SE, Itaya M, Kunichika M, Mori H, Shinohara A, Chiba M, Mizuno Y, Ueno T, Hattori N: Long-term oral lithium treatment attenuates motor disturbance in tauopathy model mice: implications of autophagy promotion, *Neurobiol Dis* 46:101–108, 2012.

Shimura H, Schwartz D, Gygi SP, Kosik KS: CHIP-Hsc70 complex ubiquitinates phosphorylated tau and enhances cell survival, *J Biol Chem* 279:4869–4876, 2004.

Stolz A, Ernst A, Dikic I: Cargo recognition and trafficking in selective autophagy, *Nat Cell Biol* 16:495–501, 2014.

Su V, Lau AF: Ubiquitin-like and ubiquitin-associated domain proteins: significance in proteasomal degradation, *Cell Mol Life Sci* 66:2819–2833, 2009.

Tai HC, Serrano-Pozo A, Hashimoto T, Frosch MP, Spires-Jones TL, Hyman BT: The synaptic accumulation of hyperphosphorylated tau oligomers in Alzheimer disease is associated with dysfunction of the ubiquitin-proteasome system, *Am J Pathol* 181:1426–1435, 2012.

Tan CC, Yu JT, Tan MS, Jiang T, Zhu XC, Tan L: Autophagy in aging and neurodegenerative diseases: implications for pathogenesis and therapy, *Neurobiol Aging* 35:941–957, 2014.

Tarozzi A, Angeloni C, Malaguti M, Morroni F, Hrelia S, Hrelia P: Sulforaphane as a potential protective phytochemical against neurodegenerative diseases, *Oxid Med Cell Longev* 2013:415078, 2013.

Tian Y, Chang JC, Fan EY, Flajolet M, Greengard P: Adaptor complex AP2/PICALM, through interaction with LC3, targets Alzheimer's APP-CTF for terminal degradation via autophagy, *Proc Natl Acad Sci USA* 110:17071–17076, 2013.

Tomasoni R, Mondino A: The tuberous sclerosis complex: balancing proliferation and survival, *Biochem Soc Trans* 39:466–471, 2011.

Tramutola A, Triplett JC, Di Domenico F, Niedowicz DM, Murphy MP, Coccia R, Perluigi M, Butterfield DA: Alteration of mTOR signaling occurs early in the progression of Alzheimer disease (AD): analysis of brain from subjects with pre-clinical AD, amnestic mild cognitive impairment and late-stage AD, *J Neurochem* 133:739–749, 2015.

Tumbarello DA, Kendrick-Jones J, Buss F: Myosin VI and its cargo adaptors—linking endocytosis and autophagy, *J Cell Sci* 126:2561–2570, 2013.

Ulbricht A, Eppler FJ, Tapia VE, Van Der Ven PF, Hampe N, Hersch N, Vakeel P, Stadel D, Haas A, Saftig P, Behrends C, Furst DO, Volkmer R, Hoffmann B, Kolanus W, Hohfeld J: Cellular mechanotransduction relies on tension-induced and chaperone-assisted autophagy, *Curr Biol* 23:430–435, 2013.

Vaden JH, Bhattacharyya BJ, Chen PC, Watson JA, Marshall AG, Phillips SE, Wilson JA, King GD, Miller RJ, Wilson SM: Ubiquitin-specific protease 14 regulates c-Jun N-terminal kinase signaling at the neuromuscular junction, *Mol Neurodegener* 10:3, 2015.

van Leeuwen FW, De Kleijn DP, Van Den Hurk HH, Neubauer A, Sonnemans MA, Sluijs JA, Koycu S, Ramdjielal RD, Salehi A, Martens GJ, Grosveld FG, Peter J, Burbach H, Hol EM: Frameshift mutants of beta amyloid precursor protein and ubiquitin-B in Alzheimer's and Down patients, *Science* 279:242–247, 1998.

Wang AM, Miyata Y, Klinedinst S, Peng HM, Chua JP, Komiyama T, Li X, Morishima Y, Merry DE, Pratt WB, Osawa Y, Collins CA, Gestwicki JE, Lieberman AP: Activation of Hsp70 reduces neurotoxicity by promoting polyglutamine protein degradation, *Nat Chem Biol* 9:112–118, 2013.

Wang J, Whiteman MW, Lian H, Wang G, Singh A, Huang D, Denmark T: A non-canonical MEK/ERK signaling pathway regulates autophagy via regulating Beclin 1, *J Biol Chem* 284:21412–21424, 2009a.

Wang Y, Martinez-Vicente M, Kruger U, Kaushik S, Wong E, Mandelkow EM, Cuervo AM, Mandelkow E: Tau fragmentation, aggregation and clearance: the dual role of lysosomal processing, *Hum Mol Genet* 18:4153–4170, 2009b.

Ward SM, Himmelstein DS, Lancia JK, Binder LI: Tau oligomers and tau toxicity in neurodegenerative disease, *Biochem Soc Trans* 40:667–671, 2012.

Watanabe Y, Tanaka M: p62/SQSTM1 in autophagic clearance of a non-ubiquitylated substrate, *J Cell Sci* 124:2692–2701, 2011.

Wong ES, Tan JM, Soong WE, Hussein K, Nukina N, Dawson VL, Dawson TM, Cuervo AM, Lim KL: Autophagy-mediated clearance of aggresomes is not a universal phenomenon, *Hum Mol Genet* 17:2570–2582, 2008.

Yang DS, Stavrides P, Mohan PS, Kaushik S, Kumar A, Ohno M, Schmidt SD, Wesson D, Bandyopadhyay U, Jiang Y, Pawlik M, Peterhoff CM, Yang AJ, Wilson DA, St George-Hyslop P, Westaway D, Mathews PM, Levy E, Cuervo AM, Nixon RA: Reversal of autophagy dysfunction in the TgCRND8 mouse model of Alzheimer's disease ameliorates amyloid pathologies and memory deficits, *Brain* 134:258–277, 2011a.

Yang DS, Stavrides P, Mohan PS, Kaushik S, Kumar A, Ohno M, Schmidt SD, Wesson DW, Bandyopadhyay U, Jiang Y, Pawlik M, Peterhoff CM, Yang AJ, Wilson DA, St George-Hyslop P, Westaway D, Mathews PM, Levy E, Cuervo AM, Nixon RA: Therapeutic effects of remediating autophagy failure in a mouse model of Alzheimer disease by enhancing lysosomal proteolysis, *Autophagy* 7:788–789, 2011b.

Zhang L, Liu C, Wu J, Tao JJ, Sui XL, Yao ZG, Xu YF, Huang L, Zhu H, Sheng SL, Qin C: Tubastatin A/ACY-1215 improves cognition in Alzheimer's disease transgenic mice, *J Alzheimers Dis* 41:1193–1205, 2014.

Zou J, Guo Y, Guettouche T, Smith DF, Voellmy R: Repression of heat shock transcription factor HSF1 activation by HSP90 (HSP90 complex) that forms a stress-sensitive complex with HSF1, *Cell* 94:471–480, 1998.

CHAPTER

14

Passive Immunotherapy for Tau Pathology

P. Davies

OUTLINE

INTRODUCTION

Practical experience with passive immunotherapy for tau pathology is quite new and, aside from a couple of anecdotal reports, is confined to studies in cell culture or in transgenic mice. Active immunization with tau or tau peptides is even more limited, with just a handful of papers (Asuni et al., 2007; Ando et al., 2014; Kontsekova et al., 2014; Selenica et al., 2014), and no consensus at all on efficacy or appropriate strategy. Although a section dealing with the problems inherent in active immunization is at the end of this piece, most of what follows is concerned with passive immunization. A recent review provides a fairly complete listing of publications in this area (Pedersen and Sigurdsson, 2015). Rather than dissect one by one the limited number of publications that have appeared to date, it is probably more useful to consider the conceptual and practical issues that arise in attempting immunotherapy for

Developing Therapeutics for Alzheimer's Disease. http://dx.doi.org/10.1016/B978-0-12-802173-6.00014-9

tau pathology. Illustrations of these issues as they have arisen in our work will be provided. Superficially, targeting amyloid pathology would appear much easier than targeting tau pathology, simply because the former is largely extracellular while the latter is generally considered to be intracellular (except perhaps at the very end stage, in what is called the "ghost" or "tombstone" tangle). Until quite recently, the existence of an extracellular component of tau pathology did not seem likely. However, the best evidence in favor of this—the staging of pathology described by the Braaks—has been around for more than 20 years.

SPREAD OF TAU PATHOLOGY IN THE HUMAN BRAIN

It was the seminal work of Heiko Braak and coworkers that made clear the spread of tangle pathology in Alzheimer's disease (AD) (Braak et al., 1993; Braak and Braak, 1995, 1997). This idea that the disease moved or expanded from the transentorhinal region into the hippocampus and then out to the rest of the medial temporal cortex has been very useful in staging Alzheimer's disease. Recent work has suggested that tangle pathology might have its beginnings in the locus coeruleus, and move up to the cerebrum essentially along noradrenergic fibers (Braak and Del Tredici, 2012). Regardless of where the pathology is thought to begin, it is very common to read about the movement or spread of pathology. Braak and others have suggested that the spread of the disease is along anatomically defined neuronal connections or pathways (Braak and Del Tredici, 2011, 2012). Transynaptic spread of Alzheimer's disease appears to have become a widely accepted hypothesis, but the molecular details have remained quite obscure. The suggestion that it is actually some form of the tau protein itself that is directly responsible for the spread of tau pathology is a new idea that has received much attention in the past few years (Clavaguera et al., 2009; Frost et al., 2009; Goedert et al., 2010), and if this is true, it might make immunotherapy a very attractive approach to treatment.

SPREAD OF TAU PATHOLOGY IN THE RODENT BRAIN

The first evidence for the experimentally induced spread of tau pathology is the work of Clavaguera et al. (2009). These authors describe the injection of homogenates of the brains of P301S tau transgenic mice (Allen et al., 2002) into the brains of wild-type mice or mice transgenic for a nonmutated human tau gene (the Alz17 mouse). The amount of tau pathology that normally develops in the Alz17 mouse is quite limited, but when homogenates of pathology-rich P301S mice were injected, evidence of both qualitative and quantitative changes in pathology was seen. Tau pathology developed both at the site of injection and distant to it, pathology that would not have developed in the absence of the injection. Much less obvious was the development of pathology following injection of P301S homogenates into the wild-type mouse brain. It is notable that Jucker, Walker, and others (Langer et al., 2011; Rosen et al., 2012) had suggested that beta-amyloid pathology could be accelerated in a very similar fashion. The injection of various preparations of beta-amyloid into mice transgenic for the human amyloid precursor protein (APP) did appear to speed up and exacerbate the deposition of amyloid. The real difference between the work on beta-amyloid and tau is again that amyloid deposition is an extracellular event, and it is easy to imagine how exogenous amyloid preparations could seed deposition of endogenously produced material. As tau protein and tau pathology are intraneuronal, it is much more difficult to elucidate the mechanism by which tau spreading could take place.

Since tau is expressed in the majority of neurons, it must be assumed that what is propagated is some modified, abnormal form of tau. Tau is present both in the intracellular and extracellular space of the normal brain. Tau concentrations are readily measurable in the cerebrospinal fluid (CSF) of young normal people (Fagan et al., 2009), although it remains unclear where this tau comes from. The most common explanation for its presence in CSF is that tau is produced in cell bodies and is transported down axons, where it is supposed to act to stabilize microtubules; presumably there is some release of tau at axon terminals, even in normal individuals. Levels of tau protein in CSF rise in Alzheimer's disease (de Leon et al., 2002; Fagan et al., 2009; Barten et al., 2011) and in several other degenerative diseases, and this has been thought to be due to neuronal dysfunction or death. The fact that CSF levels of tau rise early in the course of Alzheimer's disease, before there is extensive neuronal death, does not support this idea (Barten et al., 2011), and there has been a great deal of recent interest in the notion of a physiological tau release from neurons. Several publications have described cell culture systems in which tau release has been measured (Kim et al., 2010a,b; Chai et al., 2012; Wu et al., 2013; Kanmert et al., 2015), although there is very little agreement even on the basic premise that *physiological* tau release can be reliably demonstrated.

Whether or not there is an active release process for tau in the normal central nervous system (CNS), there is no doubt about the existence of tau in the extracellular space. This may be an important issue in detecting and/or blocking the propagation of tau pathology. What has been demonstrated in several studies is that the intracerebral administration of *abnormal* tau results in the appearance of abnormal tau at sites distant from the point of injection (Clavaguera et al., 2009; Sydow and Mandelkow, 2010; Sankaranarayanan et al., 2015). Evidently, there is uptake and probably transport of abnormal tau, following which there seems to be facilitation of tau pathology (Kfoury et al., 2012). The term facilitation is used because it seems that, at least in mouse models, propagation of pathology does not occur unless there is overexpression of human tau and at least a limited degree of pretangle pathology in the absence of injection. There is one paper suggesting that normal mouse tau can be induced to form pretangle pathology by injection of tau preparations (Clavaguera et al., 2013). Another publication suggests that peripheral administration of tau aggregates can facilitate the development of tau pathology in the CNS (Clavaguera et al., 2014). Thus, we have a scheme that suggests release of an abnormal form of tau from diseased neurons, uptake into vulnerable cells, and facilitation of development of more tau pathology. The molecular details of this process—the precise nature of the abnormal tau, the mechanisms of release and uptake, and the propagation of the abnormality—remain rather sketchy.

TAU CONCENTRATIONS AND ANTIBODY CONCENTRATIONS IN THE CNS

It is important to consider the relative concentrations of tau and antibodies to tau that are likely to exist in the CNS of the mouse models routinely used. As noted earlier, there have been numerous reports of CSF or interstitial fluid tau concentrations, and these are of the order of 1 ng/mL. It is not necessary to know precisely what these concentrations are for the purposes of this discussion, and this approximation is sufficiently accurate. The injection of 10 mg/kg of IgG1 into a 25 g mouse yields an approximate plasma concentration of 75 μg/mL. A typical dose used in published studies is 10 mg/kg, although up to 40 mg/kg has been given, and plasma concentrations usually scale to injected dose. It has been reported that 0.1–0.2% of plasma antibody levels are present in CSF (Freund, 1930; Bard et al., 2000; Pan et al., 2002; Atwal et al., 2011), and studies by our group have confirmed that number with tau antibodies.

This implies that CSF antibody levels are 75–150 ng/mL, and this is between 1 and 2 orders of magnitude greater than tau levels. Most of the monoclonal antibodies made in the Davies lab have apparent affinity constants of 0.1–2.0 nM (d'Abramo et al., 2013), and from what can be gleaned from other published work, many of the other antibodies being tested have similar affinities. Given these figures, it would seem likely that all the tau in the CSF was antibody bound, provided that the epitope recognized by the antibody administered was present.

This is a critical point. Most of the attempts to use immunotherapy for tau pathology assume that the target is the abnormal extracellular form of tau responsible for the spread of pathology. This has to be targeted against a background of normal tau in the extracellular space. All of the available data suggest that most of the normal tau in CSF is truncated, almost certainly missing most of the microtubule binding domain and the C-terminal sequences, and may also show N-terminal truncations (Johnson et al., 1997; Ugolini et al., 1997; Barten et al., 2011; Amadoro et al., 2014; Corsetti et al., 2015; Derisbourg et al., 2015). At least some of the antibodies tested in immunotherapy in mice [MC1 and PHF1 (Chai et al., 2011; d'Abramo et al., 2013), HJ8,5 (Yanamandra et al., 2013, 2015), and 43D (Dai et al., 2015)] recognize epitopes that are probably not present on tau in human CSF. Some potentially therapeutic antibodies [DA9, DA31 (d'Abramo et al., 2013, submitted), 5E2 (Mably et al., 2015), and 77E9 (Dai et al., 2015)] do recognize epitopes on CSF tau and indeed are used in assays of tau in this fluid (Acker et al., 2013), as well as in the blood of transgenic mice (see later discussion). As mentioned previously, the precise nature of the tau species responsible for propagation of disease through the extracellular space is unknown, but some antibodies will bind this species selectively, whereas others will also bind to the much larger amounts of normal tau present. Measurement of the normal/abnormal tau ratio in the brains of both humans and mice suggests that concentrations of abnormal tau species are likely 1 to 2 orders of magnitude lower than those of normal tau (Forest et al., 2013).

Given that CNS tau antibodies would appear to be present in a large concentration excess relative to extracellular tau, even with 10 mg/kg dosing, we predicted that there would be little evidence of dose–response effects for tau antibodies if larger amounts were given. This assumption appears to be wrong, as we found that 40 mg/kg doses of DA9 were significantly superior to 10 mg/kg (d'Abramo et al., submitted), and are at a loss to explain why this is so. Others have reported similar results (Yanamandra et al., 2015). If antibody concentration were in some way limiting efficacy, it might be reasonable to expect that the more selective an antibody was for pathological tau species, the less would be bound by the "normal" tau species in the extracellular space. Perhaps this is the case in more restricted brain compartments; the interstitial volume of the brain is small, and diffusion of IgG molecules (molecular weight 160,000) from CSF into brain tissue spaces might be quite limited. If it is possible to generalize from our present very limited experience, it would seem that almost any tau antibody might be an effective treatment if used in sufficient dose, provided it recognizes pathological species of tau. It seems that antibodies that are selective for pathological tau species are likely to be effective at lower doses than those that also recognize the bulk of tau present in the extracellular space. There are several different routes by which antibodies to tau might affect the development of pathology, and it is important to note that these are not mutually exclusive, and it seems at least possible that all are active to some extent when anti-tau antibodies are used.

DO ANTIBODIES ACT WITHIN NEURONS?

The notion that antibodies to tau could enter neurons in sufficient quantities to influence the development of pathology has been suggested, and a limited amount of evidence of antibody penetration into neurons has been published (Asuni et al., 2007; Collin et al., 2014). The efforts of other groups, including my own, have not been successful in demonstrating the presence of antibody within neurons after prolonged treatments. Mice given 10 or 40 mg/kg of mouse IgG1 once weekly for 16 weeks have consistently failed to show staining of neurons for mouse IgG1 (Chai et al., 2011; d'Abramo et al., 2013, 2015). Binding of antibodies to neurons via Fc receptors is much lower than binding to either microglia or astrocytes, and antibody uptake by glia seems much more likely. It is also somewhat unclear what would happen to antibody taken up by a neuron. In some cells there does appear to be an intracellular high-affinity IgG binding protein, which may be involved in intracellular viral protein clearance.

TRIM21 is an E3 ubiquitin–protein ligase, which appears to have several different functions (Rhodes and Trowsdale, 2007; Keeble et al., 2008; Mallery et al., 2010). Activation of the TRIM21 viral clearance mechanism requires a cell-surface receptor for the virus, and uptake of antibody-bound virus. Complex formation with TRIM21 is entirely dependent on the virus binding to the cell surface and cointernalization of antibody attached to the virus. Following TRIM21 binding, there is ubiquitinylation of viral antigen and antibody, followed by degradation of both via the proteasome. In these systems, the antibody gains entry to the cell as a passenger rather than through active uptake, and no antibody uptake is measurable in the absence of a virus and a viral receptor. It is currently unknown if the aforementioned mechanism is active in neurons. For TRIM21-mediated degradation of tau, a cell-surface receptor for tau may be required for import of tau–antibody complexes.

In some published reports, anti-tau antibody has been reported to be associated with elements of the lysosomal system, but these studies employ cultured cells and higher concentrations of antibody than are likely to be achieved in studies of intact animal (Asuni et al., 2007; Krishnamurthy et al., 2011; Congdon et al., 2013). Given that many investigators have been unable to detect significant amounts of antibody in neurons of treated mice, it is hard to accept that this is a major site of antibody action.

BLOCKING NEURONAL TAU UPTAKE

The currently popular models of tau propagation involve the release of abnormal tau from one neuron and uptake and propagation in anatomically connected neurons, and this is an opportunity for intervention if antibodies can interrupt this process. Work from the Diamond lab suggests that heparin sulfate-type cell-surface molecules may play a role in uptake of synthetic tau oligomers (Holmes et al., 2013). In vivo, neither the nature of the tau species released nor the nature of the receptors involved in uptake are known, but it is not hard to imagine that some antibodies to tau might block this process by directly binding to critical tau sequences. In studies of Abeta antibodies, Solomon and coworkers (Solomon et al., 1996; Pan et al., 2002) have suggested that certain antibodies are able to block aggregation and assembly of amyloid deposits by changing the conformation of the peptide. The ability of specific antibodies to alter the process of tau aggregation has not been comprehensively investigated, but there are a few reports suggesting such a strategy might be fruitful (Sydow and Mandelkow, 2010; Yanamandra et al., 2013; Falcon et al., 2015). It may be that simple interaction of an antibody with the abnormal tau is sufficient to reduce tau uptake into neurons. It certainly seems likely that binding of antibodies to extracellular tau would at least favor glial uptake (Adolfsson et al., 2012). While there may be Fc receptors on some neurons, levels are much lower on neurons than they are on microglia.

MICROGLIAL UPTAKE

Antibody uptake through Fc receptors on microglial cells has been described many times (Vedeler et al., 1994a; Mosley and Cuzner, 1996; Brazil et al., 2000; Hazama et al., 2005; Minami et al., 2012; Gold et al., 2013; Funk et al., 2015), and there is no reason to believe that this will not occur when tau antibodies are given to mice. There is a single report that primary cultures of mouse microglia can take up and degrade pathological tau aggregates, and that the presence of an anti-tau antibody (MC1) enhanced this process (Luo et al., 2015). Although direct evidence from in vivo studies is lacking, antibody-mediated microglial uptake and degradation of abnormal tau species are most likely how antibodies might limit the spread of pathology. What seems to be more controversial is the possible deleterious effects of activation of microglia by antibody binding to Fc receptors (Ulvestad et al., 1994; Lue and Walker, 2002; Lee and Landreth, 2010). In reports of passive immunization for treatment of Abeta deposition, microglial activation and increased phagocytosis of Abeta have been seen, along with a quite common appearance of microhemorrhages (Wilcock et al., 2003, 2004a,b). It is unclear whether this involvement of the vasculature is because Abeta appears to be actively transported across the blood–brain barrier, and often can be found deposited in small vessels (Zaghi et al., 2009). Neither case is true for tau, and to date there are no reports of vascular issues or microhemorrhage in mice treated with tau antibodies.

Over the past few years, the Davies lab has treated large numbers of mice with nine different tau monoclonal antibodies, usually for 4 months, but in some cases for as long as 9 months. In no case have we detected microhemorrhage, and the status of microglial activation is somewhat difficult to assess. It has been reported several times that P301L or P301S mice develop a microglial and astrocytic activation, perhaps somewhat in advance of the development of tau aggregates in neurons. On treatment with some anti-tau antibodies, the development of tau pathology is reduced, and it is our impression that this reduction is accompanied by reduced microgliosis and astrocytosis. There may be an analogous situation in the human brain, where there are correlations between the extent of tau pathology and the extent of the gliosis (Streit et al., 2009). In our studies, it has not been possible to show additional activation of microglia in mice treated with anti-tau antibodies as compared to the controls. It is currently unclear if functional Fc receptors are present on astrocytes in the rodent or human brain (Nitta et al., 1992; Vedeler et al., 1994b).

TAU EXPORT FROM BRAIN

As mentioned earlier, antibodies cross from blood to brain to the extent that 0.1–0.2% of the plasma level will be found within the brain and in the CSF within 24 h. It is also well established that antibodies are transported out of the CNS into the blood at a rate faster than the bulk flow of CSF and thought to be mediated at least in part by an Fc receptor at the blood–brain barrier (Carty et al., 2006; Caram-Salas et al., 2011). This transport system has been shown to participate in removal of Abeta from the brains of transgenic mice (DeMattos et al., 2001). Antibodies directed against primary amino acid sequences of tau have been shown to increase plasma tau concentrations significantly when given to tau transgenic mice (d'Abramo et al., 2016). The antibodies shown to be effective in this regard are those with epitopes in the region 20–240 amino acids. Antibodies to conformational (MC1) or phosphorylated (phosphoSer202, phosphoThr231, phosphoSer396, and phosphoSer409) sites are much less effective in this regard. That is not to suggest that MC1 and the other antibodies selective for pathology do not export pathological tau from the brain. Because pathological tau is present at 1–2% of total or extracellular tau (Forest et al., 2013), the amounts appearing in plasma will be below the sensitivity of currently available assays.

Of course, antibody-mediated transport of tau out of the CNS is only one possible explanation for elevated plasma tau levels after antibody treatment. It is also possible that tau accumulates in the blood because clearance is blocked by the presence of antibody, as some have suggested for Abeta (Mengel et al., 2013). This latter possibility seems less likely in Tg4510 mice, which express mutant human tau driven by the brain-specific Cam kinase II promoter (Santacruz et al., 2005). These mice do not have measureable levels of human tau in the blood unless treated with antibody (d'Abramo et al., 2016).

ARE EXISTING MOUSE MODELS APPROPRIATE FOR TESTING IMMUNOTHERAPY?

To date, most of the published studies in this area have used the JNPL3 P301L mouse (Lewis et al., 2000), the R5 P301L mouse (Bi et al., 2011), or one of the two available P301S mice lines. There have been a few studies in the htau mouse (Boutajangout et al., 2010; Castillo-Carranza et al., 2014), one in the 3X transgenic mouse (Walls et al., 2014), one in the J20 amyloid mouse (Mably et al., 2015), and a few in other tau transgenic models (Umeda et al., 2015). None of these models have been demonstrated to show the same spreading or propagation of tau pathology as seen in the human brain, and it is perhaps surprising that this has not been more widely discussed. In the P301L and P301S mice, as in the htau mouse, the transgene is widely expressed and is intrinsically prone to aggregation within neurons. In general terms, the highest density of pathology occurs in these mice in regions with the highest level of transgene expression. It is unclear what role propagation of tau might play in the development of pathology in these models. The success of some antibodies in blocking the development of pathology in these mice argues either for a direct effect on neurons or for an unappreciated phenomenon of propagation in the mice. More attention to discovering which neurons express the transgene in relation to the anatomy of pathology might be informative.

The variants of the P301L models that have been used by Liu et al. (2012) and de Calignon et al. (2012) use a promoter to drive transgene expression in the entorhinal cortex, and these investigators have claimed to show transsynaptic spread of pathology to the hippocampus. These mice may be better models of what appears to happen with the spread of tau pathology in human Alzheimer's disease, but their utility is greatly limited by the very long time (18–24 months) it appears to take for the spread of pathology. There have not yet been reports of immunotherapy in these mice.

The critical question is how well any of the models will perform in predicting the efficacy of tau antibodies in human disease. Experience of such prediction in the Abeta immunotherapy field is not encouraging. A variety of monoclonal antibodies to Abeta have proven remarkably effective in reducing amyloid deposition and behavioral abnormalities in a number of different mouse models. So far, the effects in human patients have been disappointing, and certainly nowhere near the level seen in the animal studies. The predictive power of the tau mouse models is likely to become clear quite soon. Although there is little published at this point, it seems likely that human trials with anti-tau antibodies are beginning as this review goes to press (http://www.alzforum.org/therapeutics/bms-986168 and http://www.alzforum.org/therapeutics/rg7345). As cognitive changes appear to be detectable at quite early stages in the spread of tau pathology (Bancher et al., 1993), antibody effectiveness might be quite readily demonstrated, if it exists. Tau imaging, covered elsewhere in this volume, will also contribute greatly if quantitative determinations of the extent of tau pathology can be made. The next few years should prove very informative.

PROBLEMS FOR ACTIVE IMMUNIZATION STRATEGIES

There seems to be a fundamental flaw in active immunization protocols that is barely mentioned in the Alzheimer's disease immunotherapy literature. This is the problem of epitope spreading, also called determinant spreading. This phenomenon occurs when a peptide from a specific region of an endogenous protein is used as an immunogen. Following the original immune response to the immunizing peptide, both antibody and cellular responses appear that are to other epitopes of the same or similar proteins. Thus, the immune response is said to have spread to other epitopes or determinants. This phenomenon has been recognized for many years, and has been seen with a variety of different proteins. Epitope spreading may play an important role in autoimmune diseases such as systemic lupus erythematosus (Arbuckle et al., 1998; James and Harley, 1998; Orth et al., 1998; Monneaux and Muller, 2002), type 1 diabetes (Zechel et al., 1998; Csorba et al., 2010), Sjogren's syndrome (Kinoshita et al., 1998; McCluskey et al., 1998), myasthenia gravis (Vincent et al., 1994, 1998; Agius et al., 1998), and multiple sclerosis (Tuohy et al., 1998; Tuohy and Kinkel, 2000; Miller and Eagar, 2001; McMahon et al., 2005; Lundberg and Venables, 2008; Quintana et al., 2014).

This is only a partial listing and a sampling of a large literature to make a point. The use of pieces of tau or APP as immunogens seems very likely to result in the development of immune responses to other regions of these and related proteins, likely with very negative consequences. The idea that we can "control" or limit the immune response to a single peptide or determinant is simply not established over the long term. As Steinman suggested, "Despite epitope spreading in the pathogenesis of autoimmune disease, highly restricted approaches to immune therapy may still succeed [with a hedge on this bet]" (Steinman, 2000).

There are perhaps two other concerns regarding active immunization that make me an opponent of this approach. The first is that active immunization is irreversible: if adverse effects occur, there is little that can be done beyond attempts at immunosuppression. Immunosuppressive treatments for autoimmune diseases are being developed and tested, but having to subject Alzheimer's disease patients to these does not seem desirable. The second issue is that participating in an active immunization trial seems very likely to bar patients from a second study, even if the immunization appears to be free of adverse events. Epitope spreading in autoimmune disease occurs over many years (Vanderlugt and Miller, 2002), and it is doubtful that future clinical trials will want to inherit potential disasters from active immunizations in the past. Immunization of humans with pieces of human proteins would seem to be a fundamentally bad idea. Despite these concerns, there are efforts to develop and test active immunization for tau epitopes in humans (http://www.alzforum.org/therapeutics/aadvac-1 and http://www.alzforum.org/therapeutics/aci-35).

From today's viewpoint, the use of passive immunotherapy directed against tau can be seen as a very exciting development. If tau pathology spreads through the extracellular space, immunotherapy offers the possibility of halting this process in its tracks. In at least some mouse models, certain antibodies virtually halt the progression of pathology. The apparent linkage of tau pathology to cognitive dysfunction raises the hope that cognitive decline can be slowed or even halted. There are many "ifs," but there are good reasons for optimism.

Acknowledgments

The author would like to thank Cristina d'Abramo, PhD, and Jeremy Koppel, MD, for a critical reading of the manuscript, and Heidy Bavara, Leslie Adrien, and Francesca Vitale for continuing assistance with immunotherapy. Christopher M. Acker contributed significantly to earlier work in this area. P.D. acknowledges long-term support from the National Institute on Aging.

References

Acker CM, Forest SK, Zinkowski R, Davies P, d'Abramo C: Sensitive quantitative assays for tau and phospho-tau in transgenic mouse models, *Neurobiol Aging* 34(1):338–350, 2013.

Adolfsson O, Pihlgren M, Toni N, Varisco Y, Buccarello AL, Antoniello K, Lohmann S, Piorkowska K, Gafner V, Atwal JK, Maloney J, Chen M, Gogineni A, Weimer RM, Mortensen DL, Friesenhahn M, Ho C, Paul R, Pfeifer A, Muhs A, Watts RJ: An effector-reduced anti-beta-amyloid (Abeta) antibody with unique abeta binding properties promotes neuroprotection and glial engulfment of Abeta, *J Neurosci* 32(28):9677–9689, 2012.

Agius MA, Twaddle GM, Fairclough RH: Epitope spreading in experimental autoimmune myasthenia gravis, *Ann NY Acad Sci* 841:365–367, 1998.

Allen B, Ingram E, Takao M, Smith MJ, Jakes R, Virdee K, Yoshida H, Holzer M, Craxton M, Emson PC, Atzori C, Migheli A, Crowther RA, Ghetti B, Spillantini MG, Goedert M: Abundant tau filaments and nonapoptotic neurodegeneration in transgenic mice expressing human P301S tau protein, *J Neurosci* 22(21):9340–9351, 2002.

Amadoro G, Corsetti V, Sancesario GM, Lubrano A, Melchiorri G, Bernardini S, Calissano P, Sancesario G: Cerebrospinal fluid levels of a 20–22 kDa NH_2 fragment of human tau provide a novel neuronal injury biomarker in Alzheimer's disease and other dementias, *J Alzheimers Dis* 42(1):211–226, 2014.

Ando K, Kabova A, Stygelbout V, Leroy K, Heraud C, Frederick C, Suain V, Yilmaz Z, Authelet M, Dedecker R, Potier MC, Duyckaerts C, Brion JP: Vaccination with sarkosyl insoluble PHF-tau decrease neurofibrillary tangles formation in aged tau transgenic mouse model: a pilot study, *J Alzheimers Dis* 40(Suppl 1):S135–S145, 2014.

Arbuckle MR, Gross T, Scofield RH, Hinshaw LB, Chang AC, Taylor FB Jr, Harley JB, James JA: Lupus humoral autoimmunity induced in a primate model by short peptide immunization, *J Investig Med* 46(2):58–65, 1998.

Asuni AA, Boutajangout A, Quartermain D, Sigurdsson EM: Immunotherapy targeting pathological tau conformers in a tangle mouse model reduces brain pathology with associated functional improvements, *J Neurosci* 27(34):9115–9129, 2007.

Atwal JK, Chen Y, Chiu C, Mortensen DL, Meilandt WJ, Liu Y, Heise CE, Hoyte K, Luk W, Lu Y, Peng K, Wu P, Rouge L, Zhang Y, Lazarus RA, Scearce-Levie K, Wang W, Wu Y, Tessier-Lavigne M, Watts RJ: A therapeutic antibody targeting BACE1 inhibits amyloid-beta production in vivo, *Sci Transl Med* 3(84):84ra43, 2011.

Bancher C, Braak H, Fischer P, Jellinger KA: Neuropathological staging of Alzheimer lesions and intellectual status in Alzheimer's and Parkinson's disease patients, *Neurosci Lett* 162(1–2):179–182, 1993.

Bard F, Cannon C, Barbour R, Burke RL, Games D, Grajeda H, Guido T, Hu K, Huang J, Johnson-Wood K, Khan K, Kholodenko D, Lee M, Lieberburg I, Motter R, Nguyen M, Soriano F, Vasquez N, Weiss K, Welch B, Seubert P, Schenk D, Yednock T: Peripherally administered antibodies against amyloid beta-peptide enter the central nervous system and reduce pathology in a mouse model of Alzheimer disease, *Nat Med* 6(8):916–919, 2000.

Barten DM, Cadelina GW, Hoque N, DeCarr LB, Guss VL, Yang L, Sankaranarayanan S, Wes PD, Flynn ME, Meredith JE, Ahlijanian MK, Albright CF: Tau transgenic mice as models for cerebrospinal fluid tau biomarkers, *J Alzheimers Dis* 24(Suppl 2):127–141, 2011.

Bi M, Ittner A, Ke YD, Gotz J, Ittner LM: Tau-targeted immunization impedes progression of neurofibrillary histopathology in aged P301L tau transgenic mice, *PLoS One* 6(12):e26860, 2011.

Boutajangout A, Quartermain D, Sigurdsson EM: Immunotherapy targeting pathological tau prevents cognitive decline in a new tangle mouse model, *J Neurosci* 30(49):16559–16566, 2010.

Braak H, Braak E: Staging of Alzheimer's disease-related neurofibrillary changes, *Neurobiol Aging* 16(3):271–278, 1995 (discussion 278–284).

Braak H, Braak E: Staging of Alzheimer-related cortical destruction, *Int Psychogeriatr* 9(Suppl 1):257–261, 1997 (discussion 269–272).

Braak H, Braak E, Bohl J: Staging of Alzheimer-related cortical destruction, *Eur Neurol* 33(6):403–408, 1993.

Braak H, Del Tredici K: Alzheimer's pathogenesis: is there neuron-to-neuron propagation? *Acta Neuropathol* 121(5):589–595, 2011.

Braak H, Del Tredici K: Where, when, and in what form does sporadic Alzheimer's disease begin? *Curr Opin Neurol* 25(6):708–714, 2012.

Brazil MI, Chung H, Maxfield FR: Effects of incorporation of immunoglobulin G and complement component C1q on uptake and degradation of Alzheimer's disease amyloid fibrils by microglia, *J Biol Chem* 275(22):16941–16947, 2000.

Caram-Salas N, Boileau E, Farrington GK, Garber E, Brunette E, Abulrob A, Stanimirovic D: In vitro and in vivo methods for assessing FcRn-mediated reverse transcytosis across the blood–brain barrier, *Methods Mol Biol* 763:383–401, 2011.

Carty NC, Wilcock DM, Rosenthal A, Grimm J, Pons J, Ronan V, Gottschall PE, Gordon MN, Morgan D: Intracranial administration of deglycosylated C-terminal-specific anti-Abeta antibody efficiently clears amyloid plaques without activating microglia in amyloid-depositing transgenic mice, *J Neuroinflammation* 3:11, 2006.

Castillo-Carranza DL, Gerson JE, Sengupta U, Guerrero-Munoz MJ, Lasagna-Reeves CA, Kayed R: Specific targeting of tau oligomers in htau mice prevents cognitive impairment and tau toxicity following injection with brain-derived tau oligomeric seeds, *J Alzheimers Dis* 40(Suppl 1):S97–S111, 2014.

Chai X, Dage JL, Citron M: Constitutive secretion of tau protein by an unconventional mechanism, *Neurobiol Dis* 48(3):356–366, 2012.

Chai X, Wu S, Murray TK, Kinley R, Cella CV, Sims H, Buckner N, Hanmer J, Davies P, O'Neill MJ, Hutton ML, Citron M: Passive immunization with anti-tau antibodies in two transgenic models: reduction of tau pathology and delay of disease progression, *J Biol Chem* 286(39):34457–34467, 2011.

Clavaguera F, Akatsu H, Fraser G, Crowther RA, Frank S, Hench J, Probst A, Winkler DT, Reichwald J, Staufenbiel M, Ghetti B, Goedert M, Tolnay M: Brain homogenates from human tauopathies induce tau inclusions in mouse brain, *Proc Natl Acad Sci USA* 110(23):9535–9540, 2013.

Clavaguera F, Bolmont T, Crowther RA, Abramowski D, Frank S, Probst A, Fraser G, Stalder AK, Beibel M, Staufenbiel M, Jucker M, Goedert M, Tolnay M: Transmission and spreading of tauopathy in transgenic mouse brain, *Nat Cell Biol* 11(7):909–913, 2009.

Clavaguera F, Hench J, Lavenir I, Schweighauser G, Frank S, Goedert M, Tolnay M: Peripheral administration of tau aggregates triggers intracerebral tauopathy in transgenic mice, *Acta Neuropathol* 127(2):299–301, 2014.

Collin L, Bohrmann B, Gopfert U, Oroszlan-Szovik K, Ozmen L, Gruninger F: Neuronal uptake of tau/pS422 antibody and reduced progression of tau pathology in a mouse model of Alzheimer's disease, *Brain* 137(Pt 10):2834–2846, 2014.

Congdon EE, Gu J, Sait HB, Sigurdsson EM: Antibody uptake into neurons occurs primarily via clathrin-dependent Fcgamma receptor endocytosis and is a prerequisite for acute tau protein clearance, *J Biol Chem* 288(49):35452–35465, 2013.

Corsetti V, Florenzano F, Atlante A, Bobba A, Ciotti MT, Natale F, Della Valle F, Borreca A, Manca A, Meli G, Ferraina C, Feligioni M, D'Aguanno S, Bussani R, Ammassari-Teule M, Nicolin V, Calissano P, Amadoro G: NH_2-truncated human tau induces deregulated mitophagy in neurons by aberrant recruitment of parkin and UCHL-1: implications in Alzheimer's disease, *Hum Mol Genet* 24(11):3058–3081, 2015.

Csorba TR, Lyon AW, Hollenberg MD: Autoimmunity and the pathogenesis of type 1 diabetes, *Crit Rev Clin Lab Sci* 47(2):51–71, 2010.

d'Abramo C, Acker CM, Jimenez H, Davies P: Passive immunization in JNPL3 transgenic mice using an array of phospho-tau specific antibodies, *PLoS One* 10(8):e0135774, 2015.

d'Abramo C, Acker C, Schachter J, Terracina G, Wang X, Forest SK, Davies P: Detecting tau in the serum of transgenic animal models after tau immunotheray treatment, *Neurobiol Aging* 37:58–65, 2016.

d'Abramo C, Jimenez H, Adrien L, Davies P: High dose of DA9, an antibody recognizing an amino acid sequence in tau, reduces soluble and insoluble tau in an animal model of tauopathy. (Submitted)

d'Abramo C, Acker CM, Jimenez HT, Davies P: Tau passive immunotherapy in mutant P301L mice: antibody affinity versus specificity, *PLoS One* 8(4):e62402, 2013.

Dai CL, Chen X, Kazim SF, Liu F, Gong CX, Grundke-Iqbal I, Iqbal K: Passive immunization targeting the N-terminal projection domain of tau decreases tau pathology and improves cognition in a transgenic mouse model of Alzheimer disease and tauopathies, *J Neural Transm* 122(4):607–617, 2015.

de Calignon A, Polydoro M, Suarez-Calvet M, William C, Adamowicz DH, Kopeikina KJ, Pitstick R, Sahara N, Ashe KH, Carlson GA, Spires-Jones TL, Hyman BT: Propagation of tau pathology in a model of early Alzheimer's disease, *Neuron* 73(4):685–697, 2012.

de Leon MJ, Segal S, Tarshish CY, DeSanti S, Zinkowski R, Mehta PD, Convit A, Caraos C, Rusinek H, Tsui W, Saint Louis LA, DeBernardis J, Kerkman D, Qadri F, Gary A, Lesbre P, Wisniewski T, Poirier J, Davies P: Longitudinal cerebrospinal fluid tau load increases in mild cognitive impairment, *Neurosci Lett* 333(3):183–186, 2002.

DeMattos RB, Bales KR, Cummins DJ, Dodart JC, Paul SM, Holtzman DM: Peripheral anti-A beta antibody alters CNS and plasma A beta clearance and decreases brain A beta burden in a mouse model of Alzheimer's disease, *Proc Natl Acad Sci USA* 98(15):8850–8855, 2001.

Derisbourg M, Leghay C, Chiappetta G, Fernandez-Gomez FJ, Laurent C, Demeyer D, Carrier S, Buee-Scherrer V, Blum D, Vinh J, Sergeant N, Verdier Y, Buee L, Hamdane M: Role of the tau N-terminal region in microtubule stabilization revealed by new endogenous truncated forms, *Sci Rep* 5:9659, 2015.

Fagan AM, Mintun MA, Shah AR, Aldea P, Roe CM, Mach RH, Marcus D, Morris JC, Holtzman DM: Cerebrospinal fluid tau and ptau(181) increase with cortical amyloid deposition in cognitively normal individuals: implications for future clinical trials of Alzheimer's disease, *EMBO Mol Med* 1(8–9):371–380, 2009.

Falcon B, Cavallini A, Angers R, Glover S, Murray TK, Barnham L, Jackson S, O'Neill MJ, Isaacs AM, Hutton ML, Szekeres PG, Goedert M, Bose S: Conformation determines the seeding potencies of native and recombinant tau aggregates, *J Biol Chem* 290(2):1049–1065, 2015.

Forest SK, Acker CM, d'Abramo C, Davies P: Methods for measuring tau pathology in transgenic mouse models, *J Alzheimers Dis* 33(2):463–471, 2013.

Freund J: Accumulation of antibodies in the central nervous system, *J Exp Med* 51(6):889–902, 1930.

Frost B, Jacks RL, Diamond MI: Propagation of tau misfolding from the outside to the inside of a cell, *J Biol Chem* 284(19):12845–12852, 2009.

Funk KE, Mirbaha H, Jiang H, Holtzman DM, Diamond MI: Distinct therapeutic mechanisms of tau antibodies: promoting microglial clearance versus blocking neuronal uptake, *J Biol Chem* 290(35):21652–21662, 2015.

Goedert M, Clavaguera F, Tolnay M: The propagation of prion-like protein inclusions in neurodegenerative diseases, *Trends Neurosci* 33(7):317–325, 2010.

Gold M, Mengel D, Roskam S, Dodel R, Bach JP: Mechanisms of action of naturally occurring antibodies against beta-amyloid on microglia, *J Neuroinflammation* 10:5, 2013.

Hazama GI, Yasuhara O, Morita H, Aimi Y, Tooyama I, Kimura H: Mouse brain IgG-like immunoreactivity: strain-specific occurrence in microglia and biochemical identification of IgG, *J Comp Neurol* 492(2):234–249, 2005.

Holmes BB, DeVos SL, Kfoury N, Li M, Jacks R, Yanamandra K, Ouidja MO, Brodsky FM, Marasa J, Bagchi DP, Kotzbauer PT, Miller TM, Papy-Garcia D, Diamond MI: Heparan sulfate proteoglycans mediate internalization and propagation of specific proteopathic seeds, *Proc Natl Acad Sci USA* 110(33):E3138–E3147, 2013.

James JA, Harley JB: A model of peptide-induced lupus autoimmune B cell epitope spreading is strain specific and is not H-2 restricted in mice, *J Immunol* 160(1):502–508, 1998.

Johnson GV, Seubert P, Cox TM, Motter R, Brown JP, Galasko D: The tau protein in human cerebrospinal fluid in Alzheimer's disease consists of proteolytically derived fragments, *J Neurochem* 68(1):430–433, 1997.

Kanmert D, Cantlon A, Muratore CR, Jin M, O'Malley TT, Lee G, Young-Pearse TL, Selkoe DJ, Walsh DM: C-terminally truncated forms of tau, but not full-length tau or its C-terminal fragments, are released from neurons independently of cell death, *J Neurosci* 35(30):10851–10865, 2015.

Keeble AH, Khan Z, Forster A, James LC: TRIM21 is an IgG receptor that is structurally, thermodynamically, and kinetically conserved, *Proc Natl Acad Sci USA* 105(16):6045–6050, 2008.

Kfoury N, Holmes BB, Jiang H, Holtzman DM, Diamond MI: Trans-cellular propagation of tau aggregation by fibrillar species, *J Biol Chem* 287:19440–19451, 2012.

Kim W, Lee S, Hall GF: Secretion of human tau fragments resembling CSF-tau in Alzheimer's disease is modulated by the presence of the exon 2 insert, *FEBS Lett* 584(14):3085–3088, 2010a.

Kim W, Lee S, Jung C, Ahmed A, Lee G, Hall GF: Interneuronal transfer of human tau between lamprey central neurons in situ, *J Alzheimers Dis* 19(2):647–664, 2010b.

Kinoshita G, Keech CL, Sontheimer RD, Purcell A, McCluskey J, Gordon TP: Spreading of the immune response from 52 kDaRo and 60 kDaRo to calreticulin in experimental autoimmunity, *Lupus* 7(1):7–11, 1998.

Kontsekova E, Zilka N, Kovacech B, Novak P, Novak M: First-in-man tau vaccine targeting structural determinants essential for pathological tau–tau interaction reduces tau oligomerisation and neurofibrillary degeneration in an Alzheimer's disease model, *Alzheimers Res Ther* 6(4):44, 2014.

Krishnamurthy PK, Deng Y, Sigurdsson EM: Mechanistic studies of antibody-mediated clearance of tau aggregates using an ex vivo brain slice model, *Front Psychiatr* 2:59, 2011.

Langer F, Eisele YS, Fritschi SK, Staufenbiel M, Walker LC, Jucker M: Soluble Abeta seeds are potent inducers of cerebral beta-amyloid deposition, *J Neurosci* 31(41):14488–14495, 2011.

Lee CY, Landreth GE: The role of microglia in amyloid clearance from the AD brain, *J Neural Transm* 117(8):949–960, 2010.

Lewis J, McGowan E, Rockwood J, Melrose H, Nacharaju P, Van Slegtenhorst M, Gwinn-Hardy K, Paul Murphy M, Baker M, Yu X, Duff K, Hardy J, Corral A, Lin WL, Yen SH, Dickson DW, Davies P, Hutton M: Neurofibrillary tangles, amyotrophy and progressive motor disturbance in mice expressing mutant (P301L) tau protein, *Nat Genet* 25(4):402–405, 2000.

Liu L, Drouet V, Wu JW, Witter MP, Small SA, Clelland C, Duff K: Trans-synaptic spread of tau pathology in vivo, *PLoS One* 7(2):e31302, 2012.

Lue LF, Walker DG: Modeling Alzheimer's disease immune therapy mechanisms: interactions of human postmortem microglia with antibody-opsonized amyloid beta peptide, *J Neurosci Res* 70(4):599–610, 2002.

Lundberg K, Venables PJ: Epitope spreading in animal models: array of hope in rheumatoid arthritis and multiple sclerosis, *Arthritis Res Ther* 10(6):122, 2008.

Luo W, Liu W, Hu X, Hanna M, Caravaca A, Paul SM: Microglial internalization and degradation of pathological tau is enhanced by an anti-tau monoclonal antibody, *Sci Rep* 5:11161, 2015.

Mably AJ, Kanmert D, McDonald JM, Liu W, Caldarone BJ, Lemere CA, O'Nuallain B, Kosik KS, Walsh DM: Tau immunization: a cautionary tale? *Neurobiol Aging* 36(3):1316–1332, 2015.

Mallery DL, McEwan WA, Bidgood SR, Towers GJ, Johnson CM, James LC: Antibodies mediate intracellular immunity through tripartite motif-containing 21 (TRIM21), *Proc Natl Acad Sci USA* 107(46):19985–19990, 2010.

McCluskey J, Farris AD, Keech CL, Purcell AW, Rischmueller M, Kinoshita G, Reynolds P, Gordon TP: Determinant spreading: lessons from animal models and human disease, *Immunol Rev* 164:209–229, 1998.

McMahon EJ, Bailey SL, Castenada CV, Waldner H, Miller SD: Epitope spreading initiates in the CNS in two mouse models of multiple sclerosis, *Nat Med* 11(3):335–339, 2005.

Mengel D, Roskam S, Neff F, Balakrishnan K, Deuster O, Gold M, Oertel WH, Bacher M, Bach JP, Dodel R: Naturally occurring autoantibodies interfere with beta-amyloid metabolism and improve cognition in a transgenic mouse model of Alzheimer's disease 24 h after single treatment, *Transl Psychiatr* 3:e236, 2013.

Miller SD, Eagar TN: Functional role of epitope spreading in the chronic pathogenesis of autoimmune and virus-induced demyelinating diseases, *Adv Exp Med Biol* 490:99–107, 2001.

Minami SS, Sun B, Popat K, Kauppinen T, Pleiss M, Zhou Y, Ward ME, Floreancig P, Mucke L, Desai T, Gan L: Selective targeting of microglia by quantum dots, *J Neuroinflammation* 9:22, 2012.

Monneaux F, Muller S: Epitope spreading in systemic lupus erythematosus: identification of triggering peptide sequences, *Arthritis Rheum* 46(6):1430–1438, 2002.

Mosley K, Cuzner ML: Receptor-mediated phagocytosis of myelin by macrophages and microglia: effect of opsonization and receptor blocking agents, *Neurochem Res* 21(4):481–487, 1996.

Nitta T, Yagita H, Sato K, Okumura K: Expression of Fc gamma receptors on astroglial cell lines and their role in the central nervous system, *Neurosurgery* 31(1):83–87, 1992 (discussion 87–88).

Orth T, Mayet WJ, Deister H, Chang S, Schmitz M, Bachmann M: Analysis of epitope spreading over an eleven-year period in a patient with systemic lupus erythematosus, *Scand J Rheumatol* 27(6):461–464, 1998.

Pan W, Solomon B, Maness LM, Kastin AJ: Antibodies to beta-amyloid decrease the blood-to-brain transfer of beta-amyloid peptide, *Exp Biol Med* 227(8):609–615, 2002.

Pedersen JT, Sigurdsson EM: Tau immunotherapy for Alzheimer's disease, *Trends Mol Med* 21(6):394–402, 2015.

Quintana FJ, Patel B, Yeste A, Nyirenda M, Kenison J, Rahbari R, Fetco D, Hussain M, O'Mahony J, Magalhaes S, McGowan M, Johnson T, Rajasekharan S, Narayanan S, Arnold DL, Weiner HL, Banwell B, Bar-Or A: Canadian Pediatric Demyelinating Disease Network: Epitope spreading as an early pathogenic event in pediatric multiple sclerosis, *Neurology* 83(24):2219–2226, 2014.

Rhodes DA, Trowsdale J: TRIM21 is a trimeric protein that binds IgG Fc via the B30.2 domain, *Mol Immunol* 44(9):2406–2414, 2007.

Rosen RF, Fritz JJ, Dooyema J, Cintron AF, Hamaguchi T, Lah JJ, LeVine H III, Jucker M, Walker LC: Exogenous seeding of cerebral beta-amyloid deposition in betaAPP-transgenic rats, *J Neurochem* 120(5):660–666, 2012.

Sankaranarayanan S, Barten DM, Vana L, Devidze N, Yang L, Cadelina G, Hoque N, DeCarr L, Keenan S, Lin A, Cao Y, Snyder B, Zhang B, Nitla M, Hirschfeld G, Barrezueta N, Polson C, Wes P, Rangan VS, Cacace A, Albright CF, Meredith J Jr, Trojanowski JQ, Lee VM, Brunden KR, Ahlijanian M: Passive immunization with phospho-tau antibodies reduces tau pathology and functional deficits in two distinct mouse tauopathy models, *PLoS One* 10(5):e0125614, 2015.

Santacruz K, Lewis J, Spires T, Paulson J, Kotilinek L, Ingelsson M, Guimaraes A, DeTure M, Ramsden M, McGowan E, Forster C, Yue M, Orne J, Janus C, Mariash A, Kuskowski M, Hyman B, Hutton M, Ashe KH: Tau suppression in a neurodegenerative mouse model improves memory function, *Science* 309(5733):476–481, 2005.

Selenica ML, Davtyan H, Housley SB, Blair LJ, Gillies A, Nordhues BA, Zhang B, Liu J, Gestwicki JE, Lee DC, Gordon MN, Morgan D, Dickey CA: Epitope analysis following active immunization with tau proteins reveals immunogens implicated in tau pathogenesis, *J Neuroinflammation* 11:152, 2014.

Solomon B, Koppel R, Hanan E, Katzav T: Monoclonal antibodies inhibit in vitro fibrillar aggregation of the Alzheimer beta-amyloid peptide, *Proc Natl Acad Sci USA* 93(1):452–455, 1996.

Steinman L: Despite epitope spreading in the pathogenesis of autoimmune disease, highly restricted approaches to immune therapy may still succeed [with a hedge on this bet], *J Autoimmun* 14(4):278–282, 2000.

Streit WJ, Braak H, Xue QS, Bechmann I: Dystrophic (senescent) rather than activated microglial cells are associated with tau pathology and likely precede neurodegeneration in Alzheimer's disease, *Acta Neuropathol* 118(4):475–485, 2009.

Sydow A, Mandelkow EM: "Prion-like" propagation of mouse and human tau aggregates in an inducible mouse model of tauopathy, *Neurodegener Dis* 7(1–3):28–31, 2010.

Tuohy VK, Kinkel RP: Epitope spreading: a mechanism for progression of autoimmune disease, *Arch Immunol Ther Exp* 48(5):347–351, 2000.

Tuohy VK, Yu M, Yin L, Kawczak JA, Johnson JM, Mathisen PM, Weinstock-Guttman B, Kinkel RP: The epitope spreading cascade during progression of experimental autoimmune encephalomyelitis and multiple sclerosis, *Immunol Rev* 164:93–100, 1998.

Ugolini G, Cattaneo A, Novak M: Co-localization of truncated tau and DNA fragmentation in Alzheimer's disease neurones, *Neuroreport* 8(17):3709–3712, 1997.

Ulvestad E, Williams K, Matre R, Nyland H, Olivier A, Antel J: Fc receptors for IgG on cultured human microglia mediate cytotoxicity and phagocytosis of antibody-coated targets, *J Neuropathol Exp Neurol* 53(1):27–36, 1994.

Umeda T, Eguchi H, Kunori Y, Matsumoto Y, Taniguchi T, Mori H, Tomiyama T: Passive immunotherapy of tauopathy targeting pSer413-tau: a pilot study in mice, *Ann Clin Transl Neurol* 2(3):241–255, 2015.

Vanderlugt CL, Miller SD: Epitope spreading in immune-mediated diseases: implications for immunotherapy, *Nat Rev Immunol* 2(2):85–95, 2002.

Vedeler C, Ulvestad E, Grundt I, Conti G, Nyland H, Matre R, Pleasure D: Fc receptor for IgG (FcR) on rat microglia, *J Neuroimmunol* 49(1–2):19–24, 1994a.

Vedeler C, Ulvestad E, Nyland H, Matre R, Aarli JA: Receptors for gammaglobulin in the central and peripheral nervous system, *J Neurol Neurosurg Psychiatry* 57(Suppl):9–10, 1994b.

Vincent A, Jacobson L, Shillito P: Response to human acetylcholine receptor alpha 138-199: determinant spreading initiates autoimmunity to self-antigen in rabbits, *Immunol Lett* 39(3):269–275, 1994.

Vincent A, Willcox N, Hill M, Curnow J, MacLennan C, Beeson D: Determinant spreading and immune responses to acetylcholine receptors in myasthenia gravis, *Immunol Rev* 164:157–168, 1998.

Walls KC, Ager RR, Vasilevko V, Cheng D, Medeiros R, LaFerla FM: p-Tau immunotherapy reduces soluble and insoluble tau in aged 3xTg-AD mice, *Neurosci Lett* 575:96–100, 2014.

Wilcock DM, DiCarlo G, Henderson D, Jackson J, Clarke K, Ugen KE, Gordon MN, Morgan D: Intracranially administered anti-Abeta antibodies reduce beta-amyloid deposition by mechanisms both independent of and associated with microglial activation, *J Neurosci* 23(9):3745–3751, 2003.

Wilcock DM, Rojiani A, Rosenthal A, Levkowitz G, Subbarao S, Alamed J, Wilson D, Wilson N, Freeman MJ, Gordon MN, Morgan D: Passive amyloid immunotherapy clears amyloid and transiently activates microglia in a transgenic mouse model of amyloid deposition, *J Neurosci* 24(27):6144–6151, 2004a.

Wilcock DM, Rojiani A, Rosenthal A, Subbarao S, Freeman MJ, Gordon MN, Morgan D: Passive immunotherapy against Abeta in aged APP-transgenic mice reverses cognitive deficits and depletes parenchymal amyloid deposits in spite of increased vascular amyloid and microhemorrhage, *J Neuroinflammation* 1(1):24, 2004b.

Wu JW, Herman M, Liu L, Simoes S, Acker CM, Figueroa H, Steinberg JI, Margittai M, Kayed R, Zurzolo C, Di Paolo G, Duff KE: Small misfolded tau species are internalized via bulk endocytosis and anterogradely and retrogradely transported in neurons, *J Biol Chem* 288(3):1856–1870, 2013.

Yanamandra K, Jiang H, Mahan TE, Maloney SE, Wozniak DF, Diamond MI, Holtzman DM: Anti-tau antibody reduces insoluble tau and decreases brain atrophy, *Ann Clin Transl Neurol* 2(3):278–288, 2015.

Yanamandra K, Kfoury N, Jiang H, Mahan TE, Ma S, Maloney SE, Wozniak DF, Diamond MI, Holtzman DM: Anti-tau antibodies that block tau aggregate seeding in vitro markedly decrease pathology and improve cognition in vivo, *Neuron* 80(2):402–414, 2013.

Zaghi J, Goldenson B, Inayathullah M, Lossinsky AS, Masoumi A, Avagyan H, Mahanian M, Bernas M, Weinand M, Rosenthal MJ, Espinosa-Jeffrey A, de Vellis J, Teplow DB, Fiala M: Alzheimer disease macrophages shuttle amyloid-beta from neurons to vessels, contributing to amyloid angiopathy, *Acta Neuropathol* 117(2):111–124, 2009.

Zechel MA, Krawetz MD, Singh B: Epitope dominance: evidence for reciprocal determinant spreading to glutamic acid decarboxylase in non-obese diabetic mice, *Immunol Rev* 164:111–118, 1998.

CHAPTER

15

Inhibition of Tau Aggregation as a Basis for Treatment and Prevention of Alzheimer's Disease

C.M. Wischik, J.M.D. Storey, D.J. Wischik, C.R. Harrington

OUTLINE

Developing Therapeutics for Alzheimer's Disease. http://dx.doi.org/10.1016/B978-0-12-802173-6.00015-0

INTRODUCTION: CHALLENGING COMMON PRECONCEPTIONS UNDERLYING THE RATIONALE IN STRATEGIES FOR PREVENTION AND TREATMENT OF AD PATHOLOGY

It is not necessary for the amyloid theory of molecular pathogenesis of Alzheimer's disease (AD) to be wrong for a treatment approach based on targeting the tau pathology of AD to have potential utility. What matters is the development of therapies that work, whatever the underlying rationale. However, the underlying theory of pathogenesis translates into the way we conceptualize the use and scope of potential treatments. Based on the genetic evidence in rare kindreds, a rather simplistic linear hypothesis has come to dominate the AD field over the past 20 years. In this view, deposition of amyloid-β in the brain is assumed to have temporal and etiological primacy in molecular pathogenesis. The expectation which follows is that an amyloid-based therapy will impact decisively on the theoretical cascade. In particular, there is a common expectation that targeting the pathological processing of APP will prevent the tau aggregation pathology: "We showed that if you use human neurons made from stem cells and you grow it in a gel that mimics the brain, that indeed amyloid causes tangles. So now there's no doubt. And if you stop the amyloid, you stop the tangles" (Tanzi, 2015).

We argue in this chapter that the poor correlation between amyloid-β load in the brain and deficits seen either clinically or by functional molecular imaging suggests that amyloid-β load is not itself the predominant substrate of dementia. The fact that numerous clinical trials at the mild/moderate stages of AD have failed (Wischik et al., 2014) has led to a repositioning of the same theory to prodromal and preclinical stages of the disease, on the assumption that the studies to date were conducted too late in the evolution of the disease. The revised view is that amyloid-β pathology triggers tau aggregation pathology, and it is the latter which drives clinical dementia and deficits on functional molecular imaging: "amyloid is the match that lights the fire, but the tangle is the fire that spreads through the brain" (Tanzi, 2015). However, the consistent failure of transgenic mouse models based on mutations in either APP or presenilin proteins to trigger robust intracellular tau aggregation pathology (Hall and Roberson, 2012) casts doubt on this view also.

We attempt in this review to set out an alternative position in which abnormal processing of APP may act merely as a contributory factor in certain individuals in an underlying cascade which has its roots in a more widespread age-related impairment in endosomal/lysosomal processing, or autophagy. On this view, the altered processing of APP leading to aggregation of amyloid-β in the brain may not be rate limiting. Therefore, therapeutic approaches targeting this pathway may have minimal effect on tau aggregation pathology and may thus have limited scope, even if there is some evidence of clinical efficacy. In other words, we argue against the proposition that an amyloid-based therapy should be considered *in principle* the first line of defense.

We set out some of the evidence that challenges the temporal, and therefore implied etiological, primacy of aggregation of amyloid-β in the brain. We review the clinico-pathological studies which show that, contrary to widely held opinion, the appearance of tau aggregation pathology in the brain is at least contemporaneous with the earliest stages of amyloid-β aggregation, if not definitely prior to it. It follows that there is no reason to prioritize therapeutic approaches targeting the APP cascade over those targeting the aggregation of tau protein as a preventive strategy. Whether during the 20 years preclinical to evident dementia or during the exponentially increasing rate of tau aggregation that occurs in the clinically evident phases of the disease, the pathological aggregation of tau protein is an entirely valid pharmaceutical target for prevention as well as treatment. We argue that there are plausible grounds for remaining agnostic as to the role of amyloid-β pathology as causative, or upstream or rate critical in the eventual evolution of clinical dementia.

If, as is now increasingly accepted, targeting the pathological aggregation of tau protein is a valid pharmaceutical strategy in its own right, the next question is how to do so. Although it is widely assumed in the field that "phosphorylated tau" and "paired helical filament (PHF) tau" are synonyms, we review the evidence questioning this identification. There have been numerous attempts to build conceptual bridges between altered processing of APP and tau aggregation pathology based on pathological phosphorylation of tau. These have formed the basis for proposing inhibition of pathological kinases as a viable therapeutic strategy. We show that less than 5% of aggregated tau is even full length, let alone phosphorylated. We review the evidence showing that "abnormal" phosphorylation of tau is inhibitory to tau aggregation and may actually be protective. We show that in tau-transgenic mouse models, it is possible to dissociate phosphorylation from aggregation of tau, and that neither behavioral deficits nor visible pathology is dependent on phosphorylation.

We develop an alternative position whereby the release of a primitive, conformationally distinct, high-affinity tau–tau binding interaction through the repeat domain is seen as the critical driver of the tau aggregation pathology of AD. The altered repeat domain forms a proteolytically stable oligomeric template which has the capacity to propagate and amplify itself at the expense of normal tau. Most likely, the primary conformational change in the repeat domain is initiated by binding to an exogenous substrate, probably a product of failed mitochondrial clearance due to age-related impairment in autophagy. Once available above a critical level, the proteolytically stable oligomers are able to transmit the pathology to otherwise healthy neurons. These induce the same conformational change in normal tau protein molecules, transmitting the pathology in a highly stereotyped neuropathological cascade which is quantitatively linked to clinical dementia.

Fortunately, the pathological binding interaction is conformationally distinct from the physiological tau–tubulin binding interaction, even though both occur through the repeat domain. This difference provides a potential therapeutic key, permitting both disaggregation of existing aggregates and prevention of further aggregation via a novel class of "tau aggregation inhibitors" (TAIs). Such compounds are selective, in that they do not interfere with the normal tau–tubulin binding interaction. They have the ability to reverse the proteolytic stability of both oligomers and polymers, thereby facilitating clearance and blocking the propagation of the pathology.

SEQUENCE OF CHANGES IN CEREBROSPINAL FLUID AMYLOID-β AND TAU BIOMARKERS

Biomarkers and their detection have assumed a particularly important role in theoretical and regulatory discussions of disease progression in AD, its treatment, and appropriate regulatory end points for clinical trials. It has come to be recognized that the development of AD pathology exists as a continuum which evolves over at least 20 years from preclinical to prodromal to mild/moderate dementia phases of the disease. However, the sequencing of cerebrospinal fluid (CSF) changes in amyloid-β and phosphorylated tau during the preclinical

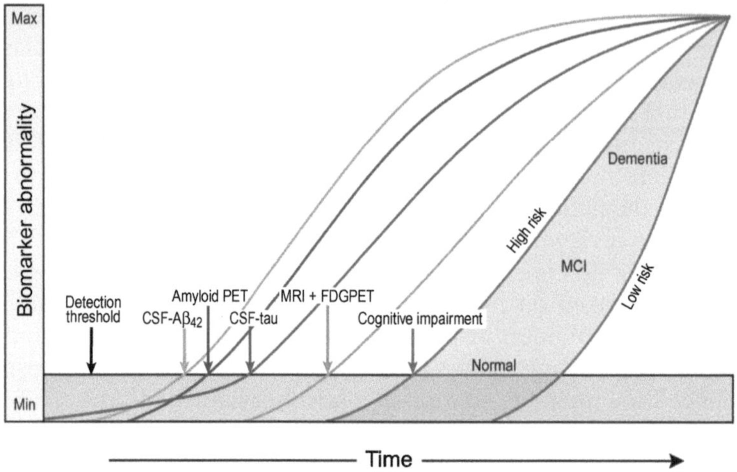

FIGURE 15.1 **Model integrating Alzheimer's disease immunohistology and biomarkers as hypothesized by Jack and coworkers.** The threshold for biomarker detection of pathophysiological changes is denoted by the black horizontal line at the top of the gray area that denotes the zone in which abnormal pathophysiological changes lie below the biomarker detection threshold. According to this figure, amyloid-β deposition precedes tau pathology in time in terms of changes in CSF markers which are detectable and detection of amyloid-β deposition by PET imaging. *Source: From Jack et al.:* Lancet Neurol *12:207–216, 2013, with permission of Elsevier.*

phases of AD has been interpreted to imply that amyloid-β pathology precedes tau aggregation pathology, and is therefore more suitable as a preventive target.

The picture generally quoted in this regard (Jack et al., 2013) emphasizes the temporal and etiological priority of changes in processing of amyloid-β (Fig. 15.1). This is, however, a diagrammatic illustration, and not a quantitative analysis of actual data.

Donohue et al. (2014) attempt to provide a quantitative picture based on long-term multivariate projection estimates calibrated to Mini Mental State Examination (MMSE) based on ADNI data in *APOE* ε4 carriers. In the Jack et al. picture (Fig. 15.1), disease markers are intended to range from 0 (absolutely normal) to 1 (absolutely abnormal) and follow sigmoidal shapes. The same concept has been applied in the Donohue et al. analysis shown in Fig. 15.2A, except that the derived trajectory is based on estimation of nonparametric monotonic functions for each variable, rather than imposing the assumption of a sigmoid trajectory. The vertical axis measures the normalized degree of abnormality, as is the intention in Fig. 15.1, and the values for the corresponding percentiles are stated explicitly in the Fig. 15.2 legend. As can be seen, CSF amyloid-β_{1-42} values begin to be abnormal at about the same time as the CSF p-tau values start to become abnormal. Fig. 15.2B shows the first derivative of the values shown in Fig. 15.2A, divided by the residual standard error (ie, an effect size expressed in terms of rate of change). Using this analysis, the earliest abnormality in CSF amyloid-β_{1-42} consists in an abrupt decrease in the rate of decline in levels and, for CSF p-tau, the earliest abnormality is an abrupt increase in the rate of increase in levels. Neither the CSF amyloid-β_{1-42} nor CSF p-tau follow a sigmoid trajectory as proposed in Jack et al. (2012).

In a recent study, in which the sequence of changes was examined for 137 cases of sporadic mild cognitive impairment (MCI) progressing to AD over a period of 9.2 years (Buchhave et al., 2012), levels of CSF amyloid-β_{1-42} were found to decrease 5–10 years before

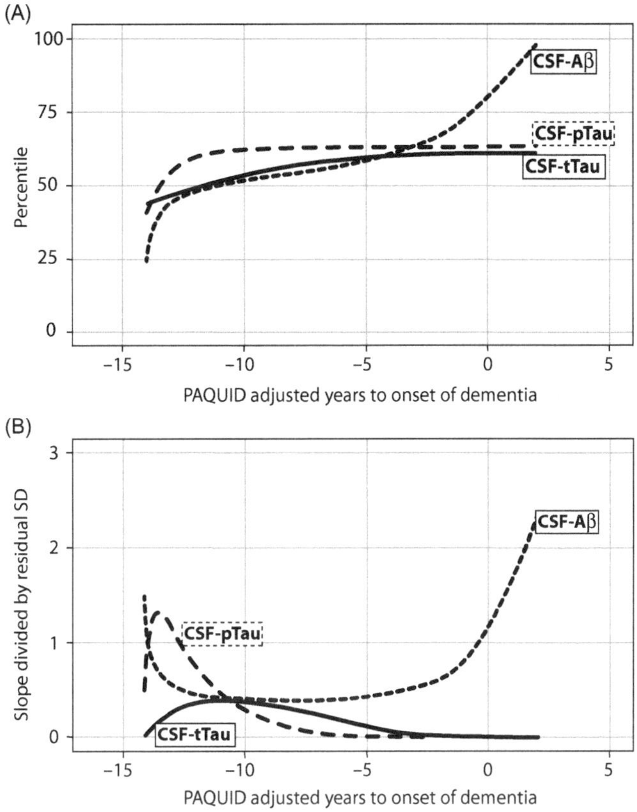

FIGURE 15.2 **The estimated mean trajectories of CSF markers determined for 570 ADNI *APOE* ε4 carriers in the 15 years preceding the onset of dementia.** Increasing percentile scores are intended to be associated with worsening of the disease, with zero representing complete normality and 1 representing complete abnormality. In (A) time has been adjusted using long-term "*Personnes Agées Quid*" (PAQUID) MMSE trajectories, so that time zero represents the estimated time to onset of dementia. The mean trajectories are shown for CSF-Aβ (CSF-amyloid-β), CSF-tau, and CSF-p-tau (phosphorylated tau) expressed in terms of estimated population percentiles according to degree of abnormality. The actual values for the 0th, 25th, 50th, 75th, and 100th percentiles are, respectively: for CSF-Aβ, 364, 181, 146, 131, 98 pg/mL; for CSF-tau, 31, 64, 90, 122, 379 pg/mL; for CSF-p-tau, 10.0, 21.6, 32.3, 42.0, 82.0 pg/mL. Thus, the percentiles given in (A) correspond to extent of abnormality, with values becoming more abnormal on the vertical axis, decreasing for Aβ and increasing tau and p-tau. This corresponds conceptually to the Jack et al. representation in Fig. 15.1. In (B), the first derivatives of the values shown in (A) are plotted, showing the corresponding rates of change in degree of abnormality. *Source: Adapted from Donohue et al.:* Alzheimers Dement *10:S400–S410, 2014, with permission of Elsevier.*

conversion to AD and then stay low, whereas CSF tau began to increase at about the same time, and continued to increase steadily during the progress to clinical dementia. In another study of 128 subjects with autosomal-dominant AD mutations, in which it was assumed that the age of dementia onset is the same in unaffected subjects as in probands, the earliest CSF biomarker to change was amyloid-β_{1-42} (Bateman et al., 2012). Unlike the studies of Donohue et al. and Buchhave et al., the selection of cases with autosomal-dominant AD mutations is likely to have biased the data. However, this was not the case in the study of Braak et al. (2013), which reports that changes in CSF amyloid-β precede those in CSF tau, whereas for the brain pathology the order is reversed, as discussed further in the next section. Overall, therefore, the picture emerging from biomarker studies is complex, is subject to a high degree of interindividual variability, and does not follow the simple model proposed by Jack et al. In relation to p-tau, the question remains as to what exactly is being measured at the molecular level in CSF, and how this relates or fails to relate to brain pathology, given the apparent dissociation between tau pathology and CSF p-tau reported by Braak et al. (2013).

NEUROPATHOLOGICAL SEQUENCE OF CHANGES IN AMYLOID-β AND TAU MARKERS IN THE NEOCORTEX

The pattern of spread of the tau aggregation pathology in the human brain is highly characteristic and stereotyped. Layer II of the entorhinal cortex is the first area to be affected in the cortex. From here, the pathology spreads via the perforant pathway to the hippocampus. Projections from the hippocampus return to layer IV of the entorhinal cortex and also to other limbic structures. From here, the pathology spreads into the isocortex, initially into temporal and parietal lobes and eventually into frontal and occipital neocortex. This pattern of progression and spread forms the basis of the six-stage Braak staging system for neurofibrillary degeneration in AD (Braak and Braak, 1991).

Braak staging has proved to be a useful tool for examining the sequence of molecular and pathological events in the brain. We reported a study in a prospectively characterized neuropathological cohort in which we examined the sequence of changes in tau and amyloid-β pathology, tau aggregation measured biochemically (as proteolytically stable PHF levels), and corresponding changes in synaptic markers that occurred in the neocortex (Mukaetova-Ladinska et al., 2000). The Braak staging "clock" can be defined, at the early stages, on the basis of histopathological changes restricted largely to entorhinal cortex and hippocampus (stages 1 and 2). The sequence of changes in parietal and frontal neocortex, which begin later in terms of histopathology (stages 3 and 4), can then be analyzed at the molecular level as they develop against an initially clear histopathological background, using the staging clock to order the sequence. These are summarized in Fig. 15.3.

In contrast to tau histopathology (measured as tangle counts), PHF accumulation reaches detection levels that are statistically significant from Braak stage 2 onward in parietal and frontal neocortex. In the neocortex, therefore, tangles are a relatively late manifestation of tau aggregation pathology that can be detected biochemically as proteolytically stable PHFs. As discussed further later, the calculated interval between onset of tau aggregation in neocortex and tangle histopathology is about 35 years. Braak stages 4–6 represent the more typically recognized stages of pathology, in which the appearance of tau tangles and tau-positive neuritic plaques appear at approximately the same time. There is a slight (nonsignificant) increase in diffuse amyloid plaques at Braak stage 2, but these increase in a statistically significant manner only at Braak stage 4, along with the histological markers of tau aggregation pathology. Thus, Braak stage 4 represents a point of neuropathological transition that is expressed simultaneously in terms of both neurofibrillary tangles and neuritic/amyloid plaques. However, further progression in Braak stages 5 and 6 is seen only for the tau markers.

It is surprising to see that the changes in levels of synaptic proteins measured biochemically in the same brain regions follow a biphasic course, with an initial *increase* at Braak

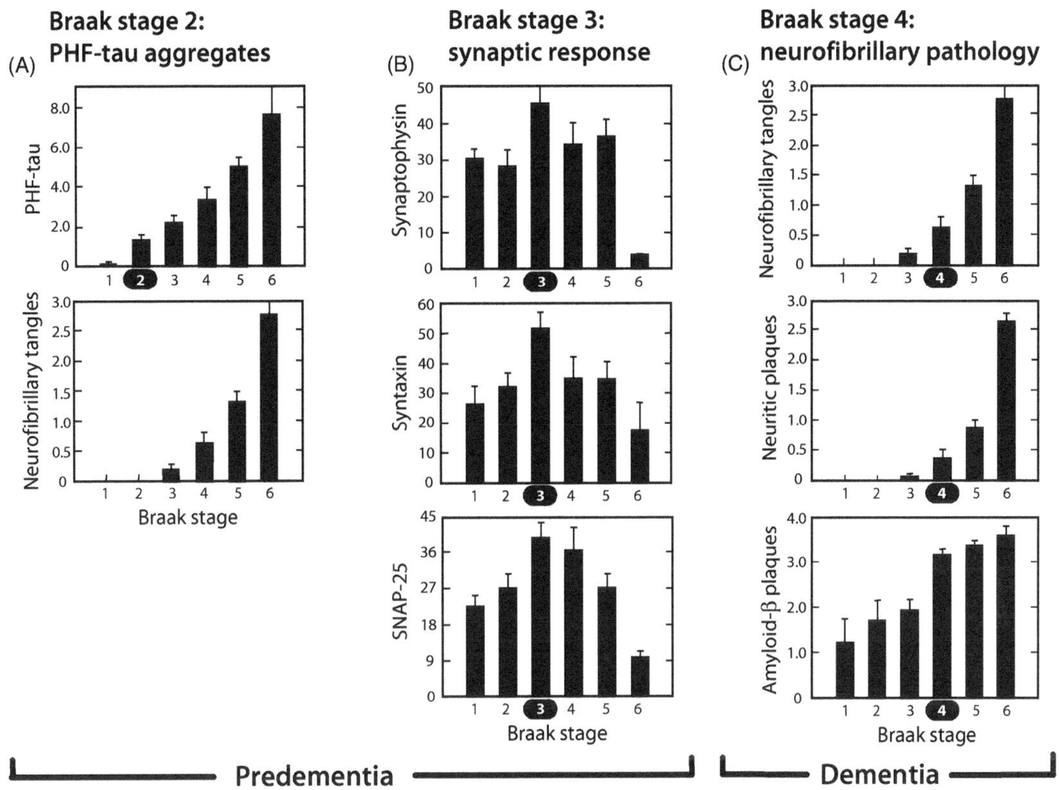

FIGURE 15.3 **Molecular characterization of Braak stages in frontal and temporal cortex.** (A) PHF-tau (upper panel) is already present by Braak stage 2, whereas significant numbers of neurofibrillary tangles are not observed until stage 4 and beyond (lower panel). (B) Immunochemical measurements of three synaptic proteins (synaptophysin, syntaxin, and SNAP-25) with respect to Braak stage. (C) Neuropathological changes in tau-positive tangles, tau-positive neuritic plaques, and amyloid-β plaques by Braak stage. *Source: Adapted from Mukaetova-Ladinska et al.:* Am J Pathol *157:623–636, 2000, with permission of Elsevier.*

stage 3, followed by progressive decrease only from Braak stage 4 onward. This implies that the appearance of measurable levels of proteolytically stable aggregated tau in the neocortex at Braak stage 2 is followed by a statistically significant *increase* in synaptic proteins at Braak stage 3. Whether this increase is a compensatory consequence of a functional impairment in pyramidal transmission or a release phenomenon resulting in loss of inhibitory tone in the pyramidal cell system is unknown at present. Either way, this provides a direct measure of a physiological impairment/disturbance consequent upon the appearance of proteolytically stable aggregated tau in the neocortex. These data also provide a neurophysiological complement to the molecular neuroimaging data, discussed further later, whereby Braak stage correlates with functional impairment shown by FDG-PET and hexa-methyl-propyl-amine-oxime single-photon emission computed tomography (HMPAO-SPECT) .

The picture that has emerged from a very large pathological study in 2332 subjects very clearly places tau pathology ahead of amyloid-β pathology by at least 20 years

(Braak et al., 2013). For this study, Braak et al. compared staging of tau aggregation pathology and staging of amyloid-β pathology, providing three levels with increasing amyloid (stages A–C). This has been compared with tau staging for 2661 consecutive autopsy cases of subjects between the ages of 25 and 95 years (Braak et al., 2013). It is clear from this that tau aggregation precedes amyloid-β deposition (Fig. 15.4), confirming earlier reports showing the same thing (Duyckaerts, 2011; Mukaetova-Ladinska et al., 2000).

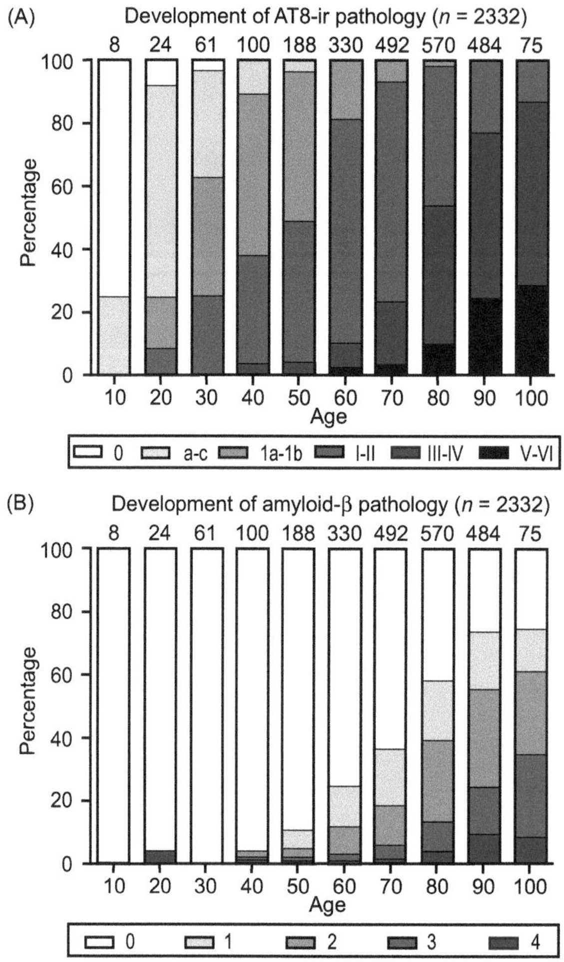

FIGURE 15.4 Intraneuronal deposits of abnormal tau and extracellular amyloid-β deposition in 2332 nonselected autopsy cases. (A) White portions of the columns represent the relative frequency of cases without abnormal tau. Increasing darkness from gray to black shows progression of neurofibrillary pathology through Braak stages 1 to 6. (B) White portions represent proportion of cases without amyloid-β pathology. Increasing darkness from gray to black represents subgroups showing the presence of amyloid-β deposition progressively affecting basal temporal neocortex (phase 1), allocortex (phase 2), and neocortical association areas of all lobes (phase 3) before affecting virtually all regions of the cerebral cortex (phase 4). Amyloid-β plaques appear relatively late and affect only a fraction of the cases, all of which also have tau pathology. *Source: From Braak et al.:* Acta Neuropathol *126:631–641, 2013, with permission of Springer.*

Similar findings have emerged from an even larger recent study from the Mayo Clinic in 3618 subjects (Murray et al., 2015). Murray and coworkers used the Thal six-stage amyloid phasing system (Thal et al., 2002), which depends on the regional distribution of thioflavin-S positive amyloid-β plaques. As can be seen in Fig. 15.5A, these begin in middle frontal and inferior temporal regions at Thal phase 1, progress to superior temporal cortex and subiculum

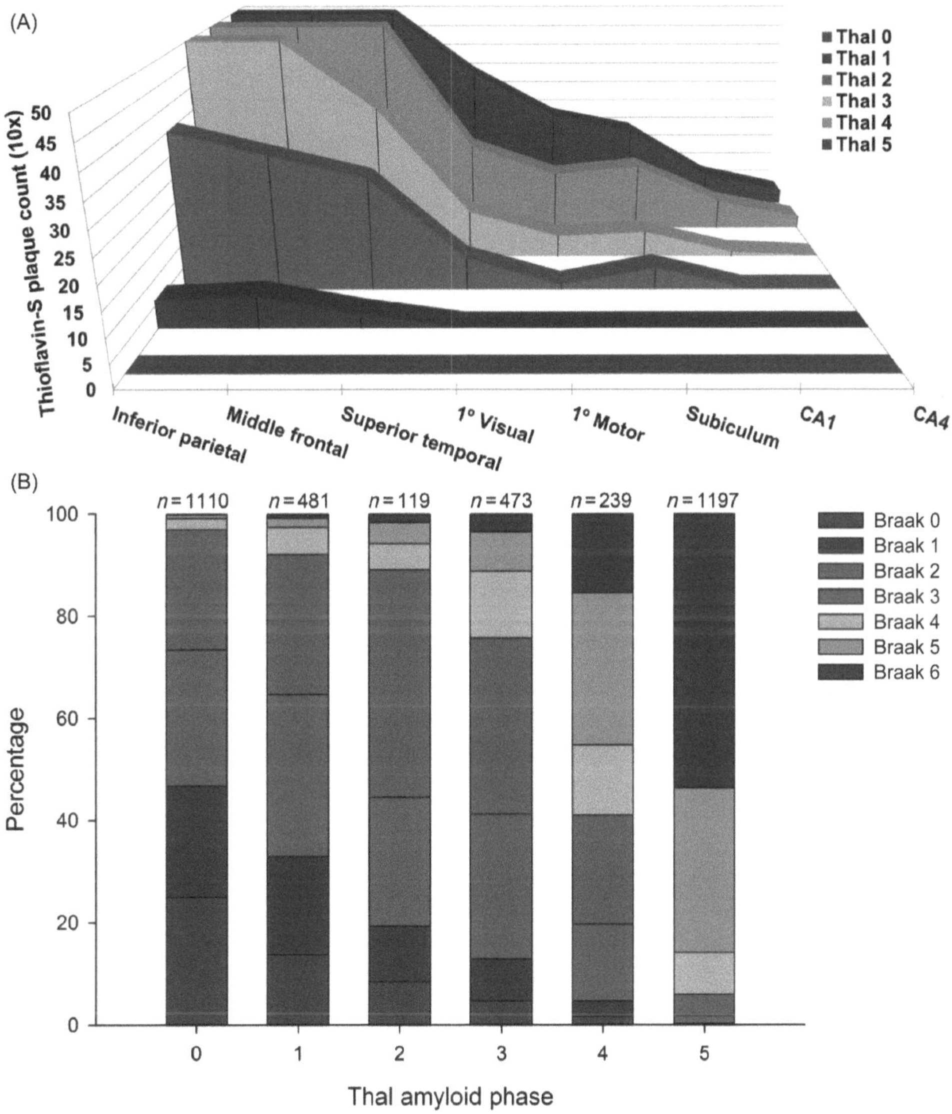

FIGURE 15.5 **Sequence of neuropathological changes in a series of 3618 cases.** (A) Stereotypic progression of thioflavin-S plaque counts by six Thal amyloid phases. There is an incremental involvement of association cortices and allocortices throughout each phase. (B) The proportion for individual Braak stages is shown for each Thal amyloid phase. *Source: From Murray et al.:* Brain, *138:1370-1381, 2015, with permission of Oxford University Press.*

at Thal phase 2, and then progress to visual and motor cortices at Thal phases 3–5. It is particularly striking in this study that at Thal phase 0, already 52% of cases are at Braak stage 2 or beyond (Fig. 15.5B). This provides independent confirmation of the neuropathological sequence provided in the 2013 study of Braak et al. In other words, the generally quoted schematic picture of events proposed by Jack et al. (2013) is not supported by the neuropathological sequence seen in the brain.

RELATIONSHIP BETWEEN TAU PATHOLOGY AND COGNITIVE IMPAIRMENT AND IMAGING DEFICITS

Numerous clinico-pathological studies have demonstrated correlations between tau pathology and the extent of clinical dementia (Arriagada et al., 1992; Bancher et al., 1993, 1996; Chien et al., 2013; Duyckaerts et al., 1997; Grober et al., 1999; Maruyama et al., 2013; Mukaetova-Ladinska et al., 2000; Okamura et al., 2014; Wilcock and Esiri, 1982). In an epidemiological study based on repeated sampling of an original population in primary care, where MMSE scores were measured 12–24 months prior to death, we were able to determine the approximate trajectory linking Braak stage and MMSE score (Mukaetova-Ladinska et al., 2000). As can be seen in Fig. 15.6, what is now referred to interchangeably as prodromal AD or MCI (ie, MMSE score >25) occurs roughly between Braak stages 2 and 3.

The relationship between tau aggregation pathology and cognitive impairment, already well established in the previous literature, has been confirmed most recently in the large Mayo Clinic study referred to earlier (Murray et al., 2015). In an unselected subset of 1375 cases where MMSE within the last 3 years prior to death and education were determined retrospectively from the case notes, postmortem findings were quantified in terms of Braak stage, Thal amyloid phase, age at death, brain weight, *APOE* genotype status, and presence or absence of Lewy body pathology. Only the Braak tangle stage was found to be a significant predictor of final MMSE score, with brain weight a further weaker factor.

There are similar strong relationships between Braak stage and functional molecular imaging deficits as shown either by HMPAO-SPECT or FDG-PET. Although FDG-PET tends to be used more widely for functional molecular imaging of the brain in the United States, both HMPAO-SPECT and FDG-PET have similar ability to demonstrate deficits due to neuropathology (Herholz et al., 2002; Matsuda, 2007). Both are nonspecific tracers that show uptake proportionate to cerebral blood flow and glucose uptake, respectively. As such, they are both indirect measures of normal brain metabolism. Their contribution to an imaging diagnosis in AD is the pattern of reduction in blood flow or glucose uptake in areas of the brain typically affected by tau aggregation pathology (Matsuda, 2007). Normal brain metabolic activities (ie, oxygen and glucose consumption, respectively) are impaired in regions typically affected by tau aggregation pathology. Both HMPAO-SPECT (Bradley et al., 2002; Jobst et al., 1992) and FDG-PET (Mosconi et al., 2009) are correlated with Braak stage.

The emergence of tau imaging ligands has made possible the direct imaging of tau aggregation pathology in vivo (Villemagne et al., 2015). This has permitted an explicit confirmation of the relationship between aggregation of tau and functional molecular imaging deficits. Functional deficit is strongly correlated with tau aggregation as shown by tau-PET imaging, but not with aggregation of amyloid-β as shown by imaging with ^{11}C-PIB (Ossenkoppele et al., 2015) (Fig. 15.7).

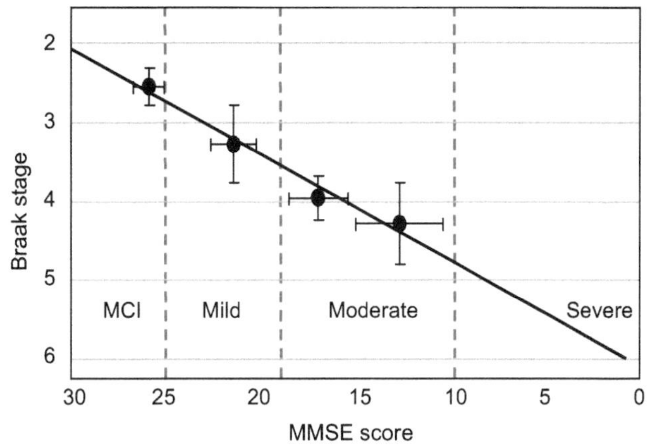

FIGURE 15.6 Correlation of Braak staging with cognitive decline measured by Mini Mental State Examination (MMSE) determined 12–24 months antemortem. *Source: From Wischik et al.:* Biochem Pharmacol *88:529–539, 2014, based on data from Mukaetova-Ladinska et al.:* Am J Pathol *157:623–636, 2000.*

It is unlikely that the functional molecular imaging deficits in the neocortex that are commonly used to support a diagnosis of AD are due to neuronal loss. Based on an analysis of neurofibrillary tangles in a prospectively characterized population of AD cases (García-Sierra et al., 2001), the extracellular neurofibrillary tangles left behind after cell death are not seen in the neocortex until Braak stages 5/6 (Fig. 15.8). This contrasts with the entorhinal cortex and hippocampus, where extracellular tangles are already prominent from Braak stage 2 onward. Thus the relationship in the neocortex between impairment in glucose utilization as shown

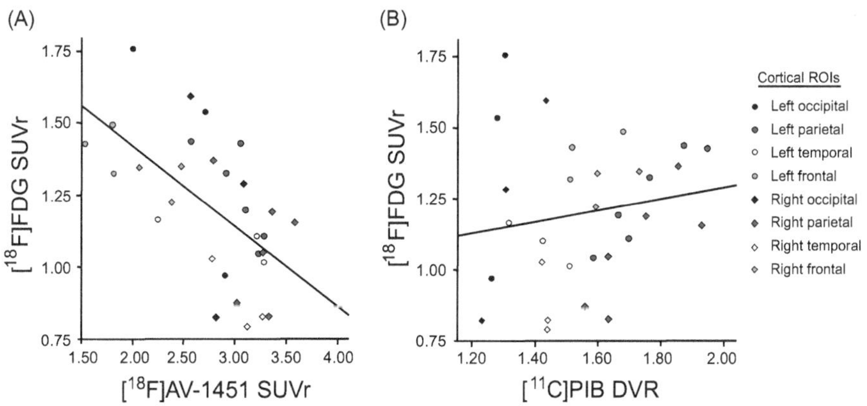

FIGURE 15.7 Correlations between [^{18}F]fluorodeoxyglucose (FDG) uptake and (A) retention of the tau ligand [^{18}F]AV-1451 ($r = -0.60$, $p < 0.001$) and (B) binding of [^{11}C]Pittsburgh compound B (PIB) binding ($r = 0.17$, $p = 0.38$) across the neocortex suggest a stronger relationship with hypometabolism for tau than for amyloid pathology. DVR, distribution volume ratio; SUVr, standardized uptake value ratio; ROI, region of interest. *Source: From Ossenkoppele et al.:* Ann Neurol *77:338–342, 2015, with permission of John Wiley & Sons.*

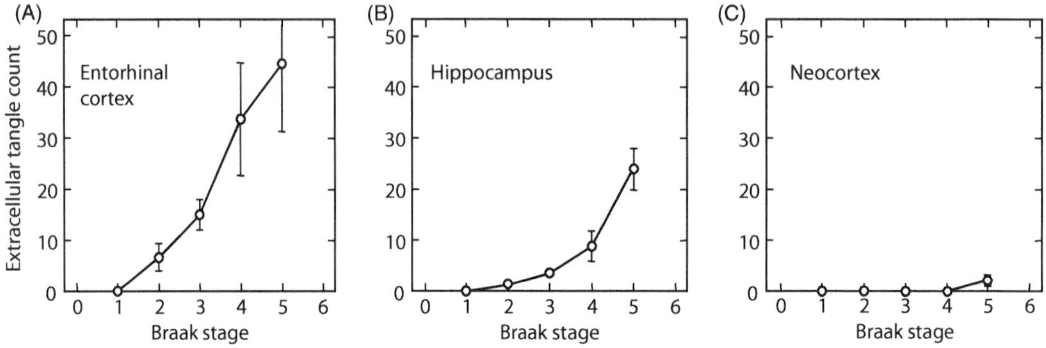

FIGURE 15.8 Counts of extracellular neurofibrillary tangles in (A) entorhinal cortex, (B) hippocampus, and (C) neocortex as a function of Braak stage.

by FDG-PET and tau aggregation as shown by tau-PET imaging is likely to be driven by functional consequences of tau aggregation in living neurons rather than loss of neurons.

TEMPORAL SEQUENCING OF TAU AGGREGATION, PATHOLOGY, AND COGNITIVE IMPAIRMENT

The relationships discussed so far are based on "pathological time" as defined by Braak tangle stage. It is possible to convert this to actual time using the Ohm data (Ohm et al., 1995), which reported Braak stage relative to age in 847 routine autopsies in subjects aged 45–95 years (17 cases per year of life) that had not been selected for presence of cognitive impairment. We have applied a Kaplan–Meier survival analysis to these data to calculate the survival probabilities for transitions from Braak stage 0 $\rightarrow$ 1 or beyond, Braak stage 1 $\rightarrow$ 2 or beyond, Braak stage 2 $\rightarrow$ 3 or beyond, and Braak stage 3 $\rightarrow$ 4 or beyond. These probabilities are shown in Fig. 15.9A. It is also possible to use the same data set to calculate an explicit relationship between Braak stage and age in years, as shown in Fig. 15.9B.

Data are also available linking direct measurements of aggregated tau (Lai et al., 1995; Mukaetova-Ladinska et al., 2000), intracellular and extracellular tangle counts in entorhinal cortex, hippocampus, and neocortex (García-Sierra et al., 2001; Gertz et al., 1996; Mukaetova-Ladinska et al., 2000), and measurement of MMSE score in the 12–24 months prior to death to Braak stage (García-Sierra et al., 2001; Gertz et al., 1996; Lai et al., 1995; Mukaetova-Ladinska et al., 2000). Since the Ohm et al. (1995) data permit a mapping of Braak stage to actual time, it is possible to put together the overall composite schema based on years since Braak stage 1, as shown in Fig. 15.10.

There are several important points to note. The first is that the entire sequence occurs over a 50-year time span. Second, the primary vertical axis shows levels of aggregated tau in the form of proteolytically stable PHFs measured in the entorhinal cortex, hippocampus, and neocortex on a logarithmic scale. In other words, the progressive accumulation of aggregated tau is exponential over time, consistent with the autocatalytic characteristics of tau aggregation through the repeat domain, discussed further later. By linking tau levels to tangle

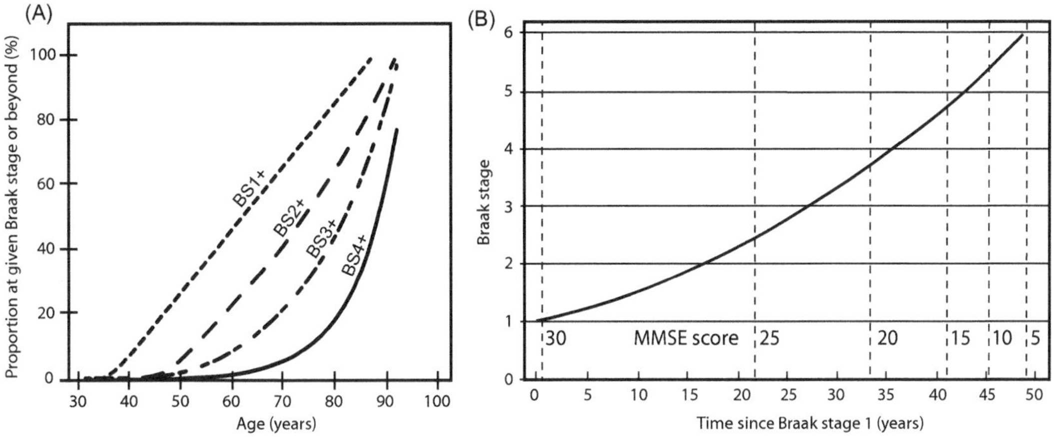

FIGURE 15.9 **Epidemiology of tau aggregation pathology.** (A) Age-specific probability of Braak stage transitions based on the Ohm et al. autopsy series. (B) Use of the same data set to determine relationship between Braak stage and age. *Source: Part A from Wischik et al.:* Biochem Pharmacol *88:529–539, 2014.*

counts, it is possible to derive a measurement for the threshold at which the accumulation of proteolytically stable PHFs, measured biochemically, becomes visible histologically as intracellular neurofibrillary tangles. This occurs at about 0.03 ng/g of PHFs for any of the three tissues measured, with entorhinal cortex being the first region where this threshold is met. This threshold is not met in the neocortex until more than 35 years later. At a PHF tissue level of about 2 ng/g, intracellular neurofibrillary tangles become extracellular. For all three regions, this transition from intracellular to extracellular tangles takes more than 25 years.

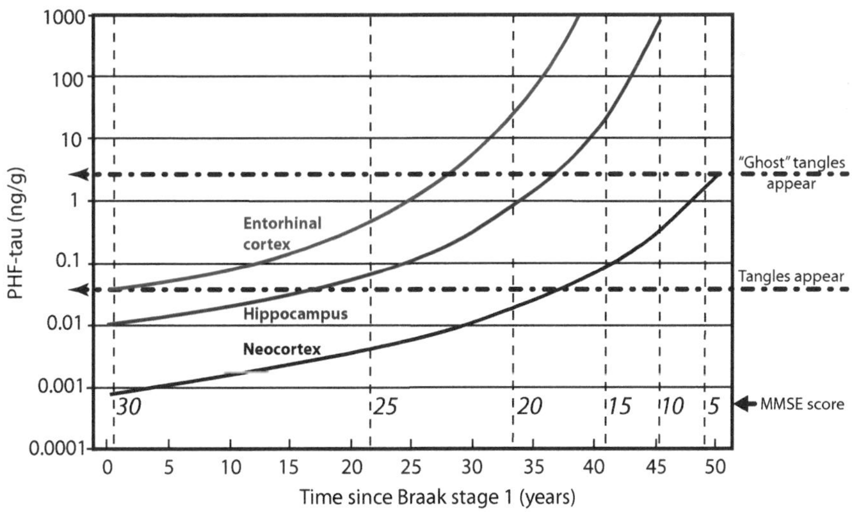

FIGURE 15.10 Measures of aggregated PHF-tau (from Lai et al., 1995; Mukaetova-Ladinska et al., 2000), intra- and extracellular tangles in entorhinal cortex, hippocampus, and neocortex (from Gertz et al., 1996; Mukaetova-Ladinska et al., 2000) according to Braak stage expressed as time in years since Braak stage 1 as depicted in Fig. 15.9B.

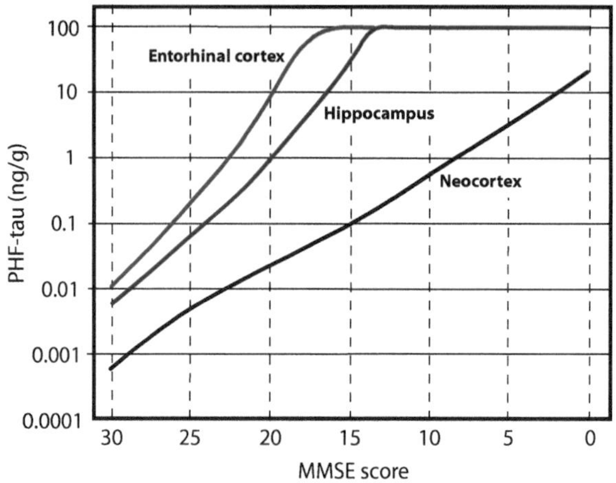

FIGURE 15.11 **PHF accumulation in entorhinal cortex, hippocampus, and neocortex increases exponentially with decline in MMSE score.** The plots are based on values truncated at a PHF level of 100 ng/g in brain tissue.

As can be seen explicitly in Fig. 15.11, the MMSE score is linearly related to the logarithm of brain PHF content; that is, MMSE score is an exponential measure of PHF load. A 4-point decline in MMSE score between 29 and 25 is associated with 15-fold (0.03–0.46 ng/g), 7-fold (0.008–0.058 ng/g), and 5-fold (0.0008–0.0042 ng/g) increases in PHF content in entorhinal cortex, hippocampus, and neocortex, respectively. Whereas these levels are sufficient to cross the threshold for intracellular tangles in the entorhinal cortex and hippocampus, this is not the case in the neocortex.

THE EPIDEMIOLOGY OF TAU AGGREGATION PATHOLOGY

The Ohm et al. (1995) data set also makes it possible to estimate population prevalence of tau aggregation pathology by Braak stage. We have applied the Braak transition probabilities by age (shown in Fig. 15.9A) to estimate the number of affected persons in the United States by age (Fig. 15.12), using WHO data for the US 2010 population. We calculate that for the population over the age of 45, there is a 50% probability of having some degree of tau pathology in the brain. This can be divided as follows: 25% at Braak stage 1, 10% at Braak stage 2, 10% at Braak stage 3, and 5% at Braak stage 4 or beyond. The age profile of the affected US population is shown in Fig. 15.12. We estimate that there are approximately 64 million people in the United States affected with some degree of tau aggregation pathology in their brains: 31 million at Braak stage 1, 13 million at Braak stage 2, 12 million at Braak stage 3, and 7 million at Braak stage 4 or beyond. It is only the latter number which is typically captured by prevalence estimates of AD in the United States (Hebert et al., 2013). The projected numbers for all affected persons in the United States are 88 million in 2030 and 105 million in 2050.

Applying the same methodology to European data, the affected population is currently estimated to be 170 million, increasing to 208 million in 2030 and 223 million in 2050. The numbers for Asia are truly staggering. We estimate that across all of Asia (including China,

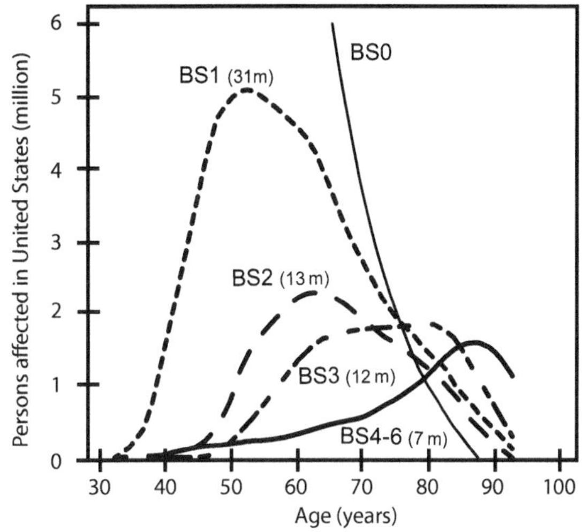

FIGURE 15.12 **Number of persons at a given Braak stage in the US population in 2010 with numbers affected for each stage, in millions.** *Source: From Wischik et al.:* Biochem Pharmacol *88:529–539, 2014.*

India, Indonesia, and Japan), there are at present 520 million persons affected by tau aggregation pathology, with 227 million at Braak stage 2 or beyond. By 2030, the total is expected to increase to 889 million, with 428 million at Braak stage 2 or beyond. By 2050, the total is expected to increase to 1.2 billion, with 665 million at Braak stage 2 or beyond.

As discussed earlier, the tauopathy of AD is not a late-life/late-stage phenomenon. The peak age for Braak stage 1 is 55 years, but it can appear as early as 38 years. Braak has suggested that the process may well begin in the 20s (Braak and Del Tredici, 2011). For those who convert to Braak stage 2, the transition can occur as early as 48 years, but the peak age for Braak stage 2 is the mid-60s. Based on the cross-sectional estimates of the population data, it appears that only half of those at Braak stage 1 progress to Braak stage 2. However, the estimated population at Braak stage 2 is equivalent to that at Braak stage 3, but shifted in age by about 10 years. This suggests that Braak stage 1 is a state of risk, from which it is possible not to progress with about a 50% probability. However, once Braak stage 2 has been reached, it appears from this cross-sectional analysis that essentially everyone at Braak stage 2 progresses to Braak stage 3 and beyond. As shown in Fig. 15.6, Braak stage 2 corresponds approximately to the maximum MMSE score of 30/30, and hence is largely invisible clinically without close attention to subjective memory impairments and more sophisticated psychometric assessments than are common in routine clinical practice, as well as without costly brain imaging.

MOLECULAR DISSECTION OF THE NEUROFIBRILLARY TANGLE

Having discussed the temporal sequencing of tau aggregation pathology over the human life span largely at the histological level, we turn now to a characterization of the pathology at the molecular level. What we now call the amyloid plaque had been described by Blocq and Marinesco (1892), whereas what we call the neuritic plaque was first described by Fischer

(1907). What Alzheimer actually discovered was the neurofibrillary tangle (Alzheimer, 1907), although he also described "miliary foci" that correspond to what we now call amyloid plaques, but did not ascribe the same pathological significance to the latter. The neurofibrillary tangle comprises a dense whorl of fibers occupying the entire perinuclear cytoplasm of cortical pyramidal cells and other large neurons in the brain stem (nucleus basalis of Meynert and locus coeruleus). These fibers were termed paired helical filaments (PHFs) by Kidd (Kidd, 1963). Structurally, the PHF is a de novo polymer of C-shaped subunits forming a left-handed helical ribbon with a periodicity of ~70 nm (Wischik et al., 1985). Neurofibrillary tangles can be labeled in situ with antibodies against a variety of neuronal proteins, including vimentin, actin, ubiquitin, MAP2, and amyloid-β. In crude preparations, PHFs can be labeled with antibodies against MAP2, neurofilament, ubiquitin, and tau (Anderton et al., 1982; Brion et al., 1985; Grundke-Iqbal et al., 1986a, b; Ihara et al., 1986; Masters et al., 1985a, b; Mori et al., 1987; Perry et al., 1987; Yen et al., 1983, 1987). It was only when we succeeded in isolating a short 12-kD protein fragment from highly enriched preparations of proteolytically stable core PHFs that it was possible to establish unequivocally that a short segment of tau protein from the repeat region of the molecule is an integral structural constituent of the PHF (Wischik et al., 1988a).

Another common misconception, which has entered the literature since the papers by Lee et al. (1991) and Goedert et al. (1992), is that PHFs are composed "almost entirely of hyperphosphorylated tau protein." The further finding that hyperphosphorylation of tau protein leads to a 20-fold inhibition of tau–tubulin binding affinity has led to a widely held view that abnormal phosphorylation of tau protein plays a critical role in the pathogenesis of neurofibrillary degeneration. The idea is that the balance between kinases and phosphatases is disturbed in AD, leading tau protein to become detached from microtubules, and secondarily to aggregate. In this scenario, a tau-based therapeutic approach would target a kinase particularly responsible for a pattern of phosphorylation causing reduced microtubule stability.

Although PHFs isolated without protease digestion can be immunolabeled by tau antibodies directed against phosphorylation-dependent epitopes located in the N-terminal half of the molecule, this immunoreactivity is lost after proteolytic removal of the fuzzy coat (Wischik et al., 1988a, b). The fuzzy coat consists of the lengthy N-terminal portions of tau molecules that cover the surface of the filaments and are readily sensitive to proteolytic digestion. Such digestion leaves intact the proteolytically stable core structure comprising the left-handed helical or straight ribbon of repeated C-shaped subunits. In other words, the fuzzy coat comprising phosphorylated tau does not contribute to the structural core of the PHF.

It is possible to deduce the relative contributions of tau protein to the structural core and the fuzzy coat. Since the mean molecular mass of the protease-resistant core of the PHF is ~65 kDa/nm (Wischik et al., 1988a), and since the only tau fragments isolated from the core of the PHF are restricted to the repeat domain with a predicted mass of ~10 kDa, there must be 6 or 7 tandem-repeat fragments per nm to account for the observed mass of ~65 kDa/nm of the PHF core (if tau is the only constituent). If these tau molecules were N-terminally intact in fuzzy PHFs, the predicted mass of the PHF would be ~210 kDa/nm, since the additional N-terminal mass is ~23 kDa per tau molecule [$6.5 \times (10 + 23) = 210$]. This would add an additional 145 kDa/nm to the fuzzy coat. However, the majority of PHFs isolated from the brain without proteases have a mass of only 80–95 kDa/nm and the maximum measured mass is 110 kDa/nm. This implies that only 1 in 7 of the tau molecules making up the PHF is N-terminally intact, the remainder being truncated and restricted to the repeat domain of the molecule. The alternative is that there is another non-tau molecule which contributes to the core of the PHF. We have shown that the latter is not the case, and that tau protein indeed accounts for at least 93% of the protein content of the PHF (Wischik et al., 1997). Indeed, biochemical studies which set out to quantify the amount of PHF-tau which is phosphorylated showed the amount to be less than 5% (Lai et al., 1995; Wischik et al., 1995), in line with the structural mass data.

A characteristic feature of the tau protein found in the core of the PHF (the PHF-core tau unit) is that it is restricted to the repeat domain but shifted by 15 residues with respect to the organization of the tubulin-binding repeats. As illustrated in Fig. 15.13A, the N-termini of the tau fragments found in the proteolytically stable structural core of the PHF are located 15 residues C-terminal to the start of the repeats, and have a characteristic C-terminal truncation at position Glu-391, which is 15 residues C-terminal to the end of the repeats (Novak et al., 1993). If one compares the alignment of the repeats in the PHF-core unit (Fig. 15.13B) with that of normal tau (Fig. 15.13C), it is striking that the core fragment and its homologs are nevertheless exactly 3 repeats in length, but shifted by 15 residues with respect to the normal repeat structure.

The characteristic Glu-391 C-terminal truncation creates a tau neo-epitope that is recognized by a monoclonal antibody (mAb 423, Fig. 15.14A) that was raised against proteolytically stable PHF preparations (Harrington et al., 1991; Novak et al., 1991) and which has been used to monitor tau pathology in vivo and tau aggregation in vitro. In AD brain tissues, this neo-epitope is available without occlusion in early pathological tau oligomers, in tau oligomers accumulating in pathological lysosomes (so-called granulovacuolar degeneration), and in end-stage extracellular PHFs (Bondareff et al., 1991; Bondareff et al., 1994; Mena et al., 1995, 1996). In intracellular PHFs, the epitope is occluded by a coating of full-length, hyperphosphorylated PHF-associated tau which constitutes the proteolytically sensitive fuzzy coat of the PHF (Wischik et al., 1988b). The underlying neo-epitope can be exposed by treatment with formic acid (Bondareff et al., 1994; Mena et al., 1995, 1996; Wischik et al., 1988b).

C-terminal truncation of tau at Asp-421 is an early event in tau aggregation (Luna-Munoz et al., 2007), and C-terminally truncated tau protein also has a greater affinity for binding full-length tau molecules (Abraha et al., 2000; Berry et al., 2003). The relationship between phospho-dependent tau epitopes located at the C-terminus with truncation at Glu-391 has been investigated to determine whether C-terminal truncation may trigger events leading to the assembly of insoluble PHFs from soluble tau aggregates present in pretangle cells (Flores-Rodríguez et al., 2015). The first abnormal event, occurring in the cytoplasm of neurons prone to degeneration in AD, is characterized by the appearance of the minimal PHF-tau core unit (truncated at Glu-391) within the cytoplasm (Fig. 15.15, stage 1). This pathological event appears to determine subsequent stages that are characterized by the binding of intact tau molecules to the PHF core. The resultant tau oligomers appear to act as a template that grows bidirectionally as further tau molecules become sequestered and structurally integrated into the proto-PHF. The toxic PHF-core tau fragment would be expected to trigger a cellular protective response, including phosphorylation of normal tau protein and activation of caspases, including caspase-3 (Fasulo et al., 2000, 2005; Gamblin et al., 2003). Once attached to a highly stable and resistant PHF core, full-length tau protein would then become phosphorylated. This additional full-length hyperphosphorylated tau

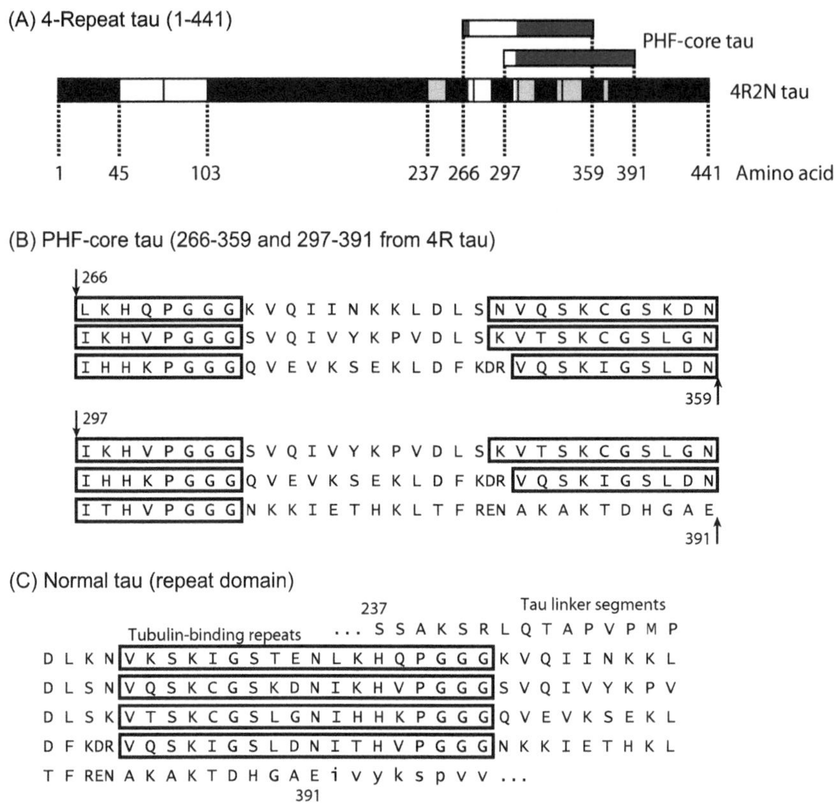

FIGURE 15.13 **Relationship of the fragments found in the PHF-core to the full-length tau molecule.** (A) Full-length tau with two N-terminal inserts (white) and 4 C-terminal repeats (4R2N); the second repeat (shown in white) is absent from the 3-repeat isoforms. The numbering corresponds to amino acid residues of the largest 441-residue tau isoform. The only species of tau found in the proteolytically stable core of the PHF are from the repeat domain. These fragments (shown as stippled) are restricted to exactly 3 repeats in length, regardless of the isoform from which they originate. There are two fragments from the 4-repeat isoforms that originate from repeats 1, 2, and 3 and from repeats 2, 3, and 4. A fragment originating from the 3-repeat isoforms, originating from repeats 1, 3, and 4, is not shown for simplicity. (B) The sequence of the two PHF-core tau units derived from 4-repeat tau. (C) The sequence of normal tau for the repeat domain. The tubulin-binding domains are shown in black boxes, separated by intervening linker segments. The PHF-core tau units have N-termini midway through the tubulin-binding segment, and extend C-terminally by 15 residues to the end of the repeats in such a way that the N- and C-termini are exactly equivalent to 3 repeats in length (B). This contrasts with the normal alignment structure of the repeat domain (C). Thus, the PHF-core unit is shifted 15 residues with respect to the normal alignment of the repeat domain. This is the consequence of the characteristic pathological tau–tau binding structure that defines the proteolytically stable footprint of the pathological binding domain.

occludes the Glu-391 epitope. This would be consistent with the idea that phosphorylation in the early stages of PHF formation may play a protective role, based on in vitro and animal models (Arendt et al., 2003). Tau hyperphosphorylation had been proposed as a protective mechanism for other reasons as well, since it is seen also in normal, nonpathological conditions, such as during development or hibernation, where tau hyperphosphorylation does

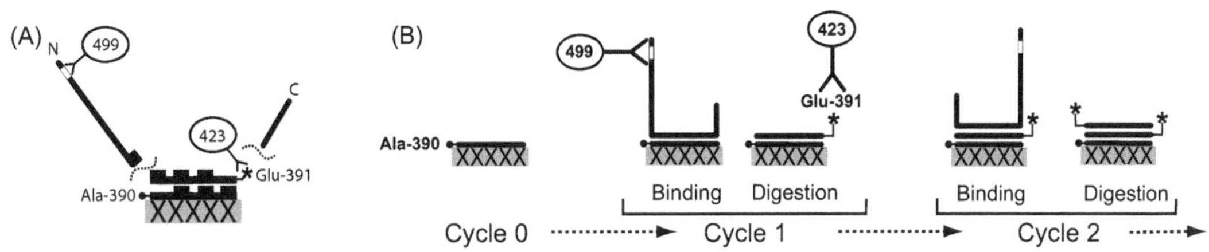

FIGURE 15.14 In vitro tau aggregation. (A) Formation of the proteolytically stable footprint of the pathological tau–tau binding domain can be demonstrated in vitro. Here a fragment with the same N-terminus as the PHF-core, but terminating at Ala-390, is allowed to bind in vitro to full-length 4-repeat tau. After digestion with a broad-spectrum exo-protease, immunoreactivity (recognized by mAb 423) associated with the characteristic C-terminus at Glu-391 appears. (B) This process can be repeated through successive binding/digestion cycles, with repeated removal of the N- and C-terminal domains of full-length tau, and increasing levels of mAb 423 immunoreactivity are detected over successive cycles. *Source: Adapted from Wischik et al.:* Proc Natl Acad Sci USA *93:11213–11218, 1996.*

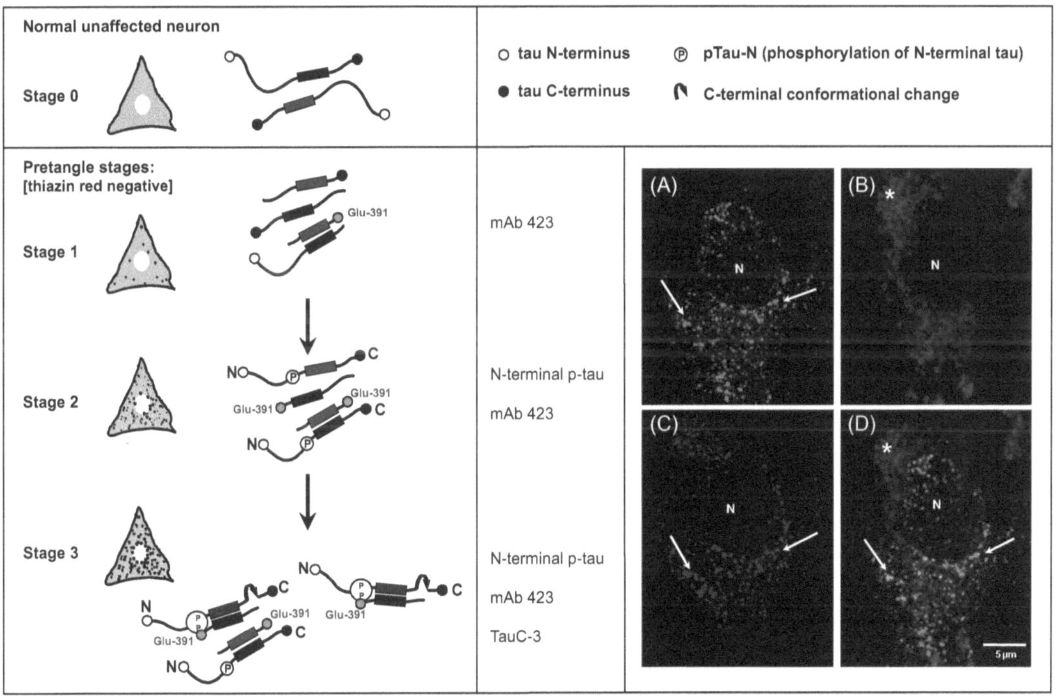

FIGURE 15.15 The C-terminal truncation of tau in early, pretangle stages in AD neurons develops in stages as depicted in the scheme. Unaffected neurons (stage 0) will have normal tau (neither truncated nor phosphorylated), whereas stages 1–3 represent early events that precede the appearance of fibrillary inclusions. Stage 1 is characterized by the appearance of the PHF core, namely a fragment of 93–95 amino acids in length corresponding to the repeat domain of tau. Stage 2 is defined by the cytoplasmic aggregation of tau molecules resulting from the binding to PHF-core fragments of full-length tau and which react with an N-terminal phospho-dependent antibody. This stage corresponds to the diffuse granular structures seen in neurons by confocal microscopy following triple immunolabeling (A–D). A pretangle cell displays granular cytoplasmic structures labeled with mAb 423 (A), the majority of which is also detected with Alz-50 (C) (*arrows*). Phospho-tau labeling of these structures (pS396, B) is not seen. Autofluorescent lipofuscin granules are also observed in the absence of antibodies (*). The merged image for A, B, and C is shown in D. N, nucleus. *Source: From Flores-Rodriguez et al.:* Front Neurosci *9:33, 2015.*

not lead to aggregation or neurodegeneration (Arendt et al., 2003). Phosphorylation of tau in its C-terminal domain appears to be associated with early stages of tau aggregation, when the formation of small tangles that can be labeled with ligands for PHFs, such as thiazin red and primulin (Resch et al., 1991), occurs. Moreover, tau phosphorylation at Ser-422 is observed from the earliest stages of tau aggregation. Previous studies suggested that tau phosphorylation at the Ser-422 can prevent the action of caspase-3, which is very active in AD and truncates tau at Asp-421 (Guillozet-Bongaarts et al., 2006). Truncated tau is present from early to late stage of tau aggregation. This is why we considered that tau truncation and phosphorylation occur through the entire process of formation and evolution of the NFTs. Two events are relevant for this process: (1) tau truncation and (2) sequestration of intact tau and its phosphorylation. This implies that the more internal epitopes of the PHF are the ones that are more stable and resistant to proteolysis.

The tau species making up the structural core of the PHF and its oligomeric precursors are derived from a mixture of fragments derived from both 3- and 4-repeat isoforms, but restricted to the equivalent of 3 repeats in length. There are two distinct species originating from the 4-repeat isoform of tau: the fragment derived from repeats 1, 2, and 3 and the fragment derived from repeats 2, 3, and 4 (Fig. 15.13B). There is also a fragment derived from the 3-repeat isoform (which lacks the second repeat), comprising the equivalent of repeats 1, 3, and 4. Since all of these fragments are restricted to the equivalent of 3 repeats in length, they all have identical gel mobility. Two of the fragments terminate at the C-terminus at Glu-391. The third, derived from the first 3 repeats of the 4-repeat isoform, has a C-terminal truncation at a homologous position, conferring upon it the same gel mobility as the other species when these are released from the PHF core (Jakes et al., 1991). These features represent the footprint of the pathological tau–tau binding interaction which locks the repeat domains into a characteristic proteolytically stable configuration.

The repeat domain tau fragment originally isolated from the core of the PHF has prion-like properties in vitro (Wischik et al., 1996). Using a relatively simple assay in which the core tau fragment of the PHF was adsorbed to a solid phase, we found that binding of full-length tau locked the repeat domain of the bound molecule into a proteolytically stable configuration which, when digested with a broad-spectrum exoprotease, reproduced a characteristic C-terminal truncation at position Glu-391 seen both in early pathological oligomers in the brain and within the core of the native PHF (Wischik et al., 1996). Surprisingly, when the bound complex was taken through repeated cycles of digestion with protease and reincubation of full-length tau, N-terminal tau immunoreactivity was eliminated in every cycle, while a progressive buildup of immunoreactivity associated with the truncated repeat-domain fragment of the PHF core was observed (Fig. 15.14B). Thus, the repeat domain of tau is able to catalyze and propagate the conversion of normal soluble tau into the aggregated and truncated oligomeric form in a cell-free setting. This is important, as it has been suggested that the kinetic barrier to tau aggregation can be overcome by a nucleation event of some kind (Arrasate et al., 1997; Friedhoff et al., 1998; Goedert et al., 1996; Hasegawa et al., 1997; Pérez et al., 1996).

We have found that the tau–tau binding interaction through the repeat domain has several unexpected properties. All of the binding data can be described in a surprisingly consistent manner by a system of typical Langmuir equations. This in turn implies that the tau–tau binding interaction is competitive, saturable, and reversible. For any given set of binding conditions, the interaction can be defined quantitatively by a binding constant (K_D) and a saturation binding value (B_{max}). For the tau–tau binding interaction to be described systematically in this way, the following assumptions must be met: (1) for any given set of conditions, individual binding sites operate independently of one another (ie, there is no positive or negative cooperativity between them); (2) the number of binding sites is finite; and (3) binding is reversible, with on and off rates that are determined entirely by the relative concentrations of the interacting species. The implied reversibility has particular theoretical importance in that it contradicts claims that the formation of covalent bonds is necessary to support tau–tau binding through the repeat domain (Akoury et al., 2013). It is further supported by a report that the formation of fibrils from a tau208-324 fragment does not depend on cross-linking between cysteine residues (Huvent et al., 2014).

Systematic binding studies in vitro where the autoaggregation of the tau repeat domain has been controlled show that, as the concentration of either truncated tau in the solid phase or full-length tau in the aqueous phase species increases, their respective binding affinities increase to asymptotic values of 21.1 ± 2.9 and 31.5 ± 22.6 nM, respectively. These results indicate that there is an avidity effect in both solid and aqueous phases, such that there is alignment of molecules at higher concentrations, which permits a one-to-many binding configuration that produces higher binding affinities.

Phosphorylation of tau profoundly disturbs the tau–tau binding affinity through the repeat domain. The inhibitory effect of phosphorylation can be shown to occur in both solid and aqueous phases, by factors ranging from 10- to 50-fold depending on the precise configuration of the measurement. In particular, if the species in the solid phase is itself hyperphosphorylated, this inhibits the binding of aqueous phase full-length tau even if the latter is not phosphorylated. This inhibitory effect can be shown to depend on regions of the tau molecule outside the repeat domain (Wischik et al., 1997; Lai et al., 2016).

In contrast to the complexities of tau–tau binding, the tau–tubulin binding interaction is much simpler (Wischik et al., 1997). First, there is no avidity effect, as providing tubulin in the solid phase at higher concentration does not enhance tau–tubulin binding, and the K_D remains 403 ± 86 nM, indicating a 19-fold lower affinity for tau–tubulin binding compared with the tau–tau binding interaction. Second, the inhibitory effect of tau phosphorylation is comparable in both tau–tubulin and tau–tau binding interactions, with a 24-fold inhibition in the case of tau–tubulin binding. There is therefore no need to invoke phosphorylation as a mechanism to explain detachment of tau from microtubules and the 80-fold redistribution of the tau pool from tubulin-bound to aggregated forms that is seen in AD (Harrington et al., 1991). Once either full-length tau or the truncated repeat-domain fragment have undergone the conformational change induced by binding to an exogenous substrate, the higher binding affinity of the tau–tau binding site thus exposed, and reproduced through repeated binding cycles, will simply drive tau protein away from physiological to pathological binding.

We have shown previously in a biochemical study of progression of tau aggregation in the human brain that the loss of soluble tau (released from depolymerized microtubules) is insufficient to explain the accumulation of aggregated tau in the AD brain. Rather, there appears to be increased synthesis of new tau to compensate for the continued loss of soluble tau through aggregation (Lai et al., 1995). This continues until a point is reached when the overall rate of aggregation exceeds the ability of the neuron to compensate by synthesis of new tau protein. As noted earlier, tau aggregation becomes visible histologically as tangles only after the mean PHF levels have reached 0.3 ng/g. It is likely that an important driver of this transition is a significant impairment of cytoskeletal and microtubule functions due to loss of normal tau which prevents transport of newly formed tau oligomers and PHFs out of the somatodendritic compartment, leaving them to accumulate as tangles visible in the light microscope.

It appears unlikely, therefore, that hyperphosphorylation of tau is necessary as a prerequisite for it either to aggregate or to dissociate from microtubules. This has important implications for pharmaceutical development programs for preventing tau aggregation in AD based on the premise that pathological phosphorylation is a critical step in the cascade. Furthermore, more general theories attempting to link abnormal processing of APP with tau aggregation using hyperphosphorylation as a bridge are unlikely to be useful. The profoundly inhibitory effects of phosphorylation on tau–tau binding add to the increasing evidence that phosphorylation may actually be protective in inhibiting tau aggregation (Crowther et al., 1992; Flores-Rodríguez et al., 2015; Lai et al., 1995; Schneider et al., 1999; Wischik et al., 1995).

A much more important factor required for conversion of tau protein from nonaggregating to aggregating states is primary induction of the conformational change in the repeat domain associated with capture of tau by an exogenous substrate. This can be shown, for example, by the observation that neonatal tau in the aqueous phase carries an endogenous state of phosphorylation which entirely prevents binding to the repeat domain in the solid phase. If, however, neonatal tau is first bound to a solid phase substrate, the binding of full-length tau presented in the aqueous phase is identical to that seen for the repeat domain fragment similarly presented (Wischik et al., 1997; Lai et al., 2016). This process does not depend on prior posttranslational modifications such as hyperphosphorylation (Alonso et al., 1994; Biernat et al., 1993) or proteolytic truncation (Fasulo et al., 1996, 1998) as essential initiating events, nor does the critical pathological interaction require stabilization by formation of a covalent bond as has been suggested (Akoury et al., 2013; Schweers et al., 1995). Once the pathological solid-phase configuration of the repeat domain has been acquired, further tau aggregation can then be driven by the inherent high affinity of the tau–tau binding interaction, which is self-replicating and self-amplifying (Wischik et al., 1996). The resulting aggregate is proteolytically stable and self-propagating (ie, prion-like) (Wischik et al., 1997). This is summarized in Fig. 15.16. The concept of prion-like aggregation, which we first proposed as underlying

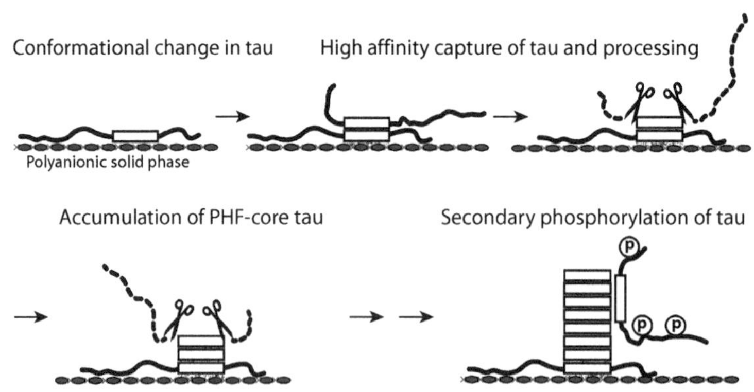

FIGURE 15.16 **Modeling tau aggregation in vitro.** Full-length tau bound to a macromolecular substrate induces a conformational change in tau. The bound tau serves to capture further tau molecules. The N- and C-termini are cleaved by proteolysis, and this further processing allows for the further capture of tau. This process results in accumulation of truncated tau to which occasional phosphorylated, full-length tau protein molecules may bind.

the formation of the PHF in AD (Wischik et al., 1996, 1997), has come to be seen more broadly as a feature shared by proteins aggregating in a number of neurodegenerative disorders (Goedert et al., 2010; Guo and Lee, 2011).

This raises the question as to the identity of the exogenous substrate which captures tau in the first place and permits self-propagation of the prion-like aggregation process thereafter. As indicated earlier, the inhibitory (ie, protective) effects of phosphorylation on the tau–tau binding interaction can be abrogated by its prior adsorption to a nonspecific substrate. For example, polyanionic substrates such as heparin or RNA which have been shown to promote tau aggregation in vitro (Goedert et al., 1996; Kampers et al., 1996; Pérez et al., 1996) or by products of mitochondrial clearance (Wischik et al., 2001). Lipofuscin deposits, composed of undigested products of mitochondrial turnover, could provide the primary substrate needed to initiate the tau aggregation cascade. Such a scenario would then locate the initiation of tau aggregation within the framework of a common age-related dysfunction, namely age-related loss of efficiency of the endosomal–lysosomal pathway which is needed to process a range of proteins, including membrane-bound proteins and mitochondria (Ihara et al., 2012; Schultz et al., 2011).

In this theoretical framework, the primary driver for the initiation of the tau aggregation cascade would be progressive failure of endosomal–lysosomal processing (ie, autophagy). This loss, combined with the triggering of tau aggregation, would have two consequences, illustrated schematically in Fig. 15.17. The first is that endosomal–lysosomal processing is, in

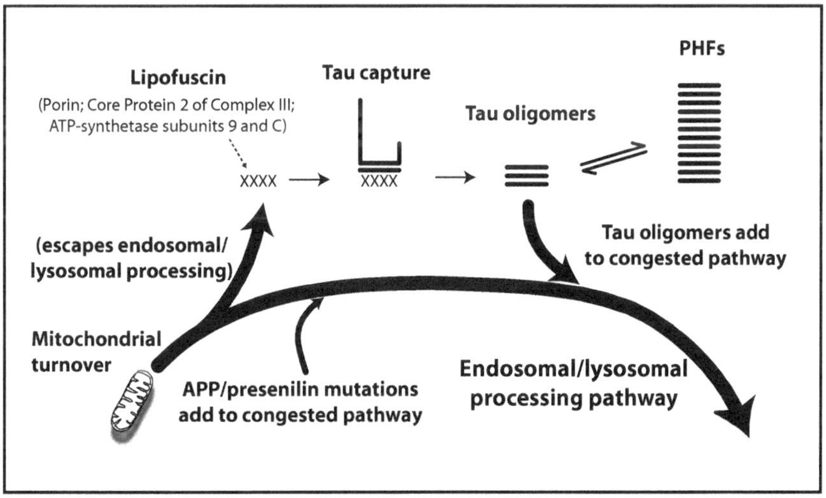

FIGURE 15.17 **Involvement of the endosomal–lysosomal pathway in removal of aggregated proteins.** Congestion of the clearance pathway associated with progressive age-related failure of normal mitochondrial turnover leads to release of products of failed clearance which become seeds for triggering tau aggregation. The resulting tau oligomers add to congestion in the pathway and themselves catalyze further tau aggregation. Abnormal amyloid processing adds to the endogenous load on endosomal processing, and brings forward the time of critical failure. It does not follow that preventing APP processing abnormalities will affect the age-related drivers of the tau aggregation cascade. The tau aggregation cascade proceeds by an autocatalytic process of binding and proteolysis of tau, initiated by its capture by products of failed mitochondrial clearance resulting from age-related failure of endosomal–lysosomal processing. *Source: From Wischik et al.:* Biochem Pharmacol *88:529–539, 2014.*

effect, the only pathway available for clearance of proteolytically stable tau oligomers once these have begun to accumulate. The oligomers are inherently resistant to cytosolic proteases once formed. However, their accumulation would only add to the load placed on an already failing system and would cause further failure/overload of the endosomal–lysosomal processing pathway. We have previously shown that one of the early pathological features of tau aggregation, namely the appearance of granulovacuolar degeneration, is linked to endosomal–lysosomal vesicles associated with tau oligomers truncated at the hallmark Glu-391 position (Bondareff et al., 1991). In other words, an early phase in the development of tau aggregation pathology is in effect a tau-lysosomal storage disease. The second consequence is that as tau oligomers continue to be formed in the cytosol but fail to be cleared by the endosomal–lysosomal pathway, they become the seeds for further autocatalytic propagation of the tau aggregation cascade.

If this process were restricted to only affected neurons, tau protein aggregation would be damaging but self-limiting. However, it has recently emerged that proteolytically stable tau oligomers are able to propagate between neurons and initiate the cascade in previously healthy neighboring neurons (Clavaguera et al., 2009, 2013; Frost et al., 2009; Frost and Diamond, 2010). Transneuronal movement of proteins and aggregates has been documented in vivo for several neurodegenerative disorders in which the aggregating pathological proteins include tau, amyloid, synuclein, prion, and polyglutamine proteins. Further elucidation of the mechanism by which the specific proteins or their aggregates bind to and enter cells may explain the differential selectivity of neurons affected in the different clinical diseases (Frost and Diamond, 2010). Whatever the mechanism of spread, the tau pathology of AD can be understood as a self-propagating "prionosis." Once the cascade has been initiated in any given neuron, it cannot be arrested by cytosolic proteases because the resulting oligomers are inherently stable to such proteases. However, the process does not stay circumscribed. Oligomers are transported by cytoplasmic flow to nerve terminals, where they damage synapses, are released, and proceed to initiate the same cascade in neighboring neurons. This also provides a basis for understanding the spread of pathology along neural networks that define the Braak staging system (Braak and Braak, 1991).

MODELING TAU AGGREGATION IN CELLS

It proves to be difficult to control the state of aggregation of the repeat-domain fragment in vitro because of a pronounced tendency to autoaggregate. It is also difficult to control tau aggregation within cells by simple overexpression, even when using inducible expression vectors, due to the inherent cytotoxicity of the core-PHF tau fragment. While the exact form of tau that is toxic in AD, and the cellular location of such toxicity, remains uncertain (Rankin and Gamblin, 2008), we have observed toxicity of both truncated tau and PHF-tau in lipofectin transfection models (Wischik et al., 2008).

We have recently reported the development of two cell-based assays which permit demonstration of prion-like processing of tau in the more physiological milieu of the cell. These models confirm that tau protein, in the absence of any posttranslational modification, is inherently able to form proteolytically resistant aggregates through the repeat domain in a physiological environment, and that this process recruits normal tau to undergo template-directed proteolytic truncation to form characteristic neofragments, including the core tau unit of the PHF. We have used for this purpose fibroblast cell lines that lack endogenous tau protein (Harrington et al., 2015). In one model, we have targeted the expression of truncated tau to the endoplasmic reticulum (ER) membrane where, at low levels, it is capable of initiating the capture and aggregation of full-length human tau. The motivation for this approach is to attempt to provide an initial substrate for tau capture by misdirecting it to the ER for export using a 17-residue signal sequence (SS). In this model, cells are able to generate two families of neofragments restricted to either 3 or 4 repeats. The oligomers formed are the equivalent of 100-mers of truncated tau neofragments. The combined expression of the truncated initiator species and full-length tau protein therefore leads to the processing of the latter to form increased levels of characteristic truncated neofragments of tau.

The generation of neofragments by directing truncated tau expression to the ER membrane is relevant in the light of evidence that early amorphous aggregates of tau in AD are associated with mitochondrial and ER membranes (Mena et al., 1996). Furthermore, there is increased contact between mitochondria and rough ER membranes in JNLP3 mice that express P301L mutant tau, and accumulation of tau was identified in ER membrane-enriched fractions prepared from both these transgenic mice and AD brain tissues (Perreault et al., 2009).

For the second model, we have found that provided constitutive expression of the PHF-core fragment is maintained at very low levels, long-term cell viability is possible without aggregation occurring. These low levels do not permit aggregation to be studied. However, when such cells were cotransfected with inducible, full-length 4-repeat tau, it was possible to induce tau aggregation and template-directed truncation of full-length tau in a controlled manner (Harrington et al., 2015). The neofragment generated in a concentration-dependent manner with respect to induced full-length tau is simply the core tau unit itself. This confirms within the physiological milieu of the cell the model of propagation of tau aggregation through the repeat domain already shown in the cell-free system (Wischik et al., 1996) and also illustrated in Fig. 15.14B. Thus the repeat domain has the ability to define a template-directed truncation of full-length tau to reproduce and amplify the proteolytically stable species characteristic of the PHF-core in AD (Fig. 15.18).

In this model, tau aggregation can be demonstrated only after induction of full-length tau (Fig. 15.18A). On induction of full-length tau, there is a concomitant increase in truncated tau fragment arising by aggregation and proteolysis of newly expressed tau (Fig. 15.18B). There is a further particularly important feature of this model that has a direct bearing on understanding the redistribution of the tau protein pool that occurs in AD. Whereas induction of full-length tau in the absence of the PHF-core fragment permits binding to microtubules (Fig. 15.18C,D), this does not occur in cells coexpressing the PHF-core fragment. Instead, newly expressed full-length tau simply aggregates as it is preferentially directed to the aggregation/truncation pathway (Fig. 15.18E,F). This is consistent with in vitro data discussed earlier, whereby the binding affinity for tau–tau binding is substantially higher than for tau–tubulin binding, although both occur through the repeat domain. This again confirms that it is the inherent autoaggregation property of the repeat domain which underlies the almost complete redistribution of the tau protein pool from microtubule-bound to aggregated forms that is characteristic of AD (Harrington et al., 1991), and further confirms that phosphorylation is not required to account for loss of microtubule binding in AD (Lai et al., 1995; Schneider et al., 1999).

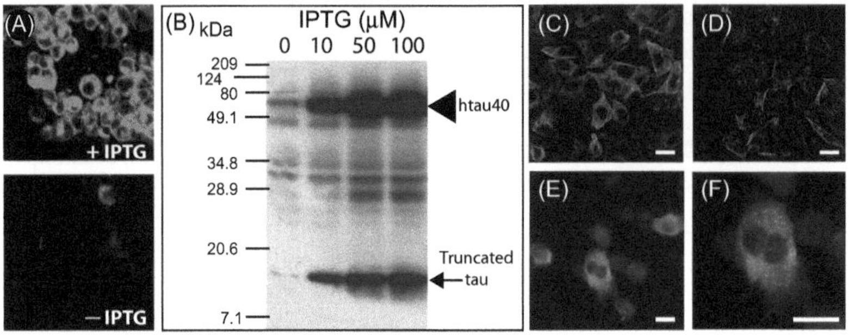

FIGURE 15.18 Cellular model of tau aggregation. (A) Fibroblasts, stably transfected with both constitutive truncated tau(295–391) and uninduced full-length tau (htau40), express both proteins at low levels. Following induction of expression of the full-length tau with IPTG, cells exhibit aggregated tau that binds a fluorescent PHF ligand. (B) SDS-PAGE and immunoblot analysis of cells shows that the induction of full-length tau with increasing concentrations of IPTG (*arrowhead*) is associated with the accumulation of a 12-kDa truncated tau neofragment (*arrow*). (C–F) Cells transfected with inducible full-length tau, in the absence of truncated tau295–391, showed normal microtubular network patterns after induction, whether labeled with mAbs 27/499 to the N-terminus (C) or 7/51 to the repeat domain (D) of tau. In contrast, cells cotransfected with both tau and truncated tau showed granular staining with mAb 7/51 in the cells, following induction of full-length tau, in the absence of microtubule labeling (E and F). Scale bars, 20 μm. *Source: From Harrington et al.:* J Biol Chem *290:10862–10875, 2015.*

The properties of the two cell models of tau aggregation can be summarized schematically as shown in Fig. 15.19. (1) Aggregation of tau is seeded initially either by the membrane-localized truncated tau or by the truncated tau itself interacting with full-length tau; (2) cleavage of the N-terminal signal peptide and/or the N- and C-termini of full-length tau; (3) leaves tau oligomers in the cytoplasm; (4) these oligomers allow further capture of full-length tau, which enters the proteolytic processing pathway; and (5) oligomers are susceptible to disaggregation by TAIs, allowing for their subsequent clearance from the cell.

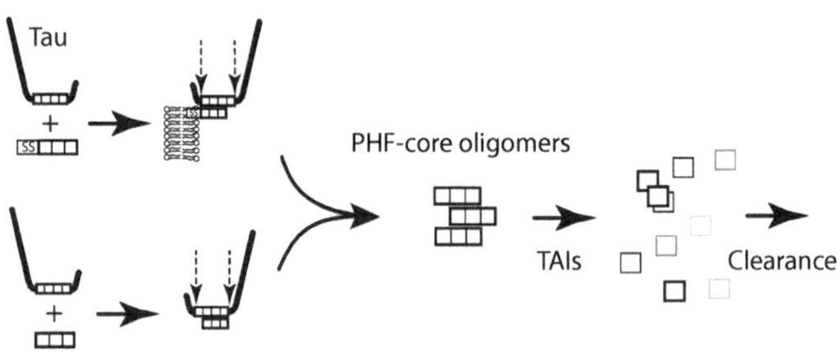

FIGURE 15.19 Schematic representation of tau aggregation in cell models of tau aggregation. The combined presence of a truncated tau fragment (either with or without a signal sequence [SS]) and a full-length molecule of tau protein, followed by proteolysis of the larger tau molecules, leads to the accumulation of truncated PHF-core tau oligomers. Formation of the oligomers needed for template-directed truncation can be blocked and their clearance can be enhanced by TAIs. *Source: From Harrington et al.:* J Biol Chem *290:10862–10875, 2015.*

Further evidence for tau aggregation in cells being seeded by truncated tau (Clavaguera et al., 2009; Frost et al., 2009) has been confirmed independently in transgenic rat studies (Hrnkova et al., 2007; Zilka et al., 2006). In the latter studies, insoluble tau aggregates formed in the brain consist of both transgenic human truncated tau and endogenous rat tau in a 1:1 ratio. This confirms, as predicted by the earlier in vitro data (Wischik et al., 1996) and the cell-based data (Harrington et al., 2015), that truncated tau coopts normal tau into a pathological aggregation pathway leading ultimately to aggregates typically formed within neurons in AD. It suggests that truncated tau oligomers are sufficient to drive neurofibrillary degeneration in the presence of full-length tau and to permit the transmission of tau pathology between neurons (Clavaguera et al., 2009, 2013; Frost et al., 2009; Frost and Diamond, 2010).

The robust cellular screening models we have described should be contrasted with an alternative approach to modeling tau aggregation within cells that has been reported recently (Choi et al., 2014). This approach is based on human neural progenitor cells carrying human APP harboring the Swedish and London familial AD mutations with or without the FAD-linked presenilin 1 mutation, PSEN1ΔE9. In order to increase the levels of toxic amyloid-β, cells were grown in an extracellular matrix gel in order to prevent amyloid-β aggregates being washed away from the cells. This approach was developed because, as the authors concede, transgenic mouse models based on APP/presenilin protein mutations have generally failed to produce somatic aggregates of tau or insoluble fibrils of tau (Hall and Roberson, 2012; Phinney et al., 2003; Radde et al., 2008). This has represented a fundamental failure in one of the founding predictions of the amyloid cascade theory for the pathogenesis of AD (Hardy and Allsop, 1991). In the absence of any experimental verification to date, it casts doubt on the widespread expectation that treatment of the APP pathology of AD will result in treatment of the tau pathology. After allowing the neural stem cells to differentiate, sodium dodecyl sulfate (SDS)-soluble phosphorylated 4-repeat tau was detected (Choi et al., 2014). Phosphorylated tau was also detected in an SDS-insoluble/formic-acid-soluble fraction, although it is unclear whether this was simply a carryover of the SDS-soluble phosphorylated tau into the formic acid fraction; occasional tau filaments were seen, and one was shown. The levels of extracellular amyloid-β generated by these cells had increased 19-fold compared with control cells lacking mutant APP, and enhanced a further 5-fold by the coexpression of PSEN1ΔE9. With these high levels of toxic amyloid-β produced, it is not clear that such a system could provide a screen for therapeutic tau aggregation inhibitors where potential inhibitors may be affecting the burden of extracellular, toxic amyloid-β. Furthermore, phosphorylation of tau is a common nonspecific response of cell systems to stressful environments (Arendt et al., 2003; Pérez et al., 2002), and its quantification may not address the aggregation process that occurs in AD.

A more relevant system has studied the seeding of the repeat domain of tau carrying the disease-associated P301S mutation (Holmes et al., 2014). Having fused two fluorescent tags to separate repeat tau fragments, the techniques of fluorescence resonance energy transfer in combination with cell sorting have been used to measure the ability of tau aggregates at subpicomolar concentrations to seed aggregation in HEK293 cells. The application of this assay to brain tissue has established the appearance of tau aggregates in the brains of P301S tau mice at least 1 month earlier than the appearance of tau pathology using standard histological stains or immunohistochemical labeling (Holmes et al., 2014). This is similar in principle to the observations noted earlier from studies of Braak-staged human postmortem tissues, where tau aggregation precedes the appearance of tangles by about 20 years (Figs. 15.3 and 15.10). It is important, however, to note that the nature of the seed for aggregation in vivo may differ from that created in vitro. Synthetic K18 aggregates that display robust seeding in vitro fail to demonstrate the induction of tau pathology in P301L mice following intrahippocampal injection (Chakrabarty et al., 2015), whereas, as discussed further later, the PHF-core unit does induce age-related propagation of tau pathology in mice, similar to Braak staging.

MODELING TAU AGGREGATION IN TRANSGENIC ANIMALS

We have used what has been learned in creating cellular models to generate a novel animal model of tau aggregation, and to shed light on poorly understood features of the tauopathies in terms of their very different clinical presentations. Whether or not linked to mutations in the *MAPT* gene, the clinical features of the frontotemporal lobar degeneration (FTLD) spectrum are generally dominated by motor and emotional/psychiatric abnormalities, whereas cognitive deficits tend to be rarer, more subtle, and present at later disease stages (Neary et al., 1998). In AD, on the other hand, the clinical features are dominated by cognitive and memory deficits occurring early in the disease, in the almost complete absence of motor abnormalities until very advanced disease stages. One possible explanation is that the difference depends on the presence of concomitant pathology linked to the amyloid-β protein pathway. Indeed, animal studies of combined APP/tau models have tended to emphasize tau as merely an aggravating or accelerating factor in what is conceptualized primarily as a disorder of APP processing (Hurtado et al., 2010). However, given that amyloid load is poorly correlated with cognitive impairment or functional molecular neuroimaging deficits, it is not clear that an abnormality in APP processing contributes to cognitive impairment in AD. An alternative possibility is that the dissociation between motor and cognitive abnormalities seen in the various clinical tauopathies is actually inherent to differences in the underlying molecular pathophysiology of tau protein itself.

Familial autosomal-dominantly inherited *MAPT* mutations have formed the basis of the majority of tau-transgenic mouse models developed to date. The majority of these models express cDNA mutated in exon 10 (P301L, P301S, N279K), exon 9 (G272V), exon 13 (R406W), or exon 12 (V337M), and these present with intracellular aggregates of tau in neurons and glial cells (Denk and Wade-Martins, 2009). Motor phenotypes are common to most mutations in exon 10, while there is some suggestion that cognitive and emotional abnormalities may have a greater association with exons 9, 12, and 13 mutations (Reed et al., 2001). We have recently reported a novel FTDP-17 mouse model, in which the longest human *MAPT* cDNA in the central nervous system (htau40; 441 amino acids), containing 4 repeats and including point mutations P301S and G335D (termed line 66), was expressed under the Thy-1 regulatory element. Clinically, the P301S mutation causes early onset and rapid progression of disease associated with lowered microtubule assembly in patients and in mouse models with different tau isoforms (4R0N, Allen et al., 2002; 4R1N, Yoshiyama et al., 2007; 4R2N, Onishi et al., 2014). The resulting line 66 mice are characterized by severe neurofibrillary pathology associated with a prominent motor phenotype occurring in the absence of any higher cognitive features despite abundant tangles being present in hippocampus and entorhinal cortex. Line 66 mice also exhibit neuropathological features characteristic of a degenerative axonopathy (Melis et al., 2015b).

Given the limitations of transgenic models based on *MAPT* mutations as models for the cognitive deficits of AD, we have developed an alternative approach based on the truncated tau fragment restricted to the repeat domain which is the principal constituent of PHFs (Wischik et al., 1988b). Cleavages at Glu-391 and/or Asp-421 result in tau fragments which appear relatively early in the disease state and induce toxicity in transfected cells in vitro (Fasulo et al., 1998; Guillozet-Bongaarts et al., 2005). Rats transgenic for a truncated human tau fragment encompassing residues tau151–391 present with symptoms of neurodegeneration, intracellular accumulation of human tau in neurons (Filipcik et al., 2009), reduced life span (Koson et al., 2008), and late-onset sensorimotor impairment (>9 months) (Hrnkova et al., 2007). We have recently reported (Melis et al., 2015b) the development of a new tau-transgenic line 1 in which mice express truncated tau296–390 similar to a fragment of tau isolated from AD PHFs (Wischik et al., 1988b) and that is targeted to the ER membrane (as in the cell model described previously). The line 1 mouse was found to manifest a strong cognitive phenotype occurring in the absence of prominent sensorimotor features. The tau pathology seen in line 1 remains at the stage of diffuse oligomeric aggregates, and does not progress histologically to tangles. This can be contrasted with the line 66 model described previously which mimics existing FTDP-17 lines by the inclusion of a P301S point mutation. Although both models are based on overexpression of tau protein, there are major differences in the resultant neuropathological and behavioral phenotypes. In common with previously reported models based on mutant forms of full-length tau, the phenotype in homozygous line 66 mice is characterized by an early onset of sensorimotor deficits, gait anomalies, and learning deficits restricted to the motor domain, all of which become more severe as mice age. It culminates in a palsy-like dyskinesia at the age of 7 months resembling parkinsonism in FTDP-17. Noteworthy is the complete absence of a higher cognitive phenotype in line 66 despite the severity of neuropathological changes present. By contrast, line 1 mice display deficits in spatial learning resembling the deficits in spatial route learning seen early in AD. These changes are associated with minimal abnormalities in sensorimotor function. There is therefore a marked dissociation between cognitive and sensorimotor expressions of tau aggregation pathology that depends solely on the form of tau which is overexpressed in the absence of APP overexpression or β-amyloid pathology.

A particularly striking feature of the tau aggregation pathology seen in line 1 is its anatomical progression out of the entorhinal cortex and hippocampus at 3–6 months of age into the retrosplenial cortex, visual cortex, and subiculum at 12–18 months (Fig. 15.20A,B). This progression from archicortex into neocortex is typical of Braak staging in AD. As discussed earlier, the highly stereotyped neuroanatomical spread of tau pathology is now understood in terms of transmission of tau aggregates at the oligomer stage between neurons. The neuroanatomical spread of pathology in line 1 is in marked contrast to the anatomically static nature of the line 66 pathology (Fig. 15.20C,D). An earlier reported model showing neuroanatomical spread similar to Braak staging was in PS19/PDAPP mice (Hurtado et al., 2010), with an early transentorhinal stage in animals under 4 months, followed by a limbic stage (4–10 months) and then an isocortical stage (>11 months). The phenotype found in line 1 shows that concomitant expression of mutant APP is not necessary for neuroanatomical spread of this kind, and that this property is inherent to the repeat domain of tau.

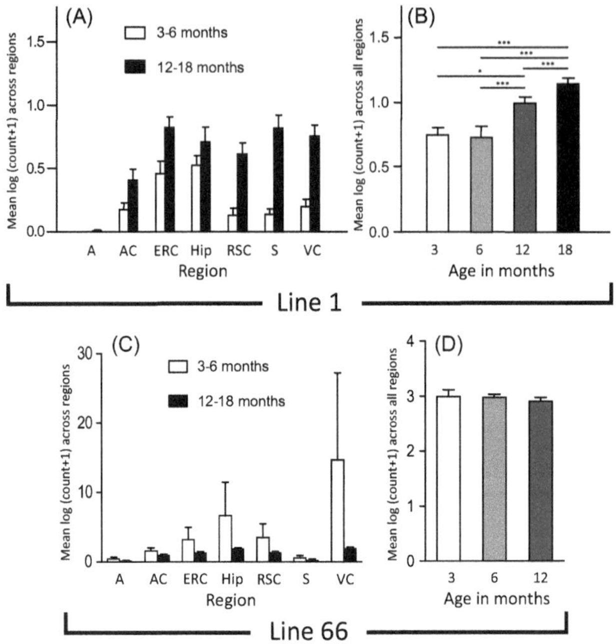

FIGURE 15.20 **Transgenic mice exhibiting both regional and age-related changes in tau immunoreactivity.** (A, B) Homozygous line 1 mice present with a significant age-related spread of tau-reactive cells from entorhinal cortex and hippocampus to neocortex that is reminiscent of Braak staging, and a corresponding increase in numbers of cells having tau pathology. (C, D) In contrast, homozygous line 66 mice exhibit strong tau immunoreactivity in all regions by 3 months of age, and the levels do not increase with advancing age. Overall, there are approximately 7-fold more tau-positive neurons in line 66 relative to line 1. A, amygdala; AC, auditory cortex; ERC, entorhinal cortex; Hip, hippocampus; RSC, retrosplenial cortex; S, subiculum; VC, visual cortex. *Source: From Melis et al.:* Cell Mol Life Sci *72:2199–2222, 2015b.*

A further interesting finding in these animal models is the dissociation between labeling for aggregated tau and labeling with phosphorylation-dependent antibodies. Although there was a general tendency for affected brain regions to be labeled by both antibodies, more detailed analysis showed that there was limited overlap between the two. This was demonstrated by double labeling in line 66 mice, where only a subset of neurons with tau aggregates was also labeled with mAb AT8. The same phenomenon was demonstrated in aged line 1 mice. Whereas no phosphorylation-dependent immunoreactivity was seen in younger animals, labeling was seen in mice at 15 months in both neocortex and hippocampus. Since the C-terminal pS404 epitope in question is lacking in the transgene, terminating as it does at Ala-390, acquisition of this immunoreactivity implies that both recruitment of endogenous mouse tau and secondary phosphorylation can occur after aggregation has been initiated. One-to-one recruitment of native tau by truncated tau aggregates has also been reported in rats expressing a longer truncated tau transgene (residues 151–391; Hrnkova et al., 2007).

The implied dissociation between tau aggregation and tau phosphorylation has important theoretical implications, since it is commonly thought that hyperphosphorylation is on the critical path to both aggregation and loss of microtubule-binding function (Iqbal et al., 2014). As noted previously, although the quantity of phosphorylated tau in PHF preparations from the AD brain is correlated with the total quantity of aggregated tau, phosphorylated tau accounts for less than 5% of the tau content of the PHF in AD. Phosphorylation of tau is likely to be a late-stage epiphenomenon in the process of tau aggregation also in AD (Lai et al., 1995; Wischik et al., 1995). In the line 1 mouse, the phosphorylation seen only after 15 months cannot explain the severe cognitive deficits that are seen from 3 months of age.

The comparison of the line 1 and line 66 phenotypes at the molecular and pathological levels demonstrates the existence of two distinct but convergent pathways for the pathological processing of tau protein. These are summarized in Fig. 15.21. In line 1, although pathology is arrested at the oligomer stage, the model demonstrates prominent cognitive impairment and age-related neuroanatomical spread of pathology of the type formalized as Braak staging. It is likely therefore that oligomers consisting of the truncated repeat domain fragment of the PHF core are the fundamental toxic species required for both phenomena. Notwithstanding this, the levels of tau pathology remain low, despite high copy number of the transgene, most likely due to enhanced clearance of the SStau296–390 via the endosomal–lysosomal pathway. This can be contrasted with line 66, in which there is early aggressive formation of filamentous neurofibrillary tangles with high levels of pathology in the entorhinal cortex and hippocampus occurring in the absence of either higher cognitive deficit or neuroanatomical spread of the Braak staging type. As reported also by others (Aoyagi et al., 2007; García-Sierra et al., 2001), this filamentous/tangle stage of tau protein aggregation is probably not a critical driver of clinical dementia, although it is linked quantitatively to dementia (Mukaetova-Ladinska et al., 2000) and eventual tangle-mediated neuronal loss at advanced stages (García-Sierra et al., 2001).

Hyperphosphorylation of full-length tau is not required for cognitive impairment, interneuronal transmission of pathology, assembly of PHFs, or formation of neurofibrillary tangles, but, in a nonaggregating form, it appears to be closely linked to disintegrative axonal degeneration. Both pathways involve recruitment of normal tau. Both pathways converge at the point of formation of aggregates in which the proteolytically stable core consisting of a repeat-domain fragment of tau which is restricted to approximately 3 repeats in length (Figs. 15.13 and 15.14), irrespective of either the transgene or the endogenous tau which is recruited. The two models make possible the demonstration of two distinct but nevertheless convergent pathways of tau molecular pathogenesis and show that aberrant processing of APP is not required to explain the differences in the clinical presentations of AD-like and FTLD syndromes.

IDENTIFICATION AND OPTIMIZATION OF TAU AGGREGATION INHIBITORS FOR TREATMENT AND PREVENTION OF AD

As discussed earlier, a characteristic feature that distinguishes the repeat-domain fragment isolated from the core of the PHF from the normal repeat domain of tau is that it is shifted with respect to the normal repeats. The overall length of the repeat domain isolated from PHF is exactly 3 repeats in length, but the positioning of the alternating tubulin-binding segments and the intervening linker segments is shifted by 15 amino acids (Novak et al., 1993) (Fig. 15.13). The repeat domain in the PHF core is therefore subject to quite precise structural

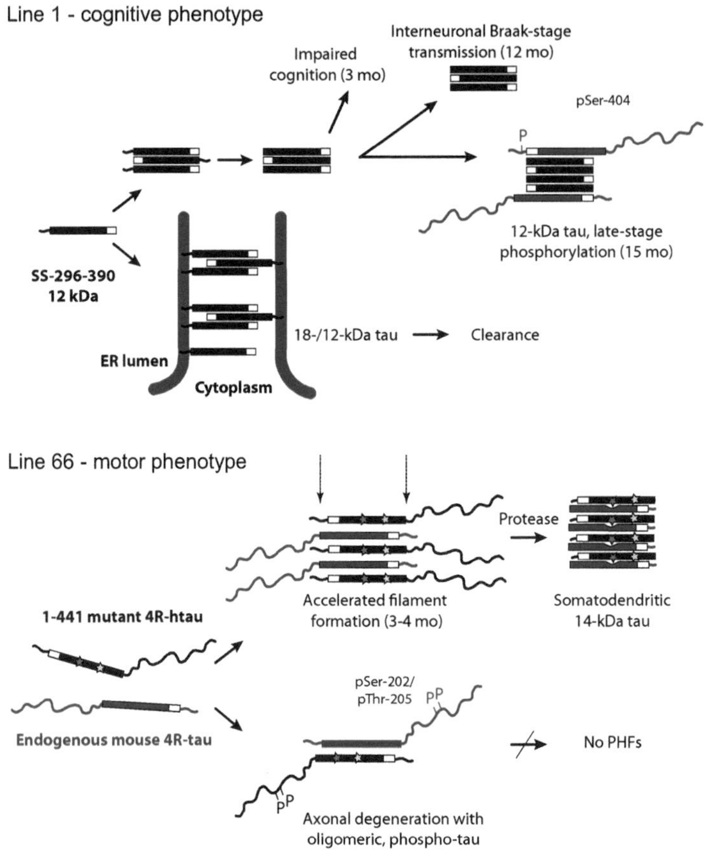

FIGURE 15.21 **Schematic representation of the molecular pathogenesis in tau-transgenic mice.** In line 1 mice, a generally toxic truncated tau species can assemble into aggregates of small oligomers of tau either on its own or via membrane-anchored species targeted to the endoplasmic reticulum membrane when expressed as a protein fused with a signal sequence. These oligomers already impair cognition at 3 months, and this progresses with age. At later stages, the aggregation pathology can be transmitted in a Braak-stage-like fashion to neighboring neurons, which spreads and amplifies the pathology. Phosphorylation of endogenous N-terminal tau that is recruited to the pathological cascade is a late-stage event. A balance between toxicity of truncated tau oligomers and their proteolysis and clearance is required by the mouse for survival. Line 66 mice are characterized by an early onset of aggregate and filament formation that is accelerated by the presence of mutations within the PHF-core domain. There are subpopulations of neurons which accumulate filamentous aggregates of tau that consist predominantly of truncated 14-kDa tau oligomers, whereas others become phosphorylated and lead to axonal degeneration but do not progress to PHFs. Line 66 mice are characterized by prominent sensorimotor deficits. *Source: From Melis et al.:* Cell Mol Life Sci *72:2199–2222, 2015b.*

constraints that distinguish the tau–tau binding interaction from the tau–tubulin binding interaction. This has important pharmaceutical implications, in that it suggests that it should be possible to distinguish between the two binding interactions with potential aggregation inhibitors. This is obviously critical, since an inhibitor of tau aggregation would be of little therapeutic use if it also impaired the normal tau–tubulin binding interaction which also occurs through the repeat domain. We showed that this pharmacological discrimination is indeed feasible for compounds based on the diaminophenothiazine scaffold that we first identified as tau-aggregation inhibitors (Wischik et al., 1996). Using the solid-phase tau–tau binding assay described previously in which autoaggregation was controlled, the K_i in vitro for inhibition of tau–tau binding was found to be 98 nM. For the corresponding tau–tubulin binding interaction, the K_i was 7.9 mM, an 80,000-fold difference (Wischik et al., 1997).

Since we first described the selective inhibition of tau–tau binding by compounds of the diaminophenothiazine class (Wischik et al., 1996), several other tau polymerization inhibitors have been reported. These include bis-thiacarbocyanine (Hall et al., 2002; Honson et al., 2007), Congo red derivatives and anthraquinones (Pickhardt et al., 2005), 2,3-di(furan-2-yl)-quinoxalines (Crowe et al., 2007), phenylthiazolyl-hydrazide (Pickhardt et al., 2007), polyphenols and porphyrins (Taniguchi et al., 2005), oleocanthal (Li et al., 2009), rhodanines (Bulic et al., 2009), cyanin dyes (Chirita et al., 2004), asperbenzaldehyde (Paranjape et al., 2014), and PE859 (Okuda et al., 2015). The methodology for identification of this activity is based on one or more of a number of measurements (eg, the relatively nonspecific emission of fluorescence from bound thioflavin T, transmission electron microscopy, atomic force microscopy, circular dichroism spectroscopy, filter assays to segregate soluble and insoluble protein, quantification of sarkosyl-soluble and insoluble proteins, X-ray crystallography, and NMR studies). These have been applied to PHFs extracted from the AD brain, and to synthetic filaments generated by the aggregation of recombinant tau proteins expressed in bacteria or short synthetic peptides based on sequences within tau protein.

For reasons discussed further later, we have had a particular interest in studying the methylthioninium (MT) moiety, and in particular developing a stabilized reduced form, leucomethylthioninium (LMT). We have recently reported the synthesis and physicochemical characterization of stabilized diprotic acid salts of LMT, and refer to them as the novel chemical entity class, LMTX (Harrington et al., 2015). X-ray crystal structure determinations of the dihydromesylate version of LMTX (LMTM) demonstrate that the nitrogen atoms at positions 3 and 7 have tetrahedral geometry, and hence the molecule is distinct both from methylthioninium chloride (MTC) and reduced-MT [LMT, sometimes referred to "methylene white" (MW)]. In MW, the corresponding nitrogen atoms are not protonated. The X-ray crystallography of these structures is illustrated in Fig. 15.22. MW is a highly unstable molecule, requiring synthesis under an inert atmosphere. Its instability in an oxygen atmosphere (where it converts to the oxidized MT^+ form) underlies its use as an oxygen sensor to monitor the security of sealed components. In contrast, LMTM can be manufactured in bulk without the need for deoxygenation and remains stable for at least 2 years when open to an air atmosphere. In addition to its stability in an oxygen atmosphere, LMTM is substantially more soluble than MTC and has a pKa more appropriate for pharmacological applications (pH 6.5 for LMTM vs pH 0 for MTC).

An important limitation of in vitro methods to identify TAIs is determination of the potential clinical relevance of the aggregates formed. For example, when we have used scaled-up versions of the solid-phase in vitro assay described earlier, it has proved difficult to control the inherent propensity of the isolated repeat domain fragment to autoaggregate. The aggregates formed are not necessarily representative of the oligomers or polymers that form in the brain in AD and in other tauopathies.

We have reported that compounds based on the diaminophenothiazine scaffold have the ability not only to block tau aggregation in a tau–tau binding assay in vitro, but also to disrupt the morphology and reverse the proteolytic stability of PHFs isolated as protease stable

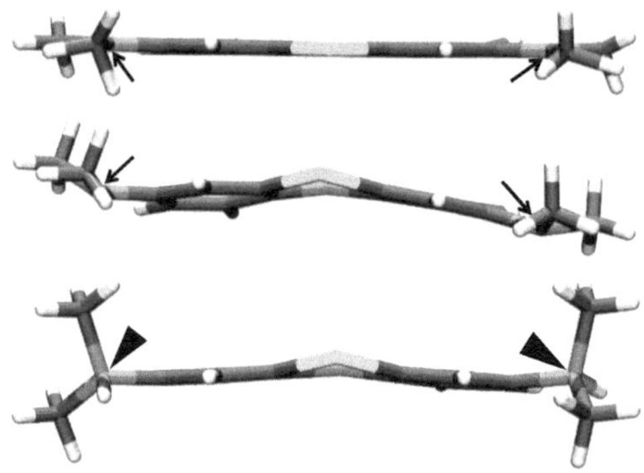

FIGURE 15.22 X-ray structures of methylthioninium chloride (MTC), methylene white (MW), and leucomethylthioninium dihydromesylate (LMTM). The nitrogen atoms at positions 3 and 7 are planar in the case of MTC or pyramidal in the case of MW (*arrows*) and tetrahedral for LMTM (*arrowheads*). *Source: From Harrington et al.:* J Biol Chem *290:10862–10875, 2015.*

polymers from AD brain tissues (Wischik et al., 1996). This activity was quantified using a fluorometric assay based on primulin. Primulin, which we have synthesized as a pure ligand, is the predominant tangle-binding constituent of the highly impure commercial preparations of thioflavin-S that are commonly used as aggregation sensors. Addition of PHFs to a primulin solution induces a PHF concentration-dependent increase in fluorescence at an excitation wavelength of 420 nm, due to the binding of primulin to PHFs (Resch et al., 1991). We had earlier used another closely related compound based on the primulin scaffold to provide the first identification and sequencing of the core tau unit of the PHF (Wischik et al., 1988b), establishing compounds of this type as PHF-core ligands. Addition of MTC produces concentration-dependent disruption of fluorescence enhancement. Dissolution of PHFs can be distinguished from competitive binding by its independence from primulin concentration. This contrasts with competitive ligands, such as thiazine red, where competition can be overcome by increasing the concentration of primulin (Harrington et al., 2015). As noted earlier, thiazin red is another ligand that binds PHFs in AD neurofibrillary tangles that we have used to monitor the transformation of pathological tau oligomers into PHFs in the brain (Mena et al., 1995). In contrast to thiazin red, MTC destroys the PHF-core structure (Wischik et al., 1996).

The activity in vitro of MTC, 1,9-dimethyl-substituted MTC (DMMTC), and leucomethylthioninium dihydromesylate (LMTM) is shown in Table 15.1, and their structures in Fig. 15.23. The P_{50} values represent the extent of disruption by the compounds on the primulin-binding capacity of PHFs. The B_{50} values denote the inhibition of tau–tau binding in the solid-phase assay described earlier in which spontaneous autoaggregation of the repeat-domain core fragment is not controlled. The B_{50} values for MTC and LMTM do not differ significantly, and DMMTC has a 48-fold higher potency than MTC in the in vitro tau–tau binding assay. Although these compounds do not differ significantly in terms of P_{50} values, the B_{50} values range between 24- and 3000-fold higher than the corresponding P_{50} values. These discrepancies illustrate the importance of defining an assay for TAI activity which has disease relevance. Differences in TAI activity between PHFs and the in vitro assay are most likely due to differences

TABLE 15.1 Inhibition of PHF Dissolution, Tau–Tau Binding, and Tau Aggregation in Cells by MTC, DMMTC, and LMTM[a]

Compound	PHF dissolution P_{50} (μM)	Tau–tau binding B_{50} (μM)	Inhibition of aggregation-dependent production of core tau unit within cells EC_{50} (μM)	Cellular toxicity LD_{50} (μM)	Therapeutic index (RxI)
MTC	0.159 ± 0.013 (4)	195.6 ± 16.1 (10)	0.59 ± 0.04 (73)	65 ± 5 (38)	110
DMMTC	0.180 ± 0.011 (3)	4.3 ± 0.5 (19)	0.041 ± 0.004 (22)	3.5 ± 0.97 (6)	85
LMTM	0.159 ± 0.007 (3)	238.2 ± 74.2 (3)	0.19 ± 0.04 (9)	34 ± 4 (8)	179

[a] *P_{50}, concentration at which there is 50% decrease of PHF-dependent primulin binding; B_{50}, concentration at which tau–tau binding in a cell-free assay is inhibited by 50%; EC_{50}, effective concentration at which aggregation-dependent production of truncated tau is inhibited by 50% in cells; LD_{50}, dose at which 50% of 3T6 mouse cells are killed (as measured by LDH release assay); and therapeutic index, RxI = LD_{50}/EC_{50}. Data expressed as the mean ± SE, with number of replicate experiments indicated in parentheses.*

in the state of aggregation of the core tau domain in vitro compared with native PHFs formed within the brain, and to lack of control of its autoaggregation in vitro. An important implication of this discrepancy is that it is not possible to define the concentrations required for clinically relevant TAI activity in vivo based solely on tau aggregation or polymerization assays in vitro (Chirita et al., 2004; Crowe et al., 2007; Hall et al., 2002; Pickhardt et al., 2005; Taniguchi et al., 2005).

The difficulties encountered in controlling tau aggregation in vitro and the discrepancies with respect to actual PHFs from AD brain indicate the need to model the process in a more physiological setting such as that within a living cell. It was primarily for this purpose that the cell-based assays described previously were developed. Since the recruitment of full-length tau and its template-directed proteolytic processing are dependent on aggregation, inhibition of intracellular amplification of the core tau unit provides a means for assaying intracellular TAI activity. Examples of the inhibitory activity of DMMTC and LMTM using two separate cell models are illustrated in Fig. 15.24.

In the second of these models, truncated tau corresponding to the core PHF tau is generated (Figs. 15.18B and 15.24B). TAI activity is expressed in terms of reduction in the ratio of the truncated 12-kDa species to induced full-length tau, permitting control for different background expression levels. The EC_{50} values are the concentrations required for 50% inhibition. DMMTC, MTC, and LMTM all inhibited conversion of full-length tau to the 12-kDa species following IPTG induction of full-length tau (Table 15.1). DMMTC is potent as an intracellular inhibitor. LMTM is 3-fold more potent than MTC in the cell assay ($p < 0.0001$). Using the K_D value (21.1 ± 2.9 nM) determined in vitro for binding of full-length tau in the aqueous phase

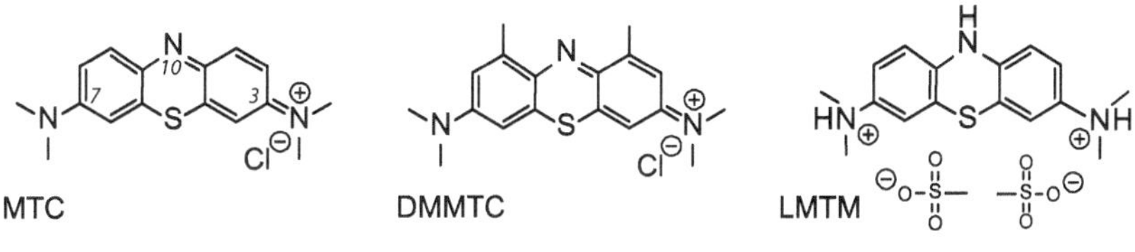

FIGURE 15.23 **Structures of tau aggregation inhibitors.** Methylthioninium chloride (MTC), dimethyl methylthioninium chloride (DMMTC), and leucomethylthioninium dihydromesylate (LMTM).

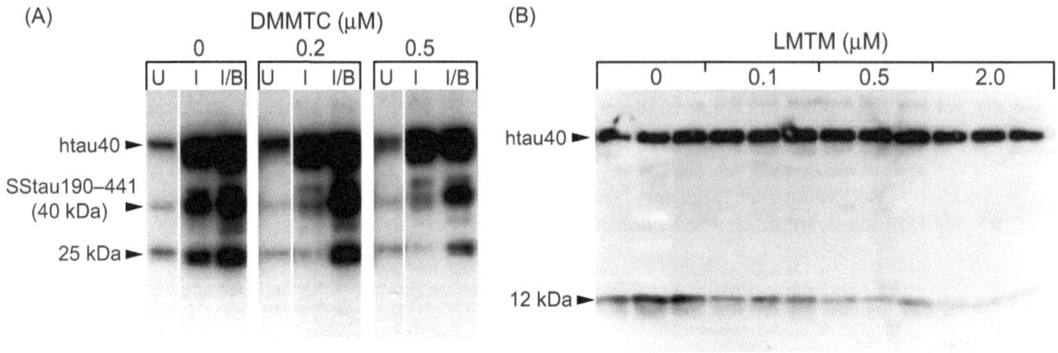

FIGURE 15.24 **Effect of tau aggregation inhibitors in cellular models.** In the first model, (A) DMMTC is a potent inhibitor of tau aggregation in cells coexpressing constitutive truncated tau fused with a membrane-targeting sequence (SStau190–441) and inducible, full-length tau (htau40). When induced with IPTG alone, htau40 expression is increased together with the amount of the 40- and 25-kDa tau truncation products. Butyrate induction alone or induction with both IPTG and butyrate increased the level of the 25-kDa truncation product. The capture of full-length tau and its conversion to the 25-kDa species is inhibited by DMMTC. (B) With an alternate model, as described in Fig. 15.18, LMTM is inhibitory over the concentration range 0.5–2.0 μM. The positions of full-length and truncated tau are indicated by arrowhead and arrow, respectively, and the 12-kDa fragment corresponds to the size of the PHF-core tau. U, uninduced; I, IPTG-induced; B, butyrate-induced. *Source: From Harrington et al.:* J Biol Chem *290:10862–10875, 2015.*

to the PHF-core fragment in the solid phase described previously, in which autoaggregation was controlled (Wischik et al., 1997), and assuming an intracellular concentration of tau to be 500 nM, the K_i values for MTC and DMMTC were estimated as 123 nM and 4.4 nM, respectively (Harrington et al., 2015).

The cellular toxicity (LD_{50}) for diaminophenothiazines was used to estimate their therapeutic indexes (ie, LD_{50}/EC_{50}, Table 15.1). These indicate that LMTM had the best profile in this series and DMMTC the poorest profile, notwithstanding its higher potency as a TAI in cell-free and cellular assays.

From the data provided earlier, these in vitro model systems make it possible to define the critical concentrations of the MT moiety required for dissolution of PHFs isolated from AD brain tissues (0.16 μM, Table 15.1), and activity as a TAI in the physiological milieu of the cell noted earlier (K_i 0.12 μM) (Harrington et al., 2015). These values are compared in the following with the brain concentrations of MT required for TAI activity in the tau-transgenic mouse models described earlier, and ultimately in the human brain.

There have been several studies that have sought to explain the potential clinical efficacy of MTC in AD (discussed further later) in terms of a range of non-TAI activities. For example, it has been argued by Crowe (Crowe et al., 2009) that MT has a potentially broad pharmacology and a potential to induce microtubule disassembly. However, from the data provided, the concentration required for this activity (ie, 50% diminution of microtubule assembly) is 50 μM. This 280-fold difference is therapeutically irrelevant if MT can be shown to be effective in the concentration range required for TAI activity. Similar considerations apply to other proposed effects of MTC. For example, it has been claimed that MTC could potentially reduce endogenous production of tau protein (Dickey et al., 2006). However, the EC_{50} for this effect is 10 μM. Another claim has been that MTC might potentially exert a therapeutic effect via Hsp70 ATP-ase inhibition (Jinwal et al., 2009), thereby affecting tau degradation. However, the EC_{50} for this effect is 83 μM. Congdon et al. and O'Leary et al. have reported that MTC increases proteasomal and autophagic degradation of tau in vitro (Congdon et al., 2012; O'Leary et al., 2010). However, the claimed brain concentration of MT required for this effect is ~250 μM.

Other effects reported in vitro which are outside the range required for TAI activity include acetylcholinesterase inhibition (1 μM, Pfaffendorf et al., 1997); nitric oxide synthase inhibition (5 μM, Mayer et al., 1993); inhibition of β-amyloid aggregation (2.3–12.4 μM, Necula et al., 2007a, b; Taniguchi et al., 2005); monoamine oxidase B inhibition (5.5 μM, Ramsay et al., 2007); glutamatergic inhibition (5–50 μM, Vutskits et al., 2008); noradrenaline uptake inhibition (50 μM, Chies et al., 2003); and guanylate cyclase inhibition (60 μM, Deutsch et al., 1996). There are a limited number of activities of MT in vitro which occur in a concentration range comparable to its TAI activity. These are enhancement of mitochondrial β-oxidation (0.3 μM, Visarius et al., 1997) and inhibition of monoamine oxidase A (0.16 μM, Ramsay et al., 2007). These activities are for the oxidized MT^+ form, and their relevance to the situation in vivo is unknown. A further activity which has potential relevance for the treatment of frontotemporal dementia (FTD) is inhibition of aggregation of TDP-43 by MT (0.05 μM, Yamashita et al., 2009). The latter is of interest, since the pathology of FTD typically involves aggregation of either tau protein or TDP-43 in roughly equal proportions of cases (ie, approximately 45% each); TDP-43 proteinopathy is also the predominant form of amyotrophic lateral sclerosis (Irwin et al., 2015).

ACTIVITY OF TAIs IN TAU-TRANSGENIC MOUSE MODELS

There have been several reports of MTC having activity in transgenic mouse models of tauopathy. Global attenuation of tau pathology in a mouse model based on overexpression of full-length mutant tau (JNPL3, expressing the P301L mutation) was reported following 5 months of exposure to MTC in drinking water or 2 weeks of daily oral gavaging in mice (Congdon et al., 2012; Hosokawa et al., 2012), although there were no corresponding behavioral studies. Another P301L mouse model with tau expression under the control of the tetracycline-operative responsive element and producing a very strong pathological phenotype (rTg4510) was found to show benefit from treatment with MTC administered through an osmotic mini-pump into one hippocampal hemisphere (O'Leary et al., 2010; Ramsden et al., 2005). In another study, MTC provided in drinking water was found to lower normal tau levels, but did not affect preestablished tau aggregation pathology (O'Leary et al., 2010; Spires-Jones et al., 2014). Other models with weaker pathology, for example, 3xTg-AD mouse (Medina et al., 2011) or P301S mouse (Stack et al., 2014), showed reduction in tau pathology, although there have been contradictory findings (Spires-Jones et al., 2014). Although generally supportive, studies in which MTC is administered via drinking water do not control dose adequately, and investigators have not determined the effective brain concentration of MT required to produce benefit. There are significant technical difficulties in measurement of MT in tissues, and some claims regarding brain concentrations achieved after oral dosing are implausible and inconsistent with results of studies using radiolabeled MT (Baddeley et al., 2015).

Although some models of tauopathy have been examined in water maze tests (O'Leary et al., 2010), we have adopted more refined protocols to capture subtle improvements that can occur after short-term treatments. We have used a spatial problem-solving task that encompasses both reference memory and behavioral flexibility, which reflects the clinical problems in switching between tasks and cognitive inflexibility that are early indicators of cognitive impairment in AD. We have examined particularly MTC and LMTX in these models (Melis et al., 2015a). Both compounds rescued this learning impairment and restored behavioral flexibility. Following treatment, the performance of line 1 mice became indistinguishable from wild-type controls. MTC was required at a dose of 35 mg-MT/kg[a] to produce benefit, whereas with LMTX recovery was already evident at 9 mg-MT/kg (Melis et al., 2015a). Spatial learning and memory were normalized after 8 weeks of treatment at these doses. After 19 days of treatment, the 35 mg-MT/kg dose of MTC produced an overall reduction of 60% of tau-reactive neurons, and in subiculum the reduction was 83%. It does not appear that a reduction of this magnitude is necessary for behavioral improvements, since with LMTX at 9 mg-MT/kg, the reduction in tau-positive cells was 11% overall and 28% in hippocampus after 19 days of treatment. Cortico-hippocampal processing is critical for working memory and behavioral flexibility. Therefore, the reduction in the tau immunoreactivity of neurons in hippocampus, subiculum, and entorhinal cortex reflects a common effect on the underlying tau aggregation pathology. It is therefore likely that this explains the behavioral efficacy of MT in line 1 mice.

Since deficits in motor performance are the most prominent phenotypic feature of transgenic models of the line 66 type, we have used the rotarod to examine the effects of treatment. Line 66 is associated with a reliable motor learning deficit that manifests as a failure to improve performance over repeated trials without any difference in baseline performance (Melis et al., 2015b). The motor learning deficit, as measured by the difference in time on the rotarod between the first and last trial, was corrected at all doses tested, including the lowest dose of 4 mg-MT/kg. Both drugs produced equivalent benefit (Melis et al., 2015a). However, it was possible to distinguish between MTC and LMTX on the basis of task memory as measured by difference between first trial pretreatment and first trial posttreatment. Line 66 mice receiving LMTX at 15 mg-MT/kg between pre- and posttreatment testing periods were better able than vehicle-treated controls to retrieve motor learning acquired during the initial testing period. The effect of treatment at a dose of 45 mg-MT/kg for 19 days in line 66 mice was to reduce the number of tau-positive neurons overall by 40% with MTC and by 23% with LMTX. For both drugs, the effects were widespread, including hippocampus and cortex.

We have been able to establish a consistent dose–response relationship between MT levels measured in the brain and mean rotarod performance in line 66 mice for both MTC and LMTX (Melis et al., 2015a). The rotarod provides a technically more tractable paradigm in which to establish such relationships than the problem-solving version of the water maze paradigm. At the lowest effective dose (4 mg-MT/kg), the mean brain concentrations of total MT were 0.154 ± 0.012 and 0.199 ± 0.022 μM for MTC and LMTX, respectively. As shown in Fig. 15.25, there was increasing performance benefit over a 10-fold concentration range of brain MT (0.13–1.38 μM). Therefore, the lowest brain concentration of MT at which benefit

[a] The molecular weights of different salt forms of MT differ significantly, since they take into account the counterion and also water of crystallization, where present. Therefore, doses are not generally expressed as mg/kg, but rather mg-MT/kg to state explicitly the basis of the dosage statement, and to permit dose comparisons to be made with respect to different dosage forms of the same active moiety.

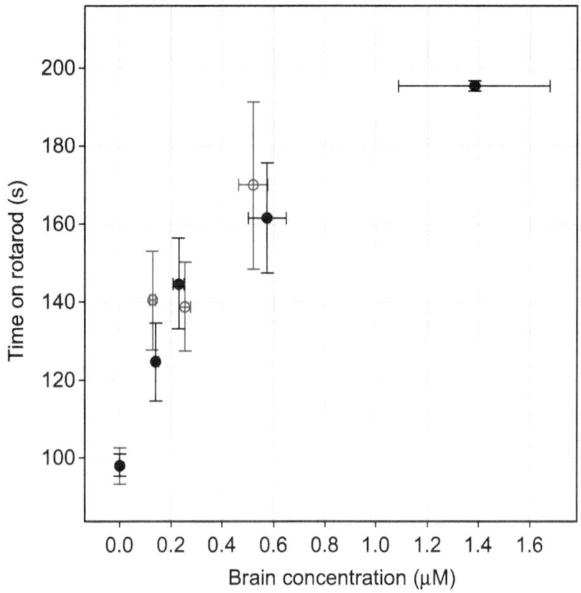

FIGURE 15.25 **Motor performance of line 66 mice treated with MTC and LMTX as a function of brain MT concentration.** The performance, measured as time spent on rotarod for line 66 mice treated with, respectively, 3.7 or 11 mg-MT/kg of MTC (○) or LMTX (●) is plotted as a function of brain MT concentration. Performance at corresponding brain concentrations of MT is similar, whether compound is delivered as MTC or LMTX. There is nonlinear improvement in performance over a 10-fold MT concentration range, with evidence of a plateau at MT concentrations of 0.6 μM (MTC) and 1.4 μM (LMTX). *Source: From Melis et al.:* Behav Pharmacol *26:353–368, 2015a.*

could be demonstrated corresponds closely to the K_i value (0.12 μM) for MT activity as an inhibitor of tau aggregation in cells (Harrington et al., 2015) and the concentration required for dissolution of PHFs isolated from AD brain tissues (0.16 μM).

Thus, LMTX appears to have a superior pharmacological profile compared with MTC based on similar efficacy at a quarter of the dose of MT in line 1. However, detailed examination of the relationship between brain concentration of MT and behavioral effect in line 66 mice demonstrates that MT produces the same effect at the same brain concentration whether dosed as LMTX or MTC. The apparent differences in potency are therefore explained by differences in absorption, metabolism, and distribution. We have shown that LMTX produces 3-fold higher concentrations of MT in mouse brain at similar doses (Baddeley et al., 2015). Importantly, the behavioral and pathological effects we have been able to measure occur at brain concentrations which are consistent with the concentrations required for TAI activity in vitro.

POTENTIAL CLINICAL EFFICACY OF TAI THERAPY IN MILD OR MODERATE AD

MT, as the chloride salt (oxidized MT^+, MTC, "methylene blue"), has a long history of safe use, both as an approved treatment for methemoglobinemia (Mansouri and Lurie, 1993) and experimentally in urolithiasis and bipolar disorder, among others (Boyce et al., 1967; Naylor et al., 1986; Wein et al., 1976). As summarized previously, MT inhibits tau aggregation in vitro and dissolves PHFs from AD brain tissue (Harrington et al., 2015; Wischik et al., 1996).

We have recently reported the results of the first phase 2 clinical trial of a TAI in 321 subjects with mild/moderate AD (Wischik et al., 2015). The trial was designed as an exploratory double-blind, randomized, placebo-controlled, 24-week dose-finding study of MT as monotherapy in AD. Treatment could be extended in a blinded fashion in two sequential extension phases. In addition, a nested HMPAO-SPECT substudy was conducted in 135 of the participating subjects to explore whether treatment could prevent progression of molecular imaging deficits. The primary aim of the study was to determine whether treatment with a TAI has potential utility in the treatment of AD and, if so, to determine the minimum safe and effective dose and likely treatment effect size for further investigation.

The primary efficacy analysis at 24 weeks showed that treatment with MT 138 mg-MT/day is the minimum effective dose required to prevent disease progression in subjects with baseline disease of moderate severity. Efficacy was confirmed in an independent population using more sensitive imaging measures in subjects with baseline mild disease. Specifically, in the prespecified primary efficacy analysis model, treatment with 138 mg-MT/day produced statistically significant benefit with respect to placebo on the ADAS-cog scale [effect size = –5.42 units, CI = (–9.44, –1.41), nominal $p = 0.008$, corrected $p = 0.047$] at 24 weeks in patients with moderate AD at baseline, even after correcting conservatively for multiple comparisons. Significant effects were also seen on the ADCS-CGIC scale and the MMSE [effect size = 3.79 units, CI = (1.16, 6.41), nominal $p = 0.0048$, corrected $p = 0.028$] secondary outcome scales. A significant treatment effect was seen at the same dose on the overall functional molecular imaging outcome in a separate population (mild subjects) at approximately 24 weeks after applying similar corrections [effect size = 1.97%, CI = (1.02, 2.92), nominal $p < 0.001$, corrected $p < 0.001$]. Similar conclusions are drawn if one uses the statistical analysis methodology favored by the US Food and Drug Administration, and used as the primary outcome analysis in recent phase 3 clinical trials of antiamyloid agents (Doody et al., 2014; Salloway et al., 2014). This comprises a linear mixed effects analysis with an unstructured correlation matrix, and does not impute values that are missing. Such an analysis model has the advantage of estimating the relevant parameters from only the data available from each individual and makes no assumptions as to the nature of underlying correlations. In similar analyses, the treatment effect at the 138 mg-MT/day dose was significant in moderate subjects at 24 weeks ($p = 0.023$) and in the combined mild/moderate AD population at 50 weeks ($p = 0.0073$).

Because of the similarity of pharmacokinetic handling of MT in minipigs and humans, a ^{14}C-MTC study was conducted in minipigs to estimate the likely brain concentration in humans at the minimum effective dose of 138 mg-MT/day (Baddeley et al., 2015). Mean total radioactivity in brain homogenates obtained 2 h after oral administration of ^{14}C-MTC (30 mg-MT/kg) was 0.595 μg equivalent per g, a level comparable to that found in pooled red blood cells (0.618 μg equivalent per g) at the same time. Samples were extracted and profiled by LCMSn for identification of MT and its metabolites. A mean of 0.214 μg equivalent per g was identified as MT and a further 0.073 μg equivalent per g as desmethyl derivatives of MT. The latter have lost either one or two methyl groups but retain TAI pharmacological activity similar to MT (Taniguchi et al., 2005). The minimum effective clinical dose in humans for treatment of AD at the nominal dose of 138 mg-MT/day, given as 60 mg MTC capsules administered three times per day (ie, a total daily dose of 180 mg MTC, or 138 mg of the MT moiety), is associated with an accumulation factor of 1.65 [based on comparison of day 1 and day 15 peak total MT plasma concentrations (Cmax)] due to repeat dosing. At this dose, the calculated steady state trough concentration of parent MT and its active metabolites in the human brain is estimated to be 0.051 μg equivalent per g (0.18 μM).

This concentration overlaps the concentrations required for the TAI activities discussed previously. In particular, the concentration required for dissolution of PHFs is 0.16 μM, the K_i of MT for inhibition of aggregation-dependent template-directed proteolysis of tau protein in the physiological milieu of the cell is 0.12 μM, and the concentration range over which behavioral deficits are reversed and tau pathology reduced is 0.13–1.38 μM (Harrington et al., 2015; Melis et al., 2015a). It is therefore plausible that the clinical benefit seen in the phase 2 trial is due to TAI activity in the human brain. This is further supported by the anatomical pattern of reduction in functional molecular imaging deficits as determined by HMPAO-SPECT in the nested imaging substudy. Fig. 15.26 is a difference map between placebo- and MTC-treated subjects of change in regional cerebral blood flow between baseline and week 24, determined by statistical parametric mapping. The regions where the difference is statistically significant (shown either as a surface projection on the left or as a coronal projection on the right) correspond closely to the regions known to be particularly rich in neurofibrillary tangles (ie, the Braak staging regions).

Surprisingly, none of the clinical, imaging, or overall safety effects increased monotonically with respect to the nominal dose. A considerable body of work was required to understand the unexpected failure of the 228 mg-MT/day nominal dose recently reported in Baddeley et al. (2015). In summary, MT is a redox molecule and, depending on environmental conditions (eg, pH, oxygen, reducing agents), exists in equilibrium between a reduced LMT and oxidized form (MT^+). As the chloride salt (MTC) used in the phase 2 trial, MT exists entirely in

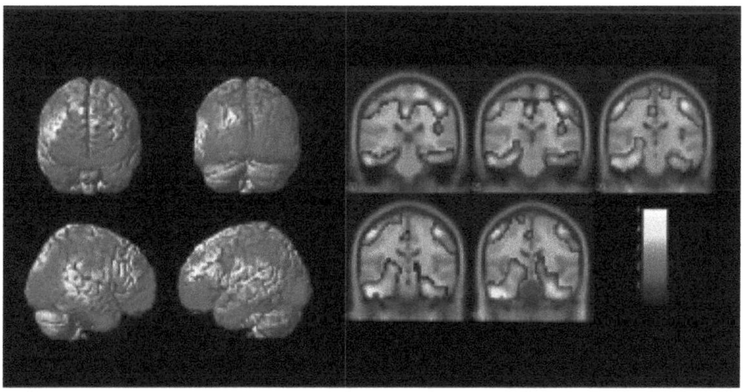

FIGURE 15.26 **Difference in HMPAO-SPECT signal from baseline over 6 months between those receiving MTC versus placebo in mild AD subjects.** The significant treatment-associated differences are in areas of the brain typically involved with neurofibrillary tangle pathology, that is, treatment with MT has resulted in significantly less loss of neuronal function as detected by SPECT (or, in some, the preservation of blood flow) (see online version showing colored regions). *Source: From Wischik et al.:* J Alzheimers Dis *44:705–720, 2015.*

the MT^{+} form in an oxygen atmosphere. Active conversion to the LMT form is required to permit absorption by passive diffusion (Baddeley et al., 2015; May et al., 2004). This conversion occurs optimally in the stomach, likely due to the pH dependence of the MT redox potential (Murthy and Reddy, 1984). MTC is therefore a prodrug, and the absorption and disposition of MT depend both on the fed/fasting status and on dissolution time of the formulation administered (Baddeley et al., 2015).

The dose-dependent impairment in absorption occurring in the presence of food proved to be an important determinant of dose response for the SPECT scan effect at 24 weeks, the ADAS-Cog effect at 50 weeks, and the frequency of adverse events (AEs) leading to dose interruption/discontinuation. The dose–response relationships taking account of the calculated dose available when the highest-dose 100 mg MTC capsules (each containing 76 mg MT) were taken with food (as subjects were instructed to do for all doses in the phase 2 trial) were monotonic and linear with correlation coefficients for mean effects all greater than 0.97. Thus, of the nominal dose of 228 mg-MT/day (given as 100 mg MTC capsules taken three times per day), only 109 mg-MT/day was available for absorption when taken with food. Therefore, the most effective dose of 138 mg-MT/day identified in the phase 2 study simply represented the highest available dose tested.

Dissolution time within or after 60 min proved to be a further contributory factor accounting, respectively, for the ADAS-Cog effect at 24 weeks ($r = 0.835$) and the hematological effect of MT ($r = 0.955$). This analysis was made possible from capsule dissolution studies conducted at the time the phase 2 study was initiated. It was found that there was a capsule strength-dependent impairment of dissolution (Baddeley et al., 2015). The calculated dose available for absorption within or after 60 min was found to predict, respectively, the cognitive or hematological effects of MT. This partial dissociation suggests that conversion of the MT^{+} form to LMT in the stomach is a further requirement for cognitive efficacy; presumably this reflects differential redox processing at different levels of the gut.

The complex factors affecting absorption and disposition of MT redox forms were entirely unknown at the time the study was designed, or for the past 100 years that MTC has been in clinical use. However, the unexpected dose-dependent limitations in the absorption of the 100 mg MTC capsule made the blinded extension phase of the study to 52 weeks more informative than would otherwise have been the case. During weeks 24–50, subjects originally randomized to placebo received a nominal dose of 152 mg-MT/day administered as 100 mg MTC capsules given twice daily with food, with poor dissolution and poor absorption. The intention was to obtain preliminary information regarding twice-daily dosing using the highest-strength capsules. Since these were particularly affected by absorption and dissolution limitations, only 73 mg-MT/day of the 152 mg-MT/day nominal dose administered during weeks 24–50 was available for absorption with food. Therefore, subjects originally randomized to placebo during the first 24 weeks and progressing to the 152 mg/day nominal dose during weeks 24–50 provided a relatively inactive control arm through to 50 weeks which permitted informative post hoc comparisons to be made with respect to subjects randomized to active doses who continued with their original randomized doses for 50 weeks.

The cognitive decline over 50 weeks seen in mild subjects originally randomized to placebo was 2.9 ± 0.7 units (mean ± SE) ADAS-Cog units. This is comparable to the mean placebo decline (3.5 ± 1.8 units [mean ± SE]) seen in a metaanalysis of studies in mild AD subjects at

12 months (Wischik et al., 2015). By contrast, the mean decline seen in mild subjects receiving the 138 mg-MT/day dose was close to zero, implying an effect size of –2.8 ± 1.1 units (mean ± SE) ADAS-Cog units, equivalent to 96% of the decline seen in the control arm and statistically significant ($p = 0.009$). Similarly, the effect size at this dose in moderate subjects (–5.2 ± 2.3 units [mean ± SE] ADAS-Cog units) was 94% of the decline of 5.5 ± 1.5 units (mean ± SE) ADAS-Cog units seen in the control arm at 50 weeks ($p = 0.025$). This indicates that notwithstanding the differences in decline relative to severity seen in the control arm, the corresponding treatment effect sizes appear to represent a constant fraction of control arm decline, as would be expected for a disease-modifying treatment.

It is intriguing that the mean effect size seen by SPECT scan in mild subjects in the absence of apparent clinical benefit at 24 weeks was highly correlated with the mean clinical effect seen on the ADAS-Cog scale at 50 weeks in mild subjects ($r = 0.99$). This suggests that the benefit seen early in the more sensitive functional molecular imaging modality is an indicator of a physiological change that takes a further 6 months to be manifest clinically on the ADAS-Cog scale, and could have potential utility as an early predictor of later clinical benefit.

The benefits first seen at 24 weeks were sustained to 50 weeks such that the overall decline in mixed mild/moderate subjects randomized to the 138 mg-MT/day dose was not significantly different from zero (0.27 ± 0.74 ADAS-Cog units [mean ± SE], $p = 0.714$) (Wischik et al., 2015). From our metaanalysis of previously reported studies, the decline expected in clinical trial populations of mixed mild/moderate AD subjects at 12 months is 4.4 ± 1.8 (mean ± SE). While the efficacy data at 50 weeks, being as they are exploratory and post hoc, cannot support an inferential claim in the same way that the 24-week data can, they are nevertheless informative as a basis for planning confirmatory phase 3 trials. They provide an empirical estimate of effect size at the minimal effective dose expected in a mixed mild/moderate population at 12 months as approximately 90% ± 35% (mean ± SE) of the expected placebo decline as a basis for planning further studies. The power of a study depends on estimating the absolute effect size. However, for a disease-modifying treatment, the results seen in the phase 2 study suggest that absolute effect size is variable, depending as it does on the placebo decline, although what we term the "effect fraction" (effect size expressed as a percentage of placebo decline) remains relatively constant. It is the effect fraction which provides the most appropriate measure of inherent efficacy. Absolute effect size, on the other hand, depends on the absolute rate of decline expected in the placebo arm. The latter depends on baseline severity profile, inherent rate of progression of the population studied, and duration of observation.

Thus the phase 2 study identified a dose of 138 mg-MT/day as the minimum effective dose required to prevent decline on three clinical outcome measures and on rCBF decline at 24 weeks. The AEs seen at the 138 mg-MT/day dose, which were predominantly mild and restricted to the gastrointestinal system and micturition, do not preclude further clinical development. While the results support further confirmatory studies with MT, these cannot be conducted using MTC because of absorption and longer-term tolerability limitations. The absorption limitations at the highest nominal dose of 228 mg-MT/day (given via the 100 mg MTC capsules) limited delivery to an available dose of 109 mg-MT/day. Therefore, the phase 2 study did not permit determination of whether greater efficacy than seen at the 138 mg-MT/day dose is achievable at a higher available dose without significant loss of tolerability or safety. Global phase 3 studies of MT have now completed recruitment in mild and moderate

AD. The studies investigate MT doses in the range 150–250 mg-MT/day using the newly developed, stable reduced form (LMTX) that directly delivers LMT without need for active gastric conversion from MT^+, is better tolerated, and does not suffer from the dose-dependent absorption limitations of MTC (Baddeley et al., 2015).

CONCLUSIONS: PRION-LIKE PROCESSING OF TAU PROTEIN AND ITS IMPLICATIONS FOR DRUG DEVELOPMENT

In this chapter we have set out an alternative position to widely held presumptions in the field regarding both the priority of the APP target for AD prevention and the potential role of aberrant phosphorylation of tau protein as a bridge between APP misprocessing and tau aggregation pathology. We have argued that the critical process underlying the initiation and propagation of tau aggregation pathology is the inherent ability of the repeat domain of tau to undergo a high-affinity binding interaction which is associated with an induced conformational change. This process is self-propagating; that is, the induced conformational change created by an initial pathological binding event creates a high-affinity tau capture site which induces the same conformational change in subsequently bound tau molecules. The process is also autocatalytic, in that the resulting aggregates are proteolytically stable in the region of the critical binding domain (ie, what we call the PHF-core tau unit), and the oligomers thus created become seeds for further tau aggregation. These twin processes result in the sequestration of normal tau protein into a toxic proteolytically stable form in which the repeat domain acts as a template for nucleation and proteolytic processing. The process is inherently exponential over time, and its progression can be mapped empirically to cognitive decline and the histological phenomena of tangle formation and tangle-mediated neuronal destruction. We show that this process can be modeled in cell-free systems in vitro and, more importantly, in cell-based models where the prion-like processing can be shown to occur within the physiological milieu of the cell.

In this view, the most appropriate target for intervention is the aggregation cascade itself, irrespective of the phosphorylation hypothesis. We show that the pharmacological viability of TAIs depends on an inherent conformational difference between the pathological tau–tau and physiological tau–tubulin interactions which both occur through the repeat domain of the molecule. Model systems based on prion-like processing of the repeat domain can be used as a platform to optimize TAIs for further clinical development. These model systems also make it possible to derive estimates of the critical concentrations of prototype TAIs required for efficacy.

We review the first exploratory clinical trial of a therapeutic approach based on the TAI strategy, and show that a surprisingly high degree of efficacy could be achieved in both mild and moderate AD at doses with an acceptable safety profile. The minimum effective dose required for efficacy on clinical and imaging end points is estimated to produce brain concentrations which overlap closely with the concentrations required for TAI activity in vitro and in tau-transgenic animals. The hypothesis that it is TAI activity which accounts for efficacy is further supported by the neuroanatomical distribution of brain regions where prevention of decline on the functional molecular neuroimaging outcome could be mapped to brain regions known to be particularly affected by tau aggregation pathology.

The results of the exploratory phase 2 trial and the theoretical rationale we have developed in this review provide the basis for the ongoing phase 3 trials of the TAI approach to the treatment of AD. The program comprises three distinct trials in mild/moderate AD, mild AD, and bvFTD, respectively. All three are now fully recruited, and the first results will be available during the first half of 2016. If these trials are successful, they will provide a basis for further studies in prodromal AD to test the viability of secondary prevention (ie, prevention of prodromal AD progressing to dementia), and thereafter studies seeking to establish whether the TAI strategy can be used for primary prevention (ie, primary prevention of prodromal AD). We have attempted in this review to provide a rationale for the tau aggregation pathology as an inherently valid target for both prevention and treatment of AD and related neurodegenerative disorders of protein aggregation.

References

Abraha A, Ghoshal N, Gamblin TC, Cryns V, Berry RW, Kuret J, Binder LI: C-terminal inhibition of tau assembly in vitro and in Alzheimer's disease, *J Cell Sci* 113:3737–3745, 2000.

Akoury E, Pickhardt M, Gajda M, Biernat J, Mandelkow E, Zweckstetter M: Mechanistic basis of phenothiazine-driven inhibition of tau aggregation, *Angew Chem Int Ed* 52:3511–3515, 2013.

Allen B, Ingram E, Takao M, Smith MJ, Jakes R, Virdee K, Yoshida H, Holzer M, Craxton M, Emson PC, Atzori C, Migheli A, Crowther RA, Ghetti B, Spillantini MG, Goedert M: Abundant tau filaments and nonapoptotic neurodegeneration in transgenic mice expressing human P301S tau protein, *J Neurosci* 22:9340–9351, 2002.

Alonso AD, Zaidi T, Grundke-Iqbal I, Iqbal K: Role of abnormally phosphorylated tau in the breakdown of microtubules in Alzheimer's disease, *Proc Natl Acad Sci USA* 91:5562–5566, 1994.

Alzheimer A: Über eine eigenartige Erkrankung der Hirnrinde, *Allg Z Psych Psych-Gerich Med* 64:146–148, 1907.

Anderton BH, Breinburg D, Downes MJ, Green PJ, Tomlinson BE, Ulrich J, Wood JN, Kahn J: Monoclonal antibodies show that neurofibrillary tangles and neurofilaments share antigenic determinants, *Nature* 298:84–86, 1982.

Aoyagi H, Hasegawa M, Tamaoka A: Fibrillogenic nuclei composed of P301L mutant tau induce elongation of P301L tau, but not wild-type tau, *J Biol Chem* 282:20309–20318, 2007.

Arendt T, Stieler J, Strijkstra AM, Hut RA, Rudiger J, Van der Zee EA, Harkany T, Holzer M, Hartig W: Reversible paired helical filament-like phosphorylation of tau is an adaptive process associated with neuronal plasticity in hibernating animals, *J Neurosci* 23:6972–6981, 2003.

Arrasate M, Pérez M, Valpuesta JM, Avila J: Role of glycosaminoglycans in determining the helicity of paired helical filaments, *Am J Pathol* 151:1115–1122, 1997.

Arriagada PW, Growdon JH, Hedley-White ET, Hyman BT: Neurofibrillary tangles but not senile plaques parallel duration and severity of Alzheimer's disease, *Neurology* 42:631–639, 1992.

Baddeley TC, McCaffrey J, Storey JMD, Cheung JKS, Melis V, Horsley D, Harrington CR, Wischik CM: Complex disposition of methylthioninium redox forms determines efficacy in tau aggregation inhibitor therapy for Alzheimer's disease, *J Pharmacol Exp Therap* 352:110–118, 2015.

Bancher C, Braak H, Fischer P, Jellinger K: Neuropathological staging of Alzheimer lesions and intellectual status in Alzheimer's and Parkinson's disease, *Neurosci Lett* 162:179–182, 1993.

Bancher C, Jellinger K, Lassmann H, Fischer P, Leblhuber F: Correlations between mental state and quantitative neuropathology in the Vienna Longitudinal Study on Dementia, *Eur Arch Psychiatry Clin Neurosci* 246:137–146, 1996.

Bateman RJ, Xiong C, Benzinger TLS, Fagan AM, Goate A, Fox NC, Marcus DS, Cairns NJ, Xie X, Blazey TM, Holtzman DM, Santacruz A, Buckles V, Oliver A, Moulder K, Aisen PS, Ghetti B, Klunk WE, McDade E, Martins RN, Masters CL, Mayeux R, Ringman JM, Rossor MN, Schofield PR, Sperling RA, Salloway S, Morris JC: Clinical and biomarker changes in dominantly inherited Alzheimer's disease, *New Eng J Med* 367:795–804, 2012.

Berry RW, Abraha A, Lagalwar S, LaPointe N, Gamblin TC, Cryns VL, Binder LI: Inhibition of tau polymerization by its carboxy-terminal caspase cleavage fragment, *Biochemistry* 42:8325–8331, 2003.

Biernat J, Gustke N, Drewes G, Mandelkow E-M, Mandelkow E: Phosphorylation of Ser262 strongly reduces binding of tau to microtubules: distinction between PHF-like immunoreactivity and microtubule binding, *Neuron* 11:153–163, 1993.

Blocq P, Marinesco G: Sur les lésions et la pathogénie de l'épilepsie des dite essentielle, *Sem Méd* 12:445–446, 1892.

Bondareff W, Wischik CM, Novak M, Roth M: Sequestration of tau by granulovacuolar degeneration in Alzheimer's disease, *Am J Pathol* 139:641–647, 1991.

Bondareff W, Harrington C, Wischik CM, Hauser DL, Roth M: Immunohistochemical staging of neurofibrillary degeneration in Alzheimer's disease, *J Neuropathol Exptl Neurol* 53:158–164, 1994.

Boyce WH, McKinney WM, Long TT, Drach GW: Oral administration of methylene blue to patients with renal calculi, *J Urol* 97:783–789, 1967.

Braak H, Braak E: Neuropathological stageing of Alzheimer-related changes, *Acta Neuropathol* 82:239–259, 1991.

Braak H, Del Tredici K: The pathological process underlying Alzheimer's disease in individuals under thirty, *Acta Neuropathol* 121:171–181, 2011.

Braak H, Zetterberg H, Del Tredici K, Blennow K: Intraneuronal tau aggregation precedes diffuse plaque deposition, but amyloid-beta changes occur before increases of tau in cerebrospinal fluid, *Acta Neuropathol* 126:631–641, 2013.

Bradley KM, O'Sullivan VT, Soper NDW, Nagy Z, King EM-F, Smith AD, Shepstone BJ: Cerebral perfusion SPET correlated with Braak pathological stage in Alzheimer's disease, *Brain* 125:1772–1781, 2002.

Brion J-P, Passareiro H, Nunez J, Flament-Durand J: Mise en évidence immunologique de la protéine tau au niveau des lésions de dégénérescence neurofibrillaire de la maladie d'Alzheimer, *Arch Biol (Brux)* 95:229–235, 1985.

Buchhave P, Minthon L, Zetterberg H, Wallin Å, Blennow K, Hansson O: Cerebrospinal fluid levels of β-amyloid 1–42, but not of tau, are fully changed already 5 to 10 years before the onset of Alzheimer dementia, *Arch Gen Psychiat* 69:98–106, 2012.

Bulic B, Pickhardt M, Schmidt B, Mandelkow E-M, Waldmann H, Mandelkow E: Development of tau aggregation inhibitors for Alzheimer's disease, *Angew Chem Int Ed* 48:1740–1752, 2009.

Chakrabarty P, Hudson VJ III, Sacino AN, Brooks MM, D'Alton S, Lewis J, Golde TE, Giasson BI: Inefficient induction and spread of seeded tau pathology in P301L mouse model of tauopathy suggests inherent physiological barriers to transmission, *Acta Neuropathol* 130:303–305, 2015.

Chien DT, Bahri S, Szardenings AK, Walsh JC, Mu F, Su M-Y, Shankle WR, Elizarov A, Kolb HC: Early clinical PET imaging results with the novel PHF-tau radioligand [F-18]-T807, *J Alzheimers Dis* 34:457–468, 2013.

Chies AB, Custódio RC, de Souza GL, Corrêa FM, Pereira OC: Pharmacological evidence that methylene blue inhibits noradrenaline neuronal uptake in the rat vas deferens, *Pol J Pharmacol* 55:573–579, 2003.

Chirita C, Necula M, Kuret J: Ligand-dependent inhibition and reversal of tau filament formation, *Biochemistry* 43:2879–2887, 2004.

Choi SH, Kim YH, Hebisch M, Sliwinski C, Lee S, D'Avanzo C, Chen H, Hooli B, Asselin C, Muffat J, Klee JB, Zhang C, Wainger BJ, Peitz M, Kovacs DM, Woolf CJ, Wagner SL, Tanzi RE, Kim DY: A three-dimensional human neural cell culture model of Alzheimer's disease, *Nature* 515:274–278, 2014.

Clavaguera F, Bolmont T, Crowther RA, Abramowski D, Frank S, Probst A, Fraser G, Stalder AK, Beibel M, Staufenbiel M, Jucker M, Goedert M, Tolnay M: Transmission and spreading of tauopathy in transgenic mouse brain, *Nature Cell Biol* 11:909–914, 2009.

Clavaguera F, Lavenir I, Falcon B, Frank S, Goedert M, Tolnay M: Prion-like templated misfolding in tauopathies, *Brain Pathol* 23:342–349, 2013.

Congdon EE, Wu JW, Myeku N, Figueroa YH, Herman M, Marinec PS, Gestwicki JE, Dickey CA, Yu WH, Duff KE: Methylthioninium chloride (methylene blue) induces autophagy and attenuates tauopathy in vitro and in vivo, *Autophagy* 8:609–622, 2012.

Crowe A, Ballatore C, Hyde E, Trojanowski JQ, Lee VM-Y: High throughput screening for small molecule inhibitors of heparin-induced tau fibril formation, *Biochem Biophys Res Commun* 358:1–6, 2007.

Crowe A, Huang W, Ballatore C, Johnson RL, Hogan A-ML, Huang R, Wichtermann J, McCoy J, Huryn DM, Auld DS, Smith AB III, Inglese J, Trojanowski JQ, Austin CP, Brunden KR, Lee VM-Y: The identification of aminothienopyridazine inhibitors of tau assembly by quantitative high-throughput screening, *Biochemistry* 48:7732–7745, 2009.

Crowther RA, Olesen OF, Jakes R, Goedert M: The microtubule binding repeats of tau protein assemble into filaments like those found in Alzheimer's disease, *FEBS Lett* 309:199–202, 1992.

Denk F, Wade-Martins R: Knock-out and transgenic mouse models of tauopathies, *Neurobiol Aging* 30:1–13, 2009.

Deutsch SI, Rosse RB, Paul SM, Tomasino V, Koetzner L, Morn CB, Mastropaolo J: 7-Nitroindazole and methylene blue, inhibitors of neuronal nitric oxide synthase and NO-stimulated guanylate cyclase, block MK-801-elicited behaviors in mice, *Neuropsychopharmacology* 15:37–43, 1996.

Dickey C, Ash P, Klosak N, Lee W, Petrucelli L, Hutton M, Eckman C: Pharmacologic reductions of total tau levels; implications for the role of microtubule dynamics in regulating tau expression, *Mol Neurodegener* 1:6, 2006.

Donohue MC, Jacqmin-Gadda H, Le Goff M, Thomas RG, Raman R, Gamst AC, Beckett LA, Jack CR Jr, Weiner MW, Dartigues J-F, Aisen PS: Estimating long-term multivariate progression from short-term data, *Alzheimers Dement* 10:S400–S410, 2014.

Doody RS, Thomas RG, Farlow M, Iwatsubo T, Vellas B, Joffe S, Kieburtz K, Raman R, Sun X, Aisen PS, Siemers E, Liu-Seifert H, Mohs R: Phase 3 trials of solanezumab for mild-to-moderate Alzheimer's disease, *New Eng J Med* 370:311–321, 2014.

Duyckaerts C: Tau pathology in children and young adults: can you still be unconditionally baptist? *Acta Neuropathol* 121:145–147, 2011.

Duyckaerts C, Bennecib M, Grignon Y, Uchihara T, He Y, Piette F, Hauw J-J: Modeling the relation between neurofibrillary tangles and intellectual status, *Neurobiol Aging* 18:267–273, 1997.

Fasulo L, Ovecka M, Kabát J, Bradbury A, Novák M, Cattaneo A: Overexpression of Alzheimer's PHF core tau fragments: implications for the tau truncation hypothesis, *Alzheimers Res* 2:195–200, 1996.

Fasulo L, Ugolini G, Cattaneo A: Apoptotic effect of caspase-3 cleaved tau in hippocampal neurons and its potentiation by tau FTDP-mutation N279K, *J Alzheimers Dis* 7:3–13, 2005.

Fasulo L, Ugolini G, Visintin M, Bradbury A, Brancolini C, Verzillo V, Novak M, Cattaneo A: The neuronal microtubule-associated protein tau is a substrate for caspase-3 and an effector of apoptosis, *J Neurochem* 75:624–633, 2000.

Fasulo L, Visintin M, Novak M, Cattaneo A: Tau truncation in Alzheimer's disease: expression of a fragment encompassing PHF core tau induces apoptosis in COS cells, *Alzheimers Rep* 1:25–32, 1998.

Filipcik P, Cente M, Krajciova G, Vanicky I, Novak M: Cortical and hippocampal neurons from truncated tau transgenic rat express multiple markers of neurodegeneration, *Cell Mol Neurobiol* 29:895–900, 2009.

Fischer O: Miliare Nekrosen mit drusigen Wucherungen der Neurofibrillen, eine regelmässige Veränderung der Hirnrinde bei seniler Demenz, *Monatsschr Psychiat Neurol* 22:361–372, 1907.

Flores-Rodríguez P, Ontiveros-Torres MA, Cárdenas-Aguayo MC, Luna-Arias JP, Meraz-Rios MA, Viramontes-Pintos A, Harrington CR, Wischik CM, Mena R, Florán-Garduño B, Luna-Muñoz J: The relationship between truncation and phosphorylation at the C-terminus of tau protein in the paired helical filaments of Alzheimer's disease, *Frontiers Neurosci* 9:33, 2015.

Friedhoff P, von Bergen M, Mandelkow E-M, Davies P, Mandelkow E: A nucleated assembly of Alzheimer paired helical filaments, *Proc Natl Acad Sci USA* 95:15712–15717, 1998.

Frost B, Jacks RL, Diamond MI: Propagation of tau misfolding from the outside to the inside of a cell, *J Biol Chem* 284:12845–12852, 2009.

Frost B, Diamond MI: Prion-like mechanisms in neurodegenerative diseases, *Nat Rev Neurosci* 11:155–159, 2010.

Gamblin TC, Chen F, Zambrano A, Abraha A, Lagalwar S, Guillozet AL, Lu M, Fu Y, Garcia-Sierra F, LaPointe N, Miller R, Berry RW, Binder LI, Cryns VL: Caspase cleavage of tau: linking amyloid and neurofibrillary tangles in Alzheimer's disease, *Proc Natl Acad Sci USA* 100:10032–10037, 2003.

García-Sierra F, Wischik CM, Harrington CR, Luna-Muñoz J, Mena R: Accumulation of C-terminally truncated tau protein associated with vulnerability of the perforant pathway in early stages of neurofibrillary pathology in Alzheimer's disease, *J Chem Neuroanat* 22:65–77, 2001.

Gertz H-J, Xuereb JH, Huppert FA, Brayne C, Kuüger H, McGee MA, Paykel ES, Harrington CR, Mukaetova-Ladinska EB, O'Connor DW, Wischik CM: The relationship between clinical dementia and neuropathological staging (Braak) in a very elderly community sample, *Eur Arch Psychiatry Clin Neurosci* 246:132–136, 1996.

Goedert M, Clavaguera F, Tolnay M: The propagation of prion-like protein inclusions in neurodegenerative diseases, *Trends Neurosci* 33:317–325, 2010.

Goedert M, Jakes R, Spillantini MG, Hasegawa M, Smith MJ, Crowther RA: Assembly of microtubule-associated protein tau into Alzheimer-like filaments induced by sulphated glycosaminoglycans, *Nature* 383:550–553, 1996.

Goedert M, Spillantini MG, Cairns NJ, Crowther RA: Tau proteins of Alzheimer paired helical filaments: abnormal phosphorylation of all six brain isoforms, *Neuron* 8:159–168, 1992.

Grober E, Dickson D, Sliwinski MJ, Buschke H, Katz M, Crystal H, Lipton RB: Memory and mental status correlates of modified Braak staging, *Neurobiol Aging* 20:573–579, 1999.

Grundke-Iqbal I, Iqbal K, Quinlan M, Tung Y-C, Zaida MS, Wisniewski HM: Microtubule associated protein tau: a component of Alzheimer paired helical filaments, *J Biol Chem* 261:6084–6089, 1986a.

Grundke-Iqbal I, Iqbal K, Tung YC, Quinlan M, Wisniewski HM, Binder LI: Abnormal phosphorylation of the microtubule-associated protein tau in Alzheimer cytoskeletal pathology, *Proc Natl Acad Sci USA* 83:4913–4917, 1986b.

Guillozet-Bongaarts AL, Cahill ME, Cryns VL, Reynolds MR, Berry RW, Binder LI: Pseudophosphorylation of tau at serine 422 inhibits caspase cleavage: in vitro evidence and implications for tangle formation in vivo, *J Neurochem* 97:1005–1014, 2006.

Guillozet-Bongaarts AL, Garcia-Sierra F, Reynolds MR, Horowitz PM, Fu Y, Wang T, Cahill ME, Bigio EH, Berry RW, Binder LI: Tau truncation during neurofibrillary tangle evolution in Alzheimer's disease, *Neurobiol Aging* 26:1015–1022, 2005.

Guo JL, Lee VM-Y: Seeding of normal tau by pathological tau conformers drives pathogenesis of Alzheimer-like tangles, *J Biol Chem* 286:15317–15331, 2011.

Hall AM, Roberson ED: Mouse models of Alzheimer's disease, *Brain Res Bull* 88:3–12, 2012.

Hall G, Lee S, Yao J: Neurofibrillary degeneration can be arrested in an in vivo cellular model of human tauopathy by application of a compound which inhibits tau filament formation in vitro, *J Mol Neurosci* 19:251–260, 2002.

Hardy J, Allsop D: Amyloid depositions as the central event in the aetiology of Alzheimer's disease, *Trends Pharmacol Sci* 12:383–388, 1991.

Harrington CR, Mukaetova-Ladinska EB, Hills R, Edwards PC, Montejo de Garcini E, Novak M, Wischik CM: Measurement of distinct immunochemical presentations of tau protein in Alzheimer disease, *Proc Natl Acad Sci USA* 88:5842–5846, 1991.

Harrington CR, Storey JMD, Clunas S, Harrington KA, Horsley D, Ishaq A, Kemp SJ, Larch CP, Marshall C, Nicoll SL, Rickard JE, Simpson M, Sinclair JP, Storey LJ, Wischik CM: Cellular models of aggregation-dependent template-directed proteolysis to characterize tau aggregation inhibitors for treatment of Alzheimer's disease, *J Biol Chem* 290:10862–10875, 2015.

Hasegawa M, Crowther RA, Jakes R, Goedert M: Alzheimer-like changes in microtubule-associated protein tau induced by sulfated glycosaminoglycans: inhibition of microtubule binding, stimulation of phosphorylation, and filament assembly depend on the degree of sulfation, *J Biol Chem* 272:33118–33124, 1997.

Hebert LE, Weuve J, Scherr PA, Evans DA: Alzheimer disease in the United States (2010–2050) estimated using the 2010 census, *Neurology* 80:1778–1783, 2013.

Herholz K, Schopphoff H, Schmidt M, Mielke R, Eschner W, Scheidhauer K, Schicha H, Heiss W-D, Ebmeier K: Direct comparison of spatially normalized PET and SPECT scans in Alzheimer's disease, *J Nuc Med* 43:21–26, 2002.

Holmes BB, Furman JL, Mahan TE, Yamasaki TR, Mirbaha H, Eades WC, Belaygorod L, Cairns NJ, Holtzman DM, Diamond MI: Proteopathic tau seeding predicts tauopathy in vivo, *Proc Natl Acad Sci USA* 111:E4376–E4385, 2014.

Honson NS, Jensen JR, Darby MV, Kuret J: Potent inhibition of tau fibrillization with a multivalent ligand, *Biochem Biophys Res Commun* 363:229–234, 2007.

Hosokawa M, Arai T, Masuda-Suzukake M, Nonaka T, Yamashita M, Akiyama H, Hasegawa M: Methylene blue reduced abnormal tau accumulation in P301L tau transgenic mice, *PLoS One* 7:e52389, 2012.

Hrnkova M, Zilka N, Minichova Z, Koson P, Novak M: Neurodegeneration caused by expression of human truncated tau leads to progressive neurobehavioural impairment in transgenic rats, *Brain Res* 1130:206–213, 2007.

Hurtado DE, Molina-Porcel L, Iba M, Aboagye AK, Paul SM, Trojanowski JQ, Lee VM-Y: Aβ accelerates the spatiotemporal progression of tau pathology and augments tau amyloidosis in an Alzheimer mouse model, *Am J Pathol* 177:1977–1988, 2010.

Huvent I, Kamah A, Cantrelle F-X, Barois N, Slomianny C, Smet-Nocca C, Landrieu I, Lippens G: A functional fragment of tau forms fibers without the need for an intermolecular cysteine bridge, *Biochem Biophys Res Commun* 445:299–303, 2014.

Ihara Y, Morishima-Kawashima M, Nixon R: The ubiquitin–proteasome system and the autophagic–lysosomal system in Alzheimer disease, *Cold Spring Harb Perspect Med* 2:a006361, 2012.

Ihara Y, Nukina N, Miura R, Ogawara M: Phosphorylated tau protein is integrated into paired helical filaments in Alzheimer's disease, *J Biochem* 99:1807–1810, 1986.

Iqbal K, Liu F, Gong C-X: Alzheimer disease therapeutics: focus on the disease and not just plaques and tangles, *Biochem Pharmacol* 88:631–639, 2014.

Irwin DJ, Cairns NJ, Grossman M, McMillan CT, Lee EB, Van Deerlin VM, Lee VM-Y, Trojanowski JQ: Frontotemporal lobar degeneration: defining phenotypic diversity through personalized medicine, *Acta Neuropathol* 129:469–491, 2015.

Jack CR Jr, Knopman DS, Jagust WJ, Petersen RC, Weiner MW, Aisen PS, Shaw LM, Vemuri P, Wiste HJ, Weigand SD, Lesnick TG, Pankratz VS, Donohue MC, Trojanowski JQ: Tracking pathophysiological processes in Alzheimer's disease: an updated hypothetical model of dynamic biomarkers, *Lancet Neurol* 12:207–216, 2013.

Jack CRJ, Vemuri P, Wiste HJ, Weigand SD, Lesnick TG, Lowe V, Kantarci K, Bernstein MA, Senjem ML, Gunter JL, Boeve BF, Trojanowski JQ, Shaw LM, Aisen PS, Weiner MW, Petersen RC, Knopman DS: Alzheimer's Disease Neuroimaging Initiative: Shapes of the trajectories of 5 major biomarkers of Alzheimer disease, *Arch Neurol* 69:856–867, 2012.

Jakes R, Novak M, Davison M, Wischik CM: Identification of 3- and 4-repeat tau isoforms within the PHF in Alzheimer's disease, *EMBO J* 10:2725–2729, 1991.

Jinwal UK, Miyata Y, Koren J III, Jones JR, Trotter JH, Chang L, O'Leary J, Morgan D, Lee DC, Shults CL, Rousaki A, Weeber EJ, Zuiderweg ERP, Gestwicki JE, Dickey CA: Chemical manipulation of Hsp70 ATPase activity regulates tau stability, *J Neurosci* 29:12079–12088, 2009.

Jobst KA, Smith AD, Barker CS, Wear A, King EM, Smith A, Anslow PA, Molyneux AJ, Shepstone BJ, Soper N, Holmes KA, Robinson JR, Hope RA, Oppenheimer C, Brockbank K, McDonald B: Association of atrophy of the medial temporal lobe with reduced blood flow in the posterior parietotemporal cortex in patients with a clinical and pathological diagnosis of Alzheimer's disease, *J Neurol Neurosurg Psychiat* 55:190–194, 1992.

Kampers T, Friedhoff P, Biernat J, Mandelkow E-M, Mandelkow E: RNA stimulates aggregation of microtubule-associated protein tau into Alzheimer-like paired helical filaments, *FEBS Lett* 399:344–349, 1996.

Kidd M: Paired helical filaments in electron microscopy in Alzheimer's disease, *Nature* 197:192–193, 1963.

Koson P, Zilka N, Kovac A, Kovacech B, Korenova M, Filipcik P, Novak M: Truncated tau expression levels determine life span of a rat model of tauopathy without causing neuronal loss or correlating with terminal neurofibrillary tangle load, *Eur J Neurosci* 28:239–246, 2008.

Lai RYK, Gertz H-J, Wischik DJ, Xuereb JH, Mukaetova-Ladinska EB, Harrington CR, Edwards PC, Mena R, Paykel ES, Brayne C, Huppert FA, Roth M, Wischik CM: Examination of phosphorylated tau protein as a PHF-precursor at early stage Alzheimer's disease, *Neurobiol Aging* 16:433–445, 1995.

Lai RYK, Harrington CR, Wischik CM: Absence of a role for phosphorylation in the tau pathology of Alzheimer's disease, *Biomolecules* 6:19, 2016.

Lee VM-Y, Balin BJ, Otvos LJ Jr, Trojanowski JQ: A68: a major subunit of paired helical filaments and derivatized forms of normal tau, *Science* 251:675–678, 1991.

Li W, Sperry JB, Crowe A, Trojanowski JQ, Smith AB III, Lee VM-Y: Inhibition of tau fibrillization by oleocanthal via reaction with the amino groups of tau, *J Neurochem* 110:1339–1351, 2009.

Luna-Munoz J, Chavez-Macias L, Garcia-Sierra F, Mena R: Earliest stages of tau conformational changes are related to the appearance of a sequence of specific phospho-dependent tau epitopes in Alzheimer's disease, *J Alzheimer's Dis* 12:365–375, 2007.

Mansouri A, Lurie AA: Concise review: methemoglobinemia, *Am J Hematol* 42:7–12, 1993.

Maruyama M, Shimada H, Suhara T, Shinotoh H, Ji B, Maeda J, Zhang M-R, Trojanowski JQ, Lee VM-Y, Ono M, Masamoto K, Takano H, Sahara N, Iwata N, Okamura N, Furumoto S, Kudo Y, Chang Q, Saido TC, Takashima A, Lewis J, Jang M-K, Aoki I, Ito H, Higuchi M: Imaging of tau pathology in a tauopathy mouse model and in Alzheimer patients compared to normal controls, *Neuron* 79:1094–1108, 2013.

Masters C, Simms G, Weinman N, Multhaup G, McDonald B, Beyreuther K: Amyloid plaque core protein in Alzheimer disease and Down syndrome, *Proc Natl Acad Sci USA* 82:4245–4249, 1985a.

Masters CL, Multhaup G, Simms G, Pottgiesser J, Martins RN, Beyreuther K: Neuronal origin of a cerebral amyloid: neurofibrillary tangles of Alzheimer's disease contain the same protein as the amyloid of plaque cores and blood vessels, *EMBO J* 4:2757–2763, 1985b.

Matsuda H: Role of neuroimaging in Alzheimer's disease, with emphasis on brain perfusion SPECT, *J Nuc Med* 48:1289–1300, 2007.

May JM, Qu Z-C, Cobb CE: Reduction and uptake of methylene blue by human erythrocytes, *Am J Physiol–Cell Physiol* 286:C1390–C1398, 2004.

Mayer B, Brunner F, Schmidt K: Inhibition of nitric oxide synthesis by methylene blue, *Biochem Pharmacol* 45:367–374, 1993.

Medina DX, Caccamo A, Oddo S: Methylene blue reduces Aβ levels and rescues early cognitive deficit by increasing proteasome activity, *Brain Pathol* 21:140–149, 2011.

Melis V, Magbagbeolu M, Rickard JE, Horsley D, Davidson K, Harrington KA, Goatman K, Goatman EA, Deiana S, Close SP, Zabke C, Stamer K, Dietze S, Schwab K, Storey JMD, Harrington CR, Wischik CM, Theuring F, Riedel G: Effects of oxidized and reduced forms of methylthioninium in two transgenic mouse tauopathy models, *Behav Pharmacol* 26:353–368, 2015a.

Melis V, Zabke C, Stamer K, Magbagbeolu M, Schwab K, Marschall P, Veh RW, Bachmann S, Deiana S, Moreau PH, Davidson K, Harrington KA, Rickard JE, Horsley D, Garman R, Mazurkiewicz M, Niewiadomska G, Wischik CM, Harrington CR, Riedel G, Theuring F: Different pathways of molecular pathophysiology underlie cognitive and motor tauopathy phenotypes in transgenic models for Alzheimer's disease and frontotemporal lobar degeneration, *Cell Mol Life Sci* 72:2199–2222, 2015b.

Mena R, Edwards PC, Harrington CR, Mukaetova-Ladinska EB, Wischik CM: Staging the pathological assembly of truncated tau protein into paired helical filaments in Alzheimer's disease, *Acta Neuropathol* 91:633–641, 1996.

Mena R, Edwards P, Pérez-Olvera O, Wischik CM: Monitoring pathological assembly of tau and β-amyloid proteins in Alzheimer's disease, *Acta Neuropathol* 89:50–56, 1995.

Mori H, Kondo J, Ihara Y: Ubiquitin is a component of paired helical filaments in Alzheimer's disease, *Science* 235:1641–1644, 1987.

Mosconi L, Mistur R, Switalski R, Tsui WH, Glodzik L, Li Y, Pirraglia E, De Santi S, Reisberg B, Wisniewski T, de Leon MJ: FDG-PET changes in brain glucose metabolism from normal cognition to pathologically verified Alzheimer's disease, *Eur J Nuc Med Mol Imaging* 36:811–822, 2009.

Mukaetova-Ladinska EB, Garcia-Sierra F, Hurt J, Gertz H-J, Xuereb JH, Hills R, Brayne C, Huppert FA, Paykel ES, McGee M, Jakes R, Honer WG, Harrington CR, Wischik CM: Staging of cytoskeletal and β-amyloid changes in human isocortex reveals biphasic synaptic protein response during progression of Alzheimer's disease, *Am J Pathol* 157:623–636, 2000.

Murray ME, Lowe VJ, Graff-Radford NR, Liesinger AM, Cannon A, Przybelski SA, Rawal B, Parisi JE, Petersen RC, Kantarci K, Ross OA, Duara R, Knopman DS, Jack CR, Dickson DW: Clinicopathologic and ^{11}C-Pittsburgh compound B implications of Thal amyloid phase across the Alzheimer's disease spectrum, *Brain* 138:1370–1381, 2015.

Murthy ASN, Reddy KS: Cyclic-voltammetric studies of some phenothiazine dyes, *J Chem Soc Faraday Trans 1 Phys Chem Condensed Phases* 80:2745–2750, 1984.

Naylor GJ, Martin B, Hopwood SE, Watson Y: A two-year double-blind crossover trial of the prophylactic effect of methylene blue in manic-depressive psychosis, *Biol Psychiatry* 21:915–920, 1986.

Neary D, Snowden JS, Gustafson L, Passant U, Stuss D, Black S, Freedman M, Kertesz A, Robert PH, Albert M, Boone K, Miller BL, Cummings J, Benson DF: Frontotemporal lobar degeneration: a consensus on clinical diagnostic criteria, *Neurology* 51:1546–1554, 1998.

Necula M, Breydo L, Milton S, Kayed R, van der Veer WE, Tone P, Glabe CG: Methylene blue inhibits amyloid Aβ oligomerization by promoting fibrillization, *Biochemistry* 46:8850–8860, 2007a.

Necula M, Kayed R, Milton S, Glabe CG: Small-molecule inhibitors of aggregation indicate that amyloid beta oligomerization and fibrillization pathways are independent and distinct, *J Biol Chem* 282:10311–10324, 2007b.

Novak M, Jakes R, Edwards PC, Milstein C, Wischik CM: Difference between the tau protein of Alzheimer paired helical filament core and normal tau revealed by epitope analysis of mAbs 423 and 7.51, *Proc Natl Acad Sci USA* 88:5837–5841, 1991.

Novak M, Kabat J, Wischik CM: Molecular characterization of the minimal protease resistant tau unit of the Alzheimer's disease paired helical filament, *EMBO J* 12:365–370, 1993.

Ohm TG, Müller H, Braak H, Bohl J: Close-meshed prevalence rates of different stages as a tool to uncover the rate of Alzheimer's disease-related neurofibrillary changes, *Neuroscience* 64:209–217, 1995.

Okamura N, Furumoto S, Fodero-Tavoletti MT, Mulligan RS, Harada R, Yates P, Pejoska S, Kudo Y, Masters CL, Yanai K, Rowe CC, Villemagne VL: Non-invasive assessment of Alzheimer's disease neurofibrillary pathology using F-18-THK5105 PET, *Brain* 137:1762–1771, 2014.

Okuda M, Hijikuro I, Fujita Y, Wu X, Nakayama S, Sakata Y, Noguchi Y, Ogo M, Akasofu S, Ito Y, Soeda Y, Tsuchiya N, Tanaka N, Takahashi T, Sugimoto H: PE859, a novel tau aggregation inhibitor, reduces aggregated tau and prevents onset and progression of neural dysfunction in vivo, *PLoS One* 10:e0117511, 2015.

O'Leary J, Li Q, Marinec P, Blair L, Congdon E, Johnson A, Jinwal U, Koren J, Jones J, Kraft C, Peters M, Abisambra J, Duff K, Weeber E, Gestwicki J, Dickey C: Phenothiazine-mediated rescue of cognition in tau transgenic mice requires neuroprotection and reduced soluble tau burden, *Mol Neurodegener* 5:45, 2010.

Onishi T, Matsumoto Y, Hattori M, Obayashi Y, Nakamura K, Yano T, Horiguchi T, Iwashita H: Early-onset cognitive deficits and axonal transport dysfunction in P301S mutant tau transgenic mice, *Neurosci Res* 80:76–85, 2014.

Ossenkoppele R, Schonhaut DR, Baker SL, O'Neil JP, Janabi M, Ghosh PM, Santos M, Miller ZA, Bettcher BM, Gorno-Tempini ML, Miller BL, Jagust WJ, Rabinovici GD: Tau, amyloid, and hypometabolism in a patient with posterior cortical atrophy, *Ann Neurol* 77:338–342, 2015.

Paranjape SR, Chiang Y-M, Sanchez JF, Entwistle R, Wang CCC, Oakley BR, Gamblin TC: Inhibition of tau aggregation by three Aspergillus nidulans secondary metabolites: 2, ω-dihydroxyemodin, asperthecin, and asperbenzaldehyde, *Planta Medica* 80:77–85, 2014.

Pérez M, Hernández F, Gómez-Ramos A, Smith M, Perry G, Avila J: Formation of aberrant phosphotau fibrillar polymers in neural cultured cells, *Eur J Biochem* 269:1484–1489, 2002.

Pérez M, Valpuesta JM, Medina M, Montejo de Garcini E, Avila J: Polymerization of τ into filaments in the presence of heparin: the minimal sequence required for τ-τ interaction, *J Neurochem* 67:1183–1190, 1996.

Perreault S, Bousquet O, Lauzon M, Paiement J, Leclerc N: Increased association between rough endoplasmic reticulum membranes and mitochondria in transgenic mice that express P301L tau, *J Neuropathol Exptl Neurol* 68:503–514, 2009.

Perry G, Friedman R, Shaw G, Chau V: Ubiquitin is detected in neurofibrillary tangles and senile plaque neurites of Alzheimer disease brains, *Proc Natl Acad Sci USA* 84:3033–3036, 1987.

Pfaffendorf M, Bruning TA, Batink HD, van Zwieten PA: The interaction between methylene blue and the cholinergic system, *Br J Pharmacol* 122:95–98, 1997.

Phinney AL, Horne P, Yang J, Janus C, Bergeron C, Westaway D: Mouse models of Alzheimer's disease: the long and filamentous road, *Neurol Res* 25:590–600, 2003.

Pickhardt M, Gazova Z, von Bergen M, Khlistunova I, Wang Y, Hascher A, Mandelkow E-M, Biernat J, Mandelkow E: Anthraquinones inhibit tau aggregation and dissolve Alzheimer paired helical filaments in vitro and in cells, *J Biol Chem* 280:3628–3635, 2005.

Pickhardt M, Larbig G, Khlistunova I, Coksezen A, Meyer B, Mandelkow E-M, Schmidt B, Mandelkow E: Phenylthiazolyl-hydrazide and its derivatives are potent inhibitors of τ aggregation and toxicity *in vitro* and in cells, *Biochemistry* 46:10016–10023, 2007.

Radde R, Duma C, Goedert M, Jucker M: The value of incomplete mouse models of Alzheimer's disease, *Eur J Nuc Med Mol Imaging* 35:70–74, 2008.

Ramsay RR, Dunford C, Gillman PK: Methylene blue and serotonin toxicity: inhibition of monoamine oxidase A (MAO A) confirms a theoretical prediction, *Br J Pharmacol* 152:946–951, 2007.

Ramsden M, Kotilinek L, Forster C, Paulson J, McGowan E, SantaCruz K, Guimaraes A, Yue M, Lewis J, Carlson G, Hutton M, Ashe KH: Age-dependent neurofibrillary tangle formation, neuron loss, and memory impairment in a mouse model of human tauopathy (P301L), *J Neurosci* 25:10637–10647, 2005.

Rankin CA, Gamblin TC: Assessing the toxicity of tau aggregation, *J Alzheimer's Dis* 14:411–416, 2008.

Reed LA, Wszolek ZK, Hutton M: Phenotypic correlations in FTDP-17, *Neurobiol Aging* 22:89–107, 2001.

Resch JF, Lehr GS, Wischik CM: Design and synthesis of a potential affinity/cleaving reagent for beta-pleated sheet protein structures, *Bioorg Med Chem Lett* 1:519–522, 1991.

Salloway S, Sperling R, Fox NC, Blennow K, Klunk W, Raskind M, Sabbagh M, Honig LS, Porsteinsson AP, Ferris S, Reichert M, Ketter N, Nejadnik B, Guenzler V, Miloslavsky M, Wang D, Lu Y, Lull J, Tudor IC, Liu E, Grundman M, Yuen E, Black R, Brashear HR: Two phase 3 trials of bapineuzumab in mild-to-moderate Alzheimer's disease, *New Eng J Med* 370:322–333, 2014.

Schneider A, Biernat J, von Bergen M, Mandelkow E, Mandelkow E-M: Phosphorylation that detaches tau protein from microtubules (Ser262, Ser214) also protects it against aggregation into Alzheimer paired helical filaments, *Biochemistry* 38:3549–3558, 1999.

Schultz ML, Tecedor L, Chang M, Davidson BL: Clarifying lysosomal storage diseases, *Trends Neurosci* 34:401–410, 2011.

Schweers O, Mandelkow E-M, Biernat J, Mandelkow E: Oxidation of cysteine-322 in the repeat domain of microtubule-associated protein τ controls the in vitro assembly of paired helical filaments, *Proc Natl Acad Sci USA* 92:8463–8467, 1995.

Spires-Jones TL, Friedman T, Pitstick R, Polydoro M, Roe A, Carlson GA, Hyman BT: Methylene blue does not reverse existing neurofibrillary tangle pathology in the rTg4510 mouse model of tauopathy, *Neurosci Lett* 562:63–68, 2014.

Stack C, Jainuddin S, Elipenahli C, Gerges M, Starkova N, Starkov AA, Jové M, Portero-Otin M, Launay N, Pujol A, Kaidery NA, Thomas B, Tampellini D, Beal MF, Dumont M: Methylene blue upregulates Nrf2/ARE genes and prevents tau-related neurotoxicity, *Hum Mol Genet* 23:3716–3732, 2014.

Taniguchi S, Suzuki N, Masuda M, Hisanaga S, Iwatsubo T, Goedert M, Hasegawa M: Inhibition of heparin-induced tau filament formation by phenothiazines, polyphenols, and porphyrins, *J Biol Chem* 280:7614–7623, 2005.

Tanzi RE: "New clarity" against Alzheimer's, *Harvard Gazette* http://news.harvard.edu/gazette/story/2015/2005/new-clarity-against-alzheimers/; 2015.

Thal DR, Rub U, Orantes M, Braak H: Phases of Aβ-deposition in the human brain and its relevance for the development of AD, *Neurology* 58:1791–1800, 2002.

Villemagne VL, Fodero-Tavoletti MT, Masters CL, Rowe CC: Tau imaging: early progress and future directions, *Lancet Neurol* 14:114–124, 2015.

Visarius TM, Stucki JW, Lauterburg BH: Stimulation of respiration by methylene blue in rat liver mitochondria, *FEBS Lett* 412:157–160, 1997.

Vutskits L, Briner A, Klauser P, Gascon E, Dayer AG, Kiss JZ, Muller D, Licker MJ, Morel DR: Adverse effects of methylene blue on the central nervous system, *Anesthesiology* 108:684–692, 2008.

Wein AJ, Benson GS, Raezer DM, Mulholland SG: Oral methylene blue and the dissolution of renal calculi, *J Urol* 116:140–141, 1976.

Wilcock GK, Esiri MM: Plaques, tangles and dementia: a quantitative study, *J Neurol Sci* 56:343–356, 1982.

Wischik CM, Crowther RA, Stewart M, Roth M: Subunit structure of paired helical filaments in Alzheimer's disease, *J Cell Biol* 100:1905–1912, 1985.

Wischik CM, Edwards PC, Lai RYK, Gertz H-J, Xuereb JH, Paykel ES, Brayne C, Huppert FA, Mukaetova-Ladinska EB, Mena R, Roth M, Harrington CR: Quantitative analysis of tau protein in paired helical filament preparations: implications for the role of tau protein phosphorylation in PHF assembly in Alzheimer's disease, *Neurobiol Aging* 16:409–431, 1995.

Wischik CM, Edwards PC, Lai RYK, Roth M, Harrington CR: Selective inhibition of Alzheimer disease-like tau aggregation by phenothiazines, *Proc Natl Acad Sci USA* 93:11213–11218, 1996.

Wischik CM, Horsley D, Rickard JE, Harrington CR: Materials and methods relating to protein aggregation in neurodegenerative disease. US Patent:7335505; 2008.

Wischik CM, Harrington CR, Storey JMD: Tau-aggregation inhibitor therapy for Alzheimer's disease, *Biochem Pharmacol* 88:529–539, 2014.

Wischik CM, Lai RYK, Harrington CR: Modelling prion-like processing of tau protein in Alzheimer's disease for pharmaceutical development. In Avila J, Brandt R, Kosik KS, editors: *Brain microtubule associated proteins: modifications in disease*, Amsterdam, 1997, Harwood Academic Publishers, pp 185–241.

Wischik CM, Novak M, Edwards PC, Klug A, Tichelaar W, Crowther RA: Structural characterization of the core of the paired helical filament of Alzheimer disease, *Proc Natl Acad Sci USA* 85:4884–4888, 1988a.

Wischik CM, Novak M, Thøgersen HC, Edwards PC, Runswick MJ, Jakes R, Walker JE, Milstein C, Roth M, Klug A: Isolation of a fragment of tau derived from the core of the paired helical filament of Alzheimer's disease, *Proc Natl Acad Sci USA* 85:4506–4510, 1988b.

Wischik CM, Staff RT, Wischik DJ, Bentham P, Murray AD, Storey JMD, Kook KA, Harrington CR: Tau aggregation inhibitor therapy: an exploratory phase 2 study in mild or moderate Alzheimer's disease, *J Alzheimer's Dis* 44:705–720, 2015.

Wischik CM, Theuring F, Harrington CR: The molecular basis of tau protein pathology in Alzheimer's disease and related neurodegenerative dementias. In Dawbarn D, Allen SJ, editors: *Neurobiology of Alzheimer's disease*, Oxford, 2001, Oxford University Press, pp 103–206.

Yamashita M, Nonaka T, Arai T, Kametani F, Buchman VL, Ninkina N, Bachurin SO, Akiyama H, Goedert M, Hasegawa M: Methylene blue and dimebon inhibit aggregation of TDP-43 in cellular models, *FEBS Lett* 583:2419–2424, 2009.

Yen S-H, Dickson DW, Butler M, Shelanski ML: Alzheimer's neurofibrillary tangles contain unique epitopes in common with the heat-stable microtubule-associated proteins tau and MAP2, *Am J Pathol* 126:81–91, 1987.

Yen S-H, Gaskin F, Fu SM: Neurofibrillary tangles in senile dementia of the Alzheimer type share an antigenic determinant with intermediate filaments of the vimentin class, *Am J Pathol* 113:373–381, 1983.

Yoshiyama Y, Higuchi M, Zhang B, Huang S-M, Iwata N, Saido TC, Maeda J, Suhara T, Trojanowski JQ, Lee VM-Y: Synapse loss and microglial activation precede tangles in a P301S tauopathy mouse model, *Neuron* 53:337–351, 2007.

Zilka N, Filipcik P, Koson P, Fialova L, Skrabana R, Zilkova M, Rolkova G, Kontsekova E, Novak M: Truncated tau from sporadic Alzheimer's disease suffices to drive neurofibrillary degeneration in vivo, *FEBS Lett* 580:3582–3588, 2006.

CHAPTER

16

Neuroprotective Strategies for Alzheimer's Disease Prevention and Therapy

D.A. Simmons, T. Yang, S.M. Massa, F.M. Longo

OUTLINE

ROLES FOR NEUROPROTECTIVE STRATEGIES

In Alzheimer's disease (AD), synaptic dysfunction and the eventual degeneration of synapses, neurites, and neurons is likely caused by a potent and highly robust combination of factors, including age-related processes, inflammatory mechanisms, and accumulation of toxic forms of amyloid-beta (Aβ) and tau along with other deleterious factors (Cameron and Landreth, 2010; Krstic and Knuesel, 2013; Morris et al., 2011; Ubhi and Masliah, 2013). The majority of AD therapeutic efforts that have advanced to phase 3 clinical trials have focused on strategies intended to lower levels of soluble or other forms of Aβ (Grundman et al., 2013; Kalra and Khan, 2015; Lannfelt et al., 2014; Sun et al., 2015; von Bernhardi, 2010).

Developing Therapeutics for Alzheimer's Disease. http://dx.doi.org/10.1016/B978-0-12-802173-6.00016-2

Each of these efforts failed to achieve primary clinical end points (Grundman et al., 2013; Lannfelt et al., 2014; von Bernhardi, 2010). While current trials aimed at lowering Aβ, which target early stages of AD, may produce small therapeutic effects, evidence that non-Aβ mechanisms may be involved in these early stages suggests that effective therapies that truly affect quality of life, even when administered at early stages, will require that additional targets be engaged (Anand et al., 2014; Longo and Massa, 2004; Selkoe, 2005). An emerging major approach involves applying antibodies directed to pathological forms of tau that might lower their concentrations and thereby reduce degeneration (Anand et al., 2014; Gotz et al., 2012; Gu and Sigurdsson, 2011; Himmelstein et al., 2012; Kumar et al., 2015; Pedersen and Sigurdsson, 2015). One limitation of this approach is that removing pathological forms of tau only after they develop may have minimal effects on deleterious mechanisms triggered by their formation. It is possible that regulation of processes enabling the pathological assembly or mislocalization of tau will be more efficacious than post-hoc removal.

Strategies intended to prevent, inhibit, or reverse degenerative mechanisms or intraneuronal signaling patterns triggered by or involving age, Aβ, tau, inflammation, and other factors can be described under the broad rubric of "neuroprotection." Given the inexorable and profound nature of the AD degenerative process, it is likely that any truly effective therapies will have to engage an adequately broad array of mechanisms that are at least as fundamental and robust. While neuroprotection is a broad term, this review will focus on harnessing neurotrophin (NT) receptor-related signaling mechanisms to inhibit or counteract degenerative signaling patterns contributing to synaptic dysfunction and degeneration in AD. Engaging strategic receptors upstream of AD-relevant signaling pathways may produce simultaneous effects on multiple degenerative mechanisms, including those modulating tau. Given that NTs, their receptors, and their downstream signaling constitute an important fundamental and robust set of pathways that participate in the forming and subsequent pruning of the nervous system, their constellation of actions offers candidate approaches for preventing or inhibiting underlying AD neural degeneration which extends beyond target areas pursued thus far.

There are two classes of NT receptors, and each regulates neuronal signaling networks that are deeply integrated with the majority of candidate mechanisms thought to promote synaptic dysfunction and degeneration in AD, including those triggered by Aβ oligomers and those leading to the accumulation of toxic forms of tau.

NEUROTROPHIN RECEPTORS AND THEIR SIGNALING PATHWAYS

The mammalian NT family includes nerve growth factor (NGF), brain-derived neurotrophic factor (BDNF), neurotrophin-3 (NT-3), and neurotrophin-4/5 (NT-4/5), each secreted from various source cells in a proform and enzymatically cleaved to a mature form (Chao, 2003; Reichardt, 2006). Pro- and mature NTs bind to and signal through two main receptor types, tropomyosin receptor-kinases (Trks) and the p75 neurotrophin receptor ($p75^{NTR}$). Trks are transmembrane receptors containing an extracellular NT-binding region and an intracellular tyrosine kinase domain. Each Trk isoform selectively binds different neurotrophins: TrkA binds NGF, TrkB binds BDNF and NT-4/5, and TrkC binds NT-3 (Barbacid, 1995;

Chao, 2003; Huang and Reichardt, 2001). Trk receptors activate the following three primary signaling pathways: phosphatidylinositol-3 kinase (PI3K)/AKT, mitogen-activated protein kinase (MAPK)/extracellular signal-regulated kinases (ERK), and phospholipase Cγ-1 (PLCγ)/protein kinase C (PKC) (Chao, 2003; Reichardt, 2006). These pathways generally support survival, neuronal and synaptic function, and various forms of plasticity (Huang and Reichardt, 2003; Reichardt, 2006). TrkB and TrkC are expressed by broad populations of neurons throughout the central and peripheral nervous systems, while TrkA is found primarily associated with basal forebrain cholinergic, dorsal root ganglion, and sympathetic neurons (Boissiere et al., 1997a,b; Gibbs et al., 1989; Huang and Reichardt, 2001; Patapoutian and Reichardt, 2001; Pitts and Miller, 1995; Vega et al., 1994). Some of the best-characterized functions of the Trk receptors include NGF/TrkA enhancement of basal forebrain cholinergic function (Levi-Montalcini, 1987; Salehi et al., 1996; Sanchez-Ortiz et al., 2012); BDNF/TrkB stimulation of synaptic plasticity (Bekinschtein et al., 2008; Kang et al., 1996; Kang and Schuman, 1995, 1996; Korte et al., 1995; Yamada and Nabeshima, 2003); and NT-3/TrkC support of peripheral proprioceptive neuron survival (Zhou and Rush, 1996).

In addition to binding to their cognate Trk receptors, each of the NTs binds to $p75^{NTR}$ and thereby recruits intracellular receptor adapters which in turn differentially stimulate either degenerative- or survival-promoting signaling networks. Pathways regulated by $p75^{NTR}$ include PI3K/AKT, MAPK, cyclic AMP/protein kinase A (cAMP/PKA), and nuclear factor-κB (NFκB), which can serve functions such as survival/antidegeneration, synaptic stability/function (Carter et al., 1996; Poo, 2001; Roux et al., 2001; Sachs and Akassoglou, 2007; Sachs et al., 2007; Volonte et al., 1993), as well as pathways triggering various degenerative processes such as loss of spines/synapses caused by activation of JUN N-terminal kinase (JNK), caspase, ceramide, and RhoA (Barrett, 2000; Casaccia-Bonnefil et al., 1996, 1999; Yamashita et al., 1999). The overall pattern of degenerative versus nondegenerative signaling stimulated by $p75^{NTR}$ is dependent on biological context and the available combinations and molar ratios of Trks present, sortilin receptors (see later discussion), and various intracellular signaling adaptors (Blochl and Blochl, 2007; Charalampopoulos et al., 2012; Le Moan et al., 2011; Longo and Massa, 2008; Roux and Barker, 2002; Sachs and Akassoglou, 2007). As described later, small-molecule ligands of $p75^{NTR}$ have been developed that shift the signaling pattern away from degeneration-induction to prosurvival.

The prodomains of proNTs bind to the vacuolar protein sorting 10 family member sortilins (also referred to as the sortilin receptor), allowing the formation of a heterotrimeric receptor complex with $p75^{NTR}$ (Feng et al., 2010; Gong et al., 2008; Nykjaer et al., 2004; Westergaard et al., 2004). In most cases, proNT binding to this receptor complex stimulates degenerative signaling (Barrett, 2000; Hempstead, 2014; Nykjaer et al., 2004) and pro-BDNF has been reported to stimulate long-term depression at certain synapses (Woo et al., 2005).

$p75^{NTR}$ RECEPTORS IN AD

The signaling networks controlled by $p75^{NTR}$ are remarkable for the extent of their overlap with signaling networks that underlie degeneration in AD (Fig. 16.1). As a potential target in AD therapeutics, it is notable that $p75^{NTR}$ is expressed by central nervous system (CNS) cell

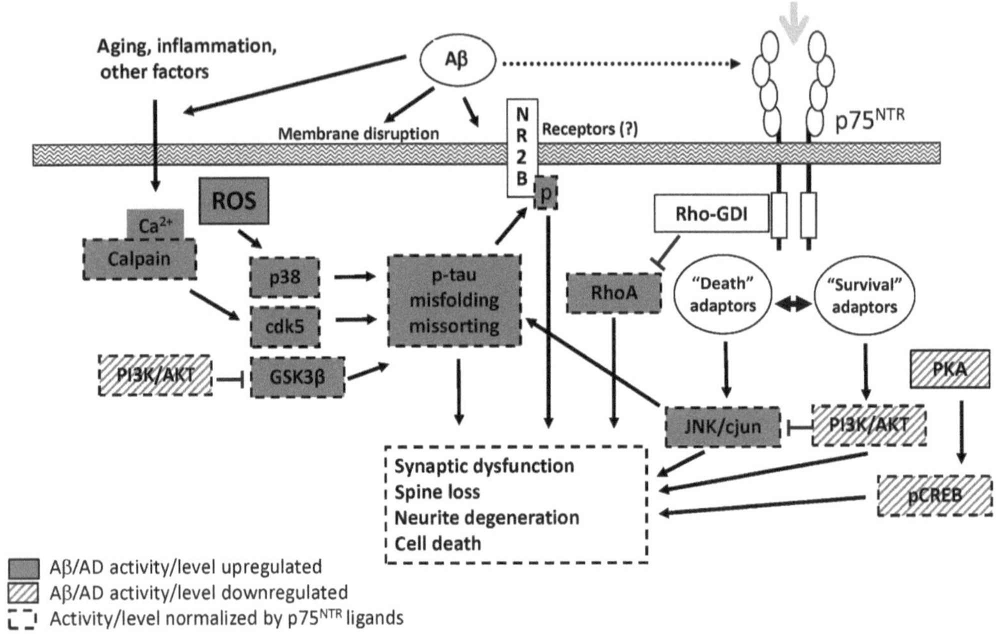

FIGURE 16.1 **p75NTR signaling pathways and pathological mechanisms in AD: effects of small-molecule p75NTR ligands.** The diagram shows a simplified schematic of the signaling pathways regulated by $p75^{NTR}$ and their overlap with AD degenerative signaling networks contributing to pathology. Neurotrophins (*light gray arrow*) bind to $p75^{NTR}$ to promote the interaction of the intracellular domains with intracellular "death" or "survival" adaptor proteins which regulate downstream signaling. In the nonliganded "default" state, $p75^{NTR}$ tends to promote degenerative signaling while different ligands such as pro- and mature neurotrophins versus various small molecules can differentially affect the balance between "death" and "survival" signaling. In cases in which a ligand favors the balance away from degenerative signaling and toward survival signaling, AD-related degenerative mechanisms would be inhibited. *Aβ*, amyloid-β; *cdk5*, cyclin-dependent kinase 5; *CREB*, cAMP response element-binding protein; *GSK-3β*, glycogen synthase-3beta; *JNK*, JUN N-terminal kinase; *NR2B*, *N*-methyl-D-aspartate (NMDA) receptor subunit B; *p*, phosphorylated; *PI3K*, phosphatidylinositol-3 kinase; *PKA*, protein kinase A; *ROS*, reactive oxygen species.

populations that degenerate in AD, including those affected in the earliest stages. These populations include neurons in the locus coeruleus, raphe nuclei, entorhinal cortex, basal forebrain, hippocampus, and neocortex (Chakravarthy et al., 2012; Hu et al., 2002; Mufson and Kordower, 1992; Yamuy et al., 2000). Moreover, a number of studies have found that $p75^{NTR}$ levels are elevated in neuropathological states, including human AD (Chakravarthy et al., 2012; Fombonne et al., 2009; Hu et al., 2002; Mufson and Kordower, 1992; Salehi et al., 2000; Treanor et al., 1991) and AD mouse models (Chakravarthy et al., 2010; Perez et al., 2011; Simmons et al., 2014). In addition, the increase in the ratio of $p75^{NTR}$ relative to TrkA in AD patients has been suggested to promote degenerative signaling in basal forebrain cholinergic neurons (BFCNs) (Diarra et al., 2009; Ginsberg et al., 2006). Levels of pro-NGF, which binds to $p75^{NTR}$ and sortilin to trigger degenerative signaling through a number of pathways, including JNK, are also elevated (Fahnestock et al., 2001; Mufson et al., 2012; Pedraza et al., 2005). The combination of elevated pro-NTs and excess $p75^{NTR}$ would be expected to generate a particularly potent degenerative signaling milieu. From the standpoint of a potential therapeutic target, it is especially notable that $p75^{NTR}$ plays a major role in enabling Aβ-induced degeneration (Coulson, 2006; Sotthibundhu et al., 2008). In in vitro studies, the addition of Aβ was shown to promote neurite degeneration of mature mouse hippocampal neurons obtained from wild-type mice; however, in cultures derived from $p75^{-/-}$ mice (extracellular domain deleted), Aβ failed to promote degeneration (Knowles et al., 2009). Furthermore, in in vivo studies, Aβ caused degeneration of BFCNs when injected into the hippocampi of wild-type but not $p75^{-/-}$ mice (Knowles et al., 2009), and when AD mice expressing amyloid precursor protein (APP) with the London and Swedish mutations ($APP^{L/S}$), in which Aβ levels are high, were crossed with $p75^{-/-}$ mice, BFCN degeneration was prevented (Coulson et al., 2009; Knowles et al., 2009).

Trk RECEPTORS IN AD

Within the CNS, TrkA receptor expression is primarily limited to BFCNs (Boissiere et al., 1997b; Gibbs et al., 1989; Huang and Reichardt, 2003; Patapoutian and Reichardt, 2001; Pitts and Miller, 1995; Vega et al., 1994), which constitute one of the key systems undergoing degeneration in AD in early and subsequent stages; however, a number of other key neuronal populations are also affected (Budni et al., 2015; Mufson et al., 2008; Teipel et al., 2005). In contrast to TrkA, TrkB and TrkC are broadly expressed by essentially all of the neurons affected in AD, including those in the hippocampus, entorhinal cortex, neocortex, basal forebrain, and key brain stem nuclei (Allen et al., 1999; Boissiere et al., 1997a; Budni et al., 2015; Connor et al., 1996; Murer et al., 2001; Patapoutian and Reichardt, 2001; Tapia-Arancibia et al., 2008). TrkB and TrkC signaling promotes synaptic maintenance, function and/or plasticity [including long-term potentiation (LTP)], as well as neuronal and neurite survival (Mattson et al., 2004; Patapoutian and Reichardt, 2001; Reichardt, 2006).

These functions and the large integration of TrkB/TrkC signaling pathways with the primary degenerative signaling networks underlying AD suggest that upregulating signaling of these receptors might counteract AD degenerative signaling patterns regardless of whether Trk signaling deficiency plays a causal role in AD (Fig. 16.2). It is of particular interest, however, that several lines of evidence indicate that deficiencies in BDNF/TrkB and NT-3/TrkC signaling might also make important contributions to AD degenerative processes and impairments of synaptic function (Connor et al., 1996; Savaskan et al., 2000; Zhang et al., 2012). BDNF brain levels decrease with normal aging (Budni et al., 2015; Hayashi et al., 1997; Liu et al., 2006; Mattson et al., 2004; Strasser et al., 2006; Webster et al., 2006), and the majority of studies examining brain tissue in mild cognitive impairment (MCI) have found decreased BDNF transcript and/or protein levels (Budni et al., 2015; Tapia-Arancibia et al., 2008). In AD subjects, reduced BDNF levels have been consistently described in cerebrospinal fluid (CSF) and serum (Forlenza et al., 2010a,b; Laske et al., 2006a, 2007; Lee et al., 2009; Li et al., 2009; Yasutake et al., 2006; Yu et al., 2008; Zhang et al., 2008) and the serum levels were associated with the severity of AD dementia (Konukoglu et al., 2012), though in two studies, increased serum BDNF was noted in MCI and early-stage AD (Angelucci et al., 2010; Laske et al., 2006b). Multiple genetic studies suggest that BDNF polymorphisms, including Val66Met, are risk factors for AD (Borroni et al., 2009a,b; Feher et al., 2009; Hashimoto et al., 2009; Kunugi et al., 2001; Olin et al., 2005; Tsai et al., 2004), and Val66Met may speed disease progression

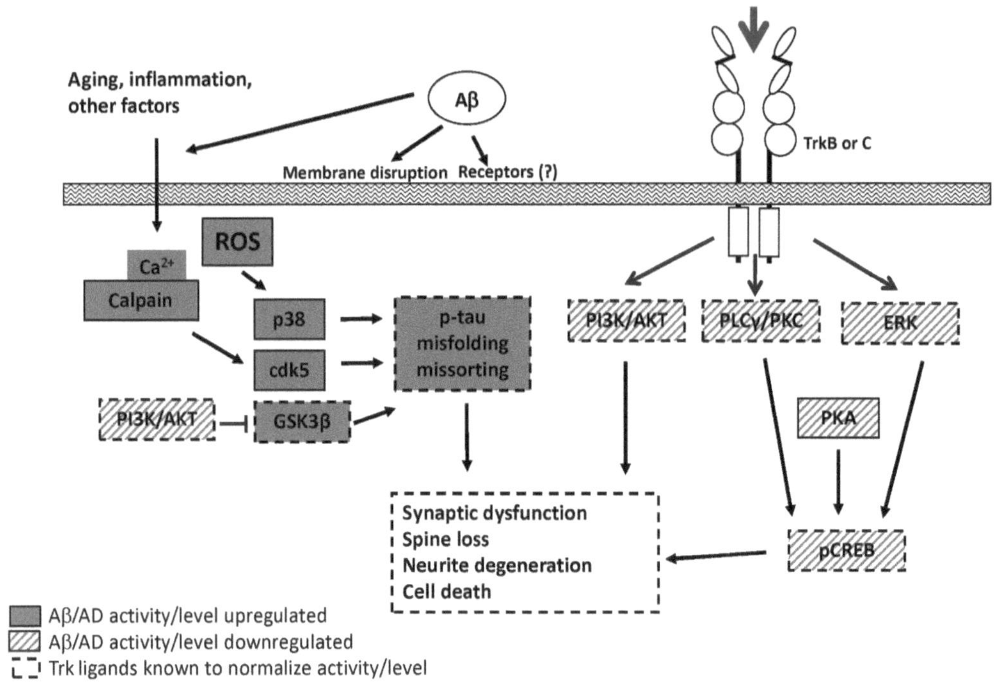

FIGURE 16.2 **TrkB and TrkC signaling pathways oppose degenerative signaling in Alzheimer's disease (AD).** The diagram shows a simplified schematic of the signaling pathways regulated by TrkB and TrkC and their overlap with AD degenerative signaling networks contributing to pathology. BDNF and NT-3 (*dark gray arrow*) bind to TrkB and/or TrkC and initiate three primary signaling pathways: phosphatidylinositol-3 kinase (PI3K)/AKT, phospholipase Cγ-1 (PLCγ)/protein kinase C (PKC), and mitogen-activated protein kinase (MAPK)/extracellular signal-regulated kinases (ERK). These pathways support survival, neuronal and synaptic function, and various forms of plasticity. Dysfunctional TrkB/TrkC signaling has been associated with AD pathophysiology, including amyloid accumulation, tau phosphorylation, and synapse loss. The high integration of TrkB/TrkC signaling pathways with the primary degenerative signaling networks underlying AD suggest that upregulating signaling of these receptors might counteract AD degenerative signaling patterns. *Aβ*, amyloid-β; *cdk5*, cyclin-dependent kinase 5; *CREB*, cAMP response element-binding protein; *GSK-3β*, glycogen synthase-3beta; *p*, phosphorylated; *PKA*, protein kinase A; *ROS*, reactive oxygen species.

(Hashimoto et al., 2009). Pro-BDNF and BDNF also interact with $p75^{NTR}$, through which they can initiate gene transcription and in some cases degenerative signaling or long-term depression. The role of NT-3 in AD pathogenesis has received relatively little attention, but several lines of evidence suggest it may be an important contributor. Reduced NT-3 levels have been found in the motor cortex (Durany et al., 2000; Narisawa-Saito et al., 1996), and levels of its TrkC receptor are decreased in the cortex and basal forebrain of AD brains (Salehi et al., 1996; Savaskan et al., 2000). Low serum NT-3 levels may predict the emergence of AD in MCI patients (Rocha de Paula et al., 2011), and an NT-3 polymorphism (Kobayashi et al., 2012) and mutation (Kunugi et al., 1998) may be risk factors for AD. Finally, NT-3-stimulated TrkC activation of AKT signaling may alleviate amyloid-induced cell death in vitro (Lesne et al., 2005).

Dysfunctional BDNF/TrkB signaling has been associated with many of the pathophysiological features of AD, including amyloid accumulation, tau phosphorylation/neurofibrillary tangles, and synapse loss. In vitro studies suggest that soluble Aβ42 downregulates BDNF expression by inhibiting phosphorylation of the transcription factor cAMP response element-binding protein (CREB) (Arancio and Chao, 2007; Fahnestock et al., 2002; Garzon et al., 2002) and disturbs NT intracellular transport (Gan and Silverman, 2015). Aβ42 also may disrupt BDNF-activated transduction pathways RAS/MEK/ERK, PI3K/Akt, and PKA/CREB (Tong et al., 2001, 2004; Vitolo et al., 2002). Moreover, BDNF ameliorates amyloid toxicity by reducing Aβ42 production via MAPK and Akt signaling to modulate APP processing (Arancibia et al., 2008; Rohe et al., 2009). BDNF may also prevent or reverse the cytotoxic effects of Aβ42 on cortical neurons via TrkB activation (Arancibia et al., 2008). Decreased BDNF levels correlate with amyloid load in multiple AD mouse models (Peng et al., 2009), and injecting Aβ42 into rat ventricles caused reduced hippocampal BDNF (Zhang et al., 2015a).

Of particular interest is that BDNF/TrkB signaling may also provide neuroprotection against AD-related tau pathology. Cortical and hippocampal neurons containing aberrantly phosphorylated tau have reduced BDNF and TrkB levels (Ferrer et al., 1999). BDNF signaling can stimulate intracellular tau dephosphorylation and redistribution, which may be important for neurite outgrowth (Chen et al., 2014). BDNF-induced tau dephosphorylation is due to glycogen synthase-3beta (GSK-3β) inhibition by TrkB signaling via the PI3K/AKT pathway (Elliott et al., 2005; Li et al., 2007), and reduction of BDNF/TrkB signaling, as seen in TrkB haplo-insufficient 5X familial AD (FAD) mice, causes GSK-3β hyperactivity (Devi and Ohno, 2015). Further, GSK-3β inhibition triggered by BDNF is disrupted by Aβ42 (Tong et al., 2004), suggesting that BDNF/TrkB signaling deficits may link tau and Aβ42 pathology in AD (Elliott et al., 2005).

Synapse loss and cognitive deficits in AD have been linked to dysfunctional BDNF/TrkB signaling. BDNF and TrkB's essential role in dendritic spine formation and functional facets of synaptic plasticity (LTP) and memory are well established (Bekinschtein et al., 2008; Kang et al., 1996; Korte et al., 1995; Lynch et al., 2007; Yamada and Nabeshima, 2003). During memory formation, BDNF is released in an activity-dependent manner and binds to TrkB at pre- and postsynaptic locations, including spines (Sui et al., 2015), initiating MAPK and PI3K signaling (Yamada and Nabeshima, 2003). BDNF/TrkB signaling leads to *N*-methyl-D-aspartate (NMDA) receptor phosphorylation, regulates their trafficking (Caldeira et al., 2007), and enhances their activity (Li et al., 1998; Matsumoto et al., 2006; Suen et al., 1997), while Aβ42 causes NMDA receptors to internalize, reducing their synaptic availability (Snyder et al., 2005). Aβ42 also perturbs LTP in cortical slices (Origlia et al., 2008, 2009) while BDNF/TrkB signaling via MAPK prevents this deficit (Criscuolo et al., 2015). BDNF also triggers protein synthesis needed for late-phase hippocampal LTP (Kang and Schuman, 1996) by increasing mRNA translation via multiple signaling pathways, including PI3K/AKT (Takei et al., 2001). Late-phase LTP is blocked by Aβ42 via PKA/CREB pathway inhibition (Chen et al., 2002; Espana et al., 2010; Vitolo et al., 2002). CREB is downstream of TrkB and is necessary for LTP and memory consolidation (Silva et al., 1998). Activated CREB and glutamate receptor expression are greatly reduced in TrkB haplo-insufficient 5X FAD mice, and these deficits are accompanied by impaired cognition (Devi and Ohno, 2015). Last, BDNF transforms functional changes into persistent structural changes in dendritic spines (Tanaka et al., 2008). Reduced TrkB expression is associated with age-related spine loss (von Bohlen und Halbach et al., 2006), and spine density is severely decreased in AD brains and mice (Kojima and Shirao, 2007;

Lanz et al., 2003; Moolman et al., 2004). Spine/synapse loss in the cortex and hippocampus is strongly correlated to cognitive deficits in AD patients and is a better indicator of the severity of these deficits than amyloid accumulation and neurofibrillary tangles (Masliah, 2001; Masliah et al., 2006; Selkoe, 2002; Terry et al., 1991). In all, restoring and/or augmenting BDNF/TrkB signaling could prevent or alleviate AD-related cognitive deficits by reversing degenerative signaling, including that involved in tau pathology and the resulting synaptic dysfunction and degeneration; reducing neuronal vulnerability to amyloid; and promoting synaptic persistence and plasticity.

NEUROTROPHIN-BASED AD THERAPIES

The application of an NT of course involves the concomitant targeting of Trk and $p75^{NTR}$ receptors. Potential limitations of NTs as therapeutic entities includes their suboptimal pharmacological profile, including poor stability in serum (with half-lives of minutes or less) and negligible oral bioavailability. Moreover, they exhibit minimal blood–brain barrier (BBB) penetration and restricted diffusion within brain parenchyma (Pardridge, 2002; Poduslo and Curran, 1996; Saltzman et al., 1999). The pleiotropic actions of NTs triggered by their multireceptor signaling networks can include neurodegeneration, upregulation of pain transmission, seizures, and weight loss (Abram et al., 2009; Bergmann et al., 1998; Dyck et al., 1997; Malcangio and Lessmann, 2003; Pezet et al., 2002; Sah et al., 2003; Shu and Mendell, 1999).

The first application of an NT to AD subjects consisted of intraventricular administration of high doses of NGF in a group of three patients (Eriksdotter Jonhagen et al., 1998). In two of the three cases, improved cognition was observed; however, all three patients experienced new onset back pain, and two sustained weight loss, resulting in discontinuation of the trial. Subsequent studies in rats found that intrathecal administration of NGF triggers sprouting of sympathetic fibers, a known contributor to pain syndromes (Jones et al., 1999; Pertovaara, 2006). Moreover, recent studies established that activating TrkA upregulates pain mechanisms (Hirose et al., 2015). More recent clinical trials employed direct CNS delivery of NGF via implantation of encapsulated NGF-producing cells in the basal forebrain, with the intent of slowing or reversing degeneration of BFCNs, which are known to express TrkA and $p75^{NTR}$ and to be responsive to NGF (Gibbs et al., 1989; Levi-Montalcini, 1987; Salehi et al., 1996; Sanchez-Ortiz et al., 2012). In an assessment of two CSF cholinergic markers, acetylcholinesterase (AChE) and choline acetyltransferase (ChAT), NGF-treated subjects demonstrated a significant increase in AChE levels, and the activity of soluble ChAT was highly correlated with cognitive responses (Karami et al., 2015). In another study, 10 patients underwent NGF gene therapy targeted to the basal forebrain using autologous skin fibroblasts transfected to express NGF or an AAV2-NGF vector. All of these patients demonstrated a trophic response to NGF, with axonal sprouting toward the NGF source. In some cases, activation of cell signaling, as detected by CREB activation, was found (Tuszynski et al., 2015). Ongoing studies will determine the extent to which NGF-based therapy affects cognitive and other clinical outcomes.

While administration of BDNF has been tested in subjects with amyotrophic lateral sclerosis (ALS), in which efficacy was unfortunately not detected (Allen et al., 2013), to our knowledge no trials in AD have been conducted. As in the case of NGF, limited CNS bioavailability, as likely occurred in application to ALS, would likely be a key issue.

p75^{NTR}-BASED AD THERAPEUTIC STRATEGIES

Our research team has developed small-molecule ligands that serve as antagonists to p75^{NTR} degenerative signaling (Longo and Massa, 2013; Massa et al., 2006) (Fig. 16.1). These compounds compete with pro-NGF for binding to p75^{NTR} and, in the absence of pro-NGF or other pro-NTs, shift the pattern of p75^{NTR} signaling away from degenerative and toward survival-promoting components (Massa et al., 2006; Tep et al., 2013). Two prototype ligands that have been particularly well characterized are LM11A-31 and LM11A-24. In in vitro studies, low nanomolar concentrations of both compounds were found to prevent Aβ oligomer-induced degeneration of hippocampal, cortical, and basal forebrain neurons (Yang et al., 2008). The compounds also blocked Aβ-induced activation of GSK-3β, calpain/cdk5, p38, and c-Jun (Yang et al., 2008), each of which directly promotes tau phosphorylation among other downstream degenerative mechanisms (Borsello and Forloni, 2007; Mazanetz and Fischer, 2007; Yoshida et al., 2004). Consistent with these actions, promotion of tau phosphorylation by Aβ was also prevented by LM11A-31 and LM11A-24 (Yang et al., 2008). In subsequent in vitro studies (Yang et al., unpublished results), we found that LM11A-31 prevented the formation of misfolded tau (MC-1 antibody) and tau oligomers (Tau22 antibody; Castillo-Carranza et al., 2015). Both small-molecule p75^{NTR} ligands also blocked Aβ-induced inhibition of AKT and CREB activation (Yang et al., 2008), two key components promoting normal synaptic function. Consistent with these molecular mechanisms, LM11A-31 and -24 blocked Aβ-induced neuritic dystrophy. Since these small molecules bind to p75^{NTR} but not Trks (Massa et al., 2006) while NTs bind to both p75^{NTR} and Trk receptors, one would expect the biological profile of these small molecules and the NT proteins to be distinct. Indeed, in these same studies, NGF failed to protect neurons from Aβ-induced degeneration (Yang et al., 2008), and other mouse studies performed in our laboratories showed that NGF increased pain (thermal) sensitivity while the p75^{NTR} ligands did not (Nguyen et al., 2014; Xie et al., unpublished results).

The molecular and therapeutic effects of small-molecule p75^{NTR} ligands have also been studied in a number of AD mouse models. In APP$^{L/S}$ mice, a 3-month, once-daily oral gavage treatment course initiated shortly after amyloid plaques are detected at age 3–4 months (Rockenstein et al., 2001) normalized deficits in novel-object recognition, Y-maze testing, contextual fear conditioning, and delayed-matching-to-place water maze (Knowles et al., 2013; Nguyen et al., 2014). Histological analysis revealed that the compounds completely blocked excess tau phosphorylation. Moreover, the accumulation of misfolded tau, as detected by the MC-1 and Alz50 antibodies, was also significantly reduced (Nguyen et al., 2014).

Excess phosphorylation and misfolding of tau are thought to play key roles in the formation of tau oligomers and various aggregate forms (Frost et al., 2015). Hence, the development of therapeutic approaches that might inhibit pathological tau phosphorylation, misfolding, and oligomer formation has become a high priority (Brunden et al., 2009; Gotz et al., 2012; Gu and Sigurdsson, 2011). There are a small number of examples of orally bioavailable small molecules capable of reducing excess tau phosphorylation or misfolding in Aβ-based AD mouse models. Oral administration of tadalafil, a phosphodiesterase type 5 inhibitor, in an AD mouse model that expresses mutant APP (Swedish and Indiana mutations; J20 line) was shown to inhibit GSK-3β-induced tau phosphorylation (Garcia-Barroso et al., 2013). Oral administration of the GSK-3β inhibitor 2-methyl-5-(3-{4-[(S)-methylsulfinyl]phenyl}-1-benzofuran-5-yl)-1,3,4-oxadiazole led to decreased tau phosphorylation in the 3xTg-AD model but also in wild-type mice (Onishi et al., 2011). Another GSK-3β inhibitor, the flavonoid morin, was also reported to inhibit tau phosphorylation in 3XTg-AD mice when given intraperitoneally (Gong et al., 2011). Finally, a dual GSK-3β-CDL5/p25 inhibitor administered intraperitoneally to 3xTg-AD mice lowered levels of tau phosphorylation and improved fear conditioning response (Zhang et al., 2013). The predominant approaches to inhibiting excess tau phosphorylation have involved the direct targeting of individual tau kinases. Potential limitations of this strategy include interference with physiological roles of the targeted kinases and the possibility that the tau sites regulated by just one kinase would not be sufficient to prevent misfolding. The $p75^{NTR}$ ligands prevent both Aβ-induced tau misfolding and activation of multiple tau kinases, without directly targeting the tau kinases, which highlights the potential broad and potent effects of targeting upstream $p75^{NTR}$ signaling.

Degeneration of BFCNs and their neurites likely underlies significant components of diminished cognitive function in AD (Coulson et al., 2009; Lad et al., 2003; Niewiadomska et al., 2011; Vana et al., 2011). $p75^{NTR}$ signaling regulates the trophic status of BFCNs, among many other neuronal populations in the CNS. Degeneration of BFCNs is also found in AD mouse models, including $APP^{L/S}$ mice (German et al., 2003; Knowles et al., 2013; Nguyen et al., 2014; Perez et al., 2007, 2011; Simmons et al., 2014). Treatment of $APP^{L/S}$ mice at midstages of degeneration with LM11A-31 and -24 once daily for 3 months was found to reduce BFCN neurite degeneration and the loss of cholinergic fibers within cortical and hippocampal target regions (Knowles et al., 2013; Nguyen et al., 2014). In addition, the formation of dystrophic cholinergic neurites in the cortex and hippocampus was also diminished. A similar LM11A-31 treatment paradigm (once daily for 3 months) also alleviated BFCN neurite degeneration in another AD mouse model, Tg2576, when initiated in mid to late disease stages (Simmons et al., 2014), after cognitive deficits and Aβ deposition occur in these mice (Irizarry et al., 1997; King and Arendash, 2002). In studies in which late-stage $APP^{L/S}$ mice received LM11A-31 once daily for 1 month only, assessment of BFCN projections at time points before and after the treatment course revealed a true reversal of neurite degeneration (Simmons et al., 2014), which is uncommon in the AD preclinical treatment literature. Of note, the in vivo effects of LM11A-31 on tau phosphorylation/misfolding, neurite degeneration, and cognitive status in $APP^{L/S}$ mice occurred without a decrease in Aβ levels (Knowles et al., 2013; Nguyen et al., 2014; Simmons et al., 2014). This further suggests that these therapeutic effects are mediated by blocking $p75^{NTR}$-enabled degenerative mechanisms, and is consistent with earlier in vitro work in which these compounds inhibited Aβ-induced degenerative signaling and neurite degeneration (Yang et al., 2008).

TrkA-BASED AD THERAPEUTIC STRATEGIES

As discussed previously, the NGF protein has limited CNS bioavailability (Pardridge, 2002; Poduslo and Curran, 1996; Saltzman et al., 1999). Thus, there has been interest in developing small-molecule ligands capable of engaging and activating TrkA expressed by CNS neurons, particularly those in BFCNs undergoing degeneration in AD. One such ligand is D3, which is a peptidomimetic TrkA partial agonist that does not bind to TrkB, TrkC, or p75^{NTR} (Maliartchouk et al., 2000). This peptidomimetic was administered intraventricularly via osmotic minipump to the APP/J20 AD mouse model for 2 weeks (Aboulkassim et al., 2011). D3 increased AKT signaling in the hippocampus and cortex and decreased cortical Aβ levels. These effects were accompanied by improved learning and short-term memory but not long-term memory in the Morris water maze; however, persistent deficits in long-term memory occurred in wild-type mice, possibly due to increased hippocampal long-term depression (Aboulkassim et al., 2011). In an in vitro rat hippocampal model of AD involving NGF deficits and amyloidogenesis, another selective TrkA agonist, MT2, increased TrkA phosphorylation, decreased APP generation, and increased cell survival (Scarpi et al., 2012). While TrkA activation produced some positive effects in cellular and mouse models of AD, it has also been reported that inhibiting TrkA could be therapeutic in AD. When GW441756, which has been shown to inhibit TrkA, was administered to APP/J20 mice, the ratio of soluble APP to Aβ was increased, suggesting that inhibiting TrkA shifts proapoptotic signaling toward nonamyloidogenic, antiapoptotic signaling (Zhang et al., 2014a). However, these results are confounded by the observation that GW441756 also inhibits TrkB and TrkC (Wang et al., 2008). Taken together, these results stress the complexity of TrkA as an AD therapeutic target since TrkA activation may have favorable as well as detrimental effects.

TrkB-BASED AD THERAPEUTIC STRATEGIES

Like NGF, BDNF is unstable and penetrates the BBB poorly (Pardridge, 2002; Poduslo and Curran, 1996). Increasing BDNF levels and/or expression centrally via ventricular perfusion, cortical gene delivery, BDNF fusion peptides for increased BBB penetration, hippocampal transplantation of BDNF-producing neural stem cells, or viral-mediated BDNF expression is neuroprotective against Aβ neurotoxicity, synapse loss, and/or cognitive deficits in rodents and primates (Arancibia et al., 2008; Blurton-Jones et al., 2009; Iwasaki et al., 2012; Nagahara et al., 2009, 2013; Wu et al., 2015; Zhang et al., 2015a). However, BDNF delivery via these routes is not clinically feasible on a large scale and, moreover, targets limited brain areas. Other treatment paradigms aimed at upregulation of endogenous BDNF via behavioral modifications (eg, dietary restriction and exercise), antidepressants and other drugs, or antioxidants (Cimini et al., 2013; Hou et al., 2010; Hu et al., 2013, 2015; Li and Liu, 2010; Paillard et al., 2015; Prakash and Kumar, 2014; Zhang et al., 2015b) only minimally and transiently increase BDNF levels so that TrkB activation sufficient for effective neuroprotection is improbable. One approach more suitable for clinical use is developing small-molecule TrkB ligands. A small-molecule TrkB agonist, the flavone 7,8-dihydroxyflavone (7,8-DHF) (Jang et al., 2010), reduced synaptic loss and improved cognition in 5XFAD mice after systemic injection, in part by alleviating amyloid accumulation (Devi and Ohno, 2012; Zhang et al., 2014b). However, more recent work raises the likelihood of limited bioavailablity of 7,8-DHF, promoting current efforts to develop a prodrug version (Ye, 2014). In addition, in a recent study, 7,8-DHF failed to reduce pathology or cognitive deficits in APP23/PS45 AD mice (Zhou et al., 2015). Additionally, the specificity of 7,8-DHF actions is unclear. Studies using a cell line lacking TrkB found that 7,8-DHF protected against glutamate-, hydrogen peroxide-, and menadione-induced toxicity while increasing glutathione levels and reducing reactive oxygen species, consistent with an antioxidant effect (Chen et al., 2011). Thus, the mechanisms of action of 7,8-DHF in a given setting may be complex, including mechanisms independent of TrkB activation.

Our laboratories have developed a series of small-molecule nonpeptide ligands for the TrkB receptor which are capable of stimulating activation of TrkB and its downstream signaling pathways. One of these compounds, LM22A-4, has been studied in the context of a number of neurodegenerative disorders (Massa et al., 2010; Schmid et al., 2012; Simmons et al., 2013). In in vitro assays using mouse hippocampal neurons, LM22A-4 achieved 85% of maximal BDNF neurotrophic activity and 30% of maximal BDNF-induced $TrkB^{Y490}$ phosphorylation, one primary indicator of TrkB activation. Its activity profile was consistent with that of a TrkB partial agonist. Consistent with its ability to activate TrkB, LM22A-4 promoted activation of ERK and AKT signaling pathways. In studies in which oligomeric Aβ was applied to mature hippocampal neurons, LM22A-4 blocked neuronal death with an efficacy equal to that of BDNF. When administered in vivo to normal mice, LM22A-4 promoted activation of TrkB, AKT, and ERK in hippocampal and cortical tissue (Massa et al., 2010). Studies in AD mouse models are under way.

Our team has also developed a small-molecule ligand that binds to and activates both TrkB and TrkC and their downstream signaling (Yang et al., unpublished results). This approach has the potential for synergistic intracellular signaling, as can occur with Trk receptors (Volinsky and Kholodenko, 2013), and combating multifaceted pathological mechanisms seen in AD. Recent drug discovery efforts for complex diseases, including AD, have focused on multitarget-directed ligands with functional synergy (Bajda et al., 2011; Buccafusco, 2009; Fang et al., 2015; Guzior et al., 2015; Luo et al., 2015).

CONCLUSIONS

As degenerative signaling patterns occurring in AD and those regulated by NT receptors continue to be identified, rationales and strategies for their therapeutic targeting will be further developed. Such approaches will include disease prevention and/or delaying, slowing, and certain elements of reversal. The advent of small molecules capable of targeting individual neurotrophin receptors will significantly accelerate progress in AD therapeutic testing.

References

Aboulkassim T, Tong XK, Tse YC, Wong TP, Woo SB, Neet KE, Brahimi F, Hamel E, Saragovi HU: Ligand-dependent TrkA activity in brain differentially affects spatial learning and long-term memory, *Mol Pharmacol* 80:498–508, 2011.

Abram M, Wegmann M, Fokuhl V, Sonar S, Luger EO, Kerzel S, Radbruch A, Renz H, Zemlin M: Nerve growth factor and neurotrophin-3 mediate survival of pulmonary plasma cells during the allergic airway inflammation, *J Immunol* 182:4705–4712, 2009.

Allen SJ, Watson JJ, Shoemark DK, Barua NU, Patel NK: GDNF, NGF and BDNF as therapeutic options for neurodegeneration, *Pharmacol Ther* 138:155–175, 2013.

Allen SJ, Wilcock GK, Dawbarn D: Profound and selective loss of catalytic TrkB immunoreactivity in Alzheimer's disease, *Biochem Biophys Res Commun* 264:648–651, 1999.

Anand R, Gill KD, Mahdi AA: Therapeutics of Alzheimer's disease: past, present and future, *Neuropharmacology* 76(Pt A):27–50, 2014.

Angelucci F, Spalletta G, di Iulio F, Ciaramella A, Salani F, Colantoni L, Varsi AE, Gianni W, Sancesario G, Caltagirone C, Bossu P: Alzheimer's disease (AD) and mild cognitive impairment (MCI) patients are characterized by increased BDNF serum levels, *Curr Alzheimer Res* 7:15–20, 2010.

Arancibia S, Silhol M, Mouliere F, Meffre J, Hollinger I, Maurice T, Tapia-Arancibia L: Protective effect of BDNF against beta-amyloid induced neurotoxicity in vitro and in vivo in rats, *Neurobiol Dis* 31:316–326, 2008.

Arancio O, Chao MV: Neurotrophins, synaptic plasticity and dementia, *Curr Opin Neurobiol* 17:325–330, 2007.

Bajda M, Guzior N, Ignasik M, Malawska B: Multi-target-directed ligands in Alzheimer's disease treatment, *Curr Med Chem* 18:4949–4975, 2011.

Barbacid M: Structural and functional properties of the TRK family of neurotrophin receptors, *Ann NY Acad Sci* 766:442–458, 1995.

Barrett GL: The p75 neurotrophin receptor and neuronal apoptosis, *Prog Neurobiol* 61:205–229, 2000.

Bekinschtein P, Cammarota M, Katche C, Slipczuk L, Rossato JI, Goldin A, Izquierdo I, Medina JH: BDNF is essential to promote persistence of long-term memory storage, *Proc Natl Acad Sci USA* 105:2711–2716, 2008.

Bergmann I, Reiter R, Toyka KV, Koltzenburg M: Nerve growth factor evokes hyperalgesia in mice lacking the low-affinity neurotrophin receptor p75, *Neurosci Lett* 255:87–90, 1998.

Blochl A, Blochl R: A cell-biological model of p75NTR signaling, *J Neurochem* 102:289–305, 2007.

Blurton-Jones M, Kitazawa M, Martinez-Coria H, Castello NA, Muller FJ, Loring JF, Yamasaki TR, Poon WW, Green KN, LaFerla FM: Neural stem cells improve cognition via BDNF in a transgenic model of Alzheimer disease, *Proc Natl Acad Sci USA* 106:13594–13599, 2009.

Boissiere F, Faucheux B, Agid Y, Hirsch EC: Expression of catalytic trkB gene in the striatum and the basal forebrain of patients with Alzheimer's disease: an in situ hybridization study, *Neurosci Lett* 221:141–144, 1997a.

Boissiere F, Faucheux B, Ruberg M, Agid Y, Hirsch EC: Decreased TrkA gene expression in cholinergic neurons of the striatum and basal forebrain of patients with Alzheimer's disease, *Exp Neurol* 145:245–252, 1997b.

Borroni B, Archetti S, Costanzi C, Grassi M, Ferrari M, Radeghieri A, Caimi L, Caltagirone C, Di Luca M, Padovani A, ITINAD Working Group: Role of BDNF Val66Met functional polymorphism in Alzheimer's disease-related depression, *Neurobiol Aging* 30:1406–1412, 2009a.

Borroni B, Grassi M, Archetti S, Costanzi C, Bianchi M, Caimi L, Caltagirone C, Di Luca M, Padovani A: BDNF genetic variations increase the risk of Alzheimer's disease-related depression, *J Alzheimers Dis* 18:867–875, 2009b.

Borsello T, Forloni G: JNK signalling: a possible target to prevent neurodegeneration, *Curr Pharm Des* 13:1875–1886, 2007.

Brunden KR, Trojanowski JQ, Lee VM: Advances in tau-focused drug discovery for Alzheimer's disease and related tauopathies, *Nat Rev Drug Discov* 8:783–793, 2009.

Buccafusco JJ: Multifunctional receptor-directed drugs for disorders of the central nervous system, *Neurotherapeutics* 6:4–13, 2009.

Budni J, Bellettini-Santos T, Mina F, Garcez ML, Zugno AI: The involvement of BDNF, NGF and GDNF in aging and Alzheimer's disease, *Aging Dis* 6:331–341, 2015.

Caldeira MV, Melo CV, Pereira DB, Carvalho R, Correia SS, Backos DS, Carvalho AL, Esteban JA, Duarte CB: Brain-derived neurotrophic factor regulates the expression and synaptic delivery of alpha-amino-3-hydroxy-5-methyl-4-isoxazole propionic acid receptor subunits in hippocampal neurons, *J Biol Chem* 282:12619–12628, 2007.

Cameron B, Landreth GE: Inflammation, microglia, and Alzheimer's disease, *Neurobiol Dis* 37:503–509, 2010.

Carter BD, Kaltschmidt C, Kaltschmidt B, Offenhauser N, Bohm-Matthaei R, Baeuerle PA, Barde YA: Selective activation of NF-kappa B by nerve growth factor through the neurotrophin receptor p75, *Science* 272:542–545, 1996.

Casaccia-Bonnefil P, Carter BD, Dobrowsky RT, Chao MV: Death of oligodendrocytes mediated by the interaction of nerve growth factor with its receptor p75, *Nature* 383:716–719, 1996.

Casaccia-Bonnefil P, Gu C, Chao MV: Neurotrophins in cell survival/death decisions, *Adv Exp Med Biol* 468:275–282, 1999.

Castillo-Carranza DL, Guerrero-Munoz MJ, Sengupta U, Hernandez C, Barrett AD, Dineley K, Kayed R: Tau immunotherapy modulates both pathological tau and upstream amyloid pathology in an Alzheimer's disease mouse model, *J Neurosci* 35:4857–4868, 2015.

Chakravarthy B, Gaudet C, Menard M, Atkinson T, Brown L, Laferla FM, Armato U, Whitfield J: Amyloid-beta peptides stimulate the expression of the p75(NTR) neurotrophin receptor in SHSY5Y human neuroblastoma cells and AD transgenic mice, *J Alzheimers Dis* 19:915–925, 2010.

Chakravarthy B, Menard M, Ito S, Gaudet C, Dal Pra I, Armato U, Whitfield J: Hippocampal membrane-associated p75NTR levels are increased in Alzheimer's disease, *J Alzheimers Dis* 30:675–684, 2012.

Chao MV: Neurotrophins and their receptors: a convergence point for many signalling pathways, *Nat Rev Neurosci* 4:299–309, 2003.

Charalampopoulos I, Vicario A, Pediaditakis I, Gravanis A, Simi A, Ibanez CF: Genetic dissection of neurotrophin signaling through the p75 neurotrophin receptor, *Cell Rep* 2:1563–1570, 2012.

Chen J, Chua KW, Chua CC, Yu H, Pei A, Chua BH, Hamdy RC, Xu X, Liu CF: Antioxidant activity of 7,8-dihydroxyflavone provides neuroprotection against glutamate-induced toxicity, *Neurosci Lett* 499:181–185, 2011.

Chen QS, Wei WZ, Shimahara T, Xie CW: Alzheimer amyloid beta-peptide inhibits the late phase of long-term potentiation through calcineurin-dependent mechanisms in the hippocampal dentate gyrus, *Neurobiol Learn Mem* 77:354–371, 2002.

Chen Q, Zhou Z, Zhang L, Xu S, Chen C, Yu Z: The cellular distribution and Ser262 phosphorylation of tau protein are regulated by BDNF in vitro, *PLoS One* 9:e91793, 2014.

Cimini A, Gentile R, D'Angelo B, Benedetti E, Cristiano L, Avantaggiati ML, Giordano A, Ferri C, Desideri G: Cocoa powder triggers neuroprotective and preventive effects in a human Alzheimer's disease model by modulating BDNF signaling pathway, *J Cell Biochem* 114:2209–2220, 2013.

Connor B, Young D, Lawlor P, Gai W, Waldvogel H, Faull RL, Dragunow M: Trk receptor alterations in Alzheimer's disease, *Brain Res Mol Brain Res* 42:1–17, 1996.

Coulson EJ: Does the p75 neurotrophin receptor mediate Abeta-induced toxicity in Alzheimer's disease? *J Neurochem* 98:654–660, 2006.

Coulson EJ, May LM, Sykes AM, Hamlin AS: The role of the p75 neurotrophin receptor in cholinergic dysfunction in Alzheimer's disease, *Neuroscientist* 15:317–323, 2009.

Criscuolo C, Fabiani C, Bonadonna C, Origlia N, Domenici L: BDNF prevents amyloid-dependent impairment of LTP in the entorhinal cortex by attenuating p38 MAPK phosphorylation, *Neurobiol Aging* 36:1303–1309, 2015.

Devi L, Ohno M: 7,8-Dihydroxyflavone, a small-molecule TrkB agonist, reverses memory deficits and BACE1 elevation in a mouse model of Alzheimer's disease, *Neuropsychopharmacology* 37:434–444, 2012.

Devi L, Ohno M: TrkB reduction exacerbates Alzheimer's disease-like signaling aberrations and memory deficits without affecting beta-amyloidosis in 5XFAD mice, *Transl Psychiatr* 5:e562, 2015.

Diarra A, Geetha T, Potter P, Babu JR: Signaling of the neurotrophin receptor p75 in relation to Alzheimer's disease, *Biochem Biophys Res Commun* 390:352–356, 2009.

Durany N, Michel T, Kurt J, Cruz-Sanchez FF, Cervas-Navarro J, Riederer P: Brain-derived neurotrophic factor and neurotrophin-3 levels in Alzheimer's disease brains, *Int J Dev Neurosci* 18:807–813, 2000.

Dyck PJ, Peroutka S, Rask C, Burton E, Baker MK, Lehman KA, Gillen DA, Hokanson JL, O'Brien PC: Intradermal recombinant human nerve growth factor induces pressure allodynia and lowered heat-pain threshold in humans, *Neurology* 48:501–505, 1997.

Elliott E, Atlas R, Lange A, Ginzburg I: Brain-derived neurotrophic factor induces a rapid dephosphorylation of tau protein through a PI-3 kinase signalling mechanism, *Eur J Neurosci* 22:1081–1089, 2005.

Eriksdotter Jonhagen M, Nordberg A, Amberla K, Backman L, Ebendal T, Meyerson B, Olson L, Seiger, Shigeta M, Theodorsson E, Viitanen M, Winblad B, Wahlund LO: Intracerebroventricular infusion of nerve growth factor in three patients with Alzheimer's disease, *Dement Geriatr Cogn Disord* 9:246–257, 1998.

Espana J, Valero J, Minano-Molina AJ, Masgrau R, Martin E, Guardia-Laguarta C, Lleo A, Gimenez-Llort L, Rodriguez-Alvarez J, Saura CA: Beta-amyloid disrupts activity-dependent gene transcription required for memory through the CREB coactivator CRTC1, *J Neurosci* 30:9402–9410, 2010.

Fahnestock M, Garzon D, Holsinger RM, Michalski B: Neurotrophic factors and Alzheimer's disease: are we focusing on the wrong molecule? *J Neural Transm Suppl* 62:241–252, 2002.

Fahnestock M, Michalski B, Xu B, Coughlin MD: The precursor pro-nerve growth factor is the predominant form of nerve growth factor in brain and is increased in Alzheimer's disease, *Mol Cell Neurosci* 18:210–220, 2001.

Fang J, Li Y, Liu R, Pang X, Li C, Yang R, He Y, Lian W, Liu AL, Du GH: Discovery of multitarget-directed ligands against Alzheimer's disease through systematic prediction of chemical–protein interactions, *J Chem Inf Model* 55:149–164, 2015.

Feher A, Juhasz A, Rimanoczy A, Kalman J, Janka Z: Association between BDNF Val66Met polymorphism and Alzheimer disease, dementia with Lewy bodies, and Pick disease, *Alzheimer Dis Assoc Disord* 23:224–228, 2009.

Feng D, Kim T, Ozkan E, Light M, Torkin R, Teng KK, Hempstead BL, Garcia KC: Molecular and structural insight into proNGF engagement of p75NTR and sortilin, *J Mol Biol* 396:967–984, 2010.

Ferrer I, Marin C, Rey MJ, Ribalta T, Goutan E, Blanco R, Tolosa E, Marti E: BDNF and full-length and truncated TrkB expression in Alzheimer disease: implications in therapeutic strategies, *J Neuropathol Exp Neurol* 58:729–739, 1999.

Fombonne J, Rabizadeh S, Banwait S, Mehlen P, Bredesen DE: Selective vulnerability in Alzheimer's disease: amyloid precursor protein and p75(NTR) interaction, *Ann Neurol* 65:294–303, 2009.

Forlenza OV, Diniz BS, Talib LL, Radanovic M, Yassuda MS, Ojopi EB, Gattaz WF: Clinical and biological predictors of Alzheimer's disease in patients with amnestic mild cognitive impairment, *Rev Bras Psiquiatr* 32:216–222, 2010a.

Forlenza OV, Diniz BS, Teixeira AL, Ojopi EB, Talib LL, Mendonca VA, Izzo G, Gattaz WF: Effect of brain-derived neurotrophic factor Val66Met polymorphism and serum levels on the progression of mild cognitive impairment, *World J Biol Psychiatr* 11:774–780, 2010b.

Frost B, Gotz J, Feany MB: Connecting the dots between tau dysfunction and neurodegeneration, *Trends Cell Biol* 25:46–53, 2015.

Gan KJ, Silverman MA: Dendritic and axonal mechanisms of Ca^{2+} elevation impair BDNF transport in Abeta oligomer-treated hippocampal neurons, *Mol Biol Cell* 26:1058–1071, 2015.

Garcia-Barroso C, Ricobaraza A, Pascual-Lucas M, Unceta N, Rico AJ, Goicolea MA, Salles J, Lanciego JL, Oyarzabal J, Franco R, Cuadrado-Tejedor M, Garcia-Osta A: Tadalafil crosses the blood–brain barrier and reverses cognitive dysfunction in a mouse model of AD, *Neuropharmacology* 64:114–123, 2013.

Garzon D, Yu G, Fahnestock M: A new brain-derived neurotrophic factor transcript and decrease in brain-derived neurotrophic factor transcripts 1, 2 and 3 in Alzheimer's disease parietal cortex, *J Neurochem* 82:1058–1064, 2002.

German DC, Yazdani U, Speciale SG, Pasbakhsh P, Games D, Liang CL: Cholinergic neuropathology in a mouse model of Alzheimer's disease, *J Comp Neurol* 462:371–381, 2003.

Gibbs RB, McCabe JT, Buck CR, Chao MV, Pfaff DW: Expression of NGF receptor in the rat forebrain detected with in situ hybridization and immunohistochemistry, *Brain Res Mol Brain Res* 6:275–287, 1989.

Ginsberg SD, Che S, Wuu J, Counts SE, Mufson EJ: Down regulation of trk but not p75NTR gene expression in single cholinergic basal forebrain neurons mark the progression of Alzheimer's disease, *J Neurochem* 97:475–487, 2006.

Gong Y, Cao P, Yu HJ, Jiang T: Crystal structure of the neurotrophin-3 and p75NTR symmetrical complex, *Nature* 454:789–793, 2008.

Gong EJ, Park HR, Kim ME, Piao S, Lee E, Jo DG, Chung HY, Ha NC, Mattson MP, Lee J: Morin attenuates tau hyperphosphorylation by inhibiting GSK3beta, *Neurobiol Dis* 44:223–230, 2011.

Gotz J, Ittner A, Ittner LM: Tau-targeted treatment strategies in Alzheimer's disease, *Br J Pharmacol* 165:1246–1259, 2012.

Grundman M, Dibernardo A, Raghavan N, Krams M, Yuen E: 2012: a watershed year for Alzheimer's disease research, *J Nutr Health Aging* 17:51–53, 2013.

Gu J, Sigurdsson EM: Immunotherapy for tauopathies, *J Mol Neurosci* 45:690–695, 2011.

Guzior N, Wieckowska A, Panek D, Malawska B: Recent development of multifunctional agents as potential drug candidates for the treatment of Alzheimer's disease, *Curr Med Chem* 22:373–404, 2015.

Hashimoto R, Hirata Y, Asada T, Yamashita F, Nemoto K, Mori T, Moriguchi Y, Kunugi H, Arima K, Ohnishi T: Effect of the brain-derived neurotrophic factor and the apolipoprotein E polymorphisms on disease progression in preclinical Alzheimer's disease, *Genes Brain Behav* 8:43–52, 2009.

Hayashi M, Yamashita A, Shimizu K: Somatostatin and brain-derived neurotrophic factor mRNA expression in the primate brain: decreased levels of mRNAs during aging, *Brain Res* 749:283–289, 1997.

Hempstead BL: Deciphering proneurotrophin actions, *Handb Exp Pharmacol* 220:17–32, 2014.

Himmelstein DS, Ward SM, Lancia JK, Patterson KR, Binder LI: Tau as a therapeutic target in neurodegenerative disease, *Pharmacol Ther* 136:8–22, 2012.

Hirose M, Kuroda Y, Murata E: NGF/TrkA signaling as a therapeutic target for pain, *Pain Pract* 16:175–182, 2015.

Hou Y, Aboukhatwa MA, Lei DL, Manaye K, Khan I, Luo Y: Anti-depressant natural flavonols modulate BDNF and beta amyloid in neurons and hippocampus of double TgAD mice, *Neuropharmacology* 58:911–920, 2010.

Hu YS, Long N, Pigino G, Brady ST, Lazarov O: Molecular mechanisms of environmental enrichment: impairments in Akt/GSK3beta, neurotrophin-3 and CREB signaling, *PLoS One* 8:e64460, 2013.

Hu S, Maiti P, Ma Q, Zuo X, Jones MR, Cole GM, Frautschy SA: Clinical development of curcumin in neurodegenerative disease, *Expert Rev Neurother* 15:629–637, 2015.

Hu XY, Zhang HY, Qin S, Xu H, Swaab DF, Zhou JN: Increased p75(NTR) expression in hippocampal neurons containing hyperphosphorylated tau in Alzheimer patients, *Exp Neurol* 178:104–111, 2002.

Huang EJ, Reichardt LF: Neurotrophins: roles in neuronal development and function, *Ann Rev Neurosci* 24:677–736, 2001.

Huang EJ, Reichardt LF: Trk receptors: roles in neuronal signal transduction, *Ann Rev Biochem* 72:609–642, 2003.

Irizarry MC, McNamara M, Fedorchak K, Hsiao K, Hyman BT: APPSw transgenic mice develop age-related A beta deposits and neuropil abnormalities, but no neuronal loss in CA1, *J Neuropathol Exp Neurol* 56:965–973, 1997.

Iwasaki Y, Negishi T, Inoue M, Tashiro T, Tabira T, Kimura N: Sendai virus vector-mediated brain-derived neurotrophic factor expression ameliorates memory deficits and synaptic degeneration in a transgenic mouse model of Alzheimer's disease, *J Neurosci Res* 90:981–989, 2012.

Jang SW, Liu X, Yepes M, Shepherd KR, Miller GW, Liu Y, Wilson WD, Xiao G, Blanchi B, Sun YE, Ye K: A selective TrkB agonist with potent neurotrophic activities by 7,8-dihydroxyflavone, *Proc Natl Acad Sci USA* 107:2687–2692, 2010.

Jones MG, Munson JB, Thompson SW: A role for nerve growth factor in sympathetic sprouting in rat dorsal root ganglia, *Pain* 79:21–29, 1999.

Kalra J, Khan A: Reducing Abeta load and tau phosphorylation: emerging perspective for treating Alzheimer's disease, *Eur J Pharmacol* 764:571–581, 2015.

Kang H, Jia LZ, Suh KY, Tang L, Schuman EM: Determinants of BDNF-induced hippocampal synaptic plasticity: role of the Trk B receptor and the kinetics of neurotrophin delivery, *Learn Mem* 3:188–196, 1996.

Kang H, Schuman EM: A requirement for local protein synthesis in neurotrophin-induced hippocampal synaptic plasticity, *Science* 273:1402–1406, 1996.

Kang HJ, Schuman EM: Neurotrophin-induced modulation of synaptic transmission in the adult hippocampus, *J Physiol* 89:11–22, 1995.

Karami A, Eyjolfsdottir H, Vijayaraghavan S, Lind G, Almqvist P, Kadir A, Linderoth B, Andreasen N, Blennow K, Wall A, Westman E, Ferreira D, Kristoffersen Wiberg M, Wahlund LO, Seiger A, Nordberg A, Wahlberg L, Darreh-Shori T, Eriksdotter M: Changes in CSF cholinergic biomarkers in response to cell therapy with NGF in patients with Alzheimer's disease, *Alzheimers Dement* 11:1316–1328, 2015.

King DL, Arendash GW: Behavioral characterization of the Tg2576 transgenic model of Alzheimer's disease through 19 months, *Physiol Behav* 75:627–642, 2002.

Knowles JK, Rajadas J, Nguyen TV, Yang T, LeMieux MC, Vander Griend L, Ishikawa C, Massa SM, Wyss-Coray T, Longo FM: The p75 neurotrophin receptor promotes amyloid-beta(1-42)-induced neuritic dystrophy in vitro and in vivo, *J Neurosci* 29:10627–10637, 2009.

Knowles JK, Simmons DA, Nguyen TV, Vander Griend L, Xie Y, Zhang H, Yang T, Pollak J, Chang T, Arancio O, Buckwalter MS, Wyss-Coray T, Massa SM, Longo FM: Small molecule p75NTR ligand prevents cognitive deficits and neurite degeneration in an Alzheimer's mouse model, *Neurobiol Aging* 34:2052–2063, 2013.

Kobayashi N, Nagata T, Shinagawa S, Nakayama R, Kondo K, Nakayama K, Yamada H: Association between neurotrophin-3 polymorphisms and executive function in Japanese patients with amnestic mild cognitive impairment and mild Alzheimer disease, *Dement Geriatr Cogn Disord* 34:190–197, 2012.

Kojima N, Shirao T: Synaptic dysfunction and disruption of postsynaptic drebrin–actin complex: a study of neurological disorders accompanied by cognitive deficits, *Neurosci Res* 58:1–5, 2007.

Konukoglu D, Andican G, Firtina S, Erkol G, Kurt A: Serum brain-derived neurotrophic factor, nerve growth factor and neurotrophin-3 levels in dementia, *Acta Neurol* 112:255–260, 2012.

Korte M, Carroll P, Wolf E, Brem G, Thoenen H, Bonhoeffer T: Hippocampal long-term potentiation is impaired in mice lacking brain-derived neurotrophic factor, *Proc Natl Acad Sci USA* 92:8856–8860, 1995.

Krstic D, Knuesel I: Deciphering the mechanism underlying late-onset Alzheimer disease, *Nat Rev Neurol* 9:25–34, 2013.

Kumar A, Nisha CM, Silakari C, Sharma I, Anusha K, Gupta N, Nair P, Tripathi T, Kumar A: Current and novel therapeutic molecules and targets in Alzheimer's disease, *J Formos Med Assoc* 115:3–10, 2015.

Kunugi H, Hattori M, Ueki A, Isse K, Hirasawa H, Nanko S: Possible association of missense mutation (Gly[-63]Glu) of the neurotrophin-3 gene with Alzheimer's disease in Japanese, *Neurosci Lett* 241:65–67, 1998.

Kunugi H, Ueki A, Otsuka M, Isse K, Hirasawa H, Kato N, Nabika T, Kobayashi S, Nanko S: A novel polymorphism of the brain-derived neurotrophic factor (BDNF) gene associated with late-onset Alzheimer's disease, *Mol Psychiatr* 6:83–86, 2001.

Lad SP, Neet KE, Mufson EJ: Nerve growth factor: structure, function and therapeutic implications for Alzheimer's disease, *Curr Drug Targets CNS Neurol Disord* 2:315–334, 2003.

Lannfelt L, Moller C, Basun H, Osswald G, Sehlin D, Satlin A, Logovinsky V, Gellerfors P: Perspectives on future Alzheimer therapies: amyloid-beta protofibrils—a new target for immunotherapy with BAN2401 in Alzheimer's disease, *Alzheimers Res Ther* 6:16, 2014.

Lanz TA, Carter DB, Merchant KM: Dendritic spine loss in the hippocampus of young PDAPP and Tg2576 mice and its prevention by the ApoE2 genotype, *Neurobiol Dis* 13:246–253, 2003.
Laske C, Stransky E, Leyhe T, Eschweiler GW, Maetzler W, Wittorf A, Soekadar S, Richartz E, Koehler N, Bartels M, Buchkremer G, Schott K: BDNF serum and CSF concentrations in Alzheimer's disease, normal pressure hydrocephalus and healthy controls, *J Psychiatr Res* 41:387–394, 2007.
Laske C, Stransky E, Leyhe T, Eschweiler GW, Schott K, Langer H, Gawaz M: Decreased brain-derived neurotrophic factor (BDNF)- and beta-thromboglobulin (beta-TG)-blood levels in Alzheimer's disease, *Thromb Haemost* 96:102–103, 2006a.
Laske C, Stransky E, Leyhe T, Eschweiler GW, Wittorf A, Richartz E, Bartels M, Buchkremer G, Schott K: Stage-dependent BDNF serum concentrations in Alzheimer's disease, *J Neural Transm* 113:1217–1224, 2006b.
Le Moan N, Houslay DM, Christian F, Houslay MD, Akassoglou K: Oxygen-dependent cleavage of the p75 neurotrophin receptor triggers stabilization of HIF-1alpha, *Mol Cell* 44:476–490, 2011.
Lee JG, Shin BS, You YS, Kim JE, Yoon SW, Jeon DW, Baek JH, Park SW, Kim YH: Decreased serum brain-derived neurotrophic factor levels in elderly Korean with dementia, *Psychiatr Investig* 6:299–305, 2009.
Lesne S, Gabriel C, Nelson DA, White E, Mackenzie ET, Vivien D, Buisson A: Akt-dependent expression of NAIP-1 protects neurons against amyloid-β toxicity, *J Biol Chem* 280:24941–24947, 2005.
Levi-Montalcini R: The nerve growth factor 35 years later, *Science* 237:1154–1162, 1987.
Li G, Peskind ER, Millard SP, Chi P, Sokal I, Yu CE, Bekris LM, Raskind MA, Galasko DR, Montine TJ: Cerebrospinal fluid concentration of brain-derived neurotrophic factor and cognitive function in non-demented subjects, *PLoS One* 4:e5424, 2009.
Li N, Liu GT: The novel squamosamide derivative FLZ enhances BDNF/TrkB/CREB signaling and inhibits neuronal apoptosis in APP/PS1 mice, *Acta Pharmacol Sin* 31:265–272, 2010.
Li YX, Zhang Y, Lester HA, Schuman EM, Davidson N: Enhancement of neurotransmitter release induced by brain-derived neurotrophic factor in cultured hippocampal neurons, *J Neurosci* 18:10231–10240, 1998.
Li Z, Tan F, Thiele CJ: Inactivation of glycogen synthase kinase-3beta contributes to brain-derived neutrophic factor/TrkB-induced resistance to chemotherapy in neuroblastoma cells, *Mol Cancer Ther* 6:3113–3121, 2007.
Liu J, He QJ, Zou W, Wang HX, Bao YM, Liu YX, An LJ: Catalpol increases hippocampal neuroplasticity and up-regulates PKC and BDNF in the aged rats, *Brain Res* 1123:68–79, 2006.
Longo FM, Massa SM: Neuroprotective strategies in Alzheimer's disease, *NeuroRx* 1:117–127, 2004.
Longo FM, Massa SM: Small molecule modulation of p75 neurotrophin receptor functions, *CNS Neurol Disord Drug Targets* 7:63–70, 2008.
Longo FM, Massa SM: Small-molecule modulation of neurotrophin receptors: a strategy for the treatment of neurological disease, *Nat Rev Drug Discov* 12:507–525, 2013.
Luo XT, Wang CM, Liu Y, Huang ZG: New multifunctional melatonin-derived benzylpyridinium bromides with potent cholinergic, antioxidant, and neuroprotective properties as innovative drugs for Alzheimer's disease, *Eur J Med Chem* 103:302–311, 2015.
Lynch G, Rex CS, Gall CM: LTP consolidation: substrates, explanatory power, and functional significance, *Neuropharmacology* 52:12–23, 2007.
Malcangio M, Lessmann V: A common thread for pain and memory synapses? Brain-derived neurotrophic factor and trkB receptors, *Trends Pharmacol Sci* 24:116–121, 2003.
Maliartchouk S, Feng Y, Ivanisevic L, Debeir T, Cuello AC, Burgess K, Saragovi HU: A designed peptidomimetic agonistic ligand of TrkA nerve growth factor receptors, *Mol Pharmacol* 57:385–391, 2000.
Masliah E: Recent advances in the understanding of the role of synaptic proteins in Alzheimer's disease and other neurodegenerative disorders, *J Alzheimers Dis* 3:121–129, 2001.
Masliah E, Crews L, Hansen L: Synaptic remodeling during aging and in Alzheimer's disease, *J Alzheimers Dis* 9:91–99, 2006.
Massa SM, Xie Y, Yang T, Harrington AW, Kim ML, Yoon SO, Kraemer R, Moore LA, Hempstead BL, Longo FM: Small, nonpeptide p75NTR ligands induce survival signaling and inhibit proNGF-induced death, *J Neurosci* 26:5288–5300, 2006.
Massa SM, Yang T, Xie Y, Shi J, Bilgen M, Joyce JN, Nehama D, Rajadas J, Longo FM: Small molecule BDNF mimetics activate TrkB signaling and prevent neuronal degeneration in rodents, *J Clin Invest* 120:1774–1785, 2010.
Matsumoto T, Numakawa T, Yokomaku D, Adachi N, Yamagishi S, Numakawa Y, Kunugi H, Taguchi T: Brain-derived neurotrophic factor-induced potentiation of glutamate and GABA release: different dependency on signaling pathways and neuronal activity, *Mol Cell Neurosci* 31:70–84, 2006.

Mattson MP, Maudsley S, Martin B: A neural signaling triumvirate that influences ageing and age-related disease: insulin/IGF-1, BDNF and serotonin, *Ageing Res Rev* 3:445–464, 2004.

Mazanetz MP, Fischer PM: Untangling tau hyperphosphorylation in drug design for neurodegenerative diseases, *Nat Rev Drug Discov* 6:464–479, 2007.

Moolman DL, Vitolo OV, Vonsattel JP, Shelanski ML: Dendrite and dendritic spine alterations in Alzheimer models, *J Neurocytol* 33:377–387, 2004.

Morris M, Maeda S, Vossel K, Mucke L: The many faces of tau, *Neuron* 70:410–426, 2011.

Mufson EJ, Counts SE, Perez SE, Ginsberg SD: Cholinergic system during the progression of Alzheimer's disease: therapeutic implications, *Expert Rev Neurother* 8:1703–1718, 2008.

Mufson EJ, He B, Nadeem M, Perez SE, Counts SE, Leurgans S, Fritz J, Lah J, Ginsberg SD, Wuu J, Scheff SW: Hippocampal proNGF signaling pathways and beta-amyloid levels in mild cognitive impairment and Alzheimer disease, *J Neuropathol Exp Neurol* 71:1018–1029, 2012.

Mufson EJ, Kordower JH: Cortical neurons express nerve growth factor receptors in advanced age and Alzheimer disease, *Proc Natl Acad Sci USA* 89:569–573, 1992.

Murer MG, Yan Q, Raisman-Vozari R: Brain-derived neurotrophic factor in the control human brain, and in Alzheimer's disease and Parkinson's disease, *Prog Neurobiol* 63:71–124, 2001.

Nagahara AH, Mateling M, Kovacs I, Wang L, Eggert S, Rockenstein E, Koo EH, Masliah E, Tuszynski MH: Early BDNF treatment ameliorates cell loss in the entorhinal cortex of APP transgenic mice, *J Neurosci* 33:15596–15602, 2013.

Nagahara AH, Merrill DA, Coppola G, Tsukada S, Schroeder BE, Shaked GM, Wang L, Blesch A, Kim A, Conner JM, Rockenstein E, Chao MV, Koo EH, Geschwind D, Masliah E, Chiba AA, Tuszynski MH: Neuroprotective effects of brain-derived neurotrophic factor in rodent and primate models of Alzheimer's disease, *Nat Med* 15:331–337, 2009.

Narisawa-Saito M, Wakabayashi K, Tsuji S, Takahashi H, Nawa H: Regional specificity of alterations in NGF, BDNF and NT-3 levels in Alzheimer's disease, *Neuroreport* 7:2925–2928, 1996.

Nguyen TV, Shen L, Vander Griend L, Quach LN, Belichenko NP, Saw N, Yang T, Shamloo M, Wyss-Coray T, Massa SM, Longo FM: Small molecule p75NTR ligands reduce pathological phosphorylation and misfolding of tau, inflammatory changes, cholinergic degeneration, and cognitive deficits in AbetaPPL/S transgenic mice, *J Alzheimers Dis* 42:459–483, 2014.

Niewiadomska G, Mietelska-Porowska A, Mazurkiewicz M: The cholinergic system, nerve growth factor and the cytoskeleton, *Behav Brain Res* 221:515–526, 2011.

Nykjaer A, Lee R, Teng KK, Jansen P, Madsen P, Nielsen MS, Jacobsen C, Kliemannel M, Schwarz E, Willnow TE, Hempstead BL, Petersen CM: Sortilin is essential for proNGF-induced neuronal cell death, *Nature* 427:843–848, 2004.

Olin D, MacMurray J, Comings DE: Risk of late-onset Alzheimer's disease associated with BDNF C270T polymorphism, *Neurosci Lett* 381:275–278, 2005.

Onishi T, Iwashita H, Uno Y, Kunitomo J, Saitoh M, Kimura E, Fujita H, Uchiyama N, Kori M, Takizawa M: A novel glycogen synthase kinase-3 inhibitor 2-methyl-5-(3-{4-[(S)-methylsulfinyl]phenyl}-1-benzofuran-5-yl)-1,3,4-oxadiazole decreases tau phosphorylation and ameliorates cognitive deficits in a transgenic model of Alzheimer's disease, *J Neurochem* 119:1330–1340, 2011.

Origlia N, Arancio O, Domenici L, Yan SS: MAPK, beta-amyloid and synaptic dysfunction: the role of RAGE, *Expert Rev Neurother* 9:1635–1645, 2009.

Origlia N, Righi M, Capsoni S, Cattaneo A, Fang F, Stern DM, Chen JX, Schmidt AM, Arancio O, Yan SD, Domenici L: Receptor for advanced glycation end product-dependent activation of p38 mitogen-activated protein kinase contributes to amyloid-beta-mediated cortical synaptic dysfunction, *J Neurosci* 28:3521–3530, 2008.

Paillard T, Rolland Y, de Souto Barreto P: Protective effects of physical exercise in Alzheimer's disease and Parkinson's disease: a narrative review, *J Clin Neurol* 11:212–219, 2015.

Pardridge WM: Neurotrophins, neuroprotection and the blood–brain barrier, *Curr Opin Investig Drugs* 3:1753–1757, 2002.

Patapoutian A, Reichardt LF: Trk receptors: mediators of neurotrophin action, *Curr Opin Neurobiol* 11:272–280, 2001.

Pedersen JT, Sigurdsson EM: Tau immunotherapy for Alzheimer's disease, *Trends Mol Med* 21:394–402, 2015.

Pedraza CE, Podlesniy P, Vidal N, Arevalo JC, Lee R, Hempstead B, Ferrer I, Iglesias M, Espinet C: Pro-NGF isolated from the human brain affected by Alzheimer's disease induces neuronal apoptosis mediated by p75NTR, *Am J Pathol* 166:533–543, 2005.

Peng S, Garzon DJ, Marchese M, Klein W, Ginsberg SD, Francis BM, Mount HT, Mufson EJ, Salehi A, Fahnestock M: Decreased brain-derived neurotrophic factor depends on amyloid aggregation state in transgenic mouse models of Alzheimer's disease, *J Neurosci* 29:9321–9329, 2009.

Perez SE, Dar S, Ikonomovic MD, DeKosky ST, Mufson EJ: Cholinergic forebrain degeneration in the APPswe/PS1DeltaE9 transgenic mouse, *Neurobiol Dis* 28:3–15, 2007.

Perez SE, He B, Muhammad N, Oh KJ, Fahnestock M, Ikonomovic MD, Mufson EJ: Cholinotrophic basal forebrain system alterations in 3xTg-AD transgenic mice, *Neurobiol Dis* 41:338–352, 2011.

Pertovaara A: Noradrenergic pain modulation, *Prog Neurobiol* 80:53–83, 2006.

Pezet S, Malcangio M, McMahon SB: BDNF: a neuromodulator in nociceptive pathways? *Brain Res Brain Res Rev* 40:240–249, 2002.

Pitts AF, Miller MW: Expression of nerve growth factor, p75, and Trk in the somatosensory and motor cortices of mature rats: evidence for local trophic support circuits, *Somatosens Mot Res* 12:329–342, 1995.

Poduslo JF, Curran GL: Permeability at the blood–brain and blood–nerve barriers of the neurotrophic factors: NGF, CNTF, NT-3, BDNF, *Brain Res Mol Brain Res* 36:280–286, 1996.

Poo MM: Neurotrophins as synaptic modulators, *Nat Rev Neurosci* 2:24–32, 2001.

Prakash A, Kumar A: Implicating the role of lycopene in restoration of mitochondrial enzymes and BDNF levels in beta-amyloid induced Alzheimers disease, *Eur J Pharmacol* 741:104–111, 2014.

Reichardt LF: Neurotrophin-regulated signalling pathways, *Philos Trans R Soc Lond B* 361:1545–1564, 2006.

Rocha de Paula M, Gomez Ravetti M, Berretta R, Moscato P: Differences in abundances of cell-signalling proteins in blood reveal novel biomarkers for early detection of clinical Alzheimer's disease, *PLoS One* 6:e17481, 2011.

Rockenstein E, Mallory M, Mante M, Sisk A, Masliaha E: Early formation of mature amyloid-beta protein deposits in a mutant APP transgenic model depends on levels of Abeta(1-42), *J Neurosci Res* 66:573–582, 2001.

Rohe M, Synowitz M, Glass R, Paul SM, Nykjaer A, Willnow TE: Brain-derived neurotrophic factor reduces amyloidogenic processing through control of SORLA gene expression, *J Neurosci* 29:15472–15478, 2009.

Roux PP, Barker PA: Neurotrophin signaling through the p75 neurotrophin receptor, *Prog Neurobiol* 67:203–233, 2002.

Roux PP, Bhakar AL, Kennedy TE, Barker PA: The p75 neurotrophin receptor activates Akt (protein kinase B) through a phosphatidylinositol 3-kinase-dependent pathway, *J Biol Chem* 276:23097–23104, 2001.

Sachs BD, Akassoglou K: Regulation of cAMP by the p75 neurotrophin receptor: insight into drug design of selective phosphodiesterase inhibitors, *Biochem Soc Trans* 35:1273–1277, 2007.

Sachs BD, Baillie GS, McCall JR, Passino MA, Schachtrup C, Wallace DA, Dunlop AJ, MacKenzie KF, Klussmann E, Lynch MJ, Sikorski SL, Nuriel T, Tsigelny I, Zhang J, Houslay MD, Chao MV, Akassoglou K: P75 neurotrophin receptor regulates tissue fibrosis through inhibition of plasminogen activation via a PDE4/cAMP/PKA pathway, *J Cell Biol* 177:1119–1132, 2007.

Sah DW, Ossipo MH, Porreca F: Neurotrophic factors as novel therapeutics for neuropathic pain, *Nat Rev Drug Discov* 2:460–472, 2003.

Salehi A, Ocampo M, Verhaagen J, Swaab DF: P75 neurotrophin receptor in the nucleus basalis of Meynert in relation to age, sex, and Alzheimer's disease, *Exp Neurol* 161:245–258, 2000.

Salehi A, Verhaagen J, Dijkhuizen PA, Swaab DF: Co-localization of high-affinity neurotrophin receptors in nucleus basalis of Meynert neurons and their differential reduction in Alzheimer's disease, *Neuroscience* 75:373–387, 1996.

Saltzman WM, Mak MW, Mahoney MJ, Duenas ET, Cleland JL: Intracranial delivery of recombinant nerve growth factor: release kinetics and protein distribution for three delivery systems, *Pharm Res* 16:232–240, 1999.

Sanchez-Ortiz E, Yui D, Song D, Li Y, Rubenstein JL, Reichardt LF, Parada LF: TrkA gene ablation in basal forebrain results in dysfunction of the cholinergic circuitry, *J Neurosci* 32:4065–4079, 2012.

Savaskan E, Muller-Spahn F, Olivieri G, Bruttel S, Otten U, Rosenberg C, Hulette C, Hock C: Alterations in trk A, trk B and trk C receptor immunoreactivities in parietal cortex and cerebellum in Alzheimer's disease, *Eur Neurol* 44:172–180, 2000.

Scarpi D, Cirelli D, Matrone C, Castronovo G, Rosini P, Occhiato EG, Romano F, Bartali L, Clemente AM, Bottegoni G, Cavalli A, De Chiara G, Bonini P, Calissano P, Palamara AT, Garaci E, Torcia MG, Guarna A, Cozzolino F: Low molecular weight, non-peptidic agonists of TrkA receptor with NGF-mimetic activity, *Cell Death Dis* 3:e339, 2012.

Schmid DA, Yang T, Ogier M, Adams I, Mirakhur Y, Wang Q, Massa SM, Longo FM, Katz DM: A TrkB small molecule partial agonist rescues TrkB phosphorylation deficits and improves respiratory function in a mouse model of Rett syndrome, *J Neurosci* 32:1803–1810, 2012.

Selkoe DJ: Alzheimer's disease is a synaptic failure, *Science* 298:789–791, 2002.

Selkoe DJ: Defining molecular targets to prevent Alzheimer disease, *Arch Neurol* 62:192–195, 2005.

Shu XQ, Mendell LM: Neurotrophins and hyperalgesia, *Proc Natl Acad Sci USA* 96:7693–7696, 1999.

Silva AJ, Kogan JH, Frankland PW, Kida S: CREB and memory, *Ann Rev Neurosci* 21:127–148, 1998.

Simmons DA, Belichenko NP, Yang T, Condon C, Monbureau M, Shamloo M, Jing D, Massa SM, Longo FM: A small molecule TrkB ligand reduces motor impairment and neuropathology in R6/2 and BACHD mouse models of Huntington's disease, *J Neurosci* 33:18712–18727, 2013.

Simmons DA, Knowles JK, Belichenko NP, Banerjee G, Finkle C, Massa SM, Longo FM: A small molecule p75NTR ligand, LM11A-31, reverses cholinergic neurite dystrophy in Alzheimer's disease mouse models with mid- to late-stage disease progression, *PLoS One* 9:e102136, 2014.

Snyder EM, Nong Y, Almeida CG, Paul S, Moran T, Choi EY, Nairn AC, Salter MW, Lombroso PJ, Gouras GK, Greengard P: Regulation of NMDA receptor trafficking by amyloid-beta, *Nat Neurosci* 8:1051–1058, 2005.

Sotthibundhu A, Sykes AM, Fox B, Underwood CK, Thangnipon W, Coulson EJ: Beta-amyloid(1-42) induces neuronal death through the p75 neurotrophin receptor, *J Neurosci* 28:3941–3946, 2008.

Strasser A, Skalicky M, Hansalik M, Viidik A: The impact of environment in comparison with moderate physical exercise and dietary restriction on BDNF in the cerebral parietotemporal cortex of aged Sprague-Dawley rats, *Gerontology* 52:377–381, 2006.

Suen PC, Wu K, Levine ES, Mount HT, Xu JL, Lin SY, Black IB: Brain-derived neurotrophic factor rapidly enhances phosphorylation of the postsynaptic N-methyl-D-aspartate receptor subunit 1, *Proc Natl Acad Sci USA* 94:8191–8195, 1997.

Sui WH, Huang SH, Wang J, Chen Q, Liu T, Chen ZY: Myosin Va mediates BDNF-induced postendocytic recycling of full-length TrkB and its translocation into dendritic spines, *J Cell Sci* 128:1108–1122, 2015.

Sun X, Chen WD, Wang YD: Beta-amyloid: the key peptide in the pathogenesis of Alzheimer's disease, *Front Pharmacol* 6:221, 2015.

Takei N, Kawamura M, Hara K, Yonezawa K, Nawa H: Brain-derived neurotrophic factor enhances neuronal translation by activating multiple initiation processes: comparison with the effects of insulin, *J Biol Chem* 276:42818–42825, 2001.

Tanaka J, Horiike Y, Matsuzaki M, Miyazaki T, Ellis-Davies GC, Kasai H: Protein synthesis and neurotrophin-dependent structural plasticity of single dendritic spines, *Science* 319:1683–1687, 2008.

Tapia-Arancibia L, Aliaga E, Silhol M, Arancibia S: New insights into brain BDNF function in normal aging and Alzheimer disease, *Brain Res Rev* 59:201–220, 2008.

Teipel SJ, Flatz WH, Heinsen H, Bokde AL, Schoenberg SO, Stockel S, Dietrich O, Reiser MF, Moller HJ, Hampel H: Measurement of basal forebrain atrophy in Alzheimer's disease using MRI, *Brain* 128:2626–2644, 2005.

Tep C, Lim TH, Ko PO, Getahun S, Ryu JC, Goettl VM, Massa SM, Basso M, Longo FM, Yoon SO: Oral administration of a small molecule targeted to block proNGF binding to p75 promotes myelin sparing and functional recovery after spinal cord injury, *J Neurosci* 33:397–410, 2013.

Terry RD, Masliah E, Salmon DP, Butters N, DeTeresa R, Hill R, Hansen LA, Katzman R: Physical basis of cognitive alterations in Alzheimer's disease: synapse loss is the major correlate of cognitive impairment, *Ann Neurol* 30:572–580, 1991.

Tong L, Balazs R, Thornton PL, Cotman CW: Beta-amyloid peptide at sublethal concentrations downregulates brain-derived neurotrophic factor functions in cultured cortical neurons, *J Neurosci* 24:6799–6809, 2004.

Tong L, Thornton PL, Balazs R, Cotman CW: Beta-amyloid-(1-42) impairs activity-dependent cAMP-response element-binding protein signaling in neurons at concentrations in which cell survival is not compromised, *J Biol Chem* 276:17301–17306, 2001.

Treanor JJ, Dawbarn D, Allen SJ, MacGowan SH, Wilcock GK: Low affinity nerve growth factor receptor binding in normal and Alzheimer's disease basal forebrain, *Neurosci Lett* 121:73–76, 1991.

Tsai SJ, Hong CJ, Liu HC, Liu TY, Hsu LE, Lin CH: Association analysis of brain-derived neurotrophic factor Val66Met polymorphisms with Alzheimer's disease and age of onset, *Neuropsychobiology* 49:10–12, 2004.

Tuszynski MH, Yang JH, Barba D, U HS, Bakay RA, Pay MM, Masliah E, Conner JM, Kobalka P, Roy S, Nagahara AH: Nerve growth factor gene therapy: activation of neuronal responses in Alzheimer disease, *JAMA Neurol* 72:1139–1147, 2015.

Ubhi K, Masliah E: Alzheimer's disease: recent advances and future perspectives, *J Alzheimers Dis* 33(Suppl 1):S185–S194, 2013.

Vana L, Kanaan NM, Ugwu IC, Wuu J, Mufson EJ, Binder LI: Progression of tau pathology in cholinergic basal forebrain neurons in mild cognitive impairment and Alzheimer's disease, *Am J Pathol* 179:2533–2550, 2011.

Vega JA, Vazquez E, Naves FJ, Del Valle ME, Calzada B, Represa JJ: Immunohistochemical localization of the high-affinity NGF receptor (gp140-trkA) in the adult human dorsal root and sympathetic ganglia and in the nerves and sensory corpuscles supplying digital skin, *Anat Rec* 240:579–588, 1994.

Vitolo OV, Sant'Angelo A, Costanzo V, Battaglia F, Arancio O, Shelanski M: Amyloid beta-peptide inhibition of the PKA/CREB pathway and long-term potentiation: reversibility by drugs that enhance cAMP signaling, *Proc Natl Acad Sci USA* 99:13217–13221, 2002.

Volinsky N, Kholodenko BN: Complexity of receptor tyrosine kinase signal processing, *Cold Spring Harb Perspect Biol* 5:a009043, 2013.

Volonte C, Angelastro JM, Greene LA: Association of protein kinases ERK1 and ERK2 with p75 nerve growth factor receptors, *J Biol Chem* 268:21410–21415, 1993.

von Bernhardi R: Immunotherapy in Alzheimer's disease: where do we stand? Where should we go? *J Alzheimers Dis* 19:405–421, 2010.

von Bohlen und Halbach O, Krause S, Medina D, Sciarretta C, Minichiello L, Unsicker K: Regional- and age-dependent reduction in trkB receptor expression in the hippocampus is associated with altered spine morphologies, *Biol Psychiatr* 59:793–800, 2006.

Wang J, Hancock MK, Dudek JM, Bi K: Cellular assays for high-throughput screening for modulators of Trk receptor tyrosine kinases, *Curr Chem Genomics* 1:27–33, 2008.

Webster MJ, Herman MM, Kleinman JE, Shannon Weickert C: BDNF and trkB mRNA expression in the hippocampus and temporal cortex during the human lifespan, *Gene Expr Patterns* 6:941–951, 2006.

Westergaard UB, Sorensen ES, Hermey G, Nielsen MS, Nykjaer A, Kirkegaard K, Jacobsen C, Gliemann J, Madsen P, Petersen CM: Functional organization of the sortilin Vps10p domain, *J Biol Chem* 279:50221–50229, 2004.

Woo NH, Teng HK, Siao CJ, Chiaruttini C, Pang PT, Milner TA, Hempstead BL, Lu B: Activation of p75NTR by proBDNF facilitates hippocampal long-term depression, *Nat Neurosci* 8:1069–1077, 2005.

Wu Y, Luo X, Liu X, Liu D, Wang X, Guo Z, Zhu L, Tian Q, Yang X, Wang JZ: Intraperitoneal administration of a novel TAT-BDNF peptide ameliorates cognitive impairments via modulating multiple pathways in two Alzheimer's rodent models, *Sci Rep* 5:15032, 2015.

Yamada K, Nabeshima T: Brain-derived neurotrophic factor/TrkB signaling in memory processes, *J Pharmacol Sci* 91:267–270, 2003.

Yamashita T, Tucker KL, Barde YA: Neurotrophin binding to the p75 receptor modulates Rho activity and axonal outgrowth, *Neuron* 24:585–593, 1999.

Yamuy J, Sampogna S, Chase MH: Neurotrophin-receptor immunoreactive neurons in mesopontine regions involved in the control of behavioral states, *Brain Res* 866:1–14, 2000.

Yang T, Knowles JK, Lu Q, Zhang H, Arancio O, Moore LA, Chang T, Wang Q, Andreasson K, Rajadas J, Fuller GG, Xie Y, Massa SM, Longo FM: Small molecule, non-peptide p75 ligands inhibit Abeta-induced neurodegeneration and synaptic impairment, *PLoS One* 3:e3604, 2008.

Yasutake C, Kuroda K, Yanagawa T, Okamura T, Yoneda H: Serum BDNF, TNF-alpha and IL-1beta levels in dementia patients: comparison between Alzheimer's disease and vascular dementia, *Eur Arch Psychiatr Clin Neurosci* 256:402–406, 2006.

Ye K: 7,8-Dihydoxyflavone and 7,8-substituted flavone derivatives, compositions, and methods related thereto, Google Patents, 2014.

Yoshida H, Hastie CJ, McLauchlan H, Cohen P, Goedert M: Phosphorylation of microtubule-associated protein tau by isoforms of c-Jun N-terminal kinase (JNK), *J Neurochem* 90:352–358, 2004.

Yu H, Zhang Z, Shi Y, Bai F, Xie C, Qian Y, Yuan Y, Deng L: Association study of the decreased serum BDNF concentrations in amnestic mild cognitive impairment and the Val66Met polymorphism in Chinese Han, *J Clin Psychiatr* 69:1104–1111, 2008.

Zhang Q, Descamps O, Hart MJ, Poksay KS, Spilman P, Kane DJ, Gorostiza O, John V, Bredesen DE: Paradoxical effect of TrkA inhibition in Alzheimer's disease models, *J Alzheimers Dis* 40:605–617, 2014a.

Zhang Z, Liu X, Schroeder JP, Chan CB, Song M, Yu SP, Weinshenker D, Ye K: 7,8-Dihydroxyflavone prevents synaptic loss and memory deficits in a mouse model of Alzheimer's disease, *Neuropsychopharmacology* 39:638–650, 2014b.

Zhang L, Fang Y, Lian Y, Chen Y, Wu T, Zheng Y, Zong H, Sun L, Zhang R, Wang Z, Xu Y: Brain-derived neurotrophic factor ameliorates learning deficits in a rat model of Alzheimer's disease induced by abeta1-42, *PLoS One* 10:e0122415, 2015a.

Zhang L, Fang Y, Xu Y, Lian Y, Xie N, Wu T, Zhang H, Sun L, Zhang R, Wang Z: Curcumin improves amyloid beta-peptide (1-42) induced spatial memory deficits through BDNF-ERK signaling pathway, *PLoS One* 10:e0131525, 2015b.

Zhang X, Hernandez I, Rei D, Mair W, Laha JK, Cornwell ME, Cuny GD, Tsai LH, Steen JA, Kosik KS: Diaminothiazoles modify tau phosphorylation and improve the tauopathy in mouse models, *J Biol Chem* 288:22042–22056, 2013.

Zhang F, Kang Z, Li W, Xiao Z, Zhou X: Roles of brain-derived neurotrophic factor/tropomyosin-related kinase B (BDNF/TrkB) signalling in Alzheimer's disease, *J Clin Neurosci* 19:946–949, 2012.

Zhang J, Sokal I, Peskind ER, Quinn JF, Jankovic J, Kenney C, Chung KA, Millard SP, Nutt JG, Montine TJ: CSF multianalyte profile distinguishes Alzheimer and Parkinson diseases, *Am J Clin Pathol* 129:526–529, 2008.

Zhou W, Li X, Huang D, Zhou W, Li T, Song W: No significant effect of 7,8-dihydroxyflavone on APP processing and Alzheimer-associated phenotypes, *Curr Alzheimer Res* 12:47–52, 2015.

Zhou XF, Rush RA: Functional roles of neurotrophin 3 in the developing and mature sympathetic nervous system, *Mol Neurobiol* 13:185–197, 1996.

CHAPTER

17

Symptomatic Cognitive Enhancing Agents

J.L. Cummings, K. Zhong

OUTLINE

Developing Therapeutics for Alzheimer's Disease. http://dx.doi.org/10.1016/B978-0-12-802173-6.00017-4

Alzheimer's disease (AD) and other dementing disorders are increasing at a rapid rate as the global population ages. Cognitive decline is the principal aspect of dementia syndromes. There is an urgent need to develop both symptomatic cognitive enhancing agents with improved efficacy as well as disease-modifying therapies (DMTs) that delay the onset or slow the progression of the disease.

Two classes of symptomatic cognitive enhancing agents have been approved for use in dementia syndromes—cholinesterase inhibitors and the *N*-methyl-D-aspartate (NMDA) receptor antagonist memantine; these are the only treatments known to be effective for dementing disorders. No DMTs have been developed successfully for neurodegenerative diseases. There are numerous clinical trials in process to develop both symptomatic cognitive enhancing agents and DMTs. In the decade 2002–2012, symptomatic agents represented 36.6% of the trials executed worldwide and captured on www.clinicaltrials.gov. Disease-modifying small molecules were tested in 35.1% of the trials, and disease-modifying immunotherapies in 18% (Cummings et al., 2014). Symptomatic therapy development is a robust aspect of drug development for AD.

In this chapter, we will concentrate on symptomatic cognitive enhancing agents being developed for AD. Contrasts to DMT programs and extension of cognitive enhancement from AD to other dementing disorders will be noted.

DEFINITION OF "SYMPTOMATIC" TREATMENT

The definition of "symptomatic" is somewhat controversial, and there are uncertainties regarding the meaning of the dichotomy between symptomatic and disease-modifying treatments. The word "symptomatic" is usually accepted to mean that the patient experiences cognitive improvement above baseline and that the intervention does not alter the underlying disease process leading to cell death. "Symptomatic" is contrasted with disease-modifying interventions from which the patient has a clinical response (usually conceived as slower decline compared to a matched placebo group without improvement above baseline) and there is a corresponding impact on the underlying disease process leading to cell death.

An impact on the underlying cell death processes can only be inferred and is not directly observed in human trials. Meeting a definition of disease modification depends on inferential data from a biomarker or a set of biomarkers. The role of biomarkers in supporting these definitions creates uncertainty. There is no regulatory guidance as to what data are needed to support a biomarker-based inference about disease modification. Biomarkers might also be less sensitive than clinical measures in some trials, or a collection of multiple biomarkers might not give consistent information regarding disease modification. In these cases, the labeling of the agent will likely be "for the treatment of AD" exactly as it is for symptomatic agents. From the regulatory perspective, labeling of a drug is less reflective of the putative mechanism of action of the agent and is determined by the outcomes of the measures included in the trial.

Symptomatic agents are disease course modifying even if they do not change the underlying disease process of neuronal loss. Mohs et al. (2001), for example, showed that donepezil, a symptomatic agent, delays predefined milestones in loss of activities of daily living (ADLs). This study also showed that a symptomatic response may be characterized primarily by delaying decline rather than improvement above baseline. A delay-to-milestone clinical trial design cannot distinguish between symptomatic and DMT effects. The course of the disease is altered by delaying decline, even though the biological criteria for disease modification are not met.

Natural history studies suggest that combination treatment with a cholinesterase inhibitor and memantine may slow the expected course of cognitive decline (Atri et al., 2013; Rountree et al., 2013). Whether this effect is mediated by an impact on neuronal death processes or results from better preservation of function and ability to participate in brain-preserving cognitive and physical engagement is unknown.

Another area of challenge in distinguishing between disease modification and symptomatic responses is the possibility that some disease-modifying agents may produce symptomatic responses. Effective intervention in removing cytotoxic proteins, restoring mitochondrial function, or achieving neuroprotection may allow recovery of dysfunctional but not moribund cell populations with a corresponding recovery of deficits. Improvement of cognitive performance in animal models treated with disease-modifying types of agents is well established (Tong et al., 2014; Yu et al., 2014). If this also occurs in patients with AD, then combined symptomatic and disease-modifying responses might occur together in patients treated with DMTs. The possible dual activity suggests that the symptomatic/disease-modification distinction may be arbitrary.

These observations indicate that the distinction between symptomatic and disease-modifying responses is not sharp, especially as seen from clinical trials and regulatory approval perspectives. DMT development programs are defined by agents with mechanisms of action that impact pathophysiology and cell death; these effects may not be demonstrable in clinical trials. All AD clinical trials use similar outcomes and trial designs, making it difficult to distinguish among drug mechanisms from a clinical trial outcome perspective.

The label of disease modification may be more important to basic science efforts or the pharmaceutical industry than for patients, families, or practicing physicians. The latter are interested in improving existing symptoms or delaying decline of cognition and function; these may be more compatible with symptomatic responses than with disease modification. The principal promise of disease modification from a patient perspective is that onset of symptoms could be deferred or the progression of disease significantly slowed for longer periods of time than with symptomatic interventions, keeping the patient functioning at a higher level for a longer period of time. Supporting these goals will require data from multiple clinical trials collected from different types of interventions across multiple stages of AD. Use of combinations of DMTs and symptomatic agents is anticipated and may best facilitate optimal patient management.

ADVANTAGES OF SYMPTOMATIC DRUG DEVELOPMENT

There are many advantages for academic investigators, federal agencies, biotechnology companies, and pharmaceutical sponsors to engage in the development of symptomatic agents for cognitive enhancement (Table 17.1). The only approved drugs for treatment of dementing disorders are symptomatic agents; these establish a model for clinical trial, biomarker, regulatory, and market approaches to drug development. Much less is known about development of DMTs and there is much greater uncertainty in DMT drug development programs.

TABLE 17.1 Comparison of Drug Development Programs for Symptomatic Cognitive Enhancing Agents and Disease-Modifying Therapies (DMTs)

Trial feature	Symptomatic	Disease-modifying
Precedent established	Approved agents to model	No approved agents to model
Outcome of the trial	Symptom reduction	Delay of onset or slowing of progression
Trial duration	Shorter trials (3–6 months)	Longer trials (12–36 months)
Trial size	Smaller trials (100–400 per arm)	Larger trials (600–1000 per arm)
Experience with trial instruments	Trial instrument performance known	Trial instrument performance unknown (eg, in patients with prodromal AD or in prevention trials; one had progressed to FDA approval)
Role of biomarkers	Biomarker role limited (eg, patient selection, receptor occupancy)	Biomarker role critical (risk genes, diagnosis, target engagement, outcome, safety monitoring)
Experience with populations	Familiar populations (mild-to-severe AD dementia)	Unfamiliar populations (individuals with normal cognition at risk for AD; prodromal AD)
Experience with targets	Familiar targets (eg, enzymes, receptors, channels, transporters)	Unfamiliar targets (eg, protein–protein interactions, cell-to-cell transmission)
Experience with formulations	Familiar delivery modalities (eg, oral, patch)	Unfamiliar delivery modalities (eg, intravenous monoclonal antibodies)
Cost of drug development	Less expensive	More expensive
Experience with payers	Approach to reimbursement known	Approach to reimbursement unknown
Regulatory history	Known regulatory pathway	Unknown regulatory pathway
Placebo response in trials	Placebo responses common	Placebo responses limited

Trials for symptomatic cognitive enhancing drugs tend to be shorter (3–6 months) than clinical trials for DMTs that are usually 12–24 months in duration. Trials for symptomatic cognitive enhancing agents also tend to be smaller (100–400 subjects per arm) than clinical trials for DMTs where there are typically 400–1000 subjects per arm. Shorter, smaller trials tend to be less expensive than longer, larger trials, and the cost of drug development for symptomatic agents is substantially less than the cost of clinical trials for DMTs.

In symptomatic drug development programs, the goal of treatment is cognitive improvement. Trials are relatively short and improvement above baseline is the usual outcome measured. In short trials, there is relatively little cognitive decline in the placebo group; most of the drug–placebo difference is generated by improvement in cognition above baseline, with little contribution from placebo decline below baseline. In the development of DMTs, trials are longer and the drug–placebo difference is generated nearly entirely through the greater decline in the placebo group compared to the treatment group. There is decline in the active treatment group, but it is less marked than in the placebo group.

Biomarkers play different roles in trials for symptomatic agents than for DMTs (see later discussion of biomarkers). Biomarkers have several roles in DMT drug development. Trait biomarkers, such as genetics, may be used for subject selection or trial stratification. The apolipoprotein E epsilon 4 (ApoE4) genotype, for example, increases the risk for AD, decreases the age of onset of AD, and accelerates the speed of cognitive decline in the prodromal phases of AD. Thus, stratification by ApoE genotype is common to facilitate analysis of trial data. An amyloid burden on amyloid imaging, or presence of an AD signature in the cerebrospinal fluid (CSF), may be used for subject identification in prevention trials or in prodromal AD trials. Biomarkers also improve the subject selection for AD dementia trials. Target engagement biomarkers are used in DMT clinical trials to demonstrate that the near-term effects of the agent are those desired. An example of a target engagement biomarker is the measurement of secretase enzyme inhibition through dynamic spinal fluid measures of amyloid beta protein (Aβ) synthesis and clearance (Bateman et al., 2006). Biomarkers have a critical role as disease outcome measures in DMT clinical trials. The standard for disease modification is to show an effect on the primary clinical outcome as well as on a biomarker reflecting maintenance of neuronal integrity in the active treatment group compared to the placebo group. A drug–placebo difference in favor of one or more biomarkers at study conclusion is key evidence in support of disease modification. Finally, biomarkers have been important in DMT trials to monitor adverse events such as amyloid-related imaging abnormalities (ARIAs) of the effusion (ARIA-E) or hemorrhagic (ARIA-H) type (Sperling et al., 2011).

In symptomatic drug development programs, biomarkers may be used to determine blood–brain penetration, receptor occupancy, and dose–response effects (Kadir et al., 2008). As with DMT drug development, biomarkers can also be used for subject selection to ensure that patient populations used in symptomatic trials have the underlying neuropathology of AD. Downstream effects such as cerebral blood flow (CBF) and glucose metabolism may also be used to ensure target engagement (discussed later).

There is much more experience with clinical outcomes in trials with cognitive enhancing agents than with clinical trials with DMTs. Cognitive enhancing drugs are used in symptomatic patients and standard clinical trial instruments such as the Alzheimer's Disease Assessment Scale—Cognitive Subscale (ADAS-Cog), Alzheimer's Disease Cooperative Study (ADCS) ADL scale, or Clinical Interview Based Impression of Change with Caregiver Input (CIBIC+) are tools whose psychometric properties and performance in clinical trials are well understood. DMT trials are often implemented in trial populations of patients with milder symptoms where there is much less experience with clinical measurements and much less certainty about sensitivity to change, psychometric properties, and performance in clinical trials. This increases the risk of drug development for DMTs.

Clinical trials of cognitive enhancing symptomatic agents have used familiar trial populations, mostly patients with mild, moderate, or severe AD. Clinical trials of DMTs have expanded to include unfamiliar populations such as prevention trials of individuals who are cognitively normal but are at increased risk for AD or populations of patients with prodromal AD who manifest episodic memory impairment and have a biomarker indicative of the presence of AD but do not meet criteria for AD dementia. The speed of progression, heterogeneity of progression, and performance of cognitive measures and biomarkers in these unfamiliar populations are less predictable and increase the risk in drug development programs.

The targets of cognitive enhancing drug development programs (see later discussion) are more familiar in the neuroscience arena than are the targets of therapy of DMT clinical trials. The targets addressed in symptomatic cognitive enhancing trials include ion channels, transmitter receptors, and transmitter transporters as well as well-known enzymes such as acetylcholinesterase. The pharmacokinetics, feedback loops, and pharmaceutical properties of these targets and small molecules that interact with them are better understood than those addressed by DMTs where protein–protein interactions and cell-to-cell transmission of proteins are evolving as major targets. Delivery systems are also more familiar in symptomatic therapies where oral agents and transdermal delivery of drugs are relatively well understood compared to unfamiliar approaches such as monoclonal antibodies in clinical trials of DMTs.

The regulatory pathway for symptomatic treatments is well understood, with five agents approved for treatment of AD and one agent approved for Parkinson's disease (PD) dementia. The dual-outcome criteria required by the US Food and Drug Administration (FDA) include the ADAS-Cog and a global (such as the CIBIC+) or functional (ADCS-ADL or Disability Assessment for Dementia [DAD]) measure are well understood. The labeling approach and requirements for approval have been defined by successful drug development programs. In contrast, there are no approved DMTs, and requirements eventually exerted by the FDA for clinical and biomarker outcomes for labeling as a DMT are uncertain.

The response of payers to newly introduced dementia therapies has also been explored with cognitive enhancing agents and not with DMTs. The payers currently cover the generic forms of cholinesterase inhibitors as a Tier 1 drug class that is readily available to nearly all symptomatic patients. No DMT has been approved by the FDA or funded by any payer, and the requirements for reimbursement, the approaches to copayments, and the degree of slowing of decline considered clinically relevant by payers remain to be defined.

One aspect of drug development that is problematic for cognitive enhancing agents and less of a challenge for DMTs is the presence of placebo responses in cognitive enhancer trials. This may be a combination of patient placebo effect, caregiver placebo effect, practice effects, and clinical trial participation benefit. Behavioral improvements are particularly marked among placebo groups in clinical trials, and this may rebound to enhance cognitive performance on commonly used cognitive assessments. Clinical trials of cognitive enhancing agents must be planned with anticipation of placebo effects.

TARGETS FOR SYMPTOMATIC COGNITIVE ENHANCING AGENTS

Approved Symptomatic Therapies

Multiple targets are being considered for symptomatic drug development (Fig. 17.1). Successful symptomatic drug development programs have been built around facilitating cholinergic and glutamatergic function (Zemek et al., 2014). Cholinesterase inhibitors block acetylcholinesterase, increasing residence times for acetylcholine in the synaptic cleft, improving the opportunity for acetylcholine to interact with postsynaptic receptors, and increasing the postsynaptic cholinergic signal. This intervention is based on the observations of loss of cholinergic neurons in the nucleus basalis of Meynert and compromise of the presynaptic cholinergic system with concomitant preservation of the postsynaptic cholinergic system for much of the disease course (Whitehouse, 1998). The presynaptic abnormality and relatively intact postsynaptic system are a unique circumstance that is not recapitulated with most other transmitter systems; it may be more difficult to induce a similarly beneficial response with these

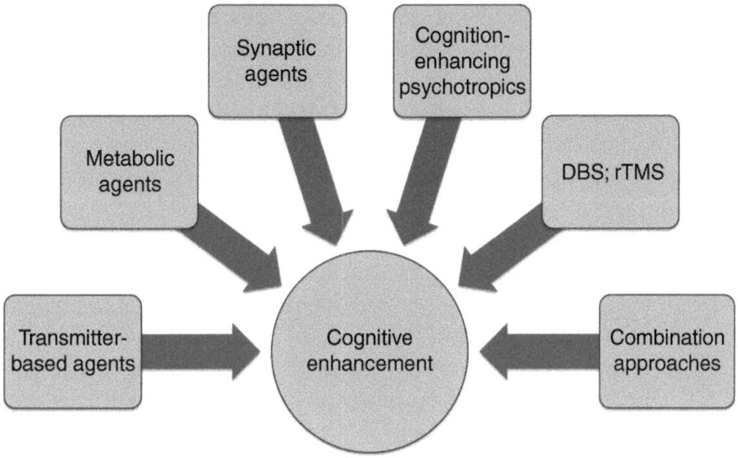

FIGURE 17.1 **Approaches currently used to achieve cognitive enhancement in Alzheimer's disease.** *DBS*, deep brain stimulation; *rTMS*, repetitive transcranial magnetic stimulation.

other systems. There are four approved cholinesterase inhibitors, three of which are actively marketed (donepezil, rivastigmine, and galantamine; tacrine is approved but rarely used).

Memantine is a competitive inhibitor of the NMDA receptor, where it competes with magnesium in the ion channel. It is easily displaced by physiological signals and is hypothesized to improve the transmitter signal-to-noise ratio, enhancing the postsynaptic glutamatergic signal (Parsons et al., 2013). In laboratory studies, memantine has neuroprotective properties (Olivares et al., 2012); these have not been supported by biomarker outcomes in clinical trials (Wilkinson et al., 2012).

Cholinesterase inhibitors and memantine are commonly used together as a dual symptomatic therapy. A fixed dose combination of the two agents has been approved (Namzaric™).

Symptomatic Treatments in Phase 3 Trials

The potential therapeutic benefits of normalizing function in a variety of other transmitter systems to improve symptoms of AD are under study. Two approaches that have reached phase 3 trials are the alpha-7 nicotinic acid agonist, encenicline (Deardorff et al., 2014, 2015; Thomsen et al., 2010), and the serotonin 5-HT_6 antagonist, idalopirdine (Wilkinson et al., 2014). Both of these compounds have positive phase 2 trials with significant drug–placebo differences on the primary outcome measure.

Symptomatic Treatments in Early Clinical Development

A variety of other transmitter systems that have deficits in AD are being explored as possible therapeutic targets. Histaminergic systems are affected and have an important influence on alertness, arousal, and attention. Histamine H_3 receptor antagonists are being explored as possible therapeutic interventions (Grove et al., 2014; Haig et al., 2014). Trials of these agents have not shown consistent benefit; further studies are anticipated.

Phosphodiesterase (PDE) inhibitors increase cAMP augmenting energy sources and may have additional effects such as reducing inflammation. Included among the PDE inhibitors of interest in AD are inhibitors of PDE1, 2, 4, 5, 7, and 9 (Devan et al., 2014; Garcia-Barroso et al., 2014; Gurney et al., 2014; Heckman et al., 2014). These PDEs have been tested in animal models with promising results; a few have been extended to early human trials with inconsistent outcomes. Repurposing PDE5 inhibitors currently approved for erectile dysfunction may present a developmental pathway for these agents.

Cannabinoid 1 (CB_1) receptor antagonists are being tested in animal models of AD mechanisms and may progress to human clinical trials (de Bruin et al., 2010). Paradoxically, however, CB_1 agonists also improve memory in some rodent models of AD (Aso and Ferrer, 2014; Aso et al., 2012), and the balance of effects of CB_1 agonism and antagonism requires clarification.

Monoamine oxidase (MAO) B inhibitors such as rasagiline have multiple central nervous system (CNS) effects and may have neuroprotective and cognitive enhancing effects (Youdim, 2006). Clinical trials of rasagiline in AD are being pursued.

Metabolic Agents

Agents that affect neuronal metabolism may have both neuroprotective and cognitive enhancing effects. Insulin resistance occurs in AD, an observation leading to trials of insulin and insulin-sensitizing agents (Dineley et al., 2014; Freiherr et al., 2013). Preliminary proof-of-concept trials support the concept that insulin improves memory in individuals with AD and mild cognitive impairment (MCI) (Claxton et al., 2014).

Peroxisome proliferator-activated receptor gamma (PPAR-gamma) agonists such as the thiazolidinediones (eg, rosiglitazone, pioglitazone) improve insulin sensitivity and may represent additional noninsulin approaches to neuronal insulin resistance in AD (Xiang et al., 2012). Metformin and liraglutide are among other insulin-sensitizing agents being studied in rodent models or have advanced to human trials of AD (Yarchoan and Arnold, 2014).

Alternatives to glucose as metabolic substrates for neuronal metabolism are also being explored as a means of enhancing cognition. Beta-hydroxybutyrate derived from the medical food Axona produced ketones that can be used for neuronal metabolism (Reger et al., 2004). This agent has been assessed in preliminary clinical trials and is being assessed in additional trials. Initial trials demonstrated cognitive benefits in patients who did not carry an ApoE4 allele.

Mitochondrial enhancing agents that increase mitochondrial respiration may have both neuroprotective and cognitive enhancing properties (Gonzalez-Lima et al., 2014). These drugs constitute a class of bioenergetic compounds that enhance mitochondrial function in energy production and function as antioxidants with improved capture of free radicals, decreasing oxidative stress at the mitochondrial level. Reduced oxidative injury is a neuroprotective approach in AD and other neurodegenerative disorders. Mitochondrial dysfunction may precede amyloid deposition and facilitate the amyloid cascade and well as lead to cell death and dysfunction (Swerdlow et al., 2014). Dimebon (latrepirdine), derived from antihistamines, was a putative mitochondrial enhancer that failed in clinical trials but has stimulated a search for effective mitochondrial agents (Bharadwaj et al., 2013; Shevtsova et al., 2014). Thiazolidinediones such as rosiglitazone and pioglitazone may improve mitochondrial function as well as functioning as insulin sensitizers.

Psychotropic Agents With Cognitive Enhancing Properties

A new developmental pathway involves agents that have psychotropic as well as cognitive enhancing activities. Vortioxetine, for example, appears to improve cognition and depression in patients with major depressive disorder (Pehrson et al., 2014). It is an agent with pleiotropic transmitter effects, including functioning as 5-HT_3, 5-HT_7, and 5-HT_{1D} receptor antagonist, 5-HT_{1B} receptor partial agonist, 5-HT_{1A} receptor agonist, and 5-HT transporter inhibitor. Such agents might be useful in AD or in AD with mood changes, and clinical trials of agents with these properties are progressing. In trials of this type of dual-function agent with behavioral and cognitive effects, the behavioral outcome might function as a coprimary outcome, substituting for a global or functional measure used in typical clinical trials for AD (discussed later).

Other agent classes that may have both psychotropic and cognitive enhancing properties include M1 muscarinic agonists, $5HT_6$ antagonists, NMDA receptor antagonists, PDE inhibitors, and histaminergic H_3 antagonists.

Synaptic Support Interventions

Synapses are compromised early in the course of AD, and loss of synapses correlates with the degree of cognitive impairment (Arendt, 2009; Spires-Jones and Hyman, 2014). Therapies that maintain or regenerate synapses could be promising interventions for treatment and may produce cognitive benefit or cognitive enhancement.

Pathological reduction of protein kinase C (PKC) epsilon in AD correlates with loss of synapses and impaired memory function in rodent models of AD. Increase in PKC epsilon with agents such as bryostatin is being explored as a means of maintaining synaptic integrity and enhancing memory function (Hongpaisan et al., 2011).

The medical food Souvenaid comprises a combination of elements designed to optimize synaptic function, including eicosapentaenoic acid (EPA), docosahexaenoic acid (DHA), phospholipids, choline, uridine monophosphate, and antioxidant vitamins. A placebo-controlled trial showed improved memory function (Olde Rikkert et al., 2014; Scheltens et al., 2012).

Combination Therapies

Impacting more than one signaling pathway in AD may optimize the opportunity to produce a beneficial effect on memory and cognition (Bansal and Silakari, 2014). Ladostigil, for example, is the combination of a cholinesterase inhibitor and a MAO B inhibitor that is being studied in AD clinical trials (Weinreb et al., 2012). Combinations may have additive or synergistic effects that produce greater or more enduring cognitive enhancement than single-agent approaches.

Devices

Devices are a means of therapeutic intervention that are not drug treatments. Deep brain stimulation (DBS) is being investigated as a means of enhancing cognition through transmitter release and increased neuroplasticity (Hescham et al., 2013). Several DBS targets have been explored, including cholinergic system nuclei (nucleus basalis of Meynert). Repetitive transcranial magnetic stimulation (rTMS) is also being explored as an alternative technique for cognitive enhancement in early AD and MCI (Nardone et al., 2014). Combinations of rTMS and cognitive training are being studied as a means of enhancing the effect of either approach alone (Bentwich et al., 2011).

OUTCOMES FOR CLINICAL TRIALS OF COGNITIVE ENHANCING AGENTS

The first "modern" trials for AD were conducted for tacrine in 1992 (Davis et al., 1992; Farlow et al., 1992). These trials and other investigations of this first-generation cholinesterase inhibitor eventually led to its approval as the first anti-AD therapy. The methodology of these trials defined the approach and instrumentation that continue to be used in AD trials today. The primary cognitive outcome was the ADAS-Cog (Rosen et al., 1984). A global scale was also incorporated as a measure of clinical meaningfulness. There are several types of global outcomes; the instrument most commonly used for this purpose now is the Clinical Global Impression of Change (CGIC) (Schneider et al., 1997). The Mini Mental State Examination (MMSE) (Folstein et al., 1975) was used to define the severity of dementia for the population entering the clinical trial and as a secondary cognitive outcome. The MMSE continues to serve this role in trials of prodromal AD and AD dementia. An ADL scale is typically used to capture functional effects in a trial. The most commonly used instrument is the ADCS-ADL scale (Galasko et al., 1997). Finally, behavior is an important outcome in clinical trials, and behavioral changes were originally included in the ADAS as the ADAS-Non-Cog. More recently, behavioral changes in response to treatment are typically captured on the Neuropsychiatric Inventory (Cummings et al., 1994).

Four outcomes constitute the principal features of a contemporary clinical trial: measures of cognition, function, and behavior, as well as a global measure. The primary outcome is cognition; functional or global measures serve as coprimary outcomes. Cognitive assessments are considered measures of the core features of AD, and global or functional measures are used to reflect the clinical meaningfulness of an induced change. A statistically significant difference between drug and placebo on a global or functional measure is considered to be an indication of a meaningful difference.

The measurement approaches used in contemporary clinical trials are based on considerations linked to measuring a symptomatic benefit produced by a cholinesterase inhibitor. In many cases, the same tools continue to be used in trials of DMTs that have different therapeutic targets. It has not yet been demonstrated whether agents from different therapeutic classes will produce different profiles of cognitive change and whether other instruments may be better suited to capturing the cognitive impact of emerging DMTs or the cognitive changes associated with new evolving symptomatic therapies that have noncholinergic mechanisms of action.

CLINICAL TRIAL DESIGNS FOR COGNITIVE ENHANCING AGENTS

The classical clinical trial design for a cognitive enhancing agent is a double-blind, randomized, placebo-controlled, parallel-group trial. The duration of such trials can be from 3 to 12 months, with most registration-type trials being 6 months in duration. The principal outcome is the change from baseline in the placebo group compared to the change from baseline of the active therapy group. There is usually a minimum or no decline in a placebo group over a 6-month period, and symptomatic benefit is shown by improvement above baseline by the test agent.

Critical to the success of an AD clinical trial is the overall measurement characteristics of outcomes in the placebo group. On average, a placebo group is expected to decline by 4–6 points on the ADAS-Cog over a 12-month period. However, up to 25% of placebo patients decline by 1 point or less even in 18-month trials (Schneider and Sano, 2009). Placebo group trajectories are variable and stable; predictable performance of the placebo group on outcome instruments is usually not achieved until there are at least 100 patients in the placebo group.

Identifying the optimal population for clinical trials is a crucial aspect of research design. Recent studies, including amyloid imaging, show that a number of patients who meet clinical criteria for AD fail to have positive amyloid imaging, indicating that they do not have a substantial amyloid burden and presumably do not have classic AD. In a trial of bapineuzumab, for example, 6.5% of apolipoprotein E-epsilon 4 carriers had negative amyloid scans, and 36.1% of ApoE noncarriers had negative amyloid scans (Salloway et al., 2014). This indicates that a substantial number of patients entering AD clinical trials do not have the classic pathologic substrate associated with AD. This observation is very important in trials of DMTs, which are often aimed at amyloid protein; but the finding that many non-AD patients may be entering AD trials also has significance for other mechanisms, including symptomatic trials, since the underlying pathophysiology and response to treatment of amyloid-negative patients is uncertain.

BIOMARKERS IN COGNITIVE ENHANCING AGENT DRUG DEVELOPMENT

Biomarkers can play important roles in symptomatic drug development. These include patient identification, target engagement, and side effect monitoring. Symptomatic drug development programs would not use biomarkers as outcomes as would be the case in DMT programs. Patient selection can best be ensured through the use of amyloid imaging or the CSF profile characteristic of AD—low CSF Aβ and elevated CSF tau or phosphorylated tau (p-tau) (Dubois et al., 2014). These features are currently considered the most specific for the diagnosis of AD and can ensure that the AD substrate is present in the patients selected.

Biomarkers have an important role in demonstrating target engagement. These biomarkers can either show direct involvement of the target or show a closely linked downstream event of target engagement. An example of a direct target engagement in symptomatic drug development is demonstration of brain cholinesterase inhibition by cholinesterase inhibitors. Studies using positron emission tomography (PET) and an acetylcholinesterase tracer show an approximately 30–40% inhibition of CNS cholinesterase (Kaasinen et al., 2002; Kuhl et al., 2000; Shinotoh et al., 2001). These studies show that there is blood–brain barrier penetration, the target is effectively engaged, and the degree of inhibition can be pushed to higher levels if peripheral side effects allow. Such target engagement demonstration is critical to ensuring that the desired drug effect observed in models is being recapitulated in AD patients, that dosage extrapolation from animals produces effective responses in humans, and that blood–brain barrier penetration in humans is comparable to that observed in animal model systems.

Examples of a downstream measure that reflects target engagement in symptomatic drug development include increased CBF or cerebral glucose metabolism determined by PET and increased connectivity as assessed by functional magnetic resonance imaging. These types of downstream effects have been demonstrated following treatment with cholinesterase inhibitors (Li et al., 2012; Mega et al., 2001, 2005; Zaidel et al., 2012). Increased regional cerebral metabolism has also been seen following 10-week treatment with memantine (Sultzer et al., 2010).

Side effect monitoring using biomarkers typically involves assessing the impact of drugs on liver and cardiac function using liver enzymes and electrocardiogram (Amacher, 2010; Assis and Navarro, 2009; Ferri et al., 2013). Progress is being made in predictive toxicology using computational, systems biology, and pharmacogenetic approaches (Russell et al., 2013).

Biomarkers can also be applied at the preclinical level to help derisk the advancement of candidate compounds from animal to human testing. Cholinesterase inhibitors, for example, have been shown to reduce CNS cholinesterase activity in nonhuman primates to levels similar to those seen in humans (Tsukada et al., 2004). Receptor occupancy studies have been used in rodents to explore target effects in widely used laboratory species (Da Costa et al., 2013).

REGULATORY ASPECTS OF COGNITIVE ENHANCING DRUG DEVELOPMENT PROGRAMS

Guidelines for antidementia drug development require the use of dual outcomes—a cognitive measure to assess the effect on core cognitive and memory symptoms and a global or functional measure to assess the clinical meaningfulness of the intervention (Leber and USFDA, 1990). The ADAS-Cog (Rosen et al., 1984) is the most widely used cognitive outcome. Recently, the Neuropsychological Test Battery has been used in addition to or instead of the ADAS-Cog (Harrison et al., 2007). The CGIC is the global measure most commonly used in trials of symptomatic drug development (Schneider et al., 1997), and the ADCS-ADL scale is a frequently used measure of function (Galasko et al., 1997).

Recently, the FDA suggested that a single primary outcome will be allowable in clinical trials of patients with prodromal AD (US Food and Drug Administration, 2013). The FDA indicated that the Clinical Dementia Rating (Morris, 1993) might function in this role, and alternatives such as the AD Composite Score are being developed.

Symptomatic drugs may be of less importance in prodromal AD than DMTs. The symptoms are mild and not severely disabling; improvement in this population would require very large sample sizes since the patients are nearly normal. This stage of the disease also progresses slowly, making a delay to milestone design difficult to implement (Wilkosz et al., 2010). Symptomatic agents are likely to continue to find their greatest application in patients with mild, moderate, or severe AD.

COGNITIVE ENHANCING DRUG DEVELOPMENT PROGRAMS

Stages of Alzheimer's Disease

Drug development programs for symptomatic agents commonly begin with patients in mild-to-moderate AD with MMSE scores in the range of 12–24 and using the ADAS-Cog as the principal measure of the core cognitive deficits. Once efficacy is established in this population, determination of the effects in moderate to severe AD is a common next step. This developmental course was followed for donepezil and rivastigmine (Cummings et al., 2012; Farlow et al., 2010). The instrument used in clinical trials involving more severe AD dementia patients is the Severe Impairment Battery (Schmitt et al., 1997). Symptomatic agents have been tested in MCI, but none have yet shown effects in this population (Jelic et al., 2006).

Non-Alzheimer Indications for Symptomatic Alzheimer Therapies

Once benefit has been established in AD, other conditions with similar pathophysiologies relevant to the drug mechanism can be included in expanded drug development programs. Rivastigmine, a cholinesterase inhibitor, for example, was tested and approved for PD dementia after approval for AD dementia (Emre et al., 2004). PD dementia has a cholinergic deficit comparable to that of AD, linking it pathologically and mechanistically to AD and cholinesterase inhibitors.

Symptomatic agents developed for AD are being assessed for trials in other related disorders such as Down syndrome, fragile X syndrome, autism spectrum disorders, multiple sclerosis, traumatic brain injury, and others.

Alternate Formulations

Drugs may be delivered as oral, transdermal, intravenous, or subcutaneous formulations. Development of one formulation may be followed by development of others in life-cycle management programs. Rivastigmine, for example, was developed as an oral agent; a transdermal formulation was then developed to reduce gastrointestinal side effects (Winblad et al., 2007).

COMMENT AND SUMMARY

Symptomatic therapies are aligned with the goal of patients—to improve their cognitive circumstances. Symptomatic agents complement the effects of DMTs that intend to forestall the appearance of AD or to slow its progression once symptoms have occurred. Development of DMTs has so far eluded AD researchers. There is a model of successful development of symptomatic AD therapies with known population definitions, outcome measure performance, regulatory pathway, and payer approaches. Several new mechanisms for symptomatic agents are being investigated in clinical trials and in preclinical development programs. Disease modification and symptomatic response definitions overlap. Further engagement in symptomatic AD drug development to enhance cognitive function of affected patients is warranted.

Disclosures

Dr. Cummings has provided consultation to Abbott, Acadia, Adamas, Anavex, Astellas, Avanir, Bayer, BMS, Eisai, EnVivo, Forest, Genentech, GSK, Lundbeck, Neuronetrix, Novartis, Otsuka, Pfizer, Prana, QR, Sanofi-Aventis, Signum, Takeda, and Toyama pharmaceutical companies, and to Avid, ExonHit, GE Healthcare, MedAvante, Neurotrax, and UBC assessment companies. He owns the copyright of the Neuropsychiatric Inventory, and has stock options in Adamas, MedAvante, Neurokos, Prana, and QR pharma.

References

Amacher DE: The discovery and development of proteomic safety biomarkers for the detection of drug-induced liver toxicity, *Toxicol Appl Pharmacol* 245:134–142, 2010.

Arendt T: Synaptic degeneration in Alzheimer's disease, *Acta Neuropathol* 118:167–179, 2009.

Aso E, Ferrer I: Cannabinoids for treatment of Alzheimer's disease: moving toward the clinic, *Front Pharmacol* 5:37, 2014.

Aso E, Palomer E, Juves S, et al: CB1 agonist ACEA protects neurons and reduces the cognitive impairment of AbetaPP/PS1 mice, *J Alzheimers Dis* 30:439–459, 2012.

Assis DN, Navarro VJ: Human drug hepatotoxicity: a contemporary clinical perspective, *Expert Opin Drug Metab Toxicol* 5:463–473, 2009.

Atri A, Molinuevo JL, Lemming O, et al: Memantine in patients with Alzheimer's disease receiving donepezil: new analyses of efficacy and safety for combination therapy, *Alzheimers Res Ther* 5:6, 2013.

Bansal Y, Silakari O: Multifunctional compounds: smart molecules for multifactorial diseases, *Eur J Med Chem* 76:31–42, 2014.

Bateman RJ, Munsell LY, Morris JC, et al: Human amyloid-beta synthesis and clearance rates as measured in cerebrospinal fluid in vivo, *Nat Med* 12:856–861, 2006.

Bentwich J, Dobronevsky E, Aichenbaum S, et al: Beneficial effect of repetitive transcranial magnetic stimulation combined with cognitive training for the treatment of Alzheimer's disease: a proof of concept study, *J Neural Transm* 118:463–471, 2011.

Bharadwaj PR, Bates KA, Porter T, et al: Latrepirdine: molecular mechanisms underlying potential therapeutic roles in Alzheimer's and other neurodegenerative diseases, *Transl Psychiatr* 3:e332, 2013.

Claxton A, Baker LD, Hanson A, et al: Long-acting intranasal insulin Detemir improves cognition for adults with mild cognitive impairment or early-stage Alzheimer's disease dementia, *J Alzheimers Dis* 44:897–906, 2014.

Cummings JL, Mega M, Gray K, et al: The Neuropsychiatric Inventory: comprehensive assessment of psychopathology in dementia, *Neurology* 44:2308–2314, 1994.

Cummings JL, Froelich L, Black SE, et al: Randomized, double-blind, parallel-group, 48-week study for efficacy and safety of a higher-dose rivastigmine patch (15 vs. 10 cm(2)) in Alzheimer's disease, *Dement Geriatr Cogn Disord* 33:341–353, 2012.

Cummings JL, Morstorf T, Zhong K: Alzheimer's disease drug-development pipeline: few candidates, frequent failures, *Alzheimers Res Ther* 6:37, 2014.

Da Costa BE, Becker G, Bouteiller C, et al: Radiosynthesis and in vivo evaluation of fluorinated huprine derivates as PET radiotracers of acetylcholinesterase, *Nucl Med Biol* 40:554–560, 2013.

Davis KL, Thal LJ, Gamzu ER, et al: A double-blind, placebo-controlled multicenter study of tacrine for Alzheimer's disease: the Tacrine Collaborative Study Group, *N Engl J Med* 327:1253–1259, 1992.

de Bruin NM, Prickaerts J, Lange JH, et al: SLV330, a cannabinoid CB1 receptor antagonist, ameliorates deficits in the T-maze, object recognition and social recognition tasks in rodents, *Neurobiol Learn Mem* 93:522–531, 2010.

Deardorff WJ, Shobassy A, Grossberg GT: Safety and clinical effects of EVP-6124 in subjects with Alzheimer's disease currently or previously receiving an acetylcholinesterase inhibitor medication, *Expert Rev Neurother* 15:7–17, 2015.

Devan BD, Pistell PJ, Duffy KB, et al: Phosphodiesterase inhibition facilitates cognitive restoration in rodent models of age-related memory decline, *NeuroRehabilitation* 34:101–111, 2014.

Dineley KT, Jahrling JB, Denner L: Insulin resistance in Alzheimer's disease, *Neurobiol Dis* 72PA:92–103, 2014.

Dubois B, Feldman HH, Jacova C, et al: Advancing research diagnostic criteria for Alzheimer's disease: the IWG-2 criteria, *Lancet Neurol* 13:614–629, 2014.

Emre M, Aarsland D, Albanese A, et al: Rivastigmine for dementia associated with Parkinson's disease, *N Engl J Med* 351:2509–2518, 2004.

Farlow M, Gracon SI, Hershey LA, et al: A controlled trial of tacrine in Alzheimer's disease: the Tacrine Study Group, *J Amer Med Assoc* 268:2523–2529, 1992.

Farlow MR, Salloway S, Tariot PN, et al: Effectiveness and tolerability of high-dose (23 mg/d) versus standard-dose (10 mg/d) donepezil in moderate to severe Alzheimer's disease: a 24-week, randomized, double-blind study, *Clin Ther* 32:1234–1251, 2010.

Ferri N, Siegl P, Corsini A, et al: Drug attrition during pre-clinical and clinical development: understanding and managing drug-induced cardiotoxicity, *Pharmacol Ther* 138:470–484, 2013.

Folstein MF, Folstein SE, McHugh PR: "Mini-mental state": a practical method for grading the cognitive state of patients for the clinician, *J Psychiatr Res* 12:189–198, 1975.

Freiherr J, Hallschmid M, Frey WH, et al: Intranasal insulin as a treatment for Alzheimer's disease: a review of basic research and clinical evidence, *CNS Drugs* 27:505–514, 2013.

Galasko D, Bennett D, Sano M, et al: An inventory to assess activities of daily living for clinical trials in Alzheimer's disease: the Alzheimer's Disease Cooperative Study, *Alzheimer Dis Assoc Disord* 11(Suppl 2):S33–S39, 1997.

Garcia-Barroso C, Ugarte A, Martinez M, et al: Phosphodiesterase inhibition in cognitive decline, *J Alzheimers Dis* 42(Suppl 4):S561–S573, 2014.

Gonzalez-Lima F, Barksdale BR, Rojas JC: Mitochondrial respiration as a target for neuroprotection and cognitive enhancement, *Biochem Pharmacol* 88:584–593, 2014.

Grove RA, Harrington CM, Mahler A, et al: A randomized, double-blind, placebo-controlled, 16-week study of the H3 receptor antagonist, GSK239512 as a monotherapy in subjects with mild-to-moderate Alzheimer's disease, *Curr Alzheimer Res* 11:47–58, 2014.

Gurney ME, D'Amato EC, Burgin AB: Phosphodiesterase-4 (PDE4) molecular pharmacology and Alzheimer's disease, *Neurotherapeutics* 12:49–56, 2014.

Haig GM, Pritchett Y, Meier A, et al: A randomized study of H3 antagonist ABT-288 in mild-to-moderate Alzheimer's dementia, *J Alzheimers Dis* 42:959–971, 2014.

Harrison J, Minassian SL, Jenkins L, et al: A neuropsychological test battery for use in Alzheimer disease clinical trials, *Arch Neurol* 64:1323–1329, 2007.

Heckman PR, Wouters C, Prickaerts J: Phosphodiesterase inhibitors as a target for cognition enhancement in aging and Alzheimer's disease: a translational overview, *Curr Pharm Des* 21:317–331, 2014.

Hescham S, Lim LW, Jahanshahi A, et al: Deep brain stimulation in dementia-related disorders, *Neurosci Biobehav Rev* 37:2666–2675, 2013.

Hongpaisan J, Sun MK, Alkon DL: PKC epsilon activation prevents synaptic loss, Abeta elevation, and cognitive deficits in Alzheimer's disease transgenic mice, *J Neurosci* 31:630–643, 2011.

Jelic V, Kivipelto M, Winblad B: Clinical trials in mild cognitive impairment: lessons for the future, *J Neurol Neurosurg Psychiatr* 77:429–438, 2006.

Kaasinen V, Nagren K, Jarvenpaa T, et al: Regional effects of donepezil and rivastigmine on cortical acetylcholinesterase activity in Alzheimer's disease, *J Clin Psychopharmacol* 22:615–620, 2002.

Kadir A, Darreh-Shori T, Almkvist O, et al: PET imaging of the in vivo brain acetylcholinesterase activity and nicotine binding in galantamine-treated patients with AD, *Neurobiol Aging* 29:1204–1217, 2008.

Kuhl DE, Minoshima S, Frey KA, et al: Limited donepezil inhibition of acetylcholinesterase measured with positron emission tomography in living Alzheimer cerebral cortex, *Ann Neurol* 48:391–395, 2000.

Leber P: USFDA: *Guidelines for the clinical evaluation of antidementia drugs: first draft*, New Canaan, CT, 1990, US Food and Drug Administration.

Li W, Antuono PG, Xie C, et al: Changes in regional cerebral blood flow and functional connectivity in the cholinergic pathway associated with cognitive performance in subjects with mild Alzheimer's disease after 12-week donepezil treatment, *NeuroImage* 60:1083–1091, 2012.

Mega MS, Cummings JL, O'Connor SM, et al: Cognitive and metabolic responses to metrifonate therapy in Alzheimer disease, *Neuropsychiatr Neuropsychol Behav Neurol* 14:63–68, 2001.

Mega MS, Dinov ID, Porter V, et al: Metabolic patterns associated with the clinical response to galantamine therapy: a fludeoxyglucose f 18 positron emission tomographic study, *Arch Neurol* 62:721–728, 2005.

Mohs RC, Doody RS, Morris JC, et al: A 1-year, placebo-controlled preservation of function survival study of donepezil in AD patients, *Neurology* 57:481–488, 2001.

Morris JC: The Clinical Dementia Rating (CDR): current version and scoring rules, *Neurology* 43:2412–2414, 1993.

Nardone R, Tezzon F, Holler Y, et al: Transcranial magnetic stimulation (TMS)/repetitive TMS in mild cognitive impairment and Alzheimer's disease, *Acta Neurol* 129:351–366, 2014.

Olde Rikkert MG, Verhey FR, Blesa R, et al: Tolerability and safety of Souvenaid in patients with mild Alzheimer's disease: results of multi-center, 24-week, open-label extension study, *J Alzheimers Dis* 44:471–480, 2014.

Olivares D, Deshpande VK, Shi Y, et al: *N* methyl D-aspartate (NMDA) receptor antagonists and memantine treatment for Alzheimer's disease, vascular dementia and Parkinson's disease, *Curr Alzheimer Res* 9:746–758, 2012.

Parsons CG, Danysz W, Dekundy A, et al: Memantine and cholinesterase inhibitors: complementary mechanisms in the treatment of Alzheimer's disease, *Neurotox Res* 24:358–369, 2013.

Pehrson AL, Leiser SC, Gulinello M, et al: Treatment of cognitive dysfunction in major depressive disorder—a review of the preclinical evidence for efficacy of selective serotonin reuptake inhibitors, serotonin-norepinephrine reuptake inhibitors and the multimodal-acting antidepressant vortioxetine, *Eur J Pharmacol* 753:19–31, 2014.

Reger MA, Henderson ST, Hale C, et al: Effects of beta-hydroxybutyrate on cognition in memory-impaired adults, *Neurobiol Aging* 25:311–314, 2004.

Rosen WG, Mohs RC, Davis KL: A new rating scale for Alzheimer's disease, *Am J Psychiatr* 141:1356–1364, 1984.

Rountree SD, Atri A, Lopez OL, et al: Effectiveness of antidementia drugs in delaying Alzheimer's disease progression, *Alzheimers Dement* 9:338–345, 2013.

Russell C, Rahman A, Mohammed AR: Application of genomics, proteomics and metabolomics in drug discovery, development and clinic, *Ther Deliv* 4:395–413, 2013.

Salloway S, Sperling R, Fox NC, et al: Two phase 3 trials of bapineuzumab in mild-to-moderate Alzheimer's disease, *N Engl J Med* 370:322–333, 2014.

Scheltens P, Twisk JW, Blesa R, et al: Efficacy of Souvenaid in mild Alzheimer's disease: results from a randomized, controlled trial, *J Alzheimers Dis* 31:225–236, 2012.

Schmitt FA, Ashford W, Ernesto C, et al: The severe impairment battery: concurrent validity and the assessment of longitudinal change in Alzheimer's disease: the Alzheimer's Disease Cooperative Study, *Alzheimer Dis Assoc Disord* 11(Suppl 2):S51–S56, 1997.

Schneider LS, Sano M: Current Alzheimer's disease clinical trials: methods and placebo outcomes, *Alzheimers Dement* 5:388–397, 2009.

Schneider LS, Olin JT, Doody RS, et al: Validity and reliability of the Alzheimer's Disease Cooperative Study–Clinical Global Impression of Change. The Alzheimer's Disease Cooperative Study, *Alzheimer Dis Assoc Disord* 11(Suppl 2):S22–S32, 1997.

Shevtsova EF, Vinogradova DV, Kireeva EG, et al: Dimebon attenuates the Abeta-induced mitochondrial permeabilization, *Curr Alzheimer Res* 11:422–429, 2014.

Shinotoh H, Aotsuka A, Fukushi K, et al: Effect of donepezil on brain acetylcholinesterase activity in patients with AD measured by PET, *Neurology* 56:408–410, 2001.

Sperling RA, Jack CR Jr, Black SE, et al: Amyloid-related imaging abnormalities in amyloid-modifying therapeutic trials: recommendations from the Alzheimer's Association Research Roundtable Workgroup, *Alzheimers Dement* 7:367–385, 2011.

Spires-Jones TL, Hyman BT: The intersection of amyloid beta and tau at synapses in Alzheimer's disease, *Neuron* 82:756–771, 2014.

Sultzer DL, Melrose RJ, Harwood DG, et al: Effect of memantine treatment on regional cortical metabolism in Alzheimer's disease, *Am J Geriatr Psychiatr* 18:606–614, 2010.

Swerdlow RH, Burns JM, Khan SM: The Alzheimer's disease mitochondrial cascade hypothesis: progress and perspectives, *Biochim Biophys Acta* 1842:1219–1231, 2014.

Thomsen MS, Hansen HH, Timmerman DB, et al: Cognitive improvement by activation of alpha7 nicotinic acetylcholine receptors: from animal models to human pathophysiology, *Curr Pharm Des* 16:323–343, 2010.

Tong LM, Djukic B, Arnold C, et al: Inhibitory interneuron progenitor transplantation restores normal learning and memory in ApoE4 knock-in mice without or with Abeta accumulation, *J Neurosci* 34:9506–9515, 2014.

Tsukada H, Nishiyama S, Fukumoto D, et al: Effects of acute acetylcholinesterase inhibition on the cerebral cholinergic neuronal system and cognitive function: functional imaging of the conscious monkey brain using animal PET in combination with microdialysis, *Synapse* 52:1–10, 2004.

US Food and Drug Administration: *Guidance for industry: Alzheimer's disease: developing drugs for the treatment of early stage disease*, Washington, DC, 2013, USFDA.

Weinreb O, Amit T, Bar-Am O, et al: Ladostigil: a novel multimodal neuroprotective drug with cholinesterase and brain-selective monoamine oxidase inhibitory activities for Alzheimer's disease treatment, *Curr Drug Targets* 13:483–494, 2012.

Whitehouse PJ: The cholinergic deficit in Alzheimer's disease, *J Clin Psychiatr* 59(Suppl 13):19–22, 1998.

Wilkinson D, Fox NC, Barkhof F, et al: Memantine and brain atrophy in Alzheimer's disease: a 1-year randomized controlled trial, *J Alzheimers Dis* 29:459–469, 2012.

Wilkinson D, Windfeld K, Colding-Jorgensen E: Safety and efficacy of idalopirdine, a 5-HT6 receptor antagonist, in patients with moderate Alzheimer's disease (LADDER): a randomised, double-blind, placebo-controlled phase 2 trial, *Lancet Neurol* 13:1092–1099, 2014.

Wilkosz PA, Seltman HJ, Devlin B, et al: Trajectories of cognitive decline in Alzheimer's disease, *Int Psychogeriatr* 22:281–290, 2010.

Winblad B, Cummings J, Andreasen N, et al: A six-month double-blind, randomized, placebo-controlled study of a transdermal patch in Alzheimer's disease—rivastigmine patch versus capsule, *Int J Geriatr Psychiatr* 22:456–467, 2007.

Xiang GQ, Tang SS, Jiang LY, et al: PPARgamma agonist pioglitazone improves scopolamine-induced memory impairment in mice, *J Pharm Pharmacol* 64:589–596, 2012.

Yarchoan M, Arnold SE: Repurposing diabetes drugs for brain insulin resistance in Alzheimer disease, *Diabetes* 63:2253–2261, 2014.
Youdim MB: The path from anti Parkinson drug selegiline and rasagiline to multifunctional neuroprotective anti Alzheimer drugs ladostigil and m30, *Curr Alzheimer Res* 3:541–550, 2006.
Yu CJ, Liu W, Chen HY, et al: BACE1 RNA interference improves spatial memory and attenuates Abeta burden in a streptozotocin-induced tau hyperphosphorylated rat model, *Cell Biochem Funct* 32:590–596, 2014.
Zaidel L, Allen G, Cullum CM, et al: Donepezil effects on hippocampal and prefrontal functional connectivity in Alzheimer's disease: preliminary report, *J Alzheimers Dis* 31(Suppl 3):S221–S226, 2012.
Zemek F, Drtinova L, Nepovimova E, et al: Outcomes of Alzheimer's disease therapy with acetylcholinesterase inhibitors and memantine, *Expert Opin Drug Saf* 13:759–774, 2014.

CHAPTER

18

Tackling Alzheimer's Disease by Targeting Oxidative Stress and Mitochondria

R.J. Castellani, S.C. Correia, P.I. Moreira, G. Perry

OUTLINE

INTRODUCTION

The strength of the amyloid cascade theory in Alzheimer's disease (AD) pathogenesis lies in the genetic underpinnings (Castellani and Perry, 2014). Amyloid-β precursor protein (AβPP) mutation, although exceedingly rare, with only some 90 families described, is associated with AD-like early-onset presentation and autosomal-dominant transmission. Presenilins 1 and 2, protein constituents of the γ-secretase complex that performs intramembrane cleavage yielding putative pathogenic amyloid-β (Aβ) fragments, also may be mutated, and also may lead to autosomal-dominant, AD-like, early-onset disease. Likewise, AD-like pathology in Down

Developing Therapeutics for Alzheimer's Disease. http://dx.doi.org/10.1016/B978-0-12-802173-6.00018-6

syndrome, although not strictly linked to pathogenic mutation, emphasizes a role for Aβ because of constitutive overexpression of AβPP. The amyloid cascade concept thus adheres closely to central dogma of molecular biology—not only genotype–phenotype relationships driven by mutation and protein expression, but also genotype–enzyme–substrate–phenotype relationships.

The extent to which this concept has been demonstrated both in vitro and in any one of a number of transgenic models is considerable (Selkoe, 2013). Most such studies have pathogenic mutation embedded somewhere in the construct. Essentially all experimental preclinical models have one or several pathogenic mutations that drive the pathological findings, as well as behavioral outcomes, at least in those models with demonstrable phenotypes. The overall approach is relatively straightforward: overexpression of mutated protein with demonstration of behavioral and pathological outcomes, and a therapeutic approach that removes the mutated protein and demonstrates improvement in, or amelioration of, behavioral and pathological outcomes. Some nuances of this approach, such as evaluation of the synapse, either electrophysiologically or morphologically, in addition to garden-variety pathological lesions, and the incorporation of putative, low-*n* assembly intermediates (oligomers) (Tanzi, 2005), have added to the complexity, sophistication, if not difficulties in reproducibility of the experiments, but the overall approach is again the same—overproduce a presumed toxic substance and then remove it.

On the other hand, the weakness of the amyloid cascade theory also lies in the genetics. The vast majority of AD subjects lack pathogenic mutation (Chouraki and Seshadri, 2014). AβPP and presenilins 1 and 2 are all wild type in sporadic AD. Indeed, even in the case of apolipoprotein E polymorphism, the most significant genetic risk factor for sporadic AD, the majority of human AD subjects lack an apoE 4 allele (Peacock and Fink, 1994). In short, the amyloid cascade as it applies to therapy is based on mutation, and yet the protein targeted in the disease process under study for therapeutic trials, sporadic AD, lacks mutation. For this basic reason, one may not be surprised now by the proof of concept that exists with respect to Aβ in AD—that one can remove Aβ from human sporadic AD subjects in vivo, and have no impact the cognitive trajectory (Holmes et al., 2008). The term "reductionism" is often invoked for such small-molecule therapy (Castellani et al., 2009), given the target which is a single, small proteolytically processed wild-type protein, produced from among thousands of other protein transcripts of diverse and essential function at any given moment. Clearly, other factors should be sought for further study.

So the question is not whether an amyloid cascade of sorts exists, but rather its role in disease pathogenesis, over and above other processes, especially in sporadic AD. Given the complexity of the human brain and the challenges inherent in blunting the progression of this disease, a broader perspective, one that acknowledges whole cell and whole organism biology, and also recognizes that biology and pathology are inextricably linked (Perry and Castellani, 2014), is necessitated.

OXIDATIVE BIOLOGY

There is perhaps no broader area of biology than oxidative metabolism. Like the genetics in the amyloid cascade, the breadth of oxidative biology is both a strength and a weakness; a strength in terms of its relevance to health and disease across all systems, including the brain, and a weakness in terms of it being able to provide a circumscribed, rate-limiting, and targetable event.

The energy required to drive life itself is derived from the electron transport chain (ETC) and the maintenance of a proton gradient across the inner mitochondrial membrane, and ultimately the acceptance of electrons by oxygen (O_2) to produce water (H_2O), which acts in concert to power ATP synthetase. It is noteworthy that interaction of inorganic O_2 with organic compounds is energetically unfavorable at the quantum level (triplet spin state) (Dumont and Beal, 2011). Organisms have overcome this energy barrier to O_2 utilization by evolving a variety of metalloenzymes that facilitate electron transfer from O_2 to redox-active metals such as iron (Fe) and copper (Cu). As the resulting so-called reactive oxygen species (ROS) are toxic, energy metabolism is tightly regulated, and likewise may become destructive when regulatory processes break down.

This process may be likened to internal combustion, where a series of small controlled explosions generates the force necessary for locomotion, following an igniting force to overcome activation energy. Similar to igniting a gas tank, the conversion of oxygen to water requires an initial igniting force, and in the absence of a controlled system would result in an inefficient burst of energy, with a degree of free radical toxicity incompatible with life. A process similar to the latter is, in fact, exploited, in bacterial defense and microbial killing via NADPH oxidase (Hampton et al., 1998). The simple fact of an O_2 requirement for energy and life, therefore, necessitates not only a controlled electron transport, but antioxidant defenses, such that oxidative stress associated with energy metabolism is exquisitely balanced with an antioxidant defense mechanism over the decades that span human life. In terms of disease, one could therefore look at excessive oxidative stress, inefficient or waning antioxidant defenses, or both, as disease mechanisms of chronic neurodegenerative disease.

Such balance is, on the other hand, the central theoretical problem relating oxidative stress to cellular cytotoxicity. An increase in free radicals should in theory be met with a compensatory increase in antioxidant defense as a biochemical imperative. Similarly, any prooxidant molecule may also serve as an antioxidant depending on the chemical microenvironment, and vice versa (Nunomura et al., 2006). Antioxidants that are reducing agents can also act as prooxidants. For example, vitamin C has antioxidant activity with respect to hydrogen peroxide (H_2O_2), but will also participate in Fenton chemistry by reducing transition metals. Moreover, ROS may have beneficial cellular functions, such as redox signaling. Thus, the function of antioxidant systems is the maintenance of optimal balance or redox homeostasis, rather than the quenching of free radicals entirely. The point at which a threshold may be reached where this multifaceted balance is disrupted and damage ensues is impossible to define by currently available methods. Oxidative stress in disease in this respect is nebulous, subject to numerous opposing forces, and measureable in vivo only indirectly and often with the presumption, rightly or wrongly, that oxidative stress end points are deleterious rather than beneficial. These collective problems and complexities are only magnified in the setting of chronic disease that occurs over many years.

Sources of Free Radicals

Mitochondria, not surprisingly, are considered a major source of ROS. The respiratory chain comprises both nucleus- and mitochondria-encoded proteins, among which are redox carriers capable of transferring unpaired, single electrons to O_2, generating toxic superoxide ($O_2^{\bullet -}$) radicals. Enzymes of the tricarboxylic acid (TCA) cycle, monoamine oxidases, and respiratory chain complexes I, II, and III are all capable of generating $O_2^{\bullet -}$[9]. Superoxide itself is of limited cytotoxicity, but conversion to the highly toxic hydroxyl radicals (OH·) may be catalyzed by transition metals. Importantly, OH· cannot be removed enzymatically and therefore is responsible for the bulk of oxidative damage in biological systems.

Transition metals provide a vast array of critical functions, and may be potent catalysts for the generation of free radicals, which may be harmful (Bush, 2013). Not only Fe and Cu, but also manganese (Mn) and zinc (Zn), function as cofactors to a variety of proteins of diverse function, including energy metabolism as noted, nucleic acid metabolism, cellular signaling, and even ROS detoxification. The chemical properties of transition metals make them ideal cofactors for enzymes. Fe and Cu are intimately associated with the ETC, indicating their requirement for life processes in most prokaryotic and eukaryotic cells. The same features again, however, render them capable of generating deleterious ROS in aerobic cells and require endogenous antioxidant balance.

The production of OH· is catalyzed by Fe and to a lesser extent Cu, in the Haber–Weiss cycle (Ravet and Pilon, 2013). The net reaction in the Haber–Weiss cycle is the reaction of $O_2^{\bullet -}$ with H_2O_2 to yield OH· and O_2. The reaction occurs in three steps (Fig. 18.1), which involve (1) the reduction of transition metal, (2) reaction of reduced metal with H_2O_2 to yield OH· and OH^- (known as the Fenton reaction when involving Fe^{2+}), and (3) the combining of O_2^- with H_2O_2 to yield OH·, OH^-, and O_2. Overall, the reaction illustrates how the presence of $O_2^{\bullet -}$ and H_2O_2 can generate toxic OH· in the presence of transition metals. The toxicity of OH· may initiate a cascade of deleterious processes, such as the oxidation of DNA and production of high mutation rates, catalysis of lipid peroxidation and membrane damage, and oxidation of proteins to produce adducts that alter diverse aspects of protein function.

(i) Iron reduction

$$Fe^{3+} + O_2^{\bullet -} \Rightarrow Fe^{2+} + O_2$$

(ii) Fenton reaction

$$Fe^{2+} + H_2O_2 \Rightarrow Fe^{3+} + OH^{\bullet} + OH^-$$

(iii) Haber–Weiss reaction, in the presence of catalytic amounts of iron

$$O_2^{\bullet -} + H_2O_2 \Rightarrow O_2 + OH^{\bullet} + OH^-$$

FIGURE 18.1 **Schematic illustration of Haber–Weiss cycle.** The Haber–Weiss cycle occurs in three steps: (i) the reduction of transition metal, (ii) the Fenton reaction, and (iii) the Haber–Weiss reaction.

Antioxidant Defense

Not surprisingly, mitochondria have elaborated potent antioxidant defenses, including superoxide dismutase (SOD), which converts $O_2^{\bullet -}$ to H_2O_2; catalase, which catalyzes the decomposition of H_2O_2 to H_2O and O_2; and glutathione peroxidase, which reduces lipid hydroperoxides to their corresponding alcohols and reduces free H_2O_2 to H_2O (Salminen and Paul, 2014). Metal chaperones, such as the Cu chaperone for SOD1, appear to limit unbound metal and resulting toxicity (Barnham et al., 2004). Other endogenous antioxidants include α-tocopherol (vitamin E), ascorbic acid (vitamin C), β-carotene (vitamin A), coenzyme Q10 (CoQ_{10}) and other ubiquinone derivatives, acetyl L-carnitine, and R-α lipoic acid, among other substances (Dumont and Beal, 2011).

Antioxidants, whether endogenous or exogenous, may be hydrophilic or lipophilic. H_2O-soluble antioxidants tend to react with oxidants in the cytosolic compartment and plasma, whereas lipid-soluble antoxidants tend to protect cell membranes from lipid peroxidation (Flora et al., 2013).

Oxidative Damage

Unpaired electrons are labile. OH·, in particular, has a very short half-life of approximately 10 s (Dumont and Beal, 2011), which in turn highlights the short reaction distance and susceptibility to neighboring molecules of various species (Sies, 1993). Indeed, free radicals are capable of damaging every major category of biomacromolecule. Nucleic acid modification is well known and may disrupt DNA transcription or foster mutagenesis. Sublethal oxidative damage to unpaired RNA may be particularly relevant to disease states with disrupted translation and its pleiotropic effects. Oxidative modification of lipids is also well characterized, with hydroxynonenal (HNE) and malondialdehyde among the better-characterized chemical modifications in human disease. Proteins may be damaged directly by carbonyl modification, and also via the Maillard reaction (advanced glycation) (Smith et al., 1995a). The latter is initiated by the condensation between amino groups of proteins and reducing sugars, which results in intra- and intermolecular cross-links, rendering proteins protease resistant, or altering protein conformation such that receptor interaction, signal transduction, and endosomal and proteasomal processing may all be perturbed.

OXIDATIVE STRESS IN ALZHEIMER'S DISEASE

While the identification and quantitation of unpaired electrons in tissues is challenging, chemical adducts of oxidative stress may appear as putative biomarkers in body compartments such as serum, cerebrospinal fluid (CSF), and urine, where they may be amenable to quantitation and correlation with disease states (Chang et al., 2014). These include biomarkers of lipid peroxidation such as serum or CSF thiobarbituric acid-reactive substances (Aybek et al., 2007); oxidized low-density lipoprotein (Aldred et al., 2010); serum or CSF protein carbonyl levels (Cristalli et al., 2012); serum antioxidants such as uric acid (Rinaldi et al., 2003); vitamins A, C, and E (Rinaldi et al., 2003; Polidori and Mecocci, 2002; Sano et al., 1997); SOD (Cristalli et al., 2012; Kharrazi et al., 2006); glutathione peroxidase (Cherubini et al., 2005);

8-hydroxyguanosine (Migliore et al., 2005); and F_2-isoprostanes (Milne et al., 2005). Each of these has been examined in AD and has shown variable results, with some showing both increases and decreases in different studies. Such imprecise association between peripheral biomarkers in disease is perhaps not surprising given the difficulties in relating these measurements to specific neurodegenerative disease mechanisms. The barriers between brain and periphery (eg, pulmonary, cardiovascular, blood–brain, olfactory mucosa, etc.), or between exposure and end organ effects within the central nervous system, are substantial. Interestingly, olfactory mucosa from AD subjects exhibits increased levels of oxidative stress, which is, to date, the closest link between the external environment and the central nervous system (Perry et al., 2003).

Oxidative damage in biomarker studies is instead inferred on the basis of the presumption of exposure to oxidative stress, empirical measurement of a chemical change attributed to oxidative disease, and presence of disease, which together fall short of a cause–effect relationship. The specific meaning of any measured differences vis-à-vis the null hypothesis is still an open question. Whether a quantitative change is physiologically relevant or represents cause versus epiphenomenon is unclear. In this respect, such studies are hampered by the aforementioned breadth of oxidation biology, lack of clarity regarding threshold levels that have meaning pathophysiologically, and compensatory mechanisms as yet unidentified that take place over decades.

In the mid to late 1990s through the early 2000s, a number of assays were developed to analyze oxidative stress in situ. Antibodies designed to detect two Maillard end products, pyrraline and pentosidine, were applied in the context of AD pathology (Smith et al., 1994a). Interestingly, both adducts colocalized with hallmark pathology in AD. This suggests that Maillard reaction-related modifications account for the biochemical and insolubility properties of the lesions of AD through the formation of protein cross-links. Around the same time, immunochemical techniques were used to identify carbonyl modification of neurofilament protein for the first time in situ (Smith et al., 1995b). In a subsequent study, a widespread nitrotyrosine-mediated damage was documented in the AD brain, which is an indicator of the presence of peroxynitrite, and consequently a source of OH•-like reactivity (Smith et al., 1997a). Peroxynitrite directly oxidizes proteins and other macromolecules with resultant carbonyl formation from side-chain and peptide-bond cleavage. Taken together, this indicated that oxidative damage is pervasive in AD, and is not restricted to long-lived polymers such as neurofibrillary tangles, but instead reflects a generalized oxidative stress.

To further assess pathology as a response to oxidative stress, the presence of heme oxygenase-1, an important enzyme involved in heme catabolism (Smith et al., 1994b), was detected. In the AD brain, heme oxygenase-1 was found to be associated with neurofibrillary tangles, senile plaque neurites, granulovacuolar degeneration, and neuropil threads, supporting the role of an oxidative stress–response induction in neurofibrillary degeneration (Smith et al., 1994b).

In another study, the role of lipid peroxidation in AD was demystified with the use of antibodies against lysine-derived pyrrole adducts formed by lipid peroxidation-derived HNE (Sayre et al., 1997). HNE-pyrrole immunoreactivity not only was identified in about half of all neurofibrillary tangles, but was also evident in neurons lacking neurofibrillary tangles in the AD cases. In contrast, few senile plaques were labeled, and then only the dystrophic neurites were weakly stained, whereas the Aβ deposits were unlabeled, suggesting that lipid peroxidation was more closely aligned with neurofibrillary degeneration—generally considered more downstream compared to Aβ, but nevertheless a more robust indicator of cognitive function in AD (Castellani and Perry, 2014). In a recent study, Bradley and collaborators also reported increased brain levels of 4-hydroxyhexenal (HHE) in preclinical stages of AD, fostering the idea that lipid peroxidation occurs early in the progression (Bradley et al., 2012). This was also seen for other markers, such as F_2-isoprostane and F_4-neuroprostane, when comparing levels in frontal, parietal, and occipital lobes between controls, individuals with mild cognitive impairment (MCI), and late-AD patients (Markesbery et al., 2005).

In still another study, N(epsilon)-(carboxymethyl)lysine (CML), the predominant advanced glycation end product that accumulates in vivo, along with its glycation-specific precursor hexitol-lysine, was evaluated in the AD brain tissue (Castellani et al., 2001). Both CML and hexitol-lysine were increased in neurons, especially those containing intracellular neurofibrillary pathology in cases of AD. The increase in hexitol-lysine and CML in AD suggests that glycation is an early event in disease pathogenesis. In addition, because CML can result from either lipid peroxidation or advanced glycation, while hexitol-lysine is solely a product of glycation, this study suggests that two distinct oxidative processes may be acting in concert in AD neuropathology, suggesting again a level of breadth and complexity to AD pathology. Additionally, protein carbonyls and 3-nitrotyrosine levels were also found to be increased in the frontal cortex of individuals with MCI, mild AD, and AD, a finding that supports the idea of oxidative stress as an early event in AD (Ansari and Scheff, 2010).

The potential role of transition metals, in particular Cu, Fe, and Zn, in oxidative stress in AD raises another avenue of in situ investigation. X-ray emission analysis of amygdala in AD (a site of both phospho-tau and Aβ pathology) suggest a three- to fivefold increase in Fe, Cu, and Zn in the AD brain compared to age-matched controls (Lovell et al., 1998). In general, these metals are found in highest concentration in brain regions most affected by neurodegeneration in AD (Barnham et al., 2004). Cu in CSF and plasma has been demonstrated to be 2.2 times that of controls (Basun et al., 1991; Squitti et al., 2002). Elevated levels of Fe and Fe-binding proteins are described in numerous studies. Using an innovative modification of a common histochemical technique that relies on mixed-valence iron complexes, Smith and collaborators identified redox-active Fe^{2+} in association with senile plaques and neurofibrillary tangles in AD (Smith et al., 1997b).

Synthetic Aβ is toxic in vitro in the presence of Cu, which in turn is inhibited by catalase, suggesting that OH· is liberated by H_2O_2 in the presence of metal (Behl et al., 1994; Opazo et al., 2002). Interaction of Aβ with Cu^{2+} and Fe^{3+} reduces the oxidation state of both metals and generates H_2O_2, which again sets the stage of toxic OH· generation. It is interesting that Aβ possesses histidine residues at positions 6, 13, and 14, which enables chemical interaction with metal ions. Spectroscopic studies have confirmed the metal binding, and in particular copper binding, of Aβ; such binding, moreover, is inhibited by methylation of histidine, providing convincing evidence of metal–Aβ interaction (Curtain et al., 2001, 2003). Additional low-affinity Aβ–metal binding is also suggested (Atwood et al., 2000). Although the precise extent of metal binding by various Aβ species requires further study, there is support for the concept that Aβ becomes hypermetallated as a function of age and disease, resists clearance via oxidative modification in disease, and serves as a reservoir for local cytotoxicity (Bush and Tanzi, 2008). Synapse-associated Zn accumulation in senile plaques is intriguing in light of these data. Indeed, genetic ablation of Zn transporter protein 3 (required for Zn transport in synaptic vesicles) reduced plaque formation in Tg2576 mice. Zn in insoluble Aβ aggregates further partially quenches H_2O_2, which may provide a basis for hypothesized enhanced toxicity of soluble Aβ species (Barnham et al., 2004). We have also found that ceruloplasmin, which regulates the distribution of both Cu and Fe, is deficient in AD (Castellani et al., 1999), consistent with the emerging evidence that the AD brain is characterized by fatigue of metal trafficking, with Aβ pathology and resulting metal sequestration occurring as a disease response. Indeed, we have also demonstrated a reduction of oxidative stress with increasing Aβ burden overall, with oxidative stress preceding Aβ pathology (Nunomura et al., 2000, 2001), supporting our hypothesis that Aβ in brain issue serves as a beneficial antioxidant that sequesters toxic metals, and our overarching assertion that AD pathology is a disease response rather than a signature of cytotoxicity per se. In addition, experimental data revealed that metal transporters such as Zn transporters and divalent metal transporter 1 are increased in the cortex and hippocampus of APP/PS1 transgenic mice; and similar to transition metals, these metal transporters are colocalized with Aβ in senile plaques in the cortex of AD brains (Zhang et al., 2008; Zheng et al., 2009). This finding leads to the speculation that metal transporters may play important roles in the aberrant metal dyshomeostasis in AD.

Although cellular RNA is subjected to the same oxidative insults as DNA and other cellular macromolecules, oxidative damage to RNA has not been a major focus in investigations of the biological consequences of free radical damage. In fact, because it is largely single-stranded and its bases lack the protection of hydrogen bonding and binding by specific proteins, RNA is more susceptible to oxidative insults than is DNA. Oxidative damage to protein-coding RNA or noncoding RNA will, in turn, potentially cause errors in proteins and/or dysregulation of gene expression. While less lethal than mutations in the genome, such sublethal insults to cells might be associated with underlying mechanisms of several chronic diseases, including neurodegenerative disease. Oxidative RNA damage has been described in several neurodegenerative diseases, including AD, Parkinson's disease, dementia with Lewy bodies, and prion diseases (Nunomura et al., 2007, 2012a). Of particular interest, oxidative RNA damage can be demonstrated in vulnerable neurons early in disease, suggesting that RNA oxidation may actively contribute to the onset of the disease (Nunomura et al., 1999). Indeed, it was recently reported that MCI subjects (but not preclinical AD) exhibit a higher burden of oxidized RNA nucleoside 8-hydroxyguanosine in the temporal cortex when compared to age-matched controls (Nunomura et al., 2012b). An increasing body of evidence suggests that, mechanistically speaking, the detrimental effects of oxidative RNA damage to protein synthesis are attenuated, at least in part, by the existence of protective mechanisms that prevent the incorporation of the damaged ribonucleotides into the translational machinery. Overall perturbation of cellular homeostasis by oxidative damage to RNA remains undefined, but in need of further study.

MITOCHONDRIAL DYSFUNCTION IN ALZHEIMER'S DISEASE

Neuronal fate is dictated by the delicate interplay between mitochondrial bioenergetics and dynamics. These fascinating organelles have been recognized as the "powerhouses of the cell," providing energy via ATP generation, which is accomplished through the TCA cycle and oxidative phosphorylation system (Correia et al., 2012). Due to their complex architecture and limited glycolytic capacity, neurons exquisitely rely on mitochondrial function and distribution to distal areas with high energy demands, such as synaptic terminals, to ensure proper synaptic function (Correia et al., 2012; Sheng, 2014; Sheng and Cai, 2012). During the mitochondrial life cycle, new mitochondria are generated from the division of preexisting organelles (mitochondrial biogenesis), whereas dysfunctional mitochondria are removed through selective degradation by autophagy (mitophagy), these two processes occurring in the soma. In between, mitochondria experience successive cycles of fusion and fission that allow the generation of a heterogeneous mitochondrial population. Fusion events are crucial for the exchange of contents between mitochondria and enable damaged mitochondria to acquire components from healthy mitochondria, while fission is essential for mitochondrial trafficking along axons and a prerequisite for mitophagy (Sheng and Cai, 2012; Westermann, 2010). Within this scenario, the mechanisms that govern mitochondrial dynamics and bioenergetics seem to be intertwined in order to control mitochondrial morphology, mass, and quality in neurons.

A critical pathological feature of AD is the development of mitochondrial abnormalities. As mentioned previously, mitochondria can be a "Pandora's box" since these organelles are one of the major hubs of ROS and the prime targets of oxidative damage, which in turn compromise mitochondrial efficiency, leading to a vicious cycle. In this sense, oxidative damage has been documented to be coupled to a progressive decline of mitochondrial function during the pathological course of AD (Moreira et al., 2010). Lessons from clinical and experimental studies revealed that oxidative damage and mitochondrial abnormalities precede the occurrence of the two classical pathological hallmarks of AD, the deposition of senile plaques and neurofibrillary tangles (Nunomura et al., 2001; Chou et al., 2011; Resende et al., 2008; Yao et al., 2009). Indeed, the early stages of AD are marked by a hypometabolic state, as noticed by hampered brain glucose metabolism (Azari et al., 1993), impaired activities of the TCA cycle enzymes (Bubber et al., 2005; Mastrogiacomo et al., 1993), and defects in the mitochondrial ETC (Bosetti et al., 2002; Cardoso et al., 2004; Kish et al., 1992; Valla et al., 2006), with the consequent depletion of ATP levels. Altered activities of TCA cycle enzymes (specifically that of the pyruvate dehydrogenase complex) are correlated with the clinical state of AD, suggesting a progressive deterioration of mitochondrial function with the severity of the disease. Notably, mitochondrial components are known to be highly susceptible to oxidative modification and are altered by exposure to a range of prooxidants (Tretter and Adam-Vizi, 2000). In the AD brain, oxidative modification of metabolic proteins, such as α-ketoglutarate dehydrogenase and pyruvate dehydrogenase complexes and cytochrome c oxidase (COX), have been demonstrated by elevated levels of protein carbonyl and nitration of tyrosine residues and indicate impaired metabolic activity (Sultana and Butterfield, 2013). Importantly, impaired COX activity, which is the most consistent mitochondrial defect documented in AD, disturbs energy metabolism and increases ROS generation, fostering the idea that mitochondrial malfunction further exacerbates oxidative stress (Mutisya et al., 1994).

Aside from compromised mitochondrial function, defects in mitochondrial morphology and dynamics have been postulated to contribute to neuronal network disruption and subsequent cognitive deficits in AD. Ultrastructural alterations in mitochondrial morphology such as reduced size and broken internal membrane cristae were reported in the AD brain (Baloyannis, 2006; Hirai et al., 2001). But what is the trigger of these defects in mitochondrial structure? An imbalance in mitochondrial fusion and fission events could in part explain the reduced size of mitochondria in AD. An exhaustive study aimed to unveil the role of the molecular machinery that controls mitochondrial fusion–fission on structural defects in AD reported reduced protein levels of optic atrophy protein-1 (OPA-1) and mitofusin-1 and -2, which are key proteins that orchestrate mitochondrial fusion, and increased mitochondria fission protein 1 (Fis1) in hippocampal tissue from AD individuals when compared with the respective age-matched controls (Wang et al., 2009). Consistently, these authors also found that AβPP overexpression in M17 neuroblastoma cells resulted in predominantly fragmented mitochondria, decreased OPA-1 protein levels, and a defect in neuronal differentiation (Wang et al., 2008). In a further step, Gan and collaborators (Gan et al., 2014) found that AD cybrids have fragmented, misshaped, and bleb-like mitochondria, which are consistent with alterations in ultrastructure observed in the human AD brain tissue. It is noteworthy that AD cybrid cells exhibited an increased translocation of the mitochondrial fission protein dynamin related protein-1 (DRP-1) to mitochondria, whereas mitofusin-2 protein levels were decreased. DRP-1 exists primarily in the cytoplasm but partially associates into foci on the outer surface of mitochondria that coalesce at sites of mitochondrial fission (Smirnova et al., 2001). Increased DRP-1 recruitment to mitochondria results in higher rates of DRP1-dependent mitochondrial division and mitochondrial fragmentation (Wang et al., 2009). Furthermore, the AD brain displays increased levels of *S*-nitrosylation of DRP-1 (Cho et al., 2009). In cell-based models of AD, *S*-nitrosylation was shown to modulate the GTPase activity of DRP-1, thus contributing to mitochondrial fragmentation, bioenergetic impairment, synaptic damage, and eventually frank neuronal loss (Cho et al., 2009). More recently, it was demonstrated that the axis oxidative stress–extracellular signal-regulated kinase (ERK)-DRP-1 has a key role in AD-related mitochondrial dynamic (Gan et al., 2014). In fact, the antioxidant probucol was found to blunt mitochondrial-derived ROS production, block ERK1/2 activation, and rescue mitochondrial morphology by suppressing mitochondrial DRP-1 levels in AD cybrids. Overall, these findings suggest that oxidative stress-mediated ERK activation augments DRP-1 recruitment to mitochondria and shifts mitochondrial dynamics toward excessive fission in AD (Gan et al., 2014).

Taking into account that the fine-tuning of mitochondrial fusion and fission events is crucial for mitophagy and mitochondrial biogenesis and motility, defects in these processes are also expected to contribute to structural and functional mitochondrial changes in AD. Mitophagy, a type of cargo-specific autophagy, acts as a mitochondrial quality-control mechanism that ensures the maintenance of a healthy mitochondrial pool through the selective degradation of damaged mitochondria (Kim et al., 2007). The first proof that mitophagy plays a role in AD comes from a study performed in postmortem AD brain tissue revealing the presence of mitochondrial DNA and COX in the neuronal cytoplasm, with mitochondrial DNA being presented in lipofuscin-containing vacuoles (Hirai et al., 2001). In the same line, elevated levels of mitochondrial components, namely COX and lipoic acid, within autophagosomes were detected in human postmortem brain tissue, suggesting an increase in the rate of mitochondrial degradation by autophagy (Moreira et al., 2007a, b). Using a rat model of AD, it was recently found that mitophagy markers reach a maximum level and return to basal level as apoptotic markers start to increase, indicating the mitophagy might be stimulated in an initial phase as a compensatory mechanism to "escape" from a neuronal energetic crisis (Shaerzadeh et al., 2014). Regarding the plausible candidates that initiate the mitophagic process in AD, it is tempting to speculate that mitochondrial-derived ROS and mitochondrial depolarization are the major players. Mitochondrial-derived ROS may act as signaling molecules and trigger mitophagy throughout redox regulation of Atg4, an essential cysteine protease in the autophagic pathway (Scherz-Shouval et al., 2007). On the other hand, mitochondrial depolarization, which reflects loss of function of the mitochondrial respiratory chain or the permeabilization of the inner membrane, can also function as an "eat me" signal. Mitochondrial fission can generate fusion-competent daughter mitochondria or fusion-incompetent mitochondria with decreased mitochondrial membrane potential. After that, depolarized daughter mitochondria are isolated and tagged to degradation by mitophagy (Twig et al., 2008; Twig and Shirihai, 2011). However, a major question persists: Is mitophagy efficiently removing damaged mitochondria in the AD brain? In a recent study, it was observed that AD is associated with a progressive decline in the cytosolic levels of Parkin, a protein that positively regulates mitophagy (Ye et al., 2015). Thus, these data indicate that the accumulation of dysfunctional mitochondria during the course of AD is in part attributable to defects in the molecular machinery behind mitophagy. However, further studies are warranted to clarify the (patho)physiological role of mitophagy during the different stages of AD progression.

Another important aspect of perturbed mitochondrial dynamics in AD is the fact that neurons need to refurnish "old" mitochondrial pools via mitochondrial biogenesis. Mitochondrial content is significantly reduced in susceptible hippocampal neurons from AD subjects, which points to a possible compromise of mitochondrial biogenesis (Baloyannis, 2006; Hirai et al., 2001). Recent breakthroughs reported a drastic reduction in the protein levels of peroxisome proliferator activator receptor gamma-coactivator 1α (PGC-1α) and nuclear respiratory factor-1 and -2 and mitochondrial DNA-to-nuclear DNA ratio in human AD brain tissue and in in vitro and in vivo models of AD (Qin et al., 2009; Sheng et al., 2012). Being considered the master regulator of mitochondrial biogenesis, PGC-1α is known to initiate the transcription of cellular programs regulating mitochondrial respiration and oxidative stress defense. Therefore, the overexpression of PGC-1α in an in vitro model of AD was shown to restore mitochondrial biogenesis and mitochondrial function (Sheng et al., 2012). Using genetic approaches to modulate the nuclear respiratory factor-2, it was found that the upregulation of this coordinator of the antioxidant pathway culminates in an improved behavioral performance and reduced Aβ burden and cell damage in transgenic mouse models of AD (Kanninen et al., 2008, 2009).

But what are the consequences of the aforementioned mitochondrial alterations? First and foremost, defects on mitochondrial bioenergetics and fusion–fission could compromise the mitochondrial movement along the microtubules tracks, leading to a defective delivery of healthy mitochondria to the synaptic terminals, and consequent synaptic "starvation" (Correia et al., 2012). Recent research advances outlined the existence of a defective mitochondrial trafficking in AD that is accompanied by mitochondrial overcrowding and mislocalization, and impaired mitochondrial function in metabolic demanding structures like synaptic terminals (Correia et al., 2012; Trimmer and Borland, 2005). In some ways this is not surprising, as the transport of mitochondria from the soma to distal axonal and dendritic regions is coordinated by two classes of motor proteins, kinesin and dynein, and requires ATP hydrolysis (Hirokawa et al., 2010). Furthermore, mitofusins interact with the adaptor complex Miro–Milton, which tethers mitochondria to kinesin motors (Misko et al., 2010). On this basis, loss of mitofusins

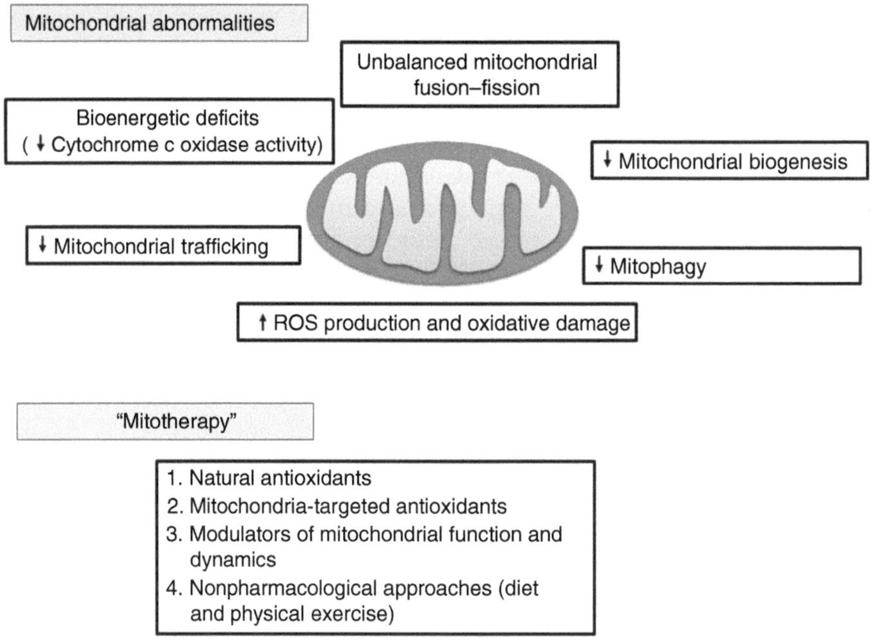

FIGURE 18.2 **Mitochondrial abnormalities and "mitotherapies" in Alzheimer's disease.** The AD brain is characterized by several abnormalities, including bioenergetics deficits, increases in mitochondrial ROS production, unbalanced mitochondrial fusion and fission events, impaired mitochondrial biogenesis and mitophagy, and hampered mitochondrial trafficking. Overall, these abnormalities contribute to faulty delivery of "healthy" mitochondria to synaptic terminals, leading to "synaptic starvation" and consequent degeneration and loss. Conversely, several strategies to "fight" mitochondrial failure in AD have been developed during the last decades. These strategies include antioxidants (natural and mitochondria-targeted) and modulators of mitochondrial function and dynamics. Nonpharmacological approaches (ie, diet and physical exercise) are also useful in counteracting mitochondrial defects and AD-related neuropathology.

during AD progression could in part represent a mechanism underlying defective axonal transport of mitochondria in this disease.

Overall, the failure at "mito-checkpoints" (biogenesis, dynamics, and mitophagy) contributes to the aggravation of AD phenotype by potentiating mitochondrial bioenergetics defects, oxidative damage, and synaptic pathology (Fig. 18.2).

OXIDATIVE STRESS AND MITOCHONDRIA AS FEASIBLE THERAPEUTIC TARGETS IN ALZHEIMER'S DISEASE

At present, there are no effective disease-modifying therapies for AD, in part because of the complex nature of this devastating neurodegenerative disease. Past therapeutic approaches focused on removing Aβ, interfering with Aβ aggregation, or directly altering AβPP metabolism have repeatedly failed in late-stage clinical trials (Feldman et al., 2014; Karran et al., 2011). Within this scenario, the presymptomatic and prodromal stages of AD, which are mainly characterized by oxidative damage and mitochondrial abnormalities, are emerging as windows of opportunity to prevent or postpone AD progression. From a therapeutic perspective, this section intends to clarify whether and how oxidative stress and mitochondria can be targeted in order to efficaciously counteract AD-related symptomatic and neuropathological features (Fig. 18.2).

Natural Antioxidants

Since oxidative stress occurs early in the course of AD pathology, several researchers have conducted studies in order to investigate whether antioxidant therapy could act as a first line of defense in the prevention of AD development. Antioxidants such as vitamins C and E have a long history as possible treatments for AD (Chen and Zhong, 2014; Di Domenico et al., 2015). Preclinical studies performed in transgenic AD models demonstrated that both vitamins C and E reduce markers of lipid peroxidation and Aβ plaque burden and restore cognitive function (Harrison et al., 2009; Sung et al., 2004). However, the outcome derived from clinical trials showed that vitamins C and E have limited benefits on cognitive performance and on delaying AD progression (Sano et al., 1997; Jack et al., 2008). For instance, a recent study revealed that the combined supplementation of AD patients with vitamins E (400 IU/day) and C (1 g/day) increases the levels of these vitamins in CSF, which were accompanied by a clear reduction of in vivo oxidation of CSF lipoproteins after 1 month (Arlt et al., 2012). However, this antioxidant supplementation was unable to significantly mitigate cognitive deterioration in AD over a period of 1 year (Arlt et al., 2012).

Lipoic acid, which acts a cofactor for the mitochondrial pyruvate and α-ketoglutarate dehydrogenase complexes, possesses robust antioxidant properties, being involved in the recycling of other antioxidants such as vitamins C and E and glutathione (Moreira et al., 2009). An elegant in vitro study from Moreira and collaborators (Moreira et al., 2007c) demonstrated that lipoic acid (1 mM) attenuates mitochondrial-related oxidative stress in fibroblasts from AD subjects and AD-like mitochondrial dysfunction triggered by *N*-methylprotoporphyrine, a cytochrome oxidase assembly inhibitor. Subsequent in vivo studies also demonstrated that lipoic acid prevents cognitive deficits and mitochondrial decay associated with aging and AD (Aliev et al., 2009; Poon et al., 2005; Quinn et al., 2007). Clinical studies reported that the treatment of AD patients with lipoic acid (in conjugation with the standard treatment with cholinesterase inhibitors) led to a stabilization of cognitive functions, fostering the idea that this antioxidant may delay the onset or slow down the progression of the disease (Hager et al., 2001, 2007). However, further studies are warranted to replicate this achievement in a large-scale trial. The use of lipoic acid in combination with other antioxidants has also been of interest in some clinical studies. The combination of lipoic acid and acetyl-L-carnitine showed beneficial effects in both clinical and psychometric tests in MCI and mild AD patients (Bianchetti et al., 2003; Montgomery et al., 2003).

Another potential candidate to "fight" oxidative stress and AD-related neuropathology is CoQ_{10}. CoQ_{10} is an essential cofactor of the electron transport chain and a potent ROS scavenger (Moreira et al., 2010). Preclinical studies highlighted the ability of CoQ_{10} to avert mitochondrial abnormalities, including loss of mitochondrial potential and mitochondrial ROS overproduction (Li et al., 2005; Moreira et al., 2005; Somayajulu et al., 2005). Furthermore, studies performed in transgenic mouse models of AD revealed that CoQ_{10} attenuates Aβ pathology and improves cognitive performance (Dumont et al., 2011; Elipenahli et al., 2012; Yang et al., 2010). Unfortunately, idebenone, a synthetic analog of CoQ_{10}, failed to slow cognitive decline in AD subjects during clinical trials (Thal et al., 2003).

Melatonin, the major secretory product of the pineal gland, is also a potent antioxidant and free radical scavenger. In 1997, a pioneering study reported for the first time the ability of melatonin to avert Aβ-induced lipid peroxidation, intracellular Ca^{2+} overloading, and cell death in vitro (Pappolla et al., 1997). Since then, several steps forward have been made in order to demystify the potential of melatonin as a therapeutic approach in AD. Using a transgenic model of AD, Olcese and collaborators (Olcese et al., 2009) documented that long-term administration of melatonin improved cognitive performance and reduced Aβ deposition. Additionally, the administration of melatonin also promoted an increase in SOD and glutathione levels (Feng et al., 2006), with the concomitant reduction in oxidative damage and proapoptotic markers (Matsubara et al., 2003) in a transgenic mouse model of AD. Furthermore, it was reported that melatonin restores mitochondrial mass and morphology and structural hippocampal neuroplasticity in a rat model of sporadic AD (Rudnitskaya et al., 2015; Stefanova et al., 2015). Surprisingly, a recent study revealed that long-term treatment with melatonin significantly reduces AD neuropathology and some associated cognitive deficits in the $A\beta PP^{swe}$/PSEN1dE9 mouse model of AD—however, in a manner that is independent of antioxidant pathways (O'Neal-Moffitt et al., 2015). The combined effects mediated by melatonin and physical exercise during the pathological course of AD were also explored in 3xTg-AD mice aged from 6 to 12 months. Notably, both treatments protected against cognitive decline, oxidative stress, and mitochondrial DNA depletion (Garcia-Mesa et al., 2012). However, only the combined treatment was effective in preserving brain mitochondrial function (Garcia-Mesa et al., 2012), suggesting a synergistic effect between an antioxidant therapy and physical exercise against the range of pathological disturbances that occur in AD. Despite the encouraging outcome derived from experimental studies, melatonin failed in preventing AD-associated symptoms in clinical trials. Two clinical trials reported no improvements in sleep disturbances, circadian rhythms, or agitation in AD patients treated with melatonin (Dowling et al., 2008; Gehrman et al., 2009).

Other antioxidants such as curcumin and *Ginkgo biloba* extract (EGb 761) also exert protective effects against AD-associated oxidative damage, mitochondrial malfunction, and neuropathological phenotype in both in vitro and in vivo models of the disease (Garcia-Alloza et al., 2007; Lim et al., 2001; Rhein et al., 2010; Smith and Luo, 2003; Wu et al., 2006; Yang et al., 2005). Nevertheless, clinical trials showed no consistent evidence of a benefit of curcumin and *G. biloba* in the treatment of AD.

At this point, the major question is why natural antioxidant therapy failed to show efficacy in clinical trials despite the positive outcomes in preclinical models. There are several possible reasons for the limited success of these natural antioxidants: (1) issues with the experimental design of the clinical trials, (2) poor ability of these natural substances to cross the blood–brain barrier, (3) inability to reach mitochondria and neutralize free radicals overproduction, and (4) most clinical trials having been conducted in the late stages of the disease (Persson et al., 2014).

Mitochondria-Targeted Antioxidants

With the purpose of enhancing the delivery and accumulation of antioxidants into mitochondria, multiple mitochondria-targeted molecules have been developed during the last decades. The most promising mitochondria-targeted antioxidants as therapeutic approaches to counteract AD pathology are MitoQ and Szeto–Schiller (SS) peptides.

MitoQ is produced by covalently binding ubiquinone, an endogenous antioxidant and component of the mitochondrial electron transport chain, to a triphenylphosphonium (TPP^+) cation. MitoQ rapidly crosses the blood–brain barrier and neuronal membranes, concentrates several 100-fold in mitochondria due to its high membrane potential, and helps to prevent lipid peroxidation. MitoQ does not react with hydrogen peroxide or hydrogen peroxide radicals but does react with superoxide radicals, among other radical oxygen and carbon species. Preventing lipid peroxidation is probably the most important thing to mention here (Murphy and Smith, 2007). MitoQ is oriented with the TPP^+ moiety near the membrane surface, accessing the membrane core to act as a chain-breaking antioxidant and allowing recycling of MitoQ to its ubiquinol form via reduction by complex II (James et al., 2007). Using primary neurons from AβPP transgenic mice and N2a cells treated with the amyloidogenic peptide $A\beta_{25-35}$, Manczak and collaborators (Manczak et al., 2010) found that MitoQ prevents the alterations in mitochondrial structure and function that occur in these in vitro models of AD. Notably, MitoQ also increased synaptic branching in primary neurons from AβPP transgenic mice, suggesting that antioxidants targeted to mitochondria boost neurite outgrowth. A subsequent study revealed that MitoQ is effective in averting cognitive decline and delaying the early neuropathological phenotype (oxidative stress, Aβ deposition, astrogliosis, caspase activation, and loss of synaptic integrity) in the 3xTg-AD mice (McManus et al., 2011). More recently, studies on a transgenic *Caenorhabditis elegans* model of AD showed that MitoQ extends life span and avoids mitochondrial cardiolipin depletion and impaired activity of complexes I and IV of the ETC (Ng et al., 2014). Hitherto, only a phase 1 clinical trial was performed in AD patients using MitoQ supplementation, in which this promising synthetic antioxidant showed good pharmacokinetic behavior with oral dosing at 80 mg (1 mg/kg), resulting in a plasma C_{max} = 33.15 ng/mL and T_{max} = 1 h (Moreira et al., 2010). Therefore, further research is required to investigate the potential of MitoQ in counteracting AD-related symptomatology and neuropathology.

The SS peptides (SS-02, SS-19, SS-20, and SS-31) belong to a novel class of small cell-permeable peptide antioxidants that target mitochondria in a potentially independent manner. Among these SS peptides, SS-31 is the most effective antioxidant molecule due to its extensive cellular uptake and selective portioning into mitochondria. By concentrating in the inner mitochondrial membrane, SS-31 is localized to the site of ROS production and protects against mitochondrial oxidative damage and further ROS production (Zhao et al., 2004). Using primary neurons from Tg2756 mice treated with $A\beta_{25-35}$, Reddy and collaborators demonstrated that SS-31 restores mitochondrial trafficking and synaptic viability, and decreases the percentage of defective mitochondria, indicating that SS-31 can protect mitochondria and synapses from Aβ toxicity (Reddy et al., 2012). Consistently, another study reported that SS-31 is able to normalize the number of mitochondria and reduce the abnormal expression of peroxiredoxins and mitochondrial structural genes in N2a cells treated with $A\beta_{25-35}$ (Manczak et al., 2010).

Modulators of Mitochondrial Function and Dynamics

Besides mitochondrial-driven ROS generation and oxidative damage, several other aspects of mitochondrial physiology have been pinpointed as potential targets to tackle AD. As mentioned previously, a decline in mitochondrial function can occur decades prior to clinical manifestation of the disease, and thus it may represent a feasible therapeutic target for AD (Swerdlow, 2009). The metabolic enhancer piracetam was shown to improve mitochondrial function in AD model systems. The first clue that piracetam is capable of restoring mitochondrial function was provided by Leuner and collaborators (Leuner et al., 2010) and demonstrated that this drug improves brain glucose uptake and utilization and ATP synthesis in a transgenic mouse model of AD. At the same time, it was observed that piracetam ameliorates mitochondrial function and reverses the diminished neuritogenesis in PC12 cells treated with the oligomeric $A\beta_{1-42}$ or expressing mutant AβPP (Leuner et al., 2010; Kurz et al., 2010). Recent breakthroughs revealed that piracetam also modulates mitochondrial dynamics by shifting mitochondrial morphology back to an elongated phenotype in SH-SY5Y cells expressing AβPP (Stockburger et al., 2013).

Another important aspect of mitochondrial physiology which plays a crucial role in the maintenance of the mitochondrial pool is mitochondrial biogenesis. By activating the master regulator of mitochondrial biogenesis PGC-1α, pioglitazone and rosiglitazone have emerged as promising therapeutic candidates for AD. In vitro evidence suggested that pioglitazone promotes mitochondrial biogenesis, as supported by increased mitochondrial DNA content and subunit proteins, and reduces mitochondrial oxidative damage (Ghosh et al., 2007). Using aged AβPP transgenic mice, pioglitazone was shown to avert cognitive deficits, cerebrovascular dysfunction, and neurometabolic "uncoupling" (Nicolakakis et al., 2008; Papadopoulos et al., 2013). Similarly, rosiglitazone also stimulates neuronal mitochondrial biogenesis and reduces cognitive deterioration in rodent models of AD (Nicolakakis et al., 2008; Escribano et al., 2009; Strum et al., 2007). A small clinical trial performed in patients with mild AD revealed that pioglitazone induces modest cognitive benefits and improves cerebral blood flow in the parietal lobes (Hanyu et al., 2009; Sato et al., 2011). Rosiglitazone preserved cognition in patients with early AD and MCI (Watson et al., 2005), but failed to show significant cognitive benefits in a subsequent larger trial performed in patients with mild-to-moderate AD (Risner et al., 2006). However, these two candidates have as a major limitation poor blood–brain barrier penetration.

Resveratrol induces the expression of sirtuin 1, a nicotinamide adenine dinucleotide-dependent deacetylase, which in turn sets in motion a cascade of PGC-1α-triggered events that ultimately lead to improved mitochondrial function and biogenesis and boost cellular ROS scavenging (Granzotto and Zatta, 2014). Experimental evidence demonstrated that resveratrol reduces cognitive impairment and the classical neuropathological features of AD, the Aβ burden and tau hyperphosphorylation, in SAMP8 mice (Porquet et al., 2013). In the same line, resveratrol also prevented AD-like phenotype in the sporadic model of AD induced by the intracerebroventricular administration of streptozotocin. In particular, resveratrol attenuated cognitive deficits, tau pathology, and oxidative stress (Du et al., 2014; Sharma and Gupta, 2002). In vitro findings demonstrated that resveratrol abolished Aβ-induced reduced mitochondrial mass and abnormal expression of mitochondrial structural genes, and preserved mitochondrial function by inhibiting cyclophilin D expression (Manczak et al., 2010). Recently, a phase 2 clinical trial on mild-to-moderate AD patients revealed that resveratrol is safe and well tolerated, and alters some AD biomarker trajectories (Turner et al., 2015).

Latrepirdine, also known as dimebolin, is a nonselective antihistamine that has the ability of modulating mitochondrial physiology and has been proposed to stabilize mitochondrial membrane potential and block mitochondrial permeability transition pore opening (Bachurin et al., 2001; Zhang et al., 2010). Compelling evidence showed that latrepirdine can protect against Aβ toxicity in cultured cells, improve cognition, and arrest progression of neuropathology in transgenic mouse models of AD (Bachurin et al., 2001; Zhang et al., 2010; Bharadwaj et al., 2012; Steele et al., 2013; Wang et al., 2011). Notably, latrepirdine was also shown to protect against the toxic effects of Aβ on mitochondrial morphology, respiratory chain complex activities, and mitochondrial mass in an in vitro model of AD overexpressing neurotoxic Aβ peptides, fostering the idea that mitochondria are a target of latrepirdrine (Eckert et al., 2012). In a phase 2 clinical trial, latrepirdine significantly improved cognitive function in patients with moderate AD (Doody et al., 2008). However, these findings were not corroborated in a subsequent larger phase 3 clinical trial performed in patients with moderate-to-severe AD (Bezprozvanny, 2010; Miller, 2010). The complex pharmacology and the interaction with several targets have been pinpointed as the major reasons underlying latrepirdine's failure in clinical trials (Okun et al., 2010).

Owing to excessive mitochondrial fragmentation and unbalanced fission and fusion events, the mitochondrial division inhibitor-1 (mdivi-1) emerged has a potential therapeutic drug for AD. Mdivi-1 inhibits mitochondrial fission by selectively preventing DRP-1 assembly and thus inhibiting its GTPase activity (Cassidy-Stone et al., 2008). A recent study revealed that mdivi-1 attenuates the degree of inflammation; reverses abnormal mitochondrial fission, mitochondrial membrane potential loss, cytochrome c release, and caspase-3 activation; and consequently suppresses mitochondrial apoptosis in BV-2 and primary microglial cells exposed to Aβ (Xie et al., 2014). Using AD cybrids, Gan et al. (2014) found that mdivi-1 eradicates the defects on mitochondrial bioenergetics and dynamics. Particularly, the pharmacological blockage of mitochondrial division with mdivi-1 improved mitochondrial length and density, restored COX activity and ATP levels, and suppressed ROS overproduction, corroborating the potential of this drug in protecting mitochondrial structure and function (Gan et al., 2014). However, there are as yet no clinical data regarding the beneficial effects of mdivi-1 in AD.

Nonpharmacological Approaches

In the context of AD complexity, scientific advances revealed that nonpharmacological interventions may also exert direct benefits on AD-related pathology by modulating oxidative status and mitochondrial physiology. Among these interventions, diet and physical exercise are now a focus of intense scrutiny as therapeutic strategies to postpone AD.

Extensive literature reported the ability of caloric restriction to activate an adaptive metabolic reprogramming leading to lower levels of oxidative damage. A common signature of caloric restriction is the induction of PGC-1α-dependent mitochondrial biogenesis and bioenergetic efficiency (Duan and Ross, 2010; Lopez-Lluch et al., 2006). Studies performed in transgenic mouse models of AD demonstrated that caloric restriction improves behavioral performance and attenuates both Aβ and tau pathologies (Brownlow et al., 2014; Wang et al., 2005; Wu et al., 2008). However, whether these benefits of caloric restriction in experimental models of AD result from an improvement in mitochondrial function remains elusive.

Physical exercise was shown to stimulate mitochondrial biogenesis, improve mitochondrial bioenergetics, and positively regulate mitochondrial fusion–fission and mitophagy in the brain cortex (Marques-Aleixo et al., 2015; Steiner et al., 2011). As expected, physical exercise was reported to repress neuronal cell death, Aβ pathology, and cognitive deficits in transgenic mouse models of AD (Adlard et al., 2005; Um et al., 2008, 2011). Interestingly, Lezi et al. (2013) observed that lactate, the most elementary product of exercise physiology, is able to reproduce the same benefits on brain mitochondria as those found during exercise. This observation raised the possibility of having "exercise-in-a-bottle" to counteract AD progression (Correia et al., 2013). Epidemiological evidence has repeatedly revealed that physical exercise is associated with reduced decline in cognitive performance in AD subjects (Archer, 2011; Venturelli et al., 2011; Winchester et al., 2013).

CONCLUSIONS

The past 30 years have seen remarkable advances in the technology and details of molecular pathogenesis that would have been impossible to imagine only a few years earlier. Nevertheless, progress in treatment of neurodegenerative disease in general, and AD in particular, has been remarkably flat. These two facts reinforce humility before nature, with the reality that treatment of these afflictions is beyond the reach of our current capabilities and perhaps will be for many years into the future. The concept of rate-limiting toxic proteins has its appeal, and the genetic foundation for such concepts is elegant in its simplicity, but more research and more knowledge are required. This is not to discount the merit of individual mechanisms, which is substantial. The modern scientific process, for better or worse, requires the artificial separation of individual mechanisms that in reality act in concert. An approach to AD therapy, just like an approach to AD biology, should instead be more broad, unless and until discernible progress is made toward disease modification.

In this sense, oxidation biology is appropriate for the study of AD pathology and a worthy subject on its own, as it embodies evolutionarily conserved physiologic processes, which are out of balance in disease, and forces the investigator to consider multiple forces acting on the intact organism. For example, molecular oxygen, free radicals derived from the interaction of oxygen and metals, and antioxidant substances are necessary to sustain life but toxic when poorly regulated. Exquisite balance persists for decades due to complex regulation. This complex control though makes it challenging to differentiate disease response from disease mechanism. For these reasons, therapeutic trials with individual substances like vitamins C and E and a narrow focus on a circumscribed pathogenic mechanism may be inappropriate. The study of oxidation biology may encourage a broader approach to the complexities of AD, with recognition of the extensive overlap between biology and pathology, not only in AD but in chronic disease in general. In this way, we might identify targetable molecular events more closely aligned with disease.

References

Adlard PA, Perreau VM, Pop V, Cotman CW: Voluntary exercise decreases amyloid load in a transgenic model of Alzheimer's disease, *J Neurosci* 25:4217–4221, 2005.

Aldred S, Bennett S, Mecocci P: Increased low-density lipoprotein oxidation, but not total plasma protein oxidation, in Alzheimer's disease, *Clin Biochem* 43:267–271, 2010.

Aliev G, Liu J, Shenk JC, et al: Neuronal mitochondrial amelioration by feeding acetyl-L-carnitine and lipoic acid to aged rats, *J Cell Mol Med* 13:320–333, 2009.

Ansari MA, Scheff SW: Oxidative stress in the progression of Alzheimer disease in the frontal cortex, *J Neuropath Exp Neurol* 69:155–167, 2010.

Archer T: Physical exercise alleviates debilities of normal aging and Alzheimer's disease, *Acta Neurologica Scandinavica* 123:221–238, 2011.

Arlt S, Muller-Thomsen T, Beisiegel U, Kontush A: Effect of one-year vitamin C- and E-supplementation on cerebrospinal fluid oxidation parameters and clinical course in Alzheimer's disease, *Neurochem Res* 37:2706–2714, 2012.

Atwood CS, Scarpa RC, Huang X, et al: Characterization of copper interactions with Alzheimer amyloid beta peptides: identification of an attomolar-affinity copper binding site on amyloid beta1-42, *J Neurochem* 75:1219–1233, 2000.

Aybek H, Ercan F, Aslan D, Sahiner T: Determination of malondialdehyde, reduced glutathione levels and APOE4 allele frequency in late-onset Alzheimer's disease in Denizli, Turkey, *Clin Biochem* 40:172–176, 2007.

Azari NP, Pettigrew KD, Schapiro MB, et al: Early detection of Alzheimer's disease: a statistical approach using positron emission tomographic data, *J Cerebr Blood F Metabol* 13:438–447, 1993.

Bachurin S, Bukatina E, Lermontova N, et al: Antihistamine agent Dimebon as a novel neuroprotector and a cognition enhancer, *Ann NY Acad Sci* 939:425–435, 2001.

Baloyannis SJ: Mitochondrial alterations in Alzheimer's disease, *J Alzheimers Dis* 9:119–126, 2006.

Barnham KJ, Masters CL, Bush AI: Neurodegenerative diseases and oxidative stress, *Nat Rev Drug Discov* 3:205–214, 2004.

Basun H, Forssell LG, Wetterberg L, Winblad B: Metals and trace elements in plasma and cerebrospinal fluid in normal aging and Alzheimer's disease, *J Neural Transm-Park Dis Dement Sect* 3:231–258, 1991.

Behl C, Davis JB, Lesley R, Schubert D: Hydrogen peroxide mediates amyloid beta protein toxicity, *Cell* 77:817–827, 1994.

Bezprozvanny I: The rise and fall of Dimebon, *Drug News Perspect* 23:518–523, 2010.

Bharadwaj PR, Verdile G, Barr RK, et al: Latrepirdine (Dimebon) enhances autophagy and reduces intracellular GFP-Abeta42 levels in yeast, *J Alzheimers Dis* 32:949–967, 2012.

Bianchetti A, Rozzini R, Trabucchi M: Effects of acetyl-L-carnitine in Alzheimer's disease patients unresponsive to acetylcholinesterase inhibitors, *Curr Med Res Opin* 19:350–353, 2003.

Bosetti F, Brizzi F, Barogi S, et al: Cytochrome c oxidase and mitochondrial F1F0-ATPase (ATP synthase) activities in platelets and brain from patients with Alzheimer's disease, *Neurobiol Aging* 23:371–376, 2002.

Bradley MA, Xiong-Fister S, Markesbery WR, Lovell MA: Elevated 4-hydroxyhexenal in Alzheimer's disease (AD) progression, *Neurobiol Aging* 33:1034–1044, 2012.

Brownlow ML, Joly-Amado A, Azam S, et al: Partial rescue of memory deficits induced by calorie restriction in a mouse model of tau deposition, *Behav Brain Res* 271:79–88, 2014.

Bubber P, Haroutunian V, Fisch G, Blass JP, Gibson GE: Mitochondrial abnormalities in Alzheimer brain: mechanistic implications, *Ann Neurol* 57:695–703, 2005.

Bush AI: The metal theory of Alzheimer's disease, *J Alzheimers Dis* 33(Suppl 1):S277–S281, 2013.

Bush AI, Tanzi RE: Therapeutics for Alzheimer's disease based on the metal hypothesis, *Neurotherapeutics* 5:421–432, 2008.

Cardoso SM, Proenca MT, Santos S, Santana I, Oliveira CR: Cytochrome c oxidase is decreased in Alzheimer's disease platelets, *Neurobiol Aging* 25:105–110, 2004.

Cassidy-Stone A, Chipuk JE, Ingerman E, et al: Chemical inhibition of the mitochondrial division dynamin reveals its role in Bax/Bak-dependent mitochondrial outer membrane permeabilization, *Dev Cell* 14:193–204, 2008.

Castellani RJ, Perry G: The complexities of the pathology–pathogenesis relationship in Alzheimer disease, *Biochem Pharmacol* 88:671–676, 2014.

Castellani RJ, Smith MA, Nunomura A, Harris PL, Perry G: Is increased redox-active iron in Alzheimer disease a failure of the copper-binding protein ceruloplasmin? *Free Radic Biol Med* 26:1508–1512, 1999.

Castellani RJ, Harris PL, Sayre LM, et al: Active glycation in neurofibrillary pathology of Alzheimer disease: N(epsilon)-(carboxymethyl) lysine and hexitol-lysine, *Free Radic Biol Med* 31:175–180, 2001.

Castellani RJ, Zhu X, Lee HG, Smith MA, Perry G: Molecular pathogenesis of Alzheimer's disease: reductionist versus expansionist approaches, *Int J Mol Sci* 10:1386–1406, 2009.

Chang YT, Chang WN, Tsai NW, et al: The roles of biomarkers of oxidative stress and antioxidant in Alzheimer's disease: a systematic review, *BioMed Res Intl* 2014:182303, 2014.

Chen Z, Zhong C: Oxidative stress in Alzheimer's disease, *Neurosci Bull* 30:271–281, 2014.
Cherubini A, Ruggiero C, Polidori MC, Mecocci P: Potential markers of oxidative stress in stroke, *Free Radic Biol Med* 39:841–852, 2005.
Cho DH, Nakamura T, Fang J, et al: S-nitrosylation of Drp1 mediates beta-amyloid-related mitochondrial fission and neuronal injury, *Science* 324:102–105, 2009.
Chou JL, Shenoy DV, Thomas N, et al: Early dysregulation of the mitochondrial proteome in a mouse model of Alzheimer's disease, *J Proteomics* 74:466–479, 2011.
Chouraki V, Seshadri S: Genetics of Alzheimer's disease, *Adv Genet* 87:245–294, 2014.
Correia SC, Santos RX, Cardoso S, et al: Alzheimer disease as a vascular disorder: where do mitochondria fit? *Exp Gerontol* 47:878–886, 2012.
Correia SC, Perry G, Castellani R, Moreira PI: Is exercise-in-a-bottle likely to proffer new insights into Alzheimer's disease? *J Neurochem* 127:4–6, 2013.
Cristalli DO, Arnal N, Marra FA, de Alaniz MJ, Marra CA: Peripheral markers in neurodegenerative patients and their first-degree relatives, *J Neurol Sci* 314:48–56, 2012.
Curtain CC, Ali F, Volitakis I, et al: Alzheimer's disease amyloid-beta binds copper and zinc to generate an allosterically ordered membrane-penetrating structure containing superoxide dismutase-like subunits, *J Biol Chem* 276:20466–20473, 2001.
Curtain CC, Ali FE, Smith DG, Bush AI, Masters CL, Barnham KJ: Metal ions, pH, and cholesterol regulate the interactions of Alzheimer's disease amyloid-beta peptide with membrane lipid, *J Biol Chem* 278:2977–2982, 2003.
Di Domenico F, Barone E, Perluigi M, Butterfield DA: Strategy to reduce free radical species in Alzheimer's disease: an update of selected antioxidants, *Expert Rev Neurotherapeutics* 15:19–40, 2015.
Doody RS, Gavrilova SI, Sano M, et al: Effect of Dimebon on cognition, activities of daily living, behaviour, and global function in patients with mild-to-moderate Alzheimer's disease: a randomised, double-blind, placebo-controlled study, *Lancet* 372:207–215, 2008.
Dowling GA, Burr RL, Van Someren EJ, et al: Melatonin and bright-light treatment for rest–activity disruption in institutionalized patients with Alzheimer's disease, *J Am Geriatr Soc* 56:239–246, 2008.
Du LL, Xie JZ, Cheng XS, et al: Activation of sirtuin 1 attenuates cerebral ventricular streptozotocin-induced tau hyperphosphorylation and cognitive injuries in rat hippocampi, *Age* 36:613–623, 2014.
Duan W, Ross CA: Potential therapeutic targets for neurodegenerative diseases: lessons learned from calorie restriction, *Curr Drug Targets* 11:1281–1292, 2010.
Dumont M, Beal MF: Neuroprotective strategies involving ROS in Alzheimer disease, *Free Radic Biol Med* 51:1014–1026, 2011.
Dumont M, Kipiani K, Yu F, et al: Coenzyme Q10 decreases amyloid pathology and improves behavior in a transgenic mouse model of Alzheimer's disease, *J Alzheimers Dis* 27:211–223, 2011.
Eckert SH, Eckmann J, Renner K, Eckert GP, Leuner K, Muller WE: Dimebon ameliorates amyloid-beta induced impairments of mitochondrial form and function, *J Alzheimers Dis* 31:21–32, 2012.
Elipenahli C, Stack C, Jainuddin S, et al: Behavioral improvement after chronic administration of coenzyme Q10 in P301S transgenic mice, *J Alzheimers Dis* 28:173–182, 2012.
Escribano L, Simon AM, Perez-Mediavilla A, Salazar-Colocho P, Del Rio J, Frechilla D: Rosiglitazone reverses memory decline and hippocampal glucocorticoid receptor down-regulation in an Alzheimer's disease mouse model, *Biochem Bioph Res Co* 379:406–410, 2009.
Feldman HH, Haas M, Gandy S, et al: Alzheimer's disease research and development: a call for a new research roadmap, *Ann NY Acad Sci* 1313:1–16, 2014.
Feng Z, Qin C, Chang Y, Zhang JT: Early melatonin supplementation alleviates oxidative stress in a transgenic mouse model of Alzheimer's disease, *Free Radical Biol Med* 40:101–109, 2006.
Flora SJ, Shrivastava R, Mittal M: Chemistry and pharmacological properties of some natural and synthetic antioxidants for heavy metal toxicity, *Curr Med Chem* 20:4540–4574, 2013.
Gan X, Huang S, Wu L, et al: Inhibition of ERK-DLP1 signaling and mitochondrial division alleviates mitochondrial dysfunction in Alzheimer's disease cybrid cell, *Biochimica et Biophysica Acta* 1842:220–231, 2014.
Garcia-Alloza M, Borrelli LA, Rozkalne A, Hyman BT, Bacskai BJ: Curcumin labels amyloid pathology in vivo, disrupts existing plaques, and partially restores distorted neurites in an Alzheimer mouse model, *J Neurochem* 102:1095–1104, 2007.
Garcia-Mesa Y, Gimenez-Llort L, Lopez LC, et al: Melatonin plus physical exercise are highly neuroprotective in the 3xTg-AD mouse, *Neurobiol Aging* 33(1124):e13–e29, 2012.

Gehrman PR, Connor DJ, Martin JL, Shochat T, Corey-Bloom J, Ancoli-Israel S: Melatonin fails to improve sleep or agitation in double-blind randomized placebo-controlled trial of institutionalized patients with Alzheimer disease, *Am J Geriat Psychiat* 17:166–169, 2009.

Ghosh S, Patel N, Rahn D, et al: The thiazolidinedione pioglitazone alters mitochondrial function in human neuron-like cells, *Mol Pharmacol* 71:1695–1702, 2007.

Granzotto A, Zatta P: Resveratrol and Alzheimer's disease: message in a bottle on red wine and cognition, *Frontiers Aging Neurosci* 6:95, 2014.

Hager K, Marahrens A, Kenklies M, Riederer P, Munch G: Alpha-lipoic acid as a new treatment option for Alzheimer [corrected] type dementia, *Arch Gerontol Geriat* 32:275–282, 2001.

Hager K, Kenklies M, McAfoose J, Engel J, Munch G: Alpha-lipoic acid as a new treatment option for Alzheimer's disease—a 48 months follow-up analysis, *J Neur Tr S*:189–193, 2007.

Hampton MB, Kettle AJ, Winterbourn CC: Inside the neutrophil phagosome: oxidants, myeloperoxidase, and bacterial killing, *Blood* 92:3007–3017, 1998.

Hanyu H, Sato T, Kiuchi A, Sakurai H, Iwamoto T: Pioglitazone improved cognition in a pilot study on patients with Alzheimer's disease and mild cognitive impairment with diabetes mellitus, *J Am Geriatr Soc* 57:177–179, 2009.

Harrison FE, Allard J, Bixler R, et al: Antioxidants and cognitive training interact to affect oxidative stress and memory in APP/PSEN1 mice, *Nutr Neurosci* 12:203–218, 2009.

Hirai K, Aliev G, Nunomura A, et al: Mitochondrial abnormalities in Alzheimer's disease, *J Neurosci* 21:3017–3023, 2001.

Hirokawa N, Niwa S, Tanaka Y: Molecular motors in neurons: transport mechanisms and roles in brain function, development, and disease, *Neuron* 68:610–638, 2010.

Holmes C, Boche D, Wilkinson D, et al: Long-term effects of Abeta42 immunisation in Alzheimer's disease: follow-up of a randomised, placebo-controlled phase I trial, *Lancet* 372:216–223, 2008.

Jack CR Jr, Petersen RC, Grundman M, et al: Longitudinal MRI findings from the vitamin E and donepezil treatment study for MCI, *Neurobiol Aging* 29:1285–1295, 2008.

James AM, Sharpley MS, Manas AR, et al: Interaction of the mitochondria-targeted antioxidant MitoQ with phospholipid bilayers and ubiquinone oxidoreductases, *J Biol Chem* 282:14708–14718, 2007.

Kanninen K, Malm TM, Jyrkkanen HK, et al: Nuclear factor erythroid 2-related factor 2 protects against beta amyloid, *Mol Cell Neurosci* 39:302–313, 2008.

Kanninen K, Heikkinen R, Malm T, et al: Intrahippocampal injection of a lentiviral vector expressing Nrf2 improves spatial learning in a mouse model of Alzheimer's disease, *Proc Natl Acad Sci USA* 106:16505–16510, 2009.

Karran E, Mercken M, De Strooper B: The amyloid cascade hypothesis for Alzheimer's disease: an appraisal for the development of therapeutics, *Nat Rev Drug Discov* 10:698–712, 2011.

Kharrazi H, Vaisi Raygani A, Sabokroh AR, Pourmotabbed T: Association between apolipoprotein E polymorphism and coronary artery disease in the Kermanshah population in Iran, *Clin Biochem* 39:613–616, 2006.

Kim I, Rodriguez-Enriquez S, Lemasters JJ: Selective degradation of mitochondria by mitophagy, *Arch Biochem Biophys* 462:245–253, 2007.

Kish SJ, Bergeron C, Rajput A, et al: Brain cytochrome oxidase in Alzheimer's disease, *J Neurochem* 59:776–779, 1992.

Kurz C, Ungerer I, Lipka U, et al: The metabolic enhancer piracetam ameliorates the impairment of mitochondrial function and neurite outgrowth induced by beta-amyloid peptide, *Brit J Pharmacol* 160:246–257, 2010.

Leuner K, Kurz C, Guidetti G, Orgogozo JM, Muller WE: Improved mitochondrial function in brain aging and Alzheimer disease—the new mechanism of action of the old metabolic enhancer piracetam, *Frontiers Neurosci* 4, 2010.

Lezi E, Lu J, Selfridge JE, Burns JM, Swerdlow RH: Lactate administration reproduces specific brain and liver exercise-related changes, *J Neurochem* 127:91–100, 2013.

Li G, Zou LY, Cao CM, Yang ES: Coenzyme Q10 protects SHSY5Y neuronal cells from beta amyloid toxicity and oxygen-glucose deprivation by inhibiting the opening of the mitochondrial permeability transition pore, *BioFactors* 25:97–107, 2005.

Lim GP, Chu T, Yang F, Beech W, Frautschy SA, Cole GM: The curry spice curcumin reduces oxidative damage and amyloid pathology in an Alzheimer transgenic mouse, *J Neurosci* 21:8370–8377, 2001.

Lopez-Lluch G, Hunt N, Jones B, et al: Calorie restriction induces mitochondrial biogenesis and bioenergetic efficiency, *Proc Natl Acad Sci USA* 103:1768–1773, 2006.

Lovell MA, Robertson JD, Teesdale WJ, Campbell JL, Markesbery WR: Copper, iron and zinc in Alzheimer's disease senile plaques, *J Neurol Sci* 158:47–52, 1998.

Manczak M, Mao P, Calkins MJ, et al: Mitochondria-targeted antioxidants protect against amyloid-beta toxicity in Alzheimer's disease neurons, *J Alzheimer's Dis* 20(Suppl 2):S609–S631, 2010.

Markesbery WR, Kryscio RJ, Lovell MA, Morrow JD: Lipid peroxidation is an early event in the brain in amnestic mild cognitive impairment, *Ann Neurol* 58:730–735, 2005.

Marques-Aleixo I, Santos-Alves E, Balca MM, et al: Physical exercise improves brain cortex and cerebellum mitochondrial bioenergetics and alters apoptotic, dynamic and auto(mito)phagy markers, *Neuroscience* 301:480–495, 2015.

Mastrogiacomo F, Bergeron C, Kish SJ: Brain alpha-ketoglutarate dehydrogenase complex activity in Alzheimer's disease, *J Neurochem* 61:2007–2014, 1993.

Matsubara E, Bryant-Thomas T, Pacheco Quinto J, et al: Melatonin increases survival and inhibits oxidative and amyloid pathology in a transgenic model of Alzheimer's disease, *J Neurochem* 85:1101–1108, 2003.

McManus MJ, Murphy MP, Franklin JL: The mitochondria-targeted antioxidant MitoQ prevents loss of spatial memory retention and early neuropathology in a transgenic mouse model of Alzheimer's disease, *J Neurosci* 31:15703–15715, 2011.

Migliore L, Fontana I, Trippi F, et al: Oxidative DNA damage in peripheral leukocytes of mild cognitive impairment and AD patients, *Neurobiol Aging* 26:567–573, 2005.

Miller G: Pharmacology: the puzzling rise and fall of a dark-horse Alzheimer's drug, *Science* 327:1309, 2010.

Milne GL, Musiek ES, Morrow JD: F2-isoprostanes as markers of oxidative stress in vivo: an overview, *Biomarkers* 10(Suppl 1):S10–S23, 2005.

Misko A, Jiang S, Wegorzewska I, Milbrandt J, Baloh RH: Mitofusin 2 is necessary for transport of axonal mitochondria and interacts with the Miro/Milton complex, *J Neurosci* 30:4232–4240, 2010.

Montgomery SA, Thal LJ, Amrein R: Meta-analysis of double blind randomized controlled clinical trials of acetyl-L-carnitine versus placebo in the treatment of mild cognitive impairment and mild Alzheimer's disease, *Int Clin Psychopharmacol* 18:61–71, 2003.

Moreira PI, Santos MS, Sena C, Nunes E, Seica R, Oliveira CR: CoQ10 therapy attenuates amyloid beta-peptide toxicity in brain mitochondria isolated from aged diabetic rats, *Exp Neurol* 196:112–119, 2005.

Moreira PI, Siedlak SL, Wang X, et al: Autophagocytosis of mitochondria is prominent in Alzheimer disease, *J Neuropathol Exp Neurol* 66:525–532, 2007a.

Moreira PI, Siedlak SL, Wang X, et al: Increased autophagic degradation of mitochondria in Alzheimer disease, *Autophagy* 3:614–615, 2007b.

Moreira PI, Harris PL, Zhu X, et al: Lipoic acid and N-acetyl cysteine decrease mitochondrial-related oxidative stress in Alzheimer disease patient fibroblasts, *J Alzheimers Dis* 12:195–206, 2007c.

Moreira PI, Cardoso SM, Pereira CM, Santos MS, Oliveira CR: Mitochondria as a therapeutic target in Alzheimer's disease and diabetes, *CNS Neurol Disord-Dr* 8:492–511, 2009.

Moreira PI, Zhu X, Wang X, et al: Mitochondria: a therapeutic target in neurodegeneration, *Biochimica et Biophysica Acta* 1802:212–220, 2010.

Murphy MP, Smith RA: Targeting antioxidants to mitochondria by conjugation to lipophilic cations, *Annu Rev Pharmacol* 47:629–656, 2007.

Mutisya EM, Bowling AC, Beal MF: Cortical cytochrome oxidase activity is reduced in Alzheimer's disease, *J Neurochem* 63:2179–2184, 1994.

Ng LF, Gruber J, Cheah IK, et al: The mitochondria-targeted antioxidant MitoQ extends lifespan and improves healthspan of a transgenic Caenorhabditis elegans model of Alzheimer disease, *Free Radical Biol Med* 71:390–401, 2014.

Nicolakakis N, Aboulkassim T, Ongali B, et al: Complete rescue of cerebrovascular function in aged Alzheimer's disease transgenic mice by antioxidants and pioglitazone, a peroxisome proliferator-activated receptor gamma agonist, *J Neurosci* 28:9287–9296, 2008.

Nunomura A, Perry G, Pappolla MA, et al: RNA oxidation is a prominent feature of vulnerable neurons in Alzheimer's disease, *J Neurosci* 19:1959–1964, 1999.

Nunomura A, Perry G, Pappolla MA, et al: Neuronal oxidative stress precedes amyloid-beta deposition in Down syndrome, *J Neuropathol Exp Neurol* 59:1011–1017, 2000.

Nunomura A, Perry G, Aliev G, et al: Oxidative damage is the earliest event in Alzheimer disease, *J Neuropathol Exp Neurol* 60:759–767, 2001.

Nunomura A, Castellani RJ, Zhu X, Moreira PI, Perry G, Smith MA: Involvement of oxidative stress in Alzheimer disease, *J Neuropathol Exp Neurol* 65:631–641, 2006.

Nunomura A, Moreira PI, Takeda A, Smith MA, Perry G: Oxidative RNA damage and neurodegeneration, *Curr Med Chem* 14:2968–2975, 2007.

Nunomura A, Moreira PI, Castellani RJ, et al: Oxidative damage to RNA in aging and neurodegenerative disorders, *Neurotox Res* 22:231–248, 2012a.

Nunomura A, Tamaoki T, Motohashi N, et al: The earliest stage of cognitive impairment in transition from normal aging to Alzheimer disease is marked by prominent RNA oxidation in vulnerable neurons, *J Neuropathol Exp Neurol* 71:233–241, 2012b.

Okun I, Tkachenko SE, Khvat A, Mitkin O, Kazey V, Ivachtchenko AV: From anti-allergic to anti-Alzheimer's: molecular pharmacology of Dimebon, *Curr Alzheimer Res* 7:97–112, 2010.

Olcese JM, Cao C, Mori T, et al: Protection against cognitive deficits and markers of neurodegeneration by long-term oral administration of melatonin in a transgenic model of Alzheimer disease, *J Pineal Res* 47:82–96, 2009.

O'Neal-Moffitt G, Delic V, Bradshaw PC, Olcese J: Prophylactic melatonin significantly reduces Alzheimer's neuropathology and associated cognitive deficits independent of antioxidant pathways in AbetaPP(swe)/PS1 mice, *Mol Neurodegener* 10:27, 2015.

Opazo C, Huang X, Cherny RA, et al: Metalloenzyme-like activity of Alzheimer's disease beta-amyloid: Cu-dependent catalytic conversion of dopamine, cholesterol, and biological reducing agents to neurotoxic H(2)O(2), *J Biol Chem* 277:40302–40308, 2002.

Papadopoulos P, Rosa-Neto P, Rochford J, Hamel E: Pioglitazone improves reversal learning and exerts mixed cerebrovascular effects in a mouse model of Alzheimer's disease with combined amyloid-beta and cerebrovascular pathology, *PLoS One* 8:e68612, 2013.

Pappolla MA, Sos M, Omar RA, et al: Melatonin prevents death of neuroblastoma cells exposed to the Alzheimer amyloid peptide, *J Neurosci* 17:1683–1690, 1997.

Peacock ML, Fink JK: ApoE epsilon 4 allelic association with Alzheimer's disease: independent confirmation using denaturing gradient gel electrophoresis, *Neurology* 44:339–341, 1994.

Perry G, Castellani R: Plaques and tangles: birthmarks of the aging soul: preface, *Biochem Pharmacol* 88:423–425, 2014.

Perry G, Castellani RJ, Smith MA, et al: Oxidative damage in the olfactory system in Alzheimer's disease, *Acta Neuropathol* 106:552–556, 2003.

Persson T, Popescu BO, Cedazo-Minguez A: Oxidative stress in Alzheimer's disease: why did antioxidant therapy fail? *Oxidative Med Cell Longevity* 2014:427318, 2014.

Polidori MC, Mecocci P: Plasma susceptibility to free radical-induced antioxidant consumption and lipid peroxidation is increased in very old subjects with Alzheimer disease, *J Alzheimers Dis* 4:517–522, 2002.

Poon HF, Farr SA, Thongboonkerd V, et al: Proteomic analysis of specific brain proteins in aged SAMP8 mice treated with alpha-lipoic acid: implications for aging and age-related neurodegenerative disorders, *Neurochem Int* 46:159–168, 2005.

Porquet D, Casadesus G, Bayod S, et al: Dietary resveratrol prevents Alzheimer's markers and increases life span in SAMP8, *Age* 35:1851–1865, 2013.

Qin W, Haroutunian V, Katsel P, et al: PGC-1alpha expression decreases in the Alzheimer disease brain as a function of dementia, *Arch Neurol* 66:352–361, 2009.

Quinn JF, Bussiere JR, Hammond RS, et al: Chronic dietary alpha-lipoic acid reduces deficits in hippocampal memory of aged Tg2576 mice, *Neurobiol Aging* 28:213–225, 2007.

Ravet K, Pilon M: Copper and iron homeostasis in plants: the challenges of oxidative stress, *Antioxid Redox Signal* 19:919–932, 2013.

Reddy PH, Tripathi R, Troung Q, et al: Abnormal mitochondrial dynamics and synaptic degeneration as early events in Alzheimer's disease: implications to mitochondria targeted antioxidant therapeutics, *Biochimica et Biophysica Acta* 1822:639–649, 2012.

Resende R, Moreira PI, Proenca T, et al: Brain oxidative stress in a triple-transgenic mouse model of Alzheimer disease, *Free Radical Biol Med* 44:2051–2057, 2008.

Rhein V, Giese M, Baysang G, et al: Ginkgo biloba extract ameliorates oxidative phosphorylation performance and rescues abeta-induced failure, *PLoS One* 5:e12359, 2010.

Rinaldi P, Polidori MC, Metastasio A, et al: Plasma antioxidants are similarly depleted in mild cognitive impairment and in Alzheimer's disease, *Neurobiol Aging* 24:915–919, 2003.

Risner ME, Saunders AM, Altman JF, et al: Efficacy of rosiglitazone in a genetically defined population with mild-to-moderate Alzheimer's disease, *Pharmacogenomics J* 6:246–254, 2006.

Rudnitskaya EA, Muraleva NA, Maksimova KY, Kiseleva E, Kolosova NG, Stefanova NA: Melatonin attenuates memory impairment, amyloid-beta accumulation, and neurodegeneration in a rat model of sporadic Alzheimer's disease, *J Alzheimers Dis* 47:103–116, 2015.

Salminen LE, Paul RH: Oxidative stress and genetic markers of suboptimal antioxidant defense in the aging brain: a theoretical review, *Rev Neurosci* 25:805–819, 2014.

Sano M, Ernesto C, Thomas RG, et al: A controlled trial of selegiline, alpha-tocopherol, or both as treatment for Alzheimer's disease. The Alzheimer's Disease Cooperative Study, *N Engl J Med* 336:1216–1222, 1997.

Sato T, Hanyu H, Hirao K, Kanetaka H, Sakurai H, Iwamoto T: Efficacy of PPAR-gamma agonist pioglitazone in mild Alzheimer disease, *Neurobiol Aging* 32:1626–1633, 2011.

Sayre LM, Zelasko DA, Harris PL, Perry G, Salomon RG, Smith MA: 4-Hydroxynonenal-derived advanced lipid peroxidation end products are increased in Alzheimer's disease, *J Neurochem* 68:2092–2097, 1997.

Scherz-Shouval R, Shvets E, Fass E, Shorer H, Gil L, Elazar Z: Reactive oxygen species are essential for autophagy and specifically regulate the activity of Atg4, *EMBO J* 26:1749–1760, 2007.

Selkoe DJ: SnapShot: pathobiology of Alzheimer's disease, *Cell* 154, 2013, 468–468.e1.

Shaerzadeh F, Motamedi F, Minai-Tehrani D, Khodagholi F: Monitoring of neuronal loss in the hippocampus of Abeta-injected rat: autophagy, mitophagy, and mitochondrial biogenesis stand against apoptosis, *Neuromol Med* 16:175–190, 2014.

Sharma M, Gupta YK: Chronic treatment with trans resveratrol prevents intracerebroventricular streptozotocin induced cognitive impairment and oxidative stress in rats, *Life Sci* 71:2489–2498, 2002.

Sheng ZH: Mitochondrial trafficking and anchoring in neurons: new insight and implications, *J Cell Biol* 204:1087–1098, 2014.

Sheng ZH, Cai Q: Mitochondrial transport in neurons: impact on synaptic homeostasis and neurodegeneration, *Nat Rev Neurosci* 13:77–93, 2012.

Sheng B, Wang X, Su B, et al: Impaired mitochondrial biogenesis contributes to mitochondrial dysfunction in Alzheimer's disease, *J Neurochem* 120:419–429, 2012.

Sies H: Strategies of antioxidant defense, *Eur J Biochem/FEBS* 215:213–219, 1993.

Smirnova E, Griparic L, Shurland DL, van der Bliek AM: Dynamin-related protein Drp1 is required for mitochondrial division in mammalian cells, *Mol Biol Cell* 12:2245–2256, 2001.

Smith JV, Luo Y: Elevation of oxidative free radicals in Alzheimer's disease models can be attenuated by Ginkgo biloba extract EGb 761, *J Alzheimers Dis* 5:287–300, 2003.

Smith MA, Taneda S, Richey PL, et al: Advanced Maillard reaction end products are associated with Alzheimer disease pathology, *Proc Natl Acad Sci USA* 91:5710–5714, 1994a.

Smith MA, Kutty RK, Richey PL, et al: Heme oxygenase-1 is associated with the neurofibrillary pathology of Alzheimer's disease, *Am J Pathol* 145:42–47, 1994b.

Smith MA, Sayre LM, Monnier VM, Perry G: Radical AGEing in Alzheimer's disease, *Trends Neurosci* 18:172–176, 1995a.

Smith MA, Rudnicka-Nawrot M, Richey PL, et al: Carbonyl-related posttranslational modification of neurofilament protein in the neurofibrillary pathology of Alzheimer's disease, *J Neurochem* 64:2660–2666, 1995b.

Smith MA, Richey Harris PL, Sayre LM, Beckman JS, Perry G: Widespread peroxynitrite-mediated damage in Alzheimer's disease, *J Neurosci* 17:2653–2657, 1997a.

Smith MA, Harris PL, Sayre LM, Perry G: Iron accumulation in Alzheimer disease is a source of redox-generated free radicals, *Proc Natl Acad Sci USA* 94:9866–9868, 1997b.

Somayajulu M, McCarthy S, Hung M, Sikorska M, Borowy-Borowski H, Pandey S: Role of mitochondria in neuronal cell death induced by oxidative stress: neuroprotection by coenzyme Q10, *Neurobiol Dis* 18:618–627, 2005.

Squitti R, Lupoi D, Pasqualetti P, et al: Elevation of serum copper levels in Alzheimer's disease, *Neurology* 59:1153–1161, 2002.

Steele JW, Lachenmayer ML, Ju S, et al: Latrepirdine improves cognition and arrests progression of neuropathology in an Alzheimer's mouse model, *Mol Psychiatr* 18:889–897, 2013.

Stefanova NA, Maksimova KY, Kiseleva E, Rudnitskaya EA, Muraleva NA, Kolosova NG: Melatonin attenuates impairments of structural hippocampal neuroplasticity in OXYS rats during active progression of Alzheimer's disease-like pathology, *J Pineal Res* 59:163–177, 2015.

Steiner JL, Murphy EA, McClellan JL, Carmichael MD, Davis JM: Exercise training increases mitochondrial biogenesis in the brain, *J Appl Physiol* 111:1066–1071, 2011.

Stockburger C, Kurz C, Koch KA, Eckert SH, Leuner K, Muller WE: Improvement of mitochondrial function and dynamics by the metabolic enhancer piracetam, *Biochem Soc T* 41:1331–1334, 2013.

Strum JC, Shehee R, Virley D, et al: Rosiglitazone induces mitochondrial biogenesis in mouse brain, *J Alzheimers Dis* 11:45–51, 2007.

Sultana R, Butterfield DA: Oxidative modification of brain proteins in Alzheimer's disease: perspective on future studies based on results of redox proteomics studies, *J Alzheimers Dis* 33(Suppl 1):S243–S251, 2013.

Sung S, Yao Y, Uryu K, et al: Early vitamin E supplementation in young but not aged mice reduces Abeta levels and amyloid deposition in a transgenic model of Alzheimer's disease, *FASEB J* 18:323–325, 2004.

Swerdlow RH: Mitochondrial medicine and the neurodegenerative mitochondriopathies, *Pharmaceuticals* 2:150–167, 2009.

Tanzi RE: The synaptic Abeta hypothesis of Alzheimer disease, *Nat Neurosci* 8:977–979, 2005.

Thal LJ, Grundman M, Berg J, et al: Idebenone treatment fails to slow cognitive decline in Alzheimer's disease, *Neurology* 61:1498–1502, 2003.

Tretter L, Adam-Vizi V: Inhibition of Krebs cycle enzymes by hydrogen peroxide: a key role of [alpha]-ketoglutarate dehydrogenase in limiting NADH production under oxidative stress, *J Neurosci* 20:8972–8979, 2000.

Trimmer PA, Borland MK: Differentiated Alzheimer's disease transmitochondrial cybrid cell lines exhibit reduced organelle movement, *Antioxid Redox Sign* 7:1101–1109, 2005.

Turner RS, Thomas RG, Craft S, et al: A randomized, double-blind, placebo-controlled trial of resveratrol for Alzheimer disease, *Neurology* 85:1383–1391, 2015.

Twig G, Shirihai OS: The interplay between mitochondrial dynamics and mitophagy, *Antioxid Redox Sign* 14:1939–1951, 2011.

Twig G, Elorza A, Molina AJ, et al: Fission and selective fusion govern mitochondrial segregation and elimination by autophagy, *EMBO J* 27:433–446, 2008.

Um HS, Kang EB, Leem YH, et al: Exercise training acts as a therapeutic strategy for reduction of the pathogenic phenotypes for Alzheimer's disease in an NSE/APPsw-transgenic model, *Int J Mol Med* 22:529–539, 2008.

Um HS, Kang EB, Koo JH, et al: Treadmill exercise represses neuronal cell death in an aged transgenic mouse model of Alzheimer's disease, *Neurosci Res* 69:161–173, 2011.

Valla J, Schneider L, Niedzielko T, et al: Impaired platelet mitochondrial activity in Alzheimer's disease and mild cognitive impairment, *Mitochondrion* 6:323–330, 2006.

Venturelli M, Scarsini R, Schena F: Six-month walking program changes cognitive and ADL performance in patients with Alzheimer, *Am J Alzheimer's Dis* 26:381–388, 2011.

Wang J, Ho L, Qin W, et al: Caloric restriction attenuates beta-amyloid neuropathology in a mouse model of Alzheimer's disease, *FASEB J* 19:659–661, 2005.

Wang X, Su B, Siedlak SL, et al: Amyloid-beta overproduction causes abnormal mitochondrial dynamics via differential modulation of mitochondrial fission/fusion proteins, *Proc Natl Acad Sci USA* 105:19318–19323, 2008.

Wang X, Su B, Lee HG, et al: Impaired balance of mitochondrial fission and fusion in Alzheimer's disease, *J Neurosci* 29:9090–9103, 2009.

Wang J, Ferruzzi MG, Varghese M, et al: Preclinical study of Dimebon on beta-amyloid-mediated neuropathology in Alzheimer's disease, *Mol Neurodegener* 6:7, 2011.

Watson GS, Cholerton BA, Reger MA, et al: Preserved cognition in patients with early Alzheimer disease and amnestic mild cognitive impairment during treatment with rosiglitazone: a preliminary study, *Am J Geriat Psychiat* 13:950–958, 2005.

Westermann B: Mitochondrial fusion and fission in cell life and death, *Nat Rev Mol Cell Biol* 11:872–884, 2010.

Winchester J, Dick MB, Gillen D, et al: Walking stabilizes cognitive functioning in Alzheimer's disease (AD) across one year, *Arch Gerontol Geriat* 56:96–103, 2013.

Wu Y, Wu Z, Butko P, et al: Amyloid-beta-induced pathological behaviors are suppressed by Ginkgo biloba extract EGb 761 and ginkgolides in transgenic Caenorhabditis elegans, *J Neurosci* 26:13102–13113, 2006.

Wu P, Shen Q, Dong S, Xu Z, Tsien JZ, Hu Y: Calorie restriction ameliorates neurodegenerative phenotypes in forebrain-specific presenilin-1 and presenilin-2 double knockout mice, *Neurobiol Aging* 29:1502–1511, 2008.

Xie N, Wang C, Lian Y, Wu C, Zhang H, Zhang Q: Inhibition of mitochondrial fission attenuates Abeta-induced microglia apoptosis, *Neuroscience* 256:36–42, 2014.

Yang F, Lim GP, Begum AN, et al: Curcumin inhibits formation of amyloid beta oligomers and fibrils, binds plaques, and reduces amyloid in vivo, *J Biol Chem* 280:5892–5901, 2005.

Yang X, Dai G, Li G, Yang ES: Coenzyme Q10 reduces beta-amyloid plaque in an APP/PS1 transgenic mouse model of Alzheimer's disease, *J Mol Neurosci* 41:110–113, 2010.

Yao J, Irwin RW, Zhao L, Nilsen J, Hamilton RT, Brinton RD: Mitochondrial bioenergetic deficit precedes Alzheimer's pathology in female mouse model of Alzheimer's disease, *Proc Natl Acad Sci USA* 106:14670–14675, 2009.

Ye X, Sun X, Starovoytov V, Cai Q: Parkin-mediated mitophagy in mutant hAPP neurons and Alzheimer's disease patient brains, *Hum Mol Genet* 24:2938–2951, 2015.

Zhang LH, Wang X, Stoltenberg M, Danscher G, Huang L, Wang ZY: Abundant expression of zinc transporters in the amyloid plaques of Alzheimer's disease brain, *Brain Res Bull* 77:55–60, 2008.

Zhang S, Hedskog L, Petersen CA, Winblad B, Ankarcrona M: Dimebon (latrepirdine) enhances mitochondrial function and protects neuronal cells from death, *J Alzheimers Dis* 21:389–402, 2010.

Zhao K, Zhao GM, Wu D, et al: Cell-permeable peptide antioxidants targeted to inner mitochondrial membrane inhibit mitochondrial swelling, oxidative cell death, and reperfusion injury, *J Biol Chem* 279:34682–34690, 2004.

Zheng W, Xin N, Chi ZH, et al: Divalent metal transporter 1 is involved in amyloid precursor protein processing and Abeta generation, *FASEB J* 23:4207–4217, 2009.

CHAPTER

19

Clinical Issues in Alzheimer Drug Development

L.S. Schneider

OUTLINE

INTRODUCTION

Formal drug development for Alzheimer's disease can be dated to the early 1980s and was informed by the cholinergic hypothesis of memory impairment, the availability of a range of cholinergic medications, and the 1984 research criteria for Alzheimer's disease (Giacobini, 2006; Schneider, 2008a). Yet, despite the evaluation of numerous potential treatments in clinical trials, only four cholinesterase inhibitors and memantine have shown sufficient safety and efficacy to allow marketing approval at a trans-national level. As far back as 2008, at least 172 drug development failures in Alzheimer's therapeutics were identified (Becker et al., 2008; Lindner et al., 2008) and the Pharmaceutical Research and Manufacturers of America, PhRMA, an industry trade group, acknowledged 101 failures between

Developing Therapeutics for Alzheimer's Disease. http://dx.doi.org/10.1016/B978-0-12-802173-6.00019-8

1990 and 2012 (PhRMA, 2012). Drug discovery in neuroscience in general is complicated and uncertain with overall failure rates greater than 95%, and very long development programs of 10–15 years from discovery to marketing approval (PhRMA, 2012).

The most probable reason for this lack of success is that the drugs tested are, in fact, ineffective. Lingering in the background, however, is the concern that inadequate clinical development methods and governmental requirements may have been responsible for some failures. In other words, effective drugs were not recognized because of errors in trial methods or regulatory constraints.

Thus, within the Alzheimer drug development milieu there is an outsized concern about methods and regulatory guidance as barriers to demonstrating effective and safe drugs. Here we consider some issues in Alzheimer drug development including potential targets, clinical trials, methods, uses of biomarkers, and regulatory considerations.

Trial methods have evolved incrementally: inclusion criteria have largely remained focused on mild-to-moderate Alzheimer's disease criteria, but are also extended to earlier or prodromal Alzheimer's disease (or the roughly equivalent "mild cognitive impairment due to Alzheimer disease"). There is also hope that a drug for prodromal Alzheimer's disease—if effective—might be considered as a "disease-modifying" product by the regulatory authorities.

The Food and Drug Administration (FDA) advisory committees in 1989, 1991, and 1993 discussed clinical trial methods, as well as the new drug application for the first cholinesterase inhibitor, and unpublished FDA draft guidelines (Leber, 1990), and considerably shaped the process by which a drug could receive marketing approval for Alzheimer's disease. In 1993 the cholinesterase inhibitor, tacrine, was the first drug approved "for the treatment of mild-to-moderate dementia of the Alzheimer's type."

The early regulatory trials used the National Institute of Neurological and Communicative Disorders and Stroke–Alzheimer's Disease and Related Disorders Association consensus criteria for Alzheimer's disease diagnoses, known as the "McKhann criteria" (McKhann et al., 1984) for identifying patients to be included; the Alzheimer's Disease Assessment Scale–cognitive subscale (ADAS-cog) (Mohs et al., 1997; Rosen et al., 1984) for assessing cognitive change; and a simple, face-valid, seven-point clinician's global impression of change (Schneider et al., 1997) for assessing clinically meaningful change. Trials generally extended to 6 months of treatment.

The durations of Alzheimer trials have tended to remain at 2–6 months for drugs intended to improve symptoms; and have been extended to 12–24 months for drugs expected to attenuate a deteriorating clinical course. Cognitive performance, activities of daily living, and global change and severity ratings continue as the primary clinically relevant outcomes. Recently, so-called composite outcomes have been employed in several trials, composed of subscales of established cognitive, functional, and severity staging scales (eg, combining the Mini-mental State Examination (MMSE) (Folstein et al., 1975) with the Clinical Dementia Rating Scale (CDR) (Morris, 1993) and selected neuropsychological tests).

Regulatory guidance and oversight have evolved to allow for "enrichment" of early-stage Alzheimer's disease trial samples by using biomarkers to enhance the likelihood that included patients have Alzheimer-related neuropathology and phase-specific outcomes appropriate for the cognitive severity of the illness. There is opportunity for substantial improvements in drug discovery and clinical development methods (Fig. 19.1).

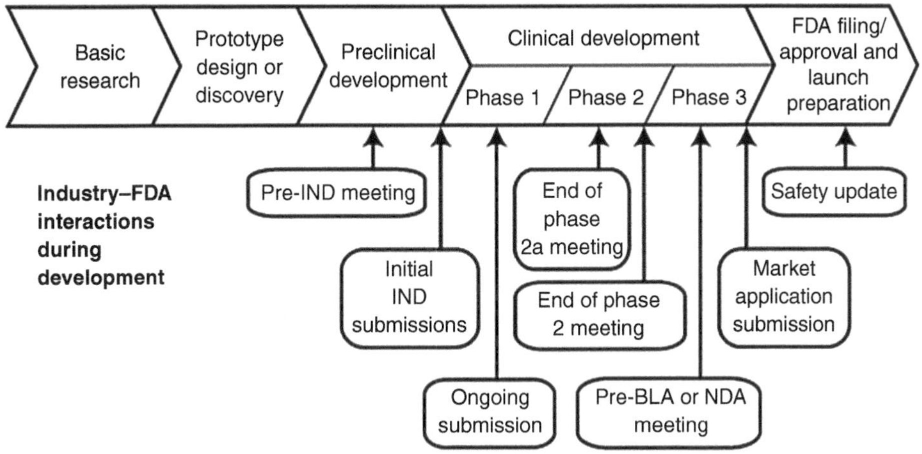

FIGURE 19.1 **The drug development process from preclinical development to approval.** Some phase 2 trials can be pivotal and serve as the basis for regulatory approval. In general, although the vast majority of phase 2a and 2 have not been successful, drugs lacking proof of concept or primary efficacy evidence have, nonetheless, been taken into phase 3 trials. Source: Modified from the FDA publication, *Innovation or Stagnation: Challenge and Opportunity on the Critical Path to New Medical Products* (http://www.fda.gov/ScienceResearch/SpecialTopics/CriticalPathInitiative/CriticalPathOpportunitiesReports/ucm077262.htm). BLA, biologics license application; FDA, Food and Drug Administration; IND, investigational new drug application; NDA, new drug application.

CLINICAL ISSUES IN DRUG DEVELOPMENT

Basic Regulatory Requirements for Alzheimer's Drugs

The basis for FDA marketing approval of the cholinesterase inhibitors, and subsequently for memantine, were the requirements of at least one 3-month and one 6-month parallel-group, randomized, placebo-controlled trial showing safety and effectiveness. The 6-month trial requirement was based on a 1989 FDA advisory committee opinion that 6 months was the minimum time needed to demonstrate a clinically meaningful effect (FDA, 1989), and on unpublished draft FDA guidelines (Leber, 1990).

Although the overall efficacy of the cholinesterase inhibitors was considered modest, the 2–3 point effect on the coprimary cognitive outcome, the ADAS-cog, and similarly small effects on global and functional assessments (Birks, 2006) became the standard expected drug effect for future drugs. Despite being statistically significant, the small size of the effects of cholinesterase inhibitors can be appreciated by considering that patients' baseline scores on the ADAS-cog are about 22–24 and so the effect represents about a 10–12% improvement compared with placebo treatment.

Development programs for newer drugs have been based almost exclusively on the original cholinesterase inhibitors programs and the 1990 draft guidelines, as the latter were the early examples of success showing cognitive and global assessment efficacy in 6-month trials in patients with mild-to-moderate Alzheimer's disease (Schneider et al., 2014).

These programs enrolled mild-to-moderate Alzheimer's disease patients and used the ADAS-cog as the primary cognitive outcome (Lindner et al., 2008; Schneider, 2008a). Nearly all failed on the basis of lack of cognitive efficacy. Often when cognitive efficacy seemed apparent in one trial, the effect was not confirmed in subsequent confirmatory trials or by other clinical ratings. Perhaps because of these past failures to meet rather minimal regulatory requirements, any improvement in cognition has been considered worthy and meaningful for a new drug for Alzheimer's disease.

Mild Cognitive Impairment Trials

A postulate for treating early Alzheimer's disease is the consideration that a risk state or predementia syndrome can be identified before the onset of the dementia syndrome. The concept of incipient cognitive impairment as detected by the mild cognitive decline stage of the Global Deterioration Scale (Reisberg et al., 1982), the "questionable dementia" or the 0.5 stage of the CDR (Morris et al., 1991), was established in the 1980s. This early stage may represent very early Alzheimer's disease before the onset of dementia, that is, not fulfilling the McKhann criteria (McKhann et al., 1984). Indeed, a point of nomenclature and research diagnostic confusion is that a 0.5 global score on the CDR is consistent with both having and not having dementia; yet the 0.5 score is sometimes used to (inaccurately) define mild cognitive impairment (MCI).

MCI and amnestic MCI were defined in the late 1990s as progressive memory impairment similar to that seen in patients with early Alzheimer's disease but with less impairment in other cognitive and functional domains. In cohort studies, patients with MCI declined on average at a greater rate than nonimpaired controls, such that about half developed dementia within 3 years (Petersen et al., 1999). The idea that amnestic MCI could be a clinical target for early treatment interventions was facilitated by the endorsement of an FDA advisory committee in 2001 (FDA, 2001). At about the same time, longer-term clinical trials of MCI used continuous treatment over 2–4 years with the main outcome of progression to Alzheimer's disease dementia and secondary outcomes of change on cognition scales. The drugs investigated included the marketed cholinesterase inhibitors, vitamin E, vitamin B complex, and rofecoxib (Feldman et al., 2007; Petersen et al., 2005; Smith et al., 2010; Thal et al., 2005; Winblad et al., 2008). The cholinesterase inhibitor donepezil was also used in 6-month (Salloway et al., 2004) and 12-month placebo-controlled trials (Doody et al., 2009).

The results of these MCI trials were null, with no benefit on clinical progression or delay in onset of dementia. Moreover, the rates of progression from MCI to dementia were lower than expected based on prior cohort studies of MCI (Petersen et al., 1999). The different rates of progression were most likely due to variations in sample ascertainment, heterogeneity of patients, and different definitions of MCI, and to the characteristics of the clinical outcomes measures. But these factors undermine the validity of the inclusion criteria and the design of these trials. Of interest to drug development in general, the trial assessing the anti-inflammatory rofecoxib showed significant cognitive-impairing effects compared to placebo. Notable, as well, was that phase 2 trials had not been performed with rofecoxib to demonstrate proof of concept or safety. (Rofecoxib was subsequently withdrawn from the market because of cardiotoxicity).

The development of rofecoxib antedated a current trend in Alzheimer's drug development that appears to bypass phase 2a proof of concept or early efficacy studies in favor of moving directly to larger, phase 2b or 3 pivotal that would more clearly demonstrate efficacy and safety (if in fact the test drug was efficacious). The following references compare the earlier MCI trials from the early 2000s: Jelic et al., 2006; Raschetti et al., 2007.

Regulatory Considerations for MCI Clinical Trials

An FDA advisory committee in 2001 helped to focus drug development for Alzheimer's disease by offering several requirements for the marketing approval of drugs for MCI (2001). The committee reflected FDA's concerns that: (1) MCI must be clearly defined in the clinical setting; (2) there must be valid criteria for its diagnosis; (3) it can be defined in terms of the future onset of Alzheimer's disease; (4) appropriate outcomes need to be used in trials; and (5) trials should be designed to assess rating scale changes, onset of dementia, and clinically meaningful effects.

Post hoc analyses of the several cholinesterase inhibitor trials for mild cognitive impairment variously suggested that one subgroup or another had potentially benefited from cholinesterase inhibitor treatment. These post hoc analyses, however, were not followed by confirmatory trials to test the various hypotheses that they generated. The failed trials led to the consideration that MCI was a heterogeneous at-risk state that did not necessarily lead to Alzheimer's disease and that it might be too early in the disease course for those particular drugs to be effective. The European Medicines Agency (EMA) (EMA, 2008) went further and stated that MCI could not be recognized as a clinical entity for which target drugs could be developed, and more work on characterizing the diagnostic criteria, possible subtypes, and the development of outcomes assessments had to be done. Finally, because a marketing claim could not be achieved for delaying onset of Alzheimer's disease or for "disease modification," that probably contributed to the lack of interest for developing drugs for MCI, as there was little commercial incentive. There was, however, continuing interest among academics in advancing the concepts of "MCI due to Alzheimer's disease" and "prodromal Alzheimer's disease."

The Amyloid Cascade Hypothesis

As amply evidenced throughout this book, the amyloid cascade hypothesis is the most-researched conceptual framework for Alzheimer's disease therapeutics. It has been the dominant influence on the development of targets and therapeutic agents (Golde et al., 2011; Mangialasche et al., 2010). At the heart of the hypothesis is the idea that aggregation of amyloid-β peptide (Aβ), produced by sequential β- and γ-secretase cleavage of the amyloid precursor protein, is an early pathological process that triggers tau hyperphosphorylation, neurofibrillary tangle formation, and neurodegeneration. Also central to the hypothesis is the concept that both the pathology and clinical expression of Alzheimer's disease result from the increased production or impaired clearance of toxic Aβ species, with oligomeric assemblies of Aβ being the leading candidates, although Aβ fibrils may also play a role.

This, in turn, has led to the development of drugs to disrupt the cascade and to clinical trials. For the amyloid hypothesis, candidate drugs have been mainly tested in early-stage Alzheimer's disease, specifically in patients with mild cognitive impairment due to Alzheimer's disease, prodromal Alzheimer's disease, or mild Alzheimer's disease (defined as Alzheimer dementia with MMSE scores (Folstein et al., 1975) from 20 to 26). Although straightforward in concept, the validation and development of amyloid drug targets has been complex in practice. For example, oligomers, protofibrils, and plaques may have distinct toxicities. Oligomers may be toxic in synapses and with certain membrane receptors, and plaque-associated Aβ fibrils may be proinflammatory and neurotoxic, thus constituting separate drug targets. Extensive preclinical and clinical research has yet to validate an amyloid-related drug target. Specifically, it is not at all clear that inhibition or modulation of amyloid precursor protein, secretases, inhibition of fibril aggregation, or the use of antibodies targeting various Aβ forms are valid strategies in affecting human Alzheimer's disease pathology. Yet, current clinical drug development is dominated by drugs and vaccines designed to affect amyloid.

Trials in Mild-to-Moderate Alzheimer's Disease Intended to Demonstrate Disease Modification

Similar inclusion criteria and outcomes have been used in 18-month-long trials that have been used in shorter length trials (Schneider and Sano, 2009). One difference is that they allow the use of cholinesterase inhibitors and memantine as concomitant medications. In fact, 80–90% of participants in current trials are using these drugs. Therefore, current trials are performed with the expectation or hope that the effects of the new drug are not substantially influenced by use of the current marketed drugs. Although most included mild-to-moderate Alzheimer's disease (allowing a maximum MMSE score of 26), the lower limit defining "moderate" severity varies. Some trials focused exclusively on "mild" Alzheimer's disease (ie, restricting the MMSE score to 20–26).

More recent phase 2 and 3 trials mainly included investigational drugs to test the amyloid hypothesis. These included trials of Aβ aggregation inhibitors tramiprosate (Aisen et al., 2007) and scyllo-inositol (ELND005) (Salloway et al., 2011), phase 3 trials of a γ-secretase modulator tarenflurbil (Green et al., 2009), trials of the γ-secretase inhibitors semagacestat (Doody et al., 2013) and avagacestat (Coric et al., 2012), a RAGE inhibitor (PF 04494700/ TTP488), and antibodies to Aβ (including phase 2 and 3 trials of bapineuzumab (Salloway et al., 2009), trials of solanezumab (Doody et al., 2013), immunoglobulin G (IVIG) [unpublished], crenezumab [unpublished], and gantenerumab [unpublished]). All yielded null results with respect to their primary and main outcomes.

The more recent trials include obtaining cerebrospinal fluid (CSF) for Aβ peptides and tau protein and amyloid positron emission tomography (PET) as biomarkers. These biomarkers were first used in subsets of patients as a potential means to understand any clinical effects that might be observed, or in the hope that a biomarker change during a clinical trial would be considered as supportive evidence of a disease-modifying effect. More recently, and perhaps influenced by EMA (2012a,b) guidelines on sample enrichment with biomarkers, these biomarkers have been used to help enrich clinical trial samples with patients having evidence of amyloid pathology, in order to more accurately identify trial participants with Alzheimer's disease pathology and perhaps select those more likely to respond to the investigational drug, although there is no empirical support for this (EMA, 2012a).

The designs of these trials have been informed by group consensus recommendations that well-established scales be used, for example, the ADAS-cog, Alzheimer's Disease Cooperative Study–Activities of Daily Living scale and Clinical Dementia Rating, due to an absence of suitable alternatives, and that a 2-point drug–placebo group difference on the ADAS-cog would be the minimally important difference between drug and placebo that would be a clinically meaningful effect (Vellas et al., 2007, 2008). Notably, this is less than the effect with cholinesterase inhibitors over 6 months and less than the difference recommended by an FDA advisory committee in 1989 (EMA, 2009).

As the required or sought-after effect becomes smaller in these longer trials, the sample sizes of 18-month trials have been increased to over 1200 patients for industry-sponsored trials in mild-to-moderate Alzheimer's disease, and to 2100 for a trial limited to participants with mild Alzheimer's disease treated with the Aβ antibody solanezumab (http://www.clinicaltrials.gov/ct2/show/NCT01900665?term=LZAX&rank=1). This trial should be able to detect less than a 2-point drug–placebo difference on the ADAS-cog.

Several characteristics of these trials and of Alzheimer's disease itself, such as slow clinical progression and the modest decline of placebo group rating scores, heterogeneity and variability of clinical course, imprecision of the outcomes, and the expectation that new drugs will only attenuate decline, when taken together, diminish the likelihood of discovering effective drugs. Therefore, as mentioned previously, biomarker enhancement, large sample sizes, and more diligent training of clinical raters are employed in efforts to improve efficiency and chances for success. The outcomes of the solanezumab trial should be known by the latter half of 2016 and should provide greater insight on these approaches.

In summary, 18-month, placebo-controlled trials have become a de facto standard for trials of mild and moderate Alzheimer's disease, even though no 18-month trial has shown statistically significant primary outcomes favoring the test drug in a priori analyses. The use of CSF Aβ and tau and amyloid PET biomarkers in longer, 18-month trials may allow demonstration of disease modification, depending on the mechanism of action of the drug, and FDA's assessment of the validity of the biomarkers at the end of the trials.

Prodromal Alzheimer's Disease Trials

As mentioned, the earlier MCI trials used varying definitions for MCI. For example, differing tests and cut-off scores were used to define the memory impairment or the criteria for amnestic MCI (Petersen et al., 2005). The advancement of trials for prodromal Alzheimer's disease followed proposed research criteria from an international workgroup (Dubois et al., 2007). Here the intent is to diagnose clinical Alzheimer's disease before dementia onset by increasing confidence that patients with amnestic MCI or an apparent episodic memory deficit have Alzheimer's disease pathology, and to increase the likelihood that participants so diagnosed would advance to clear Alzheimer's disease dementia over a short period of time (Dubois et al., 2010). In order to accomplish this, the research diagnosis requires the use of an amyloid biomarker such as amyloid PET imaging or CSF Aβ42 concentrations. Prodromal Alzheimer's disease trials theoretically allow individuals to be treated earlier in their disease course, perhaps when certain drugs may be more effective than they would be at a later disease stage.

The current trials that use "MCI due to Alzheimer's disease" or "prodromal Alzheimer's disease" as inclusion criteria have trial designs similar to the 18-month mild-to-moderate and mild Alzheimer's disease trials. Most of the recent phase 2 and 3 trials, however, include biomarker inclusion requirements that patients have positive Aβ biomarkers, specifically, low CSF Aβ42 concentrations or increased retention of an Aβ-binding ligand on amyloid PET scan. It is reasoned that such patients are more likely to have Alzheimer's disease pathology. The recent prodromal Alzheimer's disease trials also differ from the earlier MCI trials in having shorter treatment and follow-up periods of 18–24 months, compared to the earlier 2–4 years, and in the use of biomarkers as indices of change that may be interpreted as support for a disease modification of the drug being tested.

A hypothetical or model phase 2 or 3 trial in prodromal Alzheimer's disease or MCI due to Alzheimer's disease currently would have the following features: (1) use either the National Institute on Aging-Alzheimer's Association criteria for MCI associated with Alzheimer's disease (Albert et al., 2011) or the IWG-2 criteria for prodromal Alzheimer's disease (Dubois et al., 2014) for inclusion; (2) require a delayed memory test deficit threshold using the Wechsler Memory Scale Logical Memory II or the Free and Cued Selective Reminding Test (Grober et al., 2000); (3) require a positive amyloid biomarker, usually an Aβ PET scan to further define "MCI associated with Alzheimer's disease with a high level of confidence" or "prodromal Alzheimer's disease"; (4) use the CDR-sum of boxes (CDR-SB) as the primary clinical outcome; (5) use selected cognitive and functional ratings as secondary outcomes; and (6) use amyloid, tau, and MRI biomarkers as exploratory outcomes that might help support a marketing claim for "disease modification." Trials with these features should comply with the FDA's recent draft guidelines for pivotal trials in early-stage Alzheimer's disease. It should be stressed, however, that no trial with these characteristics has been positive; and the FDA has commented that diagnostic criteria and outcomes discussed in their draft guidelines may still require validation. Moreover, as with earlier trials, if a nominally significant primary outcome is not statistically robust and not supported by the secondary outcomes, the interpretation of a new drug's clinical meaning will be challenging.

Prevention Trials

Prevention trials are intended to address the fact that the pathology of Alzheimer's disease may exist and progress, perhaps two decades or longer before the onset of clinical illness (Braak and Del Tredici, 2012). From a public health point of view, prevention can be considered as primary or secondary. The former term is reserved for prevention of illness in people who do not yet have the illness in question, and who may or may not be at increased risk for illness. The term secondary prevention, however, is often used for the treatment of people who have subtle signs of illness. The shift towards recognizing presymptomatic and preclinical phases of Alzheimer's disease, before the onset of prodromal Alzheimer's disease or mild cognitive impairment due to Alzheimer's disease, has focused on the need for preventive treatment trials.

Such trials require large samples and prolonged follow-up over many years in order to be able to identify the relatively few individuals who will progress to clinical illness. They are complicated and expensive to conduct, and until recently were hindered by the lack of compelling and safe drugs or other interventions to test (Schneider, 2008b). Known and presumed risk and protective factors for Alzheimer's disease influence the design and conduct of prevention trials. Prevention trials have tended to select participants with risk factors such as family history, cardiovascular disease, relatively greater age, or with existing mild cognitive impairment in an effort to increase the numbers of individuals who progress to dementia over a typical 5-year follow-up. Newer prevention trials are selecting participants with increased risk for Alzheimer's disease based on genotype or amyloid PET scans.

Earlier prevention trials used marketed drugs and food supplements, often as an add-on or nested within a larger trial for another condition, and have assessed the preventive effects of antihypertension medications (Peters et al., 2008), conjugated equine estrogens, a 3-hydroxy-3-methylglutaryl-coenzyme A reductase inhibitor or vitamin E and selenium (Kryscio et al., 2013). Two trials used Ginkgo biloba standardized extract EGb 761 (DeKosky et al., 2008; Vellas et al., 2012), and one used nonsteroidal antiinflammatory drugs (ADAPT Research Group, 2007). These trials did not show protective effects on cognitive function or dementia onset and in some cases may have shown the opposite (Schneider, 2008b).

Multi-domain intervention trials involve the management of risk factors by encouraging lifestyle changes and using marketed pharmacological products, including food supplements. These trials include the Finnish Geriatric Intervention Study to Prevent Cognitive Impairment and Disability, Multi-domain Alzheimer Prevention Study, and Prevention of Dementia by Intensive Vascular Care (Kivipelto et al., 2013). Conducting prevention trials that involve multiple interventions can be complicated and can involve a range of issues and design considerations that are different from prevention trials that use only one drug intervention.

Current pharmaceutical company-sponsored prevention trials are components of proprietary drug development programs. Participants must have an Aβ biomarker as a risk factor, a genetic risk marker or specific *PSEN 1* or *APP* mutation in order to enter the trial. These studies include the Alzheimer's Prevention Initiative (API), the Dominantly Inherited Alzheimer Network (DIAN), the Anti-amyloid Treatment in Asymptomatic Alzheimer's Disease (the A4 study) and the ApoE/TOMM40 (the TOMMORROW study) trials; the first three tested Aβ antibodies crenezumab, solanezumab, and gantenerumab and the last a very low dose of the thiazolidinedione pioglitazone (Solomon et al., 2014).

The two trials in patients with early-onset dominantly inherited Alzheimer's disease are unusual in that there is no doubt that all participants are on the path to developing cognitive and neurological impairment and will develop Alzheimer's disease pathology in midlife. As participants show no cognitive deficiencies or impairment, they are considered to have presymptomatic Alzheimer's disease. Both trials are investigating the efficacy of anti-Aβ antibodies—crenezumab in the API and gantenerumab and solanezumab in the DIAN study. Therefore, these trials are also tests of the amyloid hypothesis.

The A4 trial (Sperling et al., 2014) is testing the concept of treating participants between the ages of 65 and 85 who have "preclinical Alzheimer's disease," which is operationally defined as having cognitive complaints, may or may not have impairments in delayed recall, but who score a 0 on the CDR, and are amyloid-PET positive (ie, who are at statistical risk of sporadic, late-onset Alzheimer's disease). The expectation is that participants treated with the Aβ antibody solanezumab will show less change on a composite, neuropsychological rating composed of tests of delayed memory, orientation, praxis, and processing speed (ie, the Free and Choice Selective Reminding Test, Wechsler Memory Scale Logical Memory II Delayed, MMSE, and Digit Symbol Substitution Test).

The TOMMORROW trial is unique in that it includes approximately 5000 noncognitively impaired participants whose increased risk for Alzheimer's disease is determined by a biomarker—defined by the chronological age of the patient and particular alleles of the *TOMM40* gene and *APOE* gene—and who are randomly treated with pioglitazone or placebo and followed over 6 years (Roses et al., 2012) (https://clinicaltrials.gov/ct2/show/NCT01931566). The goals are both to assess efficacy of pioglitazone and to qualify a biomarker for clinical prediction. Here, the outcome is not change on a scale, but the onset of "mild cognitive impairment due to Alzheimer's disease."

DIAGNOSES FOR REGULATORY TRIALS IN ALZHEIMER'S DISEASE

The 1984 McKhann criteria for possible, probable, and definite Alzheimer's disease provided a diagnostic framework for advancing drug development (McKhann et al., 1984). Severity levels for use in clinical trials were conventionally defined by reference to MMSE scores: mild severity greater than or equal to 20, mild to moderate, 10–26; moderate to severe, less than 14; and severe, less than 10.

The promotion of newer research diagnostic criteria for clinical trials reflects the change towards etiologically directed approaches compared with more clinically and phenotypically based inclusion criteria. The extent to which the proposed 2011 research diagnostic criteria for Alzheimer's disease (McKhann et al., 2011) might replace the 1984 criteria (McKhann et al., 1984) for trials is not clear. A main difference between the older and newer criteria is that CSF Aβ and tau concentrations, fluorodeoxyglucose-PET, amyloid PET, and brain volume biomarkers are integrated into the new research criteria for probable and possible Alzheimer's disease dementia (McKhann et al., 2011). This represents a change from conceptualizing Alzheimer's disease as being definitively diagnosable only postmortem, to the diagnosis being predicted with a higher level of certainty in vivo (ie, possible and probable Alzheimer's disease), to the construct of Alzheimer's disease as being reliably diagnosable in life, early in the course of illness by using prognostic biomarkers.

Inclusion criteria for mild cognitive impairment or amnestic mild cognitive impairment followed either the Mayo clinic criteria (Petersen et al., 1999) or other criteria that generally required, in part, a CDR global score of 0.5, and a Wechsler Memory Scale Logical Memory II, New York University paragraph recall score or Auditory Verbal Learning Test score below a certain critical level. The MCI criteria used in clinical trials further required relative preservation of activities of daily living such that a dementia diagnosis cannot be made. The criteria for "MCI due to Alzheimer's disease" as used in one early MCI trial (Petersen et al., 2005) is the same as the new 2011 "MCI associated with Alzheimer's disease" criteria except that the latter can be further enriched with a range of Alzheimer-related biomarkers (Albert et al., 2011). Inclusion of an amyloid biomarker makes the latter criteria essentially the same as the International Work Group criteria for prodromal Alzheimer's disease (Dubois et al., 2010, 2014).

The emerging concept of preclinical Alzheimer's disease, wherein there may or may not be evidence of cognitive impairment but biological evidence of Alzheimer's disease pathology (Dubois et al., 2010, 2014; Sperling et al., 2011) is present, partially addresses the poorly defined space between normal cognitive aging and pathological cognitive impairment. For one trial, the research criteria for preclinical Alzheimer's disease have been operationalized as: ages 65–85, MMSE 25–30, Wechsler Memory Scale Logical Memory II delayed recall, 6–18 (ie, spanning the range from normal to severely impaired), CDR global score of 0, and a positive Aβ-PET scan.

In summary, diagnostic criteria for clinical trials of Alzheimer's disease have remained largely consistent for more than 30 years, and those for MCI trials for nearly 20. The new research criteria mainly incorporate biomarkers to increase the likelihood of Alzheimer pathology in patients clinically diagnosed as having prodromal Alzheimer's disease and MCI and to delineate a preclinical or presymptomatic Alzheimer's disease state. These latter diagnoses require validation.

BIOMARKERS IN ALZHEIMER TRIALS

The consecutive failures of experimental drugs in the longer-term trials, and especially with the drugs targeting the amyloid cascade, led to explanations that the main reasons for failure were that the mild-to-moderate Alzheimer patients in the trials were too severely impaired and perhaps some did not have Alzheimer neuropathology. Consequently, the experimental drugs did not have the potential to be effective as the brain already contained too much amyloid substrate, the neurodegeneration was too advanced, or the research participants did not have Alzheimer pathology to begin with. These explanations, combined with the wish both to improve symptoms and to modify the progression of Alzheimer pathology, supported advancing especially amyloid biomarkers for diagnosis, sample enrichment, indexing disease progression, and for targeting patients in an earlier, prodromal, or mild dementia phase in clinical development programs.

Advances in molecular assay technology, MRI visualization, and amyloid PET led to the use of CSF and imaging biomarkers in clinical trials. The purposes of CSF Aβ peptides and tau protein assays in trials were as diagnostic aids and prognostic markers of illness and later as potential therapeutic, predictive, pharmacodynamic, or surrogate markers of the effects of a drug. The EMA in 2011 and the FDA in 2013 (Kozauer and Katz, 2013) recognized their potential use as markers to enrich sample selection in early-stage Alzheimer's disease. The EMA qualified both amyloid PET imaging and CSF Aβ42 and tau assays as enrichment biomarkers for enrolling participants with either prodromal or mild-to-moderate Alzheimer's disease in regulatory clinical trials (EMA, 2012a,b).

Most current longer-term, phase 2 and 3 clinical trials use a biomarker at least in a subset of patients, usually for exploratory purposes and for the possibility that a salutary change in a biomarker could help to support a disease-modification claim. Biomarkers that could be affected by the experimental drug might be used for enrichment and prediction, but are of limited use as a surrogate clinical outcome. For example, an Aβ biomarker that is affected by a test drug cannot be used as a surrogate clinical outcome but could be used as a pharmacodynamics measure.

The types of biomarkers used in Alzheimer trials include: (1) diagnostic—for determining diagnosis; (2) enrichment—for enhancing entry criteria; (3) prognostic—for forecasting illness course; (4) predictive—for determining treatment outcomes; (5) surrogate—to substitute for clinical outcomes; and (6) companion biomarkers. For the most part, biomarkers require validation for the purpose for which they are used. This requires more than correlation with diagnosis or clinical change. One method for validating a biomarker in a given development program is to observe the change in the biomarker in phase 1 studies, validate the change in phase 2 by correlation with the clinical outcomes, and use it in confirmatory phase 3 trials.

An example of the qualification of a companion biomarker is the TOMMORROW trial, described previously, for which a compound biomarker composed of a *TOMM40* genotype, *APOE* genotype, and age is intended as a prognostic biomarker for MCI due to Alzheimer's disease, and as a predictive marker for pioglitazone delaying the diagnosis of MCI due to Alzheimer's disease (Roses et al., 2012).

The hope for a surrogate biomarker is that it can measure pathological change indexing disease progression, and serve as a substitute marker of clinical effect in place of clinical ratings. To do so, however, it would have to be as accurate as and more precise than the clinical rating it is replacing. In such a scenario, the standard clinical outcomes can be wholly replaced (Vellas et al., 2008). Consideration regarding the use of biomarkers should be given to several factors, including the type of therapeutic intervention, the clinical stage of illness, and the time dependence of biomarker changes during illness.

RECENT REGULATORY CONSIDERATIONS FOR DRUG DEVELOPMENT IN ALZHEIMER'S DISEASE

In order to approve a drug for marketing, the FDA, EMA, and other regulatory agencies assess that an investigational drug is safe and effective for its proposed use, there is a favorable benefit-to-risk ratio, the prescribing information (ie, the label) accurately describes its conditions for use and is not misleading, and the manufacturing methods and quality are acceptable. In Europe, drugs for neurodegenerative disorders (and selected other conditions) are evaluated centrally by the EMA rather than separately by each country. Regulatory positions change as the clinical science changes, and regulators often facilitate drug development by issuing new guidelines for clinical development. For example, the FDA provided unofficial guidelines for trial methods for demonstrating disease modification in 1996 (Leber, 1997), and more recently proposed guidelines for early-stage Alzheimer's disease including prodromal Alzheimer's disease (FDA, 2013; Kozauer and Katz, 2013). The EMA issued detailed guidelines for disease modification (EMA, 2009), and qualified new methods, including using biomarkers for enrichment (EMA, 2012a,b).

Guidelines, however, may be inhibiting and limiting by encouraging nearly identical clinical development programs for drugs with very different actions or characteristics. Sponsors of development programs may then feel limited to using standardized clinical trial designs that might not be the most suitable for the particular drug and indication.

The EMA considers cholinesterase inhibitors as standard care; therefore, it requires that a new drug under development in phase 3 trials includes research participants already maintained on cholinesterase inhibitors. Pragmatically, for mild Alzheimer's disease and even for mild cognitive impairment due to Alzheimer's disease, it is very difficult to recruit participants to long-term clinical trials who are not taking these drugs. For example, approximately half of MCI patients in the first Alzheimer's Disease Neuroimaging Initiative cohort were prescribed cholinesterase inhibitors (Schneider et al., 2011). An issue here, of course, is that the marketed drugs could be influencing the effect of the experimental drugs.

Disease-Modification Claims

The concept of an FDA- or EMA-approved disease-modification marketing claim is driven by the pharmaceutical industry's belief that it could sell more drug and at a higher price with this claim. On the other hand, patients would welcome a treatment that was effective over a long period whether or not it is labeled as a disease modifier. In the late 1990s, the FDA informally suggested two methods to demonstrate disease modification that could support such a claim: (1) a randomized-start and (2) a randomized-withdrawal design (Leber, 1997). (The former is described shortly.)

Only the EMA offered formal guidelines that included an approach to a disease modification claim. Here, a biomarker needs to correlate with the presumed mechanism of action of the drug, and then with the clinical efficacy (EMA, 2012a). Thus far, these relationships have not been seen except in subsets of larger trials that unfortunately had negative or null primary outcomes overall. For example, the Aβ vaccine, AN1792, appeared to lower CSF phosphorylated-tau (Gilman et al., 2005) and amyloid plaque density on autopsy but with no apparent clinical effect (Holmes et al., 2008). A trial of bapineuzumab including only 29 patients showed a small decrease in fibrillar Aβ on PiB-PET and a decrease in CSF phosphorylated-tau after 18 months (Blennow et al., 2012; Rinne et al., 2010). The biomarker observations, unfortunately, were not correlated with clinical improvement, and thus do not support the use of these biomarkers as surrogate or predictive markers.

The FDA provided brief, draft guidelines for a disease-modification claim within the context of their early-stage Alzheimer's disease guidance document that are more compatible with those of the EMA (EMA, 2013; FDA, 2013). The FDA uses the term "early-stage" to include symptomatic, preclinical Alzheimer's disease (so-called stage 3 preclinical), mild cognitive impairment due to Alzheimer's disease, which it considers to be the same as prodromal disease, and perhaps mild Alzheimer's disease. The draft guidelines allow for the possibility that a disease-modification claim could be supported: (1) by evidence of a meaningful effect on a biomarker in combination with clinical benefit, or (2) through the use of a randomized-start design trial. For the latter, patients who initially received placebo and then were assigned to active drug would be expected to fail to catch up to the group initially treated with active drug for the drug to earn a disease-modification claim. The FDA prefers the latter option and first proposed this clinical trial design two decades earlier (Leber, 1997).

It was noted, however, that for the former to be the case, that is, for evidence of a meaningful effect on a biomarker:

> ...there should be widespread evidence-based agreement in the research community that the chosen biomarker reflects a pathophysiologic entity that is fundamental to the underlying disease process.... There is currently no consensus as to what particular biomarkers would be appropriate to support clinical findings in trials in early AD [Alzheimer's disease]. (FDA, 2013)

Fig. 19.2 diagrams a randomized-start design, illustrating a clinical effect that the FDA could consider as disease-modifying. Indeed, in the late 1990s, a 12-month trial of propentofylline actually designed into a phase 3 protocol a randomized-start and a randomized-withdrawal design by re-randomizing patients at 12 months and extending the trial by an additional 6 months (Kittner et al., 1997). The drug, however, showed only marginal effects and clinical development was discontinued. Recently, the potential for a delayed-start design to show disease modification was demonstrated by a reanalysis of the pooling of mild Alzheimer's disease patients (ie, MMSE scores from 20 to 26) from two large clinical trials of solanezumab (Liu-Seifert et al., 2015). Patients treated earlier may have maintained an advantage across the delayed-start time period.

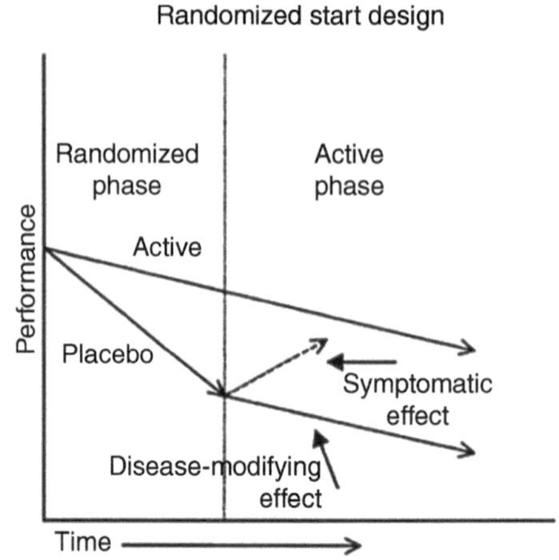

FIGURE 19.2 **Illustration of a randomized-start design for a regulatory clinical trial to demonstrate disease modification.** *Source: Reproduced with permission from Leber (1997).*

The EMA has offered further scientific advice on how a sponsor could obtain a disease-modification claim for treating patients with very early-stage disease and to develop diagnostic companion biomarkers. Here they consider prodromal Alzheimer's disease and mild Alzheimer's disease dementia (eg, MMSE 20–26) on a continuum, and that the efficacy of a treatment that delays clinical progression should be demonstrated in two trials. The first trial should randomize patients with mainly prodromal Alzheimer's disease, for example, with virtually no functional impairment; and efficacy should be demonstrated on a composite endpoint, such as the CDR, or possibly a single primary endpoint providing that it is validated in this population. The second trial should randomize patients with mild (or mild-to-moderate) Alzheimer's disease, with efficacy demonstrated on coprimary cognitive and functional endpoints. The outcomes from both trials should be robust and supported by secondary endpoints, including responder analyses and biomarkers that show delay in brain neurodegeneration.

Although the FDA and EMA guidelines address disease modification, and opinion leaders and sponsors discuss it extensively, it should be emphasized that any disease modification claim would be an extraordinarily major claim, implying that nearly all individuals at risk of Alzheimer's disease would need to take the drug (Schneider, 2014). This consideration might put the prospects for approval of a drug with a disease-modification claim in a realistic context.

DISCUSSION AND FUTURE DIRECTIONS

Clinical Alzheimer's disease is a complex, multidetermined disease with a pleomorphic phenotype. There are many potential drug targets, and so far none are validated except perhaps for cholinergic targets.

Because very few of the many negative trials give clear information about why results were null or inconclusive, current methods used to develop the drugs should be viewed with caution and critically evaluated. An important question is whether or not there are better approaches to clinical development that might enhance the likelihood of success. Explaining after the fact why trials failed is speculative. For example, one explanation for failure is that patients should have been treated earlier in the course of their illness, particularly those with milder illness and who have amyloid markers. Yet, however rational this explanation may seem, there is no supporting evidence that the approach will be effective.

The failures in late-stage phase 3 trials suggest that decisions to undertake them may not have been based on prior evidence. The earlier phase 2 trials may not be informative; inferences may have been made from valuing or interpreting post hoc analyses from these trials. As examples, the phase 2 trials of tarenflurbil and bapineuzumab did not show significant outcomes, phase 2 findings from a γ-secretase inhibitor study showed evidence for toxicity but were ignored; rather, phase 2 was used to find dosage, pharmacodynamics changes in amyloid, and to demonstrate sufficient safety for phase 3. Without prior evidence or demonstration of the potential for efficacy, the null outcomes of the subsequent phase 3 trials would have been expected. As several phase 3 trials had to have their designs changed while the trial was under way because of toxicity and other unexpected events, this further suggests that important aspects of the drugs, dosages, and targets were not known before entering confirmatory trials.

In summary, in Alzheimer's disease clinical development, phase 2 trials have not provided proof of concept nor have predicted phase 3 outcomes. Instead, they have been used as bridges to provide enough safety experience to go on to phase 3 or pivotal trials (Karran and Hardy, 2014; Schneider et al., 2014). The decision to progress a drug through clinical development appears more related to how pharmaceutical companies and academics make decisions and to business considerations about the potential for sales over the marketing life of the drug than to evidence from earlier development (Karran and Hardy, 2014; Trusheim et al., 2011). Here the high probability of failure is taken into account. But this makes these large phase 3 trials more exploratory than confirmatory.

The rather modest changes in trial methods may be a result of having no successes to build on and the perceived risk aversion of companies and academics to making changes. Therefore, only small changes are made from trial to trial: MMSE criteria ranges are expanded or contracted, trial durations are lengthened, similar or slightly different clinical outcomes are substituted, sample sizes are increased, biomarkers are used to increase diagnostic confidence, and smaller clinical effects are sought. Trials now are designed to detect drug–placebo differences of only 1–2 points on the ADAS-cog over 18–24 months. Notably, this is half the effect with more than three times the treatment duration than had been sought with the cholinesterase inhibitors (ie, 2.5–3 points over 6 months).

The enrichment and predictive markers currently used in trials have advantages and disadvantages. Sample enrichment may identify patients who might benefit from a particular drug and may lead to the identification of drug-responsive phenotypes and genotypes. Alternatively, the current amyloid and imaging markers may not be sufficiently specific and sensitive to the progression of illness or may indicate more advanced illness. In the future, newer markers such as tau imaging might prove better.

Better, smarter, phase 2 studies are needed to demonstrate proof of concept and the potential efficacy of drugs, such that phase 3 will be more likely to succeed and be confirmatory. These future trials would include fewer participants, drug-specific outcomes, and protocol designs that can be changed or adapted after randomization. Phase 3 trials may need to be more efficiently designed for clinically relevant and more precise outcomes.

Acknowledgments

LSS was supported in part by the USC Alzheimer's Disease Research Center, NIH P50 AG05142 and NIH R01 AG037561.

References

ADAPT Research Group: Naproxen and celecoxib do not prevent AD in early results from a randomized controlled trial, *Neurology* 68:1800–1808, 2007.

Aisen PS, Gauthier S, Vellas B, Briand R, Saumier D, Laurin J, Garceau D: Alzhemed: a potential treatment for Alzheimer's disease, *Curr Alzheimer Res* 4:473–478, 2007.

Albert MS, DeKosky ST, Dickson D, Dubois B, Feldman HH, Fox NC, Gamst A, Holtzman DM, Jagust WJ, Petersen RC, et al: The diagnosis of mild cognitive impairment due to Alzheimer's disease: recommendations from the National Institute on Aging-Alzheimer's Association workgroups on diagnostic guidelines for Alzheimer's disease, *Alzheimer Dement* 7:270–279, 2011.

Becker RE, Greig NH, Giacobini E: Why do so many drugs for Alzheimer's disease fail in development? Time for new methods and new practices? *J Alzheimers Dis* 15:303–325, 2008.

Birks, J. Cholinesterase inhibitors for Alzheimer's disease. *Cochrane Database Syst Rev* CD005593, 2006.

Blennow K, Zetterberg H, Rinne JO, Salloway S, Wei J, Black R, Grundman M, Liu E: Effect of immunotherapy with bapineuzumab on cerebrospinal fluid biomarker levels in patients with mild to moderate Alzheimer disease, *Arch Neurol-Chicago* 69(8):1–9, 2012.

Braak H, Del Tredici K: Where, when, and in what form does sporadic Alzheimer's disease begin? *Curr Opin Neurol* 25:708–714, 2012.

Coric V, van Dyck CH, Salloway S, Andreasen N, Brody M, Richter RW, Soininen H, Thein S, et al: Safety and tolerability of the γ-secretase inhibitor avagacestat in a phase 2 study of mild to moderate Alzheimer disease, *Arch Neurol-Chicago* 69:1–12, 2012.

DeKosky ST, Williamson JD, Fitzpatrick AL, Kronmal RA, Ives DG, Saxton JA, Lopez OL, Burke G, Carlson MC, Fried LP, et al: Ginkgo biloba for prevention of dementia: a randomized controlled trial, *J Amer Med Assoc* 300:2253–2262, 2008.

Doody RS, Ferris SH, Salloway S, Sun Y, Goldman R, Watkins WE, Xu Y, Murthy AK: Donepezil treatment of patients with MCI, *Neurology* 72:1555–1561, 2009.

Doody RS, Raman R, Farlow M, Iwatsubo T, Vellas B, Joffe S, Kieburtz K, He F, Sun X, Thomas RG, et al: A phase 3 trial of semagacestat for treatment of Alzheimer's disease, *New Engl J Med* 369:341–350, 2013.

Dubois B, Feldman HH, Jacova C, Dekosky ST, Barberger-Gateau P, Cummings J, Delacourte A, Galasko D, Gauthier S, Jicha G, et al: Research criteria for the diagnosis of Alzheimer's disease: revising the NINCDS-ADRDA criteria, *Lancet Neurol* 6:734–746, 2007.

Dubois B, Feldman HH, Jacova C, Cummings JL, DeKosky ST, Barberger-Gateau P, Delacourte A, Frisoni G, Fox NC, Galasko D, et al: Revising the definition of Alzheimer's disease: a new lexicon, *Lancet Neurol* 9:1118–1127, 2010.

Dubois B, Feldman HH, Jacova C, Hampel H, Molinuevo JL, Blennow K, DeKosky ST, Gauthier S, Selkoe D, Bateman R, et al: Advancing research diagnostic criteria for Alzheimer's disease: the IWG-2 criteria, *Lancet Neurol* 13:614–629, 2014.

EMA, European Medicines Agency: Pre-authorisation evaluation of medicines for human use. Guideline on medicinal products for the treatment of Alzheimer's disease and other dementias. CPMP/EWP/553/95 Rev. 1; 2008.

EMA, European Medicines Agency: Committee for Medicinal Products for Human Use. Guideline on medicinal products for the treatment of Alzheimer's disease and other dementias. CPMP/EWP/553/95 Rev. 1, 2009.

EMA, European Medicines Agency: Qualification opinion of Alzheimer's disease novel methodologies/biomarkers for PET amyloid imaging (positive/negative) as a biomarker for enrichment, for use in regulatory clinical trials in predementia Alzheimer's disease. EMA/CHMP/SAWP/892998/2011, 2012a.

EMA, European Medicines Agency: Qualification opinion of Alzheimer's disease novel methodologies/biomarkers for the use of CSF AB 1-42 and t-tau and/or PET-amyloid imaging (positive/negative) as biomarkers for enrichment, for use in regulatory clinical trials in mild and moderate Alzheimer's disease. EMA/CHMP/SAWP/893622/2011, 2012b.

EMA, European Medicines Agency: Qualification opinion of a novel data driven model of disease progression and trial evaluation in mild and moderate Alzheimer's disease. EMA/CHMP/SAWP/420174/2013, 2013. Available from: http://www.ema.europa.eu/docs/en_GB/document_library/Regulatory_and_procedural_guideline/2013/07/WC500146179.pdf.

FDA. United States Food and Drug Administration Peripheral and Central Nervous System Drugs Advisory Committee Meeting. Rockville, MD, 1989, Department of Health and Human Services, Public Health Service, Food and Drug Administration.

FDA. United States Food and Drug Administration Peripheral and Central Nervous System Drugs Advisory Committee, Mild Cognitive Impairment, 2001. Available from: http://www.fda.gov/ohrms/dockets/ac/01/minutes/3724m1.html, March 13, 2001.

FDA. United States Food and Drug Administration. Guidance for Industry Alzheimer's Disease: Developing Drugs for the Treatment of Early Stage Disease (FDA-2013-D-0077) DRAFT (US Food and Drug Administration, Center for Drug Evaluation and Research), 2013.

Feldman HH, Ferris S, Winblad B, Sfikas N, Mancione L, He Y, Tekin S, Burns A, Cummings J, del Ser T, et al: Effect of rivastigmine on delay to diagnosis of Alzheimer's disease from mild cognitive impairment: the InDDEx study, *Lancet Neurol* 6:501–512, 2007.

Folstein MF, Folstein SE, McHugh PR: Mini-mental state: a practical method for grading the cognitive state of patients for the clinician, *J Psychiat Res* 12:189–198, 1975.

Giacobini E: Cholinesterases in human brain: the effect of cholinesterase inhibitors on Alzheimer's disease and related disorders. In Giacobini E, Pepeu G, editors: *The Brain Cholinergic System in Health and Disease*, Oxon, UK, 2006, Informa Healthcare, pp 235–264.

Gilman S, Koller M, Black RS, Jenkins L, Griffith SG, Fox NC, Eisner L, Kirby L, Rovira MB, Forette F, et al: Clinical effects of Abeta immunization (AN1792) in patients with AD in an interrupted trial, *Neurology* 64:1553–1562, 2005.

Golde TE, Schneider LS, Koo EH: Anti-Aβ therapeutics in Alzheimer's disease: the need for a paradigm shift, *Neuron* 69:203–213, 2011.

Green RC, Schneider LS, Amato DA, Beelen AP, Wilcock G, Swabb EA, Zavitz KH: Effect of tarenflurbil on cognitive decline and activities of daily living in patients with mild Alzheimer disease, *J Amer Med Assoc* 302:2557–2564, 2009.

Grober E, Lipton RB, Hall C, Crystal H: Memory impairment on free and cued selective reminding predicts dementia, *Neurology* 54:827–832, 2000.

Holmes C, Boche D, Wilkinson D, Yadegarfar G, Hopkins V, Bayer A, Jones RW, Bullock R, Love S, Neal JW, et al: Long-term effects of Abeta42 immunisation in Alzheimer's disease: follow-up of a randomised, placebo-controlled phase I trial, *Lancet* 372:216–223, 2008.

Jelic V, Kivipelto M, Winblad B: Clinical trials in mild cognitive impairment: lessons for the future, *Neurosurg Psych* 77:429–438, 2006.

Karran E, Hardy J: A critique of the drug discovery and phase 3 clinical programs targeting the amyloid hypothesis for Alzheimer disease, *Ann Neurol* 76:185–205, 2014.

Kittner B, Rössner M, Rother M: Clinical trials in dementia with Propentofylline, *Ann NY Acad Sci* 826:307–316, 1997.

Kivipelto M, Solomon A, Ahtiluoto S, Ngandu T, Lehtisalo J, Antikainen R, Bäckman L, Hänninen T, Jula A, Laatikainen T, et al: The Finnish geriatric intervention study to prevent cognitive impairment and disability (FINGER): study design and progress, *Alzheimers Dement* 9:657–665, 2013.

Kozauer N, Katz R: Regulatory innovation and drug development for early-stage Alzheimer's disease, *New Engl J Med* 368:1169–1171, 2013.

Kryscio R, Abner E, Schmitt F, Goodman P, Mendiondo M, Caban-Holt A, Dennis B, Mathews M, Klein E, Crowley J, et al: A randomized controlled Alzheimer's disease prevention trial's evolution into an exposure trial: the PREADViSE trial, *J Nutr Health Aging* 17:72–75, 2013.

Leber P: *Guidelines for the clinical evaluation of anti-dementia drugs, 1st draft*, Rockville, MD, 1990, United States Food and Drug Amdinistration.

Leber P: Slowing the progression of Alzheimer disease: methodologic issues, *Alz Dis Assoc Dis* 11:S10–S21, 1997, discussion S37–S19.

Lindner MD, McArthur RA, Deadwyler S, Hampson R, Tariot PN: Development, optimization and use of preclinical behavioral models to maximize the productivity of drug discovery for Alzheimer's disease. In McArthur RA, Borsini F, editors: *Animal and translational models for CNS drug discovery*, San Diego, CA, 2008, Academic Press, pp 93–157.

Liu-Seifert H, Siemers E, Holdridge KC, Andersen SW, Lipkovich I, Carlson C, Sethuraman G, Hoog S, Hayduk R, Doody R, et al: Delayed-start analysis: mild Alzheimer's disease patients in solanezumab trials, 3.5 years, *Alzheimers Dement* 1:111–121, 2015.

Mangialasche F, Solomon A, Winblad B, Mecocci P, Kivipelto M: Alzheimer's disease: clinical trials and drug development, *Lancet Neurol* 9:702–716, 2010.

McKhann G, Drachman D, Folstein M, Katzman R, Price D, Stadlan EM: Clinical diagnosis of Alzheimer's disease: report of the NINCDS-ADRDA work group under the auspices of Department of Health and Human Services Task Force on Alzheimer's Disease, *Neurology* 34:939–944, 1984.

McKhann GM, Knopman DS, Chertkow H, Hyman BT, Jack CR, Kawas CH, Klunk WE, Koroshetz WJ, Manly JJ, Mayeux R, et al: The diagnosis of dementia due to Alzheimer's disease: recommendations from the National Institute on Aging-Alzheimer's Association workgroups on diagnostic guidelines for Alzheimer's disease, *Alzheimers Dement* 7:263–269, 2011.

Mohs RC, Knopman D, Petersen RC, Ferris SH, Ernesto C, Grundman M, Sano M, Bieliauskas L, Geldmacher D, Clark C, et al: Development of cognitive instruments for use in clinical trials of antidementia drugs: additions to the Alzheimer's Disease Assessment Scale that broaden its scope. The Alzheimer's Disease Cooperative Study, *Alz Dis Assoc Dis* 11:S13–S21, 1997.

Morris JC: The Clinical Dementia Rating (CDR): current version and scoring rules, *Neurology* 43:2412–2414, 1993.

Morris JC, McKeel DW Jr, Storandt M, Rubin EH, Price JL, Grant EA, Ball MJ, Berg L: Very mild Alzheimer's disease: informant-based clinical, psychometric, and pathologic distinction from normal aging, *Neurology* 41:469–478, 1991.

Peters R, Beckett N, Forette F, Tuomilehto J, Clarke R, Ritchie C, Waldman A, Walton I, Poulter R, Ma S, et al: Incident dementia and blood pressure lowering in the Hypertension in the Very Elderly Trial Cognitive Function Assessment (HYVET-COG): a double-blind, placebo controlled trial, *Lancet Neurol* 7:683–689, 2008.

Petersen RC, Smith GE, Waring SC, Ivnik RJ, Tangalos EG, Kokmen E: Mild cognitive impairment: clinical characterization and outcome, *Arch Neurol-Chicago* 56:303–308, 1999.

Petersen RC, Thomas RG, Grundman M, Bennett D, Doody R, Ferris S, Galasko D, Jin S, Kaye J, Levey A, et al: Vitamin E and donepezil for the treatment of mild cognitive impairment, *New Engl J Med* 352:2379–2388, 2005.

PhRMA. Pharmaceutical Research and Manufacturers of America. Researching Alzheimer's medicines: setbacks and stepping stones, 2012.

Raschetti R, Albanese E, Vanacore N, Maggini M: Cholinesterase inhibitors in mild cognitive impairment: a systematic review of randomised trials, *PLoS Med* 4:e338, 2007.

Reisberg B, Ferris SH, de Leon MJ, Crook T: The Global Deterioration Scale for assessment of primary degenerative dementia, *Am J Psychiat* 139:1136–1139, 1982.

Rinne JO, Brooks DJ, Rossor MN, Fox NC, Bullock R, Klunk WE, Mathis CA, Blennow K, Barakos J, Okello AA, et al: 11C-PiB PET assessment of change in fibrillar amyloid-beta load in patients with Alzheimer's disease treated with bapineuzumab: a phase 2, double-blind, placebo-controlled, ascending-dose study, *Lancet Neurol* 9:363–372, 2010.

Rosen WG, Mohs RC, Davis KL: A new rating scale for Alzheimer's disease, *Am J Psychiatry* 141:1356–1364, 1984.

Roses AD, Welsh-Bohmer KA, Burns DK, et al: A pharmacogenetics-supported clinical trial to delay onset of mild cognitive impairment due to Alzheimer's disease, *J. Nutr Health Aging*:841, 2012.

Salloway S, Ferris S, Kluger A, Goldman R, Griesing T, Kumar D, Richardson S, Donepezil 401 Study G: Efficacy of donepezil in mild cognitive impairment: a randomized placebo-controlled trial, *Neurology* 63:651–657, 2004.

Salloway S, Sperling R, Gilman S, Fox NC, Blennow K, Raskind M, Sabbagh M, Honig LS, Doody R, van Dyck CH, et al: A phase 2 multiple ascending dose trial of bapineuzumab in mild to moderate Alzheimer disease, *Neurology* 73:2061–2070, 2009.

Salloway S, Sperling R, Keren R, Porsteinsson AP, van Dyck CH, Tariot PN, Gilman S, Arnold D, Abushakra S, Hernandez C, et al: A phase 2 randomized trial of ELND005, scyllo-inositol, in mild to moderate Alzheimer disease, *Neurology* 77:1253–1262, 2011.

Schneider LS: Issues in design and conduct of clinical trials for cognitive-enhancing drugs. In McArthur RA, Borsini F, editors: *Animal and translational models for CNS drug discovery*, San Diego, CA, 2008a, Academic Press, pp 21–76.

Schneider LS: Prevention therapeutics of dementia, *Alzheimers Dement* 4:S122–S130, 2008b.

Schneider LS: Rethinking the Food and Drug Administration's 2013 guidance on developing drugs for early-stage Alzheimer's disease, *Alzheimers Dement* 10:247–250, 2014.

Schneider LS, Sano M: Current Alzheimer's disease clinical trials: methods and placebo outcomes, *Alzheimers Dement* 5:388–397, 2009.

Schneider LS, Olin JT, Doody RS, Clark CM, Morris JC, Reisberg B, Schmitt FA, Grundman M, Thomas RG, Ferris SH: Validity and reliability of the Alzheimer's Disease Cooperative Study—clinical global impression of change: the Alzheimer's Disease Cooperative Study, *Alz Dis Assoc Dis* 11:S22–S32, 1997.

Schneider LS, Insel PS, Weiner MW: Treatment with cholinesterase inhibitors and memantine of patients in the Alzheimer's Disease Neuroimaging Initiative, *Arch Neurol-Chicago* 68:58–66, 2011.

Schneider LS, Mangialasche F, Andreasen N, Feldman H, Giacobini E, Jones R, Mantua V, Mecocci P, Pani L, Winblad B, et al: Clinical trials and late-stage drug development for Alzheimer's disease: an appraisal from 1984 to 2014, *J Intern Med* 275:251–283, 2014.

Smith AD, Smith SM, de Jager CA, Whitbread P, Johnston C, Agacinski G, Oulhaj A, Bradley KM, Jacoby R, Refsum H: Homocysteine-lowering by B vitamins slows the rate of accelerated brain atrophy in mild cognitive impairment: a randomized controlled trial, *PLoS ONE* 5:e12244, 2010.

Solomon A, Mangialasche F, Richard E, Andrieu S, Bennett DA, Breteler M, Fratiglioni L, Hooshman B, Khachaturian AS, Schneider LS, et al: Advances in the prevention of Alzheimer's disease and dementia, *J Intern Med* 275(3):229–250, 2014.

Sperling RA, Aisen PS, Beckett LA, Bennett DA, Craft S, Fagan AM, Iwatsubo T, Jack CR, Kaye J, Montine TJ, et al: Toward defining the preclinical stages of Alzheimer's disease: recommendations from the National Institute on Aging–Alzheimer's Association workgroups on diagnostic guidelines for Alzheimer's disease, *Alzheimers Dement* 7:280–292, 2011.

Sperling RA, Rentz DM, Johnson KA, Karlawish J, Donohue M, Salmon DP, Aisen P: The A4 Study: stopping AD before symptoms begin? *Sci Transl Med* 6, 2014, 228fs213.

Thal LJ, Ferris SH, Kirby L, Block GA, Lines CR, Yuen E, Assaid C, Nessly ML, Norman BA, Baranak CC, et al: A randomized, double-blind study of rofecoxib in patients with mild cognitive impairment, *Neuropsychopharmacology* 30:1204–1215, 2005.

Trusheim M, Burgess B, Hu S, Long T, Averbuch S, Flynn A, Lieftucht A, Mazumder A, Milloy J, Shaw P, et al: Quantifying factors for the success of stratified medicine, *Nat Rev Drug Discov* 10:817–833, 2011.

Vellas B, Andrieu S, Sampaio C, Wilcock G: Disease-modifying trials in Alzheimer's disease: a European task force consensus, *Lancet Neurol* 6:56–62, 2007.

Vellas B, Andrieu S, Sampaio C, Coley N, Wilcock G: Endpoints for trials in Alzheimer's disease: a European task force consensus, *Lancet Neurol* 7:436–450, 2008.

Vellas B, Coley N, Ousset P-J, Berrut G, Dartigues J-F, Dubois B, Grandjean H, Pasquier F, Piette F, Robert P, et al: Long-term use of standardised ginkgo biloba extract for the prevention of Alzheimer's disease (GuidAge): a randomised placebo-controlled trial, *Lancet Neurol* 11:851–859, 2012.

Winblad B, Gauthier S, Scinto L, Feldman H, Wilcock GK, Truyen L, Mayorga AJ, Wang D, Brashear HR, Nye JS: Safety and efficacy of galantamine in subjects with mild cognitive impairment, *Neurology* 70:2024–2035, 2008.

CHAPTER

20

Molecular Imaging in Alzheimer Clinical Trials

M.E. Schmidt, D.C. Matthews, S. Staelens

OUTLINE

INTRODUCTION

Human life expectancy in developed countries has doubled over the past century largely thanks to effective prevention and treatment of childhood illnesses and infectious diseases. As these illnesses have diminished as causes of mortality, diseases of aging have emerged as a major focus of health care need, among them neurodegenerative disorders associated with loss of cognitive and functional ability captured under the rubric of dementia. A third of elders now die with dementia, most commonly attributed to Alzheimer's disease (AD),

Developing Therapeutics for Alzheimer's Disease. http://dx.doi.org/10.1016/B978-0-12-802173-6.00020-4

their deaths preceded by years of decline and progressive need for support by caregivers. The economic burden in 2013 for health care and long-term care alone was estimated to come to $203 billion. As the number of people with AD and other dementias grows, these costs could reach $1.2 trillion by 2050 (Alzheimer's Association, 2015). Our current pharmacological armamentarium against AD is limited to medications with modest effects on symptoms, none having a meaningful impact on disease onset or progression. It is no wonder that many governments are mounting research campaigns to identify means of intervening with the disease process as they ponder the scale of demand on national health care systems for care of patients with AD in the coming decades.

Several large pharmaceutical companies, numerous biotech companies, and many academic labs are pursuing the discovery and testing of therapeutics for AD. The hurdles faced in this effort include high development costs, estimated at $2 billion per compound; the long duration of trials to determine whether an effect can be observed; and the low success rate in identifying effective treatments (Paul et al., 2010). A single agent, memantine, was approved as a treatment for AD between 2002 and 2012, representing a failure rate of 99.6% of all agents tested (Cummings et al., 2014). While treatments may have failed due to the absence of therapeutic potency, the methods of clinical testing have also been questioned. Reasons thought to challenge assay performance include methods of subject selection and variability in clinical assessment and measurement. Assessment using clinical history, signs, and symptoms has reasonable sensitivity and specificity in expert hands; however, assessment in clinical trials may be compromised by the eagerness of sponsors, investigators, subjects, and families to identify relief for desperate conditions. Moreover, diagnosis in expert clinical settings can be iterative over time, whereas duration and range of screening procedures for clinical trial are highly constrained. The standard cognitive and functional measures used in AD trials have floor and ceiling effects that limit their dynamic range, especially in subjects with mild impairment, and exhibit high end-point variability within and between subjects. This translates into very large sample sizes. Moreover, if the goal is to intervene before onset of significant cognitive impairment, then treatment studies may need to be conducted for years to see an impact on clinical outcomes. The long cycle time and large trials translate to significant costs. This, along with the high failure rate, has led to a number of large companies exiting neuroscience discovery while at the same time accelerating the effort to find tools that could reduce the time to identify a signal and reduce the number of subjects required to test new agents. Objective evidence, such as a biomarker, might help this situation, by refining subject selection and providing some indication that a treatment was having an effect on the disease process, which could ultimately translate into arrest of neurodegeneration and attendant cognitive and functional decline.

Accrual of evidence of AD pathology in vivo began 40 years ago as structural imaging of the brain, first computed tomography (CT) and then magnetic resonance imaging (MRI), allowed detection of cortical atrophy. MRI has been included in AD trials for many years, although primarily for purposes of excluding subjects with vascular pathology or those with distinct non-AD atrophy such as Pick's or Huntington's disease. A challenge for structural imaging of the brain as a biomarker of AD has been specificity, as atrophy and its measurement occur at tissue level, and progressive cortical atrophy can be seen with a number of neurodegenerative diseases. More AD-specific patterns have been identified with structural MRI, such as atrophy of the medial temporal lobe and hippocampus or regional changes in cortical thickness

(Johnson et al., 2012), although thresholds of abnormality have not yet been defined. As a consequence, these more differentiating features have not been adopted for subject inclusion in clinical trials but rather as baseline covariate or a means of tracking disease progression. Moreover, atrophy and neuronal loss appear to occur years after significant brain amyloid burden has accrued, when cognitive impairment is already apparent: perhaps too late for a prevention trial (Bateman et al., 2012; Jack et al., 2010). Detection of biomarkers at the molecular level—protein abnormalities specific for AD—has developed more recently. Detection of $A\beta_{1-42}$ in human cerebrospinal fluid (CSF) required the identification of suitable antibodies for assay development (Vigo-Pelfrey et al., 1993). Amyloid PET (positron emission tomography) has been a recent entry as a molecular biomarker. The protein chemistry of fibrillar β-amyloid, developed since the 1980s (Glenner and Wong, 1984; Masters et al., 1985), has been critical for lead selection and validation of PET ligands. Biomarkers of brain amyloidosis, either amyloid PET or CSF, have been accepted as positive indicators of AD pathology and are being used for subject selection. This is redefining how clinical trials in AD are conducted.

Establishing that amyloid PET and CSF biomarkers could be collected in a multisite clinical trial setting, in elderly subjects with no signs of cognitive impairment and across a wide spectrum of symptoms and deficits up to and including dementia, is a major achievement of the Alzheimer's Disease Neuroimaging Initiative (ADNI). ADNI began enrolling subjects in 2004 and began to include [^{11}C]-PiB PET 2 years later, just a few years after the first reports that a high cortical signal had been observed in subjects with probable AD in contrast to healthy elders (Klunk et al., 2004). In the process, ADNI developed the first set of standards for acquisition of amyloid PET across multiple centers and PET camera types (Jagust et al., 2010). ADNI protocols provided the foundation for inclusion of amyloid PET in multisite trials, and the field of testing treatments for possible benefit in AD has gone from reliance on clinical assessment and recruiting subjects with significant impairments to defining cases entirely by biomarkers and recruiting subjects who are thought to be at risk of developing AD.

To illustrate the shift, the phase 3 trials of bapineuzumab and solanezumab that completed 3 years ago used the National Institute of Neurological and Communicative Disorders and Stroke criteria for probable AD as the primary basis for enrollment (Salloway et al., 2014; Doody et al., 2014). These criteria rely on a history of decline, clinical assessment of cognitive and functional impairment, and visual reading of brain MRI as "not inconsistent with AD" (McKhann et al., 1984). CSF sampling, [^{18}F]-fluoro-2-deoxy-d-glucose (FDG) PET, amyloid PET, and quantitative structural MRI were included in substudies as candidate markers of disease progression, not for subject inclusion. Even as those trials were enrolling the first subjects, the conceptualization of subjects with AD evolved, signaled by the development of the Dubois research criteria. In addition to progressive and objectively verified memory deficits, a diagnosis of probable AD required biomarker evidence of AD pathology: evidence of medial temporal atrophy on MRI, abnormal CSF amyloid and/or tau peptide concentrations, and/or bilateral temporal parietal hypometabolism by FDG PET. Amyloid PET at that time was noted to be "promising" (Dubois et al., 2007). These biomarkers were also recognized as a means for detecting the disease process prior to the development of dementia, thereby allowing better understanding of factors contributing to disease progression and opportunity for early intervention. Confidence in the ability to detect pathological changes is reflected by research criteria developed for preclinical AD (before the appearance of cognitive and functional deficits) entirely based on biomarkers: brain amyloidosis as evidenced by either low CSF Aβ42 or "positive" amyloid PET demarcate apparently healthy elderly as on the path (stage 1) to AD; otherwise, subjects were not on the path (stage 0) (Sperling et al., 2011). The recently launched "A4 study" (Anti-Amyloid Treatment in Asymptomatic Alzheimer's) illustrates the impact of this change (Sperling et al., 2014). The A4 study will screen healthy elders (ages 65–85) who have no evidence of cognitive impairment with evidence of high brain amyloid burden by amyloid PET scans. Nothing has been identified to date that can arrest the development of AD, so the decision to initiate treatment in otherwise healthy individuals identified by biomarkers is a high-risk, technically challenging, and costly undertaking. Nonetheless, identification of a treatment that could arrest the development of AD has become a social and economic imperative, and requires accepting a high-risk, if not drastic, strategy. How molecular imaging can be used, the types of probes available, and, critically, how to ensure that the data are reliable and interpretable when used in intervention trials will be reviewed in this chapter.

We will begin with some background on PET relevant to considering its use in AD clinical research among the various biomarker methods available; how AD "specific" PET tracers were developed; and how differences among the various tracers, scan acquisitions, and analyses can impact the data extracted from PET images and influence interpretation. The primary focus will be amyloid PET and tau PET as tools for clinical trials in AD, from preclinical/presymptomatic stages to dementia. In addition to these protein markers, we will review the role of FDG PET. Patterns of glucose hypometabolism can inform the differential diagnosis of subjects with impairment, and severity of hypometabolism is highly predictive of decline. The extent of deficits in neuronal activity can provide complementary information to the accumulation of amyloid and tau in the brain. The accuracy of any measurement can be judged only by understanding its variability, so we will also consider the impact of biological and technical factors that influence measurements in multisite, longitudinal trials. We will also address how amyloid and FDG PET perform in transgenic mouse models as a means of selecting treatments for testing in humans, and how these measures in preclinical models can inform us regarding expected performance in humans. As we have noted, MRI and CSF assays are also extensively used for phenotyping and following subjects in intervention trials. We will touch on the intersection of MRI and CSF with PET imaging, but not review them as end points per se. MRI and CSF end points have similar challenges regarding assay reliability, interpretation, validation, and variability, but are best addressed separately. We will conclude with how these methods can contribute to intervention trials in AD, and potential next steps.

WHY PET?

The origin of the PET signal is a γ photon. Positrons are emitted from PET isotopes as they decay to a more stable form. When a positron meets an electron in the surrounding environment, this meeting of particle and antiparticle results in a mutual annihilation event, producing a pair of γ photons as the particle masses are converted to energy. Positrons can travel up to a few millimeters after emission from the isotope, depending on their energy, and it is this variability in the potential location of the annihilation that creates one of the limits on the spatial resolution of PET. Photons are highly energetic and travel away from the annihilation site in opposite directions, where they can be detected by crystals in the PET camera, organized as opposing pairs. When a pair of detectors simultaneously detects a photon, a line of response is defined along which an annihilation event might have occurred, and an isotope atom ought to have been in the vicinity. The first form of data is the spatial recording of the emission signal intensity associated with the lines of response. These data are transformed into a frequency distribution represented as a sinogram. Representing the spatial information in frequency form significantly reduces the computational difficulty of processing the image. These emission data are corrected for signal attenuation by bone and other tissues by using a separate transmission scan for noise resulting from scattered and random counts, signals missed by the camera during the detector "dead time" and corrections for performance differences between the detectors. The corrected emission data are then reconstructed to form anatomic images (Fig. 20.1). Image reconstruction involves transforming the corrected frequency data back to spatial representation in order to create a visual image. The type of image reconstruction used can be a function of the camera type or investigator preference. These reconstructed images are often referred to as the raw PET data, although it is apparent that a number of processing steps and data transformations occur after the assembly of the sinogram that are camera and operator dependent, and potentially subject to error (Saha, 2005).

The appeal of PET is the potential for highly sensitive detection of very specific targets and for quantitation of the signal. The signal detection made possible by sensing γ photons can be in the picomolar range, readily allowing identification of protein aggregates such as fibrillar amyloid which can be present at nanomolar concentrations in human brain (Klunk et al., 2005). As indicated in Table 20.1, PET is associated with exposure to energy sufficient to free electrons from atoms—better known as ionizing radiation, which can damage tissues and generate mutations. As an example, a scan with [^{18}F] florbetapir results in an effective radiation exposure of around 7 millisieverts (mSv) using the recommended 370 megabecquerel (MBq) dose (Joshi et al., 2012; Wong et al., 2010a). The International Commission for Radiological Protection

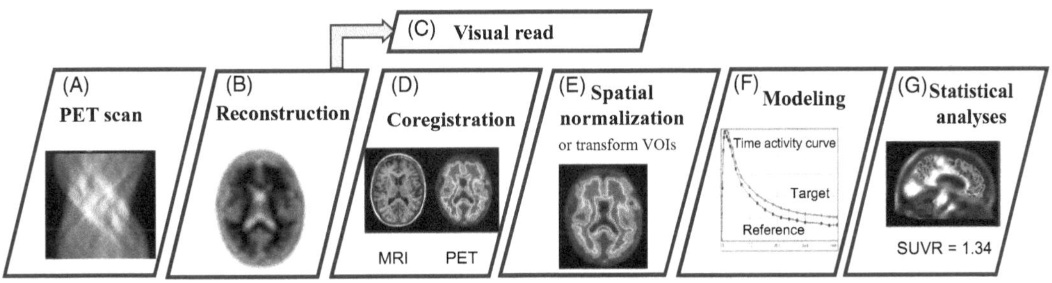

FIGURE 20.1 (A) PET image is first recorded as a sinogram; (B) the sinogram is then reconstructed into an image that is interpretable with regard to spatial and intensity information; this may be performed using methods such as filtered back-projection or iterative reconstruction, and the emission scan is also corrected for skull attenuation and scatter; (C) the scan may be visually read for a qualitative assessment; (D) reconstructed images are typically coregistered to other images, which may be anatomical MRI and/or other PET scans, in order to compare scans; (E) images may be spatially normalized, or warped, to a common spatial template in order to allow voxel-based comparisons to be made across images from different subjects, and template volumes of interest (VOIs) may be transformed onto a subject's native scan; (F) depending on the PET tracer and imaging objectives, images may be modeled using kinetic equations or simply summed time frames; and (G) a variety of quantitative analysis techniques can be applied, which may include region-of-interest measurement and calculation of standardized uptake value ratio or voxel-based comparisons.

TABLE 20.1 Comparison of In Vivo Methods

Imaging method	Temporal resolution	Spatial resolution	Sensitivity	Energy ($\Delta E = h\nu$)
MEG	1 ms	5 mm		
EEG	1 ms	10–15 mm		
MRI	100 m single slice 3 s multiple slice	3.5 mm[a] 1–2 mm[b]	10^{-5} molar	10^{7} Hz
PET	45 s[c] 20 min[d]	6.5 mm[c] 4 mm[d]	10^{-12} molar	10^{17} Hz
SPECT	>60s	6–8 mm	10^{-12} molar	10^{17} Hz

[a] *GE BOLD 1.5T.*
[b] *SE-BOLD 7T.*
[c] *$H_2^{15}O$ to measure blood flow.*
[d] *FDG to measure glucose metabolism.*
Adapted from Volkow et al. (1997), Logothetis (2008).

guidance for clinical research studies recommends that exposures should not exceed 10 mSv for adults up to the age of 50. While higher cumulative radiation doses might be acceptable in older adults if potential benefit comes from the information, this represents a strong argument for MRI for the serial and potentially frequent assessments desired in longitudinal studies.

The PET signal detected by the scanner is a composite of radioactivity from tracer present in multiple tissue compartments: the blood into which the tracer was infused and from which it will be cleared; a "free" tissue compartment in the brain, where the tracer has crossed the blood–brain barrier but is not bound; the specific binding compartment of interest; and a nonspecific binding compartment (Morris et al., 2004). Targeting highly specific binding compartments is possible using small molecules selected for having nanomolar affinity for a particular target—such as a membrane receptor, enzyme, or protein binding pocket—to which a positron-emitting radioisotope can be attached. Such ligands can be found using in vitro binding screens and medicinal chemistry approaches such as analysis of structure–activity relationships. The nonspecific contribution can be from "off-target" binding of the ligand to another protein or distribution into a large-capacity and slowly clearing compartment such as the various lipid compartments in the brain. This is a major contributor to the noise from which the specific signal must be extracted. In order for ligands to efficiently cross the blood–brain barrier, a certain degree of lipophilicity and a limited size (less than 500 daltons) are needed among the physical chemical attributes (Zhang et al., 2013). The art of selecting a useful ligand for imaging targets in the brain requires identifying chemical derivatives that demonstrate the right balance of getting into the brain and washing out "nontarget" compartments, which cannot be fully predicted by physicochemical properties or pharmacological profile and requires testing in vivo. The extent of background signal is a notable differentiating feature of the various ligands for amyloid or tau PET imaging. Another potential contributor to the noise is generation of metabolites of the tracer that bear the PET isotope and can enter into the brain, and determining the metabolic fate of a ligand is also part of the selection of a tracer for PET imaging. The PET imaging glucose derivative FDG is very hydrophilic and highly polar but enters the brain via active, glucose-specific transporters.

Due to the polar nature and selectivity of FDG as a substrate for hexokinase, there is very little nonspecific signal.

While a number of PET isotopes are available, those relevant for this chapter are [^{11}C] carbon, with a radioactive half-life of slightly more than 20 min, and [^{18}F] fluorine, with a half-life of slightly less than 110 min. The shorter half-life of [^{11}C] results in per scan radiation burden that is roughly half that of [^{18}F]-labeled tracers, permitting repeat scans to be conducted a few hours apart and more scans per subject for a given study. As a result, [^{11}C] is the preferred isotope for occupancy studies, when several scans may be acquired in a subject. However, use of a [^{11}C]-labeled probe requires production at the PET center where the scan is to be acquired by a trained radiochemist, whereas [^{18}F] labeling allows for central production of the radioligand and distribution to a number of PET centers within a few hours' travel distance. For these reasons, sponsors of all PET ligands that have or are seeking marketing authorization are using those labeled with [^{18}F] fluorine.

PET LIGANDS FOR AMYLOID IMAGING

Imaging the pathology of AD ex vivo began toward the end of the 19th century as neuropathologists reported autopsy findings of "round heaps" of a substance that stained more intensely than the neurons in the cortex of elderly subjects suffering from progressive dementia. The appearance of these "heaps," referred to as "miliary sclerosis," distinguished subjects with dementia from cases due to vascular pathology or tertiary syphilis. Miliary sclerosis was identified by exposing brain tissue to a variety of histological stains, including Bielschowsky's silver stain, favored by Oskar Fischer, who described the key features of neuritic plaques, and Alois Alzheimer, who further identified intracellular neurofibrillary tangles as unique pathological features of the disease that now bears his name (Goedert, 2009). Fluorescing small molecule dyes were subsequently found that could intensely stain these deposits. While useful at autopsy or biopsy samples, the signal detected by fluorescence is weak and requires micromolar concentrations of dyes for ex vivo/in vitro preparations, prompting efforts to develop target-specific imaging probes using radioisotopes for in vivo signal detection. Among these dyes, Congo red and thioflavin T were considered for radiolabeling but have poor brain penetration (Mathis et al., 2012). The parent structures have provided chemical scaffolds for building a series of derivatives better at crossing the blood–brain barrier. While many of these derivatives are better able to get into the brain, they also differ in metabolic stability and selective retention in plaques relative to other tissue compartments in the brain, a key determinant of the signal-to-background that can be achieved with these radioligands.

The first attempts at developing a small-molecule ligand for labeling fibrillar amyloid were the radiolabeling of Congo red, a textile dye that was found to intensely stain amyloid, and a close analog, chrysamine G. A number of derivatives were tested by the University of Pittsburgh; however, these large and somewhat polar molecules do not cross the blood–brain barrier. Efforts to reduce the size and improve the physical chemical properties led to generation of styryl derivatives referred to as "X-compounds." Many of these derivatives were tested and abandoned, although the insight offered by the styryl structures led to the testing of styrylbenzenes or stilbenes, to which we will return later. Neutral and more lipophilic thioflavin T derivatives were next pursued, and after screening a number of compounds for affinity for $A\beta_{1-40}$ fibrils, brain penetrability, and washout from the brain, 2-(4′-[^{11}C] methylaminophenyl)-6-hydroxybenzothiazole, subsequently named Pittsburgh compound B (PiB) (Table 20.2), was selected for testing in humans and was found to result in a pattern of retention much higher in cortical regions of subjects with probable AD than in healthy elders (Klunk et al., 2004).

An [^{18}F] fluorinated derivative of PiB (flutemetamol; Table 20.2) has been developed by GE Healthcare (Nelissen et al., 2009). Fluorination of a benzene ring can be a very challenging radiolabeling, although the location on an aromatic ring helps to protect the fluorine from early metabolic removal. This reduces a common risk of [^{18}F]-labeled molecules: release of free [^{18}F] that can be taken up by bone, such as the skull, where it can confound measurement of the brain signal. Addition of the fluorine also results in different kinetic behavior and white matter affinity compared to [^{11}C]-PiB, reflected in the later scan acquisition times seen in Table 20.2. A benzofuran analog (NAV4694) was selected by AstraZeneca, also incorporating fluorination of an aromatic ring. The difference between the benzothiazoles and benzofurans in chemical structure is subtle, but can be sufficient for differences in kinetic behavior in the brain. The compound was selected for faster apparent washout from white matter and potential for enhanced target-to-nontarget ratios (Cselényi et al., 2012). This tracer has been licensed by AstraZeneca to Navidea, which is undertaking its further development.

TABLE 20.2 Amyloid PET Tracers Currently Used for Research or Commercial Use

Tracer	Structure	K_i (nM)	K_d (nM)	Dose (MBq)	Acquisition time postinjection (p.i.) for static scans
[^{11}C]-PiB	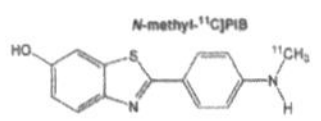	0.87 ± 0.18	1.02	500	50–70 min p.i.
[^{18}F]-Florbetaben	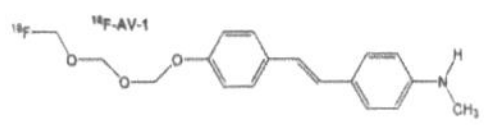	2.22 ± 0.54		300	90–110 min/ or 15–20 min scan beginning 45–130 min p.i.
[^{18}F]-Florbetapir	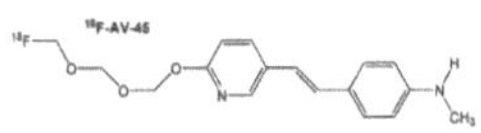	2.87 ± 0.17	3.72 ± 0.3	370	50–70 min/or 10 min scan beginning 30–50 min p.i.
[^{18}F]-Flutemetamol	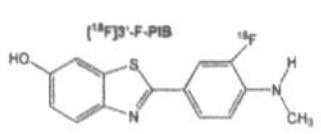	0.74 ± 0.38	1.6 ± 0.2	185	90–110 min/or 20 min scan beginning 90+ min p.i.
[^{18}F]-NAV4694	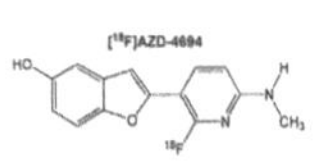		2.3 ± 0.3	200	40–70 min p.i.

Florbetaben (Amyvid®) has been developed by Avid, a subsidiary of Eli Lilly; florbetapir (Neuraceq®), by Piramal Imaging; and flutemetamol (Vizamyl®), by GE Healthcare. Each has been approved for clinical use by the US Food and Drug Administration and the European Medicines Agency. NAV4694 is in late-stage clinical development by Navidea, and [^{11}C]-PiB can be used as an investigational agent under an IND. Inhibition constants are determined against [^{18}F]-florbetapir in AD brain homogenates; dissociation constants are from $A\beta_{1-40}$ synthetic fibrils (Klunk et al., 2005; Juréus et al., 2010; Choi et al., 2009).

As noted previously, the early work with the "X-compound," as structural analogs of Congo red inspired interest in stilbene derivatives which were extensively explored at the University of Pennsylvania (Skovronsky et al., 2000). Stilbenes have proven to be a highly productive scaffold as illustrated by [^{11}C]-labeled SB13 (Thompson et al., 2009) and two [^{18}F]-labeled tracers, florbetaben and florbetapir, developed by Avid Radiopharmaceuticals, a spin-out from the University of Pennsylvania. As can be seen in Table 20.2, florbetaben and florbetapir are structurally very similar: florbetaben having a benzene ring and florbetapir replacing that with a pyridine ring. The clearance of florbetapir from the brain is faster, leading to scan acquisitions that can start 50 min postinjection (Wong et al., 2010a), in contrast to 70 min or later postinjection for florbetaben (Barthel et al., 2011).

AMYLOID PET IMAGE ANALYSIS

Amyloid PET tracers were selected first and foremost for high affinity and specific binding to fibrillar amyloid, and, as a consequence, retention ought to be higher in regions where fibrillar amyloid has accumulated. All the amyloid-specific PET tracers consistently produce images of retention of compound throughout the cerebral cortex in subjects at risk. A minimum threshold of plaque density to generate a signal may be met only after development of amyloid aggregates throughout the isocortex, or at least stage B as defined by Braak and others (Braak and Braak, 1991). High spatial resolution (voxel, or volume element level) analyses across scans in older adults have suggested an evolution of this pattern beginning in the medial frontal and cingulate cortex followed by the lateral frontal, parietal, and finally lateral temporal cortex (Villeneuve et al., 2015). Amyloid "positivity" by PET can emerge by the sixth decade in apoE ε4 carriers (Vlassenko et al., 2011; Fleisher et al., 2013) and occurs in up to 30% of healthy elders, consistent with autopsy findings (Braak et al., 2011). Evaluation of PET image data by visual reading or quantitative analysis depends on determining whether the signal in the potentially target-rich cortex is higher than would be expected if the same region has little or no fibrillar amyloid, after allowing for clearance of some of the background signal. Visual reading protocols have been established for florbetapir, florbetaben, and flutemetamol as a requirement for marketing approval as diagnostic agents. The protocols rely on readers being trained to discern whether the PET image signal intensity in gray matter regions vulnerable to accumulation of fibrillar amyloid deposits is at least as high as the signal intensity in underlying white matter, which serves as the visual reference region. Moderate signal intensity occurs in white matter for all the currently approved agents due to lower blood flow, the more lipophilic environment, and possible "off-target" binding to sites such as myelin basic protein (Stankoff et al., 2011). In subjects who do not have a high brain fibrillar amyloid burden, the faster clearance of tracer from gray matter should result in a lower cortical signal compared to white matter, while the contrast between gray and white matter is lost in subjects with high brain amyloid burden. Accuracy of visual reading has been validated against histopathology at autopsy for florbetapir (Clark et al., 2011), flutemetamol (Curtis et al., 2015), and florbetaben (Sabri et al., 2015). Each of these studies enrolled end-of-life subjects to allow amyloid imaging within a few months (Clark et al., 2011; Curtis et al., 2015) to a few years (Sabri et al., 2015), and included reading by three to five trained readers. Accuracy was determined by evaluating concordance

TABLE 20.3 Comparative Results of the Phase 3 Autopsy Studies for Validation of Visual Reading of Whole Brain Images

Tracer	Subjects	Amyloid+	Sites	Raters	Interreader κ	% Sensitivity	% Specificity[a]
Florbetapir	29	15/29	23	3	[b]	93	100
Flutemetamol	68	43/68	19	5	0.72	81–93	44–92
Florbetaben	74	47/74	15	3	0.66[c]	97.9–100	85.2–88.9

[a] *Sensitivity and specificity used dense plaque frequency score by Bielschowsky silver stain and/or β-amyloid immunohistochemistry as truth.*
[b] *Consensus ratings only.*
[c] *Estimates of interreader agreement in the florbetaben study were derived from visual readings of regions on images from 31 subjects for whom separate regional histopathology data were available. Whole brain visual readings in that study were the basis of the sensitivity and specificity estimates and were consensus readings, using plaque frequency scoring over multiple brain regions (Consortium to Establish a Registry for Alzheimer's Disease protocol) as truth.*

between the visual reading and semiquantitative scoring of plaque density in multiple brain regions (Table 20.3).

As seen in Table 20.3, visual readings identified a cortical signal that corresponded with autopsy findings of dense plaque the vast majority of the time for all these tracers, and support their use for detection of β-amyloid plaque burden in the brain in the differential diagnosis of progressive cognitive impairment. Indeed, visual reading has been accepted for subject selection in clinical trials. However, agreement with histology and between readers was not perfect. One of 15 cases of AD diagnosed at autopsy by significant plaque burden in the florbetapir study had a negative visual reading antemortem (Clark et al., 2011). False positives, which would have greater consequences for subject management, also occurred. One of the readers in the flutemetamol study tended to "overread" the cortical signal, accounting for the lower range of specificity in that report (Curtis et al., 2015). This would advise consensus reading when enrolling subjects into clinical trials, as was done in the other two autopsy studies; two pairs of eyes can be better than one. The florbetaben study also illustrates the limitations of clinical diagnosis, as 13 out of 57 subjects clinically diagnosed with probable AD in life had no evidence of significant amyloid plaque burden at autopsy or significant antemortem cortical PET signal, and likely had some other reason for their dementia (Sabri et al., 2015). Potential limitations of visual reading demonstrated by these studies are that the true positives were frequently subjects with advanced dementia and the average age of subjects was around 80. Visual reading may be less sensitive to subjects who are younger and much earlier in disease course, which is the dominant focus of current-generation intervention trials. Indeed, the majority of "false negative" readings in the flutemetamol study were subjects close to the Bielschowsky threshold for plaque density (Curtis et al., 2015). To allow for more sensitive detection of fibrillar amyloid signal as well as to detect change, quantitative analysis is necessary.

Quantitative analysis is mandatory for longitudinal observational studies and intervention trials when change in amyloid burden as measured by PET is a treatment end point. Treatments intended to remove Aβ may have modest effects on the amyloid PET signal that are not detectable by visual comparison of scans. Detecting the effect of drugs designed to modify Aβ deposition, such as secretase inhibitors, will require identifying treatment effects against the background rate of signal change, which may be slight over the 2- to 3-year duration of a clinical trial. Subject averaging and group comparisons for effect require normalization of the individual PET data to a common reference space, which can involve multiple postprocessing steps. These may include (1) motion correction by registration of the individual data frames from the PET scan to each other, (2) smoothing PET data to a level of resolution common across different camera types, (3) coregistration of the subject's PET image volume with his or her MRI scan, coregistration of within-subject serial scans, (4) segmenting the MRI image into gray matter and white matter compartments and then applying the segmentation to the coregistered PET data, and (5) spatial normalization of the subject data to common brain space, and then sampling the spatially normalized data with a reference atlas of brain regions that has been spatially normalized to the same common brain space. The choice of tools is highly dependent on the lab, and the nuances are many. Cross-modality coregistration (eg, PET to MRI) can be especially thorny due to differences in the image information shared by the data sets (Kiebel et al., 1997). Some of the implications regarding coregistration methods have been described elsewhere (Schmidt et al., 2015). While necessary for comparing PET data across and within subjects, these postprocessing steps can introduce measurement error and require regular quality control (QC) checks after the various data transformations have been applied.

PET image data can be acquired as a "dynamic" scan or a "static" scan. Dynamic scans are the gold standard method for PET tracer quantitative analysis and involve beginning data collection right after tracer injection and continuing until the time limit available for collecting sufficient emission counts is reached. Dynamic scans permit measurement of tracer kinetics from the blood and into the brain as well as providing information on blood flow. Indeed, "early frame" PET data can be used effectively as a blood flow image, and low flow areas correlate highly with regions of the brain that are hypometabolic by FDG in AD (Rostomian et al., 2011). Signal intensity in specific brain regions can be extracted from the PET image and plotted as a time activity curve (TAC) of the tracer activity in tissue. The TAC indicates how rapidly the tracer is taken up by the brain, where it accumulates, and the extent to which the tracer clears. Dynamic data on the tracer can also be obtained from frequent sampling of arterial blood to generate an "input function" TAC and to measure the rate of clearance of the tracer from blood as well as measure the appearance of metabolites that might contaminate the brain tissue signal. The two TACs can be used to build a model of how the tracer is behaving in the brain. Models can be either compartmental models that describe the movement of the tracer between blood, brain, and a specific binding compartment or noncompartmental models, also known as graphical analysis, that generate estimates of the volume of distribution of the tracer instead of the transfer rate constants from compartmental models. Arterial blood sampling is invasive, and analysis of the tracer and metabolites in plasma is complex and time-consuming. Therefore, tissue tracer activity is commonly normalized to the injected dose and subject body mass, resulting in a standardized uptake value (SUV). To simplify dynamic modeling of amyloid PET data, a reference tissue region approach has been adopted. In this method, a region of the brain is selected that is free of the ligand target and ideally free of the pathology under study, and is assumed to represent a signal associated with free and unbound tracer as well as nonspecific binding. This is used to segment out the target-specific signal seen in regions that accumulate fibrillar amyloid such as the cerebral cortex. Kinetic modeling can then be applied to TACs from these two tissue types to yield a parameter, such as the target-specific distribution volume or binding potential of the tracer that in turn ought to be an index of fibrillar amyloid burden.

Parameters derived from noncompartmental models using only brain tissue signal have been found to strongly correlate with those derived from compartmental models with arterial input functions, and are less noisy than those models using blood data (Price et al., 2005; Yaqub et al., 2008).

The acquisitions required for dynamic scans can be long, costly, and difficult for a clinical center to support given competing clinical service demands. Long periods of relative immobility can be arduous, especially for elderly patients with dementia. Excess movement during the scan prompted by discomfort can render portions of the acquisition data unusable. In clinical practice and many research studies, especially large clinical trials, image data are collected over a shorter period of time. Acquisitions begin long after the tracer has been injected, when the signal in the brain is relatively stable. Regional tissue activity is collected as a series of 5-min blocks or "frames" and then summed to generate a "static" scan. The collection time for static scans varies between the different tracers; the acquisition windows worked out by the tracer vendors for scans to be visually read are effectively the time frames best suited for quantitative static scans and are listed in Table 20.2. The same reference tissue method described for dynamic scans is used, as a ratio of a target-rich (such as individual or grouped cortical regions) to a target-poor reference tissue (such as a cerebellar gray or a white matter region). This is reported as a standardized uptake value ratio (SUVr) as a signal ratio between two tissue regions; a "true" SUV (normalization by injected dose and body size) may not be calculated if the intention is to only generate a ratio, as these factors cancel out. SUVr values have also been reported to correlate highly with parameters from dynamic modeling for [^{11}C]-PiB (Price et al., 2005; Lopresti et al., 2005) and florbetapir, although the correlation was notably lower in the occipital region ($r = 0.58$) compared to frontal cortex ($r = 0.88$) in the florbetapir study (Wong et al., 2010a). SUVr slightly overestimates tracer binding compared to compartmental or graphical analysis of dynamic scan data, as it cannot track the rate of tracer clearance (Lopresti et al., 2005; van Berckel et al., 2013). These slight differences can likely be managed in controlled studies using within-subject designs, although it is notable that SUVr was reported to be susceptible to decline in brain blood flow over time in AD subjects. The resulting reduction in SUVr signal could be misinterpreted as due to a loss of fibrillar amyloid rather than a decrease in tracer delivery (van Berckel et al., 2013).

Whether using dynamic or static imaging, the derived values depend on the signal associated with the retention of a particular tracer in target regions potentially rich with fibrillar amyloid relative to the signal in a reference region. The signal in target regions such as the cerebral cortex is complex and depends on factors such as specific and nonspecific binding within the region, spillover of signal from neighboring tissue outside the region, and the amount of tissue present. Change in the amount of tissue present is pathognomonic for AD, as progressive neurodegeneration results in significant loss in regional brain volume and decreases in cortical thickness relative to healthy elders (Lerch et al., 2005). To manage partial volume effects due to signal spillover and tissue loss, partial volume corrections can be applied. Several methods of partial volume correction (PVC) have been developed, with a current bias toward incorporating the point spread function, a characteristic of the scanner underlying its intrinsic resolution, and applying this to the gray and white matter segmented tissue compartments from the subject's MRI scan (Rousset et al., 1998). While efficient and robust, this or any method of PVC comes with a cost of increased noise associated with coregistration of PET and MRI data (Su et al., 2015), the need for additional image QC, and requirement for high-quality contemporaneous MRI for each PET scan, which may be operationally challenging in a multisite clinical trial. Moreover, the value assigned to the nonspecific signal also depends on where it is measured. Traditionally, the cerebellar cortex has been used as a reference region, as gray matter is assumed to be free of fibrillar amyloid and has blood flow more similar to that of cerebral cortical regions than white matter has, resulting in more comparable tracer tissue kinetics. While conceptually appealing, the cerebellar cortex has several drawbacks: how much to include and where to sample, signal spillover from underlying white matter, less robust representation in reference atlases used for spatial normalization, and PET imaging factors, including location near the edge of the scanner field of view; in addition, scatter correction of PET emission data of the contours of the cerebellum can be significantly challenged relative to superior brain regions (Schmidt et al., 2015). Alternative reference regions have been developed including "whole cerebellum" (gray and underlying white matter) (Fleisher et al., 2013), pons/brain stem (Lundqvist et al., 2013), and subcortical white matter segmented from whole brain MRI volumes or regions such as centrum semiovale (Wong et al., 2010b; Brendel et al., 2015). Brendel and coworkers compared cerebellar gray, brain stem, and white matter composite reference regions, with and without PVC, for their ability to discriminate between subject groups and detect change over time, using florbetapir PET data from ADNI. Composite white matter was clearly superior in test–retest analysis of florbetapir scans acquired 2 years apart in subjects who were amyloid negative compared to cerebellar gray (Pearson's $R = 0.93$ for composite white matter, $R = 0.55$ for cerebellar gray). This suggests subcortical white matter to be a more stable and reliable reference region for longitudinal studies. PVC allowed marginally better discrimination between groups and notably resulted in estimated rates of change over 2 years that were more than double those derived from a reference method (with no PVC) (Brendel et al., 2015). Whether these findings will apply to other amyloid tracers to the same extent remains to be determined, although the size of the data set and source, from the multisite ADNI study, commend these findings for consideration in clinical trial design.

Given the chemical and pharmacokinetic differences between the tracers listed in Table 20.2 and the different ways of analyzing PET images, quantitative values would be expected to differ between studies. As we have noted, each of the marketed amyloid tracers has reported the intensity of the cortical signal in the PET scan to correspond closely with the amount of dense fibrillar plaques observed at autopsy (Clark et al., 2011; Curtis et al., 2015; Sabri et al., 2015). Given the differences that might arise from subtle differences in binding affinity interacting with forms of β-amyloid aggregates (Ye et al., 2005; Lockhart et al., 2005), this convergence is notable and suggests that across all these tracers the majority of the specific signal can be accounted for by retention of the ligand to dense fibrillar β-amyloid plaques. Nonetheless, being able to map data from one tracer to another is critical for developing a more standard definition of normal and abnormal values, integration of data across studies, and comparison of findings among studies. The performance of flutemetamol, florbetapir, and florbetaben relative to [^{11}C]-PiB as a gold standard has been reported (Vandenberghe et al., 2010; Landau et al., 2014; Villemagne et al., 2012). Comparisons in each of these studies were within subject, and correlations between cortical composite SUVrs obtained with the paired tracers were high, and appeared linear across a range of values obtained in healthy elderly subjects with MCI and/or subjects with AD. Standardization was variable, with reference and comparison scans being obtained from hours (Vandenberghe et al., 2010; Wolk et al., 2012) to years (Landau et al., 2014) apart and at single (Vandenberghe et al., 2010;

Villemagne et al., 2012; Wolk et al., 2012) or multiple (Landau et al., 2014) centers, and using different analysis methods for each tracer in the ADNI study. As a consequence, the linear transformations to map SUVrs to each could differ considerably. The linear transform of PiB global SUVr (x) to florbetapir global SUVr (y) was $y = 0.60x + 0.35$ in the ADNI study (Landau et al., 2014) and $y = 0.33x + 0.72$ for the study at the University of Pennsylvania (Wolk et al., 2012). White matter SUVrs showed considerably greater variation between subjects for the [^{18}F]-labeled tracers compared to [^{11}C]-PiB, illustrating the greater retention/slower clearance of those tracers from white matter (Vandenberghe et al., 2010). To improve comparison between the amyloid PET tracers, a working group was formed after the Alzheimer's Association International Conference in 2012 to outline what has become known as the "centiloid scale" as a common metric for all amyloid tracers (Rowe, 2013). The scale has a 0 point and 100 point anchor. To generate the range of values, a group of 25 subjects is suggested, including 10 healthy young adults (under 45 years of age) to provide the values distributed around the 0 anchor, and 15 subjects likely to have amyloid burden, including ~5 "typical AD" subjects to provide the values distributed around the 100 anchor. The anchor "0" is defined as the mean of the young controls and "100" as the mean of the AD subjects. Subjects are scanned with [^{11}C]-PiB and then scanned with an [^{18}F] tracer as the comparator, to determine where SUVr values for the [^{18}F] tracer can map to the [^{11}C]-PiB centiloid as the gold standard. The SUVr values for each subject are transformed to centiloid units using the equation:

$$\mathrm{CL} = 100(\mathrm{SUVr_{IND}} - \mathrm{SUVr_{YC}}) / (\mathrm{SUVr_{AD}} - \mathrm{SUVr_{YC}})$$

CL is centiloid unit, $\mathrm{SUVr_{IND}}$ is the SUVr of an individual scan to be scaled, and $\mathrm{SUVr_{YC}}$ and $\mathrm{SUVr_{AD}}$ are the mean values from the young control and AD samples scanned with a specific tracer, respectively. An [^{11}C]-PiB centiloid scale was generated by the working group, which has made all the data publicly available as reference data for comparison of other centiloid programs or to test image analysis pipelines against those used by the group (Klunk, 2015). Centiloid scales are currently being generated by Avid, GE Healthcare, and Piramal in support of the use of their amyloid tracers in the ADNI study and should be available soon.

QUANTITATIVE AMYLOID PET FOR DIAGNOSTIC CLASSIFICATION

The end point for quantitative analysis may be for diagnosis, which requires selection of a threshold SUVr value that defines abnormality: amyloid positive or amyloid negative. Older adult samples, whether healthy or impaired, show a bimodal distribution of signal intensity, suggesting that subjects are more or less susceptible to accumulation of fibrillar amyloid plaques. The threshold SUVr for abnormality for [^{11}C]-PiB PET using a composite cortical region for the numerator and cerebellar gray as a reference region for the denominator has most commonly been 1.4 to 1.5, based on break points in the data from samples that include subjects with AD and healthy elders, lower or upper confidence limits in the distributions for either group, or derived from receiver operating characteristic curves using clinical diagnosis as the standard of truth (Vandenberghe et al., 2010; Jack et al., 2012). This approach is limited by a large partial volume effect; some subjects assigned a clinical diagnosis of AD do not have evidence of brain amyloid burden (around 10% in the ADNI data set), and up to 30% of healthy adults have significant brain amyloid burden as measured by PET (Rowe et al., 2010; Aizenstein et al., 2008). Indeed, these are the very subjects sought for "at-risk trials such as the A4 study. Such thresholds have also been used to diagnose "suspected non-AD pathophysiology" in subjects who show evidence of neurodegeneration by CSF, FDG PET, or MRI but do not have an amyloid PET SUVr that meets the threshold (Jack et al., 2012). Moreover, the probability that any adult will have a significant amyloid burden is dependent on age and risk genes, either one or more APOE e4 alleles, trisomy 21, or one of the amyloid precursor protein (APP) or presenilin mutations (Bateman et al., 2012; Vlassenko et al., 2011; Fleisher et al., 2013; Sabbagh et al., 2011). An alternative approach included in the centiloid scale is to use young healthy adults as the control for "amyloid negative." Following this approach, Villeneuve and coworkers, using four different threshold approaches, found a threshold value for a cortical composite/cerebellar gray SUVr of 1.21 (Villeneuve et al., 2015). This threshold was also validated against autopsy evidence of at least moderate plaque load, albeit few cases were available to test the validity of lower thresholds. Selection of the SUVr threshold has a major impact on who is identified as "at risk" for AD and entered into a trial for disease prevention. More thorough investigations of subjects in the lower end of the distribution for amyloid burden are needed to determine who among them progresses to AD, although the outcome of such trials could require years of follow-up. Additional biomarkers would also need to be included, to better phenotype the subjects and test as markers predictive of decline.

Screening for evidence of amyloid pathology for clinical trials in AD is also done by measuring $A\beta_{42}$ concentrations in CSF. Low concentrations of CSF $A\beta_{42}$ were found to be associated with AD long before the availability of amyloid PET (Motter et al., 1995) and were hypothesized to reflect sequestration of soluble $A\beta_{42}$ into insoluble plaques. Strong negative correlations between CSF $A\beta_{42}$ and amyloid PET signal have been found by several university groups and in the ADNI data set, and across amyloid PET tracers and CSF $A\beta_{42}$ assays (Fagan et al., 2006; Landau et al., 2013a; Palmqvist et al., 2014; Mattsson et al., 2015; Grimmer et al., 2009). Beyond differences in assays and tracers, the standards for thresholds were not uniform. Using the transforms by Landau and others (Landau et al., 2014), the concordance of florbetapir PET scans in ADNI used a "low"-threshold SUVr close to 1.21, as proposed by Villeneuve and others (Villeneuve et al., 2015), while flutemetamol used a threshold close to the PiB SUVr of 1.4 (Palmqvist et al., 2014). Amyloid PET and CSF $A\beta_{42}$ have been treated as fungible markers of brain amyloidosis for diagnosis (Weigand et al., 2011) and are used as either/or for enrollment into AD clinical trials. Concordance between these measures is high, generally around 90% across studies, although invariably discordance is seen: subjects who are "PET positive/CSF negative" or "PET negative/CSF positive." Interpretations for this discordance are many. Beyond the assay variability of each of the measures, the vast majority of comparisons are cross-sectional, and information on the longitudinal course is sparse. An apparently normal CSF $A\beta_{42}$ measure could reflect a decrease from a previously higher value; disease conditions may affect $A\beta_{42}$ levels other than AD pathophysiology; changes in CSF $A\beta_{42}$ from sequestration may precede the accumulation of enough dense plaques to support a PET signal; and the two measures may be looking at two fundamentally different forms and pools of $A\beta_{42}$, either soluble or insoluble (Mattsson et al., 2015). While it may be pragmatic and necessary to see these biomarkers as interchangeable for clinical trial enrollment, this will come at some cost of subject misclassification, and the selection of the threshold for each measure has to be thought through carefully.

EVALUATION OF TREATMENT EFFECT

While the debate on thresholds and preferred methods of analysis continues, pharma companies have had sufficient trust to adopt amyloid PET for selection of subjects and as a treatment end point: testing target engagement of amyloid-specific treatments and whether a change in brain amyloid burden correlates with clinical response. Two proof-of-concept studies using [^{11}C]-PiB PET as an efficacy end point and one using [^{18}F]-florbetapir PET have been reported, each testing for effects of monoclonal humanized antibodies targeting Aβ_{42} on brain amyloid burden. The two including [^{11}C]-PiB PET evaluated the effects of different doses of bapineuzumab and gantenerumab in subjects with mild-to-moderate AD. Each of them reported a treatment effect on the [^{11}C]-PiB PET signal—after 28 weeks (gantenerumab) or 78 weeks (bapineuzumab)—namely, a reduction in signal compared to placebo. Both were small studies with fewer than 10 subjects per treatment group, and neither reported any change in clinical end points, as would be expected from such small studies. Notably, the increase in [^{11}C]-PiB PET signal in the placebo group was quite high in both studies: 11% in the gantenerumab study in just 28 weeks and roughly the same over 78 weeks in the bapineuzumab study, which is a much greater signal increase than has been seen in any of the larger studies in AD, suggesting the apparent change could be related to the very small number of placebo subjects in both studies (Rinne et al., 2010; Ostrowitzki et al., 2012). The most recent proof-of-concept study with [^{18}F]-florbetapir PET and aducanumab was considerably larger, with more than 30 subjects per group. Dose- and time-dependent effects were seen on the PET signal that paralleled slowing of decline on the MMSE and CDR-SB, although the former was not clearly dose dependent. In this study, there was negligible change in the PET signal over 54 weeks in the placebo group, which is consistent with observations from ADNI (Sevigny, 2015). In aggregate, these studies suggest that amyloid PET can be used in small proof-of-concept studies to demonstrate target engagement for putative amyloid-clearing agents and test for dose dependence.

Has amyloid PET been scalable for larger phase 3 trials? Amyloid PET was used in the recently completed phase 3 trials for bapineuzumab and solanezumab (Salloway et al., 2014; Doody et al., 2014). Both programs enrolled roughly 2000 subjects with a clinical diagnosis of mild-to-moderate AD. Neither set of trials met their primary cognitive and functional end points. A secondary analysis of mildly affected subjects in one of the solanezumab trials suggested a modest reduction in decline on those end points, and development of solanezumab continues. Both studies included amyloid PET in roughly 10% of the subjects: [^{11}C]-PiB scans were acquired at baseline and after 45 and 71 weeks of treatment in the bapineuzumab trials, and [^{18}F]-florbetapir scans were acquired at baseline and after 80 weeks of treatment in the solanezumab trials. No treatment effect was seen on amyloid PET in the solanezumab trials. Treatment effects were seen in the Apo ε4 carrier study of bapineuzumab but not in the noncarrier study. The results in the noncarrier study were especially puzzling. An increase in the mean [^{11}C]-PiB PET signal for the placebo group appeared to occur over 45 weeks of treatment and then dropped below baseline by 71 weeks. Inspection of the individual trajectories suggests that a few subjects in the placebo with extreme changes may be driving this effect and that anomalous trajectories may also be driving the mean changes in the active dose groups (Fig. 20.2) (Liu et al., 2015). Similarly anomalous trajectories can be found in ADNI, another multisite trial involving collection over long periods of time (Schmidt et al., 2015), suggesting significant measurement error.

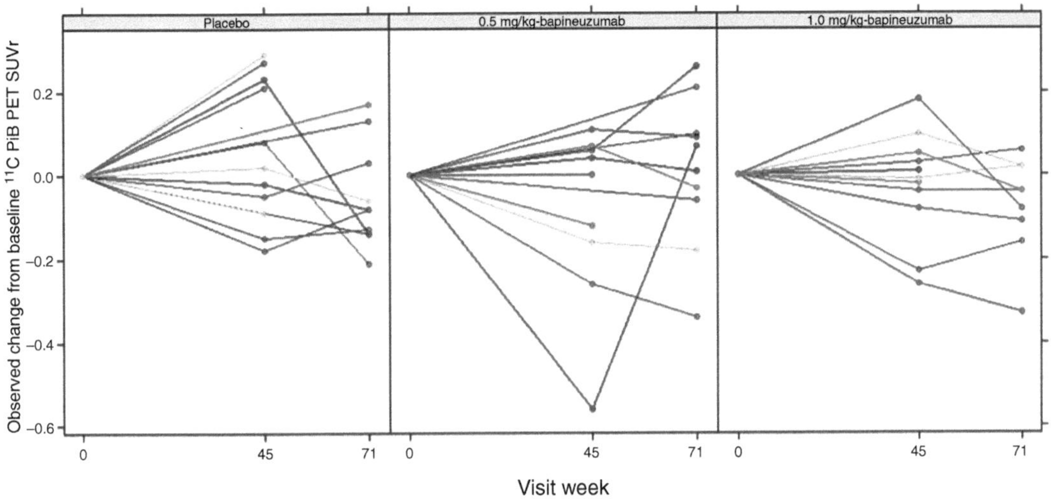

FIGURE 20.2 **Individual subject trajectories for change in the ^{11}C-PiB PET SUVr from baseline over time among the ApoE ε4 noncarriers with baseline SUVr ≥ 1.35 and one or more follow-up ^{11}C-PiB PET scans post baseline (PBO *N* = 15; 0.5 mg/kg *N* = 12; 1.0 mg/kg *N* = 12).** Shown are the individual subject tractories in change from baseline to week 71 [^{11}C]-PiB SUVr as measured by the average value of five cortical regions of interest (anterior cingulate cortex, posterior cingulate cortex or precuneus, frontal cortex, lateral temporal cortex, and parietal cortex) relative to cerebellar gray as reference region for each of the treatment groups in the Apo ε4 noncarrier substudy (Liu et al., 2015).

Multicenter trials can include imaging centers that differ markedly in scanning hardware, technical resources and capabilities, and competing clinical service demands. They are breeding grounds for measurement error, and this is a major driver for standardization of biomarker methods in AD trials. Similar standardization efforts have been and are being applied to CSF biomarkers (Mattsson et al., 2011) and hippocampal volumes (Jack et al., 2011). For PET, standardization of FDG PET/CT has long been a goal for oncology trials (Boellaard et al., 2010); however, collaborative standardization for quantitative amyloid PET has been lacking. Acquisition standards have generally relied on protocols developed for ADNI (Jagust et al., 2010) and guidance from the amyloid PET tracer vendors, although the Quantitative Imaging Biomarkers Alliance (QIBA) initiative in the Radiological Society of North America (RSNA) has recently begun work on draft guidelines for quantitative amyloid PET (https://www.rsna.org/QIBA.aspx). Two classes of variability are relevant for use of quantitative amyloid PET in intervention trials: between-center and within-subject. Management of between-center variability includes qualification of sites, standardization of protocols, and ongoing QC. There are a number of features intrinsic to scanners, such as adjustments applied to the emission data, that allow for "absolute" quantitation of the PET signal, and the impact of some of these are described elsewhere (Schmidt et al., 2015). Such scanner-dependent issues are manageable as long as a subject is scanned on the same camera throughout the trial. Intrinsic differences in PET scanner resolution can be addressed by developing "smoothing" data to a common resolution (Joshi et al., 2009), and use of a central imaging lab for analysis of all the data can also reduce variability arising between centers and subjects. What is striking in the bapineuzumab and ADNI data is within-subject variability.

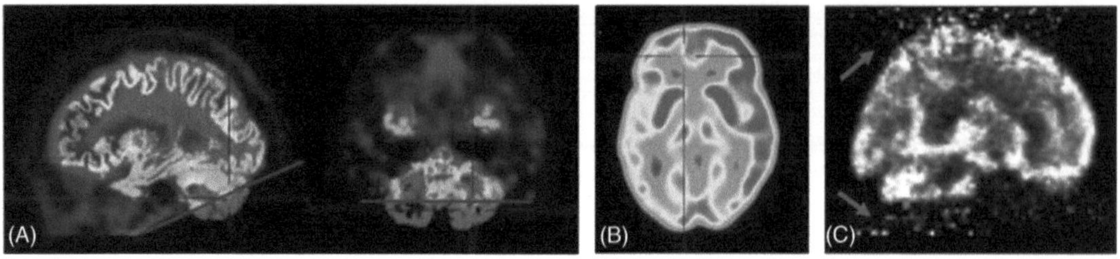

FIGURE 20.3 **Sources of artifact in PET images.** (A) Truncation of a portion of the cerebellum due to patient position out of the scanner field of view (PiB PET image superimposed over the patient's MRI); (B) right–left asymmetry in an FDG PET scan due to misalignment of the emission and transmission scans during attenuation correction; and (C) noise outside of the boundaries of a Hoffman phantom (3-D anatomical brain phantom, filled with [^{18}F] FDG that simulates a normal uptake ratio in gray and white matter in FDG PET studies) caused by amplification of low counts at the upper and lower edges of the axial field of view of the scanner. *Source: ADM Diagnostics and data from ADNI.*

The changes from baseline over time are in excess of what would be expected from test–retest comparisons of amyloid PET (generally around 5%) (Joshi et al., 2012; Sabri et al., 2015; Tolboom et al., 2009; Vandenberghe et al., 2010) and are biologically implausible. Test–retest studies are generally conducted by single centers by academic groups dedicated to quantitative imaging with short interscan intervals: hours to days apart. Estimates from test–retest studies are unlikely to provide accurate information on variability over time and are better considered as measurements of precision of the assay under ideal circumstances. The marked within-subject changes seen in these longer trials are more likely related to inconsistencies in positioning subjects in the scanner from one session to the next, resulting in differences in signal measurement in the cerebellum, the preferred reference region on those studies. Differences in signal in cerebellum can arise from the location (eg, near the noisy edge of the field of view), nonuniform scatter correction in the inferior planes, and movement during the scan (Fig. 20.3). If the subjects being studied have dementia and decline over the study, their ability to remain still for even brief acquisitions can become challenging.

It is hoped that within-subject variability can be tamed by improved attention to and standardization of scan acquisition and optimization of data analysis. Longitudinal amyloid PET appears to provide a means for demonstrating target engagement, even if it has not yet provided evidence of modifying the disease course. Moreover, the primacy of defining subjects based on brain amyloidosis has been questioned (Schneider et al., 2010; Fjell and Walhovd, 2012; Jack et al., 2013a), especially as the field has moved toward secondary prevention of AD in subjects with mild cognitive impairment and asymptomatic individuals. Evidence of brain amyloidosis has obvious value over clinical assessment alone for selecting subjects for a trial with an amyloid-targeting agent. In the bapineuzumab PET substudy, 6.1% of the ApoE e4 carriers and 36.1% of the noncarriers, enrolled using the McKhann criteria, did not have significant brain amyloid burden, suggesting that a significant number of subjects included were unlikely to show benefit of treatment. Amyloid burden as measured by PET does not correlate well with disease progression or cognitive impairment, and, while accepted as an indication of the presence of fibrillar amyloid plaques, it is a necessary but not sufficient indicator of Alzheimer's pathology. That said, healthy elderly and subjects with MCI who are "amyloid positive" have faster rates of cognitive decline and brain atrophy than those who are "amyloid negative" (Chetelat et al., 2012; Knopman et al., 2012; Jack et al., 2009;

Bourgeat et al., 2010; Morris et al., 2009) and are more likely to have CSF evidence of neurodegeneration (Fagan et al., 2009). These observations support a model of temporal ordering of AD biomarkers, with brain amyloidosis accelerating—if not initiating—the appearance of markers of neurodegeneration such as FDG hypometabolism, elevated CSF tau species, and brain atrophy followed by cognitive decline (Jack et al., 2013b). Nonetheless, subjects with evidence of brain amyloidosis, whether healthy or mildly impaired, are heterogeneous populations and can be expected to follow a number of pathways as they age, and the time interval between indications of significant amyloid burden to clinical decline in subjects with familial early-onset AD has been estimated to be at least 15 years (Bateman et al., 2012). Moreover, some subjects may develop significant amyloid plaque burden without developing neurodegeneration or cognitive impairment (Lue et al., 1999). As a consequence, additional biomarkers are needed to better identify subjects at risk for decline, and among the more promising new candidates is tau PET.

TAU PET

In addition to fibrillar amyloid plaques, the other cardinal feature of Alzheimer's disease pathology is intracellular aggregates of tau protein fibrils, also known as neurofibrillary tangles (NFTs). Pretangle tau accumulation can be identified during childhood and neurofibrillary deposits by early adulthood in brain stem neurons. Cortical NFTs first appear in the transentorhinal region and then spread laterally and dorsally through association cortex and finally to primary sensory cortices. This pattern emerges slowly over many decades, although extensive spreading is not inevitable (Braak et al., 2011). Spreading of NFT pathology beyond the temporal cortex is observed in individuals with an antemortem diagnosis of dementia, while distribution limited to the hippocampus and medial temporal/entorhinal cortex is seen in subjects who had no evidence of dementia prior to death. Moreover, the extent and density of NFT pathology correlates with severity of cognitive impairment (Nelson et al., 2010). Tau pathology might therefore be a more informative predictor of progression toward dementia than fibrillar amyloid, as well as being a target for disease interception. As a consequence, the discovery of PET radioligands for imaging tau aggregates is a highly active and competitive field.

Tau is highly expressed in the central nervous system and is associated with stabilization of microtubules, making it an essential element for intracellular structure and transport in neurons. Six different isoforms occur in the human brain with three (3R) or four (4R) repeats of the microtubule binding domain, and in the healthy brain the 3R and 4R isoforms are in equilibrium. Tau proteins undergo a number of posttranslational modifications, of which phosphorylation is considered the most important. In pathological conditions such as AD, tau protein dissociates from microtubules and is susceptible to hyperphosphorylation. Hyperphosphorylated tau can assemble into insoluble filaments, which in turn self-aggregate as NFTs within cell bodies and accumulate in dystrophic neurites (Ariza et al., 2015; Lee et al., 2011). Like β-amyloid, these tau aggregates have a β-sheet structure, and the starting points of discovery of tau PET ligands were ligands such as thioflavin T that can bind to both β-amyloid and phosphorylated tau aggregates. The similarity in binding sites is also the major hurdle for identifying ligands that are more specific for tau aggregates, especially for use in AD, where β-amyloid is 5–20 times more abundant. It is also important that tau PET agents discriminate against other β-sheeted misfolded proteins such as α-synuclein (Klunk et al., 2005; Mukaetova-Ladinska et al., 1993; Brettschneider et al., 2015).

The first tracer claimed to bind to tau aggregates was FDDNP (Shoghi-Jadid et al., 2002), a ligand first developed as an agent for in vitro imaging of cells. FDDNP has low affinity for both β-amyloid and tau aggregates (Thompson et al., 2009; Agdeppa et al., 2001) and has been surpassed by more selective agents, representatives of which are presented in Table 20.3, along with available binding characteristics. Leading scaffolds for more selective agents include quinoline derivatives championed by Tohoku University and benzimidazole pyrimidine derivatives developed by Siemens. Several quinoline derivatives have been clinically evaluated, beginning with THK523 (Villemagne et al., 2014). White matter signal with THK523 was high, and more selective and slightly less lipophilic derivatives have begun testing. Subjects with AD showed a high signal in the hippocampus, insula, and medial temporal cortex after PET scans with [^{18}F]-THK5117, whereas scans with [^{11}C]-PiB showed a low signal in the medial temporal cortex and hippocampus, but a high signal in the frontal, posterior cingulate, and lateral temporal cortices associated with dense plaques. A pyridine derivative, THK5351, is reported to have better clearance from white matter and is now being tested at a number of academic centers. The tracer first developed by Siemens, T807, was evaluated in several subjects with different levels of cognitive impairment. They observed retention of signal to be largely restricted to the hippocampus in healthy elderly, while appearing in the inferior and medial temporal cortices in a subject with MCI, and in temporal and parietal cortices in subjects with AD, neatly following the evolution of tau pathology described by Braak and others (Braak and Braak, 1991). While the sample was small, there was a strong linear inverse correlation between MMSE score and cortical retention signal associated with [^{18}F]-T807 (Schöll et al., 2016). The license for this tracer was subsequently acquired by Eli Lilly; it was renamed AV1451, and is undergoing development by Lilly's subsidiary, Avid Radiopharmaceuticals, for possible marketing approval. A follow-up tracer that had been optimized for faster clearance from white matter, T808, also showed promise for labeling tau (Chien et al., 2014), although the fluoroalkyl labeling proved too susceptible to defluorination and further development has been on hold. The phenyl/pyridinyl-butadienyl-benzothiazoles (PBBs) developed by the National Institute of Radiological Sciences (NIRS) in Chiba, Japan, are notable for testing positively in transgenic mice overexpressing human tau. In vivo imaging of these transgenic mice with [^{11}C]-labeled PBB3 was reported by the group, suggesting that this tracer could be used as a translational tool, as none of the other ligands have significant retention in transgenic mice (Maruyama, 2013). The double trans-stilbene linker in this molecule is highly susceptible to photoisomerization, rendering this a very challenging ligand for radiolabeling. The NIRS group is trying to identify more stable derivatives and ligands that can be radiofluorinated.

The potential for a tau ligand to serve as a more predictive biomarker in AD has spurred interest in developing tau PET ligands by a number of groups, and several more candidates should be entering clinical evaluation in the coming years. Optimizing the tau-related signal against white matter and off-target binding are current goals. Notably, the Tohoku and Siemens tracers show equally high signal retention in striatum in both healthy and impaired subjects, which should not have a significant NFT burden, and the target has not yet been identified. The current generation of tau tracers has been selected using brain tissue from AD in which 3R and 4R isoforms are present. Other tauopathies in which one or the other isoforms

TABLE 20.4 Candidate Tau PET Ligands That Have Been and/or are Undergoing Clinical Evaluation

Tracer	Structure	K_i (nM)[a]	K_d (nM)[a]	Selectivity tau/Aβ[b]
[^{18}F]-THK5117	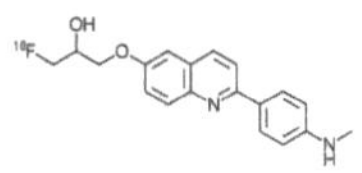	10.50	5.19	30
[^{18}F]-THK5351	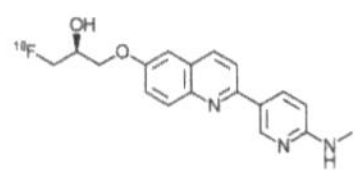	c	c	
[^{18}F]-T807/AV1451	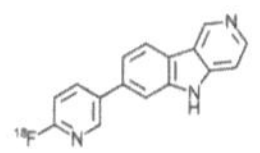		14.6	25
[^{18}F]-T808	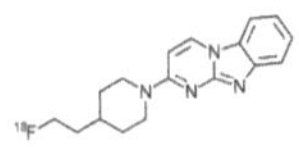		22	27
[^{11}C]-PBB3	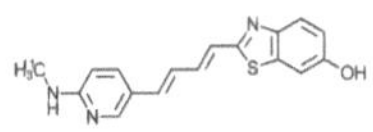			40

K_i and K_d values are based on tau paired helical filaments (PHF) from AD brain homogenates or human AD brain slices.
[a] *Ariza et al. (2015); Maruyama (2013).*
[b] *Tau/Aβ ratios are based on* K_i *or* K_d *values from PHF (tau) versus Aβ fibrils in vitro or human brain slices.*
[c] *Affinity data for THK5351 have not been published but are assumed to be similar to THK5117, while having slightly improved clearance rates from brain.*

predominate, such as Pick's disease or progressive supranuclear palsy, might show differences in affinity for these tracers (Maruyama, 2013; Villemagne, 2015). While the use of tau tracers for diagnostic use is eagerly anticipated, a more powerful research application may be to demonstrate the temporospatial spreading of tau pathology. This will be of particular interest for development of tau-based therapies, as at least some of these are intended to arrest the formation of fibrils or the extracellular/interneuronal transmission of misfolded tau proteins (Hampel et al., 2015; Jucker and Walker, 2011). To support testing of change in the distribution of the tau signal, reliable and sensitive methods for assessment of longitudinal change will be critical as well as attention to scan acquisition quality and control, as we have learned from longitudinal amyloid PET (Table 20.4).

FDG PET

Enormous strides in understanding the emergence and progression of AD during life have been enabled by amyloid PET. High amyloid burden appears to be a risk factor for progressive cognitive impairment in nondemented subjects; however, it does not correlate with disease severity and can appear decades before symptom onset. While preliminary findings suggest tau PET may offer a superior correlate of impairment, whether it can predict proximate decline is not known. Biomarkers of neurodegeneration can have greater predictive value, and to assess this, one of the earliest used and most widely available methods has been FDG PET. As a measure of glucose metabolism, FDG PET detects changes in neuronal activity that can enable differential diagnosis, prediction of clinical decline, and evaluation of treatment effect, complementing pathology-specific information such as amyloid and tau. Here we describe the tracer, its application in AD, advances increasing its benefit, and possible migration to alternate modalities to derive similar information.

Glucose provides the substrate for approximately 95% of the adenosine triphosphate energy used by the brain (Varrone et al., 2009) and is required in continuous supply (Khatri and Man, 2013). The majority of energy is derived through the complete oxidation of glucose to carbon dioxide and water, while approximately 10–12% comes from aerobic glycolysis. For glutamatergic neurons, it has been proposed that the glycolysis occurs in astrocytes, producing lactate, which then provides energy to adjacent neurons (Magistretti and Pellerin, 1996). Regardless of pathway, the energy derived from glucose is primarily used for neurotransmitter uptake and recycling in the synapse, postsynaptic receptor activation, and the maintenance of membrane potentials necessary for neurotransmission (Khatri and Man, 2013; Bélanger, 2011). With the exception of limited cases where ketone bodies may be used as an alternate energy source (Nehlig et al., 2004), the rate of cerebral glucose metabolism correlates directly with neuronal activity and, in particular, synaptic function (Bélanger, 2011).

The development by Louis Sokoloff and coworkers of 2-deoxy-D-glucose (2DG) as a biomarker for glucose metabolism significantly enhanced the opportunity to study relationships between neuronal activity, disease, and treatment response. 2DG differs from glucose only in the replacement of one hydroxyl group by a hydrogen atom. Identically to glucose, it is transported into brain tissue and undergoes phosphorylation by hexokinase to glucose-6-phosphate as a first step toward metabolism. However, the hydroxyl group substitution prevents it from undergoing glycolysis, and it becomes trapped in tissue with limited mobility, providing a measurable, spatially specific record of glucose utilization (Sokoloff et al., 1977). Use of this measurement approach in human studies was enabled by the synthesis of a fluorinated version of 2DG (FDG) suitable for PET imaging at Brookhaven Labs (Ido et al., 1978) and the derivation of kinetic modeling parameters for its quantitation (Reivich et al., 1979). FDG subsequently became the basis for numerous studies to understand neuronal function, and was made widely available for clinical use.

The uptake of FDG into brain tissue occurs primarily during first 20 min following tracer injection, although some uptake continues to occur (Schmidt et al., 1992). Once the uptake period has elapsed, subject activity, including walking from the uptake room to the scanner, does not affect the scan. In contrast to modalities that capture activation events in the range of milliseconds (electroencephalogram, EEG) to a few seconds (fMRI BOLD), the FDG signal represents the integration of all activity occurring during the uptake period. While not capable of measuring rapid events, it is well suited and a highly sensitive means to capture changes in brain state induced by disease progression or prolonged activation stimuli.

Because glucose utilization reflects all neuronal activity, FDG PET captures the effects of a wide range of causal factors, including finger tapping (Reivich et al., 1983), visual stimulation (Kushner et al., 1988), cognitive engagement (Haier et al., 1992), or changes in anxiety or mood (Mayberg et al., 1999). When subject behavior is controlled during the FDG uptake period to limit these factors, it can provide a sensitive, specific measure of the neurodegenerative effects of diseases such as Alzheimer's as well as the interventional effects of disease-modifying and/or symptomatic therapeutics.

As with other PET tracers, FDG PET data can be evaluated using kinetic modeling and the full-time activity curve from injection through relative equilibrium, preferably over a minimum time period of 60 min (Lucignani et al., 1993). However, for practical reasons, the SUVr approach is most often applied, using only later time frames, for example, from 30 to 60 min postinjection.

FDG PET in Probable Alzheimer's Dementia

FDG PET studies were conducted in persons with dementia of the Alzheimer's type soon after the introduction of the tracer. Patients with probable AD had significantly lower cerebral glucose metabolism levels than age-matched controls, and the degree of hypometabolism correlated with severity of cognitive impairment (Ferris et al., 1980; de Leon et al., 1983). Additional studies identified a distinctive Alzheimer's pattern of hypometabolism initiating in the posterior cingulate and hippocampus, then spreading to parieto-occipito-temporal association cortices followed by frontal deterioration, while cerebellum, pons, thalamus, and basal ganglia remained relatively preserved (Heiss et al., 1989; Friedland et al., 1989; Minoshima et al., 1995, 1998; Mosconi, 2010). There is variability in the extent and degree to which regions are affected, as well as the amount of symmetry (Zahn et al., 2004). Regional metabolic decline correlates with clinical worsening on a domain-specific basis, including deficits in memory (Kalpouzos et al., 2008), spatial orientation (Haxby et al., 1985), language (Josephs et al., 2010), presence of apathy (Marshall et al., 2007), and deficits in executive function (Woo et al., 2010).

The pervasive decreases in FDG PET signal observed in AD are consistent with the synaptic and neuronal losses that are fundamental to the disease (Koffie et al., 2011). Reduction in synaptic density in AD-relevant regions has been demonstrated to be highly correlated to cognitive worsening in AD, superior to that of plaques and tangles (Samuel et al., 1994; Terry et al., 1991; DeKosky et al., 1996). Factors contributing to neurodegeneration may include oligomeric Aβ and plaques (Haass and Selkoe, 2007), tau pathology (Liu et al., 2008), reductions to glucose transport and metabolism (Jagust et al., 1991), and downstream effects on cortical activity due to disconnection from directly affected regions (Drzezga et al., 2011).

FDG PET Prior to Dementia

Hypometabolism emerges very early in the AD process, long before symptoms appear. Consistent with this, it is included as a biomarker of neurodegeneration in published guidelines for the evaluation of preclinical Alzheimer's disease (Sperling et al., 2011). A study of individuals with autosomal-dominant Alzheimer's disease showed hypometabolism in precuneus/posterior cingulate and lateral parietal cortex 10 years prior to symptom onset, and 5 years prior to detectable hippocampal atrophy (Benzinger et al., 2013). Longitudinal studies of autopsy-confirmed AD subjects and additional subjects followed for 8–14 years have shown hippocampal hypometabolism several years prior to symptom onset (Mosconi et al., 2008). Decreased metabolism in posterior cingulate, parietal, temporal, and prefrontal cortex has been found in cognitively normal carriers of the Apo ε4 allele as early as in their 20s and 30s (Reiman et al., 2004), and in an ApoE ε4 dose-dependent manner in cognitively normal individuals age 47–68 years, prior to detection of hippocampal atrophy (Reiman et al., 2005).

The early signs of hypometabolism may reflect synaptic dysfunction and mitochondrial damage occurring in response to toxic levels of Aβ (Haass and Selkoe, 2007; Freir et al., 2011) or even APP (Valla et al., 2010). Soluble Aβ oligomers have been demonstrated to be toxic to neurons and damaging to synapses (Walsh et al., 2002). Even in the absence of soluble Aβ, plaques, or tangles, mitochondrial dysfunction indicated by reductions in cytochrome oxidase have been found in young Apo ε4 carriers in posterior cingulate, postulated to involve APP or related molecular pathways (Valla et al., 2010). Approximately 32% of cognitively normal subjects who were amyloid negative according to an amyloid PET threshold exhibited AD-like neurodegeneration via either hypometabolism or hippocampal atrophy, suggesting that subthreshold levels of Aβ may be biologically relevant and associated with neurodegeneration (Mormino et al., 2014). Roughly 60% of amyloid-positive subjects showed evidence of neurodegeneration.

Disease Differentiation

FDG PET can also be used to differentiate between dementia types, with the potential to increase clinical trial homogeneity. Unique signatures of relative hypometabolism and preservation are associated with different forms of dementia—for example, frontal and temporal deficits in frontotemporal dementia (Foster et al., 2007), occipital hypometabolism in Lewy body dementia (O'Brien et al., 2014), asymmetrical inferior temporal deficits in semantic dementia (Drzezga et al., 2008), multiple focal metabolic defects in the case of multiinfarct disease (Friedland et al., 1989), and striatum in Huntington's disease (Feigin et al., 2001). Metabolic differences also distinguish atypical variants of AD such as posterior cortical atrophy (Rosenbloom et al., 2011), early-onset AD (Kaiser et al., 2012), and logopenic progressive aphasia (Rabinovici et al., 2008). Regional deficits in general correspond to the observed clinical phenotype.

The ability to detect comorbidities or alternate causes of cognitive impairment using FDG can allow better assignment of treatment to a particular disease process. Even in amyloid-positive patients, a relatively large percentage of cases involve comorbid disease, particularly in older adults. Of 22 autopsied subjects from ADNI, comorbid Lewy body disease, medial temporal lobe pathology, and vascular disease were found in 46%, 40%, and 23% of patients, respectively (Toledo et al., 2013). Lewy body disease itself can be amyloid positive (Fodero-Tavoletti et al., 2007; Kantarci et al., 2012). Amyloid positivity also does not assure that clinical symptoms are primarily driven by amyloid, as evidenced by the prevalence of amyloid positivity in up to 35% of cognitively normal individuals (Aizenstein et al., 2008; Gu et al., 2015).

Methods significantly impact the utility of FDG as a diagnostic biomarker. In a retrospective metaanalysis, interrater agreement and utility in clinical diagnosis was reported to be mediocre, evidence that this method may not be appropriate for routine clinical use (Smailagic et al., 2015). Diagnostic use often relies on visual reads, and complex disease patterns and subtle differences early in disease may elude visual detection (Womack et al., 2011). However, appropriate study design, disease definition, and data analysis methods have resulted in highly accurate and useful information (Morbelli et al., 2015). A compelling body of data was successfully presented to obtain reimbursement by the Centers for Medicare and Medicaid for the use of FDG PET in discriminating AD and FTD in 2004 (Dickerson, 2012). Advances in multivariate image analysis could offer greater sensitivity for disease discrimination (Matthews et al., 2014).

Clinical Trajectory Prediction and Stratification

Subjects with clinical diagnosis of late MCI and AD vary in rate of decline, even when enriched for amyloid positivity. This challenge becomes more difficult in cognitively normal subjects, where the conversion rate to MCI has been reported at 6 and 17% at 3 and 5 years, respectively (Toledo et al., 2014). While amyloid-positive subjects have been demonstrated to decline clinically at a greater rate than amyloid-negative subjects, the amyloid-positive pool remains heterogeneous. For example, using ADAS-Cog as an outcome measure, 47% of amyloid-positive (Aβ+) MCI subjects declined as compared to 10% of Aβ− MCI subjects, while 40% of Aβ+ normal subjects worsened as compared to 5% of Aβ− controls (Doraiswamy et al., 2014). While enrichment for amyloid significantly increased the degree of worsening, a majority of amyloid-positive subjects did not decline.

Several studies have found FDG PET to add value in predicting clinical progression. FDG was a stronger predictor of conversion to AD in MCI patients as compared to CSF Aβ, hippocampal volume alone, or CSF tau when combined with Aβ measurement (Prestia et al., 2015) and episodic memory (Landau et al., 2011), and predicts substantially lower sample size estimates compared to clinical end points for detection of treatment effects (Chen et al., 2010). The concurrent presence of amyloid burden and neurodegeneration as evidenced by either FDG PET or hippocampal atrophy was predictive of accelerated cognitive decline in normal subjects as compared to those with amyloid burden alone (Mormino et al., 2014). Measurement of AD-like pattern expression using a multivariate machine learning-based FDG PET classifier has been demonstrated to be predictive of cognitive decline across all stages of disease, exceeding that by cognitive measures at baseline and amyloid burden in most cases (Matthews et al., 2014). Particularly for prevention trials, the ability to identify participants more likely to decline may be critical for demonstrating clinical effects.

Not all studies find FDG to be informative, particularly in early MCI and cognitively normal stages. This relates strongly to the analysis methods used, and it is critical to apply approaches that are optimized to detect robust signal in the target population compared to nondisease-related (eg, technical) variability. Effects of age, cognitive reserve, gender, and genotype should also be taken into account. Normal aging is associated with decreases in glucose metabolism in regions including the frontal cortex (Loessner et al., 1995), while years of education correlate with deferred cognitive decline better than the degree of hypometabolism (Garibotto et al., 2008). Age and Apo ε4 status have both been found to influence glucose metabolism in cognitively normal subjects (Knopman et al., 2014).

Evaluation of Treatment Effect

FDG PET can be used to reduce the number of subjects required to detect treatment effect through stratification by metabolic severity at baseline or as a direct outcome measure. Estimates for the number of subjects required per study arm to detect a 25% slowing of decline (2-tailed t-test, 80% power) in MCI subjects using the ADAS-Cog and CDR sum of boxes were 4219 and 1110, respectively, while an estimate using FDG PET and a statistical ROI approach was 218 (Chen et al., 2010). This may be contingent on analysis methods. A much larger required sample size of 1271 MCI subjects per study arm was estimated using a meta-ROI approach (Landau et al., 2010).

FDG PET has been included as an end point in a limited number of studies of AD-targeted therapeutics. An evaluation of phenserine, which inhibits formation of Aβ precursor protein, showed metabolic increases in frontal and parietotemporal cortices in treated patients as compared to placebo, correlating with less decline in cognition (Kadir et al., 2008). In a 1-year study of galantamine, regional glucose metabolism declined in controls but remained stable in treated patients, whose cognitive function did not decline (Keller, 2011). Glucose metabolism declined at a slower rate in subjects with moderate AD treated with memantine compared to controls (Schmidt et al., 2008).

FDG could potentially dissociate effects of target disease versus other comorbid conditions. This becomes critical when at-risk populations such as those with Down syndrome (DS) may be selected as enriched populations for AD clinical trials. DS adults typically develop amyloid plaque by their 40s, but the contribution of AD pathology to their underlying DS pathophysiology can vary greatly and is difficult to discern using cognitive measures. Using machine learning image analysis, two distinct contributing FDG patterns have been extracted from the scans of DS adults, one associated with DS and the second pattern corresponding to degree of AD progression. The latter pattern provides a potential biomarker for disease-specific treatment effect measurement (Matthews et al., 2016 in press).

In the evaluation of drugs such as amyloid-removal agents, other considerations must be taken into account. The treatment itself, clearance of amyloid, or changes to vascular integrity may affect local blood flow rates (van Berckel et al., 2013; Kile and Olichney, 2007), which could potentially affect FDG signal. Inflammation can also alter FDG signal (Buscombe, 2014). Increases in activity within reference regions, such as the cerebellum, pons, thalamus, striatum, or sensorimotor cortex, can create the appearance of worsened hypometabolism in regions referenced to those structures. Treatment may cause improvement in regions other than those typically compromised in AD. In addition, longitudinal atrophy related to disease or drug effect can create error due to partial volume effects. These challenges can be addressed with appropriate analytical approaches.

Data Acquisition Considerations

Because FDG PET measures neuronal activity arising from many different factors, special considerations apply to scan acquisitions that are not as critical with other tracers. Control of subject activity, environment, visual focus, and mental activity is vital during the uptake period in order to minimize the contribution of any factor other than the disease or drug effect. Use of sleep agents or sedatives prior to FDG uptake (Wang et al., 1996) or changes to drugs such as acetylcholinesterase inhibitors should be avoided. Glucose ingestion prior to the scan must also be minimized, as elevated glucose in the blood will compete with the uptake of FDG. Time of day should be kept relatively constant from scan to scan (van der Veen et al., 2012). As with other PET imaging, preventing head motion during scan acquisition is important.

Despite these sensitivities, FDG PET has proven to be a remarkably robust metric of neuronal changes associated with AD using an eyes open, dimly lit room, seated/reclining patient paradigm (Jagust et al., 2010).

Alternative Modalities to FDG

Despite the many potential benefits of using FDG PET, practical considerations of imaging costs and patient burden must be considered. As clinical trials are more frequently including several MRI sequences, amyloid PET, and now tau PET, it may be difficult to incorporate FDG into study design. While not a direct substitute, it may be feasible to derive similar information from these modalities.

In particular, the earliest few minutes of amyloid PET images bear strong similarity to the metabolic profiles obtained using FDG PET. This may be due to the close coupling of blood flow, reflected in the initial minutes of amyloid tracer uptake, and glucose metabolism. The potential to differentiate AD from FTD and normal controls using early-frame [^{11}C]-PiB images has been demonstrated (Rostomian et al., 2011), as has a strong correlation between early-frame florbetapir PET images and FDG PET (Hsiao et al., 2012). Studies comparing tau PET, which shows correlation to clinical decline, to FDG PET have been initiated and will evolve as tau tracers mature. Further research and development efforts are under way to achieve similar diagnostic and prognostic value from early-frame amyloid, arterial spin labeling MRI, and other modalities.

PRECLINICAL IMAGING

Given the clinical utility of [^{18}F]FDG and amyloid tracers, there is considerable interest in back-translating to preclinical investigations and determining whether preclinical models employing in vivo imaging could assist in clinical lead selection, estimation of dose–response relationships, and identification of biomarkers of treatment response for clinical studies. A number of transgenic mouse models of cerebral amyloidosis are readily available and are generally created by the manipulation of the genes involved in amyloid processing (Gotz and Ittner, 2008). While investigation of these models has led to a greater understanding of amyloid-related disease mechanisms, they were in the past limited by the primary use of ex vivo methods to assess brain pathology. The application of small-animal PET imaging (μPET) to preclinical research allows for the simultaneous longitudinal monitoring of a number of physiological processes in a subject over time. Thus, μPET can enhance the translational value of animal studies and potentially reduce the number of animals needed by allowing within-animal testing over time.

Amyloid Imaging in Transgenic Mouse Models

Amyloid PET has been applied with varying success in these animal models. Initial attempts with [^{18}F]-FDDNP and [^{11}C]-PiB failed to demonstrate differences between transgenic and wild-type mice (Klunk et al., 2005; Kuntner et al., 2009; Toyama et al., 2005). A number of subsequent studies have reported significantly higher uptake of amyloid tracers in transgenic mice versus wild-type mice (Poisnel et al., 2012a; Rojas et al., 2013; von Reutern et al., 2013), some have successfully monitored amyloidosis longitudinally (Manook et al., 2012; Maeda et al., 2007; Rominger et al., 2013; Snellman et al., 2013; Maier et al., 2014), and a few studies have shown treatment-induced reductions in plaque load with an antiamyloid antibody (Maeda et al., 2007) and a γ-secretase inhibitor (Rominger, 2014).

Differences in the composition and posttranslational modifications of amyloid-β plaques and the severity of amyloidosis between models are thought to be the main contributors to the aforementioned variation, although methodological issues may also be accountable. A unique problem in preclinical amyloid PET arises from the lower number of high-affinity radioligand binding sites on amyloid-β plaques in transgenic models (Klunk et al., 2005). Employing highly specific activity is thought to help counteract this problem through minimizing saturation of binding sites by cold ligand (Maeda et al., 2011). This is one incentive for employing [^{18}F]-labeled alternatives to [^{11}C]-PiB in small-animal imaging, as it is easier to obtain high yields and specific activity with [^{18}F]-labeling procedures. Additionally, on account of the longer half-life, [^{18}F]-tracers allow for a better signal-to-noise ratio due to improved count statistics and are more practical in terms of high-throughput imaging.

These numerous benefits for [^{18}F]-tracers are, however, counterbalanced by the generally less favorable pharmacokinetics of these [^{18}F]-labeled alternatives, predominantly the rapid peripheral metabolism and high nonspecific binding (Kepe et al., 2013). This rapid peripheral clearance makes amyloid tracers prone to flow-limited uptake (Rodell et al., 2013), a factor complicated in AD by vascular alterations (van Berckel et al., 2013; Kalaria et al., 2012). While cerebrovascular disturbances are well documented in the clinical phenotype of AD, the extent to which animal models exhibit neurovascular deficits is variable depending on their genetic mutations. Waldron et al. used the perfusion tracer [^{99m}Tc]-HMPAO to assess if their employed transgenic mouse model manifests blood flow alterations and indeed found that the TASTPM double transgenic mouse strain (APP Swedish mutation and presenilin 1 M146V mutation) exhibits significantly reduced perfusion (unpublished data). As shown by dynamic imaging, these perfusion deficits hinder early brain uptake of the tracer in TASTPM mice in comparison with age-matched wild-type mice by approximately 9%. Also, Maier et al. (2015) found an inverse relationship between [^{11}C]-PiB binding potential and regional cerebral blood flow as measured with a high-field MRI in APP23 transgenic animals and not in wild-type controls. Considering the rapid metabolism, adequate initial brain uptake when intact tracer levels are still high is crucial. In combination with the lower number of tracer binding sites (Klunk et al., 2005), inadequate tracer penetrance has been described as a contributing factor in failed detection of amyloid-β in small-animal imaging. Indeed, Kuntner et al. described a 24–26% lower maximum brain uptake of [^{18}F]-FDDNP in 13- to 15-month-old Tg2576 mice in comparison to wild-type mice (Kuntner et al., 2009). Similarly, Toyama et al. observed significantly lower peak uptake of [^{11}C]-PiB in this same model, albeit at the older age of 22 months (Toyama et al., 2005). Neither study demonstrated significant retention of amyloid tracer in transgenic mice at later time points during washout. Additionally, as cerebral blood flow deficits likely emerge in tandem with worsening amyloidosis and age, as occurs in human disease, the consequent alterations over time in the amount of intact tracer that enters the rodent brain will have repercussions on quantitative analysis of longitudinal static amyloid studies.

The high nonspecific binding issue is a particular challenge to sensitivity, as nonspecific retention dilutes signal specificity. Clinical studies have shown that fluorinated amyloid tracers have markedly decreased dynamic ranges in comparison to [^{11}C]-PiB (Vandenberghe et al., 2010; Villemagne et al., 2012; Landau et al., 2013b). In the aforementioned human studies, the lowered sensitivity did not substantially hinder amyloid-β quantification, but in the case of small-animal imaging, this lowered dynamic range could be a limiting factor in accurate detection of amyloid-β (Waldron et al., 2015a,b).

FDG Imaging in Transgenic Mouse Models

Although FDG is a better-established tracer, its ability to detect cerebral hypometabolism in amyloidosis models with μPET is debated. Early investigations of glucose utilization in transgenic models with FDG focused on the high-resolution technique of ex vivo autoradiography. With this method, a number of models were shown to have reductions in FDG uptake in brain regions with homology to those affected in clinical AD (Valla et al., 2006, 2008; Reiman et al., 2000; Dodart et al., 1999). However, when applied in vivo with μPET scanners, the majority of studies have reported either unchanged (Kuntner et al., 2009; Rapic et al., 2013) or increased (Rojas et al., 2013; Poisnel et al., 2012b; Luo et al., 2012) FDG uptake in transgenic models. Given the lower resolution of μPET in comparison to autoradiography, decreased sensitivity may indeed mask small regional decreases in FDG uptake between genotypes (Valla et al., 2002). However, these discrepancies may also be accounted for by methodological factors (Welch et al., 2013) in addition to strain differences. In that respect, the biodistribution of FDG and its uptake into target tissues is influenced by a wide variety of physiological, pharmacological, and methodological factors (Martic-Kehl et al., 2012; Wong et al., 2011). Hence, it is possible that the reported differences between the transgenic mouse models are in actuality artifacts due to methodological inconsistencies and are not representative of inherent pathological processes.

It is therefore important that these FDG imaging protocols are standardized to eliminate confounding factors, as these can potentially alter the outcome of the experiment. Most FDG imaging studies, including those in imaging for AD, make use of semiquantitative measures—the percent injected dose per gram of animal weight (%ID/g) or the SUV—thereby eliminating the need for long scan durations or invasive catheterization to obtain the plasma input function required for absolute quantification. The %ID/g represents the ratio of tissue uptake and the injected dose, while SUV additionally normalizes the %ID/g by the body weight of each individual animal. Without a standardized protocol, these measures can be biased by confounding factors, both in humans (Boellaard, 2009; Abouzied et al., 2005) and in small animals. There have been several comprehensive studies investigating potential influencing factors such as the administration route, fasting (Wong et al., 2011; Fueger et al., 2006; Wahl et al., 1992; Deleye et al., 2014), anesthesia (Fueger et al., 2006; Toyama et al., 2004; Saha et al., 2005; Flores et al., 2008; Matsumura et al., 2003), body temperature, and stress (Fueger et al., 2006; Deleye et al., 2014; Vachon and Moreau, 2001; De Boer et al., 1990; Meijer et al., 2005). Most of these influence FDG uptake by directly changing the blood glucose levels or by altering the glucose need.

To avoid all the aforementioned issues related to glucose and body weight and also with attenuation or calibration, normalization to a reference region is commonly performed. Moreover, such normalization increases statistical power by reducing variability in global flow or metabolism (Welch et al., 2013). However, this approach may yield very inaccurate results if such a reference region is compromised by disease and can thus be a confounding methodological factor. Due to its relative lack of amyloid pathology, the cerebellum is often designated as a reference region (Toyama et al., 2005; Rojas et al., 2013; Poisnel et al., 2012b). However, despite the lack of amyloid deposits, lower FDG uptake in the cerebellum of TASTPM mice compared to wild-type mice has been observed (Waldron et al., 2015b; Klupp et al., 2014). More recently, however, in vivo hypometabolism in amyloidosis mouse models has now been accurately described using reliable and consistent methodologies (Waldron et al., 2015b; Macdonald et al., 2014; Kelley, 2013).

FUTURE DIRECTIONS

Detection of the hallmarks of AD in life by means other than brain biopsy now appears feasible. As confidence and availability of biomarker methods—including PET imaging—have grown, pharmaceutical companies have embraced them for selecting subjects and detection of treatment effects. The potential benefit of biomarkers to the development of new therapeutics can be mapped to a simple formula developed by Paul and others (Paul et al., 2010):

$$P \propto \frac{\mathrm{WIP} \times p(\mathrm{TS}) \times V}{\mathrm{CT} \times C}$$

This formula describes productivity (P) as proportional to the product of ongoing research (work in progress = WIP), the probability of technical success [p(TS)], and the value of the product (V). Productivity is inversely related to cycle time (CT)—the time required to run a development cycle from discovery to decision point—and the cost (C) of development. The potential value of a biomarker that can provide an early indication of treatment efficacy and provide an end point with lower variability than clinical assessments is enormous. It means smaller and faster clinical trials and ideally more compelling evidence of impact on the disease process. If biomarker methods like PET imaging work, they could increase the probability of technical success (more suitable subjects, end points closer to disease pathology) and reduce cycle time (earlier readout and less time needed to enroll subjects) and cost.

Risks associated with amyloid PET include overemphasis of the role of amyloid in AD and, by extension, amyloid-targeted treatments (Fjell and Walhovd, 2012) and overestimation of the information provided by the biomarker (Jack et al., 2013a). This risk is implicit in the testing of the amyloid cascade hypothesis, which continues to be a valued foundation of rational discovery of new treatments for the interception of disease process of AD. Schneider and others have argued that enrichment of trials for prodromal AD with amyloidosis markers does not offer greater efficiency, as screening out the fraction of subjects with negative markers offered only a marginal increase in effect size, independent from the cost and complexity of including biomarkers as a filter during screening (Schneider et al., 2010). Their analysis may have assumed a lower prevalence of amyloid-negative subjects who might be recruited for such trials. Indeed, over a third of subjects with a clinical diagnosis of AD were amyloid negative in the bapineuzumab trials (Salloway et al., 2014). Moreover, MCI/prodromal subjects by definition manifest signs of neurodegeneration, which can be a more powerful predictor of decline than brain amyloid burden, and studies in asymptomatic subjects at risk for late-onset AD ought to consider risk factors other than age.

PET imaging is being included in AD trials for phenotyping subjects and as a treatment end point. Visual reading can be used for screening subjects, and can be made robust across centers and tracers with central reading. This may not be sufficient for trials of subjects at risk: quantitative analysis may be needed for detection of evolving amyloid burden. Quantitative analysis is needed when using PET as a treatment end point and appears to operate well in small proof-of-concept studies conducted at a limited number of sites under well-controlled conditions. As we have learned from larger multisite trials, quantitative longitudinal measurement has not scaled well and needs to be optimized. Well-controlled collection of PET data for quantitative analysis over months to years is beyond the standard practices of many nuclear medicine departments, and optimization will require a systems approach. To this end, notable efforts are being undertaken by work groups in the QIBA initiative in the RSNA for amyloid PET (http://qibawiki.rsna.org/index.php?title=PET_Amyloid_Biomarker_Ctte). These efforts would greatly benefit by contributions from pharma companies as they adopt these methods, including requiring timely feedback to sites contributing the data, to allow continuous real-time improvement. Regrettably, this type of feedback is seldom provided by sponsors to sites and investigators for assessments gathered in a clinical trial, even after the study has been completed.

Tau PET could prove essential for phenotyping of subjects for AD trials and serve as an indicator of treatment efficacy, whether or not the treatment is targeting tau protein. The qualification of these tracers is very much a work in progress, and innovation in the tools and their use needs to be encouraged and protected. While amyloid PET is becoming widely available for use in multicenter, multinational intervention trials, it may be years for tau PET to be as accessible. When it becomes available, it will be essential to adopt the lessons learned from acquiring amyloid PET in multicenter trials.

Private–public consortia have emerged as strong champions for introducing and testing of new PET imaging methods in clinical trial settings. These include ADNI in the United States, with its emphasis on open access to data (Mueller, 2005); parallel ADNI projects around the world (World Wide Alzheimer's Disease Neuroimaging Initiative); the Australian Imaging, Biomarkers and Lifestyle Flagship Study of Aging (Ellis et al., 2009); the European Prevention of Alzheimer's Dementia (EPAD); and the Critical Path Institute (C-Path) (Woosley et al., 2010). EPAD intends to develop a sizable registry of subjects for possible enrollment in AD trials, including phenotyping a cohort of subjects with amyloid PET. C-Path focuses on advocacy for acceptance of PET by health authorities for use in registration trials. These consortia have been critical for establishing protocols for data acquisition, building reference databases, and creating a community of researchers and customers of the methods as well as a means by which the needs of participants can be shared and challenged in a precompetitive environment. Such consortia are essential for risk and cost sharing, as undertaking these endeavors is far too costly and takes too long for an individual company or academic network to support. These consortia have and will continue to deliver critical information on the use of PET in AD trials but require sustained engagement and support.

The value of more functional readouts for phenotyping and following subjects in AD trials has probably been underestimated in the enthusiasm for protein biomarkers relevant to AD, such as amyloid PET which has face validity, greater stability, and less complex interpretation. This may be especially important to consider as trials move into the asymptomatic, at-risk population. The promise of considering end points indicative of neurodegeneration is illustrated by the study by Mormino and others, who identified up to roughly 60% of their amyloid-positive healthy elderly subjects as having early evidence of neurodegeneration by FDG PET or hippocampal atrophy (Mormino et al., 2014). A similar prevalence among amyloid-positive healthy elders in the ADNI database appeared to have an AD pattern on FDG PET, using a multivariate machine learning-based FDG PET classifier (Matthews et al., 2014). Notably, decline over time was observed only in amyloid-positive healthy elderly who had evidence of neurodegeneration (Mormino et al., 2014). This segment of the "at-risk" population may be those at highest risk and in greater need of disease intervention. A combination of imaging biomarkers will likely be essential for AD trials in the future.

References

Abouzied MM, Crawford ES, Nabi HA: 18F-FDG imaging: pitfalls and artifacts, *J Nucl Med Technol* 33(3):145–155, 2005.

Agdeppa ED, Kepe V, Liu J, Flores-Torres S, Satyamurthy N, Petric A, et al: Binding characteristics of radiofluorinated 6-dialkylamino-2-naphthylethylidene derivatives as positron emission tomography imaging probes for β-amyloid plaques in Alzheimer's disease, *J Neurosci* 21(24):RC189, 2001.

Aizenstein HJ, Nebes RD, Saxton JA, Price JC, Mathis CA, Tsopelas ND, et al: Frequent amyloid deposition without significant cognitive impairment among the elderly, *Arch Neurol* 65:1509–1517, 2008.

Alzheimer's Association: 2015 Alzheimer's disease facts and figures, *Alzheimers Dement* 11(3):332–384, 2015.

Ariza M, Kolb HC, Moechars D, Rombouts F, Andrés JI: Tau positron emission tomography (PET) imaging: past, present, and future, *J Med Chem* 58(11):4365–4382, 2015.

Barthel H, Gertz HJ, Dresel S, Peters O, Bartenstein P, Buerger K, et al: Cerebral amyloid-β PET with florbetaben (18F) in patients with Alzheimer's disease and healthy controls: a multicentre phase 2 diagnostic study, *Lancet Neurol* 10:424–435, 2011.

Bateman RJ, Xiong C, Benzinger TLS, Fagan AM, Goate A, Fox NC, et al: Clinical and biomarker changes in dominantly inherited Alzheimer's disease, *New Engl J Med*:795–804, 2012.

Bélanger M, Allaman I, Magistretti PJ: Brain energy metabolism: focus on astrocyte-neuron metabolic cooperation, *Cell Metab* 14(6):724–738, 2011.

Benzinger TLS, Blazey T, Jack CR, Koeppe RA, Su Y, Xiong C, et al: Regional variability of imaging biomarkers in autosomal dominant Alzheimer's disease, *Proc Natl Acad Sci USA* 110(47):E4502–E4509, 2013.

Boellaard R: Standards for PET image acquisition and quantitative data analysis, *J Nucl Med* 50(Suppl 1):11S–20S, 2009.

Boellaard R, O'Doherty M, Weber W, Mottaghy F, Lonsdale M, Stroobants S, et al: FDG PET and PET/CT: EANM procedure guidelines for tumour PET imaging: version 1.0, *Eur J Nucl Med Mol Imaging* 37(1):181–200, 2010.

Bourgeat P, Chételat G, Villemagne VL, Fripp J, Raniga P, Pike K, et al: Beta-amyloid burden in the temporal neocortex is related to hippocampal atrophy in elderly subjects without dementia, *Neurology* 74:121–127, 2010.

Braak H, Braak E: Neuropathological stageing of Alzheimer-related changes, *Acta Neuropathologica* 82:239–259, 1991.

Braak H, Thal DR, Ghebremedhin E, Del Tredici K: Stages of the pathologic process in Alzheimer disease: age categories from 1 to 100 years, *J Neuropath Exp Neurol* 70:960–969, 2011.

Brendel M, Hogenauer M, Delker A, Sauerbeck J, Bartenstein P, Seibyl J, et al: Improved longitudinal [(18)F]-AV45 amyloid PET by white matter reference and VOI-based partial volume effect correction, *NeuroImage* 108:450–459, 2015.

Brettschneider J, Tredici KD, Lee VMY, Trojanowski JQ: Spreading of pathology in neurodegenerative diseases: a focus on human studies, *Nat Rev Neurosci* 16(2):109–120, 2015.

Buscombe J: PET imaging of inflammation, *Q J Nucl Med Mol Imaging* 58(3):284–289, 2014.

Chen K, Langbaum JBS, Fleisher AS, Ayutyanont N, Reschke C, Lee W, et al: Twelve-month metabolic declines in probable Alzheimer's disease and amnestic mild cognitive impairment assessed using an empirically predefined statistical region-of-interest: findings from the Alzheimer's Disease Neuroimaging Initiative, *NeuroImage* 51(2):654–664, 2010.

Chetelat G, Villemagne VL, Villain N, Jones G, Ellis KA, Ames D, et al: Accelerated cortical atrophy in cognitively normal elderly with high beta-amyloid deposition, *Neurology* 78(7):477–484, 2012.

Chien DT, Szardenings AK, Bahri S, Walsh JC, Mu F, Xia C, et al: Early clinical PET imaging results with the novel PHF-tau radioligand [F18]-T808, *J Alzheimers Dis* 38(1):171–184, 2014.

Choi SR, Golding G, Zhuang Z, Zhang W, Lim N, Hefti F, et al: Preclinical properties of 18F-AV-45: a PET agent for Aβ plaques in the brain, *J Nucl Med* 50(11):1887–1894, 2009.

Clark CM, Schneider JA, Bedell BJ, Beach TG, Bilker WB, Mintun MA, et al: Use of florbetapir-PET for imaging b-amyloid pathology, *JAMA–J Amer Med Assoc* 305:275–283, 2011.

Cselényi Z, Jönhagen ME, Forsberg A, Halldin C, Julin P, Schou M, et al: Clinical validation of 18F-AZD4694, an amyloid-β-specific PET radioligand, *J Nucl Med* 53(3):415–424, 2012.

Cummings J, Morstorf T, Zhong K: Alzheimer's disease drug-development pipeline: few candidates, frequent failures, *Alzheimers Res Therapy* 6(4):37, 2014.

Curtis C, Gamez JE, Singh U, et al: Phase 3 trial of flutemetamol labeled with radioactive fluorine 18 imaging and neuritic plaque density, *JAMA Neurol* 72(3):287–294, 2015.

De Boer SF, Koopmans SJ, Slangen JL, Van Der Gugten J: Plasma catecholamine, corticosterone and glucose responses to repeated stress in rats: effect of interstressor interval length, *Physiol Behav* 47(6):1117–1124, 1990.

de Leon MJ, Ferris SH, George AE, Christman DR, Fowler JS, Gentes C, et al: Positron emission tomographic studies of aging and Alzheimer disease, *Am J Neuroradiol* 4(3):568–571, 1983.

DeKosky ST, Scheff SW, Styren SD: Structural correlates of cognition in dementia: quantification and assessment of synapse change, *Neurodegeneration* 5(4):417–421, 1996.

Deleye S, Verhaeghe J, Wyffels L, Dedeurwaerdere S, Stroobants S, Staelens S: Towards a reproducible protocol for repetitive and semi-quantitative rat brain imaging with 18 F-FDG: exemplified in a memantine pharmacological challenge, *NeuroImage* 96:276–287, 2014.

Dickerson BC: Diagnostic tests for Alzheimer disease: judicious use can be helpful in clinical practice, *Neurology: Clinical Practice* 2(2):154–157, 2012.

Dodart J-C, Mathis C, Bales KR, Paul SM, Ungerer A: Early regional cerebral glucose hypometabolism in transgenic mice overexpressing the V717F β-amyloid precursor protein, *Neurosci Lett* 277(1):49–52, 1999.

Doody RS, Thomas RG, Farlow M, Iwatsubo T, Vellas B, Joffe S, et al: Phase 3 trials of solanezumab for mild-to-moderate Alzheimer's disease, *New Engl J Med* 370(4):311–321, 2014.

Doraiswamy PM, Sperling RA, Johnson K, Reiman EM, Wong TZ, Sabbagh MN, et al: Florbetapir F 18 amyloid PET and 36-month cognitive decline:a prospective multicenter study, *Mol Psychiatr* 19(9):1044–1051, 2014.

Drzezga A, Grimmer T, Henriksen G, Stangier I, Perneczky R, Diehl-Schmid J, et al: Imaging of amyloid plaques and cerebral glucose metabolism in semantic dementia and Alzheimer's disease, *NeuroImage* 39(2):619–633, 2008.

Drzezga A, Becker JA, Van Dijk KRA, Sreenivasan A, Talukdar T, Sullivan C, et al: Neuronal dysfunction and disconnection of cortical hubs in non-demented subjects with elevated amyloid burden, *Brain* 134(6):1635–1646, 2011.

Dubois B, Feldman HH, Jacova C, DeKosky ST, Barberger-gateau P, Cummings J, et al: Research criteria for the diagnosis of Alzheimer's disease: revising the NINCDS–ADRDA criteria, *Lancet Neurol* 6:734–746, 2007.

Ellis KA, Bush AI, Darby D, De Fazio D, Foster J, Hudson P, et al: The Australian Imaging, Biomarkers and Lifestyle (AIBL) study of aging: methodology and baseline characteristics of 1112 individuals recruited for a longitudinal study of Alzheimer's disease, *Int Psychogeriatr* 21:672–687, 2009.

Fagan AM, Mintun MA, Mach RH, Lee S-Y, Dence CS, Shah AR, et al: Inverse relation between in vivo amyloid imaging load and cerebrospinal fluid Aβ42 in humans, *Ann Neurol* 59(3):512–519, 2006.

Fagan AM, Mintun MA, Shah AR, Aldea P, Roe CM, Mach RH, et al: Cerebrospinal fluid tau and ptau181 increase with cortical amyloid deposition in cognitively normal individuals: implications for future clinical trials of AD, *EMBO Mol Med* 1:371–380, 2009.

Feigin A, Leenders KL, Moeller JR, Missimer J, Kuenig G, Spetsieris P, et al: Metabolic network abnormalities in early Huntington's disease: an [18F]FDG PET study, *J Nucl Med* 42(11):1591–1595, 2001.

Ferris SH, de Leon MJ, Wolf AP, Farkas T, Christman DR, Reisberg B, et al: Positron emission tomography in the study of aging and senile dementia, *Neurobiol Aging* 1(2):127–131, 1980.

Fjell A, Walhovd K: Neuroimaging results impose new views on Alzheimer's disease—the role of amyloid revised, *Mol Neurobiol* 45(1):153–172, 2012.

Fleisher AS, Chen K, Liu X, Ayutyanont N, Roontiva A, Thiyyagura P, et al: Apolipoprotein E epsilon4 and age effects on florbetapir positron emission tomography in healthy aging and Alzheimer disease, *Neurobiol Aging* 34(1):1–12, 2013.

Flores J, McFarland L, Vanderbilt A, Ogasawara A, Williams S-P: The effects of anesthetic agent and carrier gas on blood glucose and tissue uptake in mice undergoing dynamic FDG-PET imaging: sevoflurane and isoflurane compared in air and in oxygen, *Mol Imaging Biol* 10(4):192–200, 2008.

Fodero-Tavoletti MT, Smith DP, McLean CA, Adlard PA, Barnham KJ, Foster LE, et al: In vitro characterization of Pittsburgh compound-B binding to Lewy bodies, *J Neurosci* 27(39):10365–10371, 2007.

Foster NL, Heidebrink JL, Clark CM, Jagust WJ, Arnold SE, Barbas NR, et al: FDG-PET improves accuracy in distinguishing frontotemporal dementia and Alzheimer's disease, *Brain* 130(10):2616–2635, 2007.

Freir DB, Fedriani R, Scully D, Smith IM, Selkoe DJ, Walsh DM, et al: Aβ oligomers inhibit synapse remodelling necessary for memory consolidation, *Neurobiol Aging* 32(12):2211–2218, 2011.

Friedland RP, Jagust WJ, Huesman RH, Koss E, Knittel B, Mathis CA, et al: Regional cerebral glucose transport and utilization in Alzheimer's disease, *Neurology* 39(11):1427, 1989.

Fueger BJ, Czernin J, Hildebrandt I, Tran C, Halpern BS, Stout D, et al: Impact of animal handling on the results of 18F-FDG PET studies in mice, *J Nucl Med* 47(6):999–1006, 2006.

Garibotto V, Borroni B, Kalbe E, Herholz K, Salmon E, Holtoff V, et al: Education and occupation as proxies for reserve in aMCI converters and AD: FDG-PET evidence, *Neurology* 71(17):1342–1349, 2008.

Glenner GG, Wong CW: Alzheimer's disease: initial report of the purification and characterization of a novel cerebrovascular amyloid protein, *Biochem Bioph Res Commun* 120(3):885–890, 1984.

Goedert M: Oskar Fischer and the study of dementia, *Brain* 132(4):1102–1111, 2009.

Gotz J, Ittner LM: Animal models of Alzheimer's disease and frontotemporal dementia, *Nat Rev Neurosci* 9(7): 532–544, 2008.

Grimmer T, Riemenschneider M, Förstl H, Henriksen G, Klunk WE, Mathis CA, et al: Beta amyloid in Alzheimer's disease: increased deposition in brain is reflected in reduced concentration in cerebrospinal fluid, *Biol Psychiat* 65(11):927–934, 2009.

Gu Y, Razlighi QR, Zahodne LB, Janicki SC, Ichise M, Manly JJ, et al: Brain amyloid deposition and longitudinal cognitive decline in nondemented older subjects: results from a multi-ethnic population, *PLoS One* 10(7):e0123743, 2015.

Haass C, Selkoe DJ: Soluble protein oligomers in neurodegeneration: lessons from the Alzheimer's amyloid [beta]-peptide, *Nat Rev Mol Cell Biol* 8(2):101–112, 2007.

Haier RJ, Siegel BV, MacLachlan A, Soderling E, Lottenberg S, Buchsbaum MS: Regional glucose metabolic changes after learning a complex visuospatial/motor task: a positron emission tomographic study, *Brain Res* 570(1): 134–143, 1992.

Hampel H, Schneider LS, Giacobini E, Kivipelto M, Sindi S, Dubois B, et al: Advances in the therapy of Alzheimer's disease: targeting amyloid beta and tau and perspectives for the future, *Expert Rev Neurotherapeutics* 15(1):83–105, 2015.

Haxby JV, Duara R, Grady CL, Cutler NR, Rapoport SI: Relations between neuropsychological and cerebral metabolic asymmetries in early Alzheimer's disease, *J Cerebr Blood Flow Metab* 5(2):193–200, 1985.

Heiss W-D, Herholz K, Pawlik G, Hebold I, et al: Positron emission tomography findings in dementia disorders: contributions to differential diagnosis and objectivizing of therapeutic effects, *Keio J Med* 38(2):111–135, 1989.

Hsiao I-T, Huang C-C, Hsieh C-J, Hsu W-C, Wey S-P, Yen T-C, et al: Correlation of early-phase 18F-florbetapir (AV-45/Amyvid) PET images to FDG images: preliminary studies, *Eur J Nucl Med Mol Imaging* 39(4):613–620, 2012.

Ido T, Wan CN, Casella V, Fowler JS, Wolf AP, Reivich M, et al: Labeled 2-deoxy-D-glucose analogs: 18F-labeled 2-deoxy-2-fluoro-D-glucose, 2-deoxy-2-fluoro-D-mannose and 14C-2-deoxy-2-fluoro-D-glucose, *J Labelled Comp-Radiopharm* 14(2):175–183, 1978.

Jack CR Jr, Lowe VJ, Weigand SD, Wiste HJ, Senjem ML, Knopman DS, et al: Serial PIB and MRI in normal, mild cognitive impairment and Alzheimer's disease: implications for sequence of pathological events in Alzheimer's disease, *Brain* 132:1355–1365, 2009.

Jack CR, Knopman DS, Jagust WJ, Shaw LM, Aisen PS, Weiner MW, et al: Hypothetical model of dynamic biomarkers of the Alzheimer's pathological cascade, *Lancet Neurol* 9:119–128, 2010.

Jack CR Jr, Barkhof F, Bernstein MA, Cantillon M, Cole PE, Decarli C, et al: Steps to standardization and validation of hippocampal volumetry as a biomarker in clinical trials and diagnostic criterion for Alzheimer's disease, *Alzheimers Dement* 7(4):474–485, 2011, e4.

Jack CR Jr, Knopman DS, Weigand SD, Wiste HJ, Vemuri P, Lowe V, et al: An operational approach to National Institute on Aging–Alzheimer's Association criteria for preclinical Alzheimer disease, *Ann Neurol* 71(6):765–775, 2012.

Jack C Jr, Barrio J, Kepe V: Cerebral amyloid PET imaging in Alzheimer's disease, *Acta Neuropathologica* 126(5): 643–657, 2013a.

Jack CR, Knopman DS, Jagust WJ, Petersen RC, Weiner MW, Aisen PS, et al: Tracking pathophysiological processes in Alzheimer's disease: an updated hypothetical model of dynamic biomarkers, *Lancet Neurol* 12(2):207–216, 2013b.

Jagust WJ, Seab JP, Huesman RH, Valk PE, Mathis CA, Reed BR, et al: Diminished glucose transport in Alzheimer's disease: dynamic PET studies, *J Cerebr Blood Flow Metab* 11(2):323–330, 1991.

Jagust WJ, Bandy D, Chen K, Foster NL, Landau SM, Mathis CA, et al: The Alzheimer's Disease Neuroimaging Initiative positron emission tomography core, *Alzheimers Dement* 6(3):221–229, 2010.

Johnson KA, Fox NC, Sperling RA, Klunk WE: Brain imaging in Alzheimer disease, *Cold Spring Harb Perspect Med* 2(4), 2012.

Josephs KA, Duffy JR, Fossett TR, et al: Fluorodeoxyglucose f18 positron emission tomography in progressive apraxia of speech and primary progressive aphasia variants, *Arch Neurol* 67(5):596–605, 2010.

Joshi A, Koeppe RA, Fessler JA: Reducing between scanner differences in multi-center PET studies, *NeuroImage* 46(1):154–159, 2009.

Joshi AD, Pontecorvo MJ, Clark CM, Carpenter AP, Jennings DL, Sadowsky CH, et al: Performance characteristics of amyloid PET with florbetapir F 18 in patients with Alzheimer's disease and cognitively normal subjects, *J Nucl Med* 53(3):378–384, 2012.

Jucker M, Walker LC: Pathogenic protein seeding in Alzheimer disease and other neurodegenerative disorders, *Ann Neurol* 70:532–540, 2011.

Juréus A, Swahn BM, Sandell J, Jeppsson F, Johnson AE, Johnström P, et al: Characterization of AZD4694, a novel fluorinated Abeta plaque neuroimaging PET radioligand, *J Neurochem* 114:784–794, 2010.

Kadir A, Andreasen N, Almkvist O, Wall A, Forsberg A, Engler H, et al: Effect of phenserine treatment on brain functional activity and amyloid in Alzheimer's disease, *Ann Neurol* 63(5):621–631, 2008.

Kaiser NC, Melrose RJ, Liu C, Sultzer DL, Jimenez E, Su M, et al: Neuropsychological and neuroimaging markers in early versus late-onset Alzheimer's disease, *Am J Alzheimers Dis* 27(7):520–529, 2012.

Kalaria RN, Akinyemi R, Ihara M: Does vascular pathology contribute to Alzheimer changes? *J Neurol Sci* 322(1–2):141–147, 2012.

Kalpouzos G, Chételat G, Landeau B, Clochon P, Viader F, Eustache F, et al: Structural and metabolic correlates of episodic memory in relation to the depth of encoding in normal aging, *J Cognitive Neurosci* 21(2):372–389, 2008.

Kantarci K, Lowe VJ, Boeve BF, Weigand SD, Senjem ML, Przybelski SA, et al: Multimodality imaging characteristics of dementia with Lewy bodies, *Neurobiol Aging* 33(9):2091–2105, 2012.

Keller C, Kadir A, Forsberg A, Porras O, Nordberg A: *Long-term effects of galantamine treatment on brain functional activities as measured by PET in Alzheimer's disease patients*, 2011, IOS Press, Contract No. 1.

Kelley J, Wintmolders C, Bottelbergs A, Waldron A-M, Wyffels L, Czech C, et al: Investigations of brain glucose utilization in three transgenic mouse strains that develop neuropathological features of Alzheimer's disease, *Alzheimers Dement* 9(4):P329, 2013.

Kepe V, Moghbel MC, Långström B, Zaidi H, Vinters HV, Huang S-C, et al: Amyloid-β positron emission tomography imaging probes: a critical review, *J Alzheimers Dis* 36(4):613–631, 2013.

Khatri N, Man H: Synaptic activity and bioenergy homeostasis: implications in brain trauma and neurodegenerative diseases, *Frontiers Neurol* 4:199, 2013.

Kiebel SJ, Ashburner J, Poline JB, Friston KJ: MRI and PET coregistration—a cross validation of statistical parametric mapping and automated image registration, *NeuroImage* 5(4):271–279, 1997.

Kile SJ, Olichney JM: Amyloid clearing immunotherapy for Alzheimer's disease and the risk of cerebral amyloid angiopathy, *Alzheimers Dis Res J* 1(1–2):5–12, 2007.

Klunk WE, Koeppe RA, Price JC, Benzinger TL, Devous MD Sr, Jagust WJ, et al: The centiloid project: standardizing quantitative amyloid plaque estimation by PET, *Alzheimers Dement* 11(1):1–15.e4, 2015.

Klunk WE, Engler H, Nordberg A, Wang Y, Blomqvist G, Holt DP, et al: Imaging brain amyloid in Alzheimer's disease with Pittsburgh compound-B, *Ann Neurol* 55(3):306–319, 2004.

Klunk WE, Lopresti BJ, Ikonomovic MD, Lefterov IM, Koldamova RP, Abrahamson EE, et al: Binding of the positron emission tomography tracer Pittsburgh compound-B reflects the amount of amyloid-beta in Alzheimer's disease brain but not in transgenic mouse brain, *J Neurosci* 25(46):10598–10606, 2005.

Klupp E, Förster S, Grimmer T, Tahmasian M, Yakushev I, Sorg C, et al: In Alzheimer's disease, hypometabolism in low-amyloid brain regions may be a functional consequence of pathologies in connected brain regions, *Brain Connect* 4(5):371–383, 2014.

Knopman DS, Jack CR, Wiste HJ, Weigand SD, Vemuri P, Lowe V, et al: Short-term clinical outcomes for stages of NIA-AA preclinical Alzheimer disease, *Neurology* 78(20):1576–1582, 2012.

Knopman DS, Jack CR Jr, Wiste HJ, Lundt ES, Weigand SD, Vemuri P, et al: 18F-fluorodeoxyglucose positron emission tomography, aging, and apolipoprotein E genotype in cognitively normal persons, *Neurobiol Aging* 35(9):2096–2106, 2014.

Koffie RM, Hyman BT, Spires-Jones TL: Alzheimer's disease: synapses gone cold, *Mol Neurodegener* 6:63, 2011.

Kuntner C, Kesner A, Bauer M, Kremslehner R, Wanek T, Mandler M, et al: Limitations of small animal PET imaging with [18F]FDDNP and FDG for quantitative studies in a transgenic mouse model of Alzheimer's disease, *Mol Imaging Biol* 11(4):236–240, 2009.

Kushner MJ, Rosenquist A, Alavi A, Rosen M, Dann R, Fazekas F, et al: Cerebral metabolism and patterned visual stimulation: a positron emission tomographic study of the human visual cortex, *Neurology* 38(1):89, 1988.

Landau SM, Harvey D, Madison CM, Reiman EM, Foster NL, Aisen PS, et al: Comparing predictors of conversion and decline in mild cognitive impairment, *Neurology* 75(3):230–238, 2010.

Landau SM, Harvey D, Madison CM, Koeppe RA, Reiman EM, Foster NL, et al: Associations between cognitive, functional, and FDG-PET measures of decline in AD and MCI, *Neurobiol Aging* 32(7):1207–1218, 2011.

Landau SM, Lu M, Joshi AD, Pontecorvo M, Mintun MA, Trojanowski JQ, et al: Comparing positron emission tomography imaging and cerebrospinal fluid measurements of β-amyloid, *Ann Neurol* 74(6):826–836, 2013a.

Landau SM, Breault C, Joshi AD, Pontecorvo M, Mathis CA, Jagust WJ, et al: Amyloid-β imaging with Pittsburgh compound B and florbetapir: comparing radiotracers and quantification methods, *J Nucl Med* 54(1):70–77, 2013b.

Landau SM, Thomas BA, Thurfjell L, Schmidt M, Margolin R, Mintun M, et al: Amyloid PET imaging in Alzheimer's disease: a comparison of three radiotracers, *Eur J Nucl Med Mol I* 41(7):1398–1407, 2014.

Lee VM-Y, Brunden KR, Hutton M, Trojanowski JQ: Developing therapeutic approaches to tau, selected kinases, and related neuronal protein targets, *Cold Spring Harb Perspect Med* 1(1), 2011.

Lerch JP, Pruessner JC, Zijdenbos A, Hampel H, Teipel SJ, Evans AC: Focal decline of cortical thickness in Alzheimer's disease identified by computational neuroanatomy, *Cerebral Cortex* 15:995–1001, 2005.

Liu Y, Liu F, Iqbal K, Grundke-Iqbal I, Gong C-X: Decreased glucose transporters correlate to abnormal hyperphosphorylation of tau in Alzheimer disease, *FEBS Lett* 582(2):359–364, 2008.

Liu E, Schmidt ME, Margolin R, Sperling R, Koeppe R, Mason NS, et al: Amyloid-β 11C-PiB-PET imaging results from 2 randomized bapineuzumab phase 3 AD trials, *Neurology* 85(8):692–700, 2015.

Lockhart A, Ye L, Judd DB, Merritt AT, Lowe PN, Morgenstern JL, et al: Evidence for the presence of three distinct binding sites for the thioflavin T class of Alzheimer's disease PET imaging agents on β-amyloid peptide fibrils, *J Biol Chem* 280(9):7677–7684, 2005.

Loessner A, Alavi A, Lewandrowski K-U, Mozley D, Souder E, Gur RE: Regional cerebral function determined by FDG-PET in healthy volunteers: normal patterns and changes with age, *J Nucl Med* 36(7):1141–1149, 1995.

Logothetis NK: What we can do and what we cannot do with fMRI, *Nature* 453(7197):869–878, 2008.

Lopresti BJ, Klunk WE, Mathis CA, Hoge JA, Ziolko SK, Lu X, et al: Simplified quantification of Pittsburgh compound B amyloid imaging PET studies: a comparative analysis, *J Nucl Med* 46(12):1959–1972, 2005.

Lucignani G, Schmidt KC, Moresco RM, Striano G, Colombo F, Sokoloff L, et al: Measurement of regional cerebral glucose utilization with fluorine-18-FDG and PET in heterogeneous tissues: theoretical considerations and practical procedure, *J Nucl Med* 34(3):360–369, 1993.

Lue LF, Kuo YM, Roher AE, Brachova L, Shen Y, Sue L, et al: Soluble amyloid β peptide concentration as a predictor of synaptic change in Alzheimer's disease, *Am J Pathol* 155:853–862, 1999.

Lundqvist R, Lilja J, Thomas BA, Lötjönen J, Villemagne VL, Rowe CC, Thurfjell L: Implementation and validation of an adaptive template registration method for ^{18}F-flutemetamol imaging data, *J Nucl Med* 54:1472–1478, 2013.

Luo F, Rustay NR, Ebert U, Hradil VP, Cole TB, Llano DA, et al: Characterization of 7- and 19-month-old Tg2576 mice using multimodal in vivo imaging: limitations as a translatable model of Alzheimer's disease, *Neurobiol Aging* 33(5):933–944, 2012.

Macdonald IR, DeBay DR, Reid GA, O'Leary TP, Jollymore CT, Mawko G, et al: Early detection of cerebral glucose uptake changes in the 5XFAD mouse, *Curr Alzheimer Res* 11(5):450–460, 2014.

Maeda J, Ji B, Irie T, Tomiyama T, Maruyama M, Okauchi T, et al: Longitudinal, quantitative assessment of amyloid, neuroinflammation, and anti-amyloid treatment in a living mouse model of Alzheimer's disease enabled by positron emission tomography, *J Neurosci* 27:10957–10968, 2007.

Maeda J, Zhang MR, Okauchi T, Ji B, Ono M, Hattori S, et al: In vivo positron emission tomographic imaging of glial responses to amyloid-beta and tau pathologies in mouse models of Alzheimer's disease and related disorders, *J Neurosci* 31(12):4720–4730, 2011.

Magistretti PJ, Pellerin L: The contribution of astrocytes to the 18F-2-deoxyglucose signal in PET activation studies, *Mol Psychiatr* 1(6):445–452, 1996.

Maier FC, Wehrl HF, Schmid AM, Mannheim JG, Wiehr S, Lerdkrai C, et al: Longitudinal PET-MRI reveals β-amyloid deposition and rCBF dynamics and connects vascular amyloidosis to quantitative loss of perfusion, *Nat Med* 20(12):1485–1492, 2014.

Maier FC, Keller MD, Bukala D, Bender B, Mannheim JG, Brereton IM, et al: Quantification of β-amyloidosis and rCBF with dedicated PET, 7 T-MR imaging and high-resolution microscopic MR imaging at 16.4 T in APP23 mice, *J Nucl Med* 56(10):1593–1599, 2015.

Manook A, Yousefi BH, Willuweit A, Platzer S, Reder S, Voss A, et al: Small-animal PET imaging of amyloid-beta plaques with [11C]PiB and its multi-modal validation in an APP/PS1 mouse model of Alzheimer's disease, *PLoS One* 7(3):e31310, 2012.

Marshall GA, Monserratt L, Harwood D, Mandelkern M, Cummings JL, Sultzer DL: Positron emission tomography metabolic correlates of apathy in alzheimer disease, *Arch Neurol* 64(7):1015–1020, 2007.

Martic-Kehl MI, Ametamey SM, Alf MF, Schubiger PA, Honer M: Impact of inherent variability and experimental parameters on the reliability of small animal PET data, *EJNMMI Res* 2(1), 2012.

Maruyama M, Shimada H, Suhara T, Shinotoh H, Ji B, Maeda J, et al: Imaging of tau pathology in a tauopathy mouse model and in Alzheimer patients compared to normal controls, *Neuron* 79(6):1094–1108, 2013.

Masters CL, Simms G, Weinman NA, Multhaup G, McDonald BL, Beyreuther K: Amyloid plaque core protein in Alzheimer disease and Down syndrome, *Proc Natl Acad Sci USA* 82(12):4245–4249, 1985.

Mathis CA, Mason NS, Lopresti BJ, Klunk WE: Development of positron emission tomography β-amyloid plaque imaging agents, *Semin in Nucl Med* 42(6):423–432, 2012.

Matsumura A, Mizokawa S, Tanaka M, Wada Y, Nozaki S, Nakamura F, et al: Assessment of microPET performance in analyzing the rat brain under different types of anesthesia: comparison between quantitative data obtained with microPET and ex vivo autoradiography, *NeuroImage* 20(4):2040–2050, 2003.

Matthews DC, Lukic A, Andrews RA, Streffer J, Liu E, Van Nueten L, et al: Detection of an FDG AD signature in early MCI and cognitively normal subjects and its potential for clinical trial enrichment, CTAD Annual Congress 2014, Philadelphia, PA, 2014.

Matthews DC, Lukic AS, Andrews RD, Marendic B, Brewer JB, Rissman RA, et al: Dissociation of Down syndrome and Alzheimer's disease effects with imaging. *Alzheimer's Dement Transl Res Clin Interv*; 2016 (in press).

Mattsson N, Andreasson U, Persson S, Arai H, Batish SD, Bernardini S, et al: The Alzheimer's Association external quality control program for cerebrospinal fluid biomarkers, *Alzheimers Dement* 7(4):386–395, 2011, e6.

Mattsson N, Insel PS, Donohue M, Landau S, Jagust WJ, Shaw LM, et al: Independent information from cerebrospinal fluid amyloid-β and florbetapir imaging in Alzheimer's disease, *Brain* 138(3):772–783, 2015.

Mayberg HS, Liotti M, Brannan SK, McGinnis S, Mahurin RK, Jerabek PA, et al: Reciprocal limbic-cortical function and negative mood: converging PET findings in depression and normal sadness, *Am J Psychiat* 156(5):675–682, 1999.

McKhann G, Drachman D, Folstein M, Katzman R, Price D, Stadlan EM: Clinical diagnosis of Alzheimer's disease, *Neurology* 34:939–944, 1984.

Meijer MK, Lemmens AG, Van Zutphen BFM, Baumans V: Urinary corticosterone levels in mice in response to intraperitoneal injections with saline, *J Appl Anim Welf Sci* 8(4):279–283, 2005.

Minoshima S, Frey KA, Foster NL, Kuhl DE: Preserved pontine glucose metabolism in Alzheimer disease: a reference region for functional brain image (PET) analysis, *J Comput Assist Tomo* 19(4):541–547, 1995.

Minoshima S, Frey KA, Kuhl DE: Cerebellar metabolic reduction in Alzheimer's disease and data normalization, *J Nucl Med* 39(2):374–375, 1998.

Morbelli S, Garibotto V, Van De Giessen E, Arbizu J, Chételat G, Drezgza A, et al: A Cochrane review on brain [18F] FDG PET in dementia: limitations and future perspectives, *Eur J Nucl Med Mol Imaging* 42(10):1487–1491, 2015.

Mormino EC, Betensky RA, Hedden T, et al: Synergistic effect of β-amyloid and neurodegeneration on cognitive decline in clinically normal individuals, *JAMA Neurol* 71(11):1379–1385, 2014.

Morris ED, Endres CJ, Schmidt KC, Christian BT, Muzic RF, Fisher RE: Kinetic modeling in positron emission tomography. In Wernick MN, Aarsvold JN, editors: *Emission tomography: the fundamentals of PET and SPECT*, Academic Press, Amsterdam, 2004, pp 499–540.

Morris JC, Roe CM, Grant EA, Head D, Storandt M, Goate AM, et al: Pittsburgh compound B imaging and prediction of progression from cognitive normality to symptomatic Alzheimer disease, *Arch Neurol* 66:1469–1475, 2009.

Mosconi L, Berti V, Glodzik L, Pupi A, De Santi S, de Leon MJ: *Pre-clinical detection of Alzheimer's disease using FDG-PET, with or without amyloid imaging*, 2010, IOS Press, Contract No. 3.

Mosconi L, De Santi S, Li J, Tsui WH, Li Y, Boppana M, et al: Hippocampal hypometabolism predicts cognitive decline from normal aging, *Neurobiol Aging* 29:676–692, 2008.

Motter R, Vigo-Pelfrey C, Kholodenko D, Barbour R, Johnson-Wood K, Galasko D, et al: Reduction of β-amyloid peptide42 in the cerebrospinal fluid of patients with Alzheimer's disease, *Ann Neurol* 38(4):643–648, 1995.

Mueller SG, Weiner MW, Thal LJ, Petersen RC, Jack C, Jagust W, et al: The Alzheimer's Disease Neuroimaging Initiative, *Neuroimaging Clin* 15(4):869–877, 2005.

Mukaetova-Ladinska EB, Harrington CR, Roth M, Wischik CM: Biochemical and anatomical redistribution of tau protein in Alzheimer's disease, *Am J Pathol* 143(2):565–578, 1993.

Nehlig A: Brain uptake and metabolism of ketone bodies in animal models, *Prostag Leukotr Ess* 70(3):265–275, 2004.

Nelissen N, Van Laere K, Thurfjell L, Owenius R, Vandenbulcke M, Koole M, et al: Phase 1 study of the Pittsburgh compound B derivative 18F-flutemetamol in healthy volunteers and patients with probable Alzheimer disease, *J Nucl Med* 50(8):1251–1259, 2009.

Nelson PT, Abner EL, Schmitt FA, Kryscio RJ, Jicha GA, Smith CD, et al: Modeling the association between 43 different clinical and pathological variables and the severity of cognitive impairment in a large autopsy cohort of elderly persons, *Brain Pathol* 20(1):66–79, 2010.

O'Brien JT, Firbank MJ, Davison C, Barnett N, Bamford C, Donaldson C, et al: 18F-FDG PET and perfusion SPECT in the diagnosis of Alzheimer and Lewy body dementias, *J Nucl Med* 55(12):1959–1965, 2014.

Ostrowitzki S, Deptula D, Thurfjell L, Barkhof F, Bohrmann B, Brooks DJ, et al: Mechanism of amyloid removal in patients with Alzheimer disease treated with gantenerumab, *Arch Neurol* 69:198–207, 2012.

Palmqvist S, Zetterberg H, Blennow K, et al: Accuracy of brain amyloid detection in clinical practice using cerebrospinal fluid β-amyloid 42: a cross-validation study against amyloid positron emission tomography, *JAMA Neurol* 71(10):1282–1289, 2014.

Paul SM, Mytelka DS, Dunwiddie CT, Persinger CC, Munos BH, Lindborg SR, et al: How to improve R&D productivity: the pharmaceutical industry's grand challenge, *Nat Rev Drug Discov* 9:203–214, 2010.

Poisnel G, Dhilly M, Moustié O, Delamare J, Abbas A, Guilloteau D, et al: PET imaging with [18F]AV-45 in an APP/PS1-21 murine model of amyloid plaque deposition, *Neurobiol Aging* 33(11):2561–2571, 2012a.

Poisnel G, Hérard A-S, El Tannir El Tayara N, Bourrin E, Volk A, Kober F, et al: Increased regional cerebral glucose uptake in an APP/PS1 model of Alzheimer's disease, *Neurobiol Aging* 33(9):1995–2005, 2012b.

Prestia A, Caroli A, Wade SK, van der Flier WM, Ossenkoppele R, Van Berckel B, et al: Prediction of AD dementia by biomarkers following the NIA-AA and IWG diagnostic criteria in MCI patients from three European memory clinics, *Alzheimers Dement* 11(10):1191–1201, 2015.

Price JC, Klunk WE, Lopresti BJ, Lu X, Hoge JA, Ziolko SK, et al: Kinetic modeling of amyloid binding in humans using PET imaging and Pittsburgh compound-B, *J Cerebr Blood Flow Metab* 25(11):1528–1547, 2005.

Rabinovici GD, Jagust WJ, Furst AJ, Ogar JM, Racine CA, Mormino EC, et al: Abeta amyloid and glucose metabolism in three variants of primary progressive aphasia, *Ann Neurol* 64(4):388–401, 2008.

Rapic S, Backes H, Viel T, Kummer MP, Monfared P, Neumaier B, et al: Imaging microglial activation and glucose consumption in a mouse model of Alzheimer's disease, *Neurobiol Aging* 34(1):351–354, 2013.

Reiman EM, Uecker A, Gonzalez-Lima F, Minear D, Chen K, Callaway NL, et al: Tracking Alzheimer's disease in transgenic mice using fluorodeoxyglucose autoradiography, *NeuroReport* 11(5):987–991, 2000.

Reiman EM, Chen K, Alexander GE, Caselli RJ, Bandy D, Osborne D, et al: Functional brain abnormalities in young adults at genetic risk for late-onset Alzheimer's dementia, *Proc Natl Acad Sci USA* 101(1):284–289, 2004.

Reiman EM, Chen K, Alexander GE, Caselli RJ, Bandy D, Osborne D, et al: Correlations between apolipoprotein E ε4 gene dose and brain-imaging measurements of regional hypometabolism, *Proc Natl Acad Sci USA* 102(23):8299–8302, 2005.

Reivich M, Kuhl D, Wolf A, Greenberg J, Phelps M, Ido T, et al: The [18F]fluorodeoxyglucose method for the measurement of local cerebral glucose utilization in man, *Circ Res* 44(1):127–137, 1979.

Reivich M, Gur RE, Alavi A: Positron emission tomographic studies of sensory stimuli, cognitive processes and anxiety, *Hum Neurobiol* 2(1):25–33, 1983.

Rinne JO, Brooks DJ, Rossor MN, Fox NC, Bullock R, Klunk WE, et al: 11C-PiB PET assessment of change in fibrillar amyloid-β load in patients with Alzheimer's disease treated with bapineuzumab: a phase 2, double-blind, placebo-controlled, ascending-dose study, *Lancet Neurol* 9:363–372, 2010.

Rodell AB, Aanerud JF, Braendgaard H, Gjedde A: Washout allometric reference method (WARM) for parametric analysis of [11C]PIB in human brains, *Frontiers Aging Neurosci* 5:45, 2013.

Rojas S, Herance JR, Gispert JD, Abad S, Torrent É, Jiménez X, et al: In vivo evaluation of amyloid deposition and brain glucose metabolism of 5XFAD mice using positron emission tomography, *Neurobiol Aging* 34(7):1790–1798, 2013.

Rominger A, Brendel M, Rötzer C, Gildehaus F-J, Baumann K, Haass C, et al: Monitoring of long-term gamma secretase modulation treatment in APP-SWE mice by means of [18F]-florbetaben PET, *Alzheimers Dement* 10(4):P149–P150, 2014.

Rominger A, Brendel M, Burgold S, Keppler K, Baumann K, Xiong G, et al: Longitudinal assessment of cerebral β-amyloid deposition in mice overexpressing Swedish mutant β-amyloid precursor protein using 18F-florbetaben PET, *J Nucl Med* 54(7):1127–1134, 2013.

Rosenbloom MH, Alkalay A, Agarwal N, Baker SL, O'Neil JP, Janabi M, et al: Distinct clinical and metabolic deficits in PCA and AD are not related to amyloid distribution, *Neurology* 76(21):1789–1796, 2011.

Rostomian AH, Madison C, Rabinovici GD, Jagust WJ: Early 11C-PIB frames and 18F-FDG PET measures are comparable: a study validated in a cohort of AD and FTLD patients, *J Nucl Med* 52(2):173–179, 2011.

Rousset OG, Ma Y, Evans AC: Correction for partial volume effects in PET: principle and validation, *J Nucl Med* 39(5):904–911, 1998.

Rowe C: The centiloid scale: standardization of amyloid imaging measures, Alzheimer's Imaging Consortium–Alzheimer's Association International Conference, Boston, MA, 2013.

Rowe CC, Ellis KA, Rimajova M, Bourgeat P, Pike KE, Jones G, et al: Amyloid imaging results from the Australian Imaging, Biomarkers and Lifestyle (AIBL) study of aging, *Neurobiol Aging* 31:1275–1283, 2010.

Sabbagh MN, Fleisher A, Chen K, Rogers J, Berk C, Reiman E, et al: Positron emission tomography and neuropathologic estimates of fibrillar amyloid-β in a patient with Down syndrome and Alzheimer disease, *Arch Neurol* 68:1461–1466, 2011.

Sabri O, Sabbagh MN, Seibyl J, Barthel H, Akatsu H, Ouchi Y, et al: Florbetaben PET imaging to detect amyloid beta plaques in Alzheimer disease: phase 3 study, *Alzheimers Dement* 11(8):964–974, 2015.

Saha GB: Basics of PET imaging: physics, chemistry and regulations [e-book], 2005, Springer.

Saha JK, Xia J, Grondin JM, Engle SK, Jakubowski JA: Acute hyperglcemia induced by ketamine/xylazine anesthesia in rats: mechanisms and implications for preclinical models, *Exp Biol Med* 230(10):777–784, 2005.

Salloway S, Sperling R, Fox NC, Blennow K, Klunk W, Raskind M, et al: Two phase 3 trials of bapineuzumab in mild-to-moderate Alzheimer's disease, *N Engl J Med* 370(4):322–333, 2014.

Samuel W, Masliah E, Hill LR, Butters N, Terry R: Hippocampal connectivity and Alzheimer's dementia: effects of synapse loss and tangle frequency in a two-component model, *Neurology* 44(11):2081, 1994.

Schmidt K, Lucignani G, Moresco RM, Rizzo G, Gilardi MC, Messa C, et al: Errors introduced by tissue heterogeneity in estimation of local cerebral glucose utilization with current kinetic models of the [18F]fluorodeoxyglucose method, *J Cerebr Blood Flow Metab* 12(5):823–834, 1992.

Schmidt R, Ropele S, Pendl B, Ofner P, Enzinger C, Schmidt H, et al: Longitudinal multimodal imaging in mild to moderate Alzheimer disease: a pilot study with memantine, *J Neurol Neurosur Psychiat* 79(12):1312–1317, 2008.

Schmidt ME, Chiao P, Klein G, Matthews D, Thurfjell L, Cole PE, et al: The influence of biological and technical factors on quantitative analysis of amyloid PET: points to consider and recommendations for controlling variability in longitudinal data, *Alzheimers Dement* 11(9):1050–1068, 2015.

Schneider LS, Kennedy RE, Cutter GR: Requiring an amyloid-b1-42 biomarker for prodromal Alzheimer's disease or mild cognitive impairment does not lead to more efficient clinical trials, *Alzheimers Dement* 6:367–377, 2010.

Schöll M, Lockhart SN, Schonhaut DR, O'Neil JP, Janabi M, Ossenkoppele R, et al: PET imaging of tau deposition in the aging human brain, *Neuron* 89:971–982, 2016.

Sevigny J: Clinical trials and translational studies targeting Abeta aducanumab (BIIB037), an anti-amyloid beta monoclonal antibody, in patients with prodromal or mild Alzheimer's disease: interim results of a randomized, double-blind, placebo-controlled, phase 1B study, AAIC 2015;Washington, DC, 2015.

Shoghi-Jadid K, Small GW, Agdeppa ED, Kepe V, Ercoli LM, Siddarth P, et al: Localization of neurofibrillary tangles and beta-amyloid plaques in the brains of living patients with Alzheimer disease, *Am J Geriat Psychiat* 10(1):24–35, 2002.

Skovronsky DM, Zhang B, Kung MP, Kung HF, Trojanowski JQ, Lee VMY: In vivo detection of amyloid plaques in a mouse model of Alzheimer's disease, *Proc Natl Acad Sci USA* 97(13):7609–7614, 2000.

Smailagic N, Vacante M, Hyde C, Martin S, Ukoumunne O, Sachpekidis C: 18F-FDG PET for the early diagnosis of Alzheimer's disease dementia and other dementias in people with mild cognitive impairment (MCI), *Cochrane Database Syst Rev*: 1, 2015, CD010632.

Snellman A, López-Picón FR, Rokka J, Salmona M, Forloni G, Scheinin M, et al: Longitudinal amyloid imaging in mouse brain with 11C-PIB: comparison of APP23, Tg2576, and APPswe-PS1dE9 mouse models of Alzheimer disease, *J Nucl Med* 54(8):1434–1441, 2013.

Sokoloff L, Reivich M, Kennedy C, Rosiers MHD, Patlak CS, Pettigrew KD, et al: The [14C]deoxyglucose method for the measurement of local cerebral glucose utilization: theory, procedure, and normal values in the conscious and anesthetized albino rat, *J Neurochem* 28(5):897–916, 1977.

Sperling RA, Aisen PS, Beckett LA, Bennett DA, Craft S, Fagan AM, et al: Toward defining the preclinical stages of Alzheimer's disease: recommendations from the National Institute on Aging–Alzheimer's Association workgroups on diagnostic guidelines for Alzheimer's disease, *Alzheimers Dement* 7(3):280–292, 2011.

Sperling RA, Rentz DM, Johnson KA, Karlawish J, Donohue M, Salmon DP, et al: The A4 study: stopping AD before symptoms begin? *Sci Translational Med* 6(228):228fs13, 2014.

Stankoff B, Freeman L, Aigrot MS, Chardain A, Dolle F, Williams A, et al: Imaging central nervous system myelin by positron emission tomography in multiple sclerosis using [methyl-(1)(1)C]-2-(4′-methylaminophenyl)-6-hydroxybenzothiazole, *Ann Neurol* 69(4):673–680, 2011.

Su Y, Blazey TM, Snyder AZ, Raichle ME, Marcus DS, Ances BM, et al: Partial volume correction in quantitative amyloid imaging, *NeuroImage* 107:55–64, 2015.

Terry RD, Masliah E, Salmon DP, Butters N, DeTeresa R, Hill R, et al: Physical basis of cognitive alterations in Alzheimer's disease: synapse loss is the major correlate of cognitive impairment, *Ann Neurol* 30(4):572–580, 1991.

Thompson PW, Ye L, Morgenstern JL, Sue L, Beach TG, Judd DJ, et al: Interaction of the amyloid imaging tracer FDDNP with hallmark Alzheimer's disease pathologies, *J Neurochem* 109(2):623–630, 2009.

Tolboom N, Yaqub M, Boellaard R, Luurtsema G, Windhorst A, Scheltens P, et al: Test–retest variability of quantitative [11C]PIB studies in Alzheimer's disease, *Eur J Nucl Med Mol Imaging* 36(10):1629–1638, 2009.

Toledo J, Cairns N, Da X, Chen K, Carter D, Fleisher A, et al: Clinical and multimodal biomarker correlates of ADNI neuropathological findings, *Acta Neuropathol Commun* 1(1):65, 2013.

Toledo J, Weiner M, Wolk D, Da X, Chen K, Arnold S, et al: Neuronal injury biomarkers and prognosis in ADNI subjects with normal cognition, *Acta Neuropathologica Communications* 2(1):26, 2014.

Toyama H, Ichise M, Liow J-S, Vines DC, Seneca NM, Modell KJ, et al: Evaluation of anesthesia effects on [18F]FDG uptake in mouse brain and heart using small animal PET, *Nucl Med Biol* 31(2):251–256, 2004.

Toyama H, Ye D, Ichise M, Liow JS, Cai L, Jacobowitz D, et al: PET imaging of brain with the beta-amyloid probe, [11C]6-OH-BTA-1, in a transgenic mouse model of Alzheimer's disease, *Eur J Nucl Med Mol Imaging* 32(5):593–600, 2005.

Vachon P, Moreau JP: Serum corticosterone and blood glucose in rats after two jugular vein blood sampling methods: comparison of the stress response, *J Am Assoc Lab Anim* 40(5):22–24, 2001.

Valla J, Chen K, Berndt JD, Gonzalez-Lima F, Cherry SR, Games D, et al: Effects of image resolution on autoradiographic measurements of posterior cingulate activity in PDAPP mice: implications for functional brain imaging studies of transgenic mouse models of Alzheimer's disease, *NeuroImage* 16(1):1–6, 2002.

Valla J, Schneider L, Reiman EM: Age- and transgene-related changes in regional cerebral metabolism in PSAPP mice, *Brain Res* 1116(1):194–200, 2006.

Valla J, Gonzalez-Lima F, Reiman EM: FDG autoradiography reveals developmental and pathological effects of mutant amyloid in PDAPP transgenic mice, *Int J Dev Neurosci* 26(3-4):253–258, 2008.

Valla J, Yaari R, Wolf AB, Kusne Y, Beach TG, Roher AE, et al: Reduced posterior cingulate mitochondrial activity in expired young adult carriers of the APOE ε4 allele, the major late-onset Alzheimer's susceptibility gene, *J Alzheimers Dis* 22(1):307–313, 2010.

van Berckel BNM, Ossenkoppele R, Tolboom N, Yaqub M, Foster-Dingley JC, Windhorst AD, et al: Longitudinal amyloid imaging using 11C-PiB: methodologic considerations, *J Nucl Med* 54(9):1570–1576, 2013.

van der Veen DR, Shao J, Chapman S, Leevy WM, Duffield GE: A 24-hour temporal profile of in vivo brain and heart PET imaging reveals a nocturnal peak in brain 18F-fluorodeoxyglucose uptake, *PLoS One* 7(2):e31792, 2012.

Vandenberghe R, Van Laere K, Ivanoiu A, Salmon E, Bastin C, Triau E, et al: 18F-flutemetamol amyloid imaging in Alzheimer disease and mild cognitive impairment: a phase 2 trial, *Ann Neurol* 68(3):319–329, 2010.

Varrone A, Asenbaum S, Borght T, Booij J, Nobili F, Någren K, et al: EANM procedure guidelines for PET brain imaging using [18F]FDG, version 2, *Eur J Nucl Med Mol Imaging* 36(12):2103–2110, 2009.

Vigo-Pelfrey C, Lee D, Keim P, Lieberburg I, Schenk DB: Rapid communication: characterization of β-amyloid peptide from human cerebrospinal fluid, *J Neurochem* 61(5):1965–1968, 1993.

Villemagne VL, Fodero-Tavoletti MT, Masters CL, Rowe CC: Tau imaging: early progress and future directions, *Lancet Neurol* 14(1):114–124, 2015.

Villemagne V, Mulligan R, Pejoska S, Ong K, Jones G, O'Keefe G, et al: Comparison of 11C-PiB and 18F-florbetaben for Aβ imaging in ageing and Alzheimer's disease, *Eur J Nucl Med Mol I* 39(6):983–989, 2012.

Villemagne V, Furumoto S, Fodero-Tavoletti M, Mulligan R, Hodges J, Harada R, et al: In vivo evaluation of a novel tau imaging tracer for Alzheimer's disease, *Eur J Nucl Med Mol Imaging* 41(5):816–826, 2014.

Villeneuve S, Rabinovici GD, Cohn-Sheehy BI, Madison C, Ayakta N, Ghosh PM, et al: Existing Pittsburgh compound-B positron emission tomography thresholds are too high: statistical and pathological evaluation, *Brain* 138(7):2020–2033, 2015.

Vlassenko AG, Mintun MA, Xiong C, Sheline YI, Goate AM, Md TLS, et al: Amyloid-beta plaque growth in cognitively normal adults: longitudinal PIB data, *Ann Neurol*, 70(5):857–861, 2011.

Volkow ND, Rosen B, Farde L: Imaging the living human brain: magnetic resonance imaging and positron emission tomography, *Proc Natl Acad Sci USA* 94(7):2787–2788, 1997.

von Reutern B, Grünecker B, Yousefi B, Henriksen G, Czisch M, Drzezga A: Voxel-based analysis of amyloid-burden measured with [11C]PiB PET in a double transgenic mouse model of Alzheimer's disease, *Mol Imaging Biol* 15(5):576–584, 2013.

Wahl RL, Henry CA, Ethier SP: Serum glucose: effects on tumor and normal tissue accumulation of 2-[F-18]-fluoro-2-deoxy-D-glucose in rodents with mammary carcinoma, *Radiology* 183(3):643–647, 1992.

Waldron A-M, Verhaeghe J, Wyffels L, Schmidt M, Langlois X, Van Der Linden A, et al: Preclinical comparison of the amyloid-β radioligands [11C]Pittsburgh compound B and [18F]florbetaben in aged APPPS1-21 and BRI1-42 mouse models of cerebral amyloidosis, *Mol Imaging Biol* 17(5):688–696, 2015a.

Waldron A-M, Wyffels L, Verhaeghe J, Bottelbergs A, Richardson J, Kelley J, et al: Quantitative μPET imaging of cerebral glucose metabolism and amyloidosis in the TASTPM double transgenic mouse model of Alzheimer's disease, *Curr Alzheimer Res* 12(7):694–703, 2015b.

Walsh DM, Klyubin I, Fadeeva JV, Rowan MJ, Selkoe DJ: Amyloid-beta oligomers: their production, toxicity and therapeutic inhibition, *Biochem Soc Trans* 30(4):552–557, 2002.

Wang G-J, Volkow ND, Overall J, Hitzemann RJ, Pappas N, Pascani K, et al: Reproducibility of regional brain metabolic responses to Lorazepam, *J Nucl Med* 37(10):1609–1613, 1996.

Weigand SD, Vemuri P, Wiste HJ, Senjem ML, Pankratz VS, Aisen PS, et al: Transforming cerebrospinal fluid Ab42 measures into calculated Pittsburgh compound B units of brain Ab amyloid, *Alzheimers Dement* 7:133–141, 2011.

Welch A, Mingarelli M, Riedel G, Platt B: Mapping changes in mouse brain metabolism with PET/CT, *J Nucl Med* 54(11):1946–1953, 2013.

Wolk DA, Zhang Z, Boudhar S, Clark CM, Pontecorvo MJ, Arnold SE: Amyloid imaging in Alzheimer's disease: comparison of florbetapir and Pittsburgh compound-B positron emission tomography, *J Neurol Neurosur Psychiat* 83(9):923–926, 2012.

Womack KB, Diaz-Arrastia R, Aizenstein HJ, et al: Temporoparietal hypometabolism in frontotemporal lobar degeneration and associated imaging diagnostic errors, *Arch Neurol* 68(3):329–337, 2011.

Wong DF, Rosenberg PB, Zhou Y, Kumar A, Raymont V, Ravert HT, et al: In vivo imaging of amyloid deposition in Alzheimer disease using the radioligand 18F-AV-45 (florbetapir [corrected] F 18), *J Nucl Med* 51(6):913–920, 2010a.

Wong KP, Wardak M, Shao W, Dahlbom M, Kepe V, Liu J, et al: Quantitative analysis of [18F]FDDNP PET using subcortical white matter as reference region, *Eur J Nucl Med Mol Imaging* 37(3):575–588, 2010b.

Wong K-P, Sha W, Zhang X, Huang S-C: Effects of administration route, dietary condition, and blood glucose level on kinetics and uptake of 18F-FDG in mice, *J Nucl Med* 52(5):800–807, 2011.

Woo BKP, Harwood DG, Melrose RJ, Mandelkern MA, Campa OM, Walston A, et al: Executive deficits and regional brain metabolism in Alzheimer's disease, *Int J Geriatr Psychiatr* 25(11):1150–1158, 2010.

Woosley RL, Myers RT, Goodsaid F: The Critical Path Institute's approach to precompetitive sharing and advancing regulatory science, *Clin Pharmacol Ther* 87:530–533, 2010.

Yaqub M, Tolboom N, Boellaard R, van Berckel BNM, van Tilburg EW, Luurtsema G, et al: Simplified parametric methods for [11C]PIB studies, *NeuroImage* 42(1):76–86, 2008.

Ye L, Morgenstern JL, Gee AD, Hong G, Brown J, Lockhart A: Delineation of positron emission tomography imaging agent binding sites on β-amyloid peptide fibrils, *J Biol Chem* 280(25):23599–23604, 2005.

Zahn R, Juengling F, Bubrowski P, Jost E, Dykierek P, Talazko J, et al: Hemispheric asymmetries of hypometabolism associated with semantic memory impairment in Alzheimer's disease: a study using positron emission tomography with fluorodeoxyglucose-F18, *Psychiat Res-Neuroim* 132(2):159–172, 2004.

Zhang L, Villalobos A, Beck EM, Bocan T, Chappie TA, Chen L, et al: Design and selection parameters to accelerate the discovery of novel central nervous system positron emission tomography (PET) ligands and their application in the development of a novel phosphodiesterase 2A PET ligand, *J Med Chem* 56(11):4568–4579, 2013.

CHAPTER

21

Fluid Biomarkers and Diagnostics

H. Zetterberg, K. Blennow

OUTLINE

INTRODUCTION

Traditionally, the neuropathology of Alzheimer's disease (AD) is considered to have three main features: (1) gross atrophy due to neuronal degeneration and loss, (2) extracellular argyrophilic accumulations called plaques, and (3) intraneuronal inclusions called neurofibrillary tangles (Blennow et al., 2006). Glenner and Wong (1984a) purified and sequenced a protein derived from twisted β-pleated sheet fibrils in cerebrovascular amyloidosis of AD

Developing Therapeutics for Alzheimer's Disease. http://dx.doi.org/10.1016/B978-0-12-802173-6.00021-6

brains. They called the protein amyloid fibril protein β. The year after, Masters and Beyreuther established the presence of an approximately 40-amino-acid-long protein, with a sequence similar to the one Glenner and Wong had reported, in plaques from brains of patients with AD and Down syndrome (Masters et al., 1985). The protein, or peptide, was originally called the A4 protein because of its 4 kDa molecular weight. This term has now virtually disappeared in favor of amyloid β (Aβ). It is now known that the predominant Aβ forms in plaques are (in descending order) Aβ4–42 (Aβ starting at amino acid 4 in the Aβ domain and ending at amino acid 42 after a stretch of hydrophobic amino acids making the protein self-adhesive), Aβ1–42, Aβ1–40, and pyro-glutamate-modified Aβ3–42 (Portelius et al., 2010a). In 1986, data were published showing that an abnormally hyperphosphorylated form of tau protein is the main component of neurofibrillary tangles (Grundke-Iqbal et al., 1986; Nukina and Ihara, 1986). Tau is a microtubule-binding axonal protein that promotes microtubule assembly and stability. Abnormal phosphorylation and truncation of tau may lead to disassembly of microtubules and impaired axonal transport with compromised neuronal function, which is believed to cause tau aggregation into paired helical filaments and neurofibrillary tangles (Mandelkow and Mandelkow, 2012). The in-depth characterization of the molecular composition of plaques and tangles constitutes the basis for modern AD biomarker research. In the fluid biomarker field, most progress has been made on cerebrospinal fluid (CSF) markers. This progress has occurred in parallel with the development of imaging techniques to detect and quantify cerebral tau and Aβ accumulations using molecular tracers. Altogether, AD biomarker research during the past 20 years has made it possible to examine the impact of AD pathology on symptoms and clinical disease progression in prospective studies of living human beings.

BIOMARKER CONCEPT

A biomarker can be defined as a characteristic that is an indicator of a normal or pathological biological process, or of a pharmacological response to a therapeutic intervention that can be objectively measured. Biomarkers can be used for several purposes: to guide clinical diagnosis (so-called diagnostic markers), to estimate disease risk or prognosis (prognostic markers), to evaluate disease stage (staging markers), and to monitor progression or response to therapy (theragnostic markers). In clinical trials, biomarkers can be used to select a specific diagnostic subgroup (ie, sample enrichment or patient stratification), to ensure appropriate therapeutic target engagement, to identify downstream effects of therapeutics on the disease process, and as a measure of clinical efficacy and/or safety.

CSF IN ALZHEIMER'S DISEASE

CSF is located in the cerebral ventricles and in the subarachnoid space that surrounds the brain and the spinal cord. It communicates freely with the brain interstitial fluid, and may thereby serve as a biochemical window into the brain. CSF investigations in AD were pioneered by Gottfries et al. (1969, 1970), who reported reduced CSF monoamine metabolite concentrations in AD, suggesting a breakdown of these neurotransmitter systems in the deteriorating brain, and elevated CSF lactate concentration as a sign of tissue hypoxia (Gottfries et al., 1974). During the 1990s, tests for proteins thought to reflect the core neuropathology of AD were developed.

CSF Aβ42

Initially, just after the identification of aggregation-prone Aβ proteins ending at amino acids 40 and 42 in plaques (Glenner and Wong, 1984a,b; Masters et al., 1985), the protein was thought to be an abnormal side product of amyloid precursor protein (APP) metabolism invariably associated with AD. The natural secretion of Aβ from untransfected primary cells therefore came as a surprise (Haass et al., 1992). Since then, it has been established that APP can enter at least three proteolytic clearance pathways: (1) amyloidogenic processing that primarily leads to production of Aβ42 and Aβ40 (but also some shorter, less aggregation-prone fragments) by successive β- and γ-secretase cleavages; (2) nonamyloidogenic processing that leads to production of sAPPα and possibly also a C-terminal fragment called p3 (this fragment should consist of Aβ17–40/42, but has been difficult to verify using modern techniques); and (3) another nonamyloidogenic processing pathway involving concerted cleavages of APP by β- and α-secretase resulting in production of Aβ1–14/15/16 fragments at the expense of longer Aβ fragments (Portelius et al., 2011). There are also additional processing pathways that result in multiple APP/Aβ fragments that extend N-terminal from the Asp1 site of Aβ, some of which are glycosylated (Halim et al., 2011; Portelius et al., 2013; Welzel et al., 2014).

The first assay for CSF Aβ42 was published in 1995 (Motter et al., 1995). Using this enzyme-linked immunosorbent assay (ELISA), AD patients were shown to have reduced levels of CSF Aβ42, a finding which has since been replicated and verified in hundreds of papers (Rosen et al., 2013). This reduction is thought to reflect Aβ42 sequestration in senile plaques in the brain, as evidenced by autopsy, biopsy, and in vivo imaging studies (Strozyk et al., 2003; Fagan et al., 2006; Forsberg et al., 2008; Seppala et al., 2012). In 1999, the first paper showing a reduction in CSF Aβ42 in patients with mild cognitive impairment (MCI) who later developed AD dementia was published (Andreasen et al., 1999). Since then, numerous studies have verified that low CSF Aβ42 levels are highly predictive of future AD, both in MCI (Hansson et al., 2006; Shaw et al., 2009; Visser et al., 2009; Buchhave et al., 2012) and in cognitively normal cohorts (Skoog et al., 2003; Fagan et al., 2009; Gustafson et al., 2007). Causal mutations aside, CSF Aβ42 remains the earliest biomarker currently available in AD, and as a result CSF Aβ42 is now incorporated into new criteria for the diagnosis of AD, also in predementia stages (Dubois et al., 2014).

Besides Aβ42, several other Aβ isoforms are present in CSF. The most abundant variant in CSF is Aβ40, which is relatively unchanged in AD. The ratio of CSF Aβ42 to Aβ40 has been suggested to have stronger diagnostic accuracy for AD compared to CSF Aβ42 alone (Schoonenboom et al., 2005), potentially by normalizing individuals according to their Aβ production level, so that low CSF Aβ42 can be more easily detected in "high Aβ producers" and vice versa (Wiltfang et al., 2007). There are also several other C- or N-terminally truncated Aβ isoforms in CSF, which may be altered in AD (Portelius et al., 2006), also in the earliest clinical stages (Mattsson et al., 2012a).

CSF T-tau

The first CSF total tau (T-tau) assay was published in 1993 (Vandermeeren et al., 1993). This was a sandwich ELISA in which a monoclonal antibody against the middomain of tau was combined with a polyclonal antitau antiserum. Two years later, the first assay based on three midregion monoclonal antibodies, which recognizes all tau isoforms irrespective of phosphorylation state, was published (Blennow et al., 1995). This assay is today known as the "innogenetics assay." Using this assay, AD patients were shown to have clearly elevated T-tau levels (Vandermeeren et al., 1993; Blennow et al., 1995), a finding that has been replicated in hundreds of papers, using several different assays, in many different clinical contexts (Rosen et al., 2013). It has been shown that CSF T-tau levels correlate with imaging measures of hippocampal atrophy (Wang et al., 2012) and gray matter degeneration (Glodzik et al., 2012), findings in keeping with the known high expression of tau in thin unmyelinated axons of the cortex (Trojanowski et al., 1989). In response to acute brain injury, CSF T-tau levels are dynamic; they increase during the first few days following injury and stay elevated for a few weeks to months until they normalize (Hesse et al., 2001; Zetterberg et al., 2006). This has led to the view that elevated CSF T-tau levels reflect ongoing axonal degeneration, which in turn may indicate disease activity. Indeed, CSF T-tau predicts the rapidity of the clinical course in AD; the higher the levels, the more rapid the clinical disease progression (Wallin et al., 2010). Accordingly, in severe and rapid neurodegeneration such as Creutzfeldt–Jakob disease (CJD), CSF T-tau elevations that are orders of magnitude higher than in typical AD are seen (Sanchez-Juan et al., 2007). Also in this disorder, the degree of tau elevation correlates with clinical disease progression; very high levels predict short remaining survival time (Skillback et al., 2014b).

Two recent discoveries have made the tau biomarker field more complex. These include preclinical studies reporting on tau secretion from cultured cells (Saman et al., 2012) and mouse neurons (Maia et al., 2013) that may be stimulated by Aβ in the absence of neuronal death (Maia et al., 2013), and patient studies reporting that most of the tau in human CSF seems to be fragmented (Meredith et al., 2013). Tau secretion in the absence of neurodegeneration is not unexpected, as it has been known for decades that tau is present in CSF of healthy individuals also (Blennow et al., 2010). Nonetheless, this raises some important issues from a practical perspective, as it suggests that tau elevation may not simply be considered a surrogate marker of neurodegeneration. Moreover, the mechanism of tau elevation in AD may well be at least partially independent of neuronal death. The latter would be consistent with tau changes seen in other forms of brain injury and the observation of intraneuronal increase in tau expression following acute experimental brain injury in animals (Uryu et al., 2007).

The finding that most CSF tau seems to be in fragmented forms is consistent with well-established evidence that endogenous tau fragments are found in tangles (Wischik et al., 1988). It may also explain why it has been important to have capture and detection antibodies located closely to each other in T-tau assays, and why combinations of distally located N- and C-terminal antibodies do not work (Meredith et al., 2013). The clinical significance of these fragments is not known, and it remains challenging to accomplish a reliable quantification.

CSF P-tau

The first CSF assay for phosphorylated tau (P-tau), the form of tau that is believed to show the closest association with neurofibrillary tangle load, was published in 1995 (Blennow et al., 1995). Since then, a variety of P-tau assays measuring different forms of phosphorylated tau proteins have been developed (Hampel et al., 2004). Broadly speaking, these assays correlate well with one another and show similar findings in AD (Hampel et al., 2004). CSF P-tau levels correlate with neurofibrillary tangle pathology in AD (Seppala et al., 2012; Buerger et al., 2006), but a major outstanding research question is why other tauopathies, including some forms of frontotemporal lobar degeneration and progressive supranuclear palsy, do not show P-tau elevation, at least not as systematically as seen in AD. It is possible that tau pathology in these disorders is less abundant than in AD, but it is also possible that these other tauopathies show disease-specific tau phosphorylation, or that tau is processed or truncated in a way that is not recognized by currently available assays. However, determining the relative specificity of P-tau elevation and AD has considerable advantages in differentiating different neurodegenerative diseases. For example, the ratio of T-tau to P-tau is a quite specific test for CJD (Skillback et al., 2014b; Riemenschneider et al., 2003).

Diagnostic Performance of Combined CSF T-tau, P-tau, and Aβ42 Tests

Multiple studies have investigated the diagnostic accuracy of combined CSF tests for T-tau, P-tau, and Aβ42 (Blennow et al., 2010). These studies collectively suggest that, in cross-sectional studies aiming to distinguish AD from controls and in longitudinal studies aiming to determine which MCI patients will develop AD, combinations of tau and Aβ markers perform better than each biomarker alone (Blennow et al., 2010). Higher diagnostic performance is typically seen in single-center studies (Hansson et al., 2006; Johansson et al., 2011), whereas large multicenter studies tend to report slightly lower sensitivities and specificities (Visser et al., 2009; Mattsson et al., 2009). The association of elevated T-tau and P-tau and reduced Aβ42 with AD neuropathology has been validated in autopsy (Shaw et al., 2009) and brain biopsy (Seppala et al., 2012) studies. The influence of AD phenotype on CSF biomarkers has been less thoroughly explored in other clinical variants of AD, including AD presenting with logopenic primary progressive aphasia (Bibl et al., 2011) or corticobasal degeneration (Borroni et al., 2011).

Longitudinal Changes in CSF AD Biomarkers in Observational and Intervention Studies

Recent data show that it is possible to identify longitudinal changes in CSF Aβ42, T-tau, and P-tau in cognitively healthy controls followed over several years (Toledo et al., 2013; Mattsson et al., 2013b; Moghekar et al., 2013), although most studies (with exceptions; Toledo et al., 2013) show that CSF AD biomarkers are essentially stable once patients have converted to AD (Mattsson et al., 2012a; Zetterberg et al., 2007; Blennow et al., 2007). This biomarker stability, at least during short-term (months to a few years) follow-up periods, may be useful in clinical trials to help identify effects of interventions on the intended biological target, such as altered Aβ metabolism in response to an anti-Aβ treatment. In pharmacodynamic studies, CSF measurements may be used to track trajectories of specific Aβ and APP metabolites (Mattsson et al., 2012b; Lannfelt et al., 2008; May et al., 2011; Portelius et al., 2010b), as well as downstream effects, such as reduced axonal degeneration as reflected by CSF tau levels in response to a disease-modifying drug (Gilman et al., 2005; Blennow et al., 2012). One of the relatively few longitudinal studies of cognitively normal individuals, where repeated lumbar punctures were made, suggests that Aβ42 and tau changes occur in parallel and predict incident cognitive symptoms better than absolute baseline levels (Moghekar et al., 2013). A recent study shows that individuals who are close to the cut point for abnormal CSF Aβ42 are more likely to drop further in CSF Aβ42 levels, suggesting that these are actively depositing Aβ42 (Mattsson et al., 2015). However, further data from clinical studies with repeated longitudinal biomarker assessments are needed to understand when in time during the preclinical period of AD the three core CSF biomarkers change from normal to AD-like levels, as well as whether they change close in time to each other and to other AD biomarkers such as amyloid and tau PET imaging.

CANDIDATE AD BIOMARKERS AND MARKERS OF OTHER PATHOLOGIES

As explained earlier, despite sharing the same core pathology, AD does show heterogeneity in terms of both phenotype and pathological comorbidities. Thus, etiologically, phenotypically, and pathologically, AD in an 85-year-old person with type II diabetes, hypertension, and sleep apnea is likely to show considerable differences compared to AD in an otherwise healthy 60-year-old with a positive family history. AD in advanced age has been suggested to be highly multifactorial, with age-related changes and multiple other pathologies contributing on top of less advanced AD pathology (plaques and tangles) to the clinical phenotype (Blennow and Wallin, 1992). There are also several other conditions that may contribute to AD-like cerebral dysfunction (Schott and Warren, 2012). A recent clinicopathologic study reported that dementia with Lewy bodies, cerebrovascular disease, frontotemporal lobar degeneration, and hippocampal sclerosis are the most prevalent AD mimics (Shim et al., 2013). Interestingly, the clinical phenotype can vary considerably, although the same brain plaque and tangle pathology can be seen, as demonstrated for the nonamnestic AD variants, including posterior cortical atrophy and logopenic or progressive nonfluent aphasia (Schott and Warren, 2012). Some of this variation may be explained by coexisting pathologies for which we need better biomarkers. For example, we currently lack well-functioning biomarkers for TDP-43 and α-synuclein (Lewy body) pathologies, which are highly prevalent in the brains of individuals who have died in the course of an AD-like disease—such pathologies are unlikely to be simply coincidental, but our ability to address any contributory effects in vivo in the absence of biomarkers is at present very limited (Nag et al., 2015; Schneider et al., 2012; Josephs et al., 2014).

CSF BACE1

As described previously, in the amyloidogenic pathway, Aβ is produced through proteolytic processing of APP by β- and γ-secretases. The major β-secretase in the brain is the β-site

APP-cleaving enzyme 1 (BACE1) (Andreasson et al., 2007). Increased BACE1 activity has been measured in postmortem samples from patients with AD (Fukumoto et al., 2002). The activity and concentration of BACE1 can also be measured in CSF, but the results have been conflicting. Holsinger et al. (2004, 2006) found an increase in the activity of CSF BACE1 in AD patients, as well as in patients with other dementias compared to nonneurological controls. The activity of CSF BACE1 was also found to be elevated in patients with MCI who progressed to AD compared to subjects with MCI who remained stable or developed other forms of dementia (Zetterberg et al., 2008). Many studies, however, have failed to show any significant difference in BACE1 activity between MCI and AD patients compared to controls (Mulder et al., 2010; Zhong et al., 2007), and one study suggested that CSF BACE1 activity may drop in advanced disease stages (Rosen et al., 2012). Altogether, the discrepant results of these studies suggest that the diagnostic value of BACE1 in AD is limited. However, the marker may still be valuable in certain circumstances, for example, as a pharmacodynamic marker in clinical trials of putative BACE1 inhibitors (May et al., 2011).

CSF sAPPα/sAPPβ

Theoretically, secreted forms of APP should be excellent fluid markers of amyloidogenic (sAPPβ) and nonamyloidogenic (sAPPα) APP processing. The proteins are readily measureable in CSF, but several studies have failed to show any differences between AD patients and controls (Johansson et al., 2011; Zetterberg et al., 2008; Olsson et al., 2003). In the context of MCI, one study reported elevated CSF sAPPβ in patients with MCI compared with controls (Olsson et al., 2003), and another study showed increased levels of CSF sAPPβ in MCI patients who progressed to AD compared to patients who remained stable (Perneczky et al., 2011). Studies that grouped patients on the basis of CSF tau and Aβ markers into those with and without biomarker support for AD found elevated levels of CSF sAPPα and sAPPβ in the group displaying AD-like changes (Lewczuk et al., 2010, 2012; Gabelle et al., 2010). However, in the absence of a cognitively normal control group, these studies did not take into account that the differences might have been driven by lower levels of sAPPα and sAPPβ among non-AD cases, and not by increase in AD. Similarly to BACE1, the results of studies exploring CSF sAPPα and sAPPβ as potential biomarkers for AD have been sufficiently inconsistent and are still not useful in clinical practice. However, these biomarkers may be valuable in clinical trials to monitor the effect of novel therapies targeting APP metabolism.

Aβ Oligomers

The correlation between amyloid plaque cerebral load and disease severity is poor (Castellani and Smith, 2011). To reconcile this observation with the amyloid cascade hypothesis, it has been suggested that most of the presumed Aβ toxicity is exerted by soluble portions of Aβ, while the plaques per se are relatively inert. Walsh et al. (2002) showed that soluble oligomers of Aβ inhibit hippocampal long-term potentiation in rats, and others have reported that they can lead to abnormal phosphorylation of tau as well as neuritic dystrophy (Zempel et al., 2010; Jin et al., 2011; De Felice et al., 2008). Not surprisingly, higher levels of oligomers have been shown in the brains of AD patients than in controls (Bruggink et al., 2013; Shankar et al., 2008), but results from several studies trying to replicate these findings in CSF have been inconsistent. Some studies have found elevated CSF Aβ oligomer levels in patients with AD (Gao et al., 2010; Fukumoto et al., 2010; Georganopoulou et al., 2005; Pitschke et al., 1998; Holtta et al., 2013) or in cognitively normal older adults with an AD-like biomarker profile (Handoko et al., 2013), whereas others have not found this relationship (Bruggink et al., 2013; Santos et al., 2007). A consistent problem when developing oligomer assays is the unreliable quantification due to their low concentration in CSF. Moreover, "oligomers" include species ranging from dimers to protofibrils, and most studies to date are using methods that cannot distinguish between these various forms.

Blood–Brain Barrier Biomarkers

The best-established biomarker so far for the integrity of the blood–brain barrier is the CSF/serum albumin ratio. Typically, this ratio is normal in patients with pure AD (Blennow et al., 1990b), whereas patients with cerebral small-vessel disease generally have an increased CSF/serum albumin ratio (Wallin et al., 1999). The same finding is often present in Lyme disease (neuroborreliosis), where typically there also is an increased number of CSF monocytes and evidence of immunoglobulin production within the central nervous system (CNS) (Tumani et al., 1995). Other less well established blood–brain biomarkers in CSF include secretory Ca^{2+}-dependent phospholipase A2 activity (Chalbot et al., 2010) and antithrombin III (Zetterberg et al., 2009). More research is warranted in this field, especially to develop assays to differentiate between specific forms of blood–brain barrier dysfunction.

Additional Biomarkers for Neurodegeneration

CSF biomarker candidates other than tau proteins that may reflect AD-like neurodegeneration are visinin-like protein 1, a neuronal protein which is elevated in AD patients and correlates with T-tau concentration (Lee et al., 2008), and trefoil factor 3, a gastrointestinal protein with unknown function in the CNS, which just emerged as a strong predictor of brain atrophy rates in the Alzheimer's Disease Neuroimaging Initiative (Paterson et al., 2014).

An established biomarker for subcortical axonal degeneration that is frequently seen in potential AD mimics, such as cerebral small-vessel disease (Rosengren et al., 1999; Agren-Wilsson et al., 2007; Wallin and Sjogren, 2001), frontotemporal lobar degeneration (De Jong et al., 2007; Landqvist Waldo et al., 2013), and HIV-associated dementia (Gisslen et al., 2007), is neurofilament light protein (NFL). NFL, as well as other members of the neurofilament group of proteins, acts as an integral part of the neural cytoskeleton, providing structural support for predominantly large-caliber myelinated axons. Elevated CSF NFL levels indicate involvement of these axons in the disease process and can help differentiate pure AD from the conditions listed earlier, as combined T-tau and NFL increases are common in mixed forms of AD and cerebrovascular disease. These mixed CSF findings are very common in unselected patients undergoing evaluation because of suspected neurodegenerative disease (Skillbäck et al., 2013) and correlate with more rapid disease progression (Skillback et al., 2014a). NFL is also a useful biomarker for damage severity in several other conditions characterized by white matter lesions and injury to subcortical brain regions such as amyotrophic lateral sclerosis (ALS) (Tortelli et al., 2012), various CNS infections (Grahn et al., 2013), and stroke (Rosengren et al., 1996).

Biomarkers for Inflammation, Oxidative Stress, and Microglial Activation

Inflammation, oxidative stress, and microglial activation in AD may be downstream phenomena of neurodegeneration, although recent genetic data suggest that they may well contribute to neurodegenerative disease in susceptible individuals (Guerreiro et al., 2013; Jonsson et al., 2013; Kleinberger et al., 2014). Possible triggers are the accumulation of abnormal proteins (aggregated Aβ in the case of AD) and/or mediators released from dying cells. Such triggers may lead to overshoot inflammation in some individuals, for example, carriers of a recently described loss of function mutation in the microglia-controlling triggering receptor expressed on myeloid cells-2 (*TREM2*) gene (Guerreiro et al., 2013; Jonsson et al., 2013)—perhaps making them more likely to develop clinical AD in response to Aβ.

Many studies have examined potential biomarkers linked to inflammatory processes. Cytokines, such as interleukin 6, transforming growth factor (TGF)-β, tumor necrosis factor α (TNF-α), and interleukin 1β (IL-1β) have been measured in CSF of AD patients, but in one metaanalysis the only consistent finding was of increased CSF levels of TGF-β in AD compared with control groups (Swardfager et al., 2010). Additional candidate inflammatory biomarkers for AD include the cytokine osteopontin, which was elevated in CSF from AD patients (Comi et al., 2010), and the TNF-α-induced proinflammatory agent lipocalin 2, which has been found at lower concentrations in CSF from MCI and AD patients compared with controls (Naude et al., 2012). Another study found that CSF lipocalin 2, also known as neutrophil gelatinase-associated lipocalin, occurred at lower levels in AD and stable MCI patients compared with patients who had AD and vascular risk factors (Rosen et al., 2011).

It should be noted that the biomarker literature contains studies reporting CSF cytokine or interleukin concentrations that are below the analytical sensitivity of the employed assays (IL-1β is just one example), and that standard clinical chemistry tests for neuroinflammation, including CSF leukocyte count and general signs of IgG or IgM production within the CNS, are generally negative in AD and other primary neurodegenerative diseases (Blennow et al., 1990a). Where the CSF shows cells or CSF-selective oligoclonal bands, non-AD pathology should be considered and should motivate further investigation of the patient to exclude infections, multiple sclerosis, and neuroinflammatory conditions that may contribute to the cognitive symptoms (Rossor et al., 2010).

Isoprostanes, in particular a subclass called F2-isoprostanes, are the most examined CSF biomarkers for oxidative stress. They are prostaglandin-like compounds produced by free radical-dependent peroxidation of arachidonic acid (Morrow and Roberts, 1997). Studies report elevated F2-isoprostane levels in AD CSF (Brys et al., 2009; De Leon et al., 2006; Grossman et al., 2005; Montine et al., 1998, 1999) in a manner that appears to be downstream of Aβ pathology (Ringman et al., 2008). CSF isoprostanes correlate to clinical disease progression in the MCI and dementia stages of AD, especially in *APOE* ε4-carrying patients (Duits et al., 2013), and may serve as damage response markers. Pilot studies suggest that the levels of oxidative DNA damage-repair products are elevated in CSF from mixed vascular and Alzheimer's dementia patients (Gackowski et al., 2008), and that reduced levels of mitochondrial DNA in CSF suggest depletion of mitochondria (Podlesniy et al., 2013), which may reflect oxidative stress, but these studies await replication.

Neuroinflammation is tightly linked to activation of the inflammatory M1 phenotype of microglia, the macrophages of the brain. Chitotriosidase is a chitinase enzyme with unknown function in mammals (in plants, fungi, worms, and arthropods, chitinases help in digesting or reshaping chitin) that is secreted by activated macrophages (Renkema et al., 1998), and its plasma levels are increased in patients with the lysosomal storage disorder Gaucher's disease (Hollak et al., 1994). Increased CSF chitotriosidase activity has been found in AD patients compared with nondemented controls (Watabe-Rudolph et al., 2012). A glycoprotein that has great homology with chitotriosidase but lacks its enzymatic activity is YKL-40 (Hakala et al., 1993). YKL-40 is expressed in both microglia and astrocytes, and elevated levels have been reported in both prodromal AD and cerebrovascular disease (Craig-Schapiro et al., 2010; Olsson et al., 2013).

Another microglial marker, the C-C chemokine receptor 2, is expressed on monocytes, and one of its ligands, C-C chemokine ligand 2 (CCL2), that can be produced by microglia is important for the recruitment of monocytes in the CNS (Sokolova et al., 2009). Higher CSF CCL2 levels have been associated with a faster cognitive decline in MCI patients who developed AD (Westin et al., 2012). CCL2 levels in CSF were increased in AD patients compared with healthy controls (Correa et al., 2011; Galimberti et al., 2006a), as well as in the MCI stage of the disease (Galimberti et al., 2006b). However, one study failed to report any significant differences between AD patients and controls (Mattsson et al., 2011b). Another study found elevated CSF CCL2 levels in AD patients compared with controls, but there was an age-dependent increase in the biomarker level that may have affected the result (Blasko et al., 2006). Moreover, one study reported elevated levels of a soluble form of CD14 in the CSF from AD (and Parkinson's disease [PD]) patients compared with healthy controls (Yin et al., 2009). CD14 is a surface protein, mainly expressed by macrophages. As a cofactor for toll-like receptors, CD14 is essential for the recognition of pathogens by the innate immune system of the brain. Another microglial biomarker that has been detected in CSF of AD patients is neopterin, a degradation product deriving from the purine nucleotide guanosine triphosphate. However, no significant differences between AD and controls have been seen to date (Engelborghs et al., 1999).

Taken together, biomarker studies support involvement of low-grade neuroinflammation, oxidative stress, and microglial activation in the AD process, but to date no single biomarker has emerged as being sufficiently robust to have clinical utility. Future longitudinal studies of healthy individuals will most likely help to determine what order these markers change in relation to plaque and tangle pathology and neurodegeneration in AD. A recent study found that CSF levels of several proteins possibly associated with microglia activity predicted longitudinal reduction of CSF Aβ42 in cognitively healthy subjects, suggesting involvement of inflammatory pathways early in the AD disease process (Mattsson et al., 2013b). Although the diagnostic utility of the biomarkers listed in the following is limited, the markers may prove useful to verify target engagement in clinical studies of drugs aimed at modulating microglial activation in AD and also as safety markers to detect overshoot microglial activation and inflammation in Aβ-targeting drug trials.

Biomarkers for Synaptic Changes

Loss of synapses is highly correlated with decrease in neurocognitive function in AD patients (Terry et al., 1991). Therefore, a biomarker that reflects this pathology has very significant potential both for diagnosis and for prognosis. Synaptic proteins such as synaptotagmin, growth-associated protein 43, synaptosomal-associated protein 25 (SNAP-25), rab3a, and neurogranin are abundant in brain tissue, but present at very low concentrations in CSF (Davidsson et al., 1999), thus presenting analytical challenges. Nevertheless, the dendritic protein neurogranin has been detected in CSF, and elevated levels in AD have been observed using a semiquantitative immunoblot method (Thorsell et al., 2010), as well as an ELISA (Kvartsberg et al., 2014). An immunoprecipitation mass spectrometry method has also shown elevated levels of the presynaptic protein SNAP-25 in AD CSF (Brinkmalm et al., 2014). More research is needed to determine the biomarker potential of synaptic proteins in the CSF. Recent breakthroughs in ultrasensitive immunochemical techniques may help in this regard (Blennow and Zetterberg, 2015).

Other Protein Inclusions

α-Synuclein is the major component of intraneuronal Lewy bodies, which are characteristic of PD and dementia with Lewy bodies (Mollenhauer et al., 2010). The α-synuclein pathology is sometimes found together with Aβ plaques and neurofibrillary tangles in AD (Guo et al., 2013), and experimental studies show that Aβ42 enhances aggregation of α-synuclein (Pletnikova et al., 2005). In PD and other synucleinopathies, CSF α-synuclein levels are typically reduced (Hall et al., 2012; Mollenhauer et al., 2011), whereas in AD and CJD the levels are elevated and correlate to T-tau, suggesting that α-synuclein may also be a nonspecific marker of neurodegeneration (Mollenhauer et al., 2011; Tateno et al., 2012; Wennstrom et al., 2013; Ohrfelt et al., 2009). Importantly, α-synuclein is highly expressed in red blood cells, a reason why blood contamination during sample collection may further limit any diagnostic value (Barbour et al., 2008; Hong et al., 2010).

Transactivation response DNA-binding protein of 43 kDa (TDP-43), encoded by the *TARDBP* gene on chromosome 1, is a major component of tau-negative and ubiquitin-positive inclusions that characterize ALS and a number of forms of frontotemporal dementia (FTD) linked to TDP-43 pathology (FTD-TDP) (Neumann et al., 2006). TDP-43 can be measured in CSF (Steinacker et al., 2008), but its levels seem to correlate more with blood levels than with CNS pathology (Feneberg et al., 2014). Truncated or modified forms of TDP-43 that better correlate with the presence of inclusions are now being actively sought. A reliable biomarker for TDP-43 would be an important tool for differential diagnosis in neurodegenerative diseases and also to assess the clinical relevance of TDP-43 pathology in AD.

AD Biomarkers in Blood

While the most successful body fluid for finding biomarkers for AD has undoubtedly been CSF, probably because of its proximity to the brain and the pathologic processes of interest, the identification of one or more blood-based biomarkers would be highly advantageous for routine clinical use. However, despite much research in this field there is still no established blood-based biomarker for AD. Several candidate biomarkers exist, the most promising of which is serum NFL level (Gaiottino et al., 2013). Plasma levels of tau are quantifiable, but their association with AD is weak and there is no correlation to CSF levels (Zetterberg et al., 2013). Aβ42 can be measured in plasma, but there is no correlation to CSF levels, and again the correlation to cerebral β-amyloidosis as measured using amyloid PET is weak (Hansson et al., 2010; Rembach et al., 2014). Brain-derived proteins occur in lower concentrations in blood than in CSF, at least partly because of the blood–brain barrier, which limits the transport of substances between blood vessels and the brain parenchyma, additional problems being binding of proteins of interest to plasma proteins in the blood and protein degradation. Recent approaches using techniques where several biomarkers are analyzed simultaneously have identified some other promising biomarkers (Doecke et al., 2012; Ray et al., 2007), but the results have so far been hard to replicate (Bjorkqvist et al., 2012; Soares et al., 2009).

CSF BIOMARKERS IN RELATION TO THE LATEST CLINICAL TRIALS

The CSF biomarkers just reviewed play several important roles in clinical trials of disease-modifying drug candidates against AD (Fig. 21.1). They may be used as inclusion criteria to verify that the included patients have the pathological changes against which the drug is targeted (Blennow et al., 2010). They may also be used as pharmacodynamic markers (markers of target engagement) to test if the drug had the desired biochemical effect in patients on active treatment and as downstream markers to detect any modifying effect by the drug candidate on the neurodegenerative process (Hampel et al., 2014). From a regulatory perspective, the use of CSF Aβ42 and tau proteins for clinical trials in AD has been qualified by the European Medicines Agency (EMA) (Isaac et al., 2011). The EMA released qualification opinions in Apr. 2011 and Feb. 2012 stating that a pathological signature based on low CSF Aβ42 and high T-tau levels in subjects with MCI was useful for identifying people at increased risk of AD dementia. Given the high sensitivity and moderate specificity, the EMA concluded that this CSF signature was useful for the purpose of enriching clinical trial populations (Isaac et al., 2011). The US Food and Drug Administration has recently released a draft guidance on clinical trials in subjects in the predementia stages of AD (http://www.fda.gov/downloads/Drugs/GuidanceComplianceRegulatoryInformation/Guidances/UCM338287.pdf). According to this guidance document, there is not enough evidence that biomarkers can be used to predict clinical benefit, although they could be used to support disease modification in combination with a clinical outcome measure.

In the context of targeted immunotherapy trials directed against Aβ pathology, two large phase 3 clinical trials in AD using the monoclonal antibodies bapineuzumab and solanezumab have recently been concluded. Bapineuzumab is a humanized monoclonal IgG1 antibody against the Aβ N-terminus (Aβ1–5), based on the murine antibody 3D6, and was intended to promote brain Aβ clearance by binding to aggregated Aβ (Salloway et al., 2009). Solanezumab, on the other hand, a humanized version of the mouse monoclonal antibody m266, raised against Aβ13–28 (Seubert et al., 1992; Siemers et al., 2010), has little or no affinity for the fibrillar form, but binds soluble Aβ (Seubert et al., 2008). In phase 2 studies, bapineuzumab had no clinical efficacy (Salloway et al., 2009), and in the phase 3 study, despite reduced CSF tau levels, the drug failed to reach its primary cognitive outcomes (Salloway et al., 2014). However, it is important to note that biomarker evidence of AD pathology was not a prerequisite for study entry, and that, of those for whom biomarker evidence of AD pathology was available, 38% did not have evidence of underlying AD. In the phase 3 study, solanezumab also did

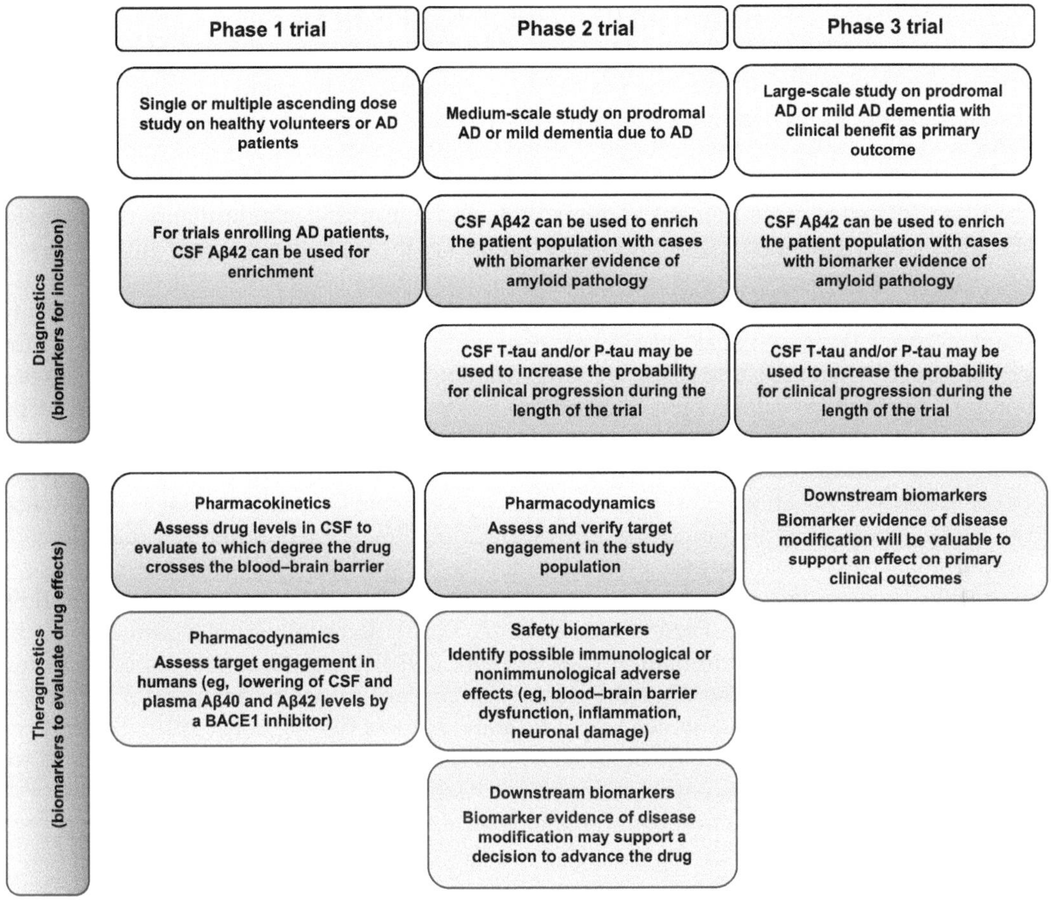

FIGURE 21.1 **Schematic representation of how CSF biomarkers may be used in different phases of AD clinical trials.** Individual biomarkers are discussed in detail in the text.

not reach its primary clinical end points (Doody et al., 2014), but in subgroup analyses, there was a small reduction in clinical progression in those with mild AD, although this was not associated with a reduction in CSF tau levels (Doody et al., 2014). As discussed elsewhere in this book, there are multiple potential explanations for the negative phase 3 trials of anti-AD drug candidates. However, most experts agree that it will be very important to ascertain that patients included in future clinical trials indeed have the pathology against which the drug is designed. Further, future phase 1 and 2 trials may benefit from using current and novel biomarkers in an attempt to demonstrate robust target engagement before later-stage studies are embarked upon. Recently presented promising phase 1 data on the Biogen anti-Aβ antibody aducanumab may be a successful example of this approach (http://www.alzforum.org/therapeutics/aducanumab).

STANDARDIZATION EFFORTS

The clinical utility of CSF tests for T-tau, P-tau, and Aβ42 is clear, and their importance for selecting patients in predementia stages of AD for clinical trials of disease-modifying drug candidates is undisputed (Hampel et al., 2010). However, most of the commercially available assays for these biomarkers are still research grade, and there is a lack of common calibrators or certified reference measurement systems that can be used for standardization (Mattsson et al., 2012c). This leads to a risk of bias in the biomarker measurements across different assay platforms. A recognizable consequence of this is that optimal CSF Aβ42 cut points for differentiating AD patients from control individuals vary from 192 ng/L (Shaw et al., 2009) to around 550 ng/L (Hansson et al., 2006; Duits et al., 2014), depending on the assay format. Furthermore, even when the same assay is used, variation in biomarker measurements between laboratories is high, as can be seen in multicenter comparisons of measurements, including the Alzheimer's Association QC Program for CSF Biomarkers (Mattsson et al., 2011a, 2013a). This program includes about 90 participants around the globe and shows that the interlaboratory coefficients of variation (CVs) for commercially available tau and Aβ assays are between 20 and 30%, whereas intralaboratory studies show that CVs of <10% should be feasible.

Important preanalytical sources of variation for the most variable AD biomarker, Aβ42, are storage tube type (polypropylene tubes are recommended, but different brands seem to show different analyte adsorption; Perret-Liaudet et al., 2012); sample aliquot volume (Toombs et al., 2013); and blood contamination (Bjerke et al., 2010). Analytical sources of variation include the composition of the diluent buffer—low concentrations of detergent increase the measured Aβ42 concentration, which has to be standardized (Bjerke et al., 2010). Several additional factors may be important in an assay-specific manner, and close adherence to kit inserts is recommended, as is participation in the Alzheimer's Association QC Program and other interlaboratory comparison programs to ensure that proper laboratory procedures are in place.

To help solve bias and variation problems, a number of standardization efforts have been initiated, all aimed at facilitating the development of standard operating procedures for preanalytical sample handling and assay procedures, as well as reference methods and materials for the key analytes. These initiatives include the Alzheimer's Association Global Biomarkers Standardization Consortium (GBSC) and the International Federation of Clinical Chemistry and Laboratory Medicine Working Group for CSF Proteins (Carrillo et al., 2013). Standard operating procedures for CSF sampling and storage have been published (Blennow et al., 2010), and candidate selected reaction monitoring mass-spectrometry-based methods for Aβ1–42 have been described (Korecka et al., 2014; Leinenbach et al., 2014; Pannee et al., 2013). Strong collaborative efforts within GBSC are under way, and updates are available on http://www.alz.org/research/funding/global_biomarker_consortium.asp.

CONCLUDING REMARKS

Three CSF biomarkers reflecting the core pathological features of AD are in common use: T-tau (broadly, but not entirely reflecting neurodegeneration), P-tau (reflecting tau hyperphosphorylation and tangle formation), and Aβ42 (which inversely correlates with plaque pathology). According to revised clinical criteria, these markers may help diagnose AD more accurately, and in a research setting open up the possibility of detecting predementia stages of the disease. At present, their most obvious utility is in clinical trials of novel disease-modifying treatments against AD. In the future, they may help in selecting the right treatment for individual patients by making it possible to assess which molecular pathology is most likely to cause the patient's symptom(s) at different stages of the disease. In addition, there is considerable promise that CSF biomarkers will be able to provide in vivo measurement of a range of additional pathophysiological processes in AD, including microglial activation and synapse loss. Depending on the mode of action, these could be useful as pharmacodynamic markers in the evaluation of novel candidate drugs against AD and other neurodegenerative diseases.

Acknowledgments

Work in the authors' laboratories is supported by the Swedish Research Council, the Knut and Alice Wallenberg Foundation, the Torsten Söderberg Foundation, the Alzheimer's Association, the Swedish Alzheimer Foundation, and Swedish State Support for Clinical Research. We wish to thank colleagues and patients and their families for generating the extensive literature that was reviewed here.

References

Agren-Wilsson A, Lekman A, Sjoberg W, et al: CSF biomarkers in the evaluation of idiopathic normal pressure hydrocephalus, *Acta Neurol* 116(5):333–339, 2007.

Andreasen N, Minthon L, Vanmechelen E, et al: Cerebrospinal fluid tau and Abeta42 as predictors of development of Alzheimer's disease in patients with mild cognitive impairment, *Neurosci Lett* 273(1):5–8, 1999.

Andreasson U, Portelius E, Andersson ME, Blennow K, Zetterberg H: Aspects of beta-amyloid as a biomarker for Alzheimer's disease, *Biomarkers Med* 1(1):59–78, 2007.

Barbour R, Kling K, Anderson JP, et al: Red blood cells are the major source of alpha-synuclein in blood, *Neurodegener Dis* 5(2):55–59, 2008.

Bibl M, Mollenhauer B, Lewczuk P, et al: Cerebrospinal fluid tau, p-tau 181 and amyloid-beta38/40/42 in frontotemporal dementias and primary progressive aphasias, *Dement Geriatr Cogn Disord* 31(1):37–44, 2011.

Bjerke M, Portelius E, Minthon L, et al: Confounding factors influencing amyloid beta concentration in cerebrospinal fluid, *Int J Alzheimers Dis* 2010:986310, 2010.

Bjorkqvist M, Ohlsson M, Minthon L, Hansson O: Evaluation of a previously suggested plasma biomarker panel to identify Alzheimer's disease, *PLoS One* 7(1):e29868, 2012.

Blasko I, Lederer W, Oberbauer H, et al: Measurement of thirteen biological markers in CSF of patients with Alzheimer's disease and other dementias, *Dement Geriatr Cogn Disord* 21(1):9–15, 2006.

Blennow K, Wallin A: Clinical heterogeneity of probable Alzheimer's disease, *J Geriatr Psychiatr Neurol* 5(2):106–113, 1992.

Blennow K, Zetterberg H: Understanding biomarkers of neurodegeneration: ultrasensitive detection techniques pave the way for mechanistic understanding, *Nat Med* 21(3):217–219, 2015.

Blennow K, Wallin A, Fredman P, Gottfries CG, Karlsson I, Svennerholm L: Intrathecal synthesis of immunoglobulins in patients with Alzheimer's disease, *Eur Neuropsychopharmacol* 1(1):79–81, 1990a.

Blennow K, Wallin A, Fredman P, Karlsson I, Gottfries CG, Svennerholm L: Blood–brain barrier disturbance in patients with Alzheimer's disease is related to vascular factors, *Acta Neurol* 81(4):323–326, 1990b.

Blennow K, Wallin A, Agren H, Spenger C, Siegfried J, Vanmechelen E: Tau protein in cerebrospinal fluid: a biochemical marker for axonal degeneration in Alzheimer disease? *Mol Chem Neuropathol* 26(3):231–245, 1995.

Blennow K, De Leon MJ, Zetterberg H: Alzheimer's disease, *Lancet* 368(9533):387–403, 2006.

Blennow K, Zetterberg H, Minthon L, et al: Longitudinal stability of CSF biomarkers in Alzheimer's disease, *Neurosci Lett* 419(1):18–22, 2007.

Blennow K, Hampel H, Weiner M, Zetterberg H: Cerebrospinal fluid and plasma biomarkers in Alzheimer disease, *Nat Rev Neurol* 6(3):131–144, 2010.

Blennow K, Zetterberg H, Rinne JO, et al: Effect of immunotherapy with bapineuzumab on cerebrospinal fluid biomarker levels in patients with mild to moderate Alzheimer disease, *Arch Neurol* 69(8):1002–1010, 2012.

Borroni B, Premi E, Agosti C, et al: CSF Alzheimer's disease-like pattern in corticobasal syndrome: evidence for a distinct disorder, *J Neurol Neurosurg Psychiatr* 82(8):834–838, 2011.

Brinkmalm A, Brinkmalm G, Honer WG, et al: SNAP-25 is a promising novel cerebrospinal fluid biomarker for synapse degeneration in Alzheimer's disease, *Mol Neurodegener* 9:53, 2014.

Bruggink KA, Jongbloed W, Biemans EA, et al: Amyloid-beta oligomer detection by ELISA in cerebrospinal fluid and brain tissue, *Anal Biochem* 433(2):112–120, 2013.

Brys M, Pirraglia E, Rich K, et al: Prediction and longitudinal study of CSF biomarkers in mild cognitive impairment, *Neurobiol Aging* 30(5):682–690, 2009.

Buchhave P, Minthon L, Zetterberg H, Wallin AK, Blennow K, Hansson O: Cerebrospinal fluid levels of beta-amyloid 1-42, but not of tau, are fully changed already 5 to 10 years before the onset of Alzheimer dementia, *Arch Gen Psychiatr* 69(1):98–106, 2012.

Buerger K, Ewers M, Pirttila T, et al: CSF phosphorylated tau protein correlates with neocortical neurofibrillary pathology in Alzheimer's disease, *Brain* 129(Pt 11):3035–3041, 2006.

Carrillo MC, Blennow K, Soares H, et al: Global standardization measurement of cerebral spinal fluid for Alzheimer's disease: an update from the Alzheimer's Association Global Biomarkers Consortium, *Alzheimers Dement* 9(2): 137–140, 2013.

Castellani RJ, Smith MA: Compounding artefacts with uncertainty, and an amyloid cascade hypothesis that is "too big to fail", *J Pathol* 224(2):147–152, 2011.

Chalbot S, Zetterberg H, Blennow K, Fladby T, Grundke-Iqbal I, Iqbal K: Cerebrospinal fluid secretory Ca^{2+}-dependent phospholipase A2 activity: a biomarker of blood–cerebrospinal fluid barrier permeability, *Neurosci Lett* 478(3):179–183, 2010.

Comi C, Carecchio M, Chiocchetti A, et al: Osteopontin is increased in the cerebrospinal fluid of patients with Alzheimer's disease and its levels correlate with cognitive decline, *J Alzheimers Dis* 19(4):1143–1148, 2010.

Correa JD, Starling D, Teixeira AL, Caramelli P, Silva TA: Chemokines in CSF of Alzheimer's disease patients, *Arq Neuropsiquiatr* 69(3):455–459, 2011.

Craig-Schapiro R, Perrin RJ, Roe CM, et al: YKL-40: a novel prognostic fluid biomarker for preclinical Alzheimer's disease, *Biol Psychiatr* 68(10):903–912, 2010.

Davidsson P, Puchades M, Blennow K: Identification of synaptic vesicle, pre- and postsynaptic proteins in human cerebrospinal fluid using liquid-phase isoelectric focusing, *Electrophoresis* 20(3):431–437, 1999.

De Felice FG, Wu D, Lambert MP, et al: Alzheimer's disease-type neuronal tau hyperphosphorylation induced by A beta oligomers, *Neurobiol Aging* 29(9):1334–1347, 2008.

De Jong D, Jansen RW, Pijnenburg YA, et al: CSF neurofilament proteins in the differential diagnosis of dementia, *J Neurol Neurosurg Psychiatr* 78(9):936–938, 2007.

De Leon MJ, Desanti S, Zinkowski R, et al: Longitudinal CSF and MRI biomarkers improve the diagnosis of mild cognitive impairment, *Neurobiol Aging* 27(3):394–401, 2006.

Doecke JD, Laws SM, Faux NG, et al: Blood-based protein biomarkers for diagnosis of Alzheimer disease, *Arch Neurol* 69(10):1318–1325, 2012.

Doody RS, Thomas RG, Farlow M, et al: Phase 3 trials of solanezumab for mild-to-moderate Alzheimer's disease, *N Engl J Med* 370(4):311–321, 2014.

Dubois B, Feldman HH, Jacova C, et al: Advancing research diagnostic criteria for Alzheimer's disease: the IWG-2 criteria, *Lancet Neurol* 13(6):614–629, 2014.

Duits FH, Kester MI, Scheffer PG, et al: Increase in cerebrospinal fluid F2-isoprostanes is related to cognitive decline in APOE epsilon4 carriers, *J Alzheimers Dis* 36(3):563–570, 2013.

Duits FH, Teunissen CE, Bouwman FH, et al: The cerebrospinal fluid "Alzheimer profile": easily said, but what does it mean? *Alzheimers Dement* 10:713–723, 2014.

Engelborghs S, De Brabander M, De Cree J, et al: Unchanged levels of interleukins, neopterin, interferon-gamma and tumor necrosis factor-alpha in cerebrospinal fluid of patients with dementia of the Alzheimer type, *Neurochem Int* 34(6):523–530, 1999.

Fagan AM, Mintun MA, Mach RH, et al: Inverse relation between in vivo amyloid imaging load and cerebrospinal fluid Abeta42 in humans, *Ann Neurol* 59(3):512–519, 2006.

Fagan AM, Head D, Shah AR, et al: Decreased cerebrospinal fluid Abeta(42) correlates with brain atrophy in cognitively normal elderly, *Ann Neurol* 65(2):176–183, 2009.

Feneberg E, Steinacker P, Lehnert S, et al: Limited role of free TDP-43 as a diagnostic tool in neurodegenerative diseases, *Amyotroph Lateral Scler Frontotemporal Degener* 15(5–6):351–356, 2014.

Forsberg A, Engler H, Almkvist O, et al: PET imaging of amyloid deposition in patients with mild cognitive impairment, *Neurobiol Aging* 29(10):1456–1465, 2008.

Fukumoto H, Cheung BS, Hyman BT, Irizarry MC: Beta-secretase protein and activity are increased in the neocortex in Alzheimer disease, *Arch Neurol* 59(9):1381–1389, 2002.

Fukumoto H, Tokuda T, Kasai T, et al: High-molecular-weight β-amyloid oligomers are elevated in cerebrospinal fluid of Alzheimer patients, *FASEB J* 28:2716–2726, 2010.

Gabelle A, Roche S, Geny C, et al: Correlations between soluble alpha/beta forms of amyloid precursor protein and Abeta38, 40, and 42 in human cerebrospinal fluid, *Brain Res* 1357:175–183, 2010.

Gackowski D, Rozalski R, Siomek A, et al: Oxidative stress and oxidative DNA damage is characteristic for mixed Alzheimer disease/vascular dementia, *J Neurol Sci* 266(1–2):57–62, 2008.

Gaiottino J, Norgren N, Dobson R, et al: Increased neurofilament light chain blood levels in neurodegenerative neurological diseases, *PLoS One* 8(9):e75091, 2013.

Galimberti D, Schoonenboom N, Scheltens P, et al: Intrathecal chemokine levels in Alzheimer disease and frontotemporal lobar degeneration, *Neurology* 66(1):146–147, 2006a.

Galimberti D, Schoonenboom N, Scheltens P, et al: Intrathecal chemokine synthesis in mild cognitive impairment and Alzheimer disease, *Arch Neurol* 63(4):538–543, 2006b.

Gao CM, Yam AY, Wang X, et al: Abeta40 oligomers identified as a potential biomarker for the diagnosis of Alzheimer's disease, *PLoS One* 5(12):e15725, 2010.

Georganopoulou DG, Chang L, Nam JM, et al: Nanoparticle-based detection in cerebral spinal fluid of a soluble pathogenic biomarker for Alzheimer's disease, *Proc Natl Acad Sci USA* 102(7):2273–2276, 2005.

Gilman S, Koller M, Black RS, et al: Clinical effects of Abeta immunization (AN1792) in patients with AD in an interrupted trial, *Neurology* 64(9):1553–1562, 2005.

Gisslen M, Hagberg L, Brew BJ, Cinque P, Price RW, Rosengren L: Elevated cerebrospinal fluid neurofilament light protein concentrations predict the development of AIDS dementia complex, *J Infect Dis* 195(12):1774–1778, 2007.

Glenner GG, Wong CW: Alzheimer's disease: initial report of the purification and characterization of a novel cerebrovascular amyloid protein, *Biochem Biophys Res Commun* 120(3):885–890, 1984a.

Glenner GG, Wong CW: Alzheimer's disease and Down's syndrome: sharing of a unique cerebrovascular amyloid fibril protein, *Biochem Biophys Res Commun* 122(3):1131–1135, 1984b.

Glodzik L, Mosconi L, Tsui W, et al: Alzheimer's disease markers, hypertension, and gray matter damage in normal elderly, *Neurobiol Aging* 33(7):1215–1227, 2012.

Gottfries CG, Gottfries I, Roos BE: Homovanillic acid and 5-hydroxyindoleacetic acid in the cerebrospinal fluid of patients with senile dementia, presenile dementia and parkinsonism, *J Neurochem* 16(9):1341–1345, 1969.

Gottfries CG, Gottfries I, Roos BE: Homovanillic acid and 5-hydroxyindoleacetic acid in cerebrospinal fluid related to rated mental and motor impairment in senile and presenile dementia, *Acta Psychiatr* 46(2):99–105, 1970.

Gottfries CG, Kjallquist A, Ponten U, Roos BE, Sundbarg G: Cerebrospinal fluid pH and monoamine and glucolytic metabolites in Alzheimer's disease, *Br J Psychiatr* 124(0):280–287, 1974.

Grahn A, Hagberg L, Nilsson S, Blennow K, Zetterberg H, Studahl M: Cerebrospinal fluid biomarkers in patients with varicella-zoster virus CNS infections, *J Neurol* 260(7):1813–1821, 2013.

Grossman M, Farmer J, Leight S, et al: Cerebrospinal fluid profile in frontotemporal dementia and Alzheimer's disease, *Ann Neurol* 57(5):721–729, 2005.

Grundke-Iqbal I, Iqbal K, Tung YC, Quinlan M, Wisniewski HM, Binder LI: Abnormal phosphorylation of the microtubule-associated protein tau (tau) in Alzheimer cytoskeletal pathology, *Proc Natl Acad Sci USA* 83(13):4913 4917, 1986.

Guerreiro R, Wojtas A, Bras J, et al: TREM2 variants in Alzheimer's disease, *N Engl J Med* 368(2):117–127, 2013.

Guo JL, Covell DJ, Daniels JP, et al: Distinct alpha-synuclein strains differentially promote tau inclusions in neurons, *Cell* 154(1):103–117, 2013.

Gustafson DR, Skoog I, Rosengren L, Zetterberg H, Blennow K: Cerebrospinal fluid beta-amyloid 1-42 concentration may predict cognitive decline in older women, *J Neurol Neurosurg Psychiatr* 78(5):461–464, 2007.

Haass C, Schlossmacher MG, Hung AY, et al: Amyloid beta-peptide is produced by cultured cells during normal metabolism, *Nature* 359(6393):322–325, 1992.

Hakala BE, White C, Recklies AD: Human cartilage gp-39, a major secretory product of articular chondrocytes and synovial cells, is a mammalian member of a chitinase protein family, *J Biol Chem* 268(34):25803–25810, 1993.

Halim A, Brinkmalm G, Ruetschi U, et al: Site-specific characterization of threonine, serine, and tyrosine glycosylations of amyloid precursor protein/amyloid beta-peptides in human cerebrospinal fluid, *Proc Natl Acad Sci USA* 108(29):11848–11853, 2011.

Hall S, Ohrfelt A, Constantinescu R, et al: Accuracy of a panel of 5 cerebrospinal fluid biomarkers in the differential diagnosis of patients with dementia and/or parkinsonian disorders, *Arch Neurol*:1–8, 2012.

Hampel H, Buerger K, Zinkowski R, et al: Measurement of phosphorylated tau epitopes in the differential diagnosis of Alzheimer disease: a comparative cerebrospinal fluid study, *Arch Gen Psychiatr* 61(1):95–102, 2004.

Hampel H, Frank R, Broich K, et al: Biomarkers for Alzheimer's disease: academic, industry and regulatory perspectives, *Nat Rev Drug Discov* 9(7):560–574, 2010.

Hampel H, Lista S, Teipel SJ, et al: Perspective on future role of biological markers in clinical therapy trials of Alzheimer's disease: a long-range point of view beyond 2020, *Biochem Pharmacol* 88(4):426–449, 2014.

Handoko M, Grant M, Kuskowski M, et al: Correlation of specific amyloid-beta oligomers with tau in cerebrospinal fluid from cognitively normal older adults, *JAMA Neurol* 70(5):594–599, 2013.

Hansson O, Zetterberg H, Buchhave P, Londos E, Blennow K, Minthon L: Association between CSF biomarkers and incipient Alzheimer's disease in patients with mild cognitive impairment: a follow-up study, *Lancet Neurol* 5(3):228–234, 2006.

Hansson O, Zetterberg H, Vanmechelen E, et al: Evaluation of plasma Abeta(40) and Abeta(42) as predictors of conversion to Alzheimer's disease in patients with mild cognitive impairment, *Neurobiol Aging* 31(3):357–367, 2010.

Hesse C, Rosengren L, Andreasen N, et al: Transient increase in total tau but not phospho-tau in human cerebrospinal fluid after acute stroke, *Neurosci Lett* 297(3):187–190, 2001.

Hollak CE, Van Weely S, Van Oers MH, Aerts JM: Marked elevation of plasma chitotriosidase activity: a novel hallmark of Gaucher disease, *J Clin Invest* 93(3):1288–1292, 1994.

Holsinger RM, McLean CA, Collins SJ, Masters CL, Evin G: Increased beta-secretase activity in cerebrospinal fluid of Alzheimer's disease subjects, *Ann Neurol* 55(6):898–899, 2004.

Holsinger RM, Lee JS, Boyd A, Masters CL, Collins SJ: CSF BACE1 activity is increased in CJD and Alzheimer disease versus [corrected] other dementias, *Neurology* 67(4):710–712, 2006.

Holtta M, Hansson O, Andreasson U, et al: Evaluating amyloid-beta oligomers in cerebrospinal fluid as a biomarker for Alzheimer's disease, *PLoS One* 8(6):e66381, 2013.

Hong Z, Shi M, Chung KA, et al: DJ-1 and alpha-synuclein in human cerebrospinal fluid as biomarkers of Parkinson's disease, *Brain* 133(Pt 3):713–726, 2010.

Isaac M, Vamvakas S, Abadie E, Jonsson B, Gispen C, Pani L: Qualification opinion of novel methodologies in the predementia stage of Alzheimer's disease: cerebro-spinal-fluid related biomarkers for drugs affecting amyloid burden—regulatory considerations by European Medicines Agency focusing in improving benefit/risk in regulatory trials, *Eur Neuropsychopharmacol* 21(11):781–788, 2011.

Jin M, Shepardson N, Yang T, Chen G, Walsh D, Selkoe DJ: Soluble amyloid beta-protein dimers isolated from Alzheimer cortex directly induce tau hyperphosphorylation and neuritic degeneration, *Proc Natl Acad Sci USA* 108(14):5819–5824, 2011.

Johansson P, Mattsson N, Hansson O, et al: Cerebrospinal fluid biomarkers for Alzheimer's disease: diagnostic performance in a homogeneous mono-center population, *J Alzheimers Dis* 24(3):537–546, 2011.

Jonsson T, Stefansson H, Steinberg S, et al: Variant of TREM2 associated with the risk of Alzheimer's disease, *N Engl J Med* 368(2):107–116, 2013.

Josephs KA, Whitwell JL, Weigand SD, et al: TDP-43 is a key player in the clinical features associated with Alzheimer's disease, *Acta Neuropathol* 127(6):811–824, 2014.

Kleinberger G, Yamanishi Y, Suarez-Calvet M, et al: TREM2 mutations implicated in neurodegeneration impair cell surface transport and phagocytosis, *Sci Transl Med* 6(243):243ra286, 2014.

Korecka M, Waligorska T, Figurski M, et al: Qualification of a surrogate matrix-based absolute quantification method for amyloid-beta(4)(2) in human cerebrospinal fluid using 2D UPLC-tandem mass spectrometry, *J Alzheimers Dis* 41(2):441–451, 2014.

Kvartsberg H, Duits FH, Ingelsson M, et al: Cerebrospinal fluid levels of the synaptic protein neurogranin correlates with cognitive decline in prodromal Alzheimer's disease, *Alzheimers Dement* 11:1180–1190, 2014.

Landqvist Waldo M, Frizell Santillo A, Passant U, et al: Cerebrospinal fluid neurofilament light chain protein levels in subtypes of frontotemporal dementia, *BMC Neurol* 13:54, 2013.

Lannfelt L, Blennow K, Zetterberg H, et al: Safety, efficacy, and biomarker findings of PBT2 in targeting Abeta as a modifying therapy for Alzheimer's disease: a phase IIa, double-blind, randomised, placebo-controlled trial, *Lancet Neurol* 7(9):779–786, 2008.

Lee JM, Blennow K, Andreasen N, et al: The brain injury biomarker VLP-1 is increased in the cerebrospinal fluid of Alzheimer disease patients, *Clin Chem* 54(10):1617–1623, 2008.

Leinenbach A, Pannee J, Dulffer T, et al: Mass spectrometry-based candidate reference measurement procedure for quantification of amyloid-beta in cerebrospinal fluid, *Clin Chem* 60:987–994, 2014.

Lewczuk P, Kamrowski-Kruck H, Peters O, et al: Soluble amyloid precursor proteins in the cerebrospinal fluid as novel potential biomarkers of Alzheimer's disease: a multicenter study, *Mol Psychiatr* 15(2):138–145, 2010.

Lewczuk P, Popp J, Lelental N, et al: Cerebrospinal fluid soluble amyloid-beta protein precursor as a potential novel biomarkers of Alzheimer's disease, *J Alzheimers Dis* 28(1):119–125, 2012.

Maia LF, Kaeser SA, Reichwald J, et al: Changes in amyloid-beta and tau in the cerebrospinal fluid of transgenic mice overexpressing amyloid precursor protein, *Sci Transl Med* 5(194):194re192, 2013.

Mandelkow EM, Mandelkow E: Biochemistry and cell biology of tau protein in neurofibrillary degeneration, *Cold Spring Harb Perspect Med* 2(7):a006247, 2012.

Masters CL, Simms G, Weinman NA, Multhaup G, McDonald BL, Beyreuther K: Amyloid plaque core protein in Alzheimer disease and Down syndrome, *Proc Natl Acad Sci USA* 82(12):4245–4249, 1985.

Mattsson N, Zetterberg H, Hansson O, et al: CSF biomarkers and incipient Alzheimer disease in patients with mild cognitive impairment, *J Amer Med Assoc* 302(4):385–393, 2009.

Mattsson N, Andreasson U, Persson S, et al: The Alzheimer's Association external quality control program for cerebrospinal fluid biomarkers, *Alzheimers Dement* 7(4):386–395, 2011a, e386.

Mattsson N, Tabatabaei S, Johansson P, et al: Cerebrospinal fluid microglial markers in Alzheimer's disease: elevated chitotriosidase activity but lack of diagnostic utility, *Neuromolecular Med* 13(2):151–159, 2011b.

Mattsson N, Portelius E, Rolstad S, et al: Longitudinal cerebrospinal fluid biomarkers over four years in mild cognitive impairment, *J Alzheimers Dis* 30(4):767–778, 2012a.

Mattsson N, Rajendran L, Zetterberg H, et al: BACE1 inhibition induces a specific cerebrospinal fluid beta-amyloid pattern that identifies drug effects in the central nervous system, *PLoS One* 7(2):e31084, 2012b.

Mattsson N, Zegers I, Andreasson U, et al: Reference measurement procedures for Alzheimer's disease cerebrospinal fluid biomarkers: definitions and approaches with focus on amyloid beta42, *Biomark Med* 6(4):409–417, 2012c.

Mattsson N, Andreasson U, Persson S, et al: CSF biomarker variability in the Alzheimer's Association quality control program, *Alzheimers Dement* 9(3):251–261, 2013a.

Mattsson N, Insel P, Nosheny R, et al: CSF protein biomarkers predicting longitudinal reduction of CSF beta-amyloid42 in cognitively healthy elders, *Transl Psychiatr* 3:e293, 2013b.

Mattsson N, Insel PS, Donohue M, et al: Predicting reduction of cerebrospinal fluid beta-amyloid 42 in cognitively healthy controls, *JAMA Neurol* 72:554–560, 2015.

May PC, Dean RA, Lowe SL, et al: Robust central reduction of amyloid-beta in humans with an orally available, non-peptidic beta-secretase inhibitor, *J Neurosci* 31(46):16507–16516, 2011.

Meredith JE Jr, Sankaranarayanan S, Guss V, et al: Characterization of novel CSF tau and ptau biomarkers for Alzheimer's disease, *PLoS One* 8(10):e76523, 2013.

Moghekar A, Li S, Lu Y, et al: CSF biomarker changes precede symptom onset of mild cognitive impairment, *Neurology* 81:1753–1758, 2013.

Mollenhauer B, El-Agnaf OM, Marcus K, Trenkwalder C, Schlossmacher MG: Quantification of alpha-synuclein in cerebrospinal fluid as a biomarker candidate: review of the literature and considerations for future studies, *Biomark Med* 4(5):683–699, 2010.

Mollenhauer B, Locascio JJ, Schulz-Schaeffer W, Sixel-Doring F, Trenkwalder C, Schlossmacher MG: Alpha-synuclein and tau concentrations in cerebrospinal fluid of patients presenting with parkinsonism: a cohort study, *Lancet Neurol* 10(3):230–240, 2011.

Montine TJ, Markesbery WR, Morrow JD, Roberts LJ II: Cerebrospinal fluid F2-isoprostane levels are increased in Alzheimer's disease, *Ann Neurol* 44(3):410–413, 1998.

Montine TJ, Beal MF, Cudkowicz ME, et al: Increased CSF F2-isoprostane concentration in probable AD, *Neurology* 52(3):562–565, 1999.

Morrow JD, Roberts LJ: The isoprostanes: unique bioactive products of lipid peroxidation, *Prog Lipid Res* 36(1):1–21, 1997.

Motter R, Vigo-Pelfrey C, Kholodenko D, et al: Reduction of beta-amyloid peptide42 in the cerebrospinal fluid of patients with Alzheimer's disease, *Ann Neurol* 38(4):643–648, 1995.

Mulder SD, Van Der Flier WM, Verheijen JH, et al: BACE1 activity in cerebrospinal fluid and its relation to markers of AD pathology, *J Alzheimers Dis* 20(1):253–260, 2010.

Nag S, Yu L, Capuano AW, et al: Hippocampal sclerosis and TDP-43 pathology in aging and Alzheimer's disease, *Ann Neurol* 77:942–952, 2015.

Naude PJ, Nyakas C, Eiden LE, et al: Lipocalin 2: novel component of proinflammatory signaling in Alzheimer's disease, *FASEB J* 26(7):2811–2823, 2012.

Neumann M, Sampathu DM, Kwong LK, et al: Ubiquitinated TDP-43 in frontotemporal lobar degeneration and amyotrophic lateral sclerosis, *Science* 314(5796):130–133, 2006.

Nukina N, Ihara Y: One of the antigenic determinants of paired helical filaments is related to tau protein, *J Biochem* 99(5):1541–1544, 1986.

Ohrfelt A, Grognet P, Andreasen N, et al: Cerebrospinal fluid alpha-synuclein in neurodegenerative disorders—a marker of synapse loss? *Neurosci Lett* 450(3):332–335, 2009.

Olsson A, Hoglund K, Sjogren M, et al: Measurement of alpha- and beta-secretase cleaved amyloid precursor protein in cerebrospinal fluid from Alzheimer patients, *Exp Neurol* 183(1):74–80, 2003.

Olsson B, Hertze J, Lautner R, et al: Microglial markers are elevated in the prodromal phase of Alzheimer's disease and vascular dementia, *J Alzheimers Dis* 33(1):45–53, 2013.

Pannee J, Portelius E, Oppermann M, et al: A selected reaction monitoring (SRM)-based method for absolute quantification of Abeta38, Abeta40, and Abeta42 in cerebrospinal fluid of Alzheimer's disease patients and healthy controls, *J Alzheimers Dis* 33(4):1021–1032, 2013.

Paterson RW, Bartlett JW, Blennow K, et al: Cerebrospinal fluid markers including trefoil factor 3 are associated with neurodegeneration in amyloid-positive individuals, *Transl Psychiatr* 4:e419, 2014.

Perneczky R, Tsolakidou A, Arnold A, et al: CSF soluble amyloid precursor proteins in the diagnosis of incipient Alzheimer disease, *Neurology* 77(1):35–38, 2011.

Perret-Liaudet A, Pelpel M, Tholance Y, et al: Risk of Alzheimer's disease biological misdiagnosis linked to cerebrospinal collection tubes, *J Alzheimers Dis* 31(1):13–20, 2012.

Pitschke M, Prior R, Haupt M, Riesner D: Detection of single amyloid beta-protein aggregates in the cerebrospinal fluid of Alzheimer's patients by fluorescence correlation spectroscopy, *Nat Med* 4(7):832–834, 1998.

Pletnikova O, West N, Lee MK, et al: Abeta deposition is associated with enhanced cortical alpha-synuclein lesions in Lewy body diseases, *Neurobiol Aging* 26(8):1183–1192, 2005.

Podlesniy P, Figueiro-Silva J, Llado A, et al: Low cerebrospinal fluid concentration of mitochondrial DNA in preclinical Alzheimer disease, *Ann Neurol* 74:655–668, 2013.

Portelius E, Zetterberg H, Andreasson U, et al: An Alzheimer's disease-specific beta-amyloid fragment signature in cerebrospinal fluid, *Neurosci Lett* 409(3):215–219, 2006.

Portelius E, Bogdanovic N, Gustavsson MK, et al: Mass spectrometric characterization of brain amyloid beta isoform signatures in familial and sporadic Alzheimer's disease, *Acta Neuropathol* 120(2):185–193, 2010a.

Portelius E, Dean RA, Gustavsson MK, et al: A novel Abeta isoform pattern in CSF reflects gamma-secretase inhibition in Alzheimer disease, *Alzheimers Res Ther* 2(2):7, 2010b.

Portelius E, Price E, Brinkmalm G, et al: A novel pathway for amyloid precursor protein processing, *Neurobiol Aging* 32(6):1090–1098, 2011.

Portelius E, Olsson M, Brinkmalm G, et al: Mass spectrometric characterization of amyloid-beta species in the 7PA2 cell model of Alzheimer's disease, *J Alzheimers Dis* 33(1):85–93, 2013.

Ray S, Britschgi M, Herbert C, et al: Classification and prediction of clinical Alzheimer's diagnosis based on plasma signaling proteins, *Nat Med* 13(11):1359–1362, 2007.

Rembach A, Watt AD, Wilson WJ, et al: Plasma amyloid-beta levels are significantly associated with a transition toward Alzheimer's disease as measured by cognitive decline and change in neocortical amyloid burden, *J Alzheimers Dis* 40(1):95–104, 2014.

Renkema GH, Boot RG, Au FL, et al: Chitotriosidase, a chitinase, and the 39-kDa human cartilage glycoprotein, a chitin-binding lectin, are homologues of family 18 glycosyl hydrolases secreted by human macrophages, *Eur J Biochem* 251(1–2):504–509, 1998.

Riemenschneider M, Wagenpfeil S, Vanderstichele H, et al: Phospho-tau/total tau ratio in cerebrospinal fluid discriminates Creutzfeldt–Jakob disease from other dementias, *Mol Psychiatr* 8(3):343–347, 2003.

Ringman JM, Younkin SG, Pratico D, et al: Biochemical markers in persons with preclinical familial Alzheimer disease, *Neurology* 71(2):85–92, 2008.

Rosen C, Mattsson N, Johansson PM, et al: Discriminatory analysis of biochip-derived protein patterns in CSF and plasma in neurodegenerative diseases, *Front Aging Neurosci* 3:1, 2011.

Rosen C, Andreasson U, Mattsson N, et al: Cerebrospinal fluid profiles of amyloid beta-related biomarkers in Alzheimer's disease, *Neuromol Med* 14(1):65–73, 2012.

Rosen C, Hansson O, Blennow K, Zetterberg H: Fluid biomarkers in Alzheimer's disease—current concepts, *Mol Neurodegener* 8:20, 2013.

Rosengren LE, Karlsson JE, Karlsson JO, Persson LI, Wikkelso C: Patients with amyotrophic lateral sclerosis and other neurodegenerative diseases have increased levels of neurofilament protein in CSF, *J Neurochem* 67(5):2013–2018, 1996.

Rosengren LE, Karlsson JE, Sjogren M, Blennow K, Wallin A: Neurofilament protein levels in CSF are increased in dementia, *Neurology* 52(5):1090–1093, 1999.

Rossor MN, Fox NC, Mummery CJ, Schott JM, Warren JD: The diagnosis of young-onset dementia, *Lancet Neurol* 9(8):793–806, 2010.

Salloway S, Sperling R, Gilman S, et al: A phase 2 multiple ascending dose trial of bapineuzumab in mild to moderate Alzheimer disease, *Neurology* 73(24):2061–2070, 2009.

Salloway S, Sperling R, Fox NC, et al: Two phase 3 trials of bapineuzumab in mild-to-moderate Alzheimer's disease, *N Engl J Med* 370(4):322–333, 2014.

Saman S, Kim W, Raya M, et al: Exosome-associated tau is secreted in tauopathy models and is selectively phosphorylated in cerebrospinal fluid in early Alzheimer disease, *J Biol Chem* 287(6):3842–3849, 2012.

Sanchez-Juan P, Sanchez-Valle R, Green A, et al: Influence of timing on CSF tests value for Creutzfeldt–Jakob disease diagnosis, *J Neurol* 254(7):901–906, 2007.

Santos AN, Torkler S, Nowak D, et al: Detection of amyloid-beta oligomers in human cerebrospinal fluid by flow cytometry and fluorescence resonance energy transfer, *J Alzheimers Dis* 11(1):117–125, 2007.

Schneider JA, Arvanitakis Z, Yu L, Boyle PA, Leurgans SE, Bennett DA: Cognitive impairment, decline and fluctuations in older community-dwelling subjects with Lewy bodies, *Brain* 135(Pt 10):3005–3014, 2012.

Schoonenboom NS, Mulder C, Van Kamp GJ, et al: Amyloid beta 38, 40 and 42 species in cerebrospinal fluid: more of the same? *Ann Neurol* 58(1):139–142, 2005.

Schott JM, Warren JD: Alzheimer's disease: mimics and chameleons, *Pract Neurol* 12(6):358–366, 2012.

Seppala TT, Nerg O, Koivisto AM, et al: CSF biomarkers for Alzheimer disease correlate with cortical brain biopsy findings, *Neurology* 78(20):1568–1575, 2012.

Seubert P, Vigo-Pelfrey C, Esch F, et al: Isolation and quantification of soluble Alzheimer's beta-peptide from biological fluids, *Nature* 359(6393):325–327, 1992.

Seubert P, Barbour R, Khan K, et al: Antibody capture of soluble Abeta does not reduce cortical Abeta amyloidosis in the PDAPP mouse, *Neurodegener Dis* 5(2):65–71, 2008.

Shankar GM, Li S, Mehta TH, et al: Amyloid-beta protein dimers isolated directly from Alzheimer's brains impair synaptic plasticity and memory, *Nat Med* 14(8):837–842, 2008.

Shaw LM, Vanderstichele H, Knapik-Czajka M, et al: Cerebrospinal fluid biomarker signature in Alzheimer's disease neuroimaging initiative subjects, *Ann Neurol* 65(4):403–413, 2009.

Shim YS, Roe CM, Buckles VD, Morris JC: Clinicopathologic study of Alzheimer's disease: Alzheimer mimics, *J Alzheimers Dis* 35(4):799–811, 2013.

Siemers ER, Friedrich S, Dean RA, et al: Safety and changes in plasma and cerebrospinal fluid amyloid beta after a single administration of an amyloid beta monoclonal antibody in subjects with Alzheimer disease, *Clin Neuropharmacol* 33(2):67–73, 2010.

Skillback T, Farahmand B, Bartlett JW, et al: CSF neurofilament light differs in neurodegenerative diseases and predicts severity and survival, *Neurology* 83(21):1945–1953, 2014a.

Skillback T, Rosen C, Asztely F, Mattsson N, Blennow K, Zetterberg H: Diagnostic performance of cerebrospinal fluid total tau and phosphorylated tau in Creutzfeldt–Jakob disease: results from the Swedish Mortality Registry, *JAMA Neurol* 71(4):476–483, 2014b.

Skillbäck T, Zetterberg H, Blennow K, Mattsson N: Cerebrospinal fluid biomarkers for Alzheimer disease and subcortical axonal damage in 5,542 clinical samples, *Alzheimers Res Ther* 5(5):47, 2013.

Skoog I, Davidsson P, Aevarsson O, Vanderstichele H, Vanmechelen E, Blennow K: Cerebrospinal fluid beta-amyloid 42 is reduced before the onset of sporadic dementia: a population-based study in 85-year-olds, *Dement Geriatr Cogn Disord* 15(3):169–176, 2003.

Soares HD, Chen Y, Sabbagh M, Roher A, Schrijvers E, Breteler M: Identifying early markers of Alzheimer's disease using quantitative multiplex proteomic immunoassay panels, *Ann NY Acad Sci* 1180:56–67, 2009.

Sokolova A, Hill MD, Rahimi F, Warden LA, Halliday GM, Shepherd CE: Monocyte chemoattractant protein-1 plays a dominant role in the chronic inflammation observed in Alzheimer's disease, *Brain Pathol* 19(3):392–398, 2009.

Steinacker P, Hendrich C, Sperfeld AD, et al: TDP-43 in cerebrospinal fluid of patients with frontotemporal lobar degeneration and amyotrophic lateral sclerosis, *Arch Neurol* 65(11):1481–1487, 2008.

Strozyk D, Blennow K, White LR, Launer LJ: CSF Abeta 42 levels correlate with amyloid-neuropathology in a population-based autopsy study, *Neurology* 60(4):652–656, 2003.

Swardfager W, Lanctot K, Rothenburg L, Wong A, Cappell J, Herrmann N: A meta-analysis of cytokines in Alzheimer's disease, *Biol Psychiatr* 68:930–941, 2010.

Tateno F, Sakakibara R, Kawai T, Kishi M, Murano T: Alpha-synuclein in the cerebrospinal fluid differentiates synucleinopathies (Parkinson disease, dementia with Lewy bodies, multiple system atrophy) from Alzheimer disease, *Alzheimer Dis Assoc Disord* 26(3):213–216, 2012.

Terry RD, Masliah E, Salmon DP, et al: Physical basis of cognitive alterations in Alzheimer's disease: synapse loss is the major correlate of cognitive impairment, *Ann Neurol* 30(4):572–580, 1991.

Thorsell A, Bjerke M, Gobom J, et al: Neurogranin in cerebrospinal fluid as a marker of synaptic degeneration in Alzheimer's disease, *Brain Res* 1362:13–22, 2010.

Toledo JB, Xie SX, Trojanowski JQ, Shaw LM: Longitudinal change in CSF tau and Abeta biomarkers for up to 48 months in ADNI, *Acta Neuropathol* 126(5):659–670, 2013.

Toombs J, Paterson RW, Lunn MP, et al: Identification of an important potential confound in CSF AD studies: aliquot volume, *Clin Chem Lab Med* 51:1–7, 2013.

Tortelli R, Ruggieri M, Cortese R, et al: Elevated cerebrospinal fluid neurofilament light levels in patients with amyotrophic lateral sclerosis: a possible marker of disease severity and progression, *Eur J Neurol* 19(12):1561–1567, 2012.

Trojanowski JQ, Schuck T, Schmidt ML, Lee VM: Distribution of tau proteins in the normal human central and peripheral nervous system, *J Histochem Cytochem* 37(2):209–215, 1989.

Tumani H, Nolker G, Reiber H: Relevance of cerebrospinal fluid variables for early diagnosis of neuroborreliosis, *Neurology* 45(9):1663–1670, 1995.

Uryu K, Chen XH, Martinez D, et al: Multiple proteins implicated in neurodegenerative diseases accumulate in axons after brain trauma in humans, *Exp Neurol* 208(2):185–192, 2007.

Vandermeeren M, Mercken M, Vanmechelen E, et al: Detection of tau proteins in normal and Alzheimer's disease cerebrospinal fluid with a sensitive sandwich enzyme-linked immunosorbent assay, *J Neurochem* 61(5):1828–1834, 1993.

Visser PJ, Verhey F, Knol DL, et al: Prevalence and prognostic value of CSF markers of Alzheimer's disease pathology in patients with subjective cognitive impairment or mild cognitive impairment in the DESCRIPA study: a prospective cohort study, *Lancet Neurol* 8(7):619–627, 2009.

Wallin A, Sjogren M: Cerebrospinal fluid cytoskeleton proteins in patients with subcortical white-matter dementia, *Mech Ageing Dev* 122(16):1937–1949, 2001.

Wallin A, Blennow K, Rosengren L: Cerebrospinal fluid markers of pathogenetic processes in vascular dementia, with special reference to the subcortical subtype, *Alzheimer Dis Assoc Disord* 13(Suppl 3):S102–S105, 1999.

Wallin AK, Blennow K, Zetterberg H, Londos E, Minthon L, Hansson O: CSF biomarkers predict a more malignant outcome in Alzheimer disease, *Neurology* 74(19):1531–1537, 2010.

Walsh DM, Klyubin I, Fadeeva JV, et al: Naturally secreted oligomers of amyloid beta protein potently inhibit hippocampal long-term potentiation in vivo, *Nature* 416(6880):535–539, 2002.

Wang L, Fagan AM, Shah AR, et al: Cerebrospinal fluid proteins predict longitudinal hippocampal degeneration in early-stage dementia of the Alzheimer type, *Alzheimer Dis Assoc Disord* 26(4):314–321, 2012.

Watabe-Rudolph M, Song Z, Lausser L, et al: Chitinase enzyme activity in CSF is a powerful biomarker of Alzheimer disease, *Neurology* 78(8):569–577, 2012.

Welzel AT, Maggio JE, Shankar GM, et al: Secreted amyloid beta-proteins in a cell culture model include N-terminally extended peptides that impair synaptic plasticity, *Biochemistry* 53(24):3908–3921, 2014.

Wennstrom M, Surova Y, Hall S, et al: Low CSF levels of both alpha-synuclein and the alpha-synuclein cleaving enzyme neurosin in patients with synucleinopathy, *PLoS One* 8(1):e53250, 2013.

Westin K, Buchhave P, Nielsen H, Minthon L, Janciauskiene S, Hansson O: CCL2 is associated with a faster rate of cognitive decline during early stages of Alzheimer's disease, *PLoS One* 7(1):e30525, 2012.

Wiltfang J, Esselmann H, Bibl M, et al: Amyloid beta peptide ratio 42/40 but not A beta 42 correlates with phospho-tau in patients with low- and high-CSF A beta 40 load, *J Neurochem* 101(4):1053–1059, 2007.

Wischik CM, Novak M, Thogersen HC, et al: Isolation of a fragment of tau derived from the core of the paired helical filament of Alzheimer disease, *Proc Natl Acad Sci USA* 85(12):4506–4510, 1988.
Yin GN, Jeon H, Lee S, Lee HW, Cho JY, Suk K: Role of soluble CD14 in cerebrospinal fluid as a regulator of glial functions, *J Neurosci Res* 87(11):2578–2590, 2009.
Zempel H, Thies E, Mandelkow E, Mandelkow EM: Abeta oligomers cause localized Ca(2+) elevation, missorting of endogenous tau into dendrites, tau phosphorylation, and destruction of microtubules and spines, *J Neurosci* 30(36):11938–11950, 2010.
Zetterberg H, Hietala MA, Jonsson M, et al: Neurochemical aftermath of amateur boxing, *Arch Neurol* 63(9):1277–1280, 2006.
Zetterberg H, Pedersen M, Lind K, et al: Intra-individual stability of CSF biomarkers for Alzheimer's disease over two years, *J Alzheimers Dis* 12(3):255–260, 2007.
Zetterberg H, Andreasson U, Hansson O, et al: Elevated cerebrospinal fluid BACE1 activity in incipient Alzheimer disease, *Arch Neurol* 65(8):1102–1107, 2008.
Zetterberg H, Andreasson U, Blennow K: CSF antithrombin III and disruption of the blood–brain barrier, *J Clin Oncol* 27(13):2302–2303, 2009.
Zetterberg H, Wilson D, Andreasson U, et al: Plasma tau levels in Alzheimer's disease, *Alzheimers Res Ther* 5(2):9, 2013.
Zhong Z, Ewers M, Teipel S, et al: Levels of beta-secretase (BACE1) in cerebrospinal fluid as a predictor of risk in mild cognitive impairment, *Arch Gen Psychiatr* 64(6):718–726, 2007.

CHAPTER

22

Nonpharmacologic Activity Interventions to Prevent Alzheimer's Disease

M.C. Carlson

OUTLINE

OVERVIEW

One-third of cases of Alzheimer's disease (AD) worldwide are estimated to be attributable to modifiable risk factors and behaviors that include low education, physical inactivity, smoking, depression, midlife hypertension, obesity, and diabetes (Norton et al., 2014). In the absence of known effective treatments to cure or delay AD progression once diagnosed,

Developing Therapeutics for Alzheimer's Disease. http://dx.doi.org/10.1016/B978-0-12-802173-6.00022-8

public health efforts have shifted to dementia prevention in cognitively healthy adults and those at elevated cognitive risk (World Health Organization, 2012). In Apr. 2015, the Institute of Medicine (IOM) issued a detailed report, *Cognitive Aging: Progress in Understanding and Opportunities for Action* (Blazer et al., 2015). This report recommended numerous activities to promote cognitive health that centered primarily around being physically, intellectually, and socially engaged, and reducing and managing cardiovascular disease risk factors (including hypertension, diabetes, and smoking). This chapter focuses on the growing number of activity-based interventions aimed at delaying cognitive decline, cognitive impairment, and AD, the most common form of dementia. It briefly summarizes the results of targeted cognitive training and physical exercise interventions, and then moves to the increasing number of multimodal lifestyle activity interventions that target multiple risk factors and neurobiological pathways to cognitive impairment and dementia, and highlights the utility of wearable technology in advancing the field toward novel intervention targets, including sleep behavior.

COGNITIVE TRAINING

Most commercial and experimental cognitive training (or, as popularly coined, "brain" training) programs are based on the premise that practicing one or more tasks leads to improved performance on other, untrained abilities. With practice, players generally become faster and more accurate at performing the trained tasks. However, with one exception (Smith et al., 2009), training on these games does not reliably lead to transfer of training or boosts in other untrained cognitive abilities (near transfer) or to improved function in real-life daily functions, such as driving, meal preparation, or financial management (far transfer) (Baniqued et al., 2013), and expectations of benefit may lead to placebo effects (Boot et al., 2013b).

The largest randomized, controlled trial to evaluate whether cognitive training improved other cognitive abilities and independent functions in older adults was the Advanced Cognitive Training for Independent and Vital Elderly (ACTIVE) trial, which randomly assigned participants to one of four training conditions: memory, reasoning, speed of processing, or a no-contact control group (Tennstedt and Unverzagt, 2013). Intervention groups received 10 training sessions over 3 months. Immediately after training, participants showed significant improvements on the tasks that they trained on, and these improvements were maintained, with the exception of memory, 10 years later (Rebok et al., 2014). However, the researchers did not observe transfer to other cognitive abilities or to self-reported daily functioning 1 and 2 years after training. By 10 years posttraining, more than 60% of those in the training arms reported less difficulty performing instrumental activities of daily living (IADLs) than nontrained participants (49%), and the speed-of-processing and reasoning groups were involved in fewer at-fault automobile crashes. Researchers attributed these modest and delayed effects to the need to observe age-related decline in perceived function in order to reveal transfer effects.

Nonetheless, there is little available evidence yet suggesting that the commercially popular Lumosity, Nintendo Brain Age, and a host of related cognitive games lead to reliable and significant cognitive benefits, and none has yet demonstrated benefits in lowering risk for

AD. Furthermore, adherence remains a concern. One recent study in healthy older adults found that computer game-based training resulted in no cognitive benefit, due to poor adherence (Boot et al., 2013a). Thus, while these games offer benefits in being easily scalable, low-cost, self-paced, and tailored to one's level of ability (Kueider et al., 2012), they may not be sustainable as stand-alone tools without incentives to play and, comparatively, they may not offer the same level of cognitive benefit as engaging in cognitively stimulating lifestyle activities, as exemplified by quilting and digital photography (Park et al., 2014), team-based problem-solving games (Stine-Morrow et al., 2008, 2014), and volunteering (Carlson et al., 2008a, 2009a, 2015), to be summarized later in the section on multimodal interventions.

PHYSICAL EXERCISE AND ACTIVITY

Physical activity is typically categorized as leisure or lifestyle activity (eg, walking, gardening) and exercise (brisk walking, running, swimming) (Caspersen et al., 1985; Caspersen and Fulton 2008; Howley, 2001). The relationship between physical activity and risk for dementia has been equivocal in epidemiologic studies. Studies comparing those who report higher versus lower daily and weekly physical activity show a reduced risk of incident AD among the more active participants (Yoshitake et al., 1995; Abbott et al., 2004; Podewils et al., 2005; Larson et al., 2006). Self-reported physical activity, however, was not protective of dementia among a sample of religious clergy (Wilson et al., 2002) or among community-dwelling older adults (Scarmeas et al., 2001; Verghese et al., 2003). More recently, when one of these studies used objective measures of physical activity, the researchers observed that higher levels of physical activity were protective against risk for AD (Buchman et al., 2012). Advances in objective measurement of daily physical activity have further reinforced its cognitive benefits (Hillman et al., 2008).

A metaanalysis of randomized, controlled trials examining the effect of aerobic training (brisk walking, jogging, and biking) on cognition among nondemented and those with mild cognitive impairment (MCI) suggest modest benefits (Smith et al., 2010). Aerobic exercise training plus strength training produced modest improvements in processing speed, executive function, and memory, with benefits being greatest for those with MCI. Similarly, low-intensity household activities and exercise of moderate to vigorous intensity were associated with improved executive function (Bixby et al., 2007). The effect of physical activity on executive function was additionally observed in adults with MCI (Scherder et al., 2005) and AD (Palleschi et al., 1996). Additionally, two large randomized trials reported improved cognitive function in older adults with MCI (Lautenschlager et al., 2008; Baker et al., 2010).

NEUROBIOLOGICAL TARGETS OF BENEFIT: THE PREFRONTAL CORTEX AND HIPPOCAMPUS

Physical exercise and activity appear to benefit the neural networks most vulnerable with aging, the prefrontal cortex (PFC), the brain's planning or executive center, and the hippocampus, a plastic region important to spatial navigation and memory formation. The PFC network helps us with executive processes involved in the initiation, planning, coordination, and sequencing of actions toward a goal. PFC maturation is not complete until one's early 20s (Gogtay et al., 2004; Garon et al., 2008) and is also more vulnerable than other brain regions with increasing age, as studies show that loss of brain volume is greater in the PFC than in posterior areas of the cortex and that declines in executive functions increase with age (Buckner, 2004; Hedden and Gabrielli, 2004; Raz et al., 1998; West, 1996; Head et al., 2004) and are also impaired in the early stages of AD (Albert et al., 2001; Buckner, 2004). In community-dwelling older adults, I and my coworkers have further found that executive function declines 3 years earlier than memory and that higher cardiovascular risk may exacerbate age-related functional changes in PFC and executive task performance (Chuang et al., 2014), a finding consistent with that observed by others using behavioral (Elias et al., 2004; Laughlin et al., 2011) and structural MRI (Raz et al., 2003).

The second neurobiologic system vulnerable to aging comprises the medial temporal lobes, which includes the hippocampus, the region functionally linked to spatial navigation and memory, and the region showing the most precipitous age-related decline (Buckner, 2004; Raz, 2000). This region is further implicated in risk for dementia (Killiany et al., 2002; Du et al., 2006; Raz et al., 2004; Raz and Rodrigue, 2006). The hippocampus provides a structural and functional juncture between memory and spatial navigation by linking movement through physical activity with the consolidation and updating of information learned as one moves from location to location.

EFFECTS OF PHYSICAL ACTIVITY ON AGE-RELATED NEUROBIOLOGICAL TARGETS

Animal and human research shows that physical activity likely mediates benefits in neurocognitive health through multiple neurotrophic and cardiovascular pathways (van Praag et al., 1999a,b; Vaynman et al., 2004; Ferris et al., 2007; Voss et al., 2014), including neurogenesis in the hippocampus (Erickson et al., 2011), upregulation of brain-derived neurotrophic factor (BDNF) and VEG-F (Lee et al., 2001), reduction of obesity (Mitchell et al., 2003) and insulin levels (Katzel et al., 1995), increased carotid wall thickness (Folsom et al., 1994), and cerebral blood flow (Pereira et al., 2007). Physical fitness and walking activity have been shown to directly influence the functional and structural properties of the PFC and hippocampus. In a randomized, controlled trial of aerobic walking exercise, Kramer and coworkers observed neurocognitive benefits in the efficiency of executive function and brain activity in the PFC (Colcombe et al., 2004, 2006). The same effects were not observed in a toning and stretching control group. Cross-sectional and longitudinal studies have also reported an inverse association between self-reported physical activity and moderation of age-related decreases in mediotemporal volume (Bugg and Head, 2011), and with mitigated rates of decline in hippocampal volume over 9–13 years (Erickson et al., 2010). Greater cardiorespiratory fitness levels have been cross-sectionally associated with greater hippocampal volume in both children (Chaddock et al., 2009) and healthy older adults (Erickson et al., 2009). Erickson et al. (2011) found that a moderate-intensity walking for exercise intervention over 1 year increased hippocampal volume by 2%. We have extended this finding to the study of low-intensity (nonexercise) walking activity in daily life, and hippocampal volume in mostly sedentary older adults. Our cross-sectional findings showed that higher levels of daily walking were associated with larger hippocampal volume, suggesting that even modest increases in low-intensity walking activity in daily life may yield neurocognitive benefits. Given that older adults who participate in physical activity interventions often revert back to their baseline, sedentary state (van der Bij et al., 2002), these data suggest that activity in day-to-day life may represent a target for intervention to delay and mitigate memory declines that may lead to dementia (Carlson et al., 2009b).

LIFESTYLE ACTIVITY, ENVIRONMENTAL ENRICHMENT, AND NEUROCOGNITIVE HEALTH

Evidence from animal models of environmental enrichment summarized by Kempermann et al. (2010) provides more detailed mechanistic support for the premise that physical activity may be necessary but not sufficient to sustain neurogenesis in adult animals. They summarize rigorously controlled environmental enrichment paradigms in animals spanning more than a decade and conclude that, while exercise helps promote and regulate adult neurogenesis (generation of new neurons), exposure to environmental complexity and novelty recruits these new cells for functional integration with existing neurons. Enriched environments are designed to provide novel challenges that combine curiosity and play with modest levels of physical activity (Sale et al., 2009). Functional activation of new neurons in these enriched environments occurs in older animals and exceeds that of younger animals (Kempermann et al., 1998, 2002).

In humans, cognitive enrichment through mid- and late-life activity appears to have beneficial effects on cognition (Raz, 2000; Blumenthal et al., 1989; Gunning-Dixon and Raz, 2003; Arbuckle et al., 1998; Baltes and Willis, 1982; Carlson et al., 2012), risk for neurodegenerative disorders (Gribbin et al., 1980; Pushkar et al., 1997, 1999; Schooler et al., 1999; Scarmeas et al., 2001; Stern et al., 1999; Wang et al., 2002), neuronal architecture (Wilson et al., 1999, 2002; Gould et al., 1999; Greenough et al., 1999; van Praag et al., 1999a,b), and cerebral perfusion (Rogers et al., 1990). The nature of cognitively enriching activity may take numerous forms in everyday life. We have observed benefits in rates of cognitive aging emerge from engaging in a variety of activities (Podewils et al., 2005), and that among male twin pairs, the male participating in a greater range of cognitively and socially engaging activities in midlife had reduced risk for AD and dementia 28 years later in a finding magnified among those at elevated genetic risk for the disease (Carlson et al., 2008a). Protective effects were most robust in monozygotic (identical) twin pairs, where genetic and early-life influences were most tightly controlled. These activities might be indicative of an enriched environment, which may provide cognitive benefits through the mechanism postulated by Kempermann et al. (2010) and elaborated elsewhere (Carlson and Varma, 2015). While there is now ample evidence that physically, cognitively, and socially enriching environments promote the emergence of new neurons in animals throughout life (Kempermann et al., 2006), little of this work has been directly translated to human physical activity interventions targeting neurocognitive health and risk for AD.

ADDRESSING THE CHALLENGES OF SUSTAINING PHYSICAL ACTIVITY IN LATER LIFE

A paradox of aging is that older adults represent the group with the most to gain from regular physical activity because of its beneficial effects on PFC, executive function, cardiovascular and diabetic risk, and a host of other health-related outcomes beyond the scope of this chapter. Unfortunately, they are also the subset of the population with the highest rates of inactivity (van der Bij et al., 2002). Exercise programs have been difficult to promote adherence to in any long-term, large-scale way (Pate et al., 1995) and have primarily been conducted in those with higher socioeconomic status (SES) (Katula et al., 2007; Stewart et al., 2001). Among those with lower SES, neighborhood factors often restrict opportunities for regular exercise (Moore et al., 2008). Lifestyle activity interventions that target changes in low-intensity physical activity may have the greatest potential for sustainability beyond the intervention period, particularly in older adults who have a high burden of chronic diseases, who are overweight, and who have osteoarthritis, which may make moderately vigorous activities painful.

YOGA AND MINDFULNESS ACTIVITIES

Derived from Eastern contemplative traditions, mindfulness practices—which include yoga and meditation—involve attending to the present moment in a sustained and receptive fashion (Brown and Ryan, 2003). Yoga is a form of mindfulness practice that involves breathing techniques and movement sequences that train balance, strength, and flexibility. Mindfulness practices have been associated with benefits to multiple components of cognition, including attention, memory, and executive functions (Gard et al., 2014; Jha et al., 2007a,b; Tang et al., 2007; Zeidan et al., 2010; Chiesa et al., 2011; Bishop et al., 2004), and to brain function and structure relevant to cognition and motor control (Allen et al., 2012; Brefczynski-Lewis et al., 2007; Holzel et al., 2007, 2011; Lazar et al., 2000, 2005; Davidson and McEwen, 2012). Randomized trials of similar meditation-based forms of physical activity, including Tai chi and Qigong, have also shown cognitive benefits (Lam et al., 2011; Taylor-Piliae et al., 2010). A review of studies comparing the effects of yoga and traditional physical exercise found that yoga may be equally or more effective as exercise for improving various health outcomes (Ross and Thomas, 2010). In a metaanalysis of randomized clinical trials, the benefits of yoga for older adults were shown to exceed those of conventional physical activity interventions (Patel et al., 2011).

However, yoga and mindfulness interventions have been evaluated primarily in those with higher SES. Among those with lower SES, additional infrastructure may be necessary to help overcome economic and neighborhood barriers to engaging in these activities (Frank et al., 2010; Saelens et al., 2003; Leslie et al., 2007; Randall and Baetz, 2001; Cole et al., 2006). Physical activity interventions that can circumvent these challenges through the proximal placement of yoga in community centers have the potential for long-term impact in large groups, particularly among those at elevated sociodemographic risk for AD (Frank et al., 2010; Cunningham and Michael, 2004; Balfour and Kaplan, 2002).

INCREASING COGNITIVE AND PHYSICAL ACTIVITY IN LATER LIFE THROUGH SOCIAL ENGAGEMENT: MULTIMODAL INTERVENTIONS

A growing body of evidence in middle-aged and older adults suggests that low social activity is associated with increased risk for AD (Kondo et al., 1994) and that midlife (Saczynski et al., 2006) and late-life social engagement is associated with better cognitive and physical health and greater longevity (Bassuk et al., 1999; Zunzunegui et al., 2003; Taylor et al., 2000) (for review, see Fratiglioni et al., 2004). Both social integration and social activity predict better functioning and reduced risk for declines in cognitive functioning (House et al., 1988; Seeman et al., 1987, 1993, 1995; La Greca et al., 1995; Wang et al., 2002; Barnes et al., 2004; Karp et al., 2006). Ironically, transitions with increasing age, such as retirement and resulting loss of routine contact with coworkers, as well as increasing tendencies for adult offspring to live remotely, make older adults a population at high risk for decreasing levels of social integration and interaction. As a result, opportunities for social activity and engagement become more restricted and sporadic (Unger et al., 1997; Everard, 1999; Everard et al., 2000).

Multimodal interventions that combine multiple activity pathways are increasing rapidly. They have typically combined physical exercise and cognitive training to explore whether benefits exceed those for either alone. The Mental Activity and eXercise (MAX) trial recruited inactive older adults with cognitive complaints to a 3-month intervention combining cognitive training with an aerobic exercise program. The study observed similar improvements in cognitive function in the combined intervention group compared to active cognitive control (DVD viewing) and exercise control (stretching and toning) groups (Barnes et al., 2013). These two control groups were used to account for the effects of factors such as interaction with a computer and social interaction during a group exercise class. The multicomponent (diet, exercise, cognitive training, vascular risk monitoring) Finnish Geriatric Intervention Study to Prevent Cognitive Impairment and Disability (FINGER) proof-of-concept trial found modest but significant intervention-related benefits over 2 years on a composite measure of cognition and specifically on tests of executive function and processing speed (Ngandu et al., 2015). Pilot results from the ThinkingFit intervention suggest potential cognitive benefits for participants with MCI (Dannhauser et al., 2014). Other activity-based trials, including the Synapse Project of digital photography and quilting, the Senior Odyssey program, and an iPad training study, have shown memory benefits from combined social and cognitive enrichment interventions (Chan et al., 2014; Park et al., 2013; Stine-Morrow et al., 2007). Of note, the Synapse Project trial included a receptive social control group that yielded limited cognitive benefits relative to the productive and social quilting and photography activities. Collectively, these findings suggest that engagement in cognitively and socially challenging activities embedded within daily life can enhance multiple domains of cognition.

Experience Corps (EC) represents just such a novel approach, offering a scalable opportunity for increasing physical, cognitive, and social activity in daily life. EC is a community-based health promotion program embedded within a high-intensity volunteer service program that has operated nationally for more than 17 years (Freedman and Fried, 1999) and, since 2011, under the direction of the American Association of Retired Persons (AARP). The goal of this program is to improve the academic performance of young children in underserved urban areas by using older adults' time, skills, and wisdom. In the Baltimore EC program, retired adults volunteer in teams of 10–15 in neighborhood elementary schools as mentors of children in kindergarten through grade 3 for 15 h a week over 1–2 academic years (Freedman and Fried, 1999; Fried et al., 2004, 2013; Glass et al., 2004; Parisi et al., 2009; Rebok et al., 2011). The EC model provides a real-world example of how increases in these activities lead to self-reported increases in physical activity (Fried et al., 2004; Tan et al., 2006) and cognitive activity (Fried et al., 2004), cognitive health (Carlson et al., 2008b), and improved brain activity in regions that support executive attention (Carlson et al., 2009a). A formal large-scale trial evaluation initiated in 2006, the Baltimore Experience Corps Trial (BECT), was among the first interventions to explore the neurocognitive benefits of simultaneously increasing physical and cognitive activity through purposeful social engagement over 2 academic years of service (Fried et al., 2004, 2013). A nested neuroimaging trial within the BECT showed intervention-specific increases in objectively measured physical activity among female volunteers (Varma et al., 2014) and dose-dependent benefits to hippocampal and total cortical volumes (Carlson et al., 2015). These findings regarding EC's benefits highlight the potential of real-world, community-based interventions for simultaneously raising low levels of physical activity and improving neurocognitive health in older adults at elevated risk for AD by virtue of low education and high cardiovascular risk (Carlson et al., 2009a).

MEASURING ACTIVITY IN DAILY LIFE AND AT NIGHT

Targeting increases in low-intensity, daily physical activity warrant improved methods for assessment. Recent advances in wearable computing open up new frontiers in neurocognitive intervention research. Digital technologies are becoming a regular part of daily life and provide us with a low-cost opportunity to transform standard practices in the assessment of cognitive, physical, and social activity. High-dimensional information obtained through wearable devices allows us to advance beyond self-report to provide finer spatial and temporal granularity with which to capture previously undetected changes in diurnal patterns that may increase lifestyle activity (Carlson MC, Varma VR, Adam A, Crainiceanu C, Zipunnikov V: Linking community activity to cognitive and brain health in older adults using wearable technology. Unpublished observation). Lifestyle activity among EC volunteers and those participating in other activity interventions, described previously, may have changed in modest but sustainable ways (Varma et al., in press). Use of accelerometers, GPS, and other wearable technology will enable us to circumvent self-report to directly evaluate how even modest changes in the dose, duration, and location of physical activity (eg, in complex community spaces vs at home) may be related to neurocognitive health and risk for AD.

Incorporation of wearable technology will also allow us to better evaluate nighttime activity or sleep patterns. At least 50% of older adults report insomnia symptoms (ie, difficulty falling to sleep or staying asleep) (Foley et al., 1995; Ohayon, 2002), and, in recent years, self-reported sleep disturbance, poorer sleep quality, and difficulty falling or staying asleep have been associated with poorer cognition, cognitive decline (Nebes et al., 2009; Tworoger et al., 2006; Cricco et al., 2001; Jelicic et al., 2002), and greater amyloid deposition (Spira et al., 2013). Studies using objective, wrist-worn measures of sleep disruptions (movement) (Ancoli-Israel et al., 2003) have found that shorter sleep duration, longer sleep onset latency, greater sleep fragmentation, and less efficient sleep were associated with poorer cognition (Blackwell et al., 2006, 2014), greater amyloid burden (Ju et al., 2013), worse physical function (Spira et al., 2010), and functional decline (Spira et al., 2012). As a result, assessment of sleep patterns warrants investigation as a mechanism through which activity-based interventions may exert impacts on cognitive impairment, neuropathology, and AD risk.

CONCLUSIONS

Data summarized here suggest that activity-based interventions seeking to slow cognitive declines and delay dementia onset are on the rise and hold promise in ongoing follow-up. Physical activity, yoga, and low-intensity physical activity embedded within one's complex social environment may affect cognitive and brain health in multiple ways that impact directly or indirectly the neuropathology and clinical symptoms of AD. Recent intervention efforts are increasingly targeting individuals in the community who may not self-identify risk but who are at elevated risk for AD based on poor cognitive function (eg, MCI) or based on the presence of known behavioral risk factors (eg, inactivity, low education). Many of these programs are scalable through existing clinical settings and community infrastructure, including schools, retirement centers, religious centers, YMCAs, and other public and private nonprofit organizations. At the same time, much remains to be learned about the specific physical and lifestyle activities that contribute to cognitive health or offer resilience to pathology, and the limits of their effectiveness. Questions that remain to be addressed in this developing field are not unlike those related to pharmacological studies, and include exposure or dosing (intensity/strength, duration), adherence, and sustainability of gains postexposure. A critical objective for studies going forward will be to explore the interactive, and potentially synergistic, effects of multimodal interventions incorporated into daily life using real-time wearable technologies that increase measurement precision.

References

Abbott RD, White LR, Ross GW, Masaki KH, Curb JD, Petrovitch H: Walking and dementia in physically capable elderly men, *J Am Med Assoc* 292:1447–1453, 2004.

Albert MS, Moss MB, Tanzi R, Jones K: Preclinical prediction of AD using neuropsychological tests, *J Int Neuropsychol Soc* 7:631–639, 2001.

Allen M, Dietz M, Blair KS, Van Beek M, Rees G, Vestergaard-Poulsen P, Lutz A, Roepstorff A: Cognitive-affective neural plasticity following active-controlled mindfulness intervention, *J Neurosci* 32:15601–15610, 2012.

Ancoli-Israel S, Cole R, Alessi C, Chambers M, Moorcroft W, Pollak CP: The role of actigraphy in the study of sleep and circadian rhythms, *Sleep* 26:342–392, 2003.

Arbuckle TY, Maag U, Pushkar D, Chaikelson JS: Individual differences in trajectory of intellectual development over 45 years of adulthood, *Psychol Aging* 13:663–675, 1998.

Baker LD, Frank LL, Foster-Schubert K, Green PS, Wilkinson CW, McTiernan A, Plymate SR, Fishel MA, Watson GS, Cholerton BA, Duncan GE, Mehta PD, Craft S: Effects of aerobic exercise on mild cognitive impairment: a controlled trial, *Arch Neurol* 67:71–79, 2010.

Balfour JL, Kaplan GA: Neighborhood environment and loss of physical function in older adults: evidence from the Alameda County Study, *Am J Epidemiol* 155:507–515, 2002.

Baltes PB, Willis SL: Plasticity and enhancement of intellectual functioning in old age: Penn State's Adult Development and Enrichment Project (ADEPT). In Craik FIM, Trehub SE, editors: *Aging and cognitive processes*, New York, 1982, Plenum Press.

Baniqued PL, Kranz MB, Voss MW, Lee H, Cosman JD, Severson J, Kramer AF: Cognitive training with casual video games: points to consider, *Front Psychol* 4:1010, 2013.

Barnes LL, Mendes De Leon CF, Wilson RS, Bienias JL, Evans DA: Social resources and cognitive decline in a population of older African Americans and whites, *Neurology* 63:2322–2326, 2004.

Barnes DE, Santos-Modesitt W, Poelke G, Kramer AF, Castro C, Middleton LE, Yaffe K: The Mental Activity and eXercise (MAX) trial: a randomized controlled trial to enhance cognitive function in older adults, *JAMA Intern Med* 173:797–804, 2013.

Bassuk SS, Glass TA, Berkman LF: Social disengagement and incident cognitive decline in community-dwelling elderly persons, *Ann Intern Med* 131:165–173, 1999.

Bishop S, Lau M, Shapiro S, Carlson L, Anderson N, Carmody J, Segal Z, Speca M, Velting D, Devins G: Mindfulness: a proposed operational definition, *Clin Psychol* 11:230–241, 2004.

Bixby WR, Spalding TW, Haufler AJ, Deeny SP, Mahlow PT, Zimmerman JB, Hatfield BD: The unique relation of physical activity to executive function in older men and women, *Med Sci Sports Exerc* 39:1408–1416, 2007.

Blackwell T, Yaffe K, Ancoli-Israel S, Schneider JL, Cauley JA, Hillier TA, Fink HA, Stone KL: Poor sleep is associated with impaired cognitive function in older women: the study of osteoporotic fractures, *J Gerontol A* 61:405–410, 2006.

Blackwell T, Yaffe K, Laffan A, Ancoli-Israel S, Redline S, Ensrud KE, Song Y, Stone KL: Associations of objectively and subjectively measured sleep quality with subsequent cognitive decline in older community-dwelling men: the MrOS sleep study, *Sleep* 37:655–663, 2014.

Blazer D, Yaffe K, Liverman C: *Cognitive aging: progress in understanding and opportunities for action*, Washington, DC, 2015, National Academies Press.

Blumenthal JA, Emery CF, Madden DJ, George LK, Coleman RE, Riddle MW, McKee DC, Reasoner J, Williams RS: Cardiovascular and behavorial effects of aerobic exercise training in healthy older men and women, *J Gerontol* 44:M147–M157, 1989.

Boot WR, Champion M, Blakely DP, Wright T, Souders DJ, Charness N: Video games as a means to reduce age-related cognitive decline: attitudes, compliance, and effectiveness, *Front Psychol* 4:1–9, 2013a.

Boot WR, Simons DJ, Stothart C, Stutts C: The pervasive problem with placebos in psychology why active control groups are not sufficient to rule out placebo effects, *Perspect Psychol Sci* 8:445–454, 2013b.

Brefczynski-Lewis JA, Lutz A, Schaefer HS, Levinson DB, Davidson RJ: Neural correlates of attentional expertise in long-term meditation practitioners, *Proc Natl Acad Sci USA* 104:11483–11488, 2007.

Brown K, Ryan R: The benefits of being present: mindfulness and its role in psychological well-being, *J Pers Soc Psychol* 84:822–848, 2003.

Buchman AS, Boyle PA, Yu L, Shah RC, Wilson RS, Bennett DA: Total daily physical activity and the risk of AD and cognitive decline in older adults, *Neurology* 78:1323–1329, 2012.

Buckner RL: Memory and executive function in aging and AD: multiple factors that cause decline and reserve factors that compensate, *Neuron* 44:195–208, 2004.

Bugg JM, Head D: Exercise moderates age-related atrophy of the medial temporal lobe, *Neurobiol Aging* 32:506–514, 2011.

Carlson MC, Varma VR: Activity and neurocognitive health in older adults. *Neuropsychology of cardiovascular disease*, ed 2, New York, 2015, Psychology Press, pp 79–108.

Carlson MC, Helms MJ, Steffens DC, Burke JR, Potter GG, Plassman BL: Midlife activity predicts risk of dementia in older male twin pairs, *Alzheimers Dement* 4:324–331, 2008a.

Carlson MC, Saczynski JS, Rebok GW, Seeman T, Glass TA, McGill S, Tielsch J, Frick KD, Hill J, Fried LP: Exploring the effects of an "everyday" activity program on executive function and memory in older adults: Experience Corps, *Gerontologist* 48:793–801, 2008b.

Carlson MC, Erickson KI, Kramer AF, Voss MW, Bolea N, Mielke M, McGill S, Rebok GW, Seeman T, Fried LP: Evidence for neurocognitive plasticity in at-risk older adults: the Experience Corps program, *J Gerontol A* 64:1275–1282, 2009a.

Carlson M, Xue QL, Zhou J, Fried LP: Executive decline and dysfunction precedes declines in memory: the Women's Health and Aging Study II, *J Gerontol A* 64:110–117, 2009b.

Carlson MC, Parisi JM, Xia J, Xue Q-L, Rebok GW, Bandeen-Roche K, Fried LP: Lifestyle activities and memory: variety may be the spice of life: the Women's Health and Aging Study II, *J Int Neuropsychol Soc* 18:286–294, 2012.

Carlson MC, Kuo JH, Chuang YF, Varma V, Harris G, Albert M, Erickson KI, Kramer AF, Parisi JM, Xue QL, Tan E, Tanner EK, Gross A, Seeman TE, Gruenewald T, McGill S, Rebok GW, Fried LP: Impact of the Baltimore Experience Corps trial on cortical and hippocampal volumes, *Alzheimers Dement* 11:1340–1348, 2015.

Caspersen CJ, Powell KE, Christenson GM: Physical activity, exercise, and physical fitness: definitions and distinctions for health-related research, *Public Health Rep* 100:126–131, 1985.

Caspersen CJ, Fulton JE: Epidemiology of walking and type 2 diabetes, *Med Sci Sports Exerc* 40(7 Suppl):S519–S528, 2008.

Chaddock L, Erickson KI, Prakash RS, Kim JS, Voss MW, Vanpatter M, Pontifex MB, Raine LB, Konkel A, Hillman CH, Cohen NJ, Kramer AF: A neuroimaging investigation of the association between aerobic fitness, hippocampal volume, and memory performance in preadolescent children, *Brain Res* 1358:172–183, 2009.

Chan MY, Haber S, Drew LM, Park DC: Training older adults to use tablet computers: does it enhance cognitive function? *Gerontologist* 54:1–11, 2014.

Chiesa A, Calati R, Seretti A: Does mindfulness training improve cognitive abilities? A systematic review of neuropsychological findings, *Clin Psychol Rev* 31:449–464, 2011.

Chuang YF, Eldreth D, Erickson KI, Varma V, Harris G, Fried LP, Rebok GW, Tanner EK, Carlson MC: Cardiovascular risks and brain function: a functional magnetic resonance imaging study of executive function in older adults, *Neurobiol Aging* 35:1396–1403, 2014.

Colcombe SJ, Kramer AF, Erickson KI, Scalf P, McAuley E, Cohen NJ, Webb A, Jerome GJ, Marquez DX, Elavsky S: Cardiovascular fitness, cortical plasticity, and aging, *Proc Natl Acad Sci USA* 101:3316–3321, 2004.

Colcombe SJ, Erickson KI, Scalf PE, Kim JS, Prakash R, McAuley E, Elavsky S, Marquez DX, Hu L, Kramer AF: Aerobic exercise training reduces brain tissue loss in aging humans, *J Gerontol A* 61:1166–1170, 2006.

Cole R, Leslie E, Bauman A, Donald M, Owen N: Socio-demographic variations in walking for transport and for recreation or exercise among adult Australians, *J Phys Activity Health* 3:164, 2006.

Cricco M, Simonsick EM, Foley DJ: The impact of insomnia on cognitive functioning in older adults, *J Am Geriatr Soc* 49:1185–1189, 2001.

Cunningham GO, Michael YL: Concepts guiding the study of the impact of the built environment on physical activity for older adults: a review of the literature, *Am J Health Promot* 18:435–443, 2004.

Dannhauser TM, Cleverley M, Whitfield TJ, Fletcher BC, Stevens T, Walker Z: A complex multimodal activity intervention to reduce the risk of dementia in mild cognitive impairment—ThinkingFit: pilot and feasibility study for a randomized controlled trial, *BMC Psychiatr* 14:129, 2014.

Davidson RJ, McEwen BS: Social influences on neuroplasticity: stress and interventions to promote well-being, *Nat Neurosci* 15:689–695, 2012.

Du AT, Schuff N, Chao LL, Kornak J, Jagust WJ, Kramer JH, Reed BR, Miller BL, Norman D, Chui HC, Weiner MW: Age effects on atrophy rates of entorhinal cortex and hippocampus, *Neurobiol Aging* 27:733–740, 2006.

Elias P, Elias M, Robbins M, Budge M: Blood pressure-related cognitive decline: does age make a difference? *Hypertension* 44:631–636, 2004.

Erickson KI, Prakash RS, Voss MW, Chaddock L, Hu L, Morris KS, White SM, Wojcicki TR, McAuley E, Kramer AF: Aerobic fitness is associated with hippocampal volume in elderly humans, *Hippocampus* 19:1030–1039, 2009.

Erickson KI, Raji CA, Lopez OL, Becker JT, Rosano C, Newman AB, Gach HM, Thompson PM, Ho AJ, Kuller LH: Physical activity predicts gray matter volume in late adulthood: the Cardiovascular Health Study, *Neurology* 75:1415–1422, 2010.

Erickson KI, Voss MW, Prakash RS, Basak C, Szabo A, Chaddock L, Kim JS, Heo S, Alves H, White SM, Wojcicki TR, Mailey E, Vieira VJ, Martin SA, Pence BD, Woods JA, McAuley E, Kramer AF: Exercise training increases size of hippocampus and improves memory, *Proc Natl Acad Sci USA* 108:3017–3022, 2011.

Everard KM: The relationship between reasons for activity and older adult well-being, *J Appl Gerontol* 18:325–340, 1999.

Everard KM, Lach HW, Fisher EB, Baum MC: Relationship of activity and social support to the functional health of older adults, *J Gerontol B* 55:S208–S212, 2000.

Ferris LT, Williams JS, Shen CL: The effect of acute exercise on serum brain-derived neurotrophic factor levels and cognitive function, *Med Sci Sports Exerc* 39:728–734, 2007.

Foley DJ, Monjan AA, Brown SL, Simonsick EM, Wallace RB, Blazer DG: Sleep complaints among elderly persons: an epidemiologic study of three communities, *Sleep Med Rev* 18:425–432, 1995.

Folsom AR, Eckfeldt JH, Weitzman S, Ma J, Chambless LE, Barnes RW, Cram KB, Hutchinson RG: Relation of carotid artery wall thickness to diabetes mellitus, fasting glucose and insulin, body size, and physical activity: Atherosclerosis Risk in Communities (ARIC) Study Investigators, *Stroke* 25:66–73, 1994.

Frank L, Kerr J, Rosenberg D, King A: Healthy aging and where you live: community design relationships with physical activity and body weight in older Americans, *J Phys Act Health* 7(Suppl 1):S82–S90, 2010.

Fratiglioni L, Paillard-Borg S, Winblad B: An active and socially integrated lifestyle in late life might protect against dementia, *Lancet Neurol* 3:343–353, 2004.

Freedman M, Fried L: *Launching Experience Corps: findings from a two-year pilot project mobilizing older Americans to help inner-city elementary schools*, Oakland, CA, 1999, Civic Ventures.

Fried LP, Carlson MC, Freedman M, Frick KD, Glass TA, Hill J, McGill S, Rebok GW, Seeman T, Tielsch J, Wasik BA, Zeger S: A social model for health promotion for an aging population: initial evidence on the Experience Corps model, *J Urban Health* 81:64–78, 2004.

Fried LP, Carlson MC, McGill S, Seeman T, Xue QL, Frick K, Tan E, Tanner EK, Barron J, Frangakis C, Piferi R, Martinez I, Gruenewald T, Martin BK, Berry-Vaughn L, Stewart J, Dickersin K, Willging PR, Rebok GW: Experience Corps: a dual trial to promote the health of older adults and children's academic success, *Contemp Clin Trials* 36:1–13, 2013.

Gard T, Holzel BK, Lazar SW: The potential effects of meditation on age-related cognitive decline: a systematic review, *Ann NY Acad Sci* 1307:89–103, 2014.

Garon N, Bryson SE, Smith IM: Executive function in preschoolers: a review using an integrative framework, *Psychol Bull* 134:31–60, 2008.

Glass TA, Freedman M, Carlson MC, Hill J, Frick KD, Ialongo N, McGill S, Rebok GW, Seeman T, Tielsch JM, Wasik BA, Zeger S, Fried LP: Experience Corps: design of an intergenerational program to boost social capital and promote the health of an aging society, *J Urban Health* 81:94–105, 2004.

Gogtay N, Sporn A, Clasen LS, Nugent TF III, Greenstein D, Nicolson R, Giedd JN, Lenane M, Gochman P, Evans A, Rapoport JL: Comparison of progressive cortical gray matter loss in childhood-onset schizophrenia with that in childhood-onset atypical psychoses, *Arch Gen Psychiatr* 61:17–22, 2004.

Gould E, Beylin A, Tanapat P, Reeves A, Shors TJ: Learning enhances adult neurogenesis in the hippocampal formation, *Nat Neurosci* 2:260–265, 1999.

Greenough WT, Cohen NJ, Juraska JM: New neurons in old brains: learning to survive? *Nat Neurosci* 2: 203–205, 1999.

Gribbin K, Schaie KW, Parham IA: Complexity of life style and maintenance of intellectual abilities, *J Social Issues* 36:47–61, 1980.

Gunning-Dixon FM, Raz N: Neuroanatomical correlates of selected executive functions in middle-aged and older adults: a prospective MRI study, *Neuropsychologia* 41:1929–1941, 2003.

Head D, Buckner RL, Shimony JS, Williams LE, Akbudak E, Conturo TE, McAvoy M, Morris JC, Snyder AZ: Differential vulnerability of anterior white matter in nondemented aging with minimal acceleration in dementia of the Alzheimer type: evidence from diffusion tensor imaging, *Cereb Cortex* 14:410–423, 2004.

Hedden T, Gabrielli J: Insights into the ageing mind: a view from cognitive neuroscience, *Nat Rev Neurosci* 5:87–96, 2004.

Hillman CH, Erickson KI, Kramer AF: Be smart, exercise your heart: exercise effects on brain and cognition, *Nat Rev Neurosci* 9:58–65, 2008.

Holzel BK, Ott U, Hempel H, Hackl A, Wolf K, Stark R, Vaitl D: Differential engagement of anterior cingulate and adjacent medial frontal cortex in adept meditators and non-meditators, *Neurosci Lett* 421:16–21, 2007.

Holzel BK, Carmody J, Vangel M, Congleton C, Yerramsetti SM, Gard T, Lazar SW: Mindfulness practice leads to increases in regional brain gray matter density, *Psychiatr Res* 191:36–43, 2011.

House JS, Landis KR, Umberson D: Social relationships and health, *Science* 241:540–545, 1988.

Howley ET: Type of activity: resistance, aerobic and leisure versus occupational physical activity, *Med Sci Sports Exerc* 33:S364–S369, 2001 (discussion S419–S420).

Jelicic M, Bosma H, Ponds RW, Van Boxtel MP, Houx PJ, Jolles J: Subjective sleep problems in later life as predictors of cognitive decline: report from the Maastricht Ageing Study (MAAS), *Int J Geriatr Psychiatr* 17: 73–77, 2002.

Jha AP, Krompinger J, Baime MJ: Mindfulness training modifies subsystems of attention, *Cogn Affect Behav Neurosci* 7:109–119, 2007a.

Jha AP, Stanley EA, Kiyonaga A, Wong L, Gelfand L: Examining the protective effects of mindfulness training on working memory capacity and affective experience, *Emotion* 10:54–64, 2007b.

Ju YE, McLeland JS, Toedebusch CD, Xiong C, Fagan AM, Duntley SP, Morris JC, Holtzman DM: Sleep quality and preclinical Alzheimer disease, *JAMA Neurol* 70:587–593, 2013.

Karp A, Paillard-Borg S, Wang HX, Silverstein M, Winblad B, Fratiglioni L: Mental, physical and social components in leisure activities equally contribute to decrease dementia risk, *Dement Geriatr Cogn Disord* 21:65–73, 2006.

Katula JA, Kritchevsky SB, Guralnik JM, Glynn NW, Pruitt L, Wallace K, Walkup MP, Hsu FC, Studenski SA, Gill TM, Groessl EJ, Wallace JM, Pahor M: Lifestyle interventions and independence for elders pilot study: recruitment and baseline characteristics, *J Am Geriatr Soc* 55:674–683, 2007.

Katzel LI, Bleecker ER, Colman EG, Rogus EM, Sorkin JD, Goldberg AP: Effects of weight loss vs aerobic exercise training on risk factors for coronary disease in healthy, obese, middle-aged and older men: a randomized controlled trial, *J Am Med Assoc* 274:1915–1921, 1995.

Kempermann G, Kuhn HG, Gage FH: Experience-induced neurogenesis in the senescent dentate gyrus, *J Neurosci* 18:3206–3212, 1998.

Kempermann G, Gast D, Gage FH: Neuroplasticity in old age: sustained fivefold induction of hippocampal neurogenesis by long-term environmental enrichment, *Ann Neurol* 52:135–143, 2002.

Kempermann G, Chesler EJ, Lu L, Williams RW, Gage FH: Natural variation and genetic covariance in adult hippocampal neurogenesis, *Proc Natl Acad Sci USA* 103:780–785, 2006.

Kempermann G, Fabel K, Ehninger D, Babu H, Leal-Galicia P, Garthe A, Wolf SA: Why and how physical activity promotes experience-induced brain plasticity, *Front Neurosci* 4:189, 2010.

Killiany RJ, Hyman BT, Gomez-Isla T, Moss MB, Kikinis R, Jolesz F, Tanzi R, Jones K, Albert MS: MRI measures of entorhinal cortex vs hippocampus in preclinical AD, *Neurology* 58:1188–1196, 2002.

Kondo K, Niino M, Shido K: A case-control study of Alzheimer's disease in Japan—significance of life-styles, *Dementia* 5:314–326, 1994.

Kueider AM, Parisi JM, Gross AL, Rebok GW: Computerized cognitive training with older adults: a systematic review, *PLoS One* 7:e40588, 2012.

La Greca AM, Auslander WF, Greco P, Spetter D, Fisher EB Jr, Santiago JV: I get by with a little help from my family and friends: adolescents' support for diabetes care, *J Pediatr Psychol* 20:449–476, 1995.

Lam LC, Chau RC, Wong BM, Fung AW, Lui VW, Tam CC, Leung GT, Kwok TC, Chiu HF, Ng S, Chan WM: Interim follow-up of a randomized controlled trial comparing Chinese style mind body (tai chi) and stretching exercises on cognitive function in subjects at risk of progressive cognitive decline, *Int J Geriatr Psychiatr* 26:733–740, 2011.

Larson EB, Wang L, Bowen JD, McCormick WC, Teri L, Crane P, Kukull W: Exercise is associated with reduced risk for incident dementia among persons 65 years of age and older, *Ann Internal Med* 144:73–81, 2006.

Laughlin GA, McEvoy LK, Von Muhlen D, Daniels LB, Kritz-Silverstein D, Bergstrom J, Cummins K, Der-Martirosian C, Jassal SK, Barrett-Connor E: Sex differences in the association of Framingham Cardiac Risk Score with cognitive decline in community-dwelling elders without clinical heart disease, *Psychosom Med* 73:683–689, 2011.

Lautenschlager NT, Cox KL, Flicker L, Foster JK, Van Bockxmeer FM, Xiao J, Greenop KR, Almeida OP: Effect of physical activity on cognitive function in older adults at risk for Alzheimer disease: a randomized trial, *J Am Med Assoc* 300:1027–1037, 2008.

Lazar SW, Bush G, Gollub RL, Fricchione GL, Khalsa G, Benson H: Functional brain mapping of the relaxation response and meditation, *Neuroreport* 11:1581–1585, 2000.

Lazar SW, Kerr CE, Wasserman RH, Gray JR, Greve DN, Treadway MT, McGarvey M, Quinn BT, Dusek JA, Benson H, Rauch SL, Moore CI, Fischl B: Meditation experience is associated with increased cortical thickness, *Neuroreport* 16:1893–1897, 2005.

Lee R, Kermani P, Teng KK, Hempstead BL: Regulation of cell survival by secreted proneurotrophins, *Science* 294:1945–1948, 2001.

Leslie E, Coffee N, Frank L, Owen N, Bauman A, Hugo G: Walkability of local communities: using geographic information systems to objectively assess relevant environmental attributes, *Health Place* 13:111–122, 2007.

Mitchell D, Haan MN, Steinberg FM, Visser M: Body composition in the elderly: the influence of nutritional factors and physical activity, *J Nutr Health Aging* 7:130–139, 2003.

Moore HJ, Ells LJ, McLure SA, Crooks S, Cumbor D, Summerbell CD, Batterham AM: The development and evaluation of a novel computer program to assess previous day dietary and physical activity behaviours in school children: the Synchronised Nutrition and Activity Program (SNAP), *Brit J Nutr* 99:1266–1274, 2008.

Nebes RD, Buysse DJ, Halligan EM, Houck PR, Monk TH: Self-reported sleep quality predicts poor cognitive performance in healthy older adults, *J Gerontol B* 64:180–187, 2009.

Ngandu T, Lehtisalo J, Solomon A, Levalahti E, Ahtiluoto S, Antikainen R, Backman L, Hanninen T, Jula A, Laatikainen T, Lindstrom J, Mangialasche F, Paajanen T, Pajala S, Peltonen M, Rauramaa R, Stigsdotter-Neely A, Strandberg T, Tuomilehto J, Soininen H, Kivipelto M: A 2 year multidomain intervention of diet, exercise, cognitive training, and vascular risk monitoring versus control to prevent cognitive decline in at-risk elderly people (FINGER): a randomised controlled trial, *Lancet* 385:2255–2263, 2015.

Norton S, Matthews FE, Barnes DE, Yaffe K, Brayne C: Potential for primary prevention of Alzheimer's disease: an analysis of population-based data, *Lancet Neurol* 13:788–794, 2014.
Ohayon MM: Epidemiology of insomnia: what we know and what we still need to learn, *Sleep Med Rev* 6:97–111, 2002.
Palleschi L, Vetta F, De Gennaro E, Idone G, Sottosanti G, Gianni W, Marigliano V: Effect of aerobic training on the cognitive performance of elderly patients with senile dementia of Alzheimer type, *Arch Gerontol Geriatr* 22(Suppl 1):47–50, 1996.
Parisi J, Stine-Marrow EAL, Noh SR, Morrow DG: Predispositional engagement, activity engagement, and cognition among older adults, *Aging Neuropsychol Cogn* 16:485–504, 2009.
Park DC, Lodi-Smith J, Drew L, Haber S, Hebrank A, Bischof GN, Aamodt W: The impact of sustained engagement on cognitive function in older adults: the Synapse Project, *Psychol Sci* 25:103–112, 2013.
Park DC, Lodi-Smith J, Drew L, Haber S, Hebrank A, Bischof GN, Aamodt W: The impact of sustained engagement on cognitive function in older adults: the Synapse Project, *Psychol Sci* 25:103–112, 2014.
Pate RR, Pratt M, Blair SN, Haskell WL, Macera CA, Bouchard C, Buchner D, Ettinger W, Heath GW, King AC, et al: Physical activity and public health: a recommendation from the Centers for Disease Control and Prevention and the American College of Sports Medicine, *J Am Med Assoc* 273:402–407, 1995.
Patel NK, Newstead AH, Ferrer RL: The effects of yoga on physical functioning and health related quality of life in older adults: a systematic review and meta-analysis, *J Altern Complement Med* 18:902–917, 2011.
Pereira AC, Heddleston DE, Brickman AM, Sosunov AA, Hen R, McKhann GM, Sloan R, Gage FH, Brown TR, Small SA: An in vivo correlate of exercise-induced neurogenesis in the adult dentate gyrus, *Proc Natl Acad Sci USA* 104:5638–5643, 2007.
Podewils LJ, Guallar E, Kuller LH, Fried LP, Lopez OL, Carlson M, Lyketsos CG: Physical activity, APOE genotype, and dementia risk: findings from the Cardiovascular Health Cognition Study, *Am J Epidemiol* 161:639–651, 2005.
Pushkar D, Arbuckle T, Conway M, Chaikelson J, Maag U: Everyday activity parameters and competence in older adults, *Psychol Aging* 12:600–609, 1997.
Pushkar D, Etezadi J, Andres D, Arbuckle T, Schwartzman AE, Chaikelson J: Models of intelligence in late life: comment on Hultsch et al. (1999), *Psychol Aging* 14:520–527, 1999.
Randall T, Baetz B: Evaluating pedestrian connectivity for suburban sustainability, *J Urban Plann Dev* 127:1–15, 2001.
Raz N: Aging of the brain and its impact on cogntive performance: integration of structural and functional findings. In Craik FIM, Salthouse TA, editors: *The handbook of aging and cognition*, ed 2, Mahwah, NJ, 2000, Erlbaum.
Raz N, Rodrigue KM: Differential aging of the brain: patterns, cognitive correlates and modifiers, *Neurosci Biobehav Rev* 30:730–748, 2006.
Raz N, Gunning-Dixon FM, Head D, Dupuis JH, Acker JD: Neuroanatomical correlates of cognitive aging: evidence from structural magnetic resonance imaging, *Neuropsychology* 12:95–114, 1998.
Raz N, Rodrigue KM, Acker JD: Hypertension and the brain: vulnerability of the prefrontal regions and executive functions, *Behav Neurosci* 117:1169–1180, 2003.
Raz N, Rodrigue KM, Head D, Kennedy KM, Acker JD: Differential aging of the medial temporal lobe: a study of a five-year change, *Neurology* 62:433–438, 2004.
Rebok GW, Carlson MC, Barron JS, Frick KD, McGill S, Parisi JM, Seeman T, Tan EJ, Tanner EK, Willging PR, Fried LP: Experience Corps®: a civic engagement-based public health intervention in the public schools. *Enhancing cognitive fitness in adults*, New York, 2011, Springer, pp 469–487.
Rebok GW, Ball K, Guey LT, Jones RN, Kim HY, King JW, Marsiske M, Morris JN, Tennstedt SL, Unverzagt FW: Ten-year effects of the advanced cognitive training for independent and vital elderly cognitive training trial on cognition and everyday functioning in older adults, *J Am Geriatr Soc* 62:16–24, 2014.
Rogers RL, Meyer JS, Mortel KF: After reaching retirement age physical activity sustains cerebral perfusion and cognition, *J Am Geriatr Soc* 38:123–128, 1990.
Ross A, Thomas S: The health benefits of yoga and exercise: a review of comparison studies, *J Altern Complement Med* 16:3–12, 2010.
Saczynski JS, Pfeifer LA, Masaki K, Korf ES, Laurin D, White L, Launer LJ: The effect of social engagement on incident dementia: the Honolulu–Asia Aging Study, *Am J Epidemiol* 163:433–440, 2006.
Saelens BE, Sallis JF, Frank LD: Environmental correlates of walking and cycling: findings from the transportation, urban design, and planning literatures, *Ann Behav Med* 25:80–91, 2003.
Sale A, Berardi N, Maffei L: Enrich the environment to empower the brain, *Trends Neurosci* 32:233–239, 2009.

Scarmeas N, Levy G, Tang MX, Manly J, Stern Y: Influence of leisure activity on the incidence of Alzheimer's disease, *Neurology* 57:2236–2242, 2001.

Scherder EJ, Van Paasschen J, Deijen JB, Van Der Knokke S, Orlebeke JF, Burgers I, Devriese PP, Swaab DF, Sergeant JA: Physical activity and executive functions in the elderly with mild cognitive impairment, *Aging Ment Health* 9:272–280, 2005.

Schooler C, Mulatu MS, Oates G: The continuing effects of substantively complex work on the intellectual functioning of older workers, *Psychol Aging* 14:483–506, 1999.

Seeman TE, Kaplan GA, Cohen R, Guralnik J: Social network ties and mortality among the elderly in the Alameda County Study, *Am J Epidemiol* 126:714–723, 1987.

Seeman TE, Rodin J, Albert M: Self-efficacy and cognitive performance in high-functioning older individuals: MacArthur Studies of Successful Aging, *J Aging Health* 5:455–474, 1993.

Seeman T, Berkman L, Charpentier P, Blazer D, Albert M, Tinetti M: Behavioral and psychosocial predictors or physical performance: MacArthur Studies of Successful Aging, *J Gerontol* 50A:M177–M183, 1995.

Smith G, Housen P, Yaffe K, Ruff R, Kennison RF, Mahncke HW, Zelinski EM: A cognitive training program based on principles of brain plasticity: results from improvement in memory with plasticity-based adaptive cognitive training (IMPACT) study, *J Am Geriatr Soc* 57:594–603, 2009.

Smith PJ, Blumenthal JA, Hoffman BM, Cooper H, Strauman TA, Welsh-Bohmer K, Browndyke JN, Sherwood A: Aerobic exercise and neurocognitive performance: a meta-analytic review of randomized controlled trials, *Psychosom Med* 72:239–252, 2010.

Spira AP, Friedman L, Beaudreau SA, Ancoli-Israel S, Hernandez B, Sheikh J, Yesavage J: Sleep and physical functioning in family caregivers of older adults with memory impairment, *Int Psychogeriatr* 22:306–311, 2010.

Spira AP, Covinsky K, Rebok GW, Punjabi NM, Stone KL, Hillier TA, Ensrud KE, Yaffe K: Poor sleep quality and functional decline in older women, *J Am Geriatr Soc* 60:1092–1098, 2012.

Spira AP, Gamaldo AA, An Y, Wu MN, Simonsick EM, Bilgel M, Zhou Y, Wong DF, Ferrucci L, Resnick SM: Self-reported sleep and beta-amyloid deposition in community-dwelling older adults, *JAMA Neurol* 70:1537–1543, 2013.

Stern Y, Albert S, Tang MX, Tsai WY: Rate of memory decline in AD is related to education and occupation: cognitive reserve? *Neurology* 53:1942–1947, 1999.

Stewart AL, Mills KM, King AC, Haskell WL, Gillis D, Ritter PL: CHAMPS physical activity questionnaire for older adults: outcomes for interventions, *Med Sci Sports Exerc* 33:1126–1141, 2001.

Stine-Morrow EA, Parisi JM, Morrow DG, Greene J, Park DC: An engagement model of cognitive optimization through adulthood, *J Gerontol B* 62(Spec No 1):62–69, 2007.

Stine-Morrow EA, Parisi JM, Morrow DG, Park DC: The effects of an engaged lifestyle on cognitive vitality: a field experiment, *Psychol Aging* 23:778, 2008.

Stine-Morrow EA, Payne BR, Roberts BW, Kramer AF, Morrow DG, Payne L, Hill PL, Jackson JJ, Gao X, Noh SR, Janke MC, Parisi JM: Training versus engagement as paths to cognitive enrichment with aging, *Psychol Aging* 29:891–906, 2014.

Tan EJ, Xue QL, Li T, Carlson M, Fried LP: Volunteering: a physical activity intervention for older adults—the Experience Corps® program in Baltimore, *J Urban Health* 83:954–969, 2006.

Tang YY, Ma Y, Wang J, Fan Y, Feng S, Lu Q, Yu Q, Sui D, Rothbart MK, Fan M, Posner MI: Short-term meditation training improves attention and self-regulation, *Proc Natl Acad Sci USA* 104:17152–17156, 2007.

Taylor SE, Klein LC, Lewis BP, Gruenewald TL, Gurung RA, Updegraff JA: Biobehavioral responses to stress in females: tend-and-befriend, not fight-or-flight, *Psychol Rev* 107:411–429, 2000.

Taylor-Piliae RE, Newell KA, Cherin R, Lee MJ, King AC, Haskell WL: Effects of tai chi and Western exercise on physical and cognitive functioning in healthy community-dwelling older adults, *J Aging Phys Act* 18:261–279, 2010.

Tennstedt SL, Unverzagt FW: The ACTIVE Study: study overview and major findings, *J Aging Health* 25:3S–20S, 2013.

Tworoger SS, Lee S, Schernhammer ES, Grodstein F: The association of self-reported sleep duration, difficulty sleeping, and snoring with cognitive function in older women, *Alzheimer Dis Assoc Disord* 20:41–48, 2006.

Unger JB, Johnson CA, Marks G: Functional decline in the elderly: evidence for direct and stress-buffering protective effects of social interactions and physical activity, *Ann Behav Med* 19:152–160, 1997.

U.S. Department of Health and Human Services: *Physical Activity Guidelines Advisory Committee report*, Washington, DC, 2008, Physical Activity Guidelines Advisory Committee.

van der Bij AK, Laurant MG, Wensing M: Effectiveness of physical activity interventions for older adults: a review, *Am J Prev Med* 22:120–133, 2002.

van Praag H, Christie BR, Sejnowski TJ, Gage FH: Running enhances neurogenesis, learning, and long-term potentiation in mice, *Proc Natl Acad Sci USA* 96:13427–13431, 1999a.

van Praag H, Kempermann G, Gage FH: Running increases cell proliferation and neurogenesis in the adult mouse dentate gyrus, *Nat Neurosci* 2:266–270, 1999b.

Vaynman S, Ying Z, Gomez-Pinilla F: Hippocampal BDNF mediates the efficacy of exercise on synaptic plasticity and cognition, *Eur J Neurosci* 20:2580–2590, 2004.

Verghese J, Lipton RB, Katz MJ, Hall CB, Derby CA, Kuslansky G, Ambrose AF, Sliwinski M, Buschke H: Leisure activities and the risk of dementia in the elderly, *N Engl J Med* 348:2508–2516, 2003.

Varma V, Chuang Y, Harris G, Tan E, Carlson M: Low-intensity daily walking activity is associated with hippocampal volume in older adults, *Hippocampus* 25(5):605–615, 2014.

Voss MW, Carr LJ, Clark R, Weng T: Revenge of the "sit" II: does lifestyle impact neuronal and cognitive health through distinct mechanisms associated with sedentary behavior and physical activity? *Ment Health Phys Act* 7:9–24, 2014.

Wang HX, Karp A, Winblad B, Fratiglioni L: Late-life engagement in social and leisure activities is associated with a decreased risk of dementia: a longitudinal study from the Kungsholmen project, *Am J Epidemiol* 155:1081–1087, 2002.

West RL: An application of prefrontal cortext function theory to cognitve aging, *Psychol Bull* 120:272–292, 1996.

Wilson RS, Bennett DA, Beckett LA, Morris MC, Gilley DW, Bienias JL, Scherr PA, Evans DA: Cognitive activity in older persons from a geographically defined population, *J Gerontol B* 54:P155–P160, 1999.

Wilson RS, Mendes De Leon CF, Barnes LL, Schneider JA, Bienias JL, Evans DA, Bennett DA: Participation in cognitively stimulating activities and risk of incident Alzheimer disease, *J Am Med Assoc* 287:742–748, 2002.

World Health Organization: *Dementia: a public health priority*, World Health Organization, 2012.

Yoshitake T, Kiyohara Y, Kato I, Ohmura T, Iwamoto H, Nakayama K, Ohmori S, Nomiyama K, Kawano H, Ueda K, et al: Incidence and risk factors of vascular dementia and Alzheimer's disease in a defined elderly Japanese population: the Hisayama Study, *Neurology* 45:1161–1168, 1995.

Zeidan F, Johnson SK, Diamond BJ, David Z, Goolkasian P: Mindfulness meditation improves cognition: evidence of brief mental training, *Conscious Cogn* 19:597–605, 2010.

Zunzunegui MV, Alvarado BE, Del Ser T, Otero A: Social networks, social integration, and social engagement determine cognitive decline in community-dwelling Spanish older adults, *J Gerontol B* 58:S93–S100, 2003.

CHAPTER

23

Prospects and Challenges for Alzheimer Therapeutics

M.S. Wolfe

OUTLINE

INTRODUCTION

Major efforts to develop therapeutics for Alzheimer's disease (AD) have been ongoing for more than 30 years. These efforts have yielded symptomatic treatments such as cholinesterase inhibitors and memantine, but more effective agents, including disease-modifying therapies for prevention or to halt or slow progression, have been elusive. Indeed, no AD therapeutic has been approved since 2003. This is despite major advances in understanding the genetic, molecular, and cellular basis of AD and the discovery of many agents that interact

Developing Therapeutics for Alzheimer's Disease. http://dx.doi.org/10.1016/B978-0-12-802173-6.00023-X

with seemingly relevant targets and pathways. The large majority of these agents target Aβ directly or indirectly, but clinical success has not been forthcoming. The possible reasons for this are many, but a major one is an incomplete understanding of pathogenesis and progression. Numerous critical questions remain that require continued emphasis on basic research into molecular mechanisms. These efforts should bear fruit in the form of new targets and pathways for drug discovery as well as better-designed clinical trials that enroll individuals appropriate for specific disease stages and drug mechanisms.

Along with a better mechanistic understanding, other key areas require attention. Numerous drug candidates have failed in clinical trials when preclinical results anticipated problems that should have been addressed before moving to large studies in humans. Improved animal models that recapitulate more closely the human AD process are needed. More effective, less expensive, and more convenient biomarkers and diagnostics are essential to identify people early and accurately, to allow the design of appropriate clinical trials for disease-modifying therapies. New targets for more effective symptomatic treatment are also important for those who already have the disease and may be beyond the reach of disease-modifying agents. Moreover, the polygenic and heterogeneous nature of late-onset AD suggests that personalized medicine and an array of agents that work by different mechanisms and in combination will be important. Furthermore, opportunities for nonpharmaceutical interventions—such as changes in diet or exercise—to prevent or delay disease onset or to slow or stop progression should be part of a comprehensive approach to tackling the otherwise overwhelming problem of AD that is projected in the coming years and decades.

This concluding chapter will provide a broad perspective on these various aspects of AD research and development, emphasizing the opportunities as well as the difficulties that lie ahead.

ADVANCES IN AD PATHOGENESIS AND PROGRESSION

Decades of intense investigation into the genetic, molecular, and cellular basis of AD have resulted in substantial advances in understanding pathogenesis (see Chapter 1). The discovery of the major protein components of the amyloid plaques and neurofibrillary tangles led to extensive efforts to elucidate the pathological changes in Aβ and tau that occur and the roles that aberrant forms of these proteins play in synaptic dysfunction and neurodegeneration. While pathogenic forms of these two proteins have not been definitively established, in both cases aggregation is closely associated with synapto- and neurotoxicity (Benilova et al., 2012; Jucker and Walker, 2011).

For Aβ, the focus has shifted away from the plaques per se and toward oligomeric assemblies. Soluble Aβ oligomers are found secreted from amyloid precursor protein (APP)-overexpressing cells (Walsh et al., 2002), in the brains of transgenic AD mouse models (Lesne et al., 2006), and in postmortem human AD brains (Shankar et al., 2008). Such oligomers can colocalize with synaptic markers such as PSD95 (Lacor et al., 2004), affect synaptic functions such as long-term potentiation (Walsh et al., 2002), and increase tau phosphorylation (De Felice et al., 2008; Jin et al., 2011; Zempel et al., 2010). The particular oligomeric state, however, remains controversial, and it is possible that no single specific assembly is alone responsible for triggering AD (Benilova et al., 2012). Rather, AD may be initiated by a heterogeneous

"Aβ soup" of various forms of Aβ and Aβ metabolites in a host of assembly states. The search for specific receptors for Aβ oligomers has led to identification of a several candidates, including the ephrin type-B receptor 2 (EphB2) (Cisse et al., 2011), the cellular prion protein (Lauren et al., 2009), and the leukocyte immunoglobulin-like receptor B2 (LilrB2) (Kim et al., 2013). A normal role, if any, for Aβ remains to be clearly established, and even putative functions of APP have not been validated (Dawkins and Small, 2014).

For tau, hyperphosphorylated forms were identified in the neurofibrillary tangles of AD (Goedert et al., 1992; Lee et al., 1991), although it remains unclear whether hyperphosphorylation is required for aggregation and neurotoxicity or is instead coincidental (Tenreiro et al., 2014) (see Chapters 12 and 15). Tau is phosphorylated in many different sites by many different kinases, and it is unclear whether any particular site or kinase is critical for tau-mediated neurodegeneration, although certain kinases such as glycogen synthesis kinase 3β (GSK3β) and cyclin-dependent kinase 5 (CDK5) are thought to be more important than others. Although tau is a component of microtubules and is involved in microtubule assembly, stability, and dynamics (Cleveland et al., 1977; Weingarten et al., 1975), it is apparently not essential, as tau knockout mice are viable and fertile, showing some mild phenotypes but not neurodegeneration (Ikegami et al., 2000). Nevertheless, loss of tau microtubule binding, as a consequence of hyperphosphorylation and intraneuronal tau filament formation, may be a secondary contributor to neuronal dysfunction in aging humans, along with gains of toxic function from the filaments themselves or other tau assemblies (Morris et al., 2011). In recent years, the discovery that aberrant tau can be transmitted across synapses in a prion-like manner suggests how tau pathology may spread within a neuronal network (Clavaguera et al., 2009). Thus, while Aβ may be the trigger of AD pathogenesis, tau may be responsible for disease progression that ultimately becomes Aβ independent.

The discovery of mutant genes associated with autosomal-dominant, early-onset familial AD (FAD) pointed clearly to Aβ as a pathogenic trigger (Table 23.1) (Tanzi and Bertram, 2005) (see Chapter 2). FAD missense mutations in APP are found in and around the small Aβ region of the protein and affect Aβ production or aggregation propensity (Tanzi, 2012). More recently, an APP mutation near the β-secretase cleavage site that leads to reduced Aβ production and is protective against AD was discovered (Jonsson et al., 2012), providing strong evidence that targeting Aβ should be at least preventive if initiated early enough. FAD mutations in presenilin-1 and -2 elevate the proportion of Aβ42/Aβ40 (Borchelt et al., 1996; Citron et al., 1997; Duff et al., 1996; Scheuner et al., 1996)—thus increasing the aggregation potential of Aβ—by altering the proteolytic functions of the γ-secretase complex, in which presenilin is the catalytic component (Wolfe et al., 1999). However, other longer forms of Aβ are also

TABLE 23.1 Major Genes of AD

Gene	Chr	Genetic effect	AD type	Effect on Aβ	Normal function
APP	21	Dominant	FAD	Production	Cell adhesion
PSEN1	14	Dominant	FAD	Production	Protease
PSEN2	1	Dominant	FAD	Production	Protease
APOE	19	Risk allele	SAD	Clearance	Lipid transport

proportionally increased by presenilin-mutant γ-secretase complexes, due to reduction in the enzyme's carboxypeptidase function (Chavez-Gutierrez et al., 2012; Fernandez et al., 2014; Quintero-Monzon et al., 2011). The biological or pathological roles of these longer forms—beyond serving as intermediates that are trimmed into shorter forms—are completely unknown at present. These findings in FAD are thought to be relevant to the much more common late-onset sporadic AD (SAD). Other than onset in midlife and the completely hereditary nature of the disease, FAD and SAD are nearly identical pathologically and clinically, following similar progressions of molecular, cellular, and behavioral changes, strongly suggesting shared pathological pathways. In the case of SAD, however, the problem appears to be insufficient Aβ clearance rather than altered Aβ production (see discussion later about the apolipoprotein E4 [ApoE4] SAD risk allele).

No AD-associated mutations in the gene encoding tau have been identified; however, dominant mutations in tau are linked to other tauopathies such as frontotemporal lobar degeneration, progressive supranuclear palsy, and corticobasal degeneration (Wolfe, 2009), demonstrating that altered tau alone can be a pathogenic trigger for neurodegeneration. Pathogenic Aβ appears to be one of several means of eliciting neurotoxic changes in tau. However, while various AD mouse models expressing FAD-mutant human APP and/or presenilin-1 develop amyloid pathology and age-dependent deficits in learning and memory, none display the characteristic tau pathology of AD (Ashe and Zahs, 2010), raising concerns about the use of these mice for elucidating AD pathogenic mechanisms. Nevertheless, crossing such mice with tau-knockout mice largely rescues the learning and memory deficits (Roberson et al., 2007), suggesting that tau is critical to Aβ-driven cognitive-cerebral dysfunction. Moreover, crossing FAD-mutant APP transgenic mice with mice transgenic for dementia-causing mutant tau exacerbates tau pathology with no increased effect on Aβ deposition (Lewis et al., 2001), providing further evidence that Aβ is upstream of tau in the pathogenic process.

In contrast to FAD, no single gene causes the much more common late-onset sporadic form of AD (SAD). However, the ApoE4 allele is a strong risk factor, with E4/E4 homozygous carriers being 12–15 times more likely to develop AD (Table 23.1) (Corder et al., 1993). Although discovered more than 20 years ago, the mechanism by which ApoE4 increases the risk of AD remains unclear. Evidence supports a role in Aβ clearance (Castellano et al., 2011); however, it is unresolved whether increases or decreases in ApoE levels stimulate clearance (see Chapter 10). The ApoE4 variant is also implicated in other changes in the brain that may be independent of Aβ (Bell et al., 2012; Huang, 2010; Kim et al., 2009). Other genetic risk factors, while not as great as ApoE, can have a cumulative effect, and taken together suggest the involvement of endocytic trafficking, lipid metabolism, and innate immunity in AD pathogenesis (Karch et al., 2014) (see Chapter 2).

THERAPEUTIC TARGETS

Because of the clear implication of Aβ as the key initiator of the pathogenic process, at least in FAD, targeting Aβ in various ways has been the major strategy in developing therapeutics. These include anti-Aβ antibodies, β- and γ-secretase inhibitors, γ-secretase modulators to selectively lower Aβ42, and Aβ aggregation inhibitors (Fig. 23.1).

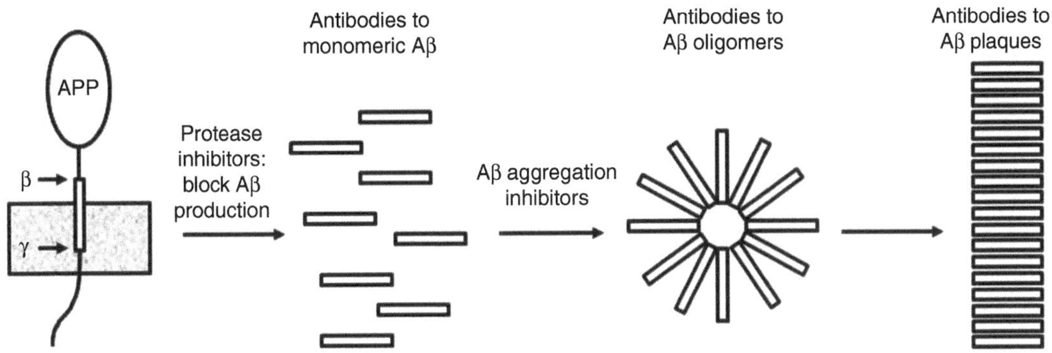

FIGURE 23.1 **Targets for pharmacological modulation of Aβ production, aggregation, and clearance.** Aβ is produced through the proteolysis of the membrane protein APP through the sequential action of β- and γ-secretases. Amphipathic monomeric Aβ assembles into soluble oligomers and ultimately amyloid plaques.

Anti-Aβ antibodies can clear Aβ plaques from the brain in animal models (Schenk et al., 1999) (see Chapter 7), and imaging results from clinical trials suggest they may do so in humans as well (Strobel, 2015). Antibodies specific to oligomeric forms of Aβ may target species that are more toxic (Kayed et al., 2003). However, the plaques, while not toxic per se, may serve as reservoirs for Aβ oligomers (Koffie et al., 2009). Therefore, specifically targeting oligomers over plaques may result in restored levels of toxic oligomers once the antibodies have cleared. A more general concern about Aβ immunotherapy is that only a very small fraction of antibodies enters the brain. However, protein engineering can improve this and may pave the way for developing more effective antibodies not only for AD but for brain disorders in general (Yu et al., 2014). Moreover, antibodies binding to Aβ deposits can lead to gradual buildup of these antibodies in the brain. Similar issues arise with Aβ aggregation inhibitors: these must not simply block plaque deposition or fibril formation, as potentially toxic oligomers may build up (Ross and Poirier, 2004), and such compounds may gradually build up in the brain despite poor brain accessibility. Although Aβ aggregation inhibitors have been under development for decades, few have passed through preclinical studies into human trials (see Chapter 6). These compounds must not only be potent and specific, but also brain penetrant, which has proved challenging.

Secretase targeting has also been a popular strategy for developing AD therapeutics. Numerous γ-secretase inhibitors have been developed, and these can be highly potent and brain penetrating; however, inhibition of Notch signaling, which requires γ-secretase, has serious toxic consequences (Wolfe, 2011) (see Chapter 4). More worrisome is the cognitive worsening seen in late-stage clinical trials with γ-secretase inhibitors (Coric et al., 2012; Doody et al., 2013), raising the concern that buildup of the APP substrates for this protease are neurotoxic (Bittner et al., 2009; Lauritzen et al., 2012; Mitani et al., 2012; Nalbantoglu et al., 1997; Oster-Granite et al., 1996; Suh, 1997; Tamayev et al., 2012). γ-Secretase modulators that selectively lower Aβ42 production are much safer, and potent compounds have been identified recently (Wolfe, 2011) (see Chapter 5), but their success depends on Aβ42 being the critical neurotoxic form of Aβ, an issue that is not entirely settled. β-Secretase inhibitors can also be highly potent (Ghosh et al., 2008), and these block production of all forms of Aβ and have the same effect as an APP mutation found to be protective from age-related cognitive decline (Jonsson et al., 2012) (see Chapter 3). Identifying compounds that enter and stay in the brain has been quite challenging, but this obstacle is being cleared with compounds currently in clinical trials. However, an important caveat is that, like γ-secretase, β-secretase has other substrates such as neuregulin (Willem et al., 2006). Blocking cleavage of these other substrates may lead to major adverse events.

Although evidence strongly implicates aberrant tau in AD pathogenesis, tau has been a challenging therapeutic target (Fig. 23.2). Several kinases thought to be important for the pathological hyperphosphorylation of tau have been the focus of screening and drug discovery campaigns (Tell and Hilgeroth, 2013) (see Chapter 12). However, as mentioned earlier, the role of phosphorylation in pathogenesis is unresolved (Tenreiro et al., 2014) (see also Chapter 15). Moreover, no single kinase or phosphorylation site has emerged as clearly critical, although a combination of sites could be involved. Even more problematic, implicated kinases, such as GSK3β and CDK5, serve important normal functions. Adding to the difficulties are the problems of selective kinase inhibition and identifying potent, selective inhibitors with good brain-penetrating properties. Other posttranslational modifications of tau, such as proteolytic truncation (Zhang et al., 2014) and acetylation (Cohen et al., 2011), are also being considered as part of the pathogenic mechanism of tau in neurodegeneration and as potential points of therapeutic intervention.

Inhibition of tau aggregation may be worthwhile if potent, selective, and brain-penetrant compounds could be identified, but this has proved challenging. Nevertheless, the dye compound methylene blue has been touted as having these properties, and derivatives thereof are being further considered (see Chapter 15). The dissociation of aberrant, hyperphosphorylated tau from microtubules in AD neurons has led to efforts to develop microtubule stabilizers to prevent any contribution that loss of normal tau function might make to AD (Barten et al., 2012) (see Chapter 11). However, such compounds must stabilize microtubules without overstabilizing them, as the dynamic assembly and disassembly of microtubules is essential to their normal function, for instance in cell replication and axonal transport.

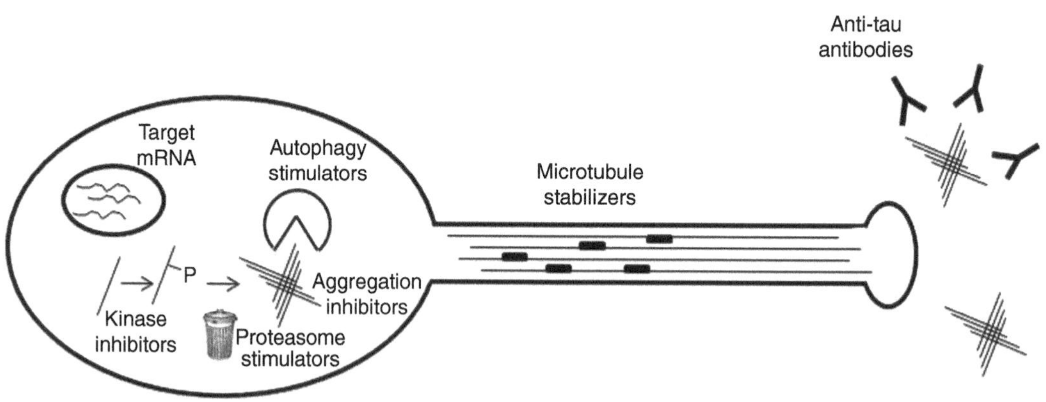

FIGURE 23.2 **Targets for pharmacological modulation of tau and tau functions.** Pathological events involving tau considered for therapeutic intervention include altered tau splicing and expression, tau hyperphosphorylation by kinases, tau aggregation and clearance, microtubule destabilization due to dissociation of pathological tau, and synaptic transmission of pathological tau.

Increasing the clearance of tau is another strategy that has been in development (see Chapter 13). One strategy seeks to stimulate the proteasome by inhibiting USP14, a component of the proteasome that inhibits protein degradation by trimming ubiquitin chains (Lee et al., 2010). However, in vivo deficiency of USP14 revealed that this deubiquitinating enzyme is essential for proper synaptic transmission and development of neuromuscular junctions (Chen et al., 2009). In addition, USP knockout mice showed no decrease in total tau, but a worrisome increase in phosphorylated tau (Jin et al., 2012). Thus, USP14 may not be a worthwhile target, although the general idea of stimulating proteasomal degradation of tau still has merit. While proteasome stimulation can clear monomeric tau, the clearance of aggregated tau likely requires autophagy (Inoue et al., 2012). A better understanding of the myriad components of autophagic degradation will be essential to revealing appropriate drug targets for AD that work through this general mechanism.

The appreciation that aberrant tau can be propagated transsynaptically (de Calignon et al., 2012; Liu et al., 2012) has opened up the possibility of preventing the spread of pathological tau and potentially slowing or halting disease progression. To target tau propagation, however, basic understanding of how this occurs is essential. Is it through secretion, exosomes, nanotubes? If it is through secretion, then anti-tau antibodies (see Chapter 14) might block this process, but not if tau pathology is transmitted while being protected inside vesicles (eg, in exosomes). If specific postsynaptic receptors are involved, this would open up the possibility of screening for small-molecule blockers of these receptors. These and other potential means of therapeutic intervention at the level of tau are relevant not only for AD but for other tauopathies, including frontotemporal lobar dementia, cortical basal degeneration, and progressive supranuclear palsy (Ballatore et al., 2007).

Other major AD therapeutic targets besides Aβ and tau are listed in Table 23.2 and include the strong risk factor gene/protein ApoE. Targeting ApoE has been even more difficult than tau and Aβ (see Chapter 10). As mentioned earlier, although ApoE appears to be involved in Aβ clearance, it remains unresolved whether up- or downregulation of ApoE is desired. For this reason, although certain transcription factors such as retinoic acid receptors can regulate ApoE gene expression, it is unclear whether agonists or antagonists to these receptors would be beneficial and whether activating or blocking these receptors would be safe. Another approach has been to identify compounds that alter the conformation of the AD-associated ApoE4 protein so that its conformation is closer to that of ApoE3 or ApoE2 (Chen et al., 2012).

TABLE 23.2 Other AD Targets

Target	Desired effect on target	Expected effect on AD biology
ApoE	Corrector	Increase Aβ clearance
α7 nicotinic receptor	Partial agonist	Increase cholinergic activity
M1 receptor	Positive allosteric modulator	Increase cholinergic activity
5-HT6 receptor	Antagonist	Increase cholinergic activity
PPAR receptor γ	Agonist	Counter brain insulin deficiency
GLP-1 receptor	Agonist	Counter brain insulin deficiency

CLINICAL TRIAL RESULTS: WHAT HAVE WE LEARNED?

Numerous clinical trials with candidate AD therapeutics have failed in the past 12 years. Not one single new agent has been approved since 2003, when memantine was introduced. But failure is not a loss in the long run if lessons learned lead to future success. What lessons have we learned, and are we applying those lessons to increase the chance of future success (Table 23.3)?

First, there must be clear evidence for target engagement. The γ-secretase modulator Flurizan (R-flurbiprofen or tarenflurbil) advanced through phase 3 clinical trials without assurance that concentrations in the brain were sufficient to expect significant lowering of Aβ42 (Green et al., 2009). In fact, Flurizan entered the brain very poorly (0.5–1.0%), as measured from cerebrospinal fluid (CSF) in an early safety trial in healthy elderly individuals (Galasko et al., 2007). Even in the plasma, only high drug concentrations showed reduction of Aβ42 levels. This should not have been surprising given Flurizan's poor potency in vitro (Eriksen et al., 2003). The decision to move forward into human trials was made based on Aβ-lowering and plaque-reducing effects in APP-transgenic mouse models (Kukar et al., 2007). Apparently promising phase 2 results showed beneficial effects in mild AD on measures of daily activity and global function (Wilcock et al., 2008), but in retrospect such results, without evidence of sufficient drug levels in the CSF, should have been viewed with skepticism. The large and long phase 3 failure of Flurizan served as a costly lesson in caution for advancing compounds that show no evidence of target engagement in the relevant organ—the brain—in humans. This lesson appears to have been learned, as illustrated by a recent small trial with the anti-Aβ antibody aducanumab, in which clearance of brain amyloid was determined via positron emission tomography (PET) imaging (Strobel, 2015). Target engagement does not ensure efficacy, but without target engagement, efficacy is highly unlikely, and any clinical evidence of efficacy should be viewed with skepticism. Identifying efficacious drugs is challenging even with a well-developed hypothesis and extensive preclinical supporting evidence. Without target engagement, the odds of observing true efficacy in human trials are reduced to pure chance.

Second, trials should be sufficiently powered and controlled to allow assessment of whether the agent was effective. A case in point is Alzhemed (tramiprosate, homotaurine), a small, soluble, and brain-penetrating compound capable of blocking Aβ fibrillization. Evidence from a phase 2 trial showed Alzhemed could lower Aβ42 levels in the CSF (Aisen et al., 2006), and a larger phase 3 trial was initiated despite no change in cognitive function compared to placebo. However, in this large trial, the control group failed to decline over the 18-month period to the degree expected and with large variations in rate of decline (Aisen et al., 2011). This was presumably because of variability in the presence or type of concurrent

TABLE 23.3 Preclinical and Clinical Issues for AD Therapeutics

- Is there clear evidence for target engagement?
- Is the trial sufficiently powered and controlled?
- Is there assurance that target engagement is safe?
- Is there clear evidence that target engagement will affect disease progression?
- Is the timing of therapeutic intervention appropriate?
- Are the biological underpinnings of drug action on AD understood?

medications being given, a problem of insufficiently controlling the trial rather than it being insufficiently powered. Thus, because of high statistical variability, no clear conclusion could be reached regarding the efficacy of Alzhemed in ADAS-cog, although a breakdown of the results suggested improved memory, language, and praxis skills (Saumier et al., 2009). Despite the equivocal findings, Alzhemed was marketed as a nutriceutical (Swanoski, 2009), which required no clinical evidence of efficacy. In this respect, the Flurizan trial was apparently a model of proper control, with a clear baseline of cognitive decline in the control group and clear evidence that the drug candidate did not work.

Third, there should be appropriate assurance that engaging the target is safe. Although this may seem obvious, candidates have gone forward with weak evidence for safety in preclinical animal model studies. Most problematic have been the γ-secretase inhibitors semagacestat and avagacestat. Both of these compounds can lower Aβ production in vivo, but they can also block essential functions of Notch receptors, which require proteolysis by γ-secretase for cell signaling (De Strooper et al., 1999). Deficiencies in Notch signaling cause immunosuppression, gastrointestinal toxicity, and skin cancers (Hadland et al., 2001; van Es et al., 2005; Wong et al., 2004; Xia et al., 2001), adverse effects that occurred with γ-secretase inhibitors in human trials (even with the putatively Notch-sparing avagacestat, which was apparently not selective enough to avoid these effects) (Coric et al., 2012; Doody et al., 2013). Studies in animals suggested a relatively small therapeutic index window with these compounds (Albright et al., 2013; Hyde et al., 2006), and yet they were advanced into clinical trials. There are now similar concerns with β-secretase inhibitors, as this protease also processes a number of other substrates besides APP (Hemming et al., 2009), the most concerning being neuregulin (Willem et al., 2006). Cleavage of neuregulin by β-secretase is essential for proper myelination of axons, although this may be most critical during development and not in adulthood. β-Secretase knockout mice also show retinal pathology due to vascular dysregulation, and similar effects were seen upon β-secretase inhibition with small molecules or RNAi (Cai et al., 2012), raising the concern of exacerbating age-related macular degeneration that commonly occurs in the elderly. This, however, has yet to emerge as a problem in human trials.

Fourth, there should be sufficient evidence that safely engaging the target will be beneficial in preventing or slowing the progression of the disease. This is perhaps the most difficult issue to address. To date, efficacy has yet to be unambiguously demonstrated in the clinic, even in the wake of numerous human trials of a variety of putatively disease-modifying agents. As many of these clinical candidates have targeted Aβ in one way or another, serious concerns are being raised about its relevance to the disease (Herrup, 2015) (see also counterpoint in same issue: Musiek and Holtzman, 2015). Certainly genetics points clearly at Aβ as the pathogenic initiator for FAD, with all mutations being in the Aβ region of APP or in the protease that produces Aβ (presenilin in the γ-secretase complex) (Tanzi and Bertram, 2005) (see Chapter 2). These mutations all alter Aβ or Aβ production in ways that increase its aggregation propensity, with the proportion of Aβ42 being considered most critical to pathogenesis for most of these mutations. As the presentation, progression, and pathology of FAD are virtually identical to SAD, and the two forms of the disease differ fundamentally only in genetic contribution and age of onset, a role for Aβ in FAD but not in SAD would seem highly unlikely. However, for both FAD and SAD, the identity of the particular assembly of Aβ that represents the neurotoxic form has been controversial (Benilova et al., 2012), and definitive direct evidence for the centrality of Aβ has been elusive. A successful clinical trial with a safe, specific, and effective Aβ-targeting agent would clearly lay these concerns to rest, but until that time lingering doubts will remain.

Fifth, the timing of therapeutic intervention appears to be crucial, certainly for Aβ-targeting agents. Decreased CSF Aβ42 can occur as early as 25 years prior to onset of FAD symptoms, and PET imaging of amyloid deposition can be observed 15 years before onset (Bateman et al., 2012). By the time of diagnosis, considerable neurodegeneration in critical brain areas, such as the hippocampus, has already occurred. Moreover, because tau pathology is apparently downstream of amyloid pathology (Lewis et al., 2001; Roberson et al., 2007) and capable of transsynaptic propagation (de Calignon et al., 2012; Liu et al., 2012), the pathogenic process may become Aβ-independent even before symptoms appear. Under this scenario, which is consistent with current evidence, none of the Aβ-targeting agents would be expected to work in any of the human trials reported to date. The hope is that enrolling at-risk presymptomatic individuals or those with prodromal AD (MCI) will lead to disease prevention, delay, or slowing of progression by an Aβ-targeting agent. This is the focus of ongoing trials such as A4, API, and DIAN (Friedrich, 2014). Even these trials, however, may not enroll people early enough, considering that the buildup of Aβ occurs so many years prior to symptoms. If this is the case, Aβ may be central to the pathogenesis of AD but nevertheless be an impractical target because a properly designed clinical trial would be too long in duration, too large, too expensive, and too difficult. In this regard, tau may be a better target, as tau pathology occurs later and more closely correlates with neurodegeneration (Bierer et al., 1995). Even so, tau pathology develops years before onset of symptoms, and devastating loss of synapses and neurons has already occurred by the time of an AD diagnosis. Targeting tau would also be better if initiated presymptomatically.

Sixth, there should be a reasonable biological understanding of how the drug should work against AD. Again, this may seem obvious, and yet much excitement, considerable effort, and great expense went into the clinical testing of dimebon (latrepirdine) without clear understanding of its potential mechanism of action. An antihistamine used clinically in Russia since 1983, dimebon was being repurposed for AD after a promising phase 2 trial, also in Russia (Doody et al., 2008). In the wake of this study, many attempts were made to understand how it might be working in AD, with suggestions that it somehow protected neurons against Aβ toxicity, that it protected mitochondria, or that it was an NMDA receptor antagonist, among other mechanisms (Bharadwaj et al., 2013). The pleotropic effects of dimebon made it difficult to confirm any of these notions. Ultimately, larger multisite phase 3 trials showed no improvement over placebo control groups (Fagan, 2010), and the compound proved to be another high-profile failure. Developing an AD drug is a high-risk endeavor in its very nature, but a lack of mechanistic understanding makes the risk even higher.

CURRENT PIPELINE

A wide variety of clinical candidates are currently in human trials, and these are directed toward a range of targets and pathways. The following sections describe advanced candidates, primarily those that have moved beyond tolerance and safety trials, categorizing them

TABLE 23.4 Current Pipeline: Selected Agents in Clinical Trials

Type	Examples	Phase
Aβ RELATED		
Vaccines	CAD106	2
Antibodies	Solenuzemab, crenezumab	2–3
γ-Secretase modulators	FRM-0762 (EVP-0962)	2
BACE1 inhibitors	Verubecestat (MK-8931), AZD3293	2–3
TAU RELATED		
Aggregation inhibitor	TRx 0237 (LMTX)	3
Microtubule stabilizer	TPI 287	1
Vaccine	AADvac-1, ACI-35	1
Calpain inhibitor	ABT-957	1
REPURPOSED (DIABETES DRUGS)		
PPAR-γ	Pioglitazone	3
GLP-1 mimetics	Exenatide, liraglutide	2
SYMPTOMATIC		
α7 nicotinic agonist	Encenicline	3
M1 receptor PAM	MK-7622	2
5HT6 receptor antagonist	Idalopirdine, PF-05212377	2–3

according to their putative mechanism of action (Table 23.4). See Fig. 23.1 for strategies for targeting Aβ, Fig. 23.2 for strategies for targeting tau, and Table 23.2 for a list of other targets.

Aβ Vaccines

The first human trial for active immunization with Aβ42 vaccine AN1792 in early AD patients was halted due to the development of subacute meningoencephalitis in 6% of the subjects. This adverse event was due to an inflammatory T-cell response (Nicoll et al., 2003). Follow-up with the participants, however, showed that in those patients who developed anti-Aβ antibodies (responders), Aβ levels and plaque counts were lowered (Holmes et al., 2008). The lack of efficacy with respect to cognitive decline was ascribed to starting the treatment too late, although a follow-up study after 4.6 years suggested some reduced functional decline in responders (Vellas et al., 2009).

Since then, active immunization has continued to be pursued, using immunogens—such as Aβ1-6 peptide—that do not elicit the toxic T-cell response (see Chapter 7) (Lemere and Masliah, 2010). These immunizations have been safe and well tolerated, while eliciting anti-Aβ antibody responses [eg, CAD106 (Winblad et al., 2012)]. Phase 2 studies have begun in some cases; however, the patients enrolled are at the mild-to-moderate stage of AD, raising the question of whether the trial design is appropriate, as amyloid plaque deposition occurs many years prior to onset of symptoms and an AD diagnosis.

Anti-Aβ Antibodies

A number of monoclonal antibodies directed at Aβ have advanced in the clinic (see Chapter 7), and this has arguably been the area of most intense focus in recent years, although nothing has yet proven efficacious enough for approval. Among the most studied clinically is Eli Lilly's solanezumab, a humanized monoclonal IgG1 antibody directed against the middle of the Aβ peptide. Although it recognizes monomeric and not fibrillar Aβ, solanezumab is thought to drive the equilibrium away from neurotoxic assemblies by shifting aggregated forms toward monomers. This antibody appears to be safe and well tolerated, and in a phase 2 trial caused increases in plasma and CSF Aβ levels, presumably through shifting equilibria from amyloid plaques (Farlow et al., 2012). However, no effects on cognitive decline were observed in this trial, and such effects were equivocal in two phase 3 studies in mild-to-moderate AD (Doody et al., 2014). A statistically significant benefit using a particular cognitive measure was seen only in mild AD patients in only one of these two studies and in a post hoc combined analysis of the two studies (Liu-Seifert et al., 2015). A third phase 3 study, called EXPEDITION-3, specifically in early AD patients, is in progress (see ClinicalTrials.gov). Also because of its safety and evidence of target engagement, this antibody was selected for trials in presymptomatic and early-stage FAD subjects with presenilin-1 and -2 mutations and for trials in very mild AD subjects over age 65 with evidence of amyloid buildup in the brain (see ClinicalTrials.gov).

Roche's gantenerumab is a fully human IgG1 antibody that binds to fibrillar Aβ, leading to its clearance through phagocytosis by microglia (Bohrmann et al., 2012; Ostrowitzki et al., 2012). In phase 1 studies, while the antibody was safe and well tolerated, the appearance of so-called Aβ-related imaging abnormalities—areas of inflammation and vasogenic edema—in some subjects has raised concern (Ostrowitzki et al., 2012), leading to close monitoring of this phenomenon in later trials. Although a phase 2–3 trial with gantenerumab in subjects with prodromal AD was halted due to the results from a preplanned interim futility analysis, two other studies, a phase 3 trial in mild AD and a phase 2/3 FAD-prevention trial, are ongoing. Roche is also developing crenezumab, a humanized IgG4 antibody that recognizes multiple forms of aggregated Aβ (Adolfsson et al., 2012). Crenezumab appears safe and well tolerated and showed results similar to those of solanezumab—a trend toward preventing cognitive decline in mild AD at high dosing—in a phase 2 clinical trial (Fagan, 2014). However, effects on amyloid deposition and Aβ and tau biomarkers were not significant in this study (Rogers, 2014). Nevertheless, crenezumab is still being tested as part of the Alzheimer Prevention Initiative (API) on presenilin mutant carriers, and the phase 2 study has informed the API trial with respect to route of administration (i.v. dosing is now preferred).

Biogen-Idec has also been pursuing two different antibodies in mid- to late-phase clinical trials. The first is BAN2401, a humanized IgG1 monoclonal antibody that recognizes Aβ protofibrils (Lannfelt et al., 2014). The antibody seems safe and well tolerated so far and is currently in phase 2 trials for early AD patients with positive amyloid PET scans. The second is aducanumab, a fully human IgG1 antibody derived from cognitively normal, otherwise healthy aged donors that binds to aggregated, but not monomeric, Aβ. The results of a phase 1 study reported in early 2015 showed substantial clearance of Aβ deposition by PET, solid evidence for target engagement (Patel, 2015; Strobel, 2015). Although primarily a safety study, the trial also examined efficacy and showed a slowing of cognitive decline in a small number of patients with MCI and early AD. However, a high number of patients in the higher-dosing groups dropped out due to complications. An earlier phase 1 study had flagged headache, diarrhea, and dizziness as adverse events at high doses. Most recently, lack of statistically significant effects on cognition at a lower dose has reduced enthusiasm for aducanumab (Sullivan, 2015). Nevertheless, this antibody is apparently headed for larger late-phase clinical trials.

It is important to remember that in all these antibody trials, even the ongoing prevention trials, there is serious concern that those enrolled already have substantial amyloid deposition and that the pathogenic process may already be Aβ independent. The field will have to await the results of long-term prevention studies to find out. Success would provide compelling evidence for the amyloid hypothesis of AD pathogenesis. Failure would suggest that while Aβ may be the pathogenic initiator of AD, it is an impractical target. Proving this suggestion would require lengthy, expensive clinical trials with large cohorts of accurately identified subjects who are likely to get AD 10–20 years later.

γ-Secretase Inhibitors and Modulators

There are no γ-secretase inhibitors currently in the clinical pipeline for AD, and the likelihood of new ones entering human trials soon seems remote. This is due to the poor performance of semagacestat and avagacestat in advanced clinical trials, in which both candidates showed unacceptable adverse events at the higher doses required to see effective lowering of CSF Aβ levels (Coric et al., 2012; Doody et al., 2013) (see Chapter 4). The adverse events—skin lesions and bloody stool—are consistent with inhibition of Notch signaling, even by avagacestat, ostensibly a "Notch-sparing" γ-secretase inhibitor. More concerning, however, was cognitive worsening observed upon treatment. While this may be attributed to a consequence of gastrointestinal distress, the possibility that this is due to elevation of APP C-terminal fragments that serve as substrates for γ-secretase cannot be ruled out. Indeed, cognitive worsening was observed in APP transgenic mice upon treatment with a γ-secretase inhibitor, effects seen at higher dosing in wild-type mice, suggesting an APP-dependent effect (Mitani et al., 2012). In the wake of the clinical trial failures, a case can be made for ruling out γ-secretase inhibition as a therapeutic strategy. However, the possibility remains that selective inhibition of γ-secretase isoforms may lead to effective Aβ lowering while avoiding the Notch-related toxicities (De Strooper, 2014) (see Chapter 4). Convincing funding agencies, companies, and venture capitalists that this is an avenue worth putting more money into will be challenging.

While inhibition of γ-secretase is fraught with difficulties, γ-secretase modulation to selectively lower aggregation-prone forms of Aβ, such as Aβ42, is still a reasonable proposition (Golde et al., 2013) (see Chapter 5). However, at the time of this writing, no such compounds are in clinical trials. Forum Pharmaceuticals (formerly EnVivo) completed a phase 1 trial for safety and tolerability with its lead compound FRM-0762 (EVP-0962). While a small, single-site two-stage phase 2 trial was completed in early 2014, no results or further studies are listed on the US Food and Drug Administration (FDA)'s ClinicalTrials.gov website. Other companies, such as Eisai and Merck, have developed second- and third-generation γ-secretase modulators with improved potency and druglike properties (Golde et al., 2013), but none appear to have advanced into the clinic. Neurogenetics (formerly Torrey Pines) Pharmaceuticals also has a class of modulators that have a different Aβ-modulating profile (Kounnas et al., 2010) and hopes to begin a phase 1 study with its lead molecule. The caveat for this approach is that it is dependent on Aβ42 being the critical neurotoxic form of Aβ.

β-Secretase Inhibitors

With γ-secretase falling out of favor as a therapeutic target, inhibition of β-secretase (aka BACE1) is currently the top anti-Aβ strategy for small-molecule drug development (see Chapter 3). Inherent difficulties with developing potent, selective, and brain-penetrating BACE1 inhibitors have been slowly overcome, and several candidates have entered into clinical trials in recent years. Eli Lilly's LY2811376, an orally available, nonpeptidic BACE1 inhibitor, entered phase 1 trials, where it appeared safe and proved capable of lowering CSF Aβ (May et al., 2011). While preparing for phase 2 trials, however, Eli Lilly researchers discovered retinal pathology in rats and halted further clinical investigation of this compound. While Lilly reported that BACE1 knockout mice developed normal retina, retinal toxicity did occur in these mice upon inhibitor administration. Since BACE1 is absent in these mice, the results suggest an off-target effect of the drug. However, other studies support inhibition of BACE1 as the reason for the retinal pathology (Cai et al., 2012). A second Lilly BACE1 inhibitor, LY2886721, advanced into phase 2 trials, but abnormal liver biochemistry was seen, again ostensibly for off-target reasons but nevertheless resulting in cessation of the trials (May et al., 2015).

Merck has moved forward with its BACE1 inhibitor MK-8931 (verubecestat). So far the drug candidate appears safe, well tolerated, and able to lower CSF Aβ levels (Menting and Claassen, 2014), and as a result MK-8931 is currently being tested in two different advanced trials (Merck, 2013). The first, the so-called EPOCH study, examined ~200 people with mild-to-moderate AD in phase 2, and after checking for safety and analyzing biomarkers, has expanded to nearly 2000 patients. The second study, called APECS, will test ~1500 people with prodromal AD. Based on other clinical trials with agents targeting Aβ, the APECS trial would appear most likely to affect cognitive decline compared to placebo control, as it targets prodromal AD rather than mild-to-moderate AD. Another compound in advanced trials is AZD3293, under joint development by AstraZeneca and Eli Lilly (AstraZeneca, 2014). This candidate also has passed safety tests and lowered CSF Aβ levels and has moved into a phase 2/3 trial called AMARANTH to test its effects in MCI and mild AD over the course of 2 years (Pamplona, 2014). The question remains whether any of the advanced trials with BACE1 inhibitors will reveal disease-modifying effects in patients who already have extensive plaque deposition in the brain (Menting and Claassen, 2014). Also unclear is whether toxicity will emerge due to chronic blocking of the proteolysis of other BACE1 substrates (Hemming et al., 2009; Kuhn et al., 2012; Willem et al., 2006).

Targeting Tau

The only agent in advanced human trials that directly targets tau is TRx 0237, a stabilized, reduced form of methylthioninium chloride or methylene blue (Baddeley et al., 2015) (see Chapter 15). Methylene blue itself had been in clinical trials in a proprietary formulation and under the name Rember from TauRx. This dye was reported to inhibit tau aggregation or dissolve existing tau aggregates (Wischik et al., 1996), although it appears to have pleiotropic effects, including induction of autophagy (Congdon et al., 2012), increase of proteasome activity (Medina et al., 2011), and regulation of gene expression (Stack et al., 2014). The compound has also been reported to prevent tau aggregation in vivo (Hochgrafe et al., 2015; Hosokawa et al., 2012), preserving cognition in tau transgenic mice (Hochgrafe et al., 2015) and preventing proteotoxicity in *Caenorhabditis elegans* (Fatouros et al., 2012); however, tau-mediated toxicity was not prevented in zebra fish (van Bebber et al., 2010). Results that were questionable—due to posttrial data manipulation—were obtained in a phase 2 trial with Rember (Wischik et al., 2015), and no efficacy studies have yet been reported with TRx 0237, which is also being tested in patients with behavioral-variant frontotemporal dementia.

The microtubule stabilizer TP1 287 from Cortice Biosciences (Fitzgerald et al., 2012) is entering phase 1 studies for mild-to-moderate AD as well as for progressive nuclear palsy and corticobasal degeneration, two other tauopathies, ostensibly to rescue loss of function due to tau dissociation from microtubules (see Chapter 11). In addition, phase 1 studies are in progress with two anti-tau vaccines, AADvac-1 from Axon Neuroscience and ACI-35 from Janssen (see Chapter 14). Also in early clinical trials is a calpain inhibitor, ABT-957, from AbbVie. Blocking calpain prevents cleavage of p35 to p25 (Lee et al., 2000), a potent activator of the tau kinase CDK5 (Patrick et al., 1999), and can also affect Aβ production (Zhang et al., 1999) and microglial activation (Nimmrich et al., 2008), events all associated with AD pathogenesis and progression.

Repurposing

There is keen interest in, and motivation for, identifying drugs approved for non-AD use that might be effective for AD treatment (Cummings and Zhong, 2014). Indeed, virtually all compound screening efforts seem to include a collection of FDA-approved drugs. Candidates found to lack efficacy in advanced clinical trials, but otherwise to be safe and well tolerated, are also considered worth retesting for possible use in AD.

In this category are agonists of peroxisome-proliferator activated receptor γ (PPARγ), the target of a number of approved drugs for the treatment of type II diabetes. The rationale for considering such agents is the overlapping risk factors for type II diabetes and AD (Barbagallo and Dominguez, 2014), as well as some evidence that PPARγ activation in microglia can facilitate clearance of Aβ deposits and reduce the release of cytokines involved in neuroinflammation (Jiang et al., 1998; Mandrekar-Colucci et al., 2012; Yamanaka et al., 2012). PPARγ agonists currently in clinical trials include pioglitazone. This drug is being tested by Takeda Pharmaceuticals in partnership with Zinfandel Pharmaceuticals in a large phase 3 trial in nonsymptomatic subjects judged to be at high risk for AD based on their ApoE and TOMM40 genotype (Rafii and Aisen, 2015).

Other agents in clinical trials for AD that are already approved for diabetes include insulin and glucagon-like peptide (GLP-1) receptor agonists. The use of insulin through nasal administration is being investigated, in part due to evidence for reduced insulin and insulin signaling in the brain in AD (Yarchoan and Arnold, 2014). Indeed, AD is considered by some to be "type III diabetes" (de la Monte and Wands, 2008; Steen et al., 2005). GLP-1 facilitates insulin release, but this peptide has other effects, including neuroprotective and antiinflammatory properties. Many GLP-1 mimetics, already in use for type II diabetes, can cross the blood–brain barrier in animal models, with protective effects such as reducing amyloid plaques, protecting against synaptic loss, preventing memory impairment, and reducing chronic neuroinflammation (McClean et al., 2011). Two such agents (exenatide and liraglutide) are in advanced clinical trials (Yarchoan and Arnold, 2014).

Symptomatic Treatments

While the emphasis in the field has been on developing disease-modifying therapies, there is still a need for new agents that temporarily improve cognition but may not affect the underlying neurodegeneration and the rate of cognitive decline (see Chapter 17). Such agents can work more quickly and provide practical benefits to patients who have already progressed to a stage in which disease-modifying therapies may not be effective. Approved drugs such as donepezil and memantine have limited benefits as well as side effects that might be avoided by agents that are more selective or directed to targets other than acetylcholinesterase or NMDA receptors.

The α7 nicotinic receptor is the target for Forum Pharmaceuticals' encenicline, a partial agonist of this receptor and a candidate in advanced clinical trials for AD as well as schizophrenia (Deardorff et al., 2015; Keefe et al., 2015). Targeting the α7 nicotinic receptor with encenicline is expected to lead to improved cognition while avoiding side effects associated with other acetylcholine receptors. In contrast, acetylcholinesterase inhibitors activate all acetylcholine receptors nonselectively by simply boosting acetylcholine levels in the synapse, albeit in a manner dependent on normal synaptic release. In a phase 2 trial, encenicline showed improvements in cognition as well as verbal fluency and executive function. Along related lines, Merck's MK-7622 is a positive allosteric modulator of the M1 receptor, another type of acetylcholine receptor. An advantage of such modulators is that they enhance signaling by endogenous acetylcholine released normally from presynaptic termini (Reid et al., 2011). MK-7622 was developed to be given with donepezil, and phase 2 trials to test this combination therapy are under way.

Finally, 5-HT6 receptor antagonists have also been considered for symptomatic treatment (Upton et al., 2008), primarily as an add-on with donepezil. Blocking this serotonin receptor subtype enhances acetylcholine and glutamate function. Lundbeck's idalopirdine is a selective 5-HT6 receptor antagonist (Arnt et al., 2010) that has shown some modest effects in phase 2 trials in moderate AD patients, with improvement of cognitive function as measured by ADAS-cog. However, other measures of cognitive function, activities of daily living, and global effects were not statistically significant (Schneider, 2014; Wilkinson et al., 2014). Nevertheless, recruitment is under way for a phase 3 trial with this candidate. Another 5-HT6 receptor antagonist, GSK's SB742457, showed mixed results in phase 2 trials and is apparently no longer being considered, while Pfizer's PF-05212377 is currently in phase 2. Interestingly, the failed dimebon was shown after the fact to be, among other things, a 5-HT6 receptor antagonist (Schaffhauser et al., 2009).

KEY UNANSWERED QUESTIONS IN AD BIOLOGY

Although much has been learned about the molecular basis of AD, many critical questions remain unresolved (Table 23.5). FAD-associated APP and presenilin mutations were discovered 20–25 years ago. Although these and subsequent findings strongly supported the central role of Aβ in AD pathogenesis, defining its role in more detail has proven extremely difficult. For instance, the basic question of the identity of the pathogenic form of Aβ has many answers, each with supporting data, but a consensus still has not been reached as to which of these, if any, is correct. The leading hypothesis is that the toxic forms are oligomers, but, as has been pointed out in a recent review, the means by which these oligomeric forms have been detected, isolated, characterized, and evaluated for biological effects have varied from lab to lab, confounding the need to reproduce results independently (Benilova et al., 2012; Teplow, 2013). The possibility that multiple aggregated forms of Aβ together "Aβ soup" are neurotoxic cannot be excluded at this point.

The neurotoxic form or forms of tau also remain unclear, not only in AD but also in cases of familial frontotemporal lobar dementia in which dominant mutations in the tau gene are clearly responsible (Wolfe, 2009). Soluble oligomers of tau are also being considered (Berger et al., 2007), as are the roles of certain posttranslational modifications such as phosphorylation (Tenreiro et al., 2014) and proteolytic truncation (Zhang et al., 2014). The problem of identifying neurotoxic forms of proteins is not unique to AD. Although aberrant protein folding, aggregation, and/or deposition are associated with other major neurodegenerative diseases, the neurotoxic form or forms of the proteins have not been definitively determined in any case (Jucker and Walker, 2011). This is even true for the prion diseases, for which it is inescapable that some form of the prion protein is responsible in all cases (Singh and Udgaonkar, 2015), as well as in Huntington's disease, which is 100% hereditary and due to mutations within a single gene (Polling et al., 2012).

The uncertainty about the pathogenic forms of Aβ and tau makes elucidating the connection between the two considerably more difficult. That pathogenic Aβ somehow elicits pathogenic tau is supported by the fact that Aβ pathology precedes tau pathology in AD

TABLE 23.5 Key Unanswered Questions in AD Biology

- What is the pathogenic form of Aβ?
- What is the neurotoxic form of tau?
- What, if any, is the connection between Aβ and tau?
- When does AD progression become Aβ independent?
- What is the mechanism of synaptic transmission of pathogenic tau?
- How are Aβ and tau cleared from neurons and the brain?
- How can synapses/neurons be protected from pathogenic Aβ and tau?
- How does ApoE4 increase AD risk?
- What factors cause age-related cognitive decline?
- What are the roles of nonneural cells in AD?

(Jack et al., 2010) and that tau pathology correlates more closely with neurodegeneration (ie, tau appears to be more proximal to neurotoxicity, both spatially and temporally) (Whitwell et al., 2008). A case could even be made that Aβ is not directly neurotoxic, that its neurotoxicity is exerted indirectly through tau, an idea consistent with the finding that tau-deficient mice overexpressing human FAD-mutant APP do not develop age-dependent cognitive deficits (Roberson et al., 2007). A leading hypothesis is that Aβ interaction with the cellular prion protein (PrP^C) results in activation of Fyn kinase and phosphorylation of tau, but this remains controversial (Kaufman et al., 2015; Um et al., 2012). Perhaps among the multitude of genes identified as AD risk factors are those encoding proteins that affect the pathogenic Aβ-tau connection. These proteins might provide clues to elucidating the Aβ-tau pathway, keeping in mind that multiple pathways may exist.

A related question is whether—and at what point—AD progression becomes primarily tau driven and Aβ independent. This is a particularly critical question with so many anti-Aβ therapeutics in the clinical pipeline. Regardless, it appears that synaptic transmission of pathological tau is a key aspect of AD progression (Clavaguera et al., 2009; de Calignon et al., 2012; Liu et al., 2012), so understanding the mechanism of transmission is critical. Moreover, it is important to keep in mind that the form of pathological tau that is transmitted across the synapse may not be the form that directly causes neurotoxicity. Such dissociation between propagation and neurotoxicity has been seen with prion diseases (Sandberg et al., 2011, 2014). The study of other tauopathies (eg, frontotemporal dementia, corticobasal degeneration, progressive supranuclear palsy) (Ballatore et al., 2007) should provide insight into these and other aspects of tau pathobiology and cross over to advance our understanding of mechanisms in AD and points of potential therapeutic intervention.

Elucidating the means by which Aβ and tau are cleared from neurons and the brain in general is also important, especially for identifying potential therapeutic targets and pathways by which levels of these proteins or their aggregates can safely and effectively be reduced. Monomeric Aβ can be cleaved by certain proteases in the brain, including neprilysin and insulin-degrading enzyme (Farris et al., 2003; Iwata et al., 2001). However, it is unclear how to activate these proteases or to specifically induce their expression. Aggregated Aβ can be cleared through the phagocytic action of microglia (Stalder et al., 1999), and there is intense interest in identifying appropriate targets for pharmacological activation of microglia, but without overactivation that would exacerbate the neuroinflammation that occurs in AD (Heneka et al., 2015; Malm et al., 2015).

Monomeric tau can be degraded through the proteasome (Chesser et al., 2013) (see Chapter 13). The recent discovery of the role of the deubiquitinating enzyme USP14 in proteasome function inspired a compound screen to identify USP14-specific inhibitors that could reduce levels of tau by increasing its proteasomal degradation (Lee et al., 2010). Further elucidation of factors and pathways that control proteasomal degradation of tau may reveal worthwhile new targets. Aggregated tau cannot be degraded by the proteasome but can be cleared through autophagy (Chesser et al., 2013) (see Chapter 13). As autophagy is a highly complex and regulated cellular process (Mizushima and Komatsu, 2011), unraveling the details of how tau is cleared in this manner may suggest specific targets for small molecules that can fine-tune autophagy for tau removal.

How synapses and neurons can be protected in the presence of pathogenic forms of Aβ and tau is another important open question. Progress on this front includes identification of putative receptors for oligomeric Aβ and neurotoxic signaling pathways ensuing from these interactions (eg, cell-surface PrP^C with activation of Fyn kinase) (see Chapter 8) and the ability of microtubule-stabilizing agents to provide protection in the presence of pathogenic tau mutations (see Chapter 11). However, a clearer understanding of the pathogenic forms of these proteins and their pathogenic mechanisms is needed to reveal new targets for neuroprotection and to suggest new assays for the discovery of therapeutic prototypes. Again, genomics and systems biology can potentially provide paths forward, with the discovery of the REST neuroprotective transcription factor (Lu et al., 2014) being a good recent illustration of the power of such approaches (see the following for further discussion of REST).

Although ApoE4 is the major risk factor for SAD, the mechanism by which it increases risk is not clear (see Chapter 10). While evidence suggests a role in Aβ clearance (Castellano et al., 2011), both reduction (Bien-Ly et al., 2012; Kim et al., 2011) and overexpression (Dodart et al., 2005; Hudry et al., 2013) of ApoE in mouse models can be protective against Aβ deposition and cognitive deficiencies, depending on the isoform, suggesting complex mechanisms at work. Moreover, Aβ-independent mechanisms appear to be operative (Huang, 2010), so a single linear pathogenic mechanism would seem unlikely. In addition to elucidating how the ApoE4 allele increases AD risk, understanding how ApoE2 is protective would seem equally important.

What factors cause age-related cognitive decline? As aging is the greatest single risk factor for SAD, efforts to identify genes, proteins, and pathways that are altered with aging and correlate with SAD and cognitive decline in general may bear fruit with respect to elucidating disease mechanisms and revealing worthwhile therapeutic targets. In this regard, the recent discovery of the transcription factor REST in SAD and age-related cognitive decline involved transcriptome analysis in the human brain (Lu et al., 2014). This approach ultimately led to the finding that REST can control Aβ production and provide neuroprotection from oxidative stress, and that its absence can exacerbate learning and memory deficits in AD transgenic mouse models.

The roles of nonneural cells remain largely undefined but are increasingly recognized as important. Glial cells in particular appear to play critical roles in AD pathogenesis (Heneka et al., 2015; Malm et al., 2015). Overactivation of both microglia and astrocytes can lead to release of factors that can cause neuroinflammation and oxidative stress. Further understanding of these mechanisms may suggest new therapeutic approaches that could alleviate these effects. While such approaches may not prevent AD, they have the potential to delay disease onset or to slow progression. In addition, microglia appear to be critical to the clearance of Aβ aggregates. Elucidating how exactly microglia accomplish this in vivo may reveal means of enhancing this process in specific ways that do not overactivate these cells.

ENABLING TECHNOLOGIES AND APPROACHES

In addition to answers to the biological questions raised in the previous section, the development of effective means of preventing and treating AD will require advances in enabling technologies and approaches, to provide platforms to discover new mechanisms and targets, identify those at risk for developing AD, match individuals to the most appropriate drug candidates, track efficacy in clinical trials, and explore the role of lifestyle in disease risk.

The issue of how to identify and evaluate druggable non-Aβ targets is critical, as targeting Aβ may be impractical: Aβ deposition begins perhaps as early as 25 years before onset of AD symptoms (Bateman et al., 2012), and Aβ-independent synaptic and neuronal degeneration may begin before diagnostics can identify people at high risk and anti-Aβ therapeutic approaches can be initiated. Tau would appear to be a high-priority target, as neurofibrillary tangles composed of aggregated tau correlate more closely with neurodegeneration than do amyloid plaques (Bierer et al., 1995), and tau aggregation can be propagated trans-synaptically in a neural network consistent with the pathological and clinical progression of AD (de Calignon et al., 2012; Liu et al., 2012). However, tau has so far been a difficult target. Progress has been slow with direct approaches (eg, aggregation inhibitors; see Chapter 15) and indirect approaches (eg, kinase inhibitors; see Chapter 12) despite many years of effort. Genome-wide and systems biological approaches may reveal new means of regulating or clearing tau or providing neuroprotection despite the presence of pathogenic tau and other factors critical to age-related cognitive decline. Such "omics" approaches may also provide insight into means of targeting ApoE, directly or indirectly, which would be worthwhile as this protein apparently contributes to AD pathogenesis through Aβ-independent as well as Aβ-dependent mechanisms. For instance, a genome-wide search in E4/E4 carriers who are nevertheless cognitively lucid in old age may reveal protective factors and suggest new targets for drug discovery. Moreover, broad searches for factors that influence age-related cognitive decline in general may suggest new potential points of intervention for cognitive enhancers, to help those who already have AD and may be beyond reach of disease-modifying therapeutics.

Another essential question is how to identify people at high risk years before the onset of symptoms. Since disease onset occurs after substantial neurodegeneration has already taken place, and regeneration of lost hippocampal and cerebral neurons is an extremely difficult proposition, the development of convenient and reliable diagnostics to identify presymptomatic individuals likely to progress to MCI and AD—and not other forms of dementia—is vitally important. Although CSF Aβ42/tau ratio is a very promising biomarker, the search for other fluid biomarkers is critical (Blennow et al., 2010). Blood-based tests would be ideal, as blood is much more conveniently accessed than CSF, although CSF is considered the closer indicator of what is happening in the brain. Perhaps an inexpensive and facile test for plasma biomarkers, in which an array of small but cumulative risk factors is examined, would be a worthwhile broad screen to narrow down those that should be further tested for CSF biomarkers (see Chapter 21 for full discussion on fluid biomarkers).

Improved imaging agents and methods are also critical for early detection. Several amyloid PET imaging agents have been approved and are being used to screen subjects for clinical trials (Blennow et al., 2015) (see Chapter 20). Moreover, amyloid PET imaging agents have helped demonstrate target engagement for anti-Aβ therapeutic candidates, for instance in the recent phase 1 trial of Biogen's aducanumab (Strobel, 2015). Such agents have also proven to be valuable tools for research, for instance in revealing that FAD-mutant carriers can deposit amyloid 15 years prior to the anticipated age of onset (Bateman et al., 2012). Corresponding imaging agents for tau are also needed, and some are advancing in the clinic (Chien et al., 2013, 2014). These would be essential for early detection, screening of subjects for clinical trials, demonstration of target engagement, and as general research tools. Therapeutic candidates targeting tau would not be expected to affect Aβ deposition, so amyloid imaging agents would not be helpful in these cases. In contrast, tau imaging agents would be useful in assessing anti-Aβ therapeutics, to demonstrate whether individuals have reached an Aβ-independent stage of the disease in which the spread of pathological tau continues despite Aβ clearance from the brain.

Continuing the search for other genetic risk factors is also worthwhile. SAD is clearly polygenic, and no single gene is responsible for initiating pathogenesis. Although the major genetic risk factors have likely already been identified (see Chapter 2), the smaller contributing factors are nevertheless important, as these can add up to substantial overall risk. Moreover, uncovering risk factors large and small provides critical clues to molecular mechanisms of the disease, especially when genes cluster into specific pathways such as cholesterol regulation, protein trafficking, or microglial activation. Advances in methodologies for genetic analysis should provide important enabling technologies for identifying new risk factors. The generation of algorithms that combine data from a variety of biomarkers and risk genes, along with such factors as family history, diet, exercise, and other lifestyle variations correlating with AD risk, will likely be needed to identify people at high risk before irreversible damage occurs.

There is a keen need for better animal models that more closely recapitulate what happens in the human AD brain (Chin, 2011; Gotz and Ittner, 2008). A number of transgenic mice have been generated that express human FAD APP and/or presenilin mutants, with age-dependent amyloid plaque pathology and learning and memory deficits. However, these proteins are typically highly overexpressed and driven by heterologous promoters. Despite the overexpression and florid plaque formation, neurofibrillary tangles with filamentous tau are not observed, apparently due to differences between mouse and human tau. Thus, tau pathology in mice requires overexpression of the human protein, typically as only one isoform and with a mutation that causes autosomal-dominant frontotemporal dementia.

The gross overexpression of these mutant proteins raises questions about whether any neurodegeneration or behavioral deficiencies occurs in the same manner as in the human disease (Webster et al., 2014). Overexpression is an understandable approach to speeding up a disease process that takes many decades in humans, but the risk of artifactual results seems high. The generation of knockin mice is preferable, as this leads to endogenous levels of expression with appropriate spatial and temporal control. This has been accomplished with APP with promising results (Saito et al., 2014). Nevertheless, the problem of the lack of tau pathology suggests that mice are not the best model. Simpler animal models, including *C. elegans* (roundworms), *Drosophilia melanogaster* (fruit flies), and *Danio rerio* (zebra fish) can provide insight into possible disease mechanisms and a platform for drug screening, but ultimately findings in these simpler organisms require confirmation in mammalian models.

No findings relevant to understanding AD mechanisms and therapeutic strategies are truly validated, however, until they are reproduced in human trials. However, this means ensuring that only those with AD, or likely to develop AD, are selected. The inadvertent inclusion of non-AD dementias in human studies confounds the results and their interpretation and dilutes any therapeutic effects that might be observed. Thus, targeting Aβ with a candidate therapeutic would not help someone with a non-AD tauopathy, so clinical trials need to be designed with rigor, for instance by prescreening with amyloid PET imaging agents. Clinical trials also require appropriate numbers in each group and a sufficient length of time to determine if a drug candidate is truly efficacious in preventing onset or in slowing or halting disease progression. Better means of assessing cognitive function are also needed to reduce variability and provide clearer indications of efficacy of drug candidates. Although substantial improvements have been made in subject selection and clinical trial design and assessment, further advances are needed to bring down the atrociously high failure rate of late-stage clinical trials for AD therapeutics (ie, no new drug approvals since 2003).

Along related lines, a better understanding of the heterogeneity of AD is needed. Different people may be at different stages and on different pathways to AD, depending on their genetic risk factors, health histories, environments, and lifestyles. Moreover, other types of neurodegenerative pathologies and presentations may occur in parallel, with increasing likelihood with advancing age. These individual differences need to be discerned and appreciated in order to increase the chances of positive outcomes in clinical trials and ultimately move AD into the realm of personalized medicine. A therapeutic approach that works in one AD patient may not work well in another, who may respond to agents that are specific for a different target in AD pathogenesis and progression. Giving an anti-Aβ therapeutic to someone whose neurodegeneration is primarily tau driven would not be appropriate, but we need the means to determine when someone is at that stage or where Aβ is not even an initiating factor. This heterogeneity also supports the need to develop a variety of agents that work by different mechanisms, targeting different proteins and pathways. As there is no single magic bullet for cancer, which is in reality a collection of myriad diseases, there will likely not be a single effective treatment for the heterogeneous diseases lumped together as AD.

The development of a variety of therapeutics should pave the way to combination therapies that work in an additive or synergistic manner to prevent or treat AD. No single agent is likely to be completely effective in most individuals. For instance, even a presymptomatic individual with cerebral amyloid deposition may benefit from targeting tau as well as Aβ, as the interneuronal spread of pathological tau would have likely already begun. Similarly, an individual who has progressed to an Aβ-independent stage may benefit from a cognitive enhancer in addition to anti-tau therapy. Combination interventions may also include nonpharmacological approaches, such as enrollment in a program to increase physical, mental, and social activity, all of which appear to delay cognitive decline and AD.

To the degree that nonpharmacological approaches can truly prevent or delay AD, these approaches should be implemented on a larger scale. Programs for stimulating cognition, increasing physical activity, and engaging in social networks all may be beneficial, and people can potentially be plugged into such programs conveniently through various community organizations (see Chapter 22). Among the most promising nonpharmacological approaches under investigation is a program to connect retired individuals as mentors to underprivileged schoolchildren in grades K-3, which has the potential to help two at-risk generations, one to aid cognitive development and the other to prevent cognitive decline. Not only might these and other programs delay onset of AD, mitigating the severe physical, emotional, social, and economic toll due to this highly prevalent disease of old age, but they should enhance other aspects of human health, for instance lowering rates of cardiovascular disease and diabetes, and improving the general quality of life in the process.

SUMMARY AND CONCLUSIONS

The past 30 years have witnessed remarkable advances in our understanding of the pathogenesis and progression of AD. The discovery of dominant genetic mutations, and elucidation of their molecular consequences, points decisively to a triggering role of Aβ, at least for familial early-onset AD. Questions remain, however, about the centrality of Aβ in the much more prevalent sporadic late-onset form of the disease. ApoE4 is a major risk factor for SAD, and this lipoprotein appears to influence the clearance of Aβ. However, the role of ApoE in AD remains unresolved, even whether it should be up- or downregulated therapeutically. Tau also seems to be a critical piece in the puzzle of AD and downstream of Aβ. Recent findings on tau seeding and spreading transsynaptically are consistent with patterns of neurodegeneration during AD progression. Much has been learned about how cells clear misfolded proteins like Aβ and tau and how these processes go awry in neurodegenerative diseases.

Despite these advances, no new AD therapeutic has been approved since 2003, and we still have only symptomatic treatments that quickly become ineffective. Every disease-modifying drug candidate has failed in advanced clinical trials. As the lion's share of these candidates has targeted Aβ one way or another, this has raised concerns about the role of Aβ in SAD. However, as cerebral Aβ deposition may begin as early as 25 years before onset of symptoms, the failures may be due to intervening too late, after AD progression has become Aβ independent. Current trials on presymptomatic and prodromal AD subjects may solve this problem, but, if not, then Aβ may simply be an impractical therapeutic target even if it truly is central to pathogenesis of most SAD. Definitively addressing this issue is of the utmost importance, and answers may be forthcoming within the next few years from the ongoing prevention trials with anti-Aβ therapeutics.

In the meantime, identification of other critical proteins and pathways, and advancing agents that work on other targets, must continue. This is not only in the event that anti-Aβ therapeutics fail, but also because agents are needed that work for those who are already symptomatic and because—even given useful anti-Aβ therapy—a multimodal therapeutic approach will likely be needed for maximal effectiveness. Tau is an obvious choice of target, and various agents with anti-tau mechanisms are in the pipeline. The discovery of synaptic transmission of tau pathology offers an exciting new possibility as a point of therapeutic intervention. However, the lack of understanding of what form or forms of tau are neurotoxic is a major reason it has been a challenging target. Genomic and systems approaches should uncover a treasure trove of potential new proteins and pathways, but ultimately clues gleaned from such studies will require drilling down into the molecular details for target validation.

Advancing therapeutic candidates will require better animal models for preclinical studies and better biomarkers for clinical trials. Current animal models recapitulate the human disease process incompletely, and overexpression of transgenes raises concerns that observed neuropathology and behavioral deficits may be artifacts, phenotypic consequences due to processes that are not part of the actual disease pathways. Naturally, targeting the overexpressed proteins with candidate therapeutics typically results in reversal of these phenotypes, with the potentially mistaken interpretation that a disease-relevant process has been inhibited. Thus, compounds can be developed that treat the disease model but not the disease.

The development of knockin mice is one way in which this problem may be averted. Better biomarkers that identify those on the path to AD and, ideally, give a sense of when disease onset might occur are needed, in order to enroll the appropriate subjects for clinical trials. In addition, these biomarkers should be useful for tracking the efficacy of drug candidates. A simple blood-based assay as a first-pass test would allow convenient and cheap mass screening, with follow-up measures of CSF biomarkers only for those who test positive. Such a blood test would likely involve an array of biomarkers, and the results could be combined and analyzed with an algorithm that also takes into account family history, environment, and lifestyle to give a preliminary risk assessment.

Beyond specific scientific developments, realizing effective AD therapeutics will take a societal effort better suited to the scope of the problem. Although AD affects over 5 million in the United States alone and is progressively debilitating, inevitability lethal, astronomically expensive, and without effective treatment, current allocations for AD research by the US National Institutes of Health amounted to only $562 million in fiscal year 2014, about $100 per AD patient. Academic investigators should be better integrated into consortia working as teams to focus on this common problem in a coordinated, multidisciplinary manner to facilitate translational research. At the same time, more support for individual exploratory projects is needed to test high-risk and unconventional ideas, often the source of major breakthroughs. Pharmaceutical and biotechnology companies likewise should move further into the formation of partnerships and consortia to avoid unnecessary duplication of efforts and to allow data sharing that will accelerate progress. Companies investing in AD drug discovery and development need to plan for much longer time lines than is typical for other disease indications and to carefully validate candidates at each stage to avoid costly failures later. Philanthropic organizations can help fill in important gaps in funding for AD research not being supported by government or industry, and expansion of these efforts will be critical to supporting basic research and translating new knowledge into the clinic. Finally, better coordination among academia, government, industry, and philanthropy would greatly streamline the discovery and development process of effective therapeutics.

It is of course difficult to predict when effective therapeutics will finally emerge. However, there is reason for optimism. Much has been learned from past failures, and new findings offer new targets and suggest new strategies for drug discovery. The improved means of identifying those at risk for AD and the design of better clinical trials likewise increases those odds. The recognition that AD is a complex and heterogeneous disease is leading to the realization that agents that work by different mechanisms are needed, and these agents will likely need to be combined into drug cocktails for maximally effective therapies. Moreover, there is recognition that different stages of the disease, even at different presymptomatic stages, will likely require different approaches. Among these approaches are nonpharmaceutical interventions, such as physical, mental, and social activity, that could be implemented for anyone in midlife who appears to be at risk. Such lifestyle modifications may prevent or delay millions of people from the scourge of AD, reducing human suffering and saving billions in societal cost. The bottom line is that there is reason for hope and for confidence that our efforts will continue to lead to advances that bring us closer to the day when AD is a preventable and treatable disease.

References

Adolfsson O, Pihlgren M, Toni N, Varisco Y, Buccarello AL, Antoniello K, Lohmann S, Piorkowska K, Gafner V, Atwal JK, Maloney J, Chen M, Gogineni A, Weimer RM, Mortensen DL, Friesenhahn M, Ho C, Paul R, Pfeifer A, Muhs A, et al: An effector-reduced anti-beta-amyloid (Abeta) antibody with unique Abeta binding properties promotes neuroprotection and glial engulfment of Abeta, *J Neurosci* 32:9677–9689, 2012.

Aisen PS, Gauthier S, Ferris SH, Saumier D, Haine D, Garceau D, Duong A, Suhy J, Oh J, Lau WC, Sampalis J: Tramiprosate in mild-to-moderate Alzheimer's disease—a randomized, double-blind, placebo-controlled, multi-centre study (the Alphase Study), *Arch Med Sci* 7:102–111, 2011.

Aisen PS, Saumier D, Briand R, Laurin J, Gervais F, Tremblay P, Garceau D: A phase II study targeting amyloid-beta with 3APS in mild-to-moderate Alzheimer disease, *Neurology* 67:1757–1763, 2006.

Albright CF, Dockens RC, Meredith JE Jr, Olson RE, Slemmon R, Lentz KA, Wang JS, Denton RR, Pilcher G, Rhyne PW, Raybon JJ, Barten DM, Burton C, Toyn JH, Sankaranarayanan S, Polson C, Guss V, White R, Simutis F, Sanderson T, et al: Pharmacodynamics of selective inhibition of gamma-secretase by avagacestat, *J Pharmacol Exp Ther* 344:686–695, 2013.

Arnt J, Bang-Andersen B, Grayson B, Bymaster FP, Cohen MP, DeLapp NW, Giethlen B, Kreilgaard M, McKinzie DL, Neill JC, Nelson DL, Nielsen SM, Poulsen MN, Schaus JM, Witten LM: Lu AE58054, a 5-HT6 antagonist, reverses cognitive impairment induced by subchronic phencyclidine in a novel object recognition test in rats, *Int J Neuropsychopharmacol* 13:1021–1033, 2010.

Ashe KH, Zahs KR: Probing the biology of Alzheimer's disease in mice, *Neuron* 66:631–645, 2010.

AstraZeneca: AstraZeneca and Lilly announce alliance to develop and commercialise BACE inhibitor AZD3293 for Alzheimer's disease, 2014. http://www.astrazenecacom/Media/Press-releases/Article/astrazeneca-and-lilly-announce-alliance

Baddeley TC, McCaffrey J, Storey JM, Cheung JK, Melis V, Horsley D, Harrington CR, Wischik CM: Complex disposition of methylthioninium redox forms determines efficacy in tau aggregation inhibitor therapy for Alzheimer's disease, *J Pharmacol Exp Ther* 352:110–118, 2015.

Ballatore C, Lee VM, Trojanowski JQ: Tau-mediated neurodegeneration in Alzheimer's disease and related disorders, *Nat Rev Neurosci* 8:663–672, 2007.

Barbagallo M, Dominguez LJ: Type 2 diabetes mellitus and Alzheimer's disease, *World J Diabetes* 5:889–893, 2014.

Barten DM, Fanara P, Andorfer C, Hoque N, Wong PY, Husted KH, Cadelina GW, Decarr LB, Yang L, Liu V, Fessler C, Protassio J, Riff T, Turner H, Janus CG, Sankaranarayanan S, Polson C, Meredith JE, Gray G, Hanna A, et al: Hyperdynamic microtubules, cognitive deficits, and pathology are improved in tau transgenic mice with low doses of the microtubule-stabilizing agent BMS-241027, *J Neurosci* 32:7137–7145, 2012.

Bateman RJ, Xiong C, Benzinger TL, Fagan AM, Goate A, Fox NC, Marcus DS, Cairns NJ, Xie X, Blazey TM, Holtzman DM, Santacruz A, Buckles V, Oliver A, Moulder K, Aisen PS, Ghetti B, Klunk WE, McDade E, Martins RN, et al: Clinical and biomarker changes in dominantly inherited Alzheimer's disease, *N Engl J Med* 367:795–804, 2012.

Bell RD, Winkler EA, Singh I, Sagare AP, Deane R, Wu Z, Holtzman DM, Betsholtz C, Armulik A, Sallstrom J, Berk BC, Zlokovic BV: Apolipoprotein E controls cerebrovascular integrity via cyclophilin A, *Nature* 485:512–516, 2012.

Benilova I, Karran E, De Strooper B: The toxic Abeta oligomer and Alzheimer's disease: an emperor in need of clothes, *Nat Neurosci* 15:349–357, 2012.

Berger Z, Roder H, Hanna A, Carlson A, Rangachari V, Yue M, Wszolek Z, Ashe K, Knight J, Dickson D, Andorfer C, Rosenberry TL, Lewis J, Hutton M, Janus C: Accumulation of pathological tau species and memory loss in a conditional model of tauopathy, *J Neurosci* 27:3650–3662, 2007.

Bharadwaj PR, Bates KA, Porter T, Teimouri E, Perry G, Steele JW, Gandy S, Groth D, Martins RN, Verdile G: Latrepirdine: molecular mechanisms underlying potential therapeutic roles in Alzheimer's and other neurodegenerative diseases, *Transl Psychiatry* 3:e332, 2013.

Bien-Ly N, Gillespie AK, Walker D, Yoon SY, Huang Y: Reducing human apolipoprotein E levels attenuates age-dependent Abeta accumulation in mutant human amyloid precursor protein transgenic mice, *J Neurosci* 32:4803–4811, 2012.

Bierer LM, Hof PR, Purohit DP, Carlin L, Schmeidler J, Davis KL, Perl DP: Neocortical neurofibrillary tangles correlate with dementia severity in Alzheimer's disease, *Arch Neurol* 52:81–88, 1995.

Bittner T, Fuhrmann M, Burgold S, Jung CK, Volbracht C, Steiner H, Mitteregger G, Kretzschmar HA, Haass C, Herms J: Gamma-secretase inhibition reduces spine density in vivo via an amyloid precursor protein-dependent pathway, *J Neurosci* 29:10405–10409, 2009.

Blennow K, Hampel H, Weiner M, Zetterberg H: Cerebrospinal fluid and plasma biomarkers in Alzheimer disease, *Nat Rev Neurol* 6:131–144, 2010.

Blennow K, Mattsson N, Scholl M, Hansson O, Zetterberg H: Amyloid biomarkers in Alzheimer's disease, *Trends Pharmacol Sci* 36:297–309, 2015.

Bohrmann B, Baumann K, Benz J, Gerber F, Huber W, Knoflach F, Messer J, Oroszlan K, Rauchenberger R, Richter WF, Rothe C, Urban M, Bardroff M, Winter M, Nordstedt C, Loetscher H: Gantenerumab: a novel human anti-Abeta antibody demonstrates sustained cerebral amyloid-beta binding and elicits cell-mediated removal of human amyloid-beta, *J Alzheimers Dis* 28:49–69, 2012.

Borchelt DR, Thinakaran G, Eckman CB, Lee MK, Davenport F, Ratovitsky T, Prada CM, Kim G, Seekins S, Yager D, Slunt HH, Wang R, Seeger M, Levey AI, Gandy SE, Copeland NG, Jenkins NA, Price DL, Younkin SG, Sisodia SS: Familial Alzheimer's disease-linked presenilin 1 variants elevate Abeta1-42/1-40 ratio in vitro and in vivo, *Neuron* 17:1005–1013, 1996.

Cai J, Qi X, Kociok N, Skosyrski S, Emilio A, Ruan Q, Han S, Liu L, Chen Z, Bowes Rickman C, Golde T, Grant MB, Saftig P, Serneels L, de Strooper B, Joussen AM, Boulton ME: Beta-secretase (BACE1) inhibition causes retinal pathology by vascular dysregulation and accumulation of age pigment, *EMBO Mol Med* 4:980–991, 2012.

Castellano JM, Kim J, Stewart FR, Jiang H, DeMattos RB, Patterson BW, Fagan AM, Morris JC, Mawuenyega KG, Cruchaga C, Goate AM, Bales KR, Paul SM, Bateman RJ, Holtzman DM: Human apoE isoforms differentially regulate brain amyloid-beta peptide clearance, *Sci Transl Med* 3:89ra57, 2011.

Chavez-Gutierrez L, Bammens L, Benilova I, Vandersteen A, Benurwar M, Borgers M, Lismont S, Zhou L, Van Cleynenbreugel S, Esselmann H, Wiltfang J, Serneels L, Karran E, Gijsen H, Schymkowitz J, Rousseau F, Broersen K, De Strooper B: The mechanism of gamma-secretase dysfunction in familial Alzheimer disease, *EMBO J* 31:2261–2274, 2012.

Chen HK, Liu Z, Meyer-Franke A, Brodbeck J, Miranda RD, McGuire JG, Pleiss MA, Ji ZS, Balestra ME, Walker DW, Xu Q, Jeong DE, Budamagunta MS, Voss JC, Freedman SB, Weisgraber KH, Huang Y, Mahley RW: Small molecule structure correctors abolish detrimental effects of apolipoprotein E4 in cultured neurons, *J Biol Chem* 287:5253–5266, 2012.

Chen PC, Qin LN, Li XM, Walters BJ, Wilson JA, Mei L, Wilson SM: The proteasome-associated deubiquitinating enzyme Usp14 is essential for the maintenance of synaptic ubiquitin levels and the development of neuromuscular junctions, *J Neurosci* 29:10909–10919, 2009.

Chesser AS, Pritchard SM, Johnson GV: Tau clearance mechanisms and their possible role in the pathogenesis of Alzheimer disease, *Front Neurol* 4:122, 2013.

Chien DT, Bahri S, Szardenings AK, Walsh JC, Mu F, Su MY, Shankle WR, Elizarov A, Kolb HC: Early clinical PET imaging results with the novel PHF-tau radioligand [F-18]-T807, *J Alzheimers Dis* 34:457–468, 2013.

Chien DT, Szardenings AK, Bahri S, Walsh JC, Mu F, Xia C, Shankle WR, Lerner AJ, Su MY, Elizarov A, Kolb HC: Early clinical PET imaging results with the novel PHF-tau radioligand [F18]-T808, *J Alzheimers Dis* 38:171–184, 2014.

Chin J: Selecting a mouse model of Alzheimer's disease, *Methods Mol Biol* 670:169–189, 2011.

Cisse M, Halabisky B, Harris J, Devidze N, Dubal DB, Sun B, Orr A, Lotz G, Kim DH, Hamto P, Ho K, Yu GQ, Mucke L: Reversing EphB2 depletion rescues cognitive functions in Alzheimer model, *Nature* 469:47–52, 2011.

Citron M, Westaway D, Xia W, Carlson G, Diehl T, Levesque G, Johnson-Wood K, Lee M, Seubert P, Davis A, Kholodenko D, Motter R, Sherrington R, Perry B, Yao H, Strome R, Lieberburg I, Rommens J, Kim S, Schenk D, et al: Mutant presenilins of Alzheimer's disease increase production of 42-residue amyloid beta-protein in both transfected cells and transgenic mice, *Nat Med* 3:67–72, 1997.

Clavaguera F, Bolmont T, Crowther RA, Abramowski D, Frank S, Probst A, Fraser G, Stalder AK, Beibel M, Staufenbiel M, Jucker M, Goedert M, Tolnay M: Transmission and spreading of tauopathy in transgenic mouse brain, *Nat Cell Biol* 11:909–913, 2009.

Cleveland DW, Hwo SY, Kirschner MW: Purification of tau, a microtubule-associated protein that induces assembly of microtubules from purified tubulin, *J Mol Biol* 116:207–225, 1977.

Cohen TJ, Guo JL, Hurtado DE, Kwong LK, Mills IP, Trojanowski JQ, Lee VM: The acetylation of tau inhibits its function and promotes pathological tau aggregation, *Nat Commun* 2:252, 2011.

Congdon EE, Wu JW, Myeku N, Figueroa YH, Herman M, Marinec PS, Gestwicki JE, Dickey CA, Yu WH, Duff KE: Methylthioninium chloride (methylene blue) induces autophagy and attenuates tauopathy in vitro and in vivo, *Autophagy* 8:609–622, 2012.

Corder EH, Saunders AM, Strittmatter WJ, Schmechel DE, Gaskell PC, Small GW, Roses AD, Haines JL, Pericak-Vance MA: Gene dose of apolipoprotein E type 4 allele and the risk of Alzheimer's disease in late onset families, *Science* 261:921–923, 1993.

Coric V, van Dyck CH, Salloway S, Andreasen N, Brody M, Richter RW, Soininen H, Thein S, Shiovitz T, Pilcher G, Colby S, Rollin L, Dockens R, Pachai C, Portelius E, Andreasson U, Blennow K, Soares H, Albright C, Feldman HH, et al: Safety and tolerability of the gamma-secretase inhibitor avagacestat in a phase 2 study of mild to moderate Alzheimer disease, *Arch Neurol* 69:1430–1440, 2012.

Cummings JL, Zhong K: Repackaging FDA-approved drugs for degenerative diseases: promises and challenges, *Expert Rev Clin Pharmacol* 7:161–165, 2014.

Dawkins E, Small DH: Insights into the physiological function of the beta-amyloid precursor protein, *J Neurochem* 129:756–769, 2014.

Deardorff WJ, Shobassy A, Grossberg GT: Safety and clinical effects of EVP-6124 in subjects with Alzheimer's disease currently or previously receiving an acetylcholinesterase inhibitor medication, *Expert Rev Neurother* 15:7–17, 2015.

de Calignon A, Polydoro M, Suarez-Calvet M, William C, Adamowicz DH, Kopeikina KJ, Pitstick R, Sahara N, Ashe KH, Carlson GA, Spires-Jones TL, Hyman BT: Propagation of tau pathology in a model of early Alzheimer's disease, *Neuron* 73:685–697, 2012.

De Felice FG, Wu D, Lambert MP, Fernandez SJ, Velasco PT, Lacor PN, Bigio EH, Jerecic J, Acton PJ, Shughrue PJ, Chen-Dodson E, Kinney GG, Klein WL: Alzheimer's disease-type neuronal tau hyperphosphorylation induced by A beta oligomers, *Neurobiol Aging* 29:1334–1347, 2008.

de la Monte SM, Wands JR: Alzheimer's disease is type 3 diabetes-evidence reviewed, *J Diabetes Sci Technol* 2:1101–1113, 2008.

De Strooper B: Lessons from a failed gamma-secretase Alzheimer trial, *Cell* 159:721–726, 2014.

De Strooper B, Annaert W, Cupers P, Saftig P, Craessaerts K, Mumm JS, Schroeter EH, Schrijvers V, Wolfe MS, Ray WJ, Goate A, Kopan R: A presenilin-1-dependent γ-secretase-like protease mediates release of Notch intracellular domain, *Nature* 398:518–522, 1999.

Dodart JC, Marr RA, Koistinaho M, Gregersen BM, Malkani S, Verma IM, Paul SM: Gene delivery of human apolipoprotein E alters brain Abeta burden in a mouse model of Alzheimer's disease, *Proc Natl Acad Sci USA* 102:1211–1216, 2005.

Doody RS, Gavrilova SI, Sano M, Thomas RG, Aisen PS, Bachurin SO, Seely L, Hung D: Effect of dimebon on cognition, activities of daily living, behaviour, and global function in patients with mild-to-moderate Alzheimer's disease: a randomised, double-blind, placebo-controlled study, *Lancet* 372:207–215, 2008.

Doody RS, Raman R, Farlow M, Iwatsubo T, Vellas B, Joffe S, Kieburtz K, He F, Sun X, Thomas RG, Aisen PS, Siemers E, Sethuraman G, Mohs R: A phase 3 trial of semagacestat for treatment of Alzheimer's disease, *N Engl J Med* 369:341–350, 2013.

Doody RS, Thomas RG, Farlow M, Iwatsubo T, Vellas B, Joffe S, Kieburtz K, Raman R, Sun X, Aisen PS, Siemers E, Liu-Seifert H, Mohs R: Phase 3 trials of solanezumab for mild-to-moderate Alzheimer's disease, *N Engl J Med* 370:311–321, 2014.

Duff K, Eckman C, Zehr C, Yu X, Prada CM, Perez-tur J, Hutton M, Buee L, Harigaya Y, Yager D, Morgan D, Gordon MN, Holcomb L, Refolo L, Zenk B, Hardy J, Younkin S: Increased amyloid-beta42(43) in brains of mice expressing mutant presenilin 1, *Nature* 383:710–713, 1996.

Eriksen JL, Sagi SA, Smith TE, Weggen S, Das P, McLendon DC, Ozols VV, Jessing KW, Zavitz KH, Koo EH, Golde TE: NSAIDs and enantiomers of flurbiprofen target gamma-secretase and lower Abeta 42 in vivo, *J Clin Invest* 112:440–449, 2003.

Fagan T: Dimebon disappoints in phase 3 trial, 2010. http://www.alzforumorg/news/research-news/dimebon-disappoints phase 3 trial?id=2387

Fagan T: Crenezumab disappoints in Phase 2, researchers remain hopeful, 2014. http://www.alzforumorg/news/conference-coverage/crenezumab-disappoints-phase-2-researchers-remain-hopeful

Farlow M, Arnold SE, van Dyck CH, Aisen PS, Snider BJ, Porsteinsson AP, Friedrich S, Dean RA, Gonzales C, Sethuraman G, DeMattos RB, Mohs R, Paul SM, Siemers ER: Safety and biomarker effects of solanezumab in patients with Alzheimer's disease, *Alzheimers Dement* 8:261–271, 2012.

Farris W, Mansourian S, Chang Y, Lindsley L, Eckman EA, Frosch MP, Eckman CB, Tanzi RE, Selkoe DJ, Guenette S: Insulin-degrading enzyme regulates the levels of insulin, amyloid beta-protein, and the beta-amyloid precursor protein intracellular domain in vivo, *Proc Natl Acad Sci USA* 100:4162–4167, 2003.

Fatouros C, Pir GJ, Biernat J, Koushika SP, Mandelkow E, Mandelkow EM, Schmidt E, Baumeister R: Inhibition of tau aggregation in a novel Caenorhabditis elegans model of tauopathy mitigates proteotoxicity, *Hum Mol Genet* 21:3587–3603, 2012.

Fernandez MA, Klutkowski JA, Freret T, Wolfe MS: Alzheimer presenilin-1 mutations dramatically reduce trimming of long amyloid beta-peptides (Abeta) by gamma-secretase to increase 42-to-40-residue Abeta, *J Biol Chem* 289:31043–31052, 2014.

Fitzgerald DP, Emerson DL, Qian Y, Anwar T, Liewehr DJ, Steinberg SM, Silberman S, Palmieri D, Steeg PS: TPI-287, a new taxane family member, reduces the brain metastatic colonization of breast cancer cells, *Mol Cancer Ther* 11:1959–1967, 2012.

Friedrich MJ: Researchers test strategies to prevent Alzheimer disease, *JAMA-J Amer Med Assoc* 311:1596–1598, 2014.

Galasko DR, Graff-Radford N, May S, Hendrix S, Cottrell BA, Sagi SA, Mather G, Laughlin M, Zavitz KH, Swabb E, Golde TE, Murphy MP, Koo EH: Safety, tolerability, pharmacokinetics, and Abeta levels after short-term administration of R-flurbiprofen in healthy elderly individuals, *Alzheimer Dis Assoc Disord* 21:292–299, 2007.

Ghosh AK, Gemma S, Tang J: Beta-secretase as a therapeutic target for Alzheimer's disease, *Neurotherapeutics* 5:399–408, 2008.

Goedert M, Spillantini MG, Cairns NJ, Crowther RA: Tau proteins of Alzheimer paired helical filaments: abnormal phosphorylation of all six brain isoforms, *Neuron* 8:159–168, 1992.

Golde TE, Koo EH, Felsenstein KM, Osborne BA, Miele L: Gamma-secretase inhibitors and modulators, *Biochim Biophys Acta* 1828:2898–2907, 2013.

Gotz J, Ittner LM: Animal models of Alzheimer's disease and frontotemporal dementia, *Nat Rev Neurosci* 9:532–544, 2008.

Green RC, Schneider LS, Amato DA, Beelen AP, Wilcock G, Swabb EA, Zavitz KH: Effect of tarenflurbil on cognitive decline and activities of daily living in patients with mild Alzheimer disease: a randomized controlled trial, *JAMA-J Amer Med Assoc* 302:2557–2564, 2009.

Hadland BK, Manley NR, Su D, Longmore GD, Moore CL, Wolfe MS, Schroeter EH, Kopan R: Gamma-secretase inhibitors repress thymocyte development, *Proc Natl Acad Sci USA* 98:7487–7491, 2001.

Hemming ML, Elias JE, Gygi SP, Selkoe DJ: Identification of beta-secretase (BACE1) substrates using quantitative proteomics, *PLoS One* 4:e8477, 2009.

Heneka MT, Carson MJ, El Khoury J, Landreth GE, Brosseron F, Feinstein DL, Jacobs AH, Wyss-Coray T, Vitorica J, Ransohoff RM, Herrup K, Frautschy SA, Finsen B, Brown GC, Verkhratsky A, Yamanaka K, Koistinaho J, Latz E, Halle A, Petzold GC, et al: Neuroinflammation in Alzheimer's disease, *Lancet Neurol* 14:388–405, 2015.

Herrup K: The case for rejecting the amyloid cascade hypothesis, *Nat Neurosci* 18:794–799, 2015.

Hochgrafe K, Sydow A, Matenia D, Cadinu D, Konen S, Petrova O, Pickhardt M, Goll P, Morellini F, Mandelkow E, Mandelkow EM: Preventive methylene blue treatment preserves cognition in mice expressing full-length pro-aggregant human tau, *Acta Neuropathol Commun* 3:25, 2015.

Holmes C, Boche D, Wilkinson D, Yadegarfar G, Hopkins V, Bayer A, Jones RW, Bullock R, Love S, Neal JW, Zotova E, Nicoll JA: Long-term effects of Abeta42 immunisation in Alzheimer's disease: follow-up of a randomised, placebo-controlled phase I trial, *Lancet* 372:216–223, 2008.

Hosokawa M, Arai T, Masuda-Suzukake M, Nonaka T, Yamashita M, Akiyama H, Hasegawa M: Methylene blue reduced abnormal tau accumulation in P301L tau transgenic mice, *PLoS One* 7:e52389, 2012.

Huang Y: Abeta-independent roles of apolipoprotein E4 in the pathogenesis of Alzheimer's disease, *Trends Mol Med* 16:287–294, 2010.

Hudry E, Dashkoff J, Roe AD, Takeda S, Koffie RM, Hashimoto T, Scheel M, Spires-Jones T, Arbel-Ornath M, Betensky R, Davidson BL, Hyman BT: Gene transfer of human Apoe isoforms results in differential modulation of amyloid deposition and neurotoxicity in mouse brain, *Sci Transl Med* 5:212ra161, 2013.

Hyde LA, McHugh NA, Chen J, Zhang Q, Manfra D, Nomeir AA, Josien H, Bara T, Clader JW, Zhang L, Parker EM, Higgins GA: Studies to investigate the in vivo therapeutic window of the gamma-secretase inhibitor N2-[(2S)-2-(3,5-difluorophenyl)-2-hydroxyethanoyl]-N1-[(7S)-5-methyl-6-oxo-6,7-dihydro-5H-dibenzo[b,d]azepin-7-yl]-L-alaninamide (LY411,575) in the CRND8 mouse, *J Pharmacol Exp Ther* 319:1133–1143, 2006.

Ikegami S, Harada A, Hirokawa N: Muscle weakness, hyperactivity, and impairment in fear conditioning in tau-deficient mice, *Neurosci Lett* 279:129–132, 2000.

Inoue K, Rispoli J, Kaphzan H, Klann E, Chen EI, Kim J, Komatsu M, Abeliovich A: Macroautophagy deficiency mediates age-dependent neurodegeneration through a phospho-tau pathway, *Mol Neurodegener* 7:48, 2012.

Iwata N, Tsubuki S, Takaki Y, Shirotani K, Lu B, Gerard NP, Gerard C, Hama E, Lee HJ, Saido TC: Metabolic regulation of brain Abeta by neprilysin, *Science* 292:1550–1552, 2001.

Jack CR Jr, Knopman DS, Jagust WJ, Shaw LM, Aisen PS, Weiner MW, Petersen RC, Trojanowski JQ: Hypothetical model of dynamic biomarkers of the Alzheimer's pathological cascade, *Lancet Neurol* 9:119–128, 2010.

Jiang C, Ting AT, Seed B: PPAR-gamma agonists inhibit production of monocyte inflammatory cytokines, *Nature* 391:82–86, 1998.

Jin M, Shepardson N, Yang T, Chen G, Walsh D, Selkoe DJ: Soluble amyloid beta-protein dimers isolated from Alzheimer cortex directly induce tau hyperphosphorylation and neuritic degeneration, *Proc Natl Acad Sci USA* 108:5819–5824, 2011.

Jin YN, Chen PC, Watson JA, Walters BJ, Phillips SE, Green K, Schmidt R, Wilson JA, Johnson GV, Roberson ED, Dobrunz LE, Wilson SM: Usp14 deficiency increases tau phosphorylation without altering tau degradation or causing tau-dependent deficits, *PLoS One* 7:e47884, 2012.

Jonsson T, Atwal JK, Steinberg S, Snaedal J, Jonsson PV, Bjornsson S, Stefansson H, Sulem P, Gudbjartsson D, Maloney J, Hoyte K, Gustafson A, Liu Y, Lu Y, Bhangale T, Graham RR, Huttenlocher J, Bjornsdottir G, Andreassen OA, Jonsson EG, et al: A mutation in APP protects against Alzheimer's disease and age-related cognitive decline, *Nature* 488:96–99, 2012.

Jucker M, Walker LC: Pathogenic protein seeding in Alzheimer disease and other neurodegenerative disorders, *Ann Neurol* 70:532–540, 2011.

Karch CM, Cruchaga C, Goate AM: Alzheimer's disease genetics: from the bench to the clinic, *Neuron* 83:11–26, 2014.

Kaufman AC, Salazar SV, Haas LT, Yang J, Kostylev MA, Jeng AT, Robinson SA, Gunther EC, van Dyck CH, Nygaard HB, Strittmatter SM: Fyn inhibition rescues established memory and synapse loss in Alzheimer mice, *Ann Neurol* 77:953–971, 2015.

Kayed R, Head E, Thompson JL, McIntire TM, Milton SC, Cotman CW, Glabe CG: Common structure of soluble amyloid oligomers implies common mechanism of pathogenesis, *Science* 300:486–489, 2003.

Keefe RS, Meltzer HA, Dgetluck N, Gawryl M, Koenig G, Moebius HJ, Lombardo I, Hilt DC: Randomized, double-blind, placebo-controlled study of encenicline, an alpha7 nicotinic acetylcholine receptor agonist, as a treatment for cognitive impairment in schizophrenia, *Neuropsychopharmacology* 40:3053–3060, 2015.

Kim J, Basak JM, Holtzman DM: The role of apolipoprotein E in Alzheimer's disease, *Neuron* 63:287–303, 2009.

Kim J, Jiang H, Park S, Eltorai AE, Stewart FR, Yoon H, Basak JM, Finn MB, Holtzman DM: Haploinsufficiency of human APOE reduces amyloid deposition in a mouse model of amyloid-beta amyloidosis, *J Neurosci* 31:18007–18012, 2011.

Kim T, Vidal GS, Djurisic M, William CM, Birnbaum ME, Garcia KC, Hyman BT, Shatz CJ: Human LilrB2 is a beta-amyloid receptor and its murine homolog PirB regulates synaptic plasticity in an Alzheimer's model, *Science* 341:1399–1404, 2013.

Koffie RM, Meyer-Luehmann M, Hashimoto T, Adams KW, Mielke ML, Garcia-Alloza M, Micheva KD, Smith SJ, Kim ML, Lee VM, Hyman BT, Spires-Jones TL: Oligomeric amyloid beta associates with postsynaptic densities and correlates with excitatory synapse loss near senile plaques, *Proc Natl Acad Sci USA* 106:4012–4017, 2009.

Kounnas MZ, Danks AM, Cheng S, Tyree C, Ackerman E, Zhang X, Ahn K, Nguyen P, Comer D, Mao L, Yu C, Pleynet D, Digregorio PJ, Velicelebi G, Stauderman KA, Comer WT, Mobley WC, Li YM, Sisodia SS, Tanzi RE, et al: Modulation of gamma-secretase reduces beta-amyloid deposition in a transgenic mouse model of Alzheimer's disease, *Neuron* 67:769–780, 2010.

Kuhn PH, Koroniak K, Hogl S, Colombo A, Zeitschel U, Willem M, Volbracht C, Schepers U, Imhof A, Hoffmeister A, Haass C, Rossner S, Brase S, Lichtenthaler SF: Secretome protein enrichment identifies physiological BACE1 protease substrates in neurons, *EMBO J* 31:3157–3168, 2012.

Kukar T, Prescott S, Eriksen JL, Holloway V, Murphy MP, Koo EH, Golde TE, Nicolle MM: Chronic administration of R-flurbiprofen attenuates learning impairments in transgenic amyloid precursor protein mice, *BMC Neurosci* 8:54, 2007.

Lacor PN, Buniel MC, Chang L, Fernandez SJ, Gong Y, Viola KL, Lambert MP, Velasco PT, Bigio EH, Finch CE, Krafft GA, Klein WL: Synaptic targeting by Alzheimer's-related amyloid beta oligomers, *J Neurosci* 24:10191–10200, 2004.

Lannfelt L, Moller C, Basun H, Osswald G, Sehlin D, Satlin A, Logovinsky V, Gellerfors P: Perspectives on future Alzheimer therapies: amyloid-beta protofibrils—a new target for immunotherapy with BAN2401 in Alzheimer's disease, *Alzheimers Res Ther* 6:16, 2014.

Lauren J, Gimbel DA, Nygaard HB, Gilbert JW, Strittmatter SM: Cellular prion protein mediates impairment of synaptic plasticity by amyloid-beta oligomers, *Nature* 457:1128–1132, 2009.

Lauritzen I, Pardossi-Piquard R, Bauer C, Brigham E, Abraham JD, Ranaldi S, Fraser P, St George-Hyslop P, Le Thuc O, Espin V, Chami L, Dunys J, Checler F: The beta-secretase-derived C-terminal fragment of betaAPP, C99, but not Abeta, is a key contributor to early intraneuronal lesions in triple-transgenic mouse hippocampus, *J Neurosci* 32:16243–16255a, 2012.

Lee BH, Lee MJ, Park S, Oh DC, Elsasser S, Chen PC, Gartner C, Dimova N, Hanna J, Gygi SP, Wilson SM, King RW, Finley D: Enhancement of proteasome activity by a small-molecule inhibitor of USP14, *Nature* 467:179–184, 2010.

Lee MS, Kwon YT, Li M, Peng J, Friedlander RM, Tsai LH: Neurotoxicity induces cleavage of p35 to p25 by calpain, *Nature* 405:360–364, 2000.

Lee VM, Balin BJ, Otvos L Jr, Trojanowski JQ: A68: a major subunit of paired helical filaments and derivatized forms of normal tau, *Science* 251:675–678, 1991.

Lemere CA, Masliah E: Can Alzheimer disease be prevented by amyloid-beta immunotherapy? *Nat Rev Neurol* 6:108–119, 2010.

Lesne S, Koh MT, Kotilinek L, Kayed R, Glabe CG, Yang A, Gallagher M, Ashe KH: A specific amyloid-beta protein assembly in the brain impairs memory, *Nature* 440:352–357, 2006.

Lewis J, Dickson DW, Lin WL, Chisholm L, Corral A, Jones G, Yen SH, Sahara N, Skipper L, Yager D, Eckman C, Hardy J, Hutton M, McGowan E: Enhanced neurofibrillary degeneration in transgenic mice expressing mutant tau and APP, *Science* 293:1487–1491, 2001.

Liu L, Drouet V, Wu JW, Witter MP, Small SA, Clelland C, Duff K: Trans-synaptic spread of tau pathology in vivo, *PLoS One* 7:e31302, 2012.

Liu-Seifert H, Siemers E, Sundell K, Price K, Han B, Selzler K, Aisen P, Cummings J, Raskin J, Mohs R: Cognitive and functional decline and their relationship in patients with mild Alzheimer's dementia, *J Alzheimers Dis* 43:949–955, 2015.

Lu T, Aron L, Zullo J, Pan Y, Kim H, Chen Y, Yang TH, Kim HM, Drake D, Liu XS, Bennett DA, Colaiacovo MP, Yankner BA: REST and stress resistance in ageing and Alzheimer's disease, *Nature* 507:448–454, 2014.

Malm TM, Jay TR, Landreth GE: The evolving biology of microglia in Alzheimer's disease, *Neurotherapeutics* 12:81–93, 2015.

Mandrekar-Colucci S, Karlo JC, Landreth GE: Mechanisms underlying the rapid peroxisome proliferator-activated receptor-gamma-mediated amyloid clearance and reversal of cognitive deficits in a murine model of Alzheimer's disease, *J Neurosci* 32:10117–10128, 2012.

May PC, Dean RA, Lowe SL, Martenyi F, Sheehan SM, Boggs LN, Monk SA, Mathes BM, Mergott DJ, Watson BM, Stout SL, Timm DE, Smith Labell E, Gonzales CR, Nakano M, Jhee SS, Yen M, Ereshefsky L, Lindstrom TD, Calligaro DO, et al: Robust central reduction of amyloid-beta in humans with an orally available, non-peptidic beta-secretase inhibitor, *J Neurosci* 31:16507–16516, 2011.

May PC, Willis BA, Lowe SL, Dean RA, Monk SA, Cocke PJ, Audia JE, Boggs LN, Borders AR, Brier RA, Calligaro DO, Day TA, Ereshefsky L, Erickson JA, Gevorkyan H, Gonzales CR, James DE, Jhee SS, Komjathy SF, Li L, et al: The potent BACE1 inhibitor LY2886721 elicits robust central Abeta pharmacodynamic responses in mice, dogs, and humans, *J Neurosci* 35:1199–1210, 2015.

McClean PL, Parthsarathy V, Faivre E, Holscher C: The diabetes drug liraglutide prevents degenerative processes in a mouse model of Alzheimer's disease, *J Neurosci* 31:6587–6594, 2011.

Medina DX, Caccamo A, Oddo S: Methylene blue reduces Abeta levels and rescues early cognitive deficit by increasing proteasome activity, *Brain Pathol* 21:140–149, 2011.

Menting KW, Claassen JA: Beta-secretase inhibitor: a promising novel therapeutic drug in Alzheimer's disease, *Front Aging Neurosci* 6:165, 2014.

Merck: Merck advances development program for investigational Alzheimer's disease therapy, MK-8931, 2013. http://www.mercknewsroomcom/news-release/prescriptionmedicine-news/merck-advances-development-program-investigational-alzheimer

Mitani Y, Yarimizu J, Saita K, Uchino H, Akashiba H, Shitaka Y, Ni K, Matsuoka N: Differential effects between gamma-secretase inhibitors and modulators on cognitive function in amyloid precursor protein-transgenic and nontransgenic mice, *J Neurosci* 32:2037–2050, 2012.

Mizushima N, Komatsu M: Autophagy: renovation of cells and tissues, *Cell* 147:728–741, 2011.

Morris M, Maeda S, Vossel K, Mucke L: The many faces of tau, *Neuron* 70:410–426, 2011.

Musiek ES, Holtzman DM: Three dimensions of the amyloid hypothesis: time, space and "wingmen", *Nat Neurosci* 18:800–806, 2015.

Nalbantoglu J, Tirado-Santiago G, Lahsaini A, Poirier J, Goncalves O, Verge G, Momoli F, Welner SA, Massicotte G, Julien JP, Shapiro ML: Impaired learning and LTP in mice expressing the carboxy terminus of the Alzheimer amyloid precursor protein, *Nature* 387:500–505, 1997.

Nicoll JA, Wilkinson D, Holmes C, Steart P, Markham H, Weller RO: Neuropathology of human Alzheimer disease after immunization with amyloid-beta peptide: a case report, *Nat Med* 9:448–452, 2003.

Nimmrich V, Szabo R, Nyakas C, Granic I, Reymann KG, Schroder UH, Gross G, Schoemaker H, Wicke K, Moller A, Luiten P: Inhibition of calpain prevents N-methyl-D-aspartate-induced degeneration of the nucleus basalis and associated behavioral dysfunction, *J Pharmacol Exp Ther* 327:343–352, 2008.

Oster-Granite ML, McPhie DL, Greenan J, Neve RL: Age-dependent neuronal and synaptic degeneration in mice transgenic for the C terminus of the amyloid precursor protein, *J Neurosci* 16:6732–6741, 1996.

Ostrowitzki S, Deptula D, Thurfjell L, Barkhof F, Bohrmann B, Brooks DJ, Klunk WE, Ashford E, Yoo K, Xu ZX, Loetscher H, Santarelli L: Mechanism of amyloid removal in patients with Alzheimer disease treated with gantenerumab, *Arch Neurol* 69:198–207, 2012.

Pamplona A: Eli Lilly, AstraZeneca launch pivotal clinical trial for early Alzheimer's disease drug, *Alzheimer's News Today*, 2014. http://alzheimersnewstoday.com/2014/12/05/eli-lilly-astrazeneca-launch-pivotal-clinical-trial-for-early-alzheimers-disease-drug/

Patel KR: Biogen's aducanumab raises hope that Alzheimer's can be treated at its source, *Manag Care* 24:19, 2015.

Patrick GN, Zukerberg L, Nikolic M, de la Monte S, Dikkes P, Tsai LH: Conversion of p35 to p25 deregulates Cdk5 activity and promotes neurodegeneration, *Nature* 402:615–622, 1999.

Polling S, Hill AF, Hatters DM: Polyglutamine aggregation in Huntington and related diseases, *Adv Exp Med Biol* 769:125–140, 2012.

Quintero-Monzon O, Martin MM, Fernandez MA, Cappello CA, Krzysiak AJ, Osenkowski P, Wolfe MS: Dissociation between the processivity and total activity of gamma-secretase: implications for the mechanism of Alzheimer's disease-causing presenilin mutations, *Biochemistry* 50:9023–9035, 2011.

Rafii MS, Aisen PS: Advances in Alzheimer's disease drug development, *BMC Med* 13:62, 2015.

Reid PR, Bridges TM, Sheffler DJ, Cho HP, Lewis LM, Days E, Daniels JS, Jones CK, Niswender CM, Weaver CD, Conn PJ, Lindsley CW, Wood MR: Discovery and optimization of a novel, selective and brain penetrant M1 positive allosteric modulator (PAM): the development of ML169, an MLPCN probe, *Bioorg Med Chem Lett* 21:2697–2701, 2011.

Roberson ED, Scearce-Levie K, Palop JJ, Yan F, Cheng IH, Wu T, Gerstein H, Yu GQ, Mucke L: Reducing endogenous tau ameliorates amyloid beta-induced deficits in an Alzheimer's disease mouse model, *Science* 316:750–754, 2007.

Rogers MB: Immunotherapy I: baby steps, but no breakthroughs, 2014. http://www.alzforumorg/news/conference-coverage/immunotherapy-i-baby-steps-nobreakthroughs

Ross CA, Poirier MA: Protein aggregation and neurodegenerative disease, *Nat Med* 10(Suppl):S10–S17, 2004.

Saito T, Matsuba Y, Mihira N, Takano J, Nilsson P, Itohara S, Iwata N, Saido TC: Single *App* knock-in mouse models of Alzheimer's disease, *Nat Neurosci* 17:661–663, 2014.

Sandberg MK, Al-Doujaily H, Sharps B, Clarke AR, Collinge J: Prion propagation and toxicity in vivo occur in two distinct mechanistic phases, *Nature* 470:540–542, 2011.

Sandberg MK, Al-Doujaily H, Sharps B, De Oliveira MW, Schmidt C, Richard-Londt A, Lyall S, Linehan JM, Brandner S, Wadsworth JD, Clarke AR, Collinge J: Prion neuropathology follows the accumulation of alternate prion protein isoforms after infective titre has peaked, *Nat Commun* 5:4347, 2014.

Saumier D, Duong A, Haine D, Garceau D, Sampalis J: Domain-specific cognitive effects of tramiprosate in patients with mild to moderate Alzheimer's disease: ADAS-Cog subscale results from the Alphase Study, *J Nutr Health Aging* 13:808–812, 2009.

Schaffhauser H, Mathiasen JR, Dicamillo A, Huffman MJ, Lu LD, McKenna BA, Qian J, Marino MJ: Dimebolin is a 5-HT6 antagonist with acute cognition enhancing activities, *Biochem Pharmacol* 78:1035–1042, 2009.

Schenk D, Barbour R, Dunn W, Gordon G, Grajeda H, Guido T, Hu K, Huang J, Johnson-Wood K, Khan K, Kholodenko D, Lee M, Liao Z, Lieberburg I, Motter R, Mutter L, Soriano F, Shopp G, Vasquez N, Vandevert C, et al: Immunization with amyloid-beta attenuates Alzheimer-disease-like pathology in the PDAPP mouse, *Nature* 400:173–177, 1999.

Scheuner D, Eckman C, Jensen M, Song X, Citron M, Suzuki N, Bird TD, Hardy J, Hutton M, Kukull W, Larson E, Levy-Lahad E, Viitanen M, Peskind E, Poorkaj P, Schellenberg G, Tanzi R, Wasco W, Lannfelt L, Selkoe D, et al:

Secreted amyloid beta-protein similar to that in the senile plaques of Alzheimer's disease is increased in vivo by the presenilin 1 and 2 and APP mutations linked to familial Alzheimer's disease, *Nat Med* 2:864–870, 1996.

Schneider LS: Idalopirdine for Alzheimer's disease: written in the stars, *Lancet Neurol* 13:1063–1065, 2014.

Shankar GM, Li S, Mehta TH, Garcia-Munoz A, Shepardson NE, Smith I, Brett FM, Farrell MA, Rowan MJ, Lemere CA, Regan CM, Walsh DM, Sabatini BL, Selkoe DJ: Amyloid-beta protein dimers isolated directly from Alzheimer's brains impair synaptic plasticity and memory, *Nat Med* 14:837–842, 2008.

Singh J, Udgaonkar JB: Molecular mechanism of the misfolding and oligomerization of the prion protein: current understanding and its implications, *Biochemistry* 54:4431–4442, 2015.

Stack C, Jainuddin S, Elipenahli C, Gerges M, Starkova N, Starkov AA, Jove M, Portero-Otin M, Launay N, Pujol A, Kaidery NA, Thomas B, Tampellini D, Beal MF, Dumont M: Methylene blue upregulates Nrf2/ARE genes and prevents tau-related neurotoxicity, *Hum Mol Genet* 23:3716–3732, 2014.

Stalder M, Phinney A, Probst A, Sommer B, Staufenbiel M, Jucker M: Association of microglia with amyloid plaques in brains of APP23 transgenic mice, *Am J Pathol* 154:1673–1684, 1999.

Steen E, Terry BM, Rivera EJ, Cannon JL, Neely TR, Tavares R, Xu XJ, Wands JR, de la Monte SM: Impaired insulin and insulin-like growth factor expression and signaling mechanisms in Alzheimer's disease—is this type 3 diabetes? *J Alzheimers Dis* 7:63–80, 2005.

Strobel G: Biogen antibody buoyed by phase 1 data and hungry investors, 2015. http://www.alzforumorg/news/conference-coverage/biogen-antibody-buoyed-phase-1-data-and-hungry-investors

Suh YH: An etiological role of amyloidogenic carboxyl-terminal fragments of the beta-amyloid precursor protein in Alzheimer's disease, *J Neurochem* 68:1781–1791, 1997.

Sullivan MG: Biogen's aducanumab stumbles on cognitive endpoints at 6 mg/kg dose, *Clinical Neurology News*, 2015.

Swanoski MT: Homotaurine: a failed drug for Alzheimer's disease and now a nutraceutical for memory protection, *Am J Health Syst Pharm* 66:1950–1953, 2009.

Tamayev R, Matsuda S, Arancio O, D'Adamio L: Beta- but not gamma-secretase proteolysis of APP causes synaptic and memory deficits in a mouse model of dementia, *EMBO Mol Med* 4:171–179, 2012.

Tanzi RE: The genetics of Alzheimer disease, *Cold Spring Harb Perspect Med* 2, 2012.

Tanzi RE, Bertram L: Twenty years of the Alzheimer's disease amyloid hypothesis: a genetic perspective, *Cell* 120:545–555, 2005.

Tell V, Hilgeroth A: Recent developments of protein kinase inhibitors as potential AD therapeutics, *Front Cell Neurosci* 7:189, 2013.

Tenreiro S, Eckermann K, Outeiro TF: Protein phosphorylation in neurodegeneration: friend or foe? *Front Mol Neurosci* 7:42, 2014.

Teplow DB: On the subject of rigor in the study of amyloid beta-protein assembly, *Alzheimers Res Ther* 5:39, 2013.

Um JW, Nygaard HB, Heiss JK, Kostylev MA, Stagi M, Vortmeyer A, Wisniewski T, Gunther EC, Strittmatter SM: Alzheimer amyloid-beta oligomer bound to postsynaptic prion protein activates Fyn to impair neurons, *Nat Neurosci* 15:1227–1235, 2012.

Upton N, Chuang TT, Hunter AJ, Virley DJ: 5-HT6 receptor antagonists as novel cognitive enhancing agents for Alzheimer's disease, *Neurotherapeutics* 5:458–469, 2008.

van Bebber F, Paquet D, Hruscha A, Schmid B, Haass C: Methylene blue fails to inhibit tau and polyglutamine protein dependent toxicity in zebrafish, *Neurobiol Dis* 39:265–271, 2010.

van Es JH, van Gijn ME, Riccio O, van den Born M, Vooijs M, Begthel H, Cozijnsen M, Robine S, Winton DJ, Radtke F, Clevers H: Notch/gamma-secretase inhibition turns proliferative cells in intestinal crypts and adenomas into goblet cells, *Nature* 435:959–963, 2005.

Vellas B, Black R, Thal LJ, Fox NC, Daniels M, McLennan G, Tompkins C, Leibman C, Pomfret M, Grundman M: Long-term follow-up of patients immunized with AN1792: reduced functional decline in antibody responders, *Curr Alzheimer Res* 6:144–151, 2009.

Walsh DM, Klyubin I, Fadeeva JV, Cullen WK, Anwyl R, Wolfe MS, Rowan MJ, Selkoe DJ: Naturally secreted oligomers of amyloid beta protein potently inhibit hippocampal long-term potentiation in vivo, *Nature* 416:535–539, 2002.

Webster SJ, Bachstetter AD, Nelson PT, Schmitt FA, Van Eldik LJ: Using mice to model Alzheimer's dementia: an overview of the clinical disease and the preclinical behavioral changes in 10 mouse models, *Front Genet* 5:88, 2014.

Weingarten MD, Lockwood AH, Hwo SY, Kirschner MW: A protein factor essential for microtubule assembly, *Proc Natl Acad Sci USA* 72:1858–1862, 1975.

Whitwell JL, Josephs KA, Murray ME, Kantarci K, Przybelski SA, Weigand SD, Vemuri P, Senjem ML, Parisi JE, Knopman DS, Boeve BF, Petersen RC, Dickson DW, Jack CR Jr: MRI correlates of neurofibrillary tangle pathology at autopsy: a voxel-based morphometry study, *Neurology* 71:743–749, 2008.

Wilcock GK, Black SE, Hendrix SB, Zavitz KH, Swabb EA, Laughlin MA: Efficacy and safety of tarenflurbil in mild to moderate Alzheimer's disease: a randomised phase II trial, *Lancet Neurol* 7:483–493, 2008.

Wilkinson D, Windfeld K, Colding-Jorgensen E: Safety and efficacy of idalopirdine, a 5-HT6 receptor antagonist, in patients with moderate Alzheimer's disease (LADDER): a randomised, double-blind, placebo-controlled phase 2 trial, *Lancet Neurol* 13:1092–1099, 2014.

Willem M, Garratt AN, Novak B, Citron M, Kaufmann S, Rittger A, DeStrooper B, Saftig P, Birchmeier C, Haass C: Control of peripheral nerve myelination by the beta-secretase BACE1, *Science* 314:664–666, 2006.

Winblad B, Andreasen N, Minthon L, Floesser A, Imbert G, Dumortier T, Maguire RP, Blennow K, Lundmark J, Staufenbiel M, Orgogozo JM, Graf A: Safety, tolerability, and antibody response of active Abeta immunotherapy with CAD106 in patients with Alzheimer's disease: randomised, double-blind, placebo-controlled, first-in-human study, *Lancet Neurol* 11:597–604, 2012.

Wischik CM, Edwards PC, Lai RY, Roth M, Harrington CR: Selective inhibition of Alzheimer disease-like tau aggregation by phenothiazines, *Proc Natl Acad Sci USA* 93:11213–11218, 1996.

Wischik CM, Staff RT, Wischik DJ, Bentham P, Murray AD, Storey JM, Kook KA, Harrington CR: Tau aggregation inhibitor therapy: an exploratory phase 2 study in mild or moderate Alzheimer's disease, *J Alzheimers Dis* 44:705–720, 2015.

Wolfe MS: Tau mutations in neurodegenerative diseases, *J Biol Chem* 284:6021–6025, 2009.

Wolfe MS: Gamma-secretase inhibitors and modulators for Alzheimer's disease, *J Neurochem* 120(Suppl 1):89–98, 2011.

Wolfe MS, Xia W, Ostaszewski BL, Diehl TS, Kimberly WT, Selkoe DJ: Two transmembrane aspartates in presenilin-1 required for presenilin endoproteolysis and γ-secretase activity, *Nature* 398:513–517, 1999.

Wong GT, Manfra D, Poulet FM, Zhang Q, Josien H, Bara T, Engstrom L, Pinzon-Ortiz M, Fine JS, Lee HJ, Zhang L, Higgins GA, Parker EM: Chronic treatment with the gamma-secretase inhibitor LY-411,575 inhibits beta-amyloid peptide production and alters lymphopoiesis and intestinal cell differentiation, *J Biol Chem* 279:12876–12882, 2004.

Xia X, Qian S, Soriano S, Wu Y, Fletcher AM, Wang XJ, Koo EH, Wu X, Zheng H: Loss of presenilin 1 is associated with enhanced beta-catenin signaling and skin tumorigenesis, *Proc Natl Acad Sci USA* 98:10863–10868, 2001.

Yamanaka M, Ishikawa T, Griep A, Axt D, Kummer MP, Heneka MT: PPARgamma/RXRalpha-induced and CD36-mediated microglial amyloid-beta phagocytosis results in cognitive improvement in amyloid precursor protein/presenilin 1 mice, *J Neurosci* 32:17321–17331, 2012.

Yarchoan M, Arnold SE: Repurposing diabetes drugs for brain insulin resistance in Alzheimer disease, *Diabetes* 63:2253–2261, 2014.

Yu YJ, Atwal JK, Zhang Y, Tong RK, Wildsmith KR, Tan C, Bien-Ly N, Hersom M, Maloney JA, Meilandt WJ, Bumbaca D, Gadkar K, Hoyte K, Luk W, Lu Y, Ernst JA, Scearce-Levie K, Couch JA, Dennis MS, Watts RJ: Therapeutic bispecific antibodies cross the blood–brain barrier in nonhuman primates, *Sci Transl Med* 6:261ra154, 2014.

Zempel H, Thies E, Mandelkow E, Mandelkow EM: Abeta oligomers cause localized Ca(2+) elevation, missorting of endogenous Tau into dendrites, Tau phosphorylation, and destruction of microtubules and spines, *J Neurosci* 30:11938–11950, 2010.

Zhang L, Song L, Parker EM: Calpain inhibitor I increases beta-amyloid peptide production by inhibiting the degradation of the substrate of gamma-secretase: evidence that substrate availability limits beta-amyloid peptide production, *J Biol Chem* 274:8966–8972, 1999.

Zhang Z, Song M, Liu X, Kang SS, Kwon IS, Duong DM, Seyfried NT, Hu WT, Liu Z, Wang JZ, Cheng L, Sun YE, Yu SP, Levey AI, Ye K: Cleavage of tau by asparagine endopeptidase mediates the neurofibrillary pathology in Alzheimer's disease, Nat Med 20:1254–1262, 2014.

Index

B

C

D

G

H

N

O

P

T

U

V

W

X

Y

Z

FSC
www.fsc.org
MIX
Papier | Fördert gute Waldnutzung
FSC® C083411

Kolibri 360 GmbH
Ferdinand-Jühlke-Straße 7
99095 Erfurt, Deutschland
produktsicherheit@kolibri360.de